The New York Times
Twentieth Century in Review

THE GAY RIGHTS MOVEMENT

Other Titles in
The New York Times 20th Century in Review

The Cold War

Forthcoming

Political Censorship
The Balkans

The New York Times
Twentieth Century in Review

THE GAY RIGHTS MOVEMENT

Editor
Vincent J. Samar

Introduction by Andrew Sullivan

FITZROY DEARBORN PUBLISHERS
CHICAGO ◆ LONDON

For information write to:

FITZROY DEARBORN PUBLISHERS
919 North Michigan Avenue, Suite 760
Chicago IL 60611
USA

or

FITZROY DEARBORN PUBLISHERS
310 Regent Street
London W1B 3AX
England

British Library and Library of Congress Cataloging in Publication Data are available.

ISBN 1-57958-225-7

First published in the USA and UK 2001

Typeset by Print Means Inc., New York, New York

Printed by Edwards Brothers, Ann Arbor, Michigan

Cover Design by Peter Aristedes, Chicago Advertising and Design, Chicago, Illinois

CONTENTS

PREFACE

This volume presents a collection of New York Times articles illustrating the development of gay and lesbian rights throughout the 20th century with respect to nondiscrimination, marriage, parenting, and so on. It would be wrong to think that the articles themselves simply chart this development, however. One must also appreciate that before the 1960's, few people, including journalists and editors at The New York Times, saw gays and lesbians as a distinct and legitimate minority. Consequently, the articles in this book are not arranged in chronological order in the first instance. Rather, the articles are placed chronologically under various headings that reflect areas of concern for gay men and lesbians. While these articles offer a rich source of documents on the subject, the reader is advised to supplement them (especially the earlier articles) with other resources in order to provide a fuller and less biased picture of this development.

For editors of newspapers, the decision to cover an event and the approach then taken often reflect individual and institutional biases, as well as wider biases in society at large. Concerning gay rights—or perhaps, more properly, the political/social/legal concerns of gay people—The New York Times was largely indifferent during the first 30 years of the century and unsympathetic between 1930 and 1980, even when compared to its competitors. This stance contrasts starkly with the sympathetic and supportive role that The Times plays today. Before the 1930's, when The Times showed indifference, it was sometimes difficult to even discern that lesbians and gay men were the subject of discussion, as euphemisms were often used. A good example is the September 9, 1928, article that talks about New York City as a Mecca for bachelors. Whether The Times was more biased during the early period or more biased today depends not only on whether one tends to agree or disagree with the reporting but also on whether the events merited the coverage they received relative to their impact on society. After all, newspapers in a free society are ideally providers of information on which people balance human rights with various views of the common good. When such information is not provided or only one point of view is presented, the public may reach faulty conclusions, and individuals' rights may be denied. This was particularly true in the context of gay and lesbian rights early in the century.

The category "homosexuality" did not show up in the index of The New York Times until mid-century. From the 1950's until the 1960's, when "homosexuality" finally appeared in the index, it was only to direct the reader to other subjects such as "U.S. Employees," "perversion," "theater," "libel," etc. In the 1960's, the word began regularly to appear as a subcategory under the subject heading of "sex." Only in 1971 did the index list articles directly under "homosexuality" as a separate category. And not until the mid-1980's did "gay rights" appear as a distinct heading. Consequently, stories about lesbians and gay men from the first half of the century, to the extent that they were reported at all, had to be found under subheadings such as "perversion," "nightclubs," "theater," "bathhouses" and "crimes involving sex." By contrast, articles after 1980, including many thousands of reports on diverse gay and lesbian issues, could be found under obvious headings. Additionally, because of technological changes in the way information is stored, these more recent articles could be found online with the help of services such as Lexis-Nexis. These services allowed for the use of key-word searches as well as subject searches.

The approach taken to gathering and selecting articles for this book was twofold. Since more stories were written about gays and lesbians in the last 20 years of the century than in the previous eight decades combined, the number of articles from the later period is correspondingly greater. With this in mind, articles published before 1980 were chosen to represent the decade from which they were drawn. These selections are meant to indicate to readers the amount and style of reporting prevalent at the time. They also demonstrate that more articles were written during the 1960's because of the influence in that decade of the civil rights movement and of the sexual revolution. Beginning in 1980, when more articles were available for inclusion, the selection was based on how well the articles reflected the development of gay rights in particular subject areas, including the efforts for and against the elimination of sodomy statutes, the adoption of antidiscrimination legislation, whether gays might openly serve in the military, same-sex marriage, and so on. These later articles reflect who was making these claims, what exactly was being argued, why the claims were made and who were the respondents of the claims. They also show that the type of self-identity one develops individually and collectively (positive or negative) is partly contingent on whether one's rights are recognized.

In various ways, the articles here illustrate how gay and lesbian rights came to be part of mainstream political and social debates, and they point to the different venues in which those debates were taking place. For example, the articles depict as important topics not only politics and law enforcement but also debates within churches and within the mainstream media over theatrical productions, films and television. There are also articles reporting that the public became aware of gay rights through crimes of hate and the responses (or lack thereof) to those crimes by politicians and others. And there are articles that show how gay men and lesbians internalized homophobia and devalued their own self-worth.

Clearly manifest within this source material is a debate over the basic morality of same-sex relations. For this reason, articles are included that treat gay and lesbian rights as part of ongoing moral discussions within the women's movement and the civil rights movement and in religion. All of these discussions illustrate a changing cultural climate in which moral positions are reexamined and lesbian and gay rights are increasingly seen as analogous to the rights of others.

The book is divided into nine parts, each addressing a key aspect of the struggle by gay men and women to win equal rights. Part I reflects the development of gay identity and gay culture. The articles are presented with an understanding that individuals both within and outside gay communities did not always share any one view. In fact, during the first 30 years of this century, to the extent gay men and lesbians were perceived at all (mostly in the large cities), the general public viewed them as a curiosity. Articles from before the 1930's are few and far between and are supplemented by recent articles discussing personalities who lived during the time or who wrote about it, as well as recent research on the period. These recent articles attest to the vibrant life that existed, especially in cities such as New York, and they show how with varying degrees of tolerance, the mainstream culture was able to accommodate lesbian and gay male life before the Depression. This section also includes a large number of post-Depression articles involving issues of coming out and the trials and tribulations associated with that; how gays and lesbians began defining themselves; and what the connection was between sexual orientation and being transsexual or transgendered. All of these articles illustrate a dynamic subculture that does not fit easily into any one mode but reflects a number of attempts to find self-identity against a non-supportive background culture.

By contrast, Part II reprints articles related to mainstream society's view of gay men and lesbians. Here, one finds articles discussing early attempts to censor information about lesbians and gay men and also articles about how the medical establishment classified them as sick and a possible danger to society. Although the backlash of the 1930's may have relaxed with the need for personnel during World War II, that reprieve did not last long. These articles also depict the various ways the media came to describe gay men and lesbians (both negative and positive) and the important effects that the Alfred C. Kinsey studies had on the general public's awareness of male and female sexuality. The Kinsey studies, although controversial, questioned how rare homosexuality actually was in society. Still, even with the sexual revolution of the 1960's, which brought many social concerns regarding sexuality to fruition, the articles from this period do not suggest that gays and lesbians were welcomed into this changing environment. Indeed, not until the AIDS crisis of the 1980's does one see a more supportive editorial attitude at The New York Times. For example, The Times now began using "gay"—the community's adopted self-description—as the preferred term over "homosexual." The paper also began to recognize same-sex spouses in obituaries and gave greater coverage and advertising space to gay social activities. Eventually, gays and lesbians would become recognized as a market by some mainstream businesses, and schools and academic institutions would take professional note of gay concerns. However, that shift would take time, and a great deal of organizing by gay men and lesbians would be needed first.

Part III concerns how the changes in attitude toward gay men and lesbians in mainstream society began to come about. The emphasis of the articles in this section is on the development of gay and lesbian organizations, such as the Mattachine Society and the Daughters of Bilitis, the impact of Stonewall, and the ways gay men and lesbians organized public displays of their own pride in themselves. The historical event that is most often credited with initiating the gay political movement was the 1969 police raid on the Stonewall Inn in Greenwich Village, New York City. In that raid, drag queens resisted police attempts to close the bar and arrest its patrons. Although The New York Times carried only a few scattered articles on the raid, knowledge of the conflict spread quickly. The result was that the Stonewall resistance became a nationwide call to gay men and lesbians to stand up and repel police raids. It also became a rallying cry for new organizations to develop outlines for anti-discrimination legislation. From a psychological standpoint, the resistance at Stonewall marked a change, too, in the direction of gay social identity, transforming it into a fully political identity. Gay men and lesbians were beginning the slow journey to civil rights. Articles about gay pride parades and achievements subsequent to Stonewall illustrate that the subculture had begun to recognize the value of its own contributions. The articles indicate how these events gave further visibility to gay men and lesbians nationwide. They also illustrate how lesbians and gay men showed others that the "standard" American family of the 1950's, depicted in *Ozzie and Harriet*, was not representative of even the average American family.

Part IV presents a number of articles on the transformations in literature, theater and other areas of the arts that gay men and lesbians were making throughout the century. Film depictions were not always supportive of the plight of gay and lesbian people, as illustrated by "The Boys in the Band," the popular 1970 made-for-Hollywood movie based on the play of the same name. Though among the earliest mainstream films to explicitly address gay themes, it presented a cast of gay characters defined by their sense of self-loathing and offered little hope that their plight could be changed. By the second half of the 1980's, greater concern had overtaken the entertainment industry, as Hollywood and the culture at large faced losses, such as the death of Rock Hudson, due to AIDS. All at once a new political and social awareness of the plight of gay men and lesbians began to take hold in various areas of the arts. There was also the now famous "Day Without Art" to show the loss society would face if AIDS were any longer ignored.

Part V presents articles about the impact of AIDS, a disease that caused the deaths of tens of thousands of gay men, young and old, and encouraged some outside the gay community to claim that gay life was dangerous. It also gave rise to heterosexual fears that the disease would not be confined to gay men, intravenous drug users, and hemophiliacs.

The tragedy of AIDS was measurable during the first five years of the decade not merely in terms of numbers of deaths in the gay male population. It could also be measured in terms of the slow and inadequate responses of government and the medical establishment to come to grips with the problem. Articles illustrating some of these responses are included here. Yet, perhaps because of these challenges, gay-focused health organizations such as Gay Men's Health Crisis were formed, forging alliances between the gay community and certain sectors of the broader society. The efforts of these organizations, combined with a heightened public awareness of the plight of gay men, brought the issue of society's treatment of gay men and lesbians more directly into the limelight.

The articles in Part VI examine issues of the family, revealing the effect of earlier periods of organizing and public disclosures. By the 1990's, courts were beginning to take seriously the claims of gay and lesbian Americans. Such claims led to public debates about whether lesbians and gay men had a right to marry, adopt children and be foster parents and guardians. They also led to more revealing discussions about what it was really like growing up in a gay household.

Part VII takes up the theme of intolerance. The articles indicate a growing number of hate crimes against gay persons as gay men and lesbians started to make progress toward securing some of their rights. As the murder of Matthew Shepherd illustrates, these rights were not secured without cost. No doubt much of this intolerance was fanned by the heightened fear of AIDS. However, the religious right, in particular, made much use of this fear to foster its own political agendas.

Part VIII includes articles concerning law, public policy and the political arena. Here one finds first a growing number of police raids on gay business establishments in the 1950's and 1960's, followed by the emergence of the post-Stonewall fight against legal harassment, including the efforts to oppose Anita Bryant's anti-gay campaign in Florida. The discrimination practiced in the greater society also took a special place in employment issues, most notably in the persecutions of the McCarthy era that led so many lesbians and gay men in the United States to conceal their identities, and more recently in the area of federal immigration policies that prevented gays and lesbians from entering the country. A major effort to combat such discriminatory practices was waged on two fronts: through the election of gay and pro-gay politicians such as Harvey Milk and Barney Frank and through legal and political challenges to the constitutionality of many of these forms of discrimination. Also of particular note here are the challenges to the U.S. military policy that continues to bar openly gay persons from serving in the military. While the 1990's was by no means a period in which all or even most of these issues were resolved, the level of attention and focus that gay men and lesbians received during this period put them at the center of mainstream politics. Illustrations of this can be found in the media's questioning of politicians about gay concerns, as well as statements and actions on gay issues by elected officials at the highest levels.

Part IX presents articles about gay male and lesbian struggles outside the United States. While these articles may not present a complete picture of events abroad, they illustrate some of the events covered by The Times. Events in one country may no longer be separable from what happens in another. On the streets of Moscow, in the heart of the former Soviet Union, Russian gay men and lesbians are now organizing and demanding their rights. Asian and Latin American gays are beginning to be noticed. South Africa's new constitution includes a clause against sexual orientation discrimination. France and the Scandinavian countries recognize various kinds of same-sex unions. Israel's Supreme Court has said that a child can have two mothers. Brazil has allowed gay spouses to inherit their partner's estate. The World Pride Parade went ahead in Rome, despite strong objections from the Vatican. And Great Britain has changed its previous policy of not allowing gays to serve in its military: the United States and Turkey are now the sole remaining NATO members to oppose this change.

Needless to say, an editorial project of this magnitude would not have been possible without the support and help of a large number of people. In particular, I want to thank my research assistant, Ryan A. Haas, a graduate student in the Philosophy Department at

Loyola University, Chicago. Ryan worked tirelessly to identify articles based on obscure entries in the Times indexes and on citations from other sources. He also researched most of the illustrations for this volume. I would also like to thank Mark Strasser and Christopher Lane for their review of my outline and for their many thoughtful comments that added to the clarity of this preface. Thanks also to Brian Donovan for helping me with the final selection of photographs. Throughout this period of time, I relied on the good graces of the Loyola University College of Arts and Sciences, especially Assistant Dean Gregory Hamill, for providing me a workspace, and I relied heavily on the Loyola University Library System. Finally, this project would not have been possible without the generosity of Fitzroy Dearborn Publishers who funded it, and the ongoing support of the series editor, David Morrow, who was ready to assist me with editing and administrative matters. To all these people and probably many more, thank you.

DR. VINCENT J. SAMAR

Vincent J. Samar is adjunct professor of philosophy at Loyola University Chicago and Oakton Community College, and adjunct professor of law at the Illinois Institute of Technology, Chicago-Kent College of Law. He is the author of "Justifying Judgment: Practicing Law and Philosophy" and "The Right to Privacy: Gays, Lesbians and the Constitution," and has written articles for the "Journal of Homosexuality," the "DePaul Law Review" and other academic publications.

INTRODUCTION

By Andrew Sullivan

One of the benefits of a newspaper announcing daily that it will publish "All The News That's Fit To Print" is that it reveals precisely what isn't. For the vast majority of the 20th century, anything to do with homosexuality was regarded by The New York Times as unfit material for a serious newspaper. The Times wasn't alone in this, of course. Like most social institutions, it reflected the culture it operated in. But that means something important in this riveting collection of articles from a hundred years of the newspaper. The most important events in the lives of most gay men and lesbians simply aren't here. Decades pass in the early part of this century, decades in which thousands of gay men and women led diverse, fascinating, ebullient and also threatened lives in New York City and beyond. But in those decades, one can scan the print of the country's leading newspaper and find nothing but the tiniest references to public morals, mental illness or police blotters. There are 'deviates' and crimes; there are occasional scandals and public spectacles. But there is no coverage of a group of people who made up then, as they make up now, a critical population in New York's teeming masses.

Then, slowly but surely, the simple reality of homosexual life begins to impinge on the extraordinary effort to deny its existence. Just as social taboos fray as the century wears on, so do those enshrined by The Times. The first, nervous references are to changes in psychiatric analysis of the 'problem.' Articles on controversies in psychoanalysis cite snippets from experts who urge a less censorious attitude toward one kind of human sexual and emotional expression. Fledgling homosexual rights groups—in particular the Mattachine Society—begin to pepper news stories. In the mid-1960's, a movement emerges to allow gay men to serve openly in the military. And then in the late 1960's and early 1970's, the New Left explodes on the scene and brings gay rights with it.

From then on, the coverage might be seen as hyper-coverage. Once the taboo against even discussion of the topic is breached, it's almost as if a dam of questions, arguments and emotions, held up for decades, if not centuries, bursts into public life. The Times goes from terse police reports to long, sprawling essays about the meaning of lesbianism, the relationship of gay rights to other civil rights battles, the impact of gay artists on American culture and cinema, the nature of homosexual relationships, the possibility of marriage rights, and on and on. And then, in the middle of this extraordinary outburst of candor comes a story so incredible and unlikely it is still hard to believe. At the very moment that homosexuality becomes a matter of public discourse, a strange virus starts spreading across gay America, bringing a plague that changes the question of homosexuality in our culture for good. Obituary pages become clogged with the early deaths of thousands of men, outed by a diagnosis. The threat of a broader public health crisis brings discussion of gay rights to a new level of urgency and importance. It is only toward the very end of the century that there is even a hint of a new public discussion of the question divorced from the exigencies and distortions of a plague that decimated at least two generations.

Reading through these articles, it is impossible not to wonder whether any other group in our society had such an extraordinary century. Women and African-Americans live in a world today unrecognizable to their predecessors at the turn of the 20th century. But both groups, even a century ago, had been organized for decades, had a clearly delineated and thoroughly self-conscious political and cultural history, a paper trail long and distinguished, and several critical moments in which history turned—the Civil War, Reconstruction, the First World War, the Suffragist movement and so on. The Times covered these stories as it did most burning issues—thoroughly, if through the lenses of its mainly privileged, white and male editors and writers. But it wasn't until the 1950's that The Times gave even passing reference to a group which now makes up 4 percent of the voting population. It wasn't until the 1960's that gay men and women began to lay claim in any larger sense to the same sort of history, politics and self-consciousness as many other social groups. As late as 1964, one can find a front page story on the arrest of Walter Jenkins, aide to Lyndon Johnson, and see no reference to the term "homosexual." Jenkins was arrested in a Y.M.C.A. for making "indecent gestures." He was hospitalized for "extreme fatigue." He is described as a "nervous type." The only clue to the real reason for the scandal is that Jenkins had had one previous arrest: for "disorderly conduct (pervert)." With that terse word, Times readers knew how to read between the lines of the rest of the story.

Certain themes, however, persist. The first is growing visibility. In the early part of the century, as historians such as George Chauncey have documented, gay life thrived in small corners of New York City—from the drag balls in Harlem to the vibrant coffee-lounge, bathhouse and bar life downtown. But gay presence was still fledgling and insecure. The Depression initiated a bout of further repression, leading to a World War that did what most wars do—shook up whole populations and accelerated social change. Many gay men, once isolated in small towns, found each other in the armed services. They found it hard to return to a completely closeted existence when they were demobilized. The post-war expansion of opportunities for women similarly gave many lesbians more economic clout and independence. As greater visibility flickered on the horizon, one begins to see homosexual rights groups emerging—from the Mattachine Society to the Daughters of Bilitis—with literature and associations typical of many political organizations. This visibility took another vault in the late 1960's, again in the wake of the social upheaval caused by the Vietnam war. Gay ghettoes emerged in New York City and San Francisco. Less established but still dogged communities grew in other cities, including Washington, D.C., Chicago and Los Angeles. But even then, the sense of shame lingered, the bifurcated lives of most gay men and women hovering in indeterminate spaces of half-acceptance, half-rejection. It was only with AIDS—and the dramatic outing of tens of thousands of gay men across the entire country—that homosexuality became as visible as race and gender.

But at each step of the way, the backlash was equally ferocious. One can see this in the pages of The Times. Homosexuals, for most of the last century, were referred to as 'deviates' at the very moment their presence was recognized. As recently as 1965, a story from Long Island quotes town officials talking of gay men as if they were vermin: "We don't want to take over police duties and responsibilities. . . . But we have been invaded by queers and dope pushers who are preying on our youngsters." Scandals and conferences on mental illness were the usual excuses for any discussion of the lives of homosexuals. But when the gay rights movement actually began to make political progress, the opposition became even more intense. From Anita Bryant in the 1970's to the birth of the religious right, the question of homosexuality galvanized social conservatives like no other issue except abortion. For every gain for gay rights, there was an equal and opposite reaction. In the decade that saw the first political gains for homosexuals and the decriminalization of sodomy in many states, the movement that Anita Bryant started gained momentum. Gay rights ordinances were repealed across the country. In the 1980's, as AIDS cemented gay unity and mobilized gay activism, the Supreme Court, in Bowers vs. Hardwick, upheld the right of states to imprison gay men for sodomy, even if it meant invading their homes with policemen. In the 1990's, as marriage rights came front and center, there were astonishing moves toward provisions for gay relationships in Hawaii, Vermont and elsewhere, but there was also the Defense of Marriage Act, outlawing any federal acceptance of gay relationships. On the military front, the first president to propose ending the ban on gay service members was peremptorily humiliated by the Pentagon and the Congress, and instead he instituted a policy that would almost double the rate of gay discharges from the military in the succeeding years.

And throughout all this, the gay world was almost always at war with itself. This was perhaps inevitable. Unlike many other minorities, gay men and lesbians inevitably come, in every generation, from a bewildering variety of backgrounds. They are born into different families in different places—from small towns to big cities. Although this is true of most minorities, other groups are typically also inducted into the established culture and politics of their communities in subtle ways from the cradle on. Not so homosexuals, who often come to their sexual orientation with their politics and personality and culture and worldview already fixed. Like most people, they find this difficult to abandon easily—for the sake of a nebulous new identity. So they strike balances that are sometimes fruitful, sometimes incoherent, but rarely dull. And everyone is a critic of everyone else's compromise.

Furthermore, the differing experiences of coming out also forge deep differences. Some homosexuals announce their orientation as a rebellion against existing norms; others do so in an attempt to adhere to those existing norms and find a way to be gay within them. Many more never publicly acknowledge their homosexuality at all. So the conservative-liberal divisions are exacerbated by the radical-assimilationist divisions, again and again throughout the century. There are the drag queens in Harlem and the closeted gay officials in Washington, D.C., in the first part of the century. There is the early, assimilationist Mattachine Society and the Gay Liberationists who supplanted them. There is currently the more mainstream Human Rights Campaign and the more leftist National Gay Lesbian Task Force. There are Log Cabin Republicans and Lesbian Avengers. There are the outers and the outed. At any Gay Pride Parade one can see only contrast: leftist radicals, sado-masochism enthusiasts, gay policemen, lesbian mothers, gay Mormons, Republican mayors, and Dykes on Bikes. Few other groups have quite this variety of viewpoints or willingness to flaunt them. The resulting internal politics can make for explosive theater.

And in the middle of a movement that is premised, according to some, on an end to prescribed gender roles, there is also unmistakable gender tension. Although lesbians and gay men live with a same-gender orientation, this is often all they have in common. Misogyny can be rife among gay men, and a suspicion of men is not far from some lesbian lives. In many cities, social life only spasmodically integrates the two groups, and their political priorities are often different. Historically, gay men have pioneered a sexual license that holds limited appeal to many lesbians; and lesbians have had to thinly veil their contempt for the way some gay men conduct their sexual and emotional lives. Lesbian women have often stressed the importance of economic security and protection from violence, rather than military integration or sexual freedom. At critical moments, to be sure, ranks have closed. The AIDS crisis was notable for prompting lesbians to become involved in ways that were neither inevitable nor demanded. Marriage rights have also brought many lesbians and gay men together. But elsewhere, tensions endure. At the beginning of the movement, gay men and lesbians had different organizations—the Mattachine Society and the Daughters of Bilitis. Today there are very few female voices on the conservative wing of the gay movement, and increasingly few male voices in the established gay political organizations. Both major national gay groups are run by women. The National Gay and Lesbian Task Force has had six consecutive women in charge. The senior staff of The Human Rights Campaign is lesbian-dominated. Even The Advocate, the main gay newsmagazine, has a lesbian editor-in-chief, although the vast majority of its readers are male. Most of the time, these differences are papered over. But the inevitable tensions simmer.

The corollary to these divisions and tensions is, of course, an often spectacularly unpredictable and diverse culture. To my ear, the details in these following stories are often the most revealing—about gay life at any particular moment in time—from the tensions about lesbianism within the women's rights movement to the new dimension of racial grievances at the Millennium March on Washington. Some of these shifts and conflicts appear in their very own stories. At other times, social shifts can be gleaned from the details. Take a story from 1977, when a fire broke out in a West Side bathhouse. Almost as soon as news of the fire broke, "[m]any [gay men] expressed concern that the inevitable publicity in the wake of the fire would force a crackdown on the homosexual world in general. . . ." Even in 1977, the instinctive response to a fire was not outrage or concern, but paranoia. Firemen were called in as a last resort: "Many empty fire extinguishers inside the building indicated that the occupants had tried to fight the blaze for some time before calling the Fire Department." Shame abounded: "Because many patrons signed in under false names, identification of the dead was expected to prove difficult." But so did diversity: "Mr. Rhone, one of the survivors, said that customers, who paid $5 for a locker or $7 for a cubicle . . . included 'your old men, young gorgeous men, your models and your successful businessmen.'" But in 1977, some openness was beginning to be more evident. Ordinary gay men are quoted with their full names in the paper; others protest the double-standards for fire precautions in gay and straight establishments. In this tiny but gripping story, a closed and furtive world was suddenly on the front page of the paper. And between the lines, the story of a social transformation can be read.

Are there lessons to be learned from this story? Perhaps the first lesson is modesty. It's clear from these stories that even some of the major actors in the gay rights movement of the last century were unaware or unsure of what they were really doing. The extraordinary contrast between the first and last few decades of the century suggests that now is not yet the time for even a partial accounting. We know that we are far too close to these events and stories to be able to see them in their full and proper context. The problem with a story that has been going on for millennia but has only been accurately and adequately described for around two decades is that true perspective is impossible. It would be too facile to talk of simple or easy progress, since so many of the dark and ugly issues of the first part of the century are still present in its closing years. It is also too easy to dismiss those who are largely invisible in these pages as somehow less real or less sophisticated or more ashamed than gay men and women are today. We are only beginning to understand their lives; and it's the job of historians not to peer into the past as if through the wrong end of a telescope, but to attempt to see the past as it was seen by those living through it. The fact that many lives were unspoken, many thoughts encoded, many loves lost or hidden does not make those lives or thoughts or loves any less authentic than ours today. In fact, given the extraordinary pressures brought to bear upon gay men and women in the past, their achievements are all the more remarkable and their rebellion all the more intense.

In other words, we have to see through these pages that the story of gay America is not like that of many other Americas. Although it is an ancient story, its telling is uniquely new, its divisions raw, its excitement and energy palpable. At the dawn of a new millennium, we can see, in fact, that the articulation of this experience has only truly just begun. In these pages, we can discern the stories of lives once lived in shadows—but also the thrill of an emerging world that has only just begun to see the light.

Andrew Sullivan is a contributing writer for The New York Times Magazine, a senior editor at The New Republic, a columnist for The Sunday Times of London and the author of several books, including "Virtually Normal: An Argument About Homosexuality."

PART I

GAY IDENTITY, GAY CULTURE

Cultural Life

September 9, 1928

THE BACHELORS OF NEW YORK

Mussolini, taxing bachelors, would collect a tidy sum if he could levy on the bachelors of New York. For the nation's bachelors this city is the Mecca. Not only is it the City of Youth, but it is the City of the Single.

They do get married in New York—more than 68,000 weddings a year is the average—but they move to the suburbs afterward. When they have run the gauntlet of City Hall they migrate to Jersey and Long Island and Westchester. New York remains the citadel of the bachelors who are too busy to marry, or too poor to marry, or rich enough to say cynically, "We don't have to marry!"

At any given moment you may expect to find about 900,000 unmarried men in New York, as compared with a mere 700,000 of single women. New York is the greatest stag city in the country. Outside of working hours, what do the bachelors do? It is certain they are not all in a Garden line-up waiting for admission to the next fight, neither are they all concentrated in speakeasies and along the docks. They are not all sitting on Bryant Park benches dreading the next job, or standing in Mr. Zero's breadline canvassing the next meal. Such men do not represent the majority of New York bachelors.

You may wander at night into the smoking gallery of a New York movie. There you will see many lonely men smoking pipes or cigarettes, satisfying their yearning for adventure and romance in the unreal world of the screen. But when you have seen them all and sympathized with their attempt to bring happiness into their lives, you have not yet discovered what New York's bachelors are doing.

If you will turn to the universities, the colleges, the evening schools of the city you will be on the track of a great discovery. New York is not merely a garment-making centre; it is an intellectual centre as well. Columbia alone turns away thousands of men students from all parts of the country, but thousands are accepted, and their lives are poured into the bachelor stream of the city. Incidentally their study furnishes an outlet for the energy of masculine youth. They fill their waking hours with work and study in order to succeed in their chosen careers. They are incredibly eager to shine as scholars, lawyers, chemists or engineers. Dance halls and cabarets do not offer lasting alternatives to classrooms and laboratories. Thousands of students in New York lay the foundations of lifelong achievement on Morningside Heights or University Heights or Washington Heights.

If all the Y. M. C. A.'s and the hall bedrooms were to toss out their young bachelors you would find fellows who believe they can succeed by brains and sweat—not the men who can afford to be friends of bootleggers, but the men who do the hard work of the city in factories, offices and stores. You would find many artists and writers, chauffeurs and mechanics, bookkeepers and stenographers. A great crowd of young scientists—in engineering, electricity and radio.

New York appeals to the nation's bachelors because it is a city where the young man can lead his life with the least interruption. If he is preparing for a revolution, like Trotsky in his east side days, he can serve his prentice years without undue hindrance. Possibly you will brush shoulders with him in the economics room of the Public Library. But that's all right. New York has catholic tastes and shelters both revolutionaries and reactionaries. If, on the other hand, he is preparing for fame and fortune in the arts, the city is one of opportunity for him.

The city has something for every kind of bachelor—for the obscure, a room in an apartment house; for the famous, an apartment in Park Avenue. New York is a young man's city. The race is to the swift.

* * *

April 6, 1975

THE ALL-GAY CRUISE: PREJUDICE AND PRIDE

By CLIFF JAHR

Two speakers the size of steamer trunks blasted rock music off the fantail deck one evening as the Renaissance lay docked in a sleepy Mexican port. Merchant seamen on a nearby Brazilian ship put down their mops and elbowed the rail to get a closer look at—olha!—boys dancing with boys. The seamen guffawed, poked each other, waved enticingly; three or four started to dance, but the parody was quickly stared down by their shipmates. Up on the Renaissance bridge, some starchy French officers watched tolerantly at first until finally they were moved to grins and restrained toetapping. Below them on the main deck, 50 boys did The

David T. Paul

cans who practice le vice Anglais? But how? "Amicably," according to Blue Flettrich, the Islanders' 32-year-old president. "If we seemed like ringtailed baboons to them, they never let on. It was always good manners and hard bargaining."

Paquet has lots of company in its pitch for the gay market in America, estimated at somewhere between 6 and 15 million adults. When the packaging is right, gay patronage can spell success for Broadway shows, films, pop singers, rock groups, magazines—even hotels and dude ranches. Group travel is a recent development.

Announcements of the Renaissance cruise were handed out on the Islanders' buses last Memorial Day and word-of-mouth spread the news. There were 300 reservations by Labor Day, but then the flow stopped. At sailing time, when 60 berths remained unsold, some said the reason was the $275 to $790 price tag (air fare to Fort Lauderdale not included) during a recession. Or the absence of help from travel agents and advertising. Flettrich thinks it was these reasons and more.

"Some figured on a week of bad taste and were just not interested," he says. "But mainly I think it was because so many 'closeted' gays could lose their jobs if newspapers and TV played it up and word got back."

Nevertheless, roughly half the passengers booked were "in the closet"—among them doctors, lawyers, designers, businessmen. The Islanders saw an obligation to protect these men's privacy. Moreover, soft drugs were sure to be on board, so the club concocted a sort of mini-coverup: A public relations man was hired to fend off inquiring reporters. A psychologist was consulted for the best "posture" to take should the cruise become public knowledge. Press releases were mimeographed and held at-the-ready for any emergency. Cruise folders in the hands of 5,000 people all over the country asked them to remember that "discretion is the better part of frolic."

Two days before sailing, The Miami Herald carried a story reporting complaints of alleged sodomy in a bus station men's room, quoting references to "queers." While it had no connection with the cruise, the Islanders held their breath for fear it might fire up local rednecks and spell trouble at the sailing. But when the big day came, 316 passengers and 28 Islanders staff darted through rain and up the gangplank without a hitch. No reporters were on hand to view the scene with its mounds of Vuitton, its smattering of passengers in head-to-toe black leather. When one husky Islanders officer took his first step on board, after the strain of eight months of planning and suspense, he burst into tears of relief.

As the ship moved out with the usual confetti and streamers excitement, three young girls at dockside waved to a pair of bearded bruisers at the rail. "S'long, Georgie and Michael," they hollered. "Happy honeymoon!" A few seconds later, a French-accented voice piped over the public address system: "Dinner for the main seating was 10 minutes ago. If you don't hurry up, you may miss it and then—won't you be sorry?"

The dining room had all the exotic air of a Kiwanis Club father-and-son banquet: penny loafers and baggy slacks, cotton pullovers and army fatigues, even Johnny Carson double-

Bump as Labelle sang "Voulez-vous coucher avec moi, ce soir?"—her invitation echoing over the village, out across the waters, deep into the jungle dusk.

We were halfway through a seven-day pre-Christmas cruise out of Fort Lauderdale, making brief stops in Guatemala and the Yucatan, with 300 homosexual passengers aboard. Most of them were men—well-heeled and under-35, from New York, California and Florida. They were new to sailing and new to each other, too; but the mixture of six-course dining, pampered loafing and casual mating—staples of more traditional heterosexual cruises—soon had the passengers feeling at home. Before the voyage was over, they had added a few outlandish touches to the annals of "special interest cruises"—and had learned something important about themselves. There are plans for a repeat cruise later this year.

It took an odd couple to invent the all-gay ocean cruise: The Islanders Club is in its seventh season of running weekend shuttlebuses to Fire Island for its 2,000 subscriber-members, most of them gay. Paquet Cruises, the Marseilles arm of a travel conglomerate, has run pleasure cruises since 1860. A sedate French provincial company reaching agreement with Ameri-

knits. One had to look hard for significant detail like a pair of acid-green lurex socks, a tiny gold earring.

Where were the clinging pants and fussy shirts once so popular with urban, middle-class gays? On pro football heroes, that's where. Since the peacock revolution, face bronzers, hair sprays and cologne have become basic survival equipment for "with-it" heterosexuals; most everyone here was close-cropped and drably attired.

Where were the "queens," those dyed and cosmetized symbols of homosexuality? Were they (a) purposely excluded, (b) unable to afford it, (c) becoming an endangered species or, (d) all of the above? Probably all of the above but especially and ironically—(a). The gay world's old guard was politely excluded. Effeminacy, seen by younger gays as a symptom of needless guilt feelings, is considered embarrassing and old-fashioned. Later in the week, some passengers were a little uneasy when a young architect with blond curls appeared at a ball in crepe dress and silver fox clutchcape. He himself confessed to feeling foolish in the "Ida Lupino look" and wore it only long enough to pose for photographs before returning to Kiwanis clothes.

Seated near the captain's table was a group of "leathermen" in black cowhide outfits that were trimmed with a virtual spare parts catalogue of chains, zippers and metal studs. They kept listlessly to themselves all week, looking as tough as a gang of Marlon Brandos. (Brando has been a kind of leatherman hero-model since his 1953 film, "The Wild One.")

A half dozen lesbian couples were on board ranging from a young dean of women at a small East Coast college, and necessarily in the closet, to Lois, in her late fifties, a blond ex-showgirl from Miami who assured us she had nothing to hide. During a ceremony at the shipboard Hawaiian luau when Lois sought to cast her lei into the sea, it was caught in an updraft and blown down a funnel where it disappeared. "It figures," she observed miserably. "My best shots always went down the bilges." Next day there appeared on the ship's message board the following note: "Will the person whose lei clogged my air vent last night please come with Roto Rooter—cabin 126."

There were a few heterosexuals on board. A Fire Island merchant and his wife, for example, who have come to enjoy the fast company of hip gays. ("Well, it doesn't upset us one way or the other.") "Straights" joined in the fun and were welcomed all around.

Everyone got to know each other with an ease born of being out adrift and bonded together with others of like tastes. Fears that the cruise could be a disaster gave way to an apparent fact: the all-gay experiment was going to "work."

At first, talk circled around movies, rock music, the newest discos and topic number one, the cruise itself. Some version of wait'll-they-hear-about-this-back-home-they're-gonna-freak-out was a surefire conversational filler. The fact that there were scores of good-looking men aboard was widely remarked. "I don't know where to start," drawled one passenger, sipping his Tequila Sunrise. "I've met three Mr. Rights before lunch."

A typical day began on the double tier of spacious aft decks with yawning and scratching passengers padding out to deckchairs and collapsing into sleep. Unlike many cruises where "Goodnight Ladies" plays before midnight, revels lasted beyond 4 A.M. and passengers were generally unresponsive before midday. Then out came backgammon sets and copies of "All the President's Men." With spirits and libidos revived there began an exchange of meaningful glances, the mating ritual called "cruising." (Once secret gay slang, the word has been picked up by many young heterosexuals to describe their own version.) "Cruising while we're cruising," observed a Laguna Beach Realtor peering over his dark glasses. "Let's hope no one makes a tacky joke about it."

A marathon poker game staked itself to a shady corner by the bar. Pots often ran up over $200, leading to a most stoic concentration ("Did I hear someone say we just passed Cuba?"). One regular usually played in the nude. Another, a Manhattan decorator, appeared during the Hawaiian party in a sarong and $20,000 worth of diamonds, announcing to the astonished table: "They're always just sitting in the goddam vault." A lesbian couple, the game's big winners, reportedly netted $1,200 by week's end.

Almost nothing disturbed the sundeck's perfect peace. A few men were uptight about overzealous picture-takers for fear of discovering themselves smiling up out from their hometown newspaper. This was solved by setting limits on the photographer employed by the ship, whom nobody knew, and trusting to the discretion of the others. The few holdout worriers learned to turn their faces away.

Daytime amusements included some optional events not likely to please a censor—they were gay versions of the stag party's moment when the girl jumps out of the cake. Example: a sado-masochistic fashion show of leather getups, including harnesses and G-strings. As pairs of models posed in master-slave tableaux trying not to laugh, and a tape recorder played the moans and shrieks of someone being savagely whipped, an announcer named Brian chirped his commentary as if the poolside were a runway at Bonwit Teller: "John is wearing a lovely two-piece vest and matching chaps combination. What lines. If the evening gets warm, he can slip out of the top . . ." Noticing the captain watching from the bridge, Brian ad-libbed: "Of course, these clothes have no interest for the crew—they're all STRAIGHT." The captain facetiously nodded his agreement and turned thumbs down, winning a big hand of applause. The ship had at least the usual complement of gay crew members.

There were, as well, the usual shipboard diversions: movies, bridge, cooking classes, jogging, bingo, calisthenics, sauna, piano concerts. One could help with the daily changing of decorations in the grand salon, an ambitious design plan built around the idea of the boat's being a "floating time capsule." Each night celebrated a 1975 holiday to come: New Year's Eve, Valentine's Day, Everybody's Birthday, Lei Day, Bastille Day, Halloween and finally, to help with decompression to reality, Christmas Eve.

Release from a week of Kiwanis clothes came on the night of the Halloween costume contest. It was a Hieronymus Bosch dress-up affair that attracted Devils, Adams, mutants, a real-life Austrian prince sporting a cardboard crown, even a five-man crepe-paper caterpillar. Clearly the audience's runaway favorite was a smiling, gray-haired entrant of dignified mien who paraded in "The Emperor's New Clothes." He was, of course, stark naked.

Some passengers opted for the land tours to Mayan ruins. Planes were chartered for a much-awaited trip to the lost jungle city of Tikal but were grounded by a low cloud ceiling; so, making the best of a gray day in port, most everyone ambled in small groups into the village's open-air market.

Round-eyed *niños,* more accustomed to sedate tourists in orthopedic shoes, clung to their mothers' skirts in fear and wonder at the sight of these fast-talking, fast-spending invaders. On the other hand, some passengers were moved by the cruel contrast between the market's wretchedness and shipboard posh. In a manner typical of some gays, true feelings were covered by firing wisecracks: "Hey, did you notice? No fleas in this market . . . that's because the flies ate them."

Two live chickens were brought back to the ship and christened Danielle and Debby Sue. When someone mischievously wafted them with a "popper" (a drug inhaled to rescue waning ardor), Danielle promptly laid an egg and Debby Sue engaged in a lust-crazed tussle with a Gucci carryall.

Dining on the Renaissance offered a pageant of courses that was elegant but bland. Referring to a showy but tasteless rack of lamb, a Broadway producer asked, "Why all this bother about fanciness instead of flavor." As compensation, one could enjoy the quite passable wines that were complimentary at all meals.

After-dinner "showtimes" on cruise ships generally run to a few musical numbers and horseplay served up by a hired baritone and a waltz team doubling as dance instructors. On this cruise the entertainment was often first-rate. Michael Greer, for example, the gay world's Jonathan Winters, achieved a kind of communion of love with the audience. Like George Burns at a Friars' Roast, these were his people and everything worked. "Have you noticed the boat lisping to one side?" he rasped, and the crowd roared.

A male singing trio named Gotham stopped the show three different nights with slick song styling and a repartee that owed a lot to Bette Midler. Each time they sang the old Andrews Sisters song, "Hold Tight," they asked the audience to shout out the answer to its line, "What is my fa-vor-ite dish?" and got back "FISH!" so loud it nearly lowered the lifeboats.

Greer and Gotham and the other professional acts all more or less concentrated on gay material. Would it ever play on a mass medium like TV? "It's coming," said Greer over a drink in the piano bar. "Take comedians. There are big stars now who avoid the sexual stuff but get big laughs doing straight material with a gay delivery."

After the show, with the flick of some switches, the grand salon became a discotheque as loud, dark and smoky as any on Manhattan's East Side. Some passengers stayed to bugaloo, some retired to cabins as singles and couples or regrouped into small pot parties. Others strolled out to the balmy decks for fellowship around the bar and a bit of cruis-

ing. Rumors had it that flash orgies might spring up in the outer deck's shadowy recesses but, judging by what anyone could report firsthand and a couple of the reporter's own forays, they were just rumors. As on a heterosexual cruise, the action was in the cabins. For those without a rendezvous, a typical day might end with a 4 A.M. nightcap and a bowl of onion soup in the taverna.

"The best week of my life," was the fairly common reaction voiced by a 26-year-old who runs his father's small construction company. "Only thing is, next time I'm going to get around and make more friends. Why, I'll bet there were 50 people I didn't meet."

Next time? With success on their hands, the Islanders have promised another cruise, "but not right away—not for eight or ten months at least," says Flettrich. "It's a huge job and we don't want a followup to flop." (Announcements of another cruise will be mailed to people sending a postcard to The Islanders Club, 322 East 34th Street, New York 10016.)

On the last afternoon, passengers assembled on the aft deck to select "Mr. Renaissance." It was not to be a muscle contest, but more like the Miss Congeniality award Bert Parks hands out every year. Twenty-five candidates lined the rail, and Mr. Renaissance, a TV actor known to soap opera fans, was chosen by applause. He blushed appropriately when a red satin robe was draped over his shoulders, and then, flashing a smile, stepped up to the microphone.

"A moment ago I thought this spelled the end of my career," he said, referring to certain firing if his sponsors heard their leading man was some kind of beauty queen. "But I'm really proud to be part of the cruise," he continued, and a hush fell over the audience. "It's nice we can do something we enjoy so much that also lets us feel righteous and good about doing it."

The audience went wild with cheers and shouts—they knew what he was talking about. Many gays, like some members of other minorities, tend to accept and believe their own bad reputation. Back home, even their friends were betting that any 300 gays together on a boat for one week would sink it with bitchery, pretension and bad manners. So they themselves were surprised when the week passed in a warm spirit of moderation and mutual respect.

"Something happened out there on the Renaissance—everyone still keeps telling me," says Flettrich. "While we were having the laughs, we were sort of changing our minds about each other."

The Growth in Group Travel

Gay people have traveled singly or in couples for years with few if any complications. But it was not until about 1969, the date of a Manhattan street protest usually cited as the start of the gay liberation movement, that gays started going in for group travel. That winter saw the formation of Gypsy Feet (1621 Second Avenue, New York), a club devoted to stretching travel dollars. Membership has grown to 2,000, mostly men in their thirties and forties, who pay $15 annual dues to choose from nearly 500 tour packages and charter flights. Examples of 1974 offerings: $209 for a four-day Thanksgiving weekend in London; $299 for Rio de Janeiro the week after Mardi Gras but before the last hurrah. (To both prices were added 10 per cent tax and service. Also, these costs were based on affinity group air fares: one must be a member for six months to take part.) Slightly older, more affluent gays are served by Hanns Ebensten Travel (55 West 42d Street, New York), a wholesale-retail organization which added just one all-male escorted tour to its regular line in 1973. Now it offers seven such packages with 13 departures. Among them, a Devil's Island (French Guiana) tour which, with some amenities, includes accommodations for 30 men in the prison's adapted guards' quarters, and a week on rubber rafts shooting the rapids of the Snake River in Idaho. "This one's popular with a lot of Marlboro Men types," Ebensten says. New this year, and his most ambitious plan to date, will be an all-male two-week Galapagos Islands cruise aboard a 66-passenger private ship leaving Aug. 22.

Gypsy Feet, Ebensten and the Islanders Club share most of the small but growing gay group market in the tristate area. There are also a few individual travel agents, like Bill Lucente of Linden Travel (41 East 57th Street, New York), who persuaded his straight employers to let him package a 14-day Greek Isles land-sea-air tour for 20 gays for late August this year. "This is a whole new thing for us," says Marilyn Carr, a Linden partner, "but the market looks wide open and we're backing Bill 100 per cent."

Thus far, few gay women have seemed to be attracted to the group idea. But there may be more women on gay packages in the future. Says Valerie Perez, president of Gypsy Feet: "When we were mentioned in a newspaper recently, you wouldn't believe how many calls we had from straight married women. They're free to go, they've heard it's a ball to travel with the guys and they figure back home their husbands won't get uptight."

Cliff Jahr is a writer who lives in New York City.

* * *

October 24, 1993

BUFFALO GALS

By JEANNINE DELOMBARD

BOOTS OF LEATHER, SLIPPERS OF GOLD: The History of a Lesbian Community
By Elizabeth Lapovsky Kennedy and Madeline D. Davis
Illustrated. 434 pp. New York: Routledge. $29.95.

History is written by the winners. If any winners have emerged from the lesbian community's internal struggle for self-representation, they are the predominantly white, well-educated lesbian feminists who have had access to the bullhorn and the media, including the publishing houses, since the late 1960's.

Their depiction of 20th-century lesbian life before the Stonewall riots in New York City in 1969 as a gay Dark Ages is a familiar one in which lesbians eked out a dreary existence in seedy bars, their internalized homophobia and sexism betrayed by their heavy drinking, barroom brawls and butch-femme role playing.

"The Persistent Desire: A Femme-Butch Reader," edited by Joan Nestle (1992), challenged this stereotype with moving personal narratives and poetry. "Boots of Leather, Slippers of Gold," by Elizabeth Lapovsky Kennedy and Madeline D. Davis, examines the working-class lesbian bar community in Buffalo in the 40's and 50's and adds some empirical weight to the claims made by Ms. Nestle and others. The 45 oral histories of white, black and Indian lesbians do not deny that fighting, drinking, seedy bars and butch-femme roles were central to pre-Stonewall blue-collar lesbian culture. But, the authors argue persuasively, these behaviors signify the community's cultural richness and capacity for resistance, not self-hatred and passivity.

Drinking and congregating in bars was—and still is—an important way for lesbians to carve out some much-needed safe social space. In the 40's and 50's, the authors say, lesbians could not socialize openly at home or in the workplace because of pervasive homophobia. Nor could they take refuge in public places like parks and beaches, where women unescorted by men were easy targets for sexual harassment and violence. Midway between public and private, the bars offered their patrons both anonymity and community. Lesbians defended and expanded this social safety zone by fighting: butch lesbians protected themselves and their girlfriends from male competitors or aggressors on their own turf, and used physical violence to gain entry into hostile straight bars.

Ms. Kennedy, who teaches American studies and women's studies at the State University of New York, Buffalo, and Ms. Davis, who is the chief conservator in the Buffalo and Erie County public library system, maintain that far from signaling a capitulation to heterosexual norms, butch-femme roles broadcast lesbians' identity in a silent yet forceful manner—but one that often left them open to verbal or physical attack. American social and political conservatism after World War II made it a difficult time to be a gay woman, and many bar lesbians responded aggressively.

Aware that it is often a quick jump from history to mythology for those who have been deprived of their heroes, the authors describe the flaws of the Buffalo lesbian community alongside its strengths. Individuals share disturbing memories of hustling drinks, prostitution, alcoholism, and violence inflicted by butches both on femmes and on one another, and the authors have checked any impulse they might have had to romanticize the lives of older lesbians. To the authors' credit, they challenge the notion that any history can tell the whole truth, even as they establish the crucial role working-class lesbians played in paving the way for the gay and women's rights movements. As one interview subject says: "The strength of gay liberation did not originate in the classrooms of middle-class students. Its strength came from those who were tired of being kicked around." They fought back.

"Boots of Leather, Slippers of Gold" is far from being a seamless narrative peopled with reliable, well-behaved characters. This is history as collaborative process, the result of 14 years of research and cooperation between the authors and Buffalo's lesbian community. Ms. Kennedy and Ms. Davis shared not only their authorship but also their authority by involving their subjects in many different aspects of their scholarly research, editing and revision. Thus some of the authors' most insightful conclusions are coupled with frank discussions of what their subjects thought were their misinterpretations and false assumptions, and the subjects' most telling anecdotes are tempered by the authors' references to their inconsistencies.

The book suffers from its dry academic tone and its uninspired organization. Because the authors move so gradually through their material, going from specific to general, the reader who drops away in the opening chapters' dense, often repetitive inventory of the Buffalo bars and their patrons will miss the illuminating, sometimes fascinating interpretations of broader issues like butch-femme roles, serial monogamy and the shifting nature of lesbian identity.

"Boots of Leather, Slippers of Gold" will probably not appeal to a wide audience. Ironically, the authors are much more likely to reach the elite lesbian feminists whose work they are writing against than the working-class bar lesbians whose lives they have so carefully reconstructed. If we have indeed entered an era in which history is no longer written solely by the winners, perhaps it is time to ask: whom is it being written for?

Jeannine DeLombard is a contributing editor at The City Paper, an alternative weekly newspaper in Philadelphia.

* * *

June 25, 1994

GAME TIME

By ANNA QUINDLEN

Several months ago the Rev. Ruben Diaz, a member of the Police Civilian Complaint Review Board, said he saw some real dangers in the Gay Games, the exuberant Olympiad for gay men and lesbians being held this week in New York.

In some fashion the Reverend was right.

The Games, which have been going on at pools, skating rinks and gymnasiums throughout the area, are a terrible threat to those who believe that America's house needs more closets. Because as men and women in warm-up clothes have stepped onto subway trains, gay cops have helped out with security and gay athletes have challenged world records, the Games have come to illustrate the myriad ways in which gay men and lesbians are now part of the mainstream.

This raises the question of why there's a need for Gay Games in the first place, which has been asked more than once as events unfolded. It reminds me of the question kids always ask about Mother's Day and Father's Day and why

there is no kid's day. Of course, we all know the answer is that every day is kid's day.

Every big athletic competition has been essentially the Straight Games. Allegedly the Olympics are open to everyone, and there have been plenty of gay athletes who have competed. But they understood that if they were to get the publicity and the endorsements—and in some countries, stay on the team—it was best to pretend.

That's one of the reasons participants in the Gay Games found cheering a message of welcome from Greg Louganis, who won gold medals in diving events in two Olympics while all around him swirled rumors about his sexual orientation. "I'm real excited to be part of an event that's all about the true Olympic ideals," said Mr. Louganis. "This is our chance to show ourselves and the world how strong we are as individuals and as a community."

"It's great to be out and proud," he concluded.

"There won't just be Liberace to look up to," said Robbie Brown, a swimmer and diver.

They're here. They're queer. They're on television, talking about their moms, their kids and their lovers. The other night Geraldo led a discussion of the issues. His guests included gay activist-athletes and a straight opponent who runs one of those organizations that's supposed to stand for family values. The gay guests were calm and courteous. The family man was obnoxious and rude, the sort of person who gives heteros a bad name. It was no contest in the humanity event.

Ever since the Evil Empire turned out to be a collection of third-world countries, Americans aligned on the far right have tried to cast gay men and lesbians as the new enemy, calculating deviants seducing the nation's young, anti-Avon ladies selling sodomy door-to-door. This simply won't wash. Just as seeing the Russians up close and personal on television humanized them, so seeing the lesbian grandmother of two little girls wearing her gold medal with pride makes the notion of otherness, much less deviance, silly and ignorant.

Civil rights movements work in predictable ways. First government outlaws egregious barriers, in employment, in housing, in education. Bias crimes are prosecuted, role models emerge, and pride becomes a linchpin of progress. The right to be treated as a human being was the essence of both Stonewall and Selma.

But the greatest moment of all comes later on, in life, not law. And that is the moment when your existence becomes commonplace, when a female cop goes the entire day without one stupid comment, when the neighborhood is inhabited by both black and white, when gay nuptials wind up in the social pages.

Mr. Diaz had something other than that in mind. He warned that the Gay Games might lead young people to conclude that there was "nothing wrong nor any risks involved" in what some people persist in calling "the homosexual life style." His warning seemed particularly hollow this week, when the national attention has been focused on the risks involved in the heterosexual life style, among them the risk of being beaten bloody by your husband.

But watching all these proud competitors gathered beneath their own multicolored flag, the risk was very real of seeing them as they really are. And that would be the most dangerous thing that could ever happen to the homophobes. Bottom line, it puts them out of business.

*   *   *

June 26, 1994

RELAXED IN A GAME OF THEIR OWN

By ROBERT LIPSYTE

"I've known world-class athletes, men particularly, who dropped away because of the stress," said Sandy Ledray last week. She gestured down at the Hunter College gym floor where two teams lunged and spiked in a Gay Games volleyball medal match. "Imagine how good they feel, how mellow. Competitive but not nasty. No one's calling the women dykes, no one's sticking tampons in the guys' lockers."

Ledray, a 35-year-old businesswoman from Seattle, agreed there could be merit in the criticism by some gays and lesbians that the Games trivialized life and death issues and blunted the thrust of confrontational politics. On the other hand, in a week of Games going, it was hard to find an athlete or serious spectator who hadn't found it a life-enhancing experience.

"It's hard to explain how thrilling it is to feel affirmed as a gay person and an athlete at the same time," said Pat Griffin, a 48-year-old triathlete. "I was an athlete in high school and college, I was a high school and college coach, and I was never totally there; I was always holding back some part of myself, keeping a secret, on guard. I was never totally free until I came out 10 years ago."

Both Griffin and 42-year-old Gary Reese, a writer from Austin, Tex., remembered the intense thrill of the opening ceremonies at their first Gay Games, in Vancouver four years ago. "That was the first time in my life I felt I could call my-

Oxlon Muhammed/The New York Times

The closing ceremonies of Gay Games IV were held last night at Yankee Stadium, where 11,000 athletes from 40 countries paraded around the field and then packed the stadium seats. The games concluded a week of sports, cultural events, fairs, parties, vigils, marches and conferences.

self an athlete," said Reese. "I'd been cycling competitively in sanctioned events for four years before that. But at a mainstream sports event, gay men always think, 'Is it showing?' and there's a loss of strength, of focus."

For Ledray, Griffin, Reese and thousands of others last week, the Gay Games were a kind of jock fantasy theme park. Professor Joan Gondola of Baruch College/CUNY, founder and chair of the first International Gay Games Congress of Athletes, Arts and Sciences, began to cry during the opening ceremonies. "There were so many of us," she said, "and we looked so good and so happy and relaxed, and you know, if you didn't know it was the Gay Games, there was no reason to believe that almost everyone there was gay or lesbian."

"All week," said Reese, "I thought about being in the envelope and what it would be like to go back."

Even within the Games there are shades of opinion; some athletes just want to compete for medals in an atmosphere without mainstream stress while others want to make a show of commonality with nongays, to create a currency of communication through sports. And, of course, some, like some athletes in the Olympics these Games are modeled on, just want to party.

"Diversity," laughed Griffin. She is an associate professor at the University of Massachusetts-Amherst, where she developed an anti-bias program called Social Justice Education.

"I hope we never lose this sense of a people's Olympics, of inclusions and love and just feeling good about yourself," she said. "Lesbian athletes my age are sad and a little angry at all those years feeling scared and thinking it was our fault. It took me a long time to find out there's nothing wrong with me."

Griffin is on the 60-member team from Northhampton, Mass., that carried a banner declaring itself from "Lesbianville," a name they took after a supermarket tabloid so dubbed their town. Griffin won a bronze medal despite cancellation of her best leg in the triathlon, swimming. Reese also won a bronze, in a cycling race dedicated to the Team Dayton captain, Tom Kohn, who was seriously injured by an automobile while training a week before the games.

"A team is about belonging," said Reese, "which is why this is so important to us. Coming out is a lifelong process and something like this deepens your sense of self. I only hope the Games don't become some nitty-gritty competition. Between these Games and Vancouver, I saw how much more sophisticated the cycling equipment got. And people got much more serious."

Sandy Ledray, sitting next to me at the volleyball, says she hopes the Games won't become too commercialized.

"We need the sponsors, but do we need the liquor companies?" she said. "With all the stress in gay life, there are already a lot of alcoholics."

Ledray, one of an estimated 500,000 Gay Games visitors, came to relax and push Brookside Soap Inc., her natural soaps and oils company. Last Wednesday, she stepped off the red-eye flight and headed toward a Broadway doubleheader—both parts of "Angels in America."

"Maybe there were four straights in the audience," Ledray said. "It was the same feeling I have here right now, the same I had when we marched in Washington last year. Community. Family. Of course, we're so diverse, nothing else binds us, so you can't get together for more than a week. Then you have to deal with laundry, relationships, the real world."

* * *

June 26, 1994

BOYS AND BOYS TOGETHER

By DAVID F. GREENBERG

GAY NEW YORK: Gender, Urban Culture, and the Making of the Gay Male World, 1890-1940
By George Chauncey.
Illustrated. 478 pp. New York: Basic Books. $25.

George Chauncey's enormously informative "Gay New York" goes far to shatter the idea that until the gay rights movement of the 1970's homosexuals lived furtive, isolated and self-hating lives. Drawing on oral histories, diaries, police records, newspaper accounts and other sources, Mr. Chauncey re-creates a New York in which homosexuals "forged a distinctive culture with its own language and customs, its own traditions and folk histories, its own heroes and heroines." Until a crackdown against "immorality" in the Roaring Twenties resulted in a backlash against them, the author argues, homosexuals successfully carved out public and private spaces for themselves, making New York a flourishing gay capital of America for decades.

Mr. Chauncey, who teaches American history at the University of Chicago, limits his study to the gay male world that existed in New York in the 50 years before the start of World War II. Lesbians sometimes patronized the cafeterias, dance halls and nightclubs where gay men congregated; yet the culture and institutions created by homosexual men were different enough from those created by lesbians to warrant independent treatment. Perhaps because sources were lacking, Mr. Chauncey scants upper-class homosexuals, but middle-class and working-class gay life are portrayed in rich detail.

The author maintains that men who sought other men as sexual partners were able to create a complex social life and subculture despite prejudice and hostility because many straight New Yorkers were either indifferent to or curious about gay life. Though legal repression could be harsh, he writes, it was too inconsistently applied to destroy the social networks and institutions of male homoeroticism.

Gay male social life can be documented for earlier periods in New York history, but Mr. Chauncey begins his narrative toward the end of the 19th century, when saloons and dance halls hospitable to gay men were largely restricted to disreputable sections of the city in the Bowery and along the waterfront (where female prostitution also thrived). There, the author writes, men who did not necessarily consider themselves homosexual but who nevertheless sought male sex partners could find cross-dressing, flamboyantly effeminate "fairies" of working-class origin. At some social clubs, he writes, as many as 500 male-male and female-female couples waltzed to live band music.

Mr. Chauncey depicts a society in which men were not "divided into 'homosexuals' and 'heterosexuals'" but rather into categories like "fairies," "queers," "trade" and "gays." "Each," he notes, "had a specific connotation and signified specific subjectivities." As used within the emerging gay subculture, these terms did not have the pejorative connotations that some would later acquire.

The "fairies," Mr. Chauncey argues, adopted effeminacy not because they read psychiatric journals linking homosexuality with effeminacy, as the French historian Michel Foucault and others have maintained, but to make themselves more acceptable to men whose usual sex partners were women. Many men who had sex with "fairies" were from the working class, he writes; at the turn of the century, a high proportion of New York's immigrant communities consisted of unattached men who could think of themselves as "normal" when they turned to a male sex partner, provided that the partner was effeminate and provided that they could define their own role in the interaction as masculine.

Restrictive immigration laws adopted after World War I reduced the influx of unmarried men deprived of women. As the imbalance in the sex ratio of the population diminished, Mr. Chauncey says, so did the number of men who had non-exclusive sexual relations with other men.

Early in the 20th century some middle-class men began to define themselves as "queer" or homosexual in the absence of effeminacy based on their erotic interest in other men. At the same time, Mr. Chauncey suggests, other men began to think of themselves as "straight" or heterosexual based on their lack of erotic interest in other men.

In private, some "queers" might draw on elements of the "fairy" style to camp it up by using feminine names, pronouns and mannerisms to subvert the rigidity of sex roles in the dominant world of "normals." Even though "queers" made up the majority of the gay world, the author writes, much of the public was completely unaware of their existence because their appearance in public did not violate the conventional expectations.

Some "queers" sought other "queer" partners, Mr. Chauncey writes; others, considering themselves psychologically feminine even though they were not effeminate in appearance or manner, sought "highly masculine 'normal'" men who held blue-collar jobs, many of whom—including quite a few who were married—responded to their solicitations. The composer Charles Tomlinson Griffes, for example, established a long-term relationship with a married Irish policeman.

Although there was little organized political activity in New York's gay world in the first half of the century, the exigencies of daily life gave a political meaning to virtually every public social encounter, Mr. Chauncey maintains. In those years gay men displayed camp behavior in restaurants and bars, they held hands and embraced in public, they developed dress codes so that they could identify one another, and they spoke in argot so that they could communicate, if they wished, without revealing their homosexuality to outsiders.

They did so at no small risk; men who were identified publicly put themselves in jeopardy of assault, arrest and loss of employment. But despite these risks, gay men socialized in public, seeking sex partners or simply companionship in places where "normals" also socialized, in addition to establishments that catered largely to gay men. Over time the gay social world expanded territorially from the Bowery, establishing enclaves in Harlem and in bohemian Greenwich Village, then in the Times Square neighborhood.

Far from being hidden, its existence was well known. Gay gathering spots were listed in guidebooks, and huge numbers of spectators attended well-publicized drag balls in Harlem and Midtown venues. A "pansy craze" developed in the 1920's, with speak-easies featuring female impersonators and other gay-oriented entertainment that drew both gay and straight audiences who prided themselves on their sophistication. Popular songs, films, plays and novels gave increasing visibility to gay life. Visitors to New York were able to find gay establishments within hours of their arrival.

But toward the end of Prohibition a backlash was mounted against such gay behavior and visibility, Mr. Chauncey writes. In 1927 the New York State Assembly barred performances of plays dealing with sexual "degeneracy" or "perversion." Threatened with a boycott by the Roman Catholic-led Legion for Decency, Hollywood agreed in 1934 not to depict homosexuality in movies. Hundreds of bars closed after the State Liquor Authority revoked the liquor licenses of establishments that had gay entertainers or served an identifiably gay clientele. Arrests for homosexual solicitation rose dramatically. A closet was being built, the author writes, and public gay life forced into it, rendering it largely invisible to those who were not gay.

Mr. Chauncey's illuminating account of these developments demonstrates that the resourcefulness, creativity and courage of modern gay activism had its antecedents in earlier generations. A sequel volume, in which Mr. Chauncey carries the history of gay New York forward to 1975, is eagerly awaited.

David F. Greenberg, a professor of sociology at New York University, is the author of "The Construction of Homosexuality."

* * *

June 28, 1994

A SLICE OF SPORTS IN DRAG

By IRA BERKOW

Gay Games IV are gone from New York, but they have left an indelible, colorful imprint, and not just pink. Other hues are red, white and blue.

The weeklong games, which ended Saturday, have suffixed themselves with a self-bloated numeral, like the Olympics and the Super Bowl. But, like much else with these games, they seemed to do so with a wink, which was frequently missed in the coverage by mainstream news organizations.

Although many of the issues raised during the games were indeed serious—from AIDS to problems in the military—the gaiety in the Gay Games was underplayed. What was left out was the full spectrum of gay life that was unabashedly demonstrated, from the irregular styles of dress to the merry spirit of competition.

The many-layered intentions of the participants were brought to my attention at the pairs figure skating at Abe Stark Recreational Arena in Coney Island.

This was to be a unique event, two skaters of the same sex in organized competition rather than the typical pairing of boy and girl sweeping about the ice entwined.

The pair of skaters I came to see, Jean-Pierre Martin and Mark Hird of Canada, were last on the program for the afternoon. And there were seven pairs ahead of them.

It turned out that, in the Gay Games, it was sometimes hard to tell the players even when you had a scorecard. The organizers and participants intended it that way, and the 600 or so spectators in the arena seemed to love it that way, including those with a variety of T-shirts that featured slogans such as "I Can't Even Think Straight!"

One of the first pairs was Tatum Blass and Brett Koop. When they skated onto the ice, one wore a formal white shirt and black pants and a black Dutch Boy's cap, and the other was bedecked in a black feather headband and black off-the-shoulder bustier and a white hoop skirt. The individual in traditional men's attire was the woman and the one in conventional female dress was the man.

During the skating routine, the woman dressed as a man playfully pulled the skirt from the man dressed as a woman to reveal a tutu not unlike the one worn by Oksana Baiul in the Lillehammer Olympics. Then that skater yanked away the pants from his partner and revealed a short white skirt like the one worn by Nancy Kerrigan.

It was a spoof compounded by a spoof. But this, as much as anything else, seemed to be what the Gay Games hoped to be about, a freedom to openly enjoy sexuality and express it without fear of reprisal or ostracism.

While the news media's reporting often centered on actual competition, with scores and placings—including legitimate world records in masters' swimming set by Bruce Hayes, a one-time Olympian—the essence of the games was participation, with no qualifying necessary and with everyone assured of getting a medal. It was what the Olympics might have been about before someone discovered big money could be made from it.

The competition was so uneven, in fact, that one pair of female figure skaters wore knee guards, a wise decision since these neophytes spent as much time sliding on the ice as skating on it. But this pair of lesbians wore red dresses cut with flowing ribbons to remind us of AIDS, which made one statement, and the song they chose, "Once I Had a Secret Love," made another. A pair of male skaters wore Army-style garb with black tape X's across their mouths to protest the ban in the military on confessing one's homosexuality. Another pair of wobbly skaters included a drag queen with a blond wig who wore a pink tubetop across his hairy chest.

Then came Martin and Hird, who skate professionally in ice shows. Their considerable skills were obvious, and, to be sure, entertaining. They were identically attired in striking unitards that bore black stripes and eye-designs on a tan-flesh-colored backdrop. Their faces were similarly marked. The costumes sought to represent ancient signs that speak of the universality of man.

"Two men skating in pairs is unacceptable in most places," said Martin. "We'd like to be able to change that. We bring a different kind of dynamic than the stereotype of the boy-meets-girl romance angle. There is a different kind of athleticism, and one that can be entertaining."

The figure skating at Coney Island was unconventional, as were the games themselves, to those who view sports conventionally. And they took place, fittingly, almost within the shadows of the Statue of Liberty, which proclaims the opportunity for all men and women to live freely, and says nothing about which one must wear a dress.

* * *

June 29, 1994

GAY GAMES ADD VISTAS FOR COUPLE

By MICHAEL T. KAUFMAN

Catherine Hughes and Jane Morrigan should have got back by now to their Nova Scotia farm after the 24-hour drive from New York. They probably will already have hung up the bronze medal that Ms. Hughes won in the 1,500-meter race at the Gay Games, and the one Ms. Morrigan received for singing with the gay and lesbian chorus during their week in New York.

"It's been a pretty wonderful time," Ms. Hughes said as she prepared for the long journey to the small dairy farm in Pictou County, where most of the 25 cows are named after the two women's feminist heroines. "We actually met the real Joan Nestle here," said Ms. Hughes, referring to the founder of the Lesbian Herstory Archives, for whom they had named one of their heifers. "That was a first."

The women have been together for seven years, working the remote farm since 1988. It has meant hard work through long days and bitter winters and, until they traveled to the New York games and the celebration of unity, they had never spent so much as a night away from the farm.

"We started planning last fall, and we were lucky enough to find another lesbian couple who were willing to look after the farm," Ms. Morrigan said. "As soon as the snow turned to mud, Catherine started training on a forest road, running with our dogs. Then, especially for the race she bought red shorts for 25 cents in our local thrift shop, tightening the waistband with a safety pin."

"But the race was only a small part of what we came for," said Ms. Hughes, who was still delighted and surprised with her third-place showing in the 18- to 29-year-old category. "What we were looking for was a sense of being with all kinds of gay and lebian people who respect diversity. Back home we know a number of lesbians who are high moral ground lesbians, quite judgmental, rigid and very eager to tell other people how they should live."

"Allies are not always obvious," said Ms. Morrigan. "We've won over some conservative farmers because they admire hard workers, and at the same time we've been betrayed by some of our sisters." She recalled how a local lesbian group threatened them with ostracism for alerting local authorities to a case of a neighbor being beaten by her husband.

"Their ideology is that real lesbians should never have anything to do with officials, no matter what, and they gave us a hard time," she said.

Ms. Hughes said that even in rural settings political battles could be nasty. "It made us hope that during the games we would find solidarity and tolerance and solidarity and diversity and that is exactly what we discovered right from the start."

Ms. Morrigan took up the conversation. "In one of the speeches at the opening ceremonies, somebody said that those of us who had come were all things, not just victims, but also victimizers, the strong and the weak, whatever was reflected in humanity, was reflected in us, and I loved that.

"I also loved being in the city, among so many different kinds of people, all of whom seemed to be getting along. New Yorkers who weren't queer were stopping to give us directions and chat. It seemed to me that for them we were just another ethnic group. I kept my credentials around my neck all the time and even though people back home warned us to be careful, particularly when riding the subways, I have to tell you after a couple of days I felt safer here than at home."

Another thing she felt happy about was what she described as a growing sense of integration among the visitors. "Even though I've been out as a lesbian for 20 years, I haven't had too much contact with gay men," said Ms. Morrigan, adding that she suspected that she was not unusual. "But during the week, lesbians and gay men were talking, greeting each other all over town. Of course, we came here as political allies, but maybe we can now get to know each other."

Of the many events that Ms. Hughes had gone to, she said, one of the best had been a drag-queen march at Tompkins Square Park.

"Until then, everybody had been pretty much on their best behavior, very proper and conservative and polite and all that," she said. "And here were these glorious, bold drag queens trying out all sorts of identities and possibilities. We put on bow ties and marched with them, but there was no way we could match what they were doing in their gowns and fantastic designs. Just being there made me feel I was part of a remarkably varied and colorful family. I think I will always remember one man with gossamer wings who kept jumping and shouting, 'I'm free, I'm free.'"

While they were in New York, two of their cows had given birth and, according to the farm-sitters who phoned, both mothers and calves were doing well. Now, the short vacation was over and the women were taking their impressions home for further consideration. But first they would have to bring in the hay.

* * *

December 8, 1996

THE GAY PARTY PLANET MOVES INTO A WIDER ORBIT

By BOB MORRIS

MIAMI, Dec. 3—They came in white stretch limos, rental convertibles and tour buses. They came on drugs and off them, to find Mr. Right or to get over Mr. Wrong, to gape or to be gaped at, for a good cause or for far more selfish impulses.

Some 2,500 revelers, mostly gay men with tans and the physiques of Calvin Klein underwear models, flocked into the Vizcaya Museum and Gardens in Miami last Sunday night for the 12th annual White Party, benefiting Health Crisis Network, the city's largest AIDS organization. They had paid $125 for tickets and were wearing everything from white dinner jackets, caftans and chinos to angel wings and devil-may-care white spandex briefs.

"This is silver, but it's a very white silver," said a sculptured young Canadian wearing not much more than a silver superhero cape and a rhinestone in his naval.

Among the smattering of single women, there was one in a white wedding gown who seemed particularly out of place and another in clinging white crocheted pants. "I'm not getting many looks tonight," she said. "But I'm not surprised."

In the ever-expanding international list of dance-until-after-dawn events called circuit parties, held mostly for AIDS charities, the White Party is considered the crown jewel.

Circuit Noise, a giveaway magazine for what it calls "crazed party boys," describes the informally linked circuit-party scene as "the chance to escape to an altered world." In that "altered world," thousands of affluent gay men convene from around the world for what amounts to several other-worldly nights packed onto pulsing, steamy dance floors.

"Circuit parties are a sociological phenomenon," said Alan Brown, a freelance reporter who covers the circuit's 50 parties a year, ranging from Hotlanta in Atlanta to the Black Party in Manhattan to Mardi Gras in Sydney, Australia. "Being in a room with thousands of beautiful gay men can be a very empowering experience. Of course, the narcissism can be intimidating, and for outsiders the debauchery is hard to understand. But only a community so acquainted with grief could sustain this level of celebration."

Witnesses to the pre-AIDS Black and White parties at the Saint disco in New York, which are credited as a model for today's circuit parties, might argue that grief is not the only inspiration.

Cindy Karp for The New York Times

They could have danced all night, and did: part of the crowd of 2,500 at the White Party at the Vizcaya Museum and Gardens in Miami last Sunday.

But then, circuit parties are many things to many people. Some see the circuit as a bonding experience and rite of passage for gay men who missed the fun of college fraternity life, or as the gay equivalent of "rave" parties for heterosexual 20-somethings. Some even see the circuit as a blueprint for the way the whole world will be evolving, given changes in post-modern values and the objectification of the male body in popular culture. Most commonly, its devotees see the circuit as a self-affirming alternative to family life, if not a radical rejection of traditional heterosexual culture.

"By being here at the White Party tonight," Mr. Brown said, "I feel like I'm spending Thanksgiving weekend with my family."

Of course, many people are not so enthusiastic about circuit parties. Last spring, Representative Robert K. Dornan, Republican of California, spoke out against the drug-taking at the Cherry Jubilee dance held in April in a federally owned building in Washington. Even some sponsors of the Morning Party last August in Fire Island Pines, an annual benefit for Gay Men's Health Crisis, questioned the value of fund-raisers where the use of euphoria-inducing drugs like ecstasy and ketamine (Special K) are considered the equivalent of L.S.D. at a Grateful Dead concert.

No matter what anyone thinks, though, one thing about the movement cannot be disputed. So much money is spent that Miller Brewing, Anheuser-Busch, Stolichnaya, American Airlines and other mainstream companies are now sponsors. Out and About, a gay and lesbian travel newsletter, wrote that $4 million to $6 million was generated last year in admission ticket sales alone. And in Miami Beach, officials estimated that $10 million was spent by visitors for the White Party week of all-night dances.

"A lot of the return of Miami Beach is because of the gay community, so we celebrate and support it, and this is their

Cindy Karp for The New York Times

The White Fantastic: Max Sanchez, who made the costumes, Jack Meharian and Cory Colton.

ultimate event," Nancy Liebman, a City Commissioner, said on Vizcaya's terrace overlooking Biscayne Bay.

Ultimate it was. Amid the Italian Renaisance fountains and rococo splendor, there was a 110-foot-yacht leased by Jules Millman, a major White Party sponsor and the owner of a telephone sex-line business. There were white twinkling lights, guests drinking milk and Absolut vodka displays set among the 35 acres of the former winter estate of James Deering, a founder of International Harvester. Barry Diller was here, Valentino there and the new Mr. South Beach everywhere.

There were also a number of heterosexual supporters of the Health Crisis Network, who find the White Party a fun and worthy addition to ballet and hospital benefits. "We're getting married here in March," said Shelley J. Kravitz, a Dade County judge, who was with her fiance, Jose Garcia-Pedrosa, the City Manager of Miami Beach. "I'll be wearing ivory, not white."

Nearby, Michael Aller, the tourism and convention coordinator for Miami Beach, was praising city politicians for their gay sensitivity. "Miami Beach has a very pro-active City Commission," Mr. Aller said. "In fact, they're here right now, looking for a date for me."

Some date-gathering was more clandestine.

In a small garden shrouded in darkness, men stood alone or walked through a topiary maze, cruising for partners. Nearby, beside a row of neoclassical statues of ancient gods, Phillip Hill and Keith Weinberg, two enormously muscular visitors from Atlanta, were causing a sensation in ancient-looking collars and cuffs they had been issued when they played temple builders at the opening ceremony for the Olympics last summer.

"Each year I come to this event," said Mr. Weinberg, a computer programmer, "and there are more beautiful men. I wonder where it's going to end. Maybe we'll become more like the ancient Greeks, who were into beautiful men, too, but also into philosophy and art. That wouldn't be so bad."

On the terrace of the 80-year-old mansion, which had become a writhing mass of groping, shirtless torsos dancing to a pounding beat, more guests were philosophizing.

"We are different," said Glenn Albin, the editor of Ocean Drive magazine in Miami Beach, "and parties like this are how we are different."

Christopher Makos, the New York photographer, whose latest book is "Makos Men," agreed. "The 21st century will be all about the individual, and at a party like this, the individual is god," said Mr. Makos, who was a friend and muse to Andy Warhol.

"Happiness is the goal," he continued. "Everybody's trying to find happiness. A mother finds happiness baking oatmeal cookies for her kids. The kids find happiness in eating them warm. For these men, working out, getting a tan, finding the right white outfit and staying up past dawn for four nights in a row makes them happy. Why should I judge that?"

Happiness may have been the goal for most guests. But for a few, health was the real issue. Last Sunday was, after all, World AIDS Day. Inside the mansion, officials from Health Crisis Network—which, at a time when government cutbacks are crippling services, raised about $500,000 from the party—were making heartfelt testimonials about AIDS.

They spoke of education, prevention and care, and they also cited a new report by the American Public Health Association about high levels of unsafe sex among visitors to South Beach.

"We are all warriors in the battle against AIDS," one speaker said.

"The Health Community Network," said another, "understands the new era of the AIDS epidemic."

Their voices were filled with intention. But they had to speak up to be heard above the insistent beat of the music outside.

It is often said that circuit parties, with their suffocatingly hot dance floors teeming with men in tight little circles of lust, defiance and perhaps fear, are ritualistic, tribal experiences. If that's so, then the drumbeats rising off the dance floor at Vizcaya might have been sending a message out to the world. But like many post-modern phenomena, that message could be interpreted in any number of ways.

Tom Cunningham, the Mayor of South Miami, who has worked on the White Party since its beginnings 13 years ago, saw the message as one of love. "I'm not a disco guy," said Mr. Cunningham, who is H.I.V.-positive and had just gotten out of the hospital earlier in the day. "But I think that anybody who would pay $125 to support this cause is doing something worthwhile."

Some shirtless men with their arms wrapped around one another passed by, seemingly oblivious to everything but getting back onto the dance floor. Mr. Cunningham shook his head almost imperceptibly.

"Of course, in my opinion," he said, "people should keep their shirts on in an elegant setting like this. But we're not put on this earth to judge people."

* * *

December 30, 1997

OFFERING THE CREAM OF A HALF-CENTURY OF NAME-BRAND GAY LIFE AND GOSSIP

By GEORGE CHAUNCEY

THE GAY METROPOLIS, 1940-1996
By Charles Kaiser
Illustrated. 404 pp. Houghton Mifflin. $27.

The "Gay Metropolis" of Charles Kaiser's title is less a place than a state of mind. We learn little in this book about the distinctly urban character of gay life or even about the bars, theaters and street corners most gay New Yorkers have frequented since the 1940's, but much about the cosmopolitan elite that made the metropolis appear glamorous. From Truman Capote and Roy Cohn to Christopher Isherwood and Paul Cadmus, this book offers a well-written and briskly paced array of anecdotes about the gay male high and mighty of postwar New York.

Although much of the gossip that animates this book is culled from previously published celebrity biographies, no other book has assembled so many such stories. Most of them are enlivened by Mr. Kaiser's own interviews with elite figures or their beaus, and many are told for the first time. Indeed, the book is less a narrative than a collection of oral histories, with some chapters gathering literally dozens of first-person stories.

Many of those stories are engaging and intriguing. It will startle many readers to learn just how pervasive the gay presence was in the postwar theater, for instance. "West Side Story," the classic postwar drama of teen-age heterosexuality, was created by four gay men: Leonard Bernstein, Stephen Sondheim, Arthur Laurents and Jerome Robbins. Mr. Kaiser's long account of their collaboration prompts one to wonder if the men's shared identity as homosexuals influenced the way they created this tale of forbidden love or affected the way they worked together. Might their collaboration tell us something about the place of gay men in the arts or gay influence on the larger culture or whether a gay sensibility exists?

Characteristically, Mr. Kaiser asks only briefly whether the play reflected a gay sensibility. After reporting that Mr. Laurents thought the fact that they were all Jewish was more significant, he moves on to the next story.

This is typical of the way the book's stories of long-ago trysts, affairs and glamour tend to take the place of historical narrative and interpretation. Curiously, Mr. Kaiser's book in many ways resembles 1940's gay folklore. Before the gay movement developed more direct tactics, homosexuals knew that spreading vicious gossip about homophobes' sexual foibles (or repressed homosexuality) was a way to undermine their stature, and Mr. Kaiser replicates this strategy in his repetition of the well-known rumors about J. Edgar Hoover and Joseph McCarthy.

At the same time, adulatory gossip about the secret homosexuality of respected figures in American culture was a way for gay men to place themselves in the pantheon of cultural heroes from which they had been excluded. "The Gay Metropolis" replicates the strengths and limitations of this tactic as well. Some readers may find it satisfying to learn that the creators of "West Side Story" were gay, but since the significance of this is nowhere analyzed, the knowledge will do little to change the way they think about American history or even gay history.

Nonetheless, the book is distinctly a product of the 1990's, which judges the past from a contemporary perspective rather than trying to understand it in its own terms. The pre-Stonewall years remain enigmatic and indecipherable in this context, as Mr. Kaiser rehashes the old saws about gay self-hatred while simultaneously regaling us with tales of gay cocktail parties, creativity and joie de vivre. The stories seem random, included because they might titillate readers rather than because they help develop a framework for understanding the past. (Thus we get three pages on the 1967 Middle East war because it lets Mr. Kaiser tell us whom Leonard Bernstein slept with after a concert in Jerusalem.)

Mr. Kaiser addresses his need for an analytic framework by adopting Allan Berube's argument in "Coming Out Under Fire" that the World War II military was, in Mr. Kaiser's words, "a great, secret unwitting agent of gay liberation by creating the largest concentration of homosexuals inside a single institution in American history." But he asserts rather than demonstrates this thesis.

Only in the 1970's does Mr. Kaiser, a former reporter for The New York Times and The Wall Street Journal, find his story line. It's an all-too-familiar morality tale of sexual hedonism leading to the AIDS calamity and a heightened compassion among gay men.

Nonetheless Mr. Kaiser's string of oral histories becomes more engrossing here, in part because he has found some wonderful raconteurs. Although the stories continue to focus on the elite (the glamorous story of Studio 54 is told again, while the funkier gay discos where most men went remain unmentioned), they have a greater depth and complexity than the stories from earlier decades.

The story line also picks up in the 1970's because of the explosion then of news coverage of gay issues, which gives Mr. Kaiser greater opportunity to bring his insider's knowledge of journalism to bear. He uses his interviews with key journalists to enliven the tale of how the nation's newspapers, and particularly The Times, came to treat gay issues more extensively and fairly. In keeping with the book's celebrity focus, Phil Donahue gets more credit for increasing gay visibility than the never-mentioned Gay and Lesbian Alliance Against Defamation does, and at times Mr. Kaiser seems simply to be settling old scores with some of his journalistic colleagues. But his dissection of anti-gay television specials and news reporting offers compelling evidence of the bias once rampant in the nation's newsrooms.

Mr. Kaiser's preoccupation with the elite, though initially fascinating, is eventually wearing and ultimately troubling. Most men in this book are rich, white and beautiful (usually "very beautiful"), or at least a beautiful date or hanger-on. It's telling that virtually the only glimpse the book gives us of Harlem comes from Philip Johnson's account of visiting the neighborhood. This is a narrow slice of gay life, masquerading as the whole.

George Chauncey is a professor of American history at the University of Chicago and the author of "Gay New York: Gender, Urban Culture and the Making of the Gay Male World, 1890-1940."

* * *

July 19, 1998

SPORTS AND THE ARTS AT GAY GAMES IN AMSTERDAM

By TRACY METZ

Amsterdam, one of Europe's gay capitals, is anticipating an influx of more than 200,000 people for the fifth Gay Games—the first to be held outside North America. From Aug. 1 to 8, 15,000 participants from 64 countries will compete in 29 sports events and take part in 14 artist's workshops.

Badminton, ice hockey, volleyball, wheelchair dancing and a marathon along the route of the 1928 Olympic race in Amsterdam are among the competitions to be held throughout the city and also in Amersfoort, a town east of Amsterdam, which will be the site of the swimming events.

According to Paul van Yperen, a spokesman for the Games, the competition will be open to both homosexuals and heterosexuals.

In addition to Government subsidies and contributions from 38 private sponsors, including KLM Royal Dutch Airlines and Kodak, the Games are also the recipient of the first contribution (about $55,000) from the European Commission to a gay event.

Even the Ministry of Defense is helping out with 3,000 cots to be set up for athletes in schools and campgrounds, although there is still hotel availability.

Three thousand volunteers are being trained to help organize the events and manage crowds. Central Amsterdam is expected to be the busiest during the games, particularly the area around Dam Square, Friendship Village and gay centers such as the Reguliersdwarsstraat.

When this event was first held in 1982 in San Francisco, the United States Olympic Committee sued to forbid the use of the name Gay Olympics; the organization subsequently changed the name. The event was last held in 1994 in New York.

In addition to the usual gold, silver and bronze medals, commissioned by the municipal Amsterdam Fund for the Arts and designed by Marcel Wanders, there is a fourth medal that all participants will receive.

Cultural events—including some 40 exhibitions—will complement the games. At the Rijksmuseum, "Olympic Gods" will feature prints and drawings of Jupiter, Adonis, Diana and other mythological beings, and at the Stedelijk Museum for Modern Art, lesbian and gay artists will display their sculptures, paintings, photographs and other works.

Many theaters are putting on special shows, among them two performances on Aug. 3 and 4 by Harvey Fierstein in the Municipal Theater.

There will be free concerts on Dam Square, open-air theater in the Vondelpark, and presentations of recent gay-themed films on an outdoor screen every evening after 10 on Nieuwmarkt Square. The opening ceremony in Amsterdam Arena, on Aug. 1 at 8 P.M., will include performances by Dana International, the Israeli transsexual who won this year's Eurovision song contest, and the Weather Girls accompanied by a hundred dancers in sailor outfits.

Most of the sports events are free; the swimming, dancing, body-building and ice hockey competitions and a number of finals will cost between about $6 and $12.

For tickets, call (31-20) 420 0200; for accommodations, call (31-20) 427 1998 or (31-35) 542 9333.

On the Web: www.gaygames.nl.

* * *

August 1, 1998

EVENT FOUNDED TO FIGHT BIAS IS ACCUSED OF IT

By KIRK JOHNSON

The Gay Games, founded 16 years ago as a way to bring together through sports competition people who were being excluded from mainstream life, have found themselves on the eve of the fifth "Gay Olympiad" in Amsterdam being accused of the very thing they were created to fight: sexual discrimination.

From within the Games' ranks, newly vocal sexual minorities—led by athletes who have changed their sex—have arisen to denounce what they say is bias against them by tradition-minded Gay Games organizers.

The problems are in many ways a result of success. The Games began in San Francisco in 1982 as a purely local event with 1,300 athletes and a budget of $120,000, and they have evolved into perhaps the most visible vehicle for gay pride and identity in the world—an institution of sport and culture expected to draw 15,000 participants from 64 countries, beginning in full this weekend.

But along with growing impact has come a conflict over what the Games are meant to achieve—what face for gay culture they should present to the world, and how the complications of becoming an institution, from the protection of the event's image to the consciousness of potential legal liabilities, should be managed. Rules about gender are where that conflict plays out.

This year, for example, local organizers in the Netherlands have banned mixed-sex couples from competing in the ballroom dance competition—an event that will also be held at the 2000 Olympic Games in Sydney, Australia, as a demonstration sport. The goal, they say, is to present the event as a kind of international showcase for homosexual athletes—

men dancing with men, women with women. What that means, however, is that a lesbian schoolteacher from Brooklyn and her gay male dance partner will not be allowed onto the floor. Gay or not, they are of the opposite sex, and that has been deemed inappropriate.

The change that is drawing the most fire and discussion among the gay participants, however, is a rule that affects only a tiny minority: a requirement that athletes who have changed their sex provide, for the first time, proof of what the rules call "completed gender transition."

Organizers say that concerns over fairness and legal liability have made it imperative that so-called transgender athletes be put into the proper category, especially so that men, with their greater body strength—whether born or created—do not compete unfairly, or perhaps even dangerously, against women. A man on the path to becoming a woman, but not there yet, they say, might still have superior physical strength and weight that could prove decisive in an event like power lifting or tennis, or dangerous to opponents in single-sex women's team sports.

"On the soccer field, a 100-pound waif of a girl has the right to participate in a safe environment," said Roz Quarto, co-president of the Federation of Gay Games.

But while critics of the new policies agree that fairness and safety are important, the central issue, they say, is larger: who is allowed to participate freely in the Games without being challenged about their private lives, and who is not?

"The Gay Games were formed because gay athletes could not compete openly—how ironic that they are now forcing another group of athletes to go back into the closet or face a barrage of stigmatizing obstacles," said Riki Anne Wilchins, the executive director of Gender PAC, a public advocacy coalition for the transgender community, and author of "Read My Lips: Sexual Subversion and the End of Gender" (Firebrand Books, 1997).

Games officials said that rules about "gender transition" were initially proposed by the Federation of Gay Games, the event's governing body, when the Games were last held, in New York in 1994. The idea was ultimately scrapped in favor of a policy that let applicants simply declare their sex with no further questions asked. The re-emergence of the issue—local officials in the Netherlands, unlike their New York counterparts, decided to implement the federation's more restrictive proposals—has made the Games an object of attack even from traditional gay rights organizations.

"Where is their sense of fairness and justice—where does discrimination stop?" said Sydney Levy, research and advocacy director of the International Gay and Lesbian Human Rights Commission, a San Francisco-based organization. "Singling out transsexuals means singling out people who vary from the norm and asking a lot of private questions," he said.

Under the new policies, transsexuals must provide documentation that includes, for example, a letter from a doctor stating that the transgender applicant has undergone hormone treatments for at least two years without interruption, and other proof, through photographs, correspondence or an employer's declaration, that the applicant has lived actively in his or her new sex for at least two years.

The dance competition rules on gender, are, if anything, even more exacting. Officials have said that a man may legally dance with another man who is dressed as a woman. It is also fine if both are dressed as women. Two women can similarly compete looking like a mixed-sex or same-sex couple so long as both are, beneath their costumes, of the same gender.

"We think it is quite unique in a dance competition to have all same-sex couples—it will be one of the most interesting things in the Gay Games," said Niek van der Spek, the director of operations for Gay Games 5.

The Gay Games, which have from their inception been a mix of sport and pageantry, have 29 events this year ranging from hockey to a marathon along the route of the 1928 Amsterdam Olympic Games, plus cultural and arts workshops.

And while Games organizers say they expect only about two dozen transgender participants at this year's Games, gay rights officials say there are probably many more like Loren Cameron who were dissuaded from going at all. Mr. Cameron, a professional photographer and author who changed sex to male from female, trained for six months preparing for the bodybuilding competition. He said he felt that the gender documentation requirement was intrusive and that he could not in good conscience comply with it.

"Basically they're singling out certain people—they're not asking every competitor for proof of gender identity, and I felt that was wrong," Mr. Cameron said. "Isn't it the whole spirit of the Games to celebrate inclusivity out of the 'normal standard?'"

Lee P. Sharmat, the Brooklyn schoolteacher and erstwhile dance competitor, who was on the board of directors for 1994 Gay Games in New York, said that striking the right balance between the role of the Games as a showcase for gay culture and its function as unifying force for gay men and women was hard then, too. The games in New York, she said, were harshly criticized by some who said it had become an event for mainstream society.

Ms. Sharmat, even though she disagrees with the policy that is keeping her out of the dance competition, said she thinks that bringing the Games into broad acceptance—and thus helping break down barriers between homosexuals and heterosexuals—is important. "You do want to mainstream it—the question is, to what extent?" she said.

Ms. Wilchins, the transgender group leader, said the opposite question is more germane: what elements of the mainstream should you avoid taking with you?

"When minorities set up their own structure, they take the best—and the worst—of the majority culture with them," Ms. Wilchins said.

Testing of athletes to determine their actual sex is nothing new to sports. In the 1970's, a battle raged in the courts over whether Dr. Renee Richards, who underwent a sex change to become a woman, could legally compete in the women's division of the United States Open tennis tournament without taking a chromosome test. She won her legal case and did not have to take the test, but lost in the tournament's first round in 1977. In the Olympics, chromosome testing has been required since 1968.

Gay Games officials also said that ballroom dancing plays a bigger symbolic role in Europe, where the image of hundreds of dancers, all same-sex pairs, would be a statement that gay men and women had fully, and openly, arrived.

Games officials are divided about the gender rules, especially on the dance competition. The tradition of the Games has been to allow wide latitude by local organizers, but officials at the Federation of Gay Games said the time may have come to exercise more centralized control.

"There's a lot of people unhappy about not being able to perform—heterosexual and homosexual," said Scott Mandell, the federation's executive director. "But they are the host city, and hopefully when we move on to Sydney in 2002 it will be a different story."

*   *   *

June 11, 2000

JOURNEY TO AN OVERLOOKED PAST

By MARCIA BIEDERMAN

Michael Korie, a lyricist, has nothing against the plaque in Greenwich Village marking the site of the former Stonewall Inn. At that spot, on Christopher Street, gay men battled police in June 1969 and began the modern movement for lesbian and gay rights.

But when Mr. Korie walks the streets of New York, he sees many other places where gay New Yorkers gathered in the decades before the now-legendary Stonewall rebellion. There is no plaque on Columbus Circle to commemorate a Childs Restaurant where gay men created a "cafeteria society" in the 1920's and 30's. No engraved words mark the Bowery's turn-of-the-20th-century "fairy resorts," the nightclubs where rouged men mingled with brawny laborers and uptown swells. And how many tours to Harlem point out the site where men in sequined splendor competed for prizes at an annual drag ball that drew thousands from the early 1920's into the late 30's?

In fact, few New Yorkers realize such places ever existed.

"There's a lot of mythology about the contemporary gay rights movement," said Mr. Korie, a slim, professorial-looking 45-year-old whose credits include the libretto for the 1995 opera "Harvey Milk," a work based on the life of San Francisco's first openly gay city supervisor. "That it began with Stonewall, that gay people were in the closet until then. There have been books and articles about gay life before Stonewall. Nevertheless, that mythology persists."

Tomorrow night at 7:30 in Carnegie Hall, a new choral work with lyrics by Mr. Korie and music by Larry Grossman will try to do what the history books could not. The New York City Gay Men's Chorus will offer the premiere of "A Gay Century Songbook," a collection of songs that traces the evolu-

tion of lesbian and gay culture in New York during the first half of the 20th century. The hourlong piece, which will include a narrative read by the actor Joel Grey, explores how earlier generations of New Yorkers transformed restaurants, parks and streets from Harlem to Brooklyn into places for themselves, despite deep-seated prejudice and legal prosecution.

The song collection is intensely site-specific. "It is so related to New York and has kind of a New York attitude," Mr. Korie said. "I don't know if it will play in Dallas," he added. "I can't see them singing about Dora on the Bowery."

Songwriters have mapped New York for the world beyond its borders, saying the Bronx is up and the Battery's down, that the lights are always bright on Broadway. This work is a Baedeker to a less-well-known city.

Some of these places survive, but many were demolished decades ago. They were urban ephemera, unremarkable parts of the street vernacular, or situated in vice-ridden areas that have since been sanitized, thanks to economic upturns and civic improvements. But they made an indelible mark, said Mr. Korie. Learning where others met for nickel coffees or bootleg gin, he said, gave him a sense of his "own gay roots."

"Gays made such an impact on history that continues to linger in New York's buildings and its spirit," said Mr. Korie, who wrote for The Village Voice and edited a weekly, now defunct, called New York Guide before turning to songwriting in the 70's. His songbook follows a fictional Irish immigrant named Macklin Moran, from his arrival in New York in 1900 until 1948, the year the Kinsey report told Americans that gay men were more common than most people thought.

Seen through Moran's eyes, the Hudson piers of 1900 are where gay veterans of the Spanish-American War sing of their plans to abandon their hometowns and find lodgings in rooming houses. Gramercy Park in 1910 is the setting for lesbian "marriages," like the one between the novelist Willa Cather and Edith Lewis. By 1915, gay-only refuges had emerged in the form of Turkish baths, including the Everard Baths on 28th Street near Sixth Avenue and the Ariston Bathhouse at 55th and Broadway.

Mr. Korie's lyrics are laced with the argot and codes of an earlier subculture, in which gay co-workers found one another by discussing the Ziegfeld Follies on breaks; lesbians endured tweed suits till May; and a red tie worn on Riverside Drive was a sexual semaphore. Many tunes are joyous, reflecting what Mr. Korie calls "windows of tolerance" during which antihomosexuality laws were sporadically enforced. Before the 1930's, the point at which political change led to a sharp escalation in arrests, a bemused or indifferent public allowed visible lesbian and gay enclaves to develop in Greenwich Village, Times Square and Harlem.

But there are also musical reminders of the clouds that hung over the same-sex dance partners in the ballroom of the Hotel Astor near Times Square, the campy kaffeeklatsches at the Horn & Hardart Automat near Bryant Park, and the winter encampments of gay hobos on the Lower East Side. At the prompting of antivice groups, the police occasionally raided even cafeterias.

Still, Mr. Korie said, the point of the songbook is that even in the New York of a century ago, "gay people had an existence that wasn't reflective of fear. They weren't all routinely arrested."

When the Bowery Was In Flower, Resplendently Gay

Certainly the phrase "only in New York" could find no greater relevance than in the Bowery of 1905. One recent morning, Mr. Korie took a visitor to Cooper Square in Lower Manhattan—home to Cooper Union and the offices of The Village Voice—a place where gay life flourished at the turn of the 20th century.

An auto parts store that faces a strip of well-groomed commercial buildings is a reminder of the days before the most recent wave of gentrification. But nothing remains to suggest the time when the Third Avenue El rattled over bars, dance halls and other pleasure palaces for working-men. These included "fairy resorts," nightspots whose attraction was the presence of effeminate men. Known among themselves and to others as "fairies," these entertainers tweezed, powdered and perfumed themselves, fashioning their hair into stylish marcelled waves. Women's apparel—low-cut dresses and high boots—sometimes completed the look, although strict laws against cross-dressing made full drag a rarity.

For profit, or sometimes just pleasure, these men sang and danced with each other and with male patrons, offering sex in rooms behind the bar. At their zenith in the 1890's, at least half a dozen such establishments lined the Bowery, and an equal number could be found in the area known as the Tenderloin, along Sixth Avenue and Broadway between 23rd and 40th Streets.

Crowds of society folk, both men and women, came from all over New York to gawk. "The whole idea of slumming originated not in Harlem but here," said Mr. Korie, "because it was chic to come down here and see the fairies dance."

He lingered in front of 32 Cooper Square, a six-story Georgian-style brick building that now houses several film companies. No. 32 was the site of Columbia Hall, one of the most notorious fairy resorts and one that earned the nickname Paresis Hall, after a medical term for a disease caused by late-stage syphilis.

Mr. Korie's bouncy song "That Way" is set in Paresis Hall. It is a catalog song, containing a seemingly endless list of humorous topical references about Alice B. Toklas, the Ziegfeld Follies' men's lounge and a strip of Coney Island beach along which gay men sometimes paraded in dresses and hats fashioned from beach towels.

"The Committee of 14 would lead 'fleshpot tours' to Paresis Hall and tell people how bad it was," Mr. Korie said, referring to a moral-purity society of the era. Tongue-clucking, he added, was probably accompanied by sexual titillation.

Just a Bar With Patrons Named Truman, Tennessee and Rudolf

The Bowery was also temporary home to the gay hobos who wintered in the cheap lodgings during an era in which crowds of transient workers moved in and out of New York by rail. Older and younger men often paired off in couples of "wolves" and "lambs" The older man helped the younger one find shelter in a Skid Row hotel, and the younger one performed "wifely" domestic duties. Mr. Korie recalls this world in the moody and wistful song "Nothin' Is as Open as the Road."

Whither goes the railway track,
South with Johnny or north with Jack,
Nothin' owned is nothin' owed,
And nothin' is as open as the road

Mr. Korie's next stop was Julius', a bar at Waverly Place and 10th Street. It is not far from the site of the Stonewall Inn and in some eyes nearly as legendary; it played itself in the 1970 film "The Boys in the Band." In the 60's, it was the site of a challenge to state laws forbidding gay bars from obtaining liquor licenses.

"It's well known that Julius' is the oldest gay bar in the city," said Mr. Korie, who learned of the place when he was growing up in Teaneck, N.J. Soon after moving to New York in 1974, he made a pilgrimage to the famed saloon.

The bar dates from 1864, said Tracy O'Neill, the current bartender. Ray Silvano, 74, who was having an early drink, recalled stopping by as a child in the 1930's to plunder the cracker bowls. With its spartan decor, wagon wheel fixtures and chalkboard notices detailing practice schedules for the Barbarians, the bar's softball team, Julius' looks more sports bar than shrine.

But one wall of this nontrendy neighborhood gay bar is plastered with newspaper clippings recalling its days as a gay speakeasy, a favorite of Tennessee Williams, Truman Capote and Rudolf Nureyev. Another wall is a gallery of yellowed celebrity photographs with faded signatures. The hardwood bar is carved deep with generations of initials and messages.

Mr. Korie chose Julius' as the setting for his song "Kieran McHugh Remained Abroad," in which gay veterans of World War I who gathered at the bar during Prohibition describe their return from the battlefield.

Merrily played the marching bands
Welcoming home the straight.
Avenues teemed with patriots
Who now crusade for hate
Saturday nights at Julius'
Drinking to comrades lost—
Our hairy-chested widowhood
Gets sentimentally sauced

But the age of Julius', Mr. Korie said, "doesn't jibe with the popular lore, that we were all closeted until 1969."

Two other famous outposts of early gay society, the Life Cafeteria and a low-priced restaurant called Stewart's, faced each other across Sheridan Square. (The building once occu-

'Fickle and foolish, moody at moments/Hardly a neutral hue./God must have made me/Lavender So I would match with you.'

pied by Stewart's, on Seventh Avenue South between Christopher and West Fourth Streets, now houses a General Nutrition Center.) Men with long hair, light makeup and stylized mannerisms used to meet behind the large plate-glass windows, observed like tropical fish by curious tourists.

It was an era in which the city abounded in rooming houses—several in Manhattan, as well as the St. George Hotel in Brooklyn Heights, were rumored to be predominantly gay—whose single tenants took their meals at inexpensive restaurants like these. Word soon spread about which cafeterias were tolerant of gays, at least at certain times of day.

"They worked on shifts," said Mr. Korie, referring to the late-night hours during which gays could safely gather at certain branches of Childs and Horn & Hardart, two major restaurant chains.

Horn & Hardart Automats were distinctive for dispensing food from little metal compartments. Their outposts were largely unsupervised, and thus attractive to gays.

In some cafeterias, owners tolerated only gays who did not draw attention to themselves. In others, customers were allowed to let their hair down. Notable for its permissiveness was the Childs on 59th Street near Columbus Circle, nicknamed "Mother Childs" because of its prime location

on the gay compass, between Central Park and the theater district.

Another freewheeling Childs, at least in the wee hours, was in the Paramount Theater Building at Broadway and 43rd Street. Mr. Korie owns an illustration of a man decked out in what the lyricist imagines as the "Childs look": peroxided hair, a brightly colored tie and a little lip rouge. In a narrative that is part of the Carnegie Hall program, a middle-aged character describes the Childs crowd:

"At midnight, when I am in bed with a book, they 'drop hairpins' and 'camp' on the tabletops at Childs Restaurant in Times Square. I go only to order pancakes. I must lose weight."

Harlem Takes the Drag Ball To New Heights

In the 1920's, a daring new form of masquerade party was becoming popular in Greenwich Village, Midtown Manhattan and the area near the Brooklyn Navy Yard. But the most spectacular and celebrated of these events, a resplendent annual drag ball, was held in Harlem.

"These made Wigstock look like an Off Off Broadway show," said Mr. Korie, as he headed north by cab in search of 280 West 155th Street, the former site of the Rockland

Palace, where the Hamilton Lodge of the Odd Fellows fraternal society held annual drag balls in the 1920's and 30's. At their height in the late 30's, the balls drew 8,000 dancers and onlookers, blacks from Harlem and whites from throughout the city.

The site is now a parking lot beneath an overpass leading to the Macombs Dam Bridge. A sign advertises parking for Yankee Stadium, just across the Harlem River. Mr. Korie inspected the asphalt for vestiges of the past. "There are no tiaras lying around," he reported.

"This must have been a glamorous location, near the river," he added. In the gospel-tinged number "Sister Hallie Lujah," he imagines the grand entrances made at these events:

Sister Hallie Lujah
You're quite the nun tonight
There in your sequined wimple
You've got that 'inner light'

Another Harlem landmark in the history of gay New York is the Salem United Methodist Church. Now 97 years old, the brick building with a magnificent arched front window still stands at Adam Clayton Powell Jr. Boulevard and 129th Street. It was there, in 1928, that the poet Countee Cullen entered into a brief marriage with Yolanda Du Bois, daughter of W. E. B. Du Bois. (Cullen then went on a honeymoon with the best man.) Cullen, like several members of the Harlem Renaissance, felt compelled to hide his sexual identity.

Well Before Bette Midler, The Baths Were the Place to Be

Mr. Korie's tour reached its coda as he stopped for a bite at the Broadway Diner at the southeast corner of 55th Street and Broadway. The building, mostly occupied by a Best Western Hotel, has no gay historical significance, but its lost twin, the Ariston apartment hotel just to the north, has a rich past. Its basement housed the Ariston Baths, which served an all-gay clientele in the early 20th century. As described in the song "Lunch at the Turkish Baths," this gathering place was a key stop:

My dining club isn't Ivy League,
Although it's exclusively male.
A haven of health and athletics
Devoted to manly aesthetics
Since one has to lunch,
I lunch with the bunch
Who lunch at the Turkish Baths
Commuters contentedly doze off.
A number I know with their clothes off.
How many men hide a nature belied
At lunch at the Turkish Baths?
Pleasantly passes the working day

Rested of body and brain.
Stopping to pick up a rose bouquet,
I race for the Westchester train.
A chap on the opposite aisle
Exchanges a sad little smile
Averting our eyes we assume our disguise
With our newspapers raised in denial

Over a salad at the diner, Mr. Korie recalled that his interest in New York's gay past intensified while he was writing "Harvey Milk" (with the composer Stewart Wallace) and interviewed Scott Smith, one of Milk's lovers, who died of AIDS in 1995. Mr. Smith told Mr. Korie that in the 50's, when Milk was a teenager living in Woodmere, N.Y., he had been arrested for cruising in the Ramble in Central Park. In Mr. Korie's eyes, ordinary gay people, as well as martyrs like Milk, are worthy of attention.

"When I walk the streets here," Mr. Korie said, "I feel that history, that those who came before me, engaged in the same issues that are still important to me today. There's hope for an answer here, and that's what entices other disenfranchised people, not just gays, to come to New York.

"It's in the air, even if the buildings aren't there anymore. That's why I'll always live in New York."

Reading List

In reseaching "A Gay Songbook," Michael Korie consulted several books on gay life in New York. Here are some of the major titles.

"About Time: Exploring the Gay Past," by Martin Duberman.
"Becoming Visible: An Illustrated History of Lesbian and Gay Life in 20th Century America," by Molly McGarry and Fred Wasserman.
"Completely Queer: The Gay and Lesbian Encyclopedia," by Steve Hogan and Lee Hudson.
"The Gay Metropolis: The Landmark History of Gay Life in America Since World War II," by Charles Kaiser.
"Gay New York: Gender, Urban Culture and the Making of the Gay Male World, 1890-1940," by George Chauncey.
"Hidden From History: Reclaiming the Gay and Lesbian Past," edited by George Chauncey, Martin Duberman and Martha Vicinus.
"Out for Good: the Struggle to Build a Gay Rights Movement in America," by Dudley Clendinen and Adam Nagourney.
"Stepping Out: Nine Walks Through New York City's Gay and Lesbian Past," by Daniel Hurewitz.
"Stonewall," by Martin Duberman.
"Terrible Honesty: Mongrel Manhattan in the 1920's," by Ann Douglas.

* * *

Defining Oneself

March 28, 1971

THE DISCIPLES OF SAPPHO, UPDATED

By JUDY KLEMESRUD

As recently as a year ago, most members of the New York chapter of the Daughters of Bilitis, the country's oldest and largest lesbian organization, knew each other only by first names, which were usually false. Meetings, in a small, stuffy, sublet room on West 38th Street, were uninspiring and poorly attended. Younger, more radical lesbians referred to D.O.B., as it is called, as "the N.A.A.C.P. of lesbian groups," and to its members as "Aunt Tabbies."

Today, although they are still in the "Establishment" lesbian group, many Daughters of Bilitis are on the verge of emerging from the closet. A growing minority are using their real names (first and last), marching in protest demonstrations, testifying at hearings on discrimination against homosexuals, appearing on television talk shows and lecturing on college campuses.

This new turn of events so angered 31 D.O.B. members that they recently bolted from the mother organization to form a conservative splinter group that meets monthly in Brooklyn. D.O.B. regulars refer to the new group as "The Bagels" because the dissidents spent much of the first meeting arguing about who would bring the bagels for the next get-together.

What changed D.O.B.? Leaders point to several events in 1970 that moved the organization to alter its traditional way of doing things. In the summer, a younger group of women known as Radicalesbians marched in women's liberation and gay protest parades, carrying banners that identified them as lesbians.

Then, in October, two uniformed policemen burst into D.O.B. headquarters during a meeting and threatened to arrest the president, Ruth Simpson, because there was no occupancy sign on the wall. The officers failed to appear in court two weeks later, but about 50 members from various homophile organizations did, to protest the summons D.O.B. had received.

In December, nine leaders of the women's liberation movement held a press conference in the Washington Square Methodist Church in Greenwich Village at which they issued a statement supporting their homosexual sisters. Several women publicly identified themselves as lesbians, and urged their sisters to do so, too.

"People must speak up as lesbians," said Barbara Love, a comely blonde. "I am a lesbian. We've got to come out of the closet and fight, because we're not going to get anywhere if we don't."

But perhaps the most significant event for the Daughters of Bilitis occurred on Jan. 3, when members opened the first exclusively lesbian center in New York, one of two in the country (the other is in Los Angeles). The center, at 141 Prince Street, in a block of shabby buildings in the lower Village, is a cavernous, second-floor loft with 4,000 square feet of space that has been partitioned into a meeting hall, kitchen and library for lesbian-oriented books. The loft is decorated in the D.O.B. colors: white walls and bright red fireproof curtains. All of the remodeling, with the exception of the plumbing, was done by D.O.B. members.

There was no secrecy about the opening. Press releases invited coverage, saying that photographs and video tapes could be taken of principals. (The only reporters who showed up were women from WBAI-FM, several underground newspapers and this magazine.) The guest speakers were Ti-Grace Atkinson, one of the more radical members of the women's movement, who suggested that heterosexual women wear "I Am a Lesbian" buttons as a sign of support for their lesbian sisters, and Florynce Kennedy, a lawyer and movement activist, who drew laughter when she said: "I dig lesbians. Some of them are my best friends."

The loft was jampacked with women, most of them wearing pants. One man who straggled in was asked to leave, and did. There were teenagers with frizzy Janis Joplin hair; gray-haired grandmotherly types toting shopping bags; black women with Afros; mannish-looking women wearing caps and heavy boots, and a few extremely beautiful women who looked as though they had spent at least an hour applying make-up. Some of the lesbian couples held hands as they sat on wooden folding chairs, listening to the speakers. Everybody seemed to laugh a lot.

Ruth Simpson, a petite 44-year-old public relations woman with a big voice and a pixyish quality reminiscent of Claudette Colbert, called the meeting to order by stomping on a black wooden platform at the front of the meeting hall. She was wearing a camel-colored pants suit and a cameo necklace given to her for Christmas by Miss Atkinson, whom she describes as "my best friend—personally and politically."

"I'll start with an analogy of what I think this center means," Miss Simpson said. "For many years, black women went and had their hair straightened, but underneath they really knew that it was outrageously gay, and not straight at all.

"Is gay proud?" she shouted. "Right on!" the audience yelled back.

"If we get enough gay people to say that," Miss Simpson continued, "then we have no fears for the future."

She gestured toward what appeared to be a closet directly behind the speaker's platform. The sliding black door was partially open. "That's to facilitate traffic in either direction," she said as the audience howled. (Later, she said that the closet hadn't been specifically built by D.O.B. members; it just happened to be there.)

Then Miss Simpson read several letters from young lesbians asking for help in "coming out." One of them, from a 16-year-old, said: "I had been using drugs as a cover-up until I realized I was a homosexual. My high school counselor told me to tell my parents, but I just couldn't. My parents still haven't accepted the fact that my older brother is gay. I would like to come out because then I think it would relieve all these tensions I have."

Miss Kennedy, the guest speaker, said her answer to anxieties like those was "honesty." "I suspect that the more lesbians come out, the freer the whole society will be," she said. "And here's a little bit of primitive analysis. If you tell your parents you will keep your sexual life private, just as they keep theirs private, your mother just might say, 'Oh, that's all right, honey, I've had a lesbian relationship with Mrs. Parker across the street for years.'"

What is a lesbian? Even a lot of lesbians don't know for sure. "A lesbian is a woman who has slept with men and still prefers women," said a bleached-blonde D.O.B. member at the center's opening. Another said that a woman was a lesbian merely if she preferred the company of women to that of men. According to a study on female homosexuality conducted in 1967 by the Society of Medical Psychoanalysts, a lesbian is "any adult female who is having repetitive overt homosexual activity." This is the definition the mental health profession seems to prefer.

The Daughters of Bilitis was founded in San Francisco in 1955 by Phyllis Lyon and Del Martin, two lesbians now around the age of 50 who have lived together for 17 years. Miss Lyon, a secretary with the Council on Religion and the Homosexual in San Francisco, and Miss Martin, a freelance writer, are working on a book about their experiences. They said they founded D.O.B. as an alternative to the gay bars, which many lesbians find degrading because of the inflated prices and often condescending attitudes of bartenders.

The name Bilitis (pronounced "buh-LEE-tus") was taken from the poem, "Songs of Bilitis," written in the late 19th century by Pierre Louys, the French poet. Bilitis was a heterosexual woman who became a disciple of Sappho, the lesbian poet of ancient Greece. But the name was used mostly, Miss Simpson said, "because it was a nice obscure reference."

"If we were doing it today," she added, "we'd probably call ourselves Sappho's Sisters."

Three years ago, D.O.B. had only three chapters, in New York, Los Angeles and San Francisco. Today, there are 14 chapters, the new ones in Boston, Detroit, Cleveland, Denver, New Orleans, Reno, Portland, Ore., North Lake, Ill., El Cajon, Calif., Mattapan, Mass., and Sydney, Australia. National membership is estimated at about 1,500.

According to Miss Simpson, the New York chapter has around 400 members, up 50 per cent from last year. About 60 of them are black. They range in age from 18 to 65, and pay dues of $12 a year. (Some younger lesbians are angry about the age requirement, and one said: "You don't have to be 18 to be gay.") There is an official handshake, so obscure that even Miss Simpson hasn't learned it yet, and an official button: two red interlocking medical symbols for woman on a white background.

The New York membership includes college professors, scientists, unemployed women on welfare, editors, singers, ac-

tresses, secretaries, students, doctors, nurses, certified public accountants, housewives and city employes. Some members are married to men; others have been. Several have been through marriage ceremonies with women and wear wedding bands. At least five members say they are heterosexual and joined either because they had questions about their sexual orientation or because they wanted to support their lesbian sisters.

Miss Simpson said she thought the New York D.O.B. membership represented only a tiny fraction of lesbians in the city. She believes there are as many lesbians as there are male homosexuals, and that the frequently given estimate of 800,000 homosexuals of both sexes in New York is only "the tip of the iceberg." (According to the Kinsey report, 4 to 6 percent of men and 2 to 3 percent of women in the United States are homosexuals.)

The D.O.B. center is open almost every night of the week, and during the day on Sundays. Men are banned except during occasional get-togethers between the D.O.B. and such homosexual groups as the Mattachine Society and the Gay Activists' Alliance. Business meetings are held on Monday nights, and on Thursdays there are "action meetings" for the more militant members who want to keep abreast of protests being planned in the homophile movement.

Other evenings are devoted to yoga classes, art shows, rap sessions, communal dinners and a feminist workshop led by Ti-Grace Atkinson. What are billed as "the best women's dances in town" are held on Saturday nights, with the proceeds (admission is $2, and beer and soft drinks cost 25 cents) going to pay the loft's hefty $500-a-month rent.

At a recent business meeting, Miss Simpson told about 80 members, again a very diverse group, what she hoped the center would accomplish: "We will provide social events, dances and open discussions for our sisters who are afraid to come out of the closet, for our sisters who remain in the closet but work behind the scenes in civil rights, and for those 'out front,' public lesbians who are active in the forefront."

She told about the problems the officers had encountered in finding a loft. They looked at about 70, she said, before they found "a beautiful, mad, sculptor-landlord" who was willing to rent to them. "When we told him it was for lesbians," Miss Simpson said, "he said, 'Oh, you can get 1,000 lesbians in there.'"

And then came problems with the telephone company. "They were giving me a lot of trouble about installing a phone," she told the women, "until I said, 'Let me speak to the supervisor. I am sick of your anti-Semitism. Daughters of Bilitis is a Jewish organization, and I have highly placed contacts in all of the media.' After that, we got our phone in quick order."

(While the D.O.B. does have a sizable minority of Jewish members, their percentage of the total membership is no more than one-third.)

There were two visitors at the meeting—a well-dressed black woman and her teenage daughter. "We get that quite often," Miss Simpson said later. Does the mother come along to give her daughter reassurance and support? "Sometimes,"

Miss Simpson said. "But sometimes they are both lesbians. And we have yet to have a mother bring a daughter who was not a lesbian."

Women who attend D.O.B. meetings are quickly made to feel at home; they are greeted at the door by the chapter's unofficial "kissing squad," Ellen Povill, 32, the D.O.B. vice president, and her partner of 11 years, Eileen Webb, also in her 30's, who edits the chapter's Lesbian Letter. I found this constant kissing rather cloying, and the two women finally sensed that and started shaking my hand.

Ellen, a slender, ethereal brunette from Brooklyn, met Eileen, a cherub-faced blonde Philadelphian who was once a fashion model—before she stopped smoking and gained 30 pounds—in a gay bar in Manhattan. They were "married" in a Woolworth's store by a clerk who sold them 50-cent rings and told them, "My daughter is married to a woman, too."

The two are constantly together. They share an apartment not far from the lesbian center, and together run a typing service. One of their few lengthy separations came when Ellen suffered a nervous breakdown and was hospitalized for $3\frac{1}{2}$ months after learning that she and Eileen had been turned down on their application to adopt a child.

(There is no law prohibiting lesbians from adopting a child, but those who do rarely go through adoption agencies. Their adopted children are generally "black market" babies. Or they may be the offspring of one of the partners during a previous heterosexual marriage or during a brief heterosexual relationship entered into so the homosexual partners could raise a child together.)

Although many lesbian couples take a dim view of "role playing" because they think it mocks heterosexual marriage, Ellen and Eileen prefer it in their relationship. "I'm the poppa," Eileen said heartily. "And I'm the feminine one," Ellen said in her whispery, Marilyn Monroe voice. "I do most of the cooking and things like that."

Ellen and Eileen have been interviewed on radio programs, and recently appeared on a Detroit television talk show billed as "a happily married couple." They regard their relationship as permanent. Although they have occasional fights, and one sometimes leaves the other behind in the apartment for a day or two, they have always managed to get back together.

"Our families know and approve," Eileen said. "Once I said to my brother, 'How do you like my fabulous treasure, Ellen?' And he said, 'Fine . . . but she's Jewish.'"

The two women have been active in homosexual demonstrations, or "zaps," as they call them. Recently, they joined Ruth Simpson, two other lesbians and about 30 male homosexuals in a Gay Activists' Alliance march on Fidelifacts of Greater New York, a company at 122 East 42d Street that investigates present or prospective employes for other businesses.

The company's president, Vincent Gillen, a former F.B.I. agent, recently told a Manhattan businessmen's association that in trying to determine if an employe is homosexual, he

usually goes by the rule of thumb: "If one looks like a duck, walks like a duck, associates only with ducks and quacks like a duck, he is probably a duck."

The demonstrators marched in a circle outside the Fidelifacts office carrying placards ("I Got My Job Through The New York Times; I Lost My Job Through Fidelifacts") and chanting: "Hey, hey, hey, hey/Try it once the other way" and "3, 5, 7, 9/Lesbians are mighty fine." One man wore a fuzzy duck costume.

Several of the "zappers" invaded the Fidelifacts office, saying they wanted Gillen investigated to find out what he does in his bedroom. Two gay men were shoved by employes of the company, but the protesters left after the policemen on the scene called for reinforcements, and no one was arrested.

As many D.O.B. members see it, demonstrations like this will be helpful in obtaining passage of the Clingan-Burden bill, filed in January by City Councilmen Eldon R. Clingan and Carter Burden to extend the city's Human Rights Law to ban discrimination in housing, public accommodation and employment based on sexual orientation.

It is not illegal to be a lesbian in New York State, but it is illegal to perform a lesbian act. In recent years, bills have been introduced in the State Legislature that would make legal any "deviate sexual acts" performed in private between consenting adults. Most of them have been defeated or have died in committee.

Three similar bills were introduced on Feb. 9 by two Democratic Assemblymen, Stephen J. Solarz of Brooklyn and Antonio G. Olivieri of Manhattan, who recently held a one-day hearing on discrimination against homosexuals. The bills, if passed, would strike down existing laws against sodomy and make it illegal for employers or landlords to discriminate against anyone on the basis of sexual preference.

"Unspoken prejudices and archaic laws restrict the rights and lives of homosexuals in this city," the Assemblymen said after the hearing, at which Miss Simpson and leaders of male homosexual organizations testified. Many of them wept as they told of what they described as police harassment, brutality, entrapment and bribery.

In general, lesbians seem to be less rejected by society than their male counterparts. Two women can share an apartment without raising eyebrows, whereas two men over the age of 30 who do so are suspect. Many lesbians seem to be able to function well in a heterosexual marriage. Lesbians have fewer of the "gay" characteristics that heterosexuals often find offensive, and nobody seems to worry that lesbians will seduce little girls.

Although the medical profession still largely maintains the "sick theory" regarding homosexuality, it is hard to find a lesbian who considers herself sick. But she is likely to tell you about her three nervous breakdowns, or that she can't get through-the day without tranquilizers, or that seven different psychiatrists haven't been able to help her. D.O.B. has a referral service that recommends psychiatrists or psychologists, most of them women who pooh-pooh the "sick theory."

Dr. Harvey E. Kaye, a Manhattan psychiatrist who headed the Society of Medical Psychoanalysts' study that defined lesbianism in 1967 and who is one of the few acknowledged experts on lesbianism, refuses to use the word "sick" when discussing women homosexuals. He prefers to call them "abnormal."

"In our society, 'sick' is so pejorative," he said, sitting in his opulently decorated apartment on East End Avenue. "I consider lesbianism an inhibitory aspect of the heterosexual drive. If you want to treat an inhibition, you can treat it. But you don't have to treat it. It's like arthritis; if someone has an arthritic finger, you can treat it if you want to."

Kaye said he had found nothing in his research to distinguish the mother of a heterosexual woman from the mother of a lesbian. However, he said there were certain noteworthy characteristics among the fathers of lesbians. He said they tended to be puritanical, overly possessive, close-binding and covertly seductive—a trait that he also calls "inverted Oedipal striving." "They frequently tend to block off their daughters' relationships with other people," he said, "and they frown upon their daughters' use of cosmetics and playing with dolls."

A tendency to dislike dolls, Dr. Kaye said, is one of the traits a woman homosexual often displays in her childhood. (He believes that homosexuality is determined by the eighth year.) He said lesbians also tend to seek physical fights in childhood and early adolescence, prefer to play boys' rather than girls' games, view themselves as tomboys, enjoy playing with guns and develop strong crushes on women during puberty and adolescence.

Kaye said he believed that 35 to 50 percent of lesbians who sought treatment could be helped; the best candidates are those who are young and have had some heterosexual experience or fantasies. "I don't think a 40-year-old confirmed lesbian should be treated," he said.

Kaye bemoaned the lack of research on female homosexuality: "There is no other area in psychiatry where less clinical work has been done. It's been rather a taboo subject. You can talk about the sexual misadventures of the male, but the sexual misadventures of the female raise more hackles."

A Manhattan psychiatrist who recently made a study of adolescent lesbians and who has many lesbian patients, Dr. Malvina W. Kremer, said she thought women homosexuals were "very troubled individuals."

"I have yet to see a problem-free lesbian," she said in her office-apartment on West End Avenue. "Invariably, they have serious, deep-seated personality problems in which lesbianism is an integral part. In treatment, they make defensive rationalizations. They do not necessarily recognize the obvious connection between the lesbianism and their depression and suicide attempts."

She said she disagreed with Kaye's findings that the fathers of lesbians tended to be close-binding and overly possessive. In her study of 25 girls in New York public schools serving predominantly lower socioeconomic groups, she found that the fathers were "hostile, exploitative, detached and absent." The mothers were not dominant, but mainly overburdened and hardly adequate for their responsibilities. "The mothers often conveyed negative attitudes toward men," she said.

Both Dr. Kaye and Dr. Kremer said they thought lesbian relationships were more stable than those of male homosexuals, and that sex was not as important to the women as it was to the men. "What the women seem to want is a lot of hugging and holding—sort of a mother-child relationship," Kaye said. "They're not looking for one-night stands. They're more interested in an emotional involvement. There is usually some initial sexual contact, but after that it generally boils down to who's taking care of whom."

Dr. Sharon London, a Manhattan psychologist whose name is on the D.O.B. referral list, disavows the "sick theory." "People are people, and you can't define a person's health or pathology by what they do in bed," she said.

"But there are qualifications," she added. "Lesbianism may be an acceptable form of adjustment for certain people to life and themselves, and I'm just one of those people who is not going to try to change them."

Mrs. Pamela O., a divorced, 45-year-old Manhattan psychotherapist who is one of D.O.B.'s heterosexual members, believes it is healthy for lesbians to admit their homosexuality publicly. "Those who don't often have many emotional problems because they've internalized society's negative attitudes," she said, "and as a result they have a great deal of self-hatred. Besides, young people are much more tolerant today, and a lot of people probably suspected that the woman in question was a lesbian, anyway."

Ruth Simpson, the D.O.B. president, has never seen a psychiatrist. "I've never felt the need," she said sardonically, "which is probably a sign of great illness on my part."

She was sitting in the living room of her one-bedroom apartment, filled with early American furniture, on Central Park West near 100th Street. She shares the apartment with a black cat named Vixen and a calico cat named Pied.

Miss Simpson was born in Cleveland to "extremely liberal" parents who were active in the labor movement. She graduated from Western Reserve University, then moved to New York, "under the delusion that I was going to be an actress." After one bit role Off Broadway, she went into public relations, where she has remained for 18 years.

"Although my first sexual relationship was with a man," she said, "I knew at least by the time I was 16 that I was a lesbian. If you begin feeling happier around women than you do around men, then it's a pretty good bet you're a lesbian."

Miss Simpson said she had had a seven-year relationship with a woman that ended 14 years ago, and since then has had brief relationships with several women. She prefers to live alone. "A live-in situation is difficult," she said, "even for heterosexuals, who have nothing to be ashamed of. An individual needs time and space to herself, especially if she's confronting problems out there in the world."

For the last four and a half years, Miss Simpson has worked for Harshe-Rotman & Druck, Inc., a Manhattan public relations firm. She told her supervisor of her homosexuality last summer, adding that she planned to represent D. O. B. in public. The supervisor, a woman, replied: "I admire your courage." Other co-workers had different reactions. Shortly after Miss Simpson was interviewed on a radio program, a woman she used to chat with in the elevator said: "Ruth, I'm going to have to ask you not to speak to me."

Miss Simpson said the police interruption at the old D.O.B. headquarters had made her more of an activist in the homophile movement. She said policemen had walked into the headquarters once before, at a meeting at which Kate Millet, the author of "Sexual Politics," told D.O.B. members about her lesbian experiences, and once later on. "The last time they said they would be back the next night, but no one showed," Miss Simpson said. "It's all part of the harassment picture."

A spokesman at the 14th Precinct, which includes the site of the old center, said the visits were "normal police procedure" and that all public meeting halls were required to have occupancy signs posted.

What are the most common heterosexual myths about lesbians? Miss Simpson smiled. "That all lesbians are man-haters," she said. "Some lesbians do hate men, but so do some heterosexual women. And then you get the 'lesbians are sick' people, and those who think we stomp around in Army boots and buy our shirts at Brooks Brothers, and those who think lesbians are lesbians because they can't get a man. A great preponderance of our members have been to bed with men."

She doesn't think too highly of the growing number of films dealing with lesbianism. "They follow a pattern," she said. "One of the women commits suicide, or sees the error of her ways, or meets Mr. Right, or ends up in a mental institution, or else is involved in a butch-femme relationship like in 'The Killing of Sister George.' The average lesbian does not go around smoking cigars and making her partner drink her bath water."

As far as children are concerned, Miss Simpson said she liked them well enough but didn't want any of her own. Many other D.O.B. members said they would like to be mothers and raise children.

Later that evening, Miss Simpson and about 200 other women attended D.O.B.'s first dance in the new center. A juke box and flashing lights had been rented for the occasion, and balloons had been strung across the ceiling, festooned with such slogans as "Peter Pan is a Lesbian," "Which is Better—D.A.R. or D.O.B.?" and "Lesbians are Lovable." There was an ink stamp for those who wanted to leave for a while and return. It read: "LOVE."

During the slow dances, there was much kissing, with many arms entwined around necks and waists. During the fast dances, many of the women danced in circles rather than with just one partner. "A lot of us come from where we've been rejected all our lives," one dancer explained. "In a circle dance, nobody's rejected."

Besides D.O.B. members, the dance also drew women from the three other New York groups that have lesbian members: Radicalesbians (also known as "Radishes"), Gay Liberation Front and Gay Activists' Alliance. Their meet-

ings are generally held in a small "lesbians only" room in the rear of the Gay Community Center, at 130 West Third Street. Members say there is no rivalry among the four groups; in fact, some women hold memberships in more than one.

The Radicalesbians and G.L.F. women are generally younger than the Daughters of Bilitis and much smaller in number; they identify primarily with Marxism and political revolution. Most of them are "out of the closet." Women of the G.A.A., like D.O.B. members, want to make changes within the system.

One of the most attractive women at the dance was Lyn Kupferman, 24, a green-eyed blonde who resembles Tricia Nixon and who is a secretary-reader at Doubleday & Company. She was with her partner of 18 months, Maricla Moyano, 32, a sultry, dark-haired college student who was married to a man for two years.

"He's been at our house for dinner," Maricla said. "I told him Lyn and I were married, and he didn't seem very surprised. My relationship with Lyn is completely different. I love her more than I did him. There are fewer fights, and it's much calmer than my marriage to him was."

Like many lesbians, Lyn and Maricla think straight men find them intriguing, titillating. "We're a challenge to them," Lyn said, smiling. "They all think that they're the ones who are going to be able to straighten us out."

The recent support of lesbians by women's liberation movement leaders at the church press conference seems to have been accepted by most, but not all, gay women. "They have to include us," Miss Simpson said, "because lesbianism is the vanguard of the feminist movement. A woman who says she is a lesbian is saying, in effect, that she's a woman who's going to make it as a woman, without a man."

Roni S., a 22-year-old former high school cheerleader and sorority member who was radicalized at City College of New York and is now a member of the Gay Liberation Front, said: "If the women hadn't come out and supported their sisters, the whole concept of sisterhood would have been laughable. Besides, there are so many lesbians in the women's movement that it's ridiculous to ignore them."

One of the dissenters was Mrs. Betty J., 45, of Larchmont, N. Y., a silver-haired nurse with two adolescent sons ("They both like girls") who has been a lesbian since she was a teen-ager.

"I really don't care for this women's lib business," she said recently before a D.O.B. meeting. "I think they should stay on their side and take care of their day care centers. I mean, either you're a lesbian or you're not."

Mrs. J. was divorced from her husband 10 years ago, she said, "because I was never completely happy—I just kept thinking of women." Whenever she attends D.O.B. meetings she tells her sons she is going to the theater or shopping at Bloomingdale's. She said she was wary of forming a lesbian relationship because she is afraid of getting venereal disease. "I see it all the time in my job," she said. "It's almost as common as the common cold."

There has been more rancor about the press conference among leaders of the women's liberation movement. Betty Friedan, mother of the movement, refused to attend the press conference and tried to talk the nine women out of holding it.

"I think it was a terrible mistake," she said. "The C.I.A. couldn't have thought of anything worse. It did not represent the majority of women in the movement. I think everybody's sex life is their private business. I'm opposed to sexual politics, and I don't think we should have a sexual red herring diverting us. Trying to equate lesbianism with the women's liberation movement is playing into the hands of the enemy."

Gloria Steinem, the journalist, who did attend, said: "Lesbians are women, and the movement can't deny women. What the press conference said to me was that we aren't going to react to this [the lesbian issue] in fear any more."

One movement leader, who asked that her name be withheld, said that the mere mention of the word lesbian scared straight women away from the movement and gave ammunition to male detractors who are fond of characterizing the movement as "a lesbian plot" and its members as "a bunch of dykes."

"Some lesbians actually prey on lonely and confused women who are new to the movement," the leader said. "I'm not saying that a lot of women have been seduced, but some lesbians are looking for partners. And let's face it, in the women's movement there is an open field for partners. Many women are looking for a human relationship, and they can't have it with a male chauvinist."

According to Ruth Simpson, most lesbians aren't interested in proselytizing. "There is no way you can convince a woman who is not a lesbian to become a lesbian," she said firmly. Then, she added: "But it is possible to gentle a lesbian out of the closet." A 19-year-old Radicalesbian, on the other hand, said she often tried to convert heterosexual women to lesbianism. "Why not?" she asked. "Straight people are always trying to change us, aren't they?"

Dr. Kremer said she thought that proselytizing was quite common among lesbians. "They try to get others involved," she said, "because they have doubts and questions about their homosexuality, and they're not firmly convinced that it's the right thing. So they feel that they need support from others."

Friction between lesbians and heterosexuals in the women's movement had been mounting since last summer. In August, Jill Johnston, a writer for The Village Voice, disrupted a benefit cocktail party for the Aug. 26 Women's Strike for Equality when she jumped into a swimming pool and swam several laps, nude to the waist, while speeches were being given. One of the reasons for her swim, said Miss Johnston, a self-professed homosexual, was that the women's movement was ignoring lesbians.

And at a Bryant Park rally following the women's march down Fifth Avenue on Aug. 26, a Radicalesbian made a plaintive plea for support from her straight sisters in the movement. She charged that the police were harassing lesbians, and that other women in the movement were ignoring their plight.

"We're your sisters, and we need help!" the speaker cried.

But what actually prompted the press conference was an article in the Dec. 14 issue of Time magazine that said Kate Millett's public disclosure that she was bisexual "is bound to discredit her as a spokeswoman for her cause." Miss Millett—along with 30 women from such groups as the National Organization for Women, Daughters of Bilitis, Radicalesbians, Columbia Women's Liberation and New York Radical Feminists—then helped draw up the statement supporting homosexuals.

Whether a woman can actually be bisexual is a question often debated among D.O.B. members. It was the topic of discussion after a recent Monday night meeting at which the guest speaker, an actress, read from the Songs of Sappho. (One of the poems, which mentioned that lesbians of ancient Greece dyed their hair gold, caused a woman in a blue windbreaker to remark: "Even then, blondes had more fun.")

Miss Simpson spoke first. "In my experience," she said, "if someone says they're bisexual, they're hanging on to their insurance policy of a husband or something."

Young woman in red sweater: "It's like saying you're only half-black. In our society, if you're half-black you're black."

Attractive, angry olive-skinned brunette: "I consider myself bisexual. I'm a homosexual when I'm in a homosexual relationship, and a heterosexual in a heterosexual relationship. I think you can get things from everybody, even men."

Older woman in pigtails: "I'd like a definition of heterosexual, homosexual and bisexual."

Miss Simpson: "If you don't know that, what are you doing here?" (Laughter)

That meeting was the last function I attended at D.O.B., and afterward I tried to make some nonprofessional judgments about the women I had met in my several weeks of research. Most were friendly; others were hostile, like the round-faced coed who yelled, "You are my oppressor!" after I told her I still preferred men. What I found most interesting was the wide assortment of women who were at every event, instead of just the "bull dykes" you read and hear about. I found the constant kissing, the hand-holding and other displays of affection a bit disgusting at first, but after a while it became routine, and my reaction changed to "So what. It's their business." I thought about the women talking of their breakdowns, their tranquilizers and their "shrinks," but then many of my heterosexual friends talk that way, too.

What bothered me most was the thought that these women are discriminated against in jobs, housing and public places simply because they prefer to love a member of their own sex. At the very least, they need decent places (like the D.O.B. center) to meet so they won't have to continue frequenting lesbian bars.

With seven Daughters of Bilitis, I spent one evening in two of the most popular lesbian bars, both of them on the northern perimeter of Greenwich Village. My seven companions agreed that they didn't like the bars. They thought the places were Mafia-controlled; the drinks were overpriced, and the employes were rude.

Both bars were ornately decorated in Victorian brothel style, with small dance floors in the rear. Customers were required to check their coats at the door before they were admitted, and drinks ($1.50 each) had to be paid for in advance.

"That's an old custom in case the bar is raided," said Marty Stephan, 36, of Manhattan, a stocky woman in a ski sweater, blue jeans and Army boots who sells subway tokens for the Transit Authority. "This way, the management gets its money either way."

Miss Stephan, who is the masculine or "butch" type of lesbian, said she came out at the age of 18, while a student at Hunter College. "One day I went to classes wearing a man's suit and tie," she recalled wryly. "I had decided I wanted to be the first president of U.S. Steel in drag. Later, I found out there weren't a whole lot of jobs available to women who dressed like men."

The second bar on the tour was run by a hard-looking blonde who was openly hostile. She kept strolling to the back of the bar, where we were sitting, to make sure that everybody was drinking. "If you don't have a drink in front of you," she said gruffly, "you'll have to leave." The bar was almost empty.

About 10 minutes later, when we appeared to be talking more than we were drinking, the blonde returned with her swarthy male bouncer and said: "This isn't a gay liberation meeting. If you want to just sit around, go to church."

We got up, paid 25 cents each to get our coats and walked out into the cold clear night. "That's exactly why we need centers of our own and groups like D.O.B.," one young lesbian said as we walked east on 14th Street. "A lot of people make you feel less than human in this world, but no place is as bad as a gay bar."

Judy Klemesrud is a staff writer for The Times.

* * *

April 13, 1988

PARTY CELEBRATES CLUB
FOR GAY AND GRAY

By RON ALEXANDER

The first time Gean Harwood, 79, and Bruhs Mero, 77, went to Radio City Music Hall together was the opening night in 1932. Last night, the two men, who have been together 58 years, were there again. They joined more than 200 men and women of all ages for a fund-raising dinner celebrating the 10th anniversary of Senior Action in a Gay Environment. The organization's goal is to provide services and programs for elderly homosexuals.

There was lots of applause and a Grand Foyer-full of reminiscences. It was a happy evening. Margaret Whiting, Dolly Dawn and Paula Laurence entertained, singing popular standards from the 30's and 40's.

"We had a good life but we were reaching that stage when we were losing many of our friends," Mr. Harwood said dur-

ing the cocktail hour on the first mezzanine level before the sit-down dinner. "We were very lonely people. Then we heard about SAGE and found a new family."

SAGE, with 3,500 members and more than 250 active volunteers, offers assistance to over 600 elderly gay men and women each month. Among the services provided are home, hospital and institutional visiting, transportation to doctors, weekly workshops and discussion groups, and monthly parties. The offices are open each weekday afternoon as a social drop-in center. SAGE receives support from the Greater New York Fund/United Way and the New York City and New York State Departments of Aging.

'Our Beginnings Were Tentative'

Barbara L. Emmerth, executive director of SAGE, said she expected last night's dinner (most tickets were $200, sponsors and patrons paid $500 and up) would net around $20,000.

Douglas C. Kimmel, remembered the early days of SAGE. "It began as the dream of a handful of professional gerontologists, social workers and psychologists concerned about the special problems and social isolation of senior gays," said Dr. Kimmel, a professor of psychology at City College of CUNY. "Our beginnings were tentative indeed." Today SAGE is a respected mainstream organization with rented space in the New York City Lesbian and Gay Community Services Center at 208 West 13th Street.

Arlene Kochman, the coordinator of social services for SAGE, called it "a symbol in the age of AIDS that gay people can live happily to a ripe old age." "These people have been closeted for years," she said. "The most important thing when one gets older is reminiscing. When straight people are talking about their children and grandchildren, who is there for gay people to talk to? Think of the energy wasted on fear and the hiding of secrets in what should be your golden years."

A 79-year-old woman who asked to be identified only as Gerry, said that when she confessed to her daughter about her secret life, her daughter told her grandchildren, "Grandma's gay." Gerry said the kids looked at their mother and remarked: "So what else is new?"

Gerry smiled and said, "It made me feel like I was only 70 years old."

* * *

April 6, 1991

MILITANTS BACK 'QUEER,' SHOVING 'GAY'
THE WAY OF 'NEGRO'

By ALESSANDRA STANLEY

"Queer," a word long bandied in schoolyards and bars as a taunt, has acquired a new meaning: it has been adopted, proudly and defiantly, by a new generation of young militants. Their use of the word has created a rift in the gay community, alienating many older members haunted by its pejorative connotations.

Ben Thornberry

The epithet "queer" has been adopted with pride by a new generation of young gay militants. Last year, a group calling itself "Queer Nation" protested violence against homosexuals in New York City.

"We've fought 20 years to get 'gay' accepted and it has been a total success," said a middle-aged man who attended a forum on the word held in Greenwich Village on Tuesday. His voice shook as he addressed the crowd of 200. "I just don't get it—'queer' is the word they used to torture us with."

The word is gaining currency in New York, San Francisco and other major cities, and the attendant controversy underscores a growing generation gap within the gay community. It divides youthful, self-described "separatists," roused to a new militant rage by the AIDS epidemic, from those who came of political age in the 60's, and for whom political struggle has long focused on issues like privacy and tolerance.

Those who define themselves as "queer" say they are reclaiming the term from bigots who use it as a slur, and turning it into an ironic badge of honor, not unlike the pink triangle that homosexuals were compelled to wear in Nazi Germany, which is now proudly worn by gay marchers and demonstrators.

The word's shock value gives it political potency. Like the movement that embraced it, "queer" is confrontational.

"It is an in-your-face kind of thing—that's what I liked about it," said Liz Powers, 34 years old, of Queer Nation, a group formed a year ago to combat gaybashing. "Using a word that is so offensive is a way of showing your anger."

Queer Nation, whose motto is "We're Here/We're Queer/Get Used to It," has chapters in cities across the country but no appointed or elected leaders, and does not refer to adherents as members. Ms. Powers calls herself a Queer Nationalist.

'Queer' Signifies Activist Spirit

"Gay, to me, has a very specific meaning," she said. "A certain kind of white, middle-class, assimilationist homosexual."

Dave Fleck, also of Queer Nation, put it this way: "Queer signifies a rebirth of energy, the spirit of activism that happened in the '70s. This is a newer, hipper generation."

Steven Miller, chairman of the media committee of the Gay and Lesbian Alliance Against Defamation, observed that the consternation over the word was in fact "a linguistic facade" covering what he called "deep divisions" between lesbian and gay militants and moderates.

'I Wouldn't Use The Word'

Yet it is more of an issue of sensibility than overt ideology. More established gay and lesbian organizations, like the National Gay and Lesbian Task Force, work closely with firebrand groups like Act-Up, an AIDS lobbying group, or Queer Nation.

Few of the Task Force's leaders expressed strong objections to "queer" or to those who use it. Tom Stoddard, the director of the Lambda Legal Defense Fund, said, "I wouldn't use the word myself, but I fully understand those who do."

Advocates of "queer" point out that when the gay liberation movement arose in the late 1960's, its use of the word "gay" also pitted radicals against those who were reluctant to replace the term preferred in mainstream society, "homosexual." It took two decades for gay to win widespread acceptance.

"The word 'queer' startles the way the word 'gay' once startled, and no longer does," Mr. Stoddard observed.

Yet "queer," to many, carries far more damaging connotations than "gay" ever did. Campion Reed, a member of the politically moderate Stonewall Democratic Club, argued that use of the word by homosexuals would only give greater license to heterosexuals to employ degrading language. "Should politicians discuss 'queers' and 'faggots' on the Senate floor?" he asked.

Anger Over 'Homo' Remark

The Gay and Lesbian Alliance Against Defamation is seeking the removal of a Federal judge in Washington, Oliver Gasch, who in a recent hearing referred to a plaintiff fighting dismissal from the Naval Academy for being homosexual as a "homo."

Outweek, a brash two-year-old New York-based gay and lesbian news magazine, ran a cover story last May entitled, "Queer Fashion." Such prominent use of the word generated heated debate among readers and within its editorial offices. "We talked a lot about it at first," said Gabriel Rotello, the editor. "We're still discussing it."

The word's meaning in the magazine has evolved over the ensuing year. "Originally it denoted a certain type of radical gay or lesbian activist," Mr. Rotello explained, "Now, it encompasses all sexual minorities."

Mr. Rotello said that part of the word's appeal was journalistic expedience. "When you're trying to describe the community, and you have to list gays, lesbians, bisexuals, drag queens, transsexuals (post-op and pre), it gets unwieldly. Queer says it all." The New York Native, an older, more established gay newspaper, does not use the term.

To Richard Goldstein, the executive editor of The Village Voice, who has begun using the word in his column, queer covers all sexual minorities, but also carries another nuance. "It's also a word that connotes militance: activists who are fervent or outrageous. It means the assertive homosexual."

'At 47, I'm Too Old to be Queer'

Mr. Goldstein also thought it suggested youth. 'I'm 47, too old to be queer—I'm gay."

And there are those who call themselves queer, yet do not relish the prospect of having the word spread beyond their community. "I am not for any straight writer using the word 'queer' in a mainstream publication," said Donna Minkowitz, a writer for The Village Voice. "This is our word," she explained. "I can say it, but you can't."

But Mr. Reed and others argue that homosexuals cannot limit use of the word and point to a recent column by the right-wing columnist Pat Buchanan, who denounced gay participation in last month's St. Patrick's Day parade. Noting that the gay group's marshal wore a 'Queer Boy' T-shirt, Mr. Buchanan wrote: "In cavorting with Queer Boy, David Dinkins showed an utter lack of respect for the Catholic families at the parade and for the Church."

Many advocates of "queer" draw parallels to the Black Power movement and the resistance that greeted its leaders' efforts to substitute "black" for "Negro."

'I Loathed the Word'

Ronald Gans, 45, a computer analyst who was active in the Gay Liberation Front in the late 60's and attended Tuesday's forum, vehemently objected to "queer" and to analogies to the civil rights movement. "Blacks, Jews and women never defined themselves with derogatory words," he insisted. "The reason is obvious, just obvious: could you imagine a group calling itself 'Kike Nation?'"

Yet many leaders of gay organizations are more sanguine about the new word, and the movement that has rallied behind it. "For so many years I loathed the word," said Larry Kramer, 55, a writer who is also a founder of Act-Up. "But these youngsters have come along and effectively and usefully defused it."

* * *

June 28, 1992

OUT OF THE CLOSET AND INTO HISTORY

By JEFFREY ESCOFFIER

MAKING HISTORY: The Struggle for Gay and Lesbian Equal Rights,1945-1990: An Oral History
By Eric Marcus
Illustrated. 532 pp. New York: HarperCollins Publishers. $25.

ODD GIRLS AND TWILIGHT LOVERS: A History of Lesbian Life in Twentieth-Century America
By Lillian Faderman
Illustrated. 373 pp. New York: Columbia University Press. Cloth, $29.95. Penguin. Paper, $12.

Historical research has radically changed how we think about homosexuality. From the end of the 19th century up until about 20 years ago, psychology was the dominant intellectual framework for understanding it, and lesbian or gay history often consisted of little more than lists of famous homosexuals. Then, starting in the 1970's, a new generation of historians, including Jonathan Katz, Jeffrey Weeks, Michel Foucault, John D'Emilio, James Steakley, Joan Nestle and Martin Duberman, made it clear that while homosexuality as a form of sexual behavior was found in every society and in every historical period, the idea of a homosexual as a type of person first appeared in North American and European societies of the 19th and 20th centuries.

A lesbian bar in San Francisco during World War II.

The discovery that the homosexual identity is a recent historical phenomenon has generated a vast literature in sociology, cultural studies, anthropology, political theory and psychology. Scholars and activists alike have long debated whether homosexual identity and desire are natural and transcend historical influences, a position that has been labeled "essentialist," or whether they are socially and historically constructed, a position that is now widely held.

Two recent histories, by Eric Marcus and Lillian Faderman, will significantly add to our knowledge of recent gay and lesbian history. While both are devoted to the immense changes that have taken place in the period since World War II, they approach the period from very different perspectives. Mr. Marcus's "Making History," in the style of Studs Terkel's oral histories, uses interviews to tell the little stories that link the intimate to the historical, while Ms. Faderman's "Odd Girls and Twilight Lovers" is a grand narrative synthesis of the cultural, social and political history of lesbian life since the late 19th century.

In "Making History" Mr. Marcus, the author of "The Male Couples Guide," offers us a rich portrait gallery of women and men, both gay and straight, who have participated in the political struggle for lesbian and gay rights since the late 1940's. These 45 oral histories give some measure of the achievement of this relatively new civil rights movement. And they span a range of lives including such prominent figures as the writer Larry Kramer, who became a prophet of doom during the AIDS epidemic; the former Republican Congressman Robert Bauman, whose marriage was destroyed by his secret homosexuality and alcoholism; the former football player David Kopay, who was the first professional athlete in the United States to disclose his homosexuality; and the advice columnist Abigail Van Buren, who has supported gay rights. The book also tells the stories of lesser-known people like Jeanne Manford, whose support of her son's coming out led her to help found Parents and Friends of Lesbians and Gays; Ann Northrop, a television journalist who has devoted much of her time to educating the public about homosexuality; and Joyce Hunter, one of the founders of New York's Harvey Milk High School for lesbian and gay students who encounter difficulties in traditional schools.

The interviews in "Making History" are roughly divided into five periods of political activity—1945-61, 1961-68, 1968-73, 1973-81 and 1981-91—each of which has a markedly different style from the others. The early period has, for instance, a kind of rabble-rousing tone that contrasts rather strikingly with the anguish of the last period, plagued by AIDS. But there are also some remarkable constants in these accounts of lesbian and gay experience. Central to the tale of almost every person, with the exception of those activists who are not gay, is the coming-out story—the account of how each man or woman realized his or her homosexual desires, acknowledged them, and then began the process of communicating that discovery to family, friends and the world at large.

Most of the people Mr. Marcus interviewed carried their public disclosures to the point of political action. Coming out is a moment of personal transformation that continues to demonstrate that for lesbians and gay men the personal is, in the widest sense of the term, the political. The intimate power of these coming-out stories, matched as they often are by the courage of each person's political struggles, can be both inspiring and heart-wrenching.

The problem is that "Making History" lacks the cumulative power it might have had if Mr. Marcus had provided more of a framework for integrating such a large number of stories, which range over a period of 45 years. The first section of the book suffers most from this lack of context. We need more historical background to make the early period intelligible than we do to understand the oral histories of those who were active in the 80's and 90's. For instance, in order to understand the personal animosities of the 50's and 60's, it helps to realize that there was an intense controversy about attempts to organize lesbians and gay men into a unified political force. One also wonders how significant it is that many of those interviewed, particularly in the sections dealing with the 70's and 80's, seem somewhat disgruntled and unhappy with how the lesbian and gay communities have responded to their personal efforts. More background information would have allowed us to evaluate their impressions.

In contrast to Mr. Marcus's book, "Odd Girls and Twilight Lovers" pulls together memoirs, literary work, personal correspondence, journalism and 186 interviews to create a social history. Lillian Faderman, the author of "Surpassing the Love of Men: Romantic Friendship and Love Between Women From the Renaissance to the Present," uses her sources to show us how lesbian identity has changed over the last 100 years—from the "romantic friendships" of college-educated women in the early 20th century to the rural communities of lesbian separatists of the 1970's and the fashion consciousness of the so-called lipstick lesbians of the present.

Her grand narrative also identifies definite cycles of improvement and decline in the status of lesbians; she sees tolerance in the 1920's and 60's and periods of repression in the 10's, 30's and 50's. She also finds that the forms of lesbian experience differ strikingly in different classes and different racial communities. For instance, in the 40's, working-class lesbians tended to meet in bars, whereas upper-middle-class women would meet on college campuses and at gatherings of formal social organizations.

One limitation of Ms. Faderman's sweeping interpretation is that it often overwhelms the rich material she has gathered. For Ms. Faderman, lesbianism is always primarily emotional; sexuality plays a less significant role. Even while she argues that the growth of sexual freedom is one of the conditions for the improvement of lesbian life, she maintains that it has also undercut romantic friendship, an important and publicly sanctioned kind of relationship between two women. She believes that romantic friendship—which was common in the late 19th century among middle-class educated women like the social reformer Jane Addams, the feminist leader Carrie Chapman Catt and M. Carey Thomas, who was president of Bryn Mawr College for many years—was destroyed by Freudianism in the 20th century. After Freud, it was impossible for two women to live their lives together without the public assuming they were in a sexual relationship, and censuring them for it.

Whatever failings these books might have, they give us so many fascinating ideas to think about, and so many engaging and deeply moving stories, that no one should pass either one of them by. Both illustrate the immense changes that gay and lesbian life has undergone since World War II, and both document the human happiness that has resulted.

Jeffrey Escoffier, the publisher of the quarterly Out/Look, was one of the founders of the San Francisco Lesbian and Gay History Project.

*   *   *

January 16, 1994

PRETTIFICATION PATROL

By WILLIAM SAFIRE

Let's say you're trying to peddle some fake flowers. Do you call yourself a fake-flower peddler? Of course not; you're a floral marketer, artificial-flower division.

Now you look at your product—sometimes quite beautiful, petals made of silk or whatever—and you ask yourself, "Why artificial?" That's a word that turns buyers off. You brood about that, and come up with a fresh-as-a-daisy answer: you'll create a market for permanent flowers. That not only lends longevity to your produce, but it also knocks the noxious weeds turned out in hothouses and pesticide-ridden, inorganic, fertilizer-driven gardens as temporary flowers.

That's the art, or racket, of euphemism, from the Greek eu-, "good," and pheme, "speech." And it's been gaining speed ever since environmentalists were able to transform the damn jungle into the glorious rain forest (where you can get wetlands fever).

Some objects of green wrath, lumbermen and fishermen, counterattacked with euphemisms of their own. "The timber industry speaks of harvesting trees on public lands, the fishing industry of harvesting fish from the ocean," grumps Ray Sawhill of New York. "My understanding is that in order to harvest you have to have first reaped." Maybe he means sown; at any rate, if you have planted the trees, or raised the fish from caviar, you could then harvest them, although "harvest" is not a term that goes well outside the vegetable world. Thus, I would not use the headline, as The New York Times did last summer, "Giant Maw for Fish Harvesting."

No newspaper can be held responsible, however, for the prose prettification in its advertising. If you're appealing to a snooty clientele, you hate to use the word sale; nice stores don't have sales. (In France, sale is a dirty word.) If it's cheap but it hasn't been marked down yet, call it a special purchase. Or, if you're the Artium Gallery on Fifth Avenue, "Join us for our current anniversary exhibition of master jewelers and receive a 10 percent accommodation." Hotels provide accommodations; what will they now call a lowering of rates on rooms?

Even the most innocent words, when they take on a taint, are quickly euphemized. The Miss America contest, eager to shed any hint of royalism, now forbids the use of reign to denote the period in which here-she-comes holds the title; her once-reign is now "a year of service."

No longer need Shakespeare's Edmund, in "King Lear," cry, "Now, gods, stand up for bastards!" As Ben J. Wattenberg has written of those born on the wrong side of the blanket: "It was once called bastardy. Then illegitimacy. Then out-of-wedlock birth. And now, frequently, wholly sanitized, non-marital birth." (He left out love child.)

"Do you do euphemisms?" writes Ben Bradlee, The Washington Post's vice president at-large. (In my view, the hyphen makes the words mean "not confined to a specific assignment"; without the hyphen, it would mean "sought after by the police.") He cited a broadcast by Peter Jennings of ABC when Yasir Arafat's plane was missing: "if something has befallen him in a terminal way. . . ."

Because the word lying is off-putting to some, we have seen some prettification under oath. Oliver North denied lying to Congress, but admitted he had "provided input which differed radically from the truth." And Roger Le Locataire notes from Ponders End, London, that British officials caught telling half-truths or otherwise deceiving the court admit they have been economical with the truth.

In the general derogation of politically correct terms, some euphemism has been parodied: nobody seriously uses vertically challenged for "short," or holds that a bad speller is orthographically impaired; Clyde Haberman of The New York Times was writing tongue-in-cheek when he described a rotund Turkish political figure as kilogramically endowed. But some writers have rejected prostitute for the less pejorative "sexual worker," and the person in charge of waste disposal (formerly garbage) for the township of Montclair, N.J., refers to herself as "Senior Sanitarian."

In politics, the Clinton Administration has made it linguistic policy to refer to the taxes necessitated by its health plan as premiums, which most people associate with insurance policies. Others say that if the payment is mandatory, it's a tax, which has become a political dirty word.

Almost as dirty as guns. When Richard Nixon came out with "Guns are an abomination," advocates for unrestricted sale of the things that shoot bullets searched for a euphemism. A reader of a Minneapolis city magazine, Mpls. St. Paul, wrote to the editor to assert that "thousands have saved themselves, contrary to the myth of the danger of a home-protection weapon." Jason Zweig of Forbes magazine objects to this euphemism: "I don't think it can transform a gun into

a mom-and-apple-pie product. You can call a bullet a criminal-impairment projectile, but that will never blind the mind's eye to the ferocious furrowing of metal through flesh and bone." (Mr. Zweig, an old-school Hyphen Harry, agrees, however, with the letter-writer's use of the hyphen in home-protection weapon.)

We cannot leave today's subject without a look at dysphemism, defined in the Random House Unabridged, revised second edition, as "the substitution of a harsh, disparaging or unpleasant expression for a more neutral one." It turns euphemism on its head.

When Dick Gregory titled a book "Nigger," he bit down hard on a painful slur, turning it to his advantage. In the same way, the word queer—like queen and fairy, long used as a derogation—is being stolen by homosexuals for their own use.

"The vivid representation of identity," Edmund White said in a speech to the Center for Lesbian and Gay Studies in New York, "is especially important for the queer community." As reprinted in The New York Times, the word seemed shocking until Mr. White repeated it: "Until recently, there were few openly queer films or publications."

Is gay passe? If queer is now acceptable, its etymology deserves a look: Hugh Rawson's "Devious Derivations" tracks Queer Street, a condition of financial impecunity, to the 1811 edition of Grose's Classical Dictionary of the Vulgar Tongue, meaning "Wrong. Improper." Before that, the word queer—perhaps rooted in the Greek for "oblique, off-center"—was used by pickpockets and con men to mean "out of order," as in "queer as Dick's hatband." Until recently, bent was the term many homosexuals preferred as the antonym to straight, but the new usage has queered it.

* * *

June 26, 1994

UNDER MANY BANNERS: VARIED VOICES IN GAY LIFE NOT ALWAYS IN CHORUS

By LAURA MANSNERUS

We're a nation of joiners, which goes a way toward explaining the many lesbians and gay men in New York this weekend. But the movement that is marking its 25th anniversary, being as fractured and indescribable as any bunch of Americans, has spun off a thousand more specialized interest groups, joined in turn by homosexuals of disparate identities.

Newsstands decked out for the celebration pitch to every erotic niche that's been thought of, and they show that gay people have organized around a lot of nonsexual interests, too—like Marxism and Catholicism, dentistry and model railroading. Visitors' guides list Manhattan bars, but you can also find in them the phone number of the Gay/Lesbian Scrabble Club. And because there's a publication for everyone, gay America's subcultures and sub-subcultures have written their own versions of what they bring to the table this weekend. A few examples follow.

What a thrill to be writing to you on the eve of the Stonewall/Gay Games celebration in New York City. With all of those activists, socialites and girljocks on hand, marching may not be the only workout you'll get.

> — *Heather Findlay, editor, writing in* On Our Backs, *a bimonthly for lesbians published in San Francisco.*

Are you tired of being represented in the news media by Luke Sissyfag, Act Up and Nambla (the National Man-Boy Love Association)?

Yes, Virginia! It's O.K. to be gay and Republican! It's O.K. to care about high taxes, crime, excessive government, as well as human and gay rights and aggressive funding for the fight against AIDS. It's even O.K. to care about values which will preserve and strengthen our gay relationships, homes and spiritual lives.

> — *Message accompanying membership form in the newsletter of the Log Cabin Club of New York, an affiliate of the national Log Cabin Federation, for gay Republicans.*

When the Apostle Paul declared: "In Christ there is neither male nor female, Jew nor Gentile, slave nor free," this was a liberating message that proclaimed equality and justice. However, the proclamation that we are all "one" can sometimes blur our differences and reinforce the norms of the majority.

Thus, in our church communities, we might reword Paul's declaration by saying, "In Christ, there is male and female, old and young, disabled and temporarily able-bodied, lesbian, gay and heterosexual."

We are seeking new theological "wineskins" that can adequately hold and convey the good news of God's love and justice for our day, as well as recovering the old language and imagery when it is life-giving and can convey to people in our times the heart of the message.

> — *The Rev. Melanie Morrison, in* Open Hands, *published by Protestant organizations welcoming gay men and lesbians.*

Like responsible heterosexuals, we have the choice of whether (and, yes, when) to parent. But unlike heterosexuals, we and our communities still remember the time when to be gay was to preclude parenting. Because of this, we are less likely to believe that we "have to" parent, that it "makes us truly" men or women or adult. These and other myths are central to the socialization of most heterosexual women and men. As a consequence, we are uniquely able to "consider parenthood."

Lesbian and gay parents DO have an advantage: we KNOW that there is more to life than we were first led to believe from our families. Since we weren't fooled then, perhaps we won't be now. We need not be fooled by some of the social myths about parenting—that it's a "woman's instinct," or that it just requires that you be "a good person."

> — *Valory Mitchell and Diane Wilson, psychotherapists, writing in* The Family Next Door, *a newsletter for lesbian and gay parents and their friends.*

The world is not an easy place for Muslims. We are viewed with great suspicion, constantly discriminated against, and openly called barbaric warmongers and oppressive tyrants. Those of us who know better find this incredible. Most Muslims are gentle, noble, peaceful people, and our societies are tolerant and charitable.

Gay people are very familiar with this same paradox, and as a gay Muslim man I have found that, by and large, the same people who would discriminate against me because of my sexuality would also do so because of my religion.

It is usually my lesbian sisters and gay brothers who are the first to stand by me when others accuse me of belonging to a religion that advocates the subjugation of women or terrorist bombing attacks. They understand that prejudice and ignorance are universal adversaries, whether the issue is religious freedom or sexual freedom.

Sadly, many leaders within the Muslim community have not made the same connection.

> — *Shaffiq Essajee, writing in* Trikone *magazine, for gay and lesbian South Asians.*

In a small and esoteric community such as ours, a little prejudice and intolerance can do a lot of damage. I've met people of color who have dropped out of the scene because their fantasies or partners were unacceptable to the groups they were in.

I've known people who have hidden the fact that they enjoyed cross-dressing, acted "too feminine" or "too masculine" in public, or liked to sleep and play with people of the "wrong" sex or gender, in a community that claims to cherish the sexual outlaw.

This seems even more incongruous and ironic in the year celebrating the 25th anniversary of the Stonewall riots, which were carried out by the very people who are looked down upon now: drag queens, effeminate gay men and diesel dykes, most of whom were people of color.

> — *Antoinette, editor,* BlackLeather, Leather on the Cutting Edge for People of Color and Their Friends.

Until more aviators with H.I.V. and AIDS are visible, we'll miss opportunities to learn and share and support. And yes, to be supported, too.

Maybe that's the hardest part for a pilot . . . admitting you need (or may need) support—that you're not in control. Pilots are taught to be independent, strong, brave, always in control. How many times have we boasted (or bemoaned) the fact that the PIC bears ultimate responsibility for the flight, no matter who else may be involved in a supportive role?

Losing control is perceived as the ultimate humiliation for a pilot. But that's exactly what H.I.V. does—pilots lose control of their careers and their health. Fortunately, my faith and a great set of friends made it easy for me to learn to let go.

> — *Ron S., writing in* NGPA News, *the quarterly of the National Gay Pilots Association.*

On June 26, New York City is going to witness a massive gathering of gays, lesbians, bisexuals and transgendered people. This gathering, Stonewall 25: International March on the United Nations to Affirm the Human Rights of Lesbian and Gay People, marks the 25th anniversary of the Stonewall riots. There is, however, a lot of controversy surrounding this celebration.

Bisexuals and transgendered people are feeling excluded because they aren't part of the title. Stonewall organizers have said that the words "transgendered" and "bisexual" cannot be understood or translated on an international level. Transgendered activists feel that is perhaps the lamest excuse the committee could have come up with.

So we urge you to come to New York City to show your pride in who you are, whoever you consider yourself to be. The important thing is to be proud. Remember that!

— *BiFocus, a newsletter for Philadelphia's bisexual community*

* * *

August 20, 1995

AGAINST ASSIMILATION

By KARLA JAY

"Queer theory" may be the hottest new area in academia, but once you get past the racy titles of conference papers and books, the subject is anything but sexy or sexual. As Leo Bersani describes it in the prologue to "Homos" (Harvard University, $22.95), queer theory is a discipline in which "gay men and lesbians have nearly disappeared into their sophisticated awareness of how they have been constructed as gay men and lesbians" by the larger society. Denouncing both the invisibility that assimilation and poststructuralist theory have brought—"de-gaying gayness can only fortify homophobic oppression"—and the traditional "homo-heterosexual dyad," Mr. Bersani is at his best when he focuses instead on the most controversial and marginal elements of gay male sexuality. In so doing, he engages in a broad inquiry into the nature of desire and power, which offers insights that apply well beyond the gay male community.

Declaring that "gay life styles cannot be dissociated from an authentically new organization of the body's pleasures," Mr. Bersani persuasively separates genital pleasure from sexuality. The most radical function of sadomasochism is not that it exposes the "centrality of erotically stimulating power plays in 'normal' society," he writes, but rather "the shocking revelation" that for the sake of stimulation "human beings may be willing to give up control over their environment." Though Mr. Bersani is not likely to win any friends within the S&M community by asserting that the master-slave pairing is akin to Nazism, this pursuit of the concept of "self-shattering" daringly takes up where Michel Foucault's "History of Sexuality" left off.

Unfortunately, other sections of "Homos" are neither so original nor so successful. Mr. Bersani is a professor of French at the University of California, Berkeley, whose previous books include "The Culture of Redemption," an examination of what Freud had to say about narcissism, sublimation and the psychoanalysis of culture. In "Homos," he presents an analysis of "the gay presence"—the heightened visibility in the general culture of male homosexuals in the wake of AIDS—that testifies to the isolation of the academy. "Straight America can rest its gaze on us, let us do our thing over and over in the media," he writes, "because what our attentive fellow citizens see is the pathos and impotence of a doomed species"; he sees AIDS as a "boon" to homophobes—"it might even be counted on to keep killing the damnably inevitable gays of future generations." These are interesting, if familiar, jumping-off points. But his analysis as a whole, especially his discussion of Federal AIDS policy and the psychology of the homophobe, remains frustratingly abstract.

"Homos," unfortunately, is written with a humorless turgidity and reads more like a collection of four essays than a cohesive whole. In the last chapter, "The Gay Outlaw," as he did in "The Culture of Redemption," Mr. Bersani turns to a literary analysis. His subjects include Marcel Proust's Charlus and other "inverts" in "Remembrance of Things Past," who are secretly women in search of real men, Andre Gide's pederast Michel in "The Immoralist" and Jean Genet's treacherous, betraying criminals in "Funeral Rites." While these may indeed be prototypical "gay outlaws," they no more represent homosexuals per se than the imaginings of the Marquis de Sade or Stephen King represent all heterosexuals.

* * *

June 27, 1999

RIGHT OUT OF THE CLOSET

By DAVID BROOKS

PARTY CRASHER: A Gay Republican Challenges Politics as Usual
By Richard Tafel
253 pp. New York: Simon & Schuster. $25.

During the 1980's it appeared the Republican Party was about to grow a gay wing. There were a number of talented gay conservative writers working their way through the ranks. There were several more or less openly gay members of the Reagan Administration. George Bush is said to have won around 40 percent of the gay vote in 1988. It seemed only a matter of time before some foundation would shell out for a gay conservative journal, a gay conservative think tank, dull but worthy conferences and all the other accouterments that go with being a bona fide faction on the American right.

But it hasn't worked out that way. In 1996 Bob Dole returned a donation from gay Republicans. The Senate leader, Trent Lott, told an interviewer that homosexual sex was sinful. And most significant, several of the prominent gay conservative writers have broken, often bitterly, with their former soul mates.

So now the question is: Is it even possible to be a gay Republican, or are the two labels inimical? In his lively book, "Party Crasher," Richard Tafel argues that the breach can be healed. Tafel is the executive director of the Log Cabin Republicans, the gay organization that tried to give that $1,000 check to the Dole campaign. Now he spends his days as a campus speaker, press releaser, television talking head and grass-roots organizer. His book is part memoir—how he emerged from the Harvard Divinity School into his quixotic role—and part political statement.

The best sections of the book simply describe what it is like to be a gay Republican, which seems to be akin to standing in the middle of a field with a hurricane hitting you from one side and a tornado slamming you from the other, while you look up hopefully for blue sky. From the right comes complacent prejudice. It seems that every gay Republican has found himself with a group of conservative types in which somebody starts referring to "queers." From the gay left comes public demonization. Apparently, every gay Republican has had a gay friend tell him that voting for the Republicans is like a Jew voting for the Nazis.

Why would anybody volunteer for such abuse? Many Log Cabin members, Tafel writes, were aware of themselves as Republicans before they became aware of themselves as gay. Most believe in limited government, and many admire the way Ronald Reagan fought the cold war. But for many there is a special fervor, as if they were on some gay Peace Corps mission to the country clubs. They want to make sure homosexual voices are heard in both major parties, and to make sure that homosexuals in turn hear Republican ideas about economic liberty. One of Tafel's colleagues tells him: "From the day I accepted Harvard's scholarship I have never forgotten the words of one of my interviewers: 'You will be expected to give back in your life what we are giving you today.' . . . I am giving much more of my time and money to Log Cabin than I had ever expected to, but I consider my work in the gay community as part of my solemn duty to make this world a better place."

It certainly takes thick skin. "I didn't get involved in politics to be liked," Tafel quotes himself saying. And it is clear that one reason Tafel can take the abuse is that he is generously coated with self-esteem. This book could have been called "Arguments I Have Won," for all the passages in which Tafel describes himself coming back with just the right retort, or scoring yet another klieg-light conquest. Living in Washington, I thought I was inured to self-admiration, but passages here would leave Narcissus gaping and applauding.

The important issue is whether there is actual intellectual ground for a gay Republican to stand on, or are gay Republicans just another set of oxymoronic oddities for talk show bookers? Tafel argues that gay political thinking falls into three main strains. There are the assimilationists, who hold black-tie dinners and hope to establish that gay men and lesbians are just like everyone else. Then there are the liberationists, heavily influenced by Marxism, who view gay issues as "one of a cluster of social justice issues that required comprehensive societal change." Finally, there are libertarians, who see sexual orientation as one facet of their lives, but rarely the most important one. Libertarians reject group labels, believing each person is responsible for his or her own destiny. And of course libertarians are suspicious of the state, believing government should stay out of economic as well as private life. Tafel is a libertarian.

He makes an outstanding case that some homosexuals should call themselves libertarian and maybe sometimes vote for Republican candidates. He doesn't make a good case that homosexuals should call themselves Republicans. Because the Republican Party, for all its commitment to limited government, has never been and never will be a libertarian party. It is a conservative party, believing that government should shore up middle-class moral standards. If gay people are to become a vital fixture in the Republican coalition, somebody will have to demonstrate that being gay is not an affront to middle-class morality, a case that should be possible to make.

Tafel seems to sense this, and yet the large and maybe most revealing failing of "Party Crasher" is that he can't bring himself to endorse middle-class morality, or to defend its institutions. One section of his book is entitled "Understanding the Religious Right," but nowhere does he really try to understand the religious right, or its concerns about family breakdown. And in his section on the limits of moral relativism, he pats himself on the back for daring to say that it is immoral knowingly to infect another with the H.I.V. virus. This is the start of a morality, one supposes, but it's not a very ambitious start.

Tafel seems unable to make comprehensive judgments about different life styles: to say that homosexuality is not a choice, but how you live is; to say that monogamy is better than promiscuity, and that anybody—straight or gay—who has more than five sex partners in a year is probably doing something sleazy. In short, Tafel has a developed set of arguments to champion the cause of economic liberty, but only apologetic, half-formed instincts when it comes to the moral demands of gay life. The person who can write compellingly about liberty and traditional morality will have laid the foundation for a principled gay Republicanism, ground that will be worth defending against homophobes and amoralists alike.

David Brooks is a senior editor at The Weekly Standard.

*   *   *

SURVIVING IN A CLOSET

September 20, 1964

May 3, 1987

'I WEEP . . .'

To The Editor:

I am one of the homosexuals who had domineering, protective mothers and hostile, uninterested fathers whom Dr. Irving Bieber describes in "Speaking Frankly on a Once Taboo Subject" (Aug. 23).

I was particularly glad that he stated that most homosexuals are "desperately unhappy about it" because recently The New York Times carried a headline to the effect that most homosexuals are pleased with their plight and would not change.

Heterosexuals can never know the horror of the life—the utter, gnawing loneliness of it. Sometimes when the four walls seem to close in, I walk the streets seeking a companion, not for dissolute, abnormal sex, but really someone to talk to, some human contact. Oh, it is a lovely life, never knowing when the last moment is coming, never knowing when the police will knock, never knowing when blackmailers will seek to do their work.

Why are there no laws to punish parents who have caused this condition? There are all sorts of societies to prevent parents from hurting their children physically. But, as far as I know, parents can ruin the lives of their offspring with impunity, so long as there is no deprivation physically.

Let all these parents be tried for murder. To take a poor innocent child and make him into an unhappy, miserable, wretched person, to ruin his life—there is no punishment harsh enough. If a father hates a son, let him at least put on an act and pretend that he likes him. My father ridiculed me constantly. He even ridiculed the very few things I was good at. I was making $40 a week and paying $40 a week to the psychiatrist (four sessions a week at $10 each). I was living at home, full of doubt each time I went to the doctor, wondering if it would do any good at all, needing some kind of encouragement. But did I get it? No. When leaving for the doctor's, I was frequently given this parting remark: "Oh, going to the lunatic doctor again?" Three times I told my father I was going to commit suicide and each time he sarcastically said, "Let me know your plans."

When I see a movie in which the father puts his arm around his son, or when I read a book which describes a happy father-son relationship, I weep for the lost father I never had.

NAME WITHHELD
New York

* * *

ON TOUR WITH ROCK HUDSON

By SARA DAVIDSON

Do we need to know the truth about Rock Hudson? Would he have wanted it known?"

The reporter gave me a reproachful look, and I stared back in disbelief. Wasn't it a writer's job to seek out the truth?

It was the first day of my tour to promote "Rock Hudson, His Story." The book contained information never published before about the disparity between Rock Hudson's image on screen and his private life as a homosexual. Three other books about Hudson were published at approximately the same time, but mine was a project that Hudson himself initiated with the publisher, William Morrow, and the book carries our joint byline.

I had expected the book to arouse interest and controversy, but I had not anticipated that it would be received with hostility and suspicion by the media. Nor had I expected that I would spend months campaigning for tolerance for homosexuals and freedom for gay actors to be themselves. This was not a role I had envisioned for myself. But in June of last year, I was sent across the country, dangled like bait on a hook, to sell Rock Hudson at a time when people were coming to grips with the terrifying reality of AIDS. And I had underestimated how devastating it would be for many to learn that a star they had cherished as a symbol of manliness was gay.

Even before I could start my tour, people began snapping. The columnists Liz Smith and Marilyn Beck went on "Good Morning America" and questioned whether Rock Hudson could ever have authorized this book or wanted it written. Though neither had seen Hudson in the last months of his life, they said he "wasn't lucid" and was too ill to have known what was happening. Marilyn Beck wrote in one of her columns that the book "desecrated" Hudson's memory. So I started on the defensive. In the first few days, all of the reporters asked the same questions: How much time did you spend with Hudson? How many interviews did you do? How many minutes was each interview? What was Hudson's mental state?

I said I had not spent a great deal of time with Hudson. I met him on Sept. 4, 1985, and he died on Oct. 2. We conducted two taped interviews and had seven informal visits. During this period, Hudson had good days, when he was able to walk downstairs, was cogent, witty, full of zest and vinegar. On other days, he was too weak to get out of bed. I asked Hudson why he wanted to undertake a book at that time, and he said: "So much bull has been written about me. It's time to set the record straight. Just tell the whole story, and write it well." Hudson knew he would not have time to complete the task of collaboration, so he asked those in his closest circle—

people he had previously instructed not to speak to the press—to work with me.

After his death, I spoke with his friends, colleagues and the six major people—all but one of them male—with whom he had been romantically involved.

There was no question in my mind that Hudson wanted the book written. Why else would he spend some of his last hours talking with me? Many biographies are authorized by the family after the subject has died. The writer has never met the subject, and yet no one questions whether the truth ought to be told. But again and again, I was asked: "Would Rock have consented to these revelations?"

On June 24, Paul Sherman, Hudson's lawyer, and Wallace Sheft, his business manager, went on "Good Morning America" to answer the critics and underscore that Rock's share of the proceeds was going for AIDS research."I'm here to set to rest this issue about whether Rock wanted this book," Sherman said. But the issue was not set to rest. Reporters kept suggesting that I had betrayed Hudson and should have let him rest in peace. The publicity director at Morrow said to me, "Why is no one talking about the content of the book, what it tells us about Rock and our society?"

It was not until I reached the Midwest, where people were more frank about their feelings, that I began to understand. The issue was not whether Rock had authorized the book; the issue was his homosexuality. If Rock had been a straight movie star, people would have expected to read about the key women in his life, but because he was gay, many felt uncomfortable at the disclosure of the men he had loved.

What astonished me was that people felt free to express their distaste for homosexuals in a way that no one today would publicly express a dislike of Jews or blacks. In St. Louis, a woman in the audience said on television, "If you go against nature, you deserve to suffer the consequences." In Cleveland, a reporter told me he thought homosexuals were a "menace" and should be "locked up in camps." A radio interviewer in Detroit said: "I find the whole gay life style repulsive. They've ruined one of our most beautiful cities—San Francisco. Now they're going to ruin the country." The host of another show confided, "I'm the station redneck, and I'm real weird about homosexuals. I liked it a lot better when they were in the closet!"

I tried to point out what the book had revealed: the terrible cost of forcing people to stay in the closet. For Rock Hudson, protecting his secret was so critical that all other considerations came afterward. This led him to make—and justify—some questionable decisions. It led him, when he learned he had AIDS, in 1984, to tell no one except three people who had proved their loyalty. It meant not telling his most recent lover, Marc Christian, that he might have been exposed to the disease, because Rock feared Christian would tell others. It meant taking a role in "Dynasty" to maintain the illusion that everything was fine. It meant kissing Linda Evans on screen. It meant kissing Doris Day, a treasured friend, in a show

taped just days before Rock collapsed in Paris in 1985. Doris had begged Rock, when she saw how sick he looked, not to do the show. But Rock insisted he had merely caught the flu and lost weight.

Rock was determined to protect his secret, even if it meant being false with friends and overlooking the rights of others to be informed. He was criticized for these actions, but they would arise naturally from a lifetime of being forced to conduct himself with hypocrisy.

In addition to the outright bigotry I encountered, there was another, more complex response, which came from people who said they were accepting of homosexuals, who had gay colleagues and friends, yet found it disturbing to learn that an object of their romantic fantasy was gay. This is irrational, of course. If Dustin Hoffman plays a murderer, no one expects him to be slaying people offscreen.

Rock's work demonstrated that a good actor, gay or straight, can portray a lover and move us. While I was doing my research, watching Rock Hudson's films, I had often felt aroused, even though I had heard, by then, graphic reports of Rock's sexual preference for men. In one film, "Pretty Maids All in a Row," Rock played a rogue high school teacher who slept with all his students. There was a scene in which he seduced Angie Dickinson, and the sexual excitement Rock gave off was so palpable that my husband turned to me and said, "This is very confusing."

Yet many people I encountered on my tour felt Rock's homosexuality was a betrayal. In St. Louis, members of the audience on the "Sally Jessy Raphael" show said they had been "distraught" to learn Hudson was gay, and could not forgive him. One woman said she couldn't watch his movies anymore. "I can't look at him the same way," she said.

The low point of my tour came in Detroit. Halfway through my appearance on "Kelly & Company," the producers brought on Shirley Eder, an entertainment columnist, who implied, in a derisive voice, that the book was "fiction" and that Rock wasn't gay. She said she knew Rock and his companion of 10 years, Tom Clark. "We were together a lot, and I think they were more masculine than anything else," she said. "They were always watching football. With me, they were men." The audience cheered. I held my hands together to stop them from shaking. I had never before been scorned and ridiculed on a stage. I got up to leave, but a young woman in the front row said, "If Rock asked you to write the book, he would have wanted you to stay and defend it." So I stayed, but I returned home feeling bruised and shaken.

Why is it important to know the truth about Rock Hudson? In Hollywood, it is still assumed that the public would not accept a gay actor in a romantic role—that people cannot suspend their disbelief.

If, by some miracle, Rock Hudson had survived AIDS, I suspect he could have gone on acting and played romantic parts. It would have been difficult, but he was so beloved, so secure in his standing with his fans, that had he asked for their support, I believe he would have received it. Rock might have been able to broaden attitudes, in a way that no lesser known actor could, but it will remain for another star, perhaps in a more enlightened era, to take that step.

Sara Davidson is the author of four books, including "Loose Change" and "Friends of the Opposite Sex."

* * *

September 21, 1992

THE OLD MEN SIT AND TALK OF A VIRUS WITHIN

By JAMES BENNET

As dusk settled beyond the windows, the slow-talking, balding men leaned back in their metal chairs and, competing just a bit, bragged about their children.

Bob, 64 years old, was looking forward to the autumn wedding of his youngest girl (the older two remain "unclaimed blessings"). He was a little worried, though, about how the groom's family—and his ex-wife and ex-in-laws—would treat him now that he was out of the closet. And H.I.V.-positive.

"Gosh," he said with a timid smile. "I don't know what to expect."

"I'd run out the back door," said Jim, 61, clearly a little horrified at his friend's prospects.

"It'll be all right," put in Robert Wheeler, 66, the third member of the support group for H.I.V.-positive older men—even though he had reason to doubt the kindness of family. After all, he said, his brother, a World War II veteran fighting cancer, refuses to see him.

Just as young people in general will reject the elderly for being slow or out of touch, young people with H.I.V. often have little patience or empathy for old people with H.I.V. So in the cavernous room in the West Village where they gather once a week, the members of the tiny group find comfort in one another, recalling Rock Hudson and other old stars they secretly lusted after as boys, describing the charades they kept up during marriage, planning their obituaries and swapping tales of afflictions they have trouble distinguishing from the symptoms of aging.

The disease tends to run more quickly through an older body, said Dr. William H. Adler, chief of Clinical Immunology for the National Institute on Aging, part of the National Institutes of Health.

"For people infected with H.I.V., the development of AIDS is more rapid the older you are, and then the progression of AIDS to death is shorter as well," he said. "One of the big problems I'm having with our older AIDS patients is these people get suicidal. They get depressed as hell."

In addition to feeling shame and isolation, some older people with H.I.V. said they were tortured by a special kind of guilt: remorse at using resources they feel should go to the young, those who did not have much of a chance at life before H.I.V. came crashing down.

Nancy Siesel/The New York Times

It took 65 years and an AIDS diagnosis before Robert Wheeler came out of the closet, and then it took him almost another year to compose the letter he sent to his family and close friends in January.

At the same time, others feel overlooked when attention focuses on the epidemic. About 11 percent of the people with AIDS in New York City, and 10 percent nationally, received their diagnoses after they turned 50, the age classified as older by those who track the disease. They far outnumber babies born with the virus, or people under 25 who have developed AIDS, and yet their deaths in the epidemic seem somehow less tragic. After all, they are so much older—a fact that, to them, can be pretty cold comfort.

H.I.V., the virus that causes AIDS, compounds the pains, loneliness and fear that can come with growing old. Illnesses strike more swiftly and withdraw more grudgingly, if ever. Old friends—the ones who have not died or moved away—stop calling.

Women, who account for about 12 percent of the AIDS diagnoses in New Yorkers over 50 and 11 percent of those over 50 nationally, can feel particularly isolated, said Karen Solomon, H.I.V. consultant at Elder Family Services in Brooklyn, which recently received a $120,000 Federal grant to help old people with AIDS and educate the elderly about H.I.V.

Talking Openly Is Difficult

Ms. Solomon's mother died at 63 from AIDS, after contracting H.I.V. from a blood transfusion. "That was my mother's biggest concern—what people were going to think about this," she said. "As soon as she learned about H.I.V., she said, 'I can't deal with this, I give up.'"

But many gay and bisexual men who came of age before the sexual revolution, who account for most of the elderly people with AIDS, also have difficulty talking openly about having H.I.V. They had enough trouble acknowledging they were gay.

Among gay men, a cultural divide often separates those who came of age in the furtive 40's and 50's, and those who came later. Partly because of that divide, a group called Senior Action in a Gay Environment runs three support groups for older men with H.I.V.

SAGE, which started its H.I.V. support services with 12 clients in 1989, serves more than 200 men who are 50 and older. The organization's support groups for older people are the only ones of their kind, said Arlene Kochman, the executive director.

Fallout of Persecution

Mr. Wheeler was the only member of the support group who would let his last name be used. "I don't mind," he said with a chuckle. "I'm going to die." Others members would allow themselves to be identified only by their first names. But even Mr. Wheeler told his companions that sometimes he felt uncomfortable talking about AIDS.

"Our whole age group still suffers from that, because we were so persecuted for so long we don't know how to express ourselves," Jim said. "But the young people do."

Mr. Wheeler said: "They don't understand—they can't. They didn't live it."

It took 65 years and an AIDS diagnosis before Mr. Wheeler came out of the closet, and then it took him almost another year to compose the letter he sent to his family and close friends in January. As he became sicker, he could no longer keep his secrets.

'No More Running Back'

"I kept my secret to myself, which at times caused stress in hiding and lying," the letter read, in part. "And so having lived 65 glorious years with the closet door just open enough to run back if I should so desire, now Robert has taken the door off its hinges—no more running back."

He regrets having had to wait so long to be honest. "It's a shame," he said. "You know, the young people today don't have to do that."

Among older men, "there's a shorthand we use, whereas you can drop all kinds of references with the younger people and they have no idea what you're talking about," said Patrick Daniels, a 56-year-old blind writer with AIDS who attends a mixed-age support group at the Gay Men's Health Crisis, in addition to a group at SAGE. "The young men don't understand what it's like to be a criminal—the older men were criminals."

Although young people in his group "sass" him, he said, he enjoys playing the fatherly role (he has no children) and loves being surrounded by the creative energy of younger men.

Mr. Daniels was married for eight years, through the late 60's. "Gay was not really an option, as far as I was concerned," he said. "It was too unwholesome and repressed."

Experiences like that color older men's approach to dealing with AIDS, often compounding their sense of shame and encouraging them to remain silent and alone. Older men "tend to be somewhat reserved and almost alienated from the rest of the group," said Patrick Moriarty, a 60-year-old psychiatric social worker who has H.I.V. and leads a support group at G.M.H.C.

Young people, he said, are often angry at the old, revealing "the kind of attitude of 'You're almost 60, you've lived a full life, and here I am, 20 years old, and I'm being robbed.'"

Still Dreaming

That's an attitude that many older people with H.I.V. say they understand, which may be why they speak so searingly about subjects often touched on when old people who do not have the virus contemplate their futures: guilt over using scarce resources; nostalgia for their younger days; occasional, unconvincing acceptance of their fate, and a yearning to live.

"I still have a couple of dreams, at 63," said Sidney Morris, a playwright who is now largely homebound. "I'd like to get rid of some of my pain and travel." Mr. Morris has sketched out two plays he hopes to write, but a drug he must take has shattered his concentration.

In his small Manhattan apartment, Mr. Morris had prepared for a reporter's visit by pulling out a 1954 black-and-white photo of the playwright as a young man, showing a slim, confident 25-year-old sitting with legs crossed, a cigarette perched all too casually between two fingers. "I thought I was going to be a Jewish Noel Coward," Mr. Morris said.

He had made some notes to remind himself of subjects he wanted to discuss: "Medical bills" on one line, "Confusion age-H.I.V." on another.

Before his illnesses drove him indoors, Mr. Morris worked for four years as a volunteer helping people with AIDS at a Bronx hospital. In the brown notebook he still keeps, the name of each who died is crossed out.

He used to read Emily Dickinson to "the kids" or tell them his "1930's gay jokes," which remain, six decades later, unprintable. Now Mr. Morris returns to the hospital only as a patient, and when he walks into his doctor's waiting room he no longer feels useful, only guilty.

"I walk into his office and it looks like central casting for, you know, 'Beverly Hills'—what is it?— '9021.'" he said. Those kids' deaths from AIDS, he said, would be tragedies. His would not be. "I feel like I'm taking up space."

Grew Up with Fear

Mr. Morris, who spent his 17th birthday in a Pennsylvania jail courtesy of the vice squad, wrote a play in 1989 about tensions between young and old gay men called, "The Wind Beneath My Wings."

"They are from different planets," he said of the two main characters. "The kid accuses the older guy of leaving him a legacy of filth."

But asked to describe the differences between the old and the young, Mr. Morris abruptly leaned forward and declared that, in a terrible way, AIDS was closing the gap.

"I grew up afraid that the vice squad was going to arrest me," he said. "I grew up thinking that part of me was insane.

The guys who grew up with the specter of the epidemic over them—my God! I got a call from a 26-year-old saying, 'I don't know how to make a date.'"

* * *

June 26, 1994

A GAY WORLD, VIBRANT AND FORGOTTEN

By GEORGE CHAUNCEY

It would have been unthinkable 25 years ago for thousands of openly gay fans to cheer openly gay athletes at Yankee Stadium, for openly gay artists to perform to the acclaim of openly gay audiences at Carnegie Hall, or for the mainstream media to provide extensive and sympathetic coverage of it all. Today's march and the Gay Games and Cultural Festival are testimony to the legacy of the Stonewall rebellion of June 28, 1969—when a police assault on a Greenwich Village gay bar turned a small civil rights campaign into a mass liberation movement.

But the enshrinement of Stonewall as the genesis of gay culture threatens to deny the richness and resiliency of gay and lesbian life before the late 60's and to obscure the long history of gay resistance that made the gay-rights movement possible.

Pre-Stonewall lesbians and gay men are often held up as passive victims of social hatred who lived solitary lives (in the "closet") that kept them vulnerable to anti-gay ideology. Many gay people blame previous generations for not having had the courage to come out of the closet. Or they condescendingly imagine that their predecessors internalized society's hatred of homosexuality and became self-loathing.

But the systematic suppression of the gay community was not due to some age-old, unchanging social antipathy, nor was it a sign of passivity and acquiescence by gay people. Anti-gay forces created the closet in response to the openness and assertiveness of gay men and lesbians in the early 20th century.

Beginning in the 1890's, an extensive gay world took shape in the streets, cafeterias, saloons and apartments of New York City, and gay people played an integral role in the social life of many neighborhoods. Openly gay men drank with sailors and other working men at waterfront dives and entertained them at Bowery saloons; well-known gay people casually mixed with other patrons at Harlem's basement cabarets; lesbians ran speakeasies where Greenwich Village bohemians—straight and gay—gathered to read their verse.

These men and women, who saw themselves as part of a visible, largely working-class gay world, forged a culture with its own language, customs, folk histories, heroes and heroines. In the 1920's and early 30's, gay impresarios organized drag balls attracting thousands of gay dancers and straight spectators. Gay writers, actors and musicians produced a distinctive gay literature and performance style. This cultural outpouring was so popular by the late 20's that gay performers moved from the margins of the city and briefly became the darlings of Broadway.

This flourishing gay world has been forgotten. It was wiped into historical oblivion by a fierce backlash in the 30's—part of a wider Depression-era condemnation of the cultural experimentation of the 20's, which many blamed for the economic collapse. With millions of male breadwinners losing their jobs, people were fearful of any additional threats to traditional family hierarchies.

In New York, laws were enacted prohibiting homosexuals from gathering in any state-licensed public place. Bars, restaurants and cabarets were threatened with loss of their liquor licenses if they employed homosexuals, allowed them to gather on the premises or served them drinks—and the State Liquor Authority closed hundreds of establishments for tolerating a gay presence. This continued for decades: nearly every gay bar in the city was closed in the winter of 1959-60 in response to an anti-gay campaign by the newspaper columnist Lee Mortimer, and again in 1964 in a pre-World's Fair "cleanup."

The public discussion of gay issues was also censored. In the early 30's, after a generation of films had dealt with gay images, the new Hollywood production code prohibited gay characters and even talk of homosexuality in films. In the theater, the backlash had started even before the Depression: after the appearance of a lesbian drama on Broadway and Mae West's threat to stage a farce about transvestites called "The Drag" in 1927, a state law was passed prohibiting the representation or discussion of homosexuality on the stage.

In the 30's, the New York City police, using a 1923 state law that made it a criminal act for one man to invite another to have sex, began sending good-looking plainclothes officers into gay bars to strike up conversations with men, lead them on and arrest them if the victims suggested going home. (Between 1923 and 1967, when gay activists persuaded Mayor John V. Lindsay to end most entrapment, more than 50,000 men had been arrested on this charge.)

Anti-gay policing around the country intensified in the 40's and especially the 50's, when Senator Joseph McCarthy claimed that homosexuals in the State Department threatened national security. Thousands of gay Federal employees were dismissed. Equally without substance, police departments and newspapers around the country began to demonize homosexuals as child molesters; arrest rates increased dramatically.

The degree to which gay men had to fear arrest—and the subsequent exposure of their homosexuality to their families and employers—is almost impossible to understand today. Although New York's gay world grew in the post-war years, gay life became less visible and gay meeting places more segregated and carefully hidden from the straight public. The state built the closet in the 30's, and the isolation of homosexuals made it easier for them to be demonized.

Still, some gay people fought for their rights. In the 1930's, gay bars challenged the prohibitions against them in the courts (unsuccessfully), and in the 1950's a handful of courageous souls organized political groups, such as the

Mattachine Society and the Daughters of Bilitis, to advocate the homosexual cause. Although most did not speak out so openly, taking this as evidence that they accepted the laws against them misinterprets silence as acquiescence. It construes resistance in the narrowest of terms—as only the organization of formal political groups or protests.

Threatened with police raids, harassment and the loss of their jobs, families and reputations, most people hid their participation in gay life from their straight associates. But this did not necessarily keep them hidden from one other. They developed a sophisticated system of subcultural codes of dress, speech and style that enabled them to recognize one another and to carry on covert conversations. "Gay" itself was such a word until the 60's, when its homosexual connotations began to be known to nongay New Yorkers.

The tactics gay people devised for communicating, claiming space and affirming their self-worth did not directly challenge anti-gay repression in the way the post-Stonewall movement would, but they allowed many gay people to form a supportive community despite the larger society's injunc-tion against their doing so. This enabled many lesbians and gay men to build happy, self-confident, loving lives.

That the openness of gay life in the early 20th century was brought to an end after a few decades, and that the memory of it was systematically suppressed, reminds us that the growth of tolerance in recent years cannot be taken for granted. Then as now, increased gay visibility produced a powerful reaction.

But the relative tolerance of homosexuality in the early 20th century also shows that America has not been monolithically and inevitably homophobic, and that social conventions of sexuality are no more natural or timeless than those of race or gender. Attacks on gay men and lesbians have often resulted from broader anxieties in American culture as much as from fears about homosexuality itself. Above all, the last century shows us that attitudes toward gay people can change—and can be changed.

George Chauncey teaches American history at the University of Chicago and is author of "Gay New York."

* * *

COMING OUT

May 8, 1977

BEHIND THE BEST SELLERS: DAVID KOPAY

By HERBERT MITGANG

Passing by the sports department at The Times, David Kopay remarked, "I once had my picture in your paper—when I was co-captain of the 1964 University of Washington Rose Bowl Team."

His picture is making the papers again for an altogether different reason—the 10-year veteran running back for the San Francisco Forty-niners, Washington Redskins, Detroit Lions, New Orleans Saints and Green Bay Packers is the first professional athlete to admit publicly his sexual preference for men.

He and his co-author, Perry Deane Young, a writer and former United Press International correspondent, are both homosexuals. Both hope that their book, "The David Kopay Story," published by Arbor House, will help to create greater understanding because they believe that state laws against homosexuality are laws against nature.

"All we are saying is that we exist and nothing we do in private is as unnatural as forcing a person to live as a heterosexual when he knows he is not," Young says. "The societal questions come down to how humanely the people in power will deal with human beings such as David Kopay and myself."

When an article appeared in the Washington Star in December 1975, about homosexuals in sports, Kopay called up the paper and decided to go public about his sexuality: "It was game time, the National Anthem was playing." That was the genesis of the idea for the book, which eventually was auctioned among several publishers.

Donald I. Fine, the Arbor House publisher, received "a very respectable commitment" in advance from Bantam Books, which will bring out the paperback edition next year. Then Fine decided to go all out in promoting the book. Unlike one of the conglomerate-owned publishers, when he goes for broke it can almost literally happen. Fine is known in the trade as an independent character, with strong links to the paperbacks, who takes chances on controversial themes where other publishers fear to tread.

"The book appealed to me because of two of my interests—football and identity," Fine said. "This isn't just a football hero story. It's about a man's whole life and about attitudes in the country as well. I was particularly moved by the passages about his family."

In telling the world about the book, Fine says he published it like any other on his list with one additional factor: "We assumed that the gay community would be interested in the story. We advertised in some of the gay magazines, such as The Advocate, Mandate and In Touch, as well as in the standard book places. His television appearances—everybody wanted Kopay—also helped greatly. My hunch is that, at the start, the gay readers contributed very strongly. Then, later, as people took to it, so did some of the book clubs."

"Don wanted it to be called "The Dave Kopay Story" but I thought David would be more dignified in the title," Kopay said. "Funny, now that it's all out in the open, I feel more like Dave."

* * *

December 5, 1981

A TOUGH MONTH IN THE NEW LIFE OF A POLICEMAN

By ANNA QUINDLEN

Charles H. Cochrane Jr. has been a police officer for 14 years, and it is apparent even when he is not in uniform. He talks of "the department" as though it is his life, not his work. He lapses in conversation into the convoluted, polysyllabic style that leads policemen to call thieves "perpetrators" and fights "altercations." Even in describing the events of his life, he uses the stuff of which official reports are made—exact date, time, place of the occurrence. In just that way, Sergeant Cochrane remembers the events of the last month.

Nov. 5: He meets with nine friends and acquaintances to discuss the consequences should he testify before a City Council committee that is going to consider a proposal to ban discrimination against homosexuals.

Nov. 8: He sits down with his parents in the living room of the home he shares with them in Canarsie, hands them a copy of a book entitled "Loving Someone Gay" and says the three of them need to have a long talk.

Nov. 15: He writes to Police Commissioner Robert J. McGuire to inform him that he plans to testify. And on Nov. 20, he enters the Council chamber, sits down at the witness table, begins to read his prepared statement and by so doing becomes the first member in the history of the New York City Police Department to announce publicly that he is a homosexual.

Two weeks have passed. The Council committee has defeated the proposal, and Sergeant Cochrane, a member of the Manhattan South Task Force, is supervising his men on peddler patrol.

As he walks up and down 34th Street, the 38-year-old sergeant, a wiry man with close-set eyes and an easy grin, meets them and they salute.

He has received 15 letters, many of them from other police officers, nearly all applauding his candor. He has received dozens of calls, all supportive. His parents, whom he told of his homosexuality only after he decided to testify, have been accepting.

When he was on duty at the Thanksgiving Day Parade, a man standing next to him stared, then looked away, stared, then looked away. Finally, Sergeant Cochrane could stand it no longer.

"Yes, it was me," he said. "I thought so," said the man jubiliantly. One of the black officers engaged him in conversation about prejudice. One of the younger men felt compelled to confide that he liked the ballet.

"The funny thing is, I don't even like the ballet," Sergeant Cochrane said. "Everyone I talked to within the department felt I probably would meet a lot of negative response," he added. "But I could not believe the support. Even the biggest clowns had nothing to say. Now maybe some of those cops who are already suspect and are teased a bit may finally say, 'Hey, knock it off, I am gay.'"

Of course, not all the response has been positive. The president of the Sergeants Benevolent Association, Harold Melnick, says, "I just think sometimes it's better left as it is, without talking about it."

But some of the men who serve under Sergeant Cochrane do not agree. "It took a lot of courage," said Officer Robert Sena, who served with Sergeant Cochrane in the Manhattan Neighborhood Stabilization Unit, where the sergeant was assigned until October. "I respected him before. I respect him even more now."

"Well, subordinates will be reluctant to make negative comments," Sergeant Cochrane said. "You should know that."

Sergeant Cochrane loves police life, and so it is somehow fitting that the first person he ever told of his homosexuality was his partner in the 71st Precinct in Brooklyn.

"Five minutes after midnight, Nov. 6, 1977," he said. "He's married, 2.7 kids, a wife, a mortgage, the whole bit. I was at his home for dinner, and when I was leaving, he came around to the other side of the car, got in and said, 'I gotta ask you something.'

"Then he said, 'Man, I love you as a friend, I love you as a partner, but I have to ask you something.' Then I knew in my mind. And before he could even ask the question, I said, 'Yes, I am gay.' That was my coming out. Just the privilege of telling someone else what I was."

It was the beginning of a new life, a life in which he told a number of his colleagues that he was a homosexual. Before then, he had been "gay in my mind, but asexual in my life," hoping he was "just a late bloomer."

He knows other homosexuals in the department, but says they tend to adopt a form of exaggerated machismo to hide what they are, to protect themselves. Sergeant Cochrane, on the other hand, says it is sometimes more difficult for him to tell his homosexual acquaintances that he is a police officer.

"Sometimes I have to come out as a cop," he said. He especially remembers one day in 1979, when there was a march by homosexuals to protest the movie "Cruisin'." During the day, Sergeant Cochrane had been working on the Gay Switchboard, providing information on the demonstration to callers. During the march, he happened to be the police officer assigned to the head of the line of demonstrators.

"I didn't feel that it was a conflict," he said. "It helped me to do a better job. I was a valuable resource to the department." Sergeant Cochrane is planning to take the test for lieutenant in June. He hopes someday to form a Gay Officers Action League. He was infuriated when an officer of the Patrolmen's Benevolent Association testified at the Council hearings that consensual sodomy was against the law, when, in fact, that statute has been overturned by the courts.

"I wasn't upset because I'm gay, but because I'm a cop," he said. "Suppose that guy brought a collar in, I would have to order an immediate release. A cop should know the law better than that."

* * *

June 17, 1985

'MY SON'S GAY. THAT'S ALL RIGHT.'

By ZELDA PILSHAW FRIEDMAN

In September 1981, my son Elliot, a singer and guitarist, wrote me: "I don't want to keep this from you any longer. In case you wondered why I have been secretive and retreated from the family, I'm going to tell you: I am gay and have been all of my life."

This couldn't be true! I wept for days, and in phone calls to Los Angeles, where Elliot had lived for eight years since he left home for college, tried to persuade him to come East, see a psychiatrist—at least attempt to change. We spoke of guilt; he tried to assure me that parents are not responsible for their children's sexual preference. He wrote: "I'm looking forward to a new kind of honesty between us now that I don't have to hide my real self from you. Yet I still fear your rejection, a fear that has kept me locked up for so many years."

So many years of searching! First, he would become a psychologist. Then, a teacher. Then, a black studies expert. He dropped out of college and moved to Boston. Then followed a return to yet another college in California and the absolutely certain decision to become a rabbi. But religion didn't work either. Nothing would have worked. Elliot had to trudge up and down many dead ends before finding himself and his vocation. Society does not make it easy for a man or woman to stand up and say, "I am gay."

Nor does society make life easy for the parent of a homosexual. I realized that I could either get to know my son or lose him. I had no choice but to educate myself.

Elliot mailed me books that dispelled myths about homosexuals. I clipped news articles. Men and women were coming out daily at home and on their jobs. Yet, I confided my secret to few. Unwittingly, I discovered other parents in the same predicament. One acquaintance had a lesbian daughter and was proud of it. Proud! Could I ever reach that point?

When Elliot invited me to fly out to meet his friends, I had to work up courage. At a supper party in Los Angeles, I talked with homosexual men and women who were artists, builders, lawyers, psychologists, social workers. Some said they wished their mothers and fathers would make the effort I had. Others said they had completely broken off from their families or had been thrown out.

Being homosexual forces young people to develop surrogate families, further separating them from the mainstream. But many don't make it.

I've heard heart-rending tales of pain, rejection, homelessness, threatened suicide. Someone quoted a Vietnam veteran whose words resounded in my ear: "I was given a medal for killing a man but excommunicated for loving one."

Though I returned to New York more enlightened, I still had trouble with the idea. Elliot helped me. Often, I could not even use the word "gay."

In my letters, I kept referring to "his situation." He corrected me: "Being gay isn't 'my situation' any more than being a women is yours. It's who I am."

I said I couldn't face our relatives, that I was embarrassed. He said:

"When you're convinced that you don't have to apologize for my being gay, you won't have to hide it. You're under a lot of pressure, Mom."

Once in the elevator, I stood beside a man I thought might be homosexual and wanted to say, "I know." Soon afterward, when a dinner companion told a nasty story, I said: "I'd appreciate your not telling jokes about gays. They're not funny to me. I have a gay son. These stories are based on stereotypes, not the truth." To my amazement, in months that followed, I opened up, even to my own parents.

"But Mom," I said, "heterosexual marriage isn't the only way. Elliot is happy. He has fine friends. His life is respectable, even though it is different from ours."

"No, Dad, it wasn't my divorce. No, it wasn't 'bad company.' Ten percent of the population is gay—it's no one's fault." Last year, Elliot decided to move East for good. "I don't have to run away any more," he told me.

Once, it was a disgrace to be a divorced woman or to live with someone outside of wedlock. That seems like ancient history now. Maybe some day it will be acceptable for Elliot and his courageous peers to be homosexual. On June 30, I'm marching in the Gay and Lesbian Pride Day parade to let people know where I stand: My son's gay. That's all right.

Zelda Pilshaw Friedman is a writer and photographer.

* * *

February 3, 1989

HOMOSEXUAL LAWYERS KEEP FIGHTING BARRIERS

By E. R. SHIPP

Richard Failla had kept his private life under wraps as he rose through the ranks of the Manhattan District Attorney's office to become one of the most respected members of the elite homicide bureau.

But in 1970 a defense lawyer, angry at a position Mr. Failla had taken in court, warned him, "I know you're a faggot, and I'm going to get you."

To be gay or lesbian and to be a lawyer in those years meant walking on tenterhooks. There was no choice. If one's homosexuality became known, it could be grounds for exclusion from the profession.

The Case of Harris Kimball

Every homosexual lawyer had heard of Harris L. Kimball, or someone like him. In 1955, when he was 29 years old, Mr. Kimball, a civil rights attorney, was arrested for lewd and lascivious conduct after he and another man were caught having sex on a deserted stretch of beach one midnight in Orlando, Fla.

Within 30 days, the Florida bar began disbarment proceedings against him, on the ground that he had violated a state law prohibiting homosexual relations. His legal career seemed over. Once he was identified as a homosexual, he found it difficult to find work even as an insurance claims adjuster.

So for Mr. Failla the warning from his adversary was a serious matter. "It was easy for me to assume at that point," he said in a recent interview, "that I could lose my license, lose my job, lose my ability to practice law—something I had worked so long for."

But Mr. Failla took a bold step. "That's when I decided, come what may, I'm not going to live under this kind of oppression and I will come out. I will not deny it to anybody. I'm not going to shout it from the rooftops, but I will not deny it to anybody and I will live my life the same way I see my friends living. No one can accuse me of denying what I am or trying to fool anybody any longer."

Bias and Stigma Remain

The step that Mr. Failla took 19 years ago is still being taken with trepidation by gay men and lesbians each day. Discrimination and stigma, lawyers say, are still the reality in many instances.

But it is a measure of how far the profession has come that a once invisible minority is being seen and heard in law firms, in public defenders' offices, in prosecutors' offices, in Congress and in a wide array of government agencies.

Homosexuals have formed scores of local bar associations across the nation, and last fall 600 lawyers meeting in San Francisco launched the National Lesbian and Gay Law Association.

Richard Failla recently became the first openly gay person to be elected to the New York State Supreme Court, joining about two dozen other elected or appointed judges around the country who have made their homosexuality known.

Major law schools like the one at New York University offer courses in gay rights. A national conference on sexual orientation and the law has been held at the University of Chicago Law School, where money is being raised to establish a scholarship fund for students who are likely to use their legal education to advance gay and lesbian causes.

"More and more people are finding it O.K. to be openly gay," said Abby Rose Rubenfeld, a Nashville lawyer who chose to be open with her colleagues because, she said, "I wanted to have my lover's picture on my desk; I wanted to be able to talk about my life."

A.B.A. Resolution Expected

It is also a measure of change within the profession that the American Bar Association, at its convention next week in Denver, is widely expected to adopt a resolution condemning discrimination on the basis of sexual orientation.

The measure lost by 24 votes in 1983 and 9 in 1985. It still faces some opposition, but when it comes up for a vote by the A.B.A.'s House of Delegates next Monday morning, it will have the support of the state bar associations of New York, Massachusetts, Wisconsin and Oregon; the New York City and Los Angeles County bar associations; the A.B.A.'s Young Lawyers Division, and three of the A.B.A.'s specialized sections: family law, litigation, and individual rights and responsibilities.

The New York Times

Richard Failla, who recently became the first openly gay person to be elected to a judgeship in New York.

Leonard L. Loeb, a former president of the A.B.A.'s family law section who is now president of the Milwaukee Bar Association, will be among those urging adoption of the resolution.

"Everyone is entitled to life, liberty and the pursuit of happiness," Mr. Loeb said. "That's a basic right."

'Forbidden Subject 20 Years Ago'

To even have a debate on homosexuality and discrimination in such a forum is in itself noteworthy. "It was a forbidden subject only 20 years ago," said Thomas B. Stoddard, executive director of the Lambda Legal Defense and Education Fund, a gay rights organization. "No lawyer ever spoke publicly in a sympathetic way about lesbians and gay men."

But in 1969 courts in the District of Columbia and California held that homosexuality could not be an automatic bar to Federal employment or to teaching. And in 1973 the New York Court of Appeals became the first high court of any state to hold that homosexuality was not a basis for denying admission to the bar. The ruling came in the case of Harris Kimball, who, taking heart from the growing gay rights movement, had applied for admission to the New York bar more than 15 years after being disbarred in Florida.

Subsequent judicial decisions, the repeal of sodomy laws and 50 jurisdictions' passage of laws barring discrimination against homosexuals have all brought about what Mr. Stoddard calls a "revolution in the law."

A 'Fear Even Now'

Yet many homosexual lawyers still see a need to remain in the closet if they are to be successful in the competitive world of the advocate.

Even finding a job can be difficult for the law school graduate who does not disguise his homosexuality, as Ben Schatz, a cum laude graduate of Harvard Law School, discovered a few years ago. "One interviewer from a major San Francisco firm said to me, 'Don't we have a legitimate concern that you might ruin the reputation of our firm?'" Mr. Schatz said. He is now a staff lawyer for National Gay Rights Advocates, a legal organization in San Francisco.

"The fear even now is that somebody will blackball you," said Craig Davidson, the executive director of the Gay and Lesbian Alliance Against Defamation. "To fit in, gay and lesbian lawyers lie a lot about their social lives, or at least keep them totally quiet."

One ambitious young prosecutor in New York City, repelled at the thought of ever being known merely as "the gay assistant district attorney" and fearing that his career would be stymied if his homosexuality were known, chose to remain silent.

"I've walked a fine line in terms of avoiding questions," he said. "You don't have to lie, but if you're gay it's easier if it's private."

An informal grapevine exists to inform lawyers which firms are more hospitable to homosexuals than others. But even at such firms, where it is known that certain partners and associates are homosexual, great care is taken to keep that information from leaking to clients who may not be so tolerant. "No firm wants the reputation for being a haven for gay people," Mr. Stoddard said. Even if a lawyer's homosexuality is accepted among colleagues, efforts must be made to assure that this is not used against a client. Ms. Rubenfeld said that because she is so well known, many people assume that her clients are also homosexual. So in a child custody case, for instance, if there is a chance that homosexuality could become an issue, "we don't put my name on the papers."

* * *

April 30, 1989

BEING ACCEPTED: GAY STUDENTS ATTEND A PROM

URBANA, Ill.—It might have looked like the average fraternity formal, but to the students in tuxedoes and evening gowns at the University of Illinois it was an "Alternative Prom"—a dance co-sponsored by the Lesbian and Gay Illini and the Illini Union Board, which organizes university-sponsored events.

For many of the 100 or so men and women who attended the gala, the first university-sponsored dance for gay people at Illinois, it was a chance to turn back the clock and go to the "prom we never had," said Steen Lawson, a senior in education from Ashton, Ill., who came up with the idea.

People at the dance said that if they had taken a gay partner to their high school proms, they might have been harassed, ostracized, even threatened with violence. Most of those interviewed said they went to those proms with a straight date or they did not go at all. Some recalled the 1981 book, "Reflections of a Rock Lobster" by Aaron Fricke, which described how a gay teen-ager sued his high school in 1980 for the right to bring a male date to a prom.

'The Lights Hit Them'

At Illinois, those interviewed at the dance said there was no place for them at the school to socialize and openly express their affection. Peter McDowell, a senior majoring in French from Champaign, Ill., said he and his companion did not feel comfortable doing things most people take for granted, like dancing in bars or holding hands in public. Joining a fraternity, he added, is out of the question. "You cannot be openly gay and join a fraternity," he said.

Many people at the dance said they still felt harassed, especially by the media. They noted, for example, that local television stations sent camera crews to cover the event. Some people asked that the cameras be turned away. "Four women got off the elevator and bam! The lights hit them," said a member of the Lesbian and Gay Illini, who asked not to be identified. "One student hid her face and screamed 'No, no, no, stop it!'"

They also said they resented an article about the dance published the day before the event in The Daily Illini, the campus paper. The article quoted John Gurney, a freshman from Downers Grove, Ill., secretary of the College Republicans, who said "most of the members consider the alternative prom foolish."

"If the Black Chorus had a dance, should the press interview the Ku Klux Klan for balance?" said Daniel Savage, an Illinois graduate in theater from Chicago who attended the dance.

A few heterosexuals said they were afraid to go into the Illini Union the night of the dance because some thought homosexuals would try to pick them up. Some who did go stood near the staircase that led up to the prom and made fun of people walking by.

Despite the heckling, people who attended the dance said they had a great time. "I'm really happy," said one woman who asked that her name not be used. "Everyone accepts me as I am. I can kiss my lover on the dance floor without feeling ashamed."

* * *

May 27, 1992

NO CLOSET SPACE

By ANNA QUINDLEN

It was 20 years ago next month that an elementary-school teacher named Jeanne Manford made history. She walked down a street in New York City carrying the sort of poster paper her students sometimes used for projects, except that printed on it were these words:

PARENTS of Gays UNITE in SUPPORT for our CHILDREN

At her side during the Gay Pride march was her son, Morty, her golden boy, the one a teacher once told her would be a senator someday. When he was in high school he said he wanted to see a psychologist, and the psychologist called the Manfords in and told them that the golden boy was gay. But it never changed his mother's mind about his glow.

Morty's story, and his mother's, too, are contained in a new oral history of the gay rights struggle, "Making History," by Eric Marcus. The cheering thing about the book is how far we have come since the days when newspaper editors felt free to use "homo" in headlines.

The distressing thing is how far we have to go, not in the world alone, where homophobia remains one of the last acceptable bigotries, but in our homes, where our children learn that the world is composed exclusively of love and sex between men and women. Even when Mom and Dad have gay friends and raised consciousness, there is too often a silence that surrounds other ways of life and love. And silence begets distance.

Distance between parent and child is one of the saddest things in "Making History": the parents who try to commit their gay children to mental hospitals, the ones who erect a gravestone and send an obituary to the paper when they discover their daughter is a lesbian, or simply the ones who were told nothing because their children considered the truth untellable.

Greg Brock, a newspaperman, describes how he came out to his parents the day before he was to appear on Oprah's show. Thirty-five years old and the man had never spoken to his mother and father of his central reality. "I was about to destroy my dad's life," he recalled.

Is this really what we want, to obsess about ear infections and reading readiness and then discover many years too late that we were either unaware or unaccepting of who our children were? To keen "What will I tell my friends?" when our kids try to talk about their lives?

In the same borough in which Morty Manford grew up and his mother taught, a Queens school board has rejected a curriculum that encourages respect for all families, including those headed by gay and lesbian parents. Consider that decision, not in terms of gay rights, but in terms of the children.

Given statistical estimates, the board is telling 1 out of 10 kids that the life they will eventually lead is not part of the human program. Among their students are surely boys and girls who will discover they are gay and who, from their earliest years, will have learned that there is something wrong with that, and therefore with them. Learned it from classmates, from teachers. Worst of all, from their own mothers and fathers.

Actually, it's probably the mothers and fathers who need that curriculum most. All parents should be aware that when they mock or curse gay people, they may be mocking or cursing their own child.

All parents should know that when they consider this subject unspeakable, they may be forever alienating their own child and causing them all enormous pain. Paulette Goodman, president of the Federation of Parents and Friends of Lesbians and Gays, likens it to her experience as a Jew in occupied Paris. "I know what it's like to be in the closet," she recalled. "I know all too well."

Jeanne Manford didn't want a closet. Her Morty was the same golden boy after she found out he was gay as he was before. She was with him at the Gay Pride march and with him in the gay rights movement.

And she was with him when he died a little more than a week ago of AIDS, almost 20 years to the day after she wrote her unconditional love on poster paper for all the world to see. She does not reproach herself. She loved and accepted her child the way he was. In a perfect world, this would be the definition of "parent" in the dictionary. The point is not what you'll tell your friends at the bridge table. It is what you'll tell yourself at the end.

* * *

April 28, 1993

THE POWER OF ONE

By ANNA QUINDLEN

Now we have the numbers game. How many gay people are there in the nation? Ten percent? One percent? Four percent? It depends upon whom you ask, what survey you read, how statisticians and sex experts crunch the numbers, which respondents tell the truth and which don't. How many marched in Washington on Sunday for the civil rights of gay men and lesbians? Three hundred thousand? Half a million? A million or more? It depends on whether you ask the Park Police or the march organizers.

But at some level none of it matters at all.

I know that gay men and lesbians have ample reason to believe their political clout in America, the most quantifying of countries, will be measured by their numbers. I know, too, that those who want to prove that homosexuality is a "deviant life style" are anxious to show that the demands are disproportionate to the number of demanders, as though the right to be treated fairly depended on a head count.

But it's the power of one that really brings change. No one's head is truly turned around by a faceless sea of folks seen from a distance marching on the capital, or by numbers on sexual behavior from a research center.

It's the power of one that does it.

It's the power of one man like Sgt. Jose Zuniga, who was the Sixth Army's 1992 soldier of the year and a medic in the gulf war. Before the march he stood before the television cameras and so before the world and said, with a chestful of medals, that he was proud to be a soldier, and he was proud to be gay.

Right that minute, maybe, some fellow vets and fellow Americans wrote him off. But there have to be people who have worked with him, trained with him, fought with him, who are now forced to re-examine their attitudes toward gay men, to compare their prejudices with what they know of this one individual.

Maybe in the beginning those people will decide that Sergeant Zuniga is the exception, and that the rule is that gay men are predatory, effeminate, unfit for service. They may embrace the old "O.K., but . . ." analysis, which we have seen with blacks, with Latinos, with women and now with gay people. It goes like this: "Jose is O.K., but the rest of them . . ."

Stereotypes fall in the face of humanity. You toodle along, thinking that all gay men wear leather after dark and should never, ever be permitted around a Little League field. And then one day your best friend from college, the one your kids adore, comes out to you. Or that wonderful woman who teaches third grade is spotted leaving a lesbian bar in the next town.

And the ice of your closed mind begins to crack.

Day by day, this is how the world will change for gay men and lesbians, with the power of one—one person who doesn't fit into the straight world's fact pattern and so alters it a tiny bit, irrevocably. A revered actor who was typecast in tough-guy roles. A beloved female friend who cannot be transformed into a hate object. Coming out is a powerful thing.

It is why the march, one of the biggest civil rights demonstrations in the history of this country, was most powerful when it reflected not quantity, but quality. A sunburned man in chinos. Two silver-haired women hand-in-hand, smiling. A woman pushing a stroller. Sure, there were men in lipstick and women in buzz cuts. And women in lipstick and men in buzz cuts. Like straight people, gay people are a diverse group. To paraphrase Gloria Steinem on turning 50, this is what gay looks like.

In recent years gay men and lesbians have moved purposefully ahead in the civic arena, putting money behind candidates, crafting anti-discrimination legislation, demanding that their relationships be formally recognized. No matter what their numbers, they've become a formidable political force.

But a veneer of tolerance atop a deep pool of hatred, distrust and estrangement is no more than a shiny surface, as civil rights leaders can testify from decades of experience. The numbers in Washington were not as important as the faces, the sheer humanity of one person after another stepping forward, saying: Look at me. I am a cop, a mother, a Catholic, a Republican, a soldier, an American. So the ice melts. The hate abates. The numbers, finally, all come down to one.

* * *

September 19, 1993

LOUGANIS APPROACHES THE EDGE OF THE STAGE, AND LEAPS

By ROBERT LIPSYTE

Outside the subculture of competitive diving, where he was simply the best of all time, Greg Louganis has never received the attention his four Olympic gold medals, his discipline, his performing beauty seemed to deserve. His face never smiled from a cereal box, he never spoke for a major corporation, and he never starred in a network comedy special, a movie, a sitcom. He never even wrote a book. Was it because of the whispers that he was gay?

"I can't look back anymore, it's destructive," said Louganis. Then he laughed. "I was supposed to be living with the head of a major Hollywood studio, a guy I actually met only twice in my life. Head of a studio. You can see how much good he did me."

We were sitting in the orchestra of the Minetta Lane Theater Wednesday night before Louganis went on stage in "Jeffrey," the brilliant and funny award-winning affirmation of life in the age of AIDS. Since Sept. 7, in his New York stage debut, Louganis has acted the role of Darius, a dying chorus boy in the Broadway show "Cats," with a skill and joy that evokes the pleasure he gave as an athlete.

"You really liked it?" he asked, at 33 as sweet and coy and cunning as the character he plays.

"I bought my own ticket," I said. "I wasn't going to interview you unless I thought you were terrific." I waited until he was smiling to ask, "So, does this mean you're out?"

"Out?" He became, briefly, zoned, as if he were on the edge of the diving board, gathering himself for that leap into space. "Didn't we have this discussion before?"

"Five years ago in a Sizzler restaurant outside L.A.," I said. "You said then that your sexuality was a totally private matter."

"I still sort of feel the same," he said, stretching out the sentence, inflecting words, as if it were the three seconds from board to water. There was no suggestion that the topic was taboo or even discomforting; in fact, he seemed to enjoy confronting it, playing with it, as I took notes for the next 25 minutes.

"It's different now. I asked the question then because there were so many rumors, and I didn't include the answer in my report because it ultimately had nothing to do with the story of you preparing for Seoul."

"But now," I gestured at the empty stage, "you are in a gay role in a gay play. It's so New York, the way you seem to be saying 'Drop dead' to anyone who ever called you a name."

Louganis laughed and squirmed and nodded. The first name was "nigger," when Louganis was growing up in

Southern California, the dark-skinned adoptive son of Greek-Americans. His biological father, whom he never knew, was a teen-aged Samoan. Louganis drank and smoked as a kid to be accepted, but he also danced and dived, keeping all his worlds separate, becoming, sometimes, a spy in his own life.

The second word was 'retard.' He was out of high school before it was discovered that his reading problems were caused by dyslexia.

"I hated those names," he said carefully, "not because of what they represented but because people could attach hate to them."

"Nigger, retard, gay," I said.

"You know," said Louganis, "The way I deal with my feelings is that if I'm afraid of something, I'll face it. When I was growing up, I had nightmares about snakes biting me. So when I was around 10, I got a boa constrictor. The pet shop guy said it was a girl. We named her Rosie. She was only about 4 feet long, she lived in my room. And my sister, my sister was really terrible about this, she would come in and bother Rosie, and Rosie would start biting me. So I've been bitten, oh, countless times by a snake, my worst nightmare."

"Is this some kind of metaphor for me to figure out?"

A door opened and a woman signaled Louganis to come for makeup. The audience was drifting into the lobby.

"I'm working on things," he said.

"But why this particular play?"

He explained it as the emotionally logical progression of a five-year journey. On Sept. 19, 1988, in Seoul, in the perfect example of grace under pressure, Louganis hit his head on the board while qualifying for the springboard final. "I was so embarrassed, I wanted to disappear," he said.

But all he did was pause for four stitches and go back up to nail his final dive. He went on to win gold medals in the springboard and 10-meter platform competition. And then he quit.

"I was five years past my peak," he said. "The Chinese are probably still debating whether their diver should have won, and maybe he should have, maybe the judges were giving me points. Anyway, it was time to move on."

For the past five years, Louganis has taken acting, singing and dancing lessons, and appeared with increasing success in regional theater, including roles as the Prince in "Cinderella" and as Tony in "The Boyfriend" at the Long Beach (Calif.) Civic Light Opera.

But it was the slow death of his father, whom he helped nurse in his apartment, and a chance visit to "Jeffrey" while auditioning for something else in New York that led him to ask his new representative, Mitch Weiss, to pitch for the role of Darius.

"His message is my message," said Louganis. "You hate the disease, not life."

The woman's signal was more urgent now, and Louganis apologized and rose. We shook hands and I said, "We'll just leave it that you're working on things."

He gestured at the empty stage. "I guess you could also say this is my Rosie."

* * *

February 23, 1995

LOUGANIS, OLYMPIC CHAMPION, SAYS HE HAS AIDS

By RICHARD SANDOMIR

Greg Louganis, the 1984 and 1988 Olympic gold medal diver, who publicly acknowledged his homosexuality for the first time at last year's Gay Games in New York, has said he has AIDS.

In an interview with ABC's "20/20" that will be broadcast at 10 P.M. tomorrow, Louganis said he knew he was H.I.V.-positive before the 1988 Summer Olympics in Seoul, South Korea, and was greatly concerned when he hit his head on the board during a dive and shed blood in the pool.

Since the Seoul Games, Louganis's infection has developed into AIDS, according to the definition established by the Centers for Disease Control. "According to the C.D.C., I have AIDS versus H.I.V.," Louganis told Barbara Walters. "I do have AIDS."

Louganis, 35, joins two other major athletes who said they had AIDS or were infected with H.I.V., the virus that causes AIDS. Magic Johnson left the Los Angeles Lakers in 1991 after saying he was infected with H.I.V. Arthur Ashe, the tennis star, died two years ago of AIDS-related causes.

Louganis has written a book, "Breaking the Surface" (Random House), which will be released next week, in which he discusses his career, including winning four Olympic gold medals, as well as his upbringing and his sexuality.

In the television interview, Louganis told Walters that six months before the 1988 Olympics, he found out that a former companion of his was dying of AIDS. Louganis underwent testing and was found to be H.I.V.-positive. He immediately began treatment with the drug AZT, taking powerful doses every four hours.

He said he went to Seoul fearing discovery of his condition. "Dealing with H.I.V. was really difficult for me because I felt like, God, the U.S. Olympic Committee needs to know this," he said. "U.S. Diving needs to know it because what if I get sick at the Olympic Games and am unable to compete?"

Louganis said he was discouraged from telling the United States Olympic Committee about his condition by his doctor and his coach, Ron O'Brien.

O'Brien, who was also interviewed by "20/20," encouraged Louganis's silence, he said, "because our sport is such that you don't ever come close to anybody."

On the reverse two-and-half pike, a qualifying dive in the springboard competition in which Louganis hit his head, he said: "I heard this big hollow thud, and then I found myself in the water. I just held my head in hopes, to, I didn't know if I was cut or not. But I wanted to hold the blood in, or just not anybody touch it."

He said he was paralyzed with fear that there would be blood in the water.

"I knew there was not too much of a chance, you know, because it takes a while if you cut yourself on the head, usually it takes a minute to start bleeding," Louganis said. "And there is chlorine in the pool all over, the deck's wet with chlorinated water."

He said he thought the blood would be diluted by the water.

In a telephone interview last night, Dr. James Puffer, the physician who stitched Louganis's scalp wound without using latex gloves, referred to a 1993 National Football League study that estimated the chances of transmitting H.I.V. from coming into contact with blood were one in a million.

"If the chances of transmission are one in a million in the N.F.L., imagine how infinitesimally small they are in a non-contact sport like diving," Puffer said.

Dr. Gary Cohan, an internist with Pacific Oaks Medical Group in Los Angeles, the nation's largest private AIDS practice, told The Associated Press yesterday: "Even if the pool was not chlorinated and somebody dove in after him, there would be a minimal to zero risk that any other athlete would contract H.I.V. through swimming in the same pool that contained Greg's H.I.V.-positive blood."

In explaining why he did not tell the doctor he was H.I.V.-positive, Louganis said: "I was so stunned. This had been an incredibly guarded secret. You could throw the entire competition into a state of alarm."

At the time, O'Brien said, he told Louganis: "If you want to quit right now, Greg, that's fine."

Since 1989, the United States Olympic Committee has had strict procedures for dealing with open wounds, such as the wearing of latex gloves, but those policies were not in place for the Seoul Games. Voluntary testing for H.I.V. is made available for Olympic athletes. The U.S.O.C., along with other sports organizations, has no policy requiring H.I.V.-positive athletes to announce that they are infected.

In the interview, Louganis said he had sensed he was different from the time he was a young boy and began to accept his homosexuality during the 1976 Olympics. He said he did not try to hide his sexuality from his teammates, adding: "Nobody would room with me. I mean, I was lucky to find one person on that team that would room with me."

Louganis, the son of a Samoan father and a northern European mother, said in the interview that he was given up for adoption at the age of 9 months to Peter Louganis, a bookkeeper who died in 1991, and his wife, Frances, of El Cajon, Calif.

He told of a troubled upbringing, saying he was dark-skinned, dyslexic and was called "sissy, nigger, retard." Frances Louganis told Walters that her husband "wasn't a role model for my son" and "had nothing to do with Greg until Greg started winning first place."

Sad and depressed, Louganis said he took pills in an attempt to commit suicide. "They didn't work," he said, laughing. "Damn it, you can't do anything right."

He said his salvation was diving "because I would focus on that, and unfortunately, I mean, if I had a bad workout, I had a bad day. If I had a good workout, I had a good day. I could deal with anything."

Since retiring from diving after the 1988 Olympics, Louganis has tried to make an acting career. Last year, he appeared in "Jeffrey," an off-Broadway play about life in the age of AIDS, in which he played a dying chorus boy.

In a short video that played during the opening ceremony of last June's Gay Games, Louganis told the crowd: "As an Olympian and as a gay man, I'd like to welcome you to the Gay Games."

He later said that it felt good "to be out and proud."

*   *   *

March 31, 1996

ACCEPTING AND LOVING

To the Editor:

As the parent of a lesbian, I would like to see Hollywood dramatize the story so often told by my fellow members of the support group Parents, Family and Friends of Lesbians and Gays (Pflag). Upon learning that a son or daughter is homosexual, each parent struggles first to understand, then to accept and finally to join with other parents to help better the lives of their beloved gay and lesbian children. This, too, is an American tale, one that shows the American family at its best: inclusive, loving and truly loyal to its members.

RUBY KOPPELMAN
Pomona, N.Y.

*   *   *

GAY YOUTH

November 24, 1992

CHRONICLE

By NADINE BROZAN

Another curtain lifts: Chelsea House Publishers is planning a series of books on gay and lesbian topics for teenagers, and Martin Duberman, the author and historian, is deep in the throes of matching subjects to authors for 40 projected books. Thirty will be biographies and the other 10 will be on health, social and cultural issues.

His title is editorial consultant, but that does not begin to describe the responsibilities he has undertaken. "I will be doing pretty much everything, including choosing which authors will write which books, who will be the biography subjects and what will be the issues," said Professor Duberman, who is Distinguished Professor of History at two branches of the City University of New York, Lehman College and the Graduate Center. He is also the founder of the Center for Lesbian and Gay Studies at the Graduate Center and the author of numerous books and plays, including "In White America," first produced in 1963.

The first two books in the series will be a biography of James Baldwin by Randall Kenan, a young gay black writer, and a study of gay and lesbian culture by Donna Minkowitz, a writer for The Village Voice.

"I had too full a plate already, but Chelsea House appealed to my missionary side," Professor Duberman said. "The gay teen suicide rate is three times that for straights. Gay teens live in isolation never dreaming that anyone in the world faces similar sexual issues. For them to read about 30 notable gay and lesbian lives is an enormous boon."

Among the prospective subjects: Walt Whitman, Liberace, Gertrude Stein, Willa Cather, Elton John, Noel Coward, Gabriel Garcia Lorca, and Audre Lord, the poet who died last week. The first three titles are planned for fall 1993.

* * *

June 13, 1993

OUT AND ORGANIZED

By JESSE GREEN

In big, loopy letters, Mary Hansen wrote the word "homosexual" on the blackboard, then turned to face the 25 unruly students in Anne Corey's ninth-grade humanities class at the High School of Telecommunications Arts and Technology in Brooklyn. "Who's the babe?" one boy asked. A few others hooted. Ms. Hansen, unfazed, asked them to divide into groups and make lists of words that came to mind when they thought about the one she had just finished writing. "And don't censor yourself," she said. "Seriously, we can handle it."

This was Ms. Hansen's ninth such "peer training" session—designed to promote tolerance of homosexuals among straight teen-agers and to provide role models for gay ones. Her supervisor, David Nieves, who accompanied her, had led more than 100 peer trainings at other high schools and colleges. There wasn't much they had not seen before: students unwilling to touch the paper on which the words were written; others reduced to shrieks when the lists were read aloud. Ms. Hansen just smiled and copied their replies onto the board.

AIDS was the first; then dyke and homo; then oral sex, anal sex, sexless, switch-hitter, butch, fags, crazy, Village, Ru Paul, fun, domineering, nasty, weird, disgusting, sodomizing, unnatural, gross and nonhuman.

"Are these mostly nice words?" Ms. Hansen said, dusting the chalk off her hands.

"No," some students said.

"Now let's say you were talking about an African-American, or a Latino person, using equivalent terms." She named some. "And you walked into a class like this one, where some African-Americans or Latinos were sitting. What would you do?"

"Stop," they answered.

"Right. But let's say you were using some of the words on the board and you walked into a room where a homosexual was sitting. What would you do then?"

"Stop," they answered, less certainly.

"Really?" she said. "But how would you know? People assume gay men and lesbians have big light bulbs above their heads. But the truth is"—she paused—"we don't."

The class, as one, gasped and fell silent.

Not that it should have come as such a surprise. Mr. Nieves had begun the presentation by explaining that he and Ms. Hansen represented the Hetrick-Martin Institute, a nonprofit New York organization dedicated to the special needs of young homosexuals, and that Ms. Hansen was in fact a graduate of its Harvey Milk High School. Still, as Mr. Nieves said later, "kids like this never expect a homeboy like me, or someone who looks like Mary, to be gay." But one other fact about Ms. Hansen might have shocked even a veteran of the gay liberation movement: she is 17 years old.

Within the gay community, which has often faced accusations of recruitment, the subject of gay youth has long caused anxiety. "The leaders of the national movement have been very afraid to touch youth issues," said Jenie Hall, director of the American Friends Service Committee's Bridges Project, which coordinates the efforts of gay-youth agencies. Even within her own organization, which had supported gay causes for more than a decade, the youth issue was divisive. "Some of the Friends meetings renounced financial support," Ms. Hall said.

If the liberal Quakers are divided on the subject, the general public has been more openly antagonistic, as was seen in the some of the opposition to the New York City Board of Education's Rainbow Curriculum, which teaches tolerance of nontraditional life styles, including homosexuality. Nevertheless, financed by a patchwork of public and private grants, Hetrick-Martin in Manhattan, the Los Angeles Gay and Lesbian Community Services Center and the Sexual Minority Youth Assistance League in Washington—among 170 such agencies in the United States and Canada—have been quietly providing everything from hot meals for youths kicked out of their homes to hot lines, pen-pal programs, counseling, companionship and high-school diplomas.

But John P. Hale, a sometime legal adviser to the Archdiocese of New York, objected to these programs. "This is extremely destructive," Mr. Hale said. "In order to give comfort to that 1 out of 100 who may ultimately choose a homosexual life style, they are willing to put at risk the other 99 by encouraging them to experiment in their formative stages of adolescence. If a man in his early 30's invited the neighborhood children over to tell them about their sexual options, parents would call the cops; the school system is just

Mary Hansen delivered a speech at the Youth Empowerment Speakout and gave interviews.

substituting young emissaries for the man next door. I call it proselytizing."

Responding to Mr. Hale's statement, Frances Kunreuther, executive director of Hetrick-Martin, said: "We are trying to help young people have happy, productive lives. To be accused, still, of something so heinous—it's disgusting."

Teresa DeCrescenzo, executive director of Gay and Lesbian Adolescent Social Services in Los Angeles, which runs the country's only licensed long-term residential program for gay and lesbian minors, said: "If you tell me at the age of 13 that you're gay, then you're gay. If you come in 15 months later and you say that was only a phase, that's great, too."

There has been no update to a 1973 study, which appeared in the journal Male and Female Homosexuality, that found that most gay males realized their orientation by age 16 and most females by 19. Experts assume that the gay youth population has remained steady, though they can only hazard a guess, based on the results of a recent Harris poll, of perhaps 2 million. But the number of gay youngsters availing themselves of the existing services has certainly mushroomed.

At Hetrick-Martin, the number has grown from a handful when it opened its doors in 1983 to 1,500 today. Most of the clients "already have a very good sense of who they are," said Debra Haffner, executive director of the Sex Information and Education Council of the United States, or Siecus, the country's pre-eminent clearinghouse for information on human sexuality. "Even for those who don't, there is absolutely no evidence that orientation can be changed due to exposure to other people and educational messages. If it could, everyone would be straight. And while I do have reservations about some teen-agers coming out in the media—I'm not sure that they think through the possible outcomes—over all, affirming one's identity can only be helpful to one's self-esteem."

The teen-agers know this, too: that's why they show up. In fact, it's not the agencies recruiting the youth, but the youth

recruiting the agencies—sometimes in the process, becoming political creatures before they are even adults. For Ms. Hansen and others like her, it has been a voyage farther out, at an earlier age, than their predecessors would ever have believed was possible.

Scanning the traffic through the bus's green windows, some of the kids tried to guess which of the cars heading south with them on the New Jersey Turnpike contained homosexuals. This being the weekend of the Gay and Lesbian March on Washington, most of them did. Had passengers in those other cars been playing the same game, however, they might have guessed wrong: a glance at the faces pressed up against the windows of the dingy, unmarked bus would more likely have suggested a field trip to Six Flags Great Adventure amusement park than a gay-youth contingent. And yet, there they were: two dozen, ages 15 to 21, scrutinizing the passing cars for signs of solidarity.

As conventional as it all seemed—the shared food, the eruptions of giggles, the familiarity of limbs—beneath every joke and gesture the politics of sexuality was rumbling. "I want Amendment 2 in Colorado overturned," said Pietro Scorsone, a senior at Brooklyn Friends School. "And I read an article that said 18 other states are trying to pass similar laws."

Mr. Scorsone, 18, scratched at his sketchy beard and added: "See, when you're gay, you have to make your own politics. If mine came from my family, I'd be bashing myself, which I used to do. Now that I'm older I can be a warrior. A warrior for gay people. Also I want to be able to walk arm in arm with a boyfriend and not get harassed. Not that I have one . . ." He trailed off plaintively. "Maybe in Washington."

Mr. Scorsone has an agenda that freely mixes the personal and the political. Many of the young people on the bus—who had learned about the march at Hetrick-Martin's drop-in center, where they sometimes gather on weekday afternoons—had signed up as much for the weekend away as for the destination. But even those who wore no buttons or sloganeering T-shirts were articulate about their cause.

"In Haiti, where I come from, no way I could be open," said an 18-year-old woman who spoke on the condition of anonymity. "I would be asking for violence." She turned down the volume on her Walkman, from which Tracy Chapman could still be heard singing about the revolution to come. "Here it's different. Only six weeks ago, I came out to my mom, and today I'm already on this march. Coming from an oppressed country, believe me, it feels like a privilege. But it is really a duty. Because that's how we'll make change."

Responsibility for change is a concept foreign to most teen-agers. But gay youth say they have much to fight for. "They realize that they haven't had a place in the community, except as commodities," said Ms. Hall of the Bridges Project, who, though only 23, has been lobbying Congress about gay youth for years. "They are saying: I'm not your future, I'm the present, and I deserve to be respected here and now. I am not important solely because of what I will be when I am an adult—if I even get there."

Two dozen youths from the New York area attended the Gay and Lesbian March on Washington in April.

Ms. Hall spelled out the gay youth agenda specifically: safe schools, suicide prevention, AIDS education. In fact, AIDS was largely responsible for the gay youth movement. In 1980, Aaron Fricke, winning the right in court to bring a male date to his high school prom in in Cumberland, R.I., became the only widely known gay youth. Young lesbians did not exist in the public mind at all.

In the 13 years since, AIDS has changed everything, turning the movement for the first time toward its children, biological and otherwise. Today's gay teen-agers were toddlers when AIDS first struck in the early 80's; they were at the brink of adolescence when protest organizations like Act Up, at least in large cities, made public awareness of homosexuals unavoidable. By the time these youths began dealing with their sexuality, the first two gay marches on Washington (in 1979 and 1987) were legend.

By 1990, Queer Nation, an offshoot of Act Up, was holding kiss-ins in the streets, a few celebrities were taking tentative steps—or being pulled—out of the closet, and kinder images of homosexuals were making their debut in popular culture. And this year, with gay issues argued everywhere, the once unspoken subject has become noisily public.

Still, some on the bus can't be bothered with an agenda. "I wasn't going to come at first," said Luna Ortiz, a 20-year-old graduate of Harvey Milk High School. "I'm glad that the older people put us where we are now, that they had their faces broken to open the doors for us. But I just didn't feel like going."

Tall and self-possessed, with short-cropped hair and a little mustache, Mr. Ortiz had an air of stillness about him.

"With my health situation, I mean," he continued. "I've been H.I.V.-positive for seven years. I'm still healthy, but it's been hard. I used to do every AIDS march, but I'm tired of screaming." He looked out at the highway. "I'm just going along for the ride," he said.

The trip, which had begun with chants of "We're here, we're queer, get used to it!" ended five hours later with a pathetic lament: "We're late, we're lost, someone please help us!" By the time the bus arrived at the Youth Empowerment Speak-out at Hine Junior High School in Washington—the first national gathering of gay youth—the event was over.

Perhaps even more disappointing to the Hetrick-Martin contingent was the dance that night at the school. "What's that music?" one boy scoffed as he entered the cafeteria. But when the deejay spun Ru Paul's "Supermodel," the New York group came running onto the dance floor like a street gang securing its turf. The other kids stood back, amazed. Though they shared common ground, it was clear that class and geography cut even deeper than sexuality.

"They were as different as straight people would have been," Rene Cotto, 16, said a little sadly. "And maybe more."

One of the paradoxes of the emerging gay youth movement—and of gay liberation in general—is that it attempts to unify people only glancingly alike. Perhaps, as such, it is designed for obsolescence. Karina Luboff, 19, a sophomore at

Evergreen State College in Olympia, Wash., who has been working for lesbian and gay causes since she was 16, envisions a day when gay youth activism will be less of a movement than a hobby. "I don't see any reason," she said, "why there couldn't be a Queer Club at high school like there's a Latin-American culture club or a math club."

Ms. Kunreuther of Hetrick-Martin said that mainstream organizations are getting better at acknowledging and caring for the gay youth in their midst. "Over the next 10 years, the trend will be toward kids less often having to leave their neighborhoods and families to get help," she said. "That's what we'd love to see. It's slow, and we still need separate services, but it's a beginning."

In the meantime, it appears that the movement will grow a lot bigger before it shrinks. In September, thanks to grants from Vogue magazine and others, Hetrick-Martin will relocate to smart new quarters on Astor Place, leaving behind its ramshackle home above a garage near the West Side Highway.

Changed by the activism of the 1980's, today's gay youth are in turn changing others—young gay men and lesbians nowhere near New York who may catch a glimpse of Mary Hansen on C-Span, or read about her friends in the paper. But as the activists get younger, do they get stronger? "I think that dealing with being a lesbian—and part of that is by being politically active—has caused me to have a less carefree adolescence," Ms. Luboff said. "But I don't think that's a bad thing. It has its rewards."

For Ms. Hansen, the reward is self-confidence. "So what if people say terrible things?" she said, perhaps remembering the words she wrote on the blackboard in Brooklyn. "Whatever they call me, I say 'Yes, and my name is Mary.' I refuse to be afraid. And I do this out of an obligation not to the community but to myself." She smiled and pushed some tendrils of hair out of her face. "Nobody should have a say in who I am."

* * *

November 14, 1999

THE INVISIBLE POPULATION, THE GAYS NEXT DOOR

At Work, Home and School, a Minority Often Under Attack

By ELSA BRENNER

WHITE PLAINS—"Either our neighbors have figured it out, and they're still friendly to us—or they think we're just sisters," Karen Carr, a lesbian living with her companion in a suburban neighborhood of this city, said last week.

Ms. Carr, 41, who is the president of the board of directors of the Loft, a gay and lesbian community services center here, and Yvette Christofilis, 42, have lived together for 23 years—most recently in a white clapboard home they bought on one of the city's tree-lined streets, with mostly heterosexual couples and families.

Unlike some other lesbian couples, the two take part in community affairs, greet their neighbors over the backyard fence and are frank about their homosexuality.

"We're very fortunate, in comparison to some of the sad stories I hear," Ms. Carr said.

Most people who do not follow the traditional heterosexual patterns often live low-profile lives—avoiding mainstream activities for fear of being found out, Ms. Carr said, losing their jobs and becoming the subject of harassment.

On Friday, organizations addressing gay issues will sponsor a conference at Westchester Community College in Valhalla entitled, "Healing the Hurt: Westchester Learns About Its Invisible Population," which will be the first forum of its kind in the county.

The conference will focus primarily on issues affecting young people. According to a survey by the National Youth Advocacy Coalition in Washington, 69 percent of lesbian, gay, bisexual and transgender students report verbal, physical or sexual harassment in school. One student interviewed recently said that her classmates daily call her "dyke," "lesbo" and other names and that they have scratched those names into the paint on her car.

"It's tough enough being a kid today, and if you're gay, it's that much tougher," Ms. Carr said.

Because of their social isolation and feelings of low self-worth, gay students have a suicide rate that is four times higher than that of their heterosexual counterparts, according to a 1995 study of 59 Massachusetts high schools by the American Academy of Child and Adolescent Psychiatry based in Washington.

Before the conference, interviews were held with several gay and lesbian students who are trying to find their place in the world; with a sponsor of the conference whose adult daughter announced three years ago that she is a lesbian, and a gay Episcopal priest.

Gays and the Bible

"We can bless animals, battleships, cars and homes," said the Rev. Rayner (Rusty) Hesse Jr., a gay priest at St. John's Episcopal Church in New Rochelle, "but we're not allowed to bless two people who are gays or lesbians and who are in love without the benefit of marriage."

Father Hesse, a part-time priest who also owns Memory Lane Auctioneers in White Plains, said he ministers to his congregation "out of my own pain, my own experiences and the isolation that I have known."

"One of the reasons that I became a priest," he said, "was that I wanted to heal some of the hurt that I experienced."

At the conference on Friday, Father Hesse said he will answer the question, "What does the Bible have to say about homosexuality?" with the answer, "Very little."

"What people get mixed up about," he explained, "is that the church has a lot to say on the subject of homosexuality. There are a lot of shalt nots in religion, but they don't necessarily come from the Scriptures."

Looking ahead to his talk at the conference, he said: "Jesus had a lot to say about divorce, about women, about almost everything. Therefore, if homosexuality was an issue for him, how come we don't know about it?"

In fact, although Saint Paul disapproved of sex between men, and in Leviticus, men lying down with men is listed among the Abominations, it was not until the Puritans and the late Middle Ages that there was a word for homosexuality, Father Hesse said.

Troubled by reports that gay teenagers still get beaten and raped by family members who want "to set them straight," and are kicked out of their homes, he said: "People come to me with those kinds of stories, and they tell me that no other church will accept them. As gay people, they feel that God has abandoned them."

"My job," he said, "is to help them feel better about themselves."

Growing Up Gay

At the Loft, a group of students in an after-school program for gay, lesbian, bisexual and transgender youths, who spoke on the condition of anonymity, said they realized by the time they were 6 that they were different from other children.

"I was always a tomboy," one lesbian said. "I never liked hanging out with girly girls, and I knew early on that I didn't fit in."

That was confirmed again for her at lunch one day in the school cafeteria, when other girls in the seventh grade were discussing which boys they had crushes on. "I wanted to say I loved Jane," the young lesbian said. "Instead I lied and told them I liked John."

Many gay and lesbian students are regularly called "faggots" and "dykes," and one teacher reportedly told a boy with pink hair that he looked "faggy," the students said. Often, gays become social outcasts when they first divulge their sexuality, usually during their teenage years—and many said they attempted suicide because they thought they were "freaks." About 28 percent drop out of school because of fear and anxiety in school, according to the National Gay and Lesbian Task Force, a nonprofit civil rights group based in Washington.

School personnel sometimes aggravate their problems, gay and lesbian youths say. For example, many students at the Loft said that while their teachers rarely tolerated racial epithets in their classrooms, they often ignored terms of abuse directed at gay classmates.

"Kids today who hear the word 'faggot' hurled at them all day long realize that the world is not a safe place to be," said Dr. Paul Bloom, a pediatrician in Haverstraw in Rockland County who counsels gay youths at the Loft here.

When they told their parents that they were gay, the students in the Center Lane drop-in program at the Loft, which is run by Westchester Jewish Community Services, reported encountering various reactions.

Often parents experience shame when learning that their children are homosexuals, with fathers blaming the mothers for being poor role models—and vice versa. As Parents and Friends of Lesbians and Gays, a national advocacy group in Washington, says, "Sometimes when the kids come out, parents go in the closet."

More than a fourth of gay youths are evicted from their homes because of their sexual orientation, the Gay and Lesbian Task Force has reported, and many turn to prostitution to survive, placing them at high risk for H.I.V. and other infections.

Some parents, though, accept their children's differences—it is estimated that about 10 percent of the population is gay—and their offspring's announcement only confirms what they had suspected. "I finally told my mother I was bisexual, and she said 'forget bisexual, you're gay,'" another student at the Loft said. "She gave me a hug and said she accepted me for who I was."

A Father's Experience

Three years ago, when Charles M. Benjamin's 27-year-old daughter Tamar told her parents she was a lesbian, the retired school psychologist sprang into action.

Knowing that gays are the only minority that frequently does not have family support, Dr. Benjamin and his wife, Florence, joined the local chapter of Parents and Friends of Lesbians and Gays, a national organization based in Washington with affiliates in 360 communities nationwide.

Using his professional training, Dr. Benjamin, whose private practice is in Tarrytown, developed the idea (which is based on a model used in Houston and Washington) for a Healing the Hurt conference to educate those who work with young people about the struggles and needs of gay and lesbian youths.

Teaming up with the Manhattan-based Gay, Lesbian and Straight Education Network, another advocacy group with regional affiliates, Dr. Benjamin, who is a co-sponsor of the conference, brought together school administrators, teachers, social workers, juvenile justice personnel, the clergy and other mainstream organizations for the event.

In Westchester, the list of co-sponsors for Friday's conference includes, among others, the County Departments of Social Services and Health, Community Mental Health and the Westchester Parent Teachers Association.

Mary Jane Karger, a co-chairwoman of the Hudson Valley Gay, Lesbian and Straight Education Network, which meets in White Plains, and also co-sponsor of the Healing the Hurt conference, said, referring to gay and lesbian youths, "There's a population out there that we are missing and who are very much at risk."

The workshops will focus on parenting issues, religion and homosexuality, legal issues of homosexuality in the schools and how gays can remain safe in what has traditionally been hostile environments for them, said Ms. Karger, a school social worker in Carmel.

For more information, contact Dr. Benjamin at 332-9494 or Ms. Karger at 962-7888.

* * *

April 2, 2000

GAY YOUTH DISCOVER THERE'S A SAFE PLACE TO BE THEMSELVES

By ALICE SPARBERG ALEXIOU

NORTH BELLMORE—It was Friday night at the Pride for Youth coffeehouse, and the blare of music competed with the sounds of 70-plus teenagers noisily socializing. As they talked, shot pool and danced, Carmela Murphy, 44, served soda, juice and cookies behind a non-alcoholic bar.

Ms. Murphy is a volunteer, but there are four full-time staff members at the center, which is publicly financed. One, Andrew Peters, 30, led a group discussion later in the evening. The topic? AIDS education.

Mr. Peters is a certified social worker and Pride for Youth is an outreach program aimed at gay and lesbian adolescents. Its managers are seeking a higher profile after years of lying low in fear of a possible backlash from local residents who might object to using taxpayer dollars to support local youth in a gay lifestyle.

So far, the program has caused barely a ripple of dissent.

Pride for Youth is part of the 24-hour Long Island Crisis Center, which was set up in 1971. The Pride for Youth program, started in 1994, offers the coffeehouses on Friday and Saturday nights and operates its own hot line and counseling and support groups.

Pride for Youth moved to its present location in May from Farmingdale. Its site, in an office building at 2050 Bellmore Avenue, is marked with a large sign that includes a logo of two stick figures holding hands. The old Farmingdale location was unmarked.

The decision to publicize was deliberate, said Mr. Peters, the program's director. "We are making a statement that we are not ashamed of who we are," he said.

Linda Leonard, director of the Long Island Crisis Center, said outreach to gay and lesbian youths had been a challenge.

Kevin P. Coughlin for The New York Times

Gay and lesbian teenagers are welcome at the Pride for Youth coffeehouse in North Bellmore, where they have a chance to socialize. From left, Melissa Cohen, Matthew Tighe and Simone Sneed.

"You don't want to offend the community," she said, but it is important that the public know the center exists.

"Our purpose is to assist families who are struggling with gay family members whom society marginalizes," she said. She cited the recent headlines about the Dix Hills man who committed suicide after the dismembered body of his gay stepson was discovered in a Queens park.

Mr. Peters said coffeehouse attendance has been increasing and approximately 800 people a year use Pride for Youth services.

"Here, gay youth can be themselves and be with others like them, which is essential to their development as healthy adults," he said. "They need a place that can reinforce them after they go through a day of being called names or ignored or physically intimidated. They need to come to a place where they are told it is O.K. to be as they are."

Posters celebrating gay themes festoon the freshly painted walls; one commemorates "National Coming Out Day," with pictures of James Baldwin, Michelangelo and Eleanor Roosevelt. (Only Baldwin publicly acknowledged his homosexuality.) Copies of Out, published by the gay civil rights organization Lambda, and The Advocate, the gay magazine, lay neatly on the coffee table.

The project began in 1994 with a $10,000 grant from the Rapoport Foundation, a Texas-based group that focuses on education. Public funding began in 1995 from the state Department of Health, which remains the major source of support. This year the program is getting $240,000 from the state; other support comes from private donors.

Public funding for the Long Island Crisis Center comes mostly from the Nassau County Youth Board, although this year assistance has been cut 39 percent, to $162,000. Some of the center's services occasionally apply to Pride for Youth. For example, Ms. Leonard said, last year the county allotted $5,000 for crisis center community education, which included homophobia-awareness workshops that Pride for Youth presented in 16 of the county's 56 school districts.

Serving gay and lesbian youth is a politically sensitive matter. Ms. Leonard, who has been at the crisis center since 1974, explained:

"The staff of the Youth Board knew that gay and lesbian kids needed services and that they were at risk," an allusion to their high rates of suicide, homelessness and substance abuse. "But the political climate of Nassau County was not ready to accept a project that openly served gay and lesbian youth."

In 1983, she said, the youth board, which finances programs for youth in trouble, gave the center a nod to do gay peer counseling. "But we were told to do it with a low profile," Ms. Leonard said, and an official at the board told her not to display material aimed at gay youth on its bulletin board.

The low profile was to avoid reactions like that of the Rev. Richard Williamson, pastor of the United Methodist Church in nearby Seaford, who opposed public financing of

Kevin P. Coughlin for The New York Times

Pride for Youth. "Providing that kind of support to young people whose identity has not solidified," he said, "makes about as much sense as providing drugs to those who choose to be addicts." Several county politicians refused to comment on the Pride for Youth program, and a reticence is still evident at the youth board, which is grappling with a halving of its budget, from $8.6 million to $4.3 million. Ramona Battle, a spokeswoman for the board, denied that the county money had ever gone to Pride for Youth. She did, however, praise the program.

But many community leaders expressed support for the program. "It's something that is so badly needed," said Robin Karp, executive director of the Bellmore Chamber of Commerce.

John Didden, principal of Mepham High School in North Bellmore, arranged for Pride for Youth to conduct two teacher workshops. "When you see needs, you are supposed to rise to the occasion," he said. Serving the needs of gay students, he said, is part of helping all students deal with diversity.

Caryn Banks, 19, a North Bellmore resident who runs peer education groups at Pride for Youth, recalls hearing homophobic remarks "every single day" when she was a student at Mepham.

"Walking through the halls, I constantly heard the word 'fag,'" said Ms. Banks, who is now a student at Nassau Community College. "People would spit on me, throw pennies at me."

In her senior year, she founded a Gay-Straight Alliance student club at Mepham, one of five established at Nassau high schools.

"I was terribly scared," she said. "I remember thinking, 'I guess this confirms that I am gay. All the kids and their parents and the whole entire school knows.'"

In the months following, students sometimes defaced or ripped down posters announcing meetings of the club. But today, said Bernard Stein, one of the two faculty advisors, the club is part of the school culture. Mr. Stein said that in recent months two nearby high schools—Kennedy, in South Bellmore, and Wantagh—had called him for advice on starting their own chapters.

Teenagers interviewed at the Pride for Youth coffeehouse said that education was the key to combating homophobia.

"I think kids need to learn about homosexuality when they are young," said Matthew Tighe, 18, of Floral Park. He said he knew he was gay by the time he was 12, but didn't tell his parents until he was 15. "I was so lonely between the ages of 12 and 15," he said.

Erik Laing, 18, of Huntington, said he thought of suicide when he was 13 because of all the harassment at school. He did not talk about it with his guidance counselor, he said, because he did not want his mother to find out.

Mr. Peters estimated that about half the youth who come to the coffeehouse do not tell their parents. Janee Harvey, a 22-year-old staff member, said five of the coffeehouse regulars live in group homes; their parents kicked them out, she said, because they are gay. A van driven by one of the staff members picks up these teens and a few others every week.

Mr. Peters says Pride for Youth tries to reach out to parents through a weekly support group. Sometimes he sets up individual appointments with families. "But we're not always successful in reaching them," he said. "Some forbid their kids to come here at all."

Yet some parents drop their kids off. Jennifer Sneed of East Northport said she and her husband drop off their daughter, Simone, 15, every week. When Simone told them she was a lesbian, Mrs. Sneed said, they had recently moved to Long Island and did not know what services there were. They found Pride for Youth by chance.

"P.F.Y. is one of the best resources for young people I've seen," Mrs. Sneed said. "They're professional, they provide support and educational information. I can't speak highly enough about them."

The increased visibility of Pride for Youth has also increased its vulnerability. According to staff members, teenagers regularly drive by shouting anti-gay slurs. In February, a 15-year-old boy who had just left the coffeehouse was beaten up by another teenager who had pulled up in a car. The accused attacker is 17, and has been charged with assault.

Nevertheless, said Melissa Cohen, 18, a senior at Oceanside High School and another Pride for Youth regular, such incidents do not scare her. "Here I feel safe," she said.

Carmela Murphy, who tends the juice bar every Friday, said she chose to volunteer specifically because it served young homosexuals. Ms. Murphy, a supervisor for the Postal Service, lives in Wantagh with her partner and is studying for a degree in psychology at Molloy College.

"It's important for these kids to see that I have a regular life," she said. "And the kids are so free, so outspoken. And they're so kind to each other."

As she was speaking, a girl came behind the bar and gave Ms. Murphy a big hug. "This woman," she said, "is my role model."

Is it easier for these youngsters than it was for her?

"It was much harsher when I was younger," Ms. Murphy said. "People in this generation are a little more understanding. But you'll always have people who are bigoted. It's never easy."

*   *   *

THE TRANSGENDERED AND THE TRANSSEXUAL

September 8, 1996

SHUNNING 'HE' AND 'SHE,' THEY FIGHT FOR RESPECT

By CAREY GOLDBERG

LOS ANGELES, Sept. 7—In Boston, Nancy Nangeroni is helping arrange a courthouse vigil for a slain male-to-female transsexual. In Washington, Dana Priesing lobbies for laws that would ban discrimination against "transgendered" people. And in Southern California, Jacob Hale and the rest of the local Transgender Menace chapter occasionally pull on their black Menace T-shirts and go for a group walkabout, just to look people in the eye with collective pride in who they are.

All see themselves as part of a burgeoning movement whose members are only now, nearly two decades after gay liberation took off, gathering the courage to go public and struggle for the same sort of respect and legal protections.

The name that scholars and organizers prefer for this nascent movement is "transgender," an umbrella term for transsexuals, cross-dressers (the word now preferred over transvestites), intersexed people (also known as hermaphrodites), womanish men, mannish women and anyone whose sexual identity seems to cross the line of what, in 1990's America, is considered normal.

That line has certainly blurred. Dennis Rodman preens in his bridal gown, Ru Paul puckers for MAC cosmetics, and viewers flock to movies like "The Crying Game."

But members of the movement say they still cannot escape the feeling that in a society that has grown more responsive to other minorities, they are among the last pariahs. When they give up the old dream of simply "passing" as their desired sex, they face painful battles both in everyday life and in the political arena, where they are roundly condemned as deviants by religious conservatives and often spark controversy among more mainstream gay and lesbian groups.

Their very existence, they say, is such a challenge to universal gut-level ideas about a person's sex as an either-or category—as reflected in everything from binary bathrooms to "he" and "she" pronouns—that they are often subjected to scorn, job discrimination and violence.

"There's finally a voice saying, 'Enough,'" said Riki Anne Wilchins, a Wall Street computer consultant and organizer in the movement. "We pay taxes. We vote. We work. There's no reason we should be taking this. When you have people in isolation who are oppressed and victimized and abused, they think it's their own fault, but when you hit that critical mass that they see it happening to other people, they realize it's not about them. It's about a system, and the only way to contest a system is with an organized response."

Mariette Pathy Allen

Members of the group Transexual Menace on a Washington subway car in October of 1995. The group joined others in a protest to draw attention to the concerns of people who call themselves "transgendered."

No one knows exactly what that critical mass is. Experts say that in the more than 40 years since George Jorgensen emerged from the operating room as Christine, several thousand Americans have undergone sex-change surgery; they are believed to include nearly even numbers of men and women. Perhaps as many as 60,000 Americans consider themselves valid candidates for such surgery, based on what psychiatrists call "gender identity dysphoria," according to the Harry Benjamin Gender Dysphoria Association, the leading medical association of specialists—including sex-change surgeons—that sets guidelines for treating transsexuals. But that is only the tip of a far larger iceberg, organizers say, of cross-dressers—many of whom are het-erosexual men—and people who live as the opposite sex but never undergo surgery.

The movement's growth, however, is easy to discern. Scores of participants rallied as part of a new advocacy group called Gender PAC for the first time in Washington last fall and plan to do the same in May, and transgender conventions now draw hundreds of people and number nearly 20 a year. Increasingly, a "T" can be found tacked onto the "G, L and B" of gay, lesbian and bisexual events and groups, from community centers to pride parades.

In San Francisco, which a survey has shown is home to about 6,000 of the movement's constituents, the San Francisco Human Rights Commission has formed a Transgender Community Task Force, and the protest group Transexual Menace now counts 46 chapters nationwide, some of which are called Transgender Menace. There is even a new national group, Transgendered Officers Protect and Serve; members act as marshals at events when needed.

The movement's coalescence, which members say began over the last five years and accelerated in recent months, has gained particular momentum from the Internet, with its ability to connect far-flung people and afford them a sense of safety. On-line groups that began by swapping tips on using makeup and obtaining hormones now also spread word of the latest victims of violence and the next political protest.

But "the fundamental building block of the whole movement," said Dr. Barbara Warren of the Gender Identity Project at New York City's Lesbian and Gay Community Services Center, "is the willingness of transgender folk to put themselves out there and be visible." That takes more than the courage to face funny looks in the checkout line. The most painful of rallying points is the frequency with which they are attacked and even killed.

"I know so many people who've suffered from vilification in their daily lives just because people have heard they're transsexual, not because they look weird or act weird," said James Green, a female-to-male transsexual and head of FtM International, the biggest group for what many members call "transmen." "As soon as the fact is known, they're just targets, and people are still being murdered."

Since last year, Ms. Wilchins and Transexual Menace have taken to organizing vigils after the slayings of transsexuals. In May 1995 they protested outside the Lincoln, Neb., courthouse where the rapist and killer of Brandon Teena, a young woman living as a man, was coming to trial. Since then, they have marked the deaths of several transsexual women who were killed by men they dated. The next will come on Sept. 16 in Lawrence, Mass., where Deborah Forte, a transsexual, was killed.

"We're so invested in being men or women that if you fall outside that easy definition of what a man or woman is, a lot of people see you as some kind of monster," said Susan Stryker, a male-to-female transsexual with a doctorate in history whose book on changing sex is to be published by Oxford University Press next year.

Gender PAC, the advocacy group, is lobbying to have crimes against "transgendered people" included in the Hate Crimes Statistics Act, which lets the Justice Department track crimes based on race, religion, ethnicity and sexual orientation. (These crimes do not fall under the orientation category because "transgenderism" concerns sexual identity, not sexual practices, Gender PAC says; some male-to-female transsexuals are lesbians, for example.)

Gender PAC's other priority, said Dana Priesing, its main lobbyist—and a prominent Washington litigator until she began her sex change—is to get the group's constituency included in the Employment Nondiscrimination Act, a bill in the House of Representatives that would protect gay people from job discrimination.

Employees currently have no recourse if they are dismissed because they reveal their sexual identity or undergo "transition" except in a handful of cities—including San Francisco, Seattle and Santa Cruz—and the state of Minnesota.

If Nancy Nangeroni is any judge, transsexuals still need help in the workplace. A 42-year-old, M.I.T.-educated computer designer, she found she could not get a job if she volunteered that she was a male-to-female transsexual, but had no problem if she kept silent. Ms. Nangeroni is not only open about her identity but also runs "Gender Talk," a radio talk show every Wednesday evening on WMBR-FM, a Boston-area station.

"There's a widespread discontent with gender roles," she said, "and transgenderism is trying to speak to that in a compassionate way, speaking only liberation and not doctrine. It's kind of like shooting fish in a barrel sometimes. People are very ripe for it."

Not everybody. Christian conservatives and advocates of traditional family values condemn the movement as decadent and unhealthy.

"This is yet another social pathology," said Robert H. Knight, cultural studies director for the Family Research Council, a think tank in Washington. "This is deviant behavior that seeks legitimization in the social, legal and political realms. It is part of a larger cultural movement to confuse the sexual roles and to usher in a relativistic mindset concerning sexuality itself."

The movement has also created some friction within the gay and lesbian groups that have generally accepted and aided it. Some gay and lesbian organizers have balked because its issues do not concern sexual orientation but rather identity. Others argued, usually sotto voce, that flamboyant "drag queens" and "stone butches" would further alienate straight America and belie their claims that gay people are really just like everybody else.

But "transgendered people" have long been at the heart of the gay rights movement, said Kerry Lobel, deputy director of the National Gay and Lesbian Task Force. Now, she said, "they're seeking and have found their own political power."

"All of a sudden a lot of people feel, 'Hey, I am proud,'" said Alison Laing, director of the International Foundation for Gender Education in Waltham, Mass. "It's like gay pride. People say, 'I didn't choose this, but I do choose my behavior and my attitude.'"

Alison Laing's life demonstrates the kind of freedom the movement espouses. A husband and father, "M. Laing" (to use the honorific proposed as an ungendered alternative to Mr. and Ms.) spends about 80 percent of the time dressed in women's clothes and 20 percent as Al, in men's clothing, showing that "we don't have to live in gender boxes."

* * *

December 2, 1996

PLEA FOR THE TRANSGENDERED

By ANDY NEWMAN

NEW BRUNSWICK—People who do not identify with the sex they were born into are lobbying Rutgers University for protection against discrimination and harassment, The Associated Press reported yesterday.

Rutgers has forbidden discrimination on the basis of sex and sexual orientation since 1981. But members of the school's "transgendered" community, which includes transsexuals and transvestites, want explicit protection. "This isn't about my sexual orientation," said Ben Singer, a female-to-male transsexual graduate student. "It's about my gender identity."

The University Senate, an advisory body of faculty, students and administrators, is expected to vote on the issue in February.

* * *

July 28, 1998

WHEN MEDICINE GOES TOO FAR IN THE PURSUIT OF NORMALITY

By ALICE DREGER

I realized recently that I suffer from a genetic condition. Although I have not actually had my genome screened, all the anatomical signs of Double-X Syndrome are there. And while I could probably handle the myriad physiological disorders associated with my condition—bouts of pain and bleeding coming and going for decades, hair growth patterns that obviously differ from "normal" people's—the social downsides associated with it are troubling.

Even since the passage of the Americans With Disabilities Act, people with Double-X remain more likely than others to live below the poverty line, more likely to be sexually assaulted, and are legally prohibited from marrying people with the same condition. Some potential parents have even screened fetuses and aborted those with Double-X in an effort to avert the tragic life the syndrome brings. Perhaps you know Double-X by its more common name: womanhood.

This fact of my "genetic condition" came to me one evening as I sat in a conference room of our local hospital participating in a community dialogue sponsored by the Human Genome Project. Our group had just finished reading a rather bleak description of the anatomy and life of the "average" woman with Turner's syndrome: "webbed neck, short stature, no chance for bearing children" and so on. Turner's syndrome, which affects roughly one in 2,500 girls born each year, arises when a person is born with a single X chromosome and no Y. It is, essentially, a "single-X syndrome."

Our group was discussing the genetic screening of pre-implantation embryos, and given the depressing description of Turner's provided to us, no wonder most everyone in the room, pro-choicers and pro-lifers alike, saw Turner's as a sad genetic disease.

But I had by then been studying human intersexuality—anatomical sexual variations, including Turner's—for several years, and had talked with and read the biographies and autobiographies of many people born intersexed. I knew that women with Turner's would describe their lives with more balance. So I began to think about how a woman with single-X and a sense of humor could describe the life of those of us women with double-X, and came up with the above portrayal.

My point is not that people with unusual genetic conditions do not suffer more than those without them; clearly, many do. But I am troubled that I see ever more cases in which psychosocial problems caused by stereotypes about anatomy are being "fixed" by "normalizing" the anatomy. There are serious downsides to this, both for the person being "normalized" and for those around her.

Take for example the "treatment" of short stature. Some pharmaceutical companies and physicians have advocated giving human growth hormone injections to very short children in an attempt to help them grow taller than they otherwise would. Profound short (and tall) stature may lead to disorders like back problems because our culture structures the physical world for average-height adults. But no one advocates using the hormone to prevent back problems.

Hormone treatments are used because of the presumption that an adult of short stature will not fare as well socially as one of average size. Indeed, statistically, taller men are more likely than shorter men to be hired, given a raise or elected President. Average-sized people see short people and tend to feel sorry for them. Getting short children to grow more seems pretty beneficent.

The same kind of intended beneficence drives the medical management of children born intersexed. Many physicians assume that intersexed children, with their unusual genitalia, will be rejected by family and peers. So they recommend early cosmetic surgery to try to erase the signs.

What's wrong with these "normalization" technologies? First, it isn't clear that they work. It seems that if an unusual anatomy leads to a psychosocial problem, "normalizing" the anatomy should solve the problem. But of the few follow-up studies that have been done on intersex surgeries, none examine the psychological well-being of the subjects in any real depth. Most simply report on the status of the postsurgical anatomy, while a very few report on whether the subjects are married (psychological health is presumed from this).

Psychological follow-up on the growth hormone treatments is similarly lacking. A study published in the March 28 Lancet reported that a randomized trial of the hormone in "short normal girls" resulted in the treated girls' averaging a final height of almost three inches more than the control group, but added that "no significant psychosocial benefits have yet been shown."

Perhaps we should not expect measurable psychological benefits from a gain of about three inches. Yet recall that the entire "normalization" treatment for short stature was designed to produce psychological benefits.

More worrisome than the loss of focus in these studies is the fact that these treatments often backfire. Children subjected to these kinds of treatments often report feelings of inadequacy and freakishness as a direct result of their parents' and doctors' attempts at normalization. And the treatments are not without physical risks. For example, intersex surgeries all too frequently leave scarred, insensate, painful and infection-prone genitalia.

So anatomy-focused have we become that children with unusual conditions are often not provided any professional psychological counseling. Nor are their parents, who are dealing with their own feelings of confusion, shame, grief and worry. The result is the message that the problem is primarily anatomical and, by consequence, a "fault" of the child and perhaps also the parents.

By extension, a dictate then kicks in: If you can fix it, you should. A friend of mine recalls the time a plastic surgeon came up to him at a party, looked at his nose and said, "You know, I can fix that." When my friend said, "No thanks," the plastic surgeon appeared to think my friend a little crazy. As normalizing technologies become more accessible, people are expected to be bothered by their "unusual" features and expected to want to fix them.

Some surgeons say they normalize intersexed children because it is too hard to be different. One points out that we still live in a nation where dark-skinned people have a harder time than light-skinned people do. But would he suggest we work on technologies to "fix" dark skin? Would we call people who refuse to lighten their children cruel Luddites?

The funny thing is, when I ask people with dark skin if they would change their color, they tell me no, and when I ask women if they would rather be men, they tell me no, and I get the same response when I ask people with unusual anatomies if they would take a magic pill to erase their unusual features.

They tell me, instead, that they would support an end to social stereotypes and oppression, but that they would not trade themselves in for a "better" model. This sentiment even comes from conjoined twins. Chang and Eng Bunker, the conjoined brothers born early in the 19th century and dubbed the Siamese twins, confessed that they preferred their state because it enabled them to bring a "double strength and a double will" to each purpose. Similarly, women born with big clitorises confess to liking their unusual anatomy. But this is the absolutely forbidden narrative—not only rejecting normalization but actively preferring the "abnormal."

What do I suggest? First, a few basic realizations. In spite of medical advances, unusual anatomies generally cannot be fixed in any significant way without significant risk, and that risk, when medically unnecessary, should be approved by the person at risk.

We also need to remember that just because it makes sense that you ought to be able to fix anatomically based psychosocial problems anatomically, that doesn't mean it is so. Working to eliminate social stereotypes would be more effective and better for everyone in the long run. I do not wish to see options entirely withdrawn from mature patients; I am suggesting we slow down the normalization of children, many of whom are likely to gain much more from acceptance and psychological support than injections and scalpels.

But how do we fix the social problems? When I talk about intersex, people ask me, "But what about the locker room?" Yes, what about the locker room? If so many people feel trepidation around it, why don't we fix the locker room? There are ways to signal to children that they are not the problem, and normalization technologies are not the way.

Instead of constantly enhancing the norm—forever upping the ante of the "normal" with new technologies—we should work on enhancing the concept of normal by broadening appreciation of anatomical variation. Show potential parents, medical students and genetic counselors images of unusual anatomies other than the deeply pathologized ones they are typically given. Allow those with the unusual anatomies to describe their own lives in full and rich detail. Even let them tell the forbidden narrative of enjoying their Double-X Syndromes.

Alice Dreger, professor of science and technology at Michigan State University, wrote "Hermaphrodites and the Medical Invention of Sex," (Harvard University Press, 1998).

* * *

September 26, 1999

FOR TRANSSEXUAL, SMALL ELECTION VICTORY IS A 'BIG STEP'

By DAVID KIRBY

"It may be a small position, but it is a very big step," said Melissa Sklarz. Ms. Sklarz, who is openly transsexual, was elected as a delegate to the Democratic Party's Manhattan Judicial Convention, which was held Thursday. No one can recall the last time a transsexual was elected to any position in the city.

A collections manager for the Actors Federal Credit Union, Ms. Sklarz, 48, and 109 other delegates nominated Democratic candidates for State Supreme Court in Manhattan. Of 33 who ran in her district in the West Village, 11 were elected delegates. Because the borough is heavily Democratic, the candidates they picked are likely to win.

Ms. Sklarz said she appreciated being able to talk to the civil and criminal court judges seeking Supreme Court seats. "Judges know absolutely nothing about conflicts transgendered people go through," she said. "Now we're going right to the judges and educating them."

She said her biggest concerns were stemming violence and discrimination against transsexuals, and preserving the quality of life in the Village, which she said has been "a welcoming place" for her.

But it has not been so welcoming to all transgendered people, some advocates say. Richard Haymes, executive director of the Gay and Lesbian Anti-Violence Project, said police antiprostitution sweeps had rounded up law-abiding transsexuals too.

Lieut. Stephen Biegel, a police spokesman, said, "Officers make arrests based on probable cause, and not based on how people are dressed or their appearance."

Mr. Haymes said his group was working with the police on sensitivity training. The police academy's director of training, Dr. James O'Keefe, said transgendered people give seminars to instructors.

Ms. Sklarz can also help, Mr. Haymes said. "With these judges meeting Melissa," he said, "she's going to shoot their stereotypes out of the water."

Sloan Wiesen of the Gay and Lesbian Victory Fund, which supports gay candidates, said no transgendered people had sought its aid. "That's not to say that there aren't any out there," he said, "but there's been none to our knowledge."

Kevin Finnegan, president of the Gay and Lesbian Independent Democrats, which supported Ms. Sklarz, said she was the first openly transgendered person to win an election in New York.

*   *   *

September 27, 1999

AFTER SEX CHANGE, TEACHER IS BARRED FROM SCHOOL

By EVELYN NIEVES

ANTELOPE, Calif., Sept. 24—By all accounts, David Warfield was an excellent teacher.

He came to Center High School in this Sacramento suburb for his first teaching job nine years ago and soon made a name for himself, developing a program for unmotivated students that became the award-winning Media Communications Academy. Students routinely called him one of the best teachers they had had or expected to have, the one most likely to be remembered as a major influence in their lives. He was awarded an $80,000 grant for his program, won the school's Stand and Deliver award for the teacher who most inspires students and received a standing ovation from the district's staff at its annual meeting last September.

Given this backdrop, when David Warfield wrote a letter to colleagues in May explaining that he was undergoing a sex change and planned to return to school as Dana Rivers, shock quickly turned to sympathy. In June, after the school board sent a letter disclosing Mr. Warfield's decision to all 1,500 families in the district, only four parents wrote back in protest.

But Dana Rivers has yet to walk through the doors of Center High. Weeks before classes started, the school board voted 3 to 2 to place her on paid administrative leave pending a formal dismissal, which is expected soon. What might have been a quiet if difficult adjustment at Center High to get to know the person some students once called Mountain Man for his love of macho sports has instead become the sole subject of board meetings and a growing, rancorous debate in this ethnically diverse, middle-class town.

At its core lies the question: Why would Dana Rivers be fired? To her supporters, the answer is obvious.

"The board members didn't want a transsexual teacher," said Ray Bender, a board member who voted against dismissal proceedings. "They said they didn't want to create confusion for the students."

The Dana Rivers case, Mr. Bender said, has become a cause for religious conservatives assisted by the Pacific Justice Institute, a local conservative legal organization that demanded that the school board fire the teacher or face a lawsuit.

"One board member," he said, "was heard telling a parent that this is a holy issue."

But board members who voted to begin dismissal proceedings say their position has nothing to do with transsexualism, the Pacific Justice Institute or religious conservatives.

Before a sex change, Dana Rivers, left, won teaching awards at her California school. Now she has been placed on leave and could lose her job. Right, students rallied in support of the teacher on Friday.

"That is the furthest thing from the truth," said Scott Rodowick, the board president. "This is about parental rights. This is about issues that the board became aware of that have nothing to do with the teacher's being transgendered. There are things I know that I would love to talk about, but I have to respect the rights of an employee. It's a personnel issue."

The majority on the board refused to discuss the case, but the members who voted for Ms. Rivers said the others wanted an excuse to fire her. They found it, the board members say, in a few parents who complained that the teacher had improperly discussed her condition, known as gender dysphoria, with their children.

"One parent stood up at a board meeting and said that her daughter was traumatized," Mr. Bender said. "But right after that, her daughter stood up and told the board that her mother was wrong."

But Donna Earnest, whose son is a junior at Center High School, said she was not the only one who believed her parental rights had been taken from her.

"My position is that this teacher acted totally unprofessionally," Ms. Earnest said. "My child was not in the class, but kids talk all over the school, and according to the kids, he said he had been sodomized as a youth and that he always felt he was a woman trapped in a man's body and that he was going to be changing into a woman in the fall. He should have gotten permission from the parents to say this."

Brad Dacus, founder of the Pacific Justice Institute, said he filed administrative complaints on behalf of more than a few parents who felt that their children had been traumatized.

"One student had to be pulled from the school," Mr. Dacus said, "and two children have had to be put in counseling."

Ms. Rivers, on the advice of the teachers union, would not discuss the details of the case. But her colleagues say that students learned of her plan when teachers read Ms. Rivers's letter to their classes. Ms. Rivers said that as rumors began circulating throughout the school and students began asking about them, she agreed to an interview with the school newspaper. The 2,600-word profile was printed the week before school ended in June.

"I didn't have to send a letter to everyone telling them what I was doing," Ms. Rivers said. "I could have just walked into school. But what confusion would that have led to?"

In a way, the debate is reminiscent of arguments about gay teachers who come out of the closet. But unlike gay men or lesbians, Ms. Rivers said, there was no way she could hide as she underwent a gender transformation. Her hair is long and auburn now, with bangs. She wears eye shadow, pink nail polish and skirts. She has trained her vocal cords to deliver a soft, feminine tenor.

"If there was a way that I could have gone on the way I was, believe me, I would have, because this is the hardest thing I have ever done," she said.

Until age 44, David Warfield had been a Navy electronics expert, a political consultant and school board member in Huntington Beach, a baseball coach and a white-water rafting instructor. Ms. Rivers says she is still proud of that resume,

but is happier personally now. Like many other people with gender dysphoria, which the International Center for Gender Education describes as extreme discomfort with one's sex, Ms. Rivers said her condition led her to alcoholism, thoughts of suicide and three failed marriages.

"I've been able to lead a successful life, but personally it's been a real struggle," she said. "Since I started taking hormones last January, I've been happier because I'm getting to be who I am for the first time. I'm going to be a better teacher for it. It's not about being a transsexual; it's about not always pretending and hiding."

She stepped near the school for the first time this school year on Friday. Classes were not in session, but in an annual staff day 40 students and 200 teachers held a lunchtime rally for Ms. Rivers across the street from the school. Students chanted "Two, four, six, eight, we demand a reinstate."

Angela Duvane, 17, a senior in the Media Communications Academy, said students missed their teacher.

"In her former state as Mr. Warfield, she was awesome," Miss Duvane said. "We all love her. Even students who never had her as a teacher."

* * *

February 4, 2000

THEIR GENDER WILL BEND EVERY WHICH WAY IT CAN

By A. O. SCOTT

GENDERNAUTS
Written, directed and produced by Monika Treut; director of photography, Elfi Mikesch; edited by Eric Schefter; music by Georg Kajanus, with additional music by Veronica Klaus and Pearl Harbour; released by First Run Features. At the Cinema Village, 22 East 12th Street, Greenwich Village. Running time: 86 minutes. This film is not rated.
WITH: Sandy Stone, Texas Tomboy, Susan Stryker, Max Valerio, Jordy Jones, Stafford, Tornado, Hida Viloria and Annie Sprinkle.

"Nature can be more inventive than culture," observes Monika Treut, musing on the sex lives, and the sex organs, of the African spotted hyena. But aside from the hyenas, which show up only in a precredit sequence, "Gendernauts" seems devoted to a contrary proposition. Hyenas, after all, don't design Web sites devoted to Gertrude Stein, or organize talent shows for drag queens and drag kings, or participate in hormone therapy.

"Gendernauts," which opens today at Cinema Village, might have been called "Sexual Ambiguity in San Francisco." The subjects of Ms. Treut's earnest new documentary—although this sounds like a coldly anthropological description of people who are, in fact, her friends—like to think of themselves as artists. Some make videos or photographs, but what unites them is the sense that their gender identities, and indeed their bodies, are works in progress.

Ms. Treut, a chirpy, sympathetic presence whose curiosity is always balanced by tact, introduces us to a few Bay Area residents who defy assimilation to the usual categories: gay or straight, male or female. Texas Tomboy, for instance, is biologically a woman. "She has a womb," explains Tornado, a former Penthouse model who sees herself as Tomboy's surrogate mother. But Tomboy sports blond stubble on her chin and prefers to be called he.

A blue-eyed, crew-cut, six-foot photographer named Stafford, on the other hand, doesn't care what pronoun people use so long as they use it respectfully. And Hida Viloria, a voluble hermaphrodite with exquisite cheekbones, can pass effortlessly from ravishing femininity to sullen machismo. Having lived credibly as a woman and as a man, Hida, like Stafford, now seems happiest occupying "the middle ground" between them.

The idea that there is a middle ground—that gender is not a fixed category, but a fluid domain of expression and experimentation—has been a staple of academic discourse for some time. So it's not surprising that Ms. Treut should have appointed a professor, Sandy Stone of the University of Texas at Austin, as our cicerone on this tour of transgender San Francisco. But Professor Stone, who aside from her teaching and scholarship performs unspecified duties as the self-declared "goddess of cyberspace," is not entirely a happy choice. She speaks in slow, didactic cadences and peppers her speech with cultural-studies jargon and New Age psychobabble.

It is left to the others—to Hida, Stafford and Tomboy, along with Max Valerio, a female-to-male transsexual, and Annie Sprinkle, who calls herself "a sex artist"—to flesh out, as it were, Dr. Stone's abstractions. The glimpse into their lives that "Gendernauts" offers is interesting, but it is only a glimpse.

Ms. Treut's intention was clearly to affirm the humanity of the intersexed, transgendered and transsexual individuals she encountered, and she has succeeded. (She also helpfully clarifies the differences among these terms.) But because human experience is by nature complex and ambiguous, it requires more than simple affirmation: there is more to these people, one suspects, than ambiguous sexual characteristics, but Ms. Treut declines to pry.

What results is a movie that, for all its candor, feels oddly decorous, even prim. The exhilarating, scary mutability of gender identity has recently inspired brilliant investigations like the Off Broadway musical "Hedwig and the Angry Inch" and the film "Boys Don't Cry," but those are passionate and troubling works of art, to which "Gendernauts" might be seen as a useful set of footnotes.

* * *

June 11, 2000

NEW BIAS FRONTIER: A COUNCIL BILL AIMS TO PROTECT THE TRANSGENDERED

By DENNY LEE

When Donnie Vargas switched sexes and became Diana, her masculine wardrobe was not the only thing to go. She lost her job waiting on tables and was evicted from her apartment in Providence, R.I.

So Ms. Vargas did what many outcasts before had done: she moved to New York in search of more "diversity and greater opportunities," she said. But two years and dozens of job interviews later, she is still looking for work.

"Some places chuckled at me," said Ms. Vargas, 30, who now lives in Astoria, Queens. "Others told me they don't hire my kind," including one restaurant that advertised itself as owned and operated by gays, she said.

On Monday, members of the City Council introduced legislation to broaden the city's human rights law to protect Ms. Vargas and others like her. The bill would insert the words, "gender identity or expression," into existing language that bars discrimination in employment, public accommodations, housing, credit and education.

"Transgendered or gender variant people have no protection under city law," said Pauline Park, legislative coordinator of the New York Association for Gender Rights Advocacy, a nonprofit group formed in 1998. "Without protection from discrimination, we can be and are routinely fired or simply denied the opportunity to work."

The bill has 22 co-sponsors, said Peter Rider, a legislative aide to Councilwoman Christine Quinn, who is leading the effort along with five other Council members: Margarita Lopez, Philip Reed, Bill Perkins, Ronnie Eldridge and Stephen DiBrienza.

If the bill is enacted, New York will join 26 other cities, including San Francisco, Seattle and Atlanta, with similar laws.

While the bill's supporters say they have not encountered much opposition, they expect an uphill battle before the Council. The city's gay civil rights bill, they note, took 15 years before it was passed in 1986 and signed into law. The Giuliani administration has not taken a position on the new measure.

Meanwhile, transgender advocates have been speaking before community groups to build support. "People respond to me just as another middle-aged woman," said Melissa Sklarz, 46, who became the city's first transgendered officeholder last November when she won a judicial delegate seat.

"I keep forgetting that I'm different," Ms. Sklarz said. "In my own head, I'm no different at all."

PART II

THE MAINSTREAM VIEW

THE MEDICAL COMMUNITY

May 2, 1937

PARENTS ARE BLAMED
FOR SEX CRIME WAVE

*Magistrate Brill Tells Hunter Class Young Are Not Taught
Hygiene in Their Homes*

Blaming mothers and fathers for the current sex-crime wave, City Magistrate Jeanette G. Brill informed members of the Hunter College class of '04 yesterday that sex offenders "don't need a prison; they need a doctor."

Magistrate Brill, who sits in both the Women's Court and the Adolescent Court, was the guest of honor at the annual re-union luncheon of the class at the Essex House.

She said that, in the case of normal boys, parents do not give their children sufficient information on the subject of sex.

"In our high schools we don't give our boys as much sex hygiene as they can manage," she declared. "They pick up what they know on the streets."

Speaking of the mental defective type of criminal, who originates in the ungraded classes of the public school and who eventually turns both to regular and to sex crimes, Magistrate Bill stressed the need for hospitalization and re-adjustment.

Magistrate Brill said of the mentally defective criminals that "magistrates can't do anything but send them to State penal institutions, where they get a criminal record."

The luncheon was presided over by Mrs. Samuel Bitterman, class president, who announced that Mrs. Ruth Helen Davis, a member of the class, had been awarded Les Palmes Academiques and an associate membership in the French Academy by the French Minister of Education for her translations and adaptations of French classics.

About eighty members of the class were present.

* * *

April 23, 1938

BODY CHANGES LAID TO MENTAL REVOLT

*Psychiatrists Say 'Rejection of Femininity' by Women
May Alter Their Appearance*

PSYCHIATRY A BEAUTY AID

*Its Achievements Are Reviewed by Symposium
at Dinner to Dr. S. E. Jelliffe*

Emotional and mental activities of everyday life play an important role in physical disease, and in extreme cases may actually induce changes in the structure of the human body, according to six of the nation's neurologists and psychiatrists who yesterday took part in a symposium on neuropsychiatry at the Academy of Medicine.

An adverse environment can no longer be considered as the sole cause of disease, and destructive forces within man may reduce the environment to secondary importance as a factor in maintaining health, it was pointed out. The six authorities called psychiatry a potent new tool in curbing ill health and in increasing the beauty, happiness and general welfare of human beings.

The symposium, which was followed by a dinner at the academy, was in the nature of a tribute to Dr. Smith Ely Jelliffe, neurologist and psychiatrist, in token of the thirty-fifth anniversary of his editorship of The Journal of Nervous and Mental Diseases.

Participants in Symposium

In addition to Dr. Jelliffe, those taking part in the symposium were Dr. George Draper, Associate Professor of Clinical Medicine of the College of Physicians and Surgeons, Columbia University; Dr. Oscar Diethelm, Professor of Psychiatry at Cornell University; Dr. Adolph Meyer, former president of the American Neurological Association; Dr. Earl D. Bond of the Institute of the Pennsylvania Hospital and Dr. Karl A. Menninger, director of the Menninger Clinic in Topeka, Kan.

Dr. Draper asserted that although man has had sixty million years to adapt himself to space and time, it is only within recent years that "we have begun to rationally face the humiliating realization that even the camouflage of an outraged Deity is no longer sufficient to obscure the truth that man's most destructive forces are within his own soul."

Dr. Draper explained that a person's susceptibility to a particular disease may be determined by his individual make-up. Gradations in differences of personal identity often paralleled the varying severity of an attack of infantile paralysis in each child, he pointed out. Two entirely different types of mankind are susceptible to the two diseases of cataract and peptic ulcer, he said.

Varying Degrees of Sex

Sex, he said, was not a fixed character, and the strength of the maleness or femaleness of an individual may determine that person's susceptibility or immunity to some particular ailment.

Dr. Menninger explained that among many women there was a marked hostility to their own sex and that this emotional revolt affected their appearance and metabolism. This "rejected femininity" usually resulted from the woman's inability to become satisfactorily adjusted to her environment, he explained.

Physical mannerisms, in addition to mental and emotional habits, are frequently traced to this feeling of "rejected femininity," he added. In extreme cases, the physical structure of a girl may change under this influence. Dr. Menninger asserted that psychiatric treatment was valuable in restoring such a person's femininity and frequently added to her beauty.

Dr. Diethelm urged the need of studying the philosophical, religious and ethical aspects of both normal and sick persons in order to guide medical and psychiatric treatment. There is increasing recognition of the importance of considering the integrated personality as a whole in prescribing treatment, he declared.

Dr. Bond declared that student health work in colleges had indicated that one or two psychiatric interviews often cleared up many serious troubles. This work should be extended and organized, he declared.

Dr. Meyer, who opened the symposium, described psychotherapy as one of the most valued tools of medical science and praised Dr. Jelliffe as a pioneer in urging the gospel of mental hygiene. Others who joined in paying tribute to Dr. Jelliffe were Dr. A. A. Brill, Dr. Louis Casamajor, Dr. Henry A. Riley and Dr. Richard H. Hutchings. Dr. Foster Kennedy was toastmaster. Dr. Jelliffe was chairman of the symposium.

* * *

September 5, 1941

CHALLENGES POLLS OF PUBLIC OPINION

Psychologist Tells Session in Chicago Many Give Answers Not Knowing Their Minds

DANGER OF METHOD CITED

Types of Maladjustment Are Discussed—Popular Girls Are Called Better Adjusted

Special to The New York Times

CHICAGO, Sept. 4—The validity of public opinion polls was challenged today before the American Psychological Association, meeting at Northwestern University.

The challenge was made by Dr. Henry C. Link, vice president of the Psychological Association, whose article was read in his absence by Dr. A. D. Freiberg, his collaborator.

Dr. Link argued that the poll taker could never be sure that he was getting valid information, that actual behavior rather than attitude was the only reliable criterion for polls and that many persons answered poll questions without knowing their own minds. Yet a gullible and eager public, he said, awaited poll results like heaven-sent manna.

As instance of invalidity, he cited a test in which 500 persons were asked what brand of tires they used on their automobiles. When the interviewers checked the tires actually used they found the discrepancy to be so large that the question was abandoned.

In August, he said, 5,000 persons were asked, "Do you think the government should do something to keep prices from going up?" Immediately after this they were asked, "Do you think the government should do something to keep wages and salaries from going up?"

In answer to the first question, 85 per cent said yes and 5 per cent said no. But to the second question only 27 per cent said yes and 35 per cent said no, he stated.

Poll Contradictions Stressed

These opinions were obviously contradictory, he said, as have been opinions expressed in some recent war polls.

"Yet in spite of such contradictions, issues of national and international importance are being discussed and decided with reference to polls results," Dr. Link pointed out. "Thus, the question of validity no longer is merely a scientific problem, but a public problem of major importance."

If polls were made with 1,000,000 interviews and almost perfect reliability, the validity of results would still be as doubtful as they now are in respect to many questions, he said.

Their great danger lies not in the small number of interviews made or the inadequacy of the sample, but in "the readiness and even eagerness of many people to take their results at face value."

"The fact that the popular polls have had to meet the touchstone of actual election results, both in respect to reliability and validity, has been extremely fortunate from the standpoint of scientific psychology," he said. "Had it not been for this harsh periodic test, the serious task of measuring the public mind might as well have become a popular pastime, a journalistic plaything, or the device of unscrupulous propagandists."

Family Situations Discussed

Femininity in men and masculinity in women is often the result of poor family situations, Leonard Ferguson, instructor of psychology at the University of Connecticut, stated. Mr. Ferguson said:

"If, for example, the parents taught a culture which was different from that of the community in which the subject grew up; if the cultures represented by the two parents were dissimilar; if the subject suffered from irrational discipline; if the parents were separated; or if one of the parents was absent from home a good deal, the subject, if a man, would tend to become more feminine; if a woman would tend to become more masculine."

His results were based on a survey of 326 students at the University of Connecticut.

Dr. Graydon L. Freeman and Ernest Haggard of Northwestern University reported that the person who flares out in a sudden burst of anger gets over it much more quickly than the person who remains outwardly calm but seethes within. They reached their conclusion in a study of emotional arousal among twenty boys.

Dr. J. H. Elder of the University of Virginia reported in another paper that if a person made up his or her mind to awaken at a certain time he probably would, but that he would not sleep well.

Girls who are "dated" frequently are better adjusted socially than those who are not, Dr. J. E. Janney of Western Reserve University declared on the basis of a survey of fifty of the most frequent and fifty of the least frequent feminine "daters" in his university.

Dr. Calvin P. Stone of Stanford University was elected president of the association. Other officers elected were: Secretary, Dr. Willard C. Olson of the University of Michigan; treasurer, Dr. Willard L. Valentine of Northwestern University.

* * *

January 4, 1948

CONCERNING MAN'S BASIC DRIVE

By HOWARD A. RUSK

SEXUAL BEHAVIOR IN THE HUMAN MALE
By Alfred S. Kinsey
804 pp, New York, W. B. Saunders Co. $6.50.

Just as this was a difficult study to make and a difficult book to write, so is it also a difficult book to review. Difficult, because of the magnitude of the subject—difficult, because it deals with man's basic drive to reproduce, a drive as strong as that for survival—difficult, because of our prejudices, taboos and preconceptions, preconceptions colored by personal experience which gives the individual the microscopic rather than the total concept. Now, after decades of hush-hush, comes a book that is sure to create an explosion and to be bitterly controversial.

The book is "Sexual Behavior in the Human Male," by 53-year-old Alfred S. Kinsey, Professor of Zoology at Indiana University. Although it is by far the most comprehensive study yet made of sex behavior, it has been preceded by hundreds of others. The author lists 500 titles in his bibliography. However, there are only nineteen articles on sex in that literature which have the "taxonomic" approach (measurement of the variation in a series of individuals that represent the species). The approach of this specific study is the taxonomic one of the trained scientist, and is based on over 12,000 personal interviews, each encompassing over 300 questions. It has required eight years to complete this first phase, "Sexual Behavior in the Human Male." The complete study, for which Dr. Kinsey plans to secure a hundred thousand interviews over a twenty-year period, will include sex behavior of the female, sex factors in marital adjustment, legal aspects, sex education and other problems.

Professor Kinsey began this study due to the frustrating experience of attempting to answer the sex queries of students when there were no adequate facts on which to base such answers. He is a brave man, for to publish this book took real courage, courage to fight taboos and prejudices, preconceptions based on ignorance and the confusion that comes from translating one's personal experience as universal practice.

That it took courage not only to publish this report, but to gather the data, is well evidenced by the fact that the author withstood violent opposition from medical groups and school boards, psychiatrists and sheriffs, scientific colleagues and politicians. In one city the president of the school board, a physician, dismissed a teacher because he had assisted in getting histories outside of the school, but in the same city. But for every individual or group that opposed the study, hundreds cooperated, ranging from Harvard and Columbia Universities to the Kansas State police and the Salvation Army's Home for Unwed Mothers. The auspices of the National Research Council, and the financial underwriting of the Rockefeller Foundation, bespeak the scientific solidarity of the project.

The 12,000 subjects interviewed in the study by Professor Kinsey and his colleagues represented every level in our social strata—bootleggers and clergymen, professors and prostitutes, farmers and gamblers, ne'er-do-wells and social registerites. The final result—800 pages of text, with hundreds of charts and graphs analytically evaluated and statistically sound—is cold, dispassionate fact, starkly revealing our ignorance and prejudices.

These facts are presented with scientific objectivity, and without moralizing—but they provide the knowledge with which we can rebuild our concepts with tolerance and understanding. Here are a few of the significant findings:

Human sex patterns are established by three factors: physiological, psychological and social, the social being by far the most predominant. Using as a yardstick the educational level of eighth grade, high school and college, wide variations in sex concepts and behavior were found. "Most of the prejudices that develop in sexual activities are products of this conflict between the attitudes of different social levels."

We understand little of the range of human sex behavior. On the graph showing sexual frequency each individual differs only slightly from those next on the chart. This brings up the point of what is "normal" and "abnormal," and where such terms fit in a scientific study.

Dr. Kinsey points out that homosexual experience is much more common than previously thought. He indicates, however, that this is an extremely difficult problem to analyze "as very few individuals are all black or all white," and that one homosexual experience does not classify the individual as a homosexual. He decries the use of the noun, and finds that there is often a mixture of both homo and heterosexual experience.

To have or not to have premarital intercourse is a more important issue for a larger number of males than any other aspect of sex. Individuals in our American society rarely adopt totally new patterns of sex behavior after their middle teens. The peak of sex drive and ability comes in the late teens rather than in the late 20's or 30's as heretofore believed.

The theory of "sex conservation" so commonly taught as reason for continence, is refuted. Boys who attain early puberty and begin sex activity earlier have the highest rate of sex activity and continue such activity to the older age level.

Comparing the sexual activities of older and younger generations evidences the stability of our sexual mores and does not justify the opinion harbored by some that there are constant changes in such mores.

The above are only a few of the revealing findings of the study.

Because we are all human, every individual is bound to interpret this study in terms of personal experience. For some it will be clarifying. Others it will confuse. Some will be alarmed, others will be shocked; a few will interpret the general findings as grounds for personal license. After the initial impact, when time permits sober reflection and analysis the end results should be healthy. They should bring about a better understanding of some of our emotional problems, and the bases for some of our psychiatric concepts.

We can reorganize some of our attitudes and methods of sex education on the basis of need as dictated by experience rather than preconception, and we must surely re-examine the legal criteria by which we renounce and condemn individual sex behavior. Professor Kinsey states this well when he concludes:

To each individual, the significance of any particular type of sexual activity depends very largely upon his previous experience. Ultimately, certain activities may seem to him to be the only things that have value, that are right, that are socially acceptable; and all departures from his own particular pattern may seem to him to be enormous abnormalities. But the scientific data which are accumulating make it appear that if circumstances be propitious, most individuals might have become conditioned in any direction, even into activities which they now consider quite unacceptable.

There is an abundance of evidence that most human sexual activities would become comprehensible to most individuals, if they could know the background of each other's individual behavior.

Dr. Alan Gregg, in his concluding paragraph of the Preface to this study, has brilliantly summarized the many facets involved in this study as follows:

Certainly no aspect of human biology in our current civilization stands in more need of scientific knowledge and courageous humility than that of sex. The history of medicine proves that in so far as man seeks to know himself and face his whole nature, he has become free from bewildered fear, despondent shame, or arrant hypocrisy. As long as sex is dealt with in the current confusion of ignorance and sophistication, denial and indulgence, suppression and stimulation, punishment and exploitation, secrecy and display, it will be associated with a duplicity and indecency that lead neither to intellectual honesty nor human dignity.

These studies are sincere, objective and determined explorations of a field manifestly important to education, medicine, government and the integrity of human conduct generally. They have demanded from Dr. Kinsey and his colleagues very unusual tenacity of purpose, tolerance, analytical competence, social skills and real courage.

The findings of Dr. Kinsey's report provide us with the material for sober thought, and a new basis for the personal understanding of our individual sex problems. It presents facts that indicate the necessity to review some of our legal and moral concepts. It gives new therapeutic tools to the psychiatrist and the practicing physician. It offers a yardstick that will give invaluable aid in the study of our complex social problems. It offers data that should promote tolerance and understanding and make us better "world citizens."

After recovery from the original impact due to the explosion of many of our preconceptions, this study should be most valuable if, in the words of Dr. Gregg, "the reader will match the authors with an equal and appropriate measure of cool attention, courageous judgment and scientific equanimity."

*   *   *

March 7, 1948

SCIENCE IN REVIEW

The Now Famous Kinsey Report Is Criticized On Statistical and Sociological Grounds

By WALDEMAR KAEMPFFERT

It was hardly to be expected that the chorus of praise that greeted the remarkable report on "Sexual Behavior in the Human Male," by Drs. A. C. Kinsey, W. B. Pomeroy and C. E. Martin, would not be offset by some caustic comment. Though this department believes that Professor Kinsey and his colleagues have performed an important service by showing how unrealistic and even barbarous is the legalistic conception of sex relations which has prevailed for centuries, it also believes that the public ought to know what sociologists and statisticians think of the now famous report. So a summary is here presented of a critique by Profs. A. H. Hobbs and R. D. Lambert of the University of Pennsylvania.

Kinsey and his colleagues draw these broad conclusions: Of the male population of this country, 85 per cent have had premarital intercourse; nearly 70 per cent have had relations with prostitutes; between 30 and 40 per cent are unfaithful to their wedded consorts, and 37 per cent have had some homosexual experience between adolescence and old age. Yet Dr. Kinsey is far from holding that our sexual morals are loose and that the world is going to the dogs. He thinks that even scientists have wrongly accepted as valid the "biological notions of ancient jurists and theologians or the analyses made by the mystics of two or three thousand years ago."

Sampling Method Criticized

In their dissection of these conclusions Hobbs and Lambert condemn Kinsey's method of procedure, specifically his method of sampling the population. To obtain a fair random sample of anything, from the heat value of a carload of coal to the patriotism of a community, is not easy. Kinsey knows it and takes what are to him the proper precautions. His men asked white males questions that covered 300 to 500 items. Thus 5,300 case histories were compiled. To obtain homogeneous samples, the histories were classified according to sex, race, marital status, age, educational level and either rural-urban background or religious background. Kinsey intends eventually to break down his cases into twelve groups.

We cannot here list all the pitfalls into which Hobbs and Lambert maintain that Kinsey has fallen in sampling the population. A few examples will have to suffice.

Each case was treated as if it fell not only within its own but also within a previous age category. A married man of 30 who was interviewed would thus provide material for youths who were single. Kinsey justified the procedure on the score that sexual patterns persist, so that practices which the 30-year-old man engaged in during his youth were assumed to be the same as those of youth in general today. Any change in the pattern of sexual behavior or any selectivity of older age groups will thus distort findings for younger groups. The procedure also classified persons in sexual categories on the basis of isolated instances rather than on the basis of patterns of behavior. The adults of today would be labeled as criminals if as boys they had ever swiped apples and as gangsters if they ever belonged to a boys' gang.

Common Statistical Procedure

Kinsey is well aware of the difficulty of getting a fair random sample and of using it correctly. So he weights his figures to accord with what is known to hold good for the general population. This is a common and a necessary statistical procedure. But, say Hobbs and Lambert, "weighting is not applied for other admittedly significant categories, such as religious affiliation, degree of adherence to religion and rural-urban differences." Those who are 20 years of age or older constitute 75 percent of the population, but only 20 percent of the sample. Only 30 percent of the total population, 20 years or over, is single, but this group of single males constitutes 78 percent of the sample. So Hobbs and Lambert take up one item after another of the sample and show that few correct conclusions can be drawn from them.

"Stratified Samples"

Kinsey justifies his disproportions by calling them "stratified samples." Hobbs and Lambert retort that "this procedure demands more or less equal samples from each of the ultimate groups" and that Kinsey accepts "the principle of the stratified sample only in setting a lower limit to the number of cases (fifty) which will be included in each subgroup."

As sociologists Hobbs and Lambert object to the method of treating the sexual behavior of man as biologists treat it in animals. Kinsey happens to be an entomologist, which may explain his attempted disregard of all sociological values. He found it impossible to abide by his principles. In discussing "Religious Background and Sexual Outlet" he is up to his neck in social and moral interpretations. Hobbs and Lambert find that this applies to ten out of eighteen chapters.

Kinsey is so very much the biologist that he contrasts various types of sexual behavior with "normal mammalian behavior," which is the "basis in the human animal" and "normal among other anthropoids," and dwells on the effect of "tyranny of the mores" on the "victims of the mores." If we are to accept this kind of reasoning, say Hobbs and Lambert, we shall have to consider speech, abstract thought, writing, driving an automobile, wearing clothes and making studies of sexual behavior as reprehensible in the sense that they are not "normal" among lower animals. Sexual behavior happens to be a matter of social concern. If we were to judge sexual practices in terms of "normal mammalian behavior," all culturally affected behavior would be "abnormal," Hobbs and Lambert point out.

Social Conditions

Just because Kinsey tried to avoid social interpretations of his data, Hobbs and Lambert think that he has erred: A sociologist would say that behavior under one set of social conditions would be wrong, under another condoned, even applauded. Killing is generally condemned; in war it is commended. The man who catches his wife in adultery and shoots her paramour stands a good chance of being acquitted by a jury. A policeman who kills a fleeing murderer is not regarded as a criminal. A college boy who necks and pets is just sowing his wild oats, but the college girl who goes as far with the boys may find herself an outcast.

"The situations are quite different biologically as well as economically and socially," say Hobbs and Lambert. Boys cannot become pregnant and thus add an illegitimate child to the burden their families must carry. All this Hobbs and Lambert adduce not to commend or condemn human sexual behavior but to indicate that man, being a social creature, must be treated as such in any study of his mores.

The human species reproduces itself much as all higher animals do, but what is normal sexual behavior for grizzly bears in a forest or for cattle in a pasture is not necessarily normal for men and women in New York or London. In fact, animals are not given to nearly as many departures from what we call "normal" sexual behavior as are human beings. Much cruelty and injustice are to be, found in laws that govern sexual behavior, but it does not follow that everything that a beast of the field may do is "normal" for members of a human society.

* * *

June 5, 1948

DR. KINSEY DEFENDS STATEMENTS IN BOOK

Dr. Alfred C. Kinsey replied yesterday to critics, chiefly psychiatrists and sociologists, who have attacked his book, "Sexual Behavior in the Human Male."

The attacks were made principally because he described as "normal" and "natural" practices they maintain are abnormal and the result of individual emotional disturbances.

This was the first public answer made by the Indiana University professor to charges brought by social scientists against parts of the book that has aroused such controversial discussion. He addressed 200 members and guests at the opening session of the thirty-eighth annual meeting of the American Psychopathological Association at the Commodore Hotel.

He asserted that most of the sexual behavior called abnormal in our particular culture is "part and parcel of our inheritance as mammals and is natural and normal biologically."

"In their training medical men take courses in comparative anatomy or comparative embryology in order to interpret what we find in the human structure," he declared. "In the same fashion it is scientifically sound to look to mammalian background as sources of human behavior."

On the basis of the data in his book, he said he would agree with those who claim that the majority of persons who engage in abnormal behavior were emotionally disturbed. He added that he believed, however, that such disturbances were primarily the result of the individual's fear of society's reaction to his behavior because of existing taboos.

Another speaker, Dr. Frank A. Beach of Yale University, supported Dr. Kinsey's statements in a talk on "Sexual Activity Common to Man and Other Mammals," saying that many practices that are called unnatural in humans "appear to be natural in the lower animals."

An appeal for the development of more emotionally mature adults capable of living together rationally and content to "accept with good will" the limitations essential to successful communal life was made by Dr. Donald J. MacPherson, president of the association, which is composed of psychiatrists, psychologists and biologists.

* * *

June 6, 1948

DR. KNIGHT ASSAILS 'STRONG-ARM CURE'

Psychiatrist Scores 'Beating Illness Out'—Urges 'Gentle' Approach to Patients

By LUCY FREEMAN

The indiscriminate use of "strong-arm" methods of psychotherapy such as electro-shock, injections of sodium amytol and lobotomy were attacked yesterday by Dr. Robert P. Knight, one of the nation's leading psychiatrists.

He condemned as "pernicious" what he called "the therapeutic attitude that the patient's illness must be beaten out of him," in addressing the closing session of the thirty-eighth annual convention of the American Psychopathological Association at the Commodore Hotel.

Dr. Knight, formerly chief of staff of the Menninger Clinic, Topeka, Kan., is now medical director of the Austen Riggs Foundation, which maintains a voluntary hospital and clinic for the study and treatment of psychoneuroses and training of psychiatrists at Stockbridge, Mass. He is also active in the National Committee for Mental Hygiene.

In his condemnation of "strong-arm" techniques, he also included the practice of "intimidating psychoanalysis."

Sees Methods 'Prostituted'

Dr. Knight charged that some of the therapeutic methods in psychiatry have become "prostituted" by psychiatrists who "know no other methods except the shock techniques and who think only of making the patient give up his complaints and subside."

These therapists operate on the theory that they "must do something vigorous to the patient, do it quickly, make it magical, and concentrate on doing something to the symptoms," he continued.

He declared that he wanted to make it clear that he was not condemning the use of these therapies as a whole because "each one has its place and purpose."

"But because some of these therapies gain support in certain types of cases and because they can be learned without too long a period of training, they come to be focussed on as the chief therapeutic method of many men," he said.

One of the dangers is that these methods are then presented to the public as the newest and most progressive kind of therapy, he warned.

He issued a plea for the use instead of what he called "the gentle arm of psychiatry" which tended "to elicit from the patient his potentialities and to teach him something about further living."

Urges Rational Programs

He asks psychiatrists to "get acquainted with their patients, learn their capabilities and then develop a psychiatric program that is rational, rather than going from one strong-arm therapeutic method to another."

Dr. Ernest W. Burgess of the University of Chicago called on sociologists for further study of the change in sexual behavior in this country brought out by the findings in the book "Sexual Behavior in the Human Male" by Dr. Alfred C. Kinsey.

He said the Kinsey report showed there had been "significant" although not "sweeping" changes over the years.

Dr. Gustav Bychowski, psychoanalyst, of New York, called Dr. Kinsey's remarks on sublimation "highly controversial." Declaring that certain drives cannot be satisfied "since we no longer are living in the jungle," he said it was up to the psychiatrists to help highly inhibited persons to become less inhibited, channeling those drives into highly satisfactory cultural activities and thus providing sublimation.

* * *

October 24, 1951

DOCTOR ASKS HELP FOR SEX OFFENDER

Special to The New York Times

BILOXI, Miss., Oct. 23—The spirit of revenge so dominates the problem of sex offenses that medical criminologists are hindered seriously in their efforts to provide treatment for offenders, the eighty-first annual Congress of Corrections was told today.

Dr. Lowell S. Selling, president of the Medical Correctional Association, said that from the standpoint of both diagnosis and treatment there was no justification for the general public practice of grouping all types of sexual deviation under one classification. It results, he said, in "bringing down on sex offenders a certain amount of conditioned responses by the police or public which very definitely hinders our efforts to treat them."

The congress, sponsored by the American Prison Association, is holding a four-day meeting attended by 700 of the nation's leaders in the fields of penology and crime and delinquency prevention.

Elizabeth M. Kates, superintendent of the State Industrial Farm for Women at Goochland, Va., said that the sex problem "is the most menacing problem persistently confronting all prison officials."

Homosexuality is not a rare affliction, Miss Kates noted, and yet its victims "have been hounded as criminals and punished as such." Any recognizable physical disease that afflicted as many persons and caused such acute unhappiness, she added, would have attracted hundreds of scientific workers and huge research funds long ago.

* * *

August 21, 1953

KINSEY RELEASES REPORT ON WOMEN

Study Reveals Many Popular Ideas Are Wrong and That No Person Is Average

BLOOMINGTON, Ind., Aug. 20 (AP)—Dr. Alfred C. Kinsey's scientific look at women's sex lives finds that many popular ideas are wrong.

He also finds that women stay younger than men in sex activity, and that the only basic difference between men and women is mental—in how they react to psychological stimuli. These two things are the cause of much maladjustment and trouble in marriages, he declares.

Dr. Kinsey authorized advance publication today of findings in the new, 842-page book, "Sexual Behavior in the Human Female," to appear Sept. 14. It is based not only upon interviews with nearly 6,000 females, but also upon many other experts' studies.

Traditional ideas that Dr. Kinsey terms wrong are:

That women are slower to respond sexually; that girls develop sexually earlier than boys; that there are any basic differences in the nature of sexual satisfaction in men and women; that the sex response is more emotion-packed for a wife than a husband.

Another important point, he adds, is that sex lives of humans are like fingerprints—no two exactly alike. No person fits all the averages that Dr. Kinsey and associates have found in their work at the Institute for Sex Research, Inc., at Indiana University.

Sharp Change in Habits

The post-war nineteen-twenties witnessed a sharp change in women's sex habits, and there has been little change since then, the report shows. More women began engaging in pre-marital affairs and "petting," and frigidity in marriage has declined by one-third to one-half of what it had been among wives born before 1900.

The statistics also indicate:

• Half of women have sex relations before they marry, with two-thirds of them experiencing full sexual satisfaction.

• About 26 per cent of wives at some time during marriage have affairs with one or more other men. Not infrequently, their husbands encourage them to seek such affairs.

• About 10 per cent of wives go through life never knowing what sexual satisfaction is. And about 28 per cent of older single women have never experienced satisfaction.

• About a third of women have never experienced satisfaction, by any method, by the time they marry. But almost all men have.

Two Findings Stressed

The report, written by all fourteen members of the institute, points up two findings that bear on many marriages—the effects of aging and psychology.

Most women, it finds, do not reach a peak of sex activity until they are about 27 years old or 28, though the peak may come earlier or later.

But once they reach this individual peak, women maintain that degree of activity to the age of 50 or 60, with no sharp decline as they grow older.

Men, though, usually reach a peak at about 16 to 18. Then their activity steadily declines with the years. The male peak is usually so much higher than the female that most men remain more active sexually throughout life than most women.

Difficulties often arise because men show this aging effect while women do not. Wives often are becoming more interested and less inhibited about sex when their husbands' interest may be lessening, especially with a wife who had objected earlier in marriage to the frequency of the husband's requests.

Most women are not stimulated as men are, or as often as men, by psychological stimuli, such as nude pictures, thoughts of sex or anticipation of it.

Dr. Kinsey said the findings in the new book were probably typical of many American women, but that they did not mirror the actions of all women, and certainly not women of other countries.

Dr. Kinsey also declared in his book that frustrated and inexperienced single women could do "considerable damage if given the power to direct the behavior of other people."

He said that "unresponsive or unresponding females" interviewed included grade and high school and college teachers, directors of youth organizations and not a few women who had "had a part in establishing public policies."

Profits Go to Institute

As with the book on men, all profits from the new book, selling for $8 and published by W. B. Saunders Co., Philadelphia, will go to the institute to finance continuing research. Other volumes are planned on sex laws, sex education, marriage problems and other subjects. Drs. Wardell B. Pomeroy, Clyde E. Martin and Paul H. Gebhard are principal co-authors of the report on women.

The latest report draws on interviews with 5,940 females aged 2 to 90, of various religions, education and occupations.

Information on the 2-year-olds came from their mothers. The report excludes Negro women because not enough had been interviewed.

Of the women represented, 69 per cent lived in ten states possessing about 47 per cent of the total United States population—New York, Pennsylvania, Illinois, Indiana, California, New Jersey, Ohio, Florida, Massachusetts and Maryland.

Of his sample, only 17 per cent had not gone beyond some high school education, 56 per cent had had some college education, and 19 per cent some graduate work. But Dr. Kinsey finds that educational level has less effect upon women's sex lives than men's.

Of women in this book, 58.2 per cent had never been married when interviewed, 41.8 per cent had been or were then married, and 13.2 per cent were widowed, separated or divorced. Sixty per cent were Protestant, 12 per cent Roman Catholic, and 28 per cent Jewish. Dr. Kinsey said more Catholic and devoutly Jewish women needed to be represented.

* * *

December 11, 1961

WOMEN DEVIATES HELD INCREASING

Problem of Homosexuality Found Largely Ignored

By EMMA HARRISON

The problem of homosexuality in women is increasing, a psychologist said here yesterday.

Yet, said Dr. Charles Socarides, the New York analyst, this psychic problem of women has been largely ignored both by psychiatry and by society in general.

Even the legal injunctions imposed by some societies on overt male homosexuality do not pertain to the female, he observed. The attitude probably rests in the "archaic unconscious morality of men," he said.

Part of the rise in female homosexuality may be accounted for, he said, in the increase of the problem among men. Although figures are scanty in the field, he said that the fact that male homosexuality had risen some 600 per cent in England since World War II indicated the possibility of some compensating drive in women. Also, he observed, such aberration is often a consequence of a disordered and confused society.

Symposium on Subject

Acknowledgement of the extent of the problem was indicated by the fact that the American Psychoanalytic Association held its first symposium on overt female homosexuality before its annual session ended yesterday at the Biltmore Hotel. Dr. Socarides participated in the panel discussion and summarized the findings of the group.

The problem of child-rearing plays a distinct role in female homosexuality, according to Dr. Judith S. Kestenberg of Sands Point, L. I. The homosexual woman "wastes nothing except, of course, her motherliness," she said. In the homosexual relationship, women "play out the mother-child relationship," she said.

There is no better description of these women, she said, than that of the poet Sappho, whom she quoted as saying "I shall remain eternally maiden." All homosexual women, Dr. Kestenberg said, "are young virginal girls at heart." They play, she said, with "life dolls."

She, too, commented on the role that society played in the kind of permissive attitude toward this form of sexual deviation. "We adults," she said, "look upon them with indulgence, pity and amused smilings."

Dr. David Beres, a New York psychoanalyst, was named president-elect of the association at the final business session.

* * *

May 19, 1964

HOMOSEXUALS PROUD OF DEVIANCY, MEDICAL ACADEMY STUDY FINDS

By ROBERT TRUMBULL

Homosexuals have gone beyond the plane of defensiveness and now argue that their deviancy is "a desirable, noble, preferable way of life," according to a report issued yesterday by the Committee on Public Health of the New York Academy of Medicine.

The report is the first authoritative study of homosexuality by a recognized organization representing all branches of medicine, a spokesman for the committee said. Public comment on sexual variance has been confined heretofore to the psychiatric branch of the profession, he declared.

Homosexuality is an "illness" that can be treated successfully in "some cases" but is more easily dealt with by early preventive measures, the report concludes.

The study takes strong issue with the contention of spokesmen for homosexuals that their aberration makes them merely "a different kind of people leading an acceptable way of life."

Organized homosexuals now go even further than this, the committee found.

"They would have it believed that homosexuality is not just an acceptable way of life but rather a desirable, noble, preferable way of life," the report goes on. "For one thing, they claim that it is the perfect answer to the problem of the population explosion."

The committee's findings were said to apply to homosexuals everywhere, not just in New York. Various authorities have estimated the number of sexual deviants in this city at between 100,000 and 600,000.

"There is . . . an impression that at the present time the practice of homosexuality is increasing among the population at large," the report says. "Certainly, if there is not more homosexuality than in the past, it appears to be more open and obstrusive.

"More plays and books are having homosexual characters, and more homosexuals seem to have taken to writing autobiographies. Furthermore the homosexuals seem to have become more formally organized, with a central office and a magazine of their own."

Allusion to Organization

This was apparently an allusion to the Mattachine Society, a national organization of homosexuals with headquarters in San Francisco and branch offices in New York and other cities. The group publishes a monthly magazine, Mattachine Review, devoted to problems of sex inverts.

"These developments," the report continues, "stand out in sharp contrast with the situation which existed in New York 30 years ago, when the subject was less frequently and less openly presented and its votaries rallied once a year to hold their well-known Fairy Ball."

The study on homosexuality was a by-product of the committee's investigations of two other public health problems—the increases in salacious literature and venereal disease. The committee found that "a substantial portion" of the objectionable publications were of a homosexual nature and that homosexuals were apparently "playing a larger role in transmitting" venereal disease.

'Indeed an Illness'

Society, including the medical profession, "has not really confronted" the problem of homosexuality, the report asserts.

"The Committee on Public Health believes that of all groups the medical profession should state clearly its position," the report says. "It should declare what homosexuality is and what can be done about it."

"Homosexuality is indeed an illness," the medical committee declared. "The homosexual is an emotionally disturbed individual who has not acquired a normal capacity to develop satisfying heterosexual relationships.

"Consequently overt homosexuality may be an expression of fear of the opposite sex and of inability to accept adult responsibility, such as marriage and parenthood."

In other words, the report says, the homosexual is a victim of "arrested development."

As main factors in early environmental life leading to deviation from customary sexual behavior, the report lists "neglect, rejection, overprotection, overindulgence" by parents.

Homosexual inclinations begin earlier in life than is generally realized, and their appearance is often motivated by defective parental relationships, the report states.

Psychotherapy Urged

Recognition of deviant tendencies may be difficult, the committee found. Personal mannerisms and characteristics can be deceptive.

"Although treatment is difficult and prognosis is guarded, it can be successful and of value," the report continues. "Psychotherapy offers the greatest probability of benefit. There is little valid evidence that other treatment is effective."

Treatment works better the earlier it is started, the report states, and it is a prerequisite to success that the deviant possess a genuine desire to correct his condition.

"There is a widespread need and desire for proper and authoritative sex education," the report goes on. "But here the reaction of society manifests an interesting ambivalence."

This ambivalence is illustrated by a prevailing "superficial, immature and artificial attitude toward sex" in the midst of general "preoccupation with sex as a symbol," the report says.

"The argument most commonly advanced is that sex education belongs in the home. But if the home is not providing that education, where will it be found?" the report asks.

The medical committee recommended that sex education in the United States be "examined realistically."

* * *

January 31, 1965

THERARY IS FOUND CURING DEVIATES

Psychiatrist Urges Positive Attitude on Treatment

A psychiatrist who reports that he has been successfully treating homosexuals for 10 years has urged his colleagues to take a strong stand against the view that homosexuality does not respond to therapy.

Dr. Samuel B. Hadden, associate professor of psychiatry at the University of Pennsylvania School of Medicine, reported his findings to the 22d annual conference of the American Group Psychotherapy Association. The association's four-day meeting and training institute, held in San Francisco ended yesterday.

Dr. Hadden said that of 32 patients who had attended at least 20 therapy sessions in groups composed entirely of homosexuals, "12 have progressed to an exclusive heterosexual pattern of adjustment and other neurotic traits have improved or disappeared."

Most of the patients had been referred to Dr. Hadden by other psychiatrists rather than by courts or community agencies.

When compared with the results of other studies, Dr. Hadden's success is unusual. Although the psychiatric literature has taken a less pessimistic tone about treating male homosexuality in recent years, previous reports have noted success in treating about a quarter of homosexual patients.

According to an authoritative report last spring by the New York Academy of Medicine, homosexuality can be treated successfully in "some cases," but is more easily dealt with by early recognition of "neglect, rejection, overprotection or overindulgence" by parents.

Contrary to the findings of the Academy and individual researchers, Dr. Hadden found that his homosexual patients were not at all proud of their deviancy.

"I have never observed a group in which homosexuality as a way of life was not fiercely attacked when a member tried to present it as desirable," he said.

Dr. Hadden found that all-homosexual therapeutic groups were most successful because the members did not have to face the hostility that often drives them from mixed groups.

More important, he said, a homosexual's insistence that his condition is a happy one is constantly challenged by older members of the group, creating enough anxiety to make the patient want to and try to change.

Dr. Hadden deplored pessimistic attitudes toward change as only helpful to the organized homosexual groups that try to influence public opinion and promote legislation "to improve the legal and social status of the homosexual."

* * *

February 10, 1971

HOMOSEXUALITY: PARENTS AREN'T ALWAYS TO BLAME

By JANE E. BRODY

Scrawled in large black letters on a subway wall:

"My mother made me a homosexual."

And beneath it, in a somewhat more timid hand:

"If I get her the wool, will she make me one, too?"

The graffiti have long since been erased by whitewash, but mother remains in the public mind as the butt of the not-very-funny homosexual joke. Among professionals, however, more careful studies-of the roots of homosexuality are beginning to take mother—and father—somewhat off the hook.

While a child's parents obviously play a substantial role in whatever kind of person he eventually becomes, a number of experts now say that to give parents the sole blame—or credit—for his sexual development is simplistic and misleading.

"With perhaps 20 million American men who practice some form of homosexuality," says Dr. Lawrence J. Hatterer, psychiatrist at New York Hospital's Payne Whitney Clinic, "it's inconceivable that all should have emerged from the same set of causes—the stereotype of the domineering, overprotective, feminizing mother and the weak or absent father."

Dr. Hatterer has evaluated more than 1,000 homosexual men and treated more than 200 of them in the last 15 years. He says:

"I've heard well over 10,000 life stories of homosexuals, with every combination and variation of parental history that you can imagine—from the most hostile, aggressive, hypercritical mother and rejecting, emasculating father to the dominating, loving, attentive father and the gentle, almost too submissive mother."

Eda LeShan, New York psychologist and expert on child rearing, believes that the psychoanalytic emphasis on how parents affect their child's sexuality has made many parents "self-conscious and uneasy."

"I have seen mothers who are hysterical with fear when their perfectly normal 4-year-old sons wanted to wear high heels, and affectionate fathers who are ashamed that they like to have their children climb into bed with them on a

Sunday morning," Mrs. LeShan relates in her book, "Natural Parenthood."

"It is important to remember," she continues, "that for every aggressively seductive mother and passive or emotionally absent father whose son turns out to be a homosexual, there are other mothers and fathers with exactly the same qualities who get to be grandmas and grandpas in the traditional fashion."

Psychiatrists agree that it is by no means easy to turn a child into a homosexual, and most children seem able to resist even the worst combination of influences.

David D. is a case in point. His mother was an overpowering, overprotective, emasculating woman who clearly wore the pants in the family. His father, although physically "there," played almost no role in the boy's upbringing. The parents had frequent violent arguments.

The boy himself was pretty, overweight, clumsy, always lagging behind in physical activities, and often ridiculed by his playmates for his ineptness.

Yet, through all this, his masculine self-image remained intact. Today, at the age of 26 after a number of heterosexual affairs, he is about to be married to a lovely, feminine girl.

Since cases like David's rarely come to psychiatric attention, professionals really know very little about what enables one youngster to resist strong homosexualizing influences while another succumbs to relatively innocuous forces.

At least one study indicates that a young boy's effeminate behavior (which sometimes but not always evolves into homosexuality) may be the cause, not the result, of how his parents treat him.

In a long term study of boys, most of whom first showed effeminate characteristics as early as age 2, 3 or 4, Dr. Bernard Zuger, child psychiatrist at Greenwich Hospital in Connecticut, found that the effeminate boys were no more likely than noneffeminate boys to have dominant mothers, their parents were no more likely to have wished for a girl, they were just as likely to be affectionate toward the child and there was no greater incidence of marital conflict.

Two important differences did emerge however. While the noneffeminate boy solicited his mother's attention and sympathy, the effeminate boy aligned himself with her interests and activities. He had no interest in his father's activities. In fact, a careful analysis of the family relationships indicated that it wasn't the father who rejected his son, it was the son who rejected his father.

In many cases that Dr. Hatterer and others have investigated, the parents of homosexuals have not been such bad folks, but other members of the family—such as a brother or sister the boy repeatedly lost out to or who continually bullied him, or an older relative, male or female, who consistently exploited the boy sexually—might have "homosexualized" him.

Dr. Martin Hoffman, psychiatrist at Mount Zion Medical Center in San Francisco, who summarized his study of homosexuals in a book, "The Gay World," also deplores the emphasis on parental influences.

While parent-child interactions are a "crucial factor" in the development of sexual feelings, he says, "a full explanation of any given adult's sexual patterns must take into account the vital years between the beginning of schooling and the end of adolescence. It is during these years that the individual learns a great deal about who he is, what he can and cannot do, and how his age-mates will respond to his actions."

Dr. Hoffman recalls the case of a 47-year-old business executive who had a "happy childhood," a close, satisfactory relationship with his father and a passive mother who was devoted to her husband.

The boy's troubles began when he entered high school. His clumsiness and lack of interest in athletics isolated him from his peers. He was also afflicted with a severe case of acne, which made him unattractive to girls.

Doubting his masculinity, he befriended another boy outcast with definite effeminate mannerisms. After a while, they began experimenting sexually with one another and soon came to regard themselves as "gay." The result: a lifelong commitment to homosexuality.

If the unspoken rejection of a boy's peer group can have such a profound effect, certainly such shattering taunts as "sissy," "Mama's boy," "fatso," "fag," and the like can seriously undermine the sexual identity of a boy who may already be questioning his masculinity.

Dr. Hatterer believes that environmental and cultural factors are becoming increasingly important contributors to the development of homosexuality.

He notes, for example, that "youngsters today are under more and more pressure to perform sexually well and early in life. Some boys may avoid heterosexual encounters because they're afraid they will be inadequate, others may fear the responsibility, still others may be afraid that their physical endowments will make them subject to ridicule or unable to satisfy a woman.

"Let's face it, for a young boy who wants sex, it's much easier and faster and often less threatening to make a homosexual contact than to pick up a girl."

Sometimes, Dr. Hatterer adds, parents inadvertently encourage such behavior by explicitly forbidding sexual encounters with girls but saying nothing explicit about other boys.

Other environmental influences Dr. Hatterer has encountered in dealing with homosexuals include the following:

• "The $1-billion hard core homosexual pornography industry" and the proliferation of homosexual movies. "For the vulnerable male, it's very stimulating and may be the thing that pushes him over the line."

• The growing public tolerance of homosexuality, which may make some men feel, "Maybe it's easier, and why not?"

• The blending of traditional male and female roles that can lead to confusion in a boy's mind as to what is male and what is female, especially if the families of his friends are structured differently from his.

• The value that our society places on sexual as well as material success. "For some young people failure, or imagined failure, in both these respects may lead to homosexuality."

"Often," Dr. Hatterer remarks in his recently published book, "Changing Homosexuality in the Male," "the family can do nothing to counter outside influences of this kind." He is critical of his psychiatric colleagues who, he says, "have given very little attention to such environmental influences on male homosexuality."

Dr. Albert Ellis, New York psychologist and author of many books on sex and marriage, shares this view. "The Freudians," he says, "highly exaggerate the part that family patterns play . . . and neglect the part that general culture patterns play."

He notes, for example, that some young men may be more interested in arts and music than they are in athletics, and a boy whose predominant interests are esthetic is a cultural outcast in current American society.

In their book, "Growing Up Straight," Peter and Barbara Wyden describe a boy who became a homosexual largely because he was physically unable to match the masculine ideal of our culture. Instead, he developed his excellent singing voice and sang in the church choir.

Strangely enough, when he traveled to Europe where the prevailing concept of masculinity encompasses esthetic interests, he had no difficulty with heterosexual relations, but upon returning to the United States, his homosexuality flared up again.

Dr. Hatterer's advice to parents: "Maybe your child is artistic and not such a good ball player. Give him a chance to develop his other strengths, even if they don't fit the lines of our stereotyped view of masculinity. Don't push him and make him feel like a failure if he can't do things that are constitutionally difficult for him."

Parents can help counter the damage that may be done by the boy's peers, Dr. Hatterer believes, by conveying to their son that he fits their image of masculinity and by showing him that they themselves are comfortable in their respective roles, regardless of who does the dishes or the cooking.

Many homosexuals are also beginning to realize that the roots of their problems go beyond their parents. As one former homosexual, who is now married and leading a completely heterosexual life, remarked: "The day I stopped blaming my parents for my condition and accepted responsibility for my acts was the day I began to grow up."

*   *   *

February 28, 1971

MORE HOMOSEXUALS AIDED TO BECOME HETEROSEXUAL

By JANE E. BRODY

"You are a sad and pathetic man," says Harold in Mart Crowley's play "The Boys in the Band." "You're a homosexual and you don't want to be. But there is nothing you can do to change it."

The widely held view that once a homosexual, always a homosexual, expressed in Mr. Crowley's drama, is being challenged by specialists around the country.

Therapists, using a variety of psychological approaches, have found that the young homosexual who is strongly motivated to change his sexual orientation has an excellent chance of success.

Furthermore, the therapists report that they have helped between 25 and 50 per cent of all their homosexual patients—regardless of age or original motivation—to make a heterosexual adjustment.

While the vast majority of homosexuals are not interested in psychiatric treatment and while most of those who do enter therapy do not want to become heterosexual, the therapists say that growing numbers of dissatisfied male homosexuals are seeking to change their sexual orientation, or at least make a better adjustment to it.

Biologically Normal

"The minute the word gets around that we are treating homosexuality with some success, we are literally besieged with requests for help," remarked one New York psychiatrist who has written widely on the subject.

Dr. William Masters and Mrs. Virginia Johnson, the St. Louis specialists in sex research and therapy whose findings in their work with homosexuals are still unpublished, report that they are receiving an increasing number of referrals of homosexual patients as word gets around in professional circles that they are involved in such research.

Approaches to treatment range from the traditional psychoanalytic method to directed psychotherapy, group therapy, behavior therapy and any combination of these. Chemical treatment has not worked since studies have shown that homosexuals are biologically normal males.

The doctors say that their techniques would apply equally to male and female homosexuals. But they note that Lesbians rarely seek treatment and, when they do, they are usually not interested in changing their sexual orientation.

Male homosexuals who want to become heterosexuals usually enter therapy with a problem directly related to their homosexuality—such as break-up in a love affair, disenchantment with the homosexual life style, fear of exposure or loss of employment, fear of growing old and undesirable or desire for a family.

Doctors who treat homosexuality believe that many who might want and benefit from treatment never seek it because of the deep pessimism about prospects for change that prevails in both the public and the professional mind.

The first turn away from this pessimism came with the publication eight years ago of a study by a team of psychoanalysts who reported that 27 per cent of 106 homosexual patients who had undergone analysis had shifted to exclusive heterosexuality.

The team, headed by Dr. Irving Bieber of the New York Medical College, called them "the most optimistic and promising results thus far reported."

The analysts, who view the main goal of therapy as ridding the homosexual of his fears of heterosexual activity, found that a shift to heterosexuality was most likely to occur if the total number of therapy hours exceeded 350—usually three years of more. Among those who underwent the therapy, nearly half achieved a complete heterosexual adjustment.

Habit Reconditioning

More recently, a New York Hospital psychiatrist, Lawrence J. Hatterer reported that, by combining the psychoanalytic method, in which he was trained, with some of the new habit reconditioning techniques of behavior therapy, he "can achieve in 50 sessions what it often takes regular psychoanalysis 350 sessions to do."

In a recently published book, "Changing Homosexuality in the Male," Dr. Hatterer documents his work over the last 15 years with more than 200 homosexual patients, a third of whom made a stable heterosexual adjustment.

Like the analysts, Dr. Hatterer tries to help his patients understand the origins of their homosexual behavior by exploring their family relationships and childhood experiences. At the same time, he tries to change the homosexual habit by asking his patients to identify and avoid those aspects of their life that trigger homosexual episodes, replacing them with heterosexual stimuli and relationships.

He might, for example, tell a patient to stop frequenting "gay" bars and go to "straight" ones instead and to substitute Playboy magazine and images of women for homosexual pornography and images of men.

Dr. Hatterer also uses capsulized tape recordings of relevant therapy sessions, which the patient listens to at home when he feels inclined to revert to the sexual activity he is trying to avoid.

One 30-year-old patient made a complete heterosexual adjustment within three months of treatment, the doctor reported. The man, who had never before had any heterosexual experience, entered therapy on the verge of suicide, having just broken up with the man be had been living with for two years.

"After just nine 45-minute sessions and 27 listenings to the tapes, the man was engaged to be married and having successful sexual intercourse with his fiancée several times a week," Dr. Hatterer said.

Dr. Hatterer, Dr. Bieber and others who have treated many homosexuals cite the following characteristics of patients as favorable to a heterosexual adjustment:
• Strong motivation to become heterosexual.
• Late introduction to homosexuality (late in adolescence or in adulthood).
• Therapy beginning before the age of 35.
• Some heterosexual interest or experience in the past.
• A liking for women at least on a social level.
• A work and living pattern not dominated by constant homosexual contacts.

Yet, Dr. Hatterer says, some patients with few or none of these characteristics have greatly benefited from therapy. A critical aspect of treatment, he maintains, is to convey to the patient that some form of help for his problem is possible.

Dr. Samuel B. Hadden, a Philadelphia psychiatrist who 15 years ago helped pioneer the group-therapy approach to redirecting homosexuals, deplores the "hopeless attitude" that he says "prevails in the minds of many psychiatrists."

Dr. Hadden feels he has reason to be hopeful. Working with all-male homosexual groups, he has found that "about one-third of those who persist in treatment [usually for several years] reach an effective heterosexual adjustment" and another third become better adjusted to their homosexuality.

The group approach, he says, gives patients a feeling of acceptance and hastens catharsis, since group members often have shared similar life experiences and reactions.

Each group member, eager for success, supports and reinforces the successes of every other member and, in turn, each successful member provides living proof to the others that sexual reorientation can be achieved.

Group therapy, like psychoanalysis, is a long-term proposition and many doctors believe that, if the many thousands of homosexuals who might benefit from treatment are ever going to get it, a faster way will have to be found.

At Temple University's Behavior Therapy Institute, Dr. Joseph Wolpe and his colleagues are attempting to treat homosexuals solely by reconditioning them through behavioral techniques.

Three-Sided Attack

Their three-sided attack works on the homosexual's fear of physical contact with females, his attraction to males and his general interpersonal fears. For example, to remove their anxieties about women, patients are placed in a state of deep relaxation and then told to conjure up images of women. To erase their sexual interest in men, patients are also subjected to such "aversive" stresses as mild electric shocks when shown pictures of naked men.

Since this combined behavioral approach is relatively new, Dr. Wolpe says he does not yet have enough cases to collate results or evaluate their long-term effectiveness. However, his "impression" is that "about 75 per cent" of patients become heterosexually oriented after about six months of therapy.

A number of therapists believe that some homosexuals are able to become heterosexuals without professional help—through will power, deep religious experience or the adoption of a new philosophical system.

But for the many homosexuals who want to change their life style and cannot do so on their own, treatment can be costly, time-consuming and difficult to find.

A National Institute of Mental Health study group on homosexuality recently called for an "expansion of efforts to develop new therapies and to improve the efficiency of current therapeutic procedures."

"While it cannot be assumed that a large portion of homosexuals will go into treatment," the study group said, "we hope and expect that, as treatment methods improve and expand, more and more persons will seek treatment voluntarily."

Noting that "another 5,000 psychiatrists would be needed to help all the homosexuals who might want it," Dr. Hatterer suggests the establishment of "sexual mental health clinics," staffed by paraprofessionals. And as the ranks of former homosexuals grow, he envisions the development of a Homosexuals Anonymous, a self-help approach that could do for homosexuals what Alcoholics Anonymous has done for many alcoholics.

* * *

February 28, 1971

THE CHANGING VIEW OF HOMOSEXUALITY

A decade ago, the concept of homosexuality as an illness to be treated medically was considered an enlightened view in a society that regarded homosexuals as criminals to be punished for acting on their sexual inclinations.

Today, a sharp debate is going on within the medical community as to whether homosexuality, practiced by millions of Americans, is really an illness or merely a form of behavior at one extreme of the continuum of normal human sexuality.

In recent years, the debate has been fed by the vocal segment of the homosexual population—such groups as the Gay Liberation Front, the Mattachine Society and the Daughters of Bilitis. Proclaiming their behavior to be within the range of normal, these groups maintain that the "sickness" one finds in the homosexual community is largely a result of society's "sick" attitude toward this form of sexual expression.

The kinds of sexual acts performed by homosexuals are still illegal in 48 states and the District of Columbia (illegal for heterosexuals, too, but the laws are not enforced against them). As a National Institute of Mental Health study group on homosexuality noted, the threat of discovery is anxiety-producing, and laws against homosexuals hardly contribute to their mental health.

Irving Bieber, a New York psychoanalyst who has evaluated many hundreds of homosexuals, and many of his colleagues regard homosexuality as "pathological." Dr. May E. Romm, a Beverly Hills analyst, says that the label "gay" is "a defense mechanism against the emptiness, the coldness, and the futility" of the homosexual life.

All Seeking Therapy

However, Dr. Judd Marmor, director of psychiatry at Cedars-Sinai Medical Center in Los Angeles, points out that "the concepts of psychoanalysts are all derived from the study of homosexuals who have sought psychoanalytic therapy."

Dr. Evelyn Hooker, a Los Angeles psychologist who is chairman of the National Institute's study group, reports that many of the homosexuals she has studied reveal, on psychological testing, no "demonstrable pathology" that would differentiate them in any way from a group of relatively normal heterosexuals.

Lawrence LeShan, a New York psychologist, views homosexuality as "a way of loving, not a pathology. The therapist's job is not to go along with the prejudices of the culture, but to help a person adjust to himself so that he can deal adequately with the culture."

"The Gay Liberation movement," he says, "is the best therapy the homosexual has had in years."

* * *

October 9, 1972

THERAPY SCORED BY HOMOSEXUALS

'Aversion Cure' Is Protested at Psychiatrists' Meeting

Members of the Gay Activists Alliance yesterday assailed a group of psychologists and psychiatrists meeting here, charging that "aversion therapy" for homosexuals amounts to brainwashing.

Contending that aversion therapy—which is sometimes used by behavior therapists in helping homosexuals become heterosexual—was a "form of torture" and a "downright cruel joke on gay people," the homosexuals, who numbered about 100, demonstrated in front of the New York Hilton hotel, at Sixth Avenue and 53d Street, shouting slogans and distributing pamphlets. The sixth annual convention of the Association for the Advancement of Behavioral Therapy was meeting inside.

To dramatize their accusation, the homosexuals performed a "guerrilla theater" display in which heterosexual volunteers were asked to submit to aversion therapy to "cure" them of their heterosexuality.

This "curing" consisted of flashing pictures of women before male heterosexuals. In actual aversion therapy, the doctor or psychologist uses external stimulants—such as pictures of male nudes—along with shock treatment and other processes in treating homosexuals. This process continues until the patient finds a person of the opposite sex more desirable than one of his sex. Aversion therapy in different form is also used to cure smokers and alcoholics of their addiction.

Demonstration Fizzles

But the demonstration fizzled out in about an hour, largely because not many passers-by seemed to take notice. The protesters then marched into the hotel where, in dozens of suites, the delegates were participants in seminars. In Suite 507, the homosexuals confronted about 50 delegates, and a shouting match developed.

"Aversion therapy is Clockwork Orange!" one demonstrator, whose jacket was decorated with buttons advertising his sexual preference, yelled. He was referring to a scene in "A Clockwork Orange," a film made by Stanley Kubrick, in which the central figure is forcibly made to watch scenes of rape and violence, so that he will learn to abhor and thus be cured of his propensity for violence.

Many delegates—both in the suite and elsewhere in the hotel—felt that the homosexuals had misunderstood the nature of aversion therapy.

"They're picketing the wrong group," said Dr. Robert Liberman, of the faculty of the University of California at Los Angeles, who served as program chairman for the convention. "The therapists here have no moral quarrel with homosexuality. All we want to do is to offer assistance for homosexuals to lead a more comfortable, spontaneous and creative life."

Therapy Voluntary

Another delegate, who asked not to be identified, said: "Aversion therapy is entirely voluntary. No one is forcing the homosexual to come to us and be transformed into a heterosexual. How can it be like 'A Clockwise Orange'? There's no compulsion here."

However, Ron Gold, a spokesman for the Gay Activists Alliance, declared that aversion therapy was a "form of social engineering."

"It is brainwashing," Mr. Gold declared. "You can't deal with an individual homosexual's problem without also dealing with the antiquated mores of society. Change must come at a broader, societywide level."

Later in the afternoon, at the final session of the three-day convention, Mr. Gold's contention was supported by Charles Silverstein, director of Identity House, a counsel center for the homosexual community in New York. In an address that was applauded frequently by homosexual members of the audience, Mr. Silverstein said:

"We must refuse to use aversion techniques. We must refuse to change homosexuals. It is a technique of violence and I don't believe it works."

*   *   *

June 22, 1980

DEVOTED TO SEX

By STEVEN MARCUS

HAVELOCK ELLIS: A Biography
By Phyllis Grosskurth
Illustrated. 492 pp. New York: Alfred A. Knopf. $16.95.

Havelock Ellis is an exemplary figure in the momentous transition from Victorian culture to modernity. His life and work help us to understand in part how we have come to be what we are. Between 1897 and 1910 he published six volumes under the title "Studies in the Psychology of Sex" (a seventh supplementary volume came out belatedly in 1928). These works were the first relatively successful serious and scholarly effort in English to achieve the open-minded, liberal, tolerant, positive and encouraging view of human sexual behavior in its many varieties that is essentially characteristic of the modern spirit.

Born in 1859, Ellis represents both chronologically and in attitude a middle point between Thomas Hardy (b. 1840) and D. H. Lawrence (b. 1885) in the development of English (and Anglo-American) conscious moral culture. Ellis died in 1939. His dates, therefore, correspond almost exactly to those of Freud (1856-1939), that intellectual presence in the wider con-

text of the evolution of modern Western civilization to whom he must inevitably be compared. For a number of quite clear reasons, Ellis compares badly, and he has been effectively eclipsed by the shadow cast by the ever-larger figure of Freud.

Nevertheless, Ellis should not be forgotten. He is one of those writers in whose work the impulsions to move out of the historical past and into the light cast by science, reason and the forces of the modern century were expressed most distinctly. Insofar as writers bear a certain responsibility for the changing climate of moral sensibility, he may be assigned some genuine share for influencing the course taken by a number of our attitudes. In this valuable and fascinating new biography, Phyllis Grosskurth carefully demonstrates how Ellis's important work came about and suggests some of the things that it means.

Ellis's parents were an upstanding and respectable Victorian couple. His father was a merchant sea-captain, away from home for months at a time; his mother was an earnest, evangelically religious and strong-willed woman, both slightly eccentric and entirely conventional. She was very serious and altogether literal-minded, characteristics which her son inherited—throughout his life, Ellis had no sense of humor at all and was chronically unable to appreciate it in others.

From the very outset, the temperament with which he confronted the world was self-contained, intractable, reclusive and remote. Although he was sent to school, he was like so many other outstanding individuals of his time and culture essentially an autodidact. A great reader, he was also a precocious taker of notes and keeper of notebooks. By the age of 10, he had acquired the 19th-century historical habit of memorializing everything: His notebooks were indexed and passages in them coordinated; whatever he read, saw and felt he treated as "data" to be compiled, sorted and set down in logical order. This "natural history method," as he described it, of accumulation and classification of material of every possible kind was the fundamental procedure he was to follow throughout his career. (He was, again characteristically, an equally prodigious writer of letters; in addition to his published correspondence, Professor Grosskurth estimates that she has read more than twenty thousand letters written by Ellis.)

At school, Ellis was maltreated and miserable. The suffering that he endured, he wrote, had an "evil influence on my nervous system." At the age of 13 he began to experience "copious seminal emissions . . . during sleep, once or twice a week, always without dreams or any sensations . . . (which) continued whenever I was alone, for some thirty years." He was deeply bewildered by these events, since he was at the time, he reports, entirely innocent of any sexual thoughts. Yet he felt ashamed of and guilty about these emissions, and "constantly dreaded their occurrence and feared their detection." Utterly confused, ignorant and unhappy, he nonetheless refused to admit that anything was bothering him or was amiss—a device of equivocation that he was to practice continually throughout his life. This defense, a kind of bland, pervasive denial, permitted him to exist with himself and to function.

In uncertain health, restless and wretched, Ellis was taken in hand at the age of 16 by his seafaring father. Captain Ellis transported his son to Australia and more or less simply deposited him there. For the next four years young Ellis was employed in a number of places as a schoolmaster. With the exception of those relations required by his pedagogical duties, he led a life of uninterrupted isolation; he occupied his solitary hours with constant reading and writing.

Two other occurrences marked these years of growth and exile. Shortly after his arrival he decided one evening, as Professor Groskurth reports, "to devote his life chiefly to an investigation of the problem of sex," but that project was to be pursued without succumbing to any tendencies toward what Ellis stereotypically called "morbid self-analysis"—he was permanently and successfully to resist all such impulses toward self-examination. He also experienced the loss of his religious beliefs and went through the spiritual crisis of deconversion that was as central and critical to the culture of the 19th century as the crisis of identity seems to be to the culture of our own era.

He was delivered from his interior wasteland by the writings of one of that multitude of obscure messiahs who were left beached, as it were, along the seashore of 19th-century history, as the sea of faith retreated. James Hinton was a physician and mystagogue who preached the incomprehensible revelation that man "is simply a limitation of the divine spirit and can attain true life through unselfishness" (what this in fact turned out to mean, Ellis was only later to learn, was the practice of polygamy, in which man became an "artist in love" in order to "serve" women). His sense of purpose and integration with the universe reconstituted by the opaque claptrap of Hinton's "Life in Nature," he also restored himself by reading Arnold, Herbert Spencer and Pater and sailed back to England to make himself a career.

Ellis started out on his return at the age of 20 as a medical student, but he devoted most of his energies in the decade of the 1880's to becoming a man of letters—a journalist, editor, literary critic, popularizer of science, and pundit at large on matters of public concern. He was by nature a rebel and a pioneer, and he joined with others of the time in London in trying to conceive of a larger personal and social life that might be guided by the ideals of empirical science, rationality, freedom of choice and experiment, decency of conduct without reference to a deity, socialism, goodness, truthfulness and progress. Meetings at which Ibsen's "A Doll's House" was read alternated with meetings at which the future of communal organizations and sanitary reform were debated. Groups such as the Fellowship of the New Life would organize, split and give hatch to, on the one hand, crackpot grouplets that encouraged salvation through bizarre dietary regimens and the wearing of sandals, and, on the other, to such equally improbable circles as the Fabian Society, whose middle-class socialism was to have such a profound effect on English political life. Ellis soon became a prominent advocate in print for a large number of these advanced causes. He was throughout his career an undeviating cultural radical.

The secret or trick that he shared with a number of his colleagues was the ability to write about threatening, disturbing or less than respectable matters in the simplest, most disarming and most apparently blameless way. This apostle to the Victorians, this virtuous adversary of the philistines, believed that a new age of clarity and emancipation was about to dawn, that prudery and hypocrisy and double-dealing had had their day. Yet in order to get away in print with saying this, Ellis further cultivated his equivocating habit of, as Professor Grosskurth pointedly observes, "saying and un-saying the same thing," of putting forth a radical proposition and then at once retracting it in a qualifying remark, so that he could never be easily accused of taking a clearly defined or formulated position. At the same time, high-minded talk and language had a way of consorting with less than high-minded motives and actions. Sex and spirituality kept getting confused with and mistaken for one another. Ellis and his friends talked nobly about relations that would transcend sexuality, and at the same time habitually sought out situations in which the sexuality they talked about transcending might be in some measure expressed.

Although Ellis was a natural cultural radical and strove continuously to be possessed of and to advocate the latest and most advanced views on just about anything, he was not personally a bohemian—he cannot even be said to have been genuinely adventurous. His own sexuality was too precariously secured to take such risks with it. His first sexual experiences of any adult account occurred when he was 25; they were part of the passionate friendship he formed with the South African writer, Olive Schreiner, whose novel "The Story of an African Farm" is still intensely readable.

Schreiner was fiercely determined to be what was thought of as the New Woman of the period; with great force of will she behaved sexually in an emancipated way and then with an equally great force of unconscious will tortured and tormented herself with guilt over her liberated conduct. Ellis was unwilling and/or unable to pay such heavy and exacting dues. He appears to have suffered from disturbances of potency all his life; he had difficulties in maintaining an erection, suffered from premature ejaculation, and it seems doubtful that he ever effected satisfactory coital union with a woman. He and Olive Schreiner caressed one another, practiced mutual masturbation when they were together and nonmutual masturbation when apart, and discussed their problems, habits and feelings openly and at great length.

It was Schreiner who first confessed to guilt and wretchedness as a result of their incompatibility and was impelled to move on—not that she ever found what she was seeking, and the remainder of her life was mostly suffering and extreme neurotic unhappiness. Ellis, who was by contrast impassive and recessive and not particularly passionate, found the relation adequate; at the same time he was certainly not devastated when Schreiner sought fulfillment elsewhere. Indeed they remained good friends for years thereafter; for another part of Ellis's peculiar, and perhaps fortunate, disposition is that he had almost no access to aggressiveness and anger; he bore no grudges and claimed, with pride, that he had never lost a friend.

He had need of all the sanguine temperament he could find to deal with his next affair with a woman. It was the most important relation of Ellis's life and had a profound effect on his intellectual career. In the late 1880's he became acquainted with Edith Lees. She too was in every sense a New Woman; she belonged to the appropriate advanced societies, gave lectures on approved radical topics and contributed to a journal, founded by members of the Fellowship of the New Life, called "Seed-Time." She and Ellis soon became close companions; they agreed that conventional marriage—the foundation upon which so much of the structure of Victorian life was based—had become an impossibility. At the same time both desired a permanent relationship. Edith wanted both security and complete freedom; it never becomes entirely clear what Ellis wanted. What was clear was that neither ever felt any passion for the other. Ellis described it in his high-minded way as "a union of affectionate comradeship, in which the specific emotions of sex had the smallest part." They aimed at a companionate marriage, in which both would spend time together and apart, and neither would give up separate living establishments or careers.

It was all very modern, as was the circumstance that Edith was a lesbian. Ellis knew this, but preferred to believe that it didn't matter. He seemed to be convinced that Edith's love for him would "rule out female rivals." In other words, the man who was to become the sage of sexuality in English got married knowing nothing and understanding less about sex. They also agreed that there were to be no children; instead each treated the other as a permanent baby, and they took turns at playing mother to one another. Within this relationship, which provided both connection and remoteness, Ellis could get on with the pursuit of his work, for which he required solitude. He believed that tenderness, talk and understanding were enough to deal with whatever problems marriage might confront him with.

That belief was tested within a few months of their marriage when Ellis received, as if out of the blue, a letter from his wife telling him that she had contracted a passionate attachment to a woman. Ellis was shocked and surprised by this turn of events; somehow he had in his extraordinary ingenuousness not expected it. He was also hurt and aggrieved and felt betrayed by Edith. Yet true child of Victorian rationalism that he was, what he did not feel, what he never permitted himself to feel let alone express, was anger or outrage. He learned to accept with good nature this lover and the succession of passionate "friendships" that Edith was to develop during the course of the following decades. He also had to accept the fact that all his hifalutin and adolescent theorizings about marriage were so much eyewash. The marriage of Ellis and Edith, though it was real and enduring, was also a tragic failure. They needed each other, they supported each other (when they were together, which was rather less than half the time), but they did not find fulfillment in one another. And in due time Ellis learned to turn to other women and to find in them whatever sexual satisfaction he was capable of.

But this embroiled union had a further consequence, for it contributed to the decisive turn in Ellis's career as a writer. Reeling beneath the impact of his "discovery" of his wife's lesbian nature, and understanding nothing about homosexuality, Ellis decided to undertake an objective and "scientific" study of the subject.

He was assisted in this resolve by John Addington Symonds, the subject of Professor Grosskurth's previous work, one of the leading English men of letters of the time, who was living in self-imposed permanent exile in Switzerland. Symonds's efforts to suppress his own homosexuality while he was still living in England had led him repeatedly to nervous collapse, and he was determined to try to affect public opinion on this matter, to mitigate some of the ferocious intolerance of British official attitudes toward homosexuality. He became Ellis's collaborator on the book; he supplied Ellis with the majority of the case histories that are central to it (while maintaining the polite fiction that they had been brought to his attention by an assortment of people largely unknown to him, when they in fact almost exclusively involved himself and his lovers), and he influenced Ellis's attitudes toward the impartiality and openmindedness that they already tended to favor.

Finally published in 1897, "Sexual Inversion," as the volume was called, appeared at a critical moment in the history of modern English moral and cultural life. In 1885 the enactment of an especially punitive law had brought about the full criminalization in England of male homosexuality; Oscar Wilde was the most celebrated victim of this new act and had just been released from prison when the volume came out. At the same time, never had the public prestige of science, medicine and "reason" been higher, and Ellis's work purported to speak with the voice and the authority of all three. But it purported as well to speak with the voice of modernity, which is to say that although it regarded itself as advocating the values of openness, realism and liberalism, it was regarded by the majority at the time as a deliberate incitement to vice, obscenity, degradation and degeneracy.

It was indeed an apologia and a polemic. As Ellis himself wrote unguardedly in a letter, "We want to obtain a sympathetic recognition for sexual inversion as a psychic abnormality which may be regarded as the highest ideal, and to clear away many vulgar errors—preparing the way, if possible, for a change in the law." In insisting that homosexuality was neither a disease nor a crime (although he did believe that it was congenital), Ellis was making revolutionary proposals. Yet he made these proposals in simple, straightforward and decent language and with relative detachment.

The reasonability and balance of Ellis's perspective did nothing to prevent the appearance of "Sexual Inversion" from stirring up a storm. There was publicity in the form of newspaper stories, prosecution and the trial of someone who sold a copy of the volume, from all of which Ellis shrunk in fear and nervousness. After the uproar had subsided he returned to his reclusive existence, and by 1910 had completed those five other volumes of "Studies in the Psychology of Sex" which are his best and most important works.

In them Ellis continued to write as the evangel of sexual tolerance and freedom to the late Victorians. For example, after homosexuality, masturbation seemed to be the most distressing form of sexual behavior to Ellis's contemporaries; Ellis coined the neutral term "Auto-Erotism" for it, and went on to discuss the subject in his usual calm and measured way. He also was an early pioneer in his recognition of female sexuality and in his advocacy of women's right to a fulfilled sexual life. These studies helped considerably to promote the acceptance of sexuality as a topic for open and candid discussion. Written in a clear and graceful prose, they did as much as any works can be expected to do in denaturing, detoxifying and defusing a subject that was at the time extremely sensitive and sometimes downright dangerous to discuss.

Ellis was a follower of Darwin and Spencer, a late 19th-century amateur expert-on-things-in-general. His "method" was to accumulate bits of data, classify this material and then recite it descriptively back at the reader with quotation marks and long footnote-like citations. This procedure made in his mind for both scholarly sobriety and scientific reliability. In point of fact it often made for pedantic aridity and solemn foolishness. At the time he wrote the "Studies," Ellis was a sexual innocent who had managed to remain, in Professor Grosskurth's words, "largely uncontaminated by experience." The credulousness with which he accepted some of the materials in his case histories as "facts" was equalled only by his lack of inwardness. His belief that public knowledge of sexuality was a social good has to be regarded within the qualifications created by his excessively simple notion of knowledge.

In this, as in so much else, he forms a focused and instructive contrast to Freud. Ellis himself was acutely sensitive to the contrast and chafed beneath it. He resented the fact that Freud was accepted as the leading conquistador of the modern spirit, and he was puzzled by it as well. It is not too much to say that Ellis was unable to understand Freud at all. Freud's insights into human irrationality and his psychological and metapsychological grand conceptual schemes meant nothing to Ellis. And Freud's literary gifts—his metaphoric powers and immense expository skills—meant if possible even less. If a useful comparison to Ellis and his work is to be instituted, it is to Sir James Frazer and "The Golden Bough" that we should turn. Ellis was really an old-fashioned anthropologist of sexuality, a collector, compiler and classifier of anecdotes, stories, accounts and practices.

He was also the direct ancestor of Alfred Kinsey and his collaborators, and he is hence the spiritual ancestor of all those people who teach courses in sex education in our schools and courses in "human sexuality" in our colleges and universities. These activities have almost certainly been a source of good in the world. They persist as part of our legacy from the 18th and 19th centuries, part of the faith which our culture has inherited that there is nothing that cannot be rationally understood and thus taught and learned, and furthermore that there is almost nothing that cannot, if properly handled, be explained and taught to children. Our culture is probably incorrigible in this virtually dogmatic innocence, and indeed it is difficult to imagine our own existence if we try to subtract from it the conviction that it is really highly preferable to live in the light we continue to generate rather than in the darkness we have cast out and replaced.

After 1910 Ellis's important work was done. His international fame as a guru for humanity's perplexities continued to grow throughout the remainder of his long days. He learned to accommodate himself to his own sexual peculiarities—his particular quirk was a permanent fascination with women's urine—and in later life had a series of relations with women, among them Margaret Sanger, in which he found comfort, release, satisfaction and contentment. Professor Grosskurth skillfully represents these experiences as rewards well-earned, and when one finishes her book with Ellis dead in 1939, one has a strongly renewed sense of what heroic efforts were involved in the passage of Western culture from the 19th century into modernity. Ellis was an important figure in this evolutionary transformation, and it is right that his work should not be forgotten.

Steven Marcus is the author of "The OtherVictorians," "Representations" and other books. He is the George Delacorte Professor in the Humanities at Columbia.

*   *   *

January 26, 1982

PSYCHIATRISTS ON HOMOSEXUALITY: VIGOROUS DISCORD VOICED AT MEETING

By JANE E. BRODY

Nearly a decade after American psychiatry deleted homosexuality from its list of mental illnesses, the profession remains polarized in its views, to judge by the vigorous debate at a major symposium on homosexuality last weekend.

Some professionals, primarily classical psychoanalysts, insist that homosexuality is inherently abnormal; others, more sociologically oriented, maintain it is a normal variant of human sexual behavior. Some say dissatisfied homosexuals should be offered therapy to help them become heterosexuals; others, especially homosexual psychiatrists, say unhappy homosexuals should be helped only to become happier with their sexual orientation.

Whatever their views, nearly all denounced homophobia (fear and hatred of homosexuality) and prejudice, which they said pervades the psychiatric profession as well as society at large. Dr. Judd Marmor, a Los Angeles psychiatrist who is a professor emeritus at the University of Southern California, asserted that homosexual physicians were still denied residency training in psychiatry by most hospitals and that no psychoanalytic institute would knowingly accept a homosexual trainee.

Despite the continuing controversy within the profession, several trends that could have major effects on society were apparent at the two-day meeting, "Homosexuality: A Decade of Developments," sponsored by New York Medical College.

For one, the "sickness" model, which portrays homosexuality as arrested development fostered by malignant parenting, appears to be rapidly yielding to an ever-growing accumulation of evidence and opinion that sees same-sex attraction as biologically normal behavior with complex and varied origins.

Dr. Marmor, who presented an overview of the problem, said: "We must stop thinking of homosexuality as a singular phenomenon. It is diverse in character, various in its manifestations and has multiple roots—genetic, hormonal, psychodynamic and sociodynamic."

Other trends described at the meeting included the following:

Research into the origins of homosexuality, long dominated by studies of unhappy homosexuals who sought psychotherapy, is now focused on nonpatient homosexuals with diverse life styles. The newer studies indicate that homosexuals, as a group, are not mentally less healthy than heterosexuals and that the same bad parent-child relationships that are characteristic of many unhappy homosexuals also are found among unhappy heterosexuals.

The new studies show that the childhood factor most often found among homosexual men and women is gender nonconformity—that is, behavior typical of the opposite sex—which may be biological in origin. This nonconforming behavior, "sissiness" in boys and tomboy behavior in girls, influences the way parents and peers treat the child, possibly fostering a homosexual orientation. The predominance of men among homosexuals may reflect parental and societal tolerance of tomboy girls but open disdain for effeminate boys, Dr. Marmor suggested.

Though no consistent hormonal differences between adult homosexuals and heterosexuals have been defined, animal studies indicate that hormonal influences on the fetal brain may predispose some children to gender nonconformity and homosexuality. In an ongoing study of feminine boys by Dr. Richard Green and his colleagues at the State University of New York at Stony Brook, half have become bisexual or homosexual as adults.

However, gender nonconformity is not a necessary prelude to homosexuality because many homosexual men were masculine during their boyhoods and many lesbians were feminine as girls, according to the recently published results of a study of 1,500 homosexuals and heterosexuals done by Dr. Alan P. Bell, Martin S. Weinberg and Sue Kiefer Hammersmith under the auspices of the Kinsey Institute for Sex Research.

Determination of a person's sexual orientation may lie more in emotional responses than in choices of sexual partners. Dr. Bell, a psychologist at Indiana University, said: "Sexual orientation goes far beyond sexual matters. It is a deep emotional situation—falling in love—that we've just begun to explore." Dr. Bell told of a woman who prefers male sexual partners but describes herself as a lesbian because of her deep emotional responses to women, which are lacking with men.

Homosexuals who are distressed about their sexual orientation and wish to adopt a heterosexual way of life can often, though not always, be helped through therapy that first makes them become more comfortable with their homosexuality and then focuses on overcoming their fear of relationships with the opposite sex. Among selected patients, one-third to two-thirds are able to function heterosexually after therapy, researchers reported.

Debate Over 'Conversion' Therapy

Though several homosexual psychiatrists spoke against such "conversion" therapy, Dr. Mark F. Schwartz, a psychologist representing the Masters and Johnson Institute of St. Louis, where such therapy is being offered, said it was "a disservice to refuse to help patients who are unhappy as homosexuals and want to live as heterosexuals."

According to Dr. Schwartz and Dr. Helen Kaplan, a psychiatrist who is a sex therapist at New York Hospital-Cornell Medical Center, distressed homosexuals commonly suffer from "intimacy disorders" that are no different from those seen in heterosexuals who have difficulty getting close to people, sharing emotions, trusting others and making a commitment to a lasting relationship.

Dr. Schwartz and others noted that when therapy helps distressed homosexuals overcome their self-loathing, they may then be able to move comfortably into heterosexuality. By the same token, Dr. Robert E. Gould, a Manhattan psychiatrist who is affiliated with New York Medical College, said that sometimes therapy for sexually distressed heterosexuals results in their adopting a homosexual orientation.

Even Dr. Irving Bieber, a New York psychoanalyst who has concluded from his studies that homosexuality is an abnormality, said: "The therapist should have no stake in the sexual outcome of a patient being treated. The therapeutic goal is to make people as comfortable as can be with whatever they are sexually."

Dr. Marshall Forstein, a psychiatric resident at the Massachusetts General Hospital in Boston, who is a homosexual, said that many homosexuals with emotional problems unrelated to their sexuality avoid psychiatric therapy "because they fear that they will be more damaged than helped and asked to face issues of sexual orientation when these are not relevant."

Although homosexuality per se was dropped from the diagnostic manual of the American Psychiatric Association when it was revised in 1973, the manual still lists distress about one's homosexuality as an illness. Dr. Green, Dr. Marmor and Dr. Gould and a number of homosexual psychiatrists who addressed the meeting deplored this listing, saying it fosters continuing prejudice and discrimination against homosexuality and suggests to parents that they should seek therapy for their homosexual children rather than accept and love them as they are.

Dr. Gould called upon psychiatrists to help reduce societal homophobia and enhance homosexual self-esteem "so that whatever sexual pathway a person follows will be more natural and healthy."

Dr. Forstein said it was "a miracle" that any homosexuals become stable and happy individuals, since they grow up lacking social validation of what they are. "Unlike women and blacks who can at least identify with one another, gays have no one to counteract the negative societal assault on their egos," he said in an interview. "It's no wonder that at times of stress, gay people are much more prone to severe depression."

* * *

December 11, 1988

NAVIGATING THE STRAITS OF OEDIPUS

By RICHARD GREEN

THE PSYCHOANALYTIC THEORY OF MALE HOMOSEXUALITY
By Kenneth Lewes
301 pp. New York: Simon & Schuster. $19.95.

Freud did not believe that homosexuality was a mental illness. He saw little prospect for converting homosexuals into heterosexuals. He argued that a homosexual could become a psychoanalyst. None of these views characterize today's psychoanalytic community. What happened? The psychoanalyst Kenneth Lewes has tracked the politicized, moralistic and occasionally objective evolution of psychoanalytic theories of male homosexuality from the enlightened flexibility of Freud to the benighted dogmatism of his disciples.

Freud, in his admiration for Plato, Michelangelo and da Vinci, concluded that exceptional creativity and social achievement could coexist with homosexuality. With his heritage in medicine, he remained realistic about the potential of psychoanalysis for understanding homosexuality. "It is not for psychoanalysis to solve the problem of homosexuality," he wrote. "It must rest content with discovering . . . and tracing the paths of psychical mechanisms.

There its work ends, and it leaves the rest to biological research." And although he believed that psychoanalysis had much to offer the homosexual patient, his goals were modest: "In general to undertake to convert a fully developed homosexual into a heterosexual is not much more promising than to do the reverse." But when Freud stopped short of developing a theory of the healthy homosexual, and his ambitious progeny misunderstood and misapplied his insights, psychoanalytic theories of homosexuality were dislocated from Freud's stance of humaneness, objectivity and humility to the "Freudian" posturings of cruelty, bias and arrogance.

A major fault in the bedrock of analytic theory has been, according to Mr. Lewes, a monumental misunderstanding of the Oedipus complex, long considered the rite of passage to normal, healthy heterosexuality. This misunderstanding created a false dichotomy between heterosexual wellness and homosexual sickness. Examining the convoluted psychological mechanisms that affect the child in his earliest years with mother and father, Mr. Lewes finds that there is more than one "natural," heterosexual resolution. Navigating the young boy through an arcane course down the siren-baited straits of Oedipus, Mr. Lewes sets him ashore at 12 ports of call. Six of the ports are homosexual. While the intricacies of the voyage defy simple description, and account for the book's only table, the telling message is that nothing about either the temptations of the voyage or the defenses of the child assures healthy sanctuary only within the heterosexual six. "The mechanisms of the Oedipus complex are really a series of psychic traumas, and all results of it are neurotic," Mr. Lewes writes. "All results of the Oedipus complex are traumatic, and, for similar reasons, all are 'normal.'" The 12 ports are simply alternative resolutions.

Freud's imprecise charting in another direction also caused his followers to lose course when he confounded biological reproductive potential with psychological destiny. In a rare display of passion, Mr. Lewes writes, "I throw up my hands in admiration and exasperation" when Freud contrasts the "ancients" who emphasized the quality of sexual expression with contemporaries who stress the object of sexual instinct. Thus Freud approached the idea that the quality of loving took psychological precedence over whether it passed between persons of the same or opposite sex. But he progressed no farther. This was because for Freud "the act of procreation was the central fact of human existence." Still the physician, he attempted to "ground human psychology in biology and all higher activities in the act of reproduction," and "turned the course of psychoanalysis away from the individual's experience."

"Gynophobia," in the service of this male-dominated profession, further contaminated the analytic intellect as it evolved into "homophobia." The same traits that were assumed to characterize neurotic women were imputed to male homosexuals—"the conviction of having been castrated, the search for the lost penis in the father, the attempt to be loved instead of striving actively to love." More disturbing than the intellectual absurdity of ascribing a "constellation of mechanisms that were normative for half the race" to psychopathology for another group was a fundamental political distinction in the writings about homosexuals. Men's jaundiced views of women could be challenged by female psychoanalysts. But there was no opposition from homosexuals. Because psychoanalysis barred homosexuals from membership, Mr. Lewes was unable to find a single paper on homosexuality written by a psychoanalyst identifying himself as a homosexual.

Two prolific New York psychoanalysts are singled out by Mr. Lewes for their homophobic and vulgar views. Edmund Bergler, who purportedly treated or evaluated 1,000 homosexuals, set forth his "bilious ridicule" in the 1940's and 1950's: "Homosexuals are essentially disagreeable people, regardless of their pleasant or unpleasant manner . . . which contains a mixture of superciliousness, false aggression, and whimpering." They were also "merciless" and "unscrupulous." Although Bergler is generally discredited today, his views were published in the major psychoanalytic journals of the time, whose editors, Mr. Lewes charges, "helped provide sanction for his bigoted and ignorant opinions." Charles Socarides, who has asserted that "homosexuality . . . is a masquerade of life," has rivaled Bergler "in intemperateness, though he lacks Bergler's smugness and cruelty." Dr. Socarides, a celebrity among contemporary analysts, continues to publish voluminously on homosexuality. He is a leader in the retrogressive action to reverse psychiatry's deletion of homosexuality from its list of mental disorders (a decision he derides as the result of "propaganda"). Yet he gets off remarkably lightly at Mr. Lewes's hand.

Two Los Angeles analysts saw the emperor nude. Robert Stoller denied that homosexuality was any more or less an "illness" than the range of heterosexualities, concurring with Freud's statement that "in the psychoanalytic sense the exclusive interest of the man for the woman is also a problem requiring an explanation." And Judd Marmor castigated his colleagues for "the cruelty, the thoughtlessness, the lack of common humanity in their attitudes," which he called "a disgrace to our profession."

Although Freud supported civil rights for homosexuals in Germany and Austria, homosexuals' rights have been hurt in this country by the statements of some analysts. The 1952 Immigration Act barred "psychopathic personalities" from entry or citizenship. That diagnosis characterized persons who were amoral or antisocial and who acted irresponsibly without anxiety or guilt. When Bergler observed "the great percentage of homosexuals among . . . lawbreakers of all sorts," national prejudice against homosexuals could find support in psychoanalytic "science."

Today, two tenaciously held analytic positions work to frustrate homosexuals' claim to equal rights: that homosexuality is not innate but acquired, and that it is amenable to change. Groups that have been discriminated against can receive special legal protection if the trait for which they are stigmatized is an immutable one (such as race). In defensively contradicting the growing evidence for innate contributions to homosexuality, and in tautologically asserting that homosexuals can be converted to heterosexuality if they really want to change, psychoanalysis has stalled social progress by placing these two roadblocks in the path of equal protection.

Dust-jacket rhetoric aside, this book is not for the general reader. The condensed packaging (dehydrated, really) of psychoanalytic theories, bumps on theories and blemishes on bumps provides a recondite review for the professional, but is hardly relaxed reading for the amateur. Professional readers, however, are in great debt to Mr. Lewes for his superb synthesis, which will richly serve future scholars.

The history of how the single most influential school of psychology and psychiatry abused its power and mishandled the most politically and morally controversial of behaviors constitutes the telling impact of Mr. Lewes's work.

As psychoanalytic parochialism consumed some of the brightest medical intellects, we were, according to Mr. Lewes, "no longer dealing with a system of free scientific inquiry, but with a closed, propagandistic set of social norms." But Mr. Lewes remains a psychoanalyst and, believing that his profession has a unique value for the homosexual, yearns for a return to the noble spirit of Freud.

Richard Green is professor of psychiatry and professor of law at the University of California, Los Angeles. His most recent book is "The 'Sissy Boy Syndrome' and the Development of Homosexuality."

* * *

December 17, 1991

GAY MEN IN TWIN STUDY

By The Associated Press

CHICAGO, Dec. 16—A new study of twins provides the strongest evidence yet that homosexuality has a genetic basis, researchers say, though they say other factors like social conditioning may be important.

The study, published in the December issue of The Archives of General Psychiatry, adds to evidence that sexual orientation does not result from a maladjustment or moral defect, one author said.

"We found 52 percent of identical twin brothers of gay men also were gay, compared with 22 percent of fraternal twins, compared with 11 percent of genetically unrelated brothers," said J. Michael Bailey, an assistant professor of psychology at Northwestern University in Evanston, "which is exactly the kind of pattern you would want to see if something genetic were going on." By "unrelated," Dr. Bailey was referring to brothers by adoption.

"The genetically most similar brothers were also the ones most likely to be gay, by a large margin," he added.

The study examined 56 identical twins, 54 fraternal twins and 57 adoptive brothers recruited through advertisements in gay-interest publications.

Identical twins are genetic clones, having developed in the womb from a single egg that split after being fertilized by a single sperm. Fraternal twins develop simultaneously from two separate eggs fertilized by two separate sperm cells, making them only as similar as non-twin siblings.

"This is the first real genetic study of sexual orientation in about 40 years," said Dr. Bailey, whose co-author was Dr. Richard C. Pillard, a psychiatry professor at Boston University School of Medicine.

Dr. Bailey estimated that the degree of the genetic contribution to homosexuality could range from 30 percent to more than 70 percent, depending on varying assumptions about the prevalence of homosexuality and how well the sample represents twins in the general population.

Gregory Carey, an assistant professor of psychology at the University of Colorado, called the work very important.

"I'm not terribly surprised at the conclusions," he said. "I think they're very well founded. Some of the earlier evidence suggested there was genetic effect, but the studies were not well done. This is something that really sort of clinches it."

* * *

July 16, 1993

REPORT SUGGESTS HOMOSEXUALITY IS LINKED TO GENES

By NATALIE ANGIER

Ushering the politically explosive study of the origins of sexual orientation into a new and perhaps more scientifically rigorous phase, researchers report that they have linked male homosexuality to a small region of one human chromosome.

The results have yet to be confirmed by other laboratories, and the chromosomal region implicated, if it holds up under further scrutiny, is almost surely just a single chapter in the intricate story of sexual orientation and behavior. Nevertheless, scientists said the work suggests that one or several genes located on the bottom half of the sausage-shaped X chromosome may play a role in predisposing some men toward homosexuality. (The researchers have begun a similar study looking at the chromosomes of lesbians.)

The findings, which appear today in the journal Science, indicate that sexual orientation often is at least partly inborn, rather than being solely a matter of choice. But researchers warn against overinterpreting the work, or in taking it to mean anything as simplistic as that the "gay gene" had been found.

The researchers emphasized that they do not yet have a gene isolated, but merely know the rough location of where the gene or genes may sit amid the vast welter of human DNA. Until they have the gene proper, scientists said they had no way of knowing how it contributes to sexual orientation, how many people carry it, or how often carriers are likely to become gay as a result of bearing the gene.

And even when they do have this gene on the X chromosome pinpointed, scientists said they will continue to search for other genes on other chromosomes that may be involved in sexual orientation.

"Sexual orientation is too complex to be determined by a single gene," said Dr. Dean H. Hamer of the National Cancer Institute in Bethesda, Md., the lead author on the new report. "The main value of this work is that it opens a window into understanding how genes, the brain and the environment interact to mold human behavior."

In the new work, the scientists studied the genetic material from 40 pairs of gay brothers and found that in 33 of the pairs, the brothers had identical pieces of the end tip of the X chromosome. Under ordinary circumstances ruled by chance alone, only half of the pairs should have shared that chromosomal neighborhood in common, a region designated Xq28. The odds of Dr. Hamer's results turning up randomly are

less than half a percent, indicating that the chromosomal tip likely harbors a genetic sequence linked to the onset of the brothers' homosexuality.

Passed Through Maternal Line

In men, the X chromosome pairs with the Y chromosome to form the so-called sex chromosomes, the final set of the 23 pairs of chromosomes found in all cells of the human body. A man's X chromosome is always inherited from the mother, who bestows on her son a reshuffled version of one of her two copies of the X chromosome. The latest results indicate that the newly reported genetic factor is passed through the maternal line, a curious twist given that in the past psychiatry has held women at least partly responsible for fostering their sons' homosexuality.

The gene could work by directly influencing sexual proclivity, perhaps by shaping parts of the brain that orchestrate sexual behavior. Or it might affect temperament in a way that predisposes a boy toward homosexuality. At the moment, researchers said, all scenarios are mere speculation.

Despite the cautionary notes, the latest study is likely to add fuel to the debate over gay rights in the military and civilian realms.

If homosexuality is shown to be largely inborn, a number of legal experts say, then policies that in any way discriminate against homosexuals are likely to be shot down in the courts.

"We think this study is very important," said Gregory J. King, a spokesman for the Human Rights Campaign Fund in Washington, the largest national lesbian and gay lobbying group. "Fundamentally it increases our understanding of the origins of sexual orientation, and at the same time we believe it will help increase public support for lesbian and gay rights."

Not all gay rights leaders have a sanguine view of the work. Some denounce it as yet another attempt to draw a reductionist and implacable line between homosexuality and heterosexuality, while others see in it the dangers of attempts to "fix" homosexuality, perhaps through gene therapy.

"I don't think it's an interesting study," said Darrell Yates Rist, co-founder of the Gay and Lesbian Alliance Against Defamation. "Intellectually, what do we gain by finding out there's a homosexual gene? Nothing, except an attempt to identify those people who have it and then open them up to all sorts of experimentation to change them."

The study appears in the same journal that two years ago unleashed a furious debate when it published a report asserting to have found an anatomical difference between the brains of gay and straight men. Other recent reports have also weighed in on the possible biological basis of homosexuality in both men and women, and all have been subjected to volleys of scientific and political attack.

Other attempts to make a genetic link to behavior, like alcoholism, manic depression and schizophrenia, have thus far all been disappointing. By contrast, today's study is considered to be impressive science even by many who denounced the previous studies.

'Merits Being Followed Up'

"It's a good piece of work," said Dr. Anne Fausto-Sterling of Brown University, a geneticist who has been one of the most outspoken critics of the genetic studies of human behavior. "Hamer is appropriately cautious about the meanings you can glean from it, and he admits that there may be more than one path to the endpoint of homosexuality."

Dr. Eric Lander of the Whitehead Institute for Biomedical Research in Cambridge, Mass., said, "From a geneticist's point of view, if you strip away the nonscientific considerations, it's an interesting finding that merits being followed up in a larger sample."

Dr. Simon LeVay, chairman of the Institute of Gay and Lesbian Studies in West Hollywood, Calif., who did the 1991 study comparing gay and heterosexual brains, was considerably more ecstatic in his appraisal of the latest report.

"For so long people have been thinking there is some genetic element for sexual orientation and this is by far and away the most direct evidence there has been," Dr. LeVay said. "It's the most important scientific finding ever made in sexual orientation."

In the latest experiments, the researchers began by taking the family histories of 114 men who identified themselves as homosexual. Much to their surprise, the researchers discovered a higher than expected number of gay men among the men's maternal uncles and male cousins who were the sons of their mothers' sisters. The ratio was far higher than for men in the general population, suggesting a gene or genes that is passed through the maternal line and thus through the X chromosome.

The scientists then focused on gay brothers, on the assumption that if two boys in a family are homosexual, they were more likely to be so for genetic reasons than were those homosexual men without gay brothers. Using a well-known genetic technique called linkage mapping, they scrutinized the X chromosome in the brothers and other relatives by the application of DNA markers, tiny bits of genetic material that can distinguish between chromosomes from different people. The researchers found that more than three-quarters of the brothers had inherited identical DNA markers on the Xq28 region of the chromosome.

"I was surprised at how easy this was to detect," Dr. Hamer said. "Part of that ease was because we were working with the X chromosome," the most extensively studied chromosome in the human genetic blueprint. So far the study has been limited to men who said they were gay, eliminating the ambiguity that would come from considering the genes of men who called themselves heterosexual.

Nonetheless, the region is about four million bases, or DNA building blocks long, and hence holds hundreds of genes, meaning the scientists have much work ahead of them to sort out which gene or genes is relevant. The researchers are also trying to perform a similar linkage study on lesbian sisters, but so far they have not managed to find a chromosomal region that is consistently passed along in families.

* * *

August 2, 1993

THE SEARCH FOR SEXUAL IDENTITY; FALSE GENETIC MARKERS

By RUTH HUBBARD

WOODS HOLE, Mass.—Gay genes are back in the news. Researchers from the National Cancer Institute announced in the July 16 issue of the journal Science that they have found a set of genetic markers shared by a number of gay brothers, indicating genetic roots of homosexuality. This study, like similar previous findings, is flawed. It is based on simplistic assumptions about sexuality and is hampered by the near impossibility of establishing links between genes and behavior.

The authors of the article claim to have found that 33 of the 40 pairs of gay brothers in their study shared certain DNA sequences on their X chromosome, the chromosome men inherit only from their mothers. The implicit reasoning is that if brothers who have specific DNA sequences in common are both gay, these sequences can be considered genetic markers for homosexuality.

There are problems with this reasoning. Of the relatively small number of siblings in the survey, almost a quarter did not have these markers. Also, the researchers did not do the obvious control experiment of checking for the presence of these markers among heterosexual brothers of the gay men they studied. It is surprising that the correlation found in this research warranted publication without these controls, especially in as influential a journal as Science.

Past claims of the discovery of genetic markers for behavioral traits such as schizophrenia, manic depression and alcoholism have not withstood further investigation. The reason the gay gene "discovery" is big news is not that it is any more promising than the others but that the debate on homosexual rights is hot. The Science article comes fast on the heels of the gays-in-the-military debate and controversial referendums on gay rights in Colorado and Oregon.

The new findings, which have been heralded as a striking breakthrough in our understanding of sexuality, conform to a long-established pattern. Although people have been sexually attracted to their own sex throughout history, our current perception of homosexuality is rooted in the late 19th century.

At that time, sexual activities were first used to define the people who engaged in them. Any sexual act that deviated from the "missionary position" could lead to its practitioner being stamped a "pervert." Masturbators, it was said, could be recognized on sight by their sallow and nervous appearance.

Homosexuality stopped being what people did and became who they were. As the French philosopher Michel

Foucault wrote, "The sodomite had been a temporary aberration; the homosexual was now a species."

This way of categorizing people obscured the accepted fact that many people do not have sexual relations exclusively in one way or with either sex. Turn-of-the-century sex reformers such as Havelock Ellis, while understanding that the categories could blur, began viewing homosexuals as biologically different from heterosexuals. They argued that homosexuals should not be punished for their acts because their orientation was biological, not a matter of choice.

Similarly, in the face of virulent homophobic attacks, some homosexuals and their allies now argue that if sexual orientation is not a choice but is biologically determined, discrimination against homosexuals would best be covered by civil rights laws.

But the use of the phrase "sexual orientation" to describe only a person's having sex with members of their own gender or the other sex obscures the fact that many of us have other strong and consistent sexual orientations—toward certain hair colors, body shapes, racial types. It would be as logical to look for genes associated with these orientations as for "homosexual genes."

Still, many people believe that homosexuality would be more socially accepted if it were shown to be inborn. The gay journalist Randy Shilts has said that a biological explanation "would reduce being gay to something like being left-handed, which is in fact all that it is."

This argument is not very convincing. Until the latter half of this century, left-handed people were often forced to switch over and were punished if they continued to favor their "bad" hand. Grounding difference in biology does not stem bigotry. African-Americans, Jews, people with disabilities as well as homosexuals have been persecuted for biological "flaws." The Nazis exterminated such people precisely to prevent them from "contaminating" the Aryan gene pool. Despite claims to the contrary, this attitude hasn't disappeared: The Daily Mail of London reported the article in Science with the headline "Abortion Hope After 'Gay Genes' Findings."

Social movements can generate interest in and support for science. Just as the civil rights movement led to research on racial differences and the women's movement to research on male-female differences, the search for gay genes comes directly out of the successes of the gay rights struggle. But studies of human biology cannot explain the wide range of human behavior. Such efforts fail to acknowledge that sexual attraction depends on personal experience and cultural values and that desire is too complex, varied and interesting to be reduced to genes.

Ruth Hubbard, professor emeritus of biology at Harvard, is co-author of "Exploding the Gene Myth" with Elijah Wald, who contributed to this article.

* * *

April 23, 1999

STUDY QUESTIONS GENE INFLUENCE ON MALE HOMOSEXUALITY

By ERICA GOODE

Underscoring the difficulty scientists face in finding genes that underlie complex human behaviors, a team of researchers reported today that they had been unable to confirm a widely publicized study linking male homosexuality to a small region of one chromosome.

Experts in behavioral genetics say the new report, which appears in the journal Science, does not invalidate the notion that genes influence sexual orientation, which many scientists believe is the case, on the basis of other types of studies. Nor do the new results completely rule out the possibility that a gene or genes for homosexuality lie on the chromosome in question, the X-chromosome.

But the failure to replicate the earlier study is typical of the zigzagging course of research efforts to ferret out genes that influence complicated traits, or that contribute to illnesses with a behavioral component, like schizophrenia, manic depression, alcoholism and hypertension.

And since the question of whether homosexuality is innate is politically charged, the new findings will very likely revive discussion of the issue.

In the new study, a team of Canadian researchers tried to replicate work by Dr. Dean Hamer, a geneticist at the National Cancer Institute. In a 1993 study of 40 pairs of homosexual brothers, Dr. Hamer reported that in 33 of the pairs—more than would be expected by chance—an area on the bottom half of the X-chromosome was identical, indicating that one or more genes in that region, called Xq28, could be connected to the brothers' sexual orientation.

In men, the X-chromosome is inherited from the mother. It pairs with the Y-chromosome to form the so-called sex chromosomes, the last of the 23 pairs of chromosomes that appear in all cells of the human body.

A second study by Dr. Hamer's laboratory, published in 1995, also found evidence for such a link, though the effect seen was smaller.

But the Canadian researchers, who studied 52 pairs of homosexual brothers, concluded that their results "do not support an X-linked gene underlying male homosexuality."

"I feel these findings need to be taken seriously," said Dr. Neil Risch, professor of genetics and statistics at Stanford University, who performed the statistical analysis of the data for the new study, and is a co-author on the paper. "If there is an effect there, it is pretty small, and this study casts doubt on there being something there in particular. I don't think the evidence for there being an X-linked gene was very strong to begin with."

Other scientists greeted the new findings with interest and caution. Dr. Kenneth Kendler, the Banks Distinguished Professor of Psychiatry at Virginia Commonwealth University, said none of the studies so far were large enough for scientists to reach a firm conclusion about whether such a gene is present on the X-chromosome.

"There are now three reports that produce data relevant to this question," Dr. Kendler said, "one strongly positive, one modestly positive and one strongly negative. Does this new report show conclusively that there is no evidence? No, that is too strong."

Detecting genes that influence complicated traits is a formidable task, he said, and current technology is limited. "Fifty years from now we're going to look back at this and say we were toddlers stumbling around in a playpen," Dr. Kendler said. "This is a raw science at this stage."

It is also a highly contentious one. As news of the research spread this week, Dr. Hamer, the author of the original report, and the Canadian investigators offered conflicting interpretations of the results.

Dr. Hamer contended that the Canadian team, led by Dr. George Rice at the University of Western Ontario, did not find the gene linkage because the families of the brothers they studied were not representative of those likely to have an X-linked gene, as indicated by the number of homosexual relatives on the mother's side. The researchers, Dr. Hamer said, identified 182 families, but only obtained DNA from 48. These families "were not a random subset," he said, and had the others been included the gene linkage might have been found.

The new study, Dr. Hamer contended in a telephone interview, shows only "that not every case of male homosexuality is linked to the X-chromosome."

"I think the question of whether there is a gene on the X-chromosome will be ultimately resolved by either finding the gene or not finding the gene," Dr. Hamer said.

Dr. Rice responded in an E-mail that selection of the study's participants was "totally random." He said that only 48 families were included because "we could not get blood samples from the rest." And the researchers said the families in their study were "not very different" from those studied by Dr. Hamer.

David M. Smith, a spokesman for the Human Rights Campaign in Washington, the largest national gay and lesbian lobbying group, said that although studies indicated there was a biological basis for sexual orientation, the evidence was still inconclusive.

"In the final analysis," Mr. Smith said, "we don't believe these studies should have a significant influence in the public policy debate on whether to treat gay and lesbian people fairly and equally, whether they conclusively prove a 'gay gene' or not."

* * *

January 15, 2000

BIGOTRY AS MENTAL ILLNESS OR JUST ANOTHER NORM

By EMILY EAKIN

In 1851, Dr. Samuel A. Cartwright, a Louisiana surgeon and psychologist, filed a report in the New Orleans Medical and Surgical Journal on diseases prevalent among the South's black population. Among the various maladies Dr. Cartwright described was "drapetomania" or "the disease causing slaves to run away."

Though a serious mental illness, drapetomania, wrote Dr. Cartwright, was happily quite treatable: "The cause, in the most of cases, that induces the negro to run away from service, is as much a disease of the mind as any other species of mental alienation, and much more curable. With the advantages of proper medical advice, strictly followed, this troublesome practice that many negroes have of running away can be almost entirely prevented."

A particularly absurd chapter in the annals of racist 19th-century science? Without question, but for Alvin Poussaint, a clinical professor of psychiatry at Harvard Medical School, Cartwright's hopelessly unscientific diagnosis is of more than just historical interest. It is a vivid illustration of how definitions of normal and abnormal behavior are shaped by the values of the society that makes them. "The culture influences what you consider pathology," says Dr. Poussaint. "Cartwright saw slavery as normative. So when slaves deviated from the norm, he called them mentally ill. The business of deciding what's normal and what's psychopathology gets influenced by culture and politics. It's not hard science."

Dr. Poussaint says that when it comes to understanding racism, contemporary psychiatry is as in the dark about its own biases as the benighted Dr. Cartwright. Dr. Poussaint's argument is not with racist psychiatrists but with the psychiatry of racism. Is racism a mental disorder?

The debate is decades old, but was recently reignited when John Rocker, a pitcher for the Atlanta Braves, made bigoted statements about blacks, homosexuals and foreigners last month in the pages of Sports Illustrated. Last week Mr. Rocker was ordered by the commissioner of major league baseball to undergo a psychological evaluation. Since then, fans, therapists, pundits, sports figures, talk show hosts and columnists have all weighed in on the degree to which his comments and the league's decision were based on science, stupidity, financial concerns and spin control.

For most psychiatrists, the answer is clear: racism is unacceptable social behavior, but not evidence of a mental disorder. There is no entry for racism in the latest edition of the Diagnostic and Statistical Manual, a compendium of mental illnesses known as D.S.M.-IV.

"If psychiatry were to define racism as a mental disorder, you'd have to include the Nazis, and the Serbs who hate Muslims—there would be no end," says Dr. Robert Spitzer, a psychiatrist at the New York State Psychiatric Institute and a consultant on the D.S.M.-IV. "Almost everyone would be ill."

Nevertheless, Dr. Spitzer concedes that prevalence alone does not negate a need for diagnosis. To meet the American Psychiatric Association's criteria for a distinct mental disorder, he says, psychiatrists would have to show that a racist's mental processes interfered with normal functioning.

Dr. Poussaint says he can do that. Arguing that racism can sometimes—though not all the time—be a mental disorder, he says that racists frequently exhibit symptoms associated with major psychopathology, including paranoia (feeling threatened unrealistically by a particular group), projection (imbuing this group with traits that have negative associations) and fixed beliefs (categorical opinions like "all foreigners are dumb"). The real reason the psychiatric association hasn't made racism a mental health issue, he argues, is because "it hasn't been a mental health issue for them." To pathologize racism, he said, would require its members "to look at their friends, their relatives, and themselves" in an uncomfortable light.

It's true that the A.P.A. is predominantly white and male. Of its current 38,200 members, only 865, or 2.3 percent, are African-American and 1,720, or 4.5 percent, are Hispanic. Some 12,000, or 31 percent, are women. And there is no doubt that psychiatry has been susceptible to some of the same biases harbored by the society at large, most notably toward women and homosexuals. Until well after World War II, instruction in now-discredited Freudian concepts like "penis envy" and "castrating female" was a routine part of psychiatric training. More egregious was the theory of the schizophrenic mother, whose bad parenting was supposedly to blame for her child's schizophrenia. Widely accepted well into the 1970's, the theory has been supplanted by explanations focusing on brain chemistry and biology.

Homosexuals fared little better. Until the early 1970's, the A.P.A. regarded homosexuality as a pathology. After heavy lobbying from gay rights activists, including a psychiatrist who was a member of the A.P.A. and who spoke at the 1972 annual meeting, his face concealed by a mask to preserve his anonymity, the board of trustees voted to remove homosexuality from the D.S.M.-IV. The membership followed suit in 1974. (One bemused observer labeled it "the single greatest cure in the history of psychiatry.")

Dr. Poussaint credits politics—the women's movement and gay rights activists—not better science, for overturning faulty psychiatric doctrine. His own politicking to change the association's opinion on racism has so far been less successful. In the mid-1960's, Dr. Poussaint joined other civil rights workers in Mississippi, where he helped desegregate the hospitals. The bigotry he witnessed among the region's white psychiatrists as well as a spate of racist killings convinced him to act.

Along with seven other black psychiatrists, Dr. Poussaint appealed to the organization to add racism to the D.S.M.-IV. Their request was turned down. "Let's say that group of black psychiatrists had been in control of establishing what the diagnoses should be in the D.S.M.," Dr. Poussaint says now. "In some way, racism would be in that book."

Perhaps. Today, many of Dr. Poussaint's black colleagues say a D.S.M. label would actually be counterproductive. "Racism is so deeply ingrained in our culture that to try to identify individuals who are racist is in some ways to trivialize the depth and breadth of the problem," says James Jones, a professor of social psychology at the University of Delaware and the director of the minority fellowships program at the American Psychological Association. Others believe that pathologizing racism would inadvertently give racists a legal defense for hate crimes.

On the whole, psychiatrists were probably more disposed to treat racism as a mental illness 50 years ago than today. In the 1950's, the profession even flirted with a quasi-medical definition of racism, although at the behest of the American Jewish Committee, not American blacks. In 1950, four scholars published an influential study titled "The Authoritarian Personality." Three of the authors were Jewish. Two of them, including the philosopher Theodor Adorno, were refugees from Nazi Germany.

Their goal was to explain Hitler's genocidal anti-Semitism. Based on their evaluations of more than 2,000 American adults, the authors concluded that extreme racist tendencies were associated with an abnormal "personality syndrome" that they labeled authoritarian. Not a D.S.M.-IV diagnosis exactly, but almost.

By the end of the decade, however, the theory underlying "The Authoritarian Personality" had been substantially revised. The book was found to have serious methodological problems, and efforts to test the hypothesis yielded mixed results. The Harvard psychologist Thomas Pettigrew struck a decisive blow. Mr. Pettigrew examined racist attitudes in eight American towns, four in the North, four in the South. In the Northern towns, he found some correlation of racist attitudes with the syndrome described in "The Authoritarian Personality." In the South, however, he found that racism was so common it was merely a social norm. "You almost had to be mentally ill to be tolerant in the South," says Mr. Pettigrew, now a retired professor at the University of California at Santa Cruz. "The authoritarian personality was a good explanation at the individual level but not at the societal level."

By the dawn of the civil rights era, psychiatrists had largely abandoned racism to social psychologists like Mr. Pettigrew who helped formulate today's model. "Racism has very much been depathologized," says Janet Schofield, a social psychologist at the University of Pittsburgh who studies racial attitudes among children. "There's been a major shift from being influenced by things like the authoritarian personality to thinking of stereotyping and prejudice as a consequence of normal psychological processes."

Bombarded with information, she says, people tend to rely on general concepts. Just as Americans divide daybeds, settees and chaise longues into "chairs" and "sofas," they divide people into categories based to a degree on stereotypes.

"Racism," says Ms. Schofield, "may be the result of inevitable processes."

This is an explanation for racism, not an excuse. But Dr. Poussaint's final appeal is to common sense: "If you have a mental process that leads some people to commit genocide, how can you not think that's a mental disorder?"

* * *

THE NEWS MEDIA

July 16, 1962

RADIO: TABOO IS BROKEN

'Live and Let Live' on WBAI Presents Homosexuals Discussing Problems

By JACK GOULD

Last night's discussion of homosexuality was handled with candor and tact on radio station WBAI, the frequency modulation outlet supported by the subscriptions of its listeners. The ninety-minute program was by far the most extensive consideration of the subject to be heard on American radio, and it succeeded, one would think, in encouraging a wider understanding of the homosexual's attitudes and problems.

The eight practicing homosexuals who participated in the taped roundtable covered such matters as their sexual drives, the patterns of their social and professional existences and the prejudices they encounter in a heterosexual society.

Since the program, entitled "Live and Let Live," was intended to give the homosexuals an opportunity to be heard without interruption, there was no challenge to their viewpoints. Perhaps on a sequel the subject could be explored with somewhat more penetrating questions. One area left hanging was the matter of a civilized legal approach to homosexuality, particularly in the distinction to be drawn between cases limited to consenting adults and those involving minors.

But from the standpoint of broadcasting, the chief significance of the evening lay in the illustration of the value of the independent station's catering to a specialized following. Such a station, knowing the composition of its audience, can offer subject matter that, if addressed to coast-to-coast masses of all ages, might pose difficulties for a network.

Not only WBAI but also many independent stations financed through advertising are playing a very considerable role in wiping away old taboos in the arena of discussion. And in each instance the result has demonstrated that the contemporary public seems ready to accept almost any subject matter so long as it is presented thoughtfully.

* * *

March 8, 1967

TV: C.B.S. REPORTS ON HOMOSEXUALS

Growing Social Problem Soberly Considered

By GEORGE GENT

"C.B.S. REPORTS" finally unveiled its long-awaited study on homosexuals last night. It was not the program originally planned more than two and a half years ago, which was said to stress the more sensational aspects of the gay life. It was more a sober, intelligent discussion of a growing social problem that only recently has reached the public forum.

To be sure, nothing really new was disclosed. There were interviews with various types of homosexuals—those who had come to terms with their sexual proclivity and those who had not. There were some fuzzy shots of homosexual bars and poolrooms, and a rather heartrending sequence about a 19-year-old soldier being arrested for the first time, for committing a lewd act in public.

By and large the program concentrated on the social, medical, sexual, legal and moral dimensions of the problem. Psychiatrists believe that the first three years of a child's life are crucial in determining his sexual orientation. The paramount importance of the mother and father in the homosexual's life was adverted to time and again on the program. Homosexuals, who are under cruel pressures from a condemning society—most Americans want to keep homosexual acts illegal—are crusading to legalize homosexual acts between consenting adult males.

Federal Judge James Braxton Craven of Charlotte, N. C., questioned whether any public purpose was served by imprisoning homosexuals. In some states they can be sentenced to terms twice as long as those served by second-degree murderers, six times as long as the terms for abortionists and twice as long as those for armed robbers.

The persons interviewed included a young college teacher, a representative of the homosexual Mattachine Society, a compulsive homosexual who had been arrested three times and was undergoing therapy, and a married psychology professor with two children, who said his wife knew that he was a homosexual and that his marriage would probably end as a result of it. There was an interesting debate on the role of the homosexual in the arts, between Dr. Albert Goldman of Columbia and Gore Vidal, the novelist.

Visually the program was disappointing. The faces of most participants were screened, and the discussions could just as well have been done on radio. It also might have been better to give the minority viewpoint that homosexuals are just as normal as anyone else a chance to speak for itself.

Otherwise, the program was a good example of how a difficult subject can be treated with fairness and dignity without sacrificing repertorial depth. Mike Wallace did a solid job on the interviews. "The Homosexuals" was produced for "C.B.S. Reports" by Harry Morgan.

* * *

Note: Following is one of the first New York Times obituaries to acknowledge a surviving homosexual partner of the deceased, using the phrase "longtime companion." Although a few earlier Times obituaries included similar acknowledgements, the practice did not become editorial policy until the mid-1980's.

May 8, 1987

PAUL POPHAM, 45, A FOUNDER OF AIDS ORGANIZATION, DIES

By ANDREW ROSENTHAL

Paul Graham Popham, a decorated Vietnam veteran and a founder of the Gay Men's Health Crisis, died of complications from AIDS yesterday at the Memorial Sloan-Kettering Cancer Center. He was 45 years old.

Mr. Popham was president of the Gay Men's Health Crisis, an educational, advisory and advocacy organization for AIDS patients, from 1981 to 1985. He also helped found the AIDS Action Council, a lobbying organization in Washington, and was chairman of the group.

Mr. Popham was born in Emmett, Idaho. He graduated from Portland (Ore.) State College.

In 1966, as a first lieutenant in the Fifth Air Cavalry in Vietnam, he was decorated with the Bronze Star for valor after his platoon had served as a lure for North Vietnamese soldiers. In the firefight, a North Vietnamese unit was destroyed, according to Mr. Popham's brother, David, of Boise, Idaho.

Paul Popham retired as a Special Forces major in the Army Reserve in 1969, after having led a psychological warfare unit in the United States, his brother said.

From 1969 until 1980, Mr. Popham worked for the Irving Trust Company, leaving as a vice president, He joined McGraw-Hill Inc., where he was general manager of a division.

David Popham and friends of Paul Popham said Mr. Popham never took an active political role until he read a newspaper article in 1981 about the disease that became known as AIDS.

"His history had been quite the opposite from a gay activist," the president of the Gay Men's Health Crisis, Richard D. Dunne, said. "It was only an issue like AIDS that galvanized people like Paul."

Mr. Popham was one of a half-dozen founders of the group and remained active in that organization and in the lobbying group until his illness, diagnosed in February 1985, became too severe, friends said.

Also surviving are his mother, Muriel Wood of Sun City, Calif., and two sisters, Nancy Veenker and Marilyn Jones, both of Portland. His longtime companion was Richard Dulong.

Services will be held in Portland.

* * *

April 24, 1993

COVERING GAY RIGHTS: CAN JOURNALISTS BE MARCHERS?

By ELIZABETH KOLBERT

The gay-rights march in Washington tomorrow has prompted many news organizations to re-examine the line between journalists' professional conduct and their private lives.

In preparation for the rally, many newspapers and television networks have reviewed or reissued their policies governing reporters' participation in activities with political overtones.

Some news organizations, including The Washington Post and ABC News, are essentially forbidding staff members to participate in the march. Others, including The New York Times and NBC News, have no objections to staff members' marching as long as their jobs do not involve covering or supervising the coverage of gay issues.

"If people wish to participate in their free time as individuals, they can," said Peggy Hubble, a spokeswoman for NBC News. "But those who cover and report on these issues shouldn't march."

Policy Issues, Personal Issues

At least one news organization, The Associated Press, has found how difficult it can be to try to frame a policy about such a personal issue.

Late last week, in response to questions from reporters about attending the rally, the A.P.'s executive editor, William E. Ahearn, issued an electronic memorandum saying that staff members "should not participate in activities—be it a gay-rights parade, anti-abortion or pro-abortion protest, anti-war demonstration, etc.—that are partisan and compromise or give the appearance of compromising their ability to be objective."

The memorandum further stated that "because A.P. staffers cover such a wide variety of news events and are used in various editorial tasks, they should not take part in any partisan activity even though the topic of that activity is one they do not directly cover."

Several reporters argued that the policy was so broad it could be construed to prohibit employees from joining a political party or religious group. In a letter to A.P. management dated Monday, Kevin Keane, the president of the union that represents A.P. reporters, the Wire Service Guild, asserted that the policy conflicted with employees' rights under collective bargaining. He warned that if the A.P. moved to enforce it, the union would take legal action.

Stance Is Defended

"It is overly broad to say, for example, that a sportswriter would compromise his or her objectivity by participating in a gay-rights parade, pro-abortion or anti-abortion protest or anti-war demonstration," he wrote.

Mr. Ahearn was out of town and could not be reached for comment. But Darrell Christian, managing editor of The Associated Press, defended the policy, arguing that it would not prevent reporters from supporting political causes as long as they did not do so in public.

Such questions received widespread attention four years ago when several journalists participated in an abortion-rights rally in Washington.

At one end are news organizations like The Washington Post, which prohibits reporters from engaging in "any partisan causes," including "community affairs" and "social action." Recently, Leonard Downie Jr., the executive editor of The Post, issued a memorandum reminding staff members that they could not participate in tomorrow's rally.

The Hometown Newspaper

In an interview, Mr. Downie said it was particularly important for reporters at The Post to avoid partisan activities because they work for the hometown newspaper of the nation's capital. "It is stricter than many other newspapers'," he said of The Post's policy, "but we feel it's important to our credibility and our relationship to our readers."

Many other news organizations, including The New York Times, do not object to their staff members' supporting causes, as long as they do not cover related topics. The Times's policy, for example, requires reporters to avoid any activity "that creates or appears to create conflict of interest with their professional work," and Times editors said the policy would not prevent reporters who cover, say, the stock market, from marching in tomorrow's rally.

The Los Angeles Times has a similar policy. "We have decided not to try to issue blanket edicts on the premise that the common sense and good judgment of the staff can be relied on," said Norman C. Miller, the paper's national editor.

Still, defining the border between the public and the private can be extraordinarily difficult for journalists, whose work does not always fall into neat categories. Any reporter who covers education in New York City, for example, would have spent much of the last few months dealing with the proposed gay-rights curriculum. Would such a reporter's work be compromised if he or she had marched in a gay-rights rally?

'I Want a Good Reporter'

An easier question for virtually all of the news executives interviewed was whether they would take a reporter's own sexual orientation into account when deciding who should cover the march tomorrow. They said it should not be a factor.

"It doesn't make any difference," said Heath Meriwether, executive editor of The Detroit Free Press. "I want a good reporter; I want one that has some expertise in the subject."

Out of concern that it could compromise its standing in the journalistic community, the National Lesbian and Gay Journalists Association has decided not to participate in the rally as an organization, although the association's president, Leroy Aarons, said many members of the group would be participating as individuals.

* * *

November 3, 1996

DON'T ASK, DON'T PRINT

By ABE PECK

STRAIGHT NEWS: Gays, Lesbians, and the News Media
By Edward Alwood
Illustrated. 386 pp. New York: Columbia University Press. $29.95.

Mainstream journalism proudly honors objectivity, balance and accuracy. But its execution often sifts those values through the filters of prevailing opinion, new knowledge, old prejudices and standard assumptions about who's worth quoting. In "Straight News," Edward Alwood examines how the relationship between gay men, lesbians and the American news media has evolved since World War II. Mr. Alwood's useful history follows a trail of derision and dismissal that gives way to an upbeat march toward the mainstream—at least until the book's end. But the title also is a journalistic double-entendre: the news media are dominated by heterosexuals—"straights"; the book's reportage is straight ahead and, at times, constrained by its earnestness.

Bulwarked by analyses of news articles, interviews and a raft of footnotes, Mr. Alwood's story begins with homosexuals, justifiably timid, emerging from World War II to request—politely—civil rights in the face of invisibility or vitriol. The watershed Stonewall rebellion of 1969, the clash between police and drag queens at a Greenwich Village gay bar that mutated from mainstream crime story into the gay Alamo, produced a 70's of self-liberation, publication and the first few declared gay reporters working in the mass media. Starting in 1981, AIDS and (not independently) a more visible gay presence created a broader acceptance of issues and journalists.

Before Stonewall, macho ruled in the newsroom: "Sexual inverts have colonized three areas of the city" is just one of the newspaper excerpts Mr. Alwood cites. In response, the Mattachine Society and the Daughters of Bilitis began in the 1950's and expressed tentative gay and lesbian identities in their publications, One and The Ladder. Their initial hesitant activities led some journalists to include homosexuals among their sources, but Mr. Alwood cites harrowing images: one television program featured a gay man wearing a hood, fearing both public identification and anti-sodomy laws.

Then came Stonewall. Routine harassment and descending nightsticks at a gay bar were met with resistance, bottles and chants of "Kill the cops"—and "Gay power." The Daily News headline was "Homo Nest Raided, Queen Bees Are

Stinging Mad." But the then-liberal New York Post's second-day story explored "The Gay Anger Behind the Riots."

Homosexuals—now self-defined as gay men and lesbians—spoke through their own press. They also picketed and disrupted, from mainstream newspaper offices to the set of "Marcus Welby, M.D." Stories were defended, editorial freedom was cited and, Mr. Alwood writes, some demonstrators regretted that rage had precluded a chance to meet with network standards-and-practices officials. But coverage began to shift—especially after the American Psychiatric Association delisted homosexuality as an illness in 1973. "In essence," Mr. Alwood notes wryly, "the decision meant that millions of homosexuals had been cured of mental illness overnight."

Still, in 1974, a Los Angeles Times front-page story denigrated the gay patrons of an all-night grocery as "fags," and the 1977 Anita Bryant flap over gay-rights legislation led to anti-gay stories, columns and editorials. Mr. Alwood also criticizes The New York Times, noting a 1963 front-page article that continued inside the paper to describe "deviates" who were mostly "condemned to a life of promiscuity." He says elsewhere that Times executives reportedly spoke of "faggots" and questioned stories deemed too declasse or too prominent. The Times prohibited the use of "gay" to mean homosexual from 1975 to 1987, except in quotations or within the name of an organization. (The word still is not used as a stand-alone noun.)

Nevertheless, timid visits by reporters to gay bars expanded into attempts to get inside the subculture and look out at the society its members faced. Some mainstream stories exploited the rough edges of gay eros, but others shaved those edges out of sympathy for gay rights.

AIDS changed everything. Mainstream newspapers were slow to cover the story even as casualties grew, out of ignorance, primness and the fact that the first victims were considered "outsiders." But as the disease became epidemic, ethical issues were slowly reconsidered: whether to mention AIDS in obituaries (cancer had been "a long illness" for years), how to weigh the rights of surviving lovers vis-a-vis blood family—and were those lovers acknowledged homosexuals? Meanwhile, the gay press itself split over whether anonymous sex in bathhouses was the expression of a life style or a health risk, and over the outing of famous closeted homosexuals. Mr. Alwood cites one confused straight reporter who asked: "Are you gay or are you queer? Is outing O.K. or is it not? If you guys can't figure it out, how can we figure it out?"

Gay and lesbian reporters themselves gained a place within mainstream newsrooms. Some were fired, others were suspected of bias or not considered for general assignments. But their numbers, and profiles, grew, and several reporters with AIDS wrote first-person stories that put a face on the disease for their colleagues and their readers. By the 1990's, big-city newspapers were including gay men and lesbians as part of an (affluent) audience that required a diversity of reporting. The Times's publisher, Arthur Sulzberger Jr., told a 1992 convention of gay and lesbian journalists that the paper must offer its readers coverage of the broad gay community, its people and its issues.

Mr. Alwood, a former CNN reporter who now works in media relations, finds today's mainstream coverage far more nuanced than before. But in his epilogue he shifts from reporting to advocacy. An "undercurrent of bias," he submits, should be countered by everything from fair employment to more profiles of gay people. Mr. Alwood also equates interviewing "antigay zealots" in the name of balance to taking Klansmen or Nazis seriously. Still, his proposals are based on what he sees as a more accepting mainstream; ironically, it is now the right that feels excluded.

Mr. Alwood's brick-by-brick exposition makes a reasonable case but limits opportunities to narrate the fear of exposure, the joys of a demonstration, the fun of dancing the night away. Nor does he contend with a commercially oriented gay press that can mirror fashion-magazine preoccupation with perfect-looking people.

"Straight News" is an important book. At the same time, there are chapters yet to be written.

Abe Peck is a professor at Northwestern University's Medill School of Journalism and the author of "Uncovering the Sixties: The Life and Times of the Underground Press."

* * *

RELIGION AND GAY RIGHTS

March 25, 1971

CHURCHES ASSAILED HERE AS FOES OF HOMOSEXUALS

By ELEANOR BLAU

The pastor of the United Church of Christ in Newark, charged yesterday that the "church historically and hysterically has been the greatest antihomosexual force," but that "one does not have to be a heterosexual before he can be a Christian.

"The homosexual," he declared at a conference, "is no longer content to sit at the door of the church singing Psalm 88" and waiting for those inside to invite him in. Verse 8 of the psalm says, in part, "Thou hast made me an abomination."

The pastor, the Rev. Robert W. Wood, said that too often churches in effect tell the homosexual, "You can come and worship here and receive our sacrament provided you can pass for a heterosexual." Yet, he added, the homosexual is "part of the same love of which our Saviour spoke."

Mr. Wood spoke at what was described as the first national conference on religion and the homosexual, at the Interchurch Center, 475 Riverside Drive.

Seventy representatives of church and homosexual organizations are attending the conference, which ends today.

Lack of Recognition

Dr. Louis Crompton, representing the Lincoln-Omaha Council on Religion and the Homosexual, said only two national church denominations—the Lutheran Church in America and the Unitarian Universalist Association—have issued public statements supporting homosexual rights. He called on other religious groups to take a stand on such matters as law reform and employment rights.

"We need an American counterpart of the Vatican statement on the Jews," he said.

On the matter of "passing as a heterosexual," the Rev. Robert Clement remarked that he had been a "good queer" until he decided to stop hiding the fact and set up a church specifically for homosexuals: the Church of the Beloved Disciple, at Ninth Avenue and 28th Street.

In that church, he said, there is "an outpouring of love like I've never seen before."

"We have found an identity and found something about what Christianity is about," he added.

Hiding Deepest Emotion

The Rev. Thomas Maurer of the National Drug and Sex Forum in San Francisco reported that he had "removed the mask" for the first time not long ago, at age 52, and subsequently had cried for the first time since he had been a child. "I had been hiding all my life some of my deepest emotions," he explained.

"We've got to have churches that will free people to be themselves," Mr. Maurer continued. To impose a life-style, he said, is to destroy the individual's uniqueness.

Mr. Maurer recommended that churches declare their acceptance of homosexuals, admit them to seminaries, have "gay" socials and encourage contacts between homosexuals and heterosexuals.

He remarked that if all homosexuals were to wake up one morning colored green, the social climate would change, because many ordinary and respected people would be revealed as homosexual, and their "straight" friends and relatives would say, "Gee, they seem pretty normal."

Mr. Maurer concluded: "Homosexuality as a way of life has come of age. Either the church will recognize it or die."

* * *

October 6, 1979

POPE FIRMLY DEFENDS CHURCH RESTRICTION ON CONTRACEPTION

DENOUNCES 'PERMISSIVENESS'
Addressing Bishops, He Reaffirms Teachings, Rejecting Divorce and Homosexual Actions

By KENNETH A. BRIGGS
Special to The New York Times

CHICAGO, Oct. 5—Pope John Paul II, deploring "onslaughts of materialism, rampant secularism and moral permissiveness," today issued the staunchest defense of Roman Catholic teachings on sexuality that he has made in his current visit to the United States. Included in that defense was the church's ban on artificial birth control.

While the Pope had voiced agreement with most of these teachings before his visit, his unequivocal reaffirmation of his positions on a broad range of moral issues took on added significance because so many American Catholics have dissented from the church's sexual guidelines. The Pope, apparently aware of these deep divisions, acknowledged that church law must be taught despite inevitable criticism.

Fidelity to Catholic Doctrine

The Pope's views were consistent with his theme of the need for unity in the face of growing pluralism in the American branch of the church, as reflected in divisions among the hierarchy. Today's views were presented to the 250 United States Catholic bishops, meeting in closed session at Quigley South Seminary. The meeting was part of an itinerary that took the Pope to a small Polish-language mass and another mass attended by hundreds of thousands of people on Chicago's lakefront.

In the longest address so far on his journey, the Pope emphasized fidelity to Catholic doctrine and underscored the authority of the bishops while appearing subtly and gently to rebuke them for failing to uphold church law firmly enough.

Quoting from recent statements by the National Conference of Catholic Bishops, the official arm of the American hierarchy, the Pontiff counseled the bishops to teach "the sacred deposit of truth" by defending such stands as the church's rejection of divorce, homosexual practice, premarital and extramarital sexual relations and artificial contraception.

No Mention of Annulments

"In exalting the beauty of marriage," the Pope said, "you rightly spoke against both the ideology of contraception and contraceptive acts, as did the encyclical Humanae Vitae. And I myself today, with the same conviction of Paul VI, ratify the teaching of this encyclical, which was put forth by my predecessor 'by virtue of the mandate entrusted to us by Christ.'"

The Pope referred to the pastoral letter by the bishops three years ago, "To Live in Christ Jesus," as a basis for his defense of these traditional moral teachings. Observers noted that he did not comment on granting of marriage annulments, which has become a more frequent practice in recent years. Last year, an estimated 30,000 annulments were granted by church tribunals.

While the Pope did not directly criticize the actions of the bishops, he held their own official statements up to them and implicitly suggested that stronger efforts to promote them were in order. There had been much speculation that the Pope would attempt to instill greater discipline in the American hierarchy because of alleged liberalizing trends that have crept into the church in the United States in recent years.

Even at the time that the pastoral letter was approved by the Catholic bishops, by a vote of 172 to 25, there was unexpectedly strong opposition from many of the laity and from bishops who argued that it lacked sufficient compassion for those Catholics who experience difficulty obeying church proscriptions on birth control, divorce and abortion.

Archbishop John R. Roach of Minneapolis, vice president of the conference of bishops, conceded that the Pope may have sounded negative but denied that the Pope had intended that result. "You can take a portion of this statement and perhaps consider it scolding," Archbishop Roach said. "I don't think it was."

The Pope's statement to the bishops, combined with his strong backing for the rules of celibacy and an all-male priesthood earlier this week, portray him as a strict constructionist on church law. By contrast, he has been widely considered left of center on social issues, particularity in his support for human rights, impressed most forcefully on this visit by his speech at the United Nations.

In other parts of today's speech, the Pope noted the need for ecumenical progress but ruled out, for the present at least, intercommunion among churches. "We must pray and study together," he said, "knowing, however, that intercommunion between divided Christians is not the answer to Christ's appeal for perfect unity." Though the Pope has expressed support for the principle of ecumenism from the start of his reign, many of those involved in interfaith relations await concrete signs of what initiative he might take.

Services of Reconciliation

In his statement, he also urged the bishops to reverse the sharp decline in participation in the sacrament of penance or confession and appeared to chastise those bishops who have held services of "reconciliation" whereby divorced and remarried Catholics have received general absolution.

Under church rules, there are very few circumstances that allow for the granting of general absolution—forgiveness to an entire group without prior individual confession to a priest. Some bishops have been moving toward greater flexibility, but the Pope seemed to oppose this move.

He also seemed aware of the challenge to the authority of bishops in recent years through widespread defections from the church and disagreement with official teachings, many of them in the area of sexuality. In addition, the bishops have been in tension with theologians who contend that traditional views must change in response to new, historical factors.

The Pope said that fidelity to church law would entail difficulty. "Brothers in Christ," he said, "as we proclaim the truth in love, it is not possible for us to avoid all criticism; nor is it possible to please everyone. But it is possible to work for the real benefit of everyone."

* * *

August 18, 1980

ON HOMOSEXUAL PRIESTS

By MICHAEL STEPHEN

Hate the sin and tolerate the sinner" best expresses the Roman Catholic Church's attitude toward homosexuals. Characteristically, ecclesiastical actions and thinking are not only behind the times but also against the tide. While the last several years have witnessed progress in accepting homosexuality in the arts, news media, psychiatry and publishing, and in accepting homosexuals' legal and public rights, the church has reversed the few hopeful signs that compassion might displace discrimination.

The 1975 Vatican "Declaration on Sexual Ethics" continued to classify homosexual behavior between individuals as sinful. (The church's position is that the condition of homosexuality is not sinful, that only homosexual acts are.) The Jesuits, instigated by the Vatican, ordered the Rev. John J. McNeill, author of "The Church and the Homosexual," to stop speaking publicly and to stop writing on the subject—his book maintains that homosexual behavior can be morally good and should be measured by the same standards as heterosexuality. Humberto Cardinal Medeiros, the Archbishop of Boston, transferred to a quiet suburban parish the Rev. Paul R. Shanley, a priest who pioneered an effective ministry to homosexuals. The Jesuits expelled Thomas P. Sweetin, a seminarian who spent 13 years preparing for the priesthood, for publicly admitting his homosexual orientation, though he said that he was sexually inactive. Not content with policing its own house, the Archdiocese of New York has vehemently and successfully lobbied against civil rights legislation for homosexuals, dooming its passage by the City Council. These and other, unpublicized actions indicate the extreme homophobic attitudes harbored by the church's hierarchy, seminary faculty and many clergy despite the possibly sizeable number of homosexual clergymen, practicing and latent, in the church.

To the average Catholic, this assessment is unbelievable; to most clergy, it is "dirty laundry"—not for public viewing. Officials in positions of power, exhibiting inadequate and inaccurate knowledge of homosexuality, hide behind the Vatican's intransigence.

Seminarians would be foolish to confess homosexual proclivities and activities regardless of whether they were confined to the past or not. The church in effect demands not veracity but duplicity from its clergy: Lie to move to the next seminary year, to be ordained. Furthermore, the topic receives scant seminary treatment except for administrative admonitions and lectures on sexual morality. Seminarians who voice support of homosexuals' rights, who challenge the church's teaching, who exhibit pastoral sensitivity to the subject are singled out and may find their opinions questioned during their annual evaluation.

Although change will not emanate from the Vatican or the church hierarchy, and although confrontation would likely backfire in such a closed society as the church's, hopeful trends are emerging. Bold statements may garner headlines but quiet action produces change. With the clergy's ranks being depleted from retirements, laicizations and a dearth of priesthood candidates, and with more celibate or active homosexuals assuming influential posts in dioceses and parishes, individuals can effect grassroots change in small, subtle ways and begin to eradicate blatantly un-Christian discrimination in their own ranks. In addition, with fewer candidates for the priesthood, seminary and diocesan officials may be reluctant to dismiss students.

As the church moves further from its emphasis on act-centered morality to one that centers on the person, homosexuality will correctly be seen as one of many aspects of the total person. Homosexual bishops and other clergymen have served the church faithfully and well for centuries in schools, hospitals, universities, and in myriad apostolic endeavors—various kinds of ministries. The phenomenal achievements of church institutions in which homosexuals have played a role bolster the belief that homosexuals' only abnormality is the burden of inferiority and the labels that society, its institutions, and the church place upon them.

If homosexual clergymen creatively and compassionately educate and minister to their people, homosexual and heterosexual, they will effect change in the church not as Vatican institution but as a pilgrim people of God, and possibly they will spur society to grant homosexuals the full legal and civil rights due them.

Since the time that Jesus challenged the hypocrisy of the Pharisees, great leaders from Saints Peter and Paul to Pope John XXIII have led the church through difficult times into new eras. Today's challenge for homosexual and "straight" clergy is to take the risk of faith and welcome homosexuals, without stigmatizing them and without regarding them as morally defective, in daily ministry and all apostolates, ushering in a new age of Christian compassion and love. The church needs true Christians, not Pharisees. Deceiving the authorities may be necessary for ordination, but living a lie is unconscionable.

"Michael Stephen"— this is a pseudonym—is a seminary student.

* * *

ARCHDIOCESE SEEKS ACCORD WITH CITY

By DAVID W. DUNLAP

The Roman Catholic Archdiocese of New York is negotiating with New York City to resolve church concerns that a mayoral ban on discrimination against homosexuals by agencies doing business with the city may violate church teachings.

The archdiocese has about $60 million in contracts with the city to provide such services as caring for disabled and emotionally disturbed children and those from broken homes. The contracts, which are subject to Mr. Koch's antidiscrimination order, are up for renewal this month.

Earlier this year, the city refused to renew seven contracts worth $4 million with the Salvation Army for child-care services because the group refused to adopt the city's ban on discrimination against hiring homosexuals.

Optimism on Negotiations

The Salvation Army's divisional commander in the New York area said yesterday that his organization and the city were still trying to resolve the impasse.

Archbishop John J. O'Connor has said he supports efforts to fight discrimination as long as it is clear that this does not include condoning homosexual activity or the teaching of homosexuality. The archdiocese, according to a spokesman, does not condemn chaste homosexual "inclination." Both Mayor Koch and a spokesman for the Archbishop expressed optimism yesterday that the negotiations would answer this concern and avoid a disruption in services. Mr. Koch also said the city's Law Department was reviewing his power to issue such antibias orders.

The possibility that the archdiocese would refuse to renew its contracts with the city came to light in the latest issue of Catholic New York, the archdiocesan weekly newspaper.

"We would rather close our child-care agencies than violate church teaching," the Archbishop was quoted as saying in an interview. At the same time, he described the Mayor as "deeply interested in trying to respect the position of the Catholic Church."

Mr. Koch said yesterday he was "very hopeful that we're not very far apart" with the archdiocese. Speaking for Archbishop O'Connor, the Rev. Peter G. Finn said, "We're optimistic that a resolution will be able to be worked out."

At issue is the Mayor's two-year-old Executive Order 50, which requires that private groups doing business with the city must state that they will not discriminate in employment or hiring because of "race, creed, color, national origin, sex, age, handicap, marital status, sexual orientation or affectional preference."

Father Finn said that the Archbishop "is simply reiterating, without in any way condemning anyone for being inclined homosexually, that we cannot and will not promote active homosexual behavior.

"Actively practiced," Father Finn said, "it is not a right, it's an evil. It's a wrong way of behaving, just as a married man committing adultery."

After reading the Catholic New York article yesterday afternoon, Mayor Koch said in a telephone interview that he was "hopeful we will be able to resolve this" because "what we're talking about is sexual orientation—this language would indicate a common ground."

"Executive Order 50 does not permit homosexual activity any more than it permits heterosexual activity on the job," Mr. Koch said. "It simply says you can't discriminate on the basis of sexual orientation."

Mayor Sees a Compromise

"If they're concerned as it relates to contacts with children," he said, "they have the right to designate who, if anyone, can discuss sexuality with children. If anyone were to violate that sanction, they could be fired."

The Mayor said he is leaving the negotiating to Deputy Mayor Stanley Brezenoff and Frederick A. O. Schwarz Jr., the Corporation Counsel.

But he also said, "I would have no objection to making a statement which sets forth clearly that an acceptance of the conditions in any agreement to perform city service in no way is condoning or accepting of homosexual activity or life style, and that no one on the job has a right to engage in homosexual or heterosexual activity."

Father Finn said he could not comment on the "many nuances of legality" in the mayoral order. Speaking generally, he said, "What we are specifying is that we would not be able to accept the promotion of active homosexual behavior as acceptable."

He said the contracts were routinely renewed before the beginning of the city's fiscal year. His understanding was that the relatively recent ban on bias against homosexuals "got by everybody but the Salvation Army, which questioned it" earlier this year.

In March, the Mayor told the Salvation Army that it would lose its city contracts if it did not adopt a hiring policy that was not biased against homosexuals.

Lieut. Col. Wallace C. Conrath, divisional commander of the Salvation Army of Greater New York, said yesterday that "Even though we came to a very serious impasse a few months ago, during this period before the contracts end, we have been endeavoring to reach common ground if we can do so without sacrificing our religious principles." City contracts with the Salvation Army will expire on June 30.

Mayor Koch said he had asked Mr. Schwarz to review his authority to implement Executive Order 50 in whole or in part, following a State Court of Appeals decision last week that struck down another order, No. 53, as unconstitutional.

That order specifies that 10 percent of all subcontracting work in the construction of municipal projects must go to companies that employ people who are, as the Mayor described them, "hard-core unemployed, which in New York City are overwhelmingly black and Hispanic."

'Usurpation of Power'

On Thursday, the court, the state's highest tribunal, found unanimously that the executive order was an "unconstitutional usurpation of legislative power" by the Mayor.

"The reasoning of the Court of Appeals," Mr. Schwarz said, "is that this whole general subject of affirmative action—frankly, I don't agree—is reserved only for the legislature—whether the City Council or the State Legislature they don't say."

The Mayor said it had not been decided yet whether to seek authority to continue the provisions of Executive Order 53 from the Council or in Albany. He said he expected to hear from the Law Department on Tuesday as to whether Executive Order 50 fell in the same category. Mr. Schwarz estimated that billions of dollars in contracts were covered by Executive Order 50. He said that some companies that do business out of state had complained about applying the antidiscriminatory clause to their operations elsewhere. Aside from those companies, the archdiocese and the Salvation Army, he said, "We have not heard any other arguments about Executive Order 50."

The Archbishop's remarks on the order were made on June 8, after a mass that he celebrated with Courage, described by the archdiocese as "a support group for homosexuals who are committed to leading celibate lives."

According to Catholic New York, Archbishop O'Connor told the group that he wanted "to expand the church's ministry to homosexuals and offer assistance to victims of AIDS," or acquired immune deficiency syndrome. He was quoted as saying, "We have no right to ignore them in justice and charity."

After the mass, during what Father Finn called a "private interview," the Archbishop spoke about "this business of contracts to the tune of millions of dollars."

"I cannot change church teaching," he said. "I can't fudge on it. I can't be ambiguous."

* * *

February 9, 1986

NEW YORK CHURCH LEADERS DIVIDED OVER HOMOSEXUAL-RIGHTS MEASURES

By JOSEPH BERGER

The issue of homosexual-rights legislation has divided New York City's religious leaders and led to an uncommonly sharp exchange between John Cardinal O'Connor and Paul Moore Jr., the Episcopal Bishop of New York.

The conflict between the two religious leaders reflects a wider dispute within religion generally, over how literally the Bible should be interpreted and what attitudes one should adopt given some of the realities of contemporary society and the Bible's call for compassion.

"We are dealing with whether you take certain passages in the Bible literally or take the spirit of the Bible and apply it to our time," Bishop Moore has said.

Cardinal O'Connor, the Archbishop of New York, has assailed a bill pending in City Council that would forbid discrimination in housing and employment based on a person's "sexual orientation," which the bill defines as "heterosexuality, homosexuality or bisexuality."

He had also strongly opposed a mayoral directive, Executive Order 50, that prohibited discrimination against homosexuals by agencies, like those of the Roman Catholic Church, holding contracts with the city. That order was voided last year by the New York State Court of Appeals.

Bishop Endorses Bill

Bishop Moore has strongly endorsed the City Council bill and supported the executive order, publicly criticizing Cardinal O'Connor for his stands. He has called the Cardinal "morally wrong" for initiating a lawsuit that successfully challenged the executive order. And last month, the Bishop said he "deeply regretted" the Cardinal's approach to the executive order.

"I think it is the more conservative approach, whether Jewish, Catholic or evangelical, against the more compassionate approach," he said.

"The funds which were being used are being raised from taxes from everybody, including the gay community," the Bishop said in a recent interview. "If we accept public funds then we must go along on the criteria by which public funds are administered. And I think trying to change the criteria is immoral. Anything that sets back the rights of an individual is not right."

Cardinal O'Connor, in an interview Tuesday, offered a cool response to the Bishop's remarks. "The Bishop feels the need to make public comments about my sense of morality," the Cardinal said. "I don't feel the same need. I can only assume he's following his conscience."

"My inclination is not to call people I think are wrong immoral," he said.

Church Groups' Attitudes

The Old and New Testaments contain at least five passages condemning homosexual behavior. The Roman Catholic Church asserts that having homosexual inclinations is morally neutral, while acting on those inclinations is sinful. Conservative Protestants essentially take the Biblical passages literally, and more liberal Protestant denominations emphasize the Bible's call for compassion.

A few liberal denominations have taken public stands opposing discrimination against homosexuals in hiring and housing. Although Bishop Moore supports the ordination of homosexuals, the Episcopal Church has refused to pass a forceful statement supporting that idea. Almost every sect endorses marriage between men and women as the moral ideal.

The range in Jewish thought is also wide. Orthodox and Conservative Jews in varying degrees condemn homosexuality, while Reform Judaism believes in equal rights for homosexuals, including ordination as rabbis.

The Cardinal argues that the Roman Catholic Church does not discriminate against homosexuals and is prepared to employ people who have a homosexual orientation or have practiced homosexuality in the past.

'Human Weakness'

"I am prepared to consider such people for employment because it is a human weakness just as I would employ someone who practiced illicit heterosexual behavior in the past," Cardinal O'Connor said. "But I cannot accept the premise that anyone must engage in homosexual behavior any more than I must accept that someone must engage in heterosexual behavior."

Moreover, the Cardinal argues that support of the City Council bill would place the church in the position of sanctioning homosexuality. Last week, he and Bishop Francis J. Mugavero of the Roman Catholic Diocese of Brooklyn issued a joint statement condemning the City Council bill for placing homosexuality and bisexuality on an equal footing with heterosexuality.

"Such a result would seriously undermine the moral education and values of our youth and the stability of families in our society," the statement said.

Bishop Moore has for years supported bills banning discrimination against homosexuals, testifying in favor of the bills at legislative hearings. "The principle here is that a person should not be discriminated against because of something he or she cannot help," the Bishop said. "If I'm black, a woman or old, or made gay, I should not be discriminated against."

Bias Because of AIDS Cited

The need for antidiscrimination legislation, he said, is more imperative than ever because men thought to be homosexual are increasingly facing discrimination in hiring and housing as a result of the public fears caused by the epidemic of AIDS, or acquired immune deficiency syndrome.

The Cardinal says current laws protect people from discrimination when the reasons for discrimination are not related to job qualifications or performance. What greatly worries him, he said, is that the new bill could lead to a civic sanctioning of homosexual marriages and to a requirement that teachers in sex-education classes espouse homosexuality as a morally valid sexual option.

Bishop Moore has pointed out that the new City Council bill excluded religious groups from its strictures. The Cardinal argued that his experience during the period that Executive Order 50 was in effect led him to believe that city agencies could still harass church groups.

* * *

October 31, 1986

VATICAN REPROACHES HOMOSEXUALS WITH A POINTED ALLUSION TO AIDS

By ROBERTO SURO
Special to the New York Times

ROME, Oct. 30—In what appeared to be a clear allusion to the AIDS epidemic, the Vatican said today that "advocates" of homosexual rights seem undeterred by the realization that "homosexuality may seriously threaten the lives and well-being of a large number of people."

The reference came in a new document that reinforced previous church teachings on homosexuality.

Although acquired immune deficiency syndrome was not mentioned in the document by name, a senior Vatican official said the document was "certainly" referring to the deadly virus in a passage that severely criticizes the pro-homosexual movement.

The Vatican official, who asked not to be identified, said, "In 1986 AIDS cannot be ignored in any consideration of the moral and ethical issues raised by homosexuality."

Task Force Is Outraged

In Washington, the passage in the Vatican document drew an angry reaction from Jeffrey Levi, executive director of the National Gay and Lesbian Task Force in Washington.

"That is outrageous," Mr. Levi said. "A church that is supposed to be showing compassion and caring for those who suffer from the horrible disease instead is furthering bigotry and hatred. The hostility of the Catholic Church to gay men and lesbians has made solving this problem more difficult. A statement like this from the Vatican is only going to worsen the AIDS crisis, not resolve it."

The document said: "Even when the practice of homosexuality may seriously threaten the lives and well-being of a large number of people. Its advocates remain undeterred and refuse to consider the magnitude of the risks involved."

"The church can never be so callous," it added.

Inclination Now Condemned

In the document, which was a letter to all Roman Catholic bishops, the Vatican for the first time explicitly condemned the mere inclination toward homosexuality as an "objective disorder." Previous Vatican statements spoke primarily of the sinfulness of homosexual acts.

Noting that "increasing numbers of people today, even within the church, are bringing enormous pressure to bear on the church to accept the homosexual condition," the document calls on the Catholic authorities to resist "an effort in some countries to manipulate the church by gaining the often well-intentioned support of her pastors with a view toward changing civil-statues and laws."

The document made public today was issued by the Congregation for the Doctrine of the Faith, the Vatican office charged with preserving the orthodoxy of Catholic belief. It had been approved by Pope John Paul II.

Senior Vatican officials, who asked not to be identified, said the letter had been issued partly in response to increasing activity by homosexual groups in Western nations including the United States.

Clarifying the Doctrine

The officials said the Vatican was trying to clarify its position while countering what the document called "deceitful propaganda" used by pro-homosexual groups. Concern over erroneous interpretations of the church's position on the subject by some pastors and theologians was another reason for producing the document, they said.

Publication of the Vatican's letter follows two disciplinary actions against prominent American churchmen who were accused, among other things, of lax attitudes toward homosexuality. The Vatican document in effect offers strong support to bishops in New York and Chicago who have recently spoken out against legislation aimed at preventing discrimination against homosexuals.

While deploring crimes against homosexuals, the letter says that "when civil legislation is introduced to protect behavior to which no one has any conceivable right," people should not be surprised when "irrational and violent reactions increase."

The letter, sent to more than 3,000 bishops around the world, also offers a series of recommendations on how priests can assist a homosexual "by affirming that person's God-given dignity and worth." But it insists on a recognition of the sinfulness of homosexual acts as a first step.

* * *

September 17, 1987

AIDS ISSUE AT FORE AS POPE VISITS SAN FRANCISCO TODAY

By ROBERT REINHOLD
Special to the New York Times

SAN FRANCISCO, Sept. 16—Probably no issue more boldly underscores the complex divisions within the Roman Catholic Church than the church's evolving approach to AIDS. It is an issue that will burst forcefully to the surface Thursday when Pope John Paul II meets 100 Catholic AIDS patients here, including two priests, and confronts what are expected to be noisy protests against him by San Francisco's gay community.

Even as gay leaders revile the Pope for the Vatican's pronouncements on homosexuality, they praise the Archbishop of San Francisco for his ministry to AIDS patients. Even as the Vatican's spokesman, Archbishop John Foley, calls the disease a "natural sanction" against immoral behavior, a Catholic church in a Houston suburb houses and cares for two dying AIDS patients, one a 19-year-old boy rejected by his Catholic family.

And even as John Cardinal O'Connor of New York forbids a gay Catholic group to meet on church property, the California Catholic Conference, made up of all the bishops in the state, is preparing to do battle against 54 bills pending in the State Legislature that the conference regards as punitive toward AIDS patients and those infected with the virus that causes the disease.

Such are the ambiguities that confront the church as it struggles to reconcile its historic moral revulsion against homosexuality with the fact that so many of its faithful, including not a few priests, have contracted the deadly disease.

Two Different Talks

In the first formal comments he had ever made about acquired immune deficiency syndrome, the Pope told health care workers in Phoenix on Monday that they were obliged to "show the love and compassion of Christ and His church" to AIDS sufferers and that the workers were living out the parable of the good Samaritan.

But in earlier words to reporters on his plane, the Pope bended none on moral principle. "The church is doing all that is possible," he said, "to heal and especially to prevent the moral background of this"—a remark widely taken, by both critics and suppottyers of his stand, to mean that AIDS is rooted in immorality.

Among Catholics suffering from the disease, the church has evoked mixed feelings.

R. Daniel LaFleur, a 31-year-old native of the East Bay area who will meet the Pope on Thursday, harbors no resentment. "He's not trying to make everybody happy," Mr. LaFleur said of the Pontiff. "He's saying these are the rules. That's not attacking gay people. He's just making a stand on what the church is. I personally have found a priest that has helped me tremendously get through this crisis."

Some Welcoming, Some Not

Mr. LaFleur, whose mother was a teacher in a Catholic parochial school, said he looked forward to meeting the Pope, an encounter he described as a "lifetime experience."

But other AIDS sufferers are less welcoming. Leonard Matlovich, who pressed a lawsuit against the Air Force a dozen years ago for discharging him when he proclaimed himself gay, said he was "outraged" by the Pope's plans to see AIDS patients.

"Seven years into this crisis, and he has not uttered a word about AIDS," Mr. Matlovich said in an interview before the Pope's speech in Phoenix. He termed the papal appearance planned for Thursday at Mission Dolores, a basilica situated near the largely homosexual Castro district here, as a "deliberate slap in the face."

"The Pope says the church must be compassionate toward the dying," said Thomas Carroll, regional director of Dignity, a nationwide organization of gay Catholics. "The church deals very well with the dying. It's the living and breathing they have problems with."

Outrage Over Letter

The Vatican stirred outrage among American homosexuals, and even among many Catholic theologians, with its

Associated Press

Mike Smith, manager of the Names Project, holding a quilt memorializing eight AIDS victims. The quilt is to be on display today when Pope John Paul II visits Mission Dolores in San Francisco.

letter to all the church's bishops last October on "the pastoral care of homosexual persons."

The letter appeared to harden the church's stand against homosexuality, saying the mere "inclination" was "a more or less strong tendency ordered toward an intrinsic moral evil." It added, in an allusion to AIDS, "Even when the practice of homosexuality may seriously threaten the lives and well-being of a large number of people, its advocates remain undeterred and refuse to consider the magnitude of the risks." Finally, the letter told bishops to withdraw support from "any organizations which seek to undermine the teaching of the church" on homosexuality.

The Rev. Richard McCormack, a professor of Christian ethics at the University of Notre Dame, said the Vatican letter had gone beyond previous teachings by calling the homosexual orientation, as opposed to practice, "disordered." That, he said, is "open to serious question" on both medical and philosophical grounds.

"It was a poorly worded document from a public relations and political point of view," said the Rev. Bill Wood, an official of the California Catholic Conference. However, he added, there "has always been a tradition that the sin is condemned but the sinner is embraced."

In an effort to soften the Vatican letter, Archbishop John R. Quinn of San Francisco, president of the conference, issued a letter in December attempting, in Father Wood's words, to "redeem" the Vatican document by explaining its philosophical words. This was followed by "A Call to Compassion," a pastoral letter from the conference, saying AIDS sufferers "deserve to remain within our communal consciousness and to be embraced with unconditional love."

The efforts of the San Francisco Archdiocese have won the plaudits of gay leaders. The Most Holy Redeemer Parish, led by the Rev. Anthony McGuire, has set up a "buddy" system to run errands for the ill. The parish has also raised funds for and rented space at low cost to the Coming Home Hospice, which houses 15 AIDS patients. A group of women, called Open Hands, cooks hot meals for the ill. Catholic Charities here has an active "outreach" program, which raises funds to bring relatives to visit AIDS patients.

"The church has been with us from day one," said Chris Sandoval, assistant director of the Shanti Project, which provides home care for AIDS patients. He called Archbishop Quinn "a man of great courage."

Mr. Carroll, of Dignity, also had praise for the Archbishop but lamented the "ignorance and bigotry" of the Vatican. "There are people in his own diocese in Rome who are dying of AIDS, and he has not ministered to them," Mr. Carroll said of the Pope.

Meanwhile, though, in dioceses across the country, the church is begining to come to grips with the human rather than the theological crisis. In Houston, for example, the Rev. Alcuin Greenburg, director of the Catholic Chaplain Corps, counsels the dying and holds memorial services to comfort the bereaved homosexual lovers of the dead.

And at St. Mary's Parish in the Houston suburb of Humble, Tex., in a house next door to the church, the parish cares for two destitute AIDS patients, 19 and 34 years old. The pastor, the Rev. Adam McClosky, makes no moral judgments.

"I respect and honor the teachings of the church," Father McClosky said. "I know people who are in homosexual relations who are good Catholics. It is not an issue how they got AIDS. I never ask. My counsel is, God can forgive all, that He understands. They do not have to make apologies."

* * *

September 18, 1987

PROTEST IN SAN FRANCISCO IS LARGEST OF POPE'S TRIP

By ROBERT REINHOLD
Special to the New York Times

SAN FRANCISCO, Sept. 17—Pope John Paul II knelt at the altar of Mission Dolores here this evening in silent prayer, his fist against his forehead. Outside a group of gay and feminist demonstrators shouted, "Pope go home."

Moments later, the Pope blessed 62 patients suffering from AIDS and related diseases in the adjoining basilica, and said, "Christ Jesus came into the world to save sinners."

At the same time demonstrators shouted, "Nazi Pope."

The Pope's visit to San Francisco was the most problematic so far of his American tour. The demonstrators—homosexuals, feminists and some Jews—gathered about 2,000 strong behind metal barricades near the 196-year-old mission to protest the Pope's conservative theology and social agenda.

They carried placards with such slogans as "Curb your dogma" and "Catholic homophobia is bigotry."

For all the noise and theater, there was no violence, no untoward events, no arrests. While the Pope might have heard the shouting, the protesters did not confront him directly. Reporters outside the mission watching the Pope on a television monitor could hear both his remarks and the protesters'.

Small Turnout

Despite glorious weather, the police estimated that only 100,000 people lined the Pope's parade route this evening, a tenth of the 1 million the police were prepared for. "For whatever reason, people did not turn out," said Officer David Ambrose, a police spokesman.

At the demonstration, on 16th Street about 300 feet from the front of the church, San Francisco Supervisor Harry Britt, a homosexual, said: "To be told in the name of God that we should be ashamed of what we are is an abomination. The Pope has as lot to learn in San Francisco about humanness and trust and responding to people. We are not on trial. It is the church that must learn if they are going to be relevant in the centry ahead."

In an adjoining street a much larger and friendlier crowd watched the Pope silently. They were mostly Hispanic residents of the nearby Mission District of the city.

The police estimated that section of the crowd at as many as 25,000 people. They were kept separate from the protesters.

The patients who met with the Pope seemed receptive to his blessings. One of them, David Glassberg, diagnosed with AIDS-related complex last December, said he had given the Pope a letter telling him that "all gay people were deserving of God's love."

Signs of Change

"His visit here changed him," Mr. Glassberg said. "His words today were very soft. Perhaps this is the begining of change.'

Meanwhile other Roman Catholics in less confrontational protests gathered for a 17-hour prayer vigil at St. Boniface Church sponsored by Dignity, a national gay Catholic group.

Dignity also sponsored a candelight procession this evening and a mass at the Palace of Fine Arts across town. Five priests celebrated the mass with women assisting.

From the beginning, San Francisco promised to be the most contentious of the stations on the Pope's pilgrimage across America. With the city's history of political assassination, and with strident protests against the Pope planned by separate groups of homosexuals, feminists and Jews, Draconian security measures were planned for the 21-hour visit.

The Secret Service had originally demanded that all residents along the parade route keep windows shut and shades drawn, but an avalanche of complaints to City Hall forced them to back down. Still, residents were not allowed to open their garages.

The security involved 1,270 San Francisco police officers, 200 sheriff's deputies, 250 Highway Patrol officers and 200 Secret Service agents—at a cost of $1 million.

At the urging of Mayor Dianne Feinstein, many businesses let their employees off early this afternoon to ease traffic problems.

There was a crescendo of complaints today among San Franciscans over the disruption caused by the Papal parade, scheduled for the evening rush hour. Geary Boulevard, a main commuter artery, was closed at 11:30 this morning, more than five hours before the 20-minute motorcade from the Golden Gate Bridge to Mission Dolores.

Protesters Line Up

Among the groups protesting papal policies were the National Organization for Women, Catholics for Free Choice, the Women's Ordination Conference, two Jewish groups and numerous gay groups.

Survivors of the Holocaust, a Northern California group of survivors and their children, spent today sitting shiva, saying the prayer for the dead, in St. Mary's Cathedral, where the Pope ended his day today with an address to members of religious orders.

The Holocaust survivors' groups were protesting the Pope's recent audience with President Kurt Waldheim of Austria, who during World War II belonged to a German army unit that has been implicated in the deportation of Jews to death camps.

* * *

October 11, 1987

HOMOSEXUALS AND THE CHURCHES

By EDWARD TIVNAN

It is no one's image of what homosexuals do in New York City on a Friday night. Every week, 30 men, most of them in their 20's and 30's, meet in a therapist's office on Manhattan's Upper East Side where, for an hour and a half, they study the Bible. "Book by book," says Ralph Blair, a professional therapist with a master's degree in religious studies and a doctorate in counseling.

In 1976, Blair founded an organization to help conservative Christians integrate their religion with their homosexuality. He called it Evangelicals Concerned, and it now has 20 chapters coast to coast. "For most, the possibility of being a

homosexual and a good Christian comes as a great relief," says Blair. It must also come as a relief to his Bible students that Ralph Blair himself is gay.

Some of the participants in Blair's study group are from strict Christian backgrounds, and, to remain faithful to their church's teachings, they spent years denying their homosexuality. Many tried celibacy, heterosexual dating, even marriage. Blair tries to help them see that the Bible is not as hard on homosexuals as they have been told.

"When I came here," explains a member of the group who once studied for the ministry and whose father is a Dutch Reformed minister, "my attitude was that if my homosexuality could fit my Christian life style, fine; but otherwise it would have to go or be sublimated. My identity was more rooted in being a Christian than a homosexual." Says another, "A gay Bible-study group has given me confidence about my acceptability in God's eyes."

Getting accepted by other Christians and by their own churches is another matter. Traditionally, Christian denominations condemn homosexual behavior as sinful and, throughout history, most Christian homosexuals have acted accordingly by hiding their feelings and their actions. More and more, that is changing.

Soon after the gay rights movement began in the early 1970's, Christian homosexual groups began sprouting around the country: Lutherans Concerned; Evangelicals Concerned; for Roman Catholics, an organization called Dignity; for Episcopalians, Integrity. (While Orthodox Judaism opposes homosexuality, Jewish homosexuals have formed their own groups and synagogues. But the antihierarchical nature of most of Judaism—and an increasingly secular American Jewish community—has kept homosexuality from becoming a major issue for Jews.) Many of these groups will be participating in today's National March on Washington for Lesbian and Gay Rights, which could well turn out to be the largest such demonstration ever.

In recent months, faced with friends and lovers dying of AIDS—and the likelihood that they, too, might be struck down by the same disease—many homosexuals have turned to religion. They have done so not only out of fear or self-interest, but also, says Blair, in a spirit of "extending oneself to help others as well."

"What AIDS is doing for spirituality in the church is extraordinary," says the Rev. John J. McNeill, the bearded, soft-spoken author of "The Church and the Homosexual." Early this year, he was expelled from the Society of Jesus because of his public opposition to the Vatican's position on homosexuality.

AIDS is testing the attitudes of all Christians toward homosexuals who, along with intravenous drug users, have been the primary victims of the disease. Some Christian leaders have been quick to show compassion toward AIDS sufferers. Although he has been an outspoken critic of gay rights, New York's Archbishop John Cardinal O'Connor last summer did a stint as a volunteer in the AIDS section of St. Clare's Hospital in Manhattan.

But others share the sentiment of Philadelphia's Catholic leader, John Cardinal Krol. Echoing Protestant fundamentalist preachers, the Archbishop said to a reporter last year, "The spread of AIDS is an act of vengeance against the sin of homosexuality." Views like this have stiffened the backs of Christian gay activists, who call on the churches to prove their commitment to Christ's own concern for society's poor, sick and outcast.

"The AIDS medical crisis challenges us profoundly to be a church in deed and in truth; to be a church as healing community," says Kevin Gordon, a former Christian Brother who teaches human sexuality and biomedical ethics at Brooklyn College, City University of New York. Gordon is also founder and director of the Consultation on Homosexuality, Social Justice and Roman Catholic Theology, a think tank that grapples with theological issues of special relevance to homosexual Christians. "It is AIDS that will judge the church," he says.

Churches have responded to the homosexual issue with compassion and with fire. A sympathetic analysis of "issues concerning homosexuality" was published last year by the Lutheran Church in America. Episcopal dioceses in New York and San Francisco have reached out to homosexuals.

The Episcopal Diocese of Newark, headed by Bishop John S. Spong, earlier this year issued its own report on family life and sexuality. "The church," said the report, "must learn how to continue to affirm the conventional without denigrating alternative sexual and family arrangements. . . . The church must find ways genuinely to affirm persons as they faithfully and responsibly choose and live out other modes of relationship." The diocese has agreed to study a proposal allowing priests to bless homosexual "marriages."

Last spring, a debate between two Episcopal bishops on changing sexual patterns and ethics packed Grace Church in Madison, N.J. Arguing that homosexual activity and sex outside marriage were sinful was the Rev. William C. Wantland, Bishop of the Diocese of Eau Claire, Wis. Bishop Spong, on the other hand, framed the issue of homosexuality in a way that drew both applause and ire. If, he said, one has no choice in being homosexual, as research seems now to indicate, and if, as many psychologists believe, homosexuals are as psychologically "normal" (or crazy) as the rest of us, injured more by prejudice than their sexual orientation, then that might require "a corporate quest for forgiveness for the harm and destruction that the church has helped to heap upon these people throughout history."

During the question-and-answer period, members of the audience took the microphone to differ with Bishop Spong, a low-keyed prelate who has declared it his job to raise major moral issues for discussion. His views on homosexuality have drawn hostile, even threatening, letters.

Within the Episcopalian Church, resistance to an open acceptance of homosexuality continues. Apparently in response to the Newark diocese's report, 13 Episcopal bishops in the Southwest signed a formal statement affirming that heterosexual marriage, monogamous and lifelong, is "one of the nearest approaches to God's intention for his human creatures," and that "chastity, by which is meant faithfulness in marriage and abstinence apart from marriage, is the sexual moral standard for all Christian people."

For its part, the Roman Catholic Church has taken a hard line. More than a year ago, the Vatican publicly criticized Raymond Hunthausen, the Archbishop of Seattle, for, among other things, supporting gay groups. Last fall, the Vatican released a "pastoral letter" (dubbed the "Halloween Encyclical" by its critics) strongly condemning homosexuality. Being homosexual was not a sin, the letter said, but being homosexual inclined one toward acting homosexually—and therefore sinfully. Homosexuality, the pastoral letter concluded, must be considered an "objective disorder." As a result, Catholic dioceses around the country have been discouraging local parishes from renting their facilities to homosexual groups like Dignity.

During his recent visit to the United States, Pope John Paul II discovered for himself how explosive an issue homosexuality is among American Catholics. In San Francisco, 2,000 demonstrators, most of them gay, greeted John Paul with cries of "Pope Go Home." The Pope, however, left no doubt in his remarks that he viewed homosexual relations as sinful.

No one is expecting the churches to change their official positions in the near future. But homosexuals continue to insist that an essential Christian doctrine is "love your neighbor as yourself." The effort has gained them significant support among pastors, theologians and church leaders. Above all, they seem to be gaining the understanding of ordinary churchgoers who, 20 years ago, did not even know (or did not want to know) that homosexuals were sitting in the same pew.

They were, of course, and still are, but the difference now is that an increasing number of Christians are discovering that it does not make any difference. According to a New York Times/CBS poll taken before the Pope's recent visit, for instance, 55 percent of all American Catholics believed someone who "engages in homosexual relations can still be a good Catholic."

If the basic tenet of Christianity is love, the religion has also always been concerned with sex, or, more precisely, the absence of sex. Early Christians quickly separated themselves from their contemporaries by their enthusiasm for chastity and virginity. "From its very beginnings, Christianity has considered an orderly sex life to be a clear second to no sex life at all," points out the Oxford historian Robin Lane Fox in his new book "Pagans and Christians." The earliest followers of Christ strived for a human perfection unencumbered by the desires of the flesh; they tried, as Lane Fox puts it, to live like angels.

It is, therefore, not surprising that the early Christians took a dim view of homosexuality. But not everyone resisted temptation. Homosexuality thrived among the large Christian communities in Rome and Antioch. In the fourth century, St. John Chrysostom, a contemporary of St. Augustine, found to his dismay that his rebukes to Christian homosexuals were "refuted with a thousand arguments."

On the basis of such evidence, the historian John Boswell argued in his controversial 1980 book "Christianity, Social Tolerance and Homosexuality" that, until the end of the 12th century, Christian moral theology treated homosexuality "as, at worst, comparable to heterosexual fornication but more often remained silent on the issue." According to Boswell, the church was more adamantly opposed to usury than to homosexuality.

No one is quite sure what happened over the next century to wipe out such relatively widespread tolerance. The best guesses are that efforts by the state and church in the late Middle Ages to centralize authority, as well as the growth of class conflict and the popularity of religious asceticism, brought hard times to many minorities, including homosexuals. Efforts to crack down on married clergy also might have made the church more vigilant about sexual alternatives.

Whatever its causes, the crackdown was swift and severe. The 13th-century Christian theologian Albertus Magnus, the first to comment extensively on homosexuality, condemned it as the most serious of sexual sins that offended "grace, reason and nature." His most famous student, Thomas Aquinas, whose "Summa theologiae" became the standard reference work on Catholic theology, agreed. Aquinas set the tress "natural"—by which he meant conjugal sex—as the measure of sexual ethics.

By the 14th century, death was the common punishment for homosexuality throughout Europe, and burning at the stake was the execution of choice. In the 17th century, the Puritan divines of Plymouth Plantation agreed that the Bible ordained the death penalty for "carnal knowledge" between two men. By the time of the American Revolution, Thomas Jefferson and a group of liberal reformers of Virginia law proposed replacing the death penalty for sodomy with castration.

Violence against homosexuals continues to be justified by references to the Bible. A decade ago, when the actress Anita Bryant waged a one-woman war against homosexuality, cars in the South bore "Kill a queer for Christ" bumper stickers.

Both the old and New Testaments, the traditional argument goes, are quite clear in their opposition to homosexuality. Are they? Many homosexuals don't think so. They find emotional affinity in the Old Testament stories of Ruth and Naomi and David and Jonathan. They cite Jesus' friendships with Lazarus and the apostle John, as well as St. Paul's attachments to Timothy and Titus, as evidence that the Scriptures do contain examples of love between members of the same sex—even though the love is not expressed carnally. They take comfort in the Old Testament's message of hope: "My house shall be a house of prayer for all people."

Many biblical scholars are equally unconvinced that the Bible unequivocally condemns homosexuality. They base their arguments on close analysis of the six passages where homosexuality seems to be mentioned, and draw upon what we now know about the customs and religious practices of the ancient Jews and early Christians. Their work is complicated, however, by the fact that there is no one word in the Greek in which the New Testament was written for "homo-sexual," itself a word devised by 19th-century doctors, combining the Greek for "same" and the Latin for "sex."

The most famous passage associated with homosexuality is in the Old Testament story of the destruction of Sodom and Gomorrah (Genesis 19:4-11). These cities were once believed to have been destroyed because of their rampant homosexuality. The new and widely accepted scholarly interpretation of this passage is that the sin of Sodom and Gomorrah was primarily one of inhospitality to strangers. As confirmation of this interpretation, many point to 21 other passages in the Old Testament that refer to the Sodom story and mention inhospitality or pride or idolatory, but never homosexuality.

Two passages from Leviticus—18:22 and 20:13—are also often quoted, where "lying with a man as with a womankind" is described by a Hebrew word usually translated as "abomination." Close readers point out that Leviticus - a list of proscriptions according to ancient Jewish law—also uses the same word, "abomination," to describe sexual intercourse during menstruation and other ritually unclean practices, such as eating pork.

The New Testament includes three direct references to homosexuality, all by St. Paul. The most quoted is Romans 1:26, where homosexuality is described in the Greek as "against nature." Paul's use of "nature" (the Greek word is physis) conjures up all sorts of Freudian and social taboos to the modern mind. Yet, as John Boswell contended in his book, for the Stoics, who dominated Roman philosophy in the first century, the word "nature" was often interchangeable with the word for "custom." In I Corinthians 11:14, Paul, sounding like a school principal in the 1960's, asks, "Doth not even nature itself teach you, that, if a man have long hair, it is a shame unto him?"

"There is no condemnation of loving homosexual actions anywhere in Scripture," contends the Rev. John McNeill, the ousted Jesuit, gesturing in frustration at the packed bookshelves that surround his dark Manhattan study. "If it is such a heinous sin, why isn't it mentioned as one, clearly—like rape and adultery?"

Eau Claire's Bishop Wantland, on the other hand, insists, as he did in his debate with Bishop Spong earlier in the year, that "what the church fathers understood from Scripture in the earliest days of the church is still what we understand today"; that "homosexual activity is clearly prohibited as inappropriate for a Christian in I Corinthians 6:9, Romans 1:27, I Timothy 1:10 and Jude 7."

The scriptural debate will undoubtedly continue, but it is ultimately a limited one. "In the final analysis," writes the Rev. Foster McCurley, head of Church in Society, a division of the Lutheran Church in America, and a member of its task force on homosexuality, "the Bible does not relieve us of the awesome responsibility to search for theological truth and for pastoral care to all persons."

Textual argument aside, many observers see homosexuality as an issue that has been enmeshed in a web of complex ethical questions facing Christian churches today—questions that result from recent scientific advances. What should be the churches' stand on test-tube babies, for example, or surrogate motherhood, or artificial insemination? Pope John Paul II has condemned all three practices, but many Catholics would still like him to convene a "Vatican III" devoted solely to the issue of sexuality.

"Homosexuals are bearing the brunt of moral turmoil for something that is much wider," says Peter Steinfels, editor of the liberal Catholic biweekly Commonweal. He sees the current change in cultural mores as comparable to such epochal events as man's move from hunter-gatherer to farmer or the industrial revolution. "Christian ethics—and society at large—can no longer take its basis from nature and the need for reproduction," says Steinfels. "And that's very scary."

The Vatican's pastoral letter of last October reinforced the church's position that the only alternative for the homosexual Catholic is a life of celibacy. Homosexuals were enjoined to liken their "sufferings and difficulties" to "the sacrifice of the Lord's cross."

"Who says anyone has a right to homosexual intercourse?" asks the Rev. John F. Harvey, a theologian and psychologist who has worked with homosexuals for 35 years. In 1980, he founded the organization Courage to help homosexuals live a life of prayer, self-discipline and close, nonsexual friendships. "Celibacy is a gift, as Augustine says," notes Father Harvey. "But nowhere in the Scriptures does it say it is given only to the religious."

Indeed, some homosexuals seem to manage, even thrive, with the pressure of sex turned off. "I've never felt more sane or peaceful," says Vera Sabella, 36, whose easy smile and personal candor hardly suggest the sexual confusion and spiritual anxiety of her past. She drifted from the Catholic church in her teens, faced up to her own homosexuality in her 20's, proceeded to have affairs with several women, but soon returned to the religion of her childhood.

Ms. Sabella was attracted to Courage's brand of self-discipline. She now runs the New York chapter out of a musty office in a Catholic church rectory in mid-Manhattan. The rent is paid by the archdiocese. "With our group you can feel the struggle," says Ms. Sabella. "There's a kernel of sanctity in the group where people are genuinely trying to live a chaste life."

John McNeill, the former Jesuit, admits that celibacy works for some people, but, he insists, "for the vast majority of homosexuals, living celibately is psychologically destructive. You can't save your soul by committing psychological suicide." According to McNeill, most good Catholics who happen to be homosexuals try celibacy but tend to backslide, usually while drunk or on drugs. He insists that the best (and these days the safest) alternative for homosexuals is a stable, loving relationship—in short, a homosexual "marriage."

This may strike traditionalists as revolutionary, but because the alternatives—celibacy or promiscuity—are unacceptable to one side or the other, the notion of homosexual marriage is beginning to look like a promising point of compromise to some theologians and homosexual activists. With AIDS now an epidemic, many homosexuals who once believed that promiscuous sex was proof of their liberation are urging monogamy.

Advocates of homosexual unions argue that they stand the test of current Catholic teaching on marriage, except for the issue of children (and not even the hardest liners are suggesting that childless marriages are by definition sinful). They point out that Vatican II declared that sexual intimacy between a loving couple is as important as procreation; therefore, they say, homosexuals have a right to erotic attraction and its consequences. They also argue that because few seem to have the talent for celibacy, Christianity's prejudice against stable homosexual relationships only encourages promiscuity.

"The Vatican seems intent on reducing all gay sexual expression to lust," contends John McNeill, who notes that many "procreational marriages" can be judged immoral on such grounds as wife or child abuse.

Newark's Episcopal Bishop, John Spong, has said that he finds it "difficult to believe that a church that blesses dogs in a Virginia fox hunt can't find a way to bless life-giving, lasting relationships between human beings." The authors of the Lutheran report on homosexuality noted that while they were not yet sure homosexual relationships could meet the "standard of a covenant of fidelity" of marriage, "it is impossible not to be moved by the authenticity" of the relationships they had seen among male and female homosexuals.

As more and more people confront the reality of having homosexuals in their families, they, too, have found their attitudes changing. When Elinor M. Crocker, a 57-year-old manager of a credit union in Washington, discovered her lesbian daughter had broken up with her live-in lover, she was relieved and hoped "she would go back to being 'normal.'" But she quickly saw that her daughter was more upset over the breakup than another daughter had been when she and her husband divorced.

"For the first time, it dawned on me," says Ms. Crocker, a devout Catholic, "that it was love, not just sex; that it was nothing abnormal, but the same thing I had felt for my husband and my other kids had felt for their spouses." Ms. Crocker became an active member of Dignity.

Traditionalists, however, wonder about the moral consequences of such a radical change. "The real difficulty with proving even a stable homosexual relationship good—and I question that 'stability'—is that it runs directly contrary to the basic principles of human sexuality and therefore cannot be true," says the theologian and psychologist John Harvey. "Once you justify it between two people of the same sex, you create moral chaos and you're off into a different future."

Another kind of future is just what some Christian liberals are embracing. Catholics like Peter Steinfels, editor of Commonweal; the psychologist Eugene Kennedy, of Loyola University, and Kevin Gordon, of City University, see sex moving inevitably from a reproductive role to a nonreproductive one. "Our codes about the ethics of sex are primarily focused on the basic questions of regulating and providing for the reproduction and upbringing of kids," says Steinfels.

Suddenly, after 2,000 years of basic agreement in the Christian world about the central role of marriage and children in society, the game seems to have changed. And the change has been brought about by such late-20th-century phenomena as population and hunger problems of awesome proportions, medical breakthroughs in the area of infertility and large numbers of financially independent women, as well as increased activism of homosexuals. The danger for the Christian churches, some liberals believe, is that if they don't come up with some answers, they could lose their moral authority.

The 1986 Lutheran report on homosexuality reminds its church members: "We must all recall that the traditions preserved about the earthly ministry of Jesus disclose his concern for those whose diseases labeled them the outcasts of their day."

"I told my mother that I don't think God really cares about one's sexual orientation," says a 32-year-old member of Ralph Blair's Friday night Bible-study group who had once believed his homosexuality doomed him to fire and brimstone. "He cares how we lead our lives. And sex is not the point."

But how to ignore sex? The interplay of emotions and physical desire remains one of the greatest human mysteries—the reason, one suspects, that the ancients had trouble distinguishing between sex and religion. To this day, the cleverest among us understand neither. "You don't have to argue that homosexuality is a good," declares the psychologist Eugene Kennedy, "to say, 'Let us examine it and see if we cannot understand it and ourselves more deeply at the same time.'"

Edward Tivnan is the author of "The Lobby: Jewish Political Power and American Foreign Policy."

* * *

June 17, 1988

SOUTHERN BAPTISTS CONDEMN HOMOSEXUALITY AS 'DEPRAVED'

By PETER STEINFELS
Special to the New York Times

SAN ANTONIO, June 16—Delegates to the Southern Baptist Convention today condemned homosexuality as "a manifestation of a depraved nature" and "a perversion of divine standards."

The resolution of homosexuality was passed overwhelmingly after about 10 minutes of debate here at the annual meeting of representatives from the country's largest Protestant denomination.

Only one speaker, Kathleen Armstrong of Fort Worth, voiced any objections, saying, "I have the deep concern after reading this resolution that we as Southern Baptists are becoming so obsessed with condemning sins we have forgotten persons."

The resolution stated that "while God loves the homosexual and offers salvation," homosexuality is "an abomination in the eyes of God."

Strikingly Strong Language

It also called homosexuality "a chosen lifestyle" linked to a general problem of "moral decline" in modern society. The resolution, using language more vivid than several statements the convention has made over the past decade condemning homosexuality, said "homosexuals like all sinners can receive forgiveness and victory" through faith in Jesus.

Resolutions passed by the Southern Baptist Convention, which represents 37,000 churches, are not binding on Southern Baptists, who believe in the primacy of the local congregation. Resolutions do carry weight with many of the denomination's 14.7 million members, however, and guide the many activities and agencies of the Convention itself.

The language in the Baptist resolution runs against current beliefs about the psychology of homosexuality. For example, the American Psychiatric Association removed homosexuality from its list of mental illnesses in 1973, characterizing it instead as a normal variant of sexual expression.

Differences With Other Churches

Unlike assertions on homosexuality made recently by the Catholic Church, the United Methodists, and the Evangelical Lutheran Church in America, the Southern Baptist statement makes no distinction between homosexual orientation and homosexual conduct.

These other churches do not condemn homosexual orientation but consider homosexual conduct a sin like other extramarital sexual activity. They also bar sexually active homosexuals from ordination as priests or ministers.

The Southern Baptist Convention resolution referred to homosexual activity as "the primary cause of the introduction and spread of AIDS in the United States." The resolution said that AIDS had struck not only homosexuals "but also many innocent victims."

* * *

July 11, 1988

EPISCOPALIANS REMAIN SPLIT ON SEXUAL ISSUES

By PETER STEINFELS

After months of controversy, the leadership of the Episcopal Church has shown itself unwilling to depart from traditional church teachings about sexual morality but also unwilling to rule out change in the near future.

On the one hand, the church's General Convention, which began meeting in Detroit July 2 and will adjourn today, has reaffirmed "the biblical and traditional teaching on chastity and fidelity." On the other hand, the convention paired that affirmation with a call for "an open dialogue" on human sexuality.

The ambiguity on sexual issues did not go uncriticized, but conservative and liberal leaders alike said they were encouraged by the actions of the convention, a gathering of

Episcopal laity, clergy and bishops that takes place every three years to set policy for the 2.8 million-member church.

At the root of the Episcopalians' debate is a report, prepared for the convention by a church commission, that affirms marriage "as the standard, the norm, the primary relationship in which the gift of human sexuality is to be shared."

But the commission members found themselves unable to condemn all sexual intimacy outside marriage. They appealed to the church to undertake "a full-scale discussion of sexual ethics." Particularly in regard to homosexuality, the commission members said they hoped the church's discussion would be "nonjudgmental" rather than "our chronic adversarial posturing."

Resolutions Are Combined

The division between church leaders was reflected in the way the convention stitched together a resolution on sexual morality combining an appeal for nonjudgmental dialogue with a clause affirming the church's traditional teachings on sexual morality as an "expression of God's love for each one of us."

The same differences were apparent on other sexual questions.

One proposed change in church law ruled out "sexual orientation" as a basis for denying people "rights or status" in the church and a second proposal ruled out sexual orientation as a basis from barring people from seeking ordination. Both changes were nearly adopted at the last General Convention in 1985.

A proposal that forbade discrimination in the church on grounds of "sexual orientation" was meant to prevent homosexuals from being automatically barred from seeking ordination. The proposal was approved by the House of Bishops here Friday, with the proviso that while it guaranteed access to the study of the priesthood it did not guarantee ordination itself.

But the House of Deputies, made up of representatives of clergy and laity, voted for a different measure, effectively reaffirming the status quo and leaving local dioceses with much leeway in setting policy concerning homosexual candidates for the priesthood.

Since no measure can become church law unless bishops and deputies agree, the outcome is almost certain to be a stand-off between advocates of change and defenders of tradition.

'Appreciation' of Gay People

The bishops' cautious approach to the issue of sexual orientation had been anticipated by Edgar K. Byham, national president of Integrity, an Episcopal support group for homosexuals, who nonetheless said he was "generally pleased" with the convention. Traditionalists, he said, had been "completely unsuccessful" in winning American endorsement of the Church of England's strong condemnation of homosexual acts. "Nothing negative has passed," he said. "There's no place where there's dialogue that there hasn't been greater appreciation of lesbians and gay men in the church."

Bishop Edmond L. Browning, the presiding bishop of the Episcopal Church, led an emotionally charged prayer service at which the names of people who have died of AIDS were read aloud. He spoke of his personal pastoral relationship with a person suffering from the deadly disease, and he challenged all the bishops to "personalize this ministry of compassion" by linking themselves with at least one such person.

Sexuality Guide Is Discarded

Conservatives were also heartened by some of the convention's actions on sexual issues. For instance, the bishops decided to scrap a guide on human sexuality developed by Episcopal educators for parishes and schools.

The study guide, "Sexuality: A Divine Gift," had encountered sharp criticism in church circles for lacking attention to Scripture and traditional moral attitudes. and for eliminating conservative materials from its recommended teaching resources. "Dr. Ruth in clerical disguise," Bishop William Frey of Colorado called it.

* * *

September 28, 1989

CATHOLICS MEET ON GAY ROLE IN CLERGY

By ARI L. GOLDMAN
Special to The New York Times

GARRISON, N.Y., Sept. 27—More than 100 people from Roman Catholic institutions in the New York area gathered here today to discuss a subject rarely talked about openly—homosexuality among priests, nuns and religious brothers.

More than 100 people from Roman Catholic institutions in the New York area gathered here today to discuss a subject rarely talked about openly—homosexuality among priests, nuns and religious brothers.

An organizer of the one-day conference titled "Our Lesbian and Gay Religious and Clergy" likened the church to parents coming to terms with a child's homosexuality.

"We in the church also need a coming out," said the organizer, Sister Jeannine Gramick, a School Sister of Notre Dame from Baltimore. "Just as parents say, 'I have a gay son and I'm proud of him,' so must the church declare that it is proud of its gay sons and lesbian daughters."

The conference here, convened by an ad hoc committee of Catholics who minister to homosexuals, was careful to make the distinction between those in religious life who are sexually active and those who are not.

True to Vows of Celibacy

For example, a priest, a nun and a brother who made up one panel all said that they were homosexual but remained true to their vows of celibacy.

David Berceli, a 35-year-old Maryknoll brother from Ossining, N.Y., said it was important for him to identify as a homosexual because "that is how I encounter the whole world, as a sexual being."

He drew a distinction between sexuality and sex, saying that sexuality could express itself in tenderness or in an esthetic sensibility, while sex was the biological function of the genitals.

Like the other panel members, Brother David said his sexuality was closely tied to his spiritual relationship with God.

'To Dismember Myself'

Sister Mary Louise St. John, 46, a Benedictine sister from Erie, Pa., said, "To alienate my lesbian identity from the identity of the Godness within me would be to dismember myself."

The third member of the panel, the Rev. Richard Cardarelli, 38, a Capucin friar from Middletown, Conn., told of his struggle to reconcile his homosexuality and his love for God. It was a journey, he said, that took him from shame, to trying to find solace in alcohol, to a suicide attempt and finally to a belief that he could express both parts of himself. "I am proud and grateful to be a priest and a gay man," he said. He wore a hooded brown robe adorned with a wooden cross.

The audience was largely made up of Catholic educators and administrators who work with priests, nuns and brothers. Several religious orders were represented, some by nuns who wore the traditional veil. Also attending were the Vicars for Religious from the Archdiocese of New York, the Diocese of Brooklyn and the Diocese of Rockville Centre on Long Island. The vicars work as liaisons between the clergy and the local bishop.

None of the bishops attended or sent personal representatives. But the organization that speaks for the nation's Catholic bishops, the National Conference of Catholic Bishops, has recently convened private meetings on sexuality in the ministry.

Vows of Celibacy Ignored

The bishops are concerned both with those who identify themselves as celibate homosexuals and those who are sexually active, either as heterosexuals or homosexuals.

The conference here did not deal directly with the issue of sexually active clergy. But church experts and psychologists say there is growing evidence that vows of celibacy are often ignored. One psychologist, Eugene Kennedy of Loyola University, said in an interview that such evidence was more "anecdotal and confessional" than statistical.

The keynote speaker at the conference—held on the grounds of Graymoor, a Catholic retreat center in Putnam County—was John Boswell, a professor of history at Yale and the author of "Christianity, Social Tolerance and Homosexuality."

Dr. Boswell argued that there has always been a disproportionately large number of homosexuals entering the ranks of the Catholic clergy.

A Refuge From Marriage

Dr. Boswell also argued that the church was far more tolerant of homosexuality in the past than it is today. "Prior to the 13th century, homosexuality was not viewed negatively by the church," he said.

The convent and monastery, he said, offered homosexuals a refuge from marriage, the only other option open to men and women in medieval times.

Some of the "greatest love letters" that remain from the medieval period, Dr. Boswell said, were written from one "lovesick" nun to another.

"What gay people have given religious life is incalculable—2,000 years of cheerful service," he said.

* * *

November 19, 1989

QUAKERS LEAD WAY IN SAME-SEX MARRIAGE

To the Editor:

Your article on same-sex marriage (Ideas & Trends: "Small Steps Toward Acceptance Renew Debate on Gay Marriage," Week in Review, Nov. 5) states, "A few religious groups are already starting to recognize same-sex partnerships." You note that an Episcopalian ministry in Hoboken will soon perform ceremonies blessing couples of the same sex.

You overlook the Religious Society of Friends, also known as Quakers. Several Quaker meetings have married gay and lesbian Quakers, and many other meetings have passed minutes affirming their willingness to do so. The meeting I attend agreed to marry gay and lesbian Quakers almost two years ago.

Quakers have often appeared at the forefront of social change in the United States. Just as Quakers abolished slavery within their communities long before the Emancipation Proclamation, so have many Quaker meetings recognized gay and lesbian marriage in advance of our nation's courts. Let us hope that this time, history will not fall so far behind its conscience.

JOHN GASTIL
Madison, Wis., Nov. 5, 1989

* * *

July 18, 1992

VATICAN CONDONES GAY-RIGHTS LIMITS

By PETER STEINFELS

A Vatican office has urged Roman Catholic bishops in the United States to scrutinize laws intended to protect homosexuals and to oppose them if they promote public acceptance of homosexual conduct.

"There are areas in which it is not unjust discrimination to take sexual orientation into account," the Vatican's Congregation for the Doctrine of the Faith, which enforces matters of doctrine for the church, said in a statement sent last month to American bishops. It specified adoptions, placement of children in foster care, military service and employment of teachers and athletic coaches.

The statement was given to news organizations this week by New Ways Ministry, a Catholic gay-rights group with headquarters in Mount Rainier, Md., and was first reported by The Washington Post yesterday. The ministry called the statement an "embarrassment" and "evidence of a growing and serious gap between the Vatican" and American Catholics.

The Vatican has long opposed homosexual conduct but not homosexual orientation, and has condemned acts of bias or hate against individual homosexuals. Half of last month's 2,500-word statement simply quoted a document that the same office had issued in 1986.

Unusually Detailed

But the statement's focus on specific legislation was unusual.

"Previous documents have brought up the question of legislation," said Archbishop Rembert G. Weakland of Milwaukee, a prominent leader of the church's liberal wing, "but this is the first time I have seen anything so detailed."

Vatican statements normally prescribe general moral principles and leave their legal applications to the local bishops.

Considerable puzzlement seemed to surround the statement. The National Conference of Catholic Bishops was directing inquiries about the statement directly to the Vatican, said William Ryan, Deputy Director of conference's media office.

Mr. Ryan said that conference officials were not even sure whether the statement had been sent to bishops outside the United States. While the statement briefly mentioned Italian housing policies, many of its references seemed to fit American issues closely. John Gallagher, a theological consultant at New Ways Ministry, suggested that the statement might have been drafted in the United States and issued by the Vatican office.

Papal Involvement Uncertain

Archbishop Weakland noted that the statement carried no signature and that there was no indication that it had been seen by the Pope. He said the ultimate concern of the Vatican seemed to be the possibility that "domestic partnership" laws assuring health benefits and other protections for homosexual couples would establish such relationships as the equivalent of traditional marriages.

The American bishops have taken a variety of stances toward statutes barring discrimination on grounds of sexual orientation.

Last year, for example, the bishops in Connecticut dropped their longstanding opposition to homosexual-rights legislation after it was rewritten to confine itself to employment, housing and public accommodations, and to permit adoption officials to consider an applicant's sexual orientation.

* * *

February 28, 1993

BETRAYED BY THEIR PROTECTORS

By JAY P. DOLAN

LEAD US NOT INTO TEMPTATION: Catholic Priests and the Sexual Abuse of Children
By Jason Berry
407 pp. New York: Doubleday. $22.50.

Scarcely a week goes by without a news article reporting the sexual abuse of children, all too often by Roman Catholic priests. According to Jason Berry in "Lead Us Not Into Temptation," in the last decade approximately 400 priests and brothers were reported to church or civil authorities for molesting children, and the number of cases is probably much higher.

Such behavior has diminished the stature of the priesthood and has undermined the moral authority of the clergy. But that is only part of the story. Less well known but perhaps more shocking is the apparently determined effort of church officials to cover up such crimes and protect clerical pedophiles. Mr. Berry maintains that "the crisis in the Catholic Church lies not with the fraction of priests who molest youngsters but in an ecclesiastical power structure that harbors pedophiles, conceals other sexual behavior patterns among its clerics, and uses strategies of duplicity and counterattack against the victims."

"Lead Us Not Into Temptation" investigates recent child molestation by members of the Catholic clergy in the United States and Canada. Mr. Berry, a freelance writer in New Orleans, is the journalist most responsible for publicizing what is clearly the worst scandal in the history of the American Catholic Church. He began his investigation in 1985 in the small Cajun parish of St. John in Louisiana. What he thought was an isolated and unusual case turned out not to be extraordinary.

In the next seven years, he discovered numerous examples of the sexual abuse of children by priests in New York, Minneapolis-St. Paul, Chicago, Cleveland, Pittsburgh, Honolulu, Seattle and elsewhere, reported in the press and in court records. Just about every Catholic diocese in the United States has experienced the shock of such incidents.

The first part of Mr. Berry's book, rightly labeled "Anatomy of a Cover-Up," is an overly detailed account of the Louisiana cases involving a priest, Gilbert Gauthe, and a number of young boys in his vicinity. In June 1984, six families agreed to a $4.2 million civil damage settlement for harm done to nine boys. One family, the Gastals, pressed for a jury trial. They were awarded $1 million for the boy and $250,000 for the parents, and on appeal accepted $1,000,020. The story moves from the bayou to the courtrooms to a series of meetings at the Vatican Embassy in Washington, where high-ranking church officials discussed the implications of the spreading scandal.

Mr. Berry has great sympathy for the child victims and the priest, but not for the church officials, who, he says, attempted to cover up the incidents. The magnitude of the problem clearly paralyzed the officials, and not knowing how to respond, he writes, they "erected a wall of silence, offering scant explanation to the faithful."

"In so doing, the bishop and the vicar general engaged in a cover-up," he continues. "However, it was an anachronistic one, a sort of monarchical attempt at spin control in an impatient, democratic world."

Mr. Berry's subsequent investigation of clerical pedophilia uncovers a consistent pattern. First, the parents of the abused child, generally a young boy, notify church officials of what has happened.

Then stonewalling by church officials begins. The parents become impatient and disillusioned; they threaten legal action; the church's lawyer takes over, and the parents and the victim now become "the enemy."

The church attempts damage control; silence, secrecy and threats of countersuits ensue; judges seal court documents and prosecutors refuse to prosecute (notably in Chicago and New Orleans). The reason seems clear: to protect the church from bad publicity. In most cases, the lawyers arrange an out-of-court settlement for substantial sums of money for therapy for the abused children. (Mr. Berry cites one accounting that as of 1992 the church and its insurance companies have paid out $500 million in settlements and fees to sexual-abuse victims and their families.) While all of this is going on, the accused priest is generally sent off to an institution for therapy. After treatment he is assigned to a new parish.

According to experts, the success rate of most therapy is "disappointing . . . not more than one in three." Thus the stage is set for another case. Meanwhile, the victim, seemingly forgotten in the legal tug-of-war, struggles to cope with the scars of the traumatic experience.

In an age of Watergate, Irangate, B.C.C.I. and other Government cover-ups, such stories have become too common. But people expect more from religious leaders, who preach a message of truth and justice, compassion and understanding. The action taken by the Archdiocese of Chicago last September, establishing a review board comprising six lay members and three priests, to respond to cases of clerical sexual misconduct with minors, suggests that the hierarchy is finally learning how to deal more humanely and honestly with the victims and their families. Time will tell.

Mr. Berry's analysis of the reasons so many Catholic priests are pedophiles is not as satisfying as his reporting of the cases and the subsequent cover-ups. One reason is that there is no shared agreement among experts about the causes of pedophilia. Mr. Berry explores several arguments but rather tentatively, briefly examining the nature-versus-nurture debate and the vow of celibacy, although, he acknowledges, "most cases of child sexual abuse occur within the home."

Another reason, he suggests, is the gay culture that permeated Catholic seminaries in the 1970's and 80's. His reporting of "the new gay clericalism" in San Diego is especially shocking, detailing promiscuous behavior. Though there is evidence that homosexual men are not especially likely to be child molesters, Mr. Berry suggests that the increase in the number of gay seminarians and priests has fostered an environment among the clergy that is too tolerant of sexual abuse of children.

Any explanation of pedophilia among the Catholic clergy must take into account the church's sexual ethic. Vatican pronouncements manifest an unreasonable fear of homosexuals; Mr. Berry cites the estimate of A. W. Richard Sipe, a former priest and the author of "A Secret World: Sexuality and the Search for Celibacy," that 20 percent of the member of the American Catholic clergy are gay. The Catholic theology of marriage is focused on procreation, and this is reflected in the obsessive preoccupation of the hierarchy with upholding the condemnation of artificial birth control.

These and other positions indicate that the Catholic sexual ethic is seriously flawed. In addition, candidates for the priesthood are not adequately educated about sexuality and are unable to integrate their sexuality with their priesthood. For years the clergy have used the church's sexual teaching as a means of political power in an effort to control the private behavior of the people in the pews. The nationwide problem of clerical pedophilia, however, has undermined the moral authority of the clergy. As a result, American Catholics are now more inclined to turn a deaf ear to the clergy's pronouncements on sexual morality.

Jay P. Dolan is director of the Cushwa Center for the Study of American Catholicism at the University of Notre Dame and the author of "The American Catholic Experience: A History From Colonial Times to the Present."

* * *

June 11, 1994

A STUDY OF MEDIEVAL RITUALS IN SAME-SEX UNIONS RAISES A QUESTION: WHAT WERE THEY SOLEMNIZING?

By PETER STEINFELS

If these words, taken from a manuscript preserved in the Vatican and dating from the year 1147, were for a bride and bridegroom, no one would find them startling:

"Send down, most kind Lord, the grace of Thy Holy Spirit upon these Thy servants, whom Thou hast found worthy to be united not by nature but by faith and a holy spirit. Grant unto them Thy grace to love each other in joy without injury or hatred all the days of their lives."

That prayer, however, is part of a ritual joining two men in some kind of a solemn, personal, affectionate relationship, a ritual that, according to John Boswell, the A. Whitney Griswold Professor of History at Yale, "functioned in the past as a 'gay marriage ceremony.'"

Amid the debate about whether Christianity should bless unions between homosexuals, Professor Boswell contends that it already has.

Scouring collections of medieval manuscripts from Paris to St. Petersburg and from the Vatican to the monastery of St.

Catherine on Mount Sinai, he has turned up more than 60 texts, dating from the 8th to the 16th centuries, of Christian ceremonies for what has been variously translated as "spiritual brotherhood," "adoptive brotherhood" or what Dr. Boswell believes to be a more neutral term, "same-sex union."

Unlike the distinctly masculine and feminine references used for heterosexual marriages, the language of these ceremonies, which prominently invoke pairs of male saints, indicates that both parties are male.

The book in which he makes his case, "Same-Sex Unions in Premodern Europe," is only now being sent to bookstores by its publisher, Villard Books. But his thesis has been made public by Doonesbury. This week the comic strip's gay character, Mark, informed a fundamentalist Christian married man whom he had tried to pick up that a Yale professor had written a book saying that "for 1,000 years the church sanctioned rituals for homosexual marriages."

The reader who prefers the book to the comic strip version will discover a picture that is both more fascinating and more puzzling. There is no question that Professor Boswell has found records of ceremonies consecrating a pairing of men, ceremonies often marked by similar prayers and, over time, by standardized symbolic gestures: the clasping of hands, the binding of hands with a stole, kisses, receiving holy communion, a feast after the ceremony. Some of these ritual actions also marked heterosexual marriages, but there remained differences in both actions and words between the two ceremonies.

Professor Boswell's book will certainly provoke a sharp debate about what these same-sex ceremonies were solemnizing. From the spread of Christianity through the ancient world to the late Middle Ages, different Christian cultures stretching from Syria to Ireland featured a variety of social bonds not even vaguely paralleled in modern society.

Was this ritual, for example, a form of fraternal adoption, or something resembling blood brotherhood? Was it a commemoration of undying friendship or a strictly spiritual bonding? To what extent, in short, was it the equivalent of heterosexual marriage, either in the contemporary sense or in medieval ones?

In the book's introduction and a chapter on the vocabulary of love and marriage in ancient and medieval times, Dr. Boswell opens the eyes of anyone who thinks it simple for scholars today to decode terms that arose in very different contexts, when marriages between men and women—at least at their beginning—were matters more of family alliance, property and offspring than of romantic love.

He whittles away at all the alternative translations and interpretations of these ceremonies that would preclude a romantic and erotic dimension to the unions being celebrated. His book is an imposing achievement, with texts in Greek, Latin, Old Church Slavonic, Hebrew and Arabic.

Ultimately, however, there is a problem. As Ralph Hexter, a professor of the classics and comparative literature at the University of Colorado, put it, "We don't know what they did in bed."

What they did in bed, however, is a central issue if Dr. Boswell's findings are going to play a part in the debate over recognizing same-sex unions legally or religiously. One suspects that his book would get a very different reception if instead of suggesting that these same-sex unions tacitly were accommodating homosexual relations, he had argued that they were meant to be strictly free of any sexual acts, no matter how profound the emotional attachment of the participants, or whether that strict chastity was sometimes abandoned behind the screen of a "spiritual brotherhood."

Professor Boswell is right in warning that moral or visceral objections to homosexuality may create a tremendous resistance to any interpretations of these unions as condoning explicitly sexual behavior. It is also true that the commitments of those who advocate gay rights, who include Dr. Boswell, may create a readiness to accept those interpretations.

Had those commitments biased Dr. Boswell's 1980 book, "Christianity, Social Tolerance and Homosexuality" (University of Chicago Press), which maintained that Christianity was not originally or inherently hostile to homosexuality? That volume is treated as a definitive text by many people demanding changes in social and religious attitudes toward homosexuality. Among scholars, it is hard even to get agreement about how the book was received in their own ranks.

The mainstream of medievalists and church historians was approving, said Professor Hexter, a longtime friend of and intellectual collaborator with Professor Boswell, who is seriously ill and not available to be interviewed. But James Brundage, a professor of history and law at the University of Kansas, said the response was "interested but skeptical, very skeptical."

Professor Brundage, the author of "Law, Sex and Christian Society in Medieval Europe" (University of Chicago Press), said, "The mainstream reaction was that he raised some interesting questions, but hadn't proved his case."

Will the book be examined with the seriousness with which it was written? Not only do skeptics about Professor Boswell's thesis worry, but so does Professor Hexter. "There's going to be a flurry of reports, and people who will never read the book will repeat that it claims there were gay marriages," he said. "Others will reply, 'Not so,' and simply reject the whole argument."

"Professor Boswell's book will certainly provoke a sharp debate about what these same-sex ceremonies were solemnizing. From the spread of Christianity through the ancient world to the late Middle Ages, different Christian cultures stretching from Syria to Ireland featured a variety of social bonds not even vaguely paralleled in modern society.

"Was this ritual, for example, a form of fraternal adoption, or something resembling blood brotherhood? Was it a commemoration of undying friendship or a strictly spiritual bonding? To what extent, in short, was it the equivalent of heterosexual marriage, either in the contemporary sense or in medieval ones?"

* * *

GOVERNMENTAL INACTION

May 26, 1977

9 KILLED BY FIRE AT A WEST SIDE BATHHOUSE

By CAREY WINFREY

Nine men were killed and 10 were injured yesterday in an early-morning fire that destroyed a Manhattan bathhouse that catered to homosexuals.

Fire officials feared that more bodies would be found in the rubble, and Commissioner John T. O'Hagan said the search for bodies could go on for a week.

Scores of men, some clad only in towels or robes, fled their rented cubicles and the dormitory at the Everard Baths at 28 West 28th Street, in the wholesale flower district, as dense smoke poured out of the three-story building. By the time the fire was brought under control at 8:45 A.M., an hour and three-quarters after it started, nearly 200 firemen and 31 pieces of equipment had been called to fight the blaze. Six patrons jumped from a second-floor ledge to the pavement, and 20 were rescued with aerial ladders from the third-floor windows facing 28th Street.

Commissioner O'Hagan said that an inspection last August resulted in an order for a sprinkler system to be installed at the baths, but that the owner had until July of this year to comply. "In all probability," the Commissioner said, "a sprinkler system would have prevented this fire."

The fire was the second at the Everard in five years.

Irving Fine, 62 years old, who said he was the owner, said a sprinkler system had been installed but was not yet working. However, a spokesman for the Mayor's office said plans for a sprinkler system were rejected by the Buildings Department in January for noncompliance with codes.

Even before the fire was brought under control, homosexuals across the city rallied to give blood, help in the identification of victims and raise funds. Many expressed concern that the inevitable publicity in the wake of the fire would force a crackdown on the homosexual world in general, while others said they hoped that fire violations in similar establishments would now be corrected.

Mayor Sees a Violation

At a late-afternoon news conference on the steps of Gracie Mansion, Mayor Beame said he had asked the District Attorney "to investigate why a bathhouse would have overnight guests—this is in violation of their operating permit."

One of the survivors said the city allowed hazardous conditions to exist where homosexuals congregated.

" 'Faggots' are given a certain amount of liberty in New York City," said Michael Rhone, 26, "and most of that is to hang out in sleazy sorts of low places that are substandard. At a straight health spa you wouldn't have rooms partitioned halfway up the walls so the fire could spread."

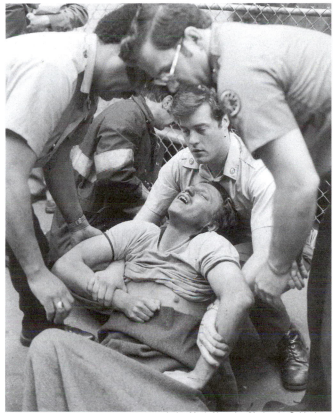

Action Movie News Inc./Kosinenke Goldenberg

A victim of the fire being aided by rescue workers outside the bathhouse.

The blaze recalled a 1973 fire in a French Quarter bar in New Orleans in which 30 persons died. That fire, in a second-floor bar called the Upstairs, which also catered to male homosexuals, was packed the evening of June 24, 1973, when flames cut off escape by both the stairs and the elevator. Although arson was widely suspected, New Orleans homosexual organizations contended that the investigation was not effectively pursued.

Bath places catering to male homosexuals, while not new, have proliferated throughout New York City over the last dozen or so years. Patrons watch television, swim, sit in sauna rooms, or "cruise" for sexual liaisons. The standard attire is a towel. Though there is a 12-hour time limit, many patrons sleep overnight, in the large dormitory room or in the cubicles, which at the Everard were barely large enough to hold a single bed.

Because many patrons signed in under false names, identification of the dead was expected to prove difficult. At the morgue, Dr. Dominick J. DiMaio, the city's Chief Medical Examiner, said none of the dead had been identified.

Officials said they believed that the four-alarm fire, which broke out shortly before 7 A.M. and tied up rush-hour traffic, started when a mattress fire, thought to have been extinguished an hour earlier, re-ignited. Many empty fire-extinguishers inside the building indicated that

Fireman aboard rescue ladder moving into position to fight fire at bathhouse at 28 West 28th Street yesterday.

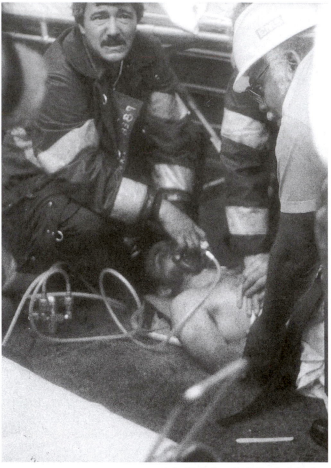

Action Movie News Inc./Kosinenke Goldenberg

A victim of the bathhouse fire being given oxygen by one fireman and a cardiac massage by another outside the building at 28 West 28th Street.

the occupants had tried to fight the blaze for some time before calling the Fire Department.

Mr. Fine estimated there had been 80 to 100 men in the bathhouse when the fire broke out. "Tuesday night was always a good night in this place," said Jeffrey Sanyour, who had come to meet a friend. "Like a bar gets known for a certain night—this place was known for Tuesdays and Thursdays."

Raymond Walsh, 20, who had paid a $7 fee for one of the 135 tiny cubicles, said he was awakened by the heat and saw an orange glow under his door. "I opened the door," he said, "and saw the room across the hall all in flames, even the wall. I started to panic and ran into the 'orgy room'—the dorm room—and yelled to everybody to wake up. I don't even know how I got down the stairs."

Michael James, 29, of Philadelphia was on the second floor when he noticed the flames. "I just saw some orange," he said. "You couldn't smell anything. Then in a matter of seconds the halls were filled with a dense smoke, the electricity went out and it was pitch dark. All you could hear was people hollering, 'This way down, this way down!' "

Miguel Agosto, 18, was trapped on the third floor, but escaped through a bathroom window. "I grabbed a bar outside the bathroom window and swung to the other roof," he said. Mr. Agosto was one of four patrons treated at Bellevue Hospital for smoke inhalation. Three others were admitted to the emergency ward, two in critical condition, one in serious condition.

Two Firemen Treated

Fireman Patrick Brown, 24, was treated at Bellevue for exhaustion. He had administered mouth-to-mouth resuscitation to unconscious victims for more than an hour. "I know two of them died," he said.

Fireman Thomas Dyer was treated for smoke inhalation.

Many of the fatalities were believed to have occurred when the roof collapsed in the rear part of the building. A fireman who tried to reach that area said the smoke was simply too intense. "I had my nose to the floor as it was. If you can't breathe, you can't move."

The fire was the second at the Everard in five years. A two-alarm fire gutted the top floor and destroyed much of the roof on March, 1972, but there were no injuries. "It was always a rat trap," said Walter LeBeau, a patron who escaped unscathed yesterday.

Built in 1890 by James Everard, an Irish brewer, the Romanesque structure enjoyed great success as a public bathhouse in the red-light and gambling district known at the turn of the century as the Tenderloin. It had catered mainly to a homosexual clientele since the 1950's. An explicitly sexual newspaper described the Everard as "well-kept and reasonably clean, attracting a kinky cross-sectional clientele from every age group."

Mr. Rhone, one of the survivors, said that customers, who paid $5 for a locker or $7 for a cubicle ($6 and $9.25 on weekends) included "your old men, young gorgeous men, your models and your successful businessmen."

Stretching the License

The building was last licensed in 1921, according to Commissioner O'Hagan, when a certificate of occupancy was issued for a facility with a "pool, baths and dormitory." While Mr. O'Hagan stopped short of calling the owner in violation of that license, he said that with 135 cubicles, "obviously he was stretching it a bit."

As the eighth body was carried out at 10:40 A.M., the scene outside the baths was one of water hoses snaked through the street littered with broken glass. The doors leading to marble stairs in the bathhouse were open, and a sign reading "Everard Baths—Men Only" was visible.

The only windows still unbroken were those on the first floor, including an ornate intertwined "EB" in a stained glass.

The last occupant to emerge alive was a cat, carried out at 11:55 A.M. by a fire marshal.

A fireman who asked not to be identified said three of the bodies were burned beyond recognition. "You couldn't even tell they were bodies," he said.

"Eight is a lot," he added. "But the way they were packed in there, it could have been a lot worse."

* * *

May 27, 1977

9 KILLED IN BATH FIRE IDENTIFIED BY FRIENDS

Morgenthau Planning Investigation Into Whether Violations of Code Might Have Led to the Blaze

By LAURIE JOHNSTON

The nine known dead in the Everard Baths fire were identified yesterday, mostly by friends rather than family members, as District Attorney Robert M. Morgenthau of Manhattan announced an investigation as to whether criminal violations of the fire and building codes might have caused the blaze Wednesday.

According to a Fire Department spokesman, rescue efforts were slowed by the small, round front windows on the third floor and by paneling and insulation that covered all windows.

Seven of the nine persons injured in the fire at the homosexual bathhouse, at 28 West 28th Street, remained hospitalized, one in critical condition. Fire officials said other bodies might be found in the rubble.

The early morning fire sent 80 to 100 men fleeing from the building, some clad only in towels. Further search of the partially collapsed ruins awaited the removal of suspended wreckage by a crane.

Patrons and former patrons of the Everard Baths said yesterday that its practice of not requiring registration made it impossible to tell whether all customers present had been accounted for.

Inspections at Issue

Amid charges by homosexual-community leaders that the city "looks the other way in protecting the safety of gays," the investigation was expected to center on whether the Everhard Baths had been improperly inspected or approved in view of their use.

The certificate of occupancy issued in 1921, when the Everhard retained some of its fashionable clientele as a Turkish bath, described it as a "bathhouse and dormitories." Since then, most of the second and third floors have been divided into cubicles, with scarcely room for a bed and coat hangers, and with plywood partitions part way to the ceiling.

Irving E. Minkin, director of operations for the Buildings Department, said yesterday that the baths had passed inspection after a fire in March 1972 made renovation necessary. But he said he could only refer to plans filed with the department.

"We had no idea of cubicles there—there was no indication to us of any use other than stated in the certificate of occupancy," Mr. Minkin said. "The question of cubicles is 'iffy'—they would not change the basic legal use but might give us cause for concern."

Crowds of spectators opposite the burned-out building yesterday could see the partially detached pipes of an overhead sprinkler system, which was installed in response to a July 1977 deadline set by the Fire Department, but which had not been connected to the street main.

Sprinkler Order Rescinded

A 1964 Fire Department order to install sprinklers was rescinded in 1965, after the owners "provided certain safety items," said the first deputy fire commissioner, Stephen J. Murphy. There was no order to install sprinklers following the 1972 fire and renovation. However, in keeping with new fire regulations, the installation was ordered again last year.

A widespread rumor, said to be "gay-community lore," that the Everard Baths were owned by either the Police Benevolent Association or the Police Athletic League, drew denials, including one from Mr. Morgenthau, who said "that it's not owned by the Police Athletic League, because I'm the president of the P.A.L."

Of the nine men who died in the fire, seven succumbed to smoke inhalation, one to respiratory burns and one—who jumped from an upper floor—to a fractured spine.

They were identified by the Medical Examiner's office as Amado Alamo, 17 years old, West 108th Street; Kenneth Hill, 38, West 4th Street; Ira Landau, 32, West 75th Street, and James Stuard, 30, East 25th Street, all of Manhattan; Anthony Calarco, about 25, 1519 Mace Avenue, the Bronx; Patrick Knott, 27, Bay Parkway, Brooklyn; Hillman Wesley Adams, 40, Scotch Plains, N.J., and Brian Duffy and Nicholas Smith, no addresses given.

One patron who jumped, Philip Osbaum, 50, was listed in critical condition at Bellevue Hospital with a fractured trachea and fractured ribs. Others there, listed as satisfactory, are Kevin Duffley, 33; Luis Figueroa, 22, and John Stanisz, 22, inhalation and multiple minor injuries, all of Manhattan; Alexander Mamon, 28, Jamaica, Queens, and Earl Hunt, 39, Long Island City, Queens, inhalation and fractured ankle.

Thomas Dyer, a fireman, remained at Bellevue Hospital suffering from smoke inhalation.

* * *

SCHOOLS AND ACADEMIC INSTITUTIONS

December 15, 1971

CAMPUS HOMOSEXUALS ORGANIZE TO WIN COMMUNITY ACCEPTANCE

By ROBERT REINHOLD

In defiance of taboos that have prevailed for generations, thousands of college students are proclaiming their homosexuality and openly organizing "gay" groups on large and small campuses across the country.

No one knows exactly how many are involved, but in growing numbers they are forming cohesive campus organizations for educational, social and political purposes, often with official sanction and with remarkable acceptance from fellow students. However, a number of psychiatrists and psychologists are somewhat uneasy about the ready availability of homosexual social activities in the presence of impressionable adolescents whose sexual identities are not fully crystallized.

By organizing, the gay students hope to build a sense of community among gay young men and women and to disabuse their heterosexual classmates and the outside community of what they feel are damaging myths about homosexuality.

From conversations with officials and homosexual students on half a dozen college campuses from Boston to Los Angeles, as well as reports from campus correspondents at 15 other schools, it would appear that the gay students have made substantial strides in changing attitudes.

To do so, they hold dances and parties, run gay lounges and offices on campus, operate telephone "hot-lines" for emergency problems and counseling services, publish newsletters, and provide speakers to address fraternity, dormitory and faculty groups.

They will, for example, provide advice and comfort over the phone to a student troubled by his attraction to his roommate. In regular meetings the students engage in discussions on such topics as the church and the homosexual and plan tactics for the repeal of sodomy laws. And in their parties they seek to provide, quite candidly, the kind of relaxed setting for "dating" and sexual contact that heterosexual students enjoy.

For the most part they are indistinguishable in appearance from their "straight" classmates. But such is their new presence that the National Student Center Association recently opened a division called the National Gay Student Center. And yesterday at Queens College in New York, more than 100 college psychologists and counselors from 30 colleges gathered to meet with gay students and discuss the delicate problems of dealing with young people who are troubled by their homosexuality.

Negligence Discerned

The counselors were told by Dr. Ralph Blair, director of the Homosexual Community Counseling Center in New York, that a national survey of deans, college counseling directors and homosexual students indicated that the schools' attitude toward their homosexual students constituted "the greatest single example of negligence" in their profession.

It was an assertion that was largely confirmed in the interviews with homosexual students.

Typical, perhaps, of the new breed is Larry, an easy-going youth with medium-length brown hair and clean-cut good looks. He was once an officer of the Interfraternity Council at the University of Southern California, where he was selected as one of the "outstanding seniors" last June for his leadership and academic abilities.

But shortly before graduation he announced to his friends, professors and family that he was a homosexual. And he began to organize the Gay Liberation Forum, a group of 30 or so homosexuals on the Los Angeles campus who will soon bring suit against the university's trustee in an attempt to gain recognition.

'Terrifying' Isolation

In organizing, Larry, now a 23-year-old graduate student, would like to save others from the eight months of "terrifying" isolation he went through as a junior when he first realized his homosexuality.

"I was isolated and I was upset—because I was looking at my own gayness through heterosexual eyes," he recalled the other day in an interview in the living room of the large, well-furnished Los Angeles apartment he shares with his lover, a U.C.L.A. student.

"I wanted to change it, but I didn't feel I could tell anybody—and the school really offered no counseling. But when I began reading on the subject I realized that there were millions of men and women who were gay and were indistinguishable—and that it was not a sickness."

"We have to reach the general student and explode the myths," he went on, "and we have to reach the gays in a supportive way. We are cut off from our church, family, jobs, our friends, not because we are gay but because of society's attitude toward gays."

As college organizations, the gay groups feel they have a special function in cushioning the young homosexual from the often agonizing experience of "coming out," the emotionally wrenching period during which he recognizes his sexuality and makes tentative contact with other homosexuals. By providing a "positive" atmosphere for social contacts, they seek to provide an alternative to the harsh noisy "gay bars" where contacts are usually superficial and sex-oriented.

While the colleges have generally maintained a hands-off attitude toward the groups, some officials harbor worries.

While sympathetic with the plight of homosexuals, Dr. Benson R. Snyder, a psychiatrist who is a dean at the Massachusetts Institute of Technology said he was worried about 18-year-olds "who are uncertain about their identities getting caught in an exploitative situation."

But others disagree. Dr. Robert Liebert, a psychiatrist at Columbia University, argues that "there is simply no basis for believing that an individual who is on the path of developing a reasonably fulfilling heterosexual life prior to the emergence of the Gay Liberation Movement will be moved from the course because of a gay lounge and militant gay movement on campus."

Official Recognition

Whatever the case, gay groups have found little difficulty in achieving recognition as official campus organizations at such diverse schools as Boston University, Columbia, Cornell, Illinois, Colorado, Stanford, City College and the various University of California campuses. At the University of Minnesota, the leader of the local gay liberation group, Jack Baker, was recently elected president of the student association.

The Student Homophile League at the University of Massachusettt in Amherst, which works out of an office on the balcony of the student union, is getting $835 this year from the student activities fund. It recently attracted about 150 students from central Massachusetts colleges for a Halloween dance on the campus and several men came in drag.

At Columbia University, a group called Gay People at Columbia set up what is believed to be the first gay lounge in a dormitory—over the strenuous objections of the college's dean but with faculty and student support. Last week, two of the students occupied the office of Dean Carl F. Hovde and won an agreement for school furniture for the lounge, located in the basement of Furnald Hall.

Arm Around a Friend

And across the country at U.C.L.A., Don Kilhefner, a former Peace Corpsman who founded a Gay Liberation branch at the university, strolled across the sunny campus one recent Saturday afternoon with his arm around a male friend. They got scarcely a glance from other students.

But at a handful of schools, the homosexuals have encountered official obstacles, mostly from older administrators and trustees. Their organizations have been barred from the University of Texas at Austin, San Jose and Sacramento State Colleges in California, the University of Kansas, Pennsylvania State, the University of Florida at Tallahassee and U.S.C. At San Jose, a California judge ordered the college to accept the group, and lawyers are preparing suits in most of the other cases.

For the most part, the gay groups are not very political, although a few small factions have tried to identify the gay homosexual cause with movements for radical social change. The memberships are predominantly male; at a few institutions, such as Stanford and Colorado, women have formed separate lesbian groups.

150 Groups Reckoned

Steve Werner of the National Gay Student Center in Washington estimates that there are 150 homosexual groups on campuses and says that many more are forming. Still, the organizers agree they are reaching only a small fraction of the homosexuals in college. The Kinsey report of 1948 said that 10 per cent of American men experienced long periods of predominantly homosexual behavior.

At the root of the new movement is an assertion by the gays that, contrary to prevailing medical opinion, homosexuality is not necessarily a mental disorder. For this reason, much of their effort goes into "consciousness raising" among homosexuals to instill a sense of worth. Many of the groups have speakers who visit and "rap" with psychology and sociology classes and with counselors.

"It's difficult going through psychology classes and constantly being told you are sick and less than good," said Benjamin Hemric, a sociology major at C.C.N.Y.

The groups appear to be most successful at schools isolated from large urban areas and where there are few social outlets. Thus, strong gay organizations exist at Cornell, Massachusetts, Rutgers, Maryland and Colorado.

Other Students' Hostility

The students say that their lives on these and other campuses are made difficult not necessarily by official harassment, but the personal hostility and indifference a student may encounter when his roommates or fraternity brothers learn of his homosexuality. The rate of suicide among homosexual students is said to be unusually high.

Even the existence of formal groups has not dispelled the fear. The Stanford Gay Students Union finds almost nobody comes when meetings are held on campus, and a medical student there reports that he was warned by a doctor to be "more discreet" about discussing his homosexuality with others.

In Boston, the Student Homophile League attracts young people from many colleges in the area. Every Friday night, after choir practice clears out, they filter into the basement of an Episcopal church on Beacon Hill to hear lectures, talk, dance, listen to music and drink punch.

"So many kids are sitting in dormitories tonight. They don't know who they are or what they are supposed to do," said one of the leaders the other night. "They know they are gay and they are going through the worst crisis of their lives. Here they can come to a church and affirm their gayness openly."

Among the participants was an affable freshman from Tufts, 18 years old, who said he "just wanted a place to go— I'm really very alienated from most of the gay scene—the campiness, the tackiness."

There was also a boyish-looking M.I.T. junior, a fraternity member, who said he was "not really decided yet" about his sexuality.

To at least some college administrators, the fact that young people must flounder so during such trying periods in their lives is very much a fault of the schools. Dr. William M. Birenbaum, president of the Staten Island Community College, told the Queens College meeting that the colleges owed their homosexual students a full opportunity to learn and grow.

"If the university is embarrassed by this commitment to do what decency says it should do, then it is a sign of our weakness," he said.

* * *

December 21, 1971

PARLEY URGES COLLEGE FACILITIES FOR COUNSELING OF HOMOSEXUALS

By ERIC PACE

College counselors and student homosexuals, in a daylong conference yesterday, called for facilities to provide homosexual undergraduates with more sympathetic, skillful and specialized advice.

The 150 counselors and students heard Dr. Ralph Blair, the meeting's moderator, define the problem in a paper that he read in the faculty cafeteria of Queens College, where the meeting was held.

"Many students," he said, "must cope with homosexuality without assistance from counselors and other student personnel workers and often must contend with the apathy or the hostility of these professionals."

Termed First of Kind

Dr. Blair, the director of the Homosexual Community Counseling Center, said the meeting was the first of its kind in scope and reflected a growing awareness of the problem of campus homosexuality.

No formal decisions were taken or resolutions passed, but many participants spoke in particular of the problems of the isolated, undeclared student homosexual. The speakers agreed that such students should be put in touch with other campus homosexuals, although the possibility was mentioned that a wavering student might thereby have his homosexuality confirmed.

The anguish of many student homosexuals was expressed by a youth who identified himself as Bob Andrews, the 21-year-old chairman of the Student Homophile League at Rutgers University.

Mr. Andrews, a senior majoring in mathematics, said in an emotional interview that student homosexuals were "told they're inferior."

None of the 120 counselors present, who came from two dozen institutions, spoke publicly against taking a permissive approach to college homosexuality.

Prof. Rica Josephs, a counselor at Bronx Community College of the City University of New York, told the gathering that "people should do what they want, want what they do—and enjoy it, as long as it doesn't hurt anybody, including oneself."

Appealing for a more sympathetic counseling of homosexuals, one student, Ellen Barrett of New York University, said: "We're a sizable minority on any campus and like any minority, our needs should be met."

Miss Barrett, a 25-year-old graduate student of medieval history, said the conference had brought awareness to "a lot of people who had never really thought about the problem."

One faculty member noted that if a counselor told a student who thought he might be homosexual to seek the company of other homosexuals, "it could be construed that you're, like, pushing him." He said such encounters arose when the student "comes in and says: 'Hey, I don't know if I'm gay or not. Let's talk about it.'"

But Miss Barrett derided such suggestions, saying, "A gay student has so many negative things thrust on him [that counseling alone] is not going to turn him into an instant homosexual."

Dr. Blair's counseling center is a group undertaking by specialists, clergy and laymen who are supported by fees and donations. Its telephone number is 834-1159.

Joint Sponsorship

The center sponsored the gathering jointly with the National Task Force on Student Personnel Services and Homosexuality, and Queens College. One student participant said homosexuals were deterred from taking their problems to counselors "for fear of the counselors being old and fuddy-duddy."

He urged sympathetic counselors to make their views known so that students would be encouraged to come to see them.

* * *

June 6, 1985

NEW YORK OFFERING PUBLIC SCHOOL GEARED TO HOMOSEXUAL STUDENTS

By LARRY ROHTER

A New York City public school for homosexual high school students has opened in Manhattan.

The school, which began classes in April in a Greenwich Village church, is named the Harvey Milk School, for the homosexual activist and San Francisco city supervisor who was shot to death in 1978. Its organizers said it was the first public school in the United States to be geared specifically to homosexual adolescents and their problems.

The New York City Board of Education is operating the school in conjunction with the Institute for the Protection of Lesbian and Gay Youth. Dr. A. Damien Martin, the institute's executive director, described the organization as a homosexual advocacy and counseling group financed in part by the city and the state of New York.

At present, 20 students—14 boys and 6 girls ranging in age from 14 to 19—are enrolled in the school. All of them say they are homosexuals who have had difficulty "fitting in at conventional high schools" because of their sexual identity and had dropped out of school, said Steve Ashkinazy, director of clinical programs for the institute.

"For the most part, the males are overtly effeminate, some are transvestites, and the girls are all tough," said Fred

Goldhaber, a teacher at the school. "All of them would be targets for abuse in regular schools."

Plans for Expansion

Since its Board of Education financing began on April 1, the school has been holding classes in the Washington Square United Methodist Church, at 135 West Fourth Street. But the school's backers say they hope soon to expand both the student body and staff and to move the school into a larger space with better facilities, though no procedures for increasing enrollment have yet been established.

"A lot of kids are waiting to get in for the fall," said Mr. Goldhaber, who teaches all five subjects in the school's curriculum and who said he is a homosexual. "These are kids who are serious about getting an education."

The program at the Harvey Milk School was first suggested to Board of Education officials by the institute, which has been counseling homosexual dropouts since November 1983. A board official, Alan Hoffman, said yesterday that his records indicated the original application was "supported by representatives of the Manhattan Borough President, the City Comptroller and the Mayor's office."

Mr. Ashkinazy said there was some initial "nervousness" and "stalling" on the part of the Board of Education because of the controversial nature of the program. But he said Lee Hudson of Mayor Koch's staff and Wayne Steinman, a policy analyst for City Comptroller Harrison J. Goldin, argued in favor of the program and helped smooth its way.

Joseph Mancini, a spokesman for the Board of Education, said yesterday that the program had been approved by the board's professional staff and that a formal board resolution ratifying the action was not necessary. Schools Chancellor Nathan Quinones was unavailable to comment on the program, he said.

Board of Education officials estimate the annual cost of the Harvey Milk School program at about $50,000. They said this included salaries for one teacher, supervisory personnel and curriculum material.

Paying School's Rent

The institute is paying the school's rent, estimated at $500 a month. It also is providing what the program director, Joyce Hunter, called "a whole range of support services," including counseling, some special reading material and transportation.

The institute had a budget of about $168,000 in the 1984-85 fiscal year, according to Dr. Martin. He said the group's funds come from the New York City Youth Bureau and the New York State Division for Youth and from private donations, mostly from homosexuals.

Richard Organisciak, director of offsite education programs for the Board of Education, said the program at the Harvey Milk School had been organized to provide a standard education to homosexual teen-agers "excluded from the mainstream" at their high schools.

"If these kids don't want to go to school anywhere but this one place, what are you supposed to do?" he asked. "The im-portant thing is to get them back into a school, address their problem and get them on the diploma track."

No Recruitment Program

All 20 students in the Harvey Milk program are school dropouts or truants who have been receiving counseling at the institute. Dr. Martin said that the organization has no outreach or recruitment program of its own and that the students had come to the institute on their own initiative.

"When I started working here, I noted that we were dealing with lots of gay kids 15 or 16 years old who had been out of school for a year or more," said Mr. Ashkinazy, who is a certified social worker. "The reason they gave was that when it became known in their schools that they were gay, they were harassed verbally or even beaten up."

When the program proposal was first considered, institute officials said, there was some discussion of setting up a special program for homosexual high school students in an existing high school. But that possibility was quickly rejected.

"We wanted an environment where gay and lesbian kids would not be subject to immature teen-agers," said Mr. Goldhaber, who taught English and remedial reading for 17 years at Wingate High School in Brooklyn before being chosen to teach at the Harvey Milk School. "A gay classroom in a general high school would not be effective protection."

Mr. Goldhaber said, however, that the Harvey Milk program was "not exclusively for gay and lesbian adolescents" but was "also open to anyone else who wants to learn in this environment." In fact, he said, one heterosexual student was briefly enrolled in the program before transferring to another school. "Neither in the school nor here at the institute do we convince the kids to be one way or another," Mr. Goldhaber said.

Counseling Sessions

Nevertheless, one of the aims of the program is to teach the teen-agers, who come from all five boroughs of the city, to be comfortable with their own homosexuality. This is done, Mr. Ashkinazy said, through the classroom curriculum as well as in the after-school counseling sessions that his organization offers the students.

While the curriculum does not contain "gay studies" material, he said, it does make an effort to integrate material likely to be of interest to homosexual students into the regular subject matter.

"In citizenship lessons, the teacher brings up the idea of commitment to each other, and loving and caring," he said. "In literature classes, there would be discussion of Shakespeare as a homosexual, and in history and geography the contributions gay people have made will be brought up."

"They work in a lot on gay issues," said Dr. Emery Hetrick, a homosexual psychiatrist who is a co-founder of the institute. "They really weave it into the curriculum."

* * *

September 2, 1992

LET CIVILITY REIGN IN HOMOSEXUALITY DEBATE; REMOVING THE STIGMA

To the Editor:

Oregon voters will be asked to approve an amendment to their state's Constitution that would remove legal protection for homosexuals and mandate schools to teach that homosexuality is "abnormal, wrong, unnatural and perverse." Colorado has a similar measure.

The Oregon amendment classifies homosexuality as a psychological abnormality. Numerous studies have shown, as the American Psychiatric Association declared in 1973, that homosexuality "implies no impairment in judgment, stability, reliability or general social or vocational capabilities." For this reason the association removed homosexuality from its 1980 Diagnostic Manual; "ego-dystonic homosexuality" was removed from the revised edition in 1987. There is no effort to reinstate it in the manual.

Furthermore, homosexuality has been removed by the World Health Organization from its International Classification of Diseases, to be published in 1993.

The suppression of sexuality, whether by religion, the state or therapists who make unsubstantiated claims to be able to change homosexuals to heterosexuals, does significant damage to the self-esteem of gay men and lesbians. It subverts the capacity to express their sexuality in mutually loving relationships. Hatred and rejection contribute to the high suicide rate of gay and lesbian youth, estimated at 30 percent of all youth suicide by the 1989 report of the Department of Health and Human Services task force on youth suicide.

The European regional office of the W.H.O. stated in 1991: "Unresolved personal attitudes and social conflicts . . . are themselves important contributors to individual health problems. People who hide their sexual orientation for fear of discrimination or alienation have less fulfilling lives, encounter additional stress and are placed in situations that are not conducive to safe sexual practices."

Meanwhile, consensus grows among mental health professionals that homophobia, the irrational fear and hatred of homosexuals, is a psychological abnormality that interferes with the judgment and reliability of those afflicted.

The Oregon amendment proposes that the Department of Higher Education should "assist in setting a standard for Oregon's youth" and discourage "sadism," while at the same time the amendment implicitly encourages these same youths to commit violence against gay men and lesbians.

RICHARD A. ISAY, M.D.
New York, Aug. 17, 1992
The writer is chairman, American Psychiatric Association committee on gay, lesbian and bisexual issues.

* * *

July 4, 1993

GOV. WELD ASKS SCHOOLS TO AID GAY STUDENTS

Special to The New York Times

BOSTON, July 3—In an effort to make Massachusetts high schools safer for homosexual students, Gov. William F. Weld has announced what is believed to be the first statewide effort to train teachers to help those students.

Each school will have the option of adopting the program, which calls for training teachers to prevent violence and harassment against homosexuals and to prevent suicide. Schools are asked to adopt anti-discrimination policies to protect gay students and to form support groups to promote communication between gay and heterosexual students.

"The concept of schools as safe havens must apply to all students, including gay and lesbian students," Governor Weld told a group of teachers and homosexual students in the Arlington Street Church, where he announced his plan on Wednesday.

The recommendations, approved by the state Board of Education in May, were made by the Governor's Commission on Gay and Lesbian Youth. Mr. Weld, a Republican, formed the panel after reading a 1989 Federal report that said nearly a third of all suicides by the young were by homosexuals.

"This is not about a different way of life; it is about life itself," the Governor said. "We can take the first step toward ending gay-youth suicide by creating an atmosphere of dignity and respect for gay youth in our schools."

Harassment Described

Before the Governor spoke, two homosexuals described their experiences in Massachusetts schools.

Troix Bettencourt, 18, hid his homosexuality two years ago at Lowell High School. He was a student leader and he had a girlfriend. He often heard slurs and epithets about homosexuals.

"Maybe they weren't directed at me, but I heard them all around me," he said. "I wanted to be normal."

Stacey Harris, 24, said she had attempted suicide five times. Six years ago, she attended Lexington High School, where her sexual orientation was no secret. "We got comments in the hallway," Ms. Harris recalled. "We had rocks thrown out the windows at our cars."

The chairman of the Governor's commission, David LaFontaine, said: "The approach we're taking in Massachusetts is very different from the one taken in New York City with the Rainbow curriculum. If we had tried to force a particular curriculum on the school system, I think the results would have been disastrous."

The New York program, which ran into strong opposition, would have put a new curriculum into the schools to promote tolerance. The Massachusetts program focuses on training teachers but makes no changes in curriculum.

Range of Reaction

While some objections to the Massachusetts program have been raised, the reactions of advocates for gay rights and of the state Republican Party have been largely favorable.

C. Joseph Doyle, the executive director of the Massachusetts chapter of the Catholic League for Religious and Civil Rights, a not-for-profit, independent lay organization, said, "We are witnessing another sordid attempt to use public education to promote the homosexual agenda."

But Torie Osborn, the head of the Gay and Lesbian Task Force in Washington, said: "This is very, very pioneering. I've never known anything on a statewide level with the imprimatur of a governor."

Frances Kunreuther, the executive director of the Hetrick-Martin Institute, a not-for-profit New York organization that helps young homosexuals, said, "I applaud it—I'm thrilled by it—but there's more to do."

But she added: "It needs to be mandated. To be able to opt out of something that really is a life-and-death issue is not acceptable."

Gene Hartigan, the executive director of the Massachusetts Republican Party, said that party members believed that the Governor "has been forthright in his willingness to take on issues that others think are too sticky to touch."

"Extremely conservative voters and extremely conservative interest groups will always feel that any kind of assessment of gay and lesbian issues is offensive," he said.

* * *

December 8, 1993

GAY RIGHTS LAW FOR SCHOOLS ADVANCES IN MASSACHUSETTS

By SARA RIMER
Special to The New York Times

BOSTON, Dec. 7—Massachusetts is about to become the first state in the nation to outlaw discrimination against gay and lesbian students in public schools.

Aides to Gov. William F. Weld say he will soon sign into law a bill that passed the State Senate here after an extraordinary lobbying campaign by hundreds of high school students—gay and lesbian, as well as heterosexual.

The law is intended to affirm the rights of openly gay students to many rituals of adolescence: to form alliances and clubs, to take a date to the prom, to participate freely in sports.

Proponents of the bill say it will make it easier for gay students who suffer harassment and violence—and who are not protected by school officials—to bring lawsuits against their schools. "They will have recourse," said Byron Rushing, the Democratic State Representative who sponsored the bill in the House. "They will be able to sue."

The lobbying effort involved hundreds of gay students who told legislators emotional stories of feeling isolated and afraid at school. They told of being physically threatened, attacked and cursed at in class and in school hallways because of their sexual orientation. Supporters of the bill said the students provided faces to Federal statistics that show an alarming rate of suicide among gay and lesbian youth, as well as a high dropout rate.

Freedom to Be Themselves

In two previous years, the Senate had kept the gay rights bill in committee. What made the difference this year, said Marty Linsky, the chief secretary to Governor Weld, were the students.

"There were 1,000 young people up here endlessly," Mr. Linsky said. "And I think they were able to persuade members of the Legislature that the problem was real and that the solution was reasonable. Their stories about their own difficulties were very compelling, very persuasive."

One of the students who testified to legislators was Troix Bettencourt, 19, who told the State House about dropping out of Lowell High School after his guidance counselor informed his parents that he might be homosexual. Mr. Bettencourt said: "This bill gives every kid their freedom. It allows every kid to be themselves."

Mr. Bettencourt, who earned his high school equivalency degree and is now a freshman at Northeastern University, was one of hundreds of students who wrote letters to their legislators, staged candlelight vigils outside the State House and marched along the Freedom Trail with signs reading: "Every Student Has A Right to An Education." The students visited the offices of all 40 state senators, and spoke to every one of them, or to their aides.

The bill has been staunchly supported by Mr. Weld, a Republican who has been praised by gay rights advocates as the Governor with the best record favoring equal rights for homosexuals.

'They Spit on Me'

Mark DeLellis, a 17-year-old senior at Belmont High School, who was one of the student leaders of the lobbying effort, told the legislators about the time his soccer teammates turned on him in middle school. "They spit on me and threw things at me and called me faggot, homo," Mr. DeLellis said in an interview today, recalling his testimony.

David LaFontaine, whom Governor Weld appointed to head a commission on gay and lesbian youth nearly two years ago, helped lead this fall's student lobbying effort. "We needed to make people realize that this bill affects people's sons and daughters," he said.

After Mr. LaFontaine convened a training workshop for 25 student lobbyists, he said the students "did role playing where they would practice about what it was like to meet with a legislator—supportive and nonsupportive."

Mr. LaFontaine added: "We told them to be very forceful, never to write anyone off. We encouraged them to speak from the heart."

For their day of lobbying at the State House in October, 150 students were divided into groups, with eight team leaders. Four or five students visited the office of each senator.

Thirty students met with a top aide to the powerful State Senate President, William M. Bulger, who had previously opposed the bill. At the time of the meeting, the bill was stalled in the Senate Committee on Steering and Policy, where it had died last year. After the meeting with Mr. Bulger, the bill got out of committee. It passed the Senate on Monday by a voice vote, with no debate.

One of the student leaders, Sarah Lonberg-Lew, 17, a junior at Brookline High School, said the last time she had tried to lobby her legislators was in the fourth grade. "It was to make the corn muffin the official state muffin," she said. "We baked corn muffins for them."

Mr. LaFontaine said part of the students' appeal to legislators was their sincerity. "They understood the legislation," he said. "But they weren't slick, professional lobbyists."

Mr. Rushing said: "It was very refreshing to see so many young people use the process. It was driven by students, both gay and straight students."

'Exploiting Public Education'

The Catholic League for Religious and Civil Rights, among other conservative groups, has criticized the Governor's stand on gay rights. Today the league issued a statement opposing the new bill.

"The ultimate purpose here is to introduce homosexual programs into the public schools," said C. J. Doyle, the director of the league. "The homosexual lobby is exploiting public education in an effort to validate homosexual behavior."

Education analysts and school law experts said no other state had even approached Massachusetts in its effort to ban discrimination against gay and lesbian students. "Other states have anti-discrimination legislation," said Frances Kunreuther, the executive director of the Hetrick-Martin Institute, which runs a school for gay youth in New York City. "But there's nobody that does anything specifically for youth. When you talk about civil rights, you wonder if they apply to people under 18."

Gay students rejoiced today over the bill's passage through the Senate.

One 17-year-old girl, who says she hides her sexual orientation out of fear, celebrated privately. For her, the bill is an important symbol. "This is for me and my friends," she said.

* * *

February 28, 1996

TO BE YOUNG, GAY AND GOING TO HIGH SCHOOL IN UTAH

By JAMES BROOKE

SALT LAKE CITY, Feb. 27—For Kelli Peterson, a 17-year-old senior at East High School here, the Aztec and U.F.O. clubs held no appeal; her primary concern was intensely personal—easing the loneliness she felt as a gay student.

"I thought I was the only lesbian student in East High," she said outside school here today. "As a sophomore I was really pressured by my friends to date. I came out that year, and immediately lost all my friends. I watched the same cycle of denial, trying to hide, acceptance, then your friends abandoning you."

So last fall, she and two other gay students formed an extracurricular club called the Gay/Straight Alliance. With that, the three set off a furor that now involves national conservative leaders, the State Legislature and the local school board.

Anti-gay leaders believe that a strong stand in Utah will help turn the national tide against gay clubs in high schools, which have sprung up in the last decade from Boston and New York to San Francisco and Los Angeles. They point to Utah's precedent-setting legislation last year that formally banned same-sex marriages. Although Utah is politically more conservative than most states, this year, 15 other state legislatures are debating similar bans.

"We are going to win this battle—and Utah will again be in the forefront," said Gayle Ruzicka, president of the Utah Eagle Forum, an affiliate of Phyllis Schlafly's national organization. "Homosexuals can't reproduce, so they recruit. And they are not going to use Utah high school and junior high school campuses to recruit."

Ms. Peterson scoffs at the idea: "Nobody led me to become a lesbian. My parents are heterosexual. I was taught to be heterosexual. I was taught to get married and to have children."

Paradoxically, 12-year-old conservative-sponsored Federal legislation would have forced the district to allow Ms. Peterson's club to meet in the school. The law, the Federal Equal Access Act of 1984, was intended to allow Bible clubs to meet in schools. Sponsored by Senator Orrin G. Hatch of Utah, the law says local school boards cannot pick among campus clubs. Last week, Mr. Hatch, a Republican, fumed. "The act was never intended to promulgate immoral speech or activity," he said.

Fearing lawsuits—and loss of Federal aid—Salt Lake City's Board of Education chose last week to ban all clubs from city high schools, from the Polynesian Club to Students Against Drunk Driving.

In response, hundreds of students poured out of city high schools last Friday, marching on the State Capitol. In the protest, one 14-year-old girl was run over by a car and critically injured.

Last month, as anti-gay feelings started to crystallize, Utah's Senate violated the state's public meetings law and met in secret to watch an anti-gay video. Senators later said they were so shocked that they would vote to ban gay clubs in schools, even if it meant risking $100 million a year in Federal aid to Utah schools.

Last week, the Senate easily approved a bill forbidding teachers from "encouraging, condoning or supporting illegal conduct." An amendment to preach "tolerance" was defeated. With sodomy a misdemeanor in Utah, the bill's sponsor said the measure was aimed at keeping avowed homosexuals out of public schools.

"Young people reach their teen-age years, and their sexuality starts developing," said State Senator Craig Taylor, the sponsor. "And I believe they can be led down that road to homosexuality."

Earlier this month, a political group, Gay Lesbian Utah Democrats, pressured Democratic legislators to try to legalize sodomy. In response, the state's party leadership demanded that the group drop "Democrats" from its name.

With battle lines drawn sharply, both sides believe that a struggle of national importance is being fought in this desert state of two million people. Defenders of gay high school clubs say that Utah's opponents are fighting a doomed battle. Nationwide, the number of high school gay clubs have mushroomed from a handful in 1992 to hundreds today, according to the Gay Lesbian Straight Teachers Network, a group based in New York.

Today, a member of this group, Clayton K. Vetter, became the first Utah public school teacher to publicly acknowledge his homosexuality.

Mr. Vetter, a debate teacher, said gay issues were everywhere. "The best way to deal with them is through openness," he said, before holding a news conference at the State Capitol. Under the "illegal conduct" bill that is expected to be passed this week by Utah's House of Representatives, Mr. Vetter risks dismissal.

In Salt Lake City, the population is roughly evenly divided between Mormons and non-Mormons. In 1991, Mormon church leaders issued a statement condemning homosexuality, saying, "Such thoughts and feelings, regardless of their causes, can and should be overcome and sinful behavior should be eliminated."

At last week's school board meeting, protesters held up signs reading "Down with homophobic clergy." Calling homosexuality an "abomination," The Deseret News, which is owned by the Mormon Church, said that a ban on high school gay groups reflected community "values that have long viewed homosexual practices as a serious problem to be combatted, rather than merely pitied or tolerated, let alone abetted."

In retort, The Salt Lake Tribune, Utah's largest-selling newspaper, called the campus ban "small-minded, uncharitable and cruel."

Ms. Peterson, who is herself Mormon, says she is taking steps to formally leave the church.

But even in Salt Lake City, some gay activists say that tolerance is inexorably spreading. "I am seeing more and more public support for what the students are doing," said Charlene Orchard, a lesbian who last month founded a support group here for the high school students, the Citizen's Alliance for Hate-Free Schools.

At East High, a neo-Gothic structure that disgorged student protesters last Friday, the divisions of Utah's larger society are mirrored among the 1,400 students.

Last week, several students asked the principal for permission to form a club called "the Anti-Homosexual League." Then, at last Friday's walkout, some boys threw snowballs at their protesting classmates.

"I'd rather do away with all the clubs, than have that club," Joseph Emerson, a high school senior, said Monday in the warmth of his pickup truck in the school parking lot.

"It's against our religion," the senior, a Mormon, said as two friends nodded assent. "Ban homosexuality, not clubs—we should have a demonstration like that."

Students like Ms. Peterson say that it was precisely these sentiments that led them to form the Gay/Straight Alliance last fall. Erin Wiser, a 17-year-old lesbian, said, "When my girlfriends would talk about marriage or boys, I would feel isolated."

A 16-year-old bisexual girl who asked not to be identified said that the alliance had sought a low profile, meeting quietly in classrooms, coffee houses or family living rooms.

"All we asked for is classroom time," said the girl, a junior. "We never used the intercom at student announcement time. We didn't ask for a picture in the yearbook."

Denying accusations that they were forming a "sex club," Ms. Peterson said the alliance is not about "technique," but about "identity."

Kelli's mother, Dee Peterson, recalled Kelli's hospitalization for depression last year after realizing her orientation. "Being gay you don't have a choice," Mrs. Peterson said. "You either are or you aren't."

While state officials may succeed in keeping homosexuality out of the state sphere, gay high school students vow to keep meeting, either on campus in school hallways or off-campus in coffeehouses.

And on graduation, they will find a full-fledged gay community that has grown in recent years in this city of half a million people.

Last June, about 5,000 people attended Salt Lake City's annual gay pride march. Every month, The Pillar, a gay tabloid carries advertisements for gay bars and gay personals. A full page of "Support and Social Groups" includes gay bowling and volleyball teams, a gay square dancing club, and such groups as the Rocky Mountain Cruisers and the Utah Gay Rodeo Association.

* * *

April 19, 1996

GAY STUDENT CLUBS IN UTAH FACE A BAN

By The Associated Press

SALT LAKE CITY, April 18—The Utah Legislature voted today to ban clubs for gay students in high schools.

The bill, which cleared the Senate 21 to 7 and the House 47 to 21, is the only one of its kind in the nation to have won passage, said Jensie Anderson of the Utah chapter of the American Civil Liberties Union.

Gov. Michael O. Leavitt, a Republican, is expected to sign it.

The issue of gay clubs in Utah high schools emerged last year when students at East High School in Salt Lake City formed a Gay-Straight Alliance.

The Salt Lake School Board reacted by banning all school-sponsored extracurricular organizations, including the chess and Latin clubs, believing it was the only way it could prohibit gay groups since a 1984 Federal law prevents schools from discriminating against clubs because of the beliefs they espouse.

Supporters of the bill say it skirts the Federal prohibition. It requires schools to deny access to clubs encouraging criminal or delinquent conduct, promoting bigotry or involving human sexuality.

A backer of the measure, Representative David Bresnahan, a Republican whose gay brother died of AIDS, said, "Free speech does not include recruiting them into a homosexual lifestyle that can kill them."

Senator George Mantes, a Democrat, called the measure "another moral witch hunt in our state." Some opponents of the bill said it would do little but open the state to expensive litigation. A.C.L.U. officials said a legal challenge was certain.

* * *

September 29, 1996

A COURSE FOR ADULTS ADDRESSES GAY ISSUES

By KATE STONE LOMBARDI

The Scarsdale Adult School, established in 1938, was a ground breaker in offering classes to adults long before phrases like continuing education and lifelong learning were part of the general lexicon. This fall, in addition to more traditional offerings like computer programming, exercise classes and conversational French, the school is again staking new ground by offering a course that addresses the issue of homosexuality.

The course, "Genes, Jeans and Gender: Exploring the Interplay Between Gay and Straight Life," will meet for six evening sessions and will cover topics like biological and psychological theories of homosexuality and current research, legislation and politics, spirituality, families and social support, educational issues and societal response.

"This course is not a polemic for any cause; it is an objective course," said Anita Malina, curriculum director for the Scarsdale Adult School. "But people need to understand what being gay is, in ways other than through innuendo or by holding on to early views that might not have been informed. This is a subject that is being discussed now in the political arena. There's a need for it, and I thought the time was right."

Dr. Suzanne Kessler, a psychology professor at Purchase College, will speak at the first class, offering an analysis of different theories of the cause of homosexuality and why certain theories are popular with different groups.

A later panel of lawyers will discuss current law, proposed legislative changes and their effect on homosexuals. On the panel will be Zelle W. Andrews, the county liaison to the lesbian and gay community, who will moderate a discussion between Paula Ettlebrick, legislative counsel of the Empire State Pride Agenda, and Kelly Donovan, legal

counsel to the Loft, the lesbian and gay community services center in White Plains.

A group of local clergy—Rabbi Helene Ferris from Temple Israel in Croton-on-Hudson, the Rev. Rayner W. Hesse Jr., priest in charge at St. John's Episcopal Church in New Rochelle, and the Rev. Joseph R. Venerosa of the Maryknoll Fathers and Brothers—will discuss spirituality.

First-hand experience with homosexuality and a discussion of the psychological and physical vulnerability of young and older homosexuals will be discussed by representatives from Parents and Friends of Lesbians and Gays, Center Lane, a program for young adolescents in White Plains, and the Loft.

Educators will talk about the schools' role concerning children and homosexuality. Dr. Janet Demb, a former Scarsdale elementary school psychologist, will talk about the plight of children who appear to be tomboys or sissies. Dr. Judith Fox, principal of Scarsdale High School, will discuss the high school's role in promoting tolerance.

"The suicide rate for gay teen-agers is something that cannot be ignored," Dr. Fox said in discussing her reasons for taking part in the course. "These kids suffer. Anything that concerns making the world a little more hospitable for adolescents, who in their times have it hard enough, captures my interest."

Edith Newton, a professor in the department of anthropology at Purchase College, will discuss the State University of New York course curriculum concerning homosexuality. The final class will feature Katherine Linton, the senior producer and host of the PBS-TV series "In the Life," a program offering a variety of gay entertainers. Ms. Malina, of the Adult School, said she hoped the course would attract a general audience that wants to become more knowledgeable about homosexuality.

Dr. Kessler said: "This is an opportunity to explore issues in the news. Political discussions will include child-custody issues, marriage issues, gays in the military, what should be done in the schools. Any educated adult in the community will have the opportunity to talk in a small forum with high-level people on issues they will be hearing about in the media."

"Genes, Jeans and Gender" will meet on six Tuesdays, from 7:30 to 8:55 P.M., beginning this Tuesday at Scarsdale High School on Brewster Road. The cost of the course is $65, $55 for people 65 and older. For information, call 723-2325.

* * *

November 21, 1996

$900,000 WON BY GAY MAN IN ABUSE CASE

By The Associated Press

EAU CLAIRE, Wis., Nov. 20—A homosexual who as a boy was beaten and otherwise tormented in school for years won a $900,000 out-of-court settlement today, bringing to an end the first Federal trial of a school district for failure to protect a gay student.

The plaintiff, Jamie Nabozny, now 21, had sued the school district in Ashland, a town of 8,000 people in far northern Wisconsin, and school administrators there on the ground that their failure to shield him from the repeated abuse of other students amounted to a violation of his rights.

The settlement came a day after a Federal court jury had found that although the district as a whole was not liable, three administrators were: Mary Podlesny, principal of Ashland Middle School, and William Davis and Thomas Blauert, principal and assistant principal at Ashland High School.

The jury had been scheduled to begin considering damages today. But the settlement was announced beforehand by a lawyer who represented the defendants on behalf of the district's insurer, the Wausau Insurance Company, and by the Lambda Legal Defense and Education Fund, a gay rights organization.

During the trial, Mr. Nabozny testified that his abuse by other students had included his being shoved, spat upon, beaten and even urinated upon. He said he had been kicked in the abdomen so many times that he later required surgery.

The abuse continued, he said, from the time he entered Ashland Middle School in 1988 until he dropped out of Ashland High School as a junior in 1993. He later earned an equivalency diploma.

The three administrators found liable were hurt by the jury's verdict, said Timothy Yanacheck, the defendants' lawyer. "School administrators are sympathetic to kids who are harassed by other kids in school," he said. "But for the most part that's misbehavior that school administrators cannot prevent or control."

* * *

December 28, 1997

STUDY OF SEX EXPERIENCING 2D REVOLUTION

By ETHAN BRONNER

Half a century after a mild-mannered Midwestern biology professor named Alfred C. Kinsey essentially created a new academic discipline with publication of his best-selling tome "Sexual Behavior in the Human Male," the study of sexuality on American campuses is again being revolutionized.

Over the past five years, courses examining the origin and meaning of sexual identity have appeared in nearly every catalogue of American liberal arts colleges, and the area is still growing. Unlike the short health classes taught at colleges in the past, what is now available permits students to specialize in sexuality, especially as a cultural phenomenon.

The University of Chicago initiated a lesbian and gay studies project this past fall; the University of Iowa will offer a certificate program—short of a major but more than a minor—in sexuality starting next September; Brown University is in the fourth year of offering a full major called Sexuality and Society; the University of Minnesota is establishing, with a pledged half-million-dollar endowment, a Center for Gay, Lesbian, Bisexual and Transgender Studies;

the University of California at Riverside, the University of Wisconsin at Milwaukee, New York University and the University of Pennsylvania are among a growing number of institutions with graduate or undergraduate programs focused on sexuality.

Some of the sessions are surprisingly explicit. At the University of Virginia, undergraduates in a course called Sexuality Today gather in coeducational pairs and sculpture genitals from Play-Doh. At Brown University, the owner of a female-oriented sex shop uses a latex replica of female sex organs to demonstrate new paraphernalia. And at the State University of New York at New Paltz, sadomasochists were invited to discuss their practices, drawing criticism from, among others, Gov. George E. Pataki.

What is noteworthy about nearly all these courses is that they spring from an area of the humanities, like history or English. The fascinating cross-cultural questions they raise have invigorated these fields, given birth to journals and established scholarly conferences. For example, they ask: When was the term homosexual invented? How does society define manhood? What is the difference between sex and gender?

By contrast, what they rarely involve is pure science. As sexuality has grown into a field of keen scholarly and societal interest, the frontiers of scientific knowledge around it, while more advanced than half a century ago, have not expanded correspondingly.

"There is still a lack of good, basic research into the fundamentals of human sexualities," said Dr. John Bancroft, an English medical researcher who now heads the Kinsey Institute at Indiana University.

"We don't understand why some people are likely to engage in high-risk sexual behavior while other people sensibly keep out of trouble," Dr. Bancroft said. "It is probably sociocultural, but there may be individual differences in physiology and neurobiology. We still know very little about the orgasm physiologically, relatively little about the extent to which men and women differ in patterns of physiological sexual response. We know little about why some people abuse children."

Dr. Bancroft added: "In other important aspects of behavior, you find a much more consistent body of scientific endeavor. It is regarded as something we need to know about. Sex is not like that. There has been a longstanding fear of knowledge in that area."

Susan Tate, who teaches the three-year-old Sexuality Today course at the University of Virginia, said it was that fear that she sought to address when she had the students build genitals from Play-Doh. "If we can discuss the heart, stomach and elbow without embarrassment," she said, "we should be able to talk about the penis, clitoris and vagina without laughing."

"I'm trying to tell the students what's good about sex," she said of her weekly, 25-student course. "All they hear is what's bad about it, how it can kill you. I want them to understand how it can be fantastic. I also want them to choose their own boundaries."

Issues Evolving From Women's Studies

Some of the material offered under sexuality today on college campuses flows from women's studies. Where at one time women's studies raised issues about equal pay, today the field is often recast as gender studies and examines societal construction of sexual identity. Whole sections of campus bookstores are taking the newly coined label lesbigay, which covers lesbian, bisexual and gay topics.

Much of the scholarship is grouped under the sardonic, defiant rubric of queer theory and challenges the view that sexuality and gender are the same thing. In other words, said David Savran, an English professor at Brown and director of its sexuality courses, sexual identity and desire are socially constructed, not innate. This school of thought is known as social constructionism.

Emphasis is placed on the changed view of sex over history, on the apparent fact, for example, that men in Athens in the 5th century B.C. were not judged by whether they had sex with other men, only whether they were seen as the penetrator or penetrated. And, Professor Savran said, "Three hundred years ago, a great many women and men were having same-sex relations but they were not necessarily labeled Sodomites." Homosexuality in the animal kingdom is also brought to bear on the issue.

There is another school of thought, essentialism, which argues that one's sexual orientation is innate, biologically determined. In the academy, at least among the gay theorists, many of whom are gay, this view is typically rejected as wrong and potentially harmful. It is seen to cast homosexuality as a kind of disability that may merit sympathy but fails to challenge the faulty bases of society.

"What I really like about queer theory is that rather than looking at minority or dissident sexuality versus the mainstream, we question a lot of basic assumptions we have about sexuality," said Marshall Miller, a 23-year-old recent graduate of Brown's program who now works in a gay health center in Boston.

The curriculum for Mr. Miller and others who major in the area include a requirement to take three of four core courses: the biology of gender, an introduction to gay and lesbian literary and cultural studies, the history of sexuality and a course that is called Queers and Culture but that appears on transcripts as Identities/Communities for fear that potential employers would be put off by the real name.

Those in this field say that learning about the fringes of sexual practice, like sadomasochism and prostitution, offers insight into issues like power and money. Tania Israel, who is studying toward a doctorate in psychology and teaching at Arizona State University, focused on strippers and found them both empowered and degraded by their work, depending on several external factors.

"It is very difficult to get at people's sexuality because the issue is so taboo," she said. "But if we want to understand sexual assault, for example, we need to understand how men and women experience their sexuality, how they internalize messages."

That is not how critics see it.

Roger Kimball, managing editor of New Criterion, a conservative monthly journal, drew angry attention to a sex conference at SUNY New Paltz this fall when The Wall Street Journal published a caustic article by him under the headline, "Syllabus for Sickos."

"There is something profoundly dehumanizing about this stuff," he said in an interview. "And what a way to waste your college years. Here you have four unrepeatable years where you can spend a great deal of money to become educated. You have to make choices. Is it better to spend time learning to use dildos or reading Kant? If you look at the amazing ignorance of people in college today, it is appalling."

The 'Dark Side' Of Enlightenment

"Then there is the moral question," he continued. "Is this a good thing, to look at the sex organs as essentially a complicated piece of plumbing? Should one's sex life be treated in an objective way, turning sex into an activity like jogging? I don't think so. What worries me is the way sex studies tend to get rid of the whole element of love and affection and intimacy in the name of emancipation. The idea is to increase pleasure by divorcing it from all those customs and rituals and social embedding in which sexuality has always been understood. This removes the decent drapery of life. Enlightenment has a dark side."

Richard A. Posner, a conservative but iconoclastic legal scholar, who is chief judge of the Federal Court of Appeals for the Seventh Circuit in Chicago, is not, however, very impressed with these concerns. He says that ignorance of things sexual by members of the judiciary, and by society generally has produced woeful results.

This was brought home to him about eight years ago, Judge Posner said, when, seeking to plug a gap in his knowledge, he picked up Plato's "Symposium." He said he knew at the time only that it was about love.

"I was surprised to discover that it was a defense, and as one can imagine a highly interesting and articulate one, of homosexual love," he wrote in the book that emerged, "Sex and Reason" (Harvard University Press, 1992). "It had never occurred to me that the greatest figure in the history of philosophy, or for that matter any other respectable figure in the history of thought, had attempted such a thing."

He added that "Symposium" and a year's worth of subsequent reading made him re-evaluate much of what had been written about homosexuality into American law. His book urges decriminalization and acceptance.

"A person who knows that James I, Francis Bacon, Oscar Wilde, Henry James, Marcel Proust, Gertrude Stein, Virginia Woolf, John Maynard Keynes, E. M. Forster, Pyotor Ilich Tchaikovsky, George Santayana, T. E. Lawrence, Alan Turing and Ludwig Wittgenstein were homosexuals," he wrote, "and that Sophocles, Socrates, Plato, Shakespeare, Christopher Marlowe, Alexander the Great, Julius Caesar and Richard the Lionhearted may have been, is not so likely to believe that homosexuality is merely a ghastly blight."

Changing Views Toward Homosexuality

There appears to be good reason to attribute the growing tolerance toward homosexuality in America at least partly to changes in education. George Chauncey, a historian at the University of Chicago, is writing a book arguing that increased acceptance of homosexuals is one of the most fundamental changes of the second half of the 20th century.

Professor Chauncey says that the first American academic conference on gay and lesbian studies was held at Yale University in 1987 and drew 200 participants. Two years later, some 600 people attended. By 1991, when the conference was held at Harvard University, there were 1,600 participants and the following year, at Rutgers University, 2,000 scholars participated and 200 papers were presented, making it one of the largest academic conferences in the country, Mr. Chauncey said.

Judith R. Shapiro, an anthropologist who is president of Barnard College, has watched the growth of gender studies with some concern but also with enthusiasm.

On the one hand, she worries that because it is such a personal issue, it encourages students to turn further inside themselves. But Ms. Shapiro also sees a great value in it because by comparing what may seem like one's most natural and inherent tendencies and feelings with historical and cross-cultural practices, students are obliged to turn outward.

"Through such studies, students are forced to ask the most basic questions about how society organizes itself and that is the very essence of a liberal education," Ms. Shapiro said. "Remember what Erik Erikson told us about Martin Luther's private demons. They were fundamental to his thought. People's personal obsessions can lead to great truths."

A Sample of Courses in Sexuality

From course catalogues at colleges and universities around the nation:

"Queer Histories," at Yale:

Examination of a recent category of analysis for gender studies and the study of sexuality, situated within a historical framework. Readings examine different aspects of what is commonly regarded as "queer," including gender and sexual nonconformity, compare and contrast past and present notions of that nonconformity, and examine how a historical perspective can influence understanding of modern categories, as well as the reverse.

"Queer Lives" at Hampshire College in Massachusetts:

This course is envisioned as an introduction to thinking about the lives and work of lesbians, gay men, transsexuals, and transgendered people (groups currently allied politically under the term "queer") mainly through their autobiographies and their work as artists and political activists. The course will trace the social and cultural history of queer people from the end of the 19th century, when sexologists coined the term "homosexual," to the queer liberation movement of the present day, stressing issues of race and class as well as gender.

"Sexuality Today" at The University of Virginia:

This course will provide an increased understanding and appreciation for human sexual behavior through learning concepts, principles and facts regarding sexual health. Topics will include: human sexual behavior and relationships, reproductive systems, contraception and unintended pregnancy, sex under the influence of alcohol, regretted sex, media influences on sexual behavior, sexually transmitted infections (including H.I.V.), sexual health and sexual assault.

Lesbian, Gay And Bisexual Studies Minor at The University of California at Riverside:

The curriculum will address such issues as: sexual identity and orientation; gay, lesbian and bisexual representation; gay, lesbian and bisexual perspectives on the arts; retheorizations of gender; sexuality and cultural diversity; intersections of sexualities and ethnic identities.

* * *

September 6, 1998

A RIGHT-WING SLANT ON CHOOSING THE RIGHT COLLEGE

By WILLIAM H. HONAN

A new, frankly conservative guide to the nation's top 100 colleges excoriates Harvard University, sings the praise of the University of Dallas and criticizes many institutions for unchecked political correctness.

The book, called "Choosing the Right College," is aimed, its editors say, at exposing the political biases of academe, the prevalence of permissive sex and the lack of core curriculums to prospective students and their parents. The 672-page guide is published by the conservative Intercollegiate Studies Institute Inc., of Wilmington, Del., one of the oldest student-oriented educational organizations in the nation. The institute was founded in the 1950's with William F. Buckley Jr. as its first president. William J. Bennett, a former Education Secretary and a conservative Republican, has contributed an introduction.

The guide criticizes all the Ivy League schools but reserves the roughest treatment for Harvard, which it contends has "lost much originality and now marches in lock step with the dominant trends of the intellectual world."

Acknowledging that Harvard has "a star-studded faculty," the guide deplores its "politicized courses and departments," which it lists as African studies, social studies, the Center for Literacy and Cultural Studies, English, fine arts, anthropology, Romance languages and literatures, comparative literature and women's studies.

Alex Huppe, a spokesman for Harvard, said the university has never commented on rankings (Harvard comes up No. 1 in most others) and added only, with a laugh, that "we seem to be in pretty good company."

The University of California at Berkeley is criticized for not shaking off the legacy of Mario Savio, the leader of the free speech movement in the 1960's, and for fighting to preserve affirmative action. One professor is quoted as saying, "A Louis Farrakhan-Ronald Reagan Presidential race, if held at the U.C.-Berkeley campus, would be a dead heat."

The guide also contends that Berkeley is so permissive, students are permitted to "walk around and attend classes in the nude, so loath is the university to step on their right to free expression."

Oberlin College in Ohio is criticized because, the guide says, political correctness has become a "religion" and "the Drag Ball held every spring is easily the most popular social event on campus."

Carleton College in Northfield, Minn., comes under attack because it has "no core curriculum to speak of" and for its "energetic promotion of the gay/lesbian/bisexual/transgendered community on campus."

Pomona College and its president, Peter W. Stanley, are criticized for having "acceded to the demands of the political activists" in allowing the formation of an Asian-American studies department last year. "Why not an Italian-American studies department or a Nepalese-American studies department?" the authors ask dismissively.

Midge Decter, a neoconservative author and critic, said she was delighted by the book. "When I was shown the book I suggested that they add a final chapter entitled 'Burn Them Down,'" she said, laughing.

The darlings of the guide include the University of Dallas, a relatively new Roman Catholic institution, which is praised as "one of the few genuinely countercultural universities in the nation."

Students there are "taught to see freedom not as an opportunity for self-aggrandizement, but as the ability to pursue truth, goodness and beauty."

Another glowing report goes to Boston University, which the guide said was spared from politicization because of determination by its neoconservative president, John Silber, who recently retired, "not to reorder the university to suit passing whims of intellectual fashion." It adds he would not tolerate employing "politicized professors who'd rather indoctrinate their students than teach them."

Middlebury College in Middlebury, Vt., is praised as "a rarity in higher education today in that multiculturalist talk seems to be waning rather than gathering strength." And Pepperdine University, a firmly Christian institution in Malibu, Calif., which offered its law school deanship to the Whitewater independent counsel, Kenneth W. Starr, is admired for having "shown little interest in the current radical trends in academe."

* * *

February 10, 2000

TO OUTLAW GAY GROUP, DISTRICT MAY BAN CLUBS

By BARBARA WHITAKER

ORANGE, Calif., Feb. 9—Under the protection of a court but in defiance of a school board's wishes, a group of gay teenagers and their supporters held a long-awaited meeting today at El Modena High School here. But whether the group will ever do so again remains uncertain.

In a fight that has roiled this conservative suburban community and drawn attention across the country, the Orange Unified School District is seeking to ban the group, contending that it is inappropriate because it deals with issues of sexuality.

Now, faced with a lawsuit and a judge's preliminary injunction, the district is considering a new approach: whether to vote on Thursday to ban all 38 noncurricular clubs, including the Black Student Union and the Gentlemen's Club, as a way of halting meetings of the group, the Gay-Straight Alliance. Only one other school district, Salt Lake City, has taken such an approach, and a suit against that district is still moving through the courts.

"We have reached a point in this process where the board faces a range of options," said Judith Frutig, a board spokeswoman. "On one hand, they could stop the lawsuit or on the other they could press forward with the knowledge that this case will likely go as far as the Supreme Court. So they have a lot to consider."

As a demonstration of the passions that the dispute has inflamed, protesters who had come from as far away as Salt Lake City exchanged verbal insults with students in a melee outside the school this afternoon. The police were called in to break up the disturbance.

For supporters of club, the board's decision in December to deny its application to meet is a violation of free speech. But to opponents of the group, the primary subject matter is inappropriate for a school organization. At least one board member contends that homosexuality is a sin and that permitting a group to meet on campus condones it.

"The Bible says we're all sinners, but this, in my opinion, is asking us to legitimize sin," the board member, Bill Lewis, said at a meeting.

On Friday, in response to a lawsuit by the group's student organizers, a federal district judge, David O. Carter, ordered the board to allow the group to meet until the case could get a full hearing and he criticized the school district for failing to protect gay students from harassment.

The dispute over the club arises as gay rights issues play out across the country on several other fronts: in Vermont, legislators are considering whether to grant domestic partnership rights to gay couples, while a California ballot initiative will ask voters to reaffirm that the state should only acknowledge heterosexual marriage. Illinois is considering a law that would offer special legal status to gay victims of violence.

But while those legislative and legal fights have attracted more attention, schools across the country are increasingly

Davis Barber for The New York Times

Anthony Colin, right, a teenager who helped organize a group for gay students at El Modena High School in Orange, Calif., argued yesterday with a protester, Sandra Rodrigues, at the school. The protest against the group drew demonstrators from as far away as Salt Lake City.

wrestling with similar kinds of sweeping issues. As studies show that gay youths are revealing their sexual orientation at younger and younger ages, a growing number of teenagers are forming gay rights support groups.

According to statistics compiled by the Gay, Lesbian and Straight Education Network, more than 600 gay alliance clubs now exist in middle schools and high schools across the country. In a handful of cases, school boards have considered moves to stop the groups from meeting, but have backed down as court actions were threatened. "The average age at which students self-identify as lesbian and gay has dropped dramatically over the last 20 years," said Jon W. Davidson, a lawyer with the Lambda Legal Defense and Education Fund, the country's largest and oldest lesbian and gay legal rights organization. "High schools are having to deal with this issue whereas they didn't in the past."

In the dispute here, the school board cited the state education code in denying the group's application to meet. The board said the code strictly defined how sex education and related courses were to be taught. It said it would be inappropriate for students to lead discussions on sexuality and sexual conduct.

The school board announced its decision after the group filed a lawsuit in November charging that the board was illegally delaying action on the application. The suit cited the Equal Access Act of 1984, the Fourteenth Amendment guaranteeing equal protection and other civil rights laws. The 1984 act provides that schools allowing groups to meet in extracurricular clubs cannot deny certain groups to meet because of the content of their discussions.

The legislation was passed by Congress at the urging of conservative groups pushing for religious meetings in schools, but it has since become an effective tool for gay rights groups seeking similar privileges.

On Friday, when Judge Carter issued his preliminary injunction ordering the district to allow the students to meet as the case moves through the court, he carefully examined the students' rights under the law, ultimately finding that the board must "give plaintiffs all the same rights and privileges that it gives to other student groups."

In making his ruling, the judge also found that there was a strong indication that the students were being harmed as a result of being denied their First Amendment right to free speech.

"Plaintiffs have been injured not only by the board's excessive delay, but also by the inability to effectively address the hardships they encounter at school every day," the judge wrote. "Some students at El Modena do not even feel safe using the school's restrooms."

In the days since the judge's ruling, the atmosphere for gay students at El Modena has been tense, student organizers said. When they arrived at school on Monday, gay students said the campus was littered with prank gay-recruitment fliers. "Come on, Elmo, don't be shy! You're either gay . . . or you're bi," read the fliers, which showed two men naked from the waist up.

Anthony Colin, a 15-year-old who helped found the gay club, said the idea for the club arose from the savage beating death in 1998 of Matthew Shepard, 21, a freshman at the University of Wyoming who was targeted because of his homosexuality.

Student organizers say their goal is to promote tolerance among and for gay and straight students at the school. A survey by the Gay, Lesbian and Straight Education Network, found that 91 percent of students polled by their organization regularly heard homophobic comments at school. More than two-thirds of gay respondents said they had been verbally, physically or sexually harassed on a daily basis.

The El Modena group said it hoped to raise awareness and promote tolerance by providing a safe forum for discussion of issues related to sexual orientation and homophobia.

"We wish to stress the need for people to put aside their personal prejudice and agree to treat everyone with respect when the situation calls for it," the group wrote.

School officials, however, and some parents say they fear the club is being used to promote the agenda of national gay advocacy groups.

But Anthony Colin, the club organizer, insists that the outside groups are merely helping. As Mr. Colin looked back over the struggle to get his club recognized, he found solace in the judge's decision.

"My mother always said to me whatever is worth having is worth fighting for," he said. "I thought this was worth having, so I decided to fight for it."

* * *

BROADENING THE MAINSTREAM

July 17, 1977

HOMOSEXUALS ARE MOVING TOWARD OPEN WAY OF LIFE AS TOLERANCE RISES AMONG THE GENERAL POPULATION

By GRACE LICHTENSTEIN
Special to The New York Times

TUCSON, Ariz., July 12—On Saturday night the new Last Culture discotheque in the heart of town, its narrow-beamed lights flashing and soul beat thumping, was crowded with some 300 young men and women, most of them homosexuals.

"For the most part, you still have to spend your nights differently than your days," observed Bob Ellis, publisher, of the weekly Arizona Gay News. "It's still a double life here, but things have loosened up in the past two years."

Tucson, a liberal university town in a very conservative state, is far from San Francisco or New York in terms of an active homosexual movement. But it reflects a growing national trend toward more organized homosexual groups, more open displays of the homosexual life style and greater acceptance of homosexuals by the majority population.

Despite a successful anti-homosexual campaign in Miami that attracted nation-wide attention last month, a spot check this week by The New York Times indicated widespread outward tolerance of homosexuals, although some backlash generated by the Florida campaign was evident.

Poll Was After Florida Vote

These findings seemed to be supported by the most recent Gallup Poll, which shows that a slim majority of Americans approve of equal job rights for homosexuals:

But the poll is not altogether encouraging for homosexuals. A big majority of those sampled disapproved of homosexuals in specific professions such as the clergy and elementary school teaching.

The Gallup Poll was conducted among 1,513 adults in mid-June. That was after Dade County, as a result of a campaign led by Anita Bryant, the singer and orange juice promoter, repealed an ordinance that had banned discrimination in hiring because of a person's sexual orientation.

According to the Gallup findings, 56 percent of those questioned answered yes when asked, "In general, do you think homosexuals should or should not have equal rights in terms of job opportunities?" Thirty-three percent said no and 11 percent had no opinion.

When asked about selected jobs, however, 65 percent were against homosexuals as elementary school teachers, compared with 27 percent in favor and 8 percent with no opinion. Fifty-four percent of those polled were against homosexuals as members of the clergy, 36 percent for them and 10 percent had no opinion.

Those polls were split evenly on whether homosexuals should be physicians and 51 percent said they should be allowed in the armed forces. Sixty-eight percent approved of homosexuals as sales persons.

The poll also showed that the larger the city, the more tolerant the population was of this minority group. Residents of the Middle West and South were more apt to be against job rights for homosexuals, as were those who called themselves churchgoers and those older than 50.

The pattern of apparent tolerance is, nevertheless, complicated by much evidence of discrimination against homosexuals, state laws that make homosexual sex a criminal act and attitudes of certain religious groups, according to reports from 10 cities checked by The Times.

There is a thriving homosexual community in every city. Most have at least one men's bath, several bars catering to homosexual males, lesbians or both, and homosexual community centers, political groups and newsletters.

Tucson, for example, a rapidly growing Sunbelt city with a population of 330,000, supports all these elements. In addition, the City Council unanimously passed in February an ordinance barring job discrimination on many grounds, among them "sexual or affectional preference." There was no move to repeal it after the Dade County vote.

About 200 Tucson residents turned out for a "gay pride" picnic June 26, as thousands of marchers paraded in San Francisco and New York. There is no harassment of homosexuals by the Tucson police.

One Beaten to Death

However, a year ago a 21-year-old man named Richard Heakin was beaten to death outside a homosexual bar in Tucson by four teen-agers.

Despite objections, the youths were tried as juveniles. Thus, they were not charged with murder in adult court. A local judge found the four "delinquent" and granted them all probation. The case outraged both homosexuals and heterosexuals. The judge was assailed in The Arizona Daily Star, the city's morning newspaper.

The case served as a rallying point for homosexuals on the civil rights issue, according to Michael Cebulski and Cathy Hemlar, leaders of the Tucson Gay Coalition.

But Phyllis Sugar, the assistant city attorney who drafted the anti-discrimination code, said of City Council members: "They didn't really know what they were doing when they passed it." Neither she nor other civil libertarians interviewed would predict, if it were submitted to a public vote, that the ordinance would remain on the books.

Life is similarly complex for homosexuals in places such as Atlanta; Wichita, Kan.; Denver, Little Rock, Ark; Salt Lake City; Jackson, Miss.; Boise, Idaho, and Portsmouth, N.H.

More than 100 Jackson residents went to New York and Washington for "Gay Pride Week." Others joined New Orleans demonstrators against Miss Bryant. But the Gay Alliance lost a four-year court fight recently to allow "gay counseling" and literature ads in the Mississippi State University newspaper.

In Atlanta, homosexuals have marched each June for seven years. But instead of labeling the occasion "Gay Pride Day," as he did last year, Mayor Maynard Jackson this year merely proclaimed the entire week "Civil Liberties Days."

In Denver, several hundred people marched in a "Gay Pride" demonstration. But across the Rockies in Salt Lake City, the Church of Jesus Christ of Latter-day Saints (the Mormon church) has waged an unremitting campaign against homosexuals.

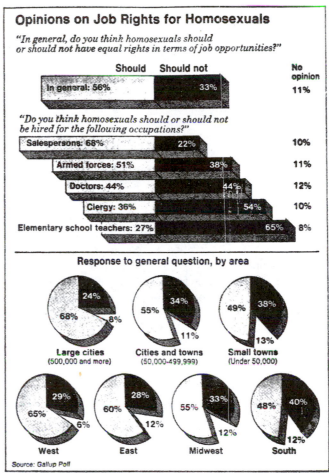

Source: Gallup Poll

The New York Times

Spencer W. Kimball, president of the church, has said that the reason for the Western drought was the Mormons' tolerance of late of too much homosexuality.

Scandal in Boise

Meanwhile, The Deseret News, Salt Lake's afternoon newspaper, editorially praised Miss Bryant this week and condemned homosexual sex as "disgusting, repulsive, severely condemned by Almighty God." The paper is owned by the Mormon church. The Hotel Utah, another church property, revoked the contract for the homosexual group that had booked a convention there in June.

Boise was the scene in 1955 of a scandal in which numerous men were sent to jail for consentual homosexual acts with youths. This year, the city has been shaken by a new scandal that began when six women were dismissed from the police department for alleged lesbian activity. None of the six have said that they were lesbians but they have been unable to find work elsewhere. They are suing the police department for damages and reinstatement.

Wichita had its first "Gay Pride Week" this year. However, the city commissioners this month postponed action on a proposed ordinance that would have banned discrimination because of sexual preference, saying it was a "very emotional issue."

In Little Rock, the Arkansas legislature has passed a law making acts of homosexuality a misdemeanor, even though a criminal code passed two years ago eliminated a similar law. The Arkansas House of Representatives also passed, by voice vote, a resolution supporting Miss Bryant's campaign.

In New Hampshire, Gov. Meldrim Thomson Jr. has criticized homosexuals. His allies in the State Senate passed an antihomosexuality law but it was killed in the House.

Despite setbacks, homosexuals in every city said that more and more men and women were "coming out of the closet." Even before the Dade County vote, their political organizations were growing more vocal on issues such as job discrimination. Now, according to one leader in Minneapolis, among the most tolerant of cities, they are getting renewed support.

Steve Endean, a member of the board of directors of the National Gay Task Force, said: "Nongays understand that this is an important civil rights issue. I think we've gained more than was lost by the Florida vote. Many gays who have never been political before now are eager to get involved with both time and money."

* * *

May 2, 1982

TAPPING THE HOMOSEXUAL MARKET

By KAREN STABINER

Major film studios made a hedged bet this season that the healthy, wealthy and/or wise homosexual was a marketable commodity. Paramount Pictures's "Partners," which opened this weekend, is a comedy about two New York cops (one's straight, the other isn't) who pretend to be lovers to solve a murder. It follows: 20th-Century Fox's "Making Love" (a doctor leaves his wife for another man); Warner Bros.'s "Personal Best" (two female Olympic teammates fall in love) and "Deathtrap" (Michael Caine and Christopher Reeve play lovers), and M-G-M/U.A.'s "Victor, Victoria," in which Julie Andrews finishes off her nun and governess image by playing a woman pretending to be a man who is a female impersonator.

The challenge was to sell these films without alienating either the general audience or the homosexual audience. Accordingly, the studios' public profile was low. Executives and film makers even denied that their projects were about homosexuality, insisting, for example, that "Personal Best" was a look at competition and friendship, while "Victor, Victoria" was alleged simply to be an updated version of an old farce.

But the investment of millions in movie-budget and movie-advertising dollars represents a radical shift in attitude, regardless of attempts to downplay it. In 1971, financial success eluded John Schlesinger's critically-acclaimed "Sunday, Bloody Sunday," about an unmarried couple attracted to the same man; audiences weren't ready for it. Only a decade later, Hollywood is gambling that they are ready for a film with a homosexual theme. Since none of the anticipated problems materialized—no pickets, no theater boycotts—Hollywood may be right. (Television took a similar chance: This season,

NBC offered "Love, Sidney," starring Tony Randall as a homosexual who finds himself with an instant family.)

The studios' wager was doubly significant in the homosexual community, which found itself both the subject of films and the object of marketing strategies.

Going beyond mainstream advertising, several studios turned to publications catering to homosexual readers, such as Christopher Street, in Manhattan, or the California-based The Advocate. When "Sunday, Bloody Sunday" flopped, the homosexually oriented press largely consisted of community newspapers eking out a marginal existence with local, mail-order and classified ads. No longer. Today, the studios advertise alongside Heublein, Seagram, Perrier, Harper & Row and others, primarily wooing an economically attractive segment of the consumer population—the white, single, well-educated, well-paid man who happens to be homosexual.

In tight-money 1982, men with high earning power and low financial obligations are making purveyors of luxury items and leisure services take a second look. While these men are a small percentage of the national homosexual population—one market researcher refers to them as "the upscale tip of the iceberg"—they are, according to The Advocate's publisher, Peter Frisch, a "recession-proof market."

However, the directing of sales campaigns at an economic elite is not necessarily accompanied by parallel changes in attitude on Madison Avenue: If profits are threatened, the corporate turtle can pull back into its shell. Billie Jean King used to do lucrative product endorsements until news of her lesbian affair surfaced last May. Although she continues to do tennis-tournament telecasts, she has not done any endorsements since.

Retailers may want the homosexual to buy, but they won't yet take a chance and let a celebrity who has confessed even to a single homosexual affair sell to a still-rejecting public.

Will the current commercial flirtation lead to a more meaningful relationship? Those who make their living seeking recognition and acceptance for homosexuals, like Frisch and Joe Di Sabato, who represents 75 newspapers claiming a combined circulation of 1.5 million, tend to be optimists. They regard economic exploitation as the first step toward social integration, and cite the parallel assimilation of middle-class blacks and single working women.

Others, mindful of black unemployment figures and women's uphill battle for the equal rights amendment, are more skeptical: If business is targeting an unrepresentative, privileged minority within a larger, diverse subculture, they believe the only motive is profits. Despite the existence of high-profile neighborhoods in many major cities—concentrations of wealthy, conspicuously consuming men—the homosexual population in this country remains largely invisible.

The Alfred C. Kinsey Institute for Sex Research states that 5 percent to 6 percent of the adult population are predominantly homosexual; 4 percent of the total adult population are male homosexuals and 1 percent to 2 percent are female homosexuals. These figures, compiled in the late 1960's, are the

These ads for 20th Century-Fox's "Making Love" (a man leaves his wife for a man) were designed for two audiences, and ended up drawing more comment than the film. The one on the left, with a bare-chested Harry Hamlin, ran in homosexual publications. The one on the right, with co-stars Kate Jackson and Michael Ontkean, left, keeping hands off a clothed Hamlin, went into mainstream publications.

only ones available and are considered conservative. The 1980 census puts the 18-and-over population at about 226.5 million, which means a homosexual population of between 11 and 14 million—a figure vastly larger than the total of the more visible populations of the nation's largest homosexual enclaves: Manhattan (estimated to be about 800,000), San Francisco (conservatively, 100,000), Los Angeles (350,000) and Washington (less than 100,000).

Little reliable information exists on the majority of this country's homosexuals, since most have not gone public. There is, however, a detailed picture of the subspecies affluent male homosexual consumer, although it comes from an obviously interested party. Most decisions and assumptions about the market can be traced back to readership surveys done for The Advocate in 1977 and 1980 by the Los Angeles marketing firm of Walker & Struman Research Inc.

The survey's 1,100 respondents were predominantly professional men residing in urban areas. Seventy percent of them were between the ages of 20 and 40, and their annual median income in 1980 was $30,000. By comparison, the national median income for the select group of men between the ages of 35 and 44—traditionally, a period of peak earning power—was $21,776. What is more, 28 percent of the respondents earned over $40,000 in 1980, while nationally, the number of men earning over $35,000 was only 6.9 percent.

Free of the financial burden of supporting a family, the homosexual consumer can afford to spend his impressive income on himself—and regularly does. As for accusations of "self-centeredness," Frisch says homosexuals are merely trying to prove that "not only can we live as well as the Joneses; we live a damn sight better."

The responses also showed a devotion to particular name brands and styles, although these vary with season and geography. Still, Peter Frisch feels confident rattling off a list of must-haves: "A convertible. A sports car, a foreign sports car. Believe me, that imported sports car shows up in our demographics. It's incredible. Some fabulous wardrobe. You take umpteen vacations and weekend trips a year. You have a second home," in a popular resort area like the Russian River, north of San Francisco, Laguna Hills or Palm Springs in Southern California, Saginaw, Mich., Fire Island or the Hamptons in New York, Key West in Florida and Galveston, Tex., on the Gulf.

"The gay man probably has a much greater interest in his physical well-being than the average man on the street," continues Frisch. "He probably belongs to a health club. Probably he subscribes to National Geographic and Time. He eats Haagen-Dazs ice cream, if he eats ice cream. He probably drinks more diet drinks than other purchasers of diet drinks—again, the health consciousness. He probably has in his closet a pair of cowboy boots, on the West Coast, and a pair of Bass Weejuns, and a pair of Adidas running shoes, if not Nike."

The composite consumer also has several pairs of Levi Strauss 501 straight-leg jeans, which were popularized more than 10 years ago by urban homosexuals who wore them as part of a uniform that signaled their sexual preference. The cigarette of choice is Marlboro because, says Frisch, "the advertising campaign emphasizes masculinity and talks about Marlboro Country as being 'open and free.' "

An updated survey of Advocate subscribers, completed in January, also reveals: 21 percent of 2,500 respondents either own or intend to purchase a personal computer this year, and 43 percent own or plan to buy a video-cassette recorder.

They are also interested in supporting the arts, which Frisch attributes to attitude as well as spendable cash. The arts seem to know it: Frisch says he gets requests "all the time" from cultural institutions like the New York City Opera that want to purchase The Advocate's mailing list, which he says is not for sale. Many groups, like the American Conservatory Theater in San Francisco, end up advertising instead. Other advertisers include American Ballet Theater, and both the Los Angeles and San Francisco Light Operas.

The standard of living Frisch describes is higher than that of most homosexual men, but it is also higher than that of homosexual women, even those with comparably impressive jobs and educational backgrounds. These women are discounted so completely, when it comes to consumer power, that most people who talk about the "gay market" make the implicit assumption that it is a male market.

The obstacles for women are twofold. Women in this country still earn on the average about 59 cents to a man's dollar, which means that a lesbian couple's combined income is likely to be less than a homosexual male couple's, and less than a heterosexual couple's. There is also the risk of possible double economic discrimination—for being a woman and for one's sexual preference. According to some women's business-group leaders, a woman who admits she has no interest in men has less chance than a heterosexual woman of success in the predominantly male workplace.

The homosexual men who enjoy high incomes are eager to spend them. If money can't buy you love, goes the theory, it could serve as a down payment on social acceptability. According to Thomas B. Stoddard, legislative counsel of the New York Civil Liberties Union and a contributor to the forthcoming guidebook called "The Rights of Gay People," living well is a matter of personal pride.

"For gays, it's a matter of showing that finally you're the 'in' group," he says. "You know how to dress and you know how to decorate your apartment. You're no longer the outsider you were in high school." The emphasis on the economic status of homosexuals represents an ideological detour: The most recent chapter of history had political and social beginnings, dating from the 1969 Stonewall riots—when patrons of that Greenwich Village bar responded with violence to repeated police harassment. And so, longtime activists and those who have advocated economic and cultural separatism for homosexuals cast a suspicious eye on the new effort to exploit homosexuals' buying power, and regarded its promoters as little more than capitalist carpetbaggers.

Ironically, a politically charged issue—Anita Bryant's 1977 campaign against homosexual rights in Dade County, Fla.—was what drove many homosexuals out into the open, into the business community's line of sight.

Retailers felt they could no longer ignore the fact that the mainstream population was adopting styles, in dress, decorating and even drinks, from affluent homosexuals. The male

homosexual with money was doubly attractive: He spent, and his selections seemed to influence others who spent.

"It was true in the 1930's, the 40's, the 50's and the 60's that we had more discretionary income than other men," says Michael Denneny, an editor at St. Martin's Press and an associate editor of Christopher Street. "But it wasn't until the 1970's that style began being heavily exported from the gay world to the rest of the culture."

One observer, surveying the Los Angeles bar scene, predicts that the sweet drinks currently in favor at bars frequented by homosexuals will be next year's major trend. In fashion, Frisch lists cotton housepainters' pants and aspects of "the western look" as crossovers.

"They're the first to do things," says Barry Lorie, Fox senior vice president, publicity and promotion, who worked on the "Making Love" campaign. "That's a given."

Joe Di Sabato, in addition to serving as an advertising representative, calls himself a "gay-marketing consultant," and is president of Rivendell Marketing. He devotes his professional life to the perpetuation of a particular, if narrow, group image.

"The old image of the gay," he says, "was gay radicals and transvestites. Now it's someone who drives a Maserati and has an Advent TV screen." Gordon Weaver, senior vice president of worldwide marketing for Paramount, says that using the homosexually oriented press is simply good business because its readers go to the movies frequently (twice a month, according to The Advocate survey). Paramount and Universal advertise most of their films in The Advocate.

Seagram advertises its Boodles Gin with a "famous men of history" campaign, and Robert Hinton, product manager for Boodles, explains that "the men pictured are purported to be gay." A bar mirror with portraits of historical figures—all safely deceased—such as Oscar Wilde and Walt Whitman was extremely popular.

Seagram is also increasing its advertising in the homosexual press this year. But company policy prohibits discussing the decision in detail, a not unusual posture among agencies and their clients. Many advertisers are ill at ease with such a decision, despite the seductive demographics, nervously referring to themselves as "groundbreakers" and "pioneers."

Roger Stone, a vice president of the Marshalk Agency, usually gets worse than silence in response. "When I make a recommendation to a client for even a modest expenditure for the gay market," says Stone, "I get six hours of conversation and two hours of elbows-in-the-ribs giggling."

"A man is going to come at this with one of three different attitudes," says Joe Di Sabato, assuming that the product is appropriate for the market. "Either he's had thoughts of homosexuality and is scared to death of confronting them, so he doesn't want to deal with it. Or he's gay and he's closeted, so he doesn't want to deal with it. Or he's straight and has no problem with it, in which case he can deal with it." Di Sabato complains that there "aren't many" of the straight executives who fit into the "no problem" category.

J. David Enright 4th worked with Roger Stone on the Smirnoff de Czar vodka account and admits, "as a young single fellow," that he was worried about guilt by association if he suggested advertising in The Advocate. But working with Stone, a family man, lessened his anxiety and the pragmatism of the move was inescapable: Many upscale male homosexuals use a bar as a social center and have money for indulgence products. Enright and Stone got Heublein, the parent company, to try a one-year "test situation."

The advertisements began last August and, while Enright refused to say how much the experiment costs, or what percentage of the account's entire magazine-advertising budget it represents, he was cautiously optimistic. The sales force reports from Los Angeles, San Francisco, New York, Chicago and Houston that the homosexual consumer seems to respond to the direct appeal.

"We've been able to use our advertising schedule as leverage," said Enright, "for getting placement in gay bars. If we show our ad to the owner of a gay bar, he'll be more willing to buy because he feels he's been supported by us."

Another direct-advertising success story comes from Pfizer Inc., a pharmaceutical company, which knew a target audience when it saw one. Lynn Gaudioso, product manager, and Joe Nolan, group product manager, got their hands on some medical research that showed homosexual men having a greater number of sexual contacts than the rest of the population, as well as a greater sophistication about dealing with resultant medical problems. Pfizer manufactures RID, an anti-crab/louse medication; the risk of infestation by these tiny pests increases with the number of sexual contacts.

Gaudioso and Nolan checked public-health clinics that treated venereal disease in neighborhoods known to have a high concentration of homosexuals and confirmed their suspicions: The creatures RID was designed to dispose of showed up there more often than at other clinics.

Pfizer hired Joe Di Sabato to pinpoint ZIP codes for target neighborhoods, and the company sales force moved in nationwide, drugstore to drugstore, with education material and a spiel. Pfizer spent $23,000 advertising RID in homosexually oriented newspapers in 1981, and will increase the budget by 20 percent to 25 percent in 1982 because salespeople reported an increase in sales.

Film makers find the path is a bit murkier, since they face a compound problem. They have to reach the homosexual audience and they have to reach the general audience with a homosexual theme. Fox felt that running a standard ad in the homosexually oriented press was not enough for "Making Love," and created a special color poster which ran in The Advocate. The studio also distributed posters and match books in bars popular among homosexuals.

The straight audience got a more subdued ad—and a promise: "'Making Love' is not sexually explicit; it is a love story that deals sensitively and candidly with a timely issue that audiences will want to discuss."

Barry Lorie realized early on that there was nothing to be gained by pushing the more controversial aspect of the film.

"If you go right ahead," he asked rhetorically, "what's your downside?"—referring to possible, but not entirely predictable, negative responses from the general audience.

Now that the film has completed its initial eight-week run, Lorie believes that Fox was successful in keeping a low profile. He blames the film's relatively modest performance ($12 million gross) on the fact that it didn't get good comments, not on audience reluctance to see a film with homosexual characters. "Personal Best" has earned less than half that, although it is still getting theater bookings after three months. One industry observer says that neither film will make back its cost on domestic rentals alone, as most succesful films do. The studios will have to depend on overseas rentals and sales to network and subscription television to recoup their investment.

No one is blaming the homosexual aspect of the stories, though—at least not publicly. Richard Kahn, head of advertising and publicity at M-G-M/U.A., says he doesn't think the theme of "Victor, Victoria" is a turnoff; rather, he says, "it plays old," meaning its middle-aged stars appeal to a middle-aged audience, which doesn't go to the movies very often. Paramount's Gordon Weaver points out that "there were no problems, no pickets" on "Making Love" and "Personal Best." He expects "Partners," like the others, "to be judged on its own merits in the marketplace."

It seems that the homosexual segment of that marketplace has responded to the advertising: "Making Love," "Personal Best " and "Victor, Victoria" did better in urban centers, where there are "gay ghettos," than in general release. (On the small screen, "Love, Sidney"—one of NBC's most successful shows—was the first of that network's new series to be renewed for the fall.)

No matter how many ad inches homosexually oriented publications tallied in 1981, the advertisements they haven't got represent many times the amount of space they have filled. Warner Bros., unconvinced by The Advocate's presentation, would not advertise for "Personal Best" or "Deathtrap." Major airlines, automobile companies and manufacturers of home-entertainment equipment—from video recorders to stereo components and cameras—have been approached by the papers, some of them more than once, and have turned them down.

Jerry Della Femina, chairman of Della Femina/Travisano & Partners, a New York advertising agency, says that most advertisers refuse to budge, all economic arguments notwithstanding. Whatever prejudices an advertiser may have personally, he still sees the economic wisdom of advertising to women and racial minorities. Homosexuals remain a special case because, as many advertisers see it, they have chosen to belong to a disenfranchised group.

"It certainly would make sense for someone to say the gay market is a potential market to look at," he says. "It's at least 10 percent of the audience. In major cities, it's up to 15 percent of the market, and that's conservative. Probably in major cities it's 20 percent to 22 percent. And yet nobody has ever said, 'Let's segment that market,' like they'll say, 'Let's reach the black market,' or 'Let's reach the ethnic market,' by which they mean Jews and Italians.''

Accusations of homophobia come quickly from within the homosexual community. Some members of the advertising profession, like Della Femina and Enright, believe that the prejudice does exist. But it is impossible to tell the extent of the problem, impossible to judge how many turn-downs are simply considered prudent business decisions.

What confuses the issue even more is the very marketing survey that makes these consumers look attractive in the first place. Some advertisers complain that The Advocate's 1,100 sampling is too small to be taken seriously, and Frisch has now formed Avanti Communications to mount national marketing surveys—surveys that have already elicited interest from a list of possible subscribers, including, says Frisch, "several large ad agencies' research staffs."

The Advocate survey also showed that members of this market read more publications than do most people, so advertisers can decide not to advertise directly because they're reaching the market through their general outlets.

According to Hank Koehn, a vice president at the Los Angeles-based Security Pacific National Bank, the nation's 10th-largest commercial banking institution, "If you're marketing properly, you'll reach the gay market anyhow. It's part of a generally affluent group we call 'singles, mingles and never-nesters.' The mingles are two adults living together, regardless of what sex they are, and the never-nesters are two people who are married but have decided never to procreate."

This way, the advertiser also avoids an unwanted return on his investment—the possibility that his product will come to be identified with the homosexual community.

"There are two ways in which an advertiser can be tainted by openly appealing to a gay market," says Tom Stoddard. "First, he can turn off straight men . . . who don't want to be identified as being homosexual. If, for example, Marlboro advertised to gay men and a straight man was smoking Marlboros, he might be afraid that he would be identified as being gay. And then there's the new phenomenon, which is the Moral Majority phenomenon, the fear that advertisers now have—the quite legitimate fear—that they will be boycotted by people who feel that it's wrong, somehow, to advertise to, or recognize, homosexuality. So they will not now, whether they are tempted to or not, openly advertise to gay people." There is an alternative, however, midway between the open appeal of direct advertising and no advertising at all: Laud Humphreys, a sociologist at Pitzer College and author of "Tearoom Trade: Impersonal Sex in Public Places," calls it "gay window advertising," and David Enright says it is "probably the most prevalent response right now" to the question of how to reach the market.

The idea is to speak to the homosexual consumer in a way that the straight consumer will not notice. "It used to be that gay people could communicate to one another, in a public place, if they didn't know one another, only by glances and a sort of code behavior," says Tom Stoddard, "to indicate to the

other person, but not to anybody else, that you, too, were gay. Advertisers, if they're smart, can do that too."

Calvin Klein's jeans advertisements are a frequently mentioned example of mainstream messages allegedly aimed at the homosexual male. One billboard for his men's jeans featured a young, shirtless blond man lying on his stomach. Another in the series showed another young, shirtless blond man lying on his side, holding a blue-jeans jacket. A simultaneous magazine campaign utilized a double-page spread of a young, shirtless blond man, shown on his stomach and on his back, sprawled on a shiny black floor.

Peter Frisch's evaluation: "You have to be comatose not to realize that it appeals to gay men." Lisa Rosen, marketing director for Puritan Fashions, which markets Calvin Klein jeans, seemed to agree, at first. After last fall's fashion shows, she admitted, she was "looking for some criteria" on how to reach homosexual men, who seem to cling to their predesigner, Levi-Strauss straight-leg, button-fly jeans despite the prevalence of newer models like Klein's.

The fashion shows proved to Lisa Rosen that this was a market worth pursuing. "We have videotapes taken during men's wear shows in San Francisco and Los Angeles," she said, offering to display the evidence. "You look at the type of man on the runway, and in the crowd, and you know there's a gay element."

But her willingness to discuss the market did not last. "I thought it over," she said, when it came time to look at the tapes. "I don't want to touch this with a 10-foot pole. I don't think it's politically smart for the company to be talking about this. I don't think that a spokesperson from Calvin Klein, other than Calvin Klein, should be taking a position on this."

Calvin Klein was unavailable on numerous occasions. Rochelle Udell, creative director at CRK Advertising, which handles all Calvin Klein fashions, had this to say about the shirtless ads: "We did not try not to appeal to gays. We try to appeal, period. With healthy, beautiful people. If there's an awareness in that community of health and grooming, then they'll respond to the ads. You really want to reach a bigger market than just gays, but you don't want to alienate them."

Paco Rabanne men's cologne, Pour Homme, is another product that comes up in any conversation about "gay window" advertising, primarily because of a magazine advertisement showing a man lying in a rumpled bed talking on the phone to someone the dialogue vividly portrays as a just-departed male lover. Among others, the novelist Felice Picano, who runs the independent Seahorse Press, says the visuals so strongly reflect popular styles ("It is a gay man's apartment") that he is convinced the ad is meant to have a dual appeal. Even the fact that the televised version of the advertisement gives the unseen lover a woman's voice does not dissuade him.

Both C. Michael Newbrand, the account executive, and the creative director who work on the account at the Ogilvy & Mather advertising agency deny any conscious effort to reach the market. But Newbrand, for one, knows that "prestige fragrances" sell in urban areas. He is aware that "gays represent a good market."

So: "If we have a high percentage of gays using the product," says Newbrand, "we certainly don't mind." Especially if the rest of the consumers don't notice the subtext in the ad. The only evidence of "gay window" advertising is in the eye of the beholder: The whole beauty of the concept, for advertisers, is in being able to do something without confessing it.

In some cases, the advertiser may not even be aware of the reaction a campaign might evoke. Jerry Della Femina dismisses the notion that cigarette companies are making a covert play for the homosexual market with advertisements that feature single, attractive men wearing what is commonly referred to as the "logger look," a popular style among homosexual men that includes a plaid lumberjack shirt and blue jeans. "These companies are located in North Carolina," he says. "Their closets aren't closets. They're fortresses. Reinforced bunkers. When they tell you they had no idea—believe me, they had no idea."

But this sidesteps the issue. The link between a company and its public is the advertising agency, where people know the demographics, recognize the attractiveness of the market and don't mind going after it if they can do so without exposing their clients to potential backlash.

There are enough examples of the phenomenon, in fact, to lead Friends Publishing to launch what could be considered a "gay window" magazine. Bicoastal, a slick monthly publication with a $3.25 price tag, is scheduled, after several delays, to make its debut this month, and its editor, Charles Codol, predicts that "nine out of 10 of our readers will be gay." The magazine's advertising strategy boils down to accentuating the positive and eliminating the negative: Codol stresses his readers' buying power and vows there will be no nudity, no sexually explicit personal ads, nothing to upset a mainstream advertiser.

"You can appeal to advertisers with discriminating tastes," he says, "if you don't visualize, pictorially, any activity that goes against the grain of American society." Until now, homosexuals have been condescendingly portrayed in movies primarily as troubled, unhappy neurotics or benign, frivolous supporting characters. In the new films, though, they are treated with an almost deferential courtesy and affection. The old images are giving way to what is, essentially, an image drawn from that segment of the homosexual population that shares a devotion to comfort with the straight middle class.

If the American Dream is material comfort, professional success and satisfying personal achievement, suddenly the homosexual is being allowed to dream it, on the silver screen, along with everybody else.

Is this an indication of growing acceptance? The question divides the homosexual community. "There is a whole ideological debate," says the sociologist Laud Humphreys, "between those who want to be considered the same as everyone else, except for whom they sleep with, and those who want to maintain their own culture."

The debate centers on whether homosexuals lose more than they gain by becoming cogs in the wheel of commerce—be it Madison Avenue or the entertainment conglomerates. Members of the community who have never aspired to sameness say the battle for recognition takes a toll: All the homosexual consumer gets is pressure to deny that he is different, sort of an economic variation on the "Invasion of the Bodysnatchers" theme.

Stuart Byron, a former Village Voice film columnist, believes that what may seem to be a superficially attractive image is merely another incomplete stereotype that will, in the end, do more damage than good.

"Sidney Schorr conforms to every stereotype people have of gay people," he says. "They can watch that program and say, 'We're right. Once a gay person reaches 45, they don't know about bars and sex. They sit at home. They're lonely. Deep down, all they're good for is to be a baby sitter. And deep down, they all want a family with a woman and a child—just like us.' " Brandon Tartikoff, president of NBC Entertainment, would prefer to believe that Sidney's homosexuality does not even exist. In fact, he is banking on references to it being so subtle that many viewers will not realize they're watching a landmark in prime-time programming. "There are a couple of those double-entendre references," Tartikoff has said, referring to the ever-present photograph of Sidney's estranged lover, Martin. "Those who are smart enough to know do know. Those who aren't smart enough aren't puzzled."

The culture produced by the homosexual community itself—the books, plays, art, music, independent films—is so young and fragile at this point, according to Michael Denneny, that it cannot withstand assimilation. "Everybody comes out sexually before they come out socially," he says. "Then there's a level where people are out socially—even their co-workers know they're gay—but their imagination is still straight-oriented. They don't buy gay magazines and novels. They subscribe to The New Yorker or Architectural Digest and they read the best sellers. If there isn't a demand from the community, the writers will dry up or die out except for the heroes. It's like being in the middle of the desert. Eventually, the writers will just start censoring themselves. They just write what will be published. Women understood that, for their identity, a separate feminist culture had to be supported. But gays are not yet buying a lot of books about gays."

Charles Ortleb, publisher of Christopher Street and The New York Native, has hung on for six years, supported primarily by local businesses, and thinks the economic as well as the cultural focus has to remain within the community. "I have always said the trick is to get political people to be rich," says Ortleb in his underendowed offices in downtown Manhattan. "I believe we waste a lot of time trying to get Bloomingdale's and Macy's to advertise. We should try to build businesses of our own in the city."

Other members of the community, who see trouble in any economic definition of progress, take an even more reluctant stance. David Rothenberg, a member of the New York Human

Rights Commission, believes that homosexuals are "the only audience they try to woo and hold in contempt at the same time," and worries that the image "of men who are economically elite and morally reprehensible to the majority of the American people" is a dangerous one because it fosters resentment and exaggerates the existing isolation.

Laud Humphreys agrees. "Right now, in a working class economy," he says, "I can imagine a lot of people reading about the gay market and saying, 'We should give them their rights? We're starving. They're buying a Mercedes.'"

As the co-author of a study of homosexual victims of violent crime, Humphreys has evidence of how that resentment is sometimes expressed. The gentrified urban ghetto may be a safe place, psychologically, but its existence can give antihomosexual violence a convenient focus. There is another drawback to living in a concentrated island of homosexual population—a distortion of one's perception. What happens to, and in, a ghetto takes on an unreal significance, and tends to eclipse what is not happening in the rest of the country.

For all the talk of economic inroads, regardless of the debate as to where those roads lead, a crucial point is often ignored. Advertisers still insist on relating to the homosexual consumer within the confines of his newspapers, unnoticed by the rest of the population, or, if "gay window" advertising is as widespread as some believe, within the confines of a homosexual's psyche.

What advertisers have yet to do is construct a homosexual prototype to take his or her place in the family of national-advertising characters. McDonald's does television commercials with all-black casts. Stouffer's frozen foods have a long-running series that features a harried career woman. On television and in print, ethnic characters sell everything from Italian food products to Pentax cameras.

We no longer see Billie Jean King, but we do see black celebrities and female celebrities selling. Once the Los Angeles Dodger pitcher and 1981 Cy Young award winner Fernando Valenzuela sifts through the mountains of endorsement offers, a Mexican celebrity who barely speaks English will have been legitimized.

But a television commercial has yet to portray two childless, attractive men as they turn off their dual alarm, or brush their teeth side by side at double sinks, or discuss the aroma of the morning's coffee or the crunch of their breakfast cereal and imitation low-cholesterol bacon. One man does not kiss another man goodbye as he gets behind the wheel of his low-mileage car.

Will they ever—or is this to continue as a secret courtship? Roger Stone of the Marshalk Agency takes the good-business approach to the issue of two men and toothpaste in television's future. "Of course, you'll have gay men," he says. "In terms of dollars, it's a bigger market than the black market."

"Definitely, you'll see it," says Ortleb. "But it is going to be another 10 or 15 years." "I doubt it," says Peter Frisch, "because two men brushing their teeth together would not appeal to most people." "Not an identifiable gay," opines Ken Struman, the market researcher who designed The Advocate surveys, "but you can put a less obvious . . . . A lot of male models don't exactly ooze masculinity."

Jerry Della Femina pronounces judgment without hesitation. "Not in our lifetime," he says. He is likely right. There is an analogy to be made, however uncomfortable the business community might be about the connection, between the homosexual population and business's attitude toward it. The highly visible, ghettoized male homosexual lives apart from other homosexuals in this country; he is a distinct minority, as are the advertisers who go after him. Like the still-closeted homosexual population—fearful of the ramifications of a public declaration, and unconvinced of the benefits—most providers of goods and services choose either to deny their interest or evade the issue altogether.

Karen Stabiner is a West Coast freelance writer.

* * *

March 26, 1992

'HOT EDITOR' PHENOMENON BENEFITS THE NEW REPUBLIC

By STUART ELLIOTT

When The New Republic became the first mainstream national magazine with an openly gay top editor, it was something of a publishing milestone. It now seems that the appointment might be a kind of advertising milestone as well.

In October, when Andrew Sullivan was named editor of the Washington-based opinion journal, there was widespread talk among advertising, marketing and media executives that some advertisers would prove leery of him, in much the same manner that sponsors withdraw from television programs with plots centering on homosexuality or other controversial issues. That was intensified by the fact that many of The New Republic's advertisers are military contractors, corporate associations and similarly traditionally minded concerns.

Instead, The New Republic finished last year, a poor one for magazine advertising over all, with an ad-page gain of 3.6 percent. And Jeffrey L. Dearth, the weekly's president, expects ad pages this year to rise by as much as 20 percent from 1991.

"The thought is always in the back of your mind" that Mr. Sullivan's sexuality would discourage advertisers, Mr. Dearth said in a telephone interview. "But no, thank God, it hasn't, and I'm delighted."

A primary reason why Mr. Sullivan's appointment has apparently not dissuaded advertisers is a phenomenon in magazine publishing known as "the hot editor." Advertisers and their agencies prize the titles whose editors can generate excitement via word of mouth and national publicity, whether because of who they are, what they write, whom they hire, or all of the above.

And Mr. Sullivan is heating up, not only because he is openly gay, but also because he is young (28 years old), a foreigner (British) and religious (Roman Catholic). He has been the subject of profiles in several leading publications, including Time magazine. On April 6, he is scheduled to receive an award for outstanding magazine editing from the Gay and Lesbian Alliance Against Defamation at its third annual media awards ceremony.

Perhaps most typical of the hot editor is Mr. Sullivan's compatriot, Tina Brown, who since becoming editor in chief at Vanity Fair in 1984 has transformed a failing revival into one of the nation's most-talked-about, and most successful, magazines. Indeed, Mr. Dearth has sent reprints of some of Mr. Sullivan's articles to "Vanity Fair-type" advertisers in chic categories underrepresented in The New Republic, like fashion, liquor and fragrances.

"It's nice when a magazine on your schedule is doing well and is, in quotes, 'hot,'" said Christine Farley, assistant vice president of advertising at the Aetna Life and Casualty Company in Hartford, which in January added The New Republic to the lengthy list of magazines in which it advertises via Ammirati & Puris, New York.

While "it is not the driver for making those decisions" about advertising in a magazine, she added, "it's a bonus."

Paula Brooks, executive vice president and director of media services at Margeotes Fertitta & Weiss in New York, is considering The New Republic for a number of clients. "The fact they have a new editor, and he's 28, and his sexual preference is what it is, and he's much publicized as well, makes you want to pick it up and look at it," she said.

And Mr. Sullivan's opinions are of "a more moderate slant," she added, "that make The New Republic more appropriate for a broader base of advertisers."

Indeed, while another gay journalist might have put off advertisers by advocating radical opinions, Mr. Sullivan opposes "outing," the practice of disclosing the homosexuality of prominent individuals, and the idea of changing the word "queer" from an epithet into a label of proud self-identification, a move popular with some gay men and lesbians.

His attitudes toward advertising are similarly inclusive. He has called it an "art form" and has participated in presentations made to advertisers, meeting executives from companies like General Motors and Lockheed.

"He's a wonderful spokesman for the magazine," said Jim McCabe, director of joint sales for The New Republic and The National Review, which in August left the Leadership Network, a sales consortium for small "opinion leader" magazines, and formed their own network called the Balance of Power.

Presentations are planned later in the spring, he added, at which Mr. Sullivan and John O'Sullivan, editor of The National Review, will speak to advertisers in Boston, Chicago and New York.

*   *   *

February 21, 1993

GAY OFFICERS FIND ACCEPTANCE ON NEW YORK'S POLICE FORCE

By RALPH BLUMENTHAL

Before agreeing to "partner up" in Manhattan's Sixth Precinct, Police Officer Emma Llaurado took her fellow officer Debra Martinez aside.

"Look, Debbie," she warned, "I came here as an open lesbian; you may get labeled."

Officer Martinez was practically insulted. She knew homosexuality was not catching, she said. And besides, she was a black woman with a Hispanic surname. "I collect labels," she said.

The buddy team of the two 39-year-old New York City policewomen—one straight, one gay, and both mothers—is a symbol of the decline of sexual stereotypes that is further diversifying the nation's largest police department.

'We Are Everywhere'

Following efforts to erase barriers to women and racial minorities, the growing receptivity to homosexuals marks a particularly striking turnabout for a department long reviled in the gay community for its 1969 raid on a Greenwich Village homosexual bar, the Stonewall Inn, which helped ignite the gay rights movement.

Now, interviews with dozens of officers and gay advocates throughout the city indicate, the New York Police Department is successfully integrating gay and lesbian officers into virtually every policing function.

Other city and state justice agencies, from corrections to district attorneys' offices, have also shown a new hospitality to gay employees, gay advocates say. The more insular Fire Department has been more resistant, although seven present and former members recently started Fire-FLAG, an organization for Firefighters, Lesbian and Gay.

At a time of sharp national debate over the Clinton Administration's commitment to lifting the military's traditional ban on homosexual troops, officers of all sexual persuasions at different levels of the Police Department say the transition to equal opportunity for gay officers, if hardly flawless, carries lessons for other organizations.

"We are everywhere," said Sgt. Edgar Rodriguez, a community policing training supervisor in the Sixth Precinct and a board member of an association of gay and lesbian police and law-enforcement officers called the Gay Officers Action League. GOAL puts its New York City membership at 1,000, about 800 of them police officers.

New York's approach stands in particular contrast to that of the Los Angeles Police Department, the nation's second largest, which for years barred homosexuals. Only this month the department settled a bitter lawsuit by agreeing to open its ranks to gay men and lesbians.

Change is coming to other departments around the country. GOAL says it recently opened chapters in Springfield, Mass.,

San Francisco, Seattle, Chicago, Denver and Marlboro, Md., and has affiliates in London and Amsterdam.

Still a Macho World

At the same time, homophobia remains widespread in the macho world of the police in New York, as elsewhere, and most gay and lesbian officers remain closeted, keeping their homosexuality secret for fear of ostracism or ridicule.

For example, the department is aware of two gay officers, as well as one heterosexual officer, who have AIDS but pay extra to buy their medication outside the department to avoid notice.

Many in law enforcement, both closeted and out, say they have suffered slurs.

When his lover died, for instance, Mike DeCicco, assistant deputy warden of the city Corrections Department's brig at the Flushing Navy Yard, said that when he returned to work, he heard that other officers had made fun of his grief. "I was infuriated," he said.

Another officer in Queens, who said he was not yet ready to come out, said someone had painted "fag" on his locker and maliciously reported him as being suicidal. He said he had rebuffed a bisexual male supervisor who had solicited him for sex.

Those who do proclaim their sexual orientation tend to do so in the few precincts where they feel comfortable, such as the Sixth in Greenwich Village, the Ninth in the East Village, the 10th in Manhattan's Chelsea section and the 78th in Brooklyn's Park Slope. Gay men are more likely to come out than lesbians, advocates say, because women, a tenth of the force, already feel under pressure.

Many Signs of Change

While it is impossible to know whether more gay men and lesbians are joining the police now than in previous years, a new receptivity to gay members is undeniable in the 30,000-member department.

The signs of change are many. Gay and lesbian officers pose for department recruiting posters, serve openly at headquarters and the Police Academy, lead precinct community policing units and train rookies.

Male officers, gay and straight, routinely share showers, locker rooms and cramped overnight billets with few reported problems, as do female officers, gay and straight.

GOAL is recognized by the department and drew Commissioner Raymond W. Kelly to its holiday party last December.

"The experience here is that there has been no experience here," said Capt. Stephen Kennedy of the Sixth Precinct, his way of shrugging off anything unusual about his heavily gay outpost at West 10th and Bleecker Streets.

The policy has been clearly set from the top after the state Court of Appeals in 1980 overturned the sodomy law that had criminalized homosexuality and thereby made it difficult for a law-enforcement agency to welcome gay men and lesbians.

By 1981 the department had added a psychologist and sex researcher who is gay, Patrick Suraci, to its staff. When Irish and Jewish fraternal police organizations balked at accepting GOAL as a member of their coalition called Brotherhood in Action, Benjamin Ward, then the Commissioner, ordered the coalition disbanded.

"We just want good cops," said Suzanne Trazoff, the deputy commissioner for public information. "We don't draw lines that exclude people because of sexual orientation or race or anything else."

The Chief of Department's special liaison officer to gay men and lesbians, Detective Vanessa Ferro, who came out as a lesbian four years ago, agreed. "This is a great place for gays to work," she said. "It's a safe environment to be who you are."

Certainly sexual orientation is not a big issue in the Sixth Precinct, where Officers Llaurado and Martinez have been partners for two years, linked more by confidence in each other's police instincts than separated by "what you do in the privacy of your bedroom," as Officer Llaurado put it.

Cold Beer and 'Fort Bruce'

Both, moreover, say they are bound by being mothers. Officer Martinez is the single parent of a daughter, age 12. Officer Llaurado has a son, 2, fathered by an anonymous sperm donor, whom she is raising with her companion of nine years, Frances DeBenedictis, an officer who trains instructors at the Police Academy.

Many of the precinct's 220 members turned out not long ago for a talent show that included a popular drag queen performer. Straight officers often stop for drinks after work at nearby gay bars.

"They don't care," said Sgt. Leslie Hanley, a community policing supervisor who said she came out last year. "If the beer is cold, they'll drink it."

With mordant police humor, officers recently debated whether to add a "Fort Bruce" T-shirt to the station house's collection of uniforms.

Captain Kennedy credited the cooperative spirit in the station house for helping cut precinct robberies by nearly a third since 1990 and for cutting nuisance offenses.

Gay officers around the city said they were not surprised by the Sixth Precinct's experience.

"There's a perception that gays and lesbians are obsessed with sex and can't control themselves," said Colleen Meenan, a retired police sergeant who now practices law and is executive director of GOAL. But she and other GOAL members said heterosexuals were more often arrested for rape and child-molestation.

Sergeant Rodriguez said he resented it when heterosexual male officers asked why he made an issue of his homosexuality. He said he replied that they were the ones who usually broadcast sexual conquests of women and that he reminded them: "I never told you anything about my sex life."

Several gay officers said they found it ludicrous that straight colleagues might fear a sexual advance in the shower or locker rooms. "Why does anyone think we want them so badly?" asked Mr. DeCicco, the corrections officer.

When complaints by officers are investigated, Detective Ferro said, they often turn out to involve personality disputes beyond the issue of sexual orientation.

Many officers said the Pentagon should take a cue from the Police Department. "This is a good house; everybody gets along," said Sgt. John Argenziano, a training supervisor in the Sixth Precinct who is straight. If it were the Army, he said, "it would be a fine fighting machine."

* * *

July 8, 1995

BENEFITS GIVEN COORS WORKERS' GAY PARTNERS

By KENNETH N. GILPIN

The Coors Brewing Company, considered by many a bedrock of conservative views, has decided to offer full benefits to employees' unmarried domestic partners, including homosexual companions.

The proposal to extend such benefits was made by a group of Coors employees known as the Lesbian and Gay Resource Group, or Lager. The company's board approved the change, by unanimous vote, on May 11. The change was disclosed to Coors employees on June 21.

The change was the latest in a series at Coors, which in the past had been boycotted by minorities over its employee relations and support of conservative causes through foundations created with the Coors fortune.

Coors joins dozens of other companies nationwide that offer full benefits to unmarried partners, including Apple Computer, the Xerox Corporation and Levi-Strauss.

In addition to recognizing the lesbian and gay employee association, Coors offers sensitivity training on minority issues and has a nondiscrimination clause to protect gay employees.

The company's new policy allows unmarried, live-in partners of company employees to be added to health and life insurance policies, pensions and other benefits.

The Coors move was hailed by gay-rights advocates.

"We absolutely applaud the victory Lager has won, and think it is a great step forward for Coors Brewery employees," said Kerry Lobel, deputy director of the National Gay and Lesbian Task Force in Washington. "We hope other employers will follow suit.

"However, we are still concerned about the relationship between the Coors Brewing Company, the Coors Family Foundation and members of the Coors family who fund social policies that are not in the interests of gays and lesbians in this country."

Among other organizations the Coors Foundation and Coors family members have contributed to, Ms. Lobel said, is the Heritage Foundation, the conservative Washington organization she contends is an advocate of anti-gay policies.

Joe Fuentes, a Coors spokesman, said there was no connection between the company's social policies and those supported by the Coors Foundation or by members of the Coors family.

* * *

August 20, 1995

THE POLITICS OF HOMOSEXUALITY

By DENIS DONOGHUE

VIRTUALLY NORMAL: An Argument About Homosexuality
By Andrew Sullivan
209 pp. New York: Alfred A. Knopf. $22.

Andrew Sullivan is, in no particular order, the following: the editor of The New Republic, an Englishman settled in the United States, a homosexual, a graduate of Oxford University in modern history and modern languages, a Ph.D. in political science from Harvard, a student of the conservative political philosophy of Michael Oakeshott and—so far as I know—a practicing Roman Catholic. In "Virtually Normal" he outlines a politics of homosexuality:

"This is not a book about how a person deals with his or her sexuality," he writes. "It is a book about how we as a society deal with that small minority of us which is homosexual. By 'homosexual,' I mean simply someone who can tell a similar story to my own; someone who has found in his or her life that he or she is drawn emotionally and sexually to the same gender, someone who, practically speaking, has had no fundamental choice in the matter."

Not much of Andrew Sullivan's own story is to be found in "Virtually Normal." He told a little more of it in an earlier version of the first chapter, which appeared last year in a special issue of South Atlantic Quarterly called "Catholic Lives/ Contemporary America." There he spoke of growing up in a Catholic family in East Grinstead, south of London, and of coming to realize that he was emotionally and sexually different from most of the boys in his school. The essay dealt with the anxiety and pain connected with that difference, and it ended with a plea to the church to permit homosexual acts on the analogy of permitting heterosexual acts to married infertile couples. Mr. Sullivan didn't pursue the matter far. He might well have quoted Pope Pius XI's encyclical "Casti Connubii" in its reference to such couples, but he let his plea speak for itself.

Most of that essay, including the plea, turns up again in this book, but the context is now worldly and secular. According to the essay, the church cannot yet see homosexuals "as it sees sterile heterosexuals: as people who, with respect to procreation, suffer from a clear, limiting condition, but who nevertheless have a potential for real emotional and spiritual self-realization, in the heart of the church, through the transfiguring power of the sacraments." In the book there is no reference to the heart of the church or the sacraments; sterile heterosexuals now have "a potential for as complete a human fulfillment as their condition will allow."

After the first chapter of "Virtually Normal," the church is mentioned only as one source of the belief that homosexual acts are to be deplored.

This belief, so far as it arises—however vaguely—from Judaic and Christian teaching, is largely based on the two stories of human creation in Genesis. One of these tells of the creation of men and women with a view to procreation: "Be fruitful and multiply." This, added to the image of Christ's Holy Family, guarantees the privilege of respect for the ideal social form: father, mother and children. The other story in Genesis tells of marriage and companionship: "It is not good that the man should be alone: I will make him a helper fit for him. . . . Therefore a man leaves his father and mother and cleaves to his wife and they become one flesh." Objection to male homosexual acts is also based on Leviticus 20: "If a man has intercourse with a man as with a woman, both commit an abomination." The objection is intensified by the story of the destruction of Sodom and Gomorrah, "cities of the plain," if their fate is interpreted as divine punishment. Some scholars of the Bible claim that the men of Sodom were punished not for sexual depravity but for refusing hospitality to strangers. But that interpretation makes it hard to understand why Lot tried to fend off the men and appease their concupiscence by letting his virgin daughters loose to them. Another element in the common attitude arises from a sense of nature or natural law that the church teaches on the authority of revelation and tradition, as these are enunciated by Aquinas and other fathers of the church.

Mr. Sullivan regards this attitude as a major obstacle to his proposed politics. It is not the only one. He distinguishes four stances, each of which is fallacious. Mr. Sullivan calls them prohibitionist, liberationist, conservative and liberal, using these words not as they are used in ordinary political discourse but in special senses. The prohibitionist thinks that the homosexual condition is an illness and that homosexual acts "are transgressions which require legal punishment and social deterrence." The liberationist thinks "that the notion of 'homosexuality' does not refer to something tangible and universal; it is a definition of a particular way of being as defined by a particular culture." Human nature, according to liberationists, "is socially constructed or infinitely malleable." A conservative is "a variety of liberal: someone who essentially shares the premises of the liberal state, its guarantee of liberty, of pluralism, of freedom of speech and action, but who still believes politics is an arena in which it is necessary to affirm certain cultural, social and moral values over others." As for liberals:

"Unlike conservatives, whose first recourse is to ask how society's interests are affected by this phenomenon—and therefore what social effects would be incurred by a relaxation of the anti-homosexual taboo—liberals ask first how the individual is affected. And by this, of course, they mean primarily the individual homosexual.

"They see the homosexual's rights infringed in several areas: the right to individual privacy, where anti-sodomy laws exist; the right to free expression, where social oppression largely intimidates homosexuals from disclosing freely who they are; and, most significantly, the right to employment and housing, where anti-homosexual prejudice results in homosexuals being fired or never hired because of their sexual orientation, or being refused housing."

Mr. Sullivan argues with notable force and cogency against each of these positions, clearing a space for his own program. He describes this as "a politics that can reconcile the best arguments of liberals and conservatives, and find a way to marry the two." The metaphor of marrying is perhaps more revealing than he knows. Further:

"This politics affirms a simple and limited principle: that all public (as opposed to private) discrimination against homosexuals be ended and that every right and responsibility that heterosexuals enjoy as public citizens be extended to those who grow up and find themselves emotionally different. And that is all."

The examples he takes are homosexuals in the military and equal access to marriage. On these, he feels strongly. He thinks the Pentagon's "don't ask, don't tell" policy is a wretched compromise, a blatant piece of hypocrisy. For the question of equal access to marriage, he reserves most of his eloquence. But he has a rather sentimental idea of marriage in the modern state: "In the contemporary West, marriage has become a way in which the state recognizes an emotional commitment by two people to each other for life."

That recognition seems to me the least of the state's interests. Marriage exists in the state, like one's Social Security number, to facilitate the enforcement of rights and responsibilities in relation to children, property, money and taxation. It enables the state to keep track of those rights and responsibilities even through the thickets of divorce.

Mr. Sullivan ends his book by asking, "What are homosexuals for?" He answers: "a more highly developed sense of form, of style," "a sense of irony" and a gift for "the estheticization of pain." I'm not sure that this last emphasis is wise. Many readers will recall that the Marxist critic Walter Benjamin described Mussolini's Fascism as "the estheticization of the political." It is a further attribute of homosexuals, according to Mr. Sullivan, that "they can transfer their absent parental instincts into broader parental roles: they can be extraordinary teachers and mentors, nurses and doctors, priests, rabbis and nuns; they can throw themselves into charity work, helping the needy and the lonely; they can care for the young who have been abandoned by others, through adoption." Yes. But I don't think Mr. Sullivan is prudent in offering a characterization of "the homosexual" at all: it merely adds a type, ostensibly stable, to the stock of types already in the hands of sociologists.

The characterization may cause him a further problem: that of being called an assimilationist, and a tame one. Mr. Sullivan's advocacy of equal access to marriage puts homosexuals in the position of miming the venerable social orthodoxy of which marriage is a crucial part. It also implies that he endorses without question the values of family and community as heterosexuals have defined them. I don't quarrel with him on these grounds, but Leo Bersani would. In his recent book, "Homos," Mr. Bersani, a literary critic, a professor of French and "a white, relatively prosperous gay man," proposes to enact "an alternative to the straight mind," and to question not only the values of family and community but the nearly universally accredited sanctity of the person. He endorses "a desire indifferent to the established sanctity of personhood."

I am not, in my own person, directly caught in this dispute. But I should declare an interest. My youngest daughter, the writer Emma Donoghue, is a lesbian. This does not darken my love for her, or qualify the joy I take in her being, her personality, her immense gifts. On the hypothetical dispute between Andrew Sullivan and Leo Bersani, I hope Emma will agree with Mr. Sullivan and continue to make her life, as far as possible, within a society that is indeed largely ordained, for better or worse, by heterosexuals. She is doing this with every sign of accomplishment and, I trust, with satisfaction. Mr. Sullivan, I imagine, would find her success worth celebrating, as I do. But I don't think Mr. Bersani would; he would regard Emma as melting into a world she has not made. His program in "Homos" seems to me a regression to apartheid, and one enforced this time round by homosexuals. I hope that Emma will have nothing to do with it.

Denis Donoghue is the University Professor of English and American Letters at New York University. His most recent book is "Walter Pater: Lover of Strange Souls."

* * *

September 1, 1996

'GAY FRIENDLY' FUND HAS BLUE-CHIP FOCUS

By REED ABELSON

The first mutual fund to invest in gay-friendly companies tries not only to identify those that already have progressive policies but also to persuade other companies to meet its criteria.

"We like to think of ourselves as socially proactive," said Shelly J. Meyers, a 37-year-old lesbian who manages the new Meyers Sheppard Pride fund in Beverly Hills, Calif.

The fund has pressed two companies to adopt an explicit policy of not discriminating against gay people in its hiring and promotion practices, Ms. Meyers said. And it has invested in one of those companies, a small software outfit that Ms. Meyers declined to name. The fund also plans to encourage companies to become even more gay-friendly, by taking measures like allowing domestic partners of same-sex couples to receive health insurance benefits.

"It was important that Disney did not give an inch when it was criticized for its health benefits" to domestic partners of same-sex couples, Ms. Meyers said. "I think it's very, very important for Disney to take a stand."

Ms. Meyers is as passionate about investing as about her social agenda. "The love of my life is the stock market," she said.

She previously managed private accounts at the Boston Company and worked as an international audit analyst with Chevron before founding Meyers Sheppard & Company with Leslie C. Sheppard. Begun in June, the fund has garnered $500,000 in assets, its management says. It invests only in blue-chip companies that it says have progressive attitudes toward gay people.

Ms. Meyers emphasized that any company in her portfolio must also be a good investment. "I am not going to buy a single company because I enjoy its social perspective," she said.

So what does she consider a good investment? Ms. Meyers says she looks for stocks that are bargains and that seem as if they could take off.

Her portfolio of 37 stocks resembles that of other growth-stock funds. Her top 10 holdings include well-known names like AT, Merck, Time Warner, Amgen and the Limited. She says she has found roughly 375 companies that meet her criteria of being blue chips and gay-friendly.

Once you factor out AT's other businesses, Ms. Meyers said, "you're getting long distance at a great bargain." The company also has a policy of not discriminating against gay people. The stock, which closed Friday at $52.50, trades at just 14 times this year's estimated earnings per share.

Mobil is an old favorite from "way back when, when I came out of the oil patch," Ms. Meyers said. Like AT, it has a policy not to discriminate against gay people. Although the stock is trading at a discount to many of its peers, Ms. Meyers says Mobil is the best run of the big oil companies. The stock closed Friday at $112.75.

Investors have to take Ms. Meyer at her word that she is not "hamstrung" by the fund's social objective. Although she worked as an analyst and assistant portfolio manager for the Boston Company, she has never managed a socially conscious fund.

The fund is sold without a sales charge, but investors should take note of its high expenses—estimated at 2.25 percent of assets, compared with 1.4 percent for the average growth fund, according to Morningstar Inc., the fund researchers. As the fund becomes larger, Ms. Meyers expects the expense ratio to fall.

While it is much too early to judge the fund, its performance has equaled the overall market. From the start of July through Thursday, it has lost 1.64 percent after management fees are deducted, Ms. Meyers said, the same decline posted by the S.& P. 500. (The fund is not yet followed by Morningstar.) "Any year I do not beat the S.& P. 500," Ms. Meyers said, "I will not be a happy camper."

* * *

April 21, 1997

DRAWING RAVE REVIEWS AFTER YEARS OUT OF SIGHT

By JOHN J. O'CONNOR

We've heard enough about the race card so deftly played by smooth Johnnie L. Cochran Jr. in that Los Angeles trial most of us would rather forget. Less obvious, though just as entrenched and sometimes at least as insidious, is what might by called the gay card.

Gay and lesbian history is rooted in decades when the mere whisper that one was not staunchly heterosexual could wreck careers and lives. Keepers of public morals kept so-called transgressors firmly in their place, preferably in ominous shadows. Then in 1969 came the Stonewall uprising, in which gay customers at a Greenwich Village bar fought back against the police, who were often raiding such places. The sea change began. It would accelerate with the advent of AIDS and years of harrowing headlines.

Today the gay card is no longer an automatic trump for bigots. When still another celebrity is found to be gay, the prevailing reaction borders on ho-hum. In fact, ABC has been using the once-feared card to drum up publicity for the episode of "Ellen," on April 30, in which the title character played by Ellen DeGeneres, who herself recently came out officially in Time magazine, will announce that she is a lesbian. "Ellen" is produced by Disney. The times, they really are a-changin'.

On television, back in 1985, the movie "An Early Frost" was justifiably praised as an all-too-rare attempt to deal with the subject of AIDS. It would remain rare for years. But pay cable, not subject to advertiser pressures, was instrumental in altering the content landscape. Home Box Office, for instance, won numerous awards with the documentary productions "And the Band Played On" and "Celluloid Closet." Now HBO has produced "In the Gloaming," the story of a young man reconciling with his family as he dies of AIDS, and nobody, apart from the usual naysayers, bats an eye as the rave reviews pour in.

In fact, something new is happening, not just in American society but in gay and lesbian circles. The gay image is edging away from the old urban cliches of kinky bars and unbridled promiscuity. Obviously, AIDS hovers over these changes. But the vibrations are unmistakable.

In his new book, "Sexual Ecology: AIDS and the Destiny of Gay Men," Gabriel Rotello, urging a new life style of limiting partners and restricting sexual acts, offers what will no doubt be a controversial suggestion that gay men "reward self-restraint and end the pervasive belief that those who are living at the most extreme fringes of gay sexual life are somehow the most liberated and the most gay."

In fact, as with any other group, gay and lesbian images cannot be reduced to one stereotype. This is one of the messages being hammered home by "In the Life," the magazine program examining gay and lesbian issues and culture every other month on national public television. The latest installment, which can be seen on Channel 13 in New York at 10 to-

Jim West/"In the Life"

Workers at Chrysler in Detroit demanding equal rights for gay and lesbian workers. They won a "sexual orientation" clause in the contract.

night (check local listings for broadcasts on other public stations), takes an "as American as apple pie" approach to gay and lesbian lives. Viewers, even many gay viewers, may be surprised.

With Katherine Linton as host, the program first goes to Detroit, where gay and lesbian workers press the big auto makers for gains. "They're going to live with me just as I have to live with them," says one man, who ends up a delegate to the United Auto Workers convention. Chrysler reluctantly agrees to include a "sexual orientation" clause in its contract. One significant development is the mutual support of gay and straight co-workers. As someone observes, management has "an attitude of contempt toward hourly workers, people who work with their hands."

The hourlong program also has sections on several other gay and lesbian viewpoints:

• A ringmaster of the Ringling Brothers and Barnum & Bailey Circus, a gay man who praises the company's support over the years.

• Various employees of the Disney Corporation who, even while recalling Walt Disney as conservative and anti-gay, firmly endorse the company's progressive policies, including domestic partner benefits.

• Several gay couples who are not into bars and flamboyance but run farms in Wisconsin and Iowa. One of them confesses that while growing up, "I don't think I could spell lesbian, much less know what one was."

The canvas is clearly broad and varied.

But the old-style gay card will still be played. A Wisconsin state senator has attacked the "gay agenda" that he detects in "In the Life." Increasingly, however, there is a difference. One of the program's staff members, John Catania, moved quickly to debate the politician on local radio, pointing out that some of the material was filmed in his district and that the gay and lesbian farmers were his taxpaying, law-abiding constituents. Mr. Catania grew up in Wisconsin. Things are not as easy as they once were for shoot-from-the-hip politicians.

Meanwhile, television prime time has been playing the gay card with startling frequency. On "Friends," speculation continues that Joey and Chandler are gay, with bemused interest, not indignation. If Niles on "Frasier," constantly fussing in the absence of the invisible Maris, isn't gay, he should be. And even the Michael J. Fox character in "Spin City" can loosen up enough to take a gender-bending spin in good humor. See Wednesday's repeat. And the great bulk of the mass audience is apparently unfazed. Once again, Americans seem more sophisticated and tolerant than hatemongering fringe groups would dare admit.

* * *

May 17, 1997

DEMOCRATS GIVE HEALTH BENEFITS TO GAY COUPLES

By The New York Times

WASHINGTON, May 16—Following in the footsteps of many top American companies, the Democratic National Committee said today that it would offer same-sex partners the same health benefits available to spouses of its employees.

Single-sex marriage has not been legalized, so such benefit offerings are not required by law. Nevertheless, approximately 500 companies, including Microsoft, the International Business Machines Corporation, the Walt Disney Company, Apple Computer and Time-Warner, offer health benefits to domestic partners of their employees. In addition, numerous cities, counties and universities offer similar programs.

The Democratic National Committee said it had decided on the policy because it was sound business sense.

"It's a way to attract and retain a talented staff," said a spokeswoman, Melissa Bonney. "We're following the lead of the business communities that already do this."

Among Fortune 500 companies, about half have policies barring discrimination against homosexuals; among Fortune 1000 companies, half have domestic partnership health benefits similar to the policy the committee is adopting, according to the Human Rights Campaign, a Washington group that lobbies on gay and lesbian issues.

The committee's new benefits policy will cover single-sex partners of its 150 employees and will take effect on July 3. Single-sex couples must have lived together for 12 consecutive months before being eligible for these benefits. How domestic partnership will be verified has not been decided yet.

"This is a way of providing equal compensation for equal work," said David M. Smith, a spokesman for the Human Rights Campaign. "Non-gay people have the ability to marry and have access to these benefits. Because gay people do not have the option of marrying, they do not have access to these benefits."

A spokesman for the Republican National Committee said he was not familiar with the Democratic committee's policy, and therefore could not comment on it.

* * *

June 30, 1997

HOMOSEXUAL IMAGERY IS SPREADING FROM PRINT CAMPAIGNS TO GENERAL-INTEREST TV PROGRAMMING

By STUART ELLIOTT

As more mainstream companies aim sales pitches at homosexuals as part of efforts to reach segments of the general consumer market, images associated with gay men and lesbians have become increasingly prevalent in print advertisements for products as disparate as Absolut vodka, American Express travelers checks, Subaru automobiles and Gardenburger vegetable patties.

Now, such images are also beginning to turn up on television, too, in commercials aimed at general audiences as well as gay and lesbian consumers. The spots feature same-sex couples, celebrities known to be homosexuals, drag performers and even a transsexual or two.

The imagery that viewers watch may often be less overt than what magazine and newspaper readers see. For instance, what is the nature of the relationship between two 20-something men who drive around aimlessly in commercials for Volkswagen of America? And there may be more stereotyped characters like effeminate fashion designers in television spots than in print ads.

But the visibility of homosexual imagery in spots shown on broadcast and cable television, locally and nationally, is growing faster than had been anticipated.

"Advertisers are a conservative bunch, but advertising likes to think of itself as a mirror reflecting the values out there," said Michael Wilke, a reporter for the trade publication Advertising Age who has collected about 100 commercials from around the world that feature or evoke homosexual imagery.

"And the reality is that gay men and lesbians are part of the consumer culture," said Mr. Wilke, who presented the collection in a lecture during the recent ninth New York Lesbian and Gay Film Festival.

The premise of many of the commercials is, as Mr. Wilke put it, "seeing a lot of people you never expected to see in women's clothes," from Fred the Dunkin' Donuts baker to the basketball player Larry Johnson to male beer drinkers who seek ladies' night discounts on Bud Light.

Some spots go beyond cross-dressing to transsexuality. One was created by the Sydney, Australia, office of Ammirati Puris Lintas, a unit of the Interpublic Group of Companies, for Domestos, a spray cleaner sold by Unilever P.L.C. That spot, with a character who resembles the transsexual in the film "Priscilla, Queen of the Desert," ends with the character declaring a bathroom cleaned with Domestos as "fit for a queen."

Another commercial in the collection shared the Grand Prix for best television and cinema work that was awarded on Saturday at the 44th International Advertising Festival in Cannes, France. It was one of two spots for Diesel jeans that won the top prize for Paradiset DDB, a unit of Omnicom Group in Stockholm.

The commercial is centered on a training class at a make-believe Scout camp. As a handsome young man gives his older, bearded scoutmaster mouth-to-mouth resuscitation, images of a pretty young woman flash on screen. The spot ends, however, with the Scout and the Scoutmaster galloping off together on horses—and the older man winking at the camera.

A second commercial that was in contention at Cannes, and also part of the collection, promotes Imperial Car Hire, a South African auto-rental company. That spot, by the Hunt Lascaris/TBWA unit of Omnicom in Sandton, South Africa, depicts two men driving along a highway. One exclaims: "I love you. I need you. I have to have you." The other man looks askance. Then these words appear on screen: "Hands-free phones, soon in all our cars."

In this country, the spots about two men randomly roaming the roads in a Volkswagen Golf—created by Arnold Communications in Boston—have proved particularly popular. When Mr. Wilke showed them during his presentation, the audience burst into applause.

"We've had such a response, we didn't anticipate it," said Liz Van Zura, advertising and marketing director for Volkswagen of America in Auburn Hills, Mich., "hundreds of inquiries on our Web site and our '800' number."

But "it never crossed our minds," she added, that viewers would infer the two men are not just friends.

"There was never any intention" other than to present them as "two college guys on a Sunday afternoon with nothing going on," Ms. Van Zura said. "It's interesting that people read more into it."

Mr. Wilke said he believed that happened because the spots are emblematic of a genre he called "gay-vague advertising, when it's not clear what the relationships are." Other examples he cited included a commercial for Quaker Toasted Oatmeal cereal featuring two men together at breakfast.

Another reason the Volkswagen men may have been perceived as a couple, Mr. Wilke said, was because the spots were introduced during the episode of the sitcom "Ellen" in which the character Ellen Morgan said she was a lesbian.

Commercials that can be read in different ways may become more common, he added, when "Ellen" returns in the fall. "You'll have, for the first time, a television program that allows advertisers to target a gay and gay-friendly audience," he said.

Even as homosexual imagery increases in commercials, Mr. Wilke said, "it all won't go smoothly; there'll be two steps forward and one step back."

For example, British and Canadian spots with kissing male and female couples, for Guinness and Molson Dry beers, have not run. The Canadian spot, though, may be seen soon, the trade publication Marketing Magazine reported.

PART III

ORGANIZING FOR CHANGE

Stonewall

June 29, 1969

4 POLICEMEN HURT IN 'VILLAGE' RAID

Melee Near Sheridan Square Follows Action at Bar

Hundreds of young men went on a rampage in Greenwich Village shortly after 3 A.M. yesterday after a force of plainclothes men raided a bar that the police said was wellknown for its homosexual clientele. Thirteen persons were arrested and four policemen injured.

The young men threw bricks, bottles, garbage, pennies and a parking meter at the policemen, who had a search warrant authorizing them in investigate reports that liquor was sold illegally at the bar, the Stonewall Inn, 53 Christopher Street, just off Sheridan Square.

Deputy Inspector Seymour Pine said that a large crowd formed in the square after being evicted from the bar. Police reinforcements were sent to the area to hold off the crowd.

Plainclothes men and detectives confiscated cases of liquor from the bar, which Inspector Pine said was operating without a liquor license.

The police estimated that 200 young men had been expelled from the bar. The crowd grew to close to 400 during the melee, which lasted about 45 minutes, they said.

Arrested in the melee was Dave Van Ronk, 33 years old, of 15 Sheridan Square, a well-known folk singer. He was accused of having thrown a heavy object at a patrolman and later paroled in his own recognizance.

The raid was one of three held on Village bars in the last two weeks, Inspector Pine said.

Charges against the 13 who were arrested ranged from harassment and resisting arrest to disorderly conduct. A patrolman suffered a broken wrist, the police said.

Throngs of young men congregated outside the inn last night, reading aloud condemnations of the police.

A sign on the door said, "This is a private club. Members only." Only soft drinks were being served.

*   *   *

June 30, 1969

POLICE AGAIN ROUT 'VILLAGE' YOUTHS

Outbreak by 400 Follows a Near-Riot Over Raid

Heavy police reinforcements cleared the Sheridan Square area of Greenwich Village again yesterday morning when large crowds of young men, angered by a police raid on an inn frequented by homosexuals, swept through the area.

Tactical Patrol Force units assigned to the East Village poured into the area about 2:15 A.M. after units from the Charles Street station house were unable to control a crowd of about 400 youths, some of whom were throwing bottles and lighting small fires.

Their arms linked, a row of helmeted policemen stretching across the width of the street made several sweeps up and down Christopher Street between the Avenue of the Americas and Seventh Avenue South.

The crowd retreated before them, but many groups fled into the numerous small side streets and re-formed behind the police line. The police were not withdrawn until 4 A.M.

A number of people who did not retreat fast enough were pushed and shoved along, and at least two men were clubbed to the ground.

Stones and bottles were thrown at the police lines, and the police twice broke ranks and charged into the crowd.

Three persons were arrested on charges of harassment and disorderly conduct.

The crowd had gathered in the evening across the street from the Stonewall Inn at 53 Christopher Street, where the police staged a raid early Saturday. The police were denounced by last night's crowd for allegedly harassing homosexuals. Graffiti on the boarded-up windows of the inn included: "Support gay power" and "Legalize gay bars."

Saturday's raid took place when about 200 people were in the bar. Plainclothes men, with a warrant authorizing a search for illegal sales of alcohol, confiscated cases of liquor and beer.

A melee involving about 400 youths ensued, a partial riot mobilization was ordered by Police Headquarters, and 13 persons were arrested on a number of charges. Four policemen were injured, one suffering a broken wrist. Among those arrested was Dave Van Ronk, a folk singer.

*   *   *

147

June 25, 1989

HOMOSEXUALS SEE 2 DECADES OF GAINS, BUT FEAR SETBACKS

By JAMES BARRON

Twenty years after a police raid on a gay bar in Greenwich Village unleashed the pent-up anger of the homosexual community and started the modern gay-rights movement, homosexual men and lesbians say that laws, court decisions and changing attitudes have helped them move closer to the mainstream of society.

But obstacles remain, along with doubts about when, or if, they will fall. Some homosexuals see what they consider disturbing signs that 20 years of gains are being rolled back under pressure from conservatives and the religious right.

Demonstrations in New York this weekend—a rally in Central Park yesterday, and the annual Lesbian and Gay Pride march today—commemorate the riot at the Stonewall Inn on Christopher Street. That incident, many homosexuals say, awakened lesbians and gay men to the idea that they were being attacked as a group. That, in turn, awakened them to the idea that they needed to organize as a group.

Advocacy and lobbying groups mushroomed after Stonewall, and now include everything from nonprofit groups mounting anti-discrimination advertising campaigns to political action committees.

"For the first time, I think more people are saying, 'I am a human being, I want to take my rightful place in society, I want to be mainstream and I want this aspect of my life to be one of many things of which I am proud,'" said Stephanie Blackwood, a public-relations executive who is leading an advertising campaign to foster greater tolerance toward homosexuals. "I'm about as mainstream as they come, and that's what we want."

Legal Victories

To many homosexuals, the last 20 years have seen legal victories, new tolerance by some religious denominations, greater understanding on the part of some heterosexuals and sometimes, action by government.

In 1985, for example, New York City opened the Harvey Milk School in Greenwich Village for teen-age students who say they are homosexuals. And last week, the United States Postal Service announced a special cancellation with the postmark, "Stonewall Sta./20 Years 1969-89/Lesbian and Gay Pride."

But the evidence is divided on whether society as a whole is now more accepting. Lesbians and gay men say they are still turned down for jobs and housing, even though such discrimination was outlawed in New York City three years ago, and they complain that they must still endure bias and hatred.

The National Gay and Lesbian Task Force reported earlier this month that homosexuals were the victims of more assaults in 1988 than in each of the preceding three years and that anti-homosexual violence was "alarmingly widespread." Nineteen percent of those incidents occurred on college campuses, and

The New York Times/Eddie Hauener

The Stonewall Inn, a gay bar on Christopher Street. A police raid on the bar 20 years ago initiated the gay-rights movement.

17 percent were classified as AIDS-related, "indicating that hatred and blame associated with the epidemic continue unabated," the task force said.

Some gay-rights advocates are concerned that the Republican-controlled New York State Senate, for the third straight year, blocked a bill that would have toughened the penalties for bias-related violence, including crimes against homosexuals as well as against blacks, Hispanic people, women, resident aliens and the elderly.

And a nationwide poll taken in March by The Los Angeles Times found that when asked if they approved of "homosexual rights"—the term was not defined—51 percent of the 3,583 men and women questioned said they disapproved, while 29 percent said they approved.

That finding was consistent with a nationwide Gallup Poll in the spring of 1987, when Gallup last explored this subject. The survey found that 55 percent were against the legalization of homosexual relations, while 33 percent favored it. Those percentages were about the same as in a 1986 poll that marked the first time a majority had opposed legalization since Gallup started asking the question in 1977, before the AIDS epidemic.

The Movement Today: Sense of Unity in Face of AIDS

In contrast to the isolation they felt 20 years ago, homosexuals and lesbians now have their own political-action committees, nonprofit foundations and support networks to promote what they feel the heterosexual world is denying them. They have opened community centers with everything from Alcoholics Anonymous to a gay Welcome Wagon. The Lesbian and Gay Community Services Center in Manhattan has a $1.5 million annual budget and 20 meeting rooms.

On the eve of the Stonewall riot there were 50 gay and lesbian organizations nationwide, said John D'Emilio, a historian and a co-author of "Intimate Matters: A History of Sexuality in America," published by Harper & Row. By 1973, there were 800, Mr. D'Emilio said. Now there are more than 3,000. But some gay-rights advocates are concerned that the growth is leveling off. "There's a saturation," Mr. D'Emilio said. "I mean, how many groups can you form?"

Many homosexuals say that all their support groups have helped the movement to downplay the differences among gay people caused by race and gender. So has AIDS.

By pressing lawmakers to allocate money for research on acquired immune deficiency syndrome, homosexuals have become an accepted part of the political landscape, as a bloc of voters if not as elected officials themselves. The staffs of major political figures like Mayor Edward I. Koch and Gov. Mario M. Cuomo now include representatives to the homosexual community. "Gay people are taking their place in the American panoply," said Richard Burns, the executive director of the Lesbian and Gay Community Services Center.

Some now live openly, and comfortably. "I'm more at ease with myself, whereas 20 years ago one had to be much more guarded about how one appeared," said Eric Washington, a waiter and a member of the AIDS Coalition to Unleash Power, or Act-Up. "These days I don't really think about that at all."

The Reality of Stonewall: Out of the Bar; Into the Streets

At the time of the Stonewall raid, a handful of gay bars, mostly in Greenwich Village, were among the few places where gay men and women socialized. "We'd carved out a small little world for us, populated by young gay people, which was a happy place, very hip," said Martin Robinson, a

co-founder of the Gay Liberation Front in 1969 and of Act-Up in 1987.

The Stonewall Inn was a black-walled bar owned by organized crime. Like a Depression-era speakeasy, it had a peephole in the door and a bouncer who was not afraid to turn people away.

"This was not the polite professional middle-class clientele that worries about making a scene," Mr. D'Emilio said. "Many of them were drag queens, maybe even runwaways, so they had less to lose by fighting back."

On June 27—two months before the rock concert at Woodstock, N.Y., and one month before Neil A. Armstrong became the first person to walk on the moon—the police raided the Stonewall for violations of liquor laws.

"When the police came in," said Mr. Robinson, who was there, "quite to their surprise, we were no longer self-effacing, we were no longer guilt-ridden. We were offended at their bullying. We didn't put up with it. As soon as the police got inside the bar, we surrounded the bar, made it difficult for them to get out."

Michael Scherker, who is writing a history of the events that night, says some people in the crowd threw pennies at the police. Others uprooted a parking meter to use as a battering ram.

"It wasn't a rebellion; it was a plain old spontaneous-combustion riot," Mr. Scherker said. "They weren't thinking of gay rights; they just wanted to get back in the bar. It wasn't until the next day or the day after that or the week after that that a lot of people realized what it was really about was gay rights."

Aftermath of the Raid: Changes in Law and in Language

Since Stonewall, even the words society uses to describe homosexuality have changed. The headline on an article that appeared in The Daily News shortly after the riot said, "Homo Nest Raided, Queen Bees Are Stinging Mad."

Now, said Sherrie Cohen, the executive director of the Fund for Human Dignity, "both in the media and society, it's becoming less acceptable to use slang words like homo and faggot against gays." She said the media have begun to reflect "a growing understanding" of lesbians and gay men and issues that concern them.

"This is all to the best in promoting tolerance in society," she said.

The church, too, has struggled with homosexuality. The Roman Catholic Church has not softened its opposition to it, and most Protestant denominations have yet to resolve whether gay men and lesbians can be ministers. But many have tried to bring them into their churches and to make them feel comfortable.

Some homosexuals say nothing illustrates the changes of the last 20 years better than their relationship with government.

"We began by fighting representatives of government," said Virginia Apuzzo, deputy executive director of the New York State Consumer Protection Board. "We still are, in a sense, but I think our demands have changed. The demand at

Stonewall was to get off our back. The demand today is not that government should get off our back, but that government should be involved in helping. Now we're saying, 'Government, give us the protections we need to live safely in this society.'"

Some of those protections have come from anti-discrimination statutes that have been passed in more than 50 jurisdictions, including most major cities, said Thomas B. Stoddard, the executive director of the Lambda Legal Defense and Education Fund. And in the 20 years since Stonewall, he said, Federal and state courts have generally supported homosexual plaintiffs in cases in which their rights were challenged. In 1962, seven years before Stonewall, Illinois became the first state in the nation to drop its sodomy law. Since the Stonewall uprising and the evolution of the gay-rights movement, 24 other states have invalidated or repealed their sodomy laws.

The old laws did not prohibit homosexuality per se, but did ban certain sexual acts that Mr. Stoddard said were "rightly or wrongly identified" with gay people, and thus prompted discrimination. In New York, the state's highest court, the Court of Appeals, struck down the sodomy statute in 1980.

But gay-rights advocates are worried about the long-term results of a 1986 Supreme Court decision that upheld the constitutionality of Georgia's sodomy law, saying there was no legal protection for homosexual acts between consenting adults, even in the privacy of their own homes. The Court said the Georgia law forbidding people from engaging in oral or anal sex could be used to prosecute homosexuals who engaged in such acts.

Homosexuals are also concerned that 25 states still have sodomy laws, and that there is no longer much momentum for repeal.

"It's not a good thing it has ground to a halt," Professor D'Emilio said, "but my informed guess is there are far fewer prosecutions. It may not be possible to get a repeal bill through a state legislature, but it is possible to exert pressure on state and local police to keep them from enforcing."

Mr. D'Emilio also argues that the Federal court system is more conservative now because of judges appointed during the Reagan administration, and is less likely to find in favor of homosexuals in discrimination cases.

A Shift in Focus: From the Courts to the Candidates

For that reason, Mr. D'Emilio said, the focus of the gay-rights movement has shifted from the courts to the political system.

"AIDS is an issue of such urgency that it has upped the level of organizing within the gay community and it has opened doors to the gay movement that were not open before," he said. "When the issue was gay rights, if you tried the Federal bureaucracy, the door stayed closed. When the issue is AIDS, the door opens. Gay activists have access to policy-makers in ways that they didn't have 20 years ago."

They also have the Human Rights Campaign Fund, a political action committee that describes itself as the nation's ninth-largest. "Increasingly, congressmen are recognizing the power gay greenbacks provide in tough elections," said Vic Basile, the executive director of the fund. "Not long ago there was the fear it would be a liability. Now they are more likely to call a press conference." In the first few years after Stonewall, "politically, we were whipping boys," said Martin Algaze, a former aide to Assemblyman Jerrold Nadler, a Manhattan Democrat.

"Now we are so powerful politically," Mr. Algaze said. "Everybody takes us seriously now. They may not like us, but they know we fight back."

In New York, Ms. Apuzzo moderated a mayoral candidates' night last month at the Lesbian and Gay Community Services Center. Four candidates appeared—Mayor Koch; Richard Ravitch, the former chairman of the Metropolitan Transportation Authority; David N. Dinkins, the Manhattan Borough President, and Harrison J. Goldin, the City Comptroller.

As she faced the audience of 400 people last month, Ms. Apuzzo thought about how different the forum was from its beginnings 12 years ago, when over a period of several weeks, the candidates met with a small group of lesbians and gay men, not in a public place, but in a penthouse apartment. Some of the people who were there, she recalled, "didn't use their last names and wouldn't appear at a press conference when we announced who we were supporting."

One generation witnessed Stonewall. Now it is 20 years later and some homosexuals say Stonewall's most enduring legacy will be felt by the next generation. Donna Lee, a 16-year-old sophomore at the Harvey Milk School shares that view. She said she thinks homosexuals will face less discrimination during her lifetime than they have in the past.

"Now we don't have undercover cops coming into our clubs and arresting us, and that's very good," she said. "I feel like I can walk down the street holding my lover's hand."

* * *

June 26, 1989

THOUSANDS MARCH TO COMMEMORATE 20 YEARS OF GAY PRIDE

By SARAH LYALL

Thousands of lesbians and gay men marched down Fifth Avenue yesterday to celebrate gay pride and to commemorate the confrontation that began as a routine police raid on a gay bar 20 years ago and has come to signify the beginning of the gay-rights movement.

They came singly, in pairs and as members of hundreds of groups, exuberant and somber, quiet and flamboyant, ranging from the Radical Faeries to the Asian Lesbians of the East Coast to the Harvard Business School Gay and Lesbian Alumni Association. Organizers said more than 150,000 people took part, making it the largest gay-rights parade in the history of New York City.

The New York march was one of several held around the country yesterday. In San Francisco, 300,000 people, many of them members of AIDS-related organizations, marched through the streets in their annual gay-rights parade. Other parades were held in Chicago and Los Angeles.

Special Signficance

But in New York City, the site of a violent melee between gays and the police 20 years ago at the Stonewall Inn, the march had a special significance. Participants—representing social, academic, athletic, religious, and service organizations—looked back on 20 years of gay rights.

Michael Weyand, 38 years old, remembered reading about the Stonewall confrontation in The Village Voice when he was a freshman in college. The article described how the police raid on the bar on June 27, 1969, escalated into a violent clash between its patrons and the police. The incident touched off pent-up anger in the gay community, and within a few days, 500 people showed up for the city's first gay-rights rally.

After years of "not owning up to who I was and hoping I would get over it," Mr. Weyand said, news of the Stonewall raid electrified him, and he made up his mind to come out of the closet. It took him more than a year.

"These people were like me," said Mr. Weyand. Yesterday, he marched next to his mother, Martha, 68, who lives in Cincinnati and is a member of Parents and Friends of Lesbians and Gays.

There were few disturbances as the marchers moved from Columbus Circle, across 59th Street, down Fifth Avenue to Washington Square Park and down Christopher Street to Hudson Street. Several shouting matches erupted between the marchers and a group of about 100 counterdemonstrators, many holding rosary beads, who had positioned themselves in front of St. Patrick's Cathedral. As the marchers passed, they jeered, shouted, sang and pleaded with them to change their life styles.

One member of the antigay contingent was charged with disorderly conduct, the police said, after he threw what appeared to be a bottle of holy water at the crowd.

The participants ranged from those who had come to celebrate quietly with their companions to men who were flamboyantly dressed as women. Some were joyous; others, notably those from AIDS-related service or political groups, were angry. In the middle of the afternoon, the parade was stopped for about three minutes, and everyone observed silence for those who have died from or are suffering from AIDS.

'My Daughter Is Gay'

Marie Varvaro, a 32-year-old lesbian from Brooklyn, was surrounded by her family, in homemade purple tie-dyed T-shirts. Ms. Varvaro's mother, Toni Sorrentino, who said she "almost had a nervous breakdown" when her daughter announced 15 years ago that she was gay, waved a placard that said, "My daughter is gay and it's okay."

Anne Beckmann of Chicago marched with her arm around her son, Mark Fotopoulos, who has AIDS.

"I'm happy and proud to take part in this march," she said, and the crowd cheered as the two walked by.

"I'm hoping this will promote awareness of what they have to contend with," Mrs. Beckmann said. "They've lost so many lovers and friends."

'Doubly Invisible'

Gay men outnumbered lesbians, and a section of the parade was devoted to women's groups. One was the Women's Herstory Archives, which compiles women's artifacts.

"For us, this is not so much a celebration as a demonstration," said Joan Nestle, who teaches writing at Queens College and is a co-founder of the project.

"As lesbians, we're doubly invisible," she said. "As gay women, we exist only in other people's fantasies or in dirty jokes."

There were young gay people, hundreds of them from college campuses or gay alumni associations. There were people in their 70's and 80's, on foot and in cars, from a group called SAGE, which represents gay elderly people. An elderly woman rode atop a stretch limousine with a sign that said, "Grandma for Gays."

Some marchers said that the gay movement had lost sight of its original ideals. When she first marched, 20 years ago, "it was militant," said Mickie Zacuto, a lesbian. "Now, people don't remember what we're about, that we're fighting for our existence."

But most were joyous in their honesty yesterday. Amy Ashworth, the mother of a gay man and a co-founder of Westchester Parents of Lesbians and Gays, a support group that marched behind a banner, said it is hard for parents in the group to come to terms with their children's homosexuality. But most finally come around, she said.

"The biggest thing they realize is that people don't choose to be gay," Mrs. Ashworth said. "You choose to hide it, or you choose to be open about it."

* * *

June 27, 1994

GAY MARCHERS CELEBRATE HISTORY IN 2 PARADES

By JANNY SCOTT

Tens of thousands of gay men and lesbians surged through Manhattan yesterday, celebrating a civil-rights movement that took its first steps during a police raid on a gay bar 25 years ago and seemed in the last week to have come of age.

The participants in the commemoration of what is now known as the Stonewall rebellion had their own reasons for being there. Some came to honor pioneers in the gay movement, to support one another, to protest, to rejoice, to remember the dead or to offer a beacon for the living.

Above all, they came to affirm the legacy of Stonewall: their very openness. Among them were a Marine lance corporal in dress uniform, a former F.B.I. agent, a New York City firefighter, a police officer and an Eskimo from Alaska wearing a buffalo-horn choker, eagle-claw necklace and tie-dyed denim shorts.

"We will never turn back," said Franklin Fry, a march organizer. "We will never be invisible again."

They marched in not one but two parades—an officially sanctioned one on the East Side of Manhattan demanding that the United Nations protect the rights of homosexuals worldwide, and a smaller, unofficial one up Fifth Avenue from Greenwich Village, organized by several dissenting groups that broke ranks with the others to make the point that the most urgent problem facing gay people is AIDS.

Yet a remarkable aspect of the day was the loose cohesion that seemed to occur, bringing together gay Republicans and drag queens and all the diverse elements of the gay-rights movement. That diversity, many say, is both a mark of the movement's success and an impediment to achieving the single-minded focus needed to force social change.

It was a less flamboyant event than a traditional gay-pride march, but more lighthearted and festive than a political rally. There were men in gowns, and topless women, but shorts and T-shirts predominated. And when the two parades met at Fifth Avenue and 57th Street, the authorized marchers halted respectfully to allow the rebel contingent to join.

They then converged in a vast river of humanity that continued to pour up the Avenue of the Americas and into Central Park from 1:15 P.M. until 5:15 P.M.—including a one-minute moment of silence at 3 P.M. memorializing people who have died of AIDS, followed shortly by a "moment of rage." Once inside the park, the marchers settled in amid the dust and crabgrass of The Great Lawn for a rally of speeches and music, dodging dragonflies and hunting for shade against a fierce sun before dispersing about 8 o'clock.

There was little agreement on how many people turned out. The organizers of the authorized march estimated the total crowd at 1.1 million. The Police Department put the figure closer to 100,000, saying The Great Lawn was known to hold 180,000 and it appeared to be half-full.

Unlike the event being commemorated, yesterday brought no clashes between marchers and police officers, and no arrests were reported. A police spokesman, Lawrence F. Loesch, said the 6,200 officers on duty made up the largest number ever assigned to a single event.

The marches and rally served as a finale to the separately organized, Olympic-style competition called the Gay Games and to a festival of gay and lesbian culture that had taken place over the past week. It came at a time when homosexuals have achieved unprecedented visibility in American life.

But many gay men and lesbians see a backlash occurring in the United States. In a half-dozen states, constitutional amendments have been proposed to repeal or prevent laws that affirm homosexual rights.

'Still a Struggle'

"Stonewall is still a struggle all over the country," said Edwin Greene, 41, from Cincinnati, where voters last year passed an initiative that removed all references to sexual orientation from a city human-rights law. "There are these ballot initiatives all over the country. This is the battle we are fighting today."

Five years in planning, the official march was led by a milelong, 30-foot-wide, rainbow-colored flag intended to symbolize gay and lesbian unity. Hundreds of volunteers had paid for the privilege of carrying the 7,550-pound flag. Their donations are to go to pay for AIDS services.

Among those near the front carrying the flag were Peter King, a 23-year-old bank employee from Sydney, who had chosen for his footwear a new pair of black patent-leather pumps, size 12 ½, and Lary Campbell, a 38-year-old nurse in the AIDS unit at Roosevelt Hospital, who said he acknowledged his homosexuality to his family at age 18 "directly as a result of Stonewall."

And there was was Rose Walton, 57, who started Long Island's first AIDS education program for health providers in 1983. A multiple sclerosis patient, she carried the flag in one hand, a cane in the other. Walking behind her was Marge Sherwin, Ms. Walton's partner of 17 years, who won a bronze medal as a 10-kilometer runner at the Gay Games.

Like many who attended, the two women are seeking legal recognition for their domestic partnership so they might share Ms. Sherwin's health benefits.

Tiaras and Gloves

Behind the flag, which billowed its way up First Avenue from the United Nations, apparently without any significant hitch, came the parade's organizers, including a few drag queens in glittering gowns, tiaras and satin gloves. Behind them came the politicians, including Mayor Rudolph W. Giuliani, surrounded by a tight knot of police officers and security guards.

Mr. Giuliani's presence was, for the most part, received politely. A few onlookers booed from the sidelines, but others were pleased to see him, waving and trying to get his attention. "He shows up," marveled Kit Stewart of Bayport, L.I. "That's a start."

Slightly farther back came the Stonewall veterans, mostly men in their 40's and 50's, who had seen their impromptu rebellion at the Stonewall Inn in Greenwich Village on June 27, 1969, not only transform their own lives, in some cases, but also become a rallying cry for a worldwide movement.

"That moment changed fundamentally how I saw myself and how I saw lesbians and gays around the world," said Jim Fouratt, who went on to help organize the first Gay Liberation Front. "Our young people, my lesbian and gay children, need to know what life was like only 25 years ago."

Meanwhile, the unauthorized march set off from Sheridan Square, the site of the Stonewall Inn, led by a red Mustang convertible and a 1969 blue convertible Cadillac that was used and impounded during the Stonewall clash. Ensconced on the Cadillac's back seat was "Queen" Allyson Allante of

Long Beach, L.I., who at age 14 had been arrested at the Stonewall Inn.

One of the passengers in the Mustang was John Paul Ranieri of Milwaukee, who said he was on his first return visit to New York since the Stonewall clash, during which, he said, he was beaten two nights in a row and had to receive five stitches after a police officer hit him with a flashlight.

"The only way I can describe this experience is that it is like a Vietnam vet going back to Saigon for a reunion," he said. "It's not exactly a pleasant experience." Asked how he felt to see police officers lining the route, he said, "I still cringe. But what I find amazing is that they're protecting us today."

Visual Extremes

There were topless women and a few men running naked up Fifth Avenue. At the New York Public Library, a man in a white chiffon skirt performed pirouettes on the steps. "The impressive thing is the visual extremes," said Roger Pretto, a tourist from Miami taking photographs with his wife, Judy.

The Giuliani administration had refused to issue a permit for the march up Fifth Avenue, saying one parade should be sufficient. The route was designed to take the participants past St. Patrick's Cathedral, where some of the marchers increased their volume and began chanting, "Tell the Cardinal we're here."

A group of hundreds at the front of the march stopped and lay down in the street for two minutes in an organized "die-in."

At a Mass earlier, John Cardinal O'Connor of the Archdiocese of New York warned worshipers as they prepared to leave St. Patrick's Cathedral that they might "encounter situations today we regret in our faith," adding that his congregation "should not condemn any human person."

* * *

June 27, 1994

FROM THE GAY WORLD'S EVERY REACH, A SEA OF MARCHERS, ALL WITH STORIES

By JAMES C. MCKINLEY JR.

They marched for any number of reasons.

Barbara and Sal Deldeo of Wilmington, Del., joined the throngs of gay and lesbian people in the Stonewall 25 parade for their son, Thomas Gerald, who died in April after a 10-month battle with AIDS. Neither had ever marched before, not against the Vietnam War, nor in marches against nuclear weapons, not even on Memorial Day.

They carried a picture of their son—a San Francisco actor and yoga instructor—on a placard, like so many others carrying photographs of the dead. Their son, who died at age 31, looked like a perpetually young movie star: twinkling eyes, straight teeth, strong jaw.

"You just feel like you are sharing him with so many, like his death wasn't in vain," Mrs. Deldeo said as they turned with the march onto 57th Street and deafening cheers rose

from the predominantly gay crowd of onlookers. "You don't get this kind of support in Wilmington."

She grew teary telling of how her son came home to die, how he finally reached an understanding with his father, how he went peacefully one day, his clothes no longer fitting his gaunt frame. "He was my only one," she said. "Explain that karma."

Foreign and Fearless

From the corner of First Avenue and 42d Street, Pavel Masalsky could see the future.

For blocks and blocks, he saw a river of singing, dancing, laughing gay people, not just unafraid of the city around them, but defiant, joyous. One day, he said, he believes it will be the same on his street in Moscow.

"I have never even imagined anything like this," said Mr. Masalsky, 31, who said he was in a labor camp in northern Russia from 1984 to 1987, jailed under Article 121, which prohibited sex between men. Other marchers, particularly those from countries where being openly gay is either illegal, unsafe or unwise, walked for at least a while without fear.

The marchers were people like Ming Wei of Taiwan, who said there was no problem being gay in his country "as long as you keep it quiet," and Juan Pablo Ordonez of Colombia, who said lower-class homosexuals in his country were treated by the police and army as "disposable people."

Sidewalk Condemnations

Along the route there were a handful of hecklers and counter-demonstrations, but they barely ruffled the sea of gay and lesbian marchers.

The Westboro Baptist Church of Topeka, Kan., sent 19 people to confront the marchers as they passed the corner of 51st Street at First Avenue. The protesters held up signs with messages like "Sodomy Is No Human Right," "Turn or Burn" and "Fear God, Not Fags."

The Rev. Fred Phelps, 64, called the parade "a threat to the moral fabric of our society" and added that "the Bible clearly denounces this lifestyle."

The tiny band of counter-demonstrators was drowned out by the marchers, who taunted them, blowing kisses and shouting, "Shame, shame, shame." One colorful group, Pagans and Witches, danced a sexually suggestive shimmy in front of them.

A Veterans' Honor Guard

One part of the march resembled a small-town Memorial Day parade, with dozens of veterans and a few active soldiers and sailors in uniform marching behind an honor guard. Among them was Jose Zuniga, the former Army soldier of the year who was discharged after making his sexual orientation public.

David Legion marched in his Navy dress whites, a uniform he has not worn since 1985, when he was discharged from the United States Navy submarine service after his superiors discovered he was gay. On his chest was an insignia for good conduct.

"I want to show people what the military threw away—the best and the brightest," said Mr. Legion, who is 37. "I've made a life for myself, but people have a stereotype."

Another veteran, Donald MacIver of Dallas, wore the same camouflage fatigues he wore as a Green Beret in 1969, when he ventured behind enemy lines in Vietnam, a world away from Sheridan Square.

A bullish man with a mustache and hard eyes, he received a Bronze Star and dozens of other commendations before retiring from the Army, he said. But he never whispered a word about his sexuality.

"These men and women are still being kicked out for utter stupidity," said Mr. MacIver, a former sergeant.

Protest and Politicking

Politicians love a parade, even an illegal one.

Representative Jerrold Nadler, a Manhattan Democrat, positioned himself and his supporters somewhere near the front of the smaller, unauthorized march and began furiously passing out literature to the crowd. A parade marshal sneered at Mr. Nadler and shouted, "This is not a Nadler march, this is an Act Up march."

Thomas K. Duane, an openly gay City Councilman who is seeking to unseat Mr. Nadler, made sure his campaign stickers were distributed as well. But his volunteers jogged beside the marchers unaccosted.

Bratton Keeps Quiet Watch

He could have almost gone undetected by most people at the unauthorized march, such was his demeanor and dress. Police Commissioner William J. Bratton, however, was there. He was first spotted on Waverly Place in sunglasses, wearing tan pants and a light-blue casual shirt. Standing behind him were two bodyguards, also dressed casually in khaki and sneakers.

He said that everything was going as planned and he offered a recollection of where he was 25 years ago during the Stonewall clash. He said he was in the Army at a missile site.

"Twenty-five years ago, I was sitting in the Everglades, swatting at mosquitoes," he said. Asked if back then it would have been impossible to imagine himself standing where he was now, watching a gay march, he said, "You could certainly say that."

* * *

June 28, 1994

INVISIBLE PEOPLE, MADE VISIBLE

June has been an enlightening, and enlightened, month in New York City. Gotham's citizens could hardly turn on their television sets or ride the subways without encountering some aspect of the astoundingly large gay presence that had converged on the city.

Gay Games IV brought 11,000 athletes and tens of thousands of sports fans from 40 countries. More than 130 cultural events celebrated gay themes. And on Sunday, tens of thousands of gay men and lesbians marched to commemorate the evening in 1969 when police, harassing patrons of a gay Greenwich Village bar called the Stonewall Inn, met fierce resistance for the first time.

The gay rights struggle has often been likened to the the struggle of blacks or women for equality. But there was one crucial difference. It was nearly always clear when a black person or a woman had entered the room. Gay Americans, by contrast, have lived largely as an indistinguishable minority. Bigots insulted them to their faces without knowing it, and were often unaware of just how many gay people there were. And homosexuals whose orientation became known were easily isolated as "abnormal."

Stonewall taught that while invisible people had no rights, gay people who stood together had a far better chance of achieving recognition. The growing gay components in both the Democratic and Republican Parties provide ample evidence today that the lessons of Stonewall have been taken to heart. So did the recent celebrations in New York.

Police estimated the final crowd in Central Park at 100,000, although organizers insist it was far larger. Along the main parade route, marchers unfurled a 20-block-long rainbow-colored flag. They were a splendidly diverse multitude: Democrats and Republicans; moderates, radicals and conservatives; drag queens in glittering gowns; a Marine lance corporal in dress uniform; a former F.B.I. agent; a police officer; an Eskimo from Alaska.

Many participants found the experience profoundly liberating, a mass statement that their movement had arrived and could never be shoved back into the closet. As one organizer said: "We will never turn back. We will never be invisible again."

* * *

Speaking Out

October 18, 1963

HOMOSEXUAL GROUP ASKS UNDERSTANDING

The public relations director of the Homosexual League of New York called yesterday for public acceptance of homosexuals as a legitimate minority group.

The director, Randolfe Wicker, addressed a group of 350 students at City College. His appearance was sponsored by the college's WBAI club, an organization supporting the WBAI-FM listener-financed radio station.

"We are only interested in educating the public, not in converting anyone to homosexuality," Mr. Wicker said, referring to the Mattachine Society, which recently absorbed the Homosexual League.

The society, he said, is a legally incorporated organization that includes six psychologists and psychiatrists among its members. It sponsors lectures on homosexuality, aids in research projects and provides employment, psychological and legal referral services.

Acceptance of the homosexual is a "question of education," he said. "Attitudes are changing, and, with organizations such as ours, the issue can be approached legitimately."

Mr. Wicker compared his organization's recruiting problems to those of organizations representing minority racial groups.

"Most homosexuals live fearful, ghettoized lives," he said. "The homosexual's biggest problem is the lack of adequate communication with others."

According to Mr. Wicker, mattachine is an Italian word used to refer to "court jesters of the Middle Ages who always told the truth despite great opposition."

* * *

August 19, 1968

HOMOSEXUALS ASK CANDIDATES' IDEAS

Seek Views on Penalties—'Bill of Rights' Urged

Special to The New York Times

CHICAGO, Aug. 18—The North American Conference of Homophile Organizations has proposed that all political candidates be asked this year for their views on penalties imposed upon homosexuals.

At the closing session of the five-day conference here late last week, the 75 delegates recommended that the 40 local organizations of homosexuals forward questionnaires to aspirants for office.

The conference also adopted a "Homosexual Bill of Rights." Major contentions are that laws dealing with homosexuality should be modified and that employment should not be denied anyone solely because he is a homosexual.

Cleric Is Chairman

Local organizations were urged to exert pressure on police officials, state legislatures, and the Federal Government to put provisions of this "bill of rights" into effect.

The conference chairman was the Rev. Robert Warren Cromey, vicar of St. Aidan's Episcopal Church in San Francisco. He said it had been estimated that over the nation there were 15 million homosexuals, most of whom sought to conceal their homosexuality from the public for obvious reasons.

The local homosexual organizations have about 2,000 members, he said.

Most homosexuals, he asserted, are normal except for their homosexuality and are responsible members of society. Many, he said, hold important positions in business and the professions.

To subject them to legal harassment and exclude them from employment solely because of sexual orientation is a denial of their constitutional rights, he declared.

Mr. Cromey, 37 years old, is married and has three daughters. He said he was one of the few heterosexuals who attended the conference. Until assuming his present pastorate three years ago he was executive assistant to the Episcopal Bishop of California.

In many states homosexuality is a crime, and in some, homosexuals are prosecuted under sodomy laws, Mr. Cromey noted.

He said that known homosexuals were denied employment in any position requiring security clearance in the Federal Government or in private businesses doing Government work.

In the "bill of rights" adopted by the conference, the following "basic rights" are outlined:

• Private sex acts between consenting persons over the age of consent shall not be offenses.

• Solicitation for any sexual act shall not be an offense except upon filing of a complaint by the aggrieved party, not a police officer or agent.

• A person's sexual orientation or practice shall not be a factor in the granting of Federal security clearance, visas and citizenship.

• Service in and discharge from the armed services, and eligibility for veterans' benefits, shall be without reference to homosexuality.

• A person's sexual orientation or practice shall not affect his eligibility for employment with Federal, state or local governments.

Under "areas for immediate reform," the conference declared that the police should cease entrapment of homosexuals, not notify employers of those arrested for homosexual offenses, keep no files solely to identify homosexuals, and refrain from harassing business establishments catering to homosexuals.

* * *

November 17, 1969

THE WOMAN HOMOSEXUAL: MORE ASSERTIVE, LESS WILLING TO HIDE

By ENID NEMY

The young homosexual woman, to an increasing degree, is refusing to live with the limitations and restrictions imposed by society and is showing a sense of active resentment and rebellion at a condemnation she considers unwarranted and unjust.

She considers herself part of what many refer to as the "current sexual revolution." When the necessity arises, she is now more frequently willing to risk open discrimination and prejudice—in jobs and with friends and acquaintances ("some people won't talk to us; they think it's catching.")

The new assertiveness and increasing visibility has resulted in:

• A rise in attendance at the weekly meetings of the New York chapter of the Daughters of Bilitis, a national Lesbian organization. Several years ago, 20 to 40 was considered average; today the figure ranges between 60 and 125, a threefold increase.

• Active participation in some of the newer homosexual organizations, including the Student Homophile League and the Gay Liberation Front. Although these groups are supported primarily by homosexual males, a woman is chairman of the New York University Student Homophile League and there are women executive members at Cornell University and at Columbia, where the organization was founded three years ago.

• A marked increase in the number of women picked up by New York City Police for "loitering," a charge applied "for soliciting another for the purpose of engaging in deviate sexual intercourse." Ten women were picked up under this charge in 1968 and a police spokesman estimated that the ratio of men to women was, at the time, 12 to 1. A total of 49 women and 69 men have been apprehended on the same charge in the first nine months of 1969.

Homosexual League Has Been Expanding

One of the aims of the Daughters of Bilitis, founded in 1955 and named after 19th century song lyrics glorifying Lesbian love, is to explore the possibility of changing present laws. The organization, with headquarters in San Francisco, now has four official and five probationary chapters; until last year the only chapters were in San Francisco, Los Angeles and New York.

In addition to social activities, self-discussion and providing a forum for professional advice (legal and psychological), the organization is prepared to assist in what it terms "responsible" studies and research.

"We are a civil liberties organization," said Joan Kent (a pseudonym), national vice-president, Eastern division.

It is not illegal to be a Lesbian in New York State but it is illegal to perform a Lesbian act. A Temporary State Commission on Revision of the Penal Law recommended, in November, 1964, that "deviate sexual acts privately and discreetly engaged in between competent and consenting adults should no longer constitute a crime."

Decisive votes in both houses of the State Legislature rejected the proposal. Subsequent bills have gotten no further than committee, although John V. P. Lassoe Jr., one of the men who testified before the commission, said that he intended to see another bill introduced at the next session in January.

"But I don't expect it to move," he conceded. "I expect it will wither and die, but I will work for it."

Religious Groups Gave No Support

Mr. Lassoe, who was director of Christian social relations of the Episcopal Diocese of New York at the time of his testimony, and is now an assistant to the Diocesan Bishop, the Right Rev. Horace W. B. Donegan, thought that the most significant reason for the defeat was "the absence of support from religious bodies in New York State."

"To the best of my knowledge," he said, "my department and the Department of Christian Social Relations of the Protestant Council of the City of New York endorsed the proposed change . . . other religious groups either opposed it, or, more commonly, remained silent."

Many Lesbians have rejected the church but almost all are encouraged by the increasing dialogue between religious leaders and homosexuals. Many theologians are inclined to agree with a statement made by Rabbi Norman Lamm, the spiritual leader of the Jewish Center in New York and professor of Jewish philosophy at Yeshiva University.

"Homosexuality between consenting adults should not be treated as a criminal offense," Rabbi Lamm said, "but to declare homosexual acts as morally neutral and at times as a good thing is scandalous." The statement, made last year and repeated recently, has been both supported and attacked by other rabbis.

Whatever the general feeling on the morals and ethics of homosexuality (a recent Louis Harris poll reported that 63 per cent of the nation believes that homosexuals are "harmful to American life"), there is apparently increasing support from public bodies for a change in the laws.

A task force of 14 experts, appointed by the National Institutes of Mental Health, last month issued a majority report (three members expressed reservations on some of the recommendations) urging states to abolish laws that make homosexual intercourse a crime for consenting adults in private. Two states have such laws. The Illinois measure was passed in 1961 and Connecticut approved one last summer, to take effect in 1971.

A recent poll conducted by Modern Medicine, a publication, reported that 67.7 per cent of the 27,741 doctors polled were in favor of allowing homosexual acts.

'Sexual Backlash' May Be Produced

There is, on the other hand, some belief that the proliferating number of articles and reports and increased public awareness of homosexuality has produced a "sexual backlash."

"The general public assumes that to remove an inappropriate law is to vote for lawlessness," said Robert Veit Sherwin, a lawyer who specializes in domestic relations and is the author of "Sex and the Statutory Law."

Despite the increasing activities of the homosexual female, many experts in the field define her relationships as "generally more discreet" than those of the homosexual male.

"With many women, a homosexual relationship evolves or devolves into a kind of companionate pair," according to Dr. Charles W. Socarides, a medical psychoanalyst and author of "The Overt Homosexual." "They protect each other and depend on each other; there is often very little actual sexual contact."

Dr. Socarides, who has treated many homosexuals, believes that "women are much more emotionally committed; they can't have one-night stands and leave."

At the Daughters of Bilitis, the relationship between Doris and Terry, two women in their 50's who have shared a home in the suburbs for 20 years, is held up as an example of Lesbian stability. Both women are scientists by profession, but Terry now stays home and keeps house.

"We don't run around and do wild things," commented Terry, who thinks there is no doubt that the neighbors know of their relationship. "If you behave yourself, pay your bills and don't offend, the community accepts you."

There are others like Doris and Terry but, according to many Lesbians, "the male-female aping of marriage is changing."

"The majority of the young Lesbians interchange responsibilities," said Miss Kent. "Alice [her friend] and I consider ourselves involved in a commitment, not husband and wife but partners."

Not Having Children Is Difficult to Accept

Miss Kent, who had a heterosexual relationship (her engagement was broken because "our religious backgrounds were different and the families disapproved") before she became a Lesbian, said it took her "three or four years to adjust to the idea of not having children."

Other Lesbians went through similar periods of adjustment but some said they had no desire for children ("I like them but I wouldn't want to be a mother; I might want to be a father," said one).

A few Lesbian couples adopt children.

"Of course, they don't announce what they are," Miss Kent explained.

(There is no law against the placement of a child with Lesbians but, in divorce cases, there are generalities about the moral atmosphere in the home. Most judges would not place a child in a home shared by Lesbians, according to Carl

N. Tuck

Homosexuals, male and female, picketing in Washington last July 4.

Zuckerman, lawyer for the Community Service Society, "but if there were no better alternative, the child would be placed with a homosexual parent.")

Women with children, who enter into a homosexual relationship, rarely live with their partners.

"We have our own apartments," said Justine, a tall, 28-year-old black Lesbian with a master's degree, who is having an affair with the mother of a 5-year-old child.

Although "an act of deviate sexual intercourse" was added in 1966 to New York State's divorce law, it is still rarely used as a basis for action, according to Geraldine Eiber, a lawyer who has handled several such cases. Most parties prefer to use other grounds.

Jean and Ruth, Long Island matrons, each maintain a residence, one with three children (aged 8 to 20) and the other with two (aged 10 and 12). Both women are divorced. Neither divorce was granted under the deviate law despite the fact that the homosexual propensities of one of the women was known to her husband throughout their 14-year marriage.

"I had had an affair with a girl while my fiancé was in the service," said Ruth, a pleasant-looking woman with intense brown eyes and cropped brown hair. "I married him when he returned because of pressure from my family—I loved my mother very much—and I felt, too, that with marriage would come respectability."

Ruth continued her relationship with the other woman for a year after marriage. When she broke it up, "the girl told my husband." He was "shocked and angry," but the marriage continued and she immediately began a relationship with another woman that continued for 13 years.

Both Left Their Jobs And Stayed at Home

"We both had jobs," she recalled. "When I had a baby, I persuaded her to have children so she could stay home too. We lived within walking distance of one another."

She ended her long-time affair after meeting Jean, an encounter she described as "like the old cliché—bells started ringing."

"I felt that any time I had, I wanted to spend with her. My husband thought he would frighten me by leaving. It didn't work out that way."

Ruth is comfortable in her role; Jean is not. She is in her 40's and had been married for more than 20 years, but was separated from her husband when she met Ruth. She had never had, or thought of having, a homosexual relationship.

"When I met Ruth, she was just another woman, another mother," she said. "We had lunch together occasionally and I found that I had extremely warm feelings toward her which I had never experienced before. It evolved from there."

The carefully made-up face beneath the bouffant hair looked troubled.

"I have a guilt complex because I'm living a lie," she said. "I lived for a long time in an unfeeling existence and I felt there must be something more. I had affairs with men while I was married, all of them satisfactory sexually, but I was always looking for someone to care for. This came to me late in life. When I see young girls who know they are Lesbians, I'm very glad for them because they have found out in time to avoid a series of traps."

Jean is an example of what Dr. Socarides terms "the consciously motivated homosexual"—people who become homosexuals or engage in homosexual acts for many reasons—power, extra thrills and kicks and, in women, often at times, "despair, disappointment or fright."

"Women can easily regress to a mother-child relationship with another woman who will take care of them at times like first menstruation, first intercourse, a disappointing love affair or a divorce," he explained.

Dr. Socarides characterizes as "ill" the true "obligatory" homosexual who is "obliged" to carry out the homosexual act and afterwards "feels restored, the way a narcotics addict takes a shot."

"It is quite a severe illness but amenable to therapy in a great majority of cases," he said. His own estimate of the number of homosexuals in New York City is about 200,000 and "in my opinion, the percentage of females is the same as males." (To Miss Kent, the number of known or suspected Lesbians "is like the tip of the iceberg.")

Dr. Socarides, who rates the incidence of suicide and alcoholism as "high" among Lesbians, insists that "a vocal minority of society is trying to sell a bill of goods that the homosexual is normal."

"The homosexuals themselves know it is not normal," he asserted.

An opposing view is taken by Dr. Lawrence Le Shan, a research psychologist with a doctorate from the University of Chicago. He believes "it is not a disease; it is a choice and everybody should be allowed to choose."

Dr. Le Shan and his wife, Eda, also a psychologist, said that the homosexual "arouses terrible anguish and enormous psychological fear in society" but that "the goal, the hope, the dream of society is the sense of the miracle of individuality."

Mrs. Le Shan thought that the change would come through the younger generation.

"Young people make no value judgments about homosexuality," she said. "They have the attitude that there are many different ways of loving and that it's no one's business. They are a tremendously moral generation. They care only about how people feel about each other."

One area where the homosexual woman appears to have made little headway is with her parents. The umbrella of parental understanding shelters few Lesbians.

"Nothing frightens parents more than the possibility that their children might become homosexuals," one psychologist said.

"I told my two brothers that I was a Lesbian," said Audrey, a diminutive, 28-year-old brunette. "The 21-year-old asked, 'Are you happy?' and the 18-year-old shrugged his shoulders and said, 'It's your bag.' But most parents won't believe it, won't discuss it and think it will go away."

Organization Purports Dual Educational Aim

The dual purpose of the Student Homophile League is, according to Helen, one of its executives, "to educate homosexuals that they have nothing to hide and to educate heterosexuals what it means to be discriminated against for something so minor as sexual orientation."

Last May, the league held "New York's first gay mixer" dance at the Church of the Holy Apostle. Six hundred students, instructors and friends ("some of them were straight, we don't discriminate") attended.

"I knew the mixer was to be a gay dance—for homosexuals," said Rev. Robert O. Weeks, the rector, who was "very proud" of the event. "It was a real revelation to me, a very pleasant scene. There was no rowdy behavior, no bad vibrations."

Father Weeks, an Episcopalian, had three students from the General Theological Seminary attend, wearing clerical collars.

"Homosexuals should be free to have social gatherings in places other than gay bars and the church's attitude should be one of compassion in accordance with the strictures of Jesus Christ," Father Weeks said.

Father Weeks admitted that there had been some negative reactions on the part of his parishioners but he chose to make the facilities available "to show that the church cares about homosexuals as people and that it is an un-Christian idea that they be shunned."

The Daughters of Bilitis (who answer their telephone on meeting nights with "D.O.B. Can we help you?") holds meetings in unprepossessing quarters on an unprepossessing street in midtown Manhattan.

Women under 21 are not allowed to join the organization, a proviso that prompts some of the younger Lesbians to inquire "do they think you have to be 21 to be a Lesbian?"

The national membership is now about 500 but, according to Rita Laporte, the national president (who uses her real name), there are many more who are interested and come to meetings but are "afraid to get on our mailing list."

The homosexual woman can, if alone, find friends in the long, narrow red-walled room, illuminated with globe-shaped bulbs. She can also, if she is with a woman friend, reach out to touch her arm or hold her hand without exciting comment. The physical demonstrations, are generally mild and infrequent.

Not Many in 'Drag' At One Popular Bar

There is notable absence of the "drag dykes," the women who imitate men in their dress and manner, at both D.O.B. and at one of the most popular Lesbian bars, a retreat of pleated red velvet walls and crystal chandeliers.

There, its portals guarded by two men who extract a minimum $3 for two drink tickets, and who are said to look unkindly on any male patronage (male homosexuals are passively, and straight males more actively, discouraged), the girls gather, young and middle-aged, white and black, miniskirted and pants-suited.

The "femmes" (the more feminine Lesbians), and the "butches" (the more aggressive and domineering Lesbians, with both masculine and feminine characteristics), talk, drink and dance to juke box records, usually with arms around each other's waist or neck.

There are also a few "dykes," the women with masculine clothing and mannerisms, who are more easily identifiable as homosexuals but do not imitate men to the same degree as "drag dykes."

Most of the Lesbians count male homosexuals among their friends "because you can feel relaxed with them—there are no sexual tensions." A number of them said that although they preferred women, they also like men and had had heterosexual relationships. A small minority were leading a bisexual life.

Almost all of them thought that straight men were generally intrigued by Lesbians. "Straight men feel challenged by us," said one Lesbian.

Many Lesbians undergo therapy; some because they have a genuine desire to belong to a heterosexual community and others because of the pressures of society. But many resent being called "sick."

"I don't think homosexuality is an illness," said one. "If I am capable of loving someone, a woman, and I feel good, why am I sick?"

"I don't think there is anything unnatural about it," Audreysaid. "I wish that some day people would consider it another form of normality. I just feel dirty when I hide.

"We all wonder why we are the way we are. Other people have the same experiences and it doesn't add up to the same total. But I can't imagine being what I'm not."

* * *

July 5, 1970

THE 'GAY' PEOPLE DEMAND THEIR RIGHTS

By LACEY FOSBURGH

André Gide once wrote that he was "obsessed and haunted . . . expending [himself] crazily to the point of utter exhaustion." Other homosexuals have described the terrible shame and loneliness that shadowed their existence. No such complexes interfered with the march in New York last Sunday of thousands of men and women who hoisted their silk banners high and chanted, "Say it loud, Gay is proud."

Singing their songs as they marched up Sixth Avenue to Central Park, they proclaimed to anyone who would listen the "new strength and pride of the Gay People."

Not long ago the scene would have been unthinkable, but the spirit of militancy and determination is growing so rapidly among the legions of young homosexuals that last weekend thousands of them came from all over the Northeast—eager to participate in the demonstration and to serve notice on the straight world that the passive climate of guilt and inferiority that has long subdued the homosexual world is changing.

Out of the Closets

"We're probably the most harassed, persecuted minority group in history, but we'll never have the freedom and civil rights we deserve as human beings unless we stop hiding in the closets and in the shelter of anonymity," said 29-year old Michael Brown, a founder of the Gay Liberation Front, one of the many activist organizations which have sprung up during the last year in response to this new aggressive mood.

The focus of the protest, which brought together almost two dozen divergent groups, was both the laws which make homosexual acts between consenting adults illegal and the social conditions which make it difficult for homosexuals to behave romantically in public, get jobs in government, corporations, banks, airlines, schools or utility companies, or even in some cases rent apartments together.

Such widespread discrimination and inequality, the new homosexual contends, is patently unfair. Now, at a time when blacks, Puerto Ricans, Indians and young people are all refusing to acquiesce in the social values that relegate them to nether worlds, many homosexuals are standing up and saying "I'm proud too. I'm equal and I demand my rights."

Those subscribing to such aggressive tactics include all the groups who marched last weekend, from the "Queens"—

The New York Times (by Michael Evans)

Treading in the steps of all the other minority groups that have been pressing their demands with demonstrations, homosexuals held a mass parade in New York last week to protest the discriminations they suffer.

men who wore lipstick and dresses—to the Lavender Menace, 30 lesbian members of the Women's Liberation Movement. They included politically oriented groups such as the Homosexual Law Reform Society and, the socially oriented like the Institute of Social Ethics and Human Enlightenment, the more collegiate, such as Gay People at Columbia and Yale, and even the revolutionary socialist, such as the Red Butterfly.

Their program, according to Michael Kotis, 28, president of the 15-year old, 700-member Mattachine Society, is defiance. "We're going out in the streets. We're going to protest against every form of bias and discrimination that holds us back."

Mood Is Explained

Bob Kohler, a leading member of the Gay Liberation Front, explained the new mood of militancy this way: "This generation of homosexuals knows that the only way to loosen up society and eliminate the fear and disgust we arouse in people is through open confrontation. We're going to get loud and angry and then more loud and angry until we get our rights."

Although leaders of the movement firmly believe that such aggressive tactics are the only way to win their legal and social rights, they admit the task is difficult.

"Many people can truly identify with the black civil rights movement or other oppressed minorities, but they still can't accept us," said Mr. Kotis. "The issue of homosexuality hits close to home because it involves the touchy matter of sex. For many people it's too personal and controversial because in their hearts they have secret doubts about their own sexual desires." He pointed out that according to the Kinsey Report 50 percent of the male population and somewhat less among females are capable of homosexual response.

"We don't belong in the closets any more and people shouldn't be afraid of what we represent," said Becky Irons, a past president of the Daughters of Bilitis, the oldest lesbian organization, with 300 members in New York. "There's just nothing wrong with us, nothing queer or freaky and as soon as everybody in the Gay World and the straight world recognizes this everything will be all right."

* * *

August 24, 1970

HOMOSEXUALS IN REVOLT

By STEVEN V. ROBERTS

Steve Gerrie wears a well-trimmed mustache, works as an accountant in a Wall Street brokerage and lives with his lover in a neat but threadbare apartment in the West Village here. His roommate, Jack Waluska, is a former welfare case worker now studying for a master's degree in sociology.

One evening recently a friend asked Mr. Gerrie if he would publicly identify himself as a homosexual. Mr. Gerrie said he would, and the friend worried that he might lose his job.

"I don't give a damn," Mr. Gerrie almost shouted. "If it means all that much to my employer, I don't want the job."

Steve Gerrie's reaction reflects a new mood now taking hold among the nation's homosexuals. In growing numbers they are publicly identifying themselves as homosexuals, taking a measure of pride in that identity and seeking militantly to end what they see as society's persecution of them.

Their feelings could be summed up by two of their popular slogans. One is "Out of the closets and into the streets," an allusion to the "closet queen" who passes for "straight" and conceals his homosexuality. The other says, "Gay is good."

This new attitude has its critics, both among "straights" and among homosexuals. Many doctors believe that, while homosexuals should have full legal rights, "gay" is not necessarily "good." Dr. Lionel Ovesey, a professor of clinical psychiatry at Columbia College of Physicians and Surgeons, said:

"Homosexuality is a psychiatric or emotional illness. I think it's a good thing if someone can be cured of it because it's so difficult for a homosexual to find happiness in our society. It's possible that this movement could consolidate the illness in some people, especially among young people who are still teetering on the brink."

As part of a recent pro-homosexual parade organized by the Gay Liberation Front, participants gathered in Central Park.

Most of the new militants refuse even to discuss the causes of their homosexuality. The inevitable reply to the question is, "Why are you a heterosexual?" They insist that their condition cannot be "cured," but Dr. Ovesey reports that about one of every four homosexuals who seek psychiatric help can lead a heterosexual life.

One widespread reaction among "straights" to "gay liberation" is a snicker, a refusal to take it seriously. And that, say the militant homosexuals, is an indication of the contempt in which they are held by society.

But homosexuals themselves are not unanimously in favor of the movement. The vast majority remain unidentifiable and uninvolved in "gay" activism. Some are openly hostile, contending that the young people are "rocking the boat" and making it harder for homosexuals to exist.

There is virtually unanimous support in the "gay" community for attempts to gain legal equality for homosexuals. But many have worked hard to be accepted by "straight" society as "no different from anybody else," and they resent the militants' attempt to set homosexuals apart in a distinct group.

A recent survey for the National Institute of Mental Health estimated that between three and four million Americans were predominantly homosexual. Many more display occasional homosexual tendencies.

Hundred Organizations

Three years ago there were only about 25 organizations serving this community. Today there are more than a hundred, ranging from old line "homophile" groups that concentrate on legal reform to self-proclaimed "revolutionaries" who have adopted the style and rhetoric of the New Left.

Some include only men, some only women, a few both sexes.

Probably the major new force in the homosexual community is the Gay Liberation Front, which started last year in San Francisco and now has about 60 loosely connected chapters from Billings, Mont., to St. Louis to Tallahassee, Fla.

It was the front that organized parades of homosexuals in New York and Los Angeles last June 28, and for the first time made the public fully aware of what had been happening in the "gay" community.

The parades commemorated the first anniversary of the "Stonewall incident," the Boston Tea Party of the "gay revolution." On that occasion the police raided a homosexual bar in Greenwich Village and the patrons, for the first time within anyone's memory, fought back, throwing bricks through the bar's windows and forcing the police to call for reinforcements.

Want to Be Seen as Equal

The incident crystalized an idea that had been growing slowly among homosexuals for years, an idea, as one said, "whose time had come." Simply put, it is that homosexuals want to be treated as equals.

The historical roots of the current ferment reach back to the Kinsey Report of 1948, which said that 10 percent of American men experienced long periods of predominantly homosexual activity. Those figures, which some researchers now feel might have been inflated, helped make homosexuality slightly more familiar and acceptable to the public.

"There has been a more open discussion of all types of sex in recent years," added Michael Kotis, president of the New York Mattachine Society, one of the oldest homosexual organizations. "People are more open-minded about it and try to find out more."

This new public attitude toward sex has fused with the new militancy of blacks, women, and other groups that feel oppressed by society. Civil disobedience by blacks, particularly, seems to have served as a model.

"We are all fighting for equal rights as human beings," explained Mr. Kotis, who had a picture of the Rev. Dr. Martin Luther King Jr. above his desk in the society's cramped offices on West End Avenue. "The philosophical ideals on which this country was founded have yet to be realized. We owe a great debt to the blacks—they were the pioneers."

Iconoclasm Of Youth

The third source of inspiration, especially among more radical elements, was the endemic iconoclasm of the young. "People my own age have been running scared all their lives," said Bob Milne of the Mattachine Society, who is 49. "The younger people just won't take anything any more."

The movement spawned by these influences has a basic goal: to enable homosexuals to overcome the feeling—nurtured and reinforced by society—that they are "queer" and inferior.

"Being homosexual per se does not create emotional problems," said Dr. Joel Fort, a San Francisco psychiatrist and an expert on homosexuality. "It is the way society reacts to the concept of homosexuality which produces the problems."

"The first job we have is to decondition ourselves, to undo all that self-contempt we have," said Don Kilhefner, a graduate student who started a Gay Liberation branch at the University of California at Los Angeles. "We've gone through the same kind of conditioning blacks have gone through. We believe the myth society tells about us, consciously or unconsciously."

"Homosexuality is not an illness; it's a way of expressing love for someone of the same sex, and any form of love is beautiful and valid," said Karla, a leader of the Lavender Menace, a lesbian organization in New York, who would not give her full name.

Popular Play Resented

Many homosexuals resented the popular play and movie, "The Boys in the Band," because they felt that its anguished, self-pitying characters were too close to the old cliches. "No one ever writes about happy homosexuals" is a frequent complaint.

Mr. Kilhefner, in his beard and blue jeans, hardly conforms to the popular image of the lisping, effeminate homosexual. In fact, most homosexuals are indistinguishable, even to other homosexuals. They come from every socio-economic group and hold jobs in every profession and industry.

For that reason, it has been relatively easy for most homosexuals to pass as "straight." But the leaders of the Gay Liberation movement feel that homosexuals should make a full disclosure of their identity to family, friends and employers.

"It's a tremendous strain leading a double life," said Mr. Kotis, who uses another name at his job with a publishing house. "You're always trying to please other people, you can never be yourself. You have to be so careful."

This is particularly true in smaller towns, which generally have fewer homosexuals and less tolerant attitudes than big cities. One New York homosexual, who finds himself completely accepted by his friends, said: "They're still suffering in Kankakee."

"Before I joined Gay Lib I was ashamed of being a lesbian. I thought there was something wrong with me," said Karla, who wore jeans, a red shirt, and earrings decorated with the peace symbol. "The first time I told somebody I was a lesbian I had a real trauma. I couldn't get the word out of my mouth. But in Gay Lib I saw other people saying they were gay and proud. They were so beautiful and free—I was really touched by their contagious pride."

Campaign for Rights

The effort to change the homosexual's self-image, to help him accept himself, is tied in with a broader campaign to secure full civil rights for the homosexual community. Adopting the tactics of other groups, homosexuals have picketed "gay" theaters for charging high prices, newspapers for not printing "gay" advertisements, and even the Army for excluding homosexuals.

Only half jokingly, they note that they are in the vanguard of the ecology issue, since few of them have children. As one slogan puts it: "More deviation, less population."

In every state except Illinois and Connecticut homosexual acts are still illegal, even if practiced in private by consenting adults. The laws in many states even make certain acts illegal if they are performed by husband and wife. Although the police in some cities, particularly New York, have significantly decreased their harassment of homosexuals, the threat remains.

"Being a homosexual is dangerous," said one man. "You're always liable to being beaten up or arrested, and when you are, you can't defend yourself, unless you want everyone to find out you're homosexual. Often police arrest you just to shake you down. They know most people would rather pay than get a morals charge on their record."

Pressure has been building to change the laws. The report to the National Institute of Mental Health recommended eliminating criminal penalties for all sexual acts between consenting adults. Homosexuals are pressing for reform in New York, California and other states. A court case that tests the sodomy laws in Texas is now being appealed to the Supreme Court.

"But changing the laws won't help much unless you also change attitudes," Mr. Gerrie said. "Sodomy isn't a crime in Illinois but they still find reasons to pick you up for vagrancy or disorderly conduct or something like that."

Homosexuals also continue to suffer discrimination in employment. Few school systems will hire homosexuals as teachers and the Federal Government refuses to employ them. Homosexual organizations complain that certain businesses, such as airlines, also exclude them.

As a result, people like Karla, despite her devotion to the movement, are still afraid. "I still face the possibility that I might have to make it in the 'straight' world," she said, in explaining why she would not give her full name. "And there are a lot of things you still can't do if they know you're 'gay.'"

In answer to these problems, "gay" organizations provide legal counsel, offer advice on job hunting, and lobby for legislative reforms. But probably the biggest complaint among homosexuals involves social life.

"Gay" Bars Expensive

Most cities of any size are said to have "gay" bars. New York reportedly has more than 50. But they are often run by disreputable characters, some say mobsters, who charge exhorbitant prices.

"It usually costs $3 to get in and a dollar for every beer. Who can afford to be gay at those prices?" asked one lesbian.

"Bars are very dehumanizing, but they are usually the only place to go," said Don Kilhefner. "You're forced into a situation where you have to look at other people as sex objects. The syndrome is that you go in, cruise around, and look for a sex partner."

In some cities, Gay Liberation has started organizing its own dances to answer the social needs of its members. Mattachine runs its own travel agency and the Society for Individual Rights in San Francisco organizes everything from ice skating parties to cookouts. In Los Angeles, a church has been formed to cater mainly to homosexuals, and several dozen homosexual "marriages" have been performed there.

But homosexuals are still irritated that the public generally disapproves of their showing affection toward each other. "You stand in line for a movie, and there are all these heterosexual couples with their arms around each other," said one. "The homosexual couples just stand there. It makes you feel there's something wrong with you."

There are sharp disagreements within the homosexual community. People such as Michael Brown of Gay Liberation in New York Identify with a broader radical movement.

"The older groups are oriented toward getting accepted by the Establishment," he said, "but what the Establishment has to offer is not worth my time. We're not oriented toward acceptance but toward changing every institution in the country—male domination, capitalist exploitation, all the rest of it."

Even among radicals there are differences. Some lesbians have found it difficult to work with men. "Homosexuals are even more chauvinistic than most males," said Karla. "They feel that they have sex with their equals, not their inferiors."

"I dig the Black Panthers," she added, "but they're going to have to stop calling people 'faggots' when they want to insult them. The same goes for Jerry Rubin and Abbie Hoffman."

On the other side are organizations such as the Tangent Group in Los Angeles, headed by a brisk, middle-aged man named Don Slater. He agreed that homosexuals should have more pride in themselves, but he added:

"People should stop thinking of homosexuals as a class. They're not. We have spent 20 years convincing people that homosexuals are no different than anyone else, and here these kids come along and reinforce what society's thought all along—that homosexuals are different, that they're 'queer.' 'Gay' is good! To hell with that. Individuals are good."

A man like Mr. Slater, who believes in "total integration" for homosexuals, is scorned by Mr. Brown as an "Auntie Tom." But older homosexuals tend to be a cautious lot. They remember a time when police harassment was far worse than it is now—the vice president of the New York Mattachine Society spent a year in jail—and they cannot help worrying about a possible backlash.

Indeed, most Americans apparently continue to despise homosexuals. According to a recent survey by Louis Harris, 63 percent of the population regards homosexuals as "harmful" to society, even though there is no evidence that they commit more sex crimes or other antisocial acts than heterosexuals.

"It's part of the American culture that anything nonmanly is looked upon with disgust," said Dr. Ovesey.

To many, however, this makes the movement all the more necessary. "The more overt demonstrations are just the tip of the iceberg," said Dr. Fort. "The movement is getting to the hidden homosexuals as well. They're becoming more comfortable in their identity and feeling a greater sense of self."

"Most homosexuals have felt very much alone," said Steve Gerrie. "You have no one to talk to. The priest gives you the sin side of it and your parents give you the sick side of it. But when you find other people like you, you don't feel so desperately alone."

* * *

December 18, 1970

THE LESBIAN ISSUE AND WOMEN'S LIB

By JUDY KLEMESRUD

The Lesbian issue, which has been hidden away like a demented child ever since the women's liberation movement came into being in 1966, was brought out of the closet yesterday.

Nine leaders of the movement held a press conference at the Washington Square Methodist Church, 133 West Fourth Street, to express their "solidarity with the struggle of homosexuals to attain their liberation in a sexist society."

The conference was prompted by an article in the Behavior section of the December 14 issue of Time magazine, which said that Kate Millett, author of "Sexual Politics" and one of the chief theoreticians of the movement, had probably "discredited herself as a spokeswoman for her cause" because she disclosed at a recent meeting that she was bisexual.

Prepared Statement Is Read

The 36-year-old Miss Millett, sitting in the center of the leaders at a table in the front of the church, read a statement that she said had been prepared last Monday night at a meeting of about 30 women representing such groups as the National Organization for Women (NOW), Radical Lesbians, Columbia Women's Liberation and Daughters of Bilitis.

The statement said, in part:

"Women's liberation and homosexual liberation are both struggling towards a common goal: A society free from defining and categorizing people by virtue of gender and/or sexual preference. 'Lesbian' is a label used as a psychic weapon to keep women locked into their male-defined 'feminine role.' The essence of that role is that a woman is defined in terms of her relationship to men. A woman is called a Lesbian when she functions autonomously. Women's autonomy is what women's liberation is all about."

Standing behind Miss Millett as she spoke were about 50 women supporters, who frequently interrupted her statement with cheers. Other leaders in the group were Gloria Steinem, the journalist; Ruth Simpson, president of the New York chapter of Daughters of Bilitis; Florynce Kennedy, a lawyer; Sally Kempton and Susan Brownmiller, journalists and members of New York Radical Feminists; and Ivy Bottini, Dolores Alexander and Ti-Grace Atkinson of NOW.

"It's not quite my position," Miss Atkinson, a tall, slender blonde in blue sunglasses said afterwards. "It's not radical enough. If men succeed in associating Lesbianism with the women's movement, then they destroy the movement."

The Lesbian issue had been festering for several months, especially since the Women's Strike for Equality last August 26.

At a rally at Bryant Park following the August 26 march down Fifth Avenue, a member of the Radical Lesbians made a plaintive plea for support from her "straight" sisters in the movement. The speaker charged that the police were harassing Lesbians, and that other women in the movement were ignoring their plight.

"We're your sisters, and we need help!" the speaker cried.

The church had been decorated for the press conference with posters that read, "Kate is Great," "We Stand Together as Women, Regardless of Sexual Preference," and "Is the Statue of Liberty a Lesbian, Too?"

During the question period, Miss Alexander said she thought the movement had taken an overly long time to deal with the Lesbian issue because many women in the movement were afraid to confront it.

'Such an Explosive Issue'

"It's such an explosive issue," she said. "It can intimidate women. Many women would be reduced to tears if you called them Lesbians."

She added that the movement represented women who were "heterosexuals, homosexuals, tall, short, fat, skinny, black, yellow and white."

"People must speak up as Lesbians," said Barbara Love, of the Gay Liberation Front. "I am a Lesbian. We've got to come out and fight, because we're not going to get anywhere if we don't."

Miss Kennedy, the only black woman among the leaders, called for a total "girlcott" of the products of the major advertisers in Time magazine.

Although they weren't present, supporting statements were distributed from Bella Abzug, Democratic Representative-elect of the 19th Congressional District; Caroline Bird, author of "Born Female," and Aileen C. Hernandez, national president of NOW, who called the attempts to use Lesbianism as a weapon against the women's liberation movement "sexual McCarthyism."

Betty Friedan, high priestess of the women's liberation movement and a conservative on the Lesbian issue, did not attend the press conference. Leaders said they had tried to contact her, but that she was "out of town."

* * *

December 12, 1973

'GAY RAIDERS' INVADE CRONKITE NEWS SHOW

C.B.S. Evening News was disrupted briefly last night when a demonstrator from an organization called "The Gay Raiders" ran in front of the camera and held up a yellow sign saying "Gays Protest CBS Prejudice."

The incident occurred about 14 minutes into the first "feed" of the C.B.S. News program, which is anchored by Walter Cronkite and broadcast live at 6:30 P.M. from the studios in New York over most of the network's affiliates.

The demonstration was rerun as a news item on the second "feed" of the show, which is broadcast at 7 and seen on the network's local affiliate, Channel 2, and on a few other stations on the East Coast.

A spokesman for C.B.S. News said the demonstrator, who identified himself as Mark Allan Segal, had called the network last week. Using a different name and pretending to be a reporter for the Camden State Community College newspaper in New Jersey, he secured permission to watch the show from within the studio.

* * *

October 25, 1977

HOMOSEXUALS IN NEW YORK FIND NEW PRIDE

By GRACE LICHTENSTEIN

It was Yom Kippur at Congregation Beth Simchat Torah, Manhattan's four-year-old self-proclaimed "gay synagogue," and the temple facilities in Westbeth apartments in Greenwich Village were over flowing with more than 350 worshipers.

As the Kol Nidre services proceeded, the congregants, a majority of them in suits, prayer shawls and yarmulkes, joined the rabbi as he recited a special holiday "petition" for "gay liberation," which ended: "Fulfill your promise to lift the oppressed from degradation. Remove affliction and suffering from all gay people."

Four years ago, the synagogue consisted of a small band of homosexuals who gathered at irregular intervals for services. Now, it is a part of New York life, involved in United Jewish Appeal fund-raising efforts, tree-plantings in Israel and offering classes in Hebrew. It is one of many symbols of what some homosexual New Yorkers call "the new gay pride."

Gains Are Enormous

The city's homosexual population, which only a few years ago began to "come out of the closet" and into the street, has developed markedly in recent months into a cohesive, open and organized force.

Despite national setbacks, such as a recent unfavorable ruling by the United States Supreme Court on the dismissals of homosexual teachers, gains by homosexuals in New York and elsewhere have been enormous.

Many people still think of homosexual life in terms of interior decorators, Fire Island and bars with a leather motif. This world does indeed exist and flourishes in some neighborhoods.

There have always been bars catering to homosexuals, where much socializing goes on and much information about homosexual concerns is exchanged.

But, increasingly, the homosexual community is very much one of lawyers, physicians, teachers, politicians, clergymen and other upper-class professional men and women. Aside from their sexual preference, many tend to live like their heterosexual counterparts.

One trustee of the synagogue for homosexuals, for instance, mentioned off-handedly, "My lover and I keep a kosher home now. We met at the synagogue. Everybody laughs because this is one of the traditional roles synagogues have always played."

Much More Open

Homosexuals are now showing a greater willingness to identify themselves. Homosexual neighborhoods, for example, are growing in parts of Greenwich Village, Chelsea, the Upper West Side and Brooklyn Heights. A variety of organizations, such as Parents of Gays and Salsa Soul Sisters, are proliferating, along with homosexual religious congregations.

No one claims to have accurate statistics on how many homosexuals there are in the city—10 percent of the population is the most-often cited figure—or how to identify them. But leaders of the community all contend their ranks are swelling and becoming visible.

"If the demographics are true," said Robert L. Livingston of the New York Political Action Council, "we ought to be able to make a Mayor."

H. Gerald Schiff, an accountant who helped found the Greater Gotham Business Council returned to New York in 1975 after a five-year absence and found the change striking.

"I came back to an entirely different city," he said. "It was very much more openly gay, more willing to seek out gay professional people, gay clients, gay customers, more conducive to 'coming out.'"

Ronald Gold of the National Gay Task Force said: "I can get my windows washed by a gay person, get my television repaired, do anything and never see a straight person again."

The reason is that a network of homosexual-oriented services and enterprises has evolved over recent months, many of them listed in Greater Gotham's directory or the Gay Yellow Pages, a national and local publication, so that bars are no longer the sole source of information.

There is a Gay Switchboard and a Lesbian Switchboard, a Gay Men's Health Project; publications such as Gaysweek, Christopher Street and Lesbian Tide; the Gay Teachers Association; Dignity, a group of homosexual Roman Catholics; Integrity, a similar group of Episcopalians; a program "Gay Rap" on WBAI radio; travel agencies, as well as numerous clothing, accessory and book stores.

In addition to getting involved in these services and enterprises, the homosexual community has become active politically, and the growing political consciousness, activists in the community say, will be a factor to be reckoned with.

Many homosexuals became involved politically when they battled for passage by the New York City Council of a measure that would have barred discrimination in housing and employment. Its passage has failed six times, most recently in September 1975.

But, as was the case nationally, with Anita Bryant's campaign in Florida, the defeats only strengthened the homosexuals' resolve to organize their forces better and to fight harder next time.

Candidates Evaluated

The Democratic mayoral candidates this summer acknowledged homosexuals' strength by appealing for their vote in interviews conducted by the New York Political Action Council. Edward I. Koch, the Democratic mayoral candidate and long a supporter of homosexual rights in Congress, got a "preferred" rating, as did Bella S. Abzug, Herman Badillo and Percy Sutton. Mario M. Cuomo, who is now the Liberal Party candidate, was rated "acceptable," Mayor Beame and Joel Harnett "unacceptable."

In the Democratic primary, Kenneth Sherrill, a candidate of the Gay Independent Democrats and other clubs, won the post of district leader in the 69th Assembly district on Manhattan's Upper West Side, becoming, he said, "the first openly gay man to be elected to any party or public office in New York State."

Meanwhile, according to Mr. Livingston, the Political Action Council signed 12,500 new voters during a three-week homosexual-oriented registration drive in June. "What you're seeing this year is a logical first step, politically," he said.

One factor contributing to the growing self-awareness of homosexuals has been the generally tolerant attitude of the city in the past few years. "People who never before thought of living their lives openly, people in important positions, are now being sanctified by the liberals," said Arthur Bell, a Village Voice columnist and long-time activist.

Alongside this apparently growing tolerance is what many leaders perceive to be the more subliminal influence of homosexual taste-makers in New York.

"Gays have a higher economic level," said Mr. Schiff, who founded the Greater Gotham Business Council with a group of professional men almost two years ago. "Gay men easily learn to socialize. So they save less, spend more on high-luxury items, have nicer apartments."

Thus, he said, a disproportionate number of homosexual trend-setting men set styles for stores, advertising campaigns and customers.

"Your major stores are catering to gay taste, certainly in fashion," he said.

Meanwhile, thousands of New York homosexual professional people are choosing to cultivate economic, political and social ties among themselves.

"I speak the same language as my patients," said Dr. Kenneth W. Unger, a physician who has had a largely homosexual practice in Greenwich Village for almost four years.

"It's something I believe in," he continued, sitting in his Sheridan Square office. "The gay community can do best by buying gay." Many patients had come to him, he said, after suffering humiliation from "straight" physicians.

Outbreaks of Disease Found

As a result of the new freedom homosexuals have found in dealing with homosexual doctors, outbreaks of diseases have been recognized in a way they might not have been even a year ago.

Earlier this month, the New York City Health Department announced that in a study done with the Gay Men's Health Project, it had found "a significant number of cases" of sexually transmitted intestinal infections in the homosexual community. A sample of 100 sexually active men showed 26 percent harbored intestinal parasites.

Dr. Yehudi M. Felman, director of the Bureau of Venereal Disease Control called on "the medical and gay communities" to help fight this "so-far silent epidemic" with more frequent examinations and treatments.

Lawyers, too, have discovered that homosexuals have special needs that they appreciate being tended to by homosexual attorneys.

"I'm getting to be quite an expert at drawing up gay wills," said George Terzian, who has had his own practice for nearly two years.

Clients often start out thinking they merely need wills, then progress to more complicated property, insurance and tax matters. As do unmarried heterosexual couples, homosexual couples need legal contracts more than married ones do precisely because married people are covered by laws that they are not.

Thus, lawyers draw up wills in which a lover becomes the heir and also designs statements of joint ownerships of week-

end homes, among other things. In life insurance, special provisions are made for a lover.

Why would homosexuals choose him over an equally competent "straight" lawyer?

"It's like any minority group," Mr. Terzian said. "There's a tremendous bond. Psychologically, it's more important than the law part. They don't understand when they first get here how much legal help I can give them. But they feel they can be much more open about themselves."

Male Indifference Cited

The same kind of services and businesses have blossomed recently among lesbians as they have among homosexual men. (Many women prefer the term lesbian, arguing that the slang "gay" is usually thought of as meaning male.)

Thus there is a lesbian switchboard, newsletter, bookstores, restaurants and political groups, as well as a word-of-mouth list of doctors, lawyers, psychiatrists and stock brokers.

Nevertheless, some lesbian leaders admit they have a larger problem of "invisibility" to overcome than homosexual men have.

The network has "really escalated in the past three years," said Ginny Apuzzo of the National Gay Rights Lobby, a Washington-based group. Yet, "fewer prominent women have come out because they have more to lose and less to gain. They can gain as much by being just feminists."

Major groups such as the National Gay Task Force have made it a point to have equal male and female leaders. Nevertheless, while lesbians may support male homosexual groups and causes, they do not always agree.

"All we have in common is same-sex preference," noted Adrienne Scott, a leader of the year-old Gay Rights National Lobby and a former editor of Blueboy, a slick magazine sometimes referred to as "Playboy for Gays."

"There are many gay men who can't relate to women and lesbians who can't relate to men," she said. There are lesbian separatist groups that will not join in "gay pride" demonstrations.

Some lesbians have also been distressed at male indifference to the women's movement.

"We come into the gay movement with an intellectual and emotional perspective that comes out of the feminist movement," said Ginny Apuzzo. "There's a real problem with many lesbian feminists when men choose to live and die with gay rights alone."

"It's an uphill struggle for the women to be heard" in the homosexual rights movement, she acknowledged.

Many Said to Stay Silent

Moreover, according to Betty Powell, a member of the New York State Advisory Committee to the United States Commission on Civil Rights, "lesbians still threaten many women in the feminist movement. That's still not resolved."

Indeed, there are serious divisions within the homosexual population in New York, not just between men and women, but between old and young, moderates and radicals, the wealthy and the poor.

Beyond this, there is what's thought to be the huge reservoir of "closet gays," men and women who still will not write out a check to an organization with "gay" in the title, who insist newspapers be sent in plain brown wrappers, or who simply feel that disclosing their sexual preference to the general public will endanger their jobs, home and family.

In addition, there are those, such as the priest from an Episcopal church, the trustee of Congregation Beth Simchat Torah, the homosexual father engaged in a custody battle over a child, who participate in "gay rights" activities but prefer not to have their names published. Too much exposure, they fear, would hurt their reputations because of still-existing biases in the "straight" world.

Often, in recent months, homosexuals who come out have been pleasantly surprised about the benign response. "Six months ago you wouldn't have caught me on television for anything," Mr. Schiff said.

He did appear, his neighbors in the small town in Connecticut where he has a weekend house saw him, "and the postmistress thought it was simply interesting," he related, laughing.

However, Mr. Schiff's willingness to accept the new activism is not universal. "There's a whole generation in their 40's and 50's that has always played the role of trying to assimilate in the straight world," he noted.

Militant groups like the Gay Activist Alliance continue to stage demonstrations—more than a dozen in the last month—which some moderates feel are counterproductive.

The group marched recently to protest portrayals of homosexuals on the television series "Soap"; an antihomosexual sign in Geordie's, an East Side singles bar; and President Carter's stand on human rights, since it failed to mention homosexuals.

"When all the polite tactics fail, we have to do the more confrontational things," Mr. Kennedy argued. The point is "to show people who offend the gay community that they can't get away with it."

Despite the relative freedom homosexuals have in New York, all believe more needs to be done.

Both Mr. Kennedy and Mr. Livingston want either a homosexual group or city government inspectors to crack down on bars, bathhouses and after-hours clubs that are fire-traps. (Nine men were killed May 25 in a fire at the Everard Baths in Manhattan.)

Everybody is optimistic that the antidiscrimination ordinance can be passed by the City Council, since its principal opponent, Councilman Matthew J. Troy, Jr. was defeated in the Democratic primary. The measure has the enthusiastic support of Mr. Koch.

Other activists are talking about homosexual addiction, alcoholism and venereal-disease centers sponsored by the government for poor people who feel uncomfortable in heterosexual clinics. A developer in California is planning what is billed as the first male homosexual retirement home. Lesbians

in New York envision a "lesbian Workman's Circle" for the same purpose.

Even so, concern lingers about an antihomosexual backlash, which activists see as part of a national conservative backlash also aimed at school desegregation, the Equal Rights Amendment and abortions.

"Gay teachers honestly feel oppressed," said Marc Rubin of the Gay Teachers Association, a week before the United States Supreme Court refused to review two state rulings allowing teachers to be dismissed on grounds of homosexuality. "It's almost a paranoia."

The American Psychiatric Association denounced the court decision, strengthening its stand, first taken only four years ago, that same-sex preference is not a sickness. "The efforts to frighten citizens into fear of the influence of homosexuals on our children are utterly without scientific foundation and the efforts should be combated by all citizens of good will," Jack Weinberg, president of the association said.

* * *

June 28, 1993

BLACKS REJECTING GAY RIGHTS AS A BATTLE EQUAL TO THEIRS

By LENA WILLIAMS

Ronald Prince has lived a gay life since his mid-teens. Now 43, he readily recalls moments when he hid his homosexuality rather than face public ridicule.

"In high school, when students would poke fun at 'faggots' or 'sissies,' I wouldn't speak up," he said. "I'd go along with the crowd." The facade he kept up included disguising what he considered potentially effeminate mannerisms.

He could conceal his homosexuality. He could not conceal his race. Mr. Prince, who lives in Manhattan, is black.

"A lot of times when you're black and gay, you don't know whether the discrimination is due to your blackness or your gayness," said Mr. Prince, who grew up in Birmingham, Ala., when it was segregated. He said he was called "nigger" and spat upon in white sections of town in the mid-1960's.

Mr. Prince said he had learned to live with the dichotomy that is his life. But like many other blacks, he is angry that leaders of the gay rights movement and some prominent blacks draw parallels between the civil rights struggle of the 60's and homosexuals' fight now for legal and social equality. The debate has intensified since the gay rights march in Washington in April.

Although some conservative blacks oppose homosexuality on religious grounds, many other blacks support legislation to guarantee equal rights for homosexuals. Still, many blacks draw the line at likening racism to anti-gay sentiment.

"A lot of blacks are upset that the feminist movement has pimped off the black movement," said Lou Palmer, who is black and has a call-in show on radio station WVON-AM in Chicago. "Now here comes the gay movement. Blacks resent it very much, because they do not see a parallel, nor do I."

Leonard Smith, 8, second from left, watching a march pass through his neighborhood in northeast Washington last month. About 3,000 people marched to the Mall, where several speakers appealed to Congress to reinstate a 1948 law prohibiting sodomy in the District of Columbia.

In more than two dozen interviews with people on all sides of the issue, several blacks said that the discrimination that homosexuals experience was not on a level with racism.

Many homosexuals say, almost apologetically, that they do not mean to trivialize the black experience in America by likening the two groups' histories. But they argue that discrimination is discrimination.

'Oppression Has Many Faces'

"I am a white gay man," said Thomas B. Stoddard, a leading gay-rights lawyer and the coordinator for the Campaign for Military Service, a group lobbying to allow homosexuals in the military. "I know I've had privileges that black gay men do not have."

He added, however, "I also know as a person who feels the scorn and discrimination of others that oppression has many faces."

But by comparing the two groups' sufferings, some blacks said, homosexuals are misappropriating the spirit and legacy of the black civil rights movement.

"I consider it offensively disrespectful of the recorded and unchronicled sufferings of millions of my people who were kidnapped, chained, shipped and sold like livestock," Vernon Jarrett, who is black and a columnist for The Chicago Sun-Times, wrote in an April 25 column. "Gays were never declared three-fifths human by the Constitution."

Social historians say that there are similarities in the struggles against discrimination, but that there are also very real differences. Andrew Hacker, a professor of political science at Queens College and the author of "Two Nations: Black and White, Separate, Hostile, Unequal" (Scribner's, 1992), said: "By every measure I have seen, race runs deeper and does more damage than any other bias. While some white Americans may have cause for complaints, they still have the built-in advantage of not being black." Mr. Hacker is white.

Roger Wilkins, a professor of history at George Mason University in Fairfax, Va., who was an Assistant Attorney General in the 1960's, said many of the arguments used to fight the integration of the military in 1948 are being used today against homosexuals.

"They said we were too promiscuous, were cowardly and lazy," said Mr. Wilkins, who is black. "Some of the same things are being said about gays. There are all kinds of soldiers who are lazy, cowardly and promiscuous, and it has nothing to do with race or sexual orientation."

Hiding from Discrimination

Mary Frances Berry, a member of the Federal Commission on Civil Rights and a professor of history and law at the University of Pennsylvania, said that anti-gay bias was clearly discrimination, but that being black in America was not the same as being gay. "When people try to equate the two," said Ms. Berry, who is black, "all they do is offend some black folks who recognize that it is not the same thing and might be willing to be supportive."

Even some blacks who acknowledged a common bond with the plight of homosexuals said they were unsympathetic to gay people, especially gay white men, who hid their sexual orientation as long as it was politically, economically and socially beneficial to do so.

"I can't go in a closet and hang up my race when it's convenient," said Vernetta Adams, a 24-year-old history major at the University of the District of Columbia. Ms. Adams is black and heterosexual. "Gays hid in the closet when they wanted to advance. Now they're out and demanding rights and yelling 'discrimination.'"

Religious Questions

For years, many blacks, including members of the clergy, have, because of religion and race, distanced themselves from homosexuals and their struggle for acceptance. Among them are those who view homosexuality as deviant and morally wrong, and others who hold that the gay rights movement has been led by whites.

"They are asking to be recognized lawfully as a minority because homosexuality is immutable," said the Rev. Lester James, pastor of Zion Hill Baptist Church in Washington. "We say, 'No.' We will not agree to them saying they're just like us. Yes, Dr. King talked about loving everybody. We have not abdicated that. I believe God loves the individual homosexual, but He hates the homosexual life style."

Some view the comparison to racism as an act of desperation among homosexuals, who lack the strength in numbers of other groups subjected to discrimination, like women and blacks. Many sociologists estimate the size of the country's gay population at roughly 4 percent, though that and other estimates have been subjects of much debate.

Several blacks said insult was added to injury when prominent blacks like the Rev. Jesse Jackson and civil rights groups like the National Association for the Advancement of Colored People not only voiced support for homosexuals but also stood before the marchers last April and referred to the 1963 march on Washington led by the Rev. Dr. Martin Luther King Jr.

Mrs. King's Letter

But many of those who marched on Washington 30 years ago, including Coretta Scott King, argue that failing to speak out against bigotry dishonors King's name and legacy. Mrs. King, for example, recently wrote a letter to Congress calling the military's ban on homosexuals "un-American."

And Mr. Jackson, speaking at the gay rights march in April, said: "Discrimination is discrimination. We're not talking about behavior; we're talking about status."

Dr. William Gibson, chairman of the N.A.A.C.P., who also addressed the marchers, echoed Mr. Jackson's sentiment. "I felt it was right for the N.A.A.C.P. to be represented there," he said, "because our tradition, objective and constitution is the elimination of segregation and discrimination in all walks of life, for all citizens of this country."

The Rev. Lou Sheldon, an outspoken critic of homosexuality who heads the Traditional Values Coalition, which says that it is affiliated with 27,000 churches nationwide, said many of its black members were "absolutely outraged" that black civil rights leaders had endorsed the gay rights movement.

'Not a Civil Rights Issue'

"The reason gays are making parallels," Mr. Sheldon said, "is that it may bring empathy from white men like me, who feel a collective sense of guilt about the way blacks have been treated. The fact remains that this is not a civil rights issue but a moral issue."

Caught in the middle of the argument are black homosexuals.

"There's always this debate within the lesbian and gay community: 'Are you black first or are you gay first?'" said Nadine Smith, an organizer of the April gay rights march who is black. "You can't stop being one. We've done that too long. Saying: 'I'm going to be black when I go to the N.A.A.C.P. meeting, so I'll stop being gay right now.' Or, 'I'm going to sit in on the Gay Pride community meeting, so I'm going to stop being black.'"

Racism Among Gays

Black homosexuals also recognize that there is racism among homosexuals themselves. "There are all-white gay clubs, all-black gay clubs, Latino gay clubs," said Perry Watkins, a former Army sergeant who was one of two grand marshals of New York's gay pride parade yesterday. "Racism within the gay community is a big problem. The primary reason is that we are a direct reflection of the society from which we come, which is controlled by white males. When the gay community was formed and became political, the leaders were white men, and they brought their prejudices with them."

Mr. Watkins said none of the "anointed leadership" within the gay movement had asked him to lend his voice and support to the fight to allow homosexuals in the military, even though he was the only openly gay serviceman to have successfully challenged the military's anti-gay policy. He acknowledged his homosexuality when he was drafted in 1967 and was twice allowed to re-enlist before being discharged in 1984, after regulations were changed to bar all homosexuals from the military. In 1991 Mr. Watkins won a landmark lawsuit against the Army that resulted in his reinstatement, a promotion and his retiring with credit for 21 years of service.

Despite their differences with homosexuals on issues of civil rights, many blacks, including nearly all those interviewed for this article, support guarantees of equal rights for gay people. According to a New York Times/CBS News Poll of 1,154 adults conducted Feb. 9-11, 53 percent of blacks thought such legislation was necessary, as against only 40 percent of whites. The poll had a margin of sampling error of plus or minus three percentage points.

Many homosexuals see such support as a sign that on some level, blacks do understand the gay struggle and relate to their cause.

As Mr. Stoddard put it: "To a large degree we are bound together by our opponents. Those who hate blacks hate gay people, hate Jews and abuse women, and fighting on behalf of any of us will ultimately lead to the liberation of all of us."

* * *

July 10, 1993

GAY CAUSE IS THE SAME AS BLACK CAUSE

To the Editor:

Re "Blacks Reject Gay Rights Fight as Equal to Theirs" (front page, June 28) and your news article of the same day on New York's gay pride march: Your coverage of the human rights issue in the black and gay communities deals a severe blow to the hard-fought legal advances that civil rights groups have made in the last 20 years.

The inference that a false dichotomy exists between the black and gay communities is misleading and offensive. One of the most striking aspects of the gay pride march was the tremendous mix of cultures and races among the men and women who took part. The day was a celebration of multiculturalism of our community, as people of all colors came together to celebrate not only gay rights, but also human rights.

Oppression, no matter what its shape, does harm to all of humanity. How unfortunate that one had to read well into the body of your front-page article to find the Rev. Jesse Jackson's words that "Discrimination is discrimination." And buried even further in the article were Coretta Scott King's words from a letter to Congress calling the ban on homosexuals in the military "un-American."

Hatred in any form is un-American, no matter what our color, sexual preference or religion. It is time for you and the public to embrace the principle that gay rights, black rights and women's rights are all human rights.

KEVIN M. CATHCART
Executive Director,
Lambda Legal Defense and Education Fund
New York, July 1, 1993

* * *

July 31, 1998

FINDING COURAGE AND ANGUISH ALONG THE ROAD TO GAY PRIDE

By STEPHEN HOLDEN

OUT OF THE PAST
Directed and produced by Jeff Dupre; written by Michelle Ferrari; director of photography, Buddy Squires; edited by George O'Donnell and Toby Shimin; music by Matthias Gohl; released by Zeitgeist Films/Unapix Films.
WITH: Linda Hunt (Narrator) and Barbara Gittings.
Shown with a 27-minute short, Todd Haynes's "Dottie Gets Spanked." At the Screening Room, 54 Varick Street, at Laight Street, TriBeCa. Running time: 64 minutes. This film is not rated.
WITH THE VOICES OF: Stephen Spinella (Michael Wigglesworth), Gwyneth Paltrow (Sarah Orne Jewett), Cherry Jones (Annie Adams Fields), Edward Norton (Henry Gerber) and Leland Gantt (Bayard Rustin).

When Kelli Peterson, an articulate, likable lesbian high school student in Salt Lake City, founded an extracurricular organization called the Gay-Straight Alliance three years ago, she had no inkling of the storm of hysterical outrage that would erupt in her conservative hometown.

The organization's opponents went so far as to as pressure the Utah State Legislature to pass a law banning all extracurricular high school clubs. (The ban was later overturned.) At the same time, Ms. Peterson's cause was taken up by thousands of sympathetic students who marched in the streets to demonstrate their support.

Her story, told largely in her own words, is the centerpiece of "Out of the Past," a solemn, well-paced documentary written by Michelle Ferrari, directed by Jeff Dupre and narrated by Linda Hunt (in her best grand manner), which compares Ms. Peterson to several unsung heroes of the gay liberation movement. The film, which opens today at the Screening Room, is a conscious attempt to extend the historical pantheon of gay and lesbian luminaries to include political and literary voices that have been largely forgotten.

Interwoven with Ms. Peterson's story are concise biographies of five men and women who prefigured the modern gay liberation movement. The most mysterious and debatable for inclusion is Michael Wigglesworth, a 17th-century Puritan cleric who kept a tormented diary of his own homosexual longings.

From here, the movie jumps ahead two centuries to the novelist Sarah Orne Jewett, whose posthumously collected love letters to her partner, Annie Adams Fields, in what was then known as "a Boston marriage" were suppressed by her publisher. The film goes on to remember Henry Gerber, a Chicago postal clerk who in 1924 founded America's first known gay rights organization. One night the police raided Gerber's home, confiscated his typewriter and other materials, and jailed him for several days without formally charging him with a crime. Upon his release, he was dismissed from his job for "conduct unbecoming" a postal worker.

A more recent unsung hero was Bayard Rustin, the charismatic black, gay civil rights leader and chief organizer of the 1963 March on Washington, known as "the lost prophet," whose homosexuality was considered such a potential embarrassment to the civil rights leadership that he never ascended to his rightful place alongside the Rev. Dr. Martin Luther King Jr. in the movement. Finally, there is Barbara Gittings, a president of the early lesbian organization Daughters of Bilitis, whose efforts were instrumental in persuading the American Psychiatric Association to remove homosexuality from its list of mental disorders.

The efficiently edited 64-minute film has no loose ends. The actors reading the words of these historical figures include Stephen Spinella (Wigglesworth), Gwyneth Paltrow (Jewett), Cherry Jones (Fields), Edward Norton (Gerber) and Leland Gantt (Rustin). Ms. Gittings, who is still active in gay politics, speaks for herself, with a clipped, composed eloquence.

* * *

July 5, 1999

TRACING THE RISE OF THE GAY RIGHTS MOVEMENT

By STEPHEN O. MURRAY

OUT FOR GOOD: The Struggle to Build a Gay Rights Movement in America
By Dudley Clendinen and Adam Nagourney
Illustrated. 716 pp. Simon & Schuster. $30.

At its best, "Out for Good" vividly reports the activism and intramural conflicts of the 1970's gay and lesbian movement. The middle of this book is superb, but its frame weakens it. To end with the funeral of a Los Angeles political patron, Sheldon Andelson, in 1987 is peculiar. An epilogue about Bill Clinton's campaign promises of 1992 is even stranger.

Neither phenomenon makes sense as the climax of the gay and lesbian movement. Was the goal of the historical figures discussed in this book only to be a rarely greased cog in the Democratic Party? For some, it was. But there were and are gay and lesbian congeries of activist sex radicals, socialists and gay libertarians, not just caucuses of the Democratic Party. The authors, Dudley Clendinen, an editorial writer for The New York Times, and Adam Nagourney, a metropolitan reporter for The Times, largely ignore the many disparate groups of gay and lesbian advocates seeking broad social or political changes to dote on those seeking to be part of one political party.

Starting the book with the Stonewall Inn "riot" may make sense for an account of New York gay politics, but other than a symbol, little developed from it. (Even for New York City, another raid—on the Snake Pit later in the summer of 1969—was more consequential for political organizing.) Before Stonewall, San Francisco provided models and precedents both of impolite public protests and of working with and within government for recognition and protection.

There is certainly plenty in the book about San Francisco and Los Angeles politics in the 1970's and 80's, but the foundational role of gay organizing in those cities is ignored to re-

peat the familiar tale of what was a false start in New York. Perhaps the best indicator of New York's nonleadership is one the authors note. The first municipal gay rights ordinance in the nation was introduced in the New York City Council on Jan. 6, 1971. One was enacted 15 years, 2 months and 14 days later—following 3 states, 11 counties and 48 other cities.

After the unfortunate choice of an opening point, "Out for Good" is actually less New York-centered than other histories of the gay and lesbian movement during the 70's and 80's. It includes richly detailed accounts of battles in Minnesota and Miami and of a 1973 fire bombing in New Orleans, though the major focal points are California, Boston, New York and Washington. After detailed accounts of the 1977 repeals of gay rights ordinances in Miami and St. Paul, the authors mention but do not tell the story of the first success in combating such a campaign (in Seattle in 1978).

The authors also provide the perspectives of many female leaders, both lesbian separatists and those eager to take over organizations and to control resources mostly supplied by men. Yet there is hardly anything about lesbian mobilizations around such issues as child custody.

The multiple narratives within the book are character-driven. This makes it engaging reading. There are plenty of villains (most of them egomaniacs), some heroes and heroines, and strong plot lines about particular battles. The overall line of development is obscure, not least because the book's two endings are so arbitrary.

With so many would-be leaders and so few followers of any particular one, the authors' focus on those who commanded some media attention at one time or another is predictable. Most of the figures of the gay and lesbian movement who were prominent burned out from infighting, were singed by attacks (often very personal ones) or faded away from exhaustion. Many have died since 1992, when work on this book began. Anyone interested in the perspectives of earlier prominent figures in the gay and lesbian movement has to be grateful for the prodigious efforts the authors made in interviewing 330 people (some multiple times), and to hope that their records will be available to future researchers.

A truly definitive history, which the authors twice claim in the introduction to have produced, has to look beyond celebrities and leaders to those who worked out of the spotlight and to the "free riders"—that is, the many people who gained from movements to which they contributed no time or energy. A definitive history would also have to provide a clearer analytical framework.

Along with individual profiles, a definitive history of the American gay and lesbian movement needs to compare this movement with those in other countries and with other contemporary movements in the United States. The civil rights movement and the Christian right are two with direct relations to the gay and lesbian movement, and offer useful comparisons of relative success, amount of infighting, frequency of schisms and so on. This lack is especially surprising because Mr. Clendinen has written extensively about the Christian right.

But systematic comparisons would make the book even longer and might not interest those who thrive on gossip about celebrities (even mostly forgotten minor-league ones). Instead of jettisoning background before Stonewall, the authors should have removed the account of mobilizations around AIDS. Their account is more reliable and far better substantiated than Randy Shilts's, but there are other, better analyses of AIDS activism (e.g., the second half of Steven Epstein's "Impure Science"). The authors dwell at inordinate length on David Goodstein, who published The Advocate for most of the years between 1975 and 1985 and repeatedly failed to shape gay movement strategy.

As prodigious as their interviewing efforts were, as interesting and reliable and well documented as their reporting is, and as well written as this book is, a more sweeping history not only of gay politics but also of gay culture can be found in "The Other Side of Silence," by John Loughery. "Out for Good" is the best history of gay mobilizations during the 1970's and useful on the early 80's, but Mr. Loughery's more analytic history, with its longer time frame, remains the best book so far available on the emergence of 20th-century American gay culture and politics.

Stephen O. Murray is the author of "American Gay" and a dozen other books.

* * *

PARADES AND MARCHES

June 29, 1970

THOUSANDS OF HOMOSEXUALS HOLD A PROTEST RALLY IN CENTRAL PARK

By LACEY FOSBURGH

Thousands of young men and women homosexuals from all over the Northeast marched from Greenwich Village to the Sheep Meadow in Central Park yesterday, proclaiming "the new strength and pride of the gay people."

From Washington, Boston and Cleveland, from Ivy League colleges, from Harlem, the East Side and the suburbs, they gathered to protest laws that make homosexual acts between consenting adults illegal and social conditions that often make it impossible for them to display affection in public, maintain jobs or rent apartments.

As the group gathered in Sheridan Square before marching up the Avenue of the Americas to hold what the participants described as a "gay-in" in the Sheep Meadow, one of the organizers said a new militancy was developing among homosexuals.

"We're probably the most harassed, persecuted minority group in history, but we'll never have the freedom and civil rights we deserve as human beings unless we stop hiding in closets and in the shelter of anonymity," said 29-year old Michael Brown. He is a founder of the Gay Liberation Front, an activist homosexual organization that has held small demonstrations in Greenwich Village in the past year.

"We have to come out into the open and stop being ashamed, or else people will go on treating us as freaks. This march," he went on, "is an affirmation and declaration of our new pride."

Then, chanting, "Say it loud, gay is proud," the marchers held bright red, green, purple and yellow silk banners high in the warm afternoon air and began to move up the avenue.

At the head of the line, which extended for 15 blocks, were about 200 members of the Gay Activists Alliance. They were followed by people representing the Mattachine Society,

The New York Times (by Michael Evans)

MARCH AGAINST ANTI-HOMOSEXUAL CONDITIONS: The Gay Liberation Day parade entering Central Park on the way to the Sheep Meadow yesterday. Demonstration by groups from Northeast area started in Greenwich Village.

women's liberation groups, the Queens and 14 other homosexual organizations.

Crowd Estimates Vary

Estimates of the size of the demonstration ranged from that by one police officer, who said casually there were "over a thousand," to organizers who said variously 3,000 and 5,000 and even 20,000.

"We've never had a demonstration like this," said Martin Robinson, 27, a carpenter who is in charge of political affairs for the Gay Activities Alliance. He walked with the others past crowds of people standing in silence on the sidewalks.

"It serves notice on every politician in the state and nation that homosexuals are not going to hide any more. We're becoming militant, and we won't be harassed and degraded any more," Mr. Robinson said.

Throughout the demonstration, first along the Avenue of the Americas and later in the park, where the group sat together, laughing, talking and waving their banners, hundreds of on-lookers gathered.

Some eagerly clicked their cameras, others tittered, many were obviously startled by the scene. There was little open animosity, and some bystanders applauded when a tall, pretty girl carrying a sign, "I am a Lesbian," walked by.

Michael Kotis, president of the Mattachine Society, which has about 1,000 members around the country, said that "the gay people have discovered their potential strength and gained a new pride" since a battle on June 29, 1969, between a crowd of homosexuals and policemen who raided the Stonewall Inn, a place frequented by homosexuals at 53 Christopher Street.

"The main thing we have to understand," he added, holding a yellow silk banner high in the air, "is that we're different, but we're not inferior."

* * *

June 27, 1971

MILITANT HOMOSEXUALS TO STAGE MARCH TO CENTRAL PARK TODAY

By JOSEPH LELYVELD

Thousands of homosexuals are expected to march from Christopher Street in Greenwich Village to the Sheep Meadow in Central Park this afternoon to mark the second anniversary of a movement known to them as "the Gay Revolution."

In part, the march is intended as a celebration of the movement's progress since its riotous beginning on Christopher Street on June 27, 1969 when homosexuals, instead of slinking off into the night, threw bottles and cans at policemen who raided a homosexual bar called the Stonewall Inn.

But beyond celebration, the march will have a calculated political purpose—to force society at large, and local lawmakers in particular, to recognize homosexuals as a well-organized, purposeful minority with a serious issue that requires attention. That issue is the legal status of homosexuals.

Prosecutions Are Rare

Although prosecutions here are rare, homosexual acts are still listed as crimes on the statute books of New York and 46 other states. Thus the homosexual is virtually defined as a criminal, a definition that lends an appearance of legitimacy to the scorn and prejudice of which he has long been an object.

Those militants here who have, as they say, "come out of the closet" in the last two years have built an efficient lobby to press for the repeal of the law against homosexual acts between consenting adults.

They have also sought amendments to the antidiscrimination statutes of both the city and state that would make it illegal to discriminate in jobs, housing and public accommodations on grounds of "sexual orientation."

In the past, when homosexuals have been bold enough to seek changes in public policy, they have done so in a manner that was deferential, even apologetic, saying they were not responsible for the condition that set them apart.

The New York Times

Picket at a City Hall demonstration last Friday.

The new militants do not go in for apology. "We do not ask for any respectability or sympathy from straight people," Jim Owles, the 24-year-old president of the Gay Activists Alliance, declared in an open letter to all members of the State Legislature in February.

"Their private opinions of us as individuals or as members of a group are of no interest to us except to the extent that these private bigotries are allowed to become public policy."

Among themselves, some members of the City Council refer to the antidiscrimination bill being sponsored there by Councilmen Eldon R. Clingan, Manhattan Liberal, and Carter Burden, Manhattan Democrat, as the "fag bill." But the persistence with which the homosexual lobbyists have marshaled their arguments and support has been a signal to most politicians to receive them with cautious respect, if not enthusiasm.

Numbers in Doubt

Estimates of the city's homosexual population usually range from 300,000 to 800,000. No one really knows, just as no one knows how many of these people vote, or whether they are inclined to vote as homosexuals.

But the idea of a "homosexual vote" is slowly gaining ground. "Register and Vote Gay," urged handbills passed out during the last campaign by the Gay Activists Alliance, the homosexual group that has been most active on the legislative scene.

Of the 37 members of the City Council, only two have since refused to meet the group's representatives. "Usually when we first approach politicians, they are completely dumfounded," Mr. Owles said. "This is one time they don't have a pat answer."

Mr. Owles was one of nine homosexual activists arrested on the steps of City Hall on Friday when they attempted to stage a sit-in in the office of the Council's Democratic Majority Leader, Thomas J. Cuite. Confrontation tactics are necessary, the activists believe, to make politicians act in public on assurances many of them freely dispense in private.

The activists assert that a majority of the Councilmen have promised to vote for the antidiscrimination measure if it ever reaches the floor. The catch is that few of them are taking any steps to see that it gets there.

A clear indication that the militants have made an impression on some local legislators can be found in the fact that 14 separate bills affecting the rights of homosexuals were introduced in the two houses of the State Legislature at the last session.

One of these, an antidiscrimination measure sponsored by Assemblyman William F. Passannante, a Greenwich Village Democrat, was debated on the floor and then turned down by a vote of 84 to 61.

Not Just a City Issue

Reform for the sake of homosexuals was generally regarded as a bizarre New York City issue in Albany, but the homosexual organizations managed to give a number of upstate legislators pause by making sure they were visited by homosexual voters from their own constituencies.

In 1965, the last time the Assembly voted on a measure affecting homosexuals, the margin was much wider. On that occasion, the vote was 115 to 16 in favor of putting a provision forbidding homosexual acts back into the penal code after a special commission had recommended its removal as part of a general reform.

Then there was active opposition to the reform from Roman Catholic churchmen and no lobbyists represented homosexuals. By contrast, Mr. Passannante said he was aware of no organized opposition to his bill.

The lack of organized opposition may reflect a subtle shift in social attitudes, but it also indicates how far the homosexual groups still have to travel merely to bring the issue of homosexual rights into the open as a matter of general debate.

"It's the kind of issue that's still being talked about in whispers," Assemblyman Passannante observed.

Until it came to the floor, the bill, he said, was regarded by a number of assemblymen as an occasion for friendly bantering about his own inclinations. "I'd tell them," he said, "'I'm not worried about my manhood. What are you afraid of?'"

Little Notice Attracted

In debate, opponents of the bill noted that the measure would make it illegal to refuse employment as a camp coun-selor to a homosexual on grounds of his deviancy. "If we pass this bill here today, we're nuts!" declared Assemblyman Charles Jerabek, a Suffolk County Republican.

The debate attracted little attention, except in homosexual publications. Indeed, there has been nothing here to match the 10-year controversy in Britain that followed the publication in 1957 of the Wolfenden Report, which asserted that homosexual acts between consenting adults should not be regarded as illegal. After a huge outpouring of pamphlets and editorials, Parliament finally accepted the recommendations in 1967.

The Gay Activists Alliance came into existence here in December, 1969, calling itself a "one-issue organization" of "liberated homosexual activists." Most of its members were in their 20's and defiantly—they say proudly—"out of the closet."

The organization, which has spawned numerous committees to pressure particular branches of government and the media, says it has about 200 members regularly engaged in its activities. Inactive members are not accepted, it says.

Until the organization came on the scene, homosexual interests were represented mainly by the Mattachine Society, many of whose members were middle-aged, used pseudonyms within the organization and led double lives.

Discrete approaches by Mattachine to the Lindsay administration in 1966 helped persuade the city to call a halt to the practice of entrapment of homosexuals by policemen. This led, the newspaper Gay later declared, to "an era of unprecedented sexual freedom" for homosexuals here.

The night Mayor Lindsay was re-elected in 1969, it is said, many homosexual bars dispensed free drinks to their customers who believed that his victory protected homosexuals against a return to repressive policies.

But the young militants, seeking something more than non-enforcement of the law, did not exempt the Mayor from their confrontation tactics. Four times in the spring and fall last year they "zapped" him—to use their word—by accosting him in public with shouted taunts and slogans to wring from him an endorsement of the Clingan-Burden Bill.

The harassment of Mr. Lindsay was finally called off, an officer of the Gay Activists Alliance conceded, when it became clear "it wasn't doing us any good with the gay community."

Last month, with a minimum of fanfare, the Mayor's office gave in to the organization's persistent lobbying and released a statement supporting the antidiscrimination bill.

In the 1970 election, the organization managed to get statements generally supporting its legislative aims from more than 40 candidates running in the city.

In an Assembly race on Manhattan's East Side, a Democrat who had taken a strong stand for homosexual rights, Antonio Olivieri, narrowly defeated a Republican incumbent, Stephen Hansen, who refused to take any stand at all. The Gay Activists Alliance had passed out leaflets calling attention to the difference and claimed that a "gay swing vote" was a major factor in the result.

By now, the militants are in regular contact with a number of liberal politicians here. Mr. Owles speaks of "our friends in Washington," meaning the few members of Congress who have shown they take the movement seriously.

The politicians assure them that the legislation they seek is bound to pass in the next few years. Mr. Owles, who says he expects to be a full-time activist in the movement "till I die," predicts that its attention will then shift to the problem of enforcement of antidiscrimination acts.

Last week, at the dedication of a former firehouse at 99 Wooster Street in the Soho section that his organization has opened as a center of "gay culture," he spoke of a future in which homosexuals would be able to "show straights and themselves that being gay means something more than the baths and the bars."

His Movement's goals of self-acceptance and self-expression for homosexuals cannot be achieved by the passage of laws, Mr. Owles says. But he regards the marches and laws as a necessary start.

According to Mr. Owles, 10 homosexuals will stay home out of fear for every one who parades up the Avenue of the Americas this afternoon. "It's a lot more difficult to march out of the closet than to march for peace," he said. "It can cost you your job or your career."

* * *

June 28, 1971

5,000 HOMOSEXUALS MARCH TO CENTRAL PARK FOR A RALLY

By PAUL L. MONTGOMERY

About 5,000 homosexual men and women marched in a happy parade from Greenwich Village to Central Park yesterday afternoon in a demonstration of gay pride and solidarity.

The good-humored throng, flying yellow and lavender balloons and chanting at curious bystanders, were participating in the second-birthday celebration of the Gay Liberation Movement. The movement aims at curbing harassment of homosexuals and discrimination in jobs and housing.

"We are united today through the strength of our love for each other, in affirming our pride in ourselves and in our life-style," said a statement by the Christopher Street Liberation Day Committee, the organizers of the march. "As individuals, we may have political and social differences; as members of the gay community, we are here today, united as sisters and brothers. This is the commitment that draws us together today."

Bigger Crowd Than 1970's

The group, a coalition of eight homophile groups in the city, held a similar march last year. Those who observed both said that this year's crowd appeared to be about double last year's.

The marchers, most of them under 30 years old, gathered in Sheridan Square in the Village. Most were dressed casually, as though for the beach. There were a few men dressed as women who posed cheerfully for the dozens of amateur photographers who crowded the route. About one-third of

the demonstrators were women belonging to various lesbian groups.

The police had set off one lane of the Avenue of the Americas with barricades for the march to the Sheep Meadow in Central Park. The policemen controlling the flow of traffic looked on without expression as the marchers passed. Bystanders on the hot sidewalks looked on with curiosity but little apparent hostility. There appeared to be a number of homosexuals who stood on the sidewalk to watch but were too shy to join.

Politics Minimal

While some of the chants and posters had political content ("Out of the closets, into the streets" and "I'm honest, kind, human—Why not equal?"), most were frankly sexual ("2-4-6-8, Gay is twice as good as straight," "3-5-7-9, Lesbians are might fine" and "Heterosexuality can be cured.")

Among the placards identifying groups were ones from Canada, Austin, Tex., Bridgeport and Hartford, Conn., Ithaca and Rochester, N.Y., Boston and Washington, D.C. There were a number of university groups, including ones from the University of Maryland, Rutgers, Penn State and Kutztown, Pa., State College.

At the Sheep Meadow, the participants lounged on the dusty grass and marveled over the strength of their numbers gathered in one place. Next year, the group plans to march in Washington.

* * *

August 21, 1977

500 HOMOSEXUALS MARCH TO THE U.N. IN A RIGHTS PROTEST

By LENA WILLIAMS

Five hundred homosexual men and women yesterday marched on United Nations headquarters in New York to "alert the world that gay men and women are still denied basic civil and human rights."

"The United Nations itself currently makes no recognition in any of its policy documents of the rights of homosexuals to live their lives free of discrimination and persecution," David Thorstad and Chery Adams of the Coalition for Lesbian and Gay Rights wrote in a letter to the United Nations Secretary General, Kurt Waldheim.

When the letter was read at a rally at Dag Hammerskjold Plaza, the crowd applauded and often interrupted the reading with a chant of "gay rights now."

Earlier, the demonstrators had walked 40 blocks from Washington Square to the United Nations, growing more vociferous as they went along.

Anita Bryant Criticized

By the time they reached Second Avenue and 40th Street, they had criticized Anita Bryant, who led a successful campaign to revoke homosexual rights legislation in Dade County,

Fla., and assailed the Carter Administration and the New York City Council for inactivity on the rights bill.

"The fight here today is part of the whole fight for human rights and dignity," said Councilwoman Miriam Friedlander, Democrat of Manhattan.

Many of those attending the rally had traveled from as far as West Germany and Quebec City to denounce worldwide harassment and discrimination of homosexuals.

Speaking through an interpreter, 27-year-old Winfried Kuhn, a student from West Berlin who had come to New York to participate in the rally, said that people in West Germany could lose their jobs if they were homosexuals.

Growing in Germany

"The gay movement in Germany is not strong, but it is growing," said Mr. Kuhn, who attended the rally with Jim Steakley, who had met Mr. Kuhn in Germany two years ago and had invited him to New York.

Jeanne Manford, a founder of the Parents of Gays of Greater New York, encouraged parents of homosexual children to "fight for the human rights of your children."

"My son is gay and I'm proud of him and I love him," she told the crowd, her speech invoking cheers and applause. "I will fight with him and with you to save homosexuals from biogtry and discrimination."

Organizers of the march said they had received the support of more than 50 groups, such as the Greenwich Village-Chelsea chapter of National Association for the Advancement of Colored People, the National Organization for Women of New York, the Socialist Workers Party, the Church of the Beloved Disciple and several homosexual alliance groups.

* * *

October 15, 1979

75,000 MARCH IN CAPITAL IN DRIVE TO SUPPORT HOMOSEXUAL RIGHTS

By JO THOMAS
Special to The New York Times

WASHINGTON, Oct. 14—An enthusiastic crowd of at least 75,000 people from around the country paraded through the capital today in a homosexual rights march and gathered afterward on the grounds of the Washington Monument to marvel at their own numbers and to urge passage of legislation to protect the rights of homosexuals.

"Almost 30 years ago I thought I was the only gay person in the world," said the keynote speaker, Betty Santoro, of New York, as the looked out over a sea of banners that proclaimed "Alaska," "Wyoming," "Gay Mormons United."

"There are still gay people who feel alone and isolated," she said. "We are here today because we refuse, we refuse to allow this kind of suffering to continue. Our message is today they need not be alone, not ever again. Our very presence here is living proof we are, indeed, everywhere."

Most of the marchers were young, although all age groups were represented. Most were white, and it appeared that men slightly outnumbered women. Many of the marchers were parents and there was much talk about family.

'Sharing' and 'Flaunting'

"When a heterosexual person shows a picture of his family, it's called sharing," Robin Tyler, a lesbian feminist comedian told the crowd. "When we show a picture of our lover, it's called flaunting. We want to share."

"We are family," said Howard Wallace, a homosexual activist and candidate for city office in San Francisco. "A new day is coming. It will come so much sooner if we cast out the great authoritarian father figures housed in our minds; if we shed our self-hatred and shame; if we stop assuming that the President, the governor, the mayor, the official, knows better than we."

Estimates of the number of people in the crowd varied. The United States Park Police first put the number at 75,000 but later said between 25,000 and 50,000 showed up. Eric Rofes, an organizer of the march, said he thought there were "more than 100,000."

Speaker after speaker cited an estimate that there were 20 million homosexuals in the United States, a sizable minority group.

The demonstrators and speakers called for legislation to amend the Civil Rights Act of 1964 to protect homosexuals against discrimination. They also have urged that President Carter sign an executive order banning discrimination in the military, civil service and among Government contractors.

While the demonstration was under way, a coalition of ministers met on Capitol Hill to organize a National Day of Prayer on Homosexuality to ask God "to deliver them from their lives of perversion," a spokesman for the group said.

The Rev. Richard Zone, executive director of the religious group, Christian Voice, said that the coalition had asked 40,000 ministers to urge their congregations to petition the President to resist efforts to give homosexuals special consideration under the law.

"God didn't create Adam and Steve, but Adam and Eve," said the Rev. Jerry Falwell, a television evangelist from Lynchburg, Va. He called homosexuality "an outright assault on the family."

* * *

June 25, 1990

THRONGS CHEER AT GAY AND LESBIAN MARCH

By JOHN TIERNEY

Tens of thousands of people marched down a lavender-striped Fifth Avenue yesterday in the 21st annual Gay and Lesbian Pride March, a parade distinguished by its diversity, its broad sense of style and its lack of marching bands. It has never needed majorettes to generate festivity.

Sara Krulwich/The New York Times

Members of Act-Up joining the tens of thousands of people who marched down Fifth Avenue in the 21st annual Gay and Lesbian Pride March.

This year's parade was the largest so far, bringing together a remarkably wide array of people. A delegation from the Union Theological Seminary was a few steps ahead of the Witches and Pagans for Gay Rights. Mayor David N. Dinkins, wearing white shoes and a short-sleeved white suit, walked a block behind the Lavender Jane Gang of lesbian motorcyclists dressed in black leather.

"This is the best day of my life—better than Christmas, better than New Year's," said Jeanne Dehauski, a 30-year-old lab technician from Fairlawn, N.J., who was riding with the Lavender Jane Gang. "I get to stand up tall and proud for my rights and for the dignity of being a lesbian."

The parade, which began at Columbus Circle and ended at Christopher Street in Greenwich Village, featured close to 300 groups. The range included the Brooklyn Women's Flag Football Team, New York City Gay and Lesbian Judges, Gay Male S/M Activists, the Libertarian Party of New York, the Knights Wrestling Club, a group from Riverside Church and the New York Aquatic Homosexuals.

The parade's organizers, Heritage of Pride Inc., estimated there were 200,000 marchers. The police estimated there were 65,000 marchers and 120,000 spectators. "Every year it's beautiful, and this year it seems even bigger and more fabulous than ever," said Robin Byrd, the host of a sexually-explicit program on cable television, who was at the reviewing stand on 42d Street judging the floats and greeting her many fans. As a member of one group of marchers, the Radical Faeries, came over and pasted a star on her shoulder, she said it was difficult to choose a winner.

"All the groups are so great," she said, and turned to watch the small contingent of a half-dozen men from the North American Man/Boy Love Association march by. "I'm for every group. Freedom of expression!"

The floats featured figures in sequined gowns and tiaras, most of them male, and they made special efforts to pucker their lips and issue the tight beauty-queen wave when they passed a group of 100 protesters standing near St. Patrick's Cathedral. The protesters, a group of Catholics and others who described themselves as born-again Christians, held up rosaries, crucifixes and signs.

"Excommunication Now!" read their main banner, and there was another sign with a picture of Jesus saying, "I shall not allow science to find a cure for AIDS." Vincent McDowell, who organized the group of Catholic protesters from Bayside, Queens, said that this quotation was revealed in 1985 to a woman he knew. But recently, he said, the woman had received word of a change.

Sara Krulwich/The New York Times

Marchers carrying panels from the AIDS quilt on Fifth Avenue during a moment of silence in the Gay and Lesbian Pride March.

"She got a message last Monday," said Mr. McDowell, "that if they repent and give up their sin of homosexuality, there will be a cure for AIDS."

Some of the protesters chanted, "Perverts on parade, someday you'll get AIDS." The marchers responded with cries of "shame, shame" and held up a sign, "You should fear the hate in your souls, not the love in our hearts." Marchers of Dignity, a group of Catholic homosexuals, staged a "kiss-in" in front of St. Patrick's Cathedral to protest the church's policies toward homosexuals.

Lavender Fireworks

Most of the marchers wore pink ribbons on which they wrote the names of people with AIDS. At 2:30, as the motorcycles at the front of the parade reached Washington Square, all the marchers stopped for a moment of silence to honor those who suffered from AIDS. Then an announcer said, "Thank you. Now let's party."

After the parade came a dance on the Christopher Street pier in Greenwich Village, and the organizers promised to cap it with a display over the Hudson River of "the first gay and lesbian fireworks ever choreographed to music." It was to feature plenty of lavender fireworks.

This year, for the first time, the Empire State Building was lighted lavender to mark the Gay and Lesbian Pride weekend. Bill Anderson, the media director for Heritage of Pride, said it was just one more sign of how far the movement for homosexual rights has come in the 21 years since police raided the Stonewall Inn gay bar in Greenwich Village. The raid on that June night started a riot and helped begin the movement.

"This is our weekend to commemorate that event," Mr. Anderson said, "and to show that we're a force to be reckoned with. This year our theme is 'Family, Friends, and Lovers,' because as we enter the 90's we're redefining what a family is. We're showing that gays and lesbians can establish stable relationships."

* * *

April 26, 1993

MARCH FOR GAY RIGHTS

Gay Marchers Throng Mall in Appeal for Rights

By JEFFREY SCHMALZ
Special to The New York Times

WASHINGTON, April 25—At once defiant and festive, hundreds of thousands of gay and lesbian Americans and their supporters rallied in the capital today, celebrating the right to be homosexual and demanding freedom from discrimination.

"Make no mistake, America," David B. Mixner, a long-time gay friend of President Clinton, who has lately been critical of him, told the crowd. "We won't compromise our freedom. We won't go back. We will win."

Several speakers, including Senator Edward M. Kennedy, Democrat of Massachusetts, who spoke by way of a taped audio message, likened the rally to the 1963 civil rights march on Washington: "We stand again at the crossroads of national conscience."

Temperatures in the 70's

At 4 P.M. on a sparkling day with temperatures in the 70's, the Mall, from the Washington Monument to the Capitol, was packed—a sea of marchers, rainbow flags, banners, signs, red ribbons and pink triangles. Chants welled up: "Act Up! Fight Back! Fight AIDS!"

Although the marchers came with a broad civil rights agenda, the ban on homosexuals in the military dominated the tone of the day. "End the Ban Now!" the crowd chanted. "End the Ban Now!" Gay Vietnam veterans received thunderous applause. Speaker after speaker repeated, "Our time has come."

By 5 P.M., groups of marchers were still streaming past the White House. The march route took them from the Ellipse, past the White House to end up at the Mall. Organizers said they had reached their goal of a million marchers, a figure supported by the Mayor's office.

Generally Peaceful Mood

But the United States Park Police's estimates often conflict with those of organizers, and that agency put the total at

Jose R. Lopez/The New York Times

Thousands of gay and lesbian Americans and their supporters marched yesterday by the White House.

Michael Geissinger for the New York Times

Thousands attended yesterday's march for gay rights. On display in the foreground was the AIDS quilt.

300,000. That made it, by the park police estimate, larger than the 1963 civil rights march but smaller than a 1992 march for abortion rights.

The mood of the march was generally peaceful, with the Park Police reporting only five arrests for disorderly conduct. The police presence was minimal.

Clinton Letter Is Read

President Clinton, who chose not to attend the rally or make a video or audio presentation, going instead to Boston to speak before newspaper publishers, sent a five-paragraph letter that was read to marchers by Representative Nancy Pelosi, Democrat of California.

"I stand with you in the struggle for equality for all Americans, including gay men and lesbians," the President wrote. "In this great country, founded on the principle that all people are created equal, we must learn to put aside what divides us and focus on what we share."

Mr. Clinton reminded the crowd that he had asked for a report by July 15 on how to put into effect an end to the ban on homosexuals in the military. And he reaffirmed his commitment to increasing spending for AIDS research.

Reaction to the letter was moderate applause mixed with boos.

With a few exceptions, Mr. Clinton generally came off well during the day. A slight majority of marchers said in dozens of conversations that they thought he was doing all he could for gay rights. But AIDS organizers were less kind. Larry Kramer, the playwright, asserting that Mr. Clinton had not kept his AIDS promises, including one to name a Government AIDS overseer.

At precisely 2 P.M., hundreds of men and women under the banner of the Gay Men's Health Crisis of New York lay down in front of the White House in silence, symbolizing the number of AIDS deaths. Other protesters passed by shouting, "Where's Bill?"

"He's all talk on AIDS," said Marilyn Hipp, a 24-year-old teacher from upstate New York.

"It's not the numbers," said Wilber Janeway, 56, from Chapel Hill, N.C. "It's the feeling of brotherhood, of being together." Indeed, many marchers were accompanied by small children and parents.

Indeed, that feeling seemed pervasive. Planning for the march began two years ago, when George Bush was in office. But the numbers were clearly swelled by reaction to recent anti-gay measures in Oregon and Colorado, by increased opposition to homosexuality from religious groups and by the sharply anti-gay comments in the fight over ending the ban on homosexuals in the military.

Feelings of Pride

The overall tone at the march today was one of pride, of feeling part of a larger gay community and not being afraid to march down the street to proclaim it. Increasingly, homosexuals have come to feel they are the only group still acceptable to hate. And today was their chance to chant: "We're here. We're queer. We're not going away."

One of the throatiest roars from onlookers went up shortly before 2 P.M., when the Colorado contingent stepped onto 17th Street. The state has been an intense political battleground, with the passage last year of Amendment 2, which prohibits local anti-discriminatory laws that are designed to protect lesbians and gay men.

The Coloradans' black banners, one of them proclaiming "Under Siege," stretched almost the full width of the thoroughfare

Hundreds of Coloradans passed by. "Did they send the whole state, or what?" asked Karen Bilsing, of Portland, Ore., who was waiting with two friends on the sidewalk to join the Oregon group, which was next in line.

Certain chants were heard again and again during the march—with variations appropriate to the given contingent. From the gay parents' group: "Ho, ho, hey, hey, we are in the P.T.A." From the vicinity of Oklahoma: "Ho, ho, hey, hey, even farmers can be gay." From North Carolina: "Hey, hey, ho, ho, Jesse Helms has got to go."

A thin line of counterdemonstrators stretched along Pennsylvania Avenue, between 13th and 14th Streets. Their signs declared: "Sodomy is no civil right" and "God hates fags" and "Fags burn in hell" and "Fag equals AIDS." Some of the marchers responded in silence. Others took to chanting, "Shame," over and over again as they passed.

The Christian Action Network, a conservative religious group that opposes homosexual rights, labeled the march "a wake-up call to the silent majority of Americans whose individual rights are at stake."

For march organizers, the day was a chance to show off much-needed support from leaders of other civil rights groups, including the Rev. Jesse Jackson, president of the Rainbow Coalition, and Patricia Ireland, president of the National Organization for Women.

Series of Short Speeches

There was no one single galvanizing speech. Instead, the day consisted of a series of short speeches by dozens of figures. Politicians speaking, from Mayor David N. Dinkins of New York to Mayor Sharon Pratt Kelly of the District of Columbia, from Representative Patricia Schroeder, Democrat of Colorado, to Senator Paul Wellstone, Democrat of Minnesota.

The military issue surfaced repeatedly at the march. Service men and women discharged for homosexuality, who have become heroes among gay people, lined up in uniform on the stage before the crowd, setting off thunderous applause, tears and screams. But all was quiet when Dorothy Hajdys, the mother of Allen R. Schindler, a 22-year-old Navy radioman beaten to death last October near the United States Navy base in Sasebo, Japan, expressed fear for every gay and lesbian service member.

The march—officially called the 1993 March on Washington for Lesbian, Gay and Bi-Equal Rights and Liberation—called for the meeting of several demands, including passage of a civil rights bill and other antidiscrimination measures; more money for AIDS education, treatment and research; the inclusion of lesbians, gay men, bisexuals and transgender people in the educational system; reproductive freedom; and an end to discrimination and violent oppression based on sexual orientation, race, religion, sex, disability, age, class or H.I.V. infection.

But the demands could be summed up in one word—acceptance.

"We want to be left alone, to just be ourselves," said Mark Connor, 42, a St. Louis businessman. "There's no mystery to being gay. We're just like everybody else in America."

* * *

April 30, 2000

GAY MARCHERS WILL FLEX POLITICAL MUSCLE IN CAPITAL

By ELAINE SCIOLINO

WASHINGTON, April 29—Throngs of gay men and lesbians and their supporters will march on Washington on Sunday to demand public legitimacy and to mobilize as a voting bloc this November.

The "Millennium March" is the fourth national gay march since one in 1979, which was attended by 25,000 people and marked the coming out of the gay rights movement on the political stage. It is also the first to be held in an election year. The last march, held in 1993 shortly after President Clinton took office, brought 300,000 to the Mall.

"Every kind of group is represented—from the leather community to the parents," said Dianne Hardy-Garcia, 34, the head of the Lesbian/Gay Rights Lobby of Texas and an organizer of the march. "We have teenagers and veterans, farmers and ranchers and city dwellers."

One primary goal of the march, Ms. Hardy-Garcia said, is to turn out the largest gay vote in American history "and prove that we are 5 percent of the vote."

Aware of the political ramifications of the march, Mr. Clinton and Vice President Al Gore are expected to deliver videotaped remarks of support to the crowd during the six hours of speeches and entertainment on the Mall. Included in the dozens of scheduled speakers are Democratic Representatives Barney Frank of Massachusetts and Tammy Baldwin of Wisconsin, both of them gay; Mayor Anthony A. Williams of Washington and Senator Paul Wellstone, the Minnesota Democrat.

The families of Matthew Shepard, a gay student from Wyoming who was beaten to death by two men in 1998, and of James Byrd Jr., a black man dragged to death behind a truck by three whites in Jasper, Tex., that same year, will attend the march to lobby for laws against hate crimes.

Although tens of thousands are expected at the march on Sunday, one of the first events of the weekend, a protest today of the military's "don't ask, don't tell" policy, drew only a handful of demonstrators to the Pentagon, including some who said they were on active duty or former military personnel and their partners.

Bob Kunst, president of Oral Majority, one of the groups involved in the march, attributed the turnout of about 10 people to poor planning by organizers, who he said placed the protest well down the official list of march activities.

Other gay groups have criticized the march, including a number of groups who are boycotting it, saying that its organizers have commercialized the event, have been exclusive in its planning and have failed to adequately turn the spotlight on AIDS and other pressing issues.

"National marches can be a very powerful tool to raise issues," said Bill Dobbs, who has organized the Ad Hoc Committee for an Open Process. "Unfortunately the purpose and timing of this one are fuzzy. This has become a marketing event in search of a political purpose. This is supposed to be a civil rights struggle, not a corporate marketing event."

In particular, Mr. Dobbs said his group was protesting the visible sponsorship of the march by corporations like United Airlines, Showtime Network and Planet Out.

Ms. Hardy-Garcia countered, saying, "We have obligations to our community to be financially responsible and to find ways to fund these important events." She said the march cost "less than $2 million" to organize.

One focus of this march will be to underscore the family values of gay men and lesbians, organizers said. A number of speakers will call for legislation to help gay and lesbian couples legalize their unions and adopt and provide foster homes for children.

A rally for gays ages 15 to 24 this afternoon will emphasize the need to help them avoid substance abuse and suicide.

On Friday night, the march organizers held a $250 to $500 black tie dinner honoring the entertainer Sir Elton John, the comedian Ellen DeGeneres and her partner, the actress Anne Heche. The dinner included a tribute to Jerry Herman, the composer of the musicals Hello Dolly, Mame and La Cage aux Folles, who has been diagnosed as H.I.V.-positive.

Other planned events today included a demonstration and ceremony celebrating same-sex marriages called "The Wedding," with a $25 entry fee for those who wanted a certificate, was held on the steps of the Lincoln Memorial. The Rev. Troy Perry of Los Angeles, the founder of a Christian Church called the Metropolitan Community Church with branches throughout the country, was to preside.

C-SPAN will present six hours of live coverage of the march on Sunday. The march will also be shown on a global Webcast. "I'm hoping that maybe somebody in Pakistan who's gay will be watching and say, 'Wow, I'm not alone in the world,'" Ms. Hardy-Garcia said.

* * *

OUTING

September 26, 1975

HOMOSEXUAL CONTROVERSY ERUPTS ABOUT MAN WHO DEFLECTED PISTOL

By LACEY FOSBURGH
Special to The New York Times

SAN FRANCISCO, Sept. 25—The husky former marine who emerged as a hero at the alleged attempt to assassinate President Ford here Monday has since become the focus of a controversy over whether he is a homosexual.

The latest development came late today when Oliver Sipple held a news conference to denounce the press and others for raising the question of his sexual preferences. The 32-year-old Vietnam veteran maintains that his sexual orientation is irrelevant.

"My sexual orientation has nothing at all to do with saving the President's life," said Mr. Sipple, who lunged at Sara Jane Moore and deflected her arm as she allegedly fired at Mr. Ford when he left the St. Francis Hotel here.

In the aftermath of the shooting episode, inquiries about Mr. Sipple have produced reports that he is associated with the large community of homosexuals in this city.

Member of 'Court'

Although Mr. Sipple has refused to say whether he is a homosexual, he has said that he is a member of the "court" of Mike Caringi, who has been elected by the city's homosexual community as "emperor" of San Francisco.

Mr. Sipple, who said he had not heard from the President or any other official since the alleged assassination attempt, added, "I would love to have a call from the President, but I understand he's a very busy man."

Today, clearly upset and angry about the persistent interest by some local newsmen in his sexual orientation, Mr. Sipple said:

"My sexuality is a part of my private life and has no bearing on my response to the act of a person seeking to take the life of another. I am first and foremost a human being who enjoys life and respects life."

* * *

September 29, 1975

BIG WEEK FOR GAYS

By WILLIAM SAFIRE

WASHINGTON—How do you thank an alleged homosexual for saving the life of a President just after a military panel decides that homosexuals are unfit to protect the nation by serving in the armed forces?

"You acted quickly and without fear for your own safety," President Ford wrote to Oliver Sipple a few days ago, after the alert 32-year-old former Marine had spoiled the aim of a would-be assassin. "By doing so, you helped to avert danger to me and to others in the crowd. You have my heartfelt appreciation."

But by doing his duty as a citizen, Mr. Sipple stepped into the white circle of pitiless publicity that surrounds the President and his party. It was soon reported that he is supported by a disability award for the aftereffects of combat experience in Vietnam, and hangs around with the "gay community" in the homosexual bars of San Francisco.

"What's he trying to hide?" demanded one gay militant, sensing a propaganda coup if a genuine hero could be presented as a man proud to be homosexual. Another leader, with more sympathy, said: "If in fact he is homosexual it would be beneficial to the community if he would come forth and state such, but I cannot condemn him for not doing so."

Under obvious strain, Mr. Sipple appeared at a press conference. Evidently the news not only of his bravery but of his reputed homosexual associations had reached his mother in Detroit, and he had suffered through a difficult family telephone call.

His prepared statement contained a sentence of considerable dignity: "My sexuality is a part of my private life and has no bearing on my response to the act of a person seeking to take the life of another."

Mr. Sipple is guilty of committing heroism in public, and is trying to hold on to the last shreds of the privacy that was stripped from him as a consequence of his selfless act. He is probably under family pressure to go one way, and under peer-group pressure to go the other, with publicity stakes fairly high. He will think twice before he does any good deed again.

The saving of the President by someone who might be a gay took place three days after the decision of a military panel in the case of T. Sgt. Leonard Matlovich. The bemedaled Air Force sergeant was testing the armed forces regulations against homosexuality, and argued that he could be both a good airman and a gay. He lost; the military judges recommended that he be given a general discharge, neither honorable nor dishonorable.

Most Americans would agree that the Air Force acted wisely, and a practical argument can be made that morale in the armed forces would suffer if homosexuality there were to be publicly tolerated. Moreover, such official toleration might lead to its unwelcome increase.

However, I think the decision is wrong. Homosexuality is a sin and not a crime. To practice it is to break all moral codes but no constitutional laws. The prattle of gay leaders that homosexuality is a beneficial "alternative lifestyle" strikes me as foolish, and the unsupported assertion of a psychologist that bisexual switch-hitting is the wave of the future is intellectually dishonest.

* * *

October 1, 1975

MAN IN FORD CASE SUES NEWSPAPERS

Says Homosexual Report Alienated His Family

SAN FRANCISCO, Sept. 30 (AP)—Oliver W. Sipple, the ex-Marine credited with thwarting an apparent attempt to assasinate President Ford, filed a $15-million lawsuit today against the press for reporting that he was homosexual.

Mr. Sipple's lawsuit said that through news reports, "his brothers and his sisters learned for the first time of his homosexual sexual orientation, and accordingly and consequentially abandoned the plaintiff."

In addition, the suit said, he "was exposed to contempt and ridicule, causing him great mental anguish, embarrassment and humiliation."

The suit, alleging invasion of privacy, named seven newspapers and their parent companies as well as 50 unnamed "Does" identified only as publishers of newspapers, magazines or news service.

The only writer specifically named as a defendant was a San Francisco Chronicle columnist, Herb Caen, who first alluded to Mr. Sipple's status in his daily column.

Newspapers named were The Chronicle, The Los Angeles Times, The Chicago Sun Times, The Denver Post, The San Antonio Express and The Indianapolis Star.

The Los Angeles Times and The Chronicle had no immediate comment.

Mr. Sipple's attorney, John Wahl, who filed the suit in San Francisco Superior Court, said that Mr. Sipple, 32 years old, had been admitted to a veterans' hospital earlier today suffering from "the pressure of this whole business which has messed up his life."

Mr. Sipple, who retired from the Marine Corps on permanent disability, became widely known on Sept. 22 when the police said he had reached out and knocked the hand of Sara Jane Moore as she allegedly aimed at the President outside the St. Francis Hotel. Miss Moore is charged with attempting to assassinate Mr. Ford, who has sent a letter of thanks to Mr. Sipple.

* * *

May 9, 1987

FRIENDS SAY McKINNEY HAD HOMOSEXUAL SEX

By CLIFFORD D. MAY
Special to the New York Times

WASHINGTON, May 8—Friends and political associates of Representative Stewart B. McKinney said today that the Connecticut Republican, who died Thursday of an AIDS-related infection, had had homosexual relationships.

On Thursday, Mr. McKinney's physician, Dr. Cesar Caceres, said the 56-year-old Congressman had contracted AIDS from blood transfusions he received during heart bypass surgery in early 1979.

Today, some associates of Mr. McKinney said they feared that attributing his illness to blood transfusions, without saying he may also have been exposed to the AIDS virus through homosexual sex, could mislead and frighten people who have had or may be in need of transfusions.

AIDS, acquired immune deficiency syndrome, is transmitted by sexual fluids or blood. More than half the people in the United States identified as having the disease have been homosexuals, according to the Federal Centers for Disease Control. The second-largest risk group is intravenous-drug users, who make up 34 percent of the total.

People who contracted AIDS through blood transfusions, by contrast, make up 2 to 3 percent of the total, according to health officials. Since 1985, blood supplies in this country have been screened, virtually eliminating transfusions as a cause of the disease.

Wife's Response

Mr. McKinney's wife of 37 years, Lucie, declined today to comment on reports about her husband's sexual orientation.

"Stewart told me that he wanted his death to focus attention on the need to find a cure for AIDS, not on the causes," she said. "He knew there would be some who would whisper how AIDS is often contracted, and his children and I are prepared for that. But his life to the end was one of looking forward, not back and we will honor that legacy."

On Thursday, a spokesman for the Greater New York Blood Program, which provided the blood for Mr. McKinney's bypass operation at St. Luke's Hospital in Manhattan, said the odds of contracting AIDS through a transfusion in 1979 were 10,000 to 1. Today, the director of the blood program, Dr. Johanna Pindyck, said: "Unless a very careful risk history is taken, it is very difficult to interpret an AIDS case as transfusion-related because the risk of getting AIDS from a transfusion is very, very small. And that was so especially in 1979 because the virus had just entered the community."

Dr. Caceres could not be reached for comment today.

The director of the Gay and Lesbian Task Force in Washington, Jeffrey Levi, said: "I don't think it's anyone's business whether Mr. McKinney was or was not a homosexual. There seems to be a subtle homophobia underlying all the curiosity, a suggestion that he would be somehow less innocent if he got the disease because he was a homosexual rather than a result of a transfusion.

"AIDS can be heterosexually transmitted, too. You can have multiple risk factors as well. Just because a person is a homosexual is no guarantee that he got AIDS as a result."

The Senate passed a bill today changing the name of the 144.5-acre Connecticut National Wildlife Refuge to the Stewart B. McKinney National Wildlife Refuge.

* * *

April 12, 1990

IS 'OUTING' GAYS ETHICAL?

By RANDY SHILTS

SAN FRANCISCO—In more polite times, gay organizers and journalists generally agreed that homosexuals in the closet had a right to stay there if they didn't choose to publicly acknowledge their sexuality. It was an unspoken rule.

With the AIDS epidemic now causing a significant depopulation of gay men in major urban areas, however, the times have become less congenial for covert homosexuals. Both gay newspapers and militant AIDS activists have launched a campaign of "outing": publicly revealing the sexual orientation of people who'd rather keep it quiet.

The controversy over outing recently erupted in force when the sexual activities of a famous, deceased millionaire were documented in a New York City gay newspaper. Over the past year, various AIDS groups have also circulated fliers announcing that several national and local politicians were gay. They did this after the officials took actions that the activists considered inimical to the fight against AIDS.

For journalists and gay leaders themselves, these tactics present a panoply of ethical quandaries.

Most mainstream daily newspapers have refused to name those exposed in gay newspapers and AIDS protests. In most cases, this has made sense. The outings of the politicians, for example, were based on nothing more than gossip and did not contain the factual substantiation that would warrant reporting in a legitimate news story.

Moreover, none of the politicians thus far exposed by outings have engaged in rabidly anti-gay politicking. By the standards of most journalists, such hypocrisy would warrant a public outing, because the politicians themselves would have already asserted that homosexuality was an issue that demanded intense public scrutiny.

The outing of the dead presents a different dilemma. There are no privacy issues here: under American law, the dead have no right to privacy. That's how it should be.

Some newspaper editors maintain that they would not reveal even a deceased person's homosexuality because they always refrain from discussing sex lives. But that just isn't so. In the most recent case, the late millionaire's heterosexual affairs with some of the world's most celebrated women were the stuff of news coverage for more than a decade. Many newspapers included the information in their obituaries.

It seems then that the refusal of newspapers to reveal a person's homosexuality has less to do with ethical considerations of privacy than with an editor's homophobia. In my experience, many editors really believe that being gay is so distasteful that talk of it should be avoided unless absolutely necessary.

This has left us with newspapers that often are more invested in protecting certain people than in telling the truth to readers. In Hollywood and New York, hundreds of publicists make their living by planting items in entertainment columns about whom this or that celebrity is dating. Many of these items are patently false and intended only to cover up the celebrity's homosexuality.

Moreover, many newspaper writers and editors know full well that this is the case and merrily participate in the deceptions. Editors who would never reveal a public figure was gay are routinely lying to their readers by implying the same person is straight.

It is in rage against this hypocrisy—and in desperation over the ravages of AIDS—that the trend of outing was born. In major urban areas around the country, the homosexual community must watch helplessly as AIDS decimates the gay male population. Meanwhile, just about every eminent body studying the Government's response to the AIDS crisis has agreed that it is woefully inadequate.

Just about everyone also agrees that the response to the epidemic is so pathetic because gay men comprise the largest population struck by AIDS—and gay men are largely viewed as degenerate reprobates. In truth, of course, lesbians and gay men are to be found among the most respected public figures in every field of American society.

Gay organizers hope that if more Americans knew this, the nation might see a better response to the AIDS epidemic. Fewer people might die. That's a major reason why outing started. That's also why it will become more pronounced, as more people die and frustration among AIDS activists grows.

At the same time, outing presents gays with their own moral quandaries. In outing politicians, gay activists often have acted more from vindictiveness over a particular vote than from a genuine desire to enlighten the public. Outing threats are political blackmail. And what happens if religious conservatives threaten to reveal a politician's homosexuality if he or she doesn't vote a certain party line? Outing is a powerful political weapon that can cut both ways.

Gay activists counter that young gay people have a right to role models of successful gay adults. That's true, but someone who is only public because he or she has been hauled from the closet is certainly no paragon of psychological integration.

As a journalist, I cannot imagine any situation in which I would reveal the homosexuality of a living person who was not a public official engaged in voracious hypocrisy.

Yet, as someone who has chosen to be open about being gay, I have nothing but disdain for the celebrated and powerful homosexuals who remain comfortably closeted while so many are dying. Most of these people have nothing to lose by stepping forward and they could do much to instruct society about the contributions gays daily make to America.

As I watch my friends die all around me, a certain part of me hopes against all hope that the outing stories now appearing in the press may do something to stop the avalanche of death around me.

Randy Shilts, national correspondent for The San Francisco Chronicle, is author of "And the Band Played On."

* * *

April 25, 1993

CLOSETS ARE OUT, BUT OUTING IS NOT

By DEGEN PENER

NAME: Michelangelo Signorile.

IDENTITY: Irascible advocate of "outing," the practice of revealing the names of "closeted" homosexuals—those who do not publicly reveal that they are gay. Writer for Out magazine.

NEW BOOK: "Queer in America: Sex, the Media and the Closets of Power" (Random House, $23). The book chronicles Mr. Signorile's days as the media coordinator for Act Up and as a columnist for the now-defunct magazine Outweek

and discusses the role of the closet in the lives of gay men and lesbians.

HOME: Lower East Side.

Q. I understand you're obsessed with going to the gym.

A. I like going. I mean, I go every day. I get a lot of thinking done. I confess, I'm part of this whole body-obsessed culture.

Q. In the book, you talk a lot about bingeing and gaining lots of weight while you were in the closet. Is there a connection?

A. My whole life has been a thing about bettering myself and fixing all of these problems that the closet created. One of the problems was this bingeing out of control and starving and then bingeing.

Q. Why don't you out anyone in the book?

A. Up front, I gave all the reasons why some people are not named, and all of them have to do with protecting people who are victimized by closeted individuals or with obtaining information I couldn't have obtained if I said I was going to out someone. I felt the mission of this book was to show the closet. In this outing debate in the last two years, we've been presenting the solution without showing the problem.

Q. Do you regret outing anyone?

A. I don't regret anything I wrote that was the truth. Perhaps sometimes my tactics were a bit too strident. But I realize, too, that if I didn't rail the way I did, I would have never gotten any attention. It was necessary.

Q. You have a chapter about a closeted Congressman who has sexually harassed staff members. Wouldn't you have outed him at Outweek?

A. No. I wouldn't have unless I had developed more information that was independent. I spoke to three men who were harrassed by him, but none of them would come forward unless I didn't name him. They have a very strange kind of sympathy for him because they see him as a victim of the closet.

Q. You give yourself a lot of credit in the book, especially for calling attention to the military's ban on gay men and lesbians with your article outing a Pentagon official in the Aug. 27, 1991, issue of the Advocate.

A. Unfortunately, the way the media operate, especially around the Pentagon, the issue was just a nonstory. Nobody was really on top of it. The outing made this a media story. It suddenly focused enormous attention on the policy. Newspapers across the country called for the lifting of the ban, and Dick Cheney was forced to distance himself from it.

Q. You really blow your own horn.

A. My feeling is, the way I've been treated, I have to. They want to look at me as some sort of monster. I don't think I'm blowing my own horn. I feel like I'm blowing the horn of all the people on the edge of this movement, of everyone who is doing a lot more of the work on the street.

Q. What's the one point you most want to get across?

A. I think people, even gay people, have the tendency to believe that the closet is a place we chose to go into and we have a right to be there. It's really the opposite. We were forced into the closet as children with no choice, and the rest of our lives are spent wrestling with that.

* * *

September 2, 1993

NEW CHANCELLOR'S FIRST 24 HOURS IN NEW YORK

By SAM DILLON

Ramon C. Cortines came to New York City carrying his own bags, and he schlepped them all the way through Kennedy International Airport, smiling patiently as reporters grilled him about his plans for sex education and for confronting the asbestos crisis.

The car carrying the new schools chancellor into the city bogged down in traffic in shirt-drenching heat Tuesday evening, and when he reached his midtown hotel, a television crew blocked his way into the lobby with questions about his sexual identity.

And the television in his hotel room was carrying a live broadcast from Board of Education headquarters, where the board's formal vote hiring him as chancellor was virtually drowned out by the howls of protest.

It was not exactly a warm welcome that New York City extended to Mr. Cortines, but he seemed to shrug off the often disagreeable tone of his first 24 hours in town. And in a series of meetings with school and city officials, union leaders and the press before flying back to California yesterday, he appeared to set the city and its leaders at ease about his intentions. He offered order for a chaotic system.

"What this community needs, relative to its schools, is to feel a calm and stability," the 61-year-old Mr. Cortines said.

One important rapprochement came at City Hall, where a smiling Mayor David N. Dinkins—who had vigorously lobbied for another candidate—clasped his hands and said, "He is my chancellor." Other educational leaders also spoke warmly of Mr. Cortines after making his acquaintance.

"He seemed like a gentle person," said Donald Singer, president of the principal's union, who met Mr. Cortines. "The system needs healing, and I sense he could be a healer."

Chosen Amid Politicking

Several details about Mr. Cortines's first hours on New York's stage invited comparison with his predecessor, Joseph A. Fernandez. Whereas Mr. Fernandez used his first day to outline an agenda for sweeping change, Mr. Cortines promised tranquillity after a tempestuous period.

Mr. Fernandez bargained hard for a contract that included a $195,000 salary plus severance benefits totaling some $475,000; Mr. Cortines accepted a contract with the same salary, but stripped of several of those benefits, without hiring a lawyer to quibble over the details. Mr. Fernandez encouraged the board to buy for his use a $1 million official residence in Brooklyn Heights. Mr. Cortines said he would open up the ground floor of that residence, which the board still owns, for community meetings.

Mr. Cortines, who was the School Superintendent in San Francisco from 1986 through 1992, was awaiting confirmation as an Assistant Secretary of the United States Department of Education when the board selected him on Monday for the chancellorship. That put him at the center of a long feud between the board's two factions that had surrounded the six-month search for a chancellor with election-year politicking.

In a quiet moment Tuesday evening at his suite in the Doral Tuscany hotel, Mr. Cortines conceded that many of his friends had warned him against taking the job.

"I haven't had much encouragement from my friends," he said. "People in California and in Washington and many of the people who know me here have said, 'Do you really want this, with all the politics and problems? Is it really worth the sacrifice?' And I have said, 'Yeah, it is.' I'm delighted to be here."

It was a triumphal evening for Mr. Cortines; the board was crowning his 30-year career in education by appointing him to head the nation's largest system. But it was a moment of melancholy, too, for Mr. Cortines, isolated in his hotel, warned away from the board's proceedings by predictions that they would turn chaotic.

His mood, however, later that evening was enthusiastic as he dined with Priscilla A. Wooten, the Brooklyn Councilwoman who heads the City Council's education committee.

Mr. Cortines rose early yesterday, had breakfast at his hotel, and traveled to Astoria, Queens, for a 7:50 A.M. meeting with Peter F. Vallone, the Council Speaker.

"I told him, 'There's every single ethnic group here, and these people couldn't care less about the politics of the school board,'" Mr. Vallone said. "People want somebody who can take charge. Don't be worried by the extremists who scream at board meetings."

The morning heat was building fast when Mr. Cortines reached the board headquarters in Brooklyn Heights that will be his domain, for meetings with the interim chancellor Harvey S. Garner, several board members, and Amy Linden, the chief executive for school facilities.

Goals and Realism

Minutes later, downstairs in a conference room, Mr. Cortines met the press.

"I want to help bring this system back to its former pre-eminence," he said.

He promised progress toward that goal, soon, but conceded, "I know there are some areas where we just won't be able to make progress." He said he would seek productivity and efficiency from the bureaucracy.

He said he would meet with the city's 32 community superintendents this month, and with parents and teachers in all 32 districts by Dec. 1.

He then took questions, and one of the first came from a television reporter, "Some have raised the question as to whether you are gay and haven't disclosed it."

Even before his arrival in the city, members of gay advocacy groups were calling news organizations with claims that Mr. Cortines was a closet homosexual. In San Francisco, Mr. Cortines faced criticism from some gay advocates because he modified their proposals for school counseling and other programs for gay and lesbian students.

"When I have not recommended things that that community wanted, they have gone after me personally," Mr. Cortines said. "I understand that, and that's their point of view. But I'm not going to be intimidated. I'm not going to be blackmailed. As it relates to me, personally, I've said previously that I'm not going to discuss that. And I won't discuss it now."

After the news conference, Mr. Cortines went back upstairs and had a lunch of tuna sandwiches with Sandra Feldman, president of the United Federation of Teachers. He congratulated her on her union's new contract and talked at some length about his respect for teachers, she said.

"He doesn't seem to be coming in with a set agenda except to bring some order to the system and to provide leadership," Ms. Feldman said. "And I think that's good. We've come through two very chaotic years in this system, with tremendous conflict between board members, between the board and the chancellor, between the chancellor and the districts. So he's saying, 'Let's have some order and get on with education.' That seems right to me."

Even before his arrival, Mr. Cortines had been seeking to schedule a meeting with the Mayor, whose support for another candidate turned Mr. Cortines's selection into an awkward moment.

"I want to assure the Mayor that he is my mayor," Mr. Cortines said several times publicly before the two men finally met, privately, at City Hall yesterday afternoon. Both men were smiling cordially when they emerged.

"He is an educator of experience and commitment and we will be working together," Mr. Dinkins said. "I know we will."

"He called you 'his mayor,'" a reporter noted.

"Well, he's my chancellor, there is no doubt about that," Mr. Dinkins said.

* * *

PART IV

THE ARTS

THEATER

BAYONNE BARS "THE DRAG"

Performance Canceled as Crowds Wait—Owners to Seek Writ

Special to The New York Times

BAYONNE, N. J., Feb. 10.—Five hundred persons were waiting to buy tickets at the Bayonne Opera House tonight for the opening performance of "The Drag," when A. Louis Finnegan, the house manager, announced that the show would not take place. Earlier in the day 800 persons had entered the theatre for the matinee of the play when Chief of Police Cornelius J. O'Neill announced that the show would not be permitted to open. Police reserves kept order on two lines, each a block long, of persons waiting to buy tickets, while Chief O'Neill explained to the promoters of the show that Assistant Prosecutor Aloysius McMahon of Hudson County had forbidden the performance. It had previously been announced that at least one performance would be given, in order that Chief O'Neill and the Hudson County Grand Jury might view it and determine whether it violated the law.

C. William Morganstern and James Timoney, part owners of "The Drag," as well as "Sex," a play which was raided by the New York police last night, declared while the patrons' money was being refunded this afternoon that efforts were being made to obtain an injunction to prevent police interference with the play.

* * *

RAIDED SHOWS PLAY TO CROWDED HOUSES

*One, Expiring, Is Brought Back to Life by
Police Campaign—May Seek Bigger Theatre*

PRODUCER DROPS 'THE DRAG'

No Further Effort Will Be Made to Present It, He Declares

Speculators were busy on the sidewalks selling tickets yesterday afternoon and last night for the three shows which were raided by the police on Wednesday night for alleged indecency.

Last night's show had been scheduled to be the final performance of "The Virgin Man" at the Princess Theatre because of the poor attendance before the police raids. The show, however, has played to capacity since the raid and will continue for an indefinite run. William Francis Dugan, author and manager of the show, said that the management was planning to move from the Princess, which seats only 300, to a house seating 1,100 or 1,200. He said that he was pleased with the police action, and added:

"We are willing to fight it out on this line if it takes all Summer."

Others Play to Full Houses

"The Captive" and "Sex" also played to full houses, but they had been well attended before the police raids. It was only in the case of "The Virgin Man" that attempted police censorship acted as a powerful administration of oxygen to a moribund production.

At the Sixty-third Street Theatre, where "Sex" is playing, the management said that their business had been boosted about 20 per cent by the raid and its publicity. This play has been performed to approximately full houses for the eleven months of its run, but the rear rows had been sold over the cut-rate ticket counter for many performances, and at times there have been empty seats at the matinees. Now, however, it has been possible to withdraw the tickets from the cut-rate brokers and to dispose of them at the box office at the regular price.

Since "The Captive," at the Empire, has been attracting capacity audiences throughout its run, the increased demand since the raid has been discernible only in a slight increase in the number of standees and a greater activity on the part of ticket speculators near the theatre. Speculators were offering seats yesterday for several times the box office price, and at the hour of the matinee only a few upper box seats were on sale at the box office. There was a row of standees in the rear of the auditorium at both performances yesterday.

Court Hearings Tomorrow

Whether the police resurrection of "The Virgin Man" will be of long or short duration may be decided tomorrow by Supreme Court Justice Bijur. The police have been ordered to appear and show cause why they should not be permanently restrained from interfering with performances. The cases of the two other shows also come before Justice Bijur. The city will be represented by the Corporation Counsel's office, which will argue against the continuation of the injunctions on the ground that such injunctions would prevent officers of the law from enforcing the law.

Hearings in the cases of the actors, managers and producers who were arrested in the police raids will begin in Jefferson Market Court tomorrow. The Magistrate may dismiss or hold the defendants for the Grand Jury. If the Grand Jury then brings in indictments the cases automatically go to Special Sessions for trial before the three Judges of that court. Lawyers for the defendants have declared, however, that if the cases get that far they will ask for transfer to General Sessions and trial by jury.

Acting Mayor McKee vetoed plans for nightly raids on the accused productions last week on the ground that a prima facie case should be established in court first. If the Magistrate holds the defendants, the city authorities will claim the right to make raids every time further performances of the shows in question are attempted. The question of repeated raids, however, will be one to be decided by the Supreme Court in relation to the injunctions proceedings.

Seven Women Arrested

General orders to the police to deal with nudity by arresting on sight were construed drastically in Brooklyn yesterday. Seven young women were arrested for not wearing stockings. Arrested at the Strand Gardens, 61 Ashland Place, early yesterday morning, they were arraigned in the Gates Avenue Court on charges of disorderly conduct. The detectives who made the arrests alleged that the dancing had been done with bare legs, although the dancers were otherwise more or less clad in satin. The defendants were released in bail of $500 each for hearings on Feb. 24.

C. W. Morganstern, producer of "The Drag," abandoned further efforts to produce it yesterday, because of the attitude of the authorities in New Jersey and New York. He paid off the company at Bayonne and disbanded it. He said last night that he would make no further effort to produce this show.

Earl Carroll, producer of the "Vanities," who is awaiting action by the Supreme Court of the United States on his plea to escape serving a sentence to Atlanta Penitentiary for perjury in the recent "bathtub case," took offense yesterday at the London dispatch to The New York Times quoting George White, producer of the "Scandals," as saying, "Look at the 'Vanities,' for instance, and you'd better look quick. As things are going it may be padlocked before you get across. New York won't stand that sort of revue much longer."

Mr. Carroll said that large audiences of women and children at the matinees of 'Vanities' proved its wholesomeness.

"George White's tactless condemnation of my work in the theatre is the first public expression of those unseen hands which have been working so hard to remove me from the field of competition," he said. "Even if it were true, as Mr.

White told the London correspondent for The New York Times, that the 'Vanities' should be padlocked and that New York would not stand that sort of revue much longer, surely it reveals a great lack of the human touch to broadcast such an opinion at a time when I need friends so badly."

* * *

November 5, 1961

NOT WHAT IT SEEMS

Homosexual Motif Gets Heterosexual Guise

By HOWARD TAUBMAN

It is time to speak openly and candidly of the increasing incidence and influence of homosexuality on New York's stage—and, indeed, in the other arts as well.

The subject is too important to be left forever to the sly whisperers and malicious gossips. Criticism, like playwriting, is crippled by a resort to evasions. The public is deluded and misled if polite pretenses are accepted at face value.

The infiltration of homosexual attitudes occurs in the theatre at many levels. It is noticeable when a male designer dresses the girls in a musical to make them unappealing and disrobes the boys so that more male skin is visible than art or illusion require. It is apparent in a vagrant bit of nasty dialogue thrown into a show or in a redundant touch like two unmistakably mannish females walking across a stage without a reason or a word of comment.

These intrusions are private jokes turned public in a spirit of defiance or in the fun-and-games exuberance of a mischievous student testing a teacher's patience and acumen. They may be nuisances, deserving the flick aimed at a pestiferous insect, but do not merit serious discussion.

What demands frank analysis is the indirection that distorts human values. Plays on adult themes are couched in terms and symbols that do not truly reflect the author's mind. Characters represent something different from what they purport to be. It is no wonder that they seem sicker than necessary and that the plays are more subtly disturbing than the playwright perhaps intended.

Exaggeration

The unpleasant female of the species is exaggerated into a fantastically consuming monster or an incredibly pathetic drab. The male is turned into a ragingly lustful beast or into a limp, handsome neutral creature of otherworldly purity. No doubt there are such people and it is the dramatist's business if he is fascinated by them. But where his emphases are persistently disproportionate, it is because he is treating a difficult, delicate problem in the guise of normality.

The insidious result of unspoken taboos is that sincere, searching writers feel they must state a homosexual theme in heterosexual situations. They convince themselves that what they wish to say will get through anyhow. But dissembling is unhealthy. The audience senses not at the drama's core.

The taboos are not what they used to be. Homosexuality is not a forbidden topic. In "The Best Man" it was the dark secret used to destroy a ruthless, young politician, and in "Advise and Consent" it was a sympathetically described aberration of a Senator. In both cases it was a facile dramatic device, used without compelling force or overriding need.

As long ago as in "The Children's Hour" Lillian Hellman dealt honestly and powerfully with a lesbian theme. There have been a number of works in which problems of homosexuality were probed with directness and integrity. Tennessee Williams' "Cat on a Hot Tin Roof," Robert Anderson's "Tea and Sympathy" and Peter Shaffer's "Five Finger Exercise" did not dissimulate, and in "A Taste of Honey" a homosexual was portrayed without meanness or snickers.

Although these are examples of successful plays on delicate themes, there can be no blinking the fact that heterosexual audiences feel uncomfortable in the presence of truth-telling about sexual deviation. And there can be no denying that playwrights interested in such themes continue to attach them tangentially, even disagreeably and sneakily.

Falsehood

That is why the work of some talented writers seems tainted. That is why studies ostensibly devoted to the tensions between men and women carry an uneasy burden of falsehood. One suspects what is wrong. But how can one question a writer's professed intentions *or* impugn motivations hidden in his heart, if not his subconscious?

What, if anything, is to be done? A writer's way may be oblique. Art, in any case, is often an ordering and articulation of unknowable and indefinable pressures. But where the writer knows what is in his mind and would like to expose it uncompromisingly, it is a great pity if he fails to do so.

Homosexuality has been a fact of history for thousands of years. It is a fact of life, even if a generally concealed one, in our society. Nothing human should be alien to an enlightened theatre. But even such a theatre must face up to the rules of commerce. Playwrights no doubt will continue to take what they regard as the safe way of smuggling a touchy subject onto the stage by heterosexual masquerade.

Hugh Wheeler is a playwright whose first plays have tried to speak out. In "Big Fish, Little Fish" he described at least one homosexual in rich, crotchety, affectionate detail. This was forthright writing. But the central character was ambiguous, and at least one other man posed questions. Rightly or wrongly, one felt that these two did not fully sum up the author's conception of them.

Explicit

In "Look: We've Come Through" Mr. Wheeler was explicit. There was no doubt about the homosexual predilections of the boy, Bobby. His mother encouraged effeminacy and urged him to take up with an older man. A brutal sailor

sought to abuse him. The boy admitted his impotence. He wanted only to be a friend of Belle, the girl with learning, culture and no sex appeal.

Why then find fault with a play that did not obfuscate? Why not acclaim without reservation a writer of humor, warmth and acute sensibility?

It is painful to mention flaws in a work of aspiration while one approves a superficial, expertly made entertainment like "Write Me a Murder." But each type of play must be judged by its own laws.

The fundamental flaw of "Look: We've Come Through" was that one did not believe in the pivotal boy-and-girl relationship as the thing it looked to be. Bobby was revealed with sympathy as a sad, passive homosexual in spite of himself. It was suggested that he was changing, but everything about him said he would not. The girl was made to appear sexless. Her first joust with sex was an intellectual experiment. While the end was touching as the maimed youngsters found security in each other, one was sure that it would not last. It could not last while she remained a woman and he the sort of man he was.

For all its virtues, the play was lamed. For all his courage, had Mr. Wheeler dared enough? Did inhibitions imposed by the theme lead to a sense of troubling incompletion?

Mr. Wheeler has been brave to go as far as he has in writing about homosexuality with probity. His way is infinitely preferable to the furtive, leering insinuations that have contaminated some of our arts.

* * *

June 23, 1966

HOMOSEXUAL DRAMA AND ITS DISGUISES

By STANLEY KAUFFMANN

A recent Broadway production raises again the subject of the homosexual dramatist. It is a subject that nobody is comfortable about. All of us admirably "normal" people are a bit irritated by it and wish it could disappear. However, it promises to be a matter of continuing, perhaps increasing, significance.

The principal complaint against homosexual dramatists is well-known. Because three of the most successful American playwrights of the last twenty years are (reputed) homosexuals and because their plays often treat of women and marriage, therefore, it is said, postwar American drama presents a badly distorted picture of American women, marriage, and society in general. Certainly there is substance in the charge; but is it rightly directed?

The first, obvious point is that there is no law against heterosexual dramatists, and there is no demonstrable cabal against their being produced. If there are heterosexuals who have talent equivalent with those three men, why aren't these "normal" people writing? Why don't they counterbalance or correct the distorted picture?

But, to talk of what is and not of what might be, the fact is that the homosexual dramatist is not to blame in this matter.

If he writes of marriage and of other relationships about which he knows or cares little, it is because he has no choice but to masquerade. Both convention and the law demand it. In society the homosexual's life must be discreetly concealed. As material for drama, that life must be even more intensely concealed. If he is to write of his experience, he must invent a two-sex version of the one-sex experience that he really knows. It is we who insist on it, not he.

Two Alternatives

There would seem to be only two alternative ways to end this masquerading. First, the Dramatists' Guild can pass a law forbidding membership to those who do not pass a medico-psychological test for heterosexuality. Or, second, social and theatrical convention can be widened so that homosexual life may be as freely dramatized as heterosexual life, may be as frankly treated in our drama as it is in contemporary fiction.

If we object to the distortion that homosexual disguises entail and if, as civilized people, we do not want to gag these artists, then there seems only one conclusion. The conditions that force the dissembling must change. The homosexual dramatist must be free to write truthfully of what he knows, rather than try to transform it to a life he does not know, to the detriment of his truth and ours.

The cries go up, perhaps, of decadence, corruption, encouragement of emotional-psychological illness. But is there consistency in these cries? Are there similar objections to "The Country Wife," "Inadmissible Evidence," "The Right Honourable Gentleman" on the ground that they propagandize for the sexually unconventional or "corruptive" matters that are germane to them? Alcoholism, greed, ruthless competitiveness are equally neurotic, equally undesirable socially; would any of us wish to bar them arbitrarily from the stage?

Only this one neurosis, homosexuality, is taboo in the main traffic of our stage. The reasons for this I leave to psychologists and to self-candor, but they do not make the discrimination any more just.

Fault Is Ours

I do not argue for increased homosexual influence in our theater. It is precisely because I, like many others, am weary of *disguised* homosexual influence that I raise the matter. We have all had very much more than enough of the materials so often presented by the three writers in question: the viciousness toward women, the lurid violence that seems a sublimation of social hatreds, the transvestite sexual exhibitionism that has the same sneering exploitation of its audience that every club stripper has behind her smile. But I suggest that, fundamentally, what we are objecting to in all these plays is largely the result of conditions that we ourselves have imposed. The dissimulations and role-playings are there because we have made them inevitable.

Homosexuals with writing ability are likely to go on being drawn to the theater. It is the quite logical consequence of the defiant and/or protective histrionism they must employ in their daily lives. So there is every reason to expect more plays by talented homosexuals. There is some liberty for them, limited, in café theaters and Off Broadway; if they want the full resources of the professional theater, they must dissemble. So there is every reason to expect their plays to be streaked with vindictiveness toward the society that constricts and, theatrically, discriminates against them.

To me, their distortion of marriage and femininity is not the primary aspect of this matter; for if an adult listens to these plays with a figurative transistor-radio simultaneously translating, he hears that the marital quarrels are usually homosexual quarrels with one of the pair in costume and that the incontrovertibly female figures are usually drawn less in truth than in envy or fear. To me, there is a more important result of this vindictiveness—its effect on the basic concept of drama itself and of art in general.

Homosexual artists, male and female, tend to convert their exclusion into a philosophy of art that glorifies their exclusion. They exalt style, manner, surface. They decry artistic concern with the traditional matters of theme and subject because they are prevented from using fully the themes of their own experience. They emphasize manner and style because these elements of art, at which they are often adept, are legal tender in their transactions with the world. These elements are, or can be, esthetically divorced from such other considerations as character and idea.

Thus we get plays in which manner is the paramount consideration, in which the surface and the *being* of the work are to be taken as its whole. Its allegorical relevance (if any) is not to be anatomized, its visceral emotion (if any) need not be validated, and any judgment other than a stylistic one is considered inappropriate, even censorious. Not all artists and critics who advance this theory of style-as-king are homosexuals, but the camp has a strong homosexual coloration.

What is more, this theory can be seen, I believe, as an instrument of revenge on the main body of society. Theme and subject are important historical principles in our art. The arguments to prove that they are of diminishing importance—in fact, ought never to have been important—are cover for an attack on the idea of social relevance. By adulation of sheer style, this group tends to deride the whole culture and the society that produced it, tends to reduce art to a clever game which even that society cannot keep them from playing.

But how can one blame these people? Conventions and puritanisms in the Western world have forced them to wear masks for generations, to hate themselves, and thus to hate those who make them hate themselves. Now that they have a certain relative freedom, they vent their feelings in camouflaged form.

Doubtless, if the theater comes to approximate the publishing world's liberality, we shall re-trace in plays—as we are doing in novels—the history of heterosexual romantic love with an altered cast of characters. But that situation would be self-amending in time; the present situation is self-perpetuating and is culturally risky.

A serious public, seriously interested in the theater, must sooner or later consider that, when it complains of homosexual influences and distortions, it is complaining, at one remove, about its own attitudes. I note further that one of the few contemporary dramatists whose works are candidates for greatness—Jean Genet—is a homosexual who has never had to disguise his nature.

* * *

June 1, 1969

HOW ANGUISHED ARE HOMOSEXUALS?

By DONN TEAL

"Why?" is a question that will immediately come to mind. Why, when "Rosencrantz and Guildenstern Are Dead," "Plaza Suite" and other long-running Broadway hits past and present have not been recorded, has Mart Crowley's The Boys in the Band—an Off Broadway drama about the neurotic homosexual—joined the ranks of tragedies and comedies immortalized on disks?

Beyond doubt, "The Boys" is a deftly fabricated, sharp-angled monument of tragicomedy. Furthermore, it is having an unprecedentedly successful run for an Off Broadway production. But the reason "The Boys" achieved a recording derives simply from a circumstance for which it currently has no competitors, except nudity: the interest in homosexuality that has over-taken New York and other major cities. Thanks to A & M Records' original-cast album (6001), this interest may soon spread to the smallest prairie town that has no local movie house where its populace might have seen "The Fox" or "The Sergeant."

Homosexuals greet this interest with mixed feelings, for we are not sure whether it stems from a broadminded, Now Generation empathy with those who love, no matter whom they love (poet Rod McKuen's closing encouragement to his recent Carnegie Hall audience), or from the desire for a new stage and screen scapegoat, producers having exhausted plot variations based on hetero sex. We homosexuals greeted "The Boys" with the same mixed emotions when it opened to raves on April 14, 1968, at Theater Four on West 55th Street: though it was our true dramatic debut in heterosexual society, it was a debasing one, as if we had arrived at our own Coming Out Party dressed in rags.

Yet Crowley's well- (if over-) wrought drama is a satanic gem, a veritable black diamond. It is set at an all-male, surprise birthday party given for Harold, a bitchy "32-year-old, ugly, pockmarked Jew fairy," in the apartment of Michael, his crony and equal in vindictiveness. Five friends arrive, plus a hustler—Emory's gift to Harold—and, unexpectedly, Alan, an old college friend of the host's who is in the depths after a rift with his wife. Alan's confrontation with the gay retinue, acid exchanges of camp humor, and a self-destroying "game" in which each guest must telephone the one person he has always loved best, soon transport the audience from a breezy first-act to a finale of absinthial tragedy.

Freidman-Abeles

Frederick Combs and Kenneth Nelson in "The Boys in the Band"
"A defenseless, emasculated Michael, trembling and weeping"

In the recording, Michael's (Kenneth Nelson) caustic wit blazons forth as predatorily as onstage. Harold (Leonard Frey) fails only at times to sustain the bitchiness he displayed in the theater, and his convulsive, near-psychotic laughter and sword-crossing with Michael in Act Two come off magnificently. Emory (Cliff Gorman) is as fey—and endearingly human—as he was before the footlights. Technically, the recording is praiseworthy. Stereo effects are good, and even sighs and cigarette puffs are audible. Director Robert Moore and Gil Garfield, producer of the album, duplicated the stage setting in the recording studios, complete with furniture, props, and all sound effects. The cast seems quite at home.

A special problem, however, even for the listener who has viewed the play, is the seeming competition among the cast to hurl out their lines, evident notably at the beginning and, most disturbingly, in scenes where non-connected conversations are run together; the rapid-fire repartee frequently forces the auditor to guess what was said and who said it. The similarity of several male voices in the womanless cast contributes to the confusion. A text would have helped.

A & M Records already reports high sales for the album. It is to be hoped that an overwhelming majority of these are to homosexuals themselves, since the heterosexual buyer may not realize that "The Boys in the Band" presents a distorted picture of a subculture about which he may know merely a trifle. Crowley's characters in "The Boys" are, in the main, immature: Michael's line, "What you see before you is a 30-year-old infant," is the truest in the play. The average among us are appalled that the heterosexual (and maladjusted homosexual) may believe our typical soirée founders on—or flourishes by—self-degrading confessions like "The Truth Game"; that we store up barbiturates as Harold does for "the long winter of his death"; that our parents have all been "killer whales"; and that we regularly address each other as "fairy" and "fag." "The Boys" exude self-ishness, self-absorption, and self-indulgence. Worst of all, they not only bespeak, they proclaim, guilt feelings through every utterance Crowley has given them. Though we grant that the New York playgoer may not be so blithely duped into accepting the stereotypes of this show, we wonder what will be the thoughts of, say, less up-to-date Kansas Citians when, turntables revolving, they hear Michael's second-act wail: "If we could just learn not to *hate* ourselves so much!"

Self-hate and a feeling of guilt are not typical of today's homosexual, though it has been a labor to shake these left-overs of Judaeo-Christian puritanism, and many of us are still wrestling with the inferiority complex which society has been only too glad to foist upon us. Then how to explain the fact that dozens—scores?—of homosexuals have returned to see "The Boys" twice, even three times, and will probably purchase the recording? Primarily because, although few of us can see ourselves therein—just as few heterosexuals could really picture themselves in "Who's Afraid of Virginia Woolf?"—many homosexuals can find a *bit* of their story and struggle in Michael, Harold, and Emory. And though we have overcome, we can nevertheless sympathize—as can every member of a "Boys" audience—with a defenseless, emasculated Michael, trembling and weeping in his friend's arms, in one of the most affecting conclusions in recent theater.

Realizing that the author's attempt was not to epitomize the normal American homosexual in "The Boys," any more than Albee's was to apotheosize the average (child-less) American marriage in "Virginia Woolf," we are angry still that an ugly misrepresentation has been broadcast by an excellent play. If, however, audiences can gain a deeper understanding of the *minority* of homosexuals represented by Michael, Harold, and Emory and if, above all, legislators can be persuaded to take steps to legalize male/male and female/female adult sexual relationships in this country, then Crowley would deserve not only the accolades but even the adulation of the world he has so one-track-mindedly described.

Donn Teal wrote an article, "Why Can't 'We' Live Happily Ever After, Too?" in these pages last winter under the pseudonym Ronald Forsythe.

* * *

January 23, 1972

WHY DO HOMOSEXUAL PLAYWRIGHTS HIDE THEIR HOMOSEXUALITY?

By "LEE BARTON"

My play "Nightride" has as its main character, a prominent playwright whose life has been spent concealing his homosexuality from the public. When the play opened several weeks ago, I was astounded by the swarm of criticism that was aimed at me because I had written it under a pen name, Lee Barton. Why, I was asked, in this age of freedom did I need to sign a

false name? And, in signing a false name, was I any different from the character in my play, whose concealment of his homosexuality I so obviously disapproved?

The answer seemed to me to be self-evident: only the rich, the self-employed or the social outcast has nothing to fear from being labeled a homosexual. Freedom, even in 1972, is something one must be able to afford. No one who has a regular desk job in industry—as I do—can be startled by my action. They know that instant dismissal, as well as investigation of their friends, would follow as a matter of course.

And sometimes it is not merely the wage-earner who must be afraid of exposure. One of my playwright friends, who is black, has chosen to have an Off Off Broadway run of his first homosexual play under a different name. Not because of his job, but because he is afraid that the black community will reject his other plays if he is discovered to be gay. Yet the play itself is perhaps the first significant attempt at dealing with a black-white homosexual marriage, and herein lies my real point about all this false-name criticism.

One work of art dealing truthfully with homosexual life is worth a hundred breast-beating-personal confessions. Who really gives a damn that Tennessee Williams has finally admitted his sexual preferences in print? He has yet to contribute any work of understanding to gay theater, and with his enormous talent one of his works would indeed be worth any amount of personal data. And several others of his generation of writers, as well as some younger ones, all of them gay, have failed again and again to come forth with anything, under *any* name, that would make a valid case for the homosexual in society. In fact, if anything, their concealment has at times been so gross and so ill-thought out that some critics have called it repeatedly to the public's attention.

If anything can damage the homosexual's image further, it is this vile art of substituting women for men as characters in plays. No wonder the female leads in so many plays are grotesque! My happy 20-year-plus homosexual marriage would be pretty grotesque, too, if I chose to pretend it didn't exist, or that marriage was impossible to obtain without a woman. In my play, I have tried to come to honest grips with two homosexual marriages—one between a great man, fallen from grace, and a younger man who seeks personal salvation in the ashes of his greatness; the other, between a famous and liberated rock-singer and a mute boy whose grip on life is so tenuous he has trouble just staying alive. Both of these liaisons are successful for many different reasons, but if the men involved in them were translated into heterosexual couples, then the very emotional foundations they rest upon would have to be—in the real sense of the word—perverted.

I would be the first to welcome a fresh, new writing talent from the "freed" generation that can say what must be said in better terms than I have. One whose "Gay Pride" comes at a time when it would do the most good in the world. Meanwhile, I can only say what I feel I must. My real name is indeed worth my job. My art, used in behalf of the homosexual, is worth much more under *any* name. Would that the gay artists of earlier generations might have thought the same and backstopped us all with many works of value. But they have not. Therein lies the rub. The homosexual as a person will never know freedom until his artists stand up for him.

*   *   *

March 28, 1985

AIDS DEATHS PROMPT WAVE OF PLAYS

By SAMUEL G. FREEDMAN

When William Hoffman began writing a play about the mysterious disease called AIDS nearly three years ago, he thought he was alone in the calling. He was writing out of a personal pain—the death of a friend who only months before had been robust enough to run a marathon—and he was facing a subject that seemed far too grisly for the stage.

By the time Mr. Hoffman's "As Is" opened this month at the Circle Repertory Company, it was part of a wave of plays about acquired immune deficiency syndrome. Moreover, "As Is" has become a critical and financial success that is likely to transfer to a Broadway or a commercial Off Broadway theater.

The first New York play about AIDS—the often-fatal disease that weakens the body's resistance to infection and that disproportionately afflicts homosexual and bisexual men, intravenous drug users, hemophiliacs and recent immigrants from Haiti—was Robert Chesley's "Nightsweat," which played last May at the Meridian Gay Theater. Four months later, Stephen Holt's "Fever of Unknown Origin" opened at the Theater for the New City. Performances of Larry Kramer's "Normal Heart" are to begin April 2 at the Public Theater. A play currently at the Public, "Coming of Age in SoHo" by Albert Innaurato, also refers to the fear of AIDS among homosexuals.

All these plays share a sense of mission that goes beyond art. While writing "Fever," for instance, Mr. Holt took the Gay Men's Health Crisis training course for "buddies" who support AIDS victims. One of the major characters in the play is a "buddy." In the case of "As Is," the Glines—an organization that produces works by homosexual artists, like Harvey Fierstein's "Torch Song Trilogy"—put up half the budget of about $100,000.

'Tragedy Is So Immediate'

"If there's any topic people don't want to see onstage, it's AIDS," Mr. Chesley said. "But this tragedy is so immediate. Writing a play about AIDS now is comparable to Euripides writing about a current war that was affecting his audience."

Each play was born in death—the death of a friend or lover, the fear of one's own death. From there, however, the plays represent extremely different approaches, from the personal "As Is" to the political "Normal Heart," from the black comedy of "Nightsweat" to the deathbed realism of "Fever." The plays also indicate the divisions within the homosexual community about the relationship between AIDS and the casual sex available in bars and bathhouses.

"When I found out other people were writing about AIDS," Mr. Hoffman said, "I was relieved. It's such a large area, such a gigantic story we're dealing with. One person can't do it."

Mr. Holt put it: "The enormity of the tragedy is so great that there will be many artistic responses."

The common problem for anyone writing about AIDS is how to convey the disease without trivializing it, how to humanize a tragedy without sugar-coating it. "The subject itself is so horrifying," Mr. Innaurato said, "that it's hard to do it justice. It's also so mysterious it doesn't lend itself to the traditional ways you would write about a disease."

Mr. Hoffman's solution was to write not about the disease, but the reaction to it. "As Is" charts the relationship between Richard, a novelist who contracts AIDS, and Saul, the lover he left before becoming ill. In "As Is," as in "Nightsweat" and "Fever," it is the jilted lover who returns to comfort the dying man.

Critics lauded the play's humanity, as well as the performances and the direction of Marshall Mason. But several critics also complained that "As Is" described Richard's sexual adventures, from leather bars to a Marrakesh graveyard, in rather elegiac terms. There was little indication that he might have developed AIDS through sexual promiscuity.

"I think some critics wanted me to be moralistic," Mr. Hoffman said, "And I'm not inclined to be. I don't think people need to be told what to do or what not to do. I don't think bawling people out has ever stopped anyone from doing anything."

Mr. Chesley, in "Nightsweat," defended sexual freedom as a cornerstone of the homosexual life style. When a character with AIDS cries out, "I'm going to die," another responds: "Yes, yes. But meanwhile you're going to live! Live until the very moment you die! And make love in every possible, safe and sensible way!"

"AIDS isn't just a question of losing young lives," Mr. Chesley said. "It's meant reneging on our eroticism. People for the first time in their lives were at home with themselves and were expressing themselves through eroticism. It was not simply a question of having fun."

Mr. Holt argues the other side of the same issue in "Fever." When an exercise teacher is hospitalized, one of his friends suggests that "if he hadn't been into all these heavy sex scenes he never would have gotten AIDS."

"My play stood for a lot of values that were unfashionable in the promiscuous 70's," Mr. Holt said. "I've seen that life style do nothing but cause torment, disease and heartbreak. I've tried to raise the consciousness of gay people so that love and fidelity become more important than casual sex."

"The Normal Heart" promises to be the most political of the AIDS plays. Its producer, Joseph Papp, has refused to provide the press with advance copies of the script—reportedly because Mr. Kramer attacks Mayor Koch, The New York Times, the National Institutes of Health and segments of the New York homosexual community for their purported inaction in the early stages of the AIDS epidemic.

"My play is very angry and accusatory," Mr. Kramer said. "I got involved in the AIDS mess early on—I lost two friends and someone I was in love with—and I knew it was the saddest thing I'd ever know. And it was obscenely difficult to get anyone to pay attention to AIDS. There's a line in the play in which the young man who's dying says, 'There's not a good word to be said for anybody in this entire mess.' It seems to me that was what had to be said."

* * *

June 21, 1987

AIDS ON STAGE: COMFORT, SORROW, ANGER

By DON SHEWEY

When William Hoffman sat down to revise his award-winning 1985 drama "As Is" for its recent revival at the Circle Repertory Theater, he ended up making only one major change. The original script contained a scene in which the six members of the play's informal Greek chorus recalled the first time they had heard about AIDS—from a doctor, from a friend, from a newspaper. In the new version, the playwright extended the scene with a speech in which one character reminisces about the first memorial service he had attended for someone who had died of AIDS.

"Since that time," the man says, "I've been to how many memorial services? Seth . . . Robby . . . Phil . . . Neil . . . " The other characters begin to chime in with the mournful litany of friends they've buried, and as the list grows longer and longer, members of the audience silently add the names of loved ones they've lost to the AIDS epidemic.

"People are using the play to express publicly their grief," says Mr. Hoffman. "With AIDS, grief is often in the closet. People don't want others to know they have AIDS or a friend has AIDS. But they can go to a play and learn that other people feel exactly the same way. I think it's important for people to know that feeling terrible is a normal response to sadness. Laughter is also a normal response. A work of art can give validation to our human responses."

Mr. Hoffman's "As Is" and Larry Kramer's "Normal Heart," produced two years ago at the Public Theater, took the lead in promoting education on AIDS and concern for the afflicted. As time goes on and the death toll from this mysterious disease mounts, there still have been no major novels or films dealing with AIDS (aside from independent features such as Bill Sherwood's "Parting Glances" and the German film maker Rosa von Prauheim's work "A Virus Knows No Morals"). Although network television has produced one drama ("An Early Frost") and scattered episodes about AIDS, it is theater artists who remain at the forefront in addressing the subject.

Along with the revival of "As Is" (currently playing in Boston, Philadelphia and Washington), this theater season has also seen Harvey Fierstein's "Safe Sex" at La Mama and on Broadway and Stuart Spencer's "Last Outpost at the End of the World" in the Ensemble Studio Theater's one-act marathon, both portraying people affected by the AIDS epidem-

ic. Currently running Off Broadway is Robert Chesley's "Jerker, or the Helping Hand" at the Sanford Meisner Theater, in which two men conduct a sexual relationship by telephone. Most recently Alan Bowne's "Beirut," the first play to address the impact of AIDS on a heterosexual relationship, opened at the Westside Arts Theater. Consciousness about AIDS outside of New York is also being reflected in plays that have originated in Atlanta, Los Angeles, Boston, Toronto, London and elsewhere.

These plays are significant in that they assert the theater's ancient function as a public forum in which a community gathers to talk about itself. What's happening onstage and what's happening in the audience is sometimes so similar that the script seems to disappear. It often becomes a mere pretext for an assembly of individuals collectively seeking information, seeking an outlet for anger, anxiety and grief, seeking to bolster a shaky sense of communal identity in order to face medical horrors and political backlash still to come. However history may judge their literary merits, plays about AIDS have an immediate social value in dealing with an issue so close to home.

"Theater deals with relationships between people, and that's where AIDS has struck most deeply," says the playwright Stuart Spencer. "Although AIDS is terrible and is completely changing the way all of us live, especially the gay community, the fact that someone is dying or has died of AIDS is not inherently dramatic. It's the fact that you've lost someone that's so large and inexplicable. It could be AIDS, it could be the Holocaust—anything that's big and powerful and confusing to all of us."

While AIDS has become a global concern—"a social phenomenon, not just a public health issue," in the words of New York City Health Commissioner Dr. Stephen Joseph—it struck first and deepest in the gay communities of New York and San Francisco, which have high populations of creative artists. Undoubtedly, it was this personal contact with AIDS that triggered such an immediate response from theater artists. "The Normal Heart," Larry Kramer's report from the front lines about the formation in 1981 of Gay Men's Health Crisis (the primarily volunteer organization that has become the model for AIDS service agencies around the world) is an impassioned call to political action. The play, which has been seen worldwide and will soon be made into a film by Barbra Streisand, has directly inspired many theatergoers to join the volunteer ranks of Gay Men's Health Crisis.

"It always moves a writer to think that he is able to provoke people," says Mr. Kramer. "But I don't personally think that I accomplished what I hoped to do. We're entering the seventh year of the epidemic, and we still have a government, a Mayor and a President who are all very ignoble on the AIDS issue."

Plays about AIDS are sometimes as much an education about the lives of gay men as about the disease. "Lots of people don't think gay people are human, in a literal sense," says William Hoffman. "They think they're animals. When they come to a show like 'As Is' and see gay people portrayed like them, they see that AIDS is like the cancer their mama had or the heart failure their son had, and they start to be able to translate it into something they know. At one performance on Broadway, an obviously straight guy was crying in the lobby afterwards, and I heard him say over and over again, 'I didn't know. I didn't know.' In a way, that's my deepest wish—to make AIDS more ordinary, to make people understand that it's not a moral affliction, it's another disease."

Theater continues to play a significant role in AIDS education in the gay community. "There's a big push in the media to emphasize that it's not a gay disease but a virus that affects everyone. That's great," says Doug Holsclaw, whose romantic comedy "The Life of the Party"—a spinoff of "The AIDS Show," a revue first performed at San Francisco's Theater Rhinoceros in 1984 and broadcast on PBS earlier this year—is simultaneously playing in San Francisco and Los Angeles. "But in San Francisco, after four or five years, we're dealing with AIDS on a possibly permanent, certainly indefinite basis. Urban gay men have been so ravaged and devastated by AIDS in every aspect of their lives that it's not possible to write a play about gay men without dealing with it. So 'Life of the Party' is what I'd call a second-generation AIDS play. I wrote it as propaganda. I wanted to show four healthy, attractive, respectable men openly discussing the difficulties and advantages of safe sex."

Unlike other AIDS plays, Alan Bowne's "Beirut" eschews any educational role. Rather than being a realistic portrait of heterosexuals dealing with AIDS, "Beirut" dramatizes the life force that drives two people to risk death to be together. Approached by a couple of young actors two years ago to write a play that they could perform in an East Village club, the playwright adapted "Romeo and Juliet" as a nightmarish fantasy set in the near future when New York is overrun with an unnamed plague. So-called "blood-positive" individuals are tattooed on the buttocks, quarantined on the Lower East Side and inspected for symptoms daily by a Lesion Patrol.

Although the play freely borrows medical terminology from AIDS literature, the playwright says, "I didn't feel responsibility for education because I thought the disease I created was worse than AIDS." Subsequent developments gave the play macabre overtones. "Not long after I wrote the play, William Buckley came out suggesting tattooing people who tested positive for the AIDS virus," he said, referring to an op-ed piece in The New York Times by Mr. Buckley, which appeared in March 1986. "After that, Lyndon LaRouche got on the ballot in California with a referendum calling for quarantining. Right away, life started imitating art."

As a grotesque fantasia inspired by AIDS, "Beirut" resembles Robert Chesley's 1984 play "Night Sweat." Set in a sex club for the terminally ill, it was the first play about AIDS seen in New York. Mr. Chesley's latest work, "Jerker," belongs to Mr. Holsclaw's category of second-generation AIDS dramas. The play's subtitle—"A Pornographic Elegy with Redeeming Social Value and a Hymn to the Queer Men of San Francisco in 20 Telephone Calls, Many of Them Dirty"—makes it sound raunchier than it really is. The dialogue between JR and Bert, strangers who conduct their entire relationship on the telephone, begins with sexual fantasies, but as the men become closer they share complete personal histories.

Departing from their usual masturbatory fantasies, toward the end of the play JR enchants Bert with a bedtime fairy tale about two young boys who battle their way through the Forbidden Forest to arrive at the castle of a handsome prince. "He questions us about each adventure, peril and sorrow," JR recounts, "and from the answers he brings forth from us we understand that each one, even the most terrible, was a lesson on our journey to the palace; and we understand that we ourselves were lessons for others whose paths crossed ours in the Forest."

The playwright is less concerned that the audience share his characters' specific sexual fantasies than that they cherish the vitality of the sexual imagination in the face of death. "I think it's important to remove the stigma against sex that AIDS has created, and it's important to remove the stigma against gay men," he says. "What I'm talking about is humanizing lives which are otherwise disregarded or despised or destroyed. As the epidemic goes on, we don't really know what is happening or what will happen, but it's important to tell our stories before they're gone for good."

Don Shewey is the editor of "Out Front: Contemporary Gay and Lesbian Plays," an anthology to be published by Grove Press in the spring of 1988.

* * *

November 10, 1992

MARCHING OUT OF THE CLOSET, INTO HISTORY

By FRANK RICH
Special to The New York Times

ANGELS IN AMERICA
Part 1: Millennium Approaches
Part 2: Perestroika
By Tony Kushner; directed by Oskar Eustis with Tony Taccone; sets by John Conklin; costumes by Gabriel Berry; lighting by Pat Collins; sound by Jon Gottlieb; fight director, Randy Kovitz; original music by Mel Marvin; production stage manager, Mary K. Klinger; stage managers, James T. McDermott and Jill Ragaway; associate producer, Corey Beth Madden. Presented by Center Theater Group/Mark Taper Forum, Gordon Davidson, artistic director and producer; Charles Dillingham, managing director, and Robert Egan, associate artistic director, in association with the New York Shakespeare Festival, JoAnne Akalaitis, artistic director; Jason Steven Cohen, producing director. At the Mark Taper Forum, Los Angeles.

Hannah Pitt	Kathleen Chalfant
Belize	K. Todd Freeman
Joe Pitt	Jeffrey King
Roy Cohn	Ron Leibman
Harper Pitt	Cynthia Mace
Louis Ironson	Joe Mantello
The Angel	Ellen McLaughlin
Prior Walter	Stephen Spinella
Heavenly Attendants	Pauline Lepor and Eve Sigall

Jay Thompson/Angels in America

Stephen Spinella and Cynthia Mace in "Angels in America," Tony Kushner's two-part epic subtitled "A Gay Fantasia on National Themes," which had its United States premiere in Los Angeles on Sunday.

LOS ANGELES, Nov. 9—Some visionary playwrights want to change the world. Some want to revolutionize the theater. Tony Kushner, the remarkably gifted 36-year-old author of "Angels in America," is that rarity of rarities: a writer who has the promise to do both.

As a political statement, "Angels in America," a two-part, seven-hour epic subtitled "A Gay Fantasia on National Themes," is nothing less than a fierce call for gay Americans to seize the strings of power in the war for tolerance and against AIDS. But this play, by turns searing and comic and elegiac, is no earthbound ideological harangue. Though set largely in New York and Washington during the Reagan-Bush 80's, "Angels in America" sweeps through locales as varied as Salt Lake City and the Kremlin, and through high-flying styles ranging from piquant camp humor to religious hallucination to the ornate poetic rage of classic drama.

When was the last time a play embraced intellectual poles as seemingly antithetical as Judy Garland and Walter Benjamin, Joseph Smith and Mikhail Gorbachev, Emma Goldman and Nancy Reagan? Almost anything can happen as history cracks open in "Angels in America." A Valium-addicted Washington housewife, accompanied by an imaginary travel agent resembling a jazz musician, visits a hole in the ozone layer above Antarctica. An angel crashes with an apocalyptic roar through the ceiling of a Manhattan apartment to embrace a dwindling, Christ-like man spotted with Kaposi's sarcoma. A museum diorama illustrating the frontier history of the Mormons comes to contentious life. Ethel Rosenberg returns from the dead to say kaddish for her executioner, Roy Cohn.

No wonder the audience is somewhat staggered as it leaves the Mark Taper Forum, where the complete "Angels in America" had its premiere in a day-and-night marathon on Sunday. (It is scheduled to travel to the New York Shakespeare Festival in February.) The show is not merely mind-bending; at times it is mind-exploding, eventually piling on more dense imagery and baroque spiritual, political and historical metaphor than even an entranced, receptive audience can absorb in two consecutive sittings.

Part 1 of "Angels in America," titled "Millennium Approaches" and a sensation at the Royal National Theater in London this year, remains a dazzling, self-contained piece. While the new, at times stodgy Taper production, directed by Oskar Eustis with Tony Taccone, does not yet reach the imaginative heights of Declan Donnellan's London staging, the work's alternate chords of deep grief and dreamy wonderment still produce exhilaration for the heart, mind and eyes. Part 2, titled "Perestroika" and never before seen in a full production, seems a somewhat embryonic, occasionally overstuffed mixture of striking passages, Talmudic digressions and glorious epiphanies. Mr. Kushner is by no means exhausted, but he may have to harness his energies more firmly to keep his audience from feeling so by the final curtain.

Huge as the playwright's canvas is, both parts of "Angels" focus intimately on two couples, one gay and one nominally heterosexual, in which one partner abandons the other. Louis Ironson (Joe Mantello), a Jewish leftist and legal cleric, runs out on his AIDS-stricken lover, a WASP esthete named Prior Walter (Stephen Spinella), once the disease's ravages leave blood on the floor. Joe Pitt (Jeffrey King), an ambitious Republican lawyer clerking in Federal court, deserts his loyal but long-suffering wife, Harper (Cynthia Mace), once his homosexual longings overpower his rectitudinous Mormon credo. Whether intact or fractured, the couples intersect throughout the play, brought together by chance events, by interlocking fantasies (erotic and mystical) and, indirectly, by the machinations of Roy Cohn.

As written by Mr. Kushner with a witty, demonic grandeur worthy of a Shakespearean villain, and played with maniacal relish by the braying Ron Leibman in high, red-faced dudgeon, Cohn is the Antichrist of "Angels in America": the witchhunting accomplice of Joe McCarthy is seen in his final guise as an unofficial Mr. Fixit in the Ed Meese Justice Department and New York City's most famous closeted gay AIDS patient. In one brilliant passage, Cohn argues that he is a heterosexual who has sex with men rather than a homosexual because gay men, unlike him, are "men who know nobody and who nobody knows, men who have zero clout." It is Mr. Kushner's sly point

that gay people could learn something from the despicable Cohn about the amassing of political power, and it is one of the play's most provocative strokes that this cutthroat often has the funniest and smartest lines. For Mr. Leibman, the vindictive, cadaverous Cohn may be the role of his career, and his performance need only shed some Don Rickles shtick to realize it.

His theatrical power is matched by Mr. Spinella's Prior, another kind of AIDS patient entirely. It is the abandoned, delusional Prior who is visited by an Angel at the end of Part 1 and becomes a heaven-sent prophet of survival for his people in Part 2. Mr. Spinella, a bone-thin young man with a boy's open face and an extravagant spirit, is triumphant in this mammoth part, creating an ethereal but tough-spined sprite who fills the theater with his transcendent will to live even as his body is gutted by "inhuman horror." He is the ideal heroic vessel for Mr. Kushner's unifying historical analogy, in which the modern march of gay people out of the closet is likened to the courageous migrations of turn-of-the-century Jews to America and of 19th-century Mormons across the plains.

None of the other performances are in this league, although Mr. Mantello's cowardly Louis shows a lot of promise and K. Todd Freeman sizzles in the comic role of a one-time drag queen who ends up as Cohn's private nurse. Among the rest, the only one that does damage comes from Ms. Mace, whose lost wife exudes brash sitcom brio rather than the disorientation and vulnerability that might make the play's one major female character touching.

In their staging of Part 1, Mr. Eustis and Mr. Taccone have not departed radically from the London choreography of the overlapping scenes and celestial revelations. But the execution can be plodding, and the fabulousness of Mr. Kushner's writing, so verdant with what one line calls "unspeakable beauty," is sometimes dimmed. While the appropriately chosen set designer is John Conklin, the artist who brought so many levitating dreams to the Metropolitan Opera's "Ghosts of Versailles," his central set here, a stylized Federal building emblematizing a decaying body politic, confronts the audience with a visually heavy blank wall and, like the direction, sometimes lumbers when it might spin or shatter.

When the going gets truly heavy in Part 2, Mr. Kushner must share responsibility. The writing retreats to conventionality as he sorts out the domestic conflicts of his major characters. Long debates about the Reagan ethos and the hypocrisies of gay Republicans seem unexceptional after this year's Presidential campaign. But just when "Angels in America" seems to bog down in the naturalism and polemics Mr. Kushner otherwise avoids, it gathers itself up for a stirring cosmic denouement in which Mr. Spinella's Prior, having passed through a spiritual heaven and five years of physical hell, addresses the audience directly from the Bethesda Fountain in Central Park. Envisioning a new age of universal perestroika in which "the world only spins forward," Prior foretells a future in which "this disease will be the end of many of us, but not nearly all," in which "we will not die secret deaths anymore," in which love and "more life" will be the destiny of "each and every one."

Above him hovers the statue of the angel Bethesda. Angels, as Prior explains, "commemorate death" but hold out the hope of "a world without dying." It is that angelic mission of mercy that seems to inform the entire universe of this vast, miraculous play.

* * *

June 28, 1994

WHY OZ IS A STATE OF MIND IN GAY LIFE AND DRAG SHOWS

By BEN BRANTLEY

Consider this scenario: A teen-ager, growing up in a drab, flat part of the Midwest that is strictly American Gothic, feels out of place and misunderstood and fantasizes about a more colorful, exotic world. Well, the kid finds that world: a land of magnificent artifice filled with strange, enchanting companions, all united by a pungent feeling of incompleteness. The kid has many exciting adventures but continues to yearn with a bottomless pang for the idea of something called home.

Yes, that is the plot of "The Wizard of Oz." It is also the life story of countless numbers of gay men and lesbians who fled what Tina Landau, the writer and director, describes in the play "1969" as the "vast map of normalcy" that is much of America. Many of them found their own Oz on a northeastern island called Manhattan. And for an important subset of those people, Emerald City took the form of an all-inclusive land of make-believe known as the New York theater.

Many of today's gay-rights advocates who emphasize progressive political engagement over escapist nostalgia may consider "The Wizard of Oz" an unhealthy frame of reference. Still, the spirit of the classic L. Frank Baum tale, especially in its incarnation as a 1939 MGM musical, hovered over the cultural festival celebrating the 25th anniversary of the Stonewall uprising. Talismanic lines from the movie showed up in everything from Tony Kushner's epic "gay fantasia" on Broadway, "Angels in America," to "Charles Busch's Dressing Up!," a one-night drag revue at Town Hall.

And the film provided a metaphoric center for two plays that dealt specifically with the 1969 rebellion: Thomas O'Neil's "Judy at the Stonewall Inn" and En Garde Arts' ambitious production of Ms. Landau's "Stonewall: Night Variations."

Nonetheless, the ways in which Oz was evoked went way beyond tear-stained sentiment and camp. If there was a subtext that united these varied works, it seemed to be that Oz was a nice place to visit but that you really couldn't live there forever. Correspondingly, the plays by Mr. O'Neil and Ms. Landau symbolically laid to rest the spirit of Judy Garland, the actress who played Dorothy on screen and whose funeral took place on the day of the Stonewall uprising (and probably helped provoke it).

Oz was a cornerstone in gay mythology for at least five decades, and characters and phrases from the movie became a coded legend for a subculture. Homosexuals in the United States military identified themselves as "friends of Dorothy," just as "I have the feeling we're not in Kansas anymore" was a traditional opening line for out-of-towners making their debuts in metropolitan gay bars.

For audiences watching "The Wizard of Oz" in its immensely popular television broadcasts from the 1950's on, the image of the ingenuous, wistful younger Garland was overlaid with an ironic awareness of the tortured, self-lacerating creature she turned into. Her version of "Somewhere Over the Rainbow" became an anthem of pain for homosexuals who perceived themselves as belonging to a despised minority. Her interpretation of the song seemed, as a character in "Judy at the Stonewall Inn" puts it, to embody "all the suffering voices of the world twisted into one spectral shape."

Last week in "Dressing Up!," the veteran female impersonator Charles Pierce (attired as Gloria Swanson playing Norma Desmond) chanted, "When you're down in the dumps, pray for Judy's red pumps," and segued into a riff of Garland's Dorothy praying for another tornado to deliver her from Kansas. In Ms. Landau's "1969," at the Humana Festival in Louisville, Ky., last March, a persecuted small-town high school student dreamed of attending his senior prom as Dorothy, and, after running away, found his own Glinda the Good Witch waiting for him in Greenwich Village in the form of a motherly drag queen.

In the current "Stonewall: Night Variations," the sequel to "1969," there's still a yellow brick road running through the Village. And Billie Burke's Glinda is evoked again, as a barker who summons gay men to the Stonewall Inn by singing Ms. Burke's fabled call to the Munchkins: "Come out, come out, wherever you are."

A white coffin, representing the dead Garland, figures prominently in the play. And a choir of angels sings an elegy to the fallen star, which includes the lines, "We were never sure whether you would fall into the abyss or soar into the sky." Implicitly, the same alternatives are available to the gay men and lesbians at Stonewall. And when the bar is raided, they choose to soar by fighting back.

The same conceit is given more explicit form in "Judy at the Stonewall Inn," where the ghost of Garland materializes to a pill-popping Judy impersonator just before the police raid. She is not the spirit of despair but of hope. While Jimmy the drag queen wails that Garland made a world that "does not like me" bearable, the ghost admonishes him to stop feeling sorry for himself and to abandon "Over the Rainbow" for the more militant song that was sung at her funeral, "The Battle Hymn of the Republic." She also tells Jimmy, in fluent Oz-ese: "You've always had the power to get home. You just had to learn it for yourself."

The notion of home and homelessness echoed through other works with gay themes last week. In a revival of her most recent performance piece, Holly Hughes spoke of the sense of exile and of the "fairy tale" that ends in banishment from the family hearth, both known to many lesbians in America. Nicky Paraiso, in the autobiographical "Asian

Boys" at P.S. 122, concluded a series of tales of displacement by saying, "I'm telling you these things here because it's the only place I feel at home."

Sir Ian McKellen, the great English actor and gay rights advocate, once described the theater as "the one place in the world I've taught myself to be at home." Last week, in his disarmingly intimate one-man Broadway show, "A Knight Out," he spoke of the pleasures in discovering the warm sanctuary provided for gay men by "the half-open closet of the theater." His show was a sustained, engaging argument for opening that door all the way.

This is a process that's happening by degrees. The last 15 years have seen more plays and performance pieces by openly gay and lesbian writers dealing directly with gay and lesbian themes. "Angels in America" is a hit on Broadway. And cross-dressing performances have moved from the margins of downtown drag shows into mainstream houses.

Indeed, one of the highlights of the cultural festival, "Charles Busch's Dressing Up!," celebrated drag with both gay female impersonators and heterosexual stars well known to American television audiences. Beatrice Arthur showed up to deliver her own version of Bette Davis saying, "What a dump!" And 85-year-old Milton Berle, who memorably donned dresses for his 1950's television variety series, swaggered out in a spangled, floor-length red gown, high heels and a blond wig.

Mr. Berle, clearly delighted by the enthusiasm with which he was greeted, proceeded to doff his wig ("It's me, Milton!") and hold the stage for half an hour with a series of Borscht Belt jokes that this audience might have been less enchanted by in another context. Finally, Bette Davis, in the person of Mr. Pierce, had to remind the actor it was time to sign off.

Mr. Berle appeared a bit annoyed. But it did seem time to let the gay version of drag reassert itself. The evening ended with a lineup of Bette Davises and Mr. Busch, in a stunning second-skin orange dress, commenting, "I suppose we have to realize how far we have to go, but I think we can all be very proud of where we've been."

Outside the theater, a middle-aged man with a boyish face observed a coterie of leathery, muscular guys in tulle and chiffon and exclaimed happily to a friend, "Hey, we're in Oz!"

* * *

December 5, 1999

TALKS WITH GAY PLAYWRIGHTS OFFERED IN COURSE AT PURCHASE

By ALVIN KLEIN

Ask Craig Lucas what a gay play is and he is likely to, purposefully, reel off flip definitions, often heard by some people:

"A gay play is a play written by a gay playwright." Or, "It sleeps with another play of the same gender."

William M. Hoffman, who wrote "As Is," a so-called gay play, and one of the American theater's two trailblazing ones

about AIDS—the other is "The Normal Heart" by Larry Kramer—perceives and emphasizes gay elements in a vast reach of plays through the ages, including Shakespeare's "Edward II," two obscure comedies by Mae West (not including "Sex") and "God of Vengeance," a Yiddish classic of 1903. Not to mention "Cat on a Hot Tin Roof" by Tennessee Williams, "Streamers" by David Rabe, "The Dying Gaul" by Mr. Lucas and "The Well of Horniness" by Holly Hughes.

In his role as director of the dramatic writing program at Purchase College, Mr. Hoffman has assigned all these plays. And he holds conversations with gay and lesbian playwrights as an offshoot of the course, "Lesbian, Gay and Bisexual Theater."

"I don't have to come in and do a manifesto—or possibly I will at the slightest provocation," said Ms. Hughes, who is Mr. Hoffman's conversationalist on Dec. 14. Not to worry, Ms. Hughes, provocation awaits.

Mr. Hoffman fully expects Ms. Hughes to "do a performance," one could say a piece of a performance piece—10 minutes or so. Ms. Hughes's new work, "Preaching to the Perverted," by her description a "low-tech show on an almost bare stage" is to be performed at Public School 122 on the Lower East Side in April and May.

It is about her Supreme Court confrontation of 1998, a case arising over a National Endowment for the Arts grant. Ms. Hughes's grant was withdrawn because of sexually explicit content, language and gesture. It was then reinstated.

"I focused on the Supreme Court hearing as a piece of theater," Ms. Hughes said.

"Judge Judy did not prepare me for this. In retrospect, I would rather have had Ed Koch, who represents more respect for the rule of law than the United States Supreme Court."

Given Ms. Hughes's gift for candor, not to mention ineffable charm and wit, one would not reasonably expect from an artist with an agenda in response to restrictive, oppressive powers—Senator Jesse Helms, Republican of North Carolina, is one of her most acerbically and humorously used adjectives—a conversation with Ms. Hughes is sure to elicit funny and dazzling rejoinders; it is not possible to believe that listeners will not jump to be participants. Once quoted as having a "mission to change the world," Ms. Hughes will be expected to explain just what a performance artist—her designation—is or does.

"I can expound on that," she said. "I will entertain the questions, if not necessarily answer them."

Although she was inspired by such seminal underground theater and avant-garde influences as the great Charles Ludlam and his legendary Ridiculous Theater Company, Ms. Hughes said:

"In the 70's, a lot of what is called performance art was coming from visual artists; Laurie Anderson started out as one. Her photos were accompanied by tapes, and she put on a headset. It is not coming out of the theater artists but was intended to push the limitations of various media to produce a hybrid art."

What started out as an anti-theatrical movement, "in the ensuing 30 years, has become autobiographically driven, like Spalding Gray, more than questioning forms of theater," she said.

Of the present arts scene, Ms. Hughes said: "We are in a cynical comodified moment where the big impact is economic. Theater is a commodity to be consumed. It is not about asking questions or about who we are. With less funding, it has to be concerned with the bottom line."

Despite the lessening of fringe movements and spaces for emerging theater artists, Ms. Hughes still spoke of going "where the excitement and energy is"—in the South Bronx, in Dumbo the acronym for Down Under Manhattan Bridge Overpass, a section in Brooklyn—which even has a performance group that calls itself Dumba.

But it is all in the cause of theater, "which will never be able to compete with the spectacle of movies," Ms. Hughes said. "What theater has to offer is unmediated human presence. That is its strongest, wonderful, irreplaceable fact."

She continued: "The need for gay and lesbian courses is almost hilarious. So many works in the canon have been disguised by closeted writers.

"And there is now a wealth of interest in gay and lesbian writers who have a particular sensibility and explicitly gay characters, but it is located in a larger world, as it exists in a larger community.

"A play like Christopher Durang's 'Betty's Summer Vacation' of last season is not a gay play. It follows a tradition of gay male sendups of heterosexuals, of gender, of family relationships—without a gay character in it. I'll ask Bill, who comes out of a more naturalistic tradition (he edited a gay play anthology) some questions. 'Why is he offering this class?' 'Why is he inviting riffraff like me?'"

A conversation with Mr. Lucas is to take place on Thursday. The playwright, who lives in Putnam County with his male companion—the couple intend to adopt an infant—is best known for, "Prelude to a Kiss" and "Reckless," neither of them ostensibly gay.

But most recently, "The Dying Gaul," which he considers his most highly praised work, was a decidedly homosexual play. A gender changed—two men instead of one man and one woman—version of "Marry Me a Little," a revue based on songs by Stephen Sondheim, which was developed by Mr. Lucas and Norman Rene, is a hit in Hollywood, where it opened last month to rave reviews.

Mr. Lucas said: "I balk at being called a gay playwright. It marginalizes you. I can imagine a straight woman, a black boy, an old Jewish man. I live in the real world, not in a gay village. My job is to imagine, not report on some factoid of my life. It would be odd if Shakespeare had written only what he 'knew.' I'm a white gay male in America. That's one of the reasons I want to talk to students, as an out person who speaks candidly about experience informed by art. No one has ever told them the truth about anything. To hear an adult talk about any aspect of life from a lived perspective shocks and means something to them."

Ms. Hughes, as teacher, is on the Purchase College semester list for January. The course is gay and lesbian performance art. It will be offered under gay and lesbian studies and "cross listed with dramatic studies," she explained, trying to avoid the academic jargon of complicated, overlapping departmental structures where, in this case, courses are identified as belonging in either a division (humanities) or a conservatory (theater arts and film). It is sufficient to say that the "lesbian, gay and bisexual theater" course, five years old and being conducted by Mr. Hoffman for the first time, is "an open course; it's out there."

Describing it that way, Mr. Hoffman intended neither a wordplay about being openly gay or gay outing. It is an elective, open to everyone. Major and dramatic writing, however, is required in order to be a member of that department, and the other two courses he is teaching this semester (dramatic writing and script analysis) go under the heading conservatory program for freshmen and sophomores, leading to a bachelor of fine arts degree. Of the students in Mr. Hoffman's dramatic writing course, he said: "We don't offer false encouragement. You have to be obsessed and you better be someone who wants it. It's not for the casual."

On the origins of gay and lesbian drama as a course, Mr. Hoffman said: "I don't have a clue, but it must be taught." In "Conversations With," as he prefers to call the series at the Neuberger Museum of Art, "I want to get the best playwrights and directors of national repute," he said, although his focus is on playwrights who are gay: Lanford Wilson, Christopher Durang, Terrence McNally, Nicky Silver. This year's conversations began with Mr. Kramer and then went to Maria Irene Fornes, whose body of work is being seen Off Broadway this season at the Signature Theater.

The conversations with Mr. Lucas and with Ms. Hughes are being held on Thursday and on Dec. 14, respectively, at the Neuberger Museum of Art at Purchase College at 4 P.M. Admission is free, but the capacity is about 75. For more information, the number to call is 251-6113.

Mr. Hoffman, who has also written the libretto for "The Ghosts of Versailles," with music by John Corigliano, has taught on various aspects of theater at Arizona State University in Tempe, at Juilliard (on the art of the libretto), at the University of Massachusetts in Amherst, and the New School.

"But I'm beginning to have an academic home here," he said.

* * *

LITERATURE

February 23, 1969

WHY CAN'T 'WE' LIVE HAPPILY EVER AFTER, TOO?

By RONALD FORSYTHE

Film critic Judith Crist has called 1968 "the year of the Third Sex"—and 1969 promises perhaps even more revealing plays and films about the homosexual. Over the past 15 years, in novels and on stage and screen, the American public has been learning about this neglected segment of its population; but 1968 was a banner year. Some of its films—notably "The Killing of Sister George" and "The Queen"—dealt compassionately with the homosexual as a human being. Others—"The Fox," "Therese and Isabelle," "Les Biches" and "The Sergeant"—insisted either that he die . . . or change his sexual attraction. 1968 even made some advances toward giving the homosexual a happy ending—"Staircase" on Broadway last spring (and soon to be seen on film) made the greatest steps in that direction. But, by and large, writers and producers still feared to let the public see two homosexuals happily in love.

A film such as "The Sergeant," graced as it may be by Rod Steiger's talents, harks back to an interpretation of the homosexual and his due that characterized plots of an earlier day, novels such as "Trio" (Dorothy Baker, 1945), in which the rejected Lesbian puts a bullet through her head. Based on the 1958 novel by Dennis Murphy, "The Sergeant" reflects attitudes more common in the 1940's and 50's. It should have been filmed 10 years ago. Realistic, more knowledgeable audiences of 1968 had no need for this decade-old melodrama.

Much like the American Negro of 20 to 30 years ago who saw himself on stage and screen—and read about himself in novels—as Ole Black Joe or Prissy or Shoe Shine Boy, the American homosexual has a complaint: He does not believe his life must end in tragedy and would like to see a change in his image reflected in the entertainment he pays to see and the books he buys to read. Like any minority group, he, too, would like his "Place in the Sun." He has been striving for it in *life* by seeking the revocation of laws that harass him unjustly; he would like also to achieve it in the creative worlds of the novel, plays, films, music, art, and television.

What picture of the homosexual do these creative worlds present now, when they deal with him? To answer this question, the writer will assume—correctly—the first person; and he will begin interrogatively . . .

Where are Our great books, Our classics? Works such as an "El Cid," showing Our bravery—for We are brave, We have to be. Epics such as "Les Misérables," testifying to Our love—which can be as enduring as Valjean's. Books such as "Seventeen," laughing sympathetically at Our puppy loves— for We have them, too. Legends such as "Tristan and Isolde," showing We would die for love—yes. We are too often willing to do so. Where are Our classics? We have none. One might almost say We have no literature, classic or modern; at least We have no *triumphant* literature, no great story where love conquers all (perhaps even despite general tragedy which overtakes the lovers) . . . and therefore We have little to turn to for inspiration or for consolation or for that blissful feeling that what We are is Right.

Who are We? We are the American homosexual.

We can sense something of ourselves in the works of great homosexual writers, such as Wilde, and can sometimes even read about ourselves—briefly, as in Proust or Sartre. But no great writer has yet given us a whole, triumphant masterpiece. Though it is said that some of the world's masterworks, written to heterosexual themes, are but our stories in disguise, in them we can find only an incomplete self-recognition and cannot convince the world that it is we pictured therein.

Over the past five decades, as the 20th century has become more open-minded, we have accumulated a literature of homophile "classics." Needless to say, we have read them eagerly and hopefully: "The Well of Loneliness" (Radclyffe Hall, 1928)—in the touching denouement of which "Stephen" loses her sweetheart to a man; "The City and the Pillar" (1948)—with its (until Gore Vidal's recent, heroic revision) murder and suicidal ending; "Finistère" (Fritz Peters, 1951)— in which Matthew's footprints, discovered by his lover, lead to the sea; "Never the Same Again" (Gerald Tesch, 1956)— whose 13-year-old hero's life is wrecked, then lost, through contact with a thirtyish pederast; "Giovanni's Room" (James Baldwin, 1958)—whose Negro hero, left alone when the police claim Giovanni, chooses homosexuality as his path, but has grave doubts about his future. A happy literature! And the foregoing do not comprise a complete list.

Jean Genet's works of homosexual genius ("Our Lady of the Flowers," trans. 1963; "The Thief's Journal," trans. 1964; "Miracle of the Rose," trans, 1966) bravely espouse our way of life—and he is our greatest living writer. But their picture of homophile love as a sex-dominated, master-slave relationship—perhaps too often true—seldom convinces us that we are Right to be what we are.

A few brave attempts have been made, in our literature, to give us a happy ever after: "Quatrefoil" (James Barr, 1950), in which—though an air crash takes his "teacher's" life—a homosexual novitiate finally knows what path he will tred and that *he will find love;* "The Charioteer" (1953), in which Mary Renault's World War II mutilé rediscovers a love for his former dorm master, which perseveres through a troubled romance and blossoms into a successful relationship; "The Last of the Wine" (1956), Miss Renault's evocation of a homosexual, yet manly, ancient Greece; "Totempole" (Sanford Friedman, 1961), whose Korean War infantry-man discovers—with an Oriental on those war-ravaged hills—that homosexual love can be fulfilling; "Sam" (Lonnie Coleman, 1962), where the heterosexual, for once, is the sinner, loses *his* mate, and ends up haunting gay bars; "A Single Man"

(1964), Christopher Isherwood's novel of a sensible homosexual growing old, tinged as it is, however, with sadness; plus a few other novels whose attempts at portraying ultimate happiness are unfortunately overshadowed by their calculations to excite the reader sexually.

With the exception of these few generally available "classics," where must we find our reading material—if we wish to keep reading about ourselves? In cheap-thrill magazine shops on 42d Street, not in the marble-halled public libraries of the nation.

Often we pick up a copy of Dickens to bask for a while in his eternal optimism and kindness, an F. Scott Fitzgerald to experience the dizzy happiness—and sadness—of his Lost Generation youth (for we like sad stories as well as pleasant ones), a sizzling John O'Hara or John Updike to feel its pulse and experience vicariously (as many readers must) its vivid sexual pleasures. Yet in none of these do we see ourselves as hero or heroine. Most of us have grown used to this, much as the Negro on countless Saturday nights has had to don sunglasses mentally if he wanted to see himself and his girl up there on the screen. In reading classic or current best sellers, most of us have ultimately this feeling of being left out, of not "qualifying"—certainly of not finding anything of ourselves therein which we might fall back on in sickness or loneliness.

We cannot even find consolation in the Bible, as can Negroes and other groups who feel put upon. The more foolish of us search in vain for some confirmation that David and Jonathan felt as we do, or hope that Jesus' disinclination for women might just indicate "something." But when mentioned in the holy writ, we are only described in contemptuous terms. Perhaps, as some social historians have concluded, it is from this original condemnation in the Jewish scriptures that we gained our low status (certainly we do not owe it to the Greeks or Romans). But, oddly enough, the Jewish lawmakers have been misinterpreted by Christian theologians, for, when proscribing homosexual contacts (and even onanism), the patriarchs were not really anti-homosexual (or anti-masturbation) but were mainly opposed to decreasing the birth rate in their small, post-Exodus nation, determined as it had to be to withstand many aggressors and create a new homeland for itself. Nevertheless, we find little solace in the Bible.

That we have no painting or sculpture is obvious; no opera equally so. Classical music, by happy chance, is generally asexual and gives us some feeling of belonging, since in every sense it belongs to all. But popular music generally does not. Can we turn on the FM when in romantic or melancholy mood to hear a masculine voice croon about his fella? Or hear a feminine one sing the praises of "Laura" or "Maria"? (Yes, we anticipate your chuckles at such a thought, for we, too, have been guilty of unwillingness to "understand" the Other Side.) Is it any wonder that "There's a Place for Us" from "West Side Story" has such a homosexual appeal?

If we see ourselves portrayed on stage or screen, it is always in an unfavorable or qualified light. We are never given a happy ending, except in some offbeat Off Broadway productions which, again, usually cater more to the sensations than to the ideals of their homosexual audiences. Of the relatively few homosexual plays and films yet produced, what heterosexual spectator has been able to detect—or would want to detect, as yet—a triumphant conclusion? (Remember that by "triumphant" we do not rule out death—surely Romeo and Juliet are ultimately triumphant to their audiences! And we would *not* call "triumphant" the disappointed Major's vengeance on his sleeping wife's voyeur in the 1967 shocker "Reflections in a Golden Eye.") "The Children's Hour" (1962) had Shirley MacLaine hang herself; in "A Taste of Honey" (1962), poor faggot Geoffrey was finally rejected and set adrift again in a London that seemed to have no place for him; "Fortune and Men's Eyes" (Off Broadway, 1967), frequently campy and humorous, witnessed rape, then near-rape and possible breakdown as it reached its conclusion; "The Boys in the Band" (Off Broadway, 1968), for all its funniness, ends in a game of self-flagellation, damaged friendships, and a feeling of utter frustration—personally, the writer and most of his friends have never attended such a masochistic gathering. In "The Killing of Sister George" (Broadway, 1967) Beryl Reid, brave as she was when she began her new life as a Cow, stood as an example—the public must have been led to believe—that Lesbian marriage cannot last; Essy Persson in the screen's "Therese and Isabelle" muses for an afternoon on the truest love of her life, an unforgettable Lesbian schoolmate—then jumps in a Citroen and drives off with her husband-to-be; "Les Biches" (like "Reflections") ends in murder—this time the "straight" girl guns to death the older woman who calculatingly seduced her.

Almost every one of us—and every honest psychiatrist—knows that Tom Lee in "Tea and Sympathy" was probably deeply and completely homosexual and that the privilege Laura Reynolds bestowed would have put him in shock rather than have "cured" him. Nevertheless, in 1953, simply the characterization on stage of a "queer" was a novelty we will still praise. A few years later, Paul Newman in Tennessee Williams's screen "Cat on a Hot Tin Roof" (1958) *had* to be mistaken, didn't he? How could any male have preferred his football buddy to the charms of then-in-her-most-beauteous-prime Liz Taylor? We fully believe, however, that even heterosexual spectators were horrified, with us, at what happened to Sebastian in the film "Suddenly, Last Summer" (1960). In a later Williams great, the film audience was again expected to feel only pity for the Lesbian schoolmate of "Night of the Iguana" (1964); though, indeed, the play's most wonderful line, spoken by wanderer Hannah Jelkes, does seem to discourage any audience disgust at the teacher's mentality: "Nothing human disgusts men unless it's unkind, violent!" Surely a line which all Us cherish.

"The Third Sex," a 1959 German-import film, salvaged its teen-age hero for heterosexuality, but did so in a way that may have left some in its audiences rocking with laughter: suspecting her son's tendencies, a wealthy Frau arranges to be away for a while, cues in the attractive maid to utilize this time with Junior, then later goes on trial and is condemned for her machinations—happy to have done a mother's duty!

"Victim," a 1961 British release, was a landmark in homosexual films; but it saw fit finally to reconcile its parliamentary hero to his embarrassed wife (What were the really beautiful words she spoke to him at the end, however? "It is a greater thing to be needed than to be loved"?) and did not give him any lasting homophile happiness. In his story "The Fox," published in 1923, D. H. Lawrence was extremely bold even to introduce a subject like Lesbianism, and the plot's mixed-tragic, ending reflected the feelings of the times. But 45 years later, when it reached the screen, film audiences still may have felt that Keir Dullea came along just in time to save Anne Heywood from All That and that it was perhaps after all best for Sandy Dennis to be killed by a falling tree—and she even seemed to want to die! On the few occasions when a man-to-man kiss has flashed across the screen it has been for pure shock value (as in the current "The Brotherhood") or has been used to create shame—as when Raf Vallone amazed film audiences of "A View From the Bridge" (1962)—or to justify suicide—as when Rod Steiger busses John Phillip Law in "The Sergeant." One might begin to believe in a "kiss of death"—or many unthinking spectators might. Most of us whose lips have met those of our own sex, however, have felt nothing but the tenderness and communion of human contact.

A plethora of plagues is upon us! In books and plays and films we seem to have to commit suicide, murder one another (or be murdered, as in "The Detective"), die à la Camille, or at lest break off the relationship lest insanity be the result. The following is a plot which would surely sell tickets. Widowed father comes home after night in a House, finds teenage son in bed with sailor, shoots sailor, then son, then self. Moral? Who knows? We begin to feel that especially filmmakers—who reach the widest public—should begin such epics as "The Sergeant" with an informative brochure passed out to the audience or should revert to the printed or spoken screen prologue of the 1930's and 40s, saying that:

"The following is the story of an un-average homosexual, who could not cope with his problem or find happiness in life. His story is a sad one, and is fortunately not a common one."

(We trust that such advice would not have been necessary, recently, to audiences of "The Queen.") Or, Broadly speaking:

"Any similarity between the characters and actual homosexuals, living or dead, is purely coincidental."

Almost alone among plays, "Staircase" seemed to go furthest toward pleasing the homosexuals in its audiences. The tribulations of Charles and Harry were really just the marital squabbles common to many couples. But even in this play, Charles' unfortunate conflict with a then unsympathetic British law promised embarrassment and possible problems for their future. We must conclude that writers and producers are unwilling to let the homosexual come off happy—or homosexual—at the end of the show.

But lest the reader believe we advocate only La-Vie-en-Rose entertainment, we insist that we would be the last to want to rule out the homosexual tragedy. Tragedy, one might say, is our middle name. How many teenage homosexuals are disinherited each year by their families, thrown out of the

house, made to leave town, or forced to endure a traumatic sexual experience under Daddy's supervision? If what the public wanted was a more up-to-the-moment "Subject Was Roses," writers might have tried out one of our real domestic tragedies. Our only hope would be that audiences were made to realize who was wrong.

We have appreciated the increasing attention given us by talented writers and producers in novels and on stage and screen—despite the uniform morbidity. The public has at least become cognizant of us and how we are forced to live. A far cry from the situation 30 years ago, when, according to rumor, the producer of "These Three," the original (1936) version of "The Children's Hour," was advised he shouldn't make a film about Lesbians, and replied: "We'll make 'em Americans!" (The story was completely revamped, and the Lesbianism disappeared!) In "The Detective" last year, we were delighted to see the industry's and law's concern about punishing our enemies. We have no complaint about such films. We merely would like to be able to smile sometimes when leaving the theater.

Unless art has no effect on those it portrays, the American Gay Boy and Lesbian must certainly view themselves, at least subconsciously, as second-class citizens, whose birthright to happiness in love and marriage has been denied them through no fault of their own.

We are therefore a people who walk in darkness. We must create our own happiness in and of ourselves. It has not been prepared for us, we cannot seek it out among the classics. And among the great modern creations, we still look in vain for the happy ending.

At this point—if not long before—the heterosexual will insist: "How can you expect to see lasting love, marriage, the happy ending, in books and plays and music when these things don't exist for you in life?" We might counter in anger with, "For the most part, we did not make life as it is for us or the laws as they exist against us" but, more supplicatingly, we would add: "We do not expect triumphs in law and complete acceptance from society to come merely from happy endings in novels and on the stage. There is no sure cause-effect relationship between life and art. And we admit that writers might find difficulty devising paradisial homosexual plots, though we do have happiness to be written about by those bold enough to want to do so. If our ultimate life goals have not yet been achieved, is this to prevent writers from fantasizing them? Haven't there always been artists who dreamed, who romanticized, who envisioned a better life—only to have some of those dreams come true?"

The American heterosexual, later than his European counterpart, has finally begun—at least in major cities, where the fear of the unknown or un-understood is not so great—to laugh at and in other ways accept, even as friends, the average homosexual and his lover. But as long as "And they lived happily ever after" cannot be tolerated for two amorous homosexuals in any of the better novels, plays, films, operas, art, in song or on television, perhaps many gay love affairs will end in murderous violence, the desperation of suicide, trans-sexualism or transvestism, free-for-all orgies, or endless sexual searchings along Central Park West. To those who would call such alternatives immoral, we say: Give us the rewards for morality, and we will be moral!

In sum, there seems today to be no homosexual happy ending in art or in life. Except in our own, frequently trashy novels, which most of us *do not believe.* Perhaps when we can see ourselves the victors in some Broadway play or snugly triumphant in some major-publishing-house romance—goals the American Negro has now achieved—we will have already found similar happiness in life: Laws may by then have been passed to protect us and grant us privileges, and society may have learned not to fear us because we are different. But, indeed, MUST the happy ending in life precede the one in art?

Ronald Forsythe is a pseudonym.

* * *

December 10, 1972

HOMOSEXUAL LITERATURE

By MARTIN DUBERMAN

Emerson once remarked that "people would stare to know on what slight single observations those laws were inferred which wise men promulgate and which society receives later and writes down as canons." After months of reading the "scientific" and "movement" literature on homosexuality, I'm convinced that no one is in possession of sufficient knowledge at this point in time (though almost no one concedes this) to warrant the confident generalizations heard on all sides—and especially on the scientific side. I write as one who has not only read the literature, but lived the life.

The deepest morass is found in discussions of the "causes" of homosexuality. Much of the scientific literature concentrates on this question, though homosexuals, sensibly, are learning to eschew it as presently unanswerable, as a political tactic designed to perpetuate barbaric legal and social discriminations, and as a convenient intellectual outlet for heterosexual condescension. It's currently possible to cite expert opinion "proving" that sexual orientation results from prenatal hormonal programming, the psychodynamics of the family structure, or an innate bisexual potential variably activated or repressed according to individual experience (such as confinement in prison) and social climate (in our country, sex-negative and homo-phobic).

The Columbia psychiatrist, Robert Liebert, in a fine article, "The Gay Student: A Psychopolitical View" (Change, Oct., 1971), points out that "to discover psychodynamics . . . is not to be confused with discovering psychopathology." Even if the experts could agree on the causes of homosexuality, they would not have thereby demonstrated that it is a "sickness." The medical criteria employed to establish the presence of "disease" relate to measurable physio-chemical phenomena. Not only has such pathology not been adduced for homosexuality, but the behavioral traits often employed

as substitute proofs of illness—self-contempt, protective clowning, guilt, dependence and passivity—have been drawn primarily from clinical sources, from homosexuals who present themselves for "treatment." These traits—as the sociologist Evelyn Hooker's "Final Report of the Task Force on Homosexuality" for the National Institute of Mental Health and the psychiatrist George Weinberg's "Society and the Healthy Homosexual" (St. Martin's, $5.95) reveal—are far less characteristic of homosexuals not in treatment, and in any case, reflect a pattern of "victim" symptomatology regularly found among all oppressed minority groups.

Most scientists bring to their research a culturally derived model of "normal" behavior that influences the nature of their findings. The model, basic to the Judeo-Christian heritage, assumes that human development, psycho-sexual as well as physical, follows ascertainable curves: certain instinctive biologic forces propel all individuals through similar "stages" which (unless "destructive" environmental forces intervene) culminate in the "healthy" end product of genital and monogamous heterosexuality.

The model is a moral, not a scientific construct—as even a cursory glance at cross-cultural data reveals. Clellan S. Ford and Frank A. Beach in "Patterns of Sexual Behavior" (Harper & Row, cloth, $6.50; paper, 95 cents) and Wainwright Churchill in "Homosexual Behavior Among Males" (Hawthorne, cloth, $8.95; Prentice Hall-Spectrum, paper, $2.45) may, as some anthropologists argue, have exaggerated the extent of homosexuality and the degree of its social acceptance in other cultures. Perhaps so, but the Judeo-Christian model of "normal" sexuality can hardly accommodate the evidence that Arab women in certain Red Sea areas take black female lovers, that among the Keraki anal intercourse is thought essential to the health and character of the growing boy, and that prominent Siwan men in Africa lend their sons to each other for purposes of sodomy.

Kinsey is reported to have said "the only kind of abnormal sex acts are those which are impossible to perform." Distinctions need to be made between sexual "acts" and sexual "identity," but, like Kinsey, the psychiatrist Ernest van den Haag has argued in Henrik M. Ruitenbeek's fine anthology of recent scientific work, "The Problem of Homosexuality in Modern Society" (Dutton, paper, $2.25), that homosexuality is "as natural as heterosexuality and not less, even if less frequent; nor would homosexual acts be 'unnatural' if confined to the human species (which they are not). Religion and art are, and the wearing of shirts . . . Moral distinctions are not made by (or in) nature, but about it—they are parts of culture, and must be justified within it."

Yet as Thomas S. Szasz has written in Joseph A. McCaffrey's useful collection of essays, "The Homosexual Dialectic" (Prentice-Hall, cloth, $6.95; paper, $2.95), "the characteristic tendency of modern psychiatry is to brand as sick that which is merely unconventional." The tendency is endemic to the culture, not merely the psychiatric profession. Differences of all kinds have come to be equated in our society with "deficiences," and deficiences—for we are rigorously rational and ameliorative—must be "explained" and "cured." Sexual deviations have come in for far more scrutiny than have deviations from other behavioral norms—like not wanting to own an automobile.

Arno Karlen's indispensable book "Sexuality and Homosexuality" (Norton, $15) traces, with almost comic result, the missionary zeal with which the causes and cures of homosexuality have been pursued through time. It has been variously ascribed to possession by devils, to self-abuse and to neurological or glandular disorders; and its "cures" have ranged from being burned alive, to chastity, to "transference," to electric shock. If the causes of shifting social reactions to sexual deviation had been studied with anything like the fervor invested in searching for the causes of deviation itself, we may have had relief long before now from punitive laws and moralistic vocabularies.

The gay liberation movement that has surfaced in the past three years is understandably angry at this history of oppression. The Gay Activists Alliance has recently issued a sophisticated pamphlet entitled "Twenty Questions About Homosexuality" (G.A.A., P.O. Box 2, Village Station, N.Y.C.; 75 cents) that deals with the most common myths necessary to the perpetuation of that oppression. But its chief author, Ronald Gold, stresses, with fine indignation, that "the questions themselves offend and oppress us, for they are not asked of other groups in our society, and they have little or nothing to do with our lives." When, indeed, did one last hear a debate on whether heterosexuality, *by its nature,* involved promiscuity and child-molestation, or whether heterosexuals are easy to identify by appearance and behavior, or whether, through proper treatment, they can be "converted"?

Not that all the literature is angry. The dominant quality of John Murphy's "Homosexual Liberation" (Praeger, $5.95) is gentle inoffensiveness—though the personal odyssey he describes and the views he expresses could more appropriately be the stuff of passion. I would guess that the polite elements in gay liberation will discover, as did so many blacks in the early phases of their struggle, that courtesy and earnestness succeed neither in maximizing outside support nor in accommodating internal rage.

Where Murphy's book is gentle, Lige Clarke and Jack Nichols's "I Have More Fun With You Than Anyone" (St. Martin's, $5.95) is merely nonchalant, even in its self-congratulation. Their "heterosexual inclinations petered out," Clarke and Nichols tell us, because their "aesthetic sense had been insulted. . . . Could we get excited about a gender which seems to prefer a security provided by morons to their own autonomy?" The sexism of the comment is perhaps less obvious than its smugness—and lends some credence to the argument of psychiatrist Irving Bieber ("A Psychoanalytical Study of Male Homosexuality," Basic, $8.50) that fear of women is both a cause and a symptom of male homosexuality.

Peter Fisher's "The Gay Mystique" (Stein & Day, $7.95) is marked much less by anger, inoffensiveness or self-congratulation than by sheer exuberance. He deals with psychoanalytical theories of homosexuality with charming—and lucid—insouciance: "Why is the 'active' role in anal intercourse an indication of 'phallic fixation' while the 'active' role in vaginal intercourse is a sign of 'genital maturity'? Why is it 'oral fixation' if a man [performs fellatio with] a man, but a 'harmless regression' if a woman does so?" And "just where is the homosexual who also enjoys heterosexual intercourse fixated?" Fisher argues that the individual with the narrowest range of sexual experience is the one most "fixated"—which puts at the top of the list "the heterosexual who never strays beyond genital intercourse."

In offering "exclusivity" as a new norm against which sexual "abnormality" might be measured, Fisher's book represents the radical challenge to traditional sex roles more characteristic of the gay liberation movement in its first two years (1969-70) than currently. Before the famed "Stonewall Riot" in 1969 (in which a New York City police attempt to raid a gay bar was met with resistance for the first time), the homophile movement in this country and its chief organizations, The Mattachine Society and The Daughters of Bilitis, were small and discreet. The new movement inaugurated by the Riot, was initially typified by The Gay Liberation Front, an organization stressing fluidity and spontaneity, anti-authoritarianism and decentralization. It stressed, too, that sexual liberation, gay and otherwise, had to be fought for in conjunction with a variety of social reforms. This meant alliance with the radical representatives of other oppressed minorities (like the Panthers), and (as the first editorial in Come Out!, the newspaper published by a G.L.F. collective) argued, the rejection in general of a "bourgeois" life style.

In calling for basic inquiries into sex, love and gender, G.L.F. seemed to embody Herbert Marcuse's prophetic suggestion in "Eros and Civilization" (1955; Beacon, cloth, $8.95; Random House-Vintage, paper, $1.65) that homosexuals, because of their explicit "rebellion against the subjugation of sexuality under the order of procreation" and their implicit rejection of genital tyranny, might provide a social critique of immeasurable significance.

No such expectation seems justified by recent developments. Today, G.L.F. no longer exists as an organization—though many of its impulses do survive in scattered consciousness-raising groups and small collectives. The history of its disintegration and the gradual secession of those who believed in more orderly procedures and more single-minded concentration on gay rights, can be followed in a number of recent books. The best is Arthur Bell's witty, vulnerable "Dancing the Gay Lib Blues" (Simon & Schuster, $5.95), but valuable additional information is in Donn Teal's "The Gay Militants" (Stein & Day, $7.95), Jack Onge's "The Gay Liberation Movement" (Alliance Press, paper, $1.50) and the collection of interviews with activist leaders gathered by Kay Tobin and Randy Wicker in "The Gay Crusaders" (Paperback Library, $1.25). The two best sources on the somewhat different emphases of the lesbian movement and life style are Sidney Abbott and Barbara Love, "Sappho Was a Right-On Woman" (Stein & Day, $7.95) and Phyllis Lyon and Del Martin, "Lesbian/Woman" (Bantam, paper, $1.50).

In the New York area, the most influential homophile organization is now The Gay Activists Alliance, a structured, Roberts-Rules group that considers political ideology divisive—and therefore irrelevant—and is, in the words of its constitution, "completely and solely dedicated" to effecting changes in the present, to "implementing and maintaining" gay rights. Just as portions of Peter Fisher's "The Gay Mystique"—those calling for a wider range of sexual expressiveness—represent the early iconoclasm of G.L.F., so the absence in the book of social analysis reflects the current ideological neutrality of G.A.A.

The one book to appear on gay liberation thus far that tries to grasp all its strands is Dennis Altman's "Homosexual" (Outerbridge & Lazard, cloth, $6.95; Avon, paper, $1.65, to appear next month). His is the only work that bears comparison, in terms of sustained analysis and theoretical complexity, with the best to appear from Women's Liberation (from Shulamith Firestone, Kate Millett, Alice Rossi, Naomi Weisstein, Robin Morgan, Roxanne Dunbar and Anne Koedt). The gay movement in its new incarnation is, to be sure, barely three years old, and fertile if fragmentary material is beginning to emerge elsewhere—in Kenneth Pitchford and Steve Dansky's essays in The Double-F Journal (Templar Press, P.O. Box 98, F.D.R. Station, N.Y.C.; 50 cents), organ of the Revolutionary Effeminism Movement, and Arthur Evans's unpublished manuscript, "The Oppression of Homosexuals."

To date, though, Altman's book is easily the outstanding work, its tone as impressive as its contents. Recognizing that current divisions within the movement may well represent healthy diversity (and in any case serve expressive if not instrumental ends), Altman tries to understand each position and to abstain from accusations. Though G.A.A. may seem "middle-class," "reformist," even "sexist" to those in the radical wing of the movement, it is doing essential work in civil rights and consciousness-raising, and while Revolutionary Effeminism may seem "adventurist," violence-prone and opaque to members of G.A.A., it is formulating basic questions on gender. In his nonjudgmental discussion of the various groupings in gay liberation, Altman comes close to approximating that ideal spirit of "fraternal criticism"—the loving, supportive discussion of differences between people of roughly similar persuasions—that up to now has been more a part of the rhetoric than the practice of the Left.

Nor does Altman's generosity of spirit come at the expense of intellectual rigor. He manages to combine the two chief approaches—autobiographical and analytical—that have thus far characterized the literature of homosexuality, without succumbing to the occasional exhibitionism of the former or the frequent over-statements of the latter. Indeed he surpasses the best thus far available in either genre. His personal testimony is as moving as Merle Miller's "On Being Different" (Random, cloth, $4.50; Popular Library, paper, 95 cents) but not as sentimental. And although Altman's command of the research literature is as firm as that of any social scientist, unlike most of them, he openly acknowledges the gaps in the evidence (and we have more gaps than fill), resisting the familiar impulse to raise speculation to the dignity of fact, repudiating the notion that one can "command" quicksilver.

He repudiates, too, the easy assertions sometimes found in gay liberation circles (indeed, throughout the counter-culture) that promiscuity and the ability to appreciate varieties of human eroticism are the equivalents of liberation. In doing so Altman perhaps shies too far away from the possibility that selective promiscuity and cycles of erotic variety may be necessary concomitants of any relationship free of possessiveness. At any rate, the touch of primness in his book seems a by-product of his refusal to celebrate, in Dr. Pangloss fashion, the imminent arrival of the best of all possible worlds, one in which "no special or different feelings," (to quote Fisher) exist between homosexuals and heterosexuals.

Altman knows that centuries of oppression have left identifying marks, that many homosexuals bear deep hostility to straight people and that in ways we may not yet even understand, we homosexuals have certain unique testimony to give on the human condition. Since basic inquiries, moreover, originate on the margin not from the center, we should be cautious—for society's sake as well as our own—in announcing that our lives are identical with everyone else's. As other oppressed minorities have learned, it may not be possible, at least at this moment in time, both to proclaim that we are "just folks" and to develop our outsider's special insights into socio-sexual norms.

In place of easy celebration, Dennis Altman's book presents the gay liberation movement with a set of difficult, even stern challenges. He asks homosexuals to remember that if Freud's belief in the inherent bisexuality of human beings is correct (and like all assumptions about sexuality, that one, too, is subject to revision, as the writings of Sandor Rado and Leon Salzman—unmentioned by Altman yet readily available in Judd Marmor's provocative collection, "Sexual Inversion" [Basic, $8.95]—already suggest), then homosexuals must add to the slogan "everyone is gay," the concession that "everyone is also straight"—and in addition, attempt to realize that fact in their own lives. Only thus, Altman argues, can homosexuals fulfill what may be their historic function: to undermine our culture's damaging insistence on sexual exclusivity.

Altman also challenges the sexual liberation movements to remember that there are basic racial and class inequalities in American life, and that if gay (or black or female) separatism now seems an essential stage in consciousness-building, it is not in itself the optimal goal, that eventually—and the difficulties here can hardly be over-estimated—a coalition of the oppressed must be forged.

Finally, Altman challenges gay liberation to resist the temptation (spawned by the desire for quick self-confirmation) to replace an older set of myths about sexuality with a new set. He warns that "to generalize is to lose the texture of reality"—a warning hardly applicable to homosexuals alone. Kinsey sounded the same note two decades ago when he pointed out that "nature rarely deals with discrete categories." It is human beings who invent those, forcing a variety of experience into neat classifications—thereby eliminating its enigmas.

Sixty years ago, Andre Gide wrote, "How strange! One has the courage of one's opinions, but not of one's habits." Now that we are learning the courage of our habits, perhaps we might find, too, the strength to question our opinions.

Martin Duberman's most recent book is "Black Mountain: An Exploration in Community." He is Distinguished Service Professor of History at Lehman College, C.U.N.Y.

* * *

November 4, 1990

THE BOYS IN BERLIN: AUDEN'S SECRET POEMS

By KATHERINE BUCKNELL

W. H. Auden was 21 years old when he went to live in Berlin in the autumn of 1928. He had recently graduated from Oxford and he was engaged to be married. Despite his notoriety as an undergraduate poet, the Oxford years had been something of a failure for Auden. He had taken a disappointing third-class degree in English, his first collection of poems had been rejected by T. S. Eliot at Faber & Faber and his love for several undergraduate men had gone largely unrequited. He had attempted to develop heterosexual traits and to improve his inferiority complex through psychoanalysis, but neither this nor a year of self-imposed celibacy brought much satisfaction.

In Berlin, everything was to change; he abandoned self-denial for self-indulgence. He soon wrote to friends about the police-controlled male brothels and the boys available for money in the bars and streets. For a time he believed that gratifying his homosexual desires would enable him to outgrow them, but after nearly 10 months in Berlin, during which he traveled some in Germany and returned twice briefly to England, his new freedom had produced moments of happiness but no permanent transformation. A journal he kept in 1929 shows that, instead, continual self-examination was bringing him to a clearer understanding of his sexual nature. At the end of July 1929 he returned to England and broke off his engagement. Eventually, in 1930, he took up a teaching post at Larchfield Academy, a boys' school in Helensburgh, Scotland.

Auden occasionally returned to Berlin, partly to see his life-long friend Christopher Isherwood, now settled there, and partly for the boys. His first visit, during his summer holiday from Larchfield in July 1930, was such a success that he felt miserable returning home. He missed the Berlin life, the Cosy Corner (a gay bar he and Isherwood frequented), and probably a boy called Willi with whom he had apparently begun a new affair. Already he was planning another visit at Christmas time. And it was almost certainly after this July visit that Auden wrote, during August and September, six love poems in German.

The poems are inspired by the kind of love affairs Auden had in Berlin and the kind of boy he now longed for. He had rejected promiscuity, yet guilt about his homosexuality continually drove him in search of new lovers. He noted in his 1929 journal that he liked to suffer and that he regarded suf-

fering as part of his identity as an artist. He also observed in the journal that the torment of his homosexuality was, for him, one of its attractions; he associated mutual love with despair. The German poems, freighted with the themes of faithlessness, transience and loneliness, reflect his characteristic relish for unrequited longing. One poem looks forward with joyful appetite to the lover's return to his boy, but otherwise the tone is melancholy, unillusioned, even cynical. Everyone is for sale; love is selfish, sometimes brutish, always short. The poems play on the language of commercial transactions, work and travel, very much in the style of Shakespeare's sonnets, and several of them hint at love triangles, a situation Auden elsewhere also associated with the sonnets.

Auden may have been cheering himself up by exercising his virtuosity in a new language, and perhaps even by measuring his talent against that of T. S. Eliot, who had written some early poems in French. Auden's spoken German was never accurate, though his comprehension eventually came to be perfect. According to David Constantine, who has translated the poems, their awkward syntax and occasionally painful grammar are not the result of stylistic choice but of linguistic backwardness. Still, after he had spent less than a year altogether in Berlin, Auden's feeling for the dialect and the sexy slang of the gay bars is impressive; Mr. Constantine suggests that his use of the vernacular may have been influenced by Bertolt Brecht, with whose work he was already a little familiar. "Poems"—Auden's first commercially published book, which appeared in September 1930, roughly while he was writing the German poems—was widely criticized for its obscurity, but the German poems are remarkably direct, perhaps because Auden never meant them to be published. Also, working in a foreign language, with its offer of both challenge and disguise, apparently freed him to speak more openly on the difficult and, for him, perennial theme of love.

Auden had some continuing interest in the poems; in 1936 he turned about half a dozen individual lines into English for the poems "Night covers up the rigid land" and "Journey to Iceland" and for "The Ascent of F6," a play he wrote with Isherwood. The poems may have been brought back to his attention by Isherwood when Auden joined him in Portugal that March to work on "F6," and it is certainly thanks to Isherwood that they have survived. Since the mid-1920's, Auden had been sending his work to Isherwood for comments and advice, and Isherwood preserved it all with his own letters and papers, which are now in private hands in Santa Monica, Calif.

The six German poems, along with English translations and commentary by David Constantine, are to be published for the first time early next year, together with letters, critical essays and bibliographical materials, in "W. H. Auden: 'The Map of All My Youth.' Early Works, Friends and Influences," edited by Katherine Bucknell and Nicholas Jenkins (Oxford University Press).

The following selection from the poems, in Mr. Constantine's English translation, concludes with the original German version of the final one, "It's raining on me in the Scottish lands."

I'm in an idle brute stupidity
For in your absence what is there to do?
I cannot learn unless you tutor me
And all my business dealings are with you.

I've never had to earn a living wage.
Others kept me. I was on my own.
But if you have employment I'll engage
To be your menial without a moan.

Have fun then with the rich and clever crowd.
Give me the heavy work. I'll hump your stuff,
I'll wash and clean for you. If I'm allowed
To do your bidding that will be enough.

For when you look at me you make me feel
I own the Ruhr with all its coal and steel.

I know you've gone. You left me vegetating.
The vacant season bores me worse and worse.
The yokels here are busy copulating.
Our local hero's travelling (in a hearse).

But what your body's doing now I don't know
Nor why the hours are slowing down today
Nor when tonight my dream of you should go
To meet your dream of me somewhere halfway.

Don't be afraid: time won't abandon you
And doubtful things will pass beyond a doubt.
Your narrow bed is wide enough for two.
We'll have the kisses we have done without.

And I shall know that you are with me then
And not know when you'll go away again.
So we can sit and stand around a bit.
I'll drink my coffee and you drink your wine.

Then say goodbye. Let's make the most of it:
An hour of yours that's still an hour of mine.

For every love has its contingency
And puts itself first. Loves of all kinds do.
I've got no money so you'll not want me.
You love your life and what I love is you.

They're waiting for you in the posh places.
Hurry along now or you'll miss your chance.
They are the loaded men, they feed their faces.
My dream of you is an irrelevance.

And if I'm sad that makes you laugh, I know.
But never mind: I'm not your business now.
The time we might have called it love has gone.
You've had as much of love as you can stand.

We use a boy who hasn't any friend
But comes and goes when someone takes him on.

The gifts and names he bears are not his own.
He goes between, and we get more remote
And though he kisses us we keep him out
And we are not together and not alone.

We have no love to give. It's time he went.
There's nothing for us now in his misery.
The kisses we give are a formality.
The names we speak are not the ones we meant.

We cannot be together unless we know
We are alone with nowhere else to go.

It's raining on me in the Scottish lands.
I'm in a place where you have never been.
There's arty conversation at weekends.
I'm home again. I'm not still in Berlin.

But things like this, they always end the same.
We've said "Auf Wiedersehen" for good, I know.
It can't be helped and you are not to blame.
Don't lose your beauty sleep. I wonder though

On Sundays when you all meet up to catch
Some little local train and you're about
To climb aboard, whether you'll turn and watch
The big transcontinentals pulling out.

But then: go with the gent who's kissing you.
I haven't paid. Do what you have to do.

Es regnet auf mir in den Schottische Lande
Wo ich mit Dir noch nie gewesen bin
Man redet hier von Kunst am Wochenende
Bin jezt zu Hause, nicht mehr in Berlin

So kommt es immer vor in diesen Sachen
Wir sehen uns nie wieder, hab' dein Ruh:
Du hast kein Schuld und es ist nichts zu machen
Sieh' immer besser aus, und nur wenn Du

Am Bahnhof mit Bekannten triffst, O dann
Als Sonntagsbummelzuge fertig stehen
Und Du einsteigen willst, kuk einmal an
Den Eisenbahnen die dazwischen gehen.

Sonst, wenn ein olle Herr hat Dich gekusst
Geh mit; ich habe nichts bezalt; Du must.

Katherine Bucknell is editing a volume of the juvenilia of W. H.
Auden.

*   *   *

September 20, 1998

FROM THE CLOSET OF HISTORY

By WARREN GOLDSTEIN

THE OTHER SIDE OF SILENCE: Men's Lives and Gay Identities: A Twentieth-Century History
By John Loughery
Illustrated. 507 pp. New York: A John Macrae Book/Henry Holt & Company. $35.

For many otherwise well-meaning Americans, homosexuality and its attendant controversies—gay marriage, military service, AIDS policy, sex education curriculums—make us think or talk about things we would rather treat with benign neglect. Even though most straight Americans oppose overt discrimination against homosexuals, 7 in 10 think sex between members of the same sex is wrong. A majority viscerally opposes teaching tolerance for a "homosexual life style" and seems happiest with a "don't ask, don't tell" approach to the entire subject.

"The Other Side of Silence," John Loughery's provocative history of gay male life in the United States from 1919 to the early 1990's, will have none of it. His title (from the name of a short-lived gay theater workshop in the 1970's) refers both to the millions of gay lives that have been lived according to a kind of omerta, as well as to those who refused to follow the code and thereby risked their livelihoods and, as in the case of Supervisor Harvey Milk of San Francisco, their lives. But the other side of silence (or discretion) is also speech. By using blunt, nonacademic Anglo-Saxonisms, Loughery, the art critic of The Hudson Review, insures that readers cannot pretend not to know exactly which sexual acts were being practiced, forbidden or celebrated.

The broad outlines of Loughery's story are becoming familiar to historians, if not to the general public. But Loughery goes farther. In "The Other Side of Silence" he combines original archival research, mastery of the secondary historical literature, more than 300 of his own interviews and a broad and deep knowledge of 20th-century American letters, theater and film into a narrative that is completely accessible to nonspecialists.

Despite our tendency to think of Victorian sexuality as repressed, dominated by the rigidly separated "spheres" apportioned to men and women, that very segregation encouraged a good bit of same-sex physical intimacy. How much of this activity was what our cruder age regards as the "real thing"— genital stimulation—remains less clear, though with so much smoke in the sources, the odds favor the existence of a substantial amount of fire.

Neither the terms nor the concepts "homosexual" and "heterosexual" even existed until the late 19th century, when a newly powerful medical profession began defining homoerotic behavior as "perversion" or mental illness. Still, the conceptual distinction between homosexual and heterosexual had considerably more force in the minds of clinicians than in the sexual practices of men, even the men who worked for vice squads.

In his opening chapter, for instance, Loughery recounts the juicy story of the 1919 sex scandal at the naval training station at Newport, R.I., in which the Navy ran a sting operation to entrap sailors and their civilian friends (known among themselves as the "Ladies of Newport") in homosexual conduct. The most striking part of the investigation, to modern eyes—and eventually to an embarrassed Department of the Navy—was the enthusiasm with which the presumably "normal" young detectives threw themselves into their work, enjoying (under often explicit orders) a "fairly staggering amount of oral sex," Loughery writes, and admitting, in at least two cases, to "having had anal sex to orgasm." But as long as they were on the receiving end of oral attentions, and on the giving end of anal intercourse, no one considered them "fairies." What was common knowledge within gay communities—that otherwise heterosexual men, known as "trade," could and did enjoy sex with other men—has been more or less suppressed in straight life.

The 1920's saw more cultural interest in sexuality, and if that decade's classic pantheon of writers (Hemingway, Faulkner, Fitzgerald, Dos Passos, Dorothy Parker) seemed to have all but ignored homosexuality, late-20's and early-30's vaudeville, theater and even movies experienced what Loughery calls a "pansy craze," an "implicit means of acknowledging, exploring and yet containing the specter of homosexuality." By the late 30's, however, in the grip of a national "sex crimes panic," otherwise respectable newspapers ran lurid tales of murder, abduction and molestation on their front pages, frequently implying that sexual "degeneracy"— code for homosexuality—was fueling this apparent rampage. The pansy had become a "public menace."

World War II had an immense if contradictory impact on gay life. On the one hand, an estimated 9,000 servicemen and women were discharged "on the basis of their sexual orientation," many of them entrapped and humiliated by "periodic witch hunts." At the same time, thousands of gay men and lesbians discovered one another—and the fact that they were not alone—in the military. They also learned that whatever society's prejudices about "queers" and "fairies," their "capacity to survive and function—and, for some, to excel—was in no way impaired by their sexual life." These lessons of gay men's wartime experience resembled those of black Americans, who also felt, following the war, that "the genie was not going to be forced back into the bottle."

The difference was that the postwar years witnessed the rise of a civil rights movement that transformed the country, while the witch-hunting fervor of the 1950's also attacked homosexuals in a less well-known (if in certain respects more effective) crusade than that carried out against the political left. A 1950 investigation by the Senate Appropriations Committee, known as the "pervert inquiry," netted about 200 homosexuals in Government agencies, while dismissals for sexual causes rose dramatically among Federal workers and military personnel.

Lincoln Center for the Performing Arts Library/From The Other Side of Silence

The 1933 play "The Green Bay Tree" depicted a fantasy of homosexual affluence and power; from left, Laurence Olivier, Leo G. Carroll, James Dale.

There were stirrings of dissent and protest, however, and Loughery carefully and empathetically charts the beginning of the Mattachine Society and periodicals like One magazine in the early 50's. Most of the second half of the book is an account of the growth, splintering, trials, successes and failures of the struggles on behalf of gay rights over the past 40 years.

"The Other Side of Silence" is exceptionally rich history by almost any standard. Loughery appears to have read every novel or play and seen every film in the past 75 years having anything to do with homosexuality. He consistently connects changes in gay life to larger developments in American society. And whether he is describing the Stonewall uprising, the intricacies of gay liberation political strategy, the antigay brutality of police officers in San Francisco (yes, San Francisco) or the sexual joy of the gay bathhouse scene of the 1970's, Loughery writes uncluttered, calm, controlled, exceptionally intelligent prose—no mean feat these days in a field whose scholarly literature is increasingly prone to post-modernist jargon.

While Loughery has favorites among gay activists (he admires Act Up, for example, and in two marvelous pages sums up the achievements and costs of the group's high-pressure confrontations), he treats nearly all his gay subjects with candor and empathy. Writing about issues and controversies that have called forth some of the most vitriolic rhetoric in modern politics, Loughery manages to be unfailingly, almost astonishingly, sensible. Pointedly noting the whiteness of most gay organizations in the last 30 years, for example, he also observes, quite reasonably, that there has been no reason for gay men to be any less racist than the rest of American society. And in a couple of pages Loughery deftly undoes the late-70's effort in which many gay men engaged in a "display of groundless self-congratulation" to portray themselves as wealthier and more educated

than the general population and therefore in need of no legal protection.

By giving voice to those who have been too often silenced in the past, by engaging them in a serious dialogue, by placing their words and their lives in front of modern readers, Loughery has rescued their experience from (in E. P. Thompson's memorable phrase) the enormous condescension of posterity. This extraordinary book will shame anyone who still wishes that gay issues would just go away. Loughery has added a powerful voice to the chorus making sure that speech triumphs over silence.

Warren Goldstein teaches history at the University of Hartford. He is completing a biography of William Sloane Coffin Jr.

* * *

April 18, 1999

AND SO TO BED

By CALEB CRAIN

GAY LIVES: Homosexual Autobiography From John Addington Symonds to Paul Monette
By Paul Robinson
Illustrated. 428 pp. Chicago: The University of Chicago Press. $30.

We need an antonym for "hagiography," a word for life stories worth reading only for their heroes' precocious and salutary defiance of convention. "Pornography" won't do, because it would arouse undue interest.

For homosexuals, the term is probably "case histories." In 1897, in their treatise "Sexual Inversion," the sexologist Havelock Ellis and the literary critic John Addington Symonds published one of the first collections of them. Like the lives of saints, the lives of these sinners were briefly told. After a few spare identifiers, personal ad-style ("Physician, unmarried, English, aged 60"), the story turned to sex: acts, fantasies, roles and opinions. If now and then a nonsexual detail slipped in ("He smokes freely; cannot whistle"), it served only to accentuate the facelessness of the genre. In Paul Robinson's new study of a century of homosexual autobiographies, "Gay Lives," these stories cast a long shadow. As Robinson notes, reading them helped men as diverse as the French Catholic novelist Julien Green and the American editorial clerk Jeb Alexander to recognize their sexual nature. As if to tip his hat to the master of the form, the first gay life Robinson retells is Symonds's. And he follows Symonds's case history formula in the retelling: Robinson wants to know what his subjects "did in bed, what they wanted to do, what they didn't want to do."

Symonds, however, already has a case history, as "XVIII—Englishman, independent means, aged 49," in "Sexual Inversion." His "Memoirs" were meant to tell something other than the raw facts. Robinson declares that he has selected autobiographies with "rich subjectivity" and "literary texture." But his verdicts are plain and prosy: Symonds "deserves credit for fashioning an erotic modus vivendi under unfavorable historical conditions and against great psychic odds." If all you want to make is liquor, potatoes are cheaper than chardonnay grapes.

Robinson concedes he is a historian, not a literary critic. Autobiography is nonetheless an art. Until very recently, it was an art forced on gay men, who nearly always had to fictionalize their lives. One of Symonds and Ellis's cases told his interviewer that "his chief regret in connection with his homosexual instinct is that he is obliged to lead a double life." The best gay writers have not regretted doubleness but taken it as a literary challenge. "The great problem of autobiography," Stephen Spender wrote, "is to create the true tension between these inner and outer, subjective and objective worlds."

In Spender's own "World Within World," doubleness verged on duplicity. He's probably the only figure in "Gay Lives" who would have responded to Robinson's sexual curiosity with outrage, which makes him the only one who deserves the treatment. In 1993, he famously charged that David Leavitt had recycled his life story into the sexually explicit novel "While England Sleeps." "Knowledge of what people do when they are in bed together may be true," Spender complained, "but it is not true to what we know or wish to know about them."

Robinson accurately tags Spender's philosophizing in "World Within World" as "sub-Sartrean existential blather," calling Leavitt's reimagining "a much-needed corrective" to Spender's "radical desexing" of his affairs. But with autobiographers who rise beyond the level of misrepresentation, he appears out of his depth. Quentin Crisp is heir to the Wildean art of lying, which causes Robinson to worry that he might not be telling the truth. When Crisp writes that it was "some years before I was bold enough to decline an invitation to 'Hamlet' on the grounds that I already knew who won," Robinson reels with disorientation. "Did he really decline?" he wonders. "Did he actually produce the zinger?" And who did win "Hamlet," anyway? "This is the language of self-caricature," we are instructed.

Robinson, the author of "The Modernization of Sex" and "Opera and Ideas," is awfully earnest. Where he finds unhappiness, he needs to diagnose it. His most frequent verdict is guilt by internalized homophobia, aggravated in the French case by abstraction, in the English case by fetishism of the working class and in the American case by insistence on a clear conscience. Robinson writes tickets for other offenses, too. A number of the men he profiles admit to having bought sex. "I have always held the view that the union of two hearts whose incomes are equal is a complete waste of time," writes Crisp, who sold it. Robinson disapproves. He also disapproves of Christopher Isherwood's unrepentant "ageism," Andrew Tobias's "vulgar commercialism" and J. R. Ackerley's exclusive taste for straight-acting guardsmen who didn't smell. Robinson suspects even Genet of harboring an embarrassment about his effeminacy. It is frustrating to find fear, hatred or selfishness where honesty has nearly made a hero, but as Leo Bersani once put it, "Gide's homophobia is regrettable, but the politically correct response to it—as well as to the offensive misogyny in 'Corydon'—is probably the least interesting."

Robinson deserves credit for drawing our attention to some works of real beauty. Like all of Ackerley, "My Father and Myself" is ingenious, sad, hilarious and hard to find. Robinson's extraction of just the naughty bits does not quite do Ackerley justice. "Artistically shocks should never be bunched," Ackerley asserted to justify his antichronological structure; Robinson's narrow focus rebunches them mercilessly. But he does recognize the book as "perhaps the most compellingly readable of homosexual memoirs." And he shows true insight into the unfolding Chinese box of selves in Isherwood's "Lions and Shadows," unfortunately out of print, and is able to explain why these disguises are at once more deceitful and less dishonest than Spender's.

When he reaches his American contemporaries, however, Robinson's sympathies and antipathies cloud his literary insight. Here as elsewhere, a dose of Wilde might help the literal-minded Robinson, who keeps suggesting how his subjects might have made themselves more contented, more ethical or more truthful. According to Wilde, Hamlet claims that art holds the mirror up to nature only "to convince the bystanders of his absolute insanity in all art-matters." But in fact, Wilde corrected, "life imitates art." Robinson's mistake is to put the horse before the cart. He thinks that living a happy gay life matters more than writing a good gay autobiography.

Caleb Crain is at work on a book about early American friendships.

* * *

FILM

February 3, 1965

REGENTS URGE HIGH COURT TO DECLARE FILM OBSCENE

ALBANY, Feb. 2 (AP)—The State Board of Regents asked the Court of Appeals today to declare the French-made motion picture "Twilight Girls" obscene, and ban its showing in the state.

The court reserved decision on the appeal after hearing an attorney for the film's distributor contend it was not obscene.

The film was distributed abroad under the title "Les Collegiennes."

The Board of Regents appealed a decision by the Appellate Division, Third Department, that the movie did "not constitute an appeal to prurient interest" and could be shown.

The regents have refused to license the film unless scenes of nudity and female homosexuality are deleted.

*   *   *

April 8, 1973

LET THE BOYS IN THE BAND DIE

By ARTHUR BELL

Black used to be Hattie McDaniel with a feather duster and Stepin Fetchit polishing the rump of a racehorse and Bill "Bojangles" Robinson in spic and span livery tapping up and down the mastah's staircase with little colonel Shirley. Gay used to be Franklin Pangborn as a prissy florist and Eric Blore as a primping butler and Erik Rhodes as a flouncy dress designer whom Ginger Rogers spurned for Fred Astaire in "The Gay Divorcee."

The Hattie McDaniel stereotype went with the 30's, and with the 50's came the black revolution and the evolution of a new consciousness. Hollywood became careful. No longer a shuffle or a yowsah for an easy laugh. Black servitude died and the silver screen gave birth to social films which instilled a sense of black identity in the 60's, which in turn begat the current cycle of blaxploitation films starring Richard Roundtree and Jim Brown as the foremost cats giving the orders.

But gay is something else. Our revolution came late, in 1969, but our stereotypes continue and our screen image is alive and sick and in need of an euthanasic ending and a liberated beginning.

In "Pete 'n' Tillie," for instance, Erik Rhodes lives in the body of René Auberjonois, but minus the flair and garble-tongued innocence that were Rhodes' hallmark. Now the humor is catty, with a touch of sanctimonious compassion thrown in, making Auberjonois both false and unfunny. He is the token homosexual, a well-groomed swizzle stick in a cocktail party world, who suddenly turns sympathetic because he proposes marriage to Carol Burnett after her long heterosexual liaison with Walter Matthau has hit the rocks.

"Pete 'n' Tillie" is stereotypical of the progression of films of the late 60's and early 70's, written, produced, and/or directed by homosexuals who have not been willing to come out of the closet or by heterosexuals who are either unconscious of what they're doing or homophobic enough to want to perpetuate the age-old stereotype that gay is bad, a stereotype equivalent to black is ugly, and one which the gay movement is working to obliterate.

About a year ago, I attended a screening of "J. W. Coop." Cliff Robertson, who made the film, was present to answer questions from the audience. During the course of the film, one scene stood out. Coop, a staunch defender of the rights of blacks, chicanos, hippies, Indians and aging ranch hands, beats up on some white guys after they've cast a racial slur on his black friend. The beating takes place in a men's lavatory and when the cops come, Coop responds with a cutesy remark to the effect that he had been solicited and his red-blooded duty was to preserve his male honor.

The scene was very quick, very in-passing, yet very out of character considering Coop's other right-on attitudes. Questioned about this inconsistency, Robertson replied that it had not occurred to him that someone would interpret the scene that way and he'd be more sensitive to such situations in the future.

A lack of consciousness on Robertson's part? Sure. But I wonder about the recent put-down cracks in "Shamus" and "Up the Sandbox" and the rationale that prompted screenwriter Alvin Sargent to include a short scene in "The Effect of Gamma Rays on Man-in-the-Moon Marigolds" in which Joanne Woodward yells "You homo" at her neighbor because the man has rejected her advances (and why did director Paul Newman choose to show this particular film clip on the Dick Cavett Show when he and star-wife Joanne Woodward appeared?).

Granted, the remark is within the psychological framework of the pathetically frustrated mother played by Miss Woodward. But did it add a new dimension to her character? The remark was not made in Paul Zindel's play, from which the film was adapted. So one wonders, was it a lack of awareness to include it in the film or did the "Marigolds" people choose to throw one more poison dart at a popular unpopular subject?

Another example of homophobic neurosis can be found in the aging ex-movie star that Sylvia Miles plays in "Heat." When informed of her daughter's lesbian tendencies, Sylvia goes berserk. From her mouth spews a barrage of ugliness that caused a gay liberationist at the Lincoln Center Film Festival showing to state to a panel of "Heat" experts, including Miss Miles and director Paul Morrissey, "I thought the film went out of its way to grossly underline the actress's anti-gay hangups when there were so many other ways you could have depicted her frustrations."

Practically every other film that dribbles from the sound stages these days has a "Heat" or "Marigolds" anti-homosexual reference—or a dipsy depiction of a homosexual character or an offensive secondary homosexual theme. In addition to the character played by René Auberjonois in "Pete 'n' Tillie," recent gay film gentlemen include the simpering benefactor of "Savage Messiah" and the grossly effete gentleman who watches a boxing match with Sarah Miles in "Lady Caroline Lamb." Both are gay equivalents of Stepin Fetchit at his "Yowsah, ma'am" low.

Homosexuality is the secondary theme in "Play It As It Lays." A handsome stud of a movie star tells Tuesday Weld to "dump the fags." A couple of reels later, one of the "fags," Tony Perkins, noshes a couple of handfuls of Seconals and dies in Tuesday's arms, because that's the way it is when you're depressed and talented and suppressed and suffering from an overpossessive mother, a mockery of a marriage to

Tammy Grimes, and too much money. Homosexuals have to end up unhappily or, better still, dead.

Then there's "Lolly Madonna XXX." The daughter of Robert Ryan's hillbilly clan chances upon two of the rowdier members of rival Rod Steiger's family. The boys are in the woods and they're in a playful mood and one of them, Ed Lauter, dresses up in ladies' clothes and minces and swishes out his Ozark mountain fantasies of faggotry. The young woman taunts him: "You look like a 'queer.'" To prove otherwise, Lauter rapes her.

But put-downs of homosexuals in movies are not confined to males. A special smarmy exploitation award goes to the gratuitous lesbian scene in "The Valachi Papers." Out of nowhere, the promiscuous girl friend of an organized crime figure is caught by her boss's henchman in a compromising position with another girl. The henchman's reaction to the situation is one of shock and disgust.

A steady diet of this fodder causes gay radicals to take up arms and gay inverts to stay in their closets and gay isolationists—with only the movies and television as nourishment—to consider suicide and gay activists to picket and make loud noises to stop this emotional destruction.

My least favorite depiction of a gay character among the current movies is the fashion designer played by Harvey Jason in "Save the Tiger." The man is temperamental, egotistical, one-dimensional and he's pitted against a lovely, sympathetic old garment-district cutter, who is symbolic of the good old ways. Designer and cutter argue, and cutter tells boss Jack Lemmon, "I can't be in a playpen with fairies."

In gay liberation circles, we play a game called "switch." Switch the designer to a black man, leave the cutter white, substitute "niggers" for "fairies," and would a director still dare to shoot the movie that way?

As long as filmmakers continue to be closed in by their unliberated attitudes, films will continue to repress millions of homosexuals. Yes, occasionally a breath of fresh air sweeps the screen: the enlightened relationship between Murray Head and Peter Finch in "Sunday Bloody Sunday," the healthy bisexuality projected by Michael York in "Cabaret," the delicious chess expert of Austin Pendleton in "The Thief Who Came to Dinner." But it's rare.

What would I like to see? Films in which homosexuals are treated as fully developed human beings. Films in which homosexuals are an integral part of the plot and not camp objects of scorn. Gayploitation films, eventually, where an updated Eric Blore—a hero who carries with him a scent of untainted sweetness—is the cat on top of the heap. Gay films that aren't about "the pain of homosexuality." Gay godfathers and gay heartbreak kids and gay sleuths, as well as originals from our own developing culture. Films that might be provocative and entertaining and fine.

A pipe dream? I don't think so. The movement is laying the foundations, but Hollywood isn't building yet. It's time the creative brains realized that the boys in the band are dying. But as long as the media play the sickee game, homosexuality will linger as a disease. How long before the films give birth to a new and healthier baby?

Arthur Bell is a writer and a founder of the Gay Activists Alliance.

* * *

February 21, 1982

THE NEW REALISM IN PORTRAYING HOMOSEXUALS

By LESLIE BENNETTS

A handsome 30-year-old doctor, Zach has been happily married for eight years to Claire, a successful television programming executive. But lately Zach has begun to stray. He is powerfully attracted to a young writer whom he meets as a patient but who—a lunch date and a dinner later—becomes a lover. When Zach's wife goes away for the weekend on a business trip, Zach turns up at the writer's apartment for a prolonged tryst. The resulting strains on his marriage precipitate a crisis.

Thus begins "Making Love," a new movie directed by Arthur Hiller. In some ways the film deals with familiar themes indeed: It is about "star-crossed lovers and something that comes between them that they cannot control," according to Mr. Hiller, who made the movie "Love Story" a dozen years ago. But "Making Love" is decidedly not just another film about adultery and its consequences. For Zach's new lover is another man, and what comes between Zach and his wife is his realization that he is a homosexual.

Moreover, while the depiction of homosexual characters on screen is not new, the lovers in "Making Love" are markedly different from most of their cinematic predecessors. "The film is revolutionary in concept because everyone in it is so sane and seemingly normal," observes Vito Russo, the author of "The Celluloid Closet," a comprehensive history of the portrayal of homosexuality in the movies. "These guys are matinee idols. Before this, you either got aging, bitter losers or 21-year-old leather numbers. Here you have a doctor who's going to work at Sloan-Kettering and a successful novelist."

Furthermore, not only are they professionally successful, but Zach (played by Michael Ontkean) and his lover, Bart (played by Harry Hamlin), are both good-looking, athletic, virile, sensitive, intelligent, and just plain nice. Their sole idiosyncrasy is Zach's developing sexual preference for Bart rather than his wife, played by Kate Jackson.

Nor is "Making Love" the only new movie to deal with the love that formerly dared not speak its name. "Personal Best," written and directed by Robert Towne, stars Mariel Hemingway as an Olympic athlete who falls in love with another female athlete. While filmmaker and star insist that "Personal Best" is not a movie about lesbianism, much of the plot revolves around the love affair between the two women and its impact on their competitive goals.

Several other forthcoming films feature homosexual relationships as well. Based on the long-running Broadway play, "Deathtrap" is a thriller about a successful playwright—the author of murder mysteries—who conspires with his young homosexual lover to plot the death of the playwright's wealthy wife. Starring Michael Caine, Christopher Reeve and Dyan Cannon, "Deathtrap" is directed by Sidney Lumet and will open in New York in March.

In "Partners," scheduled to open in the fall, Ryan O'Neal stars as a heterosexual policeman paired with John Hurt as a homosexual policeman; their assignment is to pose as a gay couple, infiltrate the homosexual community in West Hollywood, and catch a murderer who is victimizing homosexuals.

"Victor, Victoria"—which opens with a scene of Robert Preston in bed with a younger man—stars James Garner as a Chicago nightclub owner visiting Paris. He falls in love with Julie Andrews, who is masquerading as a Polish count. The fact that he has fallen in love with someone he believes to be another man causes Mr. Garner grave discomfort, but it gladdens the heart of his longtime friend and bodyguard, a large beefy former football star played by Alex Karras. Upon finding his employer in bed with the young Polish nobleman, Mr. Karras ecstatically announces that he, too, is homosexual and that he has been wanting to tell Mr. Garner for 15 years.

The emergence of a cluster of films dealing with homosexuality constitutes something of a milestone in the history of a topic that long was strictly taboo. The films are widely disparate in style and content, to be sure. But given the rigidly stereotypical ways in which Hollywood has traditionally portrayed homosexuals, their variety alone distinguishes these films.

Homosexual rights activists have long deplored the negative characterization of homosexuality in the movies, and many believe that Hollywood has discriminated against homosexuals to a greater extent than any other minority group. "Blacks were stereotyped in movies, but there was never any law forbidding the portrayal of blacks on the screen," notes Mr. Russo. "But from 1934 until 1961, the Production Code forbade any mention of homosexuality on screen or any portrayal of homosexual characters."

Such strictures often compelled major revisions in plot and character, as in the case of Lillian Hellman's play, "The Children's Hour." When first filmed in 1936, "the story of two teachers accused of lesbianism by a vicious child became, on the screen, an adulterous heterosexual triangle in which one teacher is accused of being in love with her best friend's fiance," wrote Mr. Russo in "The Celluloid Closet."

However, the fear of homosexuality provided a permissible theme for such classic stories as "Tea and Sympathy," which was filmed in 1956.

While the production code was revised in 1961, the resulting product was often malignant. "When homosexuality was allowed as a subject, the industry seized upon it as a dirty secret that had come out of the closet," says Mr. Russo. "They could now portray gays, but they knew the public would not accept a positive judgment on such characters. So from 1961

until the present, with very few exceptions, almost every portrayal was one which placed homosexuals in either a psychopathic or a stereotypic context, reinforcing the concept that homosexual men are effeminate and that lesbians are masculine women. The tendency has been either to make homosexuals a joke, and therefore funny and harmless, or to make them so threatening they become vicious, like the psychotic lesbian killer in 'Windows' who killed her psychiatrist with a butcher knife." In Mr. Russo's view, "What has come out on screen has been less a statement about homosexuality than a statement about the fear of homosexuality."

Indeed, at the end of his book Mr. Russo provides a startling chart showing the fate of homosexual characters in various movies. It is a grisly list, with most entries ending in suicide (by straight razor, by shotgun, by a falling tree, by leaping, by hanging, by poison) or murder (by stake through the heart, by being pushed from a balcony, by bludgeoning, by cannibalism, by stabbing, by gunshot, by castration). In Hollywood's eyes, the price of homosexuality was usually a horrible death.

To be sure, as the 1970's progressed homosexuality began to surface with increasing frequency on screen, as in the theater and on television. But while there were exceptions, usually the message adhered to traditional conventions.

Barry Sandler, the screenwriter for "Making Love," says that in writing the movie he was consciously trying to create "a positive image of gay men that we've really never seen on the screen before—an image of gays as normal, decent people that other gays could recognize, identify with and relate to," he explains. "I also wanted to allow the heterosexual audience to emerge with a positive perception of gay people."

Mr. Sandler acknowledges that in pursuit of that end he may have overcompensated somewhat in blessing all his characters with good luck and happy endings in addition to their winning personal attributes. "I feel that over-idealization was necessary," he says. "To a lot of people in Middle America, the fact that a gay person can be a doctor or a lawyer will be a major revelation."

Some viewers may also be shocked at Mr. Sandler's denouement. "The husband and wife don't fall into each other's arms, realize they can lick the situation and go off into the sunset," he says. "This is the first film to deal with this particular conflict and to resolve it in a positive way, in the sense that the man comes to terms with his homosexuality, pursues his identity as a homosexual man, and ultimately finds happiness as a homosexual man."

Doubtless the increasing social acceptance of homosexuality in recent years has contributed to Hollywood's growing willingness to tackle the subject. But this is also an era when the emergence of the Moral Majority and right-wing fundamentalism has helped to focus antipathy toward homosexuality among other segments of the population, and this season's bumper crop of homosexual themes seems sure to prompt controversy. "I am very nervous," admits Arthur Hiller. "Certain groups will be distressed because they consider homosexuality a disease and won't understand why we are showing what they would call sick people having warm human relationships."

One index of the persistence of social taboos is the fact that a number of prominent male film actors refused even to consider the lead role in "Making Love" because they were afraid of its impact on their careers. Arthur Hiller confirms that William Hurt, Michael Douglas, Harrison Ford, Tom Berenger and Peter Strauss were among those who were "sounded out" about playing the role of the doctor. "They all said, 'Don't even think about me for this,' reports Mr. Hiller.

Another measure of intolerance was the harassment experienced by the company of "Personal Best" while the movie was being filmed in Oregon. There were a number of bomb threats, says Mr. Towne, "and somebody pointed a gun at my secretary and said, 'Get out of town.' "

Some homosexual activists and other observers also object to aspects of the new movies. " 'Personal Best' has no respect for the lesbian relationship," charges Vito Russo. "It is unliberated, craven and completely dishonest. Homosexuality is considered to be adolescent in nature. Mariel Hemingway doesn't grow up until she gets herself a boyfriend. The lesbian relationship is so troubled it's never really legitimatized, and the emotional aspect of the girls' relationship is seen as dispensable. It's considered a phase she went through."

Arthur Bell, an author and a founder of the Gay Activists Alliance, has similarly harsh words for "Making Love." "It's a very negative prototype, because it portrays gay relationships as a bad imitation of middle-class straight relationships," he says. "And it doesn't work that way; imitating straight lifestyles doesn't work for homosexuals. The movie is absolutely not representative of the gay population."

Harry Hamlin, who plays Bart in "Making Love," takes a philosophical attitude toward such reactions. "The more radical elements of the gay culture are going to be disappointed by all the films coming out now sponsored by the major studios," he says. "A lot of people of that ilk feel they're way beyond where these films take us. But the more intelligent know there has to be a groundbreaking ceremony, which is what this is."

Needless to say, the motion picture studios will be watching closely to see how such movies fare. No one connected with them has any illusions about the importance of commercial success for these films. "The conventional wisdom has it that people are not interested in homosexual things and won't go to see a movie about the subject," says Sherry Lansing, president of 20th Century-Fox Productions. "When we started to do 'Making Love,' a lot of other executives, producers and directors said, 'Why are you making a movie like this— nobody will see it.' But I'm very optimistic about its commercial prospects. I would assume that if the film is reasonably successful, it will do an enormous amount to erase some of the negative cliches."

Others are less sanguine. "I don't have great hopes for the proliferation of gay characters even if these films are successful," says Vito Russo. "And if they bomb, I don't think you're going to see movies in which there are gay characters, except for incidental ones perceived as society's misfits. It will always be safe to do tried and true things like 'La Cage aux Folles.' Audiences will always come out to laugh at a man in a dress. But as for a serious attempt at drawing a character who's a human being first and happens to be gay, I don't think the effort will be made.

Hollywood isn't geared toward minority programming in general. Movies are made for white, straight teenagers, and the bottom line is money."

* * *

October 27, 1984

'THE TIMES OF HARVEY MILK,' A DOCUMENTARY

THE TIMES OF HARVEY MILK
Directed by Robert Epstein; photography by Frances Reid; edited by Deborah Hoffman and Mr. Epstein; narrated by Harvey Fierstein; music by Mark Isham; produced by Richard Schmiechen; released by Teleculture Films Inc. At the Carnegie Hall Cinema, Seventh Avenue between 56th and 57th Streets. Running time: 87 minutes. This film has no rating.

"The Times of Harvey Milk" was shown as part of the 1984 New York Film Festival. Following are excerpts from Janet Maslin's review, which appeared in The New York Times Oct. 7. The film opened yesterday at the Carnegie Hall Cinema, Seventh Avenue between 56th and 57th Streets.

"Harvey stood for something more than just him," someone remarks in "The Times of Harvey Milk," and this warm, well-made documentary makes that eminently clear. The personality of the slain San Francisco Supervisor, who along with Mayor George Moscone was shot in 1978 by Dan White, a disgruntled former Supervisor, comes through strongly, but personality is not the film's foremost concern. Robert Epstein, who co-directed the equally affecting "Word is Out," indicates the ways in which Harvey Milk was emblematic of one segment of society and Dan White of another. And he traces the clash that arose between them.

This conflict is intrinsically so dramatic that the film can rely on a simple, straightforward style without lacking momentum or emotion. Mr. Epstein uses abundant news footage of both Mr. Milk and Mr. White, and the ironies are overwhelming. Mr. White, for instance, is heard advocating neighborhood baseball teams and suggesting that maybe his district could challenge Harvey Milk's district to a game. "Dan White comes across as the kind of son any mother would be proud of," a television reporter declares.

Harvey Milk is seen as friendly, charming, intense and instinctively political; in lobbying for a law on dog droppings, for instance, he deliberately plants a specimen in the park and steps in it during a television interview to help make his point. Mr. Milk's friends and associates contribute many anecdotes to the film's portrait of him, but Mr. Epstein is generally careful to keep them in context.

Harvey Milk's political career and the victory it represented for San Francisco's homosexual community is contrasted with the first stirrings of the Moral Majority, stirrings to which Mr. White was especially responsive. The film examines the controversy surrounding Proposition 6, the proposed California ordinance barring homosexuals from teaching in public schools, an issue on which Mr. Milk and Mr. White were sharply divided.

It was four days after the proposition was defeated, thanks in large part to Harvey Milk's efforts, that Mr. White resigned his post. Five days later, Mr. White announced he had changed his mind and wanted to be a Supervisor again. It was 12 days after that, on the morning when Mayor Moscone had planned to announce that he would not reinstate Mr. White, that the shootings took place.

Since Mr. Milk's political career embodies the rise of the homosexual community's political power in San Francisco, and since the results of Mr. White's brief trial were evidence of a backlash, the film would have benefited from devoting closer attention to the trial itself. Mr. White's tearful confession, which was thought to have helped sway the jury toward its verdict of involuntary manslaughter, is heard. But his comments explaining his mysterious and abrupt resignation are not, even though they might have revealed something of Mr. White's mental state at the time and shed some light on the verdict.

If Mr. Epstein can't fully explain what happened, he can certainly tell the story with urgency, passion and, finally, indignation. Toward the end of the film, a young black man asks rhetorically what sort of sentence he might have received for such a crime. Another interviewee speculates that Mr. White's staunch support for middle-class values and opposition to the homosexual community's growing power contributed to his light sentence. (He was released from prison last January.) And a third man suggests how pivotal Harvey Milk and his cause may have been to the verdict: "I think if it were just Moscone who'd been killed, he would have been in San Quentin for the rest of his life."

* * *

March 31, 1985

IN EACH OTHER'S CLOTHING

By MOLLY HASKELL

HOLLYWOOD ANDROGYNY
By Rebecca Bell-Metereau
Illustrated. 260 pp. New York: Columbia University Press. $24.95.

How does it feel for a "real man" to be a woman? John Lithgow and Dustin Hoffman played women in "The World According to Garp" and "Tootsie" respectively, and have graciously shared their insiders' knowledge with the world at large, expressing in interview after interview their compassionate amazement at the difficulties poor women face in a sexist world.

As yet, no actresses have come forth with comparable insights into the singularities of maledom. One of the reasons may be that for a woman, dressing as a man is no big deal. Every time she puts on shorts or jeans—or top hat and tails—a woman resurrects the tomboy that still lives within her. Moreover, women can play at maleness, be slightly male, without endangering their femaleness. But men cannot become just slightly female. Styles of dress notwithstanding, for a man, putting on a skirt is to make an unequivocal gesture.

In "Hollywood Androgyny," a solidly researched study, Rebecca Bell-Metereau conducts an enlightening discussion of transvestism and sex-role exchange in motion pictures. Mrs. Bell-Metereau, who teaches English at Southwest Texas State University, points out that Barbra Streisand in the movie "Yentl" and Julie Andrews in "Victor/Victoria" were among the few women to play men in an era that featured a good number of male actors playing women. Male cross-dressing, either by transvestites or female impersonators, has figured in several films, including "Cabaret," "Dressed to Kill," "Freebie and the Bean," "The Queen," "La Cage aux Folles" (I and II), ". . . And Justice for All," "Come Back to the Five and Dime, Jimmy Dean, Jimmy Dean," "The Tenant," "Outrageous" and "The Rocky Horror Picture Show."

Though few of them have appeared in recent films, women who dressed as men or leaned toward androgyny were a staple in movies made between 1910 and the end of the 30's. One of the pleasures of Mrs. Bell-Metereau's book is the way it evokes not merely the most familiar figures—Marlene Dietrich in top hat and tails, Greta Garbo as Queen Christina, Katharine Hepburn as Sylvia Scarlett and the virginal aviator in "Christopher Strong"—but also Merle Oberon's George Sand, Louise Brooks in tramp drag in "Beggars of Life," the various serial stars and cowgirls, Calamity Janes and Tugboat Annies.

Mrs. Bell-Metereau sees the dwindling number of male impersonations in film as a sign that women have gained more power off screen. In other words, real life offers pants roles. And correspondingly, she concludes that the greater prestige women achieved during the 60's and 70's as a result of the women's movement has been responsible for the richer, rounder, stronger, more sympathetic impersonations that men now play.

Without disputing her general observations, I would argue that the reason for this phenomenon lies less with the improved status of women than with the opening up of the sexual floodgates generally. With the rock culture of the 60's and the decline of censorship, sex came out of the closet and the taboos against all forms of deviation were considerably weakened. Every permutation was suddenly possible, and men, dominant in films and the industry as never before, availed themselves of a wide range of interesting roles.

Books of this nature rarely avoid the pitfall of looking at sexual history in terms of the theory of progress, leading from the repressive inhibitions of the film farce "Charley's Aunt," which was produced four times, to the revolutionary reversals of films like "Alien" and "The Rocky Horror Picture Show."

However, it would be more accurate to see sexual history as a constant struggle between the forces of liberation and those of puritanism, often within the same decade or even the same film. American culture began in the puritan tradition, yet life in colonial times was wilder than during the Victorian pall of the 19th century. In the 20's, after a period of political and cultural innovation, puritanism reasserted itself with Prohibition. Yet at the same time, the Dionysian spirit held sway in speak-easies and movies. The films of the 20's were bolder and more casually racy than any since the earliest peep shows. Stars of the 30's, like Bette Davis, Barbara Stanwyck and of course Mae West, had a larger component of maleness than do any of today's actresses who, for all their freedom, seem to have less appetite for sexual game-playing and fewer options for maneuver and ambiguity.

"Hollywood Androgyny" is somewhat biased in favor of "open" films—those that challenge cultural conventions and censorship and that offer alternatives to the way we regard sexual roles—versus "closed" films that reaffirm the status quo. As an example of this distinction the author compares the unarguable superiority of Billy Wilder's farcical "Some Like It Hot" with Howard Hawks's end-of-the-war comedy, "I Was a Male War Bride." Howard Hawks's painfully unfunny film about the emasculation of an officer (Cary Grant) by his female superior (Ann Sheridan) does reflect many of the sexual and marital anxieties raised by the war. But the film is not an entirely reliable mirror of the times. More devious elements are at work. For example, Cary Grant, already associated with this sheepish man-in-distress role, plays a Frenchman, a figure mainstream American audiences regarded as sissified. And Ann Sheridan, who the film critic Parker Tyler once said sounded like a lady wrestler, had a butch image.

Two contexts could not be more different than the highly regulated military bueaucracy of "I Was a Male War Bride," where the presence of women is already questionable, and the mirthful, more expansive world in which "Some Like It Hot" transpires. Billy Wilder, who wrote and directed the 1959 film about two men who pose as women to escape the wrath of Chicago mobsters, admitted that he got away with this most audacious of cross-dressing movies by setting it in the wild, free-swinging 20's where, among gangsters and showgirls, flamboyant get-ups and characters would not be out of place.

Jack Lemmon and Tony Curtis in the key roles blended with the warm sexuality of Marilyn Monroe. The hilariously naughty Joe E. Brown closed the film with a shrug and the line "Nobody's perfect," leaving the way open for a boy-boy marriage without violating the conventions of farce. "Some Like It Hot" confronts homosexuality openly—but at the fade-out and in the past, where it doesn't hit too close to home, and without a carnal display that would make the audience nervous.

Calling the film "pivotal," Mrs. Bell-Metereau suggests that it paved the way for the uninhibitedly polymorphous, pansexual and bisexual movies to come. But unlike such underground films as "Flaming Creatures" or the Andy Warhol oeuvre, "Hot" stays within the boundaries—if not of good taste—of acceptability. "Charley's Aunt" was successful because the hero was forced into dressing like a woman, resisting all the way; this was also true for the protagonist-victims of "Some Like It Hot." By contrast, "Sylvia Scarlett," an androgynous classic, was a failure because the characters chose to dress as the opposite sex. Being forced to cross-dress is farce; choosing to do so is perverse . . . or pathological.

Counterculture movies are often mistakenly credited with more influence than they actually have. However, out-and-out cult movies like "Flaming Creatures" and "Something for Everyone" and even "Performance" are not sociologically significant in the way almost every movie of the 30's, 40's and 50's managed to be. In those days, everyone saw everything. Now audiences are fragmented by generation, level of sophistication, gender and sexual orientation. Explicitly homosexual movies are a world apart from "La Cage aux Folles," a square love story in titillating drag that has become the "Charley's Aunt" of the 80's.

"Hollywood Androgyny" is as complete a compendium as we are likely to get for some time of a subject that has not been dealt with as seriously since the era of the late Parker Tyler who wrote such books as "Magic and Myth of the Movies" and "The Hollywood Hallucination." His still timely forays into the mythology of sex focused on the stars' voices and the vibrations they emitted in a largely unconscious context. Mrs. Bell-Metereau, on the other hand, treats film as a conscious artistic activity and achieves her scholarly coups through an analysis of costuming.

With ideologically disinterested generosity, she quotes a wide range of film authorities, but her detachment is frustrating, because in the context of this subject objectivity is a handicap. What I miss in this book is a probing curiosity that could look more deeply into audience responses to the spectacle of cross-dressing and determine where and why the taboos still exist. Joan Crawford, Marlene Dietrich, Katharine Hepburn—the androgynous heroines of the early 30's—ended that decade as box-office poison. Are audiences any more open today? And are actresses any more able or willing to risk the taint of "masculinity"? Notions of masculinity and femininity persist and entangle us. Mrs. Bell-Metereau presents the evidence of our fears and desires without venturing to speculate on what is or is not perverse—and why. But perhaps that is a country from which no traveler safely returns.

Trading Authority With Freedom

Almost all cross-dressing films involve the relationship between authority and freedom—the extent to which the male is free to explore his female nature and the extent to which female characters are capable of establishing their own authority. . . . The last twenty years have seen, along with a decline in male impersonation, a marked absence of female characters in comparison with earlier films. Many films of the past two decades that do include female characters are fraught with unprecedented violence and hostility toward women. Here it is important to make a distinction often over-looked by feminist critics looking for sexist overtones in Hollywood films. A film that presents a likable yet powerless women is no less sexist than a film that presents a despicable yet powerful woman; in fact the latter film may carry a heavy misogynist message while implying superiority of females over males. The cross-dressing films of the sixties follow this pattern of misogyny and fear of the powerful female, but in the mid-seventies an interesting change occurs. For the first time, female impersonators become sympathetic characters—occasionally comic, yet no longer the figures of derision or harmless ridicule. In characters as dissimilar as Zaza of "La Cage aux Folles" (1978) and Frank-N-Furter in "The Rocky Horror Picture Show" (1975) we find a common link in their ability to capture the affection of audiences through wit and a peculiar brand of bitchy charm.

—From "Hollywood Androgyny."

Molly Haskell, the film critic for Vogue magazine, is the author of "From Reverence to Rape: The Treatment of Women in the Movies."

* * *

June 27, 1986

'DIFFERENT FROM OTHERS,' FILM ON HOMOSEXUALITY

By JOHN J. O'CONNOR

As part of its "Gay Pride Week" lineup of programming, Channel 13 is broadcasting tomorrow night at 10 o'clock a rare and fascinating film fragment entitled "Different From the Others." Being presented as part of the station's "Film on Film" series, this German production ("Anders als die Anderen") was released in 1919. It survives by accident, having been found in East Berlin only a few years ago.

The host for the program is Vito Russo, author of "The Celluloid Closet: Homosexuals in the Movies." He explains that, before World War I, Germany had passed a law, Statute 175, that banned certain homosexual acts between consenting adults. One result was increased opportunities for blackmail. The leader of the opposition to the statute was Magnus Hirschfeld, founder of the Institute for Sexual Science. Richard Oswald, a film director, joined Dr. Hirschfeld's crusade with "Different From the Others." In addition to being attacked in certain portions of the press as "a piece of rampant obscenity," the film prompted troublemakers to release "stink bombs" and live mice in movie theaters.

The object of this outrage is a carefully restrained plea for simple tolerance. The point is illustrated in the story of Paul Korner, played by Conrad Veidt, far better known for his performances in such classics as "The Cabinet of Dr. Caligari" and "Casablanca." Paul is first seen in boarding school where, for whatever reasons, all of the students are played by actors far beyond adolescence. Becoming too friendly with another student, Paul is dismissed by a board of teachers who

look like ominous figures out of the ballet "The Green Table." His life of unhappiness begins.

Now a university student, Paul is dragged off by his exuberant friends to a wild party where, grabbed and kissed by two lively women, his eyes begin popping in anxiety (as in most silent films, the conventions of emoting can look silly to our supposedly more sophisticated eyes). Then, in no time at all, Paul has become a successful virtuoso violinist. Young Kurt begs to become his student and is soon his favorite pupil. This idyllic and evidently platonic arrangement is shattered when Paul goes to a party and is wooed by Franz, who immediately demands money and threatens to let "the whole town know you're one of them."

Paul suffers, but the film ends on an upbeat note as an actor portraying Dr. Hirschfeld informs a public gathering: "The time will come when such tragedies will be no more, for knowledge will conquer prejudice, truth will conquer lies, and love will triumph over hatred." But, Mr. Russo says, Dr. Hirschfeld was forced to flee Germany in 1930 and the Nazis subsequently sent 250,000 homosexuals to their deaths in concentration camps.

In the final moments of the television program, produced by Bob Earing, Mr. Russo makes an effort to expand on his subject with a "historical perspective" of what has happened since 1919, but he could have used a few hours instead of a couple of minutes. Perspective of a broader sort, though, is provided in the "Cinema Thirteen" presentation immediately following at 10:30: a repeat of the Academy Award-winning documentary "The Times of Harvey Milk."

* * *

April 30, 1989

'BEFORE STONEWALL': THE ROOTS OF GAY LIFE

By ALVIN KLEIN

"Everything came together at that one moment. This is it. This is what we've been waiting for. We've had enough. We're going to fight back."

On June 27, 1969, these militant words summed up the response of the 200 or so patrons of the Stonewall Inn to what might have been just another in a series of police raids on gay bars in Greenwich Village.

What ensued was initially described as a melee and then, variously, as a riot and a wild insurrection. Beer cans, bricks, garbage and slabs of glass were hurled at police officers barricaded inside, while crowds ranging from as many as 400 to 1,000 mobilized outside for three days afterward.

The incident was historic, for it marked the beginning of an organized movement of homosexual activism. From then on, gay life would often be talked about in two categorical ways: before or after Stonewall.

To create a visual history of men and women who were stereotyped as outsiders, as living in "the world of the twilight," as those who were "that way" and, by implication, to chronicle events that led to the Stonewall uprising, the documentary "Before Stonewall" was made.

Robert Rosenberg, who grew up in Elmont, co-produced (with John Scagliotti) and co-directed (with Greta Schiller) the 90-minute film, which is subtitled "The Making of a Gay and Lesbian Community."

It was released in 1986 and later shown on public educational television, after which it received an Emmy award.

As part of a series of documentaries on the theme, "A Multicultural Society," which is being co-sponsored by the New York Council for the Humanities, "Before Stonewall" will be screened tomorrow at 7:30 P.M. at the State University of New York in Farmingdale and Tuesday at La Guardia Community College in Long Island City.

Following the screenings, Mr. Rosenberg, who is curator of the Global Village Documentary Festival, which runs through May 12 at Manhattan's Public Theater, and who recently completed a documentary about a Jewish family in Nicaragua ("Crossing Borders: A Jewish Witness for Peace"), will participate in a question-and-answer session with the audience.

In his office at the Media Studies Center of the New School for Social Research in Lower Manhattan, Mr. Rosenberg recalled the process of creating "Before Stonewall," which was five years in the making.

"As an independent film maker trying to make my way, I realized that the issues of lesbian and gay life were sidestepped," he said. "I was interested in revisionist and oral history, from new perspectives, from the standpoint of those involved.

"I thought it was possible to do visually interesting work and, at the same time, recover from the shadows our own ancestry, our forefathers and mothers.

"It had existed only in secretive form: home movies or in gay and lesbian archives around the country. It was also a fundable project, given the distance of time."

"Before Stonewall," which was produced for $250,000, begins with footage of Ronald Reagan, as an actor in a military role, commanding a sergeant "to report to wardrobe for assignment to 'Ladies of the Chorus.' "

It then goes on to explore aspects of homosexual life during World War II and the McCarthy era and then to find "deep connections" among civil rights, women's liberation and gay pride.

Emphasizing that the film is not a collection of personal stories, not propaganda and not a polemic, Mr. Rosenberg said:

"The focus is on how a community evolved. A knowledge of history empowers us as a society. These were the people who led to liberation, who had the chutzpah to demand and protect their rights.

" 'Stonewall' didn't come out of the sky. People have to decide how they would live their lives without oppression. This is not a ghettoized issue; it's not just for gays and lesbians, but designed to be accessible for the broadest possible audience. The real issue is choice."

The 33-year-old Mr. Rosenberg, whose own gay life began in what he called a "positive post-Stonewall" era, was a student at Elmont Memorial High School during the early days of gay liberation.

"The Elmont Public Library had gay-positive books, like Dennis Altman's 'Homosexual Oppression and Liberation,' " he said, "but I took that one out with terror, hiding it from my parents."

Mr. Rosenberg came to grips with his homosexual identity, "with being comfortable with who I was," during his freshman year at Hampshire College in Massachusetts.

"Then I told my parents during Christmas break," he said. "They were not too happy."

However, his mother's reaction changed to supportiveness, while his father, a clinical psychologist, remained resistant.

"He was a political liberal," Mr. Rosenberg said, "but he never acclimated to the idea on an emotional level. He was dying when I started applying for grants for 'Before Stonewall' in 1980, and among his last words to me were, 'Must you make this film?'

"When it opened, my mother said, 'Your father would have been proud,' but that was her illusion. I felt that he'd never be reconciled to it. Parents have to come out themselves as parents of gay children."

Mr. Rosenberg's mother, Bernice, who still lives in Elmont, is "now one of my best publicists," he said.

"She was an activist before I was born, and that must have been passed on subliminally. And now I've helped to reinspire her. My father died of asbestos-created cancer, and she's vice president of the White Lung Association and a member of the Older Women's League."

Although Mr. Rosenberg, who lives in Brooklyn, says that battles have yet to be won—"There is plenty of prejudice and homophobia in society, AIDS has decimated our community and it's not easy for any teen-ager coming out"—he remains an "overall optimist."

Mr. Rosenberg is the father of a 2½-year-old son, Noah, who lives with his lesbian mother, the child's custodial parent. The child was conceived by artificial insemination.

"Things are going in a positive direction," he said. "Gay people have taken more initiative in defining for themselves the possibilities of family life, having roots, raising kids.

"There's a lifetime commitment. And isn't that a belief in the future, a declaration of hope?"

* * *

June 25, 1989

'LONGTIME COMPANION' TAKES AN UNFLINCHING LOOK AT AIDS

By CHRISTOPHER MICHAUD

Any film maker will tell you his project has special meaning for him. "I really believe in this," he will declare in earnest.

In the case of "Longtime Companion," that most common of wisdoms has taken on new dimensions, as the film makers shoot a movie about a disease that has sent dozens of their friends and contemporaries to a premature death.

The disease, of course, is AIDS, and those involved with the film say the subject matter, never before examined in an American feature film, has come uncomfortably close to reflecting the tragedies occurring in their own lives.

Written by the playwright Craig Lucas ("Blue Window," "Reckless") and produced by American Playhouse, "Longtime Companion" takes as its title the phrase often used in obituaries to describe the lovers of those lost to AIDS, when they are acknowledged at all. From its title, it is clear that the film, which recently completed location shooting in Manhattan and Fire Island Pines, will concern itself with the gay community, whose ranks are being decimated.

With gay people accounting for a significant part of the film community, as well as having been the primary targets of AIDS, logic would dictate that when AIDS is before the cameras, gay people would be there as well. But it has not been so.

When the subject is AIDS, the response, it seems, is reticence—reticence to deal with the disease, or, barring that, reticence to approach it realistically.

On television, the crisis is depicted as the bane of hemophiliacs and children. Some critics have complained that film makers, by focusing on those they perceive to be the more palatable people with AIDS, have effectively whitewashed the issue.

Mr. Lucas's screenplay begins in July 1981, as eight main characters, all but one of them gay men, peruse their New York Times and discover the first article to appear about a rare, fatal cancer striking gay men in Los Angeles and New York. None of them has any inkling that the "cancer" (Kaposi's sarcoma) will evolve into a crisis of unprecedented proportion in their community.

Over the next seven years, some characters fall ill as their friends rally in support with a good-humored, determined resolve. There are laughs, even (and, perhaps, most importantly) when three friends forage in the deceased's closet, arguing about the most appropriate outfit for the mortuary.

The story wasn't an easy sell, among other things, it treats gay life as a fact of life and not open to debate. "I wanted to do something through the eyes of the gay community," Lindsay Law, executive producer of American Playhouse and of the film, said. "Television films have dealt responsibly with the subject, but always seemed to dance around the issue. You don't see the high-risk groups—it's as if AIDS is happening to everybody else."

Mr. Lucas said that after his success with "Blue Window," a drama of desperate singles in the 80's that won the Los Angeles Drama Critics Award, he was approached by several studios eager to work with him.

"I would invariably suggest I write a film about people with AIDS, and they would invariably say: 'No.' Case closed. Lindsay Law was the first and only person to be excited about the prospect," he said.

"It's dicey material in an industry that is not known for its risk taking," Mr. Lucas said. "But there's this crazy notion that people only go to the movies to be 'entertained,' i.e., di-

verted from any reality of their life. I seek to be reminded that I'm alive."

The phrase that comes up so often among those involved with "Longtime Companion" is "labor of love." Virtually everyone with the company knows someone who has AIDS or who has died of it. Mr. Lucas said the actors are working for "next to nothing, and the production assistants are literally working for nothing." According to Stan Wlodkowski, the producer, profits of "Longtime Companion," which is budgeted at between $1 million and $2 million and is expected to have a fall release, will be shared with a number of AIDS organizations.

The actors, among them Dermot Mulroney ("Young Guns"), Campbell Scott, Bruce Davison ("The Cocktail Hour") and Patrick Cassidy, gave the film priority over more commercial projects, as did its director, Norman Rene.

Such altruism in an industry rife with egoism has extended to the business community, in the form of service contributions from companies such as the film lab DuArt, Panavision and Sound One. "Everybody understood the responsibility and need for this movie to be made," Mr. Law said.

Mr. Wlodkowski said the film's subject matter has closed as well as opened some doors. Some locations became unavailable for shooting when AIDS was mentioned, and corporations limited use of donated goods to consumption by the crew, when typically they go to great lengths to get their products on screen.

For Mr. Lucas, shooting the film turned out to be more of an emotional challenge than writing it. Having spent two years working with the Gay Men's Health Crisis—an AIDS support services organization—as a buddy to a person with AIDS and having lost, by his count, 45 to 50 friends and acquaintances, including his first lover, he "felt comfortable with the setting," he said. "It was no problem writing and developing gay characters."

But recently he ended up living his own screenplay. He went to Los Angeles to see a friend, the actor Peter Evans, a few days before Mr. Evans's death in May. "After he died," Mr. Lucas said, "I dealt with the undertaker, comforted the family, took care of the obituary in The New York Times, and flew back Sunday night.

"Monday morning I came to the shoot and began to do the scene where they call the mortuary, and all the friends, and take care of the obituary in The New York Times. It was extraordinarily unreal."

At the same time, he said, he felt fortunate "to have a place to put some of those feelings, so that I don't feel totally helpless in the face of what is surely the deepest and most disturbing event of my life."

Others working on the film share his feelings. One prospective crew member wept during an interview on learning that parts of the film would be shot on Fire Island, as he recalled a group of friends with whom he had summered there for years in the 70's. He was the lone survivor among them. Such loss, as well as the strength of community, have pervaded the filming.

On a quiet afternoon in Greenwich Village, the inside of a church is somber and reverent, as a hundred people gather to remember one who has died. As individuals eulogize their lost friend, fond smiles and cheers of regret prevail, but this time it's only a movie, as the "Longtime Companion" company shoots its memorial service scene. Offstage, between takes, the conversation reverts to the weather and kitchen renovations—a reminder that in both life and art the mundane distracts from the omnipresent loss.

There is a fantasy all those affected by AIDS entertain from time to time, that it's all just a movie, or, more accurately, a nightmare from which they will one day awake. For the cast and crew of "Longtime Companion," the loss will end with completion of the film. But not really. Only the characters will see a wrap. For the actors, there will be a return to their real lives, where AIDS is very much alive and killing.

Christopher Michaud is a New York-based reporter who covers the arts and entertainment.

* * *

September 4, 1990

A MAJOR STUDIO PLANS TO TEST THE RATING SYSTEM

By STEPHEN FARBER
Special to The New York Times

LOS ANGELES, Sept. 3—In the last six months, the Motion Picture Association of America has given X ratings to half a dozen independent or foreign films, sparking a series of protests about the 22-year-old rating system. Now, a film from a major studio has been thrust into the controversy.

The director of "Henry and June," Philip Kaufman, whose other films include "The Unbearable Lightness of Being" and "The Right Stuff," says he plans to appeal the X rating. The case seems certain to rally critics who have called for a change in the system to allow seriously intended adult films to be given a rating that does not connote pornography.

A Bohemian Love Story

"Henry and June" chronicles the relationships in the early 1930's among Miller (played by Fred Ward), his wife, June (Uma Thurman), and Anais Nin (Maria de Madeiros), who at the time was a budding writer and the wife of an American banker in Paris. Based on Nin's unexpurgated diaries which were first published four years ago, the film includes many scenes of nude lovemaking and a few tender but explicit lesbian scenes. "Henry and June" also incorporates clips from controversial films of the 1930's—including Luis Bunuel and Salvador Dali's "Chien Andalou" and a German film about lesbianism, "Madchen in Uniform"—to establish the bohemian atmosphere that stimulated both Miller and Nin. "In a way, our film is about the struggle for freedom from censorship," Mr. Kaufman said. "So it's ironic that the first people to see the movie were a board of censors."

"Henry and June" was initially screened for the 10-member rating board in a rough cut about two months ago. At that time, Mr. Kaufman spoke with Richard Heffner, chairman of the rating board. "There was no question in his mind that the whole film was an X," Mr. Kaufman reported. "He urged me to release it as an X and said that the changes required to bring it into the R category would eviscerate the film." When the finished film was screened for the board last week, it was once again rated X, and the board cited five sex scenes that would have to be significantly altered for an R rating. (An R rating allows people under 17 to see a film if accompanied by an adult.) Mr. Heffner said: "I think 'Henry and June' is an absolutely beautiful, splendid film. But we believe most parents would consider this out of bounds for children. All we're saying with an X rating is that this is an adult film. We are not saying it's pornographic."

Pressure to Edit

Some of the other films rated X this year—"The Cook, the Thief, His Wife and Her Lover," "Tie Me Up! Tie Me Down!" and "Henry: Portrait of a Serial Killer"—were eventually released without a rating, which is an option for smaller distribution companies. But major studios like Universal have signed an agreement that they will not release any of their films without an official rating. Thomas Pollock, the president of Universal Pictures, explained that Universal will not release an X-rated film. About half the theaters in the United States will not show X-rated films, and television will not accept advertising for X-rated films, no matter how highly acclaimed they may be. Like most other directors, Mr. Kaufman has signed a contract that grants him the right of final cut only if the film qualifies for an R rating.

Because of these pressures on film makers, many critics have suggested either adding another rating between R and X or changing the X label to something more neutral like AO (adults only) or NC 17 (no children under 17). Jack Valenti, the president of the motion picture association, recently met with a group of directors and screenwriters who urged him to change the rating system. Sydney Pollack, the Academy Award-winning director of "Out of Africa," is one of the directors lobbying for change.

"I feel as much disgust toward gratuitous pornography and violence as any mother," Mr. Pollack said. "But there are genuine artists who make films not meant for children, and their movies shouldn't be lumped with exploitation fare. Some new approach has to be found that's more fair to potential artists."

Mr. Valenti said: "Nothing is nonnegotiable. I'm looking at the rating system now to see if improvements can be made."

Mr. Pollock of Universal said: "Eventually I believe there will be changes in the system. But I don't know if they will happen overnight." Mr. Pollock also indicated that he would be willing to release "Henry and June" with an adults-only rating, other than X.

Appealing the X

For the time being, however, with no new rating in the offing, both Universal and Mr. Kaufman said they hope to have the rating of "Henry and June" changed to R on appeal. The New York City-based appeals board, which consists of exhibitors, producers and distributors, must agree by a two-thirds majority to overturn a rating, and very few films have been able to muster the necessary votes. "I predict that we will win on appeal," Mr. Pollock said. "It is so clear that this quality film was not meant to be lumped with the hard-core stuff. I would be pleased to take my 17-year-old daughter to see the film. I think she'd get a lot out of it."

Mr. Pollock and Mr. Kaufman will argue that "Henry and June" does not deserve a stronger rating than "Wild at Heart" and "Total Recall," both rated R. "I see other films that have a combination of sexuality and violence, which I feel is far more destructive than anything in 'Henry and June,'" Mr. Pollock said. "And those films are rated R."

Mr. Kaufman noted the parallels between the film and Miller's own work. Miller's "Tropic of Cancer" was published in Europe 30 years before it was cleared of obscenity charges in the United States, where it was published in 1964.

"Henry and June" is to have its world premiere at the Venice Film Festival on Sept. 14 and then be released throughout Europe this month and next in the version designated X by the motion picture association. No American release date will be set until the rating controversy has been resolved.

Mr. Kaufman said: "I could have played games with the rating board and showed them much longer sexual scenes than I actually intended to use, and then agreed to cut them down to what I wanted in the first place. But I didn't want to play games. I wanted to make an honest film. I was trying to be faithful to the source material. I think films should be allowed to explore the same areas as literature."

Thomas Mallon's most recent novel is "Henry and Clara."

* * *

March 19, 1993

FOND RECOLLECTIONS OF A PART OF GAY HISTORY

By STEPHEN HOLDEN

LAST CALL AT MAUD'S
Directed by Paris Poirier; director of photography, Cheryl Rosenthal; edited by Elaine Trotter; music by Tim Horrigan; produced by Mr. Poirier and Karen Kiss; released by the Maud's Project. At the Cinema Village, Third Avenue at 13th Streets, East Village. Running time: 75 minutes. This film has no rating.
WITH: Gwenn Craig, Jo Daly, Sally Gearhart, Judy Grahn, JoAnn Loulan, Phyllis Lyon, Del Martin, Pat Norman, Rikki Streicher and Mary Wings.

"I can think of no place better to have suspense and a real eerie feeling of decadence than a lesbian bar, because lesbians have always been outlaws," asserts Mary Wings, an author of lesbian mystery novels, in the opening moments of the documentary film "Last Call at Maud's."

Ms. Wings is one of many women interviewed in the film who look back with a mystical nostalgia on the glory days of Maud's, a popular lesbian hangout in the Haight-Ashbury district of San Francisco. More than just a watering hole, Maud's, which flourished between 1966 and 1989, is remembered as a sort of sorority house for a generation of lesbians, most of whom are now over 50.

Besides Ms. Wings, some of the club's former habituees include the writers Judy Grahn, Sally Gearhart and JoAnn Loulan. Phyllis Lyon and Del Martin, who founded the international lesbian organization Daughters of Bilitis, reminisce, as does San Francisco's current police commissioner, Gwenn Craig. Their collective stories add up to a small but significant piece of gay history in which social life and political organizing are closely connected.

The 75-minute film, which was directed by Paris Poirier, interweaves two parallel narratives. One is an anecdotal history of the bar told largely by its owner, Rikki Streicher. The other, going back to the 1940's, is a wider-ranging story of the struggle for gay civil rights as viewed from a West Coast lesbian perspective.

The vignettes include memories of the days when gay bars were routinely raided by the police, and gay men and women visited them in groups. When a red light flashed to signal a raid, same-sex couples on the dance floor would switch partners and put on a heterosexual charade. One surprising historical tidbit is the fact that until 1973 it was illegal in California for a woman to tend bar.

The late 70's, when the hedonism of San Francisco's gay culture reached a peak, are remembered with some bitterness. Ms. Gearhart recalls the era as "a giant white gay male fraternity party" that excluded women and people of color.

If "Last Call at Maud's," which opens today at the Cinema Village, exudes a warmhearted honesty, its focus on the tightly knit social world of one bar over a 23-year period often gives it the feel of an alumni reunion film. For those who weren't there and didn't live the life, the scrapbook photos and newspaper clippings won't mean very much. And because so many of the reminiscences focus on arcane social details, significant historical events like the slayings of Mayor George Moscone and the municipal supervisor Harvey Milk in 1978 are glossed over.

For all its celebration of progress toward a wider acceptance of homosexuality, the film ultimately has its heart in the past. Almost despite itself, it longs for a bygone era of intrigue and subterfuge, when being lesbian really did mean belonging to a secret sisterhood of self-styled "outlaws."

* * *

August 21, 1994

GETTING BEYOND THE GAY GHETTO WITH GAY FILMS

By HOWARD FEINSTEIN

Back in 1982, 20th Century Fox tested the market for gay-themed movies with "Making Love." It starred Harry Hamlin as a homosexual home-wrecker who inserts himself between the happily married Kate Jackson and Michael Ontkean. "Making Love" was a critical and commercial flop.

"The picture was ready," Daniel Melnick, the movie's co-producer, says. "The public wasn't."

Not that Fox didn't try. The studio had a dual marketing campaign that would reassure heterosexuals while enticing a gay audience. Ads in mainstream publications pictured the three nicely tailored stars huddled innocently. In the gay press, Ms. Jackson placed an unwelcome hand on Mr. Ontkean, who had his arm wrapped around a shirtless Mr. Hamlin.

Twelve years later, the enormous success of Tri-Star's "Philadelphia" (a movie about AIDS that made $77 million domestically) has ignited studio interest in gay projects. "Jeffrey," based on Paul Rudnick's Off Broadway play, has just completed filming; Wesley Snipes, Patrick Swayze and John Leguizamo are playing drag queens in "To Wong Foo, Thanks for Everything, Julie Newmar," a Universal Studios film. Neil Meron and Craig Zadan are producing "Falsettos," an adaptation of the Broadway musical, for Disney, and, for Warner Brothers, "The Mayor of Castro Street," a biography of Harvey Milk, the slain San Francisco gay rights advocate. "Homophobia tends to disappear commensurate with box office gross," says Mr. Meron.

But none of these films will have the secret ingredient "Philadelphia" had: Tom Hanks, an actor who attracted mainstream audiences to a story about AIDS, an actor who could make even the slow-witted Forrest Gump a national hero. Instead they will have to rely on marketing. The question is, which way will they go? With the mainstream approach used for "Philadelphia," a film that appeared to be a courtroom drama? Or with the two-pronged approach used for "Making Love"?

Some marketing experts believe that it is increasingly difficult to market a film directly to homosexual audiences. "One of the problems with the gay market is to treat it homogeneously," says Chris Pula, president of marketing at New Line Cinema, which two years ago released "Three of Hearts," a film about a lesbian relationship. "One gay film isn't going to satisfy everybody."

Barry Krost, who with Doug Chapin is producing "Back Home," a Disney movie about a small town's response to a man with AIDS, says: "There used to be just one common denominator, and that was pornography. If you went to a gay bar, everybody looked the same. Now you go to bars or marches, and there are people dressed up, dressed down, in black tie—a whole range. It doesn't make it easy to sell to."

Richard Jennings, the executive director of Hollywood Supports, an advocacy group for gay people and for AIDS aware-

Zeitgeist Films

"Coming Out Under Fire"—Gay men and lesbians in the military during World War II.

ness at the studios, says: "It used to be that we would flock to anything that had gay characters, even if they were ice-pick murderers or people deranged because they were gay. Now, people want to see much more realistic films about their lives."

Gay men and lesbians show little interest in each other's films. "Men don't go to lesbian films," says Jon Gerrans, a partner in Strand Releasing. He cites "Claire of the Moon," which his company released last year. The film, a lesbian love story set at a women writers' conference, was not well received by critics but made back several times its cost with an almost exclusively lesbian audience.

Christine Vachon, who produced "Go Fish," a lesbian love story released last month by the Samuel Goldwyn Company, says: "Lesbians go to the gay men's films because there aren't enough lesbian films for them. But how many gay men do you know who want to see two women kissing on each other?"

Three years ago, the director Percy Adlon made a film set in Alaska that had at its center a lesbian relationship between an inarticulate orphan girl and a reclusive German woman. The film, "Salmonberries," had two things going for it. It starred the openly lesbian singer K. D. Lang, and it won the best film award at the Montreal Film Festival in 1991. But it was not until Roxie Releasing took over distribution of the film this year that it was seen outside festivals and retrospectives. ("Salmonberries" will open in New York in September.) Mr. Adlon says that studio distribution executives in 1991 were "scared to death" of a lesbian love story.

But that was then, and this is now. Mark Gill, the senior vice president for publicity at Columbia Pictures, which has four gay-themed films in development, says: "'Philadelphia' didn't open the door for gay projects. It opened the door and nailed it to the wall so it will stay open." Tri-Star, in releasing "Philadelphia," focused on a single campaign. Buffy Shutt, president of marketing for the studio, says, "We didn't want to have separate gay and straight campaigns, and maybe not get either audience clear."

Sherry Lansing, the president of Paramount, who was president of Fox when "Making Love" was produced, says: "One campaign was all they needed for 'Philadelphia.' We've come a long way since 'Making Love.'" Ms. Lansing is developing a new gay social comedy written by Paul Rudnick and produced by Scott Rudin.

Last month Universal Pictures began production in New York on "To Wong Foo, Thanks for Everything, Julie Newmar." How will the studio market the film, which is budgeted at over $30 million? "It's like that old advertising campaign: You don't have to be Jewish to love Levy's rye bread," says Bruce Feldman, the senior vice president for marketing. "We intend to reach the broadest possible audience, and to try to cultivate every sub-segment of that audience."

That has already been the case with the Gramercy Pictures release of "The Adventures of Priscilla, Queen of the Desert," another comedy about stranded drag queens (and a transsexual, played by Terence Stamp), this time in the Australian Outback. The film opened to strong reviews. According to Russell Schwartz, Gramercy's president: "It's not a gay picture. It's not about gay love. There's no sex in it. The last thing I want to do is ghettoize it. There is nothing that you'll see in the materials that we create that is necessarily gay." Posters show either a feather boa or what looks like three flamboyant females in the desert. Print ads for the film describe it as "a comedy that will change the way you think, the way you feel and most importantly, the way you dress."

But some industry mavens feel that such marketing requires film companies to be evasive. Samuel Goldwyn Jr., chief executive of the Samuel Goldwyn Company, says, "If you look at the ad for 'Philadelphia,' you'd think it was 'The Defiant Ones.'"

Peter Bart, the editorial director of Variety, says, "Hollywood has traditionally built campaigns that sidestep what a picture's really about."

Richard Natale, a Los Angeles journalist who has chronicled many gay and AIDS film projects, says that gay themes must be approached in an unthreatening way.

"Drag is probably a safe way to deal with it," he says. "As soon as you see two men kissing, it's bye-bye time." In October, Touchstone Pictures will release "Ed Wood," the story of the heterosexual schlock film maker who liked to dress up in women's clothing, particularly in angora sweaters. Ed Wood kisses only women.

When it comes to extremely low-budget films, the approach is reversed. Rather than skirt the issue of what the film is about, ads for some films make sure that audiences know there is homosexual content. If the movie's budget is low enough, the gay market alone can make the film profitable.

A company based in San Francisco, Frameline, releases and markets only gay and lesbian titles. "We always stress the gay and lesbian relevance of movies to audiences," says Mark Finch, the exhibitions director of Frameline and the director of the San Francisco International Lesbian and Gay Film Festival.

"Coming Out Under Fire," a documentary that opened this summer from Zeitgeist Films, is about gay and lesbian soldiers during World War II. The trailer for the film, says Nancy Gerstman, vice president of Zeitgeist, "highlights men and women equally, and the target group is gays over 35."

For "Go Fish"—a moderate commercial success—the ads suggest that the two young female leads are kissing. In the forthcoming "Jeffrey," the male leads will certainly be shown kissing. Mitch Maxwell, the executive producer of "Jeffrey," which stars Steven Weber as an AIDS-anxious naif trying to cope with sex and love, says: "The trials and tribulations of a gay male in the 90's are universal themes. If we're not happy with the way a distributor will sell the movie, we can distribute it ourselves."

Mr. Rudnick says: "Gay audiences are an enormous source of revenue for straight films, and have had no problem identifying with and enjoying straight people on screen. I would hope that there's starting to be a return on that investment."

The ads for "For a Lost Soldier," a love story about a Canadian soldier and a Dutch pre-teen-age boy during World War II, was one of Strand Releasing's biggest financial successes. The film was initially advertised with the man in a soldier's uniform and the boy dressed in school clothes. "After its fifth week, we switched the ad photo," says Mr. Gerrans of Strand. "We made both the boy and the soldier topless, and the grosses increased tremendously."

Mainstream publications, however, Mr. Gerrans says, "often refuse to play the sexy ad photos that run in the gay media." Ira Deutchman, president of Fine Line Features, adds that the Motion Picture Association of America's approval process for movie trailers is part of the problem. "Gay content is definitely verboten," he says. "For 'Swoon,' they just said there was no way in the world that they were going to allow us to be so overt about the gayness in the movie."

Bethlyn Hand, the senior vice president of the M.P.A.A., clarifies the ratings board's stand. "Homosexuality is not one of the things that is verboten," she says. "It depends on how it's used. The trailer has to be sanitized so that it's suitable for an audience with a G-rated movie."

The challenge then is to concoct a subtle marketing strategy that makes a film palatable to mainstream viewers and yet signals gay audiences that there is material of particular interest to them. Last year, the Samuel Goldwyn Company figured that an ad for "The Wedding Banquet"—a photo of a bride and her groom, who is holding hands with his best man—would primarily attract gay men. The distributor also hoped for a significant crossover audience. The low-budget film went on to make back its production cost many times over.

"What surprised us," says Mr. Goldwyn, the company's chief executive, "was that it also appealed to a large elderly female audience." James Schamus, co-producer of the film, says, "I now believe that there's only one niche market that's better and bigger than the gay market, and that's the mothers of gays."

* * *

January 1, 1995

OSCAR GIVES WAY TO ELEGY

By CLIFFORD ROTHMAN

One year ago, in the film "Philadelphia," Tom Hanks portrayed the gay lawyer Andrew Beckett who, at the beginning of the film, was seen at an AIDS clinic for an outpatient visit. As the IV drips, Andrew looks impassively around the room. Then the camera pans the faces: a once-handsome man, now gaunt to concentration-camp proportion, jokes about how an obtuse waitress offered him Sweet 'n' Low. "Do I look like I need an artificial sweetener, honey?" he says to the man sitting next to him.

Farther down the row, another man sits quietly. He is a gentle, sandy-haired fellow of about 30, his face littered with lesions.

Both the gaunt man, played by the New York actor Daniel Chapman, and the sandy-haired fellow, played by a novice actor, Mark Sorensen, are now dead. They are among the 43 of the 53 people with AIDS or those who were H.I.V. positive in "Philadelphia" who are now dead. The group also included Ron Vawter, the gay actor who played Andrew's straight colleague (the lone voice of compassion within the white-shoe law firm), and Michael Callen, one of the singers in the Flirtations, the a cappella singing group that performs at Andrew's costume party.

And it included Lou Digenio, who appeared as an extra in several scenes. Mr. Digenio, who was 34 when he died, did not want to be invisible in the courtroom scenes. So he dyed his hair henna red, to avoid getting lost in the crowd.

"Philadelphia" became one of the most successful dramatic films of 1993, earning an Oscar for Tom Hanks and $125 million at the box office worldwide before it was released on video. But audiences may have forgotten about the men in the film with AIDS.

Most of them had volunteered to populate the clinic, party and courtroom scenes; many played AIDS activists. The producers came to Action AIDS Philadelphia, a social services agency, for help in casting people with AIDS. "I tried to cast interesting people," said Bruce Flannery, who represents the organization. "But it wasn't very complex. In some cases, they needed people who were sick looking—in hospital scenes, for instance, where someone really robust would not have been right." By contrast, he said, "to participate in the courtroom scenes you had to be able to make the commitment to be available for a whole month, and be strong enough to withstand the grueling schedule, including long days of shooting."

The selection process was fairly democratic, with anyone able to put in the necessary hours accepted as an extra.

Jonathan Demme, the film's director, made a conscious decision to use as many people directly affected by the virus as possible. But the use of AIDS patients led to occasional tensions. One incident involved David Bertugli, an extra who had AIDS. Mr. Bertugli was washing up one day after filming and noticed that the extra standing next to him was scrubbing his own hands with alcohol. "You never know," said the man.

"He was afraid he was going to catch H.I.V.," said Gary Bailey, who lives with Mr. Bertugli and was also an extra in the film. Two years after "Philadelphia" was shot, Mr. Bertugli's T-cell count has dropped, along with his weight. Mr. Bailey reported that his family recently came to visit. "They were here to plan my funeral," he said. "Of all the conversations I've had with my parents, this one was the hardest. My father, who is politically a little to the right of Attila the Hun, cried like a baby. If anyone thinks that talking about sex is difficult, try talking to someone you care for about how they want to be buried."

Last year, Tom Hanks was Hollywood's first poster boy for AIDS. Mark Sorensen, the sandy-haired fellow in the AIDS clinic, was its real poster boy. His lesions did not come off with cold cream. Had he not become H.I.V. positive and sought help from Action AIDS Philadelphia, he would have got no closer to a movie than the 10th row of a cineplex.

By the time filming began in the fall of 1992, lesions from Kaposi's sarcoma covered Mr. Sorensen's face. His mother, Ann Sorensen, who lives in Malvern, Pa., outside Philadelphia, remembers that her son had always been vain. As a teen-ager, she said, Mark had been tremendously concerned about his complexion.

"If he got any marks on his face or anything, it would upset him terribly," she said. Mr. Sorensen's father, also named Mark, adds, "We spent many dollars at the doctors and the dermatologists."

Yet when the son was ready to appear in the clinic scene in "Philadelphia," which was shot in a single afternoon, he confided to Tom Hanks that he did not want to wear makeup to hide his lesions. "And he didn't," Mrs. Sorensen recalled. "He said he wanted people to see how it really was."

Fourteen months later, when Mr. Hanks won the Golden Globe award for best actor in a dramatic film, he remembered Mark Sorensen by name, paying tribute in his acceptance speech to his courage and humanity. Mr. Hanks went on to win an Oscar for the part as well, and to make an Oscar acceptance speech that also focused on the plight of people with AIDS.

Mark Sorensen did not live long enough to see either ceremony. Mr. Demme learned that the 31-year-old Mr. Sorensen was near death as the film makers were scoring the movie. "Jonathan immediately called his office," said Mr. Flannery of Action AIDS Philadelphia, "and had one of his assistants jump in the car with a rough, unedited videotape of the movie and drive it from Manhattan to Philadelphia."

Mrs. Sorensen remembers the day: Sept. 16, 1993. Mr. Demme's assistant arrived at the door with a copy of the movie. "She hands us the film and says: 'Take your time. Whenever you're done with the film, call me, and I will come pick it up.'" Mark Sorensen was bedridden, but he did not want to watch the movie from his bed. His mother recalled, "We physically carried him, my husband and myself and our nephew, down the stairs from his bedroom to the living room, and we all watched the movie." Mr. Sorensen died the next day.

Mr. Sorensen was on camera for only three seconds in the film. Ron Vawter, who had a much larger part, died last April on a jet while returning from Italy, where he had suddenly become gravely ill. Greg Mehrten, his partner of 14 years, remembers that the two of them had been sequestered in a cordoned-off section of the plane, with Mr. Vawter on a stretcher. "His heart just stopped," Mr. Mehrten recalled. For the next five hours, Mr. Mehrten flew with the body. "It was horrifying," he said. "I couldn't hear anyone, and I couldn't see anyone, except Ron. I had never really been with a dead person before."

Although the singer, Michael Callen, had survived for a very long time with the AIDS virus, he was forced by his illness to stop touring with the Flirtations in February 1993, shortly after filming the scene for the movie. He died in Los Angeles a year ago at the age of 38.

The emaciated Daniel Chapman was in a weakened state by the time he appeared in the clinic scene. "He would have been a star," said his mother, Lorraine. He died almost a year ago at the age of 41, after being hospitalized with a stroke.

Clifford Rothman has written about the arts for The Los Angeles Times and The Washington Post.

* * *

TELEVISION

November 26, 1978

THE PREOCCUPATION WITH SEX

By JOHN J. O'CONNOR

In "A Question of Love," tonight's ABC movie at 9, the subject is lesbianism. Clearly, television's sex bandwagon keeps rolling. As violent content is reduced, sex-related content becomes the major alternative. It can indeed be infinitely preferable, but, this being American television (the European variety has long been more sophisticated in such matters) the new phenomenon tends to generate tremors of nervousness on both sides of the small screen.

Sex, of course, can be treated seriously or wittily or even farcically, but, depending on the beholder, the result might be interpreted as exploitation or sensationalism or mere titilation. There are the borderline cases, certainly, but television is generally clear-cut in its intentions. In a tale about a prison farm for women, for example, there can be no doubt about ulterior motives when the voluptuous inmates traipse about like jiggly Daisy Mae dolls in skimpy Dogpatch togs. On the other hand, "Born Innocent," despite the inclusion of a controversial rape scene, offered a serious exploration of conditions in a reform home for young women.

Treatment, it seems, is virtually everything and is increasingly crucial as television's sex preoccupations continue to accelerate. Recent weeks have been clogged with representative examples. Big-budget mini-series—CBS's "The Word" and "The Pirate," or ABC's "Pearl"—have had their standard quotas of bed hopping and kinky implications, but the more interesting premises and variations are being developed for ordinary television movies. Titles can be almost pantingly contrived. NBC's "Thou Shalt Not Commit Adultery" was about a woman who, after her husband is accidentally paralyzed from the waist down, ponders the possibility of extramarital affairs. After some heavy experimenting with a professional golfer, she decided on a future dedicated to fidelity. Some nice performances, including Louise Fletcher's as the wife, made the Calder Willingham script seem considerably less opportunistic than it was. On ABC, the dreadful title of "How To Pick Up Girls" was given to a light comedy that managed to be surprisingly charming about the single-minded pursuits of swinging types in Manhattan. Once again, the performances, particularly those of Fred McCarren and Bess Armstrong, proved strong assets.

In a single week, NBC managed a triple-play in the new game of sex themes. Monday night featured "Betrayal," in which Lesley Ann Warren played the "vulnerable woman" in a true story about a psychiatrist luring his patient into a sexual relationship. Tuesday found Dyan Cannon as Sally Stanford, madame of a San Francisco brothel, in "Lady of the House." And, in a clever twist, Friday had Elizabeth Taylor in "Return Engagement" as an older college professor in a "special relationship" with a student (Joseph Bottoms). The affair in this case was never consummated, leaving everything in a constant state of trembling expectation.

And then there is homosexuality, which frequently seems to be little more than a fail-safe gimmick for attracting attention. Innumerable mincing types have flitted through countless situation comedies. Action-adventure formats are strewn with scenes in gay bars in which the hero in search of the villain has to interview various outlandish characters. At the other extreme, a more enlightened approach was attempted several years ago in "That Certain Summer," and the characters played by Hal Holbrook and Martin Sheen were elevated to something resembling sainthood. More recent efforts have been more effective. The British production of "The Naked Civil Servant" had the courage of Quentin Crisp's insistently non-conforming ways. And "Word Is Out," a WNET-financed collection of interviews with a wide spectrum of homosexuals, presented their liberated views of themselves candidly and without apology.

If male homosexuals have had a bumpy ride in television entertainment, lesbians have generally been treated with an ignorance. When not lurching around toughly in somebody's conception of a butch dyke, they are likely to be menacingly psychopathic. The classic TV example had several sadistic women running an old age home and murdering the patients to collect their insurance. Tonight's "A Question of Love" in some ways goes to the other extreme, becoming the lesbian equilavent of "That Certain Summer." Given the television record, however, the resulting exaggerations are not only justified but necessary.

The screenplay by William Blinn ("Brian's Song," episodes of "Roots") is based on an actual case in which the former husband of a lesbian sued for child custody on the ground that she was automatically an unsuitable mother. The drama's court proceedings are based on the actual proceedings of the case. As the story begins, Linda Ray is moving in with her lover Barbara. Linda Ray has two sons, teenaged David and young Billy. Barbara has a daughter in her early teens. The new family seems reasonably happy except for David, who is disturbed by his mother's relationship with another woman. He discovers that they have joint bank accounts and share several other things. Finally, he asks her directly if she is a lesbian. Linda Ray, who has never lied to him, says, "Yes, I am ¼ me and Barbara, we just care for each other, it's just as simple as that." As for the failure of her marriage to his father: "It just died in its sleep. No one was to blame."

The troubled David then goes to visit his father and refuses to return to his mother. She is convinced the reason is because the father has bought him a new car. Later, though, the father sues for custody of his other son, and David stays on his father's side. Linda Ray is taken to court. Barbara is publicly involved and remains loyal while realizing that "it could mean nothing, or it could mean our jobs—everything." Linda Ray is forced to confront lawyers who are either sexual bigots or afraid of controversy. Her case is taken by a young male-female team. She is interviewed by psychiatrists who are either hostile ("Do you worry about war a lot?") or timid about testifying for "an unpopular cause." Even before the trial begins, she is telling Barbara, "I wish to hell I had never met you—all I'd be is a divorced woman." Warnings that the trial will be rough turn out to be understated.

In its unabashed sympathy for Linda Ray, the script takes overly calculated liberties with what it chooses to include and exclude. Once again, virtual saintliness is courted as Linda Ray and Barbara, superbly played by Gena Rowlands and Jane Alexander, are portrayed as uncommonly sensitive people whose decency and intelligence are seemingly incomparable. They are carefully portrayed as reasonable moderates, unwillingly caught between the extremes of Bible-thumping critics and hysterical gay activists. The women's warm affection for each other is made quite clear as physical contact is kept to the barest minimum.

Conversely, the character of the husband, played by Clu Gulager, is parceled out sparingly and is too vaguely defined. With little known about him at the beginning, he seems like a strong, formidable adversary. However, in cross-examination at the trial, he turns out to be a quite ordinary airlines mechanic with a rather pathetic record. He once broke his wife's nose in a fight, he was found driving intoxicated, and, finally, he paid for an abortion performed on an 18-year-old he thought he might have made pregnant. On top of this, the screenplay makes only brief passing reference to an earlier hearing in which David, the older son, opted voluntarily to reside with his father.

Nevertheless, "A Question of Love" is a serious exploration of a complex issue. If it treads a bit too timidly at key points, it also avoids cheap sensationalizing. The film is provocative and, finally, very moving. Directed by Jerry Thorpe, the cast is outstanding. As Linda Ray, Miss Rowlands is at once marvelously strong and vulnerable. She's weary and determined, miserable and elated. Miss Alexander's Barbara is direct and unaffected, almost searingly on target. Once again on television, the subject is directly related to sex, but, once again, the treatment is admirably on target. "A Question of Love" is preceded by an announcement that "due to subject matter, parental discretion is advised."

* * *

November 6, 1985

NEWS SPECIAL ON AIDS TO FOLLOW NBC DRAMA

By STEPHEN FARBER
Special to the New York Times

LOS ANGELES, Nov. 5—NBC plans to broadcast a special news report and undertake an educational campaign in conjunction with "An Early Frost," a drama about AIDS that is scheduled to be shown Monday evening.

The two-hour drama is about a young homosexual lawyer (played by Aidan Quinn) whose family is thrown into a crisis when he tells his parents (Gena Rowlands and Ben Gazzara) that he has acquired immune deficiency syndrome. Immediately following the broadcast, NBC News will present a half-hour special report on the disease with Tom Brokaw as host.

"We hope it will amplify some of the points raised in the movie," said Lloyd Siegel, executive producer of the special for NBC News. "We want to answer specific questions that people still have about AIDS—who is at risk, what progress is being made in the search for a cure, and the measures taken around the country to attempt to control the disease."

One of the questions to be discussed in the news special, Mr. Siegel said, is the action by some state and city governments to close places frequented by homosexual men, such as bath houses, to try to stop the spread of the disease. "That seems to be the area of strongest disagreement in regard to AIDS," Mr. Siegel said, "and we will debate that point."

Advance Screenings of Film

NBC has arranged three advance screenings of "An Early Frost." On Thursday at the Kennedy Center in Washington, there will be a screening that Dr. Rosalind Schram, NBC's director of community relations, described as being primarily for health care officials and researchers.

On Friday at NBC headquarters in Rockefeller Center, a screening for health and science reporters will be followed by a panel discussion with Dr. Steven Schultz, Deputy Commissioner of New York City's Department of Health; Dr. John Martin, associate research scientist at Columbia University's School of Public Health, and Dr. Susan Tross, attending psychologist at the Memorial Sloan-Kettering Cancer Center.

Friday evening in Los Angeles, another screening will be held for members of the Academy of Television Arts and Sciences. The producer of "An Early Frost," Perry Lafferty, said that screening had been requested by the television academy because there has been so much misinformation about AIDS within the motion picture industry.

In addition, according to Dr. Schram, NBC has distributed a viewer's guide to hundreds of hospitals, social agencies and AIDS-related organizations across the country. And Gena Rowlands has recorded a 30-second public-service announcement—with a toll-free telephone number that viewers can call—that will be offered to all of NBC's local affiliates. Dr. Schram described this public-service campaign as "analogous to what we did last year with 'The Burning Bed' to educate people about wife abuse."

Some activities to raise money for AIDS research are being organized independent of NBC. Glenn Kennedy, associate director of AIDS Project Los Angeles, has proposed that individuals or organizations hold gatherings on the night the program is broadcast at which each guest will be asked to donate at least $10 to a local AIDS organization. In Los Angeles according to Mr. Kennedy, more than 100 of these gatherings have already been scheduled, and Bill Jones, director of development at the Gay Men's Health Crisis in New York, said a similar plan had drawn enthusiastic responses in Manhattan.

Mr. Kennedy said he rejected the idea of a large benefit screening in favor of the smaller, in-home gatherings. "My preference is smaller viewer groups," he said. "I'd like to encourage people to watch the show at home with friends. It's in keeping with the family emphasis of the film."

Other Programs on AIDS

Despite NBC's announcement that it would be making the first made-for-television movie about AIDS, "An Early Frost" will not be the first television program to deal with AIDS this season. The Showtime cable network's series "Brothers" showed an episode dealing with AIDS recently, and the CBS medical series "Trapper John, M.D.," broadcast an episode centering on AIDS last Sunday. In that episode, one of the regular characters in the series, the nurse played by Lorna Luft, was contacted by a former lover who revealed that he is bisexual and is suffering from AIDS.

Don Brinkley, the executive producer of "Trapper John, M.D.," said the episode had been in the planning stages for a long time.

"About two years ago we started thinking about doing an AIDS story," Mr. Brinkley said. "The problem we faced is that our show likes to give some reassurance, and with AIDS there was no reassurance to give. What we eventually came up with is that many AIDS victims lose their emotional support system and find themselves completely isolated. So in our story, our regulars band together to regenerate that support system. Lorna set out to bring back the victim's male lover, who had abandoned him on learing that he had AIDS."

Although the AIDS episode of "Trapper John, M.D." finished shooting only two weeks before it was broadcast, Mr. Brinkley denied it was rushed on the air ahead of "An Early Frost."

"At the time we first started talking about an AIDS story, we had no idea about the NBC film," he said. "And our episode was always scheduled for November."

* * *

February 23, 1997

SINCE COMING OUT IS IN, A GUIDE FOR THE TV AUDIENCE

Why are people all atwitter at the possibility that the lead character of the sitcom "Ellen," played by Ellen DeGeneres, will come out of the closet on television? What's the big deal? There have been hordes of openly gay characters before her, especially in made-for-television movies, since "That Certain Summer" in 1971. And only last month, PBS aired the BBC's production of "Breaking the Code," chronicling the life of the code breaker Alan Turing, who was gay.

More programs with gay characters are on the way, among them, "The Twilight of the Golds," about a family divided by a woman choosing whether or not to have a baby she knows will be gay, and a made-for-television movie about gay and H.I.V.-positive diver Greg Louganis.

The big deal now, according to The Advocate, a national gay and lesbian magazine, is that with the new television ratings system in place, networks may be queasier about showing gay relationships during prime time. The rating of a show, which flashes on the upper left-hand corner of the screen at the start of each program, depends on the sexual content and the violence in programs.

So far, there has not been much fallout. A January episode of "Relativity," on ABC, The Advocate noted, featured a 10-second lesbian kiss. (It got a rating of TV-14 (parents strongly cautioned), the next-to-highest warning. (The highest is TV-M, for mature audiences only.)

Right now, the magazine identified 22 recurring explicitly gay characters on network and cable television, including one cartoon character. Excerpts from The Advocate's list, which appears in the Feb. 18, 1997, issue, follow.

An Unnamed Waiter on "Cybill" (CBS). Played by Tim Maculan, this unhappy server may well be the . . . prissiest . . . gay character on TV . . . "What I like most about this character is that he's intelligent and witty," Maculan says. "It's kind of my kind of tribute to Noel Coward."

Peter and Barrett on "Ellen" (ABC). When Peter (Patrick Bristow) met Barrett (Jack Plotnick) at Ellen's 1995 Thanksgiving dinner, it was love at first bite. "I don't think Peter was written intentionally as a gay character," Bristow told the Advocate last year. "I guess what happened to Peter was this: Whatever it is in me that reads gay just became part of Peter's character."

Gil Chesterton on "Frasier" (NBC). Seattle radio station KACL's food critic, Gil has never come out on the series, but as played by openly gay actor Edward Hibbert, the character is unquestionably gay. "You can make a gay character as flamboyant, capricious, and outlandish as you want." Hibbert says. "But you have to make him smart."

Susan Bunch and Carol Wylick on "Friends" (NBC). The first lesbian couple on TV to become parents, Susan (Jessica Hecht) and Carol (Jane Sibbett), Ross Geller's ex-wife, wed in a 1995 commitment ceremony performed by Candace Gingrich. Best joke: Ross (David Schwimmer) grabs a can of beer and says, "This was Carol's favorite. She always drank it out of the can. I should have known."

Brian on "The Larry Sanders Show" (HBO). As gay production assistant to Larry Sanders's sidekick, Hank Kingsley (Jeffrey Tambor), openly gay comic Scott Thompson is less outrageous than he was as a member of the Canadian comedy troupe Kids in the Hall. But that's O.K. with him. "Brian's not like anyone I've ever played before," Thompson says. "He's duller than anyone I've ever played But I like it when I'm dull, and I mean to be dull."

Debbie and Joan on "Mad About You" (NBC). When Paul Buchman's sister, Debbie (Robin Bartlett), came out to her family last season, her mother almost jumped out a window. So did the show's producers. "They obviously thought it was risky," Bartlett (said). . . . "But if 'Mad About You' can't do it, who can?' Joan (Suzie Plakson) was introduced to the family in an episode that aired last fall.

Matt Fielding and Dan Hathaway on "Melrose Place" (Fox). By far TV's most forlorn gay character, Matt (Doug Savant) took to popping pills last season, which is how he met Dr. Dan Hathaway (Greg Evigan). "It's been an incredibly interesting trip playing a gay character," Savant told the Advocate in 1994. "You begin to see the homophobia in your own family when your parents, who are proud that their son is a star in a television show, don't want to tell their friends that he plays a gay character."

Ross on "Party of Five" (Fox). Perhaps the greatest moment of visibility for this gay music teacher (Mitchell Anderson) involved a 1994-1995 story line in which Ross came out and adopted a baby. Anderson created an even bigger stir offscreen when he came out at the 1996 Gay and Lesbian Alliance Against Defamation media awards presentation: "What's amazing is that people are genuinely touched by what I did . . . I never really realized how few visible role models the community has."

Rhonda Roth on "Relativity" (ABC). Playing the sister of lead character Leo Roth, Lisa Edelstein delivered the year's first same-sex kiss on the air. . . . "It was long—long, long, long," she says. "But that's not how they edited it." When asked if she liked the kiss despite what was left on the cutting room floor, Edelstein again responds in triplicate: "Yes, yes, yes."

Nancy Bartlett on "Roseanne" (ABC). When Rosie's white-trash buddy Nancy (Sandra Bernhard) came out, it seemed so natural. After all, wouldn't you turn to women after sleeping with Tom Arnold? "The character is nothing like me whatsoever," the always ambiguous Bernhard told the Advocate in 1992. "Well, in some ways maybe she is . . ."

Leon Carp and Scott on "Roseanne" (ABC). Hiring Martin Mull as Leon was a coup for the star. Getting Fred Willard to come on board as Carp's lover was sublime. After all, the two comics had shared top billing as co-hosts of the great 70's talk-show parody "Fernwood 2-Night." Best scene: the couple's 1995 commitment ceremony, which featured bare-torsoed muscle men, Milton Berle in a dress, Pachelbel's "Canon" set to a disco beat, and a special appearance by Rosie's on-screen lesbian admirer, Mariel Hemingway.

Bev Harris on "Roseanne" (ABC). The character to most recently come out on TV. Bev (Estelle Parsons) surprised her family at Thanksgiving last year by revealing her attraction to women. The announcement made her TV's first lesbian grandma. Best line: "By the end of my marriage," Bev told her family, "the only way I could have sex with my husband was if I stopped off at the store and bought myself a Playboy first."

Waylon Smithers on "The Simpsons" (Fox). The assistant to Springfield's patriarch, Montgomery Burns, Smithers (the voice of Harry Shearer) was a suspect in the 1995 shooting of his boss, with whom—it is rumored—he was in love. Although cleared of the crime, Smithers remains defiantly in the closet—despite the rub-on ankle tattoo of Liza Minnelli noted in his criminal profile.

Carter Heywood on "Spin City" (ABC). As the sitcom's resident gay activist, Carter (Michael Boatman) is TV's only African-American gay character. He is also the medium's most wry. Best line: "You're surprised I play basketball because I'm a gay man," he says to Assistant Deputy Mayor Stuart Bondek (Alan Ruck). "But you see, Stuart, I'm also a black man. So it's really just a battle of your archaic stereotypes."

Michael Delaney, Kevin Sheffield and Brad Phillips on "All My Children" (ABC). When high school history teacher Michael (Chris Bruno) came out on this popular soap in 1995, parents in the fictional town of Pine Valley tried to oust him from his job. During this time he befriended a student, Kevin (Ben Jorgensen), who also announced he's gay. Michael's new love interest . . . is Dr. Brad Phillips (Daniel McDonald). These are the only recurring gay characters on soaps, and as difficult as it has been to feature them, it's been even more difficult for lesbian characters. In fact, there are none. "This genre was created many decades ago and continues to serve the same purpose, which is to be predominately female romantic fantasy entertainment," says Michael Logan, contributing editor and soap-opera columnist for TV Guide. . . . "So it becomes more important to provide them with what they think they want, which is heterosexual romance."

* * *

April 13, 1997

A MESSAGE THAT'S DIMINISHED
BY THE BUILDUP

By CARYN JAMES

Nearly buried in the avalanche of hype surrounding "Ellen," the ABC sitcom in which the lead character is about to come out as a lesbian, is one especially revealing factoid. In a poll taken recently for TV Guide, 63 percent of viewers who were aware of "Ellen" said they had little or no interest in watching the supposedly special coming-out episode.

And why should they? Their lack of interest probably has less to do with attitudes about homosexuality than with the tiresome, teasing manner in which the lesbian story line has been promoted.

The hype has been relentless since word leaked out in September that Ellen Morgan, the bookstore manager played by Ellen DeGeneres, might acknowledge that she was a lesbian, becoming the first gay lead character on television. Magazines and newspapers tried to predict the public reaction; on talk shows, Ms. DeGeneres made coy jokes about her character being Lebanese and skated around the issue of her own sexuality. Finally, last week, she brought one part of this unsuspenseful story to a close by telling Time magazine that she is, indeed, gay. Now the character Ellen is ready to announce what the world already knows.

Still, ABC and Touchstone, the company that produces the show (both are part of the Walt Disney Company), are working hard to give the decisive episode the aura of a show-business event. The special hourlong episode is scheduled for April 30 (during the May sweeps period) and is loaded with mainstream guest stars. Laura Dern plays the woman Ellen falls for. Oprah Winfrey is the therapist who assures Ellen—and, more important, the middle-American viewing audience—that it's all right to be gay. Demi Moore, Billy Bob Thornton and K. D. Lang make brief appearances. Ms. DeGeneres's interview with Diane Sawyer, originally scheduled to run on "Prime Time Live" on ABC on April 23, has been

ABC

Ellen DeGeneres, left, and Laura Dern in the episode of ABC's "Ellen" that will be broadcast on April 30—A tame landmark, but a landmark nonetheless.

moved to "20/20" on April 25; the interview will now run during sweeps.

Despite the steamroller hype, though, this manufactured "event" is full of double messages. Paradoxically, six months of news, speculation and hot air have made the show seem both more and less important than it really is. Ellen Morgan's coming out reflects a changing middle-American attitude toward homosexuality. After all, by the time a network sitcom latches onto an issue, the show is merely validating what mainstream society has already absorbed, though cultural acceptance may still be uneasy. There are nearly two dozen gay and lesbian characters in supporting roles on television this season, so the fanfare makes Ellen's decision more daring than it really is.

But while Ellen's coming out may be a minor landmark, it is a landmark nonetheless. Television's validation of social change is itself important, making new attitudes more solid and acceptable. The circus atmosphere surrounding "Ellen" has overwhelmed the message, and made the character's declaration seem like just another sweeps-month stunt.

On one hand, the publicity machine has set up Ellen's coming-out as a comfy, middle-American experience, a ratings-grabber like Rhoda's wedding or the birth of Little Ricky. Yet the presence of a star like Ms. Winfrey offers a kind of cushion. Oprah's reassurance is only necessary if there is something to be nervous about in the first place. Embracing a gay character even while exhibiting skittishness about the act, the network may be sending a more accurate signal about conflicted mainstream attitudes than it intended.

Like the public lack of interest, the producers' nervous approach may not be entirely about the show's subject. During its three-year run, "Ellen" has never risen above its status as a "Seinfeld" wannabe. It used to be an unfunny show about a bookstore manager; now it can be an unfunny show about a gay bookstore manager. With its mediocre ratings, "Ellen" had little to lose by declaring its heroine a lesbian.

The coming-out show itself (its script was made available in advance) is cautious, bordering on unbelievable. Before Ellen tells her therapist and her friends that she's gay, she first has to tell herself. She's 35, she wore a tuxedo as maid of honor at her best friend's wedding, and she didn't have a clue? "I thought if I ignored it, it would just go away and I could have a normal life," Ellen tells the therapist, referring to her attraction to women.

"And what is a normal life?" Ms. Winfrey's kindly therapist replies. It is Ms. Winfrey, the all-American success story, who finally tells the reluctant Ellen: "O.K., Ellen, I'll say it. Good for you, you're gay." Ms. Winfrey offers many more positive lines about accepting homosexuality than Ellen Morgan does.

In the long run, a matter-of-fact acceptance of homosexual characters on television may be more effective in challenging prejudice than all this anxious jumping up and down. Carter, the gay mayoral aide in "Spin City," played by Michael Boatman, fits seamlessly into that cast. His character often makes political points about homosexual rights, but

his words carry weight because he is a credible individual, not merely a symbol.

And "Mad About You" offers sure-footed acceptance of lesbian characters. When Paul Buchman's sister, Debbie, introduced Joan, her lesbian lover, to the family, Paul's wife, Jamie, was elated. Jamie assumed she would no longer be on the lowest rung of the family; she was wrong. Joan instantly assumed the role of the favorite daughter-in-law, and also became Jamie's obstetrician.

Of course, the fact that Ellen is the unabashed heroine of "Ellen," not a minor player, is significant. Alan Klein, the communications director of the Gay and Lesbian Alliance Against Defamation (known as Glaad), is right to call Ellen Morgan's coming out a "turning point." Glaad is even sponsoring fund-raising "Coming Out With Ellen" parties in various cities, and offering home-party kits through their Web site.

In celebrating "Ellen," Glaad has a stronger point to make than their antagonist Jerry Falwell, who publicly urged Chrysler, Johnson & Johnson and General Motors, sometime advertisers on the show, not to support it. His comments made no real difference. All three companies said they had decided not to buy time on the coming-out episode long before Mr. Falwell's statement. Among the three, only Chrysler cited the show's content, saying it was good business to avoid a hot-potato issue. The network expects that all of the advertising time for the episode has been sold. As more gay characters appear on television, reactions like Mr. Falwell's will seem even more irrelevant.

Even if the coming-out episode is a ratings hit, there's no guarantee viewers will care enough to watch "Ellen" the next week. Inadvertently, the series may be making another equal-opportunity point: lesbian characters can lead lame sitcoms just as well or as badly as heterosexuals can.

* * *

April 25, 1998

ABC IS CANCELING 'ELLEN'

By BILL CARTER

ABC confirmed yesterday that it had canceled the comedy "Ellen," a year after the show made television history when its lead character, played by Ellen DeGeneres, declared she was a lesbian.

The news had been widely expected in light of the show's declining ratings in recent months and the stronger performance of another ABC comedy, the new "Two Guys, a Girl and a Pizza Place," in the same time slot this spring.

The cancellation attracted protests yesterday from gay rights groups, which accused ABC of pulling out because of concerns about content.

On Wednesday the network told the program's producers that it would not be back next season, an ABC executive said yesterday. ABC made no comment other than to confirm the cancellation officially.

Although three more episodes have been taped, only one, an hourlong series finale, will be broadcast on May 13, a network spokeswoman said, adding that ABC had no plans to broadcast the other two episodes.

Last May, the episode in which the show's namesake declared she was gay was the highest-rated episode of any show on the network. Ms. DeGeneres at the same time declared her own lesbianism, and photographs of her appeared on magazine covers as well as interviews in television news magazines.

But she clashed with ABC executives this season over the content of many of the show's episodes. ABC executives had asked that not every episode be on a gay theme and at one point ordered that a special viewer's advisory about content be included. Ms. DeGeneres protested, saying that shows that depicted heterosexual relationships were not required to include such warnings. She threatened to resign from the show but stayed on and finished the season.

Though she had asked last summer to be relieved of her contract, only to be compelled to produce another year of shows, Ms. DeGeneres said more recently she wanted to continue the series for at least one more year.

* * *

June 7, 1998

THE YELLOW BRICK ROAD TO 70'S SAN FRANCISCO

By STEPHEN McCAULEY

Last year, a student of mine told me he thought he had lived in San Francisco in a previous life.

"I was a folk singer," he said. "I lived there in the 60's and 70's."

You know a time and place has reached mythic status when it shows up in the establishing shots of someone's past-life regression: ancient Egypt; Machu Picchu; Petra, rose-red city half as old as time. But San Francisco?

I asked for specifics. While most former lives revolve around Hollywood-inspired delusions of grandeur, this one was touchingly modest. There was something about a group house near the Haight-Ashbury district, singing on street corners, picnics in Golden Gate Park. Admittedly, there was a little LSD thrown in and the suggestion of a couple of orgies, but it quickly became clear that the dominant themes were not wealth, glamour, drugs or sex, but freedom of expression and a longing for community. "I want to be a wild and crazy nonconformist," he seemed to be saying, "and live in a place with lots of people exactly like me." Or, to put a slightly different spin on it: "I want a family, albeit a nontraditional one."

Two television shows this week should be right up his alley: "Armistead Maupin's 'More Tales of the City'" on Showtime and the PBS documentary "The Castro." Both are set in San Francisco— "that spoiled and lovely city," to quote Alice Adams—and, despite vastly different styles and emphasis, they are perfect companion pieces. Each has much to say about the importance of community and our continuing

struggle to define "family" in a way that makes sense for the new millennium.

As you might guess from the title, "More Tales" (to be shown tonight and tomorrow night at 9) is the follow-up to "Armistead Maupin's 'Tales of the City.'" Although award-winning and hugely popular when broadcast on PBS in 1994, the original series included enough casual drug use, fleeting nudity and happy same-sex relationships to provoke the by-now-predictable bomb and assassination threats from religious groups. Under political pressure, PBS dropped plans to produce "More Tales," and Showtime stepped in. (Fortunately, Showtime has increased the casual drug use and made the nudity less fleeting, and the same-sex relationships happier and more passionate.)

"More Tales" is based on the second of the best-selling series of novels that Mr. Maupin began writing in 1976 as a daily column for The San Francisco Chronicle. The success of the books took many by surprise, Mr. Maupin included. What started out, in his words, as a kind of "inside joke on the way things work in San Francisco" has become something of an international sensation.

There is no shortage of reasons to explain the success of the "Tales" books and television series. They're funny, irreverent, endearingly innocent and just naughty enough to be mildly titillating. Even when broadly drawn, the characters are believable, and all are either lovable or irresistibly evil. (I think that's called a win-win situation.)

But the explanation for the almost cultlike following of the stories lies deeper than their entertainment value. Almost every major character in "More Tales" is an orphan of one kind or another. A gay man is rejected by his parents; a lonely mother was abandoned by her son. A transsexual's true love has died; a woman's confused lover has forgotten his past. Some characters are searching for their roots, but most have come to San Francisco hoping to redefine themselves and, in the atmosphere of relative openness and tolerance for which the city has become famous, to make a family from the ground up, one based on love and mutual respect, not genetics. In the midst of all the madcap goings-on, this is the raw nerve Mr. Maupin has touched in our late-20th-century psyches.

Unfortunately, the forces of oppression and censorship have recently won a number of battles in the high-stakes war raging on the floor of Congress, over the airwaves of talk radio and in the streets. The National Endowment for the Arts is so badly wounded, one almost longs for it to be euthanized. Despite a welcome reversal, the Manhattan Theater Club's initial decision to cancel a production of Terrence McNally's "Corpus Christi" in the face of death threats remains chilling. Violence against gay people and abortion clinics is up in many major cities around the country.

And yet, no matter what the daily body count, it's clear we can't return to the straight, narrow and dazzlingly white picture-postcard past that the religious right and its duly elected supporters demand for our future. "Family values" didn't fly as a major theme in the 1992 Presidential election because the profile of the happy, wholesome nuclear family it was trying to sell just wasn't striking enough chords of recognition. Like the characters in Mr. Maupin's San Francisco, many of us think of ourselves as orphans of one kind or another. And rather than being battered on the head with slogans that tell us we must cling to a set of shopworn mores and values in order to feel whole, we'd prefer to be shown some models for loving and positive alternatives.

This is exactly what the entire "Tales of the City" series does. "This is my family," a character declares as a group of lovers, friends and house mates escorts him to the hospital. The warmth generated by the crazy-quilt clan that resides at 28 Barbary Lane is felt by readers across the entire spectrum of sexual preference, marital status and gender, and is, I believe, the single most important reason for the enormous popularity of Mr. Maupin's work.

One of the author's more slyly subversive acts is to stitch together the lives of his gay and straight characters in a seamless way that makes moralizing and facile condemnation hard to pull off. Homosexuals are not safely confined to a ghetto but walking the city along with everyone else. These moving targets are a lot harder to hit without doing considerable collateral damage.

For an examination of the gay ghetto, and its social and political significance, there is "The Castro," a 90-minute documentary that has its national PBS premiere on Friday night at 9. The film describes how the Eureka Valley, at the geographical center of San Francisco, went from factories and dairy farms in the 1870's to an Irish working-class neighborhood in the 1930's to the heart of the city's large gay population, beginning in the late 1960's.

The filmmaker Peter L. Stein's take is that gay people resemble one more oppressed immigrant group struggling for political power and a place to live in peace. By charting the gay migration to the Castro neighborhood, he has come up with a history of the gay movement over the last 30 years.

San Francisco had become a kind of gay mecca by the end of the Second World War, but with the homosexual population spread out across the city, closeted and without leadership, arrests and raids were commonplace. The film makes it clear that like other immigrant groups, gay people needed to band together in order to establish a base of power and influence. But unlike other groups, gay men and lesbians had no ready-made structure—family, cultural identity—on which to build.

In the film, Phyllis Burke, an author and a former Castro resident, explains it this way: "Lesbian and gay people are the only people on earth who have to find their tribe. We aren't born into it. You have to have a place to go to find the tribe."

The place quickly became the Castro. In the late 1960's, gay men began buying up housing stock that had been abandoned (by middle-class families fleeing the city for suburbia) and started to open their own neighborhood businesses. Knowing where to "find their tribe," gay men and lesbians forged political clout. The decades that followed were triumphant and tumultuous. Harvey Milk, Castro resident, became California's first openly gay elected official and was assassinated for his sexuality, all within one year (1978). By the late

1970's, gay residents were experiencing unprecedented unity and freedoms. But in 1981, posters began appearing in Castro Street storefronts warning of a "gay cancer." The film uses dramatic footage to record this history, and to his credit, Mr. Stein doesn't shy away from class, race and gender conflicts within the Castro.

The documentary ends with bittersweet ambivalence. In the late 1990's, real estate in the Castro has become prohibitively expensive for young and minority gay men and lesbians. Many businesses cater to tourists, and the whole neighborhood has taken on something of a theme-park atmosphere: Gayworld.

On a more positive note, a young woman who was reared in the Castro by her gay father is shown marrying her female lover in a freewheeling outdoor ceremony that has all the warmth and charm of a scene from "More Tales of the City." After leaving the city for a time, she has returned home and is creating a family for herself on her own terms.

My student's past-life fantasy suggests that San Francisco has achieved mythic status among the disillusioned and disenfranchised from all over. Surrounded by water and frequently shrouded in fog, it has become, in our collective imaginations, a kind of real-world Oz. What these two films make clear is that unlike Oz, where Dorothy and company went to buy their tickets home, San Francisco is the home they seek.

Stephen McCauley is the author of three novels, including "The Object of My Affection."

* * *

September 20, 1998

HE'S GAY, SHE'S STRAIGHT, THEY'RE A TREND

By STEPHEN McCAULEY

One theory holds that if Monica had had a gay man for a confidant—vsomeone reliable, empathetic and capable of keeping certain secrets safely locked in a closet where they belong—her sex life would never have been splashed across the headlines. If only she'd had a pal like Will Truman, half of television's latest odd couple in "Will and Grace," a series that has its premiere on NBC tomorrow night at 9:30. Like all male homosexuals—you didn't know?—Will is good-looking, witty, has lots of disposable income and knows how to dress. Despite his many attributes, he's currently unattached, leaving him available for help with a multitude of late-night crises. (And emergency trips to the dry cleaner?) What more could any woman desire in a best friend than a man who can offer a sturdy shoulder to cry on and knows his way around a loose interpretation of penis envy? Based on the evidence of the first two episodes, he doesn't even own a tape recorder.

"Will and Grace" are the latest of a growing number of gay-guy, straight-girl couples to dance their way across both big and little screens in romantic comedies. Last year, the friendship of Julia Roberts and Rupert Everett helped pump grosses of "My Best Friend's Wedding" well above $100 mil-

Barry Wetcher / 20th Century Fox

1998 In "The Object of My Affection," Paul Rudd's character had two boyfriends as well as a close woman friend, Jennifer Aniston.

1961 In "Breakfast at Tiffany's," George Peppard's character was given a heterosexual makeover to be Audrey Hepburn's best friend.

lion. Earlier this year, Jennifer Aniston and Paul Rudd were an almost-perfect pair in "The Object of My Affection," Wendy Wasserstein and Nicholas Hytner's adaptation of my 1987 novel. Armistead Maupin's "More Tales of the City," broadcast on Showtime last June, featured Laura Linney and Paul Hopkins sharing a twin-bedded cruise-ship cabin by night and helping each other look for Mr. Right at the pool by day. Get out your pop-culture barometers; it's beginning to look like a trend.

In fact, couples of this sort are hardly new. Christopher Isherwood described one such pair (Sally Bowles and the author's alter ego, also named Christopher Isherwood) in his 1939 novel, "Goodbye to Berlin." Truman Capote wrote a Manhattan version of the same story in "Breakfast at Tiffany's." What is fresh is the unapologetic bluntness with which the man's sexual preference is now defined. The narrators of both Isherwood and Capote's stories are vivid characters, but their sexual identities are discreetly tucked between the lines. The film version of "Cabaret," based loosely on the Sally Bowles story, went so far as to make the male lead hesitantly bisexual, while the screen adaptation of Capote's book threw ambiguity to the wind and transformed the hero into a naive but resolutely heterosexual hunk.

Viewers know exactly where to place Will Truman on the Kinsey scale in the opening scene of the first episode when he sighs longingly over George Clooney. Instead of gasping in horror, the studio audience laughs appreciatively.

Almost all of these gay best friends are played with few if any of the limp-wristed affectations that have simultaneously

defined and demeaned male homosexuals, even in recent well-meaning farces like "The Birdcage" and "To Wong Foo." The characters are productive, well-adjusted men who've accepted their sexuality with apparent ease. No one in the world of Will Truman, lawyer, gives homosexuality a second thought. One macho client—"the largest manufacturer of buffalo feed in the entire Southwest"—is comfortable enough to make offhand, vaguely off-color jokes with Will. Trent Lott may not have received the message, but apparently we've come a long way. Maybe.

Some cultural critics argue that this current crop of gay-straight couples proves that a sexually viable gay male can appear as a main character in a major-studio film or as a protagonist in a sitcom on one of the big three networks only when he is safely (albeit chastely) paired with a heterosexual woman. Focusing on this relationship shoves into the background threatening topics like his romantic inclinations or, God forbid, his sex life.

Rupert Everett's character in "My Best Friend's Wedding" was bursting with bons mots and Noel Coward charm, but audiences who blinked missed the one reference to his private life (a photograph of another man propped up on a bookshelf). "The Object of My Affection" went much farther; George, played by Paul Rudd, has two boyfriends, and we even see him kiss one of them. Still, the steamiest scene in the movie is one in which Mr. Rudd and Jennifer Aniston nearly consummate their romantic friendship.

Michael Bronski, author of "The Pleasure Principle: Sex, Backlash and the Struggle for Gay Freedom," commends this new crop of films for "honorably resisting the demonization of homosexuality." But, he adds, "if the gay characters merely say they're gay and then aren't allowed the same rights to casual sexuality as straight characters, it doesn't represent much advance at all."

"Can a roommate walk in and catch Will making out with another man on the couch?" Mr. Bronski asks.

It remains to be seen how much casual sexuality Will Truman will be allowed in forthcoming episodes. But focusing exclusively on the gay content of this and similar scenarios is perhaps missing the more important point. In the end, these screen couplings of gay men and straight women may be most remarkable for what they have to say about current attitudes toward heterosexual men and romantic love in general.

In "Will and Grace," and almost every other example I've cited, these not-quite-lovers are portrayed as having charmed, unabashedly romantic relationships. They go ballroom dancing. They race across rooms to fly into each other's arms. They spend nights curled up in bed together, eating ice cream and watching television. The men and women are strangely nice to each other. Strangest of all, they understand each other.

Compare this with an army of sitcoms in which half the plots and two-thirds of the jokes involve men-are-from-Mars, women-are-from-Wherever misunderstandings and can't-live-with-'em-can't-live-without-'em resolutions.

No one can beat Will and Grace at giving each other clues in the home version of "The $25,000 Pyramid" because, like a pair of telepathic twins, they speak the same language, a shorthand lingo they seem to have invented.

Feelings about traditional male roles are so ambivalent these days. Many sitcoms feature straight men who are social bumblers, lumbering between clumsy attempts at chivalry—often interpreted by their wives and girlfriends as condescending machismo—and gushy sentimentality that's viewed as irritatingly weak. Heterosexual men are portrayed more than ever before as either offensive or ineffectual. (Part of Howard Stern's popularity among male listeners must surely have something to do with the way he has co-opted unflattering stereotypes of loutish men. His carefully crafted on-air persona is gleefully offensive and ineffectual at the same time. He's like a 12-year-old boy who has been told he's naughty and is hell-bent on proving he is.)

In the pilot for "Will and Grace," Will cautions Grace that Danny, her fiancé, isn't passionate, creative or sensitive enough for her. But when poor Danny tells his bride-to-be he can't wait to spend the rest of his life with her, she leaves him at the altar. Stripped of the emotional straitjacket of conventional masculinity, along with most of its responsibilities, Will is free to be Grace's "hero and soul mate," while Danny turns out to be "just another plot point" in the movie of her life.

Far from being a winsome wimp who's not man enough for a woman or woman enough for a man, Will Truman is a "true man." He's there for Grace to lean on, he speaks from the heart, and, according to her, makes her "a better woman"

NBC

Soul Mates Debra Messing and Eric McCormack in "Will and Grace." Their nonsexual courtship can last indefinitely.

for loving him. He offers Grace no sexual satisfaction, but doesn't present a sexual threat either. Certainly he isn't going to suffocate her with a marriage proposal the way dumb old Danny did.

Will is an updated version of the debonair "confirmed bachelor" character usually played with aloof warmth by Cary Grant or Rock Hudson, actors whose off-screen lives (coincidentally?) were teeming with sexual complications. Will's sexuality insures that there won't be the kind of too-pat ending that cynical audiences tend to balk at these days. The fact that there are so few happy marriages in literature is probably a good indication that there's not much literature in happy marriages. Viewers need not worry about wedding bells breaking up this twosome any time soon. Will and Grace can carry on an extended courtship indefinitely—romantic as they want to be, no strings attached, no secrets to hide, no ulterior motives.

A couple of weeks ago, I was having lunch at a diner in the Adirondacks. A rumor rolled down the counter, across the floor and passed from booth to booth: Monica was two towns away, vacationing at a great camp on Lower Saranac Lake. I sighed. If only she'd spent her last few summer vacations in Provincetown or the Pines, meeting the right kind of people.

Stephen McCauley is the author of three novels, including "The Object of My Affection."

* * *

January 25, 2000

'MILLIONAIRE' QUIETLY BREAKS TV BARRIERS

By BERNARD WEINRAUB

HOLLYWOOD, Jan. 24—On Sunday night a contestant on "Who Wants to Be a Millionaire" embraced his gay companion onstage after winning $500,000. The audience cheered, Regis Philbin, the host, grinned, and the network was not flooded with protest calls.

In its own quirky way, the quiz show, which is a ratings juggernaut and the No. 1 show in the nation, has quietly and quite nonchalantly broken sexual and racial barriers on television. Not only do gay couples routinely appear on the show—the word "gay" is never used—but so do racially mixed couples, which in the past television has often avoided showing.

By all accounts, the matter-of-fact presentation of these couples, without a comment from Mr. Philbin or anyone else, has altered the television landscape. The show, on ABC three nights a week, has an average audience of 28.5 million viewers and has single-handedly revived the network.

Sunday night's show stirred nervousness among the "Millionaire" staff members because it was the first time in memory that two men—a contestant and his companion in the audience—embraced before television cameras. The contestant was Rob Coughlin of Shoreline, Wash., who works for a transit company.

"We treat everyone the same way, and there's never been an issue about people's personal relationships," said Michael Davies, executive producer of the show. "If a contestant is married 25 years and white and middle-class with 2.4 kids and brings his wife to the show, that's fine. Or whether somebody brings their college buddy or mother or sister or lover, we don't care. We don't care about ethnic things, we don't care about sexual things. We treat everybody the same. The show broadly reflects society."

Mr. Davies admitted that he had been a bit anxious about Sunday night's show, which was taped late last week. When contestants win $250,000 or more, their partners, who until then are shown sitting and cheering them on, are taken onstage.

While sitcoms and dramas about racially mixed couples are rare, there have been some comedies involving gay characters. Billy Crystal played a gay man as far back as 1977 in the ABC series "Soap," which was a satire on soap operas. Even before the show was broadcast, ABC received about 32,000 letters protesting it, and some network affiliates were picketed because of the show's sexual content. The uproar died down, and the series lasted four years.

The NBC sitcom "Will and Grace," about a gay man and a straight woman living together, is one of the most successful shows on television. Max Mutchnick, who created the series with David Kohan, said he was surprised that there were no network "stop signs" for the series's writers. In fact, he said, the creators and writers can go quite far in terms of subject matter.

Shortly after the highly publicized decision by Ellen DeGeneres to announce that she was a lesbian, her show, "Ellen," started to fade. At the time network executives said that was in part because the show was aging and also because it had lost its sense of humor.

"There are no flags, no one's underlining it or remarking on it," Mr. Mutchnick said. "It's been put on its feet and being filmed, and it's going out on the air and no one's saying anything about it."

Mr. Mutchnick said it was a far cry from the NBC sitcom "Love, Sidney," from 1981 to 1983, in which Tony Randall played a gay commercial artist. But his sexuality was inferred, never mentioned. "He was only shy," said Mr. Mutchnick with a laugh. "He went to shy bars."

Earle Marsh, co-author of The Complete Directory to Prime Time Network and Cable TV Shows (Ballantine Books), said he could recall no previous quiz show in which either gay or multiracial couples were so evident. "Twenty years ago there would have been serious problems with network standards and practices, the censors," he said. "They might have worried about segments of the audience being homophobic or have other problems."

"I'm sure at one point the choice of people to go on the air might have raised red flags," Mr. Marsh said. "In today's environment we've moved beyond that."

He pointed out that interracial couples, while rare on television, are not unique. In "The Jeffersons," Norman Lear's spinoff about Archie Bunker's former black neighbors, the son is married to a mixed-race woman. Her black mother and white father were also neighbors. "It was groundbreaking," said Mr. Marsh.

On "Millionaire," Mr. Philbin introduced Mr. Coughlin's companion, Mark Leahy, as soon as the contestant walked onstage.

"Your partner, Mark, is in the audience, hey, Mark," said Mr. Philbin as the audience cheered.

As Mr. Coughlin, began answering questions correctly, Mr. Philbin asked Mr. Leahy what his partner should do if he won $1 million. "Get a new wardrobe," replied Mr. Leahy.

By the time Mr. Coughlin reached $500,000, he was stumped by the million-dollar question: In what country are all the United States major league baseballs manufactured? (The correct answer was Costa Rica.) Instead of risking the loss of most of the money to go for $1 million, Mr. Coughlin decided to halt the questioning and walk off with $500,000.

At that point, Mr. Philbin said, "Hey, Mark, come down."

Mr. Leahy bounded onto the stage and hugged Mr. Coughlin. "Hey, Mark, nice to see you," Mr. Philbin said.

ABC executives said there was no reaction from viewers to the episode.

Mr. Davies said there had been other gay contestants with their companions sitting in the audience and introduced by Mr. Philbin. "The first time there were definitely some raised eyebrows by some members of my team," Mr. Davies said. "I said to Regis, 'Just refer to his partner in the audience.' And that was it."

To be a contestant on "Millionaire" people apply by calling (800) 433-8321 from 6 P.M. to 2 A.M. Eastern Standard Time until Feb. 9. To qualify, they have to be 18 and over and a United States citizen. An elimination process follows, based on responses to questions as well as a random drawing. No personal questions are asked. About 240,000 people call daily.

Mr. Davies said that what concerned him was that contestants were not a cross section of the nation. "We do not have enough minority contestants, we do not have enough female contestants and this bothers me," he said. "I don't know what the reason is. There may be something about trivia and the amassing of knowledge of trivia that's essentially white and

male. It really bothers me that we can't get more female and minority contestants."

Lloyd Braun, co-chairman of the ABC Entertainment Group, said the show's potpourri of contestants was in some ways a breakthrough. "It's the most color-blind inclusive show you can ever have," said Mr. Braun. "It's fantastic that nothing's been made of it."

Mr. Braun said that each contestant on the show was actually a "slice-of-life, a mini-drama." "You get to not only meet the contestant when he or she is in the hot seat, but you meet their spouse or partner or 100-year-old grandmother," he said. "It's not judgmental. It's totally accepting."

* * *

MUSIC

June 27, 1994

THE GAY CONNECTION IN MUSIC AND IN A FESTIVAL

By ALEX ROSS

Statistics are not at hand to support the claim, but it seems that gay men and lesbians make a disproportionately large contribution to music. Why so? One popular and persistent explanation is that music is the most indefinite, the most ambiguous of all the arts, as Oscar Wilde declared in "The Critic as Artist," and is therefore attractive to those who find themselves out of sync with more conventional, clear-cut modes of expression. Encouraging an impersonal submersion in the arcana of tradition, music has historically been a refuge for homosexuals who were elsewhere silenced.

This is, of course, a very old-fashioned formulation. Twenty-five years after the Stonewall rebellion, gay men and lesbians are making a more direct engagement with the musical culture that is very much part of their heritage. In the program for the Gay Games cultural festival last week, one saw listings for the International Gay and Lesbian Baroque Orchestra, the New York City Gay Men's Chorus, a cantata entitled "Stonewall/Flashpoint." Ambiguity is very much out of fashion; what was once a refuge is now a platform for public affirmation.

Composers, too, have written works programmatically linked to contemporary gay life. John Corigliano's Symphony No. 1, among the most often played American orchestral works of recent years, memorializes friends who died of AIDS; next season the New York City Opera will present an opera based on the life of Harvey Milk, the San Francisco supervisor who epitomized gay political advancement before his assassination in 1978. And the musicological field has lately investigated questions of sexuality, with scholars combing the music of Schubert, Tchaikovsky and Handel for traces of gay identity.

Most of the cultural festival performances I attended last week justified themselves on purely musical terms. The best of these was the Baroque orchestra, which performed on Tuesday night at Kaye Playhouse. Marion Verbruggen, the acclaimed Dutch recorder virtuoso and conductor, led marvelously spirited performances of Telemann, Handel, Vivaldi and Bach. Her solo playing in Vivaldi's Concerto in C (RV 443) was a miracle of poetry and precision. There was nothing identifiably "gay" about the event, except for some ironic heterosexual theatrics on the part of Christine Brandes and Philip Wilder, superbly singing a love duet from Handel's "Joshua."

Ms. Verbruggen organized her group specifically for the Gay Games festival. Positive Music, a chamber-music group organized by the double-bassist Charles Tomlinson, has been performing for a year at the Lesbian and Gay Community Services Center; it concluded its season with a concert on Wednesday evening. Oriented toward those living with AIDS or H.I.V., the group provides a crucial opportunity for musicians who may have found it difficult to pursue full-time professional careers. Matt Sullivan was a superb oboe soloist in Britten's "Phantasy Quartet," Mr. Corigliano's "Aria" and Laura Kaminsky's "Interpolations on Utopia Parkway." The baritone Michael Dash sang in a moving performance of Barber's "Dover Beach."

On Sunday night at the Kaye Playhouse, the Unity Symphony Orchestra devoted an entire program to works by gay composers: Mr. Corigliano's "Gazebo Dances" Overture, Barber's "Medea's Meditation and Dance of Vengeance," Bernstein's "On the Town" dances, Chris DeBlasio's "All the Way Through Evening," Britten's "Sinfonia da Requiem" and the finale of Tchaikovsky's Fifth Symphony. Conducted by Stephen Rogers Radcliffe and Derrick Inouye, this group had messy moments, but, as with Ms. Verbruggen's ensemble, there was a thrilling commitment in the playing.

Britten's great symphonic Requiem made a particularly powerful effect: its grand sequence of emotions, from crushing despair to demented panic to peaceful resignation, seems to mirror the tragedies of the age of AIDS. There is a certain difficulty here, however; Britten did not advertise his homosexuality and looked on gay liberation with disdain in his final years. He is, so far, the only major composer to have consistently addressed homosexuality as a subject (usually in oblique fashion), and yet his wariness toward displays of sensuality and his persistent interest in adolescent boys have somewhat muted the heroic daring of his achievement. Barber and Copland were also circumspect, and even the flamboyant Bernstein never quite made the transition to public affirmation.

Works from the new generation of openly gay composers, on the other hand, are sometimes distinguished more by good intentions than sound inspiration. Stopping in at the Gay Men's Chorus concert on Thursday night at Carnegie Hall, I missed Roger Bourland's Stonewall cantata but heard Ricky Ian Gordon's "Angel Voices of Men"; this music seemed to bend over backward to be "accessible," relying on routine harmonic sequences better suited to Broadway than Carnegie Hall. There is an unbridgeable divide between classical idioms and an arena of popular music that allows much more direct assertions of gay identity. (At Kaye Playhouse on Wednesday night, I saw the Topp Twins, a guitar-playing, singing and yodeling lesbian duo from New Zealand who avoided political earnestness and performed with irresistible comic verve.)

Like it or not, most of the masterpieces of Western tradition have been written according to a code of reticence and transcendence, and they are perhaps best understood according to that same code. Some recent scholarly inquiries have tried to bring music out of the closet, with very mixed results; the musicologist Susan McClary's identification of a sort of homosexual musical dialect in the music of Schubert and Tchaikovsky relies on facile stereotypes of gay identity and fanciful interpretations of classical forms. The fact is, those who enter into the strange craft of music, from whatever background, all go into a kind of larger closet, one that discourages an open engagement with the here and now. As usual, Oscar Wilde was right: "To reveal art and conceal the artist is art's aim."

* * *

April 2, 1995

A BRASH OPERA HOLDS A MIRROR TO GAY LIFE IN AMERICA

By K. ROBERT SCHWARZ

The day after the premiere of "Harvey Milk" last January, the staff of the Houston Grand Opera seemed to be breathing a collective sigh of relief. Not that the quality of the production had ever been in doubt, but the threat of anti-"Harvey" demonstrations by right-wing activists had set the company on edge. Although extra security had been arranged, no protest had materialized.

Until then, the gestation of the production had gone anything but smoothly. David Gockley, the general director of

the Houston Grand Opera, had faced stormy board meetings, the loss of accustomed corporate sponsorship, and the wrath of fundamentalist Texans over the company's sponsorship of "Harvey Milk."

"Over the last year, I've gotten some 40 hate letters or telephone calls," he said recently. "Some of them were extremely sick. Most came from the Christian biblical point of view, and all were homophobically based."

The opera, with music by Stewart Wallace and libretto by Michael Korie, will probably not generate this kind of controversy in New York when the New York City Opera presents the first of three performances on Tuesday evening. Still, the critical reaction to the Houston run suggests that many in the opera world are uneasy with such an overtly gay subject. For "Harvey Milk" is an unflinching, in-your-face kind of opera, a work that examines not only Milk's tragedy but the awakening of gay consciousness in America.

Harvey Milk, the first openly gay elected city official in the United States, spent only 11 months on the San Francisco Board of Supervisors, but his political savvy carried him to national prominence. When he and San Francisco Mayor George Moscone were assassinated on Nov. 27, 1978, by Dan White, another supervisor, Milk was transformed into a martyr, a casualty in the continuing battle for civil rights for gay Americans. Mr. Wallace, 34, and Mr. Korie, 39, set out to place Milk's life within the larger context of the struggle for gay liberation.

"It was inescapable that in 'Harvey Milk' we would be telling the story of the emerging gay rights movement in America," Mr. Korie said. "I think of our Harvey Milk as a fictionalized character who embodies that story. We realized that this opera would be performed not before gay and lesbian audiences but before opera-going audiences, who are mostly conservative and who need to be shown the obstacles that Harvey Milk was up against."

Indeed, Mr. Korie's witty libretto paints Milk's evolution as a virtual mirror of gay life in postwar America. The first act shows Milk in the 1960's, leading the constrained life of a closeted Wall Street stockbroker; it ends with a re-enactment of the Stonewall rebellion and Milk's embracing of his dual identity as a gay, Jewish man. The second act recreates the riotous atmosphere of Castro Street in San Francisco in the 70's and includes a duet, sung in bed, between Milk and his lover. The third act finds Milk taking the reins of political power; it concludes with a candlelight march in his memory, framed as a setting of the Kaddish, the Jewish prayer for the dead.

Although Mr. Korie is gay, Mr. Wallace is not, a circumstance that had a profound impact on the libretto.

"Stewart, not being familiar with the meaning of coming out of the closet, couldn't take anything for granted," Mr. Korie said. "I found it very useful for him to say, 'What does this really mean?' In some ways his reaction reflected the questions the audience would have, and it made me get beyond political rhetoric. I also had taken the issue of sex for granted, and Stewart was the one who kept asking: 'Where is the passion? Where is the sex?'"

"Opera has always been about sex," Mr. Korie added with a wry smile, "and I was only too happy to comply."

But neither the composer nor the librettist had any desire to create a "docu-opera." Their portrait of Milk is unapologetically mythicized, making the character as much icon as man. Some critics bristled at this conception in Houston, accusing the creators of removing Milk's blemishes and recasting him as a saint. Many of the same critics praised the opera's thoughtful portrayal of Dan White, who comes across as far more than a one-dimensional villain. Mr. Wallace finds the comparison troubling.

"I think the characters were held to different standards," he said. "Dan White's character is much smaller. He doesn't really evolve; he's petulant and incapable of compromise. Harvey Milk is somebody who evolves greatly over time; the trajectory of his life is much larger. What irks me is when somebody says, 'You've made a sympathetic portrait of Dan White, but you haven't shown Harvey Milk's warts.' That says that it's laudable to humanize the murderer, but it's not laudable to humanize the gay man."

In fact, the opera's third act shows Milk to be a tough-talking, Machiavellian politician. The libretto alludes to his many lovers without emphasizing them; a scene in the baths, during which Milk campaigned clad only in a towel, was cut, for reasons of length, not hagiography. One of the most remarkable aspects of "Harvey Milk" is its uncompromising look at the range of gay life, from cruising in Central Park to brutal bashings, from leather fetishists to high-stepping drag queens.

Such honesty did not go over well with timid members of the gay community in Houston, who would have preferred that the Castro Street scene have a scrubbed-clean, mainstream facade.

"There was a big outcry in Houston from some of the more conservative gay couples who attend the opera," Mr. Korie said. "They said that they would boycott this one, because they felt that these stereotypes of promiscuous gay men and lesbians and drag queens parading down streets would not further our cause. Nonsense. I feel it's a very populist work that takes an affectionate look at the gay and lesbian community of that time, which is an era we can all be proud of."

Since the gay world of the 70's was as yet untouched by AIDS, the disease is never explicitly mentioned in the opera. Several critics took umbrage at the omission, seeming to regret a lost opportunity to drive home a moral judgment. Although Mr. Korie had been forewarned about such a response, it still makes him seethe.

"There is promiscuity in the opera, and there is no stigma attached to it," he said. "I was told: 'You don't know your audience. If you do things like this, you're going to make them blame AIDS on these characters.' And I totally rejected that. Of course you can't write anything today without an awareness of AIDS, and that awareness was very present in choosing to ignore it. I didn't want to constrict the behavior of these characters to appease some potential bias on the part of the audience. The world of Harvey Milk existed in a time before AIDS. It's as simple as that."

What tended to get lost amid this hubbub of politics and morality was Mr. Wallace's music. His score took some knocks for its gleeful eclecticism, a rousing melange of operatic lyricism, Broadway sentimentality, post-Minimalist repetition and the rhythmic propulsion of American pop. Such musical diversity flows naturally from Mr. Wallace's background.

Largely self-taught as a composer, he grew up in Houston, where he acted as his synagogue's cantor and played in a rock band.

"In Texas, all kinds of music are on a level playing field," Mr. Wallace said. "So I experienced everything from classical to Tejano to blues, jazz and rock, and I never had any sense of musical hierarchy."

Mr. Wallace's peculiarly American synthesis of high and low finds a champion in Mr. Gockley, of the Houston Grand Opera.

"Stewart's score says that we are getting into mining the tremendous reserve of musical raw material that we've created in America in the last century," Mr. Gockley said. "I think it's remarkably helpful, because it is the language that all of us are familiar with. The more that opera begins to embrace this raw material, the more identified we're going to be with opera as something that's American."

In another way, as well, "Harvey Milk" resonates with the sound of present-day America. Although the San Francisco that the opera evokes might appear to be a distant, almost Utopian place, the rhetoric Dan White spouts is indistinguishable from the hate-mongering that fills the air waves today.

"Dan White says things that we hear every day from the Newt Gingriches," Mr. Wallace said. "These are the kind of nostalgic and fictional ideas that are still being parlayed. We want people to realize that those ideas are not just on the surface, but that they mask deep-seated anger and violence."

K. Robert Schwarz is writing a dissertation on the music of Paul Bowles.

* * *

July 14, 1996

SILENT PARTNER

By WILL FRIEDWALD

LUSH LIFE: A Biography of Billy Strayhorn
By David Hajdu
Illustrated. 306 pp. New York: Farrar, Straus & Giroux. $ 27.50.

Billy Strayhorn was doubly invisible. Throughout his 30-year collaboration with Duke Ellington, Strayhorn contributed immeasurably to the most formidable body of work in all of American music. Yet being both black and gay forced Strayhorn to hide his light under the bushel of his partner's celebrity, as David Hajdu shows in "Lush Life," the first biography of the composer, orchestrator and pianist.

Ellington played his role as a black intellectual celebrity as adroitly as he played his piano, and Strayhorn's inability to share the spotlight worked to Ellington's advantage. Strayhorn had talent enough to have had a career without Ellington, either as a composer and bandleader or as a writer of musical comedies. But for Strayhorn to have stepped forward into the public eye, he would have had to cover up who he was—perhaps, like Cole Porter, to hide in a marriage of convenience. Coming out of the shadows would have entailed going into the closet, which would have been untenable to Strayhorn, who, from his childhood in Pittsburgh onward, was fiercely honest about himself and his sexuality. Ellington was therefore blessed with a silent partner who could supply his band's library with some of its most profound works yet take none of the bows.

Ellington first met Strayhorn in Pittsburgh in 1938 (Mr. Hajdu quotes an acquaintance of Strayhorn's as saying that had the young man not been granted an audience with Ellington, he would have sought one with the next bandleader playing through town—Count Basie). From that point on, according to their longtime friend Lena Horne, "their relationship was very sexual. Don't misunderstand—it wasn't physical at all. . . . Duke treated Billy exactly like he treated women, with all that old-fashioned chauvinism. Very loving and very protective, but controlling."

The myth has always been that Strayhorn and Ellington shared an identical approach to music. The most famous story from their three decades of collaboration relates to the writing of "Suite Thursday," the John Steinbeck-inspired composition that Ellington's orchestra introduced at the Monterey Jazz Festival in 1960. Ellington wrote most of the suite while on the road, and Strayhorn contributed one of the movements from his apartment in New York. As usual with Ellington, there was no time to rehearse the finished work, and both men heard it for the first time at the festival. "When they got to my part, then went into Ellington's part, I burst out laughing," Strayhorn recalled not long after. "Without really knowing, I had written a theme that was a kind of development of a similar theme that he had written. . . . It was as though we had really worked together—or one person had done it. It was an uncanny feeling, like witchcraft, like looking into someone else's mind."

Mr. Hajdu, an editor at Entertainment Weekly magazine, makes clear that this incident was the exception and not the rule in their partnership. Far from being just a ghostwriter or a pinch-hitter for the maestro, Strayhorn was his own man from the beginning. Where Ellington (as his aide and chronicler Stanley Dance has pointed out) tended to rely more heavily on the blues, Strayhorn was thoroughly schooled in impressionists like Debussy and Ravel. Part of the joy of Ellington compositions like "Rockin' in Rhythm" or "Dancers in Love" is the devil-may-care fashion in which one section almost randomly follows another, in the stop-and-start tradition of the great stride pianists. In Strayhorn's pieces everything fits together much more organically. And although Strayhorn's music could stomp, moan and swing no less con-

vincingly than Ellington's (particularly in his most famous composition, "Take the 'A' Train"), there was always a greater tenderness. "There's so much more sensitivity and complexity in Strayhorn's compositions than Ellington's," said Aaron Bell, the band's bassist in the early 1960's. "We could always tell Strayhorn's."

This remarkably rewarding professional partnership was fueled by the two men's personal differences. The most important attachment of each man's life was to his mother, but Ellington came from the black middle class, was heterosexual and, by many accounts, was highly promiscuous. Strayhorn, the abused son of a bitter and violent manual laborer, was homosexual and apparently involved only in very long-term romantic relationships.

Ellington, Mr. Hajdu says, was delighted to promote Strayhorn whenever he could—he generally announced the younger man's name when performing his work and even produced an album by Strayhorn in 1965—as long as boosting his collaborator took nothing away from him. When Strayhorn got outside offers (from Frank Sinatra, for instance), Ellington would pull strings to make sure he couldn't accept. Strayhorn worked most extensively outside Ellington's realm in the early 1950's, when the band was in a general decline and many of its stars had temporarily left. His full-time return to the fold was a key factor in Ellington's 1956 comeback, at which point Strayhorn's name began, for a time, appearing above the title alongside Ellington's, most notably in their 1960 revamping of the "Nutcracker" suite.

Throughout Strayhorn's short life, as Mr. Hajdu shows, his anonymity was the defining factor in his relationship with Ellington. Strayhorn was officially employed by Ellington's music publishing company, but never signed a contract or received a regular salary. Instead, his rent, food, clothes, travel and increasingly exorbitant bar bills were simply taken care of by Ellington, who never set a quota on the amount of output he expected from Strayhorn, the only composer-arranger besides himself whose work he featured regularly.

Denied the gratification that normally comes with recognition of one's talents, Strayhorn increasingly found solace in his lush life. These words were, unfortunately, not merely the title of his most famous ballad: they also describe the excessive smoking and drinking that contributed to his death from esophageal cancer in 1967, at the age of 51.

What makes "Lush Life" one of the finest of jazz biographies is the way Mr. Hajdu directs the readers to these conclusions through the weight of his evidence, without explicitly stating them. The detail that Mr. Hajdu has uncovered, particularly concerning the early Pittsburgh years and including the copious testimony of nearly 200 of Strayhorn's and Ellington's associates, is staggering, especially in light of how little has been previously published on Strayhorn.

Ellington, writing of Strayhorn several years after his partner's death (and not long before his own, in 1974), stated, "I only hope that my representation of him will have the dignity with which he represented me." Almost 30 years after Strayhorn's passing, this seminal figure in American music has finally found the "representation" he deserves.

Will Friedwald is the author of "Sinatra! The Song Is You: A Singer's Art" and "Jazz Singing."

*   *   *

October 15, 1998

TASTING BOOGIE-WOOGIE AND GLAM ROCK, INGREDIENTS IN AN ECCENTRIC FORMULA

By ANN POWERS

On Tuesday night, as thousands protested the Off Broadway opening of "Corpus Christi," Terrence McNally's play about a homosexual Christ figure, and people nationwide mourned the homophobia-fueled murder of 21-year-old Matthew Shepard in Wyoming, an openly gay man who writes music for Disney movies and has been knighted by the Queen of England sat behind his piano at Madison Square Garden and led a wholesome evening of fun. The spectacle raised an inevitable question: Why does Elton John get so much love while others fight back revulsion and hate?

A rock star's privilege to live outside convention has something to do with it. So does Mr. John's slow emergence from the closet, which coincided with the rise of a mainstream gay rights movement and involved enough poignant struggle to gain wide sympathy. But the key to Mr. John's unusual appeal is the musical formula he and the lyricist Bernie Taupin devised long before that drama ensued, which balanced outrageous personal expression with pure pop universality. Mr. John has always been a crossover artist, although it wasn't always obvious where he was crossing from.

This greatest-hits program clarified his sources. Two vie for the No. 1 position: boogie-woogie and glam rock. Mr. John's most lively songs rely on a rolling and rocking piano style inspired by Jerry Lee Lewis, acknowledged with an encore rendition of "Great Balls of Fire." The approach accelerates the soothing, sensual flow of Fats Domino-style boogie, bursting from its steady center into flamboyant runs and pounding chords.

Songs like "Crocodile Rock" and "Honky Cat" offered comfort with nostalgia Tuesday night while exciting with their speed. The showy moves for which Mr. John is famous, which culminated with him lying on the floor while playing with one hand, emanated naturally from his gregarious playing. His flashy longtime guitarist, Davey Johnstone, kept up only to be overshadowed by Mr. John's solos and antics.

When Mr. Johnstone did grab the spotlight, his theatrical playing invoked the glory of glam, when Mr. John first found his formula. Glam is again in vogue, its theatrical androgyny appealing to a new generation of liberationist libertines. Mr. John linked himself with the movement by dedicating "I'm Going to Be a Teen-Age Idol" to the glam originator, Marc Bolan. Unacknowledged connections could be found in "Rocket Man," his less creepy take on David Bowie's "Space Oddity," and "Bennie and the Jets," which turned glam's subversion into a Horatio Alger story.

That song, with its vision of rock-and-roll outlandishness as a force that can free average people, still defines Mr. John's essence. Even when he turned to the middle-of-the-road power ballads that have dominated his career since the 1980's (and to Disney, with "The Lion King," in the mid-1990's), Mr. John maintained a persona that made nonconformity approachable. He believes in a democracy of difference, in which shared emotions unite people beyond contradictory motivations. It is a vision as rosy as the tinted glasses Mr. John wore in the 1970's. It may not conquer hate, but it provides some relief.

*   *   *

December 15, 1999

COUNTRY BOYS (ONE IN A DRESS)

By NEIL STRAUSS

NASHVILLE—Performing for six years in New York, Y'All didn't get the respect they deserved. A cross-dressing guitar-and-ukulele country duo, they searched for their niche in West Village theaters, midtown country bars and East Village gay clubs. But wherever they performed, audiences arrived with the impression that they were a novelty act, that they were poking big-city fun at country music. But Y'All was serious. So serious, in fact, that last year they packed their bags and moved to Nashville.

Y'All—James Dean Jay Byrd and Steven Cheslik-DeMeyer—followed in the footsteps of many a country great, arriving in Nashville with nary a job nor friend, in hopes of making it. Now, one might think that a gay couple from New York with an act that involves one of them wearing a dress wouldn't even be able to get a meeting in the country music capital of the world. But that's not exactly what happened.

"It's funny because when we told people we were going to move here, their reaction was, 'Scary rednecks, you boys be careful,'" Mr. Cheslik-DeMeyer said. "But New Yorkers were close-minded in a different way about what we were doing. Here people are much more open to the performances."

They found that publishers and record labels were welcoming and attended the requisite meetings. "We thought we'd go down the high road first," Mr. Byrd said. "They took us seriously, but they said we wouldn't work as a viable mainstream country act. They said that Nashville needed some variety and excitement, however, and we were that."

There are three layers of musicians in Nashville. The first is the upper level of country stars, songwriters and overbooked session musicians. The second is the aspirants hustling around town and performing at open mikes with the dream of reaching the first rung. And then there is a third layer of performers who come to Nashville with an idealized picture of a country scene that doesn't really exist anymore, as is the case with Y'All, an act inspired as much by the harmonizing Louvin Brothers as by "Hee Haw."

In may ways it is this third layer of the music population that keeps country music's past alive in Nashville. Many of these transplants, like Katy K, who runs a popular country-and-western clothing store on Music Row, came to Nashville from New York.

Y'All's dreams lie not just in music but in television and their goal of landing a network variety show as well. To practice their art, they began a series of theme performance nights on Saturday at the Sutler club here. The first night's theme: New Yorkers living in Nashville. Though the Brooklyn Cowboys didn't make it, ex-New Yorkers like Kristi Rose, Amy Rigby and Tim Carroll did.

Y'All performed between the others, with bald, lanky Mr. Byrd in a rhinestone apron and short, bookish Mr. Cheslik-DeMeyer in overalls. They spun yarns about their families and sang songs alternately silly ("My Mama Likes the Feel of Cottage Cheese") and heartfelt (the Dolly Parton and Porter Wagoner duet "The Last Thing on My Mind").

Y'All isn't so much a band as it is a world unto itself: eight years of making music in a relationship has inspired the pair to metamorphose into an impressive home industry with its own product line (calendars, pamphlets, hand-painted rhinestone T-shirts and six albums with a seventh on the way); vocabulary (with words like "bedazzled" for their rhinestone fashion); original holiday recipes; and most impressive, a good back story, which is lovingly chronicled in a 300-page hardcover autobiography they just published.

"The Good Book: The True Story of Y'All," a product of Mr. Byrd's hyperactive imagination and boundless energy, tells the half-true story of Y'All's wacky preacher relatives, their fated meeting during a thunderstorm and the lucky green dress given to them by an uncle who advised, "You can't never tell what might happen to you if folks have a reason to stare." (The book and albums are available from their Web site, www.luckygreendress.com.)

The slightly truer story of Y'All is that Mr. Byrd arrived in Manhattan from Texas in 1988 with the ambition of writing musicals; Mr. Cheslik-DeMeyer, born in Indiana, arrived in 1990 to perform music and study painting. They met in the downtown theater world and soon had their own cabaret act, with Mr. Byrd wearing dresses to justify his presence as a nonmusician onstage and to get people talking about the act.

"I'm a little bit of a maniac," Mr. Byrd admitted of his work ethic, which most recently led to their commitment to put on a Y'All Christmas benefit at the Nashville church to which they belong (with the church choir singing backup) as a way of giving alms.

Though the pair may seem out of place in Nashville, there is a lineage of openly gay country performers. The current issue of The Journal of Country Music features an in-depth article on the subject, "Country Undetectable: Gay Artists in Country Music." Focusing on the recent formation of the Lesbian and Gay Country Music Association by the singer Doug Stevens, it also tracks everything from country's early, stereotyped allusions to homosexuality (in Vernon Dalhart's 1939 song "Lavender Cowboy") to the first albums by gay acts like the early 70's group Lavender Country.

"The gay culture has never really embraced us," said Mr. Byrd, adding that the band came more from the tradition of the cross-dressing comedians who appeared on the Grand Ole Opry than the drag cabaret of nightclubs.

"I think half the audiences we play for doesn't ever realize that we're a couple," Mr. Cheslik-DeMeyer added. "It's never been a part of what we do to be explicit. But I've always thought, 'How much more obvious can we be?'"

Mr. Byrd said he often wondered if "the cross-dressing, the country, the gay, the fact that we're from New York has all worked against us" and distracted people from the quality of the songwriting, harmonizing and Mr. Cheslik-DeMeyer's gentle, winsome lead vocals.

Even as early as their 1994 album, "The Next Big Thing," Y'All were making sweetly humorous, instantly likable songs that held up independently of the cross-dressing. One song on the album, "Are You on the Top 40 of Your Lord?," may be one of the best country gospel songs nobody knows. And the title track on their 1995 mini-album "Christmastime in the Trailer Park" deserves a place on holiday anthologies. Funny this duo may be, but they're not a joke.

"We used to cringe when people called us campy," Mr. Byrd said.

Mr. Cheslik-DeMeyer agreed. "It's hurtful for people to say that we're making fun of country music, because I love country music so much."

* * *

The NEA

April 24, 1990

THE CINCINNATI CASE: WHAT ARE THE ISSUES AND THE STAKES?

By LAURA MANSNERUS

The prosecution on obscenity charges of the Cincinnati museum where Robert Mapplethorpe's photographs are on exhibition is by all accounts a legal first. Until now, what-

ever is in museums has been presumed to be art, and in an obscenity case the First Amendment protects works of artistic value.

But if the case ends up vindicating the museum and reinforcing a larger point about the First Amendment, it also shows that the Constitution is sometimes beside the point.

"Even if the Cincinnati authorities are as wrong as I think they are, in a way it doesn't matter because throwing their weight around will have had its effect," said Stephen E. Weil, the deputy director of the Hirshhorn Museum and Sculpture Garden in Washington and author of "Beauty and the Beasts" (Smithsonian), a book on law and art. "Smart cops know that."

The touring Mapplethorpe retrospective—175 photographs of the erotic, the innocent, the lyrical and the sadomasochistic—had brought protests and even a pre-emptive cancellation at the Corcoran Gallery of Art in Washington. But no threats of criminal charges were advanced until the Contemporary Arts Center and its director, Dennis Barrie, were indicted in Cincinnati on April 7.

Museums as Sanctuaries

"I thought as long as it appeared in a museum it was safe," said Tex Lezar, a Dallas lawyer who served on the Attorney General's Commission on Pornography in the Reagan Administration.

Mr. Lezar's opinion seems to have been shared by the trustees of the Association of Art Museum Directors, who met in a specially convened session yesterday at the Cincinnati center. They praised the conduct of Mr. Barrie and of the museum, started a fund to pay any fines imposed, and offered the testimony of the association's members in behalf of the defense.

The prosecutors' principal task is to prove that "the work, taken as a whole, lacks serious literary, artistic, political or scientific value." That language is from a 1973 Supreme Court decision, Miller v. California, which established the current definition of obscenity. To find sexual material obscene is to say it is not protected by the First Amendment against government restriction.

There are two other elements the prosecution must prove: that the work appeals to prurient interests, as measured by "the average person applying contemporary community standards," and that it depicts in a "patently offensive way" conduct specifically set forth by state law.

Given the Miller rule, can the Contemporary Arts Center be successfully prosecuted?

'It's Not Even Close'

"Absolutely not," said Prof. Frederick Schauer of the University of Michigan Law School, who also served on the pornography commission during the Reagan Administration. "It's not even close. Let's take the worst case, or the best from their point of view. Take one Mapplethorpe photograph, and it shows gay men engaging in sadomasochistic acts. The very fact that it's by Mapplethorpe and it's in a museum would still lead me to say it's not even close." Other lawyers are less certain. "It's a public debate," said Karl P. Kadon, a lawyer in the City Solicitor's office who handled an earlier civil case in which a state court refused the museum's request for a ruling on whether the museum could be prosecuted for the Mapplethorpe exhibition. "As far as the police division is concerned, they've been neutral. They gathered evidence. The grand jury issued the indictment and they believed there was probable cause it's obscene."

The city solicitor, Richard Castellini, and Frank Proutty, the lawyer who is handling the criminal case, declined to comment on it.

Costly Decision, Either Way

Whatever the merits of its defense, the arts center has more immediate problems. "Even if the charges are dismissed or if we win a jury trial," said its director, Mr. Barrie, "we will have gone through the anguish and financial strain of fighting something that should not have been brought to court in the first place." He said legal costs were already in the "tens of thousands."

Mr. Barrie and the museum were each indicted on charges of pandering obscenity and showing a child "in a state of nudity," which is a crime in Ohio unless parents have approved. Both defendants have pleaded not guilty. A preliminary hearing is scheduled for Monday.

Because it has never come up in the context of a museum exhibition, there may remain some ambiguity in the requirement that a work be "taken as a whole" in deciding if it is obscene. The indictment designates only 7 of the 175 photographs.

H. Louis Sirkin, whose law firm is representing the center and Mr. Barrie, said the offending photographs could not be judged by themselves. "It might be different if you were talking about pictures for sale," he said, "but here each picture was picked out for its relation to the whole exhibit." The Supreme Court's standard, he said, was meant to resolve the debate that arose over James Joyce's "Ulysses" in the 1930's, when the Government argued unsuccessfully that a book could be found obscene on the basis of particular passages.

National Standards for Art

As for the "contemporary community standards" that are to guide the jury, they apply only to the questions of whether the material appeals to prurient interests and is "patently offensive." The Court has held that the separate issue of artistic value is to be judged by national standards, and, in Professor Schauer's assessment, "Cincinnati's community standards have nothing whatsoever to do with whether the exhibit has artistic merit."

Morever, these judgments are not entirely up to the jury; a judge may derail a prosecution by deciding that under the standards of the Miller case no reasonable juror could judge a particular work obscene. For example, a 1974 Supreme Court decision written by William H. Rehnquist as an associate justice concluded that the movie "Carnal Knowledge" could not be found obscene.

But if any community has strict standards, it is Cincinnati. After several decades of aggressive prosecutions, the city has no adult bookstores or peep shows and no place to buy X-rated videos or Hustler magazine. Mr. Sirkin, who said the Mapplethorpe prosecution had prompted refreshing anger and "productive debate" in Cincinnati, recalled that the sheriff tried to prosecute a production of the show "Oh! Calcutta!" and said a local repertory group recently had "tremendous concern about whether they'd be busted by the vice squad" for performing "Equus."

"What you're seeing here is a kind of bullying, and bullying more often than not is effective," said Mr. Weil at the Hirshhorn. "There's just a tremendously chilling effect. In the longer term, I think that's the bigger problem. The question is, what are you going to flinch from next, and are you even going to know you're flinching?"

'It's a Sad Commentary'

Professor Schauer, like other experts, said local officials had little to lose from pursuing a constitutionally dubious case and much to gain from "the perception that they tried to root out this awful stuff."

"It's a sad commentary on the American constitutional system, but it's not unique," he said. "We rely on the Supreme Court to do all our constitutional enforcement, and we do not penalize officials for ignoring constitutional values. We shouldn't be surprised when they do ignore them."

He cited the angry march by Chicago aldermen two years ago to the School of the Art Institute of Chicago, which had displayed a student's caricature of the late Mayor Harold Washington wearing frilly women's underwear. The aldermen tore down the painting.

"I don't think any of them were voted out of office for being unconstitutional," Professor Schauer said.

The school was hit again last spring when it opened a show that had an exhibit inviting visitors to tread on an American flag on the floor. Amid protests by veterans, the police arrested a tourist, visiting from Virginia for a teachers' convention, who stopped by and stepped on the flag; the charges of flag desecration were dropped last November.

The Question of Children

Both incidents, along with protests over the Mapplethorpe retrospective, fed the debate over the use of public funds for controversial art. But while there is some constitutional question about the Government's withholding of funds on the basis of content, the law is much more vigilant about outright censorship or criminal sanctions.

One well-recognized exception to free speech rights is child pornography, and some lawyers say the two pictures of children in the Mapplethorpe exhibition are the prosecutors' best bet. Coincidentally, the Supreme Court upheld Ohio's child pornography statute last week, ruling that states may make it a crime to possess as well as sell such material. But the Court's approval of child pornography laws generally is based on the government's power to protect children, not to punish those who would view the pictures.

The other charges against the Contemporary Arts Center would be subject to the Miller standards, which legal scholars say are unlikely to change even with a more conservative Supreme Court.

All along, the Court has shown little inclination for the task of distinguishing the obscene from the erotic. One of the best known lines in Supreme Court jurisprudence was Asso-

ciate Justice Potter Stewart's stab at a definition of obscenity: "I know it when I see it." It happens that Justice Stewart was from Cincinnati.

* * *

August 19, 1990

FEARS THAT HAUNT A SCRUBBED AMERICA

By DAVID LEAVITT

Put yourself, for a moment, inside the mind of Jesse Helms. Imagine a scrubbed, manicured neighborhood, a pocket of decency in the heart of our sinful land. The music is by Wayne Newton, the paintings are by Norman Rockwell, and sex takes place only between married men and women in beds at night.

Then one day a church-reared boy or girl goes to a museum and sees a Robert Mapplethorpe photograph; or goes to a library and checks out a novel by Rita Mae Brown (neither action likely to be undertaken innocently). What does Jesse Helms think happens? Does the photograph or book emit something between a magic fragrance and a sales pitch, luring this high-minded but fallible child into the back alleyways of decadence and sin? The "artist," in this story, is really nothing more than a street-corner beckoner, a wolf in smock and painters' pants, a wolf with a camera or a pen. What he or she creates, under the guise of art, is a "promotion" for sexual deviance, a tool for the "recruitment" of the young.

While the scenario I've just described may sound paranoid, even ludicrous, its dissemination has become the primary weapon in the current attack on the National Endowment for the Arts, an attack that, in fact, has little to do with the arts at all, and everything to do with the extreme right wing's determination to terrorize an already ambivalent American population by manipulating its entrenched fears of anything foreign, unfamiliar or explicitly sexual. People can argue as long as they want about the definitions of obscenity and art; in doing so, they become hopelessly sidetracked, trapped in a struggle to resolve unanswerable questions that neatly distracts them from the real crisis at hand, the way a computer can be distracted indefinitely by being asked to calculate the value of pi.

From Robert Mapplethorpe to Holly Hughes, the message is ringing out loud and clear. Gay and lesbian artists who deal frankly with sexuality are being singled out and refused grant money they were awarded by peer panels, as part of a conscious attempt to censor, humiliate and discourage all artists whose work challenges the right wing's rigid notions of "correct" sexual behavior. The N.E.A. is simply another target in an effort to legislate sexual demeanor that also encompasses attacks on abortion rights and on laws that protect homosexuals from violence and discrimination.

Consider the language of the infamous clause this year's National Endowment recipients were forced to sign: It binds the artist to guarantee that he or she will not use the grant money for works that include "depictions of sadomasochism, homoeroticism, the sexual exploitation of children, or individuals engaged in sex acts, and which, when taken as a whole, do not have serious literary, artistic, political, or scientific merit."

'Homoeroticism' in Bad Company

Is it only because I'm gay that when I read that sentence, the word "homoeroticism " leaps out at me? Or is it because there is nowhere in the clause a reference to "heteroeroticism," only to the portrayal of "individuals engaged in sex acts," which is of course an entirely different matter? "Sadomasochism" and "the sexual exploitation of children" can of course be both heterosexual and homosexual, and in any case represent just the sort of vague, fear-mongering terminology the right wing adores. Totally nonsexual photographs of nude children, taken with their parents' approval, have been appropriated by the F.B.I. under the latter heading; who's to say that one of Il Bronzino's cupids—portrayed, in the 16th century, as eroticized, chubby little boys—would not be as well?

By situating the word "homoeroticism" next to a taboo extreme of sexual behavior few would be willing to argue in favor of, the authors of the clause make their position glaringly clear: while only selective or extreme heterosexual content is to be forbidden, all homosexual content is to be forbidden. Once again, the fear that children may be molested, abused or lured to "deviant" life styles is being exploited as a tool to strong-arm Americans into approving the Moral Majority's effort to control artistic expression.

Behind this language—though unspoken—is the right wing's perpetual insistence that gay men and lesbians try to "recruit" young people to homosexuality by disseminating art and writing that "promotes" the homosexual life style. Of course, to any gay person who, as a frightened and confused teenager, searched desperately for books or films or television shows that offered even a mention of homosexual experience to latch on to, the idea of gay "recruitment" is laughable. It is also profoundly insulting.

Artists as Outsiders

Tennessee Williams, Michelangelo, W. H. Auden, Gertrude Stein—I hardly need to repeat history's long and illustrious list of gay and lesbian writers and artists. If a lot of gay people have felt the urge to produce art over time, it's probably only because our early-perceived status as outsiders in a largely heterosexual world forced us to call into question those assumptions about sexual identity that our straight brothers and sisters could simply take for granted.

Female in a world of men, Jewish in a world of gentiles, black in a world of whites: it's the same difference. It's rare to find an artist who, as a child, wasn't in some way treated as a member of some minority and therefore felt the need to refract the complications of his or her world through the prism of that "different" self; to offer untroubled people a troubling perspective; to reveal the strangeness of the ordinary and the ordinariness of the strange.

What distinguishes gay and lesbian artists is that their "difference" is located in the realm of sexuality; the assumptions they question are assumptions about sexuality; and therefore the work they create, in a culture that is both sexphobic and homophobic, becomes particularly susceptible to the charge that it is "obscene," or dangerous for young people. This last notion is especially distressing; while homoerotic art may have the power to awaken subconscious homosexual feelings in individuals who already harbor them, the suggestion that it can brainwash or corrupt chaste minds is almost medievally superstitious.

History offers some scary examples of what happens when a government tries to control a culture. Consider Hitler's now infamous 1937 "Degenerate Art" show, in which the works of such painters as Max Beckmann, Marc Chagall and Henri Matisse were jammed chaotically onto the walls of a Munich museum, along with hand-scribbled labels denouncing the artists and implying their links to "unfit" members of German society.

I attended a re-creation of that exhibit in Berlin last year; in the next room was another re-creation, of the "Great Exhibition of German Art" Hitler had set up as a contrast to the "Degenerate Art" show. Here gargantuan sculpted Aryan torsos thrust their muscled arms into the sky, while in paintings happy blond families frolicked on farms. Photographs from the opening of the exhibit show a rare smiling Hitler. A failed watercolorist, he apparently considered the show something of a high point in his career: what was the appropriation of political power in comparison, after all, to the appropriation of culture, not to mention the redemption of his ambition—thwarted by teachers who said he had no talent—to be a painter?

Now, five decades later, when history has redeemed the work of the "degenerate artists," it is frightening to see Robert Mapplethorpe's photographs being appropriated by Cincinnati sheriffs and put on trial; or to see videotapes of the performance artist David Wojnarowicz being incorporated into videos used by right-wing pressure groups to demonstrate N.E.A.-sponsored decadence and obscenity; or to try to imagine the kind of "art" a Jesse Helms-run N.E.A. might choose to give its money to.

The Side Effects Of Cultural Control

The National Endowment crisis, however—so far, at least—is not about banning art; it is about denying artists money. And what are the consequences of that going to be? Initially, at least, refusing grant money to these artists will probably result in a sudden wave of interest in their work. In England, the notorious Clause 28, which allows the Government to censor art that "promotes" homosexuality, prompted a surge of enthusiasm for gay literature, theater and film. Alan Hollinghurst's brilliant novel "The Swimming Pool Library" became a best seller, as did works by such gay American writers as Edmund White and Armistead Maupin; the BBC had a major hit with its four-hour television version of Jeannette Winterson's lesbian novel "Oranges Are Not the Only Fruit."

Here in America, meanwhile, where banning has always been a perverse form of publicity (consider Henry Miller), the brouhaha over the Mapplethorpe show in Cincinnati drew huge crowds to that show. And Karen Finley, the performance artist, is much better-known now than she was a month ago, though hardly for the reasons she might wish. Ms. Finley was the only heterosexual among the four performance artists whose grants were retracted.

Such a reaction, however, will probably be only temporary. Soon enough the really terrible side-effects of cultural control will start to manifest themselves. There may be a mass exodus of artists out of America to Europe, where state support of the arts is already much stronger, and where a booming economy has made it possible for governments to welcome foreign artists and writers as well.

Last year I spent five months in Barcelona as a guest of the Catalan Government. During my stay in Barcelona I could hardly keep count of the number of exhibitions (many of them Government-sponsored) of work by American artists and photographers, some quite avant-garde, not to mention the extraordinary publicity those exhibitions received. Jennie Livingston, a film maker who received money a few years ago from the National Endowment to work on "Paris Is Burning," a documentary about the gay culture of Harlem, ended up finishing the film with the help not of the N.E.A., but the BBC. If Europe continues to pick up the slack, the attack on the N.E.A. could result in the depletion of yet another precious American resource: our artists.

The most devastating effect of a Helms-controlled National Endowment, however, is one we won't see until a few years from now, when the furor has died down: the effect on the young novelist who cannot quit his job in order to devote a year to finishing his first novel, and therefore doesn't finish it; or on the young painter who cannot afford supplies, and therefore doesn't paint; or on the young film maker who, fearful of the strictures imposed on her by an N.E.A. run by the Republican Senator from North Carolina, censors her own creative impulses to satisfy such an organization's dubious morality.

I had my N.E.A. grant in 1985, in another time, before the infamous Mapplethorpe exhibition at the Corcoran Gallery in Washington, before the addition of that notorious clause, before people's grants started being withheld. That year a friend sent me a clipping from the editorial page of The Manchester (N.H.) Union Leader, a vehement attack on the National Endowment that questioned the Government's right to spend taxpayers' money to support artists or writers whose work those taxpayers might find offensive or obscene. To my surprise, it was me who was offered up as an example in the article; do the American people really want their hard-earned dollars going to an author of "paeans to homosexual love," the newspaper asked.

I remember laughing uncomfortably at that phrase, joking that if anything, my stories were paeans to the lack of love—homosexual or heterosexual. Apparently for The Union Leader, any piece of fiction with a gay character in it was necessarily a "paean." Thus, I dismissed the editorial as right-wing nonsense, and went on to finish a novel the financing of which, in the current atmosphere, would certainly have been questioned, and most probably retracted.

Art Slowed But Not Stopped

These days I think a lot about that editorial, and when I do, I wince at my own failure to recognize what it foreboded. Perhaps those of us who depended on the National Endowment, regularly or sporadically, got too comfortable, too complacent, cozying up as we did to a Government that handed out the money and never asked questions. In a chastening editorial in Outweek magazine, the novelist Sarah Schulman has suggested that the current crisis simply puts those few white, upper-middle-class gay and lesbian artists to whom the N.E.A. previously gave its seal of approval in the same position as the vast majority of artists who because of their race or class were never able to benefit from the N.E.A. reward system in the first place.

If the example of Hitler's "degenerate art" show teaches us anything, it is that while art can be slowed, it cannot be stopped. But the attack on the National Endowment is not simply about art, just as the "degenerate art" show was not simply about art; it is about trying to eradicate or at least suppress anything in American culture that challenges a fundamentalist Christian vision of family happiness that in its portrayal seems eerily similar to Hitler's artists' vision of Aryan farm life. Traditionally the head of state gives the opening address at the annual International AIDS Conference, no matter what country that conference takes place in; George Bush's decision this year to attend a Jesse Helms fund-raiser instead cannot be considered a coincidence.

Fear of change, fear of difference, fear of cultural erosion: all these fears of the extreme right mask, in fact, a deeper fear, a fear of the underground sexual desires every individual harbors (look at Jimmy Swaggart!) and for which homosexuals have traditionally been made into a catch-all symbol.

To say that gay men and lesbians are everywhere is only to say that sexuality is everywhere, that there are no rules other than the ones that we impose. Even in houses where Jesse Helms's picture hangs over the fireplace there are children who will grow up to be gay or lesbian, and some of them may become our greatest artists and writers. The influences that would supposedly seep into and corrupt the healthy American family landscape are in fact an integral part of that landscape already. What the N.E.A.'s opponents really seem to be fighting is the difference in themselves.

David Leavitt is the author of two novels, "The Lost Language of Cranes" and "Equal Affections." His second collection of stories, "A Place I've Never Been," will be published next month by Viking.

PART V

THE IMPACT OF AIDS

THE EVOLUTION OF AN EPIDEMIC

July 3, 1981

RARE CANCER SEEN IN 41 HOMOSEXUALS

By LAWRENCE K. ALTMAN

Doctors in New York and California have diagnosed among homosexual men 41 cases of a rare and often rapidly fatal form of cancer. Eight of the victims died less than 24 months after the diagnosis was made.

The cause of the outbreak is unknown, and there is as yet no evidence of contagion. But the doctors who have made the diagnoses, mostly in New York City and the San Francisco Bay area, are alerting other physicians who treat large numbers of homosexual men to the problem in an effort to help identify more cases and to reduce the delay in offering chemotherapy treatment.

The sudden appearance of the cancer, called Kaposi's Sarcoma, has prompted a medical investigation that experts say could have as much scientific as public health importance because of what it may teach about determining the causes of more common types of cancer.

First Appears in Spots

Doctors have been taught in the past that the cancer usually appeared first in spots on the legs and that the disease took a slow course of up to 10 years. But these recent cases have shown that it appears in one or more violet-colored spots anywhere on the body. The spots generally do not itch or cause other symptoms, often can be mistaken for bruises, sometimes appear as lumps and can turn brown after a period of time. The cancer often causes swollen lymph glands, and then kills by spreading throughout the body.

Doctors investigating the outbreak believe that many cases have gone undetected because of the rarity of the condition and the difficulty even dermatologists may have in diagnosing it.

In a letter alerting other physicians to the problem, Dr. Alvin E. Friedman-Kien of New York University Medical Center, one of the investigators, described the appearance of the outbreak as "rather devastating."

Dr. Friedman-Kien said in an interview yesterday that he knew of 41 cases collated in the last five weeks, with the cases themselves dating to the past 30 months. The Federal Centers for Disease Control in Atlanta is expected to publish the first description of the outbreak in its weekly report today, according to a spokesman, Dr. James Curran. The report notes 26 of the cases—20 in New York and six in California.

There is no national registry of cancer victims, but the nationwide incidence of Kaposi's Sarcoma in the past had been estimated by the Centers for Disease Control to be less than six-one-hundredths of a case per 100,000 people annually, or about two cases in every three million people. However, the disease accounts for up to 9 percent of all cancers in a belt across equatorial Africa, where it commonly affects children and young adults.

In the United States, it has primarily affected men older than 50 years. But in the recent cases, doctors at nine medical centers in New York and seven hospitals in California have been diagnosing the condition among younger men, all of whom said in the course of standard diagnostic interviews that they were homosexual. Although the ages of the patients have ranged from 26 to 51 years, many have been under 40, with the mean at 39.

Nine of the 41 cases known to Dr. Friedman-Kien were diagnosed in California, and several of those victims reported that they had been in New York in the period preceding the diagnosis. Dr. Friedman-Kien said that his colleagues were checking on reports of two victims diagnosed in Copenhagen, one of whom had visited New York.

Viral Infections Indicated

No one medical investigator has yet interviewed all the victims, Dr. Curran said. According to Dr. Friedman-Kien, the reporting doctors said that most cases had involved homosexual men who have had multiple and frequent sexual encounters with different partners, as many as 10 sexual encounters each night up to four times a week.

Many of the patients have also been treated for viral infections such as herpes, cytomegalovirus and hepatitis B as well as parasitic infections such as amebiasis and giardiasis. Many patients also reported that they had used drugs such as amyl nitrite and LSD to heighten sexual pleasure.

Cancer is not believed to be contagious, but conditions that might precipitate it, such as particular viruses or environmental factors, might account for an outbreak among a single group.

The medical investigators say some indirect evidence actually points away from contagion as a cause. None of the patients knew each other, although the theoretical possibility that some may have had sexual contact with a person with

Kaposi's Sarcoma at some point in the past could not be excluded, Dr. Friedman-Kien said.

Dr. Curran said there was no apparent danger to nonhomosexuals from contagion. "The best evidence against contagion," he said, "is that no cases have been reported to date outside the homosexual community or in women."

Dr. Friedman-Kien said he had tested nine of the victims and found severe defects in their immunological systems. The patients had serious malfunctions of two types of cells called T and B cell lymphocytes, which have important roles in fighting infections and cancer.

But Dr. Friedman-Kien emphasized that the researchers did not know whether the immunological defects were the underlying problem or had developed secondarily to the infections or drug use.

The research team is testing various hypotheses, one of which is a possible link between past infection with cytomegalovirus and development of Kaposi's Sarcoma.

*   *   *

August 8, 1982

A DISEASE'S SPREAD PROVOKES ANXIETY

By ROBIN HERMAN

The persistence of a serious disease whose victims are primarily homosexual men has touched off anxiety among homosexuals in New York City, where nearly half of the nation's cases have been reported.

Doctors treating homosexuals say they are being flooded with telephone calls from old and new patients with minor complaints. Clinics offering testing for the disease are over-subscribed. And homosexual men speak of great confusion over how to adjust their health habits to avoid the disease, which remains largely mysterious in its symptoms and causes.

The disease—called acquired immune deficiency syndrome, or A.I.D.S.—produces a suppression of the body's natural defenses and sets the stage for the intrusion of several deadly afflictions, including a rare form of cancer called Kaposi's sarcoma and a rare pneumonia.

The Centers for Disease Control in Atlanta have recorded 505 cases of the syndrome coupled with the cancer, pneumonia or other opportunistic infections since the national facility began gathering data on cases in June of last year. Of those people, 202 have died, or 40 percent. The cases include 243 residents of New York City.

Two New Cases a Day

Reports of the disease have not abated. About two new cases a day are recorded at the disease control center. Officials there attribute the increase both to improved reporting and to a real rise in cases. The disease has already killed more people than reported cases of toxic shock syndrome and the original outbreak of Legionnaire's disease, and it has engendered as much fear.

Dr. David J. Sencer, New York City's Health Commissioner, has termed the immune deficiency syndrome "a major health problem." He emphasized that groups other than homosexual men were involved. Groups afflicted with the syndrome include more than 60 heterosexual men and women who were drug abusers and used intravenous needles; 30 male and female immigrants from Haiti, all heterosexual, and some hemophiliacs who use blood products to combat their illness.

Cases in 27 States

Doctors theorize that the disease is an infectious agent transmitted in a complex way through sexual contact or through the blood. Yet in many cases one person in a long-time sexual relationship will get the syndrome, while the partner will not.

The disease has been recorded in 27 states; New York State's 259 cases is the largest concentration. The Centers for Disease Control, several of New York City's medical centers and the city's Health Department have been working intensely to find the syndrome's cause. Meanwhile, informational groups have sprung up among homosexuals, such as the Gay Men's Health Crisis group, which has published an exhaustive pamphlet on the syndrome and runs a 24-hour hot line.

The National Gay Task Force is coordinating a conference on the disease, and publications for homosexuals, including The Advocate, Christopher Street and New York Native, have been printing extensive articles about it.

'Feeling of Hopelessness'

"It's basically frightening because no one knows what's causing it," said John Kolman, a 28-year-old law student who went to the St. Mark's Clinic in Greenwich Village last week complaining of persistent swollen glands, thought to be one early symptom of the disease. "Every week a new theory comes out about how you're going to spread it."

Physicians say they are seeing panic-stricken patients who display skin lesions that turn out to be bug bites, poison ivy, black and blue marks or freckles of no medical consequence. One major symptom of Kaposi's sarcoma is purplish or discolored nodules or lumps on top of or beneath the skin.

"There's tremendous anxiety and it translates into panic behavior," said Dr. Roger W. Enlow, a clinical researcher at the Hospital for Joint Diseases, Beth Israel Medical Center, who helps run the all-volunteer St. Mark's Clinic.

Dr. Sencer, the Health Commissioner, said: "It's unfortunate we don't have anything positive to recommend to people at the present time. We just don't know."

Some General Advice

But he said the limiting of sexual partners was "probably good general advice" because of the number of other sexually transmissible diseases, including venereal diseases such as herpes, parasitic diseases and hepatitis.

Leaders of homosexual groups, including the National Gay Task Force, and several doctors emphasized that the immune deficiency syndrome does not result from being homosexual but rather seems to have settled on this particular group among others.

They said that no homosexual women were known to have the syndrome and that homosexual men have as many different life styles as heterosexual men. Only a segment of them, they said, are the "sexually active" men whom doctors identify as being most at risk of getting the syndrome because of their exposure to more partners.

Dr. James W. Curran, head of the A.I.D.S. project at the Centers for Disease Control, said the concern among homosexuals about the disease was "not ill-founded" because of its severity and the uncertainty about it.

"The other concern," he added, "is there are many other groups that seem to be affected with similar illnesses, and the homosexual community does not want to be blamed for this problem."

* * *

May 30, 1983

FACING THE EMOTIONAL ANGUISH OF AIDS

By GLENN COLLINS

The tragic medical consequences of Acquired Immune Deficiency Syndrome, known as AIDS, have been measured in the 558 known deaths caused by the disease. But for the living victims, AIDS has profound psychological consequences that are only beginning to be understood.

"It just hangs over your head," said Philip Lanzaratta, a 41-year-old AIDS patient in Manhattan who has been struggling with the disease for 20 months. "There is always the overriding uncertainty that on any day you'll come down with something new that your suppressed immune system can't repel."

New knowledge about the special emotional difficulties of AIDS victims is emerging as mental-health professionals develop strategies for treating these patients who live with a mysterious, often fatal contagious disorder that has no known causes or cures.

Last week the Government's chief health official said that investigating the illness was "the No. 1 priority" of the United States Public Health Service. Half the 1,450 cases reported nationally have occurred in New York, and social workers, psychiatrists and psychologists here have been treating AIDS victims for several years.

'There Were No Guidelines'

"We felt as if we were in uncharted waters," said Dr. Stuart E. Nichols Jr., a psychiatrist at Beth Israel Medical Center who began treating AIDS patients 18 months ago. "There were no guidelines and not much in the psychiatric literature for coping with anxiety about such a mysterious disease."

Subsequently, Dr. Nichols has interviewed and studied more than 100 AIDS patients, including Mr. Lanzaratta, who attended the doctor's first support group, started in April 1982. "One of the special problems for patients is the lack of hard medical data," Dr. Nichols said. "We don't know what causes AIDS, or how long the incubation period is. Such a situation can be a fertile ground for misinformation, superstitiousness and magical thinking."

"Some of the therapeutic issues are the same as with other chronically ill patients," said Noreen Russell, a social worker at New York University Medical Center who has been working with terminally ill patients for seven years now. "But the intensity of anxiety can be greater because we're dealing with a very great unknown."

Miss Russell, along with a co-worker, Virginia Lehman, started a therapy group for AIDS victims in December 1981 and began another group last June. "What's unique," said Miss Russell, "is that, in the presence of such sophisticated medical technology, we seem to be so powerless. AIDS reminds people of cancer, yet it has the sense of contagion about it. In a sense AIDS is like herpes—but herpes doesn't kill."

One of the victims' greatest fears is that they may spread AIDS to family, friends or partners. "Patients can feel terribly isolated," said Dr. Kenneth S. Wein, clinical director of Gay Men's Health Crisis Inc., a nonprofit social-service agency that has treated more than 150 AIDS patients in support and therapy groups. "Some really do feel like lepers, even though it appears that AIDS is not transmitted by simple social contact."

AIDS is believed to be transmitted through sexual or intimate contact. Most cases have involved male homosexuals, intravenous drug users and people from Haiti. However, other patients have included hemophiliacs who have received blood products, recipients of blood transfusions, and women who had sexual contact with AIDS victims.

A focal point for AIDS treatment in the city has been the Gay Men's Health Crisis office in Manhattan, which, in addition to its support and therapy groups for AIDS patients—including Haitians and intravenous drug users—runs groups for patients' parents and partners. Among its other programs, the agency sends crisis counselors and home attendants to visit AIDS victims and runs an AIDS hotline number, 212-685-4952.

The initial shock after AIDS is first diagnosed can be considerable, said Dr. Nichols, but reactions vary greatly from patient to patient. "One of the responses to any serious health insult is 'Why me?'" said Dr. Nichols, president of the Caucus of Gay, Lesbian and Bisexual Members of the American Psychiatric Association. "In the case of gays, it often seems that no matter how well they have come to terms with their gayness, when they learn they have AIDS they experience a feeling of being punished for being gay."

"For some the experience is a sort of second 'coming out,'" said Miss Russell. "They have to come to terms with their gayness all over again."

The Rev. William Sloane Coffin, senior minister of Riverside Church in Manhattan, has counseled a number of AIDS victims. "Some felt that this was in some way God's punishment," he said. "I reassured them that they have no right in the world to feel in any way that this is God's will. Being gay is not a sin. But once they get sick, it's as if when their immune system breaks down, their psychological immune system breaks down, too."

After patients' initial shock, said Dr. Nichols, many experience considerable anger. "They become angry at God, at society, at government, at government research funding levels and at doctors. We are medical people, and we're supposed to have answers. But essentially, there aren't any answers."

"Some of them believe that society is only interested in AIDS now that straight people may be at risk," said Dr. John B. Montana, an attending physician at Cabrini Medical Center who has treated many AIDS patients and counseled them at St. Marks Clinic in Greenwich Village.

Some of the patients have used their experience to examine the role that sex plays in their lives. Dr. Nichols said, "Some patients are learning to do loving things together that are totally nonsexual, and redefining the meaning of intimacy."

One of the important tasks of therapy with AIDS victims is to get them to reconnect with their families, where possible. For some homosexuals this has been difficult. "Many are not 'out' to their families, or are in a different city by choice and find it awfully hard to ask for support," said Dr. Nichols.

One AIDS patient got up the courage and told his family he was a homosexual, Dr. Nichols said: "His mother replied, 'Thank God you told us you're gay. We thought you didn't know. We figured we had to tell you, and we just didn't know how.'"

Miss Russell said that many of her patients were quite pleasantly surprised by family members who provided generous assistance unexpectedly. However, this has not always been the reaction.

'Some Real Horror Stories'

"There have been some real horror stories," said Dr. Montana. The family of one AIDS patient who died refused to accept the body. "They didn't know their son was gay, and they wouldn't accept it."

He said that patients' friends and families often rally round, but not always: "I've seen some people die in utter loneliness. I was with one patient in the hospital when he died. He was 22, and he was everybody's best friend—people loved him. He died alone. I said to him, 'Close your eyes now and go to sleep.' And then he died."

For the living, anxiety must constantly be coped with. "Having the fear, that's the worst thing," said a 45-year-old illustrator in Manhattan who has Kaposi's sarcoma, a cancer often seen in AIDS patients, and who asked that his name not be used. "I woke up with a temperature this morning, and I'm very worried right now. It could mean that I'll have to be hospitalized again."

The emotional toll of treating AIDS patients can be a problem for professionals as well. "I've wept," said Dr. Montana. "There are times when I feel like pounding my head against the wall. It's always hard on a hospital staff losing a young patient. These patients are often young and recently healthy."

"But the work can be extraordinarily rewarding, too," said Miss Russell. "I am moved again and again by my patients'

great courage in the face of life-threatening disease." Mr. Lanzaratta said, "The struggle has been difficult, but it has given me a sense of strength and a certain dignity."

* * *

February 15, 1987

FACT, THEORY AND MYTH ON THE SPREAD OF AIDS

By LAWRENCE K. ALTMAN

As AIDS continues its spread, mounting fear over the epidemic has been matched by persistent confusion over how the virus that causes the disease is transmitted.

More than 30,000 cases of acquired immune deficiency syndrome have been reported in the United States since 1981, when the disease was first identified. More than half the patients have died. Most victims in this country have been homosexual men and intravenous drug abusers.

Four percent of the cases have been attributed to the spread of the virus through heterosexual intercourse with a member of the known high-risk groups: bisexual men, drug abusers or those infected by contaminated transfusions or blood products. An unknown share of an additional 3 percent of cases with undetermined causes may have spread through heterosexual intercourse as well.

Part of the mystery and fear about AIDS arises from the fact that many carriers of the virus are not aware of it. The virus can lurk in the body without causing disease and, among those who develop AIDS, the average time between infection and diagnosis of AIDS may be five years or more.

While much remains to be learned about AIDS, scientists assert with confidence that studies of victims and disease patterns have provided a clear picture of how the virus has spread in this country, and how it has not.

Q. How does AIDS spread?

Many studies have documented the spread of the AIDS virus to an uninfected person through anal or vaginal intercourse with an infected person; through exchanges of blood, such as on contaminated hypodermic needles; from infected mothers to their infants before or during birth, and possibly through breast-feeding of infants.

Many studies have shown that people do not become infected with the AIDS virus as a result of routine, nonintimate contacts in the home or workplace.

Q. Who is now infected with the AIDS virus?

Experts estimate that up to 1.5 million Americans are infected with the AIDS virus. Most are homosexual men and intravenous drug users, but a small, perhaps growing portion are men or women who were infected through heterosexual intercourse with a drug user or a bisexual man. Each infected person is presumed to be capable of spreading the virus to others through sexual intercourse or through blood, as in sharing contaminated needles.

Anyone who has had sexual relations with a homosexual or bisexual man in the last decade, or who has used an unsterile needle to take drugs, is at risk of infection. The infection was rare in the United States in the late 1970's, then spread among homosexual men and drug users exponentially in the early 1980's.

Q. How can a person tell if he or she is infected with the AIDS virus?

The blood test for AIDS infection detects the presence of AIDS virus antibodies, substances the body produces in response to invasion by the virus. Those who fear they may be infected can get the blood test through a personal doctor or through anonymous testing centers in many cities.

Q. What proportion of those infected with the virus will develop AIDS?

Scientists believe that the infection persists for life. Only with time will scientists learn what proportion of virus carriers develop AIDS or related afflictions. According to recent estimates by the Federal Centers for Disease Control in Atlanta, from 20 percent to 30 percent of carriers will develop AIDS within five years of initial infection.

Q. Are some types of sexual intercourse more dangerous than others?

Many experts believe that the virus spreads more readily in anal intercourse than in vaginal intercourse because anal sex often involves breaks in rectal tissues, thus allowing easier entry of the virus into the bloodstream. Studies suggest that the receptive partner in anal sex is at greater risk. One study has suggested that the virus may be able to directly infect cells in the colon.

Q. Can the virus spread from an infected person in vaginal intercourse?

Several studies have clearly shown that it can, and that it can spread from a man to a woman or from a woman to a man. Some experts believe transmission occurs far less often from a woman to a man than from a man to a woman, but this point is debated. The virus has been found both in semen and in vaginal secretions of infected people.

Q. How is the virus transmitted in vaginal intercourse?

Scientists are not certain. One theory is that the virus passes through invisible breaks in the surface inside the vagina or on the penis. Some experts believe the virus may also enter through mucous membranes or other soft tissues in the genital areas. No one knows if the virus can penetrate the lining of the male urethra, the tubelike passage through which urine flows.

Q. What is the risk of getting the virus from a single act of vaginal intercourse with an infected person?

Precise data are lacking. From indirect evidence, Federal scientists judge the risk of transmission in a single encounter to be low. Quantification is complex: Some infected people have said they had only a single exposure, while other people who have had hundreds of exposures have escaped infection. Still, several studies have shown that with repeated intercourse, as many as half the sexual partners of infected men or women become infected.

In Africa, where vaginal intercourse is believed to be the major means of spreading AIDS, studies suggest that the virus may pass more easily among people who have had gonorrhea,

genital herpes or other sexually transmitted diseases, perhaps as a result of open sores in the skin of the genital area and the presence there of larger than usual numbers of the types of white blood cells that the virus invades.

Q. Can the virus spread through oral sex?

Federal epidemiologists suspect it can because the virus is present in semen and vaginal secretions and thus might enter the cells of the body through cuts or mucous membranes in the mouth or throat. However, they have not documented any cases.

Q. Is it dangerous to kiss an infected person?

Minute amounts of the AIDS virus have been found in the saliva of some virus carriers, but no cases of transmission by kissing have been documented. Experts say there is no danger in a peck on the cheek of an infected person but they recommend against any exchange of saliva and deep kissing with an infected person.

Q. Do condoms protect against the spread of the virus?

Laboratory studies show that the virus cannot pass through condoms, and condoms are believed to offer a high degree of protection. However, condoms are not foolproof: They may tear, slip or be misused, and in one study two cases were documented in which the virus passed between partners who used condoms in intercourse over an extended period. Because the virus may be present in men's pre-ejaculation emissions and in vaginal secretions, experts recommend that condoms be used throughout the sex act.

Q. Is there greater likelihood of viral spread when a woman is menstruating?

No data exist on this point, but some experts suspect this is so.

Q. Are blood transfusions and blood products safe?

Before the availability of the test for AIDS infection in early 1985, thousands of Americans became infected with the virus from transfusions of contaminated blood from infected donors. Many hemophiliacs were infected by contaminated blood products.

But now, because of rigorous testing of donated blood, the risk of AIDS infection from a transfusion is extremely low. Blood products for hemophiliacs also receive treatment to kill the virus and are now considered free of it. There is no risk of a blood donor acquiring AIDS because a new needle is used for each individual.

Q. Why has AIDS spread among drug addicts?

When intravenous drug users share unsterile needles and equipment, traces of blood contaminated with the AIDS virus may be injected into the bloodstream of subsequent users of the same needle. Experts consider repeated exposure to the virus through shared needles particularly dangerous. Studies have shown that doctors and nurses who accidentally stick themselves once or twice with needles that have been used on infected persons do not become infected.

Q. Can the virus spread from a bleeding sore or cut, or from vomit, urine or feces?

The danger to people exposed to such substances is considered slight because the contaminated substance must find an entry point into the body, such as through an open wound. However, experts advise standard hygienic precautions and greater care if someone is handling a nosebleed or or other excretions from an infected person.

Q. Can human bites transmit AIDS?

Experts say it is theoretically possible, but they know of no such cases.

Q. Can the virus be spread by insects?

Several studies in Africa and the United States have found no evidence that the virus has been spread by mosquitoes or other insects. Some laboratory studies have suggested the virus can survive in insects such as bed bugs, but studies of transmission patterns have not detected any cases spread by blood-sucking insects.

Q. Can the AIDS virus be spread in swimming pools, hot tubs or saunas?

Standard chlorination and heat are sufficient to kill the virus, so chlorinated pools and hot tubs are safe. Experts consider it extremely unlikely that the virus could spread in a sauna; no such cases have been detected.

* * *

March 16, 1987

THE DEVASTATION OF AIDS: MANY DEAD, MORE DYING

By JANE GROSS

There are pockets in this city where the extraordinary has become commonplace, where AIDS has made disease and death the focus of daily life.

Along the tree-lined streets of Greenwich Village, where vibrant young men have already lost two friends or four or six, a passing hearse routinely signals the death of someone in his prime.

In the tenements and housing projects of Harlem or the South Bronx, where violence and drug addiction have always snatched the young, mothers now grieve for children who they say died of pneumonia or leukemia or any of the diseases that are euphemisms for acquired immune deficiency syndrome.

No place outside Africa has suffered more from AIDS than New York City, home to nearly one-third of the cases in the United States. In the last six years the accelerating epidemic has struck 9,000 New Yorkers and killed 5,000 people. In the next five years, it is expected to kill 25,000 more.

On its deadly march, AIDS has become the leading cause of death among the city's young men and women and has placed a disproportionate burden on the black and Hispanic poor. Half a million New Yorkers are thought to be infected with the virus, many facing death, the rest shouldering a terrible uncertainty, their lives unalterably transformed.

These facts and numbers have recently gathered new force as the epidemic passes from one phase to another, from disbelief to inevitability.

Now city officials are bracing for an increased caseload in the very neighborhoods that are already reeling from poverty, homelessness and ignorance.

Now volunteer groups and public health educators are seeking to reach into the shadowy corners of the city where drug abusers are the main bridge to the heterosexual population.

And now some doctors are learning to comfort dying men and women, their bodies racked, their minds ruined, while others shun hospitals that seem overrun with patients they cannot cure. For some New Yorkers, AIDS is a dim reality that floats in and out of consciousness—there when Liberace dies or Federal health officials compare it to the black plague, gone the rest of the time.

But elsewhere AIDS is pervasive—sobering the homosexual community where it first struck half a dozen years ago, racing through the world of intravenous drug abusers at a new and alarming rate, infecting their sexual partners and killing their babies.

And as it kills or merely frightens, AIDS transforms the city, inexorably and painfully. It saps young talent from the professions that give New York its sparkle. It exacerbates the social and economic problems that weigh so heavily on the growing underclass. It shapes the debate about health care, sex education and drug addiction. It spreads fear among single people reared during the carefree days of the sexual revolution and casts a shadow over adolescence. And it tests the compassion and rationality of officials and ordinary citizens.

* * *

February 5, 1989

WHO'S STRICKEN AND HOW: AIDS PATTERN IS SHIFTING

By LAWRENCE K. ALTMAN

Eight years after AIDS made its startling appearance, it is changing its face. Once overwhelmingly an affliction of homosexual men, acquired immune deficiency syndrome is more and more becoming a disease of poor, black and Hispanic heterosexuals in the inner city.

People and institutions are slowly adjusting to a long-term threat requiring unrelenting vigilance and aggressive countermeasures. Already the disease has struck 85,000 Americans, and more than half have died.

Today gay men still account for most cases of AIDS and are believed to be the majority of those who carry the AIDS virus but are not ill. But health officials say there are tantalizing signs that the period of surges of new cases among gay men may be ending. Data over the last two years suggest that the rate at which gay men get AIDS has finally begun to flatten out at a level somewhat above 7,000 new cases a year.

One-Fourth Are Drug Users

Intravenous drug users and their sex partners and babies, concentrated in inner cities, now account for more than one-fourth of the AIDS cases. Evidence suggests that the virus is spreading fastest among those groups. Minority groups are disproportionately hit: 4 out of 5 AIDS cases attributed to sharing needles have occurred among the black and the Hispanic.

American success in curbing the disease among drug addicts and the urban poor will determine the disease's future course more than anything else, many experts now say.

So far, there has been no indication that AIDS is spreading explosively among the general heterosexual population. But the story is different among poor people who live amid rampant drug addiction.

'A Poor People's Disease'

"It is beginning to turn out that heterosexual AIDS is a poor people's disease," said Dr. Andrew Moss, an epidemiologist at the San Francisco General Hospital. "Historically speaking, say 50 years from now, homosexuals and drug users will not be the central phenomenon in AIDS. AIDS will be a routine sexually transmitted disease, and we have to adapt to thinking in those terms."

Although AIDS is no longer novel, it remains a public health emergency. One enormous challenge is further curbing the spread of the virus. While evidence suggests that most gay men are now aware of the dangers of unprotected sexual activity, education and warnings for homosexuals as well as heterosexuals must be unremitting.

Fighting the Virus Spread

The major problem today, many health experts assert, has been the inability to fight the spread of the virus among drug addicts and their sex partners, a task that requires many responses, from great increases in drug treatment programs to education in a form that will reach the dispossessed youth of urban ghettos.

The Surgeon General of the United States, Dr. C. Everett Koop, has said that health workers have been "singularly unsuccessful in penetrating the drug-addicted culture" with messages about the risks of injecting drugs and sharing needles.

The search for better medical treatment of AIDS remains as urgent as it is frustrating. Scores of thousands are suffering from AIDS-related diseases and scientists fear that over the coming years most of the million-plus Americans believed to be infected with the AIDS virus will become ill.

The search for drugs has met with controversy and disappointment. So far only one drug, AZT, azidothymidine, has been proved effective in fighting the AIDS virus, but it is highly toxic, cannot be taken by many patients and is no cure.

Survivals Seem Longer

But because of AZT and the improved treatment of some of the diseases that afflict those with AIDS, some patients appear to be surviving longer than patients in the past. But many current AIDS patients and advocates say the Federal program to develop new AIDS drugs is not responding fast enough. Scientists say they are still not sure whether a vaccine to prevent being infected with the AIDS virus will be possible.

Dr. Harold W. Jaffe, chief of AIDS epidemiology at the Federal Centers for Disease Control in Atlanta, said: "The initial hopes that either the number of infected people would be very small or that we would have a highly effective therapy or a vaccine in the near future all appear to be false hopes."

Federal health officials have projected that by the end of 1992, 365,000 Americans will have developed AIDS, with 263,000 deaths. In 1992 alone, according to this estimate, 80,000 new cases will occur, posing an extraordinary challenge to the health-care system. However, the uncertainties are great: total cases by 1992 could, in this projection, range from 205,000 to 440,000.

The total number of Americans infected with the AIDS virus remains poorly known, in part because of delays in obtaining results from several Federal surveys. Initial results of many surveys are due later this year, Federal officials said. The United States Public Health Service estimated very roughly in 1986 that 1 million to 1.5 million Americans carried the virus, and that estimate has not been revised.

Shift Detected in Geography

Available data indicate that more than half of those who carry the virus develop AIDS within 10 years of infection, and studies have suggested that most carriers will eventually become ill.

Homosexual and bisexual men remain the group at highest risk of developing AIDS, accounting for more than 60 percent of the cumulative national cases.

But no longer are cases so heavily concentrated in the gay communities of New York, San Francisco and Los Angeles. Now, more than two-thirds of AIDS cases reported among homosexual men occur outside these three cities.

Heterosexual users of intravenous drugs accounted for 23 percent of the new cases reported in this country in 1988, up from the 17 percent or 18 percent that had been steadily reported since 1982.

Federal health officials attribute part of the rise to improved reporting of AIDS cases. But they also say there has been a real rise in the number.

Drug Users and Gay Men

In New York City, which alone accounts for more than one-third of the country's cases spread by dirty needles, drug users have surpassed gay men in newly reported cases. The total number of AIDS patients among intravenous drug users exceeds those of gay men in several cities, including Newark, Jersey City, New Haven and San Juan, P.R., and in Lee County in Florida.

The problem of AIDS in babies is largely a curse of urban minority communities. As of Jan. 30, a total of 1,080 infants and children born with the virus had developed AIDS; 84 percent of them were black or Hispanic. Nearly all the mothers used drugs or were the sex partners of drug addicts. Thousands of additional babies have been born infected, so the toll will climb.

The AIDS virus has been slowly spreading among heterosexuals who do not use intravenous drugs, but again, the spread is mainly among the sex partners of drug abusers. The proportion of AIDS cases among people who are believed to have contracted the virus through heterosexual intercourse has risen steadily to 3.6 percent for new cases reported in 1988, as against 1 percent of a much smaller number in 1982. (These totals exclude people from Haiti and Africa, where heterosexual intercourse is the predominant means of spreading AIDS.) One remarkable thing about the epidemic is how consistent the evidence has been over the years on how the virus spreads and how it does not. Studies have shown that AIDS is spread by sexual intercourse, by virus-carrying blood entering the body, by sharing intravenous needles and syringes; AIDS is also spread from infected mothers to their babies. The studies clearly show that AIDS is not spread by casual contact or by insects.

Several studies have showed that the rate of new AIDS virus infection among gay men in New York and California has dropped sharply, presumably because of the wider practice of "safer sex." Now many epidemiologists are hotly debating whether there is also a major slowdown in the number of newly diagnosed AIDS cases among gay men.

A Stable Rate for Gay Men?

Data from the nation in general, along with statistics from New York, San Francisco and Los Angeles, suggest that after years of steeply rising, the annual number of new AIDS cases among gay men may be stabilizing. According to reports received by the Centers for Disease Control, 7,200 gay men who were not intravenous drug users were diagnosed with AIDS in the first six months of 1987, 7,354 in the second half of 1987 and 7,264 in the first half of 1988. (Data are still trickling in for the later months of 1988.) This follows several years of sharp increases. But some experts warn that the apparent leveling could be temporary or perhaps an artifact of reporting methods.

Experts speculate that the leveling of new cases, if it persists, could reflect the adoption of safe sex practices among many gay men in the mid-1980's. It might also reflect improvements in medical care of infected but still healthy men, possibly including preventive use of the antiviral drug AZT and of aerosol pentamidine, which is believed to help prevent a form of pneumonia in patients with damaged immune systems. These drugs have not been widely used until very recently.

The New York City Health Commissioner, Dr. Stephen Joseph, said he viewed with cautious optimism data showing that for gay men in the city, "the incidence began to plateau in mid-1986 and then actually began to fall in early 1988."

On the West Coast, Dr. Moss said he believed that the peak had been reached and that the number of new cases would drop in 1989 in San Francisco. But Dr. George Rutherford, an epidemiologist in the San Francisco Health Department, said he considered such predictions "premature," citing a possible slowdown in reporting of cases and a movement of gay men out of the city as possible factors.

Dr. Peter Kerndt, who heads the AIDS epidemiology program for the Los Angeles County Health Department, said he was "not convinced of a true decline or slowing" in the number of AIDS cases among Los Angeles gay men, and that any perceived lull was due to "underreporting."

Even if the annual case count has stabilized, the overall toll will continue its relentless climb. Dr. Ruth Berkelman of the Centers for Disease Control said any plateau could last for years before a real turn downward occurred.

Battlefront: Public Health

Public health workers face a great challenge in containing the AIDS epidemic among intravenous drug users to the Northeast and Florida, where most cases have occurred to date.

An estimated 50 percent to 60 percent of intravenous drug users in New York and New Jersey are infected with the virus, as against only 5 percent in Los Angeles and Seattle.

In San Francisco, where 15 to 20 percent of intravenous drug users are believed infected and only a little more than 100 AIDS cases have been reported so far among heterosexual drug users, concern is growing about an emerging epidemic, particularly among those who share needles as they inject cocaine many times a day.

As the AIDS epidemic shifts its course through the American population many things, from prevention strategies to medical services, must also be redirected.

But the changing face of AIDS also poses a political challenge, summed up by Dr. Jaffe of the Centers for Disease Control:

"While the gay community organized political clout to combat AIDS, it is not clear who will do the same and speak for the poor and disadvantaged, who are now at the highest risk."

Correction: Because of an editing error, an article on Sunday about the changing face of the AIDS epidemic misstated the rate of new AIDS diagnoses in gay men in recent years. As figures provided later in the same article indicate, somewhat above 7,000 new cases among gay men have been diagnosed every six months, not every year.

* * *

Society's Response

November 29, 1984

COURT LIMITS ACTIVITY IN HOMOSEXUAL BATHHOUSES IN SAN FRANCISCO

SAN FRANCISCO, Nov. 28—Bathhouses catering to male homosexuals, closed last month in an attempt to control the spread of AIDS, may reopen under strict limitations on sexual behavior, a Superior Court judge ruled today.

Judge Roy L. Wonder lifted the Oct. 15 temporary restraining order that closed the bathhouses. But he said bathhouse operators must hire employees to monitor sexual activity and eject patrons who engage in "high risk sexual activity" as defined by the San Francisco AIDS Foundation.

The foundation, a group formed to educate the public about the dangers of AIDS, acquired immune difficiency syndrome, defines high risk sexual activity as sex acts with multiple partners that involve the exchange of bodily fluids.

Restrictions on Bathhouses

Judge Wonder ordered that doors on bathhouse booths and cubicles be removed and said proprietors could not rent private rooms unless they were licensed by the city to operate hotel rooms.

AIDS is a usually fatal disease that medical evidence suggests is spread through sexual contact. Since 1981, 817 cases have been reported in San Francisco, most of them among homosexuals, according to the San Francisco Department of Health. The Department said that 358 of the victims had died of the disease.

At a Nov. 14 hearing, attorneys representing the bathhouse owners said their clients were willing to participate in a plan that would regulate sexual contact in public areas of the bathhouses. But they said activity in private rooms and cubicles was protected by privacy rights guaranteed under the California constitution.

But Deputy City Attorney Phillip S. Ward argued that the private cubicles amounted to "revolving closed doors" where patrons participate in multiple, anonymous sexual encounters associated with the spread of AIDS.

Dr. Mervyn Silverman, the city's health director, banned high-risk sexual activity in bathhouses last April. When an undercover investigation revealed that the ban was not being enforced, Dr. Silverman ordered 14 business establishments catering to the homosexual community, including bathhouses, bookstores and movie theaters, closed as a menace to public health.

Owners of the establishments initially defied the order, arguing that there was no proof that their businesses were a source of the spread of AIDS. On Oct. 15, the city obtained a temporary court order closing the bathhouses, but the court refused to close the bookstores and theaters, citing their First Amendment rights.

Thomas Steel, an attorney representing some of the bathhouses, said that his clients are reviewing Judge Wonder's ruling to decide whether to appeal the ordered removal of cubicle doors.

* * *

September 20, 1985

HOLLYWOOD TURNS OUT FOR AIDS BENEFIT

By ALJEAN HARMETZ
Special to the New York Times

LOS ANGELES, Sept. 19—More than 2,500 people, including Elizabeth Taylor, Shirley MacLaine and Mayor Tom Bradley, crowded into the Westin Bonaventure ballroom here tonight to raise money for AIDS victims, a cause that was far from popular a few months ago.

The sponsors of the "Commitment to Life" dinner, the AIDS Project Los Angeles, set the target of raising $1 million. The dinner had originally been scheduled in the much smaller Century Plaza Hotel ballroom, but after Rock Hudson announced last July that he was suffering from acquired immune deficiency syndrome, the deadly disorder that attacks the body's immune system, the response became so great that the dinner had to be moved to a larger hall.

"I've handled a hundred dinners and when the news started about Rock Hudson, I've never seen anything take off like this one," said Lucille Polachek of Events Unlimited, which handled sales of tickets at $250 to $500 a person.

Mr. Hudson, who bought $10,000 worth of tickets but was too ill to attend, sent a telegram to the guests that said in part: "I am not happy that I am sick. I am not happy that I have AIDS. But if that is helping others, I can, at least, know that my own misfortune has had some positive worth."

Telegram from the President

President Reagan also sent a telegram to the dinner, in which he said his Administration had made halting the spread of AIDS a "top priority."

On the entertainment bill at the dinner were such performers as Carol Burnett, Sammy Davis Jr., Rod Stewart, Cyndi Lauper and Diahann Carroll. Miss Taylor and Burt Reynolds auctioned off three small Andy Warhol paintings to the producer Jon Peters for $25,000. In an earlier, silent auction in which bids were registered on paper, two evening gowns by Nolan Miller, the designer for the "Dynasty" television series, a BMW and other items raised $56,000.

Miss MacLaine, asked why she was involved in the benefit, said: "Three of my close friends have died. The image is that Hollywood is panicked. Tonight shows most of us have made the choice of love rather than fear."

Mayor Bradley, speaking at the dinner, pledged the city's support "in this crisis that threatens the very health of this nation."

Many of the participants spoke at news conferences before the dinner. Betty Ford, wife of former President Gerald R. Ford, begged for an end to the stigma attached to people who have AIDS. When asked whether children with the disorder should be allowed to attend schools, she said, "I sympathize with parents who are frightened about their children, but I would not want my grandchildren kept out of school."

One man, Steve Peters, who has had AIDS for 18 months, said that he hoped that after the dinner, "other people won't be afraid to be in the same room with me."

Security was extraordinarily tight tonight, with guests being required to show dinner tickets at least seven different times at various posts.

Reminder of Polio Scares

One of the co-chairmen for tonight's dinner, Wallis Annenberg, the daughter of the former ambassador and publisher Walter H. Annenberg, said: "I felt it was time to make AIDS everyone's business. I remember the polio scares of years ago. Friends of mine would disappear from summer camp. We were told old wives' tales, not to let flies bite us because they might have bitten children with polio. I saw the same kind of thing happening again—don't eat onions because homosexuals are in the kitchen and their tears carry the AIDS virus. Rock Hudson deserves an Academy Award because his illness has made AIDS respectable."

AIDS Project Los Angeles, a nonprofit organization with a 1985 budget of $2.2 million, provides support services for AIDS victims, including haircuts for housebound patients, religious counseling, free movie tickets, transportation and dental care, a major problem since many dentists in southern California refuse to treat victims of the disorder. AIDS Project also distributes information about safe sexual practices for homosexuals, who, along with intravenous drug users and hemophiliacs, are considered at high risk of getting the disorder.

The entertainment industry has strongly backed the "Commitment to Life" dinner, with Mr. Reynolds, Miss Taylor, Miss MacLaine, Liza Minnelli, Bette Midler, Burt Lancaster and Maureen Stapleton among the co-chairmen.

The Los Angeles homosexual community has also strongly backed the benefit.

The actress Linda Evans, who played love scenes with Mr. Hudson on the television show "Dynasty" last year and was reported in some publications to be angry at the discovery that the actor had the disorder, asked to introduce the part of tonight's program that involves Mr. Hudson.

* * *

November 7, 1985

HOLLYWOOD IN CONFLICT OVER AIDS

By ALJEAN HARMETZ
Special to the New York Times

HOLLYWOOD, Nov. 6—Until the announcement in July that Rock Hudson was suffering from AIDS, the movie industry had been under no special pressure to address the social consequences of the deadly disease.

But his illness and death, because it sharpened Hollywood's awareness of its own vulnerability, has triggered a reaction that has created new problems for the industry. Some in the industry now expect there will be a rethinking of the way sex is depicted in movies while others fear the possibility of severe discrimination against homosexual actors.

Reflecting these new concerns, the Directors Guild of America will discuss taking an official position on AIDS, or acquired immune deficiency syndrome, at its national board meeting this month. The American Federation of Television and Radio Artists has informed its members in a letter that they "should and do have the right to refuse contact with anyone whom they believe may have any communicable disease." Since some institutions are now testing for AIDS, the federation also told members that "no company has the right to ask for blood tests as condition for employment."

The Screen Actors Guild added to the sense of alarm last week by calling open-mouthed kissing a possible health hazard and requiring actors to be told in advance if they will be asked to play such scenes.

Fear of Backlash

"I think there could be a purge against homosexuals," said the screenwriter William Goldman ("Butch Cassidy and the Sundance Kid"). "A gay actor friend of mine who has lost 11 friends to AIDS says he is already feeling a backlash."

Joseph Morgenstern, a screenwriter and columnist, added: "Gay actors are absolutely terrified by this, in the depths of despair. It's only my speculation, but I think a de facto blacklist may well emerge."

The fear is that the spread of AIDS will lead to the public identification of homosexuals. Few homosexual producers, directors, high-level studio executives and writers have publicly announced their homosexuality. In fact, homosexual actors hide their true sexuality because they are under pressure to appear to be in real life the macho lovers that they portray on screen. Lesser-known actors are unlikely to be chosen by casting directors if they admit their homosexuality, according to Michael Kearns, one of the few openly homosexual actors in Hollywood.

"Often, they'll even wear wedding rings to auditions," said Chris Uszler, president of the Alliance of Gay and Lesbian Artists.

Nationally, homosexuals have accounted for more than 70 percent of the more than 14,000 known cases of AIDS. Federal authorities have identified homosexuals, intravenous drug users and hemophiliacs as the groups at highest risk of carrying the AIDS virus, which is spread through intimate sexual contact or the blood.

Hollywood's historical insecurity and sensitivity to political and social trends has caused the industry to react with panic frequently in the past. The inability of the silent-film star Fatty Arbuckle to get a job after being tried, and acquitted, for manslaughter, the restrictive production code of the 1930's and the political blacklist of the McCarthy era are the most obvious examples. In his book "Senator Joe McCarthy," Richard H. Rovere wrote that Hollywood was vulnerable to the Senator's accusations precisely because "Hollywood has always been a hotbed of conformity."

"The panic is because all of Hollywood is based on fantasy," said Mr. Goldman. "It's not just because an actor is hiding being gay. These gorgeous men and women are supposed to be perfect."

Gilbert Cates, president of the directors guild, said: "An actor who has AIDS or suspects he has AIDS has an obligation as an act of good citizenship not to do a kissing scene. No amount of legislation will deal with that problem."

Charlton Heston went further. "I think a member of that lovely euphenism—'a high-risk group'—has an obligation to refuse to do kissing scenes."

Concern Over Love Scenes

Although not willing to be quoted, several important industry figures expressed dismay that Rock Hudson had played love scenes with Linda Evans on "Dynasty" after he knew he was ill.

But because refusing might disclose that he was homosexual, "It might be very difficult for a gay actor to refuse a part that required open-mouth kissing," said Mr. Uszler of the Gay Alliance.

The Screen Actors Guild has a clause in its contract that prohibits discrimination because of sexual preference. Some female members of the guild have expressed their concern about playing love scenes opposite gay actors because the AIDS virus has been discovered in saliva. There have been published reports that one actress in particular who plays opposite a gay actor on a primetime series has complained.

The new guild ruling attempted to prevent discrimination by not telling an actor or actress whom he or she was expected to kiss. The response has been that this is unworkable and unenforceable. "It's absurd," said Aaron Spelling, the producer of "Dynasty." "First you get a star, and then you get a leading lady. It's absurd to think you could keep Paul Newman or Tom Selleck a secret."

Although there is no documented case of the disease having been transmitted through kissing, medical experts have been unwilling to say that the disease can never be transmitted through the kinds of passionate, open-mouthed kisses that today's love scenes often require. Federal experts from the Centers for Disease Control have cautioned against intimate sexual contact, including kissing that involves the exchange of saliva, with members of the high-risk groups.

Mr. Uszler asks for a return to the "dry kissing" of the days of the motion picture industry's production code. That code, which was a frightened response in the 1930's to attacks on such screen sex symbols as Mae West, also forbade sexually tinged language and required married couples to keep one foot on the floor in any bedroom scenes.

TV Codes on Sex

Even if open-mouthed kissing were banned—at the present time the industry considers this an unlikely possibility—people here feel that movies and television would simply show sex in other ways.

According to Thomas Kersey, ABC's vice president of broadcast standards and practices on the West Coast, ABC's policies already forbid open-mouthed kissing. "We advise our producers that the French kiss is unacceptable," he said. "If we see a tongue flashing, we will edit it out."

The policies at NBC and CBS are less restrictive. "We simply make a judgment when a romantic situation gets excessive," said Ralph Daniels, vice president of broadcast standards at NBC. "We decide case by case," said George Schweitzer, vice president of communications for the CBS Broadcast Group.

"This whole thing is a tough call," said Dawn Steel, president of production at Paramount. "I think exciting sexuality is part of the fantasy, part of the entertainment of a love story. I would hope it won't be withdrawn."

A Los Angeles program to test blood samples for presence of AIDS virus antibodies, a sign of probable continuing infection with the virus, is too new to have come up with definitive statistics, according to Dr. Martin Finn, medical director for public health for the county of Los Angeles. Dr. Finn said, however, that in a men's study at the University of California at Los Angeles, in which homosexual participants were self-selected and thus worried about the possibility of AIDS, 54 percent tested positive for exposure to the virus.

Scientists presume that infected individuals, although healthy themselves, can pass the virus through sexual contact or transfers of blood.

* * *

November 8, 1985

CITY CLOSES BAR FREQUENTED BY HOMOSEXUALS, CITING SEXUAL ACTIVITY LINKED TO AIDS

By JOYCE PURNICK

New York City yesterday closed a bar frequented by homosexuals, contending that it permitted "high-risk sexual activity" linked to the spread of AIDS.

It was the first such action taken by the city since New York State enacted new rules designed to curb the growing incidence of the deadly disease by empowering local governments to shut down bathhouses, bars and other places where dangerous sex takes place.

In court papers signed late Wednesday by Justice Jawn A. Sandifer of State Supreme Court in Manhattan, the city asserts that the bar—the Mine Shaft at 835 Washington Street, near Little West 12th Street, in Greenwich Village—is not only in violation of the new anti-AIDS regulations but also is a public nuisance and has been operating without a liquor license.

At a hearing set for Tuesday, the city will ask that the bar be closed for a year. Its owners, listed in court papers as the DAJ Real Estate Management Corporation, could not be reached yesterday, and its operators were not identified.

A 'Notorious' Place

The Mine Shaft is a "notorious and well-known place," in the words of Richard Dunne, executive director of the Gay Men's Health Crisis.

In graphic depositions written by city inspectors, a portrait emerged of a dark place with black walls, back rooms, open cubicles without doors and the accouterments of sado-masochism. They reported seeing many patrons engaging in anal intercourse and fellatio—the "high risk" sexual practices cited in the state rules—and hearing sounds of whipping and moaning.

At a news conference with city lawyers, Mayor Koch said in answer to questions yesterday that by closing the place, the city was not trying to impose any restrictions on sexuality, but to save lives.

"Maybe it brings to the consciousness of those who have a predilection to engage in this suicidal behavior how ridiculous it is, how self-defeating it is and how lethal it is," he said. "Maybe it will deter them as well. We don't know. But we're going to do the best we can."

Opposition to Closing

Others, including homosexual activists, argued that closing the Mine Shaft and places like it would have no impact on sexual activity, and suggested that by closing the bar, the city had taken a step toward government regulation of private behavior.

"The Governor and the Mayor have taken us down a slippery slope that may lead to recriminalization of private sexual conduct in general," said Thomas B. Stoddard, legislative director of the New York Civil Liberties Union. "Once the government starts on that road, it is very hard to make distinctions between kinds of establishments and kinds of conduct."

City inspections will continue, said the Mayor, who also sent letters to 10 establishments believed to be in violation of the state rules, asking them to report to him by next Thursday what they have done to prevent high-risk sex on their premises.

A Call for Education

Mr. Dunne of the Gay Men's Health Crisis said he did not believe that closing the bar would have a salutary effect on sexual behavior, or on the spread of acquired immune deficiency syndrome.

"You don't get AIDS from buildings, you get AIDS from a virus that is transmitted sexually," he said. "The only thing that is going to stop it is education and the adoption of behavior changes. I don't just mean people going to the Mine Shaft and to the bathhouses. I'm talking about the whole gay male population, and I'm talking about all intravenous drug users and their contacts."

Mr. Koch, who until recently had taken the position that closing bathhouses, sex clubs and the like would not stop high-risk sex, said he thought closing the Mine Shaft might stop some of the sexual practices that had been taking place there.

"The Bible says, if you save one life, it's as though you have saved the whole world," he said, alluding to a similarly worded passage that is actually in the Talmud.

Frenetic Activity

The city was expected to act a day sooner than it did in closing the Mine Shaft. The Mayor announced early Wednesday that an establishment would be closed that morning, a pronouncement that set off frenetic activity at City Hall. According to the city's Corporation Counsel, Frederick A. O. Schwarz Jr., the Mayor was "confused" about the complexity of the process and the need to prepare detailed court papers.

A large portion of the court submission is made up of the depositions from three inspectors with the city's Consumer Affairs Department, who visited the Mine Shaft between last Friday and last Sunday.

In sparse, almost clinical language, they describe what they saw.

"The bar was approximately 20 feet long," one inspector wrote. "Near the bar in the center of the floor was a pool table covered with a sheet of plywood. To the rear of the bar was a coat room where a man was checking all coats that were not leather. Located on the floor, there were two horses which I would describe as the type used in a gymnasium. The interior of the premises was painted black."

Warning Signs

The inspectors wrote of seeing several men "in various stages of undress" fondling each other, engaging in oral and anal intercourse and doing so in the open. They said that they observed men moving from one sexual partner to another and that although signs warned of AIDS and offered to provide condoms, condoms were not being used.

Two of the inspectors said they heard sounds of whipping and moaning, but did not investigate "for reasons of personal safety," one wrote.

Mr. Koch praised the inspectors, who had the option of refusing the assignment. "It's tough stuff to read," the Mayor said. "It must be horrific, horrendous in its actuality to witness."

* * *

November 22, 1985

2 CITIES CONSIDER A BATHHOUSE BAN

Special to the New York Times

SAN FRANCISCO, Nov. 21—As New York seeks to slow the spread of AIDS, elected officials here and in Los Angeles are considering actions to close or strictly regulate bathhouses and other facilities catering to homosexuals that permit sexual activities linked to the disease.

New York State has empowered local health officials to close bathhouses and other places where "high-risk sexual activities" take place, and one establishment in Manhattan has been closed.

In San Francisco, Mayor Dianne Feinstein, who for nearly three years has advocated the closing of bathhouses to protect public health, met last week with the City Health Director and a member of the City Attorney's office to urge swift action against facilities that are under court order here to prevent unsafe sexual contact on their premises.

AIDS, or acquired immune deficiency syndrome, breaks down the body's immune system and leaves the victim vulnerable to a variety of deadly diseases. The spread of the AIDS virus has been tied to some sexual acts.

The City Attorney's office said last week that it would go to court to seek contempt citations against any facilities that were not complying with a judge's order to monitor sexual activity and eject patrons engaging in "high-risk sex."

'Throw the Book' at Them

Dr. David Werdegar, the City Health Director, said he hoped the court would "throw the book" at three to five establishments the City Attorney's office said were not in compliance.

In Los Angeles, the County Board of Supervisors is considering legislation that would permit the closing of the approximately 20 bathhouses catering to homosexuals and sex clubs in the greater Los Angeles area.

Last week the City Public Health Commission recommended that such an ordinance not be passed. Instead, it suggested that "new standards" providing for the elimination of high-risk sexual activities be drawn up and facilities be monitored for compliance by the County Department of Health Services.

Recently an influential homosexual political organization in Los Angeles called on owners of bathhouses, sexual massage parlors and similar facilities catering to either homosexuals or heterosexuals to voluntarily close for "the duration of the AIDS epidemic."

Craig R. Hume, a member of the board of directors of the Municipal Elections Committee of Los Angeles, the largest local homosexual and lesbian political action committee in the country, said that while the group believed homosexual bathhouses represented only a small portion of the problem, their voluntary closing was of "symbolic importance."

"It is important for the gay community to exercise responsibility in working with the nongay community in limiting the spread of the virus," Mr. Hume said. He said the recommendation was aimed at trying to solve the problem within homosexual circles to avoid intervention by government.

'Attack on Gay Life Style'

In San Francisco, a contrary position has been taken by the Committee to Preserve Our Sexual and Civil Liberties. Timothy M. Brace, chairman of the committee, said that closing the bathhouses was "never a public health issue but a political issue" that represented "an attack on gay life style."

Everyone, homosexual or heterosexual, should be concerned with practicing "safe sex" rather than focusing on the setting and site of sexual encounters, Mr. Brace said.

This city has been grappling with the issue of whether to close facilities that allow sexual activity on their premises for nearly three years. Last Nov. 28, in an action brought by 14 bathhouses, sex clubs and other facilities that had been temporarily closed by court order, Judge Roy Wonder of San Francisco Superior Court allowed the businesses to reopen with some restrictions.

Under the judge's order, renting of private rooms was forbidden except for facilities licensed as hotels. The hiring of monitors to observe activities on the premises and the expulsion of patrons engaging in high-risk sex were also ordered by the judge.

Attorneys for the businesses have appealed and requested a stay of the restrictions pending a decision. Phillip S. Ward, a lawyer for the city, has confirmed that some of the businesses were not in compliance with the restrictions and had been sent warning letters by his office. Unless the appellate court grants a stay, Mr. Ward said the City Attorney's office would go ahead with plans to seek contempt of court citations against any business found not to be in compliance.

* * *

March 18, 1986

CRUCIAL STEPS IN COMBATING THE AIDS EPIDEMIC

Identify All the Carriers

By WILLIAM F. BUCKLEY JR.

I have read and listened, and I think now that I can convincingly crystallize the thoughts chasing about in the minds of, first, those whose concern with AIDS victims is based primarily on a concern for them and for the maintenance of the most rigid standards of civil liberties and personal privacy, and, second, those whose anxiety to protect the public impels them to give subordinate attention to the civil amenities of those who suffer from AIDS and primary attention to the safety of those who do not.

Arguments used by both sides are sometimes utilitarian, sometimes moral, sometimes a little of each—and almost always a little elusive. Most readers will locate their own inclinations and priorities somewhere other than in the polar positions here put forward by design.

School A suspects, in the array of arguments of School B, a venture in ethical opportunism. Look, they say, we have made enormous headway in the matter of civil rights for all, dislodging the straight-laced from mummified positions they inherited through eclectic superstitions ranging from the Bible's to Freud's. A generation ago, homosexuals lived mostly in the closet. Nowadays they take over cities and parade on Halloween and demand equal rights for themselves qua homosexuals, not merely as apparently disinterested civil libertarians.

Along comes AIDS, School A continues, and even though it is well known that the virus can be communicated by infected needles, known also that heterosexuals can transmit the virus, still it is both a fact and the popular perception that AIDS is the special curse of the homosexual, transmitted through anal sex between males. And if you look hard, you will discern that little smirk on the face of the man oh-so-concerned about public health. He is looking for ways to safeguard the public, sure, but he is by no means reluctant, in the course of doing so, to sound an invidious tocsin whose clamor is a call to undo all the understanding so painfully cultivated over a generation by those who have fought for the privacy of their bedroom. What School B is really complaining about is the extension of civil rights to homosexuals.

School A will not say all that in words quite so jut-jawed, but it plainly feels that no laws or regulations should be passed that have the effect of identifying the AIDS carrier. It isn't, School A concedes, as if AIDS were transmitted via public drinking fountains. But any attempt to segregate the AIDS carrier is primarily an act of moral ostracism.

School B does in fact tend to disapprove forcefully of homosexuality, but tends to approach the problem of AIDS empirically. It argues that acquired immune deficiency syndrome is potentially the most serious epidemic to have shown its face in this century. Summarizing currently accepted statistics, the Economist recently raised the possibility "that the AIDS virus will have killed more than 250,000 Americans in eight years' time." Moreover, if the epidemic extended to that point, it would burst through existing boundaries. There would then be "no guarantee that the disease will remain largely confined to groups at special risk, such as homosexuals, hemophiliacs and people who inject drugs intravenously. If AIDS were to spread through the general population, it would become a catastrophe." Accordingly, School B says, we face a utilitarian imperative, and this requires absolutely nothing less than the identification of the million-odd people who, the doctors estimate, are carriers. How? Well, the military has taken the first concrete step. Two million soldiers will be given the blood test, and those who have AIDS will be discreetly discharged. Discreetly, you say!

Hold on. I'm coming to that. You have the military making the first massive move designed to identify AIDS sufferers—and, bear in mind, an AIDS carrier today is an AIDS carrier on the day of his death, which day, depending on the viral strain, will be two years from now or when he is threescore and 10. The next logical step would be to require of anyone who seeks a marriage license that he present himself not only with a Wassermann test but also an AIDS test.

But if he has AIDS, should he then be free to marry?

Only after the intended spouse is advised that her intended husband has AIDS, and agrees to sterilization. We know already of children born with the disease, transmitted by the mother, who contracted it from the father.

What then would School B suggest for those who are not in the military and who do not set out to get a marriage license? Universal testing?

Yes, in stages. But in rapid stages. The next logical enforcer is the insurance company. Blue Cross, for instance, can reasonably require of those who wish to join it a physical examination that requires tests. Almost every American, making his way from infancy to maturity, needs to pass by one or another institutional turnstile. Here the lady will spring out, her right hand on a needle, her left on a computer, to capture a blood specimen.

Is it then proposed by School B that AIDS carriers should be publicly identified as such?

The evidence is not completely in as to the communicability of the disease. But while much has been said that is reassuring, the moment has not yet come when men and women of science are unanimously agreed that AIDS cannot be casually communicated. Let us be patient on that score, pending any tilt in the evidence: If the news is progressively reassuring, public identification would not be necessary. If it turns in the other direction and AIDS develops among, say, children who have merely roughhoused with other children who suffer from AIDS, then more drastic segregation measures would be called for.

But if the time has not come, and may never come, for public identification, what then of private identification?

Everyone detected with AIDS should be tatooed in the upper forearm, to protect common-needle users, and on the buttocks, to prevent the victimization of other homosexuals.

You have got to be kidding! That's exactly what we suspected all along! You are calling for the return of the Scarlet Letter, but only for homosexuals!

Answer: The Scarlet Letter was designed to stimulate public obloquy. The AIDS tattoo is designed for private protection. And the whole point of this is that we are not talking about a kidding matter. Our society is generally threatened, and in order to fight AIDS, we need the civil equivalent of universal military training.

William F. Buckley Jr., editor of the National Review, is author, most recently, of "Right Reason." His syndicated column appears locally in The New York Daily News.

* * *

March 8, 1987

VERMONT PRISONS GIVE IMMATES CONDOMS ON REQUEST

By The Associated Press

MONTPELIER, Vt., March 6—Vermont prison officials say inmates can now get condoms on request to prevent the spread of AIDS and other sexually transmitted diseases in homosexual encounters.

The 660 prisoners housed in six regional jails can receive condoms through prison infirmaries, Corrections Commissioner Joseph Patrissi said.

He said the new directive should not be interpreted as a policy condoning homosexual behavior inside the prison system. Mr. Patrissi said the department would continue to enforce a long-standing prohibition against homosexual contact in the jails, which he said "does exist but isn't very prevalent."

Mr. Patrissi said the decision to dispense condoms stemmed from a recognition that steps can be taken to reduce the transmission of AIDS, the fatal disorder that is spread through intimate sexual contact.

"We have a responsibility here to make sure this thing doesn't get spread to the general population," he said. "I'm sure as heck not going to stand in the way if it's the best medical practice even though it may not be the best corrections practice."

Eleven AIDS cases have been reported in Vermont, but none has occurred in Vermont jails.

Mr. Patrissi said he was unaware of any state that had adopted a similar policy.

The issue arose last month at the Northwest State Correctional Facility in St. Albans after one inmate was treated for syphilis, Mr. Patrissi said. The superintendent there, Richard C. Turner, said he decided to make condoms available to inmates who, after meeting with the facility's medical staff, indicatedthey engaged in homosexual activity and had no intention of stopping.

* * *

June 30, 1987

U.S. RULES OUT GIVING CONDOMS TO PRISONERS AS AIDS CURB

By The Associated Press

WASHINGTON, June 29—The Reagan Administration has ruled out providing condoms to Federal prison inmates to curb the spread of AIDS and may consider separate prisons for victims of the disease, according to a key official.

The official, Robert Brutsche, an Assistant Surgeon General who heads the new AIDS testing program for Federal prisoners, said last week that there was strong sentiment in the Administration against distributing condoms in Federal prisons.

Mr. Brutsche, who also serves as medical director of the Federal Bureau of Prisons, said that, since homosexual sex is against prison regulations, it would be inconsistent for the authorities to pass out condoms.

There has been talk within the Administration of having separate prisons for inmates testing positive for the acquired immune deficiency syndrome virus. But segregation would create staffing difficulties, and it would force prison officials to group "all different classes of prisoners together with only one thing in common, AIDS," Mr. Brutsche said. Mr. Brutsche was interviewed as the Government began receiving figures from the program, begun June 15, of conducting AIDS tests on incoming and departing prisoners at the 47 Federal prisons. Initial conclusions will be made after Aug. 13.

At that time, the Administration may discontinue testing new prisoners and keep only that part of the program involving inmates about to be discharged, Mr. Brutsche said. The Administration plans to continue tests every six months on all new inmates not found this summer to be carrying the AIDS virus.

Mr. Brutsche said sex in Federal prisons is "not that prevalent."

But Urvashi Vaid, an attorney and AIDS consultant for the American Civil Liberties Union's National Prison Project, said the Government might not be realistic. Ms. Vaid said the prison environment is often devoid of good information about AIDS.

New Federal prison inmates are briefed on AIDS. Since 1981, 297 Federal inmates have been found infected with the virus, according to a prisons bureau spokeswoman, Maryellen Thoms.

* * *

November 29, 1989

'DAY WITHOUT ART' TO MOURN LOSSES FROM AIDS

By ANDREW L. YARROW

Nearly 600 arts institutions throughout the United States plan to observe "A Day Without Art" on Friday to draw attention to the effects of AIDS on the arts community.

Museums, galleries and other arts organizations plan to darken their galleries, temporarily remove or cover artworks, hold memorial services, or sponsor performances, lectures and exhibitions about AIDS. Some galleries plan to close. "It's a national day of mourning and action," said Thomas W. Sokolowski, a member of Visual AIDS, a group of arts professionals that organized the day's activities. "Some events are more activist while others are more elegiac." The day is intended to honor artists and others in the arts community who have died of AIDS, increase awareness of the epidemic's toll and call for greater support for AIDS services and research, he added.

"A Day Without Art," which will coincide with the World Health Organization's second "AIDS Awareness Day," will be marked by dozens of large museums like the Metropolitan Museum of Art, the Brooklyn Museum and the Museum of Modern Art in New York, the J. Paul Getty Museum in Malibu, Calif., the Dallas Museum of Art, the Museum of Fine Arts in Boston and the Walker Art Center in Minneapolis, as well as scores of university and private galleries, theaters and alternative performance spaces.

A Metaphor for Losses

"We want to use the prestige and credibility of cultural institutions to dramatically call attention to how widespread and serious the problem is," said Philip Yenawine, an organizer of the observance and the director of education at the Museum of Modern Art. "But 'A Day Without Art' is a misnomer in some ways. The name was chosen because we hoped there would be a moratorium, in which museums and galleries would close. But it's also an apt metaphor for the losses the art world has suffered and the specter of more losses to come."

In New York, where about 150 institutions will participate, the Metropolitan Museum will take down Picasso's portrait of Gertrude Stein for five days, and a placard will say it has been removed "to symbolize the losses the art community is currently experiencing because of AIDS."

Posters spelling "AIDS"—based on Robert Indiana's Pop Art "Love" paintings—will be installed in 3,000 New York subway cars throughout December by the Public Art Fund, a nonprofit group dedicated to presenting art in public spaces. The image, created by a Toronto artists' collective called General Idea, consists of the word AIDS in red letters on a green-and-blue field. "We're backing this because AIDS affects all neighborhoods, and the subway system communicates that connectedness," said James Clark, the fund's managing director.

Four Days of Events

Tomorrow night, a program called "A Jewish Perspective on AIDS" at the Jewish Museum will include speakers, music, performances and prayers, while a memorial service with three musical groups will be held at the Museum of Modern Art. Performances and videos about AIDS geared to children will be presented all weekend at the Brooklyn Children's Museum, and film or video programs on AIDS will be shown on Friday at the Brooklyn Museum, the Lehman College Art Gallery, the Bronx Museum and the Dia Art Foundation.

Other observances in New York include displays of parts of the Names Project Quilt, each panel of which memorializes someone who has died of AIDS, at the Cooper-Hewitt Museum, the American Craft Museum, the Museum of American Folk Art and the New York Historical Society; a reading by gay black men at the Studio Museum in Harlem, and an exhibition of AIDS-related work owned by Chase Manhattan Bank at the bank's downtown headquarters. Creative Time, a nonprofit arts group, is coordinating a census of artists who have died of AIDS. Galleries that plan to close include Leo Castelli, Mary Boone, Robert Miller, Artists Space and the Alternative Museum.

Theaters Join In

Some theater directors will also participate. Shows will be interrupted at the Theater for the New City, and La Mama will be dark. "In a lot of ways we have been closed, because 52 artists who've worked at La Mama have died of AIDS," Wickham Boyle, the company's executive director, said.

Symbolic actions are planned at museums from New England to California. Empty chairs representing Boston artists affected by AIDS will be displayed in the courtyard of the Fogg Art Museum at Harvard University; a coffin will be placed in the center of the gallery at the University of Florida at Gainesville, and at the Dallas Museum of Art, temporary black walls with panels of names of artists who have died of AIDS will block the entrance and a digital counter enumerating the worldwide AIDS death toll will be installed. In Madison, Wis., the Madison Art Center will lead a candle-lit vigil at the state Capitol, and works of art owned by the University of Wisconsin will be draped with black fabric. The Louisiana State Museum will place mourning wreaths on the historic houses it administers in the New Orleans area.

In Southern California, the Getty Museum will dim the lights in its photography galleries to honor the photography collector Sam Wagstaff, who died of AIDS in 1987, and both the Los Angeles County Museum of Art and the Museum of Contemporary Art will waive their admission fees, suggesting that money be donated to the AIDS Project Los Angeles. Panels from the Names Project Quilt will be displayed in many museums throughout the country, and posters about the day's observance will be put up on city streets in Philadelphia, Chicago, Houston, Los Angeles, San Francisco, Seattle and elsewhere.

How It Started

The idea for the observance came up a year and a half ago when about a dozen New York arts professionals met to establish what Mr. Sokolowski described as "an information-gathering service on AIDS-related programs at arts institutions."

"This spring, we started floating the idea of a day without art," he said, "but many museum people said it would be too hard to get this past boards of trustees. Others called it a negative action. So rather than closing doors, we decided to try to do something palpable and positive to focus attention on how we look at AIDS through the medium of art. We also decided to leave it open for each institution to do what they wanted."

Raising money and lobbying are not official parts of "A Day Without Art," but many institutions will have fund-raising events for AIDS-related causes, and Mr. Sokolowski encouraged people attending the events to "write a check to an AIDS organization and letters to politicians."

About 10 artists and arts professionals plan to meet on Friday with John E. Frohnmayer, the chairman of the National Endowment for the Arts, said Cee Brown, the director of Creative Time and a member of Visual AIDS. "We want to discuss how the arts community and the endowment can seriously increase AIDS awareness and education and jointly combat homophobia."

*   *   *

November 18, 1991

RELUCTANTLY, BLACK CHURCHES CONFRONT AIDS

By E. R. SHIPP with MIREYA NAVARRO

From the pulpit of the Memorial Baptist Church in Harlem, to a chorus of nods and cries of "Yes, yes" from the congregation below, the Rev. Dr. Preston R. Washington Sr. was preaching his gospel of necessity.

"When will we cry out for our young people?" he asked. "When will we cry out about the indiscriminate violence? When will we cry out for those silently walking around with the HIV virus?"

After the service, a 66-year-old woman who has been going to Memorial for 35 years explained why she had come to believe that it was her church's duty to speak up about AIDS.

'Our Duty to Help'

"I feel God made us all and He loves all of us, no matter your sexual preference or whatever," she said, then added, "It's our duty to help the fallen, and these are the fallen, aren't they?"

Painfully, haltingly, bucking a powerful mix of religious scruple, prudery and racial pride, black churches and mosques across the nation are beginning to turn their influence to the fight against AIDS. Forced to confront the overwhelming reality of the epidemic today—that AIDS is, in fact,their disease, that blacks, along with Hispanic people, account for an alarming proportion of the new cases being diagnosed—a cadre of black clergymen and women are speaking out in sermons, starting counseling and support groups, even sponsoring housing for homeless people with AIDS.

They are still the exceptions; often Baptist, mostly prominent, well-educated and relatively liberal. On the whole, these bedrock institutions of the black community—churches that have provided the leaders and the legions for the civil-rights movement, championed education and cared for the poor, mosques that have transformed hustlers and convicts into disciplined and productive people—are still wrestling uneasily with the deadly epidemic. Unlike other crises, AIDS is challenging their traditionally conservative theology, sending preachers and imams back to their holy books for guidance through a thicket of questions about sexuality, sin and the proper religious response.

"The majority of the churches are still not addressing AIDS; that's the bottom line," said Pernessa C. Seele, an administrator at Harlem Hospital and founder of the Harlem Week of Prayer for the Healing of AIDS, an annual mix of worship and workshops that is gradually gaining support among the Christian and Muslim clergy. "They're not talking about it, and they're not doing anything about it. The resistance is still there."

But like the woman at Memorial Baptist, ambivalence and all, more members of the clergy are realizing that they must do something. The signs of uneasy change, of how far black churches have come and how far they still have to go, are all around.

Last month, the third annual Harlem Week of Prayer drew support from 200 churches, mosques and synagogues, double the number last year. One pastor attending for the first time was the Rev. Gary Rhett Jr. of the Evangelistic Temple Church of God in Washington Heights. He is still not ready to preach about AIDS from the pulpit, he says, but he has sent for literature and is planning workshops.

'So Far Back'

"The time was now for me to get involved," he said. "Sometimes we're so far back that we forget to get involved with the now."

Involvement has not been easy, says the Rev. Dr. Calvin O. Butts 3d of Abyssinian Baptist Church in Harlem, who said that only three years ago, "I was talking about how immoral behavior caused the spread of AIDS."

After realizing that some people acquire AIDS through blood transfusions or sex with spouses, he began to emphasize compassion rather than condemnation. Recently, Dr. Butts did an about-face and said he would not oppose distributing clean needles to drug addicts in an effort to stem the disease. During the Harlem Week of Prayer, he stunned several hundred people when, during a sermon at St. James Presbyterian Church, he advised sexually active gay men to be monogamous and everyone engaged in sex to use condoms.

"That was absolutely revolutionary," said the Rev. Patricia A. Reeberg, executive director of the New York City Council of Churches. "I sat there and kept saying, 'He said that. He actually said that.'"

The Background: Prudish Reluctance To Face the Crisis

Until a couple of years ago, hardly anyone seemed interested in saying much of anything about an epidemic with potentially devastating consequences for blacks. Sometimes this reticence came from the clergy, sometimes from the congregations. But either way, it was largely because of the issue of sexual activity, which, along with intravenous drug use, is the primary means for the transmission of AIDS.

For though they have often led the way in matters of race, traditionally black Christian denominations have tended to be far more prudish than their white counterparts. As a largely self-taught clergy ministers to congregations who, like them, are often lacking in education, the fundamentalists' literal reading of the Bible, with its dim view of sex, has generally reigned. At the same time, some religious leaders have pulled their punches in preaching about sexual morality, afraid of offending their members. Promiscuity has been condemned in a general way but winked at because of a shortage of men in their communities.

But the resistance was far more complex. The Rev. Canon Frederick B. Williams, rector of the Church of the Intercession, an Episcopal parish in upper Manhattan, remembers the time in 1985 when he invited 50 religious leaders to a conference on AIDS and only 15 came.

"It was at a time when nobody wanted to talk about AIDS," Canon Williams said. "People didn't want to be identified with the crisis. It was seen as a gay disease or as God's retribution for bad behavior on the part of drug abusers. And it was seen primarily as a white problem, a white gay men's problem."

In churches and mosques, women pushing for AIDS education programs were rebuffed. Some blacks thought AIDS was the result of a conspiracy to kill blacks. Some even suspected that blacks were being blamed, since researchers and the press were saying that the AIDS virus had originated in Africa and the Federal Government had singled out Haitians as a "high-risk group."

Silence Prevailed

The silence prevailed even as the deaths began mounting, beginning with some of the more prominent members of the Christian congregations: church singers and musicians whose homosexuality was known but whose lives outside the church had never been discussed.

"In the beginning it was kind of a hands-off, let's-make-believe-it-doesn't-exist kind of thing," said the Rev. Carl E. Flemister, director of American Baptist Churches of Metropolitan New York. "Then we heard the condemnation, the divine retribution charges."

Sallie M. Perryman, who works for the New York State AIDS Institute as a liaison to the religious community, remembers that during her husband's two-year bout with AIDS, nothing was said in her church. At his funeral in 1986, she overheard one usher saying to another, "Did you know he had AIDS?"

"And I walked past them and they just shut up," Mrs. Perryman said. That, she added, was the extent of discussion about AIDS in that church.

But in the last couple of years, the clergy has been slowly waking from its passivity, as the epidemic unleashes its full force on blacks, extending its reach to women and children as well as young men, to heterosexuals as well as gay people. Blacks comprise nearly a third of the 36,000 AIDS cases reported in New York. And 46 percent of all AIDS cases among black women in the city have been reported in the last 18 months. Indeed, new cases among black and Hispanic New Yorkers are more than double those among whites.

Until recently, imams generally said that Muslims who follow the laws of God, avoiding all intoxicants and all sex outside of marriage, do not have to be concerned about AIDS. But death began to change that.

"When I began to bury Muslims who were dying of pneumocystis pneumonia, that brought it home," said Imam Ali Rashed of Masjid Malcolm Shabazz, referring to an opportunistic disease that kills many AIDS patients. "All the other imams, the thousands of them across this country, had to begin to deal with that reality."

That reality is expected to grow grimmer within the mosques, as AIDS strikes some of the men and women who have been the very targets of Muslim proselytizing: those on whom the rest of society had given up, people who abused drugs, peddled their sex in the streets or served time in prison, where homosexual relations are common.

In mosques and in churches, in short, a growing number of religious people are beginning to view AIDS in the context of the black clergy's activist tradition, as less a moral problem than a medical one with civil-rights implications.

"The more I think about it, the more I realize that anything we can do in a state of emergency, we've got to do it," said Dr. Washington of Memorial Baptist. "I'd rather save the life and then try to save the soul. You can't save the soul if the life is not here."

The Response: A Mission To Educate

"How much can we do?" Imam Ali Rashed asked. "This is the thing that concerns me greatly. After I send you some flowers and talk to you and help build your spirits up, now how do we deal with the problem other than that?"

That is a question that many are asking.

Some churches are supporting day-care centers for children and adults with AIDS. Many churches support Hale House, which provides shelter for infants born with AIDS or drug addictions, and the Upper Room AIDS Ministry, which serves homeless people with AIDS. Three groups—Harlem Churches for Community Improvement, Southeast Queens Clergy for Community Empowerment and the Association of Brooklyn Clergy for Community Development—are planning 60 units of housing for people with AIDS. St. Mary's Episcopal Church is now building a 40-bed hospice for homeless people with AIDS. Muslims are setting up counseling centers like the Islamic Wellness Institute in Brooklyn.

Beyond providing services, though, churches and mosques are most influential as educators. What they should tell their followers is a matter of division and debate.

The more conservative have continued to preach that AIDS is what Bishop Joseph S. Alston of the Faithful Workers Christ of God Church calls "the plague upon the land because of disobedience." They preach that homosexuality is "an abomination" and that all sex outside of marriage is forbidden. They insist that gay people be cured of their "disease" through repentance.

Moderates like Dr. Butts and Dr. Washington have begun to take a more pragmatic approach: disapproving of drug abuse, homosexuality and all sex outside of marriage, but acknowledging that these "sins" will not go away.

AIDS specialists like Debra Fraser-Howze, executive director of the Black Leadership Commission on AIDS, are hoping that influential ministers like Dr. Butts will help persuade others. The commission plans to broadcast a series of public service announcements containing excerpts from sermons on AIDS by five clergymen, including Dr. Butts and Imam Rashed.

Conservatives Are Repelled

But conservative preachers and Muslim imams are repelled by the pragmatic approach, which Imam Abdur-Rashid said certain high-profile ministers had adopted to be politically correct and avoid offending anyone.

Elder Charles E. Wright, assistant pastor of Greater Refuge Temple, said his church would not compromise. "We don't condone premarital sex so we don't teach the use of condoms to young people," he said. "As old-fashioned as it is, abstinence is still the surest way to prevent transmission."

Conservatives are particularly disturbed by the message that Magic Johnson, the basketball star, has been sending since announcing that he has the AIDS virus: safe sex. It is a message aimed especially at sexually active young people.

"Safe sex is wrong," said Imam Latif Khalid Abdul-Malik, who leads a mosque in East Orange, N.J., and is co-host of a weekly radio program heard throughout the metropolitan area. "Moral sex is right. You have to say this to the young women. You have to say this to the young men."

The slumbering giant that the black religious world represents has begun to stir, wrestling with issues that go beyond the immediacy of the AIDS epidemic and that have profound implications for the future of these institutions. But in spite of the awareness campaigns and the new sensitivity, the stigma of AIDS often mandates secrecy, even within the sheltering arms of the church or mosque.

Ms. Reeberg, who is assistant pastor at St. Paul Baptist Church, recently spoke with a middle-aged woman who has been a lifelong churchgoer and who now has AIDS.

"She can't tell anybody," Ms. Reeberg said. "She will tell them she has cancer, but she will not tell them she has AIDS. She's afraid of their response. She's afraid of what they'll think."

During a weekend of AIDS programs at St. Paul last month, a service of remembrance was held. At the end of the worship service, Ms. Reeberg rose to give the benediction. But as she stood, rather than offering the final prayer, she asked everyone to name the loved ones they had lost to AIDS. She began with names of her friends.

"At first it was total silence," she said. "Then finally folks started saying the names. It was just so powerful, and for 90 percent of them it was a total relief because they had not been able to say it before and they had all this anger. It was giving them permission to say: 'My friend died of AIDS. My relative died of AIDS.' It was breaking the silence."

* * *

June 26, 1998

EXCERPTS FROM SUPREME COURT OPINION ON H.I.V. INFECTION AS A DISABILITY

By The New York Times

WASHINGTON, June 25—Following are excerpts from today's Supreme Court ruling that people infected with H.I.V., the virus that causes AIDS, are protected from discrimination under the Americans With Disabilities Act even if they suffer no symptoms of AIDS. The opinion, Randon Bragdon v. Sidney Abbott, was written by Justice Anthony M. Kennedy and joined by Justices John Paul Stevens, David H. Souter, Ruth Bader Ginsburg and Stephen G. Breyer. A dissenting opinion was written by Chief Justice William H. Rehnquist and joined by Justices Antonin Scalia, Clarence Thomas, and Sandra Day O'Connor.

From the Decision by Justice Kennedy

Respondent Sidney Abbott has been infected with H.I.V. since 1986. When the incidents we recite occurred, her infection had not manifested its most serious symptoms. On Sept. 16, 1994, she went to the office of petitioner Randon Bragdon in Bangor, Me., for a dental appointment. She disclosed her H.I.V. infection on the patient registration form.

Petitioner completed a dental examination, discovered a cavity, and informed respondent of his policy against filling cavities of H.I.V.-infected patients. He offered to perform the work at a hospital with no added fee for his services, though respondent would be responsible for the cost of using the hospital's facilities. Respondent declined. Respondent sued petitioner alleging discrimination on the basis of her disability. . . .

We first review the ruling that respondent's H.I.V. infection constituted a disability under the A.D.A. The statute defines disability as:

"(A) a physical or mental impairment that substantially limits one or more of the major life activities of such individual;

"(B) a record of such an impairment; or

"(C) being regarded as having such impairment."

We hold respondent's H.I.V. infection was a disability under subsection (A) of the definitional section of the statute. In light of this conclusion, we need not consider the applicability of subsections (B) or (C).

Our consideration of subsection (A) of the definition proceeds in three steps. First, we consider whether respondent's H.I.V. infection was a physical impairment. Second, we identify the life activity upon which respondent relies (reproduction and child bearing) and determine whether it constitutes a major life activity under the A.D.A. Third, tying the two statutory phrases together, we ask whether the impairment substantially limited the major life activity. In construing the statute, we are informed by interpretations of parallel definitions in previous statutes and the views of various administrative agencies which have faced this interpretive question.

The A.D.A.'s definition of disability is drawn almost verbatim from the definition of "handicapped individual" included in the Rehabilitation Act of 1973, and the definition of "handicap" contained in the Fair Housing Amendments Act of 1988. Congress's repetition of a well-established term carries the implication that Congress intended the term to be construed in accordance with pre-existing regulatory interpretations. In this case, Congress did more than suggest this construction; it adopted a specific statutory provision in the A.D.A. directing as follows:

"Except as otherwise provided in this chapter, nothing in this chapter shall be construed to apply a lesser standard than the standards applied under title V of the Rehabilitation Act of 1973 or the regulations issued by Federal agencies pursuant to such title."

The directive requires us to construe the A.D.A. to grant at least as much protection as provided by the regulations implementing the Rehabilitation Act.

The first step in the inquiry under subsection (A) requires us to determine whether respondent's condition constituted a physical impairment. The Department of Health, Education and Welfare (H.E.W.) issued the first regulations interpreting the Rehabilitation Act in 1977. The regulations are of particular significance because, at the time, H.E.W. was the agency responsible for coordinating the implementation and enforcement of 504. The H.E.W. regulations, which appear without change in the current regulations issued by the Department of Health and Human Services, define "physical or mental impairment" to mean:

"(A) any physiological disorder or condition, cosmetic disfigurement, or anatomical loss affecting one or more of the following body systems: neurological; musculoskeletal; special sense organs; respiratory, including speech organs; cardiovascular; reproductive, digestive, genito-urinary; hemic and lymphatic; skin; and endocrine; or

"(B) any mental or psychological disorder, such as mental retardation, organic brain syndrome, emotional or mental illness, and specific learning disabilities."

In issuing these regulations, H.E.W. decided against including a list of disorders constituting physical or mental impairments, out of concern that any specific enumeration might not be comprehensive. The commentary accompanying the regulations, however, contains a representative list of disorders and conditions constituting physical impairments, including "such diseases and conditions as orthopedic, visual, speech, and hearing impairments, cerebral palsy, epilepsy, muscular dystrophy, multiple sclerosis, cancer, heart disease, diabetes, mental retardation, emotional illness, and drug addiction and alcoholism." . . .

H.I.V. infection is not included in the list of specific disorders constituting physical impairments, in part because H.I.V. was not identified as the cause of AIDS until 1983. . . .

In light of the immediacy with which the virus begins to damage the infected person's white blood cells and the severity of the disease, we hold it is an impairment from the moment of infection. As noted earlier, infection with H.I.V. causes immediate abnormalities in a person's blood, and the infected person's white cell count continues to drop throughout the course of the disease, even when the attack is concentrated in the lymph nodes. In light of these facts, H.I.V. infection must be regarded as a physiological disorder with a constant and detrimental effect on the infected person's hemic and lymphatic systems from the moment of infection. H.I.V. infection satisfies the statutory and regulatory definition of a physical impairment during every stage of the disease.

The statute is not operative, and the definition not satisfied, unless the impairment affects a major life activity. Respondent's claim throughout this case has been that the H.I.V. infection placed a substantial limitation on her ability to reproduce and to bear children. Given the pervasive, and invariably fatal, course of the disease, its effect on major life activities of many sorts might have been relevant to our inquiry. Respondent and a number of amici make arguments about H.I.V.'s profound impact on almost every phase of the infected person's life. In light of these submissions, it may seem legalistic to circumscribe our discussion to the activity of reproduction. We have little doubt that had different parties brought the suit they would have maintained that an H.I.V. infection imposes substantial limitations on other major life activities.

From the outset, however, the case has been treated as one in which reproduction was the major life activity limited by the impairment. It is our practice to decide cases on the grounds raised and considered in the Court of Appeals and included in the question on which we granted certiorari. We ask, then, whether reproduction is a major life activity.

We have little difficulty concluding that it is. . . .

Conception and childbirth are not impossible for an H.I.V. victim but, without doubt, are dangerous to the public health. This meets the definition of a substantial limitation. The decision to reproduce carries economic and legal consequences as well. There are added costs for antiretroviral therapy, supplemental insurance, and long-term health care for the child who must be examined and, tragic to think, treated for the infection. The laws of some states, moreover, forbid persons infected with H.I.V. from having sex with others, regardless of consent. . . .

In the end, the disability definition does not turn on personal choice. When significant limitations result from the impairment, the definition is met even if the difficulties are not insurmountable. For the statistical and other reasons we have cited, of course, the limitations on reproduction may be insurmountable here. Testimony from the respondent that her H.I.V. infection controlled her decision not to have a child is unchallenged. . . . Respondent's H.I.V. infection is a physical impairment which substantially limits a major life activity, as the A.D.A. defines it. In view of our holding, we need not address the second question presented, i.e., whether H.I.V. infection is a per se disability under the A.D.A. . . .

One comprehensive and significant administrative precedent is a 1988 opinion issued by the Office of Legal Counsel of the Department of Justice (O.L.C.) concluding that the Rehabilitation Act "protects symptomatic and asymptomatic H.I.V.-infected individuals against discrimination in any covered program." . . . O.L.C. determined further that asymptomatic H.I.V. imposed a substantial limit on the major life activity of reproduction. The opinion said:

"Based on the medical knowledge available to us, we believe that it is reasonable to conclude that the life activity of procreation is substantially limited for an asymptomatic H.I.V.-infected individual. In light of the significant risk that the AIDS virus may be transmitted to a baby during pregnancy, H.I.V.-infected individuals cannot, whether they are male or female, engage in the act of procreation with the normal expectation of bringing forth a healthy child." . . .

We conclude the proper course is to give the Court of Appeals the opportunity to determine whether our analysis of some of the studies cited by the parties would change its conclusion that petitioner presented neither objective evidence nor a triable issue of fact on the question of risk. In remanding the case, we do not foreclose the possibility that the Court of Appeals may reach the same conclusion it did earlier. A remand will permit a full exploration of the issue through the adversary process.

The determination of the Court of Appeals that respondent's H.I.V. infection was a disability under the A.D.A. is affirmed. The judgment is vacated, and the case is remanded for further proceedings consistent with this opinion.

From the Dissent by Chief Justice Rehnquist

The A.D.A.'s definition of a "disability" requires that the major life activity at issue be one "of such individual." The Court truncates the question, perhaps because there is not a shred of record evidence indicating that, prior to becoming infected with H.I.V., respondent's major life activities included reproduction (assuming for the moment that reproduction is a major life activity at all). At most, the record indicates that after learning of her H.I.V. status, respondent, whatever her previous inclination, conclusively decided that she would not have children. There is absolutely no evidence that, absent the H.I.V., respondent would have had or was even considering having children. Indeed, when asked during her deposition whether her H.I.V. infection had in any way impaired her ability to carry out any of her life functions, respondent answered "No." It is further telling that in the course of her entire brief to this Court, respondent studiously avoids asserting even once that reproduction is a major life activity to her. To the contrary, she argues that the "major life activity" inquiry should not turn on a particularized assessment of the circumstances of this or any other case.

But even aside from the facts of this particular case, the Court is simply wrong in concluding as a general matter that reproduction is a "major life activity." Unfortunately, the A.D.A. does not define the phrase "major life activities." But the Act does incorporate by reference a list of such activities contained in regulations issued under the Rehabilitation Act. The Court correctly recognizes that this list of major life activities "is illustrative, not exhaustive," but then makes no attempt to demonstrate that reproduction is a major life activity in the same sense that "caring for one's self, performing manual tasks, walking, seeing, hearing, speaking, breathing, learning, and working" are.

Instead, the Court argues that reproduction is a "major" life activity in that it is "central to the life process itself." . . . In support of this reading, the Court focuses on the fact that "major" "indicates comparative importance," . . . ignoring the alternative definition of "major" as "greater in quantity, number, or extent." It is the latter definition that is most consistent with the A.D.A.'s illustrative list of major life activities.

No one can deny that reproductive decisions are important in a person's life. But so are decisions as to who to marry, where to live, and how to earn one's living. Fundamental importance of this sort is not the common thread linking the statute's listed activities. The common thread is rather that the activities are repetitively performed and essential in the day-to-day existence of a normally functioning individual. They are thus quite different from the series of activities leading to the birth of a child.

Both respondent and the United States as amicus curiae, argue that reproduction must be a major life activity because regulations issued under the A.D.A. define the term "physical impairment" to include physiological disorders affecting the reproductive system. If reproduction were not a major life activity, they argue, then it would have made little sense to include the reproductive disorders in the roster of physical impairments. This argument is simply wrong. There are numerous disorders of the reproductive system, such as dysmenorrhea and endometriosis, which are so painful that they limit a woman's ability to engage in major life activities such as walking and working. And, obviously, cancer of the various reproductive organs limits one's ability to engage in numerous activities other than reproduction.

But even if I were to assume that reproduction is a major life activity of respondent, I do not agree that an asymptomatic H.I.V. infection "substantially limits" that activity. The record before us leaves no doubt that those so infected are still entirely able to engage in sexual intercourse, give birth to a child if they become pregnant, and perform the manual tasks necessary to rear a child to maturity. While individuals infected with H.I.V. may choose not to engage in these activities, there is no support in language, logic, or our case law for the proposition that such voluntary choices constitute a "limit" on one's own life activities.

The Court responds that the A.D.A. "addresses substantial limitations on major life activities, not utter inabilities." I agree, but fail to see how this assists the Court's cause. Apart from being unable to demonstrate that she is utterly unable to engage in the various activities that comprise the reproductive process, respondent has not even explained how she is less able to engage in those activities.

Respondent contends that her ability to reproduce is limited because "the fatal nature of H.I.V. infection means that a parent is unlikely to live long enough to raise and nurture the child to adulthood." But the A.D.A.'s definition of a disability is met only if the alleged impairment substantially "limits" (present tense) a major life activity. Asymptomatic H.I.V. does not presently limit respondent's ability to perform any of the tasks necessary to bear or raise a child. Respondent's argument, taken to its logical extreme, would render every individual with a genetic marker for some debilitating disease "disabled" here and now because of some possible future effects.

In my view, therefore, respondent has failed to demonstrate that any of her major life activities were substantially limited by her H.I.V. infection.

* * *

January 3, 2000

CLINTON OPPOSES COURT APPEAL OF H.I.V. RULING

By LINDA GREENHOUSE

WASHINGTON, Jan. 2—The Clinton administration has urged the Supreme Court not to hear an appeal in a discrimination case brought on behalf of hundreds of H.I.V.-positive prisoners in the Alabama prison system, where all inmates with the virus that causes AIDS are barred from educational and recreational programs and even from religious services where they might mix with the general prison population.

If the court takes the administration's advice, it will leave intact a sweeping ruling that bars these inmates from more than 70 programs available to other prisoners, including work-release programs that can shorten their incarceration.

The justices will decide this month whether to hear the appeal in the closely watched, nearly 15-year-old case, which presents the question of how to assess whether a disability is a "significant risk" to others that cannot be eliminated by the "reasonable accommodation" ordinarily required under federal laws that prohibit discrimination on the basis of disability.

A federal appeals court ruled last year that the categorical exclusion of the H.I.V.-infected inmates from prison programs did not violate the Rehabilitation Act of 1973, given the fatal nature of AIDS and the prospect that prisoners could transmit the virus to one another.

The administration told the court that, although the appeals court might have ruled too broadly, its approach was generally correct and its decision should not be reviewed.

The United States Court of Appeals for the 11th Circuit, in its 8-to-3 ruling last April, said, "When the adverse event is the contraction of a fatal disease, the risk of transmission can be significant even if the probability of transmission is low," adding, "death itself makes the risk significant."

The Americans with Disabilities Act of 1990, enacted after the Alabama lawsuit was filed, incorporated the same "significant risk" defense against a discrimination charge.

A coalition made up of public health organizations and AIDS specialists is supporting the appeal by the Alabama prisoners, arguing that the circuit court relied on "subjective fear and stigma" rather than the objective, scientific risk assessment that the Supreme Court insisted on in a 1998 ruling that was its first look at AIDS in the context of federal disability law.

In that case, a suit by an H.I.V.-positive woman against a dentist who refused to treat her in his office, the court said the assessment of "significant risk" should be made in light of the views of public health authorities, based on "objective, scientific information."

The brief for the coalition, filed by the Lambda Legal Defense and Education Fund, a gay advocacy group in New York, said the appeals courts had ignored the 1998 ruling by relying on a theoretical risk of transmission without regard to the particular circumstances. That approach, the brief said, "threatens to justify virtually any discrimination against persons with H.I.V. in employment, health care, education, and every other aspect of community life."

Alabama, Mississippi and South Carolina automatically segregate H.I.V.-positive inmates. The federal prison system, like those of most states, evaluates inmates individually and decides, on the basis of their history and psychological profile, whether to exclude them from particular activities.

The administration filed its brief in response to a request from the court for the federal government's views. The appeals court's ruling "may well be overbroad," Seth P. Waxman, the solicitor general, told the justices, adding that "the court should have carefully examined the circumstances and effect" of participation of inmates in the programs.

The brief said such an examination might have shown that there was no danger in permitting H.I.V.-positive inmates to participate in such activities as religious services, data processing classes, and testing for high school equivalency diplomas. Nonetheless, the brief said, there was no need for the court to take the case because the appeals court's opinion, even if questionable in the particulars, was generally correct in deferring to Alabama prison officials the assessment of the risk presented by "the violence that is an inescapable part of prison life."

The solicitor general said the case presented the question of "whether behavior that is concededly high-risk is likely to occur if H.I.V.-positive and non-H.I.V.-positive prisoners are integrated in a number of prison programs." The brief continued: "The answer to that question turns not on medical judgments about the risk inherent in certain behaviors, but on prison management judgments about the ability of prison authorities to control prisoners in various settings and programs."

In defending its policy, Alabama points to a much lower rate of H.I.V. transmission in its prison population than in states that do not segregate infected inmates. The state told the court that over eight years, out of 30,000 inmates who did not have H.I.V. when they entered prison, only two became infected while in prison.

Their decision on whether to take this case may depend on whether the justices see implications beyond the prison context and on the extent of their concern about whether their ruling in the 1998 dental patient case, Bragdon v. Abbott, had provided sufficient guidance to the lower courts.

The current case is called Davis v. Hopper, No. 98-9663. For many years, it was known as the Onishea case, but the lead plaintiff in the class-action lawsuit, Lydia Onishea, is no longer in custody, and another inmate, Arion Davis, was substituted.

The inmates, represented by the National Prison Project of the American Civil Liberties Union, have argued that deci-

sions about exclusion or inclusion should be based on individualized assessments of the inmate and the program.

* * *

G.M.H.C. and Act Up

December 5, 1983

FOR VICTIMS OF AIDS, SUPPORT IN A LONELY SIEGE

By MAUREEN DOWD

Cold in a warm hospital room, Stephen Lamb pulled his yellow blanket tighter around his emaciated body.

"My friends have abandoned me," Mr. Lamb said, his voice a tired whisper. "They're afraid of AIDS. But instead of just saying that, they would promise and promise to come and see me and then not show up. That really hurt."

Fighting a triple assault of cryptococcal meningitis, tuberculosis of the bone marrow and an intestinal infection, Mr. Lamb withered from 180 pounds to under 100. One of his few visitors at the New York University Medical Center was William Carroll, a man he barely knew.

Mr. Carroll is a volunteer with the Gay Men's Health Crisis, a nonprofit New York group that is currently helping 250 people with AIDS, acquired immune deficiency syndrome.

The story of the organization reflects the dramatic changes that have recast life in the city's homosexual community in the two years since AIDS emerged as a mysterious and frightening national epidemic. Fighting a siege of death and prejudice, the community that was once characterized by a carefree and free-wheeling spirit has evolved into a more mature and politically savvy population.

Mr. Carroll, who works in a law library, joined the Gay Men's Health Crisis after seeing its newspaper advertisement soliciting "buddies" for debilitated AIDS victims.

"I felt compassion for these guys' loneliness and despair," he said. "I heard that they had been neglected by their family and friends, even other gays, and that they had been treated badly by some hospital personnel."

He overrode the objections of his own friends and family, who worried that he might be exposing himself to the disease, which sabotages the body's immune system.

"I deeply identified with these men," he said. "I wanted to offer the support I hope that I would get if I were to come down with it. There is a sense of taking care of one's own."

He was assigned to Mr. Lamb in early September. The two men were both 40 years old, and shared a love of literature.

While Mr. Lamb was still in his East Side apartment, Mr. Carroll shopped for his groceries and ran other errands. Two months ago, Mr. Lamb entered the hospital, so weak that the smallest movement required intense effort.

Mr. Carroll continued to visit three times a week. He cut his charge's food, fixed him snacks of corn flakes and sherbet, and read him poetry by John Keats and Andrew Marvell. Mostly, though, he listened as Mr. Lamb reminisced about his job as a travel consultant and his personal life. "Stephen regarded his previous life in the fast lane as sort of a waste," Mr. Carroll said.

One recent night, as rain pelted the windows of his hospital room, Mr. Lamb talked about how much having a "buddy" had meant. "It's been tremendous," he said, reaching out a skeletal hand to clasp one of Mr. Carroll's. "Bill and I have grown to like each other. I just needed some companionship."

Four days later, on Nov. 14, Mr. Lamb died, one of 514 AIDS fatalities in the city since the epidemic began. "I tried not to become emotionally involved," said Mr. Carroll, shaken after hearing the news. "But you necessarily become involved with something like this."

Different Life Style, Different Expectations

Housed in a ramshackle Chelsea brownstone, the Gay Men's Health Crisis is a clutter of people, desks, file cabinets, ringing telephones and an always-busy computer.

The group was started two years ago by six men who had lost friends to the disease and who were worried about the lack of services for AIDS victims. It has become a sophisticated social-service organization with growing political power, 12 paid staff members, an 8-member board of directors, 500 male and female volunteers, and a 1984 budget of $900,000.

"AIDS pointed up the inequitable status of gays," said Rodger McFarlane, the group's 28-year-old director. "We were forced to take care of ourselves because we learned that if you have certain diseases, certain life styles, you can't expect the same services as other parts of society."

Members of the organization represent a broad spectrum, from judges and bankers and playwrights to students and carpenters and bartenders. Most have never been active in volunteer work before. They are drawn by a matter of life and death.

"It's ugly work," Mr. McFarlane said. "When persons with AIDS come to us, their lives are shattered and their heads are twisted. They've just been given the devastating news that they have a disease that's probably fatal with a stigma the size of Manhattan attached to it."

"They've usually been fired from their jobs and kicked out of their apartments," he added. "Often, their lovers have abandoned them. They feel like lepers. They don't know the ropes through the traditional social-service agencies and they're much too sick to pursue that route anyway. They're just a mess."

"We're there primarily to hand-hold and troubleshoot," Mr. McFarlane said, "and help these people get some control over their lives."

According to the latest statistics released by the Centers for Disease Control in Atlanta, the AIDS crisis continues at a steady rate. Nationwide, about eight people a day are diagnosed as having AIDS. A total of 2,803 cases have been reported, and of those, 1,146, or 41 percent, have died. The death rate is close to 100 percent for those who have the disease two years or more.

Of the sufferers, 71.5 percent are homosexual or bisexual; 17.3 percent use drugs intravenously; 4.6 percent are Haitians; sixth-tenths of 1 percent are hemophiliacs, and 6 percent appear to fit into none of these high-risk categories. Most victims are men.

New York City has been hardest hit, with 1,261 cases, 38 percent of the country's total. Of those, 41 percent have died.

Although there are no census or other official accounts, conservative estimates based on the work of Alfred C. Kinsey put New York's homosexual population at 350,000. City officials say they believe the number is much higher, and homosexual leaders put the figure between 1 million and 1.5 million.

A Crushing Caseload

Dr. Rand Stoneburner, an epidemiologist with the city's AIDS program, said that, although the rate of increase has slowed somewhat since last year, the number of AIDS cases rose 48 percent in the first six months of 1983 compared with the same time period last year.

At the Gay Men's Health Crisis, the caseload has spiraled at a crushing pace. There are ordinarily about 50 new cases every month. But in the last two weeks alone there have been 45 new admissions.

The organization helps all AIDS patients. Thirty-five percent of its caseload is made up of people who take drugs intravenously, most of them heterosexual, and three are Haitian. Out of a total of 420 patients the group has helped, 63 have died.

The organization runs 20 therapy groups for AIDS patients and their partners and families. To try to correct misconceptions about the disease and about homosexuals, the group sends experts to speak to hospital employees, church groups and schools.

While some homosexual activists have criticized the organization's tactic of focusing all homosexual issues around AIDS, the group has become an effective lobby for winning financing. With benefits and parties in homosexual bars, the Gay Men's Health Crisis has raised more than $600,000 in contributions.

It has also received a $200,000 grant from New York State and $24,500 from the city, and the Board of Estimate recently approved a $1.2 million contract with the American Red Cross to recruit and train home attendants for about 200 AIDS victims. Thanks in part to Health Crisis lobbying, Federal funds for AIDS research have jumped from $22 million to $40 million.

'City Has Done Little'

But officials of the group have been strongly critical of what they consider inadequate support from Mayor Koch and the city. "Considering the fact that G.M.H.C. has given $16 million worth of volunteer services this year," Mr. McFarlane said, "the city has done very little."

The speed with which the group has grown is reflected in its offices at 318 West 22d Street, between Eighth and Ninth Avenues.

One day not long ago, a man walked in, identified himself as a psychic from Madrid and announced he had learned the cure for AIDS in a dream: shrimp and bananas. "Everybody's got an idea," Mr. McFarlane said. "Everything from zither playing to Kundalini yoga to Jesuit priests."

In a ground-floor office, Barry Davidson was manning the 24-hour hot line, which receives about 1,200 calls a week. "The lesions are the size of a dime, raised or flat, red or purple," he explained to a woman who had called the number, 807-6655. "They will show up on different parts of the body and spread. There will be noticeable loss of weight in a short time and a hacking cough."

Fear of Contagion

Another caller wanted to know about contagion. "It's not spread by casual contact," Mr. Davidson said. "You can't get it by walking down the street or being in the same room or touching someone who has it. It seems that there has to be intimate contact with bodily fluids or shared needles."

In an upstairs office, Chuck Jones, an intake officer, pored over paper work. On a bulletin board next to him was a cartoon of a middle-aged woman airing her views on AIDS: "Good Christian people have nothing to fear as long as we stay a million miles away from the slimy creatures who may have it."

"A lot of people feel that gays have gotten what they deserve," said Mr. Jones, who is 28. "There's a lot of hostility."

Mr. Jones assesses the needs of new cases to see what sort of services he can offer—money to help pay the rent; a buddy to shop for food; a counselor to help them fill out forms to get welfare, Medicaid or Social Security disability funds; a lawyer to help them make a will, transfer an insurance policy to a lover or fight an eviction notice.

"My gut turns over when I talk to somebody on the phone and they die before I can even send a counselor over there," Mr. Jones said. "One week I had three people die within 10 days. I was just sitting in the chair kind of vibrating. I used to cry. Now there are no more tears."

Doing Errands While Preparing for Worst

The buddies and crisis counselors, most of them young professionals, are, as one put it, the "Mother Theresas of the organization." When they sign on, they are told not to expect a Junior League sort of volunteerism.

"It's a heavy trip to stand there and watch a 30-year-old person waste away over a period of a few months," Mr. McFarlane said. "I've seen some of these guys age 10 years, all of their illusions about good intentions destroyed."

The volunteers do whatever is necessary, from taking orange juice in the morning to serving as intermediaries with the city's social-service agencies. They clean apartments, do laundry, make dinner, pick up prescriptions, mail rent checks, walk dogs, take their patients to doctor's appointments and simply keep them company.

"You come to a total stranger and suddenly announce, 'I'm yours,'" said David Richardson, a magazine news editor. "My client watches Spanish TV. I don't speak Spanish, but if he wants to watch Spanish TV, that's what we do."

Victims Ask, 'Why Me?'

Sometimes, there are suicides. Always, the work is emotionally exhausting. "Your client may be hostile," said Joanne Tamm, 33, a psychiatric nurse at Cabrini Hospital who works for the group in her spare time. "They want to know, 'Why me?' If someone says thank you, you're lucky. And, after all your work, they may die."

Miss Tamm is one of the 50 or so volunteers who are heterosexual. "I'm not gay but I have good friends who are gay men," she said. "These people are sick and dying. You have to be concerned."

The volunteers have a litany of horror stories about the treatment of AIDS sufferers. They tell of government clerks who neglect AIDS cases because they are afraid to be in the same room to fill out forms. They tell of nurses and orderlies in hospitals who are so loath to enter the rooms of AIDS patients that they let the food trays pile up outside the door, leave trash baskets overflowing, or neglect patients lying in their own urine or excrement.

Diego Lopez, 35, a soft-spoken admissions counselor at Hunter College who trains Gay Men's Health Crisis volunteers, recalled that he went to visit a dying patient in the hospital and discovered him with blood seeping from his nose and mouth. He quickly found a doctor and asked her to look at the patient.

Feelings of Vulnerability

"She gave me the gauze and told me to clean it up," Mr. Lopez said. "I was shocked but I did it. Afterward, I looked at my hands and there was blood all over them. I realized I had to start being more careful. But when you see a person dying, you don't think about finding some gloves to wear."

Like other volunteers, Mr. Lopez said he signed on because he knew people who had died and because the work helps him cope with his own feelings of vulnerability.

"I'm a gay man and, all around me, gay men are dying," he said. "I never expected to be dealing with questions of mortality with my people my own age and younger. I was a marine in Vietnam and I dealt with fear. But then we were fighting a known enemy. With AIDS, it's so out of control. Just by the nature of my sexuality I'm at risk."

Volunteers said it is especially difficult because their patients are specters of their own worst fears. "It's strange to think that at any minute we could become one of them," Mr. Richardson said. "There's a creeping feeling of fatality.

There's something out there. I may get it or I may not. Every morning when I shave I check to see if my lymph nodes are swollen."

"You eat, drink, sleep and breathe AIDS," he continued. "Once in a while I go to the opera or the movies just so that I don't think about it for a couple of hours."

'No Success Stories'

Allan Kendric, 46, a landscape architect from Queens, used to worry that he had little to say to his patient, a 30-year-old horticulturist from Brooklyn. "My life is so full," Mr. Kendric said. "His whole experience is sitting in his bed in his lonely hospital room."

On one recent visit, as the two sat silently, the young man asked Mr. Kendric softly: "Can you hold me for a minute? Nobody ever holds me anymore."

"That just made me cry," Mr. Kendric recalled, his voice breaking. "This person has the same needs you and I do. It was so pathetic."

On Nov. 10, the young man died.

"There are no success stories," said Mitchell Cutler, 32, a dealer in rare books who runs the buddy program. "Sometimes I think if I hear about one more sick person I'll go crazy."

A New Maturity Among Homosexuals

Paved with AIDS fatalities, the fast lane became unfashionable for a time. There was a trend toward conservatism in the city's once-libertarian homosexual community.

But with the crisis going into its third year and no cure in sight, homosexual leaders have detected a backlash of apathy. "The numbers of people going to gay bars and baths is increasing again and that's depressing," Mr. Lopez said. "Those guys are insane. How many more people will get sick before there are not enough of us to help them? How many more will have to die before they stop functioning with their libido and start functioning with their intellect?"

Mr. Lopez and many others, however, have remained conservative and have developed more serious relationships.

"I'm not as active anymore out of a sense of self-preservation," Mr. Richardson said. "But it took AIDS to make some of us realize, the health issue apart, that that life style was pretty empty anyway."

Professionals Drawn Out

Kenny Weinberg, a 33-year-old sportswear merchandiser, agreed. "Gay men in New York have realized there's more than superficial sex, Bloomingdale's and upward mobility."

Homosexual leaders talked of another positive result of the crisis. They said it has drawn many young professionals out of the closet. One such case is Dr. Ken Wein, 34, a psychologist who works as the clinical director of the Gay Men's Health Crisis.

"I wouldn't have put myself on the line before," Dr. Wein said. "AIDS finally strenghtened my will to confront my boss, who was biased against gays, and quit a job at a hospital where I worked. You get enraged at the feeling that the world thinks you're disposable because you're gay."

On the whole, homosexual leaders agreed, the community has developed a new maturity in coping with the AIDS crisis. "We're more responsible," said Larry Kramer, a writer and one of the organization's founders. "Everyone realizes now that homosexuality is defined by more than what you do sexually. Being gay is a cultural tradition, a heritage to be proud of."

A Litany of Death

On a sunny afternoon not long ago, Mr. Kramer sat in his spacious Fifth Avenue apartment in Greenwich Village. The apartment was decorated with pictures of the actress Glenda Jackson in "Women in Love," a film Mr. Kramer produced and wrote.

From his bookcase, he pulled a small green notebook in which he has logged 37 names of friends who have died. "I heard about Vinny on Saturday," he said. "Ron is a black actor I know. Paul, a pianist. Gayle went to Yale with me. Ron Doud, the designer of Studio 54. Mark, I was involved with a long time ago. Peter, an architect."

Mr. Kramer stopped his litany, his hands clenched tightly around the notebook.

"Can't something be done?" he asked. "The rest of the city, my straight friends, go on with life as usual and I'm in the middle of an epidemic."

"We're dying," he said. "Why is this happening? Is it because we loved each other too much or not enough? I just don't know."

* * *

December 27, 1983

SEEKING RESEARCH FUND FOR AIDS

By DAVID SHRIBMAN

WASHINGTON, Dec. 26—Hospital wards and laboratories are not the only places where the battle is being waged against acquired immune deficiency syndrome, or AIDS.

In the past several months, as increasing numbers of victims have been diagnosed, the battle has increasingly been fought in the offices, committee rooms and legislative chambers of the United States Capitol. The goal there: research money.

The causes of and a cure for the disease, which has taken 1,225 lives since it appeared in 1979, have proved elusive, and representatives of homosexuals, who account for three-quarters of the victims, have hired a professional lobbyist to push for increased Federal research money. They say the $48 million in Federal financing currently devoted to the epidemic is far too little and that what financing there is has been spread among so many programs that its impact is minimal.

Because of the special social circumstances surrounding the epidemic, the lobbying effort has required a special approach.

Confrontation Avoided

"When you lobby for civil rights, the tactic often is confrontational and you put someone on the defensive," said Gerald R. Connor, the lobbyist who was hired to guide the push for funds. "That tactic doesn't work in this case. Here you want to develop as many friends as you can. You want people to help you or, at least, to apologize quietly on the phone when they can't help you."

Mr. Connor, a health official in the Carter Administration who has also lobbied for such organizations as the American Public Health Association, has developed a strategy for the AIDS fight that emphasizes the public health aspect of the disease rather than the fact that the rate of AIDS among homosexuals is higher than among other segments of the population.

"We cast it as a public health issue to give it the broadest appeal," he said. "I'm not running away from the fact that this is a gay issue. It would be silly to suggest otherwise. But I have to make the connections to the rest of the health lobby in town."

Other population groups with high rates of incidence of AIDS are abusers of intravenous drugs, Haitians who have entered the United States and hemophiliacs, according to the Centers for Disease Control. But the main effort for Federal funds to fight AIDS is being pushed by homosexual groups.

'Didn't Want To Be Political'

"We felt that we couldn't leave any stone unturned," Larry Kramer, a co-founder of Gay Men's Health Crisis in New York, said in explaining why a lobbyist was hired. "We had little or no experience in anything political. We didn't want to be political."

The Health Crisis organization, which is assisting some of the 2,952 people across the country who have been diagnosed as having AIDS, pooled its resources along with four dozen other groups to hire Mr. Connor. He, in turn, has searched the small print of committee reports and spent hours visiting the cubicles where little-known Congressional staff aides help make appropriations decisions involving millions of dollars.

A main problem, he says, is that so relatively little Federal money has been devoted to AIDS thus far that hardly anyone notices. "It is not something that staff people are accustomed to paying attention to," he added. "Typically in Washington you wonder about billions. We're talking about millions. The appropriations process ordinarily doesn't have room or time to focus on things that small. They don't get into that level of detail."

With the AIDS epidemic now going into its sixth year, homosexual groups are also considering broadening their efforts to provide not only more medical research but also small Federal grants to community groups that are assisting victims of the disease. "We're talking about large numbers of people dying, and research isn't going to save them," Mr. Connor said. "There has to be help for people now."

* * *

September 22, 1985

HOMOSEXUALS STEPPING UP AIDS EDUCATION

By JANE GROSS

A young man circled a table in the East Village one recent afternoon, approaching and then retreating from the stacks of AIDS literature offered by the Gays Men's Health Crisis.

"If you're sexually active, you're at risk!" shouted Anne Milano, an educator for the group, who delivered her message from beside a sign with the current AIDS statistics: 13,332 diagnosed cases since 1981 and 6,481 deaths, about 40 percent of them in New York City.

The young man shook off a proferred brochure, "Healthy Sex Is Great Sex," and instead pushed a crumpled dollar bill into a fishbowl that would hold $156 by dusk. "It's bad for my soul to hear about it," he whispered, head bowed, then bicycled away.

Some continue to resist the message at a time when the Gay Men's Health Crisis, the city's leading homosexual organization, is stepping up efforts to educate people about prevention of acquired immune deficiency syndrome, transmitted primarily through intimate sexual contact.

While the organization has been widely praised for its efforts in helping patients once they have AIDS, there is roiling debate among homosexuals, the group most at risk, about whether its directors, or other community leaders, have adequately addressed the issue of prevention and education.

These issues are complicated and emotionally charged for the homosexual community, which dates its "liberation" to a 1969 confrontation with the police at a Christopher Street bar called the Stonewall Inn. That police raid led to the formation of the Gay Liberation Front, a multi-issue New Left organization, and the Gay Activists Alliance, which—in the words of some of its members—"uncritically celebrated" sexual activity.

Both organizations are now defunct, but some in the homosexual community say they believe the political climate of that time fostered a tolerance for promiscuity that has exacerbated the AIDS crisis.

The contrast between homosexual behavior before and after the AIDS epidemic is demonstrated by a study just completed at Columbia University's School of Public Health.

So far, Dr. John L. Martin, who conducted the study, has interviewed 700 homosexuals and collated data from 100 of them. That small group, including monogamous men, averaged 64 different sexual partners a year outside the home before AIDS, compared with 18 now.

Before learning of the disease, 40 of these 100 men frequented bathhouses, with an average of 32 partners a year in such locations. In the last year 16 have visited the baths and averaged 7 partners.

"The movement of the 60's and the 70's legitimized promiscuity," said Larry Kramer, a founder of the Gay Men's Health Crisis and now one of its most abrasive critics. "To in

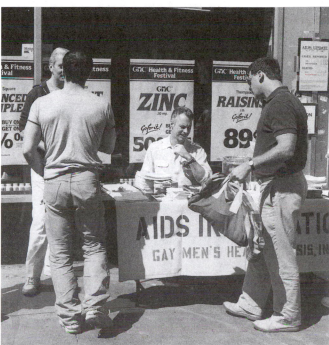

The New York Times / John Sotomayor

AIDS education: The Gay Men's Health Crisis information table outside a health food store on Sheridan Square.

any way criticize that as wrong was tantamount to heresy, and still is in certain quarters."

"Is compulsive sexuality freedom?" asked Jim Fouratt, one of the founders of the Gay Liberation Front. "I would argue it's not. All we got was a lot more alienated sexually, and a lot more disease.

"There were mistakes made and I'm not wed to the ideas I had 10 years ago," Mr. Fouratt said. "And the problem the gay AIDS leadership refused to confront until recently—the sex issue, the life-style issue—created a vacuum for the homophobic moralists."

Mr. Fouratt goes one step further, arguing that some of his fellow homosexuals profited from the fast-lane life style as owners of sex-related businesses. "The basic motivation was not freedom but profit," Mr. Fouratt said.

Efforts to Educate

It was in this context that the Gay Men's Health Crisis responded to the AIDS crisis, incorporating in 1982 as an advocacy and social-service organization that has devoted itself to the counseling and care of patients. Its earliest educational efforts were its hot line and its lectures to community groups and health-care professionals.

The group recently began sending counselors into five of the city's bathhouses, distributing so-called safe-sex literature in homosexual bars and participating in research that involves a weekend of counseling late next month for 800 sexually compulsive men.

"Had education commenced earlier, how many lives would have been saved?" asked Mr. Kramer, the author of "The Normal Heart," a play about AIDS currently at the

Public Theater. "How sad, feeble and useless those little tables are! Everything, everything, is too little, too late. By our silence we have helped murder each other."

"I don't think there's any need for us to feel defensive," said Richard Dunne, the executive director of the Gay Men's Health Crisis. "We haven't done as well as we'd like, but we haven't had the luxury of focusing on gay and bisexual men. We've had to educate health-care professionals and the general public because no one else was doing it, and we needed to get across that this wasn't merely a disease of a socially disapproved life style."

Decrease in Partners

Within the homosexual community, sexual behavior has changed radically since the start of the AIDS epidemic. The city's Health Department reports an 80 percent decline in venereal disease among homosexual men in the last two years, when sexually transmitted disease continued to increase among heterosexuals. And early results from the Columbia study show that homosexuals have dramatically reduced their number of partners and have limited certain sexual practices, particularly those involving the exchange of semen.

Dr. Martin's research, to be presented at a November convention of the American Public Health Association, indicates that sexual behavior has changed not because of education but because of contact with the sick and the dying.

"You're talking to a monk now and many of us who aren't celibate are almost celibate," said Mr. Kramer, who is no longer associated with the Gay Men's Health Crisis. "I don't think there's anybody who doesn't have a dead friend at this point—I have hundreds—so you'd have to be pretty dumb not to alter your life style."

"The two most troublesome issues in most people's lives are sex and death," said Dr. Michael Quadland, a psychiatrist specializing in sexual compulsion who is involved with the "800 Men" project. "That's very powerful and usually a deterrent to people at risk."

Ignorance About Spreading AIDS

Despite such radical changes, however, there remain people within the homosexual community who need educating. When the Gay Men's Health Crisis set up counseling tables three months ago in the bathhouses, a locus for promiscuity despite waning attendance, Jerry Johnson, the program's leader, found that half the people who approached him were ignorant about the spread of the disease.

Homosexual men who still frequent the city's 10 remaining bathhouses—before the AIDS crisis there were 15—report that AIDS patients in small numbers are among the patrons of the baths, conceivably infecting the unwary or uneducated. And on a recent afternoon at the Pleasure Chest on Seventh Avenue South, a store that sells sexual devices, the customers included a man covered with the purplish lesions associated with Kaposi's sarcoma, a cancer frequently affecting AIDS victims.

"There are people so angry they want to do to somebody what somebody did to them," said Mr. Fouratt, who argued that the handful of people knowingly spreading AIDS were doing it in dark, anonymous places like the baths during multiple sexual encounters in private cubicles.

"We've all heard those horror stories," said Mr. Johnson, "but that's not the rule because there's too much caring."

The position of Gay Men's Health Crisis on the bathhouses—that there is no need to close them because their clientele is so limited and more easily educated when centralized—seems unpopular within the homosexual community. "If you polled gay men today, 60 percent would be in favor of closing them," said one staff member at the center. "It was my feeling five years ago they should be closed, and it will remain my feeling when they have a one-tablet cure for AIDS."

Defending the Baths

"The building doesn't give you AIDS; people give you AIDS," said Barry Davidson, the center's director of community information, using the identical words as Marvin Bogner, a Health Department spokesman, to defend the continued existence of bathhouses.

"This way we've got them in a group, so we can reach them and educate them," said Victor Bender, a center volunteer, who said he stopped going to the baths when he contracted AIDS, for which there is no known cure. "It's better than having them spread all over doing it in the back of trucks."

According to Richard Berkowitz, who describes himself as a bathhouse regular, sexual habits have changed drastically in the baths in recent months. Until then, Mr. Berkowitz said, he was shunned for suggesting the use of a condom.

"Now there are condoms everywhere," said Mr. Berkowitz, who three years ago was diagnosed to have an immunological disorder but now has blood-test results within the normal range. "I have seen no unsafe sex in the last six months."

The opposition to the center's position on bathhouses has spawned several organizations, which many leaders within the homosexual community say are poorly organized, given to trading recriminative insults and inclined to defer to the Gay Men's Health Crisis and its considerable resources.

The center began on a shoestring, but now has an annual budget of $1 million, according to Mr. Dunne, its executive director—$500,000 from the state, $85,000 from the city and the rest from private donations.

Responsible Sex

There is a nine-month-old organization called the Coalition for Sexual Responsibilty, which has urged the owners of the baths to follow 13 guidelines, including distributing free condoms.

"No single bathhouse is in complete compliance, but there has been major improvement," said Michael Callen, a member of the coalition and an AIDS patient who is certain he contracted the disease in the baths.

There is also a newly formed group called the Committee for Stare Decisis, which advocates the system in place in San

Francisco. There, under court order, the baths operate with the doors removed from the cubicles and so-called lifeguards monitoring sexual practices.

According to Mathew Shebar, a lawyer formerly on the staff of the health-crisis center, the committee of lawyers would seek voluntary compliance from the owners and, if unsuccessful, would initiate a class-action lawsuit on behalf of the homosexual community. Like many homosexuals who oppose the bathhouses, Mr. Shebar prefers action by the community to Government intervention, which would raise civil-liberties questions especially troubling to those who believe their freedom was so hard won.

Trying to Dissuade Patrons

There are also what might be called guerrilla activities.

Mr. Fouratt, for one, said he has stood outside the baths with friends attempting to dissuade prospective patrons. He said he has also sprayed graffiti messages like "Sleeze Breeds Disease" on the walls of the Mine Shaft on Washington Street and other so-called backroom bars, which were decreasing in number and popularity, like the baths, but were nonetheless considered objectionable by many homosexuals.

Many of the center's detractors acknowledge that educational efforts, which require explicit discussion of sexual practices, may have been constrained by the need to win moral and financial support in all quarters of the homosexual community, and among heterosexuals.

"They've tended to be asexual," said Keith Lawrence, a member of the Coalition for Sexual Responsibility. "They're trying to deal with a disaster in a minority community, raise money from people who think we're freaks and sinners, and for their overall goals, they wanted to avoid controversy in certain areas."

No officials of the center would link their policy to a desire to win friends. But, many members said they had succeeded, in large part, because of their decorous approach. "We haven't gotten where we are by being arrogant, pushy or miserable," Mr. Davidson said.

There is also reluctance at the center to issue sexual recommendations, which are frequently updated, based on inconclusive scientific information. This sort of conservatism is applauded by Dr. Martin at Columbia.

"There's so much ambiguity that educational efforts should proceed cautiously," Dr. Martin said. "Once a policy statement is made and found to be wrong, it's hard to reinstate people's faith in the experts who made that policy."

Message Getting Across

Homosexuals seem to be getting the message, nonetheless, that certain sexual practices place them at risk. Dr. Martin's early data show a 50 percent reduction in anal intercourse and a similar reduction in oral sex, a 40 percent reduction in kissing and a 66 percent increase in the use of condoms, which was virtually unheard of several years ago and therefore is still rare.

"At one time the fast lane was the role model, and all that has changed," said Howard Welsh, the coordinator of the center's speakers bureau, who lectures to groups as varied as the Salvation Army residence on the Bowery, the Lenox Hill Neighborhood Association and the Gay Bankers Association.

"War stories—'What a weekend I had!'—you don't hear them anymore. The person who is wildly promiscuous, people tend to think he's crazy."

Mr. Welsh recently discussed the changes in the homosexual life style with a friend who is a friar.

"I said we were both active participants in a monastery," Mr. Welsh recalled. "He said, 'Yes, but mine is voluntary and yours is not.'"

* * *

January 3, 1986

LEGAL HELP TAILORED TO VICTIMS OF AIDS

By DAVID MARGOLICK

On one recent afternoon, 11 Manila file folders were lined up neatly on a glass table in Mark Senak's office at the Gay Men's Health Crisis. Each one had a man's name written on the outside. On the inside, each one contained a newly drafted will, drawn up for someone with AIDS.

For most people, writing a will is a rite of passage, an unpleasant but routine acknowledgment of mortality. But in Mr. Senak's office above the galleries, bistros and boutiques of a resurgent Chelsea, the ritual seems almost unreal.

This is so because virtually all of the 11 who entered his office this day, at roughly 20-minute intervals, were young men, most in their 30's. Most appeared healthy and, under the circumstances, reasonably calm. But if current medical wisdom holds true, all of them, along with the 700 other people whom Mr. Senak calls his clients, will be dead within two or three years.

'Gay Family Planning'

For homosexuals, particularly those with AIDS, or acquired immune deficiency syndrome, drafting a will can be of great importance. In New York as in most other states, the property of those who die without a will—or, in legal parlance, who are intestate—automatically goes to their closest blood relatives, the very people from whom many homosexuals have long been estranged.

Thus, only by drafting a will—what Mr. Senak calls "gay family planning"—can AIDS patients insure that their possessions end up with those they choose.

As a result, since the Gay Men's Health Crisis, at 254 West 18th Street, began its legal assistance program two years ago, it has drafted more than 1,000 wills, with 50 people coming in for one each month.

Fighting Discrimination

Though it constitutes fully 60 percent of the legal work at the office, drafting wills is by no means all that Mr. Senak, who directs the program, and his staff of 40 volunteer lawyers do.

Another large chunk of their energies is devoted to charges of discrimination: in housing, in medical and dental treatment, in insurance payments and in the workplace.

On one recent day, several calls came from people who had been refused treatment by dentists. One man said he was a heterosexual who had been turned away because he wore an earring; another, a homosexual, had a sore on his lip. One call was from a waiter with AIDS who had been dismissed from his job.

Many clients call when insurance companies refuse to pay benefits to them, arguing that the policyholder knew he had AIDS or a related condition when he took out his coverage.

Still other calls concern AIDS patients who return from hospitals and discover that they have been evicted for non-payment of rent. Mr. Senak or his assistant, John Mokricky, arrange emergency loans for some of them, and find new homes for others in apartments procured from sympathetic landlords and brokers.

In many instances, it takes merely one call—to the State Division of Human Rights, which enforces the law prohibiting discrimination against people with disabilities such as AIDS—for Mr. Senak to persuade landlords, employers and insurers to let up. He calls the technique "legal fist-shaking over the phone."

As the AIDS crisis spreads, however, the clientele at the clinic is diversifying and the cases are becoming more complex.

New Clients, New Issues

Increasingly, those who come to Mr. Senak's office are less often from Manhattan, less often men, and less often homosexual. Five years ago, for instance, 75 percent of those with AIDS in New York were homosexuals, according to the city's Department of Health; that number is now down to 58 percent. Most of the others are intravenous drug users or their sex partners.

This demographic switch has confronted the clinic with a whole new set of legal issues. Many mothers with AIDS, for instance, are now coming to Mr. Senak to arrange for the custody for their children after their deaths.

For Mr. Senak, a 30-year-old native of Granite City, Ill., the routine is worlds away from the Wall Street law office and Park Avenue real-estate investment concern where he once worked.

It is a task he undertook, he says, for many reasons. One of his favorite professors at Brooklyn Law School died of the disease. There was his desire to play a part in what he saw as one of the three major civil-liberties crises—along with the McCarthy era and the internment of Japanese-Americans during World War II—to confront the United States in this century.

It stemmed, too, from an effort on his part to curb whatever impulse he felt to run away from the calamity besetting his community—or, as one of his friends put it, "to manage the madness, not to be sucked into it."

"Whether you're straight or gay, you can poke your head in the sand or turn around and face the problem," he said. "And in turning around and facing AIDS, I've lost much of my fear of death and dying. To me, AIDS is no different from getting hit by a bus, or cancer. They're all threats to all of us. Right now, everyone has good reason to fear AIDS."

The Signing of the Will

Every Thursday is will day at the clinic, and those who came one recent afternoon represented a fair cross-section of Mr. Senak's clients. More than one did not keep the appointment—proving, Mr. Senak said, that for many people, drafting a will is easier than actually signing one.

Another client spoke of committing suicide, prompting Mr. Senak, who has grown used to such talk, to call the crisis hotline upstairs.

"I hate it when they do that," he said calmly.

Surprisingly, there is a matter-of-fact, almost good-natured quality to most of the signings. Mr. Senak jokes with each of his clients about the pro-forma questions which, as an attorney, he must ask them: "What is your name?" "What is this instrument before you?" "Have you read it?" "Do you understand it?" "Does it reflect your wishes?"

That completed, he poses another question: whether the "two handsome gentlemen" who have just entered the room, members of the clinic's staff, will suffice as witnesses.

He gently instructs each of those signing wills not to remove the staples from them, which could suggest tampering, or to put them in safe-deposit boxes, which are sealed at the time of death. And he explains the meaning of a "living will"—"It says, 'I don't want to be like Karen Ann Quinlan,'" he tells them.

"I now pronounce you testate," he declares as each proceeding ends. Then he shakes his client's hand. Then he prepares for his next case.

The legal clinic at the Gay Men's Health Crisis was begun by Steven Gittleson, who has since returned to private practice, and the Bar Association for Human Rights, an organization of homosexual lawyers. Many members of this bar group work part time at the clinic, sometimes without the knowledge of their principal employers.

Many of Mr. Senak's clients first heard of the service from social workers while receiving treatment.

"They came to see me in the hospital and they directed my every move for the next month or so," said one, a 39-year-old construction worker, after signing his will. "I wouldn't have known where to begin without these people."

"They made it so simple and easy," another client said. "It's something we all have to deal with, and it's better that we do it now when we're in a sound mind than when we're on our deathbeds."

Of course, not all will-signings are so serene. Two or three times a week Mr. Senak conducts them in hospitals, where he must sometimes don surgical garb—hat and mask and gloves—not to guard himself against AIDS, which apparently cannot be transmitted through casual contact, but to protect clients whose battered immunological systems can offer no protection of their own.

A year ago, for instance, it took six minutes for a patient at a Manhattan hospital simply to sign his name, which he did only after being awakened repeatedly during the procedure and Mr. Senak held the pen for him. Ten days later, the client was dead, his name appearing on a flier that circulates every week around the office. Staff members refer to it offhandedly as the "the R.I.P. sheet."

On other occasions, Mr. Senak finds himself face-to-face with clients afflicted with Kaposi's sarcoma, a condition often associated with AIDS that leaves the body covered with lesions. He recalled one such instance a few months ago in Manhattan.

"I reached out to shake his hand," Mr. Senak said. "He looked me in the eye just to see if I would flinch, and I looked back at him just as forthrightly to show him that I wouldn't."

Mr. Senak calls his current job "the most satisfying thing I've ever done in my life." He confesses, however, that it involves some things he knows he will never get used to, even though he must act as if he has.

"There are days when I come home and have a good cry, but I can't afford to lose any sleep over what I've seen," he said. "The work here is all-important to my clients, and if I agonize all night about it, I can't do any good for them the next day."

* * *

November 3, 1988

MAKING AMENDS

By WARREN LEARY and DAVID BINDER

When more than 1,200 AIDS victims and their backers staged a nine-hour protest at the Food and Drug Administration's headquarters in Rockville, Md., one day last month, hundreds of agency employees found themselves unable to get to their offices while others were in effect trapped in the building. All in all, the noisy though generally nonviolent demonstration, aimed at speeding F.D.A. approval of drugs to fight acquired immune deficiency syndrome, resulted in frayed nerves, snarled traffic and 176 arrests.

Now some of the protesters are making an effort to show the headquarters employees that the action was directed at the F.D.A. as an institution, not at them. New York members of ACT UP—for AIDS Coalition to Unleash Power—have obtained an F.D.A. telephone directory and mailed personal, "nonconfrontational" letters to 2,230 people listed as having offices in the building, including Commissioner Frank E. Young and his senior staff. Each of more than 200 ACT UP members who took part in the demonstration signed 10 copies of a letter entitled "Why I Demonstrated at the F.D.A." and added a personal salutation to the Government employees on his or her list.

"We wanted these people to understand," said Michael Miles, a spokesman for ACT UP, "that we are fighting for their lives as well as ours."

* * *

July 14, 1989

AIDS DRUG WILL BE OFFERED TO THOSE INELIGIBLE FOR TESTS

By GINA KOLATA

In an initiative intended to give AIDS patients speedier access to promising new medicines, an experimental drug will be made available to patients in September at the same time a clinical trial of its efficacy begins, the drug's manufacturer said today.

The drug, DDI, or dideoxyinosine, has slowed the progress of the AIDS virus in laboratory experiments. Researchers hope it will prove safer than AZT, or azidothymidine, the only drug now licensed for the treatment of AIDS infections.

The medicine is made by the Bristol-Myers Company, which is based in New York. The National Institutes of Health have been urging drug companies to make experimental AIDS drugs available to people who cannot or do not want to take them in clinical trials, and Bristol-Myers is the first to agree to do so.

American and Canadian advocates for people with AIDS have asked that DDI be made available to those who cannot take part in the clinical tests. Many AIDS patients cannot take part because their bodies cannot tolerate AZT, and participants in the tests will be randomly assigned to receive either DDI or AZT. Other patients may be disqualified for different reasons, like living too far from the medical centers conducting the study.

A Parallel Test Track

Dr. Anthony Fauci, director of the National Institute of Allergy and Infectious Diseases, recently proposed that such patients be allowed to receive drugs under study on what he called a parallel track, with their doctors, rather than researchers in a formal study, monitoring the effects and reporting them to the company. Dr. Fauci discussed the proposal with Bristol-Myers officials, who were also approached by Canadian physicians.

Bristol-Myers said today that the details of the parallel track had yet to be worked out. But it said any patient who did not meet the criteria for the clinical trials but for whom DDI was critical would receive the drug.

Larry Kramer, a founder of the advocacy group Act Up, the AIDS Coalition to Unleash Power, said the group was elated by the Bristol-Myers decision. He said Act Up had had daily phone conversations with the company about DDI.

* * *

December 11, 1989

111 HELD IN ST. PATRICK'S AIDS PROTEST

By JASON DEPARLE

While some 4,500 people demonstrated outside St. Patrick's Cathedral yesterday, several dozen disrupted the Mass at 10:15 A.M. to protest John Cardinal O'Connor's recent statements on abortion, homosexuality and AIDS.

Some of the protesters chained themselves to pews inside the cathedral, while others shouted or lay in aisles. "We will not be silent," a protester, Michael Petrelis, 30 years old, screamed before the police arrested him. "We will fight O'Connor's bigotry,"

The police said 111 people were arrested, including 43 inside the church. Many of the protesters were carried out on stretchers after refusing to stand up. Dozens of protesters blocked traffic on Fifth Avenue by lying in the street. One of them, Annie Hirsch, who said she was 12, leaned from a police bus and said, "I'm here to tell people that women aren't going to take it any more."

Cardinal O'Connor, who has frequently called homosexual acts a sin and has opposed the use of condoms, counseling abstinence instead, told the parishioners during the service, "Never respond to hatred." He led them in prayer that drowned out the protesters' cries and gave out a written homily in place of the regular sermon.

Cardinal Denies Insensitivity

He later said that he thought it was "kind of ironic that I'm accused of not doing enough." He said he had consistently advocated increased government spending on AIDS care and research. Cardinal O'Connor also said the archdiocese was devoting 10 to 12 percent of its health-care beds to people with AIDS, "and expanding."

The protest was co-sponsored by the AIDS Coalition to Unleash Power, or Act-Up. The Women's Health Action Mobilization, or Wham!, also joined the protest. A spokeswoman said the group is devoted to securing "reproductive freedom for all women."

By 9 A.M., about 400 police officers had lined Fifth Avenue between 48th and 51st Streets, where protesters and worshipers mixed with holiday tourists.

"O'Connor says get back, we say fight back," chanted lines of protesters marching behind police barricades on the sidewalk. "Condoms Not Prayer," read one protest sign. "Take One and Save Your Life," read another sign, with rows of condoms attached.

'Policies Are Killing People'

"The Church claims to be pro-life and their policies are killing people," said Brenda Howard, 42, a protester.

Some protesters said they had been raised in the Roman Catholic Church but could no longer support it. Among them was Arabella Ogilvie, 30, who said a Unitarian minister presided at her wedding in October. "I'm expressing spontaneous disgust," she said.

About 100 counter-demonstrators gathered to support the Cardinal and to protest what several said was an encroachment on religious freedom.

Mayor Edward I. Koch, who attended the Mass, criticized the demonstrators, saying "If you don't like the church, go out and find one you like—or start your own."

Other Protests Against Cardinal

The protest yesterday was not the first time the Cardinal had drawn the wrath of gay rights groups. In 1987 and 1988, a group of homosexual Roman Catholics, called Dignity, held regular protests at the Cathedral after Cardinal O'Connor ordered an end to a special Mass they had been celebrating at another Manhattan church.

Protesters said yesterday's action was prompted by what they said was Cardinal O'Connor's growing verbal assault on abortion and on the use of "safe sex" with condoms as a precaution against AIDS.

In October, the Cardinal expressed his admiration for Operation Rescue, an anti-abortion group that frequently blocks entrances to abortion clinics. In a speech at the Vatican in November, he restated his view that distributing condoms or clean needles was an inappropriate way to combat the spread of the AIDS virus. In a phrase frequently condemned by demonstrators yesterday, he said, "Good morality is good medicine."

The Cardinal has also denounced violence against homosexuals and against people with AIDS.

At least 20 of the people who protested outside the Cathedral marched downtown to the East Village, where they urged housing homeless people in 271 East 4th Street, an abandoned school building, the police said. Three demonstrators were arrested. An organization called the Revolution for the Homeless said at least a dozen homeless people had moved into the building. The police said last night that "two other squatters" were still inside the building but that officers had left the scene for the night.

* * *

December 12, 1989

CARDINAL SAYS HE WON'T YIELD TO PROTESTS

By TODD S. PURDUM

Responding to the arrests Sunday of more than 100 people protesting his statements on homosexuality, AIDS and abortion, John Cardinal O'Connor said yesterday that his approach could be changed only "over my dead body."

"I pray that this doesn't happen again," the Cardinal said of the demonstration at St. Patrick's Cathedral as he arrived for his annual Christmas luncheon party at the Waldorf-Astoria. "But if it happens again and again and again, the Mass will go on, or I will be dead."

"It would have to be over my dead body that the Mass will not go on, the word will not be preached orally or distributed in writing," he added. "And no demonstration is going to bring about a change in church teachings and it's certainly not going to bring about any kind of yielding on my part. I don't say that with any bravado; I'm your basic coward. But I'm the Archbishop of New York and I have to preach what the church teaches."

Jay Blotcher, a spokesman for the Aids Coalition to Unleash Power, or Act-Up, one of the protest's sponsors, said: "Unfortunately, the dead bodies that the Cardinal is stepping over are the bodies of the people with AIDS who have already passed away. And what he faces are more bodies of people who could potentially contract the disease because the church refuses to give them access to safe-sex edcuation."

'Our Tactics Are Numerous'

Mr. Blotcher said he could not say whether the group might continue such protests at the cathedral. "Our tactics are numerous, and they're very different in all cases," he said. "Negotiations are what we're looking for. If the Cardinal does not choose to change his stand on policies, that's fine, as long as he restricts his moralism to his own congregation and stops trying to foist it on the public at large."

Cardinal O'Connor has frequently called homosexual acts a sin and has opposed the use of condoms, counseling abstinence. He has also visited many AIDS patients and denounced violence against homosexuals.

Mayor Edward I. Koch, who joined the Cardinal at the party yesterday, called the protest an "excrescence." Demonstrators chained themselves to pews, shouted or lay in the aisles and one person threw a consecrated communion wafer to the floor.

'I Deplore It'

Mayor-elect David N. Dinkins, who also attended the lunch, said of the protest: "I think it was wrong. I deplore it." He added: "It's clearly improper behavior," and said "people who may be inclined to agree with the protesters in terms of philosophy, they tend to lose by the fashion in which they express themselves."

Cardinal O'Connor, asked if security at the cathedral would be changed, said: "Oh, I don't know, I leave that strictly to the commissioner of police and to the courts. If the courts give injunctions, I can't determine that."

The First Deputy Police Commissioner, Alice T. McGillion, said the department had no immediate plans to change its security detail.

At the Waldorf luncheon, the Cardinal praised the Mayor for showing support by coming to the Mass Sunday. "Mayor Koch knew where he should be and he was there, and I will die just everlastingly grateful," he said.

But the Cardinal also got in a good-humored dig at his friend and fellow author, saying, "God knows, he's disagreed with me many, many times."

At that, Mr. Koch interrupted to say, "Less and less."

That prompted the Cardinal to say, "The worst irony of all, and the worst thing that could happen to the church in New York is that he could become a Catholic." He said that people often noted that Mr. Koch is "Jewish, he's proud of it and he'd never be anything else, and I say, thank God."

* * *

December 12, 1989

THE STORMING OF ST. PAT'S

The demonstrators who stormed St. Patrick's Cathedral Sunday may have hoped to inspire sympathy for the problems of homosexuals in New York City and resistance to the Catholic Church's positions on abortion. They mostly brought discredit on themselves for demonstrating in a way that obstructs consideration of their arguments.

There is plenty of room for controversy over church positions on homosexuality, AIDS and abortion. No one can quarrel with a peaceful demonstration outside St. Patrick's, and John Cardinal O'Connor did not do so.

But some of the demonstrators turned honorable dissent into dishonorable disruption. They entered the cathedral and repeatedly interrupted the service. They lay down in the aisles, chained themselves to pews and sought to shout down Cardinal O'Connor as he said mass. One protester is reported to have disrupted even the administering of communion with an act of desecration that deeply offended worshipers.

New Yorkers generally expect protesters to respect the rights of others, even those with whom they disagree. To deny clergy and laity alike the peaceful practice of religion grossly violates a decent regard for the rights of others, let alone the law. Far from inspiring sympathy, such a violation mainly offers another reason to reject both the offensive protesters and their ideas.

Arguments over AIDS, homosexuality and abortion are not going to be advanced by hysterics, threats or the disruption of religious services. They might be advanced by serious argument that reflects conviction. The demonstrators who entered St. Patrick's Cathedral Sunday invite the public to think about a different kind of conviction.

* * *

December 26, 1989

PROTEST AT ST. PATRICK'S FOCUSED ON CARDINAL'S DANGEROUS ZEAL

To the Editor:

I'm writing in response to "The Storming of St. Pat's" (editorial, Dec. 12), about the Dec. 10 demonstration at St. Patrick's Cathedral by the AIDS Coalition to Unleash Power, or Act-Up, and the Women's Health Action Mobilization, or Wham!, to protest statements by John Cardinal O'Connor on abortion, homosexuality and acquired immune deficiency syndrome.

As a lifelong Roman Catholic, I agree with you in principle that disruption of a Mass is deplorable. However, as a gay person, I recognize that in desperate situations extreme measures may be necessary.

Cardinal O'Connor has at his disposal tremendous power to disseminate information via the diocesan network and the news media. He has done so very effectively and, until now, with little interference. He represents the most conservative element of the United States Catholic hierarchy and has not hesitated to promote his positions, which are often not universally supported by other bishops in this country. His statements condemning the use of condoms and distribution of "clean" needles to drug addicts to combat the spread of AIDS are examples of how the religious far right attempts in its zealousness to appropriate nonreligious issues. These are public health concerns that should be dealt with by the institutions that exist for that purpose. They are not the province of the church or of Cardinal O'Connor.

You say, "Far from inspiring sympathy, such a violation mainly offers another reason to reject both the offensive protesters and their ideas." You clearly do not understand the nature and importance of the issues involved. The protesters were not looking for sympathy or acceptance of their ideas. The demonstration was staged to focus attention on the actions of America's leading Catholic prelate, who has gone well beyond his religious province and is using his office and his access to the news media to promote positions that will cost lives.

MICHAEL R. VIOLANTI
New York, Dec. 12, 1989

* * *

May 22, 1990

82 HELD IN PROTEST ON PACE OF AIDS RESEARCH

By PHILIP J. HILTS
Special to The New York Times

BETHESDA, Md., May 21—More than 500 demonstrators gathered here today at the National Institutes of Health, accusing the agency of being too slow in finding and testing drugs to treat AIDS. Eighty-two of the protesters were arrested, mostly on trespassing charges. Almost all were fined $50 and released.

Twenty-one of the demonstrators briefly occupied the office of Dr. Daniel Hoth, director of the AIDS division at the National Institute of Allergies and Infectious Disease. All were arrested, fined and released without incident, the police said.

Amid brightly colored smoke bombs and costumes both grim and humorous, the demonstrators declared that officials of the institutes were among the chief enemies in the fight against AIDS. Most of the protesters were members of the AIDS Coalition to Unleash Power, or Act Up. Some carried signs reading "N.I.H.: Neglectful Institute of Death," and crowds standing outside the administration building chanted, 'N.I.H., you can't hide; we charge you with genocide.'

Mark Harrington, a leader of Act Up, said, "Publicly funded AIDS research has been murderously irrelevant to the lives of people with AIDS." He said that too few drugs were being tested and that it took too long to get drugs to those who were sick, even though a billion dollars had been spent in the effort.

Dr. Anthony Fauci, director of the National Institute of Allergies and Infectious Diseases, the leading AIDS research agency in the Government, spoke in his office as demonstrators shouted a block away. He said he knew the leaders of the protest well and was surprised to hear "irrational" language on the street from people he had worked with in meetings.

"From the time an organism has been identified as a cause of disease to the time we have an effective drug for it, this is by far the fastest ever," he said, referring to the drug AZT, which slows the progress of AIDS, although it is not a cure. "And this drug is the most effective against viruses we've had."

He said that numerous drugs had been identified as candidates to treat AIDS and its related infections, including AZT, DDI and DDC to attack the virus itself, several interferons and interleukin-2 to aid the body's response to infection. He also cited drugs that fight related infections, like Fluconazole, which combats cryptococcal meningitis.

The agency's AIDS Clinical Trial Group has also demonstrated that three drugs, once popular among AIDS patients taking unauthorized medications, were not effective in combating the virus. Those drugs are Ribavirin, dextran sulfate and AL721.

Act Up charged in a report handed out at the demonstration that few drugs had been tested to treat the infections related to AIDS, and that few of the clinical tests of drugs had been conducted in the poor, inner-city communities where the disease is spreading fastest.

Dr. Fauci said serious problems still had to be worked on, and he said the institutes were taking steps to increase the number of women and minorities in the drug trials. In addition, he said, the number of drugs being tested to fight AIDS-related infections would increase. He said in the next year 12 studies of those drugs were scheduled, as compared with only 5 studies on drugs that attack the virus itself, in a reversal of the previous priorities.

* * *

July 18, 1993

DIANA MCCAGUE; WITH ACT UP IN THE WAR AGAINST AIDS

By SI LIBERMAN

Diana McCague, a member of Act Up-New Jersey, was among five demonstrators arrested last month and charged with disrupting a State Assembly meeting by throwing packets of condoms at the legislators from the chamber balcony.

"More than six months had elapsed since the Governor's Advisory Council on AIDS submitted its recommendations, and Governor Florio and our legislators haven't done a thing," she said. "That's why we did what we did."

It was the second time in less than a year that Ms. McCague, 33, a Middlesex County restaurant worker, landed in police custody.

Last February, she and 10 others were arrested and charged with trespassing when they tried to block entry to a Hoffmann-La Roche plant in Nutley. That demonstration, also staged by Act Up, an AIDS protest group, was aimed at getting the pharmaceutical company to expedite work on an experimental AIDS virus inhibitor. Ms. McCague pleaded guilty and was fined $100.

In the Trenton case, a hearing on the charges is expected to be set in early September. Ms. McCague, released with the four others without bail, plans to plead not guilty and defend herself without a lawyer.

New Jerseyans can expect more demonstrations, Ms. McCague said. "And we'll be at the AIDS summit this month in New Brunswick."

The meeting will be on the Douglass campus of Rutgers University on July 28 and will bring together invited public officials, medical authorities and others involved in or concerned with the fight against AIDS. The session was scheduled by Gov. Jim Florio to discuss carrying out the recommendations of the Advisory Council on AIDS.

Among other things, the council recommends requiring H.I.V.-AIDS education in all schools, making condoms available to students at the ninth-grade level and above, initiating needle-exchange programs and making needles available without a prescription, making condoms available in state prisons and barring state-licensed long-term-care centers from denying access to H.I.V. patients.

As of March 31, the State Health Department had verified 15,974 cases of AIDS in New Jersey since 1981 and 10,400 AIDS-related deaths. The department estimates that 40,000 to 50,000 New Jerseyans now carry the AIDS virus. And the state has the largest proportion of AIDS cases among women and has 10 percent of the nation's cases among infants and children.

Ms. McCague's work with Act Up takes "anywhere from 5 to 30 hours a week," she said. "Lots of time is spent on the phone and driving to meetings."

Act Up is an acronmyn for the AIDS Coalition to Unleash Power. The national organization was founded in 1987.

Ms. McCague, who says she is bisexual, is a 1986 graduate of New York University who majored in history and sociology. Before she immersed herself a year ago in Act Up, she was a volunteer AIDS lecturer and helped staff an AIDS hot line for the Hyacinth Foundation, an AIDS awareness group in New Brunswick.

She was drawn to the cause after seeing a longtime friend suffer and die from the disease. "She was only 28 and got AIDS from needles," Ms. McCague said. "I knew three others who died of AIDS."

Q. What role did you play in the planning and execution of the condom tossing episode in Trenton?

A. I'm one of a handful of members who helped plan it over a period of eight to 10 weeks, volunteered to participate and got arrested. It was another member's idea to disrupt the Assembly.

Q. How were you treated by the arresting officers?

A. I was handcuffed by the state police. They were pretty rough dragging us out and took Polaroid pictures of us. I was bruised on the arm and fingers, and another demonstrator was also bruised.

Q. What impact have the demonstrations and arrests had on your life and job?

A. I've had to miss work, and I'm making less money. But my employer has been very supportive. There were some phone calls from people who read about the demonstration— some sympathetic who asked how they could help, and one caller threatened to kill me.

Of course, it interferes with my social life, but it certainly gives me something to talk about at parties. I may be a little crazy, but everything else I do takes second, third, fourth and fifth place.

Q. What's been your parents' reaction to your Act Up involvement and arrests?

A. I have two brothers who think what I'm doing is great. My mother is concerned but accepts it, and we've been very close. My father disowned me because of my political views even before I became an activist. He's very conservative.

Q. How would you define the mission of Act Up?

A. In New Jersey, it has less to do with treatment and cure than with prevention. A lot of our energy is spent on preventing AIDS and on people who should take responsibility— parents, educators, young people. During the past year, we've distributed condoms and literature to promote safer sex at 100 high schools in New Jersey.

Q. What's been the reaction of school officials and students to your condom offers?

A. It varies. We don't push them on the kids. They can take them or leave them. One angry principal tried to stop us. He called the police, but the officers did nothing, because no law was being violated. We distribute the condoms on public streets outside the high school. At another school, an official—I think she was a principal—came out, thanked us for waiting until school was over and not doing anything to disrupt classes, and then accepted a condom packet.

At Princeton, students, male and female, seemed thrilled, and many took advantage of our condom offers. At other schools, the reaction wasn't as enthusiastic. Maybe only 30 or so will accept.

Q. Do you also urge abstinence in your meetings with students?

A. No, I don't because I believe sex is as essential to life's fulfillment as any one of our senses—like seeing, feeling, smelling, tasting and hearing.

Q. Who are the officers of Act Up-New Jersey, how many members are there, and how are your activites financed?

A. We have no officers, spokespersons or dues. It's a very democratic organization. Everything is done by consensus and voluntary contributions. Right now, we have less that $1,000 in our bank account, not even enough to cover the fines we're facing.

Gay, heterosexual and bisexual members—most under 40—comprise Act Up's New Jersey membership. Each week a different member presides at our meeting. He or she is called a facilitator.

There are maybe 10 of us who attend most meetings and are very active. We have a mailing list of about 200 persons who have helped with contributions and other services.

Q. What progress in the war against AIDS, if any, can your organization take credit for?

A. I'm not sure, but pressure we applied may have contributed to the appointment of Dr. Bruce Siegel as New Jersey Health Commissioner in March. His views and support of recommendations of the Governor's Advisory Council on Aids parallel our views. And he appears tolerant of alternative behavior.

Q. How many New Jersey members of Act Up do you know who have tested H.I.V. positive or have the full-blown disease?

A. It's not my business to discuss that. I will only say that only one member that I know of has gone public with his AIDS.

Q. Have you been tested? If so, what's been the result?

A. Yes. I'm negative.

Q. If you were governor, what would you do to prevent the growing number of AIDS tragedies?

A. I would use my visibility to educate the public and to humanize the disease. I would strive to make condoms available to adolescents. I'd mandate it, in fact. I would decriminalize possession of a syringe and make clean syringes available.

I would revamp the system for prevention and treatment, and insist that the State Health Department offer anonymous testing to anyone at all its clinics. Now you have to ask to be tested anonymously, and most people don't know that.

Q. What future demonstrations or acts are you planning?

A. I'm not going to talk about that now except to say there will be more condom distributions, and we'll be running after the gubernatorial candidates. We'll be where they are, encouraging them to recognize the AIDS crisis and to really do something about it.

* * *

REEXAMINING A LIFESTYLE

June 16, 1983

HOMOSEXUALS CONFRONTING A TIME OF CHANGE

By MICHAEL NORMAN

In neighborhoods throughout the city and across a broad spectrum of New York life, the influence of homosexual men and women is being seen and felt more than ever before.

The yearly Gay Pride March, scheduled for June 26, is only one sign of the broadened awareness of homosexuality and the changes it has brought over the last decade and a half. The staffs of major political figures include representatives to the homosexual community. Homosexual churches and neighborhood groups have attracted hundreds of members. And this month a successful Broadway play about a drag queen's search for the meaning of family life won two Tony awards.

Still, there are quarters in which homosexuals encounter hostility, and many men and women continue to lead what they describe as double lives, "gay" at home and "straight" on the job. But shifts in public attitudes have prompted others to live openly.

In the last few months, however, the city's homosexual world has been shaken by the spread of a lethal disease, Acquired Immune Deficiency Syndrome, or AIDS. Its source is unknown, its cure not yet found. Half of the cases nationwide have appeared in New York, and 71 percent of them have afflicted homosexual men.

These numbers have done much more than just sour the atmosphere in the bars, baths and private clubs, where some men travel a circuit of drugs, alcohol and anonymous sex.

The epidemic has also created anxiety and caution in the homosexual community at large among those who lead a variety of life styles—individuals and couples whose lives are moored by work, home, family and friends.

The concern generated by the disease has led many people to suggest that it may change basic patterns of male homosexual life. It has already renewed a debate about homosexual morality.

Beyond all this, AIDS has focused attention on the difference in styles of life for homosexual men and women. It also has promoted a sense of unity in their community, tempering but not eliminating traditional differences caused by race, gender and social station.

Physicians Report a Spreading Fear

Ronald J. Grossman is a Manhattan physician with an office at 338 East 30th Street, a practice that includes many homosexual men. He has watched firsthand as the epidemic developed.

In recent weeks he has been charting another malady. "People are coming to see me specifically with fear," he said. "It is masked and cloaked physical symptoms of AIDS. Some of these are so trivial. You'd think people would wait to see if they would fade. This thing is scaring the hell out of them."

Other doctors echo his experience. The fear, they say, is fueled by the mystery of the disease. Most medical experts believe that AIDS may be passed on by contaminated blood or an infectious agent, possibly through sexual contact, and that Haitians, drug addicts and homosexual men, particularly those with multiple sexual contacts, appear to be most at risk. But little else is certain.

This void of information has been filled by the impressions and anecdotes of a nervous community. In the homosexual press and on the street, a few people write and talk of conspiracies by government agencies or of clandestine medical experiments.

A 'Personalized' Disease

In the main, it is a disease that, in Dr. Grossman's words, has become "personalized." Either directly or through friends, most homosexual men say they know others who have the disease or have died of it.

Although there are no census or other official counts, conservative estimates, based on the work of Alfred C. Kinsey, put the New York population of homosexual men and women aged 16 to 55 at 350,000. However, city officials and others say they believe the figure is much higher.

Nevertheless fear of disease has traveled through this large community as if it were a small town. The following account, offered by a 53-year-old man, a supplier of building materials, is typical of those reported in more than 50 interviews. Like more than half of those who agreed to talk, he asked not to be identified.

"My social life at this point is having dinner with good friends, playing backgammon and going to the theater," he said. "I had one very good friend who died of AIDS. Now I have another friend who is in the hospital with it. I know I'm clean, but I'm scared of everyone else."

Since the disease may be sexually transmitted, those who are attempting to study it have begun to look at social and sexual habits. Though there are prior studies, the homosexual community today is largely unmapped terrain. And thus most researchers and social observers say they can only report their impressions.

Diversity of Behavior Noted

Alan R. Kristal, a doctoral candidate at the Columbia University School of Public Health, has started a study to measure and characterize "gay sexual behavior." Like others in the homosexual community, he is quick to say that sexual styles among homosexuals are as diverse as they are among heterosexuals.

But he and others agree that the sexual awakening of the late 1960's and early 1970's had a particularly liberating effect on many homosexual men.

The reference point for this awakening, marked by the Gay Pride March, was June 28, 1969, the date of a police raid at the Stonewall Inn on Christopher Street, a bar for homosexual men. The raid led to a riot and the riot, many people say, gave birth to a social cause and sexual style.

"After Stonewall," Mr. Kristal said, "one thing that has been prevalent is that you socialize via sexual contact." The bars where homosexual men and women socialize range from chic disco palaces to neighborhood tap rooms. Some create an atmosphere for sexual contact. Other establishments have back rooms for private encounters. And there are the baths, with rented cubicles and large common rooms.

"There were always sleazy waterfront bars that were secret," said James M. Saslow, an editor of The Advocate, a homosexual newspaper distributed nationally. "When liberation came along, there was a proliferation of what we already had, more bars, bigger bars. What gay men wanted was easy anonymous sex with no attachments."

Early 'Euphoria' Recalled

"I can remember the euphoria of the early days," said John J. Coveney, a self-employed real-estate holder in Chelsea. "We thought we were given license to be extreme."

Sociologists, among them Martin P. Levine, an assistant professor at Bloomfield College in New Jersey, say it is difficult to document the habits of a large population of men from different generations, ethnic groups and social backgrounds.

Many men felt ill-suited to the life of a libertine, although they may have made occasional forays to the baths and back-room bars. A large number of others lived in a variety of domestic arrangements. Still, throughout the 1970's, "one set of norms called for extreme sexual activity," Mr. Levine said.

Among those who experimented with a free and open life style and among those who embraced it there evolved an amorphous group of men known as "the clones."

They were the highly visible "swinging singles of the gay world," said Mr. Levine, who is completing a dissertation called, "Gay Macho: Ethnography of the Homosexual Clone."

They adopted a uniform—work boots, blue jeans, tank tops or print shirts. They affected an air of "purely unadulterated masculinity" and celebrated the "gym body, disco, drug life in the fast lane," Mr. Levine said.

Drawn to the 'Village'

Though they lived and worked in a variety of places, many at night converged on Greenwich Village, which Mr. Levine said "symbolically represents gay space in New York."

There were risks to this kind of life. Sexually transmitted diseases, doctors say, were epidemic among homosexual men long before AIDS struck. But many men who practiced casual sex adopted casual attitudes about its consequences. This attitude, in part, was fostered by some physicians.

"We had taught people that being sexually active was an acceptable health risk," said Dr. Daniel C. William, who has a large homosexual practice on West 57th Street. "We were wrong. AIDS changed the rules. I'm very regretful that this recognition has been slow in coming."

Now Dr. William and others are counseling caution, and what they are saying has prompted critics to label them "the new moralists." "I don't consider it morality," Dr. William said. "I consider it survival." They are preaching a new health code that goes beyond the threat of AIDS. They are telling their patients to realize that indiscriminate sexual contact "turns out to be outrageously unhealthy so you have to discard it," Dr. William said.

Restraint Is Resisted

The message is not always well received. "We're taking something away," Dr. William said. "People are depressed and angry. This is a radical departure. But you don't have to throw out the culture. A lot of gay people think you can't extract the life style from being gay. I think you can have a gay identity without the risk factors."

For some, behavior has gone unchanged. "There's a big moral trip coming down," said a 32-year-old manager of a well-known bath house in the city. "They're ready to tell you, 'Don't have sex.' To me that's not an option. I've heard the line that gay men have so much more in common than sex. That's wrong. What will I do if I stop now? How will I form a relationship?"

This was also true of men that Mr. Levine studied. "They are trapped in adolescent masculinity," he said, "and they lack the social skills of forming relationships."

In other quarters, however, men are beginning to change. "I want to be a little more serious about my life," said the 32-year-old owner of a card shop in Greenwich Village. "The morality thing, I can understand that. If people change their life styles and date and care about other people, that's great. I think a lot of people are more grown up. Anonymous sex is not healthy."

Resort to Dating Reported

Most of the homosexual men interviewed report a resurgence of dating. At these lunch and dinner meetings, they often trade medical profiles. "Everyone is being careful," said one man.

Others now go through the ritual of courting, which some say is a reversal of past practice. "Gay life circumvented the courtship phase," said a playwright and novelist. "You could not pick up a boy at his house. Instead you went from sex to courtship and built the relationship backwards."

Still others have elected to be celibate. And many men have expressed a growing desire for companionship. "We are now asking ourselves the question: does one want to go into one's dotage alone," said a magazine editor.

All of this has prompted a debate about the nature of homosexual life and its social underpinnings. Some homosexuals are asking whether they should accept the behavior norms of heterosexual society.

Conversion Is Doubted

"People who think they are going to convert the gay world into monogamous couples are wrong," said Michael L. Denneny, a senior editor at St. Martin's Press. "To say that gay men are the only ones who like frequent anonymous sex is hypocri-

sy. How else do you explain the existence of prostitutes? We're just different because we have alternate institutions."

The debate predates the discovery of AIDS. "The real argument is about whether there is a need to construct some sort of an ethical system that deals with sexuality and relationships," said Dennis Altman, a Regents lecturer in politics at the University of California at Santa Cruz.

"The heterosexual model is an idealized model, and it will not apply," Mr. Altman said. "Look at the divorce rate. But the new ethics will de-emphasize the importance of sex. We need to figure out what we want from sexuality, how it relates to gay relationships."

One approach is offered by Harvey Fierstein, author of "Torch Song Trilogy," which won two Tony Awards this month. "Everyone wants the same things—a home, a job you don't hate too much and someone to share it with," he said. "We've begun our liberation, now let's liberate ourselves."

Different Approaches to Male Living

Outside the circle of researchers and theoreticians, many homosexuals either reordered their lives before this debate or have always lived by their own rules.

At 35, Matthew A. Epstein, a former vice president at Columbia Artists Management, is a special consultant to opera companies and orchestras here and in Europe. He lives alone in a suite in the Ansonia Hotel.

"I knew I was gay but wasn't active until college," he said. "I didn't want my parents and friends to know. Then I wrote a letter to a music magazine condemning a homophobic article. After that, I would never hide my own sexuality.

"The whole question of promiscuity has distressed me for 15 years. I've had a few serious relationships and I've gone without. I don't think the bars and baths are a viable way of meeting people. I felt like a square peg in a round hole. It's extremely unsettling. Being alone can be a good thing. You can't stay out all night and be productive and responsible in my profession."

Reflections of a Banker

This is true for other professionals as well. David T. Beers, 29, is an international economist for a New York bank. The image of bankers as "archetypal conservatives" amuses him.

"This respectable banker type comes along and says I'm gay, too, and that surprises people," he said. "But so far I haven't had the experience of anyone that's run screaming from the room."

Like other homosexual men who are trying to build a career, he has a desire to be open about his private life but wonders about the consequences of his candor.

"It's changing," he said. "I've never really had a professional crisis. I have colleagues who know that I'm gay. My bank has a policy against discrimination. Many companies do.

"Sometimes I've had to deal with this problem immediately. Recently some of my friends at the bank tried to hook me up with a particular girl who came along. But I'm sure that my secretary notes that most of my personal calls seem to come from men rather than women. Being discovered is not something I live in terror of."

Mr. Beers's confidence is shared more by younger homosexual men than those who are older.

'A Lot of Guilt' for One

"I worry about the attitudes of my students who won't be able to deal with it," said the principal of a public school in the city. "I have a lot of guilt and residual fear about coming out. What bothers me is that coming out now, I'll be treated like a leper."

A combat veteran of World War II who was married and divorced, he came to the city in the early 1950's from upstate New York. "There was a lot of police entrapment, but I never felt repressed," he said. "Compared to upstate, the anonymity of the city was heaven."

These days he lives alone and angry. "I'm angry because I threw myself into my career and never made the changes in my life that would have allowed me to have a sucessful marriage with a man."

It is this kind of a partnership that many men long for. "We've been living together for four years now," said a 29-year-old college professor at a New Jersey university, who, with his 25-year-old lover, a nurse, lives in a two-bedroom apartment on the upper East Side.

In many ways they are the model of domesticity. They have two dogs, share the household chores, worry about the adventures and misadventures of their families and fight over the use of the bathroom mirror in the morning. "We're really a rather boring couple," the professor said.

Both "grew up gay," he said. "When other kids were reading fairy tales and looking at damsels in distress, I was looking at Prince Charming."

Like heterosexual couples, they, too, say they suffer a certain amount of sexual tension, but it is not brought on by a classic clash of roles. The nurse explains: "In a married couple, the man has his friends and the wife has hers. Each feels safe if the other goes out with their group. We don't have that. Jealousy is a problem."

Homosexual Women: A Different View

Among homosexual women, monogamy and domestic partnerships appear to be the rule rather than the exception. "We tend to form loving connections and have loving relationships rather than affairs," said Marilyn Lamkay, an assistant professor at Bronx Community College.

"But we have some problems in sustaining those connections," Miss Lamkay continued. "One of the standing jokes among lesbians is that there are only 40 of us, and we keep changing our names. We tend to have an incestuous community."

Virginia Vida, 44, program director of the New York City Commission on the Status of Women, said she "came out" in 1970 after she had edited an anthology of lesbian articles.

"For me it was the freedom to express my emotions, to fall in love and actually do something about it," said Miss Vida, who emphasized that her comments were personal and did not reflect the attitutes of her agency.

Informal Socializing Preferred

"I don't think our freedom translated into casual sex overall," she went on. "Lesbians are less visible. We have very few bars. We prefer to meet other women though friends and informal situations. Lesbians are inclined to set up a home and to build a nest. Our life style is different from men in that respect."

Traditionally there has been a measurable amount of antipathy between homosexual men and women. This ill feeling is in part fostered by the difference in life styles. "In a way we're so much more advanced than the men," Miss Lamkay said. "Some of their behavior is really a form of social slavery."

Yet in the main the disaffection grows out of a feeling among many women that within the homosexual movement, men "tend to take the reins and play a predominent role in the decision-making process," Miss Vida said.

This too, however, is beginning to change. The executive director of the National Gay Task Force, a political advocacy and resource organization, is a woman, Virginia Apuzzo. And the AIDS crisis, although the disease has not affected lesbians, has brought much support from women for efforts to fight the disease.

Rise of Communities Within Communities

Before the disease struck, many elements of community were already in place. Throughout the city there are neighborhoods where homosexual men and women have made their presence particularly open—the East and West Village, Park Slope and Brooklyn Heights in Brooklyn, sections of Elmhurst in Queens.

Many businesses run by homosexuals cater to homosexuals—investment consultants, doctors, lawyers, even morticians and exterminators. "When I see them, there are no evasions," said Bernard Granville, an insurance broker. "They come to me and say, 'My lover and I would like . . .' Not 'my friend or my roommate and I would like . . .'"

There also is a growing list of neighborhood, social, athletic and professional groups, like the Greater Gotham Business Council. And yet despite this base, homosexual politicians are able to document their own ineffectiveness and the reasons for it. First is the problem of public image.

"There's an assumption that there is one gay life style—the frequent, anonymous sex—and this is just totally divorced from reality," said Peter Vogel, co-chairman of Lambda Independent Democrats, a political club in Brooklyn. "It's always the most exaggerated form of conduct that draws attention. The media has created this image, not us."

Mirroring Society at Large

In many ways the homosexual community mirrors the philosophical, political, class and ethnic divisions of society at large. Like other groups, it is often split by personal and political infighting.

On the most prominent political issue taken up by the homosexual community in the city, homosexual activists have a history of failure. A bill that would amend the city's human rights law to ban discrimination based on "sexual orientation" has been defeated seven times in the City Council or its committees since 1971.

The bill failed despite the personal lobbying efforts of Governor Cuomo, Mayor Koch and Council President Carol Bellamy. Now, political advocates like Mr. Vogel and Miss Apuzzo say they believe it is time to switch tactics and broaden their scope.

"We need a rallying point that has more than legislation as its agenda," Miss Apuzzo said. She said AIDS might provide that rallying point.

Social Services Now Stressed

"There are a lot of us now who feel the issue has to switch to social programs and services," Mr. Vogel said. "Politicians need to support us for getting funding for these services, and this will be our new formula for assessing political friendship and support."

Political power, of course, comes at the voting booth. "AIDS has created an emergency, but the question is can it be translated into real political muscle," said Herbert P. Rickman, a special assistant to Mayor Koch and his liaison to the homosexual community.

"I'm hoping more gays and lesbians will register," he said. "If the energy transmitted over AIDS can be turned into real organization, it will happen."

But there are skeptics, like Mr. Denneny of St. Martins Press, who feel that the future is uncertain. "It's a physical disease, not a moral cholera," he said. "How people cope with this emergency, whether there will be real changes in life styles and values, I don't know."

* * *

July 15, 1987

WHERE HOMOSEXUALS FOUND A HAVEN, THERE'S NO HAVEN FROM AIDS

By ROBERT LINDSEY
Special to the New York Times

SAN FRANCISCO, July 14—In the once-bustling Castro district here, empty storefronts are beginning to appear and "for sale" signs are adorning many of of the beautifully restored Victorian homes.

In this neighborhood that gained renown for its culture of openly expressed homosexuality, the predominant concern of the living is now dealing with death and dying. So many people have died of AIDS that many residents say they can no longer count the number of friends they have lost.

One resident, Kevin George, says that he lost count at 22. "You're always in mourning for someone," he said, "and you know there's going to be more."

Another resident, Allan Berube, said he had stopped counting at 30.

"I'm learning how to incorporate grieving into my daily life," he said, "so it's now as much a part of my life as eating and sleeping."

Ads for Mortuaries

Bart Levin, who lost track of the AIDS toll among his friends at 34, stood beside a Castro Street bar this week and pointed out a copy of The Bay Area Reporter, a newspaper that caters to San Francisco's large homosexual population.

"It's full of obituaries for people you know and ads for mortuaries, crematoriums and lawyers who warn you to write a will," he said. "I'm weary of grieving."

Since 1981, 3,402 cases of acquired immune deficiency syndrome have been diagnosed in San Francisco, a city of 725,000. And 2,030 people, almost all of them gay men, have died of the disease, almost 10 percent of the nation's total. Health experts say the AIDS death toll here could pass 10,000 by 1991.

The somber and subdued atmosphere these days in the Castro is in sharp contrast to that of a decade or so ago, when an American social revolution of sorts began here.

Thousands of men, and later women, from around the nation converged on a city noted for tolerance and, cautiously opening a secret door to their lives, acknowledged they were homosexuals.

Life out of the Mainstream

In the company of others, they sought sexual license denied them at home, a degree of political influence, pride and the right to pursue a life different from that of mainstream America.

Although the newcomers settled in many parts of the city, the Castro district, covering about six square blocks two miles west of City Hall, became the principal commercial center for San Francisco's gay population, now estimated at 70,000. Many were financially secure professionals who artfully restored deteriorating Victorian homes in the Castro and nearby neighborhoods.

As this group gained increasing acceptance and influence here, many homosexuals elsewhere would say the Castro example made it easier to acknowledge their sexual preference, and the Castro became both a symbol of success and a kind of prototype for similar gay enclaves in other cities.

The late 1970's and early 1980's were a period of anything-goes sexual liberation for San Francisco's gay community. On some nights, thousands of men, many seminude or wearing costumes, women's clothing or heavily studded leather outerwear, overflowed onto the community's sidewalks, some taunting heterosexual couples who had ventured into their neighborhood as "breeders."

Bath Houses All Shut

It was not uncommon for some men to have sexual contacts with 20 or 30 partners in a single evening at bath houses

The Castro district in San Francisco. The neighborhood, which covers about six square blocks two miles west of City Hall, long ago became the principal center for the city's gay population.

that featured "orgy rooms" and other facilities designed to encourage multiple sexual contacts.

These days, all-male crowds still congregate at the Phoenix, the Twin Peaks, the Elephant Walk and other bars that have long been fixtures in the neighborhood. Young male hustlers still cruise Castro Street, offering with a quick glance the promise of sex for a price. Not everyone practices "safe sex," regulars in the Castro concede.

But because of AIDS, the neighborhood is vastly different from what it was even three years ago.

All the bath houses, which health officials cite as a fundamental cause of the initial rapid spread of AIDS, and many of the other businesses that catered to the gay community have closed because their proprietors have died or are dying of AIDS, or they have lost too many customers to the disease.

"There's been a sort of maturation," said Ernest L. Asten, whose family has run Cliff's Variety store, a Castro Street landmark, since 1936 and who has witnessed all the changes of the last few years.

Taking Care of the Victims

"In the 70's and early 80's," he said, "people came here to come out of the closet; there was a perpetual coming out by people from all over the country—from all over the world, for that matter. They might be in their 40's, but when they came here there was still adolescent behavior."

Since then, he said, it has become easier for homosexuals around the country to pursue openly their sexual preferences on their home ground. "You don't have to make a pilgrimage here, and the very carefree promiscuity you used to have has been considerably dampened by AIDS," he said. "And I think there's more sense of responsibility in the community when it comes to taking care of the people who fall victim to this disease."

He and others pointed out that community groups had been formed to provide services to AIDS sufferers, among other things bringing food and lending solace in visits to the afflicted at their homes or in the hospital.

"It's so hard," said Mr. Berube, a writer. "So much of our lives are dedicated to dealing with death, taking care of our friends who are dying.

"Gays are feeling the importance of being alive, of saying things that might not otherwise be said. We're taking care of each other, and nothing is taken for granted."

Zohn Artman, a public relations man who has been active in Bay Area social causes for 30 years and who has AIDS, said: "We're doing everything we can to take care of our own. We're not happy, but we're not wimping out. Anybody who thinks gays are sissies should take a look. We have developed enormous strengths."

* * *

November 23, 1997

GAY CULTURE WEIGHS SENSE AND SEXUALITY

By SHERYL GAY STOLBERG

One night last May, a handful of New York City's best-known gay journalists, artists and academics called together some friends to bemoan what they viewed as a backlash against the sexual practices of homosexuals. The turnout surprised them: five dozen people jammed into an overheated room.

They swapped stories of police crackdowns on sex in public restrooms and closings of gay discos and pubs. And they complained about new books taking aim at what remains, even in the AIDS era, a central feature of gay urban life: sex clubs, bathhouses and weekend-long drug parties where men may have intercourse with a dozen partners a night.

"It sounds like a traditional sex panic," someone declared, borrowing a term historians use to describe a wave of societal prudishness. Thus the group adopted a name: Sex Panic.

Gay activist groups are hardly in short supply. What makes Sex Panic different are its enemies: three of the nation's most prominent gay authors, Gabriel Rotello, Michaelangelo Signorile and Larry Kramer. All sound alarms about the homosexual culture of sexual freedom, warning that its promiscuous pursuit by a core of gay men threatens to perpetuate epidemic AIDS.

As viruses go, H.I.V. is fragile and difficult to transmit. But in the late 70's and early 80's, Mr. Rotello writes in his new book, "Sexual Ecology" (Dutton), H.I.V. found a home in the homosexual fast lane. As their movement for sexual liberation took hold, gay men changed sex partners as often as some people changed clothes. But the very behavior favored by them—anal intercourse—was particularly conducive to the spread of AIDS. Gay men began dying.

When scientists learned that latex condoms blocked H.I.V., public health officials and AIDS activists created a "safe sex" strategy. But what Mr. Rotello calls "the condom code"—the idea that the number of partners doesn't matter, so long as you always use a condom—hasn't stamped out H.I.V., mainly because not everyone follows it. Now, two decades into the epidemic, bathhouses and unsafe sex are coming back.

"The whole culture has to change," Mr. Kramer said in an interview. "We have created a culture that in fact murdered us, killed us. What you can't help but think, if you've got any brains, is don't people ever learn anything?"

Such remarks have won him few fans at Sex Panic. "A culture doesn't kill people," retorted Kendall Thomas, a law professor at Columbia University and a founder of Sex Panic. "The virus kills people."

The volleying has deeply divided the gay intelligentsia. For the first time since the publication in 1987 of "And The Band Played On" by Randy Shilts, there is open debate among homosexuals about promiscuity's role in AIDS. For many of them, it is a terrifying discussion, one they fear could fan the flames of discrimination as it becomes public by focusing on their behavior as a cause of the epidemic. "It is something a lot of people are really afraid to speak up about," Mr. Signorile said.

A Question of Assimilation

How this argument is settled will have broad implications for all of America as the financial, social and emotional toll of AIDS continues. While death rates have been declining, studies show that men who have sex with men still account for the majority of AIDS cases, and that a young gay man has as much as a 50 percent chance of acquiring H.I.V. by middle age.

But the debate is about more than public health; it is about what it means to be homosexual. As some homosexuals press for same-sex marriage, adoption and other forms of societal acceptance, welcoming President Clinton's address this month to a gay and lesbian civil rights group (the first by a sitting President), others protest assimilation.

On one side are those like Mr. Kramer, who are beseeching homosexuals to adopt a culture rooted as much in art, literature and relationships as in "what's between our legs and what we do with it."

On the other are those like Mr. Thomas and Michael Warner, an English professor at Rutgers University and a founder of Sex Panic, who argue that promiscuous sex is the essence of gay liberation, and that any attempt to fight AIDS by changing the culture is doomed.

"It is an absurd fantasy to expect gay men to live without a sexual culture when we have almost nothing else that brings us together," Mr. Warner said.

The debate occurs against a backdrop of evidence that homosexuals are returning to what they call "bareback sex," anal intercourse without condoms. In a survey of 205 gay men in Miami's South Beach, Dr. William W. Darrow, a public health professor at Florida International University, found that 45 percent had unprotected anal sex in the past year. Gonorrhea rates are up, too. During the mid-80's, the disease—a marker for exposure to H.I.V.—all but disappeared among gay men because so many practiced safe sex. But from 1993 to 1996, the Centers for Disease Control and Prevention recently reported, a survey of clinics in 26 cities found gonorrhea among such men rose 74 percent.

The reasons aren't fully understood. Mr. Signorile blames the social scene; in his new book, "Life Outside" (Harper-

Collins), he attacks the "circuit," a national series of week-end-long bashes laden with drugs.

"What we are seeing," he said in an interview, "is a kind of live-and-let-live intense party scene that is very similar to the same scene that contributed to the AIDS epidemic exploding in the 1970's."

Invincible Youth

The myth of invincible youth is also a factor; a generation of young men has now grown up amid AIDS. Some men have simply grown weary of wearing condoms. And there is evidence that the life-saving promise of protease inhibitors is backfiring; as drugs extend the lives of AIDS patients, more people take risks.

"It is sort of like piling up wood for a bonfire in the middle of a conflagration," said Dr. Judith N. Wasserheit, who directs the C.D.C.'s prevention program for sexually transmitted diseases. "I think the gay community is at a very dangerous place."

Last year alone, the Government spent $7.3 billion for AIDS research, medical care and disability payments. And if the epidemic continues in a core of gay men in urban centers, experts say, it will thrive among all homosexuals. That, Mr. Rotello says, is what is occurring. "There is a point in epidemiology," he said, "at which any epidemic grows or shrinks. Right now we are at the replacement level."

Also, as the number of partners goes up, use of condoms goes down, said Ron Stall, a behavioral scientist at the Center for AIDS Prevention Studies at the University of San Francisco. He fears that if gay men continue to have unsafe sex in the age of protease inhibitors, drug-resistant strains of H.I.V. will spread. "We have then yielded the epidemiological nightmare," he said.

To Sex Panic, this sounds like an alarmist pretext for restricting gay civil rights. Promiscuity and safe sex can coexist, its members argue. And while it may be difficult for heterosexuals to understand anonymous sex with multiple partners, to many homosexuals it is a cornerstone of liberation. Homosexuals had been discriminated against for the way they had sex; liberation meant having as much sex as possible, as publicly as possible.

"We want to reinsert sexual liberation back in our movement," said Tony Valenzuela, an actor in gay pornographic films who organized Sex Panic's first national conference, held in San Diego this month. "For those of us who like anonymous sex, there is something very erotic," he said, adding that safe sex is standard in gay porn. "The important thing is that it can be healthy."

The debate is only likely to intensify. "In the end," Dr. Stall said, "it is a cultural fight as much as an epidemiological fight. What is the future of gay culture going to be like?"

Correction: An article on Nov. 23 about the relationship between sexual promiscuity and the AIDS epidemic referred imprecisely to the views of Prof. Kendall Thomas of Columbia University Law School. He says that while he does not believe that promiscuity is the essence of gay sexuality, he does believe, as the article stated, that any attempt to fight AIDS by demonizing the culture of sexual freedom is doomed. And he says AIDS is spread by unsafe sex, not by multi-partner sex.

* * *

September 8, 1998

DRUGS TAINT AN ANNUAL ROUND OF GAY REVELS

By FRANK BRUNI

It began in the early stages of the AIDS epidemic as a relatively modest affair, a respite for the living and remembrance of the dead that was held in daylight, so that even the ill might be able to go, and was given a double-edged title resonant of grief.

A decade and a half later, the Morning Party has evolved into a glamorous social event that attracts hordes of gay men to Fire Island and reliably raises enormous sums of money for Gay Men's Health Crisis, perhaps the country's most respected private AIDS service organization.

This year's gathering, on Aug. 16, was no different. About 4,500 men went, an estimated $450,000 was raised and a good time was had by many.

But the hangover has been formidable, underlining the way the event has become an albatross around the health group's neck and a flash point in an increasingly bitter debate over the alliances between AIDS service organizations and a network of dance-oriented fund-raisers at which a substantial number of participants are high on drugs.

In the predawn hours leading up to this year's Morning Party, a 35-year-old man from Bronxville, N.Y., overdosed and died. During the event, a security consultant who had been hired by the health group to help weed out drug use—and who had made a speech imploring partygoers to stay clean—was among 21 men arrested on charges of possessing illegal drugs.

In the three weeks since, many gay men have questioned the propriety of the group's endorsement of a party that seems to inspire the kind of drug consumption widely thought to increase the likelihood of unsafe sexual behavior and the spread of AIDS.

"It gives the organization not only money, but future clients," said Troy Masters, the publisher of LGNY, a twice-monthly newspaper for lesbians and gay men in the New York region. "In a way, it's like a self-perpetuating machine."

Criticism of this kind has been aimed at Gay Men's Health Crisis for several years. In 1996, a man was evacuated by helicopter from the Morning Party after slipping into a drug-induced coma.

But the complaints seem to be taking on a heightened urgency with the proliferation around the country of other large-scale gay dance events, some of which funnel part of their profits to AIDS service organizations and include the organizations' names in promotional materials.

These events have come to be known as "circuit parties" because they are linked by similar music and because some of them attract the same core crowd, lavishly muscled and wealthy enough to buy plane tickets and plenty of drugs like cocaine, Ecstasy and ketamine, or "special K."

In addition, the array of chemicals taken by at least a few of the men who attend circuit parties has expanded recently to include a liquid anesthetic, gamma hydroxybutyrate, or GHB, that has been implicated in a string of medical emergencies at circuit parties this year. GHB is extolled by some as an aphrodisiac.

Suffolk County law enforcement officials said that GHB appeared to cause the death of Frank J. Giordano, 35, at the Pines on Fire Island around 4 A.M. on Aug. 16, seven hours before the Morning Party officially began on a stretch of beach nearby.

Three other men at the Pines who apparently took the same batch of GHB were brought to hospitals on Long Island, treated and released, law enforcement officials said. Several people who attended the Morning Party said that one of the three men made it back to the Pines in time to join the festivities.

"People are partying harder than ever with substances that are more volatile than ever," said Alan Brown, a New Haven management consultant who annually attends about two dozen circuit parties, from Montreal to Miami, and recently sat on a panel at a gay physicians' conference in Chicago to discuss health issues relating to the events. "People have been leaving parties in ambulances routinely for three years now."

Mr. Brown and other gay men familiar with circuit parties emphasized that many men who attend the events use illegal drugs infrequently, if ever, and that a vast majority of gay men have never been to one.

Officials of Gay Men's Health Crisis, which stages (and profits from) the Morning Party, said that educating the minority of gay men involved in the party circuit about the perils of drugs is a principal reason the organization remains committed to the event, which they said would occur with or without the group's involvement.

Jeff Soref, who was president of its board when the organization began to assume full responsibility for coordinating the event in the early 1990's, said, "G.M.H.C. does need to be involved in harm reduction, and it does need to be where the community is."

Others stressed that during recent years, the organization had intensified its efforts to rid the Morning Party of illegal drugs, distributing written warnings. Many people who attended the Morning Party this year said that drug use was noticeably less prevalent and conspicuous than in the past.

Ronald Johnson, the organization's managing director for public policy, said that linking the GHB overdoses that occurred more than eight hours earlier to the event was gratuitous.

But critics said that the Morning Party, like other circuit events, has spawned several days of nonstop revelry around it, and cannot divorce itself from those often reckless festivities.

"If G.M.H.C. officials don't think they have some responsibility for the overdoses, they're kidding themselves," said Michael Trovato, 41, who spends summer weekends on Fire Island.

Many gay men said the organization could do prevention work at the party without sponsoring it, which they contended tacitly condones the drug-taking throughout the weekend. Several said they had stopped donating money to the organization because of its affiliation with the gathering and knew others who had done likewise, although Mr. Johnson said he had seen no evidence of that.

In some ways, circuit parties are nothing new. Among both heterosexuals and homosexuals, going back several decades, there have been late-night, drug-fueled dance extravaganzas.

But during the last five years, special gay events of this kind have not only multiplied—they now number in the dozens—but also clustered into an informal network with its own Internet sites, disk jockeys and preferred body type, gym-toned and sometimes steroid-enhanced.

The circuit embraces New York and New Orleans, Palm Springs and Pensacola, though many events have no connection to AIDS service organizations. It usually features shirtless men dancing all through the night, their energy and euphoria often enhanced by powders or pills.

Gay men knowledgeable about the circuit said that Viagra has also made an appearance, prompting recent seminars in San Francisco and Miami that discussed its interaction with other drugs, including protease inhibitors, the antiviral agents taken by people with AIDS.

But what most alarms many gay men and public health experts is not the drug use itself but the implications for responsible sexual conduct.

"The extent to which gay men use drugs is a strong, significant predictor of becoming H.I.V.-positive," said Ron Stall, a professor of epidemiology at the University of California at San Francisco.

Others said that some circuit parties even feature darkened back rooms and that a few men who flock to circuit extravaganzas also attend sex parties before or after the main event and may not adhere strictly to precautions against H.I.V. transmission.

That has provoked critics into greater anger at AIDS service organizations around the country for staging circuit parties or signing on as beneficiaries.

"Circuit parties got the imprimatur of their local AIDS organizations and—bingo—instant, total respectability," said Gabriel Rotello, author of "Sexual Ecology: AIDS and the Destiny of Gay Men" (Dutton, 1997). "And the irony of that is just so awesome."

To varying degrees, officials with AIDS service organizations that are involved in circuit parties are wrestling with that accusation, a process complicated by their difficulty raising money in other ways.

They said that sunny news reports about better treatments for AIDS have left many individual donors with the mistaken impression that the epidemic is waning and have discouraged them from giving as much money as in the past.

"We are more dependent than ever on special events fund-raising," said Bryan Delowery, the events coordinator for the AIDS Information Network, an organization in Philadelphia that stages a circuit party there every January. The event, called the Blue Ball, raises $125,000, more than 10 percent of the group's annual budget.

Profits from the Morning Party, for which tickets cost $100 apiece, account for a much smaller percentage of G.M.H.C.'s annual budget of $25 million. But proponents of circuit parties said the case for them transcends the economic vitality of AIDS service organizations that do crucial work.

They said that many gay men attend the events not to indulge chemical or sexual appetites but simply to bask in an environment free of the bigotry they face elsewhere in society. They noted that circuit parties are by no means the exclusive sites of risky behavior, or even the main ones.

Critics counter that circuit parties, with their special patina of glamour, have an impact beyond their perimeters, idealizing dangerous habits in a manner that has particular influence over young gay men.

The experience of Jeffrey W. supports that viewpoint. He said that when he moved to Manhattan after graduating from college a few years ago, "I had no desire to be part of a drug and intense sex culture."

But he said that the conversations of other gay men he met and the glossy ads he spotted in some gay periodicals piqued his curiosity, and even left him with the impression that the circuit scene was the very definition of gay identity.

"I figured if there were 5,000 other men who are considered the upper crust in the gay world doing this, it must be all right and it must be the norm," said Jeffrey, who spoke on the condition that his last name not be used. "I experimented quite heavily with drugs, and I began to be unsafe."

One such moment occurred in December. Several months later, Jeffrey said, he tested positive for H.I.V

* * *

Surviving AIDS

November 28, 1993

WHATEVER HAPPENED TO AIDS?

By JEFFREY SCHMALZ

I have come to the realization that I will almost certainly die of AIDS. I have wavered on that point. When the disease was first diagnosed in early 1991, I was sure I would die—and soon. I was facing brain surgery; the surgeons discovered an infection often fatal in four months. I would shortly develop pneumonia, then blood clots. I was hospitalized four times over five months. But by the end of that year, I thought differently. My health rebounded, almost certainly because of AZT. I was doing so well; I really might beat it. Now, it is clear I will not. You can beat the statistics only so long. My T-cell count, which was only 2 when I got my diagnosis, has never gone above 30—a dangerously low level. I have lived longer than the median survival time by 10 months. The treatments simply are not there. They are not even in the pipeline. A miracle is possible, of course. And for a long time, I though one would happen. But let's face it, a miracle isn't going to happen. One day soon I will simply become one of the 90 people in America to die that day of AIDS. It's like knowing I will be killed by a speeding car, but not knowing when or where.

I used to be an exception in my H.I.V. support group, the only one of its eight members who was not merely infected with the virus but who had advanced to full-blown AIDS. Now, just a year and a half later, the exception in my group is the one person who does not have AIDS. All the rest of us have deteriorated with the hallmarks of the disease—a seizure, Kaposi's sarcoma, pneumonia. Our weekly meetings simmer with desperation: We are getting sicker. I am getting sicker. Time is running out.

Once AIDS was a hot topic in America—promising treatments on the horizon, intense media interest, a political battlefield. Now, 12 years after it was first recognized as a new disease, AIDS has become normalized, part of the landscape. It is at once everywhere and nowhere, the leading cause of death among young men nationwide, but little threat to the core of American political power, the white heterosexual suburbanite. No cure or vaccine is in sight. And what small treatment advances had been won are now crumbling. The world is moving on, uncaring, frustrated and bored, leaving by the roadside those of us who are infected and who can't help but wonder: Whatever happened to AIDS? As a journalist who has written about this disease for five years, and as a patient who has had it for nearly as long, I went out looking for answers.

THE DISEASE AND THE DOCTORS

Dr. Anthony S. Fauci speaks with a hint of a Brooklyn accent, which is out of sync with the elegance of his appearance—well tailored, tidy, trim. At 52, he is scientist-cum-celebrity, ridiculed by Larry Kramer in the play "The Destiny of Me," lionized by George Bush in the 1988 Presidential debate as a hero.

Being the Government's point man on AIDS has made Tony Fauci (rhymes with OUCH-ee) famous. He professes to be solely the scientist. But in fact, he is very much the star and the politician, one year defending modest Reagan-Bush AIDS budget proposals as adequate, the next defending generous Clinton proposals as necessary. He is the activist's enemy—"Murderer!" Kramer once called him in an essay published in The Village Voice. He is the activist's friend, a comrade in arms, showing up last October at the opening of the Kramer play wearing a red AIDS ribbon.

Fauci's starring AIDS role comes from the many hats he wears—among them director of the National Institute of Allergy and Infectious Diseases and director of the National Institutes of Health's Office of AIDS Research.

"Fauci deserves a lot of the blame for where we are on AIDS," said Peter Staley of TAG, the activist Treatment Action Group. But others say that is not fair. "You can't blame any one person," said Gregg Gonsalves, who wrote TAG's report on the status of AIDS research. "We've gotten to the edge of a scientific cliff."

Whatever Fauci's faults, I have never doubted his commitment. Still, he is the face of the AIDS scientific community, and 12 years into the disease there are only temporary treatments that work for a few years at most. AIDS remains a fatal illness. Approximately a million Americans are believed to be infected with the human immunodeficiency virus, the key component of AIDS, and virtually all of them are expected to develop the disease eventually. Close to half a million Americans are expected to have full-blown AIDS by the end of next year; more than 200,000 have already died. Roughly 350,000 will have died by the end of 1994. The World Health Organization puts the number infected worldwide at more than 13 million adults and an additional 1 million or more children.

So far, the only treatments are nucleoside analogues, drugs like AZT, DDC and DDI. A fourth nucleoside analogue, D4T, is expected to be approved by the spring. Fauci has focused national research efforts on these analogues, which slow the virus by fooling it with a decoy of genetic material it needs to reproduce. But the analogues have problems. They are highly toxic, and the virus, which mutates rapidly, eventually catches on to the deception.

Everyone knew going into the international AIDS conference in Berlin in June that the nucleoside analogues were of limited use, but the horrible surprise was just how limited. A report issued just before the meeting—the Concorde Study, conducted in England, France and Ireland—found that, contrary to the recommendations of the United States Government, use of AZT before the onset of AIDS symptoms did not necessarily prolong life. (In an extraordinary action, a United States Government panel has since pulled back the earlier recommendation. AZT is still recommended for those with full-blown AIDS. But the panel left it for patients and their doctors to decide on earlier use.)

A subsequent Australian study, published in July, found that AZT, used early, did prolong life. I have always felt that it has prolonged mine. Still, what makes the fuss over AZT so stunning is not just that the drug has shortcomings—almost everyone knew that from the start. It is that AZT, flawed as it was, had become the Gold Standard of treatment, against which other therapies were being measured. The chilling message of the AZT dispute is this: Things are not just failing to get better; they are getting worse. We are losing ground.

"The fallout from Berlin has been devastating," said Martin Delaney, founding director of Project Inform, an AIDS treatment information and lobbying group. "There were no surprises. But the risk now is that AIDS gets put up on the shelf along with a lot of other long-term unresolved problems. We lose the urgency for money and the scientific momentum." The bad news has left drug companies scrambling. Last spring things were so desperate that a group of 15 announced they would pool research data. Many scientists—and activists—are fed up with the drug companies, which seem hellbent on pursuing more nucleoside analogues when the real future of AIDS treatment probably lies with gene therapy. The idea is to alter the genetic structure of cells to make them inhospitable to H.I.V. But the problem is, no one knows how to translate the occasional test-tube success into a workable treatment. In addition, most of the gene therapies are being developed by small biotechnology companies that will take years to get into full production.

So, was all the time and money spent on the nucleoside analogues wasted? Fauci, who obviously has an investment in the answer, was emphatic that it wasn't. "People say the Berlin meeting was so depressing, nothing's happening," Fauci said in his office overlooking the N.I.H. campus in Bethesda, Md. "I say that's not the way science works. There are little steps, building blocks. What's important is whether you're going in the right direction, and I am convinced that we are.

"Was it grossly inappropriate to do the extensive studies of AZT and DDI?" he continued. "No. Should we have done more with other drugs? If we had them, one could say, yes.

"Let's say a year and a half from now, nevirapine isn't working," Fauci said of an experimental drug undergoing trials in combination with the nucleoside analogues. "Somebody's going to say, 'Why did you waste all that time with it?' But you don't know it doesn't work until you test it."

If Fauci is defensive, it may be because he is still smarting from a political bruising. His Office of AIDS Research has been reorganized by the Clinton Administration and he has been, in effect, ousted—done in by the AIDS activists through their Democratic friends in Congress. And while some of his time is being diverted to playing politics, in his own laboratory research he has now returned to basics—Square 1—where many AIDS researchers are working. Fauci is studying the pathogenesis of the disease, its route through the body.

I asked him the obvious: 12 years into the disease—shouldn't we know that already? "More effort looking at pathogenesis might have been appropriate in retrospect," Fauci responded. "But we were constantly being diverted—by the activists, by Congress. It was: 'What can you give me right now? Get those drugs out there as quickly as you can.'"

Not so long ago we believed that if we just could find enough money, we could make the disease manageable, like diabetes. But in a further sign of how little hope exists these days in the scientific community, money isn't seen as the main issue anymore.

"Certainly, there are more scientific opportunities than there are resources to fulfill them," Fauci said, echoing the views of other scientists. "But should we dump billions into AIDS research now? I think we'd reach a point of diminishing returns."

Fauci presents a front of optimism, at least for me. After all, there is no cure for any virus, only vaccines to prevent them—measles is an example. By the year 2000, he predicted, "We'll be into vaccine trials that show a vaccine is much more feasible than we thought, though we may not have the best vaccine by then."

Other scientists are unconvinced. They point out that the rapid mutation of the AIDS virus and its many strains make development of a vaccine difficult.

"The public is frustrated; it says, 'You've been working on this for 10 years,' " said Dr. Irvin S. Y. Chen, director of the AIDS Institute at the University of California at Los Angeles. Chen bemoaned the lack of money for biomedical research in general, which he said was discouraging the best and the brightest from entering the field.

"We're in that in-between stage," said Dr. Merle A. Sande, an AIDS expert at the University of California at San Francisco; he was head of the Government panel on AZT use. "We know a lot about the virus, but we just don't seem able to translate that knowledge into significant treatment advances. It's incredibly frustrating."

Still, the frustration of the public and the scientists is nothing compared with the frustration of those of us living with AIDS or H.I.V. Will people still be dying of AIDS in the year 2000? Fauci didn't hesitate for a second before replying, "I don't think there's any question that will be the case."

THE ACTIVISTS AND THE GOVERNMENT

Tim Bailey was one of the Marys, and that's as close to Act Up royalty as anybody can get.

The Marys are a subgroup of Act Up, the group involved in the more radical demonstrations, like disrupting services at St. Patrick's Cathedral. When Bailey died in June at 35, stipulating that he wanted a political funeral in Washington, Act Up was obliged to comply.

So on a drizzly Thursday at 7 A.M., two buses filled with Act Up members set out from New York. They were to rendezvous with the body in Washington, then carry the open coffin through the streets from the Capitol to the White House. They would show Bill Clinton the urgency of AIDS. They would bring one of its carcasses to his doorstep.

But it was not to be. The police would not let them march, and the day turned into a sodden fiasco, as the police and activists quarreled over the body, shoving the coffin in and out of a van parked in front of the Capitol. The rage was there, but the organization was not. And when the police said no, where did Act Up members run for help but the White House, the very target of their protest, getting Bob Hattoy, a White House staff member with AIDS, to intervene. In the end, Act Up members gave up and went home, taking the body with them.

It was a perfect metaphor for the state of AIDS activism—raging in desperate but unfocused anger, one foot on the inside, one on the outside.

The AIDS movement was built on grass-roots efforts. Now those efforts are in disarray. Many Act Up leaders have died. The group's very existence was based on the belief that AIDS could be cured quickly if only enough money and effort were thrown at it—something that now seems increasingly in doubt. Besides, it is hard to maintain attacks against a Government that is seeking big increases in AIDS spending. Much of the cream of Act Up has fled, forming groups like TAG and joining mainstream AIDS organizations like the Gay Men's Health Crisis and the American Foundation for AIDS Research.

Those left behind are Act Up's hard core. Act Up was always part theater, part group therapy. Now, sadly, Act Up is increasingly reduced to burying its dead.

To say all that is not to belittle the accomplishments of the group. One reason for Act Up's decline is that it has got so much of what it wanted. Act Up forced AIDS into the Presidential race, dogging candidates. Because of Act Up the price of AZT is lower. Drugs are approved more quickly. Today it is a given that the communities affected by a disease have a voice, and must be consulted. To a great extent, Act Up deserves much of the credit for the increasing political power of the entire gay rights movement. But now even the gay movement has pushed AIDS to the sidelines.

Anyone questioning how AIDS ranks as an issue among gay groups need only look to the march on Washington on April 25. Six years earlier, in 1987, a similar gay march had one overriding theme: AIDS. If there was a dominant theme last April, it was homosexuals in the military. To be sure, AIDS was an element of the march, but just an element. Speaker after speaker ignored it.

"It's like they are waiting for us to die so they can get on with their agenda," said Dr. Nicholas A. Rango, the director of New York State's AIDS Institute, a gay man who himself has AIDS and watched the march on C-Span from his Manhattan hospital bed. [He died on Nov. 10.]

Torie Osborn, formerly executive director of the National Gay and Lesbian Task Force, argued that the shift was inevitable with the election of a Democratic President, renewed attacks from the right wing and just plain burnout. Increasingly, many homosexuals, especially those who test negative for H.I.V., do not want a disease to be what defines their community. "There is a deep yearning to broaden the agenda beyond AIDS," she said. "There's a natural need for human beings who are in deep grieving to reach for a future beyond their grieving.

"It's one thing to be fighting for treatment, believing you're going to get a cure that will have everyone survive," continued Osborn, who recently buried three friends who had died of AIDS. "But it's an incredibly depressing truth that AIDS has become part of the backdrop of gay life."

What is to some a broadening of the gay agenda, however, is to others desertion. "It's one thing for the politicians to abandon AIDS," Kevin Frost, a TAG member, said. "But for our own community to abandon the issue. . . . Who brought this issue of gays in the military out in the open? A couple of flashy queers with checkbooks. Well, what about AIDS?"

What about AIDS? Perhaps the greatest development affecting Act Up, the activist community and the entire AIDS care world is the changing face of the disease. Homosexual sex still accounts for the majority of cases, 57 percent. But that number is dropping, down from 61 percent in 1989. Meanwhile, the percentage of cases tied to intravenous drug use is beginning to climb. It is now at 23 percent, up from 21 percent in 1989.

Black and Hispanic groups are clamoring for a greater role in running AIDS care organizations. Their intentions seem genuine—what do gay groups know of inner-city drug use?—but also seem driven in part by a desire for money and power. In an age of Government cutbacks, AIDS is where the money is—"today's equivalent of the Great Society programs of the 60's," as Rango put it.

In Washington and Houston, gay groups and black and Hispanic groups are bickering over who should control the money and the programs. In New York, the largest AIDS care organization, the Gay Men's Health Crisis, is trying valiantly to be all things to all constituencies—it contributed $25,000 to the lobbying effort to allow homosexuals in the military even as it was helping to expand legal services in Harlem. Inevitably, focus is lost.

G.M.H.C. has recently changed executive directors, as have many of the more than 3,500 AIDS organizations in the United States. The average executive director of an AIDS service group lasts less than two years, burned out by depression and exhausted by the bickering among AIDS constituencies.

"We should be fighting the virus, not each other," said Dan Bross, the executive director of the AIDS Action Council. "We're eating our young."

Mary Fisher, who addressed the Republican National Convention in Houston as a woman infected with H.I.V., whom I interviewed at the time and who has since become a friend, also believes the AIDS movement is adrift. She was sitting at lunch in Manhattan with Larry Kramer, both of them bemoaning the state of AIDS activism.

"We need to agree on the goals," Fisher said.

"That's just rhetoric," Kramer shot back. "The goal is to find a cure."

Fisher sees AIDS entering a dangerous never-never land, with the day fast approaching when no one will be carrying the AIDS banner.

"The gay community is going to stop screaming," she said. "It is already stopping."

"I'm very despondent," Kramer said. "You don't know where to yell or who to yell at. Clinton says all the right things, then doesn't do anything."

Indeed, the Clinton Administration does say all the right things, at times coming close to being patronizing about it.

"I have a real understanding that the people who feel the strongest about this, they don't have time," Carol H. Rasco, the President's top domestic policy adviser, said in defense of the zealotry of Act Up. "When a bomb is ticking inside you, you have to keep pushing."

Where once Washington doors were closed to AIDS activists, they are now open. Indeed, perhaps the single biggest AIDS change in Washington under the Clinton Administra-

tion has been one of tone. AIDS sufferers are no longer treated as immoral lepers. David Barr, director of treatment education and advocacy for the Gay Men's Health Crisis, recalled a May meeting with Donna E. Shalala, the Secretary of Health and Human Services.

"She agreed to everything we wanted," Barr said. "I was amazed. We're so used to doing battle. But is it a ploy?"

Certainly Bill Clinton is a vast improvement over George Bush. The President proposed a major increase in spending on AIDS research, about 20 percent, coming up with an additional $227 million. That would raise the total N.I.H. spending on AIDS research to $1.3 billion. In aid for outpatient care, the White House proposed a giant increase in what is known as Ryan White money, named for the Midwestern teen-ager who died of AIDS in April 1990. The current appropriation is $348 million, which the Administration proposed to nearly double by adding $310 million. The House didn't add the entire amount, just a $200 million increase, but it still brought the total to $548 million. The Senate was slightly more generous, and the final appropriation was $579 million.

But is more money enough? AIDS activists say they want leadership, but they are not sure anymore what that means.

"It was much easier," said Torie Osborn, "when we could hate George Bush and Ronald Reagan, when we thought we had evil genocidal Republican Presidents who weren't doing what needed to be done to get a cure."

Still, as is so often the case with Bill Clinton, he is a victim of his own lofty campaign rhetoric. He spoke eloquently about AIDS in his pitches for the gay vote. He insisted that people infected with the AIDS virus, Bob Hattoy and Elizabeth Glaser, speak at the Democratic National Convention. On Election Night, he mentioned AIDS high in his victory speech. It all seemed so promising. David B. Mixner, a Clinton friend who helped rally the gay vote, exclaimed in the flush of a Clinton victory, "I believe thousands of my friends who wouldn't make it, who would die of AIDS, might make it now because Bill Clinton is President."

There it is: the man from Arkansas was to be not just President but savior. He's not. Bogged down early on in a battle over homosexuals in the military, Clinton has grown wary of anything that the public might perceive as a gay issue. He delayed fulfilling his campaign pledge to name an AIDS czar, finally naming her five months into his term—and only when the National Commission on AIDS was about to attack him for not providing leadership on the epidemic.

More than anything else, what the AIDS community wants from Bill Clinton is a sense of urgency. Carol Rasco maintains that Clinton is committed. "Health-care reform and AIDS are the only things I've worked on every day since I got here," said the domestic policy adviser. But others, even in the Administration, think Clinton is doing little to help.

"Other than myself, who lives with AIDS every day, there's no one at the White House for whom this is their first-tier issue," said Bob Hattoy, who, after serving six months as a White House aide often critical of the Administration's AIDS policies, was shifted to the Interior Department. He praised the President and Mrs. Clinton for having "a profoundly sensitive awareness about AIDS," but at the staff level, he said, "AIDS is not on the radar screens at the White House every day." And the political advisers? Hattoy scoffed. "I don't think they'll address AIDS until the Perot voters start getting it."

THE CZAR AND THE PRESS

There was a time when it was thought that the solution to the AIDS crisis could be found in two words: AIDS czar. One omnipotent public figure with the power to marshal funds, direct research, cut through the bureaucracy—in short, to lead a Manhattan Project-size effort to force a cure for AIDS. Kristine M. Gebbie doesn't look like a czar, and she doesn't think of herself as one, either.

At 50, she has the air of the head nurse. There is something at once no-nonsense and fussy about her—her erect posture, her precise and proper answers, her tendency to correct an interviewer's questions. She is what she is—a nurse who worked her way up through the public-health bureaucracy, a divorced mother of three children, who has willed herself to a better lot in life. In 1978 she became the chief health officer of Oregon and then, 11 years later, the chief health officer of Washington State. Her experience with AIDS is primarily as a bureaucrat, as chairman of the Centers for Disease Control's advisory panel on H.I.V. prevention and as a member of the National Commission on AIDS.

Now, she is the AIDS czar—a far cry from the stellar names that AIDS activists had fantasized about: H. Norman Schwarzkopf, Jimmy Carter, C. Everett Koop.

"We wanted 'Jurassic Park,' and we got 'Snow White,' " Larry Kramer likes to say.

"The activists wanted a war on AIDS," Gebbie said, shaking her head. "I am not one of the big names. I am someone who has struggled with systems around this epidemic since the beginning. I think I have a feel for what it takes to bring people together."

Indeed, asked to give her job description, she responded, "consensus builder."

Gebbie, whose official title is national AIDS policy coordinator, sees her job as exactly that—coordinating the various Federal agencies like Defense and Housing and Education in terms of prevention, care and research. Her goal is to have the agencies themselves take over the assault on AIDS, so she sees hers as a short-term job—3 or 5 years, "10 years tops." She expects to take no role in research other than, again, as a coordinator, but not one who independently sets priorities.

And what happened to the eagerly awaited Manhattan Project?

"Manhattan Project?" Gebbie said. "I don't know what that means. Both the Manhattan Project and the Man-on-the-Moon project involved, I think, a much more targeted goal. We know where we'd like to go—fix AIDS—but I'm not sure we can conceptualize what it would take to do that. On the other hand, if what 'Manhattan Project' conveys is: 'The Government is

behind you,' well, if I do my job right, we will target and have energy and direction. What we won't have is somebody in general's stripes who can walk around and order people, 'Drop what you're doing and work on H.I.V.' "

Gebbie advocates distributing condoms to sexually active teen-agers, though not necessarily in the schools. She supports supplying clean needles to drug addicts. She backs "in extreme cases and only as a very last resort" the isolation of people infected with H.I.V. who continue to be sexually irresponsible. "It might be in a hospital or a group home," she said. And she advocates, in theory, and with full civil rights protection, the reporting of names of those with H.I.V. as a public-health technique for making sure connections are made to their partners for counseling and possible treatment.

Kristine Gebbie was not at the top of the Administration's list of candidates for AIDS czar. Most of the medical and private-sector leaders who were approached said they had withdrawn their names for personal reasons. Yet it was clear that they did not regard the post as the all-powerful one it might have been.

"There's this contradiction," said Dr. Mark D. Smith, a San Francisco AIDS expert who discussed the job with the Administration but eventually withdrew, "between the public perception of great responsibility and the reality of no real organizational authority."

Most of those considered said, however, that they might have taken the job as AIDS adviser to the President if Clinton himself had called to convince them. But he didn't. The $112,000-a-year position, which does not require Senate confirmation, was offered to Gebbie in a phone call from Rasco. Gebbie never met the President until the morning of the June 25 news conference to announce her appointment.

To be fair, on that sunny Friday in the Rose Garden when he announced the appointment of Gebbie, the President sounded like the old Bill Clinton, the one in the campaign. He finally did what the activists wanted—he spoke out on AIDS as President. He labeled the virus "one of the most dreaded and mysterious diseases humanity has ever known" and "an epidemic that has already claimed too many of our brothers and sisters, our parents and children, our friends and colleagues."

But the trouble was, no one was listening. Newspapers and the networks reported the naming of Gebbie. But few carried the President's comments on AIDS. Newsweek magazine, in a week-in-the-life-of-the-President piece, didn't even mention the Gebbie announcement. At the news conference, there was only one question on AIDS, and that was directed to Gebbie about her qualifications. Reporters were eager to move on to the real news, like the budget and homosexuals in the military.

AIDS, it seems, had become old news.

"In the early days of AIDS, when knowledge was expanding, there were lots of very compelling things to write about," said Marlene Cimons, who covers AIDS and Federal health policy out of the Washington bureau of The Los Angeles Times. "We were in the infant stages of making policy decisions about AIDS that had unique social and political ramifications. Now it's become harder to find angles. We've written to death most aspects of the disease: AIDS in the classroom. AIDS in the workplace. Testing. They filled the front pages. Now there's a vacuum."

Stuart Shear, a reporter for "The MacNeil/Lehrer Newshour" who covers AIDS, said the conflicts that had made for good stories—the fights between Republican Administrations and AIDS advocates—were gone.

"It's become a pure science story," he said. "When it gets down to the clinical nitty-gritty, that's not what we look at. It's hard to get people to come on and complain about an Administration that's increasing funding."

For her part, Gebbie, who has a budget of just under $3 million and a staff "of four or five"—with 15 to 20 others, she said, in another office—seems to prefer being in the shadows. Her office will not be in the White House but in a building across the street that houses a McDonald's. "My guess," she said, "is that the choice of me makes clear that this isn't intended to be somebody who spends all their time outside rousing people up, but somebody who is prepared to spend a lot of time inside making it work.

"It's very clear how many people really did expect miracles," Gebbie said. "When I give what I know are appropriate answers, I know I sound like a bureaucratic stick-in-the-mud: 'This lady is not worth two bits to us; she talks about coordination and cooperation. Blah!'

"But part of my mission," Gebbie said matter-of-factly, "is to help people keep their expectations within reality."

Gebbie needn't worry. Expectations could hardly be lower. "People are weary and hopeless and sad—the researchers, the activists, the care-givers," John H. Templeton, director of AIDS educational services at Grady Memorial Hospital in Atlanta, told me. "There is this sense that no matter what you do, it's all going to turn out the same in the end."

THE PATIENT AND JOURNALIST

In my interviews for this article and others, I always ask people with AIDS if they expect to die of the disease. One reason for that is a genuine reporter's curiosity; the answer is part of the profile of who they are. But I am also searching for hope for myself. Increasingly, the answers come back the same, even from the most optimistic of Act Up zealots: Yes, we will die of AIDS.

I thought about that the other day in the emergency room at Lenox Hill Hospital. I had taken my boyfriend there for a blood transfusion to offset the anemia caused by the chemotherapy for his Kaposi's sarcoma. I realized on that Sunday morning in the emergency room that the moment of crisis wasn't coming tomorrow or the next day for my boyfriend. It was here today. And it will soon be here today for me, too.

Does that make me angry? Yes. I had such hope when I interviewed Bill Clinton about AIDS and gay issues for this magazine in August 1992. He spoke so eloquently on AIDS. I really did see him as a white knight who might save me. How naive I was to think that one man could make that big a difference. At its core, the problem isn't a government; it's a virus.

Still, in interviews with researchers and Administration officials, it was clear that we are talking from different planets. I need help now, not five years from now. Yet the urgency just wasn't there. Compassion and concern, yes; even sympathy. But urgency, no. I felt alone, abandoned, cheated.

I asked Gebbie what she says to someone with AIDS—in other words, what she says to me. And for one brief moment, there was a glimmer of realization that delay means death.

"I say, 'I hear you and I appreciate the frustration and the sorrow and the loneliness,' " she said. "That can sound trite, but it is genuine. It's inappropriate for me to hold out a false promise to you. It would be easy to say: 'There, there. It will be better soon.' That's a disservice, so I have to be honest with you. We don't have quick answers. I can't tell you when we're going to have a cure."

I am on the cutting edge of drug testing, in a trial at New York Hospital for a new combination therapy: AZT, DDI and nevirapine. That is the combination that drew so much publicity last February when researchers in Boston declared that they had found the combination was effective in inhibiting the virus. But at the Berlin conference, the formulator of the concept, Yung-Kang Chow, a Harvard medical student, reported a flaw in part of the original study. Other researchers challenged the findings after they were unable to confirm the results.

I was surprised at how jealous many of my fellow members of the support group were when I got into the trial—1 of only 25 people accepted out of more than 400 applicants. The group members felt that I had used influence. I had not. Yet admission to these trials is not purely luck, either—a point driven home when a number of leading researchers called, offering to get me into one of the nevirapine trials. I did not take them up on it. If my doctors used influence to get me in, it was not with my knowledge. But I am grateful if they did. The ship is beginning to sink; the water is lapping onto the deck. I am eager for any lifeboat, however leaky.

The letters pour in from readers who know I have AIDS, which I wrote about in this newspaper last December. A Florida woman wrote detailing her son's agonizing death from AIDS. Halfway through the letter, she caught herself, suddenly blurting out, "I don't know why I am writing this to you." Like so many of the letters, it was really not so much for me as for the writer, an excuse to open up her heart and let out the pain. She ended with a line I think of often, a line as much for her dead son, also named Jeffrey, as for me. "I intend this letter," she wrote, "as a mother's hug."

Hardly a day goes by without my getting a letter or call from someone who has the cure for AIDS. Many are crackpots. But others, I'm not so sure. Perhaps I will soon be desperate enough to pursue them.

More and more of the letters are nasty, even cruel. They are still the minority, but they make clear how deep the resentment runs against the attention given AIDS.

"As an average American," a man from Brooklyn wrote in a letter to the editor that made its way to me, "I cannot feel compassion for those who contracted AIDS through the pleasures of homosexuality, promiscuity or drug injection. The advent of the AIDS sickness in the world breaks my heart—but only for those who contracted it from blood transfusion, medical skin pricks or birth. The insipid news stories and other media accounts of AIDS pain, pneumonias and cancers attempt to reach me, but they only turn me off. And I, in turn, turn them off, as I suppose that millions of your readers do. Let's permit these pleasure seekers of the flesh to live out their years in hospices or homes at minimal cost and then die."

Am I bitter? Increasingly, yes. At the Act Up funeral for Bailey in Washington, I thought of how much the anger of the activists mirrored my own. I, too, wanted to shout—at no one really, just to vent the rage. I am dying. Why doesn't someone help us?

I didn't shout. I couldn't. All I could think about on that rainy Thursday afternoon was that a political funeral is not for me. It is at once very noble and very tacky.

What, then, is for me? I usually say that my epitaph is not a phrase but the body of my work. I am writing it with each article, including this one. But actually, there is a phrase that I want shouted at my funeral and written on the memorial cards, a phrase that captures the mix of cynicism and despair that I feel right now and that I will almost certainly take to my grave: Whatever happened to AIDS?

* * *

October 13, 1996

AIDS QUILT OF GRIEF ON CAPITAL MALL

By DAVID W. DUNLAP

WASHINGTON, Oct. 12—A carpet of grief covered the nation's front yard this weekend.

For the first time in the nine-year existence of the AIDS Memorial Quilt, a vast patchwork commemoration of those who have died, the grief was tempered by the growing hope that AIDS might be transformed into a manageable disease through new antiviral drug therapies and genetic research.

But there was no such hope for the family of Craig Steven Rowe of Woodside, Queens. "I'm very angry," said his sister, Renee, of Brooklyn. "I wish they could have found something sooner."

Moments later, she pinned a three-by-six-foot panel honoring her brother, who died last year at the age of 32, alongside those for Andrew J. Stone, who also died last year, and Peter Quinn Loughlin, who died in March.

Since the AIDS quilt was last unfurled in its entirety four years ago, around the base of the Washington Monument, it has grown to more than 39,000 panels, adorned with keenly personal memorabilia like dog tags, blue jeans and a brunette wig. It stretches 11 blocks along the Mall, from the Washington Monument to the Capitol. It is so large that visitors were directed to five different subway stations, depending on which panels they wished to see.

And the showing of the quilt was only one of dozens of events here this weekend in which gay-rights groups and AIDS service organizations demonstrated their growing visibility, even as they lamented their virtual absence from the Presidential campaign. Around the capital, they gathered under many banners.

This evening, as if the night sky had fallen to earth, the Reflecting Pool and Constitution Avenue filled with countless points of flickering light, as marchers with candles walked from the Capitol to the Lincoln Memorial.

Parents, Families and Friends of Lesbians and Gays was honoring Cher and her daughter, Chastity Bono, at its national convention while several hundred members of the National Latino/Latina Lesbian and Gay Organization gathered to discuss AIDS prevention, among other issues, and joined a large Hispanic march that took place today.

The United States Holocaust Memorial Museum celebrated the quick completion of a drive to raise $1.5 million for the study of homosexual victims of Nazism. Across town, Act Up members tried unsuccessfully to enter the Republican Presidential campaign headquarters.

Near the White House, the Human Rights Campaign held a rally to mark National Coming Out Day. AIDS groups, including Mothers' Voices, staged a demonstration today in which participants formed a human chain around the Capitol.

In a counter-event, the conservative Family Research Council marked National Coming Out of Homosexuality Day and announced the establishment of Parents and Friends of Ex-Gays, to carry the message that "no one has to be gay."

Despite all the other events, there was no question that the quilt was the focal point. The Names Project Foundation of San Francisco, which created and maintains the quilt, estimated that 750,000 people might see it during the three-day display, which ends on Sunday, and that 4,000 to 5,000 new panels would be added.

There are no plans to show it again in its entirety, said Greg Lugliani, a spokesman for the Names Project, although that has not been ruled out.

Among the first visitors on Friday were Vice President Al Gore and his wife, Tipper, who also joined in the tradition of reading aloud the names of those who have died from AIDS. Between them, they read 71 names. Then, hand in hand, they strolled slowly along the fabric walkways crisscrossing the quilt.

Later in the day, President Clinton and his wife, Hillary, visited and viewed the quilt for nearly half an hour in the company of Cleve Jones, founder of the Names Project.

It was the highest-level reception that official Washington has ever offered the quilt.

Their visits caused a brief stir but, for the most part, visitors to the quilt were as quiet as if they were at a shrine. Besides the nonstop intonation of names over loudspeakers, and the occasional caws of crows, there were few sounds louder than sniffling, sobbing and sighs.

The impact of the quilt seemed to come as much from small items as from its large scale. Baseball caps are sewn into many panels, along with berets and yarmulkes. There are

Maya Alleruzzo for The New York Times

The AIDS Memorial Quilt in Washington now has more than 37,000 panels commemorating those who have died with the disease. William Caisido, 8, of Miami remembered his aunt Cheryl Doucet yesterday.

denim jackets, leather jackets and sequined jackets and even a two-piece, glen-plaid business suit. Dozens of teddy bears inhabit the quilt, in the company of stuffed rabbits, frogs, giraffes and monkeys. Rainbow flags are much in evidence, symbolizing the gay-rights movement, but there is at least one Cleveland Indian flag, too.

Craig Rowe, the Queens man who died last year, was an artist. He is commemorated by a self-portrait showing him in a crinoline skirt and combat boots. There is also a letter to his sister from the Canadian Government, apologizing for a 1991 incident in which Mr. Rowe was removed from a Montreal-bound train and detained by customs officials who were suspicious because of all the medications he carried.

Mr. Rowe continued his battle with the Canadian immigration office even as he grew debilitated, although he did not live to receive the formal apology. "He held fast to his principles," said his mother, Jean Miller, who came here from Los Angeles.

Mr. Rowe's mother and sister submitted their panel to Names Project volunteers under a tent set up to receive new entries to the quilt.

"It's hard for me to give it up," Mrs. Miller said, "but then again, I want everybody to see it and be proud of what he did."

"There was so much he wanted to do and see," she said. "You wait for the phone to ring to hear his voice. You go to the store and see things he'd like that you want to buy. And then you remember, he's not here."

A contingent of two dozen people from Grand Rapids, Mich., waited in line with Mr. Rowe's family to submit six panels.

One of them contained the name of Scott Roberts, who died last December at the age of 62. "Up until two years ago, my father had hope, but then it was, 'Forget it,'" said Mr. Roberts's daughter, Michele Isaksen, who came with her partner, Robin Hardy.

Jack Welsh, a 61-year-old hardware and plumbing salesman at Sears, traveled from Tulsa, Okla., for the convention of the parents group. He also came to see the panels honoring his son, Michael, who died in Tampa, Fla., in 1992 at the age of 29.

"I never say in terms of his passing that we lost Michael," Mr. Welsh said. "I know where he is."

One quilt bears a lavender rose of moire fabric on a four-foot-long stem. There is a legend—"Michael Scott Welsh, June 15, 1963-Eternity"—and a poem he wrote two months before his death, ending with the exhortation: "It's not too late. I'm still alive. Let's celebrate."

*   *   *

November 10, 1996

WHEN PLAGUES END

By ANDREW SULLIVAN

I.

First, the things I resist remembering, the things that make the good news almost as unbearable as the bad.

I arrived late at the hospital, fresh off the plane. It was around 8:30 in the evening and there had been no light on in my friend Patrick's apartment, so I went straight to the intensive-care unit. When I arrived, my friend Chris's eyes were a reddened blear of fright, the hospital mask slipped down under his chin. I went into the room. Pat was lying on his back, his body contorted so his neck twisted away and his arms splayed out, his hands palms upward, showing the intravenous tubes in his wrists. Blood mingled with sweat in the creases of his neck; his chest heaved up and down grotesquely with the pumping of the respirator that was feeding him oxygen through a huge plastic tube forced down his throat. His greenish-blue feet poked out from under the bedspread, as if separate from the rest of his body. For the first time in all of his illnesses, his dignity had been completely removed from him. He was an instrument of the instruments keeping him alive.

The week before, celebrating his 31st birthday in his hometown on the Gulf Coast of Florida, we swam together in the dark, warm waters that he had already decided would one day contain his ashes. It was clear that he knew something was about to happen. One afternoon on the beach, he got up to take a walk with his newly acquired beagle and glanced back at me a second before he left. All I can say is that, somehow, the glance conveyed a complete sense of finality, the subtlest but clearest sign that it was, as far as he was concerned, over. Within the space of three days, a massive fungal infection overtook his lungs, and at midnight on the fourth day his vital signs began to plummet.

I was in the hall outside the intensive-care room when a sudden rush of people moved backward out of it. Pat's brother motioned to me and others to run, and we sped toward him. Pat's heart had stopped beating, and after one attempt was made to restart it, we intuitively acquiesced, surrounded him and prayed: his mother and father and three brothers, his boyfriend, ex-boyfriend and a handful of close friends. When the priest arrived, each of us received communion.

I remember that I slumped back against the wall at the moment of his dying, reaching out for all the consolation I had been used to reaching for—the knowledge that the final agony was yet to come, the memory of pain that had been overcome in the past—but since it was happening now, and now had never felt so unavoidable, no relief was possible. Perhaps this is why so many of us find it hard to accept that this ordeal as a whole may be over. Because it means that we may now be required to relent from our clenching against the future and remember—and give meaning to—the past.

II.

Most official statements about AIDS—the statements by responsible scientists, by advocate organizations, by doctors—do not, of course, concede that this plague is over. And, in one sense, obviously, it is not. Someone today will be infected with H.I.V. The vast majority of H.I.V.-positive people in the world, and a significant minority in America, will not have access to the expensive and effective new drug treatments now available. And many Americans—especially blacks and Latinos—will still die. Nothing I am saying here is meant to deny that fact, or to mitigate its awfulness. But it is also true—and in a way that most people in the middle of this plague privately recognize—that something profound has occurred these last few months. The power of the newest drugs, called protease inhibitors, and the even greater power of those now in the pipeline, is such that a diagnosis of H.I.V. infection is not just different in degree today than, say, five years ago. It is different in kind. It no longer signifies death. It merely signifies illness.

The reality finally sank in for me at a meeting in Manhattan this summer of the Treatment Action Group, an AIDS advocacy organization. TAG lives and breathes skepticism; a few of its members had lambasted me only nine months before for so much as voicing optimism about the plague. But as soon as I arrived at the meeting—held to discuss the data presented at the just-completed AIDS conference in Vancouver, British Columbia—I could sense something had changed. Even at 8 P.M., there was a big crowd—much larger, one of the organizers told me, than at the regular meetings. In the middle sat Dr. David Ho, a pioneering AIDS researcher, and Dr. Martin Markowitz, who presided over recent clinical trials of the new treatments. The meeting began with Ho and Markowitz revisiting the data. They detailed how, in some trials of patients taking the new protease inhibitors used in combination with AZT and another drug called 3TC, the amount of virus in the bloodstream was reduced on average a hundred- to a thousandfold. To put it another way: Most people with H.I.V. can have anywhere between 5,000 and a few million viral particles per milliliter of their blood. After being treated for a few weeks with the new drugs, and being subjected to the most sensitive tests available, many patients had undetectable levels of the virus in their bloodstreams. That is, no virus could be found. And, so far, the results were holding up.

When Ho finished speaking, the questions followed like firecrackers. How long did it take for the virus to clear from the bloodstream? Was it possible that the virus might still be hiding in the brain or the testes? What could be done for the people who weren't responding to the new drugs? Was there resistance to the new therapy? Could a new, even more lethal viral strain be leaking into the population? The answers that came from Ho and Markowitz were just as insistent. No, this was not a "cure." But the disappearance of the virus from the bloodstream went beyond the expectations of even the most optimistic of researchers. There was likely to be some effect on the virus, although less profound, in the brain or testes, and new drugs were able to reach those areas better. The good news was that H.I.V. seemed primarily to infect cells that have a short half-life, which means that if the virus is suppressed completely for two years or so, the body might have time to regenerate tissue that was "aviremic."

And since the impact of the drugs was so powerful, it was hard for resistance to develop because resistance is what happens when the virus mutates in the presence of the drugs—and there was no virus detectable in the presence of the drugs.

The crowd palpably adjusted itself, and a few chairs squeaked. These are the hard-core skeptics, I remember thinking to myself, and even they can't disguise what is going through their minds. There were caveats, of course. The latest drugs were very new, and large studies had yet to be done. There was already clinical evidence that a small minority of patients, especially those in late-stage disease, were not responding as well to the new drugs and were experiencing a "breakout" of the virus after a few weeks or months. Although some people's immune systems seemed to improve, others' seemed damaged for good. The long-term toxicity of the drugs themselves—their impact on the liver, for example—could mean that patients might undergo a miraculous recovery at the start, only to die from the effects of treatment in later life. And the drugs were often debilitating. I tested positive in 1993, and I have been on combination therapy ever since. When I added the protease inhibitors in March, the nausea, diarrhea and constant fatigue had, at first, been overwhelming.

Still, after the meeting, a slightly heady feeling wafted unmistakably over the crowd. As we spilled out into the street, a few groups headed off for a late dinner, others to take their protease drugs quickly on empty stomachs, others still to bed. It was after 10, and I found myself wandering aimlessly into a bar, where late-evening men in suits gazed up at muscle-boy videos, their tired faces and occasional cruising glances a weirdly comforting return to normalcy. But as I checked my notebook at the door, and returned to the bar to order a drink, something a longtime AIDS advocate said to me earlier that day began to reverberate in my mind. He had been talking about the sense of purpose and destiny he had once felt upon learning he was positive. "It must be hard to find out you're positive now," he had said darkly. "It's like you really missed the party."

III.

Second, the resistance to memory.

At 6 o'clock in the morning in the Roseland Ballroom in Manhattan on a Sunday last spring the crowds were still thick. I had arrived four hours earlier, after a failed attempt to sleep. A chaotic throng of men crammed the downstairs lobby, trying to check coats. There were no lines as such, merely a subterranean, almost stationary mosh-pit, stiflingly hot, full of lean, muscular bodies glacially drifting toward the coat-check windows. This was, for some, the high point of the year's gay male social calendar. It's called the Black Party, one of a number of theme parties held year-round by a large, informal group of affluent, mainly white, gay men and several thousand admirers. It's part of what's been dubbed the "circuit," a series of vast dance parties held in various cities across the country and now a central feature of an emergent post-AIDS gay "life style."

When people feared that the ebbing of AIDS would lead to a new burst of promiscuity, to a return to the 1970's in some joyous celebration of old times, they were, it turns out, only half-right. Although some bathhouses have revived, their centrality to gay life has all but disappeared. What has replaced sex is the idea of sex; what has replaced promiscuity is the idea of promiscuity, masked, in the increasing numbers of circuit parties around the country, by the ecstatic drug-enhanced high of dance music. These are not mass celebrations at the dawn of a new era; they are raves built upon the need for amnesia.

Almost nothing has been written in the mainstream media about these parties, except when they have jutted their way into controversy. A new circuit party, called Cherry Jubilee in Washington, incurred the wrath of Representative Robert Dornan because drugs had been used in a Federal building leased for the event. The annual Morning Party in August on Fire Island, held to raise money for Gay Men's Health Crisis in New York, was criticized on similar grounds by many homosexuals themselves. But in general, these parties have grown in number with a remarkable secrecy, reminiscent of the old, closeted era when completely bifurcated gay lives were the norm. But their explosion on the scene—there are now at least two a month, involving tens of thousands of gay men in cities as diverse as Pittsburgh and Atlanta—is interesting for more than their insight into party culture.

The events are made possible by a variety of chemicals: steroids, which began as therapy for men wasting from AIDS and recently spawned yet another growing sub-subculture of huge body builders; and psychotherapeutic designer drugs, primarily Ecstasy, which creates feelings of euphoria and emotional bonding, and ketamine, an animal anesthetic that disconnects the conscious thought process from the sensory body. On the surface the parties could be taken for a mass of men in superb shape merely enjoying an opportunity to let off steam. But underneath, masked by the drugs, there is an air of strain, of sexual danger translated into sexual objectification, the unspoken withering of the human body transformed into a reassuring inflation of muscular body mass.

As the morning stretched on, my friends and I stood in the recess of a bar as the parade of bodies passed relentlessly by. Beyond, a sea of men danced the early morning through, strobe lights occasionally glinting off the assorted deltoids, traps, lats and other muscles gay men have come to fetishize. At the party's peak—around 5 A.M.—there must have been about 6,000 men in the room, some parading on a distant stage, others locked in a cluster of rotating pecs, embracing one another in a drug-induced emotional high.

For a group of men who have witnessed a scale of loss historically visited only upon war generations, it was a curious spectacle. For some, I'm sure, the drugs helped release emotions they could hardly address alone or sober; for others, perhaps, the ritual was a way of defying their own infections, their sense of fragility or their guilt at survival. For others still, including myself, it was a puzzle of impulses. The need to find some solidarity among the loss, to assert some crazed physicality against the threat of sickness, to release some of the toxins built up over a decade of constant anxiety. Beyond everything, the desire to banish the memories that will not be banished; to shuck off—if only till the morning—the maturity that plague had brutally imposed.

IV.

I talk about this as a quintessentially homosexual experience, not because AIDS is a quintessentially homosexual experience. Across the world, it has affected far, far more heterosexuals than homosexuals; in America, it has killed half as many intravenous drug users as gay men. And its impact has probably been as profound on many heterosexual family members and friends as it has been on the gay men at ground zero of the epidemic. But at the same time, AIDS was and is inextricable from the question of homosexuality in the psyche of America because it struck homosexuals first and from then on became unalterably woven into the deeper and older question of homosexual integration.

In so many ways it was a bizarre turn of events. In the past, plagues were often marked by their lack of discrimination, by the way in which they laid low vast swaths of the population with little regard for station or wealth or sex or religion. But AIDS was different from the beginning. It immediately presented a political as much as a public-health problem. Before homosexuals had even been acknowledged as a central presence in American life, they were suddenly at the heart of a health crisis as profound as any in modern American history. It was always possible, of course, that, with such a lack of societal preparation, America might have responded the way many Latin American and Asian countries responded—with almost complete silence and denial—or that the gay world itself might have collapsed under the strain of its own immolation. But over the long run something somewhat different happened. AIDS and its onslaught imposed a form of social integration that may never have taken place otherwise. Forced to choose between complete abandonment of the gay subculture and an awkward first encounter, America, for the most part, chose the latter. A small step, perhaps, but an enormous catalyst in the renegotiation of the gay-straight social contract.

And an enormous shift in our understanding of homosexuality itself. Too much has been made of the analogy between AIDS and the Jewish Holocaust, and they are, indeed, deeply distinct phenomena. One was an act of calculated human evil, designed to obliterate an entire people from the center of Europe. The other is a natural calamity, singling out a group of despised outsiders by virtue of a freak of nature, and a disease that remained asymptomatic long enough to wipe out thousands before anyone knew what was happening. But in so far as each catastrophe changed forever the way a minority group was viewed by the world, the two have eerie parallels.

The hostility to homosexuals, after all, has far more in common with anti-Semitism than it does with racism. Homosexuals, like Jews, are not, in the psychology of group hatred, despised because they are deemed to be weak or inferior, but precisely because they are neither. Jews and homosexuals appear in the hater's mind as small, cliquish and very powerful groups, antipathetic to majority values, harboring secret contempt for the rest of society and sustaining a ghetto code of furtiveness and disguise. Even the details resonate. The old libel against Jews—that they would drink the blood of Christian children—has an echo today in the bigot's insistence that he has nothing against homosexuals per se, but doesn't want them allowed near his kids. The loathing for each group is closely linked to fear—and the fear is fanned, in many ways, by the distortion of a particular strain in Christian theology.

But that fear was abated, in both cases, by extraordinary contingent historic events. The Holocaust did many things to the structure of anti-Semitism, but in one hideous swoop it helped destroy the myth that Jews were somehow all powerful. The mounds of bodies, the piles of artifacts and the grotesque physical torture that the Jews of Europe suffered did not exactly indicate power. Out of that powerlessness, of course, came a new form of power, in the shape of achieved Zionism. But the idea of Jewish victimhood seared by mass murder into the Western consciousness was seared indelibly—and it remains one of the strongest weapons against the canards of anti-Semitism today.

Similarly, if on a far smaller scale, AIDS has dramatically altered the psychological structure of homophobia. By visiting death upon so many, so young, AIDS ripped apart the notion of subterranean inviolability that forms such a potent part of the fear of homosexuals. As tens of thousands of sons and uncles and brothers and fathers wasted away in the heart of America, the idea that homosexuals maintained a covert power melted into a surprised form of shock and empathy. For some, the old hatreds endured, of course, but for others an unsought and subtle transformation began to take shape. What had once been a strong fear of homosexual difference, disguising a mostly silent awareness of homosexual humanity, became the opposite. The humanity slowly trumped the difference. Death, it turned out, was a powerfully universalizing experience. Suddenly, acquiescence in gay-baiting and gay-bashing became, even in its strongholds, inappropriate at a moment of tragedy. The victimization of gay men by a disease paradoxically undercut their victimization by a culture. There was no longer a need to kick them, when they were already down.

I think this helps explain the change in the American psyche these last 10 years from one of fearful stigmatization of homosexuals to one of awkward acceptance. And it's revealing that the same thing did not really happen to the many other victims of the plague. With inner-city blacks and Latinos, with intravenous drug users, there was no similar cultural transformation, no acceleration of social change. And that was because with these groups, there had never been a myth of power. They had always been, in the majority psyche, a series of unknowable victims. AIDS merely perpetuated what was already understood and, in some ways, intensified it. With gay men, in contrast, a social revolution had been initiated. Once invisible, they were now unavoidable; once powerful subversives, they were now dying sons.

AIDS, then, was an integrator. If the virus separated, death united. But there was a twist to this tale. As the straight world found itself at a moment of awkward reconciliation, the gay world discovered something else entirely. At a time when the integration of homosexuals into heterosexual life had never been so necessary or so profound, the experience of AIDS as a homosexual experience created bonds and loyalties and solidarities that homosexuals had never experienced before. As it forced gay men out into the world, it also intensified the bonds among them; as it accelerated an integration, it forged an even deeper separation. The old question of assimilation versus separatism became strangely moot. Now, both were happening at once—and feeding off the same psychological roots.

I remember the first time I used the word "we" in print in reference to gay men. It was in an article I was writing as I witnessed my first AIDS death—of a stranger I had volunteered to help out in his final months. He was 32 years old when I got to know him, back in 1990. Without AIDS, we would never have met, and the experience changed my sense of gay identity for good. Before then, although I had carefully denied it, I had quietly distanced myself from much of what I thought of as "gay culture." Tom helped to change this.

He was the stereotype in so many ways—the 70's mustache, the Alcoholics Anonymous theology, the Miss America Pageant fan, the college swim coach. But he was also dying. His skin was clammy and pale. His apartment smelled of Maxwell House coffee and disinfectant and the gray liquid that was his constant diarrhea. I remember one day lying down on top of him to restrain him as his brittle, burning body shook uncontrollably with the convulsions of fever. I had never done such a thing to a grown man before, and as I did, the defenses I had put up between us, the categories that until then had helped me make sense of my life and his, these defenses began to crumble into something more like solidarity.

For others, the shift was more dramatic. Their own incipient deaths unleashed the unfiltered rage of the late 1980's, as decades of euphemism and self-loathing exploded into one dark, memorable flash of activism. The fire behind Act-Up was by its very nature so combustible that it soon burned out. But its articulation of a common identity—the unsustainable starkness of its definition of homosexuality—left a residue behind.

And I began to understand the pull of this identity more instinctively. Suddenly, it seemed, as my 20's merged into my 30's, everyone was infected. Faces you had got used to seeing in the gym kept turning up on the obit pages. New friends took you aside to tell you they had just tested positive. Old

flames suddenly were absent from the bars. I remember thinking that a new term was needed for something that was happening to me with increasing frequency: I would be walking along a street and see an old man coming toward me whom I vaguely recognized. And then I would realize that it wasn't an old man; it was someone I knew who had just gone through some bout with pneumonia or some intestinal parasite. Like Scott, a soldier I had got to know as a 220-pound, 6-foot-3-inch, blue-eyed, blond-haired bundle of energy. During the gays-in-the-military affair early in the Clinton Administration, I had urged him to come out to his commanders and troops, sure that the new President would protect him. He told me I had to be out of my mind, and, of course, as it turned out, I was. And then, a few weeks later, he bumped into me on the street and confided the real reason he didn't want to confront anyone. He was H.I.V.-positive and needed the Army's support. He told me with genuine anguish, as if the knowledge of his disease demanded a courage his disease would also have punished.

Then, a mere year later, I saw him with a cane (literally), his spirit completely broken, his body shrunk to 140 pounds, his breath gone after the shortest walk, his eyes welling with the bitterness of physical pain and isolation. His lover of several years somehow endured the ordeal, nursing him every inch of the way, until Scott became a 90-pound skeletal wreck, unable to walk, his hair weak and gray and glassy, his eyes sunken miserably into a scaly face. Scott never fully reconciled with his family. And after Scott died, his lover told me that his last words had been, "Tell my mother I hate her."

When I would tell my straight friends, or my work colleagues or my family, about these things, it wasn't that they didn't sympathize. They tried hard enough. It was just that they sensed that the experience was slowly and profoundly alienating me from them. And they sensed that it was more than just a cultural difference. The awareness of the deaths of one's peers and the sadness evoked and the pain you are forced to witness—not just the physical pain, but all the psychological fear and shame that AIDS unleashed—all this was slowly building a kind of solidarity that eventually eliminated my straight friends from the most meaningful part of my life. There comes a point at which the experience goes so deep that it becomes almost futile to communicate it. And as you communicate less and less and experience more and more, you find yourself gravitating to the people who have undergone the same experiences, the ones who know instinctively, the people to whom you do not have to explain.

I remember the moment when my friend Patrick told me he had AIDS. We had been friends for a long time, yet the meaning of that friendship had never been fully clear to us. But at that moment we were able to look each other in the eye and tell each other we would be there for each other, whatever it took and however hard it became. I don't think I had ever made such a commitment before—to anyone. It survived watching him waste away, seeing him buckled over on the floor, thumping the ground from the pain of his infections; it survived him messing himself in panic as he fumbled with his

IV; it survived his bloody-minded resistance to risky treatments that might have helped him; it survived the horrifying last hours in the intensive-care unit and the awkward silences with his family a year after he passed away. It survives still, as does the need to find a way to give it meaning in his absence.

For a long time I never broke down or cried about any of this—the dozens of acquaintances who have died, the handful of friends I have mourned or resisted mourning, the sudden flashes of panic at the thought of my own mortality. But late one night I caught sight of Senator Bob Kerrey on "Nightline." He was speaking haltingly of his relationship with Lewis Puller, the paralyzed Vietnam veteran who had survived the war, only to ultimately succumb to depression, alcoholism and, finally, suicide. There was in Kerrey's bitter, poignant farewell a sense that only he and a few others would fully understand Puller's anguish. Kerrey grasped, because he had experienced, what it was to face extreme danger and witness in the most graphic way possible the deaths of his closest friends and colleagues, only to come home and find those experiences denied or ignored or simply not understood. And as he spoke, I felt something break inside me. Kerrey knew, as Mark Helprin expressed so beautifully in his novel "A Soldier of the Great War," what almost every gay man, in a subtler, quieter way, has also learned: "The war was still in him, and it would be in him for a long time to come, for soldiers who have been blooded are soldiers forever. They never fit in. . . . That they cannot forget, that they do not forget, that they will never allow themselves to heal completely, is their way of expressing their love for friends who have perished. And they will not change because they have become what they have become to keep the fallen alive."

At the time of this writing, almost three times as many young Americans have died of AIDS as died in the entire Vietnam War.

V.

In Camus's novel "The Plague," the description of how plagues end is particularly masterful. We expect a catharsis, but we find merely a transition; we long for euphoria, but we discover only relief tinged with, in some cases, regret and depression. For some, there is a zeal that comes with the awareness of unsought liberation, and the need to turn such arbitrary freedom into meaningful creation. For many more, there is even—with good reason—a resistance to the good news itself because "the terrible months they had lived through had taught them prudence." The reactions to the news, Camus notes, are "diverse to the point of incoherence." Many refuse to believe that there is any hope at all, burned by dashed expectations one time too many, "imbued with a skepticism so thorough that it was now a second nature." Others found the possibility of an end too nerve-racking to bear and almost dared the plague to kill them before it was too late.

And even now, among friends, there are those who refuse to be tested for a virus that, thanks to the new treatments, might be eliminated from the bloodstream. And there are those who are H.I.V.-positive who are still waiting to take the drugs and are somehow unable to relinquish the notion that being positive is a death sentence that they can endure only alone. And there are those many who, having taken all the drugs they can, have found that for some reason the drugs will not work for them and watch as their friends recover while they still sink into the morass of sickness made all the more bitter by the good news around them. And those more who, sensing an abatement of the pressure, have returned, almost manically, to unsafe sexual behavior, as if terrified by the thought that they might actually survive, that the plague might end and with it the solidarity that made it endurable.

You can already feel, beneath the surface, the fraying of the bonds. A friend in New York, H.I.V.-positive for 10 years, contemplates breaking up with his boyfriend because he suddenly realizes he is going to live. "I felt safe where I was," he tells me. "But now I feel like an attractive person again. It's more what you're radiating inside—the feeling that, finally, you're not a potential burden. I mean, maybe I'm not a potential burden." Another positive friend, this one an AIDS advocate of hardened credentials, feels the meaning of his life slipping away. "At some point, you just have to go on," he says. "You say that was a great period in your life, but it's a big world and at some point you have to find a way to slip back into it and try and be a happy citizen. What I want is a boyfriend I love, a job that doesn't make me crazy and good friends."

But normalcy, of course, is problematic for gay America. The "normalcy" of gay life before AIDS is something few can contemplate and fewer remember. There are ways (the circuit parties) in which that history is repeated as farce, and ways (like the small revival of sex clubs) in which it is repeated as tragedy. But the solidarity of the plague years is becoming harder and harder to sustain. For the first time, serious resentment is brewing among H.I.V.-positive men about the way in which AIDS has slowly retreated from the forefront of gay politics. And among the longest-term survivors, there is a depressing sense that a whole new generation of post-AIDS gay men have no understanding of the profundity with which their own lives have become suffused.

Take John Dugdale, a 36-year-old photographer living in New York, tall and chiseled, with dark hair and even darker eyes. But when Dugdale looks at you these days, he merely looks toward you. Some time ago, he became almost blind from an AIDS-related virus. He took the new drugs, experienced euphoria as they obliterated the virus from his blood, crashed again a few months later as the virus returned, then experienced yet another high as his health improved once more. He knows his own survival is tenuous and is depressed by the shallowness of a culture that is clearly beginning to move on. As we chatted recently, he recalled with not a little edge a particular moment at the Black Party in New York earlier this year. It concerned a friend of his with AIDS, a body builder who still prized himself on being able to consort with the best of the competition. There was one problem: he had lesions on his body, lesions he refused to have treated. And when he took his shirt off that night to dance with the throng, the lesions were all too visible. Not so long ago, they might have been viewed as war medals. Now, they're something different. "This guy came up to him," Dugdale recalled, "and said: 'Would you please put your shirt on? You're ruining it for everybody else.'"

For some, of course, the ebbing of AIDS could mean that the old divisions between H.I.V.-positive and H.I.V.-negative men could heal. With a less catastrophic diagnosis, the difference in life span—and self-definition—between negative and positive men might narrow. But there is also another possibility: that with a smaller and smaller percentage of gay men having H.I.V., the isolation of those infected will actually increase, and that those with full-blown AIDS could feel more intensely alone than before.

Even at the showing of the AIDS Memorial Quilt in Washington this year, the divides were subtly present. There were those who went to see the quilt itself or went to the candlelight vigil and those who went only to the many parties that filled the weekend. (In truth, many went to all.) And the internal tensions were palpable. It is as if many H.I.V.-positive men have emerged from transformingly deep spiritual experiences only to re-enter a culture that seems, at least in part, to be returning to the superficial. And the lifting of the veil of terror has served, paradoxically, only to isolate them still further in a subculture that has less time and less energy to sympathize or understand. The good news from the laboratory has robbed them not simply of the drama and intensity of their existence but also of the recognition of that drama and intensity. And even among their own kind.

VI.

A difference between the end of AIDS and the end of many other plagues: for the first time in history, a large proportion of the survivors will not simply be those who escaped infection, or were immune to the virus, but those who contracted the illness, contemplated their own deaths and still survived. If for some, this leads to bitterness, for others it suggests something else entirely. It is not so much survivor guilt as survivor responsibility. It is the view of the world that comes from having confronted and defeated the most terrifying prospect imaginable and having survived. It is a view of the world that has encompassed the darkest possibilities for homosexual—and heterosexual—existence and now envisions the opposite: the chance that such categories could be set aside, that the humanity of each could inform the humanity of the other.

Greg Scott is a Washingtonian I've known for years. We're both in our early 30's, and as the plague has unfolded over the last decade it has affected us in different ways. Greg is from a traditional Southern family, and when he was thrown out of the Navy for being a homosexual, he threw himself into years of furious activism. When I first came to know him, he was renowned in D.C. for hanging around bars and staring wildly at passers-by as a prelude to either lecturing or seducing them. For a short period of time, he would follow me around D.C. screaming "Collaborator!" to punish me for the sin of writing or voicing politically incorrect views. But we both knew, at some level, that we were in the epidemic to-

gether, and so when I saw him slowly declining over the last two years, I felt a part of myself declining as well. My friend Pat once described Greg as "hanging by the same length of rope" as he was, so for some time I half-expected to see Greg's face in the crowded obituary columns of the local gay paper along with the dozens of other faces I had known or seen over the years. When I wrote an op-ed piece a year ago hailing the latest breakthroughs in AIDS research, Greg came up to me in a bar and regaled me. "This is not a survivable disease!" he yelled over the music. "What do you know about it, anyway?"

So I learned to avoid Greg as far as I could. I never relished our meetings. Since he didn't know I was positive, too, our conversations had this false air about them. The solidarity I felt was one I could not fully express, and it ate away at me. I occasionally spotted him walking his dog in the neighborhood, his body, always thin, now skeletal, his large, staring eyes disfigured by lesions, his gait that of a 60-year-old. When my parents visited, I pointed him out from a distance on the street, in some doomed attempt to help them understand: "See. That's my friend Greg." Read: "See. That's my friend Greg. Do you see what this is doing to us?" Last fall, Greg was taking morphine twice a day. He was on a regimen of 60 pills a day and was virtually bedridden. So when I caught sight of him five months ago, I literally jumped.

I had grown used to the shock of seeing someone I knew suddenly age 20 or 30 years in a few months; now I had to adjust to the reverse. People I had seen hobbling along, their cheekbones poking out of their skin, their eyes deadened and looking down, were suddenly restored into some strange spectacle of health, gazing around as amazed as I was to see them alive. Or you'd see them in the gym, skin infections still lingering, but their muscles slowly growing back, their skull-faces beginning to put on some newly acquired flesh. This is what Greg now looked like, his round blue eyes almost tiny in his wide, pudgy face, his frame larger than I remembered it: bulky, lumbering, heavy.

In one of those bizarre coincidences, I bumped into him the day I quit my job as editor of The New Republic. He was one of the first people I was able to tell, and from the minute I spoke to him, I could tell he was changed. The anger was somehow gone; a calm had replaced it. He seemed to understand intuitively why I might want to take time to rethink my life. As we parted, we hugged awkwardly. This was a new kind of solidarity—not one of painful necessity, but of something far more elusive. Hope, perhaps? Or merely the shared memory of hopelessness?

Since then, I've become used to Greg's describing the contours of what he calls his "second life." And he describes its emergence in a way that is shared by more people than just him. The successive physical and material losses of his illness stripped him, he recalls, of everything he once had, and allowed him, in a way that's unique to the terminally ill, to rebuild himself from scratch. "There were times I was willing to accept that it was over," he says. "But things were never fully tied up. There were too many things I had done wrong, things I wanted to amend, things I still wanted to do. I was hanging on tenaciously out of some moral judgment of myself because I knew I hadn't got it right the first time."

In his progressive illness, Greg had lost first his energy, then his ability to digest food, then his job, then his best friend and then most of his possessions, as he sold them off to pay for medications. But he hung on. "In the early days," he remembers, "I couldn't imagine going through all that to stay alive. My friend Dennis would say that I'd never go that far. But then he died. Looking back, it's absurd the lengths I went to. I'd never realized I cared so much about myself." (Greg's story brings to mind that of another friend: his illness finally threatened his sight, and he had to decide whether to pursue a treatment that involved an injection of a liquid directly into the eyeball. In other words, he had to watch as the needle came closer and closer and finally penetrated his eye. I remember asking him how on earth he could go through with it. "But I want to see," he told me.)

"When you're in bed all day, you're forced to consider what really matters to you," Greg elaborates. "When the most important thing you do in a day is your bowel movement, you learn to value every single source of energy. You go into yourself and you feel different from other people, permanently different." Some gains are subtle. "It sparked a new relationship with my grandmother. Like me, she was suddenly finding she couldn't drive her car anymore, so we bonded in a way we'd never bonded before. You suddenly see how people are valuable. I mean, if you're healthy, who has time for this old lady? And suddenly this old lady and I have so much in common. And I still have that. That's a gain. I have an appreciation and love for her that I never fully had before." Some gains are even more profound. "My grandfather would say, 'You don't squeak under the bottom wire unless you're meant to.' And I feel that there's this enormous responsibility on me that I've never felt before. And it's a pleasant responsibility. I mean, lay it on me."

Responsibility is, perhaps, an unusual word for Greg to be using, and until AIDS it was not one usually associated with homosexuality. Before AIDS, gay life—rightly or wrongly—was identified with freedom from responsibility, rather than with its opposite. Gay liberation was most commonly understood as liberation from the constraints of traditional norms, almost a dispensation that permitted homosexuals the absence of responsibility in return for an acquiescence in second-class citizenship. This was the Faustian bargain of the pre-AIDS closet: straights gave homosexuals a certain amount of freedom; in return, homosexuals gave away their self-respect. But with AIDS, responsibility became a central, imposing feature of gay life. Without it, lovers would die alone or without proper care. Without it, friends would contract a fatal disease because of lack of education. Without it, nothing would be done to stem the epidemic's wrath. In some ways, even the seemingly irresponsible outrages of Act-Up were the ultimate act of responsibility. They came from a conviction that someone had to lead, to connect the ghetto to the center of the country, because it was only by such a connection that the ghetto could be saved.

And in the experience of plague, what Greg felt on a personal level was repeated thousands of times. People who thought they didn't care for one another found that they could. Relationships that had no social support were found to be as strong as any heterosexual marriage. Men who had long since got used to throwing their own lives away were confronted with the possibility that they actually did care about themselves and wanted to survive and failed to see themselves as somehow inferior to their heterosexual peers. A culture that had been based in some measure on desire became a culture rooted in strength. Of course, not everyone experienced such epiphanies. Some cracked; others died bitter or alone. Many failed to confront the families and workplaces and churches in ways that would have helped provide the capacity to survive. But many others did. And what didn't destroy them made them only more resistant to condescension.

And as gay culture shifted in this way, so did gay politics. The radicalism of Act-Up segued into the radicalism of homosexuals in the military and same-sex marriage. From chipping away at the edges of heterosexual acceptance, suddenly the central ramparts were breached. Once gay men had experienced beyond any doubt the fiber of real responsibility—the responsibility for life and death, for themselves and others—more and more found it impossible to acquiesce in second-class lives. They demanded full recognition of their service to their country, and equal treatment under the law for the relationships they had cherished and sustained in the teeth of such terror. AIDS wasn't the only thing that created this transformation of gay demands, but it was surely linked to them at a deep psychological level.

Plagues and wars do this to people. They force them to ask more fundamental questions of who they are and what they want. Out of the First World War came women's equality. Out of the second came the welfare state. Out of the Holocaust came the state of Israel. Out of cathartic necessity and loss and endurance comes, at least for a while, a desire to turn these things into something constructive, to appease the trauma by some tangible residue that can give meaning and dignity to what has happened. Hovering behind the politics of homosexuality in the midst of AIDS and after AIDS is the question of what will actually be purchased from the horror. What exactly, after all, did a third of a million Americans die for? If not their fundamental equality, then what?

VII.

Last, the things I want to remember.

In the past six months, I have begun to believe I will live a normal life. By normal, of course, I don't mean without complications. I take 23 pills a day—large cold pills I keep in the refrigerator, pills that, until very recently, made me sick and tired in the late afternoon. But normal in the sense that mortality, or at least the insistence of mortality, doesn't hold my face to the wall every day. I mean I live with the expectation that life is not immediately fragile; that if I push it, it will not break.

It is a strange feeling this, and a little hard to communicate. When you have spent several years girding yourself for the possibility of death, it is not so easy to gird yourself instead for the possibility of life. What you expect to greet with the euphoria of victory comes instead like the slow withdrawal of an excuse. And you resist it. The intensity with which you had learned to approach each day turns into a banality, a banality that refuses to understand or even appreciate the experience you have just gone through.

Of course, I remember feeling this banality before and I remember the day it ended. I remember the doctor offering me a couple of pieces of candy, before we walked back into his office and he fumbled a way of telling me I was H.I.V.-positive. I've thought about that moment a lot in the past few months. When my doctor called recently to tell me that my viral load was now undetectable, part of me wanted to feel as if that first moment of mortality had been erased. But, of course, that moment can never be erased. And not simply because I cannot dare hope that one day the virus might be wiped completely from my system, but because some experiences can never be erased. Blurred, perhaps, and distanced, but never gone for good. And, in fact, beneath the sudden exhilaration, part of me also wants to keep the moment alive, since it allowed me to see things that I had never been able to see before.

I saw, to begin with, that I was still ashamed. Even then—even in me, someone who had thought and worked and struggled to banish the stigma and the guilt and the fear of my homosexuality—I instinctively interpreted this illness as something that I deserved. Its arrival obliterated all the carefully constructed confidence in my own self-worth. It showed me in a flash how so much of that achievement had been illusory—how, in a pinch, I still loathed and feared an inextricable part of who I was.

The diagnosis was so easily analogized to my sexuality not simply because of how I got it but also because it was so confoundingly elusive. I felt no sickness. I had no symptoms. There was nothing tangible against which I could fight—no perceptible, physical ailment that medicine could treat. So it seemed less like an illness than like some amorphous, if devastating, condition of life. Suddenly, it existed as my homosexuality had always existed, as something no one from the outside could glean, something I alone could know and something that always promised a future calamity.

For days after my diagnosis, I went through periodic, involuntary shaking spasms. My head literally sank onto my chest; I found it hard to look up or see where I was going. The fear of death and sense of failure—and the knowledge that there was nothing I could do to escape this awareness—kept me staring at the sidewalk. At night, asleep, exhaustion gave way to anxiety as panic woke me up. And then, one morning, a couple of weeks later, after walking with a friend to get some coffee and muffins for breakfast, I realized in the first few sips of coffee that for a few short seconds of physical pleasure, I had actually forgotten what had just happened

to me. I realized then that it was going to be possible to forget, that the human mind could find a way to absorb the knowledge that we are going to die and yet continue to live as if we are not. I experienced in some awful, concentrated fashion what I used to take for granted.

From then on, I suppose, I began the journey back. I realized that my diagnosis was no different in kind than the diagnosis every mortal being lives with—only different in degree. By larger and larger measures, I began to see the condition not as something constricting, but as something liberating—liberating because it forced me to confront more profoundly than ever before whether or not my sexuality was something shameful (I became convinced that it was not), and liberating because an awareness of the inevitability of death is always the surest way to an awareness of the tangibility of life.

And unlike so many others who are told they are going to die, and so many people who had been told they were H.I.V.-positive before me, I had time and health and life ahead. In one way, as I still lost friend after friend, and as others lived with griefs that would never be expunged, I experienced this with a certain amount of guilt. But also, as someone graced by the awareness of a fatal disease but not of its fatality, a heightened sense of the possibilities of living. I realized I could do what I wanted to do, write what I wanted to write, be with the people I wanted to be with. So I wrote a book with a calm I had never felt before about a truth I had only belatedly come to believe. The date I inscribed in its preface was two years to the day since my diagnosis: a first weapon against the virus and a homage to its powers of persuasion.

And for a precious short time, like so many other positive people, I also sensed that the key to living was not a concentration on fighting the mechanics of the disease (although that was essential) or fighting the mechanics of life (although that is inevitable), but an indifference to both of their imponderables. In order to survive mentally, I had to find a place within myself where plague couldn't get me, where success or failure in such a battle were of equal consequence. This was not an easy task. It required resisting the emotional satisfaction of being cured and the emotional closure of death itself. But in that, of course, it resembled merely what we all go through every day. Living, I discovered for the second, but really the first, time, is not about resolution; it is about the place where plague can't get you.

Only once or twice did I find that place, but now I live in the knowledge of its existence.

So will an entire generation.

Andrew Sullivan, a senior editor at The New Republic, is the author of "Virtually Normal: An Argument About Homosexuality."

* * *

PART VI

REDEFINING THE FAMILY

CHANGING NOTIONS OF FAMILY

April 27, 1989

HOW TO DEFINE A FAMILY: GAY TENANT FIGHTS EVICTION

By PHILIP S. GUTIS

ALBANY, April 26—For Miguel Brashi and Leslie Blanchard, two gay men who lived together for more than a decade, the one-bedroom apartment on East 54th Street in Manhattan was the focal point of their lives. Now, two and a half years after Mr. Blanchard's death, the apartment is at the center of a legal battle as Mr. Brashi fights eviction in a case that could be precedent-setting.

Beyond the immediate issue of who is entitled to live in a rent-controlled apartment after the tenant of record dies, the case before the Court of Appeals, New York State's highest court, revolves around the broader constitutional question of how to define a family.

In oral arguments before the court today, lawyers for Mr. Brashi and Stahl Associates, the owner of the building, met detailed questioning about the case, which has drawn friend-of-the-court briefs supporting Mr. Brashi from the City of New York, the City Bar Association, the Legal Aid Society, several religious leaders, AIDS-care providers and many homosexual-rights organizations. No organization filed supporting briefs for the landlord.

Shortage of Housing

City officials say the case is particularly important because of the city's housing shortage and the rapidly growing number of people with AIDS and the AIDS-related complex.

How to define a family is becoming an increasingly important issue around the country as governments struggle to determine how unrelated people living together—like gay couples, the handicapped, the elderly or group homes of single people—fit into existing laws and regulations.

Under rent-control guidelines, a landlord may not evict either the "surviving spouse of the deceased tenant or some other member of the deceased tenant's family who has been living with the tenant."

In court papers, Mr. Brashi, who is represented by the American Civil Liberties Union, said his long-term relationship as Mr. Blanchard's "gay life partner" makes him eligible to remain in the apartment. According to the court documents, the two men had entwined their lives—sharing their business,

their friends, checking accounts and vacations—until Mr. Blanchard's death of AIDS in September 1986.

'Their Family Home'

In his presentation today, William B. Rubenstein, a staff counsel for the A.C.L.U.'s Lesbian and Gay Rights Project, asked the court to protect "tenants who have made a rent-controlled apartment their family home."

In its brief, the Legal Aid Society says its civil division has faced an increasing number of eviction cases in the last decade in which many of the poor clients "live in loving and committed relationships functioning in every way as a family without regard to consanguinity or legal ceremony."

Lawyers for Stahl Associates, which owns the building on East 54th Street, assert that Mr. Brashi is not entitled to stay in his apartment because he is not related by either blood or marriage to the tenant of record, Mr. Blanchard.

In their court papers, Stahl Associates stressed a different constitutional question—whether unrelated people may, in effect, inherit property that belongs to others "such as the rent-controlled apartment at issue in this litigation."

"We submit that they may not," they said.

Dean G. Yuzek, a lawyer with Shea & Gould who is representing Stahl Associates, said the court must "balance the competing interest of landlord against tenant."

'Love and Fidelity'

Although Mr. Brashi declined to be interviewed, the court papers outline a story of a couple that, as the Appellate Division of State Supreme Court said, "had a long-term relationship marked by love and fidelity for each other."

The two men met in 1975 and Mr. Brashi soon moved into Mr. Blanchard's apartment on 54th Street.

"For more than 10 years in which Brashi and Blanchard lived together, they regarded one another, and were regarded by friends and family, as spouses," the court papers say.

The issue of gay partners and rent control has been tried in lower courts in recent years, with varying results, but this is the first time it has reached the State Court of Appeals. Although recognizing the long-term relationship between the two men, the Appellate Division in August 1988 overturned a lower-court decision that ruled in Mr. Brashi's favor. The Appellate Division's ruling said Mr. Brashi's lawyers had not persuasively proved that the Legislature intended to give protection under rent-control laws to "nontraditional family relationships."

A 1984 Decision

On the question of homosexual couples, the Appellate Division noted that gay partners "cannot yet legally marry or enter into legally recognized family relationships," like adoption. The court also referred to a 1984 decision by the Court of Appeals, in which the judges rejected a gay man's attempt to adopt his partner.

In that decision, the Court of Appeals said it was up to the Legislature "as a matter of public policy" to grant some form of legal status to a homosexual relationship.

While supporters of Mr. Brashi in the case are looking to the court to make a bold statement on gay rights, the case is in some ways more an extension of a Court of Appeals decision last month overturning a Brookhaven, L.I., zoning ordinance that prevented more than four unrelated people from living together in a single-family home.

In that decision, the court said a restriction on the number of unrelated people living together as a "functionally equivalent family" violated the State Constitution's requirement for due process.

Many organizations are hoping that the Court of Appeals will continue to move forward in broadening what qualifies as a family under state law. "While still perceived as an ideal for many, the nuclear family as the standard is now a myth," a court brief filed by religious leaders and several other interested organizations said.

'No Real Alternative'

Homosexuals cannot legally marry, which is why the issue has become a chief goal of the gay-rights movement. Although courts have been reluctant to, in effect, make a policy decision by giving gay partners certain legal rights, some advocates in the case suggest that the courts must begin to act soon because the Legislature won't.

"There may be no real alternative to a declaration of new policy from the court," said Thomas B. Stoddard, executive director of the Lambda Legal Defense and Education Fund, a gay-rights organization.

"They are dealing with a class of people who are underrepresented in the Legislature," he said, "who do not have a strong voice in the democratically elected branches of government and who need the assistance and recognition of the judicial branch to have basic necessities of life preserved for them."

* * *

November 7, 1989

GAY TEACHERS SUE FOR BENEFITS FOR LONGTIME COMPANIONS

By PHILIP S. GUTIS

When Ronald Madson applied to the New York City Board of Education to have his live-in companion covered by

The New York Times/Dith Pran

Ronald Madson, left, and his partner of 20 years, Richard Dietz, in their apartment in Brooklyn Heights. Mr. Madson joined a suit contending the city discriminated over marital status and sexual orientation after Mr. Dietz was denied coverage under Mr. Madson's health insurance.

his health insurance, the rejection arrived as a scribbled note across the top of the application, "Only married spouses can obtain these benefits."

Mr. Madson, a 43-year-old art teacher in an elementary school in Brooklyn, was not surprised. He and his companion of 20 years, Richard Dietz, knew that their request, like those of other gay couples, would be denied. The application was merely a formality necessary to join a discrimination suit by the Gay Teachers Association on behalf of two other teachers and their partners.

The suit, filed last year, contends that the city's health-benefits policies violate the State Constitution by discriminating against some workers based on marital status and sexual orientation.

"The city is being unfair," Mr. Madson said. "More important to us than the money is the recognition that gay people do form valid families."

Up to 16% of Compensation

The case, which is being watched by cities and private employers around the country, is the latest challenge to government and society's concept of what constitutes a family.

Also at issue are millions of dollars in health-insurance benefits. The benefits can amount to an average of 16 percent of an employee's total compensation, according to research groups. New York City spends $800 million a year on employees' health benefits.

For many gay couples—and their employers—the importance of health benefits has increased because of AIDS and related illnesses, which often involve long and expensive treatments.

The suit, which is before Justice Karla Moskowitz of State Supreme Court in Manhattan, may have received a boost after the Court of Appeals, the state's highest court, ruled in July that two gay men who lived together for a decade could be considered a family under the city's rent-control regulations.

In docmuents filed in the teachers' case, the city argued that the teachers did not meet state and city requirements for proving discrimination.

'We Are Constrained'

Lawyers for the city also argued that a 1936 state law, as well as a pending provision of the Federal income-tax laws, prohibited the city from offering health-insurance benefits to unmarried partners. Finally, the city lawyers argued that health benefits were arranged through collective bargaining and should not be set by the courts.

"The city has been one of the leaders in providing benefits to the gay community," a lawyer in the Corporation Counsel's office, Thomas B. Roberts, said. "In this area, we are constrained by state and Federal laws."

The Lambda Legal Defense Fund, which represents the teachers, asked Justice Moskowitz to reject the city's request for a dismissal of the case and order it to provide the health benefits.

"Clearly, civil rights are not a mere bargaining chip with which to gain leverage in labor negotiations," the teachers said in the court papers. "It is only because the city sees gay men and lesbians as a uniquely vulnerable target for irrational bias and prejudice that it would dare invite this court to countenance such patent nonsense."

Definition of Partners

The city's case has been complicated by a friend-of-the-court brief it filed in the rent-control case and an executive order that Mayor Edward I. Koch issued in July to allow city employees to take paid bereavement leaves when their unmarried partners died.

In the gay teachers' case, the city's lawyers argued that even if the city were permitted to offer insurance to the unmarried partners, it would be financially and administratively burdensome to do so. In providing such coverage, the city had argued, it would "face the impossibly difficult problem of defining 'domestic partner.'"

Since Mr. Koch's order, however, the city has backed off that position. In his order, Mr. Koch defined domestic partners as two people who have a "close and committed personal relationship involving shared responsibilities" who have lived together a year or more.

Restriction From 1936 Law

The practical considerations in the case revolve around the state insurance and Federal income-tax laws cited by the city. But because Congress is expected to kill the Federal measure, the primary question appears to be the state law. The city says the 1936 law regulating insurers offering group health policies only allows benefits for employees, their married partners and children and other possibly nonrelated people who depend on the insured person for most of their financial support.

The teachers' lawyers argue instead that the Legislature did not intend to limit the people who could receive coverage. The law just includes family members as examples, they contend.

Like the two other couples in the suit—Ruth Berman and Connie Kurtz, and a woman listed as Jane Doe and her unidentified partner—Mr. Madson and Mr. Dietz, 42, have said in court papers they would have married if the state had permitted them to do so. "We'll be celebrating our 20th anniversary together this June," Mr. Madson said.

The two men are covered by separate insurance plans. However, Mr. Madson said, that was not always the case. "Years ago, we had our own store, which Richard worked in full-time while I was teaching," he said. "Over that time we spent thousands and thousands of dollars on health insurance for Richard that a heterosexual couple would not have had to worry about."

* * *

September 21, 1990

SUIT OVER DEATH BENEFITS ASKS, WHAT IS A FAMILY?

By TAMAR LEWIN

In what is apparently the first Federal lawsuit of its kind, the surviving lesbian partner of a deceased A.T.&T. employee has charged the company with discrimination for refusing to pay her the same death benefits it would have paid to a husband.

Sandra Rovira, who filed the suit, says her life with Marjorie Forlini, an A.T.&T. manager who died of cancer two years ago, was as much a marriage as any heterosexual union. The women had even formalized their relationship in a 1977 ceremony for relatives and friends, and they exchanged rings and vows.

"Margie and I bought a house together and raised my kids together, and when she was sick, I washed her, I went to the doctors with her, I prayed with her," said Ms. Rovira, 42 years old, of New Rochelle, N.Y., who was married before she met Ms. Forlini. "She died in my arms. But when I called A.T.&T., they treated me as if I was nothing and our whole relationship was nothing. It was so humiliating. We were a family like any other family, and we deserved to be treated like one."

'Someone Who's Hurting'

A.T.&T. says its benefits are for legal spouses only, and since the law does not recognize homosexual unions, it does not either. "We recognize that this is someone who's hurting, but this was not a legally protected marriage," said Maureen Lynch, an A.T.&T. spokeswoman.

With more homosexual couples living openly in long-term relationships, the question of what constitutes a family is becoming a pressing one—for the courts and for employers, whose benefits policies are coming under attack.

Over the last five years, many cities have recognized "domestic partnerships" for some limited purposes. And many other efforts to have the benefits of marriage extended to domestic partners are under way, in legislatures and in the courts.

The changing status of domestic partnerships also affects unmarried heterosexual couples, who face similar problems in obtaining health insurance and death benefits. But unmarried heterosexual couples have the option of getting married.

"I think there will be broader recognition of domestic partnerships in the next five years, at least in large cities," said Nan Hunter, a professor at Brooklyn Law School and former director of the American Civil Liberties Union's Lesbian and Gay Rights Project. "The law is not very well developed yet, but I expect that there will be more cases in a variety of contexts, asserting that where a nontraditional couple's relationship functions as a marriage, it should be treated as a marriage."

Issues to Be Settled

But even for those sympathetic to the concept, nettlesome questions remain. For while marriage is a clearly defined status, there is no consensus about what constitutes a domestic partnership. Do the partners have to live together? And, if so, for how long? Must they contract to be responsible for each other's support? Or is a simple affirmation of a committed relationship enough? And should there be a formal process for dissolving the partnership?

The question of what constitutes a family comes up in many areas, including housing rights and sick leave plans:

In 1989, New York's highest court ruled that a gay couple was legally considered a family under New York City's rent control laws. At the same time, the city board of education is being sued by gay teachers seeking health insurance for their domestic partners.

Municipal employees in several cities, including Los Angeles, Madison, Wis., and Berkeley, Calif., are entitled to sick leave to care for a domestic partner, or bereavement leave to attend the partner's funeral. A law with similar provisions was adopted, then overturned by a referendum, in San Francisco, and will soon be back on the ballot. And in Seattle, a law was passed giving benefits to city employees' partners, but it now faces an active repeal initiative.

A few unions and municipalities, and a handful of private employers, including the American Psychological Association, The Village Voice and Ben & Jerry's Homemade Inc., the Vermont-based ice cream company, offer health insurance to the domestic partners of their employees or members. But the Internal Revenue Service recently ruled that the cost of insurance premiums is taxable income for the domestic partner.

Several places, including West Hollywood, Calif., Ithaca, N.Y., and Madison, allow all residents, not just municipal employees, to register domestic partnerships with the municipal clerks. Because private employers are not compelled by law to offer benefits to domestic partners, registering might not result in any tangible benefits, but it might help to establish the right to family membership rates at the local Y, or to visiting privileges when one partner is hospitalized.

Many experts on family law and domestic partnerships see such registrations as a necessary first step toward the widespread recognition of domestic partnerships. And, they say, homosexual partners are not the only ones who stand to gain.

"People may think of this as primarily a gay issue, but in the places where domestic partnerships are being recognized, the majority of those who take advantage of it are unmarried heterosexual couples," said Arthur Leonard, a New York Law School professor who writes a newsletter on gay issues.

Many municipalities that have been offering benefits to domestic partners agree, saying that about half the participants are unmarried heterosexuals.

Despite the new policies of a few employers and municipalities, advocates for gay people say changing something as fundamental as society's concept of a family is not quick work.

"It's a real uphill battle," said Paula Ettelbrick, legal director of the Lambda Legal Defense and Education Fund, a New York-based gay rights advocacy group, and the lawyer who is representing Ms. Rovira against A.T.&T. "We're talking about overhauling a whole system that was based on the 1930's family consisting of a male wage-earner, a nonworking wife and some kids."

Lag in Benefits Programs

Ms. Ettelbrick said the A.T.&T. case, filed last month in Federal District Court in Manhattan, is a perfect example of how changes in social realities have outpaced employer benefits.

"They have a corporate policy that, like a lot of corporate policies, says they don't discriminate on the basis of sexual orientation or marital status," said Ms. Ettelbrick. "But gay and lesbian employees can't get married, so because of their sexual orientation, they're denied the benefits that spouses get, even though, where there's a death, they have the same needs as any other family that's lost a wage-earner."

Experts say private employers have been reluctant to expand benefit packages to include domestic partners. "It's a trend in the public sector much more than in the private sector," said Stephanie Poe, a spokeswoman for the Employee Benefit Research Institute, a nonprofit research group based in Washington. "In this economic climate most employers are not expanding their benefits and would bring in domestic partners only with extensive cost controls, such as imposing waiting periods." She added that they might exclude pre-existing medical conditions, and might refuse to cover those at high risk of serious illness, like those infected with the AIDS virus.

"We talk to employers and unions and insurance companies and the question that always comes up is, where do you draw the line," said Thomas F. Coleman, who heads the Los Angeles-based Family Diversity Project, a nonprofit research and education group. "Having a registration system is very helpful in providing some evidence that the people are not just making it up at the last minute when they want something, but that they have considered themselves a family, and held themselves out as a family all along."

Ms. Forlini and Ms. Rovira clearly considered themselves a family, intermingling their lives and finances for the 12 years before Ms. Forlini's death. Frank and Alfred, Ms. Rovira's two sons, lived with them from the time they were 11 and 8, and Ms. Forlini claimed one or both of them as dependents on her tax returns for many years.

Ms. Rovira took care of Ms. Forlini while she was ill. And when Ms. Forlini died, in 1988, Ms. Rovira and Frank were the ones with her.

The A.T.&T. benefits plan for managers provides for a year's pay to the spouse and unmarried dependent children under 23 of an employee who dies of an illness. In addition, the plan says A.T.&T. may, at its discretion, pay some benefit to other relatives who have been dependent on the employee.

Ms. Forlini's lawsuit seeks damages "in excess of $75,000." The suit says the company breached its own policy of not discriminating on the basis of sexual orientation or marital status and in so doing violated the Federal pension laws.

'Not for People Like Me'

"I was Margie's executor, and when I was going through her personal things, I saw the pension and benefits book," said Ms. Rovira, who works as a lawyer for the Legal Aid Society. "At first I just put it away, but then I thought I certainly felt like a spouse, so I would call A.T.&T. and ask. Their reaction was that I was being ridiculous, that this was not for people like me. Then as I thought more, I said that even if I didn't qualify, my children probably would."

Ms. Rovira said A.T.&T. told her over the phone that there was no application for benefits and that she would not qualify. Ms. Rovira said she then sent the company a formal request for death benefits, along with extensive documentation of her relationship with Ms. Forlini. She said A.T.&T. did not acknowledge receiving her request until weeks later, when she called to inquire about its status and was told that her claim had been rejected.

A spokeswoman for A.T.&T. said the denial of benefits does not violate the company policy of not discriminating on the basis of sexual orientation or marital status.

"If we have a benefit for spouses and you don't have a spouse, that doesn't mean we've discriminated on the basis of marital status," said Maureen Lynch, of A.T.&T. "If you're single, you're not being discriminated against, you just don't have anybody who's eligible for that benefit. And from a philanthropic standpoint, A.T.&T. has done a lot for the gay community, and is widely considered a very good place for gay people to work."

* * *

March 24, 1991

VISITATION CASE COULD REDEFINE PARENTHOOD

By KEVIN SACK
Special to The New York Times

ALBANY, March 23—In a case that could set a national precedent by creating a new legal definition of parenthood,

New York State's highest court is considering whether to grant visitation rights to a lesbian who wants to spend time with the son of her former female companion.

The Court of Appeals, which was the first top state court in the nation to rule that a gay couple could legally qualify as a family, heard arguments in the case on Wednesday.

Although the seven-member court has been a pioneer in adapting the law to changes in society, several judges made it clear through their questions to lawyers that they are uneasy about the broad implications of the visitation case. They asked repeatedly whether the basic principles of child support would have to be changed if they tinker with the legal definition of parenthood.

"How would we not be fundamentally redefining the term 'parent' throughout the statutory law and the case law of the State of New York?" asked Associate Judge Judith S. Kaye.

Virginia M. and Alison D.

State legislatures have been reluctant to write new laws concerning the life-styles of unmarried couples, homosexual and heterosexual. That has increasingly left the courts to update laws on adoption, child custody, tenancy and workplace benefits.

The visitation case involves two women, known in court papers only as Virginia M. and Alison D., who jointly planned the child's conception through the artificial insemination of Virginia. The two merged their last names to create the boy's surname and reared the child in Poughkeepsie from his birth in 1981 until their separation in 1983.

When the relationship ended with Alison moving out, the women agreed to a schedule that allowed her regular visits with the child. But four years later, when Virginia became increasingly unhappy about her former companion's relationship with her son, she ended contact between the two.

In 1988, a Dutchess County Supreme Court judge ruled that Alison did not have the right to see the boy because state law limits visitation rights in most cases to parents, grandparents and siblings.

What Defines Parenthood?

Justice James D. Benson wrote that previous Court of Appeals rulings suggested that "the biological parent of the child is the parent within the meaning of the statute." The Appellate Division of State Supreme Court affirmed Justice Benson's ruling last March.

With an estimated 10,000 children nationwide being reared by lesbians, similar cases are winding through the courts in other states. In California, a midlevel appeals court ruled last week that a lesbian could not petition for custody or visitation rights to a former companion's child.

New York is the only state where a visitation case has been argued before a state's highest tribunal. Alison is asking the Court of Appeals to declare that she is functioning as a parent and to send the case back to Judge Benson for a determination of whether it is in the child's best interest for her to have visitation rights.

2 Different Opinions on Family

The New York case is of particular interest because the Court of Appeals has issued seemingly divergent rulings on issues pertaining to nonmarital relationships.

In 1989 the court broke legal ground in ruling that the term "family," as used in rent-control laws, can refer to a gay or lesbian couple. But two years earlier the court denied child visitation rights to a mother's former male companion because he was not a biological parent.

Referring to the 1989 case, Paula L. Ettelbrick, the lawyer for Alison, reminded the Court of Appeals that it previously had "recognized functional approaches to various family relationships."

"The child's best interest simply can't be served if we look only at biology as a determinant of that," she said.

But Virginia's lawyer, Anthony G. Maccarini, argued for a strict interpretation of the law. "The respondent here is a parent of her child," he said. "The appellant is not. And like any other parent, lesbian or not, the respondent has a right to raise her child as she sees fit and determine who her child can associate with."

'Domestic Partnerships'

Mr. Maccarini warned of "a steamroller effect," saying that a ruling that allows visitation rights "would allow for any person to confer legal rights on any other person, thereby possibly contravening the legal rights of the other parent." He said the issue should be left to the Legislature.

Coincidentally, Democratic members of the Legislature introduced a bill last week that while not settling the issue of parenthood, would establish nonmarital relationships as "domestic partnerships" that carry many of the legal rights of marriage.

Although some cities have such laws, which give unmarried partners rights to hospital visitation, health-care benefits and bereavement leave, New York would become the first state to pass such a measure. The law would also prohibit job discrimination and other bias against people because of marital status.

The legislation is not expected to pass any time soon. A State Senate aide said the measure "doesn't have a prayer" in the Republican-controlled chamber.

The bill, which was introduced by Assemblywoman Deborah J. Glick and Senator Franz S. Leichter, both Manhattan Democrats, would allow unmarried couples who have been together for six months to register with the local courts as domestic partners.

* * *

December 2, 1992

STUDIES FIND NO DISADVANTAGE IN GROWING UP IN A GAY HOME

By DANIEL GOLEMAN

Michael McCandlish, 12 years old, spends five nights a week with his mother and two with his stepmother. And every now and then, he spends time with his Dad.

But even in this day of ever-mutating family ties, Michael's situation stands out as unusual. While his "Mom," Dr. Barbara McCandlish, is his biological mother, the woman he calls his "Step-Mom" was his mother's lesbian lover—and co-parent—until they separated when Michael was 5. Michael's "Dad" is his biological father, a gay man who was an anonymous sperm donor at the time Michael was conceived, but whom Michael has since got to know.

Michael, a sixth-grader in Santa Fe, N.M., is on his school's basketball team, plays in Little League baseball, and is a snowboarding enthusiast.

Does Michael feel uncomfortable with his unorthodox parents? "It's never been a problem," Michael said. "I've always been pretty open about it, and I don't worry about it."

Studies Dispute Long-Held Views

And, according to a review of new studies in the current issue of the journal Child Development, children raised by gay parents are no more likely to have psychological problems than those raised in more conventional circumstances. While they may face teasing or even ridicule, especially in adolescence, the studies show that, over all, there are no psychological disadvantages for children like Michael in being raised by homosexuals.

That conclusion challenges a view long held by some mental health specialists. And the prevailing view has been reflected in court rulings in custody disputes around the country where judges, even more than psychotherapists, have assumed that being raised by gay or lesbian parents is damaging to a child's emotional and sexual development. As a result, homosexual parents have great difficulty winning custody of their children from a heterosexual partner in divorce proceedings.

In recent years, though, the scientific consensus has begun to change, as more and more experts conclude it is based on anecdotal reports and biased research rather than scientifically gathered evidence. New studies come to very different conclusions.

"What evidence there is suggests there are no particular developmental or emotional deficits for children raised by gay or lesbian parents," said Dr. Michael E. Lamb, chief of the Section on Social and Emotional Development at the National Institute of Child Health and Human Development. "The research is still relatively sparse, but it all suggests the same thing: these kids look O.K."

'Invisible' Gay Households

Estimates of the number of children being raised by homosexual parents range from 6 million to 14 million, in at least

4 million households. While those estimates, from sources like the American Bar Association, may seem high, those who make them point out that the majority of such families are "invisible," in that few outsiders realize there is a homosexual parent. Sometimes the children themselves do not know until they are teen-agers.

"The great majority of gay and lesbian parents are not out in the open about it," said Tim Fisher, director of Communications for Gay and Lesbian Parents Coalition International in Washington, which has 40 chapters in the United States and Canada. There are at least 100 other informal support groups for homosexual parents in the country, Mr. Fisher said.

In the large majority of such households the children were conceived in heterosexual marriages that ended in divorce after one parent came out as homosexual. In recent years families in which children are conceived or adopted by gay couples are growing more common.

Mr. Fisher, for example, is raising a 2½-year-old girl and a 6-month-old boy, both by surrogate mothers. His gay lover is employed outside the home, while Mr. Fisher works at home so he can care for the children.

Despite the large numbers of such families, the topic itself was largely ignored by researchers who were not themselves homosexual. Early research suggesting that homosexuals made bad parents were largely based on individual case studies of troubled children. "Early on, the studies were done by researchers with an ax to grind," Dr. Lamb said.

Unanimity of Studies

By contrast, the new studies all point in the same direction. "There is no adverse effect on any psychological measure," said Dr. Julie Gottman, a clinical psychologist in Seattle, who has done one of the best-designed studies on the topic. Her study was published in 1990 in "Homosexuality and Family Relations" (Huntington Park Press).

Dr. Gottman compared two groups of 35 adult women with 35 who had been raised by lesbian mothers after a divorce from the father. The children were 25 years old on average when Dr. Gottman studied them.

As a group, the children of lesbians did not differ from children of heterosexual mothers in their social adjustment or their identity as a boy or a girl, Dr. Gottman found. The children of lesbians were no more likely to be homosexual than those of heterosexual mothers.

"What mattered most for their adjustment was whether the mother had a partner in the home, whether male or female," Dr. Gottman said. "If so, those children tended to do somewhat better than the others in self-confidence, self-acceptance and independence. But the sexual orientation of the lesbian mothers had no adverse effects."

That conclusion was confirmed by about three dozen studies reviewed in Child Development by Charlotte Patterson, a psychologist at the University of Virginia. When children raised by homosexuals were compared with those raised by heterosexuals, no differences emerged over all on any measure of social or emotional development used in the studies.

No study found any impact on a child's feelings about being a boy or girl or sexual preference from being raised by a homosexual parent. For example, a 1983 study of 9- and 10-year-old girls and boys who were raised by lesbian mothers found that none wished to be a member of the opposite sex.

Roots of Homosexuality

There is as yet no sure scientific consensus on the roots of homosexuality. Recent studies finding differences between the brains of homosexual and heterosexual men have strengthened the position of those who argue for a biological basis. Still, "most experts assume there are both biological and social causes of homosexuality," said Dr. Greg Herek, a psychologist at the University of California at Davis, who is an editor of Contemporary Perspectives on Gay and Lesbian Psychology.

Having homosexual parents "does not cause homosexuality or gender confusion in children," said Dr. John Money, a specialist in sexual disorders at Johns Hopkins University medical school.

For example, in a 1981 study of 6- to 9-year-old children of lesbian and heterosexual mothers, there were no differences in toy and play preferences. The strongest influence on the children was not their mothers, but their playmates.

Researchers say the definitive study, which would follow the adjustment of large numbers of children over several decades, has yet to be done. And data from a study by Dr. Patterson, to be published early next year, show that the children of lesbian mothers are more likely than others to report feelings of anger and fear, as well as more positive feelings like contentment. It is unclear whether the findings reflect greater stress among the children of lesbians or a greater openness about their feelings.

Dr. Patterson concluded, "Not a single study has found children of gay or lesbian parents to be disadvantaged in any significant respect."

Even so, courts have been slow to reconcile custody decison with scientific findings. Although the data showing there are no psychological setbacks for children of homosexuals have been mounting for the last decade, "Lesbian and gay parents struggle in courts for custody and visitation rights," said Paula Ettelbrick, legal director of Lambda Legal Defense, a national legal gay and lesbian organization in New York City.

"But," Ms. Ettelbrick added, "a growing awareness of these studies is slowing down the number of outright denials. The situation is still mixed, but it's getting better."

Although there are no developmental disadvantages for children of homosexuals, Dr. Patterson acknowledged that there could be rocky times for some children of homosexual parents. "If problems occur at all, you see them in early adolescence, when kids want to be like everyone else," Dr. Patterson said.

That is the age that children of homosexual parents are likely to feel most stigmatized. "The anecdotal evidence is that if other kids know, children of gays and lesbians do meet with some ridicule, especially in the early teen years," Mr.

Fisher said. "But gay and lesbian parents are often well equipped to help them through it, since they've dealt with such problems themselves."

While there may be no discernible developmental cost for children raised by homosexual parents, there are undeniable social pressures, if only from those who disapprove of homosexuality. For that reason, many homosexual parents are cautious about the arrangement in public.

"It's clear that you need to be honest and open within the family with the kids," said Dr. McCandlish, Michael's mother. A psychologist in Santa Fe, Dr. McCandlish said that unlike Michael's "stepmother," she no longer considered herself lesbian. Dr. McCandlish added: "There may be some situations when you can't be completely open with people on the outside. Michael does not announce the situation to people, but there were never any secrets with him."

School is perhaps the most difficult arena. Heterosexual teachers and homosexual parents may have different ideas about sex roles, said Dr. Virginia Casper, a developmental psychologist at the Bank Street College of Education in New York City, herself the lesbian mother of a 7-year-old girl.

Conventional Role Models

In a study of 35 homosexual parents, their children and the children's teachers, Dr. Casper found that the teachers had far more conventional ideas about the best kind of sexual role models than did the parents. In a report of her research published in the current Columbia Teacher's College Record, Dr. Casper and her co-authors argue that teachers and administrators should acknowledge that there are children whose parents are homosexual to help remove the stigma.

* * *

January 7, 1996

HOMOSEXUAL PARENTS RAISING CHILDREN: SUPPORT FOR PRO AND CON

By DAVID W. DUNLAP

Underlying the turbulent national debate over families headed by lesbians and gay men is the contentious question of whether homosexual parents create homosexual children. A new study by two British researchers will furnish both sides with statistical ammunition.

Having followed 46 young people over 16 years, the researchers said there was no significant difference in sexual orientation between the children of lesbian mothers and those of heterosexual mothers.

The commonly held assumption that children brought up by lesbian mothers will themselves grow up to be lesbian or gay is not supported by the findings," said the researchers, Susan Golombok and Fiona Tasker, of the Family and Child Psychology Research Center at City University in London.

They said their study, published on Friday in Developmental Psychology, a journal of the American Psychological Association, was the first to trace the children of lesbian mothers from youth to adulthood.

In the study, 2 daughters of lesbian mothers identified themselves as lesbian in early adulthood, while 23 other children reared by lesbians identified themselves as heterosexual. In a comparison group of heterosexual mothers, none of their 21 children identified themselves as homosexual. The researchers said this was not a statistically significant difference between the groups.

"For the authors, it's not statistically significant, but for parents and judges and adoption agencies, it should be," said Joseph Nicolosi, executive director of the National Association for Research and Therapy of Homosexuality, whose members believe homosexuality is a disorder. "These numbers confirm our concern that lesbian parents are more likely to produce gay children."

But to Stefan Lynch, the director of Children of Lesbians and Gays Everywhere, a national group based in San Francisco, the numbers reiterated earlier findings that "you are just as likely to be straight if you have gay parents."

"For those of us who grew up in gay and lesbian families and feel fine about those families, that begs the question, 'So what?'" said Mr. Lynch. "No one has found that there's any kind of significant psychological harm incurred by kids who grow up with lesbian or gay parents. But people are more likely to listen to an 'objective' study like this than to hundreds of people like me saying, 'We're fine.'"

The study found that five daughters and one son of lesbian mothers reported having had a same-sex relationship, ranging from kissing to cohabitation, even though four of them went on to identify themselves as heterosexual. None of the children of heterosexual parents reported such a relationship.

"It seems that growing up in an accepting atmosphere enables individuals who are attracted to same-sex partners to pursue these relationships," Ms. Golombok and Ms. Tasker wrote. "But, interestingly, the opportunity to explore same-sex relationships may, for others, confirm their heterosexual identity."

The mothers and children were related. That is a major shortcoming of the study, said Dr. Richard A. Isay, a clinical professor of psychiatry at the Cornell Medical College.

"My main concern is that the study doesn't separate genetic from family influence," Dr. Isay said, "so it doesn't show very much."

The study was begun in 1976 and 1977 with 27 lesbian mothers and their 39 children, who were then an average of 9-½ years old. A comparison group of equal size was assembled, with heterosexual mothers who were then single. In the follow-up, in 1992 and 1993, 26 daughters and 20 sons were interviewed.

* * *

June 7, 1998

THE SECOND GENERATION

By DAVID KIRBY

Dan Cherubin considers himself pretty lucky. Though his father died five years ago, he still has his mother, and his other mother.

Mr. Cherubin, a music librarian who lives in the East Village, is the gay son of a lesbian who lives with her companion, and he belongs to an unusual—and, for some, unsettling—kind of family.

"We're not your average TV family," Mr. Cherubin, 33, said.

He calls himself, and other gay children of gay parents, "the second generation." For him, the experience has brought "an appreciation for things that aren't necessarily the norm." For others, it has not always been so easy.

It was only a couple of decades ago that openly gay people started rearing children. Now some of those children are teen-agers and young adults who are realizing that they, too, are gay. In some cases, having a gay parent has made it easier for them. But there are also those who came out to seemingly heterosexual parents, only to have those parents later acknowledge their own homosexuality.

Parents who have had a difficult time because they are gay often worry that their gay children will also face hardships. The children sometimes anticipate their concern and find it hard to break the news about their own homosexuality. Outside the family, some gay children of gay parents say, they may be perceived as curiosities or aberrations. Sometimes they are swept into the political and scientific debate over whether homosexuals are born or made, and whether parents influence their children's sexual orientation.

Some on the political and religious right claim that homosexuality is a choice, that it can be taught or reversed and that it does not warrant legal protections. And some conservatives maintain that gay people should not rear children because the children will likely follow their parents' "life style." In Florida and New Hampshire, it is illegal for gay people to adopt children.

But gay rights advocates have argued for years that homosexuality is genetic and unalterable, like race or ethnicity, and that gay people deserve legal protection against the discrimination that many face. They point out that numerous studies, in journals like Child Development and The Journal of Child Psychology and Psychiatry, have found that children reared by gay parents are no more likely to be gay than those brought up by heterosexual parents, and no more likely to have psychological problems.

Yet those who draw attention to the fact that both they and at least one of their parents are homosexual can make some other gay people uneasy.

Mr. Cherubin, who founded a group called Second Generation in 1991, said that when he approached other gay organizations for support, most were receptive but some "were iffy."

"They thought we were propagating stereotypes—gay people recruiting kids," he said. "Some wanted nothing to do with gay children, even if we're 30."

Mr. Cherubin remembered handing out cards at one gay pride parade referring to "gay and lesbian children of gay and lesbian parents." Some parents would look at the cards, "become horrified and hand it back," he said. "They said: 'Our kids are just like everyone else. They are not gay.'"

And last year, when he spoke at a conference for gay parents at New York University, Mr. Cherubin said, a lesbian mother who had fought for custody of her two young children told him: "Nothing personal, Dan, but you're my worst nightmare."

"People are afraid of losing their kids," he said. "It happens. And, of course, the sexuality of one's child is always an uncomfortable topic."

But April Martin, 49, a lesbian mother who is a psychotherapist in Manhattan and the author of "The Lesbian and Gay Parenting Handbook: Creating and Raising Our Families" (Harper Perennial, 1993), said that among the many families with gay parents she knows, "nobody's worried." She went on to say: "When we're in our community and we feel safe, no one worries if their kids will be gay. We're curious. We're interested in fostering whatever it's going to be. We talk about it: 'I think this one might be. I think this one probably isn't.'"

Terry Boggis, director of Center Kids, the family program of the Lesbian and Gay Community Services Center in the West Village, said: "I hear gay people say, 'Why would I want my children to be gay?' and I think 'Ouch.' Of course we want an easier, smoother path for our children. But some protest too much. They're bending over backwards about how gay people really don't want their kids to be gay."

Wayne Steinman, 48, the former president of the Gay and Lesbian Parents Coalition International, said, "Society has imposed on the gay community a sense of homophobia, that somehow we'll make our children gay."

"Unfortunately, some gay parents maintain those fears," said Mr. Steinman, who lives on Staten Island with his partner Sal Iacullo, 49, and the 10-year-old daughter they adopted as an infant, Hope Steinman-Iacullo. "It's not a particular aversion to homosexuality, but they feel their kids' lives would be easier and less frustrating if they were straight. Personally, I say who better to raise gay kids than gay parents? We allow our children to express themselves and be themselves. And we've lived through the issues."

If gay parents have reason to fear that their ability to rear children might be questioned, some of it comes from groups like the Family Research Council, a national organization based in Washington. Robert Knight, the council's director of cultural studies, said children "need to model themselves after their own sex and to get clues about treating the opposite sex by viewing their opposite-sex parent."

In households with gay parents, Mr. Knight said, "Kids see reality through a distorted lens, a frankly abnormal acting-out of sexuality." These children, he said, are more likely to have a positive view of homosexuality, making it easier for them "to develop homosexual orientations."

"If their so-called parents are doing it, and they are the most important influence on children, then common sense tells us at least some of the children will try it out," Mr. Knight said.

But in 1995, the American Psychological Association published a report on gay parents, which was prepared by psychologists who specialized in families, youth and gay men and lesbians. Charlotte J. Patterson, a professor of psychology at the University of Virginia, who did the summary for the report, pointed out that though research on the subject was "very new and relatively scarce" and had limitations, there was no evidence that homosexuals "are unfit to be parents or that psychosocial development among children of gay men or lesbians is compromised in any respect."

Still, she said, gay families were often subjected to prejudice "that turns judges, legislators, professionals and the public against them, frequently resulting in negative outcomes like loss of physical custody, restrictions on visitation and prohibition against adoption." And while courts have expressed concern that children of gay parents will become lesbian or gay, Dr. Patterson wrote, a "great majority" of the children describe themselves as heterosexual, and "the data do not suggest elevated rates of homosexuality" among such children.

"My question," Dr. Patterson said in an interview, "would be how on earth would you make your child gay, even if you wanted to?"

A Disclosure to Mom in Freshman Year

Marc M., 28, knew he was gay "since Day 1." And from the age of 10 or 11, he said, he suspected his mother might be, too. "After all, she had a roommate and no other friends' moms had roommates," he said. "I saw affection between them, but the relationship was never verbalized."

Marc, a writer who lives in Chelsea, asked that his last name not be used, for several reasons: "Is my mother out to her neighbors? No. Am I out to my grandma? No. Is my mother out to my father or brother? No, but they know about me."

He grew up in Queens in a middle-class family. His parents divorced when he was 9, and he and his brother, who is four years older, lived with their father. They saw their mother, who lived with her female companion, on weekends.

Then, when Marc was 14, his father moved out and his mother moved in. "There were always uncles and roommates and friends at the house," he said. Two uncles, his mother's brothers, were gay. Both died of AIDS.

Marc kept his homosexuality hidden for years. "I wanted badly to tell people about me. But I couldn't. One uncle was already sick, and the other got sick as I was coming out. I desperately wanted to talk to him about being gay, but he was too sick.

"My greatest fear was coming out to my mom," he said. "I could see she was gay, and I presumed what she went through—the fact she couldn't tell her kids or the people she worked with. It made me feel like I failed her, that things aren't perfect."

But during his freshman year in college, Marc decided to tell his mother. "I said, 'I need to talk to you,' and started to pace around. She started crying. I said I was gay, and she said something like, 'I have tendencies also.' And I said, 'Tendencies, mom?' And she cried and said, 'I don't want you to go through what I went through, what my brothers went through, what my best friends go through.'"

"I know what a hard life it is," Marc remembered his mother saying. "If I could push a button to make you straight when you were born, you would have been straight."

His mother, who would speak only on condition of anonymity, said: "Society doesn't accept this life style, and he's going to hit some bumpy roads along the way. It would make it easier for him if he was straight the way the world is today, even though it's a little more acceptable than it was years ago.

"That's how I feel as a mother," she said. "People have called him a freak and all kinds of names because he's gay and his mother is gay."

Marc said his mother, who is single now, "comes from a different generation, plain and simple." He went on: "She didn't move to the Village or become some lefty lesbian hippie mom. She's a bookkeeper."

"There's a weird dynamic, being gay and the kid of a gay parent," he said. "If it's nurturing, and my mom nurtured me to be like her, it doesn't make sense, because then I should like women, right?"

'I Wasn't Going To Get Kicked Out'

Two years ago, Emily Martin-Alexander, 16, called home from boarding school. She had something to tell her parents, April Martin, an author and therapist, and Susan Alexander, 53, a children's librarian at a private school. Other kids, Emily said, were saying she was a lesbian.

"I said, 'Well, what do you think?'" Dr. Martin said.

"And I said, 'Well, I think they might be right,'" Emily said.

Then, Dr. Martin said, she asked Emily what made her think she might be gay. After a long silence, Emily said she was smitten with a classmate. A female classmate.

For Emily, who said she had figured out her sexual orientation on her own the previous year, telling her mothers was relatively easy. "I knew I wasn't going to get kicked out of the house," she said.

But there were other troubles. "It was a tough year." Dr. Martin said. "A lot of hard work went into discovering and consolidating her identity, even with gay parents, who you'd think would make it totally easy. Yet people were kind of taking that away from her."

Emily said: "I got the whole shebang because I'm a lesbian and because my moms are. A lot of it was just curiosity, but some people said, 'Well, your parents did this to you.'"

"My parents didn't make me gay," she said. "I did this all by myself."

Dr. Martin said she saw being interviewed as the gay parent of a gay child as "a coming out" of sorts. "I'm out there debating the religious right, and I don't bring up the issue of my daughter being a lesbian," she said, especially "when people say 'you're going to make your kids gay,' and the best sound-bite response is the research shows that doesn't happen."

For the next edition of her book for gay parents, she said, she may add a chapter on gay kids.

Dr. Martin, and Ms. Alexander, who did not want to be interviewed, each conceived a child through donor insemination. The family lives in Chelsea. "Whatever they turned out would've been fine with us: both gay, both straight or any combination," Dr. Martin said of the children. Her son, Jesse, 13, is heterosexual, she said. "He's being raised in a household with three lesbians and no male parent, and he's grown up straight."

Helping Parents Come Out, Too

When Brook Garrett, 33, a theatrical agent who lives in Greenwich Village, told his parents he was gay 11 years ago, they were going through a difficult divorce. But, he said: "They were supportive and loving. Nobody was surprised."

What he didn't expect was that he might be paving the way for them to acknowledge their own homosexuality. "I became less the child and more the peer role model," he said. "I needed to let them come out on their own terms. They did that for me."

Brook Garrett grew up in what he called "a classic post-Eisenhower family" in New Jersey and Pennsylvania. His father, Larry, was a private-school teacher. His mother, Carole, was a nurse.

"In the early 60's, that's just what you did, got married and had kids," said Larry Garrett, who lives in Pittsburgh with his companion of five years. While he was married, he said, he had "some inkling" that he might be homosexual, but he never acted on it.

When Brook broke the news to him about being gay, he said, "I came a proverbial hairbreadth away from saying, 'Well, son, so am I.' But I didn't, and I'm not sure why."

Eventually, Brook Garrett said, he began to suspect his father was gay. "Brook and his brother forced me to come out to them about five years ago," Larry Garrett said.

Carole Garrett, who lives in Philadelphia, said she had no idea that the man she had married might be gay. And she said it was several years after her son had made his announcement that she had became aware of her own homosexuality and was able to tell him.

"I come from a family that doesn't communicate well," she said, "and these are sensitive issues."

"Had I been from a less conservative background, I might have found out about and explored things more," Ms. Garrett said. "But consciously I had no idea about myself in those days. I guess I should have, but I wasn't as socially aware back then."

Like her ex-husband, Ms. Garrett said she had no qualms about Brook's being gay. "I'm proud of him," she said. "He loves his friends, he's successful. I wouldn't have him any other way."

His father said: "Mouths drop wide open when I tell people. But that's not very often."

'Oh, My God, Dad's Gay'

Maria De la O's parents split up when she was 4 and living in San Diego. A year later, her father moved to San Francisco. She remembers her mother, who reared her, occasionally referring to her father as a "queer," though as a child, Ms. De la O said, she didn't understand why.

When she was 14, she said, he told her "how great it was" to have been at the protests over the killing of Harvey Milk, the San Francisco politician who was gunned down in 1978 by a fellow member of the city's Board of Supervisors. "And I thought, 'Oh, my God, dad's gay.'"

Ms. De la O, 29, a journalist who lives in Brooklyn, considers herself bisexual but is living with a girlfriend. After realizing her father, Bill De Lao, was gay, she said, "I thought, if he didn't know for a long time, then maybe I'm gay and don't know it.

"I asked myself: 'Am I attracted to these high-school girls? No? Good.' But then I fell in love with my best friend when I was 17.

"I didn't relish telling my mom," she continued. "She didn't take my father's being gay well at all. It threw her for a loop and affected the rest of her life. And I wanted to make absolutely sure before dropping any bombs."

So Ms. De la O didn't tell her mother. She went away to college, where she dated men and women before meeting her current girlfriend. "I dropped hints to my mom, like my dad had done. So at a certain point she just assumed. She knew, and she still loved me to death." (Her mother was not available for comment.)

Her father also seemed to make assumptions. "When I was 21, my dad and his boyfriend, Robert, invited me to Lake Tahoe for the weekend. They said, 'Bring someone, male or female.' I don't know if it was a trap or not. I think Robert was trying to open things up between me and my father. I invited my roommate, Cathy. We were just friends. When we got to Tahoe, my dad said: 'You girls will have to take twin beds, do you mind?'"

Mr. De Lao said when he realized his daughter might be gay, he was taken aback "for a few hours." He added: "But then I said to myself, 'Gee, I'm grateful to have a good daughter, and it's great she turned out to be O.K.' By the next morning, I was fine with it."

Ms. De la O said: "Maybe it was something he'd gone through. But it was so different for me. Times have changed." She credits her father with helping her be more open. "I'm a better person for it," she said.

Growing Up, Two Very Different Homes

Jamie Egan, 24, recently moved to the Upper West Side from Wisconsin, where he grew up in a small town just outside Madison.

"My mom came out to me when I was 14," he said. "I had clues. I remember not being shocked. My parents were separated, partly because my mom fell in love with her friend."

His "other mom," as he calls her, moved in when he was 16.

At the time, he assumed he was heterosexual. But two years later, he had a boyfriend. "The space was there to express what I needed to express, so coming out wasn't a problem," he said. "I would even bring my boyfriend to the house."

"My mom was thrilled when she found out," he said. "That is, thrilled at first, and then a little apprehensive later."

Mr. Egan's mother, a teacher, would speak only on condition of anonymity. "It was a bonding thing for us," she said, "but after I thought about it, it kind of scared me because it's O.K. for me, and I can handle it, but I don't want my kids to have to go through all the pain.

"I always wanted their life to be better than mine," she said. "But it's a pretty good life. It's not always easy, but it's the path I needed to be on, and if that's what he needs to do, too, then that's cool."

Mr. Egan said he had spoken with his father about his mother's homosexuality. But, he said, "He doesn't know about me. He's not quite to that point where he can handle it."

Mr. Egan grew up in two very different homes. "In one was my mom and her partner, my biological brother and my younger sister and older brother from my other mom," he said. "In a town of 2,000, it caused quite the controversy." In the other house was his father, in the same town but worlds away.

"It gave me a lot of perspective, which is a very positive thing," said Mr. Egan, an intern at the Gay, Lesbian, Straight Education Network. He now considers himself bisexual. His biological brother, he said, is heterosexual.

Sometimes, he said, he gets flak about his family. People assume he must be gay because his mother is. "But my moms didn't make me any more gay than my dad made me straight," he said. "To say gay people make people gay is a ridiculous cliche."

After a Confrontation, 'She Had to Tell Me'

Dan Cherubin grew up in what he described as a "normal" household on Staten Island, with a mother, a father, a sister and a brother.

When he was 16, Mr. Cherubin's mother, Margaret Cherubin, introduced him to a friend, Tina Fornale. "Tina made no bones about being a lesbian, and she had lots of gay friends," Mr. Cherubin said. "But I had no idea about my mom at first. I began to suspect when I was 18 and away at college."

That year his parents split up. And that year he told them he was gay. "They weren't shocked," he said. "They took it like good liberal parents."

But the divorce was nasty, and his parents' relationship was strained, Mr. Cherubin said. His mother began spending more time at Tina's house. "Then she started going to Tina's every weekend," he said, "so I really thought something was up."

When Tina moved in with his mother, Mr. Cherubin said, "I finally forced it out of her. She asked, 'How do you feel about Tina?' And I said, 'What do you mean?' And she said, 'You know what I mean!' And I said, very coyly, 'No mom, I don't.' So she had to tell me."

His first reaction was anger, Mr. Cherubin said. He had faced his own difficulties coming to terms with his homosexuality.

"How could she watch me suffer and not tell me?" he said. "But I came to understand that she comes from a different era."

Ms. Cherubin, who was married for 27 years, said she had a sense even then that she might be bisexual. "But later I realized, no, I was gay," she said.

Mr. Cherubin's father eventually remarried, and his mother and Ms. Fornale have been together for 13 years. Both think of him, and his siblings, as their children.

And as for Mr. Cherubin's being gay, Ms. Cherubin said: "I'm very proud of my son, and perfectly comfortable and proud of myself. I love the kid."

"So do I," Ms. Fornale said.

* * *

January 4, 2000

CASE ON VISITATION RIGHTS HINGES ON DEFINING FAMILY

By LINDA GREENHOUSE

WASHINGTON, Jan. 3—A Supreme Court case on whether grandparents, other relatives, and even nonrelatives should be able to gain a court-ordered right to visit with children over the parents' objection has opened the door to a profound debate over the very definition of family.

In recent years, all 50 states have adopted grandparents' rights laws, permitting grandparents, and sometimes others, to seek court-ordered visitation under various circumstances. On Jan. 12, the justices will consider one of the more far-reaching variants, a Washington law that permits anyone, without any defined relationship to the child, to petition for visiting rights and to succeed if the family court concludes that visitation would be in the child's best interest.

The Washington Supreme Court concluded in a 1998 decision that the law violated "a parent's constitutionally protected right to rear his or her children without state interference." In the absence of any indication that visitation was necessary to prevent harm to the child, the parents' rights were "fundamental" and should not be overridden, the court said, adding that "the parents should be the ones to choose whether to expose their children to certain people or ideas."

The justices' decision three months ago to review that ruling, in an appeal brought by a husband and wife seeking to regain access to their late son's young daughters, galvanized a wide spectrum of organizations and interest groups that saw implications, for good or ill, in the state court's categorical assessment of parental rights. Dozens of organizations have filed or joined briefs in Troxel v. Granville, No. 99-138, making it one of the high-visibility cases in a Supreme Court term already packed with potential landmarks.

What the briefs have in common is a focus on the centrality of families in the lives of children. What divides them are very different views of what it means to be a family.

Briefs representing the interests of the older generation, including one filed on the grandparents' behalf by the 30-million-member AARP, note that the number of children whose primary caretakers are their grandparents is growing rapidly in the face of nuclear family dissolution; for 1.4 million children today, their grandparents are their functional parents.

Briefs representing the Christian right, filed on the parents' behalf, hold up "the traditional family, consisting of married parents and their children" and "inextricably linked to the union of husband and wife"—in the words of a brief filed by the American Center for Law and Justice—as society's building block.

Gay rights groups, groups advocating parental choice in education, organizations concerned with families struggling in poverty, all have come into the case in an effort to make sure the justices at least understand the implications of a ruling one way or another.

For example, according to the Lambda Legal Defense and Education Fund, a gay rights legal organization, neither side's position is sufficiently protective of the needs of children being reared in nontraditional families where a functional parent may have neither biological nor legal ties to the child. Courts should take into account "the quality and security of the relationship between individual children and adults rather than blood ties or labels," the Lambda brief said.

Although the court could decide the case rather narrowly—by limiting its holding, for example, to grandparents or by requiring certain pre-existing conditions before the law can be invoked—"there's really no dodging the need to define family," said David D. Meyer, a law professor at the University of Illinois and the author of a recent article on the constitutional concept of family privacy.

Professor Meyer, who is not involved in the case, said in an interview today that the justices should take "a very flexible and careful approach to this case" to avoid binding the court to an analysis that fails to recognize "that families as a matter of social reality are changing dramatically."

He said that while on the surface the case presented a contrasting pair of rather easily described images of family life, one with the parents in unquestioned control and the other with grandparents involved in the children's lives, "as you peel back the layers of legal and social issues, it's an awful lot more complicated than that."

Those inclined to support the parents "are forced to deal with the implications of a hard-line decision that cuts out a lot of other interests," Professor Meyer said. For example, the main brief filed on behalf of the grandparents, Jenifer and Gary Troxel, warns that to accept the Washington Supreme Court's notion of parental control over ideas to which children should be exposed would have "revolutionary implications" for parental veto power over the curriculum in public schools.

On the other hand, Professor Meyer continued, "those who think it's a travesty to shut out the grandparents are taking a position that has a lot of implications they may find less palatable than the Norman Rockwell image of the traditional family at the Thanksgiving table."

A number of the briefs seek to focus the court's attention on implications of the case that may not be intuitively obvious to the justices. For example, a brief filed by Legal Services of Southeastern Michigan, on behalf of the parents, asserts that the family integrity of the poor is at risk under a law that "opens the door for subjective value judgments concerning the court's view of family" under a standard that appraises the best interests of the child, because "poorer, less educated parents will always look worse in relation to older, seemingly more established and settled grandparents."

Underlying the intense interest in the case is the fact that the Supreme Court will be making a constitutional ruling in an area where its decisions have been few and far between and, recently, heatedly contested. A pair of decisions in the 1920's established the right to direct one's children's education as an aspect of parental "liberty" protected against state interference by the due process guarantee of the 14th amendment.

More recently, the court has been wary of the branch of constitutional analysis known as substantive due process. Its most recent decision in the family law context was a splintered 1989 ruling, Michael H. v. Gerald D., rejecting a natural father's due process challenge to a California law's presumption that his child was legally the child of the man to whom the mother was married at the time of the birth. Justice Antonin Scalia's plurality opinion said that because there was no historic pedigree for the natural father's claim, it should not be recognized as an aspect of due process.

The case before the court now is a poignant one. The Troxels' son, who was not married to the mother of his children, committed suicide. The mother, Tommie Granville, married a man who adopted the children. The grandparents, wanting more access than the new family was willing to permit, brought suit and initially won a detailed visitation order that was overturned on appeal. In her brief, Ms. Granville said she had been obliged to spend her children's college money on the cost of "defending the fundamental right of all families not to have the state micro-manage their affairs."

* * *

June 6, 2000

JUSTICES DENY GRANDPARENTS VISITING RIGHTS

By LINDA GREENHOUSE

WASHINGTON, June 5—Declaring that parents have a "fundamental right to make decisions concerning the care, custody and control" of their children, the Supreme Court ruled today that a Washington State law went too far in permitting a judge to order visiting rights for grandparents over a mother's objection.

With a 6-to-3 vote but lacking a single rationale that could command a majority, the court stepped cautiously and appeared intent on avoiding a one-size-fits-all constitutional prescription for a world of rapidly changing family dynamics. As Justice Sandra Day O'Connor acknowledged in her opinion for a plurality of four justices: "The demographic changes of the past century make it difficult to speak of an average American family."

Consequently, the court stopped short of declaring unconstitutional a Washington law, one of the broadest regarding the rights of grandparents in terms of permitting judicial intervention in family affairs. Nor did the justices offer much guidance for judging the constitutionality of similar laws in the 49 other states.

Beginning with New York in 1966, states adopted laws on visiting rights that reflected the rising divorce rate and the impact of custody battles that caused grandparents to lose contact with their grandchildren. While most state laws make parental death or divorce a precondition for grandparents to seek visiting rights, the Washington law required no such triggering event.

The four-justice plurality found only that the law had been unconstitutionally applied to order visits by the grandparents in the case in question, a dispute between Tommie Granville, the mother of two daughters, and Jenifer and Gary Troxel, the parents of the girls' father, who had killed himself. Ms. Granville was willing to allow some visits, but not the two weekends a month the Troxels had requested when they invoked the state law and went to court. They won a modified order that was invalidated on appeal.

A fifth justice, David H. Souter, voted to strike down the Washington law in all possible applications—as had the Washington Supreme Court in a 1998 ruling that was before the court today—and a sixth justice, Clarence Thomas, suggested in a cryptic, two-paragraph opinion that he would do the same. Chief Justice William H. Rehnquist and Justices Ruth Bader Ginsburg and Stephen G. Breyer joined Justice O'Connor's opinion.

The tentative, splintered nature of the decision, with a total of six separate opinions among nine justices, all but guaranteed that challenges to other state laws would reach the Supreme Court.

Nonetheless, the court did set a constitutional bottom line that any statute would have to meet, with a balance struck clearly in favor of parental decision making while leaving the door open to upholding more carefully tailored statutes.

The decision of a fit parent to deny or limit access to a child is entitled to "at least some special weight" or "presumption of validity," Justice O'Connor said, adding that it was these characteristics that the Washington law failed to apply in this case, Troxel v. Granville, No. 99-138.

"So long as a parent adequately cares for his or her children (i.e., is fit)," Justice O'Connor wrote, "there will normally be no reason for the state to inject itself into the private realm of the family to further question the ability of that parent to make the best decisions concerning the rearing of that parent's children."

The Washington law, passed in 1994, provided that any person may petition the court for visiting rights at any time, which a court could order when visits "may serve the best interest of the child."

This was a "breathtakingly broad" invitation, Justice O'Connor said, for state judges simply to substitute their judgment for that of the parents. But, she said, "the Due Process Clause does not permit a state to infringe on the fundamental right of parents to make child-rearing decisions simply because a state judge believes a 'better' decision could be made."

In striking down the law, the Washington Supreme Court had gone considerably further, ruling not only that the parental decisions were entitled to some measure of judicial deference, but that in the absence of an unfit parent or a showing of harm to the children, parents had a constitutional right to exercise an effective veto over any request for a visit.

In other words, the state court said, a "best interests of the child" standard was never constitutionally adequate.

Justice O'Connor said today that it was unnecessary to resolve the question of whether, in order to be constitutional, a statute had to require a showing of parental unfitness or harm to the children.

"We do not, and need not, define today the precise scope of the parental due process right in the visitation context," she said, adding: "Because much state court adjudication in this context occurs on a case-by-case basis, we would be hesitant to hold that specific nonparental visitation statutes violate the Due Process Clause as a per se matter."

The court's hesitation reflected not only the novelty and emotional weight of the issue, but also the fact that in the American legal system, family law has been the province of state legislatures and state courts, with only rare occasions for Supreme Court intervention on such questions as the right of parents to choose private rather than public schools, as the court held in a case from the 1920's.

In a dissenting opinion today, Justice Anthony M. Kennedy said the court should have confronted, rather than avoided, the question of whether a law providing for visiting rights in the best interests of the child could ever be constitutional. In Justice Kennedy's view, such laws could be constitutional if directed to people who had acted "in a caregiving role over a significant period of time," whether a grandparent or a "de facto parent" of another kind.

Justice John Paul Stevens also filed a dissenting opinion that called attention to "the almost infinite variety of family relationships that pervade our ever-changing society" and warned against adopting a rule that would allow parents to exercise "arbitrary" power over their children's contact with other adults. Judge Stevens said the court should "reject any suggestion that when it comes to parental rights, children are so much chattel."

Patricia Logue, a lawyer with the Lambda Legal Defense and Education Fund, which filed a brief on behalf of the mother, said it was encouraging that justices on both sides of the case appeared eager to maintain a level of constitutional flexibility in recognizing that "there are many ways to raise children" and that significant relationships between children and people who are not their biological parents can be deserving of protection.

"The court is letting this area of law evolve to meet the families that are out there," Ms. Logue said.

Despite the variety of views the justices expressed today, the differences among eight of them appeared nuanced rather than fundamental. The lone exception was Justice Antonin Scalia, who filed a separate dissenting opinion rejecting the application of the Due Process Clause and of what he called "judicial vindication of 'parental rights' under a Constitution that does not even mention them." He warned that the court was "ushering in a new regime of judicially prescribed, and federally prescribed, family law."

One undoubtedly unexpected result of the case, which was argued in January, could be to strengthen the federal government's hand in its support of Juan Miguel Gonzalez in his effort to take his son, Elian, home to Cuba over the objection of relatives in Miami.

"The bottom line is that there is now no question that a parent decides for a child," Pamela S. Falk, a professor of international law at the City University of New York, said in an interview.

* * *

PARENTHOOD

January 10, 1983

HOMOSEXUAL VIEWS ADOPTION APPROVAL AS VICTORY

By JUDITH CUMMINGS
Special to The New York Times

RIVERSIDE, Calif., Jan. 5—Two years ago, when he was 27 years old, David Frater thought that it was time he enjoyed the satisfactions that he felt fatherhood would bring.

He decided on adoption, and a long fight ended successfully when he became the adoptive father of a 17-year-old boy. He also established something of a legal precedent. Mr. Frater is a homosexual.

His adoption of the boy, Kevin, who has taken Mr. Frater's name, is believed by some social service and homosexual organizations to represent the first legal adoption by an acknowledged homosexual. The move was approved last month by Judge George Grover of Superior Court, who said he had considered Mr. Frater's sexual orientation as he would any number of factors in a parent-child relationship.

Mr. Frater considers the adoption a major personal victory because, he says, he hopes to adopt more children. He also says he sees it as an important gain for the homosexual community, demonstrating that sexual preference is only one aspect of a life, not the dominant one.

More Seeking Family Status

The move comes as homosexuals are advancing past merely making their identity public to agitating for greater rights in family status.

Last month in San Francisco, which has a large homosexual population, the county supervisors approved a law granting homosexuals partnership rights similar to those of married people: for example, coverage of "partners" by city pension plans. But the measure was vetoed as "too vague" by Mayor Dianne Feinstein.

Homosexual activists, while they applaud the Frater adoption, note that it was not the first time a homosexual had become an adoptive parent. In the past, however, homosexuals seeking adoptions felt it imperative to keep their homosexuality secret.

"This is the first one that's gone to court, and what's significant is that when it did go to court, we won," said Tim Sweeney, executive director of the Lambda Legal Defense and Educational Fund, a 10-year-old New York organization for civil rights for homosexuals.

A 'Stereotype of Molestation'

Mr. Sweeney said the Frater case was linked with what he called "the single most emotional and irrational fear of straight people vis-a-vis gay people," adding: "What we're fighting is a stereotype of child molestation. It's absurd to say to all gay people, 'You can't adopt a child because you're going to molest him.' There are no more child molesters in the gay community than there are in the straight community."

Mr. Frater is a marketing specialist for a computer company and lives with his mother, Irma, on the arid outskirts of Riverside. He said he had long been a "surrogate big brother" to neighborhood children and finally decided to try to create a family of his own. "I like kids," he said. "It was turning out to be a major emptiness in my life." He said he had not wanted to adopt a younger child because that would put too many demands on his time and take away time from his work.

For his part, Kevin said he had lived unhappily in 14 different foster homes before the Riverside County Department of Public Social Services placed him with Mr. Frater. He said his new father's homosexuality did not concern him in the least.

When the Youth Was Told

He said he learned of it a few days after he began living with Mr. Frater and his mother. "He told me about it," Kevin said. "It really don't bother me. It wasn't no big thing to me."

He said he liked living with Mr. Frater. "We like to do a lot of the same things," he added. "He lets me do things I like to do personally, like go places with my friends or girl friends." Kevin said he was heterosexual.

Officials of the Department of Public Social Services, who have said they are legally barred from discussing adoption cases, did not respond to phone calls about Kevin Frater.

David Frater says the department subjected him to "foot-dragging" and "harassment" for two years after he applied to adopt the youth. He did not tell officials who are concerned with adoption that he was homosexual; they found out, he said, through an anonymous tip.

Mr. Frater said the members of his household, which at that time included a man who had been his companion for six years, had been put through an inordinate number of psychological and other fitness evaluations. The officials, he said, declined to approve the adoption but never gave him a reason.

Feminist Lawyer Brought In

In November he engaged Gloria Allred, a feminist lawyer, to represent him against the county. Shortly afterward, the social services department capitulated.

"They were stonewalling David," Miss Allred said. "They were refusing to consent and refusing to say why they wouldn't consent. But they never asked that the child be taken out of the home, which I found very suspicious."

She said she considered the rights of homosexuals to adopt children a feminist issue and that it involved the right to choose a style of living free of discrimination.

"I don't think a heterosexual adult who tried to adopt a child would have been subjected to such scrutiny, not even if a 27-year-old man tried to adopt a 15-year-old girl," she said.

According to the National Association of Social Workers, their profession is increasingly supporting full adoption rights for homosexuals, and there is a trend in that direction.

Backing by Psychologists' Group

A spokesman for the association, Tom Gautier, who heads its committee on homosexual issues, said the group based its attitude on a policy of the American Psychological Association.

"The A.P.A. has taken a position in support of foster care by homosexuals, and we have a general statement of support for adoption as a logical extension of that," he said. "It's the qualities of parenting and the home environment and what is in the best interests of the child that should be the determining criteria."

In May, Kevin will be 18 years old and legally an adult. If the adoption proceedings had been delayed until his birthday, the question would have become moot, Mr. Frater says. But Kevin said he wanted to go through with it anyway to establish the precedent, saying, in a reference to Mr. Frater, that he wanted "to help him—he wants to adopt more children."

Mr. Frater said he would like to adopt teen-age runaways like the hundreds on the streets of Los Angeles, who sometimes survive through prostitution.

He said he knew that this would be difficult, too. "Then they should do me one better," he said. "No one else is taking care of these kids."

* * *

January 30, 1989

LESBIAN PARTNERS FIND THE MEANS TO BE PARENTS

By GINA KOLATA

In a baby boom of unusual complexity, thousands of lesbians around the country are having children.

Most are living in lesbian relationships. Some have lived together for more than a decade, wanting children but often blocked as adoptive or foster parents. Now more and more of these women are choosing to have their own babies, most often by artificial insemination.

Although no one knows how many lesbian women are having babies, experts cite a number of indications of a boom. Hundreds of women are attending a growing number

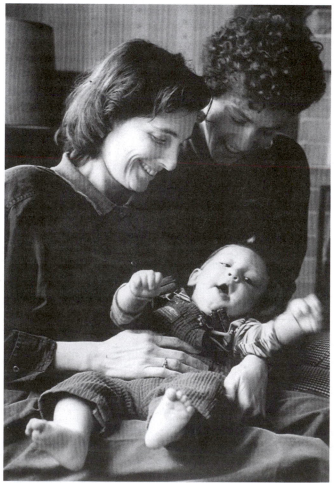

The New York Times/Terrence McCarthy

Kim Klausner, left, and Debra Chasnoff with their son, Noah, in San Francisco. The two have made a film about lesbians having babies.

of workshops for lesbians thinking of having children. Informal networks have sprung up, enabling lesbians to find sperm donors. Lawyers are formulating custody agreements to try to insure legal rights for lesbian mothers, their female partners and the fathers of their children. Support groups and social organizations are sponsoring picnics, parties and other events to keep lesbians with children from feeling isolated.

New Methods for Gay Parents

There have long been gay parents, and many homosexuals who have had heterosexual relationships maintain custody of their children from previous marriages. Other gay men and women are able to adopt, raise foster children or enter into arrangements with surrogate mothers or sperm donors to have their own children. This is the first time that large numbers of lesbians have been choosing to have children through artificial insemination, gay and lesbian groups said.

"It's phenomenal," said Rhonda Rivera, a lawyer in Columbus, Ohio, who has many gay and lesbian clients. She said she knew of at least 30 lesbian mothers in and around Columbus.

"Everybody that I know sees lots of people who are having kids, said Kevin Cathcart, a lawyer with the Gay and Lesbian Advocates and Defenders in Boston.

Dr. Richard Green, a professor of psychiatry and law at the University of California at Los Angeles, said that although psychological tests indicate that children raised by homosexuals are no more likely than other children to be homosexual themselves, the issue of children raised without a man in the family has not been sufficiently studied to be able to predict whether that could lead to other problems.

But some clinicians speculate that in the long term, girls might have difficulty in intimate relationships with men, and boys might be uncomfortable with their role as males. If lesbian parents are openly hostile toward men, these difficulties could be worsened.

Sidney Callahan, a psychologist and ethicist at Mercy College in Dobbs Ferry, N.Y., said that although it is "natural and programmed" to want children, she had "deep reservations" about lesbian motherhood through artificial insemination.

"The ethical objection is the informed-consent issue," Dr. Callahan said. "You are getting a child that is totally different from all other children. Do you have the right to do that?" She added: "As perilous as it is to be brought into the world in a normal family, this is one step beyond that."

Fears of Prejudice

Many lesbian parents say their own chief concern is that their children, whether homosexual or not, will be victims of prejudice against gay people.

But such concerns have not stopped thousands of lesbians from becoming parents. Roberta Achtenberg, a lawyer in San Francisco who specializes in issues involving gays and lesbians, said that compared to a few years ago, she gets "double,

triple, quadruple the number of calls" about homosexual parental contracts and rights. When Ms. Achtenberg conducts workshops on legal issues for gay and lesbian parents, as many as 500 people show up.

About 40 percent of the women inseminated at the Sperm Bank of Northern California, a service run by feminists in Oakland, say they are lesbians—twice as many as in 1982, when the sperm bank opened, said Barbara Raboy, the director.

Many lesbian women who use artificial insemination perform the procedure themselves.

R. James Fagelson, a director of the Gay and Lesbian Parents Coalition International, based in Washington, said a recent survey of the group's 30,000 American members revealed that 5 percent of the lesbians had babies by artificial insemination. Three years ago, the figure was 1 to 2 percent. The group's membership continues to be made up mostly of homosexuals who had children in previous heterosexual relationships.

A San Francisco lesbian said that when she and her partner went to a childbirth class at a local hospital recently, 3 of the 12 couples were lesbians.

The percentage of United States women who are lesbians remains open to question, ranging from the Kinsey Institute's estimate of 6 percent to up to 10 percent as estimated by some homosexual groups.

"It's very hard to survey a group that doesn't want to be surveyed," Mr. Fagelson said, adding that many lesbians avoid publicity.

Variety of Donors

Kim Klausner of San Francisco, who with Debra Chasnoff made a film about lesbians, said some women are entering into agreements with gay men but said many gay men could not be donors either because they carried the AIDS virus or because they did not want to be tested for the virus, which can be spread in semen. Men who are not infected sometimes serve simply as semen donors, with no involvement in rearing the child. But others sign contracts spelling out their rights and responsibilities, which can include regular visits, joint custody and child support.

Other women are going to sperm banks and using semen from anonymous donors, relying on friends to find donors or receiving sperm from relatives of their lesbian partners. Ms. Rivera said she knows one woman who used her partner's brother to donate sperm.

When Ms. Klausner, the San Francisco filmmaker, and her partner decided to have a baby, they decided they wanted to know the donor so the child's roots would be known. A gay friend agreed to be the donor. Ms. Klausner became pregnant and now has a 6-month-old boy.

A North Carolina lesbian couple, who asked not to be identified, obtained sperm from a gay man they knew. He and his lover are helping bring up the girl, now 2 years old. She spends one-third of her time with the men and two-thirds of her time with the women. "For all of us, it has been a really joyful experience," said the mother's partner.

Legal Questions

State laws recognize only the biological mother as a parent and do not allow her lesbian partner to adopt the baby. This means that if a lesbian couple breaks up or the child's mother dies, her partner can lose custody.

Another difficulty is that a man who donates his semen may want to assert rights to the child.

Custody issues aside, some lesbians say their families can be reluctant to accept their decision to become parents. One San Francisco woman, who asked not to be identified because "it would be hard for my mother," is the lover of a mother of a 5-month-old boy. The mother's mother "is the most doting grandmother," she said. But she added, "For my mother, it's more of a mixed situation. She does not know quite how to respond to the baby or how to talk about him."

Correction: Editors' Note: An article on Monday described a rise in the number of lesbians who are bearing children, usually after artificial insemination. It included the psychological speculation of clinicians, whom it did not identify, that children of lesbian parents might develop problems in intimate relationships or sexual identity. It said these difficulties could be worse if lesbian parents are openly hostile to men.

The article also quoted a psychologist and ethicist who expressed deep reservations about lesbian motherhood.

These comments were added to the article during editing. They did not fairly reflect a spectrum of views among behavioral scientists and ethicists about possible effects of being reared by lesbian parents. In the absence of evidence that hostility toward men is common among lesbian parents, the reference to such hostility was unwarranted. The article should have given lesbian parents a chance to respond to the concerns raised by others.

The article attributed to Dr. Richard Green the view that the issue of rearing children without a man in the family has not been studied enough to know whether it will lead to psychological problems. The paraphrase was imprecise. Dr. Green said that it was a particular situation, in which children are conceived with sperm from anonymous donors and reared by lesbian mothers, that has not been studied.

* * *

January 31, 1992

JUDGE LETS GAY PARTNER ADOPT CHILD

By RONALD SULLIVAN

A Surrogate Court judge in Manhattan yesterday approved the adoption of a 6-year-old boy by the lesbian partner of the child's natural mother.

The decision is believed to be the first such adoption ever approved in New York State. It comes at a time of legal attempts to provide nontraditional families greater standing in areas like housing, health insurance and child visitation.

Last May, the Court of Appeals refused to grant visitation rights to a lesbian who was not the child's adoptive parent.

Yesterday's decision would grant such visitation rights in those cases where the partner is an adoptive parent. The ruling involved a woman whose partner was artificially inseminated and gave birth to a boy in November 1985. The mother's companion subsequently filed papers to become the child's adoptive parent.

In yesterday's decision, Surrogate Eve Preminger said that: "No provision of New York law requires that the adoptive parent be of any particular gender."

Praise for the Parents

"The fact that the petitioners here maintain an open lesbian relationship is not a reason to deny adoption," she said, adding that "concern that a child would be disadvantaged by growing up in a single-sex household is not borne out by the professional literature examined by this court."

Gay rights activists said the ruling could be used as a precedent to aid the efforts of other homosexuals to adopt children.

In the ruling, the judge said the decision conferred "legal recognition of their mutual status as parents" despite the absence of a marriage certificate.

"Today a child who receives proper nutrition, adequate schooling and supportive shelter is among the fortunate, whatever the source," she said. "A child who also receives the love and nurture of even a single parent can be counted among the blessed."

"Here this court finds a child who has all the above benefits and two adults dedicated to his welfare, secure in their loving relationship, and determined to raise him to the very best of their considerable abilities," she said.

Because there are no opposing legal interests in the case, the ruling is not subject to appeal.

Supporters of gay rights called the ruling significant because New York is a magnet for gay people, and many gay couples would now be encouraged to begin adopting children.

Couple 'Thrilled'

William Rubenstein, director of the National Lesbian and Gay Rights Project for the American Civil Liberties Union, and James Marks, an A.C.L.U. lawyer who represented the couple, said the ruling was important because the court extended the legal status of a family to a gay couple.

The adoption of the boy, identified in court papers only as "Evan," grants the child several important legal rights, the judge said. It establishes the obligation of the adoptive parent to support the boy, makes him eligible for the adoptive parent's medical and Social Security benefits. It also makes the adoptive parent eligible for visitation rights in the event the couple's relationship ends.

In a statement, the couple, who were not identified, said they were "thrilled."

"We have been a family through all of Evan's life and we are relieved that the court has formalized Evan's relationship with both of us," they said.

Paula Ettelbrick, director of the Lambda Legal Defense and Education Fund, a gay legal rights' organization, hailed the ruling, saying it "will help solidify lesbian and gay family life in New York."

Last May, the Court of Appeals declined to expand the definition of parenthood to include what it called "biological strangers." In that case, a lesbian was denied the right to visit her former lover's child. As a gay couple, the two women had never tried to adopt the child.

The Court of Appeals has, however, expanded the rights of gay couples in other areas. In a ruling a year ago, the court said gay couples were legally entitled to the same legal protection as married couples under the state's rent control laws.

Before making her ruling yesterday, Surrogate Preminger said the adoption was recommended by Professor Sylvia Law of the New York University Law School, who served as the legal guardian for the boy during the court proceedings, and by two experts in social work and adoption.

The surrogate said the couple had lived together for 14 years. She said the boy's mother is a 39-year-old assistant professor of pediatrics and an attending physician at a "respected teaching hospital" and that her partner holds a doctorate in psychology and teaches at a "highly regarded private school."

She said the couple decided to have a child under an arrangement in which one of them was artificially inseminated by a mutual friend who formally relinquished any claim to the child, born in November 1985.

"Separate or together," the court said "the adoption brings Evan the additional security conferred by formal recognition in an organized society. As he matures, his connection with two involved, loving parents will not be a relationship seen outside the law, but one sustained by the ongoing legal recognition of an approved, court ordered adoption."

*   *   *

August 11, 1993

COURT BACKS LESBIAN'S RIGHT TO ADOPT A PARTNER'S CHILD

By JOSEPH F. SULLIVAN
Special to The New York Times

NEWARK, Aug. 10—A family court judge has upheld a lesbian's right to become the adoptive parent of her partner's child, in an unusually detailed opinion addressing a practice that has been growing, largely out of public view, since the mid-1980's.

The judge, Phillip M. Freedman, ruled that it would be in the best interests of the child, a 3-year-old girl, to allow her adoption by the woman who has had a "committed relationship" with her mother for 10 years.

The girl, whose mother was artificially inseminated, would have greater legal protection with the adoption, Judge Freedman said after examining New Jersey law and precedents from New York and Vermont courts.

Psychological Relationship

He said New Jersey law had long recognized a psychological parent-child relationship between a child and someone other than the child's biological parent, as well as the need "to protect the child from the emotional trauma which may be caused by terminating such psychological relationships."

Paula Ettelbrick of the National Center for Lesbian Rights said there have been 100 similar court-approved adoptions by lesbians, chiefly in California and other western states. Those uncontested private adoptions were accomplished by simple court orders that did not attract public attention.

"In the beginning of the movement, we were keeping the cases quiet," Ms. Ettelbrick said. "But as each adoption was granted, since the only question was the best interest of the child, we felt more confident and have been asking judges to write opinions comparing the adoptions with the laws in their states."

She said the only setback came in Vermont, where a lower court ruled that, under state law, the natural mother would have to surrender her parental rights if the child were adopted by another woman. Ms. Ettelbrick said her organization appealed to the Vermont Supreme Court, which ruled in June that the law allowed a "stepparent exception" and said that same-sex adoptions fell within that exception.

Provides Legal Protections

Judge Freedman said New Jersey allows a similar "stepparent exception" and said that cutting off the biological mother's parental rights would be "antithetical to the child's best interests."

Echoing a New York opinion handed down in January 1992 in the adoption of a child named Evan, Judge Freedman said he was convinced that the adoption would cause no change to the young girl's daily life and would bring some critical legal protections, such as the right to be supported by the adoptive parent and to inherit from her and her family, as well as eligibility for health insurance and Social Security benefits.

During the 16 months since the adoption request had been filed, Judge Freedman had appointed a guardian for the child, Professor Barbara Coles Bolella of Seton Hall University Law School, and had asked her and the Children of the World, an independent investigative organization, to submit reports and make recommendations concerning the adoption. He said both reports "recommended quite emphatically that granting this petition for adoption would be in the best interests of this child."

Professor Bolella, who observed the women and the child in their home, said today, "This is one very lucky child."

'Reflects Common Sense'

Judge Freedman said that although some states still maintain presumptions against granting custody to gay and lesbian parents, only two, Florida and New Hampshire, have statutes prohibiting such adoptions. He said at least 10 states have rejected presumptions against awarding custody to gay men and lesbians.

In the opinion, the biological mother is identified as E. O., an executive vice president of a large communications company. Her partner, identified as J. W. G., works part time at a cable television company and cares for the child at home.

In a telephone interview today, the adoptive parent, Joan G., said the decision would make no change in their daily routine. "We're the same family today that we were yesterday, and we believe the opinion really reflects common sense," she said.

Both women said they have long been accepted as a family in their neighborhood, their community and at their daughter's nursery school. "Truly, we've been completely accepted in town and at work," said the biological mother, Elaine O.

But they said they did not want to give their full names, identify where they live or expose their daughter to the publicity flowing from the court opinion because there is still a chance she "might be hassled in some way."

Judge Freedman said the case came at a time of great change in the thinking about what constitutes a family. "We cannot continue to pretend there is one formula, one correct pattern that should constitute a family in order to achieve the supportive, loving environment we believe children should inhabit," he said.

* * *

January 1, 1994

MOTHER FIGHTS A SON'S ADOPTION BY HOMOSEXUALS

Special to The New York Times

SEATTLE, Dec. 31—Rarely a day goes by, Megan Lucas says, that she does not regret giving up parental rights to her son, Gailen, in August 1992, when he was 2.

But she says she was 21 years old then and at a low point in her life, abusing drugs and alcohol. She had a history of trouble with the law and had abandoned the boy when he was 5 months old. It seemed like the right decision at the time.

One thing that comforted her, she says, was a photograph of her son from social workers. In it Gailen was with his smiling foster mother and father on a trip to Disneyland. She recalls hoping that the boy would be adopted by the couple.

But Gailen, now 3, was not adopted. Instead, he was moved around, spending time in at least six foster homes until, in September, he was placed with a new couple, Ross and Louis Lopton, two gay men. This time Mrs. Lucas, who says she is now devoutly Christian, objected.

Since learning of the Loptons' homosexuality, Mrs. Lucas has been fighting in court to get her son back. First she contended that she had been coerced by social workers into giving up permanent parental rights to the state. But a Whatcom County Superior Court judge rejected that argument. Now she and her husband, Wade, are trying a new tack—petitioning to adopt Gailen.

Competing Adoption Plans

On Jan. 28, the Washington State Court of Appeals will consider competing adoption plans filed by the Lucases and the Loptons. Gailen's father has not come forward.

At a time when gay rights has become a nationwide issue, the Lucas case has become a cause celebre for several small but vocal anti-gay rights groups in Washington State. Laws in most states, including Washington, do not discuss the issue of adoptions by same-sex couples. Only two states, Florida and New Hampshire, prohibit such adoptions.

In Washington, opponents of gay rights have conducted prayer vigils and letter-writing campaigns, and a conservative radio talk show in Seattle has given the case top billing.

Mrs. Lucas, meanwhile, has become an unlikely celebrity. Wearing conservative dresses and looking older than her 22 years, she has appeared on talk shows on national television to argue that homosexuals are bad role models for children.

"Every child needs a mother and a father," Mrs. Lucas said in a telephone interview from her house on Orcas Island, Wash., which is 60 miles north of Seattle. "What's going to happen to my son? He'll be ridiculed for having a father and a father. Kids can be cruel."

Plans for Legislation

In January, two conservatives in the Washington Legislature, Val Stevens, a Republican, and Thomas Campbell, a Democrat, plan to introduce a bill that would prohibit adoptions in the state except by married, heterosexual couples.

"It's lunacy that these people should be allowed to adopt," Mrs. Stevens said.

One anti-gay group, the Citizens Alliance of Washington, is using the case to gain support for a ballot initiative that would ban adoptions by same-sex couples, forbid the public schools from teaching that homosexuality is acceptable and prohibit the legalization of homosexual domestic partnerships. The treasurer of the Washington group's political action arm, Lon Maban, is also a leader of the Oregon Citizens Alliance and, with that group, drafted a ballot measure for Oregon that would have classified homosexuality as "abnormal, wrong, unnatural and perverse." The Oregon proposal was narrowly defeated in November 1992.

While Mrs. Lucas says she has no animosity toward homosexuals, she says she is opposed to their being parents. "I don't know these two men," she said. "I'm just worried about my son."

Larger Battleground

Gay rights groups say Mrs. Lucas is being used as a pawn by anti-gay groups. Her legal battles are being partly financed by the Rutherford Institute, a conservative think tank in Charlottesville, Va. The institute will provide any research Mrs. Lucas or her lawyer, Richard Kimberly, needs in fighting the Loptons, said Nancy Reynolds, a spokeswoman for the institute.

Charles Brydon, president of Washington Citizens for Fairness/Hands Off Washington, a statewide coalition organized recently to oppose anti-gay measures, said: "The radical right is using this case to instill fear in the mainstream voter. They don't give two hoots about this kid or the woman who is the mother."

Adding a twist to the story, five Seattle-area lesbians have held news conferences to assert that Mrs. Lucas had once been romantically involved with another woman. Mrs. Lucas denies ever having a lesbian relationship, her lawyer said.

In November, both the Lucases and the Loptons filed petitions for custody of the boy. The Loptons have refused to comment. Their lawyer, Brian Linn, said his clients want to shield Gailen from attention from the news media. He would say of them only that they live in Seattle and are in their 30's.

Reversal in Court

Initially, the court ordered the boy to go to the Lucases as part of a 60-day home study review, which is part of the adoption procedure. But on Dec. 10, the state won a postponement of the order, which will be reviewed by the appeals court.

That last ruling was the second setback for Mrs. Lucas in her efforts to regain custody of Gailen. The first was the Superior Court decision in September rejecting her argument that she had been coerced into giving up parental rights by social workers with the State Department of Social and Health Services. The social workers had asserted that the boy would be better off with other parents, said her lawyer, Mr. Kimberly.

Whatever the outcome, Gailen Lucas, who takes medication to control hyperactivity, will not be an easy child to handle, said Penny Vederhoff, who coordinates a support group for gay and lesbian parents in Seattle and who knows the Loptons.

And Mrs. Lucas acknowledges that she has had problems with caring for her son. In 1990, when Gailen was 5 months old, she was a single parent who was abusing drugs and alcohol. Since she was 12, she had been in and out of juvenile detention centers after arrests for larceny and burglary.

An Overwhelmed Parent

Overwhelmed with parenting, she says, she left Gailen in the care of her mother and sister in 1990. When she returned two months later, the state had taken custody of the child and placed him in the first of a series of foster homes.

Mr. Lucas, who is 30, has had his own run-ins with the law. On Feb. 24, he was given a suspended one-year jail sentence and ordered to perform 240 hours of community service for stealing a vacuum cleaner from his employer, a janitorial service, according to court records.

Mrs. Lucas says her life has now stabilized. She has taken parenting classes and has recovered from alcohol and drug abuse. She and her husband, who were married in April 1992, have a 1½-year-old daughter, Rebecca.

"I was once young and stupid and drunk," Mrs. Lucas said. "But I've changed. All we want is to have Gailen home so we can give him the love he needs."

* * *

April 22, 1995

LESBIAN'S APPEAL FOR CUSTODY OF SON REJECTED

RICHMOND, April 21—The Virginia Supreme Court today rejected a lesbian's plea for custody of her 3-year-old son, ruling that "active lesbianism practiced in the home" could stigmatize the child.

The mother, Sharon L. Bottoms, a Kmart clerk who lives in a Richmond suburb, lost custody of her son in 1993 when a local judge ruled that homosexuality "renders her an unfit parent." Ms. Bottoms's mother, P. Kay Bottoms, had sued her for custody and had kept the child, Tyler Doustou, throughout the court fight.

Today, in a 4-to-3 decision, the state's highest court said that although lesbianism in itself did not make a parent unfit, homosexual conduct remained a felony under state law and thus was an important consideration in determining custody.

Justice A. Christian Compton, writing for the majority, said, "Living daily under conditions stemming from active lesbianism practiced in the home may impose a burden upon a child by reason of the 'social condemnation' attached to such an arrangement, which will inevitably afflict the child's relationships with its peers and with the community.'"

In the dissenting opinion, Justice Barbara Milano Keenan wrote, "There is no evidence in this record showing that the mother's homosexual conduct is harmful to the child." She was joined by the court's other female justice, Justice Elizabeth B. Lacy, and Justice Henry H. Whiting.

Ms. Bottoms, 25, and her partner, April L. Wade, 29, wept when they were told of the decision. They left the Virginia office of the American Civil Liberties Union without attending a news conference their lawyers had scheduled.

In an interview on Thursday, Ms. Bottoms said she would not give up. "We don't regret this fight, but we feel it's something we shouldn't have to go through," she said. "I deserve my baby. I gave birth to him. I want him."

Leaders of gay rights groups said today's ruling gave credence to views that had already been disproved by social scientists.

"This gives the judicial stamp of approval to anti-gay prejudice," said Suzanne B. Goldberg, a staff lawyer for the Lambda Legal Defense and Education Fund. "There are countless studies demonstrating that sexual orientation is unrelated to good parenting. Under this ruling, any parent who is a member of a socially disapproved group could be vulnerable to a custody fight."

The justices overturned a decision by the Virginia Court of Appeals, which last year issued a broad opinion that gay-rights advocates hailed as giving hope to homosexual parents nationwide. But court rules required Tyler to remain with his grandmother while she appealed.

Lawyers for the A.C.L.U., which represents Ms. Bottoms, said they would seek a rehearing before the Virginia Supreme Court. They said they had not decided whether to appeal to the United States Supreme Court, but an A.C.L.U. official said his group had been deluged with offers from lawyers eager to help.

The grandmother was not available for comment today. Her lawyer, Richard R. Ryder of Richmond, said: "I'm just happy for the boy. He has a chance at a normal life. His life would have been mighty screwed up if he'd gone back with the mother."

Several lawyers who follow gay-rights issues said judges often awarded custody to one birth parent if the other is homosexual. Kate D. Kendall, the legal director for the National Center for Lesbian Rights in San Francisco, said Supreme Courts in five states had awarded custody on such a basis.

But Ms. Kendall said cases in which custody had gone to a third party for that reason were rare.

In a decision that affects couples in 10 counties in New York, a panel of the Appellate Division of the state court ruled this month that lesbians and gay men cannot adopt their partners' children, because they are not legally married.

The Virginia justices in the majority opinion cited several instances in which Ms. Bottoms had been accused in testimony of neglecting Tyler, and they noted that both women had admitted hitting him.

But lawyers for the couple disputed some of the accusations and said those factors would not have jeopardized custody for a heterosexual couple.

Celinda L. Lake, a Democratic pollster, said research she conducted in March for the Human Rights Campaign Fund showed that "the vast majority of Americans, even people who are uncomfortable with gay and lesbian issues, strongly oppose taking children away from their biological parents who happen to be gay or lesbian."

Ms. Bottoms, who is divorced, has visitation rights with Tyler Monday mornings through Tuesday nights. But he may not go to her apartment, and he may not see Ms. Wade. Ms. Bottoms said that she and her son stayed at friends' homes and that they often spent the day indulging his passion for feeding ducks.

"He's confused," she said. "I tell him he can't come to my house because Grandma and the judge-man don't want him to."

Ms. Wade said she talked to Tyler by telephone. "I sense that he feels that I've abandoned him," she said. "I told him that if we won, I'd teach him to swim this summer."

Virginia law forbids marriages between people of the same sex. Last year, Ms. Bottoms and Ms. Wade exchanged rings at a ceremony, Ms. Bottoms wearing a bridal gown, and Ms. Wade wearing a tuxedo.

"We didn't do it to spit in anybody's face," Ms. Wade said. "We did it because we love each other. My only regret about that day is that Tyler wasn't there."

* * *

November 5, 1993

FOR GAY COUPLES, RULING TO CHEER ON ADOPTION; TYPICALLY, ONLY ONE MEMBER HAD BEEN CONSIDERED PARENT

By FRANK BRUNI

There is not a scintilla of doubt in Barbara Berger's mind or heart: She is a mother to Billy Berger-Bailey, a reality played out daily when she picks out his clothes, smothers him with kisses or reads him bedtime stories. His current favorite is "Humphrey the Lost Whale," about a wayward humpback in San Francisco Bay.

But in the eyes of the law there is ambiguity aplenty, because Ms. Berger's companion of 10 years, Nan Bailey, who gave birth to Billy three years ago after donor insemination, ultimately controls all custodial rights.

That's been very frustrating," said Ms. Berger, who lives with Ms. Bailey and Billy in Larchmont, N.Y.

Ms. Bailey agreed. "She has to trust me," she said, "and even though she does, it's an ugly thing to have hanging over your head."

With a ruling Thursday by the state's highest court that couples need not be married to adopt, the two women finally hope to banish that specter. They said that within hours of the ruling, they told a lawyer to start adoption proceedings for Ms. Berger.

The two women are among what legal experts say are thousands of gay and lesbian couples in the state who are raising children together, with only one of them recognized as a parent under the law.

Many of these couples have paid rapt attention to the months of legal debate that preceded last week's decision, pinning their ardent wishes to it and plotting their families' futures around it.

A few in Manhattan, who knew that one Surrogate's Court judge was sympathetic to second-parent adoption by gay men and lesbians, scurried in recent months to file petitions with her in an effort to formalize adoptions before the State Court of Appeals ruled, in case it came down the other way.

Others, who lived in places where judges were reluctant to grant such adoptions without the clear blessing of a higher court, simply had to watch and wait.

All the while, they could not help focusing on all that was at stake. Without legal recognition of both parents, one could lose custody of a child if the other died, or could be denied visitation if the couple broke up. The child, meanwhile, had no official claim to any benefits from the parent not recognized under the law.

"There's been a collective holding of our breath around the state," said Paula Ettelbrick, legislative counsel for the Empire State Pride Agenda, a gay and lesbian lobbying organization. She and other lawyers who work with gay men and lesbians said that word of the decision on Thursday spread rapidly among gay and lesbian parents, some of whom learned about it by telephone or beeper long before hearing it on the news.

Although the court decision applies equally to heterosexual couples, it holds particular significance for homosexual ones,

Suzanne DeChill/The New York Times

Billy Berger-Bailey, 3, plays with Nan Bailey, left, who bore him, and Barbara Berger. The women, companions of 10 years, have started adoption proceedings in an effort to give Ms. Berger equal legal status as a parent.

who cannot legally marry and therefore must file for adoption as unmarried couples.

Many lesbians have had their own children through donor insemination, and gay men and lesbians have been able to adopt in this state if they applied as single parents and, in many cases, were willing to take in children who were considered least likely to be adopted.

The problem came in getting courts to grant legal rights to the other partner in each couple. Legal experts estimated that in the last decade, and particularly the last three years, between 20 and 50 homosexual couples, mostly female, have sought out sympathetic judges and secured second-parent adoptions.

Ms. Ettelbrick and other legal experts said that the exact number of such adoptions was impossible to know, because Family and Surrogate's Court records are sealed. What is clear, they said, is that the vast majority of gay and lesbian couples were so certain of failure in the courts that they didn't even try.

And not all will necessarily try or succeed now, experts said. The high court's ruling means only that a judge should not let marital status determine his decision, but it does not compel a judge to find in favor of all cases.

And advocates for gay and lesbian couples say that many will be deterred from pursuing joint legal custody of children because the court process can be invasive and costly, involving months of home visits and a price tag of more than $5,000.

What many couples have done instead is to draft stacks of documents—special powers of attorney, wills and guardianship agreements—that always represented a certain degree of wishful thinking, since none of the documents held anything approaching the legal force of a formal adoption.

That's precisely what Wayne Steinman and Sal Iacullo did to protect themselves and Mr. Iacullo's 8-year-old daughter, Hope Steinman-Iacullo. Although her name, as well as all of her school and medical forms, reflects the equal roles that both men play in her life, Mr. Iacullo is the parent listed on the adoption forms, and thus the only one recognized by law.

"It's infuriating," said Mr. Steinman, who is vice president of the parents' association at the public school that Hope attends in Brooklyn. The family lives in Staten Island.

Mr. Steinman said the arrangement was most unfair to Hope herself, who he said should be entitled to the Social Security, the medical benefits and the life insurance of both her parents. In fact, the reason that Mr. Steinman and Mr. Iacullo, who have been together 23 years, decided to have Mr. Iacullo adopt the girl is that he had the better benefits at the time.

Like many of those interviewed for this article, Mr. Steinman said that his relationship with his partner and his partner's family was strong enough that he was not overly frightened that a breakup or death would take Hope away from him.

Even so, he said he was determined to petition the court for legal recognition as one of Hope's adoptive parents. He said one reason he did not do so before now was a lower court ruling in the jurisdiction that includes Staten Island that suggested he would fail. Now, with the encouragement of the Court of Appeals ruling, he plans to file papers in two to three months.

"It's tremendously exciting, because it's finally going to bring our legal standing in line with the way we've been living the last eight years," said Mr. Steinman said. "The state is finally catching up to the reality of our home and to many like it."

The state has actually been fickle, its whims dictated by geographic and judicial happenstance. For example, Albert and Marvin Day of Belcher, N.Y., a tiny town just 20 minutes from Vermont, won an extremely rare joint-parent adoption of two H.I.V.-positive boys in August 1992 in Washington County Surrogate's Court.

But when they moved last year to adopt two retarded children, they were directed to a different judge in Family Court, and were told they could only petition for single-parent adoptions.

"It's silly," said Albert Day, who had his surname legally changed to his partner's. "We did this once. We've proven ourselves."

In Manhattan, which was not technically affected by the same lower court ruling that discouraged Mr. Steinman and Mr. Iacullo, at least three lesbian couples were granted adoptions within the last month by Surrogate Eve Preminger. The couples and their lawyers were racing to get a decision before the Court of Appeals ruling, and had carefully arranged it so that their cases were likely to be heard by Surrogate Preminger, who had made favorable decisions on such cases in the past.

A partner in one of these couples, who spoke on the condition of anonymity, said she lived in fear through September and October that a negative Court of Appeals ruling would come down before Surrogate Preminger got to her case.

Surrogate Preminger came through on Oct. 17, making the woman a legal parent of the 3-year-old girl to whom her partner had given birth.

"I didn't appreciate how much it would mean to me until the judge signed the order," she said. "What makes me her

mother isn't the legal paper—it's the bath that I give her every night, the love that I feel for her. But still, it felt like a validation, like a stamp of approval. My heart swelled."

* * *

August 31, 1996

LESBIAN LOSES COURT APPEAL FOR CUSTODY OF DAUGHTER

By MIREYA NAVARRO

MIAMI, Aug. 30—A Florida appeals court today upheld a decision by a trial judge transferring custody of a girl, now 12, from her lesbian mother to her father, who served eight years in prison for murdering his first wife 22 years ago.

In a unanimous opinion, the First District Court of Appeal said that "competent and substantial" evidence supported the trial judge's ruling last year that "conduct" at the mother's house was harmful to the girl and that she was better off living with the father. Lawyers for the mother, Mary Frank Ward, 47, of Pensacola, said they would appeal to the Florida Supreme Court.

"We are not suggesting that the sexual orientation of the custodial parent by itself justifies a custody change," the appeals court said. Rather, "as is the case when a child is inappropiately exposed to heterosexual conduct, the court's primary focus should be on what conduct is involved and whether the exposure to that conduct has had or is reasonably likely to have a direct and adverse impact on the child."

But lawyers for gay rights organizations involved in the case said that the court seemed to adopt the stereotypic and prejudicial view that gay parents expose their children to improper behavior.

"The problem is that if you have a judge who thinks negatively about a gay person having custody, it's very easy for him to say, 'I find that there are problems in this household,'" said Beatrice Dohrn, the legal director of Lambda Legal Defense and Education Fund, which filed a friend of court brief in the case. "They don't have to say very much to justify taking a child away."

Ms. Ward and John Andrew Ward were divorced in 1992, and she kept primary custody of the girl. Mr. Ward had been convicted in 1974 of the second-degree murder of his first wife, which he attributed to his "stupidity, jealousy and anger," the appeals court said. The court noted that Mr. Ward has remarried and found steady work as a building supply yard worker.

Last September, Judge Joseph Tarbuck of Escambia County Circuit Court ordered the child to move in with her father after Mr. Ward told the court that she made statements of a sexual nature, exhibited bad table manners and personal hygiene habits and preferred to wear men's cologne. Ms. Ward, who at the time lived with a girlfriend and two older daughters—one of whom is lesbian and had a live-in girlfriend—denied that she had exposed the child to any sexual behavior in her home. She noted that she had filed for increased child support shortly before Mr. Ward petitioned for custody.

In a written statement released by his lawyers today, Mr. Ward described the court's decision as one that held that "growing up in a household with a husband and wife residing together in marriage was more beneficial to an 11-year-old girl than growing up in a household with four adults engaged in homosexual relationships."

Mr. Ward said that his daughter, who he said "very much loves her mother," has made new friends and "is not embarrassed to bring them home for a visit or introduce them to her father and stepmother."

Gay rights lawyers said the case of Ms. Ward, a restaurant chef, is disappointing because there was no evidence of any improper conduct at her home.

"When a decision like this comes down, it does strike fear into the hearts of lesbian and gay parents around the country because they recognize that if it could happen to a parent like Mary Ward it could happen to them," said Kathryn D. Kendell, the executive director of the National Center for Lesbian Rights, which helped represent Ms. Ward.

* * *

September 30, 1996

ADOPTION PROPOSAL CAUSES AN UPROAR

By CAREY GOLDBERG

LOS ANGELES, Sept. 27—David G. James, a Navy transport coordinator here, adopted Patrick and Christian, 6, and 4, this winter, giving the two brothers a permanent home after rootless years in foster care and starting a single-parent family with help from his retired mother.

When Mr. James speaks of the regulations that Gov. Pete Wilson is proposing to prevent unmarried couples in California from adopting, he cannot stem his indignation, fearing that families like his would be affected by the rules: "Is it better," he demanded, "for the single parents and child to be denied one another's love and affection and nurturing and that child be kept in long-term foster care?"

The Wilson administration puts the issue differently: "The Governor believes the best interest for a child is to have a mother and father in the household," said the Governor's spokesman, Sean Walsh.

That kind of clash between proponents of traditional families like Mr. Wilson and members of less traditional ones like Mr. James erupted this month as the proposed regulations on adoption went through the public hearing process in three California cities.

At issue were rules that require social workers to spell out to the judge who decides a child's fate that if would-be adoptive couples are not married, the adoption is not "in the best interest of the child." After this month's public hearings, the rules will be reviewed by social service officials and the state's Office of Administrative Law, and could take effect a year from now.

Mr. Walsh and other state officials said the rules would merely affirm the status quo, formalizing a practice that is already in effect, under which social workers are supposed to recommend against unmarried couples but the judge can, and often does, award them the child if they seem worthy.

The Wilson administration also maintains that the rules would not prevent single people or gay couples from adopting, or reduce the number of children adopted—about 6,000 a year in California—but only protect children by bringing them into homes with more stability. The regulations specifically refer to unmarried couples.

But opponents contend that the rules would discourage would-be adoptive parents who do not fit the Ozzie-and-Harriet model, parents who are desperately needed by the thousands of children stuck in the foster care system.

The dispute has also clearly touched a nerve among non-traditional families and their backers here as well, one already raw in an election season in which both parties' conventions prominently featured babies proving their family values credentials and the Defense of Marriage Act cementing the ban on gay marriage was made Federal law.

Gay and lesbian legal groups accuse Mr. Wilson of wielding the regulations to further deprive single-sex couples of legitimacy as a family unit, and of trying to court conservatives at election-time that way. Child advocates say they are concerned that if single and gay people are discouraged from adopting, many needy children will never find parents. The American Civil Liberties Union also protested.

"It's sending a strongly anti-gay message and really a message of intolerance when there are all these children out there and loving people prepared to be parents," said Taylor Flynn, a staff lawyer who handles lesbian and gay rights at the A.C.L.U.

Virginia Weisz, a children's lawyer at Public Counsel, a pro bono law firm in Los Angeles, said that with 25 percent of the children adopted here going to single people, she worried that the pool of adoptive parents would shrink drastically if gay and single people were discouraged from applying.

"The thing about his policy," she said of Governor Wilson, "is the moral values he claims to represent are not truly child-focused. They're kind of puffing ourselves up as a righteous man and woman in a home with a white picket fence as the way we should go for all kids—and most kids don't have that choice. What the kids need is to be the apple of somebody's eye, and if they're not they'll grow up and turn into homeless or criminals, and how can we do that to kids?"

She and others noted that many single and gay parents adopted the children in least demand, those past their infancy or with AIDS or other serious problems.

Mr. Walsh and other officials said the policy was not meant to single out gay adoptive parents, but such assertions do not relieve the concern for people like Ron Rogers, a Burbank pharmacy manager who adopted 3-year-old Matthew, who has AIDS, last year.

For gay men like him who want to adopt, he said, "It will be almost impossible," because social workers will have less leeway to make their own, independent decisions, based on getting to know the unmarried would-be parents, on whether a home is a good one for children.

Gay and lesbian parents, he predicted, would have to apply as single people and hide the fact that they lived with partners. "You've got to play games with the state," he said.

The proposed rules could be especially tough on lesbian families because they also require recommendations against the "limited consent" adoptions often used when a lesbian partner legally adopts her partner's child.

Mr. Walsh, the governor's spokesman, walks a fine line in his explanation of the need for the regulations, saying they would not discriminate against gay and single adoptive parents but that they are part of a broad effort by Mr. Wilson to stem the "social pathology" caused by poor or non-existent parenting.

"You can't look at this in the micro and say he's going after gay or lesbian or unwed couples," Mr. Walsh said. "This is one element of his broader social agenda, and the governor wants to—call it old-fashioned if you want—but he wants to instill a sense of right and wrong. It's wrong for 13-year-olds to have babies. It's wrong for 12-year-olds to not have a father in the home and go into gangs. It's wrong for parents not to live up to their obligations and pay child support. He wants to say: 'No more excuses. We know what works, we know what's worked in the past, and damn it, I'm going to stand up and say it'."

Mr. James, the adoptive father, would stand up and say something different, however. "When you make rules like this, it should be for the benefit of the children because they are our focal point," he said. "This seems like regulations for the sake of regulations."

* * *

November 30, 1997

HOMOSEXUAL FOSTER PARENT SETS OFF A DEBATE IN TEXAS

By SAM HOWE VERHOVEK

DALLAS, Nov. 25—When Rebecca Bledsoe, a Texas child welfare supervisor, ordered the emergency removal of a baby boy from his foster parent, her rationale was straightforward: "We don't ordinarily license persons when we know them to be involved in any kind of crime on an ongoing basis."

The 3-month-old boy was in the care of a woman whose live-in lover, Mrs. Bledsoe learned this past summer, was another woman.

Thus began an unusual, one-woman crusade against homosexual parenting, one that has put Mrs. Bledsoe at the center of a controversy that has spotlighted a 118-year-old state statute that makes homosexual activity a crime.

Twenty states have "anti-sodomy" statutes, with Texas and five others specifically defining acts between members of the same sex as criminal sodomy. Though rarely enforced and declared unconstitutional in several states, the laws remain on the books.

Mrs. Bledsoe has added a different wrinkle to the issue by arguing that because homosexual acts are a crime in Texas, those who engage in them should not be considered fit to serve as foster or adoptive parents.

Mrs. Bledsoe also said that foster children placed with gay or lesbian couples do not have a parental "role model" of one sex or the other.

Her stance has led to a rebuke from the state's Department of Protective and Regulatory Services, which quickly overruled her decision to take the boy away from a Dallas-area woman who had disclosed her lesbian relationship to a state caseworker. And earlier this month, the department took another step against Mrs. Bledsoe, a 10-year veteran whose job evaluations had been exemplary: it demoted her to caseworker, though she retains her $35,000-a-year supervisor's salary.

Mrs. Bledsoe has counterattacked with a labor grievance in which she argues that she is being punished because she "failed to exhibit respect to the foster mother who admits to criminal sexual conduct."

Mrs. Bledsoe, whose work had never before stirred controversy, has become a heroine in some conservative quarters, and the target of withering criticism from gay rights advocates who accuse her of fostering discrimination against homosexuals.

Some members of the State Legislature have vowed to renew efforts to take the sodomy statute off the books, while others have suggested that Texas should make it illegal for homosexuals to adopt children. Only New Hampshire and Florida have such laws, said Ruth Harlow, managing attorney for the Lambda Legal Defense and Education Fund, a homosexual rights advocacy group based in Washington.

The baby boy at the center of the case was born in April to a woman with a history of drug-related crime. She is now in jail on prostitution charges. The boy remains under the care of the Dallas-area woman, a former child-care worker in her 30's who is registered as a foster parent and who, with her lesbian lover, has applied to adopt the boy.

However, there are indications that the boy may soon be moved, not because the women have been found unfit, but because a Chicago couple—the boy's uncle and aunt—have said they are willing to take him in.

The Chicago couple, located with the help of a conservative legal group that supports Mrs. Bledsoe, are already caring for 6-year-old twin girls who were born to the same mother as the infant boy. Under state guidelines, their blood relation to the baby makes them potentially more suitable parents, as does their race: they, like the baby, are black, while the lesbians are white.

The lesbian couple have not been publicly identified and have declined to speak out on the matter, but the case has forced state officials to acknowledge that some homosexuals are certified as foster parents.

The officials say that although placement guidelines give preference to a "traditional family" that includes a husband and wife, many gay men and lesbians are serving a need by taking in babies, especially those born with the AIDS virus, whom the officials describe as difficult to place.

"Sexual orientation is not mentioned at all in our policy," said Linda Edwards, a spokeswoman for the child welfare department in Austin. "If I were to summarize our policy, our agency looks for potential parents who are capable of nurturing, protecting and parenting a child who has been abused or neglected."

Technically, same-sex couples, as well as unmarried heterosexual couples, cannot jointly register as foster parents; as a matter of practice, though, both partners provide care, even if only one is registered.

There are no statistics on how many lesbians or gay men are serving as foster parents or adoptive parents. But the numbers have clearly grown over the past decade, said Joe Kroll, executive director of the North American Council on Adoptable Children, based in St. Paul, Minn., a coalition of adoption professionals and parental support groups that promote adoption.

In many ways, Mr. Kroll said, the spread of AIDS may have increased social acceptance of the practice: many gay couples go out of their way to adopt HIV-positive babies.

In the case involving the Dallas baby, the question that arose was whether Mrs. Bledsoe had exceeded her authority by calling for his immediate removal from the home. An earlier visit by a caseworker had found that the boy was flourishing under the care of the foster parent.

A report filed after that visit said the lesbian couple "appear to be very committed to each other and have a relationship based on respect and love." Mrs. Bledsoe said she thought it totally inappropriate that the state would condone the practice.

"There are two women involved, and the boy is guaranteed not to ever have a father" if he remains with them, she said. "My responsibility is to do the best I can for him, and this is not the best I can do."

Mrs. Bledsoe, who is married and has a 25-year-old son, said she was shocked to find herself overruled and then reprimanded. But Ms. Edwards, the child welfare agency spokeswoman, said Mrs. Bledsoe's effort to remove the boy from the foster mother's home was a clear violation of agency guidelines.

To justify such a decision, "There needs to be immediate risk of harm to the child," Ms. Edwards said. "Did this case meet that need? No, not in our opinion. The child was getting very good care."

* * *

December 18, 1997

ACCORD LETS GAY COUPLES ADOPT JOINTLY

By RONALD SMOTHERS

NEWARK, Dec. 17—Homosexual couples in New Jersey will for the first time be able to adopt children jointly, just as married couples can, under an agreement reached today with state child welfare officials.

Gay advocacy groups, which negotiated the agreement with the state, hailed it as an important step toward full recognition of gay and lesbian parental rights.

State regulations previously did not allow unmarried couples to adopt a child jointly in a single proceeding, requiring them instead to go through the already difficult and costly process twice.

While the settlement grew out of a challenge by gay and lesbian groups, the change also applies to cohabiting heterosexual couples, said Michelle Guhl, Deputy Commissioner of the State Human Services Department.

Michael Adams, staff lawyer with the American Civil Liberties Union's Lesbian and Gay Rights Project, represented more than 200 gay and lesbian families in a class-action suit against the state policy.

Mr. Adams lauded the decision as "historic" and one that made New Jersey the first state to say specifically in its adoption policy that gay and unmarried couples would be measured by the same standards as married couples.

But other advocacy groups around the country and experts in child welfare policies suggested that the agreement was remarkable only insofar as it explicitly allowed a category of adoptions that have been quietly taking place in a number of states in recent years.

Anne Sullivan, an adoption researcher with the Child Welfare League of America, representing state child welfare officials across the nation, said allowing such joint adoptions was significant. But, she added, "it has been going on rather discreetly" in a number of states already. Once child welfare officials and family courts in states around the country got beyond the "mythology surrounding the heated issue of homosexual adoptions" in recent years, she said, such adoptions have become more prevalent in a variety of forms, from single-parent to stepparent adoptions and joint adoptions.

Only two states, New Hampshire and Florida, have laws specifically barring gay men and lesbians from adopting children. And in 1994, courts in both Wisconsin and Colorado interpreted their state laws as barring such adoptions, said Mary Bonauto, civil rights project director for the Boston-based Gay and Lesbian Advocates and Defenders. By the same token, advocacy groups for gay men and lesbians successfully defeated legislative efforts last year to pass laws barring them from adopting children in Georgia and Missouri.

"But this issue isn't even on the radar in other states," Ms. Bonauto said. "Courts are more used to having to coerce people to take responsibility for and care for their children, and so when someone, anyone, comes in asking to be made responsible, they are very sympathetic. For these states, sexual orientation is not the issue. Parenting ability is the issue."

But to the Washington-based Family Research Council, a conservative advocacy group, the New Jersey consent decree was "a loss for children and a victory for the homosexual agenda." Kristin Hansen, a spokeswoman for the group, said, "This is bringing state government in to validate and give its stamp of approval to these practices, and it seems to have government saying for the first time that a gay environment is a good one to grow up in."

The agreement settled a lawsuit filed last June by the gay and lesbian groups and was signed by Judge Sybil R. Moses of Bergen County Superior Court in Hackensack.

Today's action follows a ruling by Judge Moses on Oct. 22 in the case of Michael Galluccio and Jon Holden, two gay men who had sought to adopt their 2-year-old foster son, Adam. State officials had prohibited the adoption, saying the law did not allow unmarried couples to adopt a child in a single proceeding, although they could go through the process twice.

While the judge had said publicly that she was allowing the joint adoption solely because it was in the best interest of the child, lawyers for both the state and the advocacy groups said she went much further in her written opinion issued in the closed adoption hearing.

Ms. Guhl, the Deputy Human Services Commissioner, said the judge's ruling had basically "cleared up the ambiguity" in the state adoption law.

"We had never had a court ruling on this issue, and suddenly Judge Moses said the law allowed us to jointly consider unmarried couples who we felt could be good parents," she said.

At a news conference here today, Mr. Holden and Mr. Galluccio reflected on the events that led to the consent decree. "This all started out with Adam and two fathers trying to protect their son," Mr. Holden said. "What we now have is a recognition that there are many different kinds of families."

Mr. Adams of the A.C.L.U. project and Lenora Lapidus, the director of the New Jersey offices of the civil liberties union, said the action today allowed gay men and lesbians to confront local adoption officials if they are told they cannot adopt and get court fees in the event that they have to go into court to enforce the decree legally.

"We expect," Ms. Lapidus said, "that many gay and lesbian couples will now apply to adopt."

* * *

April 7, 2000

RIGHTS OF GAYS AS PARENTS ARE WIDENED BY COURT

By DAVID M. HALBFINGER

TRENTON, April 6—Significantly expanding the parental rights of gay and lesbian people in New Jersey, the State Supreme Court ruled today that a lesbian who had helped raise her former partner's twins deserved visitation rights after the couple's breakup.

Gay rights advocates called the decision the clearest ruling yet that so-called psychological parents should be treated the same as biological parents in custody disputes.

"It's another nail in the coffin of the opposition's idea that we shouldn't be around children," said Wendy Berger, president of the New Jersey Lesbian and Gay Coalition.

The ruling applies not only to gay and lesbian parents but also to any unmarried couples where one partner is not a biological parent. "Our clients and other lesbians and gay men are always asking for just an equal application of the legal rules," said Ruth E. Harlow, deputy legal director of the Lambda Legal Defense and Education Fund. "And that's what we got here."

The case involved a woman who became pregnant by artificial insemination shortly after beginning a relationship with another woman. She gave birth to twins, a boy and a girl, in 1994. The two women moved in together and held a commitment ceremony in 1995. But the following year, the biological mother ended the relationship.

In its unanimous ruling, the court borrowed from a 1995 decision in Wisconsin that established a four-part test to determine whether someone had attained the status of a functional or psychological parent. He or she must have had the consent of the child's legal parent, lived with the child, taken on responsibility for the child's care and done so for enough time to forge a parental bond with the child.

"Once a third party has been determined to be a psychological parent to a child," Associate Justice Virginia Long wrote in today's decision, "he or she stands in parity with the legal parent."

The court disregarded a group called Concerned Women for America, which warned in a friend-of-the-court brief against a heavy judicial hand favoring the homosexual agenda.

The group had argued that the Legislature was the appropriate forum for the issue and said the courts were deliberately misconstruing the law to reach a politically correct result.

Legislatures in a few states, such as Connecticut, Hawaii, Massachusetts and Virginia, have already passed laws allowing judges to grant custody or visitation rights to people unrelated to a child if it is in the child's best interest. And courts in Wisconsin, Pennsylvania and Massachusetts have granted some visitation rights to nonbiological parents, said Leslie Cooper, a lawyer for the lesbian and gay rights project of the American Civil Liberties Union.

But in New York, among many states, blood lines are paramount. The Court of Appeals ruled in 1991 that state law restricted visiting rights to parents and other blood relatives of children, like siblings and grandparents.

Rejecting a lesbian's attempt to gain visiting rights to her former partner's child, the court refused to expand the definition of parenthood to include what it called "biological strangers."

Gay rights advocates likened today's ruling to a 1998 consent degree in which all legal barriers in New Jersey to joint adoption by unmarried couples, either same-sex or heterosexual, were removed.

"New Jersey has really shown itself to be a leader in recognizing the realities of parent-child relationships, instead of attempting to impose a mold that doesn't apply to everyone," Ms. Cooper said.

Ms. Berger, of the Lesbian and Gay Coalition, said the ruling "completely debunks what our opponents often say about our unfitness as parents, or teachers, or as role models."

In her ruling, Justice Long noted that New Jersey family law already provided that children should not be cut off from contact with one parent when the parents' relationship ends. That law states that the "word 'parent,' when not otherwise described by the context, means a natural parent or parent by previous adoption."

Justice Long wrote, "Although the Legislature may not have considered the precise case before us, it is hard to imagine what it could have had in mind in adding the 'context' language other than a situation such as this, in which a person not related to a child by blood or adoption has stood in a parental role vis-a-vis the child."

*   *   *

MARRIAGE AND DOMESTIC PARTNERSHIP

March 4, 1989

GAY MARRIAGES: MAKE THEM LEGAL

By THOMAS B. STODDARD

"In sickness and in health, 'til death do us part." With those familiar words, millions of people each year are married, a public affirmation of a private bond that both society and the newlyweds hope will endure. Yet for nearly four years, Karen Thompson was denied the company of the one person to whom she had pledged lifelong devotion. Her partner is a woman, Sharon Kowalski, and their home state of Minnesota, like every other jurisdiction in the United States, refuses to permit two individuals of the same sex to marry.

Karen Thompson and Sharon Kowalski are spouses in every respect except the legal. They exchanged vows and rings; they lived together until Nov. 13, 1983—when Ms. Kowalski was severely injured when her car was struck by a drunk driver. She lost the capacity to walk or to speak more than several words at a time, and needed constant care.

Ms. Thompson sought a court ruling granting her guardianship over her partner, but Ms. Kowalski's parents opposed the petition and obtained sole guardianship. They moved Ms. Kowalski to a nursing home 300 miles away from Ms. Thompson and forbade all visits between the two women. Last month, as part of a reevaluation of Ms. Kowalski's mental competency, Ms. Thompson was permitted to visit her partner again. But the prolonged injustice and anguish inflicted on both women hold a moral for everyone.

Marriage, the Supreme Court declared in 1967, is "one of the basic civil rights of man" (and, presumably, of woman as well). The freedom to marry, said the Court, is "essential to the orderly pursuit of happiness."

Marriage is not just a symbolic state. It can be the key to survival, emotional and financial. Marriage triggers a universe of rights, privileges and presumptions. A married person can share in a spouse's estate even when there is no will. She is typically entitled to the group insurance and pension programs offered by the spouse's employer, and she enjoys tax advantages. She cannot be compelled to testify against her spouse in legal proceedings.

The decision whether or not to marry belongs properly to individuals—not the Government. Yet at present, all 50 states deny that choice to millions of gay and lesbian Americans. While marriage has historically required a male partner and a female partner, history alone cannot sanctify injustice. If tradition were the only measure, most states would still limit matrimony to partners of the same race.

As recently as 1967, before the Supreme Court declared miscegenation statutes unconstitutional, 16 states still prohibited marriages between a white person and a black person. When all the excuses were stripped away, it was clear that the only purpose of those laws was, in the words of the Supreme Court, "to maintain white supremacy."

Those who argue against reforming the marriage statutes because they believe that same sex marriage would be "anti-family" overlook the obvious: marriage creates families and promotes social stability. In an increasingly loveless world, those who wish to commit themselves to a relationship founded upon devotion should be encouraged, not scorned. Government has no legitimate interest in how that love is expressed.

And it can no longer be argued—if it ever could—that marriage is fundamentally a procreative unit. Otherwise, states would forbid marriage between those who, by reason of age or infertility, cannot have children, as well as those whose elect not to.

As the case of Sharon Kowalksi and Karen Thompson demonstrates, sanctimonious illusions lead directly to the suffering of others. Denied the right to marry, these two women are left subject to the whims and prejudices of others, and of the law.

Depriving millions of gay American adults the marriages of their choice, and the rights that flow from marriage, denies equal protection of the law. They, their families and friends, together with fair-minded people everywhere, should demand an end to this monstrous injustice.

Thomas B. Stoddard, a lawyer, is executive director of the Lambda Legal Defense and Education Fund, a gay rights organization.

*   *   *

May 31, 1989

SAN FRANCISCO GRANTS RECOGNITION TO COUPLES WHO AREN'T MARRIED

By KATHERINE BISHOP
Special to The New York Times

SAN FRANCISCO, May 30—The city's Board of Supervisors today passed an ordinance giving legal recognition to the "domestic partnership" of homosexuals and unmarried heterosexual couples.

By a vote of 9 to 0, with two board members absent, San Francisco became the first major city to provide for the public registration of these relationships in the same way that other couples file marriage licenses.

The immediate impact of the measure will be to extend to domestic partnerships the same hospital visitation rights accorded to married couples. In addition, city employees in a domestic partnership will now have the same bereavement leave policy as married city workers. Both of these benefits are crucial issues to San Francisco's gay community, which has been hit hard by the AIDS epidemic.

The ordinance also mandates that the city and country, in instituting new policies or practices, cannot treat marital status differently from domestic partnership.

Mayor Art Agnos is expected to sign the ordinance within 10 days, a spokesman said.

Rules for Recognition

The ordinance defines domestic partnerships as "two people who have chosen to share one another's lives in an intimate and committed relationship." The two must live together and be jointly responsible for basic living expenses; neither may be married to anyone else. The couple must file a declaration of domestic partnership with the county clerk and pay a $35 fee. The partners must also file a notice of termination if their relationship ends.

Harry G. Britt, the president of the Board of Supervisors and a leader in the gay community here who sponsored the ordinance, predicted that other cities would now follow San Francisco's example. "There was a nervousness about this issue that needed to be overcome," he said.

Gay rights groups in Boston and New York are already organizing efforts to have such measures adopted.

Arthur Leonard, a professor at New York Law School, said a group called the Family Diversity Coalition is meeting with members of the New York City Council to find a sponsor for the measure. He also said candidates for Mayor would be questioned on the issue at a forum tonight sponsored by the Stonewall Democratic Club, a predominantly gay political group.

Veto of 1982 Measure

In 1982 the San Francisco board, by a vote of 8 to 3, passed a measure that extended health insurance coverage to domestic partners, but it was vetoed by Mayor Dianne Feinstein. Two years later she also rejected the recommendation of her Task Force on Equal Benefits to extend health benefits to the partners of city employees.

In both 1982 and this year the Roman Catholic Archdiocese of San Francisco strongly objected to the ordinances. In a statement issued May 23, Archbishop John Quinn called the current measure an attack on marriage and family life.

The current measure gives a committee 90 days to create a plan under which the domestic partners of city workers may be included in health insurance coverage. The plan would have to be adopted by the Health Services System, which administers health benefits offered to city employees.

The workers themselves would bear the cost of adding domestic partners to the plan because San Francisco does not pay for health insurance for the spouses or dependants of most city employees.

Three smaller California cities, Berkeley, Santa Cruz and West Hollywood, have already passed ordinances that to some degree recognize domestic partnerships. In 1985, for example, Berkeley extended health benefits to the unmarried partners of city workers.

Last year Los Angeles allowed unmarried city employees to use sick leave and bereavement leave upon the illness or death of a domestic partner if the couple has privately registered with the city after living together at least a year.

* * *

November 5, 1989

SMALL STEPS TOWARD ACCEPTANCE RENEW DEBATE ON GAY MARRIAGE

By PHILIP S. GUTIS

Since the early 1970's, when seven states, including New York, rejected the idea of allowing homosexual couples to marry, the issue has been all but dormant. But recently the debate has been revived. Among the most significant reasons for the renewed interest, gay-rights leaders say, is the AIDS epidemic, which has brought questions of inheritance and death benefits to many people's minds.

In September the annual convention of the influential State Bar Association of California urged recognition of marriages between homosexual couples. Some churches are also discussing whether to recognize same-sex couples who belong to their congregations.

"Nobody was even pushing that issue in the gay community in California," said Paula L. Ettelbrick, the legal director of the Lambda Legal Defense and Education Fund, a gay-rights group. "It was well meaning straight people who took the debate away from us."

Alan I. Rothenberg, the president of the California bar association said, "The message is one of fundamental fairness. It is unfair to deny people very substantial benefits solely on the basis of their sexual orientation." The group's resolution, which suggests changing the California civil code to define marriage as a "personal relation arising out of a civil contract between two people," does not become official policy unless adopted by the group's conservative board of governors. In any case, it is expected to influence other bar associations to consider similar moves.

In the meantime, opponents of homosexual marriage are preparing for a fight. "We do see this as a major battleground in the 1990's," said Gary L. Bauer, who was President Reagan's domestic affairs adviser and who now heads the Family Research Council in Washington. Same-sex marriage "would undermine deeply held and broadly accepted ideas of normalcy," Mr. Bauer said. "We have customs against such things because it has been the consensus of 2,000 years of Western civilization that such arrangements were to be discouraged."

Several European countries, including Sweden and the Netherlands, are beginning to grant rights to unmarried couples. In May, Denmark went the furthest when it became the first country to allow homosexual couples to join in "registered partnerships" giving them many of the rights of marriage.

Earlier this month, six male couples took part in civil ceremonies in Copenhagen in which they were legally joined and given certificates of partnership.

No one expects that a wave of state legislatures will follow Denmark's lead any time soon. Twenty-five states still have sodomy laws, though they are seldom enforced, and no state permits same-sex marriages.

But the issue has been rekindled by recent moves in San Francisco, Seattle, New York and several other cities toward laws that give some fringe benefits to the unmarried partners of city employees.

Also important was the recent decision by New York's highest court that two homosexual men living together for a decade could be considered a family under New York City's rent-control regulations.

'Second-Class Status'

"The marriage exclusion is offensive," said Nan D. Hunter, the director of the Lesbian and Gay Rights Project of the American Civil Liberties Union. "It carries a strong symbolic as well as a legal message that lesbian and gay Americans are relegated to second-class status."

Some gay-rights leaders and their supporters, especially women, do not think homosexuals should fight to gain entry into an institution that many feminists find oppressive.

In the current issue of Out/Look, a national gay-rights quarterly, Ms. Ettelbrick, the legal director of the Lambda Legal Defense and Education Fund, debated the issue with Thomas B. Stoddard, Lambda's executive director. "Gay relationships," Mr. Stoddard wrote, "will continue to be accorded a subsidiary status until the day that gay couples have exactly the same rights as their heterosexual counterparts."

Ms. Ettelbrick argued that marriage will not be a liberating experience. "In fact, it will constrain us, make us more invisible, force our assimilation into the mainstream and undermine the goals of gay liberation," she said.

A Better Strategy?

Some gay-rights leaders feel that it might make more strategic sense to de-emphasize the goal of homosexual marriage and push instead for laws recognizing "domestic partnerships," people who live together as families, regardless of their sexual orientation.

"We are not seeking to redefine the idea of marriage or spouse, but to conform legal policies with how people are living," said Thomas F. Coleman, the co-director of the Family Diversity Project in Los Angeles. "It's not as fraught with polarization." A few religious groups are already starting to recognize same-sex partnerships. In 1987 the bishop of the Newark Diocese of the Episcopal Church in New Jersey urged that the national Episcopal organization support the blessing of couples of the same sex.

In Hoboken, the Oasis, the diocese's new ministry for homosexual men and women, is preparing for several ceremonies this spring. The Rev. Robert Williams, the executive director of the Oasis, will perform the ceremonies. He said he would like to see the church's canon changed to allow for same-sex marriages. "If we learned anything from the 60's," he said, "separate but equal is unequal."

* * *

March 11, 1990

SIX ARE ARRESTED PROTESTING POLICY ON GAY HOUSING

IRVINE, Calif.—Six students were arrested last week at the University of California at Irvine in a demonstration protesting Chancellor Jack W. Peltason's refusal to permit gay and lesbian couples to live in family dormitories. The demonstrators blocked an entrance to the administration building.

About 100 students blocked a door after a noon rally, but most left after two warnings from the campus police. The six students who were arrested linked arms in front of the door and, after a third warning, were handcuffed and driven to the campus police station. They were charged with blocking the doorway and failing to disperse, both misdemeanors. They are to appear in court April 7. Before the crowd converged on the entrance, Melissa Soto, one of the protest organizers, said the blockade was symbolic of nontraditional couples being "locked out" of campus housing.

"With this civil disobedience, we are forcing people to look at the issue," Ms. Soto, a senior from Newport Beach, Calif., majoring in women's study, told the onlookers.

'Human Rights Now!'

Hundreds of students congregated around the administration building, holding signs protesting what the students called discriminatory university housing rules. Many chanted "Human rights now!" and sang gospel songs while the police made the six arrests.

"This is the most right thing I've done," Donald Ruth, a senior from Baldwin Park, Calif., majoring in psychology, said before his arrest. "We will not tolerate this kind of discrimination at U.C.I. any longer."

Students and administrators said the rally was so planned, the police already knew whom they were going to arrest, and had finished most of the paperwork before the demonstration. The demonstrators knew when the police would begin making arrests, and left exactly 10 minutes for "the media to record the rally," said Judith Olson, a graduate student from Anaheim majoring in English and one of the protest organizers.

Several students appeared shaken and teary-eyed as they were escorted from the administration building.

Protest Followed Ultimatum

"I'm amazed that I had to get arrested for people to notice my cause," Napoleon Lustre, a senior from Manila majoring in philosophy, said as he was driven away in a police van.

The protest followed an ultimatum last month to Mr. Peltason from a student group called the Shantytown Committee. The group demanded that the university recognize gay domestic partnerships, and that it hire openly homosexual teachers.

Unless its demands were met, the group said, it would stage demonstrations and rebuild a cardboard shantytown dismantled after a protest last month.

The Chancellor responsed to the ultimatum by pledging support for the recognition of domestic partnerships, but added that his hands were tied by state laws."The only nonstudents who may live in family housing are legal spouses and dependent children," he said.

A dozen members of the committee rebuilt the shantytown on Monday, two days before the protest.

"You must choose between justice and university policy," the committee said. "You can't be committed to working with the campus community to insure that there is a hospitable environment while supporting policies explicitly inhospitable to nontraditional families."

* * *

December 24, 1992

BENEFITS GRANTED TO GAY PARTNERS

By ANTHONY DEPALMA

Two of the country's leading universities have extended health insurance, tuition benefits, library privileges and other fringe benefits to the gay and lesbian partners of faculty and staff members and students.

Stanford University and the University of Chicago, acting independently and without arousing much controversy, voted earlier this month to give gay and lesbian domestic partners the same benefits that have been available to married couples.

The actions by the trustees of both Stanford and Chicago established the most far-reaching domestic partnership policies offered by any universities and could lead to similar actions by other universities that now are studying the issue, said George A. Chauncey, an assistant professor of history and chairman of the University of Chicago's Lesbian and Gay Faculty and Staff Organization.

Only a handful of colleges provide health insurance to gay partners. Among them are Pitzer College in Claremont, Calif., and the University of Iowa. Many universities allow gay partners to use facilities like the library and gymnasium but do not offer health insurance or tuition benefits, which can be expensive.

Stanford in early December extended fringe benefits to the long-term, same-sex domestic partners of its 9,000 active employees and 2,000 retirees.

The policy, which will take effect Feb. 1, extends health and dental benefits to same-sex domestic partners just as it does for legally married couples. Partners will also be able to audit university classes, their children will qualify for tuition grant programs, and the partners will qualify for library and athletics privileges.

Partners will be asked to sign affidavits that certify the partnership and that state that the couple's commitment includes financial responsibility for each other.

In a statement, Barbara Butterfield, vice president for faculty and staff affairs at Stanford, said the gay men, who have an increased risk of H.I.V.-related illnesses, would not drive up the cost of insurance. She said as many as 60 employees were expected to sign up for the new benefits. At the University of Iowa, only eight people enrolled under its new policy.

* * *

March 2, 1993

A LEGAL THRESHOLD IS CROSSED BY GAY COUPLES IN NEW YORK

By JONATHAN P. HICKS

Some came as if headed to a formal event, dressed in tuxedos or party dresses. Many had to go to work and wore business suits or casual slacks. All of them—the first 109 couples to register as "domestic partners" in the City of New York—left with something long withheld, an official acknowledgement of their untraditional lives.

Six weeks after Mayor David N. Dinkins signed an executive order enabling heterosexual and homosexual couples to register as unmarried "domestic partners" and receive some of the rights of married couples, the City Clerk's office yesterday began conducting the registration. In a short process in the Municipal Building, couples filled out a few forms, presented identification and received a certificate similar to a marriage license.

Demonstration of Support

"This makes us happy, because it is the closest thing we can get to the kind of acknowledgement couples get in the straight world," said Manny Lacayo, a 26-year-old accountant in an advertising firm. Mr. Lacayo and his partner, David

Sara Krulwich/The New York Times

On the first day for unmarried New Yorkers to register as domestic partners, Diane Flood Goldstick, left, and Patricia Flood Goldstick, were the second couple to do so. They combined their family names last year.

Vega, a 29-year-old hospital clerk, said they would celebrate later in the evening with a bottle of Champagne "and a toast to the future."

They began arriving in small numbers an hour before the office opened at 9 A.M. After a noon demonstration on the steps of City Hall in support of the registration, more couples streamed across the street up to the second floor of the Municipal Building, to fill out an affidavit and have it notarized, then to show identification and receive a certificate with blue borders. By the early afternoon, a line wrapped around the long corridor.

Many wore pink carnations or held bouquets. The couples were fairly evenly divided between men and women. There were three heterosexual couples. Cameras flashed as newly registered couples—some with friends and family members alongside—hugged, kissed and celebrated. Many said they would have special dinners with friends or parties in their homes.

Ruth Berman, a 59-year-old grandmother, said that registering offered another sign to her family, friends and society that her 18-year relationship with her companion, 56-year-old Connie Kurtz, was as binding as any heterosexual marriage. "We have six grandchildren between the two of us," Ms. Berman said. "And we're taking another step to make a statement. We wish we still had greater rights as a couple, but this is a start."

Under the Mayor's executive order, registered domestic partners employed by the city are entitled to the same unpaid leave that has been available to city workers who are married and wish to care for a new child. Also, registered domestic partners will have the same rights as married spouses in visiting partners at municipal hospitals and city jails.

In addition, registered domestic partners will be entitled to the same standing as married couples in qualifying for apartments and in inheriting a lease in residential buildings owned or overseen by city housing agencies, including rent-controlled and rent-stabilized apartments.

Sara Krulwich/The New York Times

Doug Anderson, left, and Michael Elsasser took their sons, Zachery, 4, and Justin, 7, to the Municipal Building in Manhattan yesterday as they registered with the city as "domestic partners."

While couples in the line to register said they considered their standing as registered domestic partners a milestone, many said the recognition did not go far enough. Some lamented that obtaining a certificate was largely symbolic and that they had a long road toward obtaining the rights of married couples.

Many couples complained that they did not have the same rights in obtaining health insurance as married couples. Nor, they noted, did they have the same tax status as married couples. Legislation is pending before the City Council that would offer the same health benefits for city workers who are domestic partners as provided to married city employees.

Similar to Marriage License

"Domestic partnerships deserve full legal recognition," said Ellen Carton, executive director of the New York chapter of the Gay and Lesbian Alliance Against Defamation. "We work. We pay taxes. We have children. We share the same responsibilities that married couples do. We deserve the same benefits."

The process for registering as domestic partners is similar to obtaining a marriage license, which is governed by the state. The major distinction is that couples getting married go through a ceremony, while domestic partners fill out an affidavit, which is notarized, unlike a marriage license. The cost for a marriage license is $30; the cost to register as domestic partners will be $20. For the moment, registration is free, under a 30-day waiting period mandated by the city charter following the beginning date of the registration, said Carlos Cuevas, the City Clerk.

Not all New Yorkers were as thrilled as the newly registered couples. One critic of the Mayor's executive order is the Roman Catholic Archdiocese of New York. "In general, the family is still the bedrock, the absolute foundation of our society," said Joseph G. Zwilling, a spokesman for the Archdiocese. "The efforts to give other living arrangements the same status as the family hurts society at large."

Can Be Terminated for $15

About 25 other cities, counties or states in the United States—including San Francisco, Washington and Minneapolis—have established some form of domestic partnerships or have offered parental leave or medical benefits for domestic partners of unmarried government workers. Under the executive order in New York City, the partnership can be terminated by filing a form with the city, accompanied by a $15 fee.

Some couples yesterday questioned whether the presence of the city's domestic partnership registration would reduce the rights of the couples who remain unregistered, particularly in tenant disputes with landlords. Some recent court rulings had validated the rights of homosexual tenants whose partners had died.

Peggy Brady, an attorney who is on the board of the New York Chapter of the Gay and Lesbian Alliance Against Defamation, said that little would likely change for unregistered couples as a result of the city's registration procedure. She said that there already are a number of factors judges use to determine the status of homosexual relationships, ranging from the number of vacations taken together to length of time partners had lived with each other.

"This would be just one more piece of evidence in showing that two people are domestic partners," Ms. Brady said. "The intention of this domestic partnership registration is that tenants should be able to still use other methods to prove that they are domestic partners."

The Procedure for Registering

To register as domestic partners, couples must fill out and submit a registration application in the City Clerk's office in the Municipal Building. Both partners must be at least 18 years old and be unmarried and unrelated. They must also attest that they have a "close and committed personal relationship."

The application must then be notarized, attesting that the couple has been living together before the date on the certificate. After verifying their identities, paying a $20 fee (which will not become effective until the beginning of April), a certificate is issued.

To terminate the domestic partnership, a couple must fill out a form with the City Clerk's office and pay a $15 fee. Couples are not allowed to register for six months after the termination of a previous registration.

*   *   *

August 1, 1993

PROUD, OFFICIAL PARTNERS

By LYNDA RICHARDSON

James D'Eramo does not care whether people like him or not. But he does care about equal rights. So in March Mr. D'Eramo stood fifth in line with his lover, Will Wake, to sign a new registry that is the City of New York's official acknowledgment of their commitment to each other.

Straight from the City Clerk's Office, where they signed a registry for unmarried heterosexual and homosexual partners, the couple went to an airline counter to put their new status to the test. In canceling an Italian vacation trip, they demanded the same bereavement benefits given to married couples. Mr. Wake's father had recently died. It took their

new certificate to persuade Alitalia Airlines to give full ticket refunds to both men.

"It is a very real way that domestic partnership protected us from being had," said Mr. D'Eramo, a medical writer who lives on the Upper West Side with his partner of eight years. "Nothing is more material than getting your money back."

Mr. D'Eramo and Mr. Wake are among nearly 1,000 couples who have sworn to their commitment as domestic partners in a registry that gives homosexual and unmarried heterosexual couples some of the rights enjoyed by married couples.

Means Different Things

In concrete and less tangible ways throughout New York City, the legal status attached to domestic partnership has meant different things to different people in their everyday lives.

More than 200 couples signed up the first week, at the beginning of March. An overwhelming majority of registrants in New York are gay and lesbian, according to a voluntary survey of the confidential registry by the City Clerk's Office. Less than 10 percent are unmarried heterosexuals, including some elderly and disabled couples, the office said.

Some couples have used their new status to obtain discount prices for health club memberships and car rentals. One woman, armed with the domestic partner certificate, confronted a funeral parlor that had refused to accept her as a close relative. She was then allowed to make future funeral arrangements for her ill partner. Many other couples have used their new status to make symbolic, political points about their sexuality.

Mr. D'Eramo said he and his partner were not looking for marriage. But he was troubled about what might happen if he "were hit by a truck." Could Mr. Wake visit him in the hospital? Could his partner lose their apartment if he died?

Same Visiting Rights

"We're still hundreds and hundreds of things behind in the privileges and rights given to heterosexual married couples," he said.

Under the new initiative, registered homosexual and unmarried heterosexual couples are granted the same standing as married couples in qualifying for apartments and in inheriting leases in residential buildings overseen by city housing agencies. They also receive the same visiting rights at city jails and hospitals. Those who work for the city may also take unpaid leave to care for newborn children. But the health benefits offered spouses of city workers are not granted to live-in partners, a benefit that the Mayor promised gay voters in his 1989 campaign.

While the registration program has come under criticism for carrying little weight on practical issues like health coverage, city officials call the program, which was created by an executive order issued in January, a significant step. Though there are no precise figures on the number of people covered by the order, everyone recognizes that many New Yorkers live in nontraditional arrangements.

"It's a major statement about the legitimacy of these families in our society," said Dennis deLeon, the Commissioner of Human Rights.

'A Binding Agreement'

"It means something," said Arlene Kochman, executive director of Senior Action in a Gay Environment in Manhattan. "The more people who say, 'We are domestic partners and we have this piece of paper,' the more it will begin to be known that this is a binding agreement and it will be respected."

But for Ellen Carton and Diane D'Alessandro, the certificate recognizing their commitment is a reminder that public acceptance of their seven-year relationship remains an elusive goal.

The couple's certificate is tucked in a manila envelope in the kitchen, nearby so that it can be easily found in the tidy clutter of their Greenwich Village apartment. The certificate has not left its envelope. It is next to their living will and other documents they have prepared for their own legal and financial protection.

"We can still be discriminated against in a way that married couples aren't, in terms of health benefits, in terms of tax returns, not to mention that our relationship is not validated by society," said Ms. Carton, 35, who directs the Gay and Lesbian Alliance Against Defamation in New York.

A Moment of Gravity

When Ms. Carton and Ms. D'Alessandro stood third in line on the first day of registration, they felt light hearted at first. They sobered as they sensed a gravity to the moment. "I thought twice; it's a serious commitment I'm making," said Ms. D'Alessandro, a 40-year-old policy analyst with a union for public employees.

But Ms. D'Alessandro says she still worries when she responds honestly to strangers asking about her relationship. And Ms. Carton said she would not have minded a Cuisinart, or any of the usual gifts that married couples receive.

"I felt like 'Why can't I get that stuff?'" said Ms. Carton, who has boycotted weddings for years. "I felt like 'Why can't it be very obvious and accepted that the relationship we have is as serious as any married couple?'"

Despite the existence of the new registry, many couples, both homosexual and heterosexual, have kept away out of fears that they have much to lose and little to gain.

Not for Gay People Only

City officials say they still have to convince many unmarried heterosexual couples that the registry can benefit them, too. They plan a campaign to inform groups for the elderly and disabled beginning this fall. Mr. deLeon says the city's research indicates that domestic partnership will not reduce government benefits, though he and others add that the issue has not been legally challenged.

Frieda Zames, 60, and her companion, Michael Imperiale, 56, are unwilling to be a test case. Both are aggressive advocates for the disabled. They picket everything from the piteous images of the disabled on Jerry Lewis telethons to the lack of lifts on more city buses and ramps into more stores.

But the couple, together for 22 years, fear that registering may jeopardize Mr. Imperiale's government benefits, including a monthly $520 check in disability and Medicaid benefits.

"Why give them a reason to take money from me?" said Mr. Imperiale, who has a genetic neurological disorder.

"Even if it's not true, people are afraid of it; they believe it's true," added his companion.

2 Fathers, 2 Sons, 4 Burgers

But Doug Robinson said he registered to prove a point. He saw it as one more step toward redefining what makes a family. Last March, Mr. Robinson, a Citibank computer programmer, was No. 44 in line with his partner, Michael Elsasser, a fabric pattern designer. They took their two sons, Justin, 7, and Zachary, 5. When it was over, they all went to McDonald's for lunch.

Since then, Mr. Robinson said, the subject of domestic partnership has not come up in their household. And the certificate with blue borders has been lost somewhere in their sunny Washington Heights apartment, cluttered with children's toys and books.

"We felt strongly that we have to do this, not only for ourselves but for our children and the greater society at large," Mr. Robinson said. "It's one more barrier that has been knocked down regarding our families and our lives."

* * *

September 30, 1993

ALBANY TO LET INSURANCE LAW COVER PARTNERS

By KEVIN SACK
Special to The New York Times

ALBANY, Sept. 29—Reversing a 54-year-old policy, the Cuomo administration today lifted New York State's prohibition against providing family health insurance that covers the domestic partners of homosexuals and unmarried heterosexuals.

The ruling, which had been sought for years by advocates for gay and lesbian rights, opens a new and untested market for the insurance industry in New York, among private companies and local governments. It also provides a major political opportunity for Mayor David N. Dinkins, who may now be able to grant insurance benefits to the domestic partners of city employees. Such a move would almost certainly energize gay and lesbian supporters in Mr. Dinkins's re-election campaign against Rudolph W. Giuliani, the Republican-Liberal candidate.

Mr. Dinkins said in a statement that the ruling "eliminates a major obstacle" to the settlement of a lawsuit filed against the city in 1988 by the Lesbian and Gay Teachers Association. The teachers charged that it was discriminatory for the city not to provide health coverage for their domestic partners while allowing coverage for the spouses of married teachers and other city employees.

The Mayor's counsel, George B. Daniels, said Mr. Dinkins would also seek to negotiate insurance coverage for domestic partners with other unions of city workers. "The Mayor's made it clear that this isn't just about settling the gay teacher's case," Mr. Daniels said. "It's a benefit that should be available to all city employees."

Opponents Question Cost to Budget

If New York City establishes health benefits for its employees' domestic partners, it will join at least a dozen municipal governments around the country. They include those of San Francisco, Seattle, Boston, West Hollywood, Calif., Ann Arbor, Burlington, Vt., Berkeley and Minneapolis.

Opponents of insurance rights for domestic partners question whether the cost would place an unmanageable burden on the New York City budget. But city officials and gay and lesbian lobbyists said that other cities had not encountered such costs.

In Seattle, for instance, insurance fees for coverage that includes domestic partners amounts to only 1.3 percent of total health insurance costs for city employees, said Sally W. Fox, Seattle's benefits manager. She said that 476 of the city's 10,000 employees were signed up for domestic partnership benefits, and that an estimated 70 percent of them were heterosexuals.

Mr. Daniels said the city was working on projections of the potential cost. Since Mr. Dinkins signed an executive order allowing domestic partners to register with the city earlier this year, 1,300 couples have registered, Mr. Daniels said. Only 150 of them include a city employee.

Until today, the State Insurance Department had interpreted the state's insurance law, which was written in 1939, as allowing family health coverage primarily for employees, their spouses and their children. It had ruled specifically that domestic partners were not covered by a clause in the law allowing coverage for "other persons chiefly dependent upon" an employee "for support and maintenance."

'Appropriate Circumstances'

In 1989, James P. Corcoran, then the Insurance Superintendent, ruled that such a change would be "wholly antithetical to the Legislature's purpose." His successor, Salvatore R. Curiale, repeated that stand in 1990.

But after reconsidering at the request of Mr. Dinkins and Gov. Mario M. Cuomo, Mr. Curiale ruled today that domestic partners can be covered "under appropriate circumstances, without a showing of complete, unilateral economic dependency." Although the state controls the kind of insurance that companies may offer, he said the state cannot require coverage of domestic partners.

Mr. Curiale wrote in a letter to Mr. Cuomo that "a showing of mutual interdependency would be sufficient under the law to permit coverage." He said that interdependency could be demonstrated by factors like "common ownership of property, common householding, shared budgeting, length of the relationship, etc."

He did not specify how the department would ultimately define a domestic partnership. But he said he would work with insurance companies and gay and lesbian representatives "to fashion a set of criteria that would make them sufficient to protect companies and encourage them to make the coverage available."

Mr. Curiale did not specify why he changed course. His spokesman, John Calagna, said he had been influenced by the Mayor's decision to allow domestic partners to register and by a 1989 ruling of the State Court of Appeals. It said a domestic partnership could be defined as a family for the purpose of determining the inheritance of a rent-controlled apartment.

But gay and lesbian advocates said the decision also clearly had a political motivation. It enabled Mr. Cuomo to provide significant—and cost-free—help for Mr. Dinkins five weeks before Election Day.

Mr. Dinkins won enthusiastic backing from gay and lesbian groups when he ran for Mayor in 1989, largely because he promised to provide insurance coverage and other standard benefits to the domestic partners of city employees. Since his election, he has said his hands were tied by the state's insurance law. Although he established the domestic partners' registry this year, gay and lesbian supporters have expressed disappointment in the Mayor for not fulfilling his pledge on the insurance issue.

Mr. Curiale's decision also may rally gay and lesbian support for Mr. Cuomo if he runs for re-election next year. One possible Republican opponent, Senator Alfonse M. D'Amato, was seen as playing to gay New Yorkers earlier this year when he expressed support for allowing homosexuals in the military.

'Cuomo Helping Cuomo'

"This is definitely Cuomo helping Dinkins, but it's also Cuomo helping Cuomo because he has not been able to deliver a gay-rights bill," said Dick Dadey, the executive director of Empire State Pride Agenda, a gay-rights lobbying group.

Mr. Cuomo said today that he did not make the decision for Mr. Curiale. But he said he was "quite content with the result."

Most of the speculation about the potential demand for the new insurance is centering on municipal governments, because they will presumably be under the most immediate pressure to provide it. Insurance executives said that their activity in the new market would depend on demand from employers, and they doubted there would be a spontaneous surge to fill the new niche.

One health maintenance organization, Oxford Health Plans of New York, already has filed an insurance department application to provide coverage for domestic partners. David B. Snow, the company's executive vice president, said the filing was made at the request of a large corporate client, which he would not name. He said his company had not had many other requests.

Kevin Heine, a spokesman for the Prudential, said: "As long as employers and health insurers can develop a reasonable definition of what constitutes a domestic partner, then we would provide coverage. But it's really client-driven. We have not seen a big demand for it."

* * *

June 29, 1994

CUOMO DECIDES TO EXTEND DOMESTIC-PARTNER BENEFITS

By IAN FISHER
Special to The New York Times

ALBANY, June 28—Gov. Mario M. Cuomo announced tonight that he would extend insurance benefits to the domestic partners of gay and lesbian state workers by the start of next year. He said he was uncertain whether the plan would include the unmarried partners of heterosexual state workers.

New York State is the second state to make such an announcement, though New York City and dozens of other municipalities around the nation already offer benefits to domestic partners. Two weeks ago, Vermont became the first state to do so when it agreed to extend health and dental insurance to unmarried homosexual and heterosexual partners.

The announcement came as Mr. Cuomo's campaign for re-election began to heat up and as gay men and lesbians demonstrated their growing political and social clout as they gathered in New York City and in Albany to commemorate the 25th anniversary of the uprising at the Stonewall Inn, which helped to spark the modern gay-rights movement.

'Something Useful'

Saying the change was long overdue, Mr. Cuomo said the step was "something useful, something that has symbolic value, but it has much more than symbolic value."

Mr. Cuomo and his aides said they did not know how much the extended insurance would cost nor how many state employees would be eligible. There are about 162,000 employees in the executive branch and in the state university system, said Joseph M. Bress, director of the Governor's Office of Employee Relations. Those employees are under Mr. Cuomo's direct control, and he does not need the Legislature's approval to make such an offer.

Mr. Cuomo said he expected the benefits to be available by Jan. 1, 1995. "It's an important step and it brings us that much closer to the all-encompassing fairness we aspire to here in the Empire State," he said at a reception here at the New York State Museum marking the Stonewall anniversary.

Dick Dadey, executive director of the Empire State Pride Agenda, an advocacy group, praised Mr. Cuomo's decision.

"This is a historic step by the Governor in recognizing gay and lesbian relationships," he said.

A Tricky Question

Mr. Cuomo offered few details, saying he had directed Mr. Bress to negotiate specifics with the six unions representing state workers. Among the issues will be the tricky question of how exactly to define a domestic partnership, what benefits to include and how to address any dependents of such a couple, Mr. Bress said.

"I don't doubt that the unions want it, that they are interested in it," Mr. Cuomo said. "Some of them have asked for it. So I anticipate no difficulty at all."

One potential obstacle, however, is whether to include unmarried heterosexual couples, which may increase the cost substantially. Mr. Dadey said the vast majority of other plans, including the one in New York City, cover heterosexual partners. "Our belief is that in the fight against discrimination against gay families, we should not create discrimination against other families," he said.

But Mr. Cuomo and at least one union have expressed reservations.

'An Open Question'

"It's an open question," Mr. Cuomo said. "That's wasn't my original thought, but I'll let them discuss that. There is a difference obviously. The heterosexuals in most cases have the opportunity to marry."

Ross D. Hanna, director of contract services for the Civil Service Employees Association, which represents Civil Service workers, said the union wrote a letter to Mr. Cuomo recently stating its opposition to including heterosexuals in any such benefits.

"Opposite-sex partners have other options," Mr. Hanna said. "They can certainly get married and take advantage of the legal aspects of dependency. Same-sex domestic partners certainly don't have that ability with the present legal status of gays and lesbians in New York State."

Numbers were not available from New York City tonight, but Mr. Dadey, whose organization has taken a special interest in the program there, said about 1,000 city workers have applied for benefits for their partners. He said cost for the first year of the program, which began on Jan. 1, was $5 million.

Mr. Bress said that to qualify for benefits, domestic partners would have to demonstrate some definable level of commitment, the specifics of which are to be made final in negotiations with the unions. New York City has required proof that a couple is financially interdependent. Under Vermont's new plan, state workers who want their partners covered must sign affidavits affirming that they are in an "exclusive, enduring relationship of at least six months."

Last year Mr. Cuomo asked the State Insurance Department to reconsider what it had interpreted as a legal ban on permitting insurance companies to extend coverage to domestic partners. The department reversed itself in time for David N. Dinkins to announce an extension of benefits to domestic partners at a time when he was courting the gay vote in his unsuccessful bid for re-election as New York City's Mayor.

*   *   *

February 3, 1995

STATE COURT RULES GAY PARTNERS CANNOT GET HEALTH CARE BENEFIT

By The Associated Press

ST. PAUL, Feb. 2—Minneapolis may not offer health care benefits to the partners of its gay employees, a state appeals court has ruled.

In a 2-to-1 decision filed on Tuesday, the Minnesota Court of Appeals upheld a district judge's decision last June striking down the city policy.

The court agreed that state law did not recognize same-sex partners as dependents or spouses and that the Minneapolis City Council acted beyond its authority when it adopted the domestic partners ordinance in August 1993.

The ordinance was challenged by a taxpayer who argued in a lawsuit that the city had no legal authority to extend health insurance benefits to same-sex partners. The suit said the ordinance violated state public policy "favoring marriage of heterosexual couples."

The city argued that the granting of employee health care benefits was a purely local matter. The court disagreed, ruling that the State Legislature traditionally defined the scope of municipal employees' benefits.

The court also noted that the state's gay rights law said Minnesota did not authorize the recognition of same-sex marriages and that the bill's sponsor told lawmakers it would not lead to benefits for domestic partners. Given that, the court said it was apparent that the Legislature did not intend to expand benefits to same-sex partners.

In a dissenting opinion, Judge Robert H. Schumacher said the question of who received domestic benefits should be left to cities.

The majority on the panel was composed of Judges Randolph Peterson and Daniel Foley.

Vermont became the first state to provide health care benefits to unmarried partners of state workers, both heterosexual and homosexual, in June 1994.

The city of Austin, Tex., had extended benefits to same-sex partners, but voters repealed the coverage in May 1994.

*   *   *

February 10, 1995

INTOLERANCE IN ALBANY

Joseph Bruno, the new majority leader of the New York State Senate, has revealed a streak of intolerance and ignorance toward New York's gay community.

Mr. Bruno, a Republican, made that plain this week when he barred unmarried Senate employees from receiving domestic-partnership health benefits available to all other state workers. He says he is concerned about the costs of the coverage, which the previous Governor, Mario Cuomo, negotiated with state employees' unions. But Mr. Bruno's real concern seems to have little to do with costs—they are likely to be modest for the Senate in any case—and everything to do with homophobia.

In his own words, spoken to a New York Post reporter, Mr. Bruno said he opposed subsidizing the "abnormal life style" of homosexuals, who he says "choose" their sexual orientation.

Mr. Bruno's decision came just days after the state's new Attorney General, Dennis Vacco, as one of his first official acts dropped homosexuals from the anti-discrimination hiring policy for his office that his two Democratic predecessors followed. Gov. George Pataki, to his credit, has said that he intends to retain the anti-discrimination protection and the domestic-partnership benefits for officials he personally appoints and that he will not attempt to renegotiate state labor contracts that allow domestic partnerships.

But it is not enough for Mr. Pataki to lead quietly by example. He needs to make some noise. So far he has shied from publicly criticizing Messrs. Bruno and Vacco. Yet as the state's top political leader his duty is to speak against bigoted statements or actions, even when the messengers are other important Republican officials.

Mr. Pataki also needs to shed some of his own anti-homosexual baggage. As a candidate, he said he opposed legislation to extend civil rights protections to gay and lesbian New Yorkers. He ought to reconsider and, while he is at it, rebuke those among his colleagues who foster intolerance.

*   *   *

July 27, 1995

FOR BETTER OR WORSE, A MARITAL MILESTONE; ITHACA OFFICIALS ENDORSE A GAY UNION

By DAVID W. DUNLAP

ITHACA, N.Y., July 20—On Valentine's Day, hoping to reverse a streak of poor romantic luck, Toshav Greene took a chance, called Phillip G. Storrs and invited him on a blind dinner date.

By the time they got to the strawberry cake, it was plain that Mr. Greene's luck had changed. The two men quickly fell in love. By mid-May, they had moved here together from nearby Elmira, hoping to marry and rear children. When they went to City Hall to apply for a marriage license, however, they expected a rejection.

Instead, much to their own surprise, they may get a license.

The Mayor and other leaders in this college town, home to Cornell University, have embraced the idea of granting a marriage license to a gay couple. They would be the first officials in the nation to do so deliberately in more than a dozen years.

Occasionally, a clerk may grant a license to a same-sex couple, particularly if the names are indeterminate. Pasha and Penny Rivers-McMahon received a license in Burlington, Vt., last August, but the clerk asked to get it back minutes later and has since refused to record the union of the two women.

Phillip and Toshav Storrs (Mr. Greene has changed his last name to that of his partner) may not hold on to their license very long, either. City clerks merely act as agents of the state in registering marriages, and Republican officials in Albany may object to such a license and try to quash it.

But that does not deter Mayor Benjamin Nichols, 74, a Democrat and 40-year veteran of the civil rights movement, who has met with the gay couple and said, "If they really want to go ahead with it, my position is that they should be granted a license."

The City Attorney expects to rule by the end of the summer on whether the Federal or State Constitutions would compel issuance without regard to a couple's sex. And on July 5, the all-Democratic Common Council unanimously endorsed the right of same-sex couples to marry.

National gay civil-rights advocates fear that a short-lived victory here could provoke judicial and legislative setbacks for their movement. Several organizations are in the paradoxical position of urging the couple to hold off.

Confessing a "totally divided heart," Paula Ettelbrick, legislative counsel of the Empire State Pride Agenda, said: "Part of me very much wants to say: 'Go for it. The question has been called.' But what would be gained if we won the right today and lost it tomorrow because we had not done the grass-roots lobbying that we needed to do?"

Evan Wolfson, senior staff attorney of the Lambda Legal Defense and Education Fund, said, "If you go to a court that is uneducated or that is going to rule in a climate that's unreceptive, you're almost certainly going to get back a decision you didn't really want."

Mr. Wolfson is co-counsel to two lesbian couples and a gay couple who were denied licenses in Hawaii. The Hawaii Supreme Court ruled in 1993 that a denial appeared to violate the constitutional guarantee of equal protection. It sent the case back to a lower court for a trial that is to begin in July 1996. A license granted to a gay couple in Boulder, Colo., was invalidated by a Federal court in 1982, Mr. Wolfson said.

Since that time, weddings and commitment ceremonies have become a more common feature of gay life, as have the limited benefits offered by some governments and companies to domestic partners. But no lesbian or gay couple has won the considerable range of economic and legal rights that come with officially sanctioned marriage.

In the eyes of many people, that is as it should be. "Marriage is for men and women," said Arthur J. Golder, a lawyer in neighboring Trumansburg who has spoken out against issuing a license. "It's not about better health-insurance premiums or credit ratings or access to bridal registries."

"We're created as male and female for a reason," he said. "It's not to enjoy sex. It's to procreate. That's nature's mandate. And nature's mandate becomes man's law."

State officials may not put it quite that way, but no one expects them to look kindly on an attempt to certify a gay marriage.

Lawyers involved with the Ithaca case say they are watching to see whether Attorney General Dennis C. Vacco will nullify the license or prevent its issuance. His office would not comment. The Legislature might amend the domestic-relations law, which does not specify sex, to state explicitly that marriage can occur only between a woman and a man.

None of this has served to dissuade the Storrses.

"It could be potentially detrimental in the short term," Toshav Storrs allowed. "But it could be potentially fantastic. From the information we have, that's a 50-50 call. If it's right on the line, I opt to move forward."

And Phillip Storrs said it would be useful for the public to see that they were "just a couple of regular people." Mr. Storrs, 36, grew up in and around Troy, Pa. He works at the Toshiba television tube factory in Horseheads, N.Y.

Toshav Storrs, 34, grew up in rural Oklahoma and came here in 1979 as a freshman at Cornell. He dropped out of school but returned to Ithaca in the 1980's and met Daniel Chiarilli. They moved to Tulsa and reared two children. Mr. Chiarilli was killed in a car accident in 1991.

Mr. Storrs came back to central New York last year and enrolled at Elmira College. This fall, he plans to return to Cornell, in human development and family studies.

When they applied for their license, the Deputy City Clerk, William Kaupe, started filling out the form but the City Clerk, Julie Conley Holcomb, returned from lunch and halted the proceeding.

She cited the domestic-relations law but the couple challenged her to find any explicit prohibition of same-sex marriage. She could not. Ms. Holcomb directed them to City Attorney Charles J. Guttman.

He took their inquiry seriously, as did Mayor Nichols, whose background is steeped in leftist progressivism. "I started out the meeting saying I didn't know whether we could do it, but that I'd like to issue the license," Mayor Nichols said.

The Mayor's support turned their application from quixotic to conceivable. "He's the one who's made this engine run," Toshav Storrs said.

The legal issue, Mr. Guttman said, centers on whether denying a license to a couple of the same sex violates the constitutional guarantee of equal protection and the fundamental right to marry.

For Ms. Holcomb, the issue is whether she might be found guilty of a misdemeanor for issuing a license improperly or, were she to refuse to grant one, end up being dismissed for insubordination.

Phillip and Toshav Storrs did not wait for the government. They exchanged vows in a private ceremony and then, on June 22, at a more public gathering. Rabbi David Castiglione presided at both.

If they get their license, a third wedding is in store. Toshav Storrs's sister, Cindy Williams, could not travel from Tulsa for the June 22 event. "She's hoping to make it to the next one," her brother said.

* * *

May 25, 1996

TOWARD A LESS PERFECT UNION

By LAURENCE H. TRIBE

CAMBRIDGE, Mass.—There is more than a little irony in the so-called Defense of Marriage Act, the proposed Federal law that would allow states to deny recognition to same-sex marriages that might be accorded full legal status in other states.

It is ironic, first, that such a measure should be defended in the name of states' rights. Our Constitution's principal means of protecting state sovereignty is to limit the national Government to certain enumerated powers—but these powers do not include any authority to invite some states to disregard the official acts of others.

And it is ironic, second, that the first such invitation ever extended by Congress should deal with marital union. The Constitution's principal device for assuring a "more perfect union" is the Full Faith and Credit Clause, which requires that each state must fully credit "the public acts, records, and judicial proceedings of every other state." More than half a century ago, the Supreme Court described the clause as "a nationally unifying force" that transformed the individual states from "independent foreign sovereignties, each free to ignore rights and obligations" created by the others, into integral parts "of a single nation, in which rights . . . established in any [state] are given nationwide application."

The Defense of Marriage Act aims to counter the possibility that Hawaii's courts will legalize same-sex marriages, prompting gay couples to flock to the islands to be wed and return to their home states to claim the benefits of civil marriage. Defenders of this novel statute are fond of quoting the 10th Amendment: "The powers not delegated to the United States by the Constitution . . . are reserved to the states respectively, or to the people."

But that very principle condemns the proposed statute, for the Constitution delegates to the United States no power to create categorical exceptions to the Full Faith and Credit Clause. To be sure, the clause does empower Congress to enact "general laws" to "prescribe the manner in which such acts, records and proceedings shall be proved, and the effect thereof." But that is a far cry from power to decree that official state acts offensive to a majority in Congress need not even be recognized by states that happen to share Congress's view.

Some claim that a law inviting states to give no effect to certain acts of other states is a general law prescribing the "effect" of such acts. But that is a play on words, not a legal argument. The Full Faith and Credit Clause cannot be read as a fount of authority for Congress to set asunder the states that this clause so solemnly brought together.

Such a reading would mean, for example, that Congress could decree that any state was free to disregard any Hawaii marriage, any California divorce, any Kansas default judgment, any punitive damage award against a lawyer—or any of a potentially endless list of official acts that a Congressional majority might wish to denigrate. This would convert the Constitution's most vital unifying clause into a license for balkanization and disunity.

Defenders of the proposed law cite judicial decisions allowing one state to decline to enforce certain determinations of another on "public policy" grounds—marriages entered in one state, for example, to evade the bigamy laws of the state where the partners live. But states need no Congressional license to deny effect to whatever marriages (or other matters) may fall within this category. They can do so on their own.

The only authority the proposed statute could possibly add to the discretion states already possess would be authority to treat a sister state's binding acts as though they were the acts of a foreign nation—authority that Congress has no constitutional power to confer.

Laurence H. Tribe is a professor of constitutional law at Harvard Law School.

* * *

July 13, 1996

HOUSE PASSES BAR TO U.S. SANCTION OF GAY MARRIAGE

By JERRY GRAY

WASHINGTON, July 12—The House of Representatives voted overwhelmingly today to bar Federal recognition of same-sex marriages and to allow each state to ignore such marriages performed in any other state.

The vote, giving passage to the Defense of Marriage Act, was 342 to 67, with 2 members voting present, and followed hours of passionate and often bitter debate spread over two days. Dozens of lawmakers who had supported gay rights measures in the past voted for the bill.

The legislation now awaits action by the Senate. President Clinton announced weeks ago that because he regarded marriage as the union of one man and one woman, he would sign the bill if it reached his desk. But Mr. Clinton also said then that he considered the measure unnecessary and divisive, and today the White House denounced it as "gay baiting."

The bill was prompted by expectation that a Hawaii court will ultimately rule, in a case now under way, that the state must recognize marriages between two people of the same sex.

Hawaii would be the first state to grant such recognition, but the bill's supporters foresee far wider consequences: Article IV of the United States Constitution requires that "Full Faith and Credit shall be given in each State to the public Acts, Records, and judicial Proceedings of every other State." The legislation is intended to give the states statutory ammunition to resist being required to recognize homosexual marriage, although opponents of the bill said today that they doubted that it could survive constitutional scrutiny.

At the same time, the bill's provision barring Federal recognition of same-sex couples would preclude spousal benefits, typically afforded partners in a heterosexual union, that are distributed by a range of Government programs, from Social Security to veterans services.

"America is not ready to change its definition of marriage," the bill's author, Representative Bob Barr, a freshman Republican from Georgia, said at a news conference after the bill had passed. "America will not be the first country in the world that throws the concept of marriage out the window and for the very first time in the history of civilization says that homosexual marriages are as important as, and rise to the level of the legal and moral equivalency of, heterosexual marriage."

In the floor debate, Mr. Barr said the bill was needed because "the flames of hedonism, the flames of narcissism, the flames of self-centered morality are licking at the very foundation of our society, the family unit."

On the other hand, Representative Patricia Schroeder, Democrat of Colorado, called the bill "an absolute outrage," adding: "If you think there isn't enough hate and polarization in America, you're going to love this bill."

The House's three openly gay members—Representatives Barney Frank and Gerry E. Studds, both Massachusetts Democrats, and Steve Gunderson of Wisconsin, a Republican— took leading roles in the debate against the bill.

"Is the relationships with your spouses," Mr. Frank demanded of the measure's advocates, "of such fragility that the fact that I have a committed, loving relationship with another man jeopardizes them?"

Although the measure has widespread bipartisan support in the Senate, three members of that chamber—James M. Jeffords, Republican of Vermont, and Joseph I. Lieberman of Connecticut and Edward M. Kennedy of Massachusetts, both Democrats—announced on Thursday that they planned to attach to it an amendment that would prohibit employment discrimination based on sexual orientation. It is not yet clear how this prospective amendment will affect the Senate chances of the same-sex-marriage bill.

The issue of gay rights has been an explosive one for the Clinton Administration ever since the controversy over homosexuals in the military arose shortly after the President's inauguration. His willingness to sign this bill will almost certainly deprive conservatives of an issue to use against him in the election campaign, while the Administration's attack on Congress for taking up the legislation in the first place may well serve to mute criticism of him from gay rights groups.

At the White House today, the President's press secretary, Michael D. McCurry, called the bill "gay baiting, pure and simple," and "a classic use of wedge politics designed to provoke anxieties and fears."

But Mr. McCurry also said that Mr. Clinton held "very strong personal views" in his belief that marriage is a hetero-

Stephen Crowley/The New York Times

After passage of the gay-marriage bill, its author, Representative Bob Barr, said, "America is not ready to change its definition of marriage."

sexual union, and that he was still committed to signing the legislation.

The bill won House passage with the backing of 224 Republicans and 118 Democrats. Sixty-five Democrats, one independent and a lone Republican—Mr. Gunderson—voted no. The two members who voted present were Representatives Sheila Jackson Lee of Texas and Major R. Owens of New York, both Democrats.

Although the bill would not outlaw homosexual marriage, it would, for the first time, create a Federal definition of marriage, regulation of which has long been left to the states. The measure specifies that marriage is a union between one man and one woman, and it defines "spouse" as a person of the opposite sex who is a husband or a wife. It is these definitions that would preclude spousal Federal benefits for homosexual couples, writing into law what is current Government practice.

The more troubling provision to some legal experts and gay rights advocates is the one that would give the states the right to refuse recognition of same-sex marriages performed in other states.

"I think there is absolutely no question that that part of the bill is unconstitutional under the Full Faith and Credit clause of the Constitution," said Matt Coles, director of the Lesbian and Gay Rights Project of the American Civil Liberties Union. "Congress can absolutely not tell states that they can ignore each other's final court decisions."

But Mr. Coles conceded that should the measure become law, it could be years before the constitutional issue was settled in court.

Representative Charles T. Canady, the Florida Republican who heads the House Judiciary Subcommittee on the Constitution, shepherded the bill through the chamber and led those in favor of it during the debate.

"Families are not merely constructs of outdated convention, and traditional marriage laws were not based on animosity toward homosexuals," Mr. Canady declared on the floor. "Rather, I believe that the traditional family structure—centered on a lawful union between one man and one woman—comports with nature and with our Judeo-Christian moral tradition."

* * *

September 6, 1996

FOES OF GAY MARRIAGE ARE FOILED IN CALIFORNIA SENATE

By DAVID W. DUNLAP

Outside Hawaii—where a court case set to begin next week may lead to the granting of marriage licenses to couples of the same sex—California is one of the most important battlegrounds in the nationwide fight over same-sex marriages. Not only is it the most populous state, it has a highly visible homosexual population and is a gateway to Hawaii.

So advocates of marriage rights for lesbian and gay couples considered it a victory, however backhanded, when the California Senate ended its session on Saturday without approving legislation to bar such unions. On the other side, those who favor the ban said that they had been victims of parliamentary maneuvering and that they would renew their efforts next year.

California is the 20th state in which bills have failed that would ban or deny recognition to same-sex marriages, or do both. Fifteen states have enacted such legislation and two Republican Governors, Fob James Jr. of Alabama and Kirk Fordice of Mississippi, recently signed executive orders to similar effect. Same-sex marriages are not legally sanctioned by any government in the nation, though the court in Hawaii may find that the state must do so, under its own Constitution, unless there is a compelling reason not to. In the Hawaii case, three couples are seeking licenses to marry.

Anticipating that decision, the United States Senate is expected to pass a bill that would deny Federal recognition and benefits to same-sex marriages and relieve states of the obligation to recognize such marriages if they are ever performed in another state, like Hawaii. The bill overwhelmingly passed the House in July, but the Senate vote was put off today, until next week, because of partisan disagreement about amendments to the legislation.

The battle in California was also largely one over amendments.

Assemblyman William J. Knight, Republican of Palmdale, introduced a bill to invalidate "any marriage contracted outside this state between individuals of the same gender." It passed the Assembly in January and Gov. Pete Wilson, a Republican, said he would sign it.

But in the State Senate the bill was amended to establish legal unions outside marriage for homosexual or heterosexual couples. The amendment, upheld in a tie vote broken by Lieut. Gov. Gray Davis, a Democrat, effectively killed the bill.

Another bill, which had been stripped of its original language and turned into a marriage measure, passed the Assembly but languished in a Senate committee until the session expired.

Mr. Knight accused the Senate's Democratic leader, Bill Lockyer of Hayward, of using "every tool of procedural manipulation to thwart the will of the people."

In reply, Mr. Lockyer's press secretary, Sandy Harrison, said the bill violated a rule that amendments must be germane and was introduced too late in the session.

Evan Wolfson, director of the marriage project at the Lambda Legal Defense and Education Fund, which represents lesbians and gay men, called the outcome in California "enormously important." "Here we had a hotly contested battle," Mr. Wolfson said, "fully joined, in a legislature with strong right-wing forces and a Governor who said he'd sign the bill—and it failed."

But Robert H. Knight of the Family Research Council, which takes a conservative approach to social issues, dismissed the significance. "California is similar to the national situation," Mr. Knight said, "in that legislation that had strong popular support has been under attack through unwarranted amendments and parliamentary stalling techniques."

* * *

September 21, 1996

CLINTON SIGNS BILL DENYING GAY COUPLES U.S. BENEFITS

By ALISON MITCHELL

BRANDON, S.D., Sept. 20—President Clinton announced tonight that he was signing a bill to deny Federal benefits to married people of the same sex and to permit states to ignore such marriages sanctioned in other states.

Mr. Clinton's approval of the legislation had not been in doubt since May when he announced that he would sign such a bill if it was approved by Congress. At the time, he sought to remove any controversy with Republicans over a divisive social issue, but it also infuriated gay rights groups that were prominent supporters of the President.

Mr. Clinton's discomfort with the legislation and the issue was made clear tonight by the way he handled the bill, not with any White House ceremony but with an evening announcement on paper, well after the evening television news programs, that he would sign the legislation upon returning to Washington early Saturday morning after a four-day campaign trip.

Asked why Mr. Clinton would sign the bill in the early morning hours, Michael D. McCurry, the White House press secretary, said, "Because the President believes the motives behind this bill are dubious, and the President believes that the sooner he gets this over with the better."

Mr. Clinton has said in the past that he has long opposed marriage between people of the same sex but that he also believed the Republicans had introduced the legislation in an effort to provoke a campaign issue.

Mr. Clinton has long supported gay rights, solicited financial support from homosexuals and paid a price for trying to end the ban on homosexuals in the military. It was his stand on homosexuals in the military that helped give him an image as a liberal Democrat in his first years in office.

The legislation's sponsors, mainly conservative Republicans, said that the institution of marriage was under assault and that the measure was necessary because of expectations that a court in Hawaii would rule that the state must recognize same-sex marriages. The bill was passed by overwhelming bipartisan majorities in both houses.

Hawaii would be the first state to grant such recognition, but the bill's supporters foresaw far wider consequences because Article IV of the United States Constitution requires that "full faith and credit shall be given in each state to the public acts, records and judicial proceedings of every other state."

The bill signed by Mr. Clinton does not ban marriages between partners of the same sex but is intended to inoculate states against having to recognize homosexual marriages performed in other states. Critics of the measure said the states already had constitutional authority to ignore laws of other states, and argued that recognition of same-sex marriage would promote stable, monogamous homosexual relationships.

The bill's provisions barring Federal recognition of same-sex marriages would preclude spousal benefits that are distributed by Government programs like Social Security and veterans services.

In his statement tonight, Mr. Clinton said he wanted to "make clear that the enactment of this legislation should not, despite the fierce and, at times, divisive rhetoric surrounding it, be understood to provide an excuse for discrimination, violence or intimidation against any person on the basis of sexual orientation."

He also called for Congress to pass a bill that would extend protection against employment discrimination to homosexuals. When it passed the law on same-sex marriage, the Senate defeated by a single vote a measure that for the first time would have banned discrimination against homosexuals in the workplace.

* * *

February 2, 1997

GAY COUPLES AND THE LAW, AT ODDS OVER THE RIGHT TO MARRY

By KIT R. ROANE

NEWARK—The gym brought them together, but it took six weeks of courting on the phone to reach the first date. Old relationships still haunted them, including one marriage, and there was a great fear of rushing things.

But that was four years ago, and now they are a couple in every sense of the word. Tim Smithhart and John Ammitzboll live together in Paterson, have bought two houses and regularly argue about rearranging the furniture. Two English bulldogs, Bette and Daphne, and two cats, Tipper and Lizzie, round out their family. They are thinking about adopting a child and would marry if they could.

They are not legally married, however, and it appears unlikely they will be anytime soon. The New Jersey Legislature is considering a bill against same-sex marriages and against recognizing any such marriages that might eventually be performed in other states.

"This is because we have to protect the sanctity of marriage," said Marian Crecco, a 65-year-old Republican Assemblywoman from Bloomfield whose bill passed out of the Assembly Health Committee late last month. "Allowing them to marry would make the institution meaningless. What if someone next wants to marry their brother or sister? Where does it stop?"

The bill, as well as another now before the Senate, would prevent gay marriages from occurring in New Jersey and ban the recognition of same-sex marriages performed elsewhere. In a small victory for gay-rights advocates, one section stating that such marriages were "against the public policy of the state" was struck from the Assembly version of the legislation but remains in the Senate bill.

While having no real effect on the current situation of gay men and lesbians in New Jersey, the law would make it necessary to fight separate court battles in New Jersey should the Hawaii Supreme Court strike down that state's ban on same-sex marriages later this year. Earlier rulings in Hawaii went against the ban.

Proponents of the bill hope it will make the New Jersey Supreme Court less likely to follow Hawaii's lead. So far, 16 states have passed measures against gay marriages, while gay-rights advocates have successfully fought these bills in 20 other states.

Lawyers specializing in constitutional and civil rights law said the legislation could be fought in two ways: either by arguing that same-sex marriages must be allowed to insure equal protection under the 14th Amendment, or by arguing that New Jersey must honor gay marriages under the "full faith and credit" clause requiring states to recognize the laws of other states.

But Earl Maltz, a civil rights specialist at Rutgers State University School of Law in Camden, said that there was little Federal law supporting intervention by the United States

Supreme Court in such a matter, and that gay rights advocates would combat the law more easily through New Jersey's state court.

He added that the Defense of Marriage Act passed by Congress and signed by President Clinton last year clearly states the Federal Government's belief that states are not obligated to recognize single-sex marriages performed elsewhere.

"Constitutionalizing this right would be a long stride, so the only recourse here appears to be in state court," he said. "But there tends to be a certain momentum to things like this, and the most difficult is getting the first state court to drop the ban. It then becomes easier for other states to follow."

The importance to homosexual couples goes far beyond an emotional desire to have their unions recognized. Currently, couples like Mr. Smithhart and Mr. Ammitzboll face financial and legal problems if one partner becomes ill or dies, including the inability to make medical decisions for a partner.

Without recognition of their union, Mr. Smithhart, 36, and Mr. Ammitzboll, 32, are also denied tax, pension and Social Security benefits that married couples have.

"We pay taxes, keep our property nice and will die in the end, like everybody else," said Mr. Ammitzboll, a hotel manager. "All we want is to be given the same rights that others now take for granted."

"Nobody should be able to legislate against my right to chose whom I love and want to spend my life with," he added.

But despite the pleas of Mr. Ammitzboll and others, passage of Assemblywoman Crecco's bill seems inevitable, political analysts said. They noted that it was an election year in a state dominated by Republican legislators unlikely to court the gay vote, and where a Republican governor known to be sympathetic to homosexuals has said she does not believe in same-sex marriage.

When the issue is framed as one of family values, said David P. Rebovich, a political science professor at Rider University, even liberal Democrats would have a hard time opposing the bill.

"This is a mischief-maker piece of legislation, a lot like flag-burning," Mr. Rebovich said. "It's symbolic and can put Democrats in a tough position because it makes them chose between the broad center of voters and their more general feelings about civil rights."

* * *

April 18, 1997

HAWAII SEEKS LAW TO BLOCK GAY MARRIAGE

By The Associated Press

HONOLULU, April 17—A proposed amendment to the Hawaii Constitution would overturn a state court ruling that it was unconstitutional to ban same-sex marriages.

State House and Senate conferees approved a plan on Wednesday evening to let voters decide on an amendment to ban same-sex marriages but give gay and lesbian couples some

rights and benefits available to married couples. The plan was expected to gain easy approval by the Legislature next week.

The measure would be put on next year's ballot, and polls leave little doubt that voters would approve it.

The state Supreme Court ruled in 1993 that banning gay marriage amounted to discrimination under the state Constitution, unless state officials could prove there was compelling public interest in doing so. This summer, the court is expected to consider rulings by lower courts that there was no such interest.

The case became a national issue because the United States Constitution says each state must recognize other state's legal actions, like marriages.

In response, Congress passed the Defense of Marriage Act denying Federal recognition of same-sex marriages and allowing states not to recognize same-sex unions licensed in other states. President Clinton signed the bill in September.

Eighteen states enacted laws not to recognize same-sex unions.

State Representative Terrance Tom, chairman of the House conferees, said the proposed amendment would address the needs of gay couples while still giving Hawaiian voters "the opportunity to reconfirm their belief that marriage, the fundamental unit of our society, is the union of one man and one woman."

The measure would let gay and lesbian couples sign up as "reciprocal beneficiaries," giving them inheritance rights, the right to sue for wrongful death, spousal benefits for insurance and state pensions, and similar rights. The proposal also would offer such rights to other pairs living together who could not marry, like a widowed mother and her unmarried son.

Gay and lesbian advocates denounced the compromise, saying it fell short of the equal rights they would receive if the state Supreme Court ruling prevailed.

Tracey Bennett, a leader of Marriage Project Hawaii, said, "We had hoped the Senate would have adhered to its desire to extend civil rights to all people, and the Senate caved."

* * *

April 17, 1998

LAWS ASIDE, SOME IN CLERGY QUIETLY BLESS GAY 'MARRIAGE'

By GUSTAV NIEBUHR

BURLINGTON, Vt.—Over a cup of coffee one blustery afternoon, Deidra Mack confessed to feeling the jitters about entering the stately brick church nearby, standing before a minister and making vows of lifetime commitment.

But minutes later, there she was, in First Unitarian Universalist Society's austerely elegant sanctuary, facing her partner, Barbara Dolores. At the Rev. Gary A. Kowalski's invitation, the two women, both 28, spoke their vows and exchanged rings. "You have made for yourselves a marriage," the minister said. "Your lives are now joined." Family members and friends applauded.

Photo by Adam Pike Riesner

Barbara Dolores, left, and Deidra Mack kissed after exchanging vows at the First Unitarian Universalist Society's church in Burlington, Vt. Same-sex religious unions like theirs are becoming more common.

Mr. Kowalski said he blessed about three same-sex unions a year, and performed 20 or more traditional weddings.

"The reason I perform same-sex ceremonies," he said, "is I think churches and other social institutions should be in the business of encouraging long-term relationships."

These days, his views are hardly unique. Religious officiation at homosexual unions, while not common, is becoming less rare. Evidence can be found across faith lines. A group of Methodist ministers declared they will perform same-sex unions, some leading Episcopalians recently called for liturgies for such ceremonies and Reform rabbis will soon consider whether to sanction the blessing of same-sex unions.

The religious debate is proceeding as legal and political battles are fought over whether gay men and lesbians should be allowed a right to civil marriage. Lawsuits filed by gay couples seeking marriage licenses have reached the supreme courts in three states, Hawaii, Alaska and Vermont, said Evan Wolfson, an official with the Lambda Legal Defense and Education Fund in New York.

Mr. Wolfson, a co-counsel on the Hawaii suit, said a decision was expected in that state soon.

But he also said there had been a backlash, in that 28 states officially barred gay marriage over the last three years.

In the Vermont case, nearly 100 Protestant, Jewish and Unitarian clergy members recently signed a resolution supporting the three homosexual couples who are suing for marriage licenses in that state.

Many major religious bodies, following their traditional teachings, assert that homosexual activity violates God's intentions for human sexual relations. But support for the ceremonies offers evidence that some clergy members take a different view.

In March, 92 United Methodist ministers declared they would perform "rites of union with all couples, regardless of gender." The statement was released during the church trial of the Rev. Jimmy Creech, an Omaha, Neb., minister charged with violating Methodist rules for having blessed the union of two women. The jury acquitted him, provoking outrage among some Methodist groups.

Last July, priests and lay people at the Episcopal Church's General Convention barely defeated a proposal that the church develop liturgies for same-sex unions. The Rev. Todd Wetzel, executive director of Episcopalians United, a conservative organization within the church, said the proposal did not represent most Episcopalians' views, but rather those of "liberal-revisionist dioceses, where the bishop and the clergy have clearly abandoned the authority of Scripture and the place of tradition."

In June, rabbis in Judaism's Reform movement will consider whether gay and lesbian unions can be affirmed in Jewish ritual.

"There's a lot of debate or discussion between rabbis who take different positions," said Rabbi Paul J. Menitoff, executive vice president of the Central Conference of American Rabbis.

He said many Reform rabbis had officiated "at some sort of same-sex ceremony," reflecting a growing acceptance of homosexuals in society.

Rabbi Eric Yoffie, president of the Union of American Hebrew Congregations, Reform's synagogue organization, said he believed "we have to find some way to give religious affirmation to monogamous, long-term relationships between gay Jews."

But he said he was uncertain that a consensus existed within the movement that religious texts and tradition would provide ground to support a resolution affirming rabbis' conducting such ceremonies.

In interviews, several ministers in mainline Protestant churches who perform same-sex unions said they officiated at one to six a year. As for gay Roman Catholics, a registry set up last July by Dignity U.S.A. has recorded two or three unions a month, typically blessed by men ordained as priests, but no longer actively serving, said Dignity's executive director, Charles L. Cox.

In addition, more than 5,000 ceremonies are performed annually within the Metropolitan Community Churches, a small denomination with 300 congregations and a predominately gay membership, a spokesman said. The 2,300-member Cathedral of Hope in Dallas, the largest of the Metropolitan Community Churches, has held about 40 ceremonies of "holy union" since Jan. 1.

"We have another 80 already on the schedule," the senior pastor, the Rev. Michael Piazza, said.

Supporters of same-sex unions say they appear to have grown along with networks of congregations that welcome gay men and lesbians. The Church of the Covenant in Boston, for example, belongs to the "More Light" network within the Presbyterian Church (USA) and the "Open and Affirming" network within the United Church of Christ. The Rev. Rosie Olmstead said she performed two or three unions annually at the church, affiliated with both denominations.

Gay couples asking her to bless their unions, Ms. Olmstead said, are seeking "a public place in the community, a community larger than their closest friends, to say we expect this relationship to last."

Same-sex ceremonies can have a ripple effect among people attending.

"It kind of snowballs," said Bob Gibeling, program director for Lutherans Concerned, which focuses on gay issues in the Evangelical Lutheran Church in America. "People hear of a ceremony or attend a ceremony, and they say, 'That's really wonderful, that's something I'd like to have.' "

Nevertheless, many say, same-sex ceremonies are controversial among some gay men and lesbians, who say homosexuals should not try to re-create an historically heterosexual model for relationships.

Same-sex unions have also prompted a larger backlash. In 1996, President Clinton signed the Defense of Marriage Act, which withholds Federal tax, pension and other benefits to partners of homosexuals.

That year, the Unitarian-Universalist Association, a creedless, theologically diverse organization, declared that homosexual couples should have a legal right to marriage. The association had already adopted a resolution supporting its ministers who conducted same-sex unions.

Its president, the Rev. John A. Buehrens, said, "There is a sense in which a traditional, biblical theology is not at all incompatible with taking this stand" supporting same-sex unions.

Although he acknowledged that several biblical verses had long been read as condemning homosexual acts, he said, "There's a much finer command to pay attention to the outcast and the despised."

But other major religious bodies take a negative view of the issue.

The Southern Baptist Convention revised its constitution in 1992 to exclude congregations that condone homosexuality, the result, partly, of a North Carolina church's decision to hold a same-sex union.

Two years ago, the National Conference of Catholic Bishops released a statement emphasizing the church's teaching that marriage was an arrangement established by God, involving "a faithful, exclusive and lifelong union between one man and one woman," and intended for love and procreation.

While saying homosexuals deserve "respect, compassion, understanding," the bishops said, "No same-sex union can realize the unique and full potential which the marital relationship expresses."

In 1993, the bishops of the Evangelical Lutheran Church in America said no basis existed in either Scripture or tradition for same-sex unions.

A similar position exists within Conservative Judaism, where the Rabbinical Assembly's committee on law and standards has issued statements that Jewish tradition does not allow same-sex unions. But the assembly has not sought a rule binding on its members.

"In terms of what's on the books, it's a kind of unambiguous no," said Rabbi Gordon Tucker of White Plains, a member of the law committee. But, he added, "I'm pretty sure there are members of the Rabbinical Assembly who have done commitment ceremonies."

Clergy members who have performed such unions can be found in many cities.

The Rev. Nancy Erickson, a United Church of Christ minister who works at a substance abuse center in Lincoln, said she had performed 10 same-sex ceremonies since graduating from Yale Divinity School in 1989.

"All of them are local people," Ms. Erickson said. "I just see it as part of my calling."

In Boston, the Rev. John P. Streit, dean of the Episcopal Cathedral of St. Paul, said he had performed two. Deciding to officiate, Mr. Streit said, has meant weighing issues of social justice and pastoral care.

"An individual says to you, 'This feels important to me, will you help with this?' " he said.

Some churches have written theological statements explaining why they bless gay couples. Discussing why it allows "services of blessing of relationships," St. Paul-Reformation Lutheran Church in St. Paul, said it understood the biblical creation story to mean that God intended no one be alone and "that all human creatures are created for the sake of mutual companionship on this earth."

Some clergy members ask gay couples to attend counseling sessions, similar to the premarital meetings they have with heterosexual couples to discuss things like compatibility, personal finances and conflict, as well as the ceremony.

Before coming to Vermont in 1989, Mr. Kowalski, a Harvard Divinity School graduate, served a congregation near Seattle. He felt a bit nervous, he said, the one time he was asked to do a same-sex union.

"No one at Harvard," he said, "ever told us, this is how you conduct a same-sex marriage service."

But as minister of the 520-member Burlington church, he has officiated at about two dozen, and also has performed more than 200 weddings. Gay unions are usually lower key.

Mr. Kowalski, 44, has been married 16 years, to a woman he met in college. They have two children. Of marriage, he said, "I wouldn't want to deny it to other people, simply because they have another sexual orientation."

Before her service, Ms. Mack said that it felt official, even if the state of Vermont did not recognize it as such.

"To me, it's legal," she said. "I'm having a ceremony, I'm in a church."

* * *

June 3, 1998

A HEATED HEARING ON PARTNER RIGHTS

By MIKE ALLEN

The City Council held its first public hearing yesterday on legislation that would give domestic partners the same rights as spouses, prompting about 150 opponents of the measure to storm out of the meeting, complaining that the bill's supporters were allowed to monopolize the time at the microphone.

By the City Council's tally, 24 people testified in favor of the bill during the three-hour hearing and eight spoke against it. But among the 200 that showed up for the hearing of the General Welfare Committee, the overwhelming number came to oppose the bill, many of them massing on steps of City Hall to continue their protest after they walked out of the meeting in frustration.

"We went upstairs and we've been waiting and waiting and waiting," said the Rev. Ruben Diaz, president of the New York Hispanic Clergy Organization, which is based in the Bronx. "The chairman is laughing in our face."

Councilman Stephen DiBrienza, a Democrat from Brooklyn and the committee chairman, said he allowed people who had pre-registered to speak first, as is customary. Many of the bill's opponents said they showed up early yesterday morning to get in line, not realizing they were already too late.

Gay and lesbian groups said the measure would provide a historic guarantee of their rights, but it would also apply to heterosexual couples who register as domestic partners with

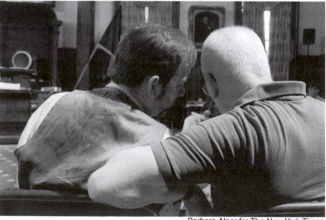

Brendan Fay, left, and Tom McLoughlin, members of Dignity New York, a gay Catholic group, observed the hearing on a partner-rights bill. Gay groups said the bill would provide a historic guarantee of their rights.

the City Clerk's Office. The bill would insure that the domestic partners of city employees would have the same rights as spouses and also guarantee the rights of domestic partners who live in city housing.

Despite fervent opposition from some religious groups, the bill has widespread bipartisan support on the Council, thanks in large part to the stances of Mayor Rudolph W. Giuliani, who proposed the legislation, and the City Council Speaker, Peter F. Vallone, its sponsor.

The committee plans to hold one more hearing on the bill before it is sent to the full Council for a vote later this month. But it was clear from the start of yesterday's hearing that there was broad support for the measure among some of the more influential Council members.

Mr. DiBrienza opened the hearing by calling the Mayor's championing of the bill "a courageous act."

The first witness was Randy M. Mastro, the Deputy Mayor for Operations, who said that Mr. Giuliani was keeping a campaign promise. Mr. Mastro also noted that most of the rights granted by the bill applied to domestic partners under executive orders already in place.

"It's about insuring that New York City law does the right thing by all of its citizens," he said. "The Mayor believes that this is the right thing to do—that as a matter of fairness and equity, we should be codifying the letter and spirit of these executive orders." As Mr. Mastro began his testimony, a man in the audience, who would not give his name, shouted, "Giuliani is a liberal turncoat."

Paula L. Ettelbrick, the legislative counsel of Empire State Pride Agenda, a statewide lesbian and gay political organization, said the measure "insures that thousands and thousands of disabled, old, gay, lesbian and straight New Yorkers and our children will receive the economic, emotional and social support necessary for our families to thrive."

In the testimony he had prepared, Mr. Diaz of the Hispanic pastors' group said: "This law diminishes the meaning and sanctity of marriage. It eliminates the incentive for a couple to marry, motivating a life that goes against that which was established by God as stipulated in holy scriptures."

Mr. Diaz handed out copies of his statement before the meeting but left without reading his text because he had to wait so long to speak.

John Cardinal O'Connor, the Archbishop of New York, used one of his Sunday homilies last month to warn of the bill's possible harm to society. No representative of the Archdiocese of New York appeared at the hearing, but at its request, the Cardinal's homily was placed in the hearing record and Mr. DiBrienza read one passage.

Councilman Thomas K. Duane, who is openly gay, was unapologetic that most of the speakers were in favor of the bill. "If on this one occasion, supporters of a civil rights bill for lesbian and gay New Yorkers got to go first, I don't think that's going to change the balance sheet in terms of public discourse," said Mr. Duane, a Democrat from Manhattan.

* * *

July 18, 1998

REPUBLICANS INTRODUCE 2 BILLS IN FIGHT AGAINST HOMOSEXUALITY

By KATHARINE Q. SEELYE

WASHINGTON, July 17—Continuing their assault on homosexuality, House Republicans are considering a proposal to deny Federal housing money to cities that require organizations doing business with them to provide health-care benefits for the unmarried domestic partners of the organization's employees.

The proposal, offered by Representative Frank Riggs, Republican of California, is aimed at San Francisco and could cost the city an estimated $265 million in Federal housing money this year.

The city last year adopted a first-of-its-kind ordinance requiring private groups that contract with it to provide benefits to their employees' domestic partners.

But Mr. Riggs wrote his proposal to cover any locality that might adopt a similar ordinance. Likely prospects could include New York and Philadelphia, which provide benefits for domestic partners of city employees but do not require their contractors to provide such benefits.

"I wanted to act now before this becomes the standard operating practice of other local governments," Mr. Riggs said today in an interview.

The measure is one of two anti-homosexual proposals moving through the House and comes during a visible, broad-based anti-gay campaign by conservatives.

The second measure, to be offered by Representative Joel Hefley, Republican of Colorado, would block President Clinton's recent directive barring job discrimination against Federal workers who are gay.

Mr. Hefley had planned to offer his amendment this week, until House leaders told him not to because the bill he was planning to attach it to was being managed on the floor by a colleague who is gay.

Representative Jim Kolbe, Republican of Arizona, publicly acknowledged his homosexuality two years ago. House leaders did not want to put him in the position of having to oppose his own bill. Mr. Hefley, who is backed by the Christian Coalition, agreed to attach his proposal to a different bill next week.

The measure would undo a May 28 executive order by Mr. Clinton that would add homosexuals to the groups that may not be discriminated against in Federal employment.

Winnie Stachelberg, political director of the Human Rights Campaign, the largest lobbying group for homosexuals, said the two measures were part of an anti-gay movement "meant to stigmatize gay people and to push us back in the closet."

"The right wing understands the political climate we're in," she said. "We're approaching an election, and the Republican Party fears their base won't show up, so to galvanize and energize them, they're feeding them anti-gay rhetoric."

Mr. Riggs said he was offering his measure because he believed that Federal money should not be used to advance a local political agenda or to force businesses to do something they found morally objectionable.

"I do feel very, very strongly that the Federal Government should not sanction that particular conduct in any way," he said of homosexuality. While the San Francisco ordinance requires benefits for unmarried partners, whether heterosexual or homosexual, Mr. Riggs said he opposed same-sex marriage and opposed giving benefits to partners because it would elevate same-sex relationships to the same status as marriage between men and women.

"Marriage is a sacred institution," he said, "and it is paramount to the protection and strengthening of the family, which is in turn paramount to building stronger communities and a better country."

* * *

October 9, 1999

GAY RIGHTS IN CALIFORNIA

California sets an admirable example for the nation by moving ahead with legislation that will help deter discrimination against gays in public and private life. Although California earlier enacted hate-crime laws to protect gays and lesbians from violence, the three bills signed into law by Gov. Gray Davis last week will help ensure that gays receive fair and equal treatment at work, in housing and at school. The movement in California, the nation's largest state, to normalize government treatment of gays is an important step toward ending anti-gay bigotry.

Under the new laws, California will create a statewide registry for domestic partners, defined as same-sex couples and unmarried couples age 62 or older, when marriage may in certain cases reduce limited retirement benefits. Domestic partners will be able to get hospital visitation rights, as family members do now, and those who are state employees will be eligible to receive health insurance benefits for their partners. Many cities in California, including Los Angeles, already provide health benefits for domestic partners under local laws. This state statute will make it easier for local governments to offer such benefits.

A second measure would outlaw harassment of gays in public schools and colleges. Violence and threats against students based on their sexual orientation are a clear danger, but many school officials have failed to take such harassment seriously or have not known how to respond. The new California law, following similar laws enacted in Wisconsin, Massachusetts and Connecticut, now prohibits discrimination based on sexual orientation. It will make school administrations accountable for combating anti-gay harassment. Another measure strengthens older state laws that ban discrimination against gays in housing and employment.

These new laws do nothing more than provide gays the basic rights that heterosexuals have without question. Still, they are an important advancement in ending discrimination as a matter of public policy.

* * *

December 10, 1999

HAWAII COURT LETS GAY MARRIAGE BAN STAND

By The Associated Press

HONOLULU, Dec. 9—The Hawaii Supreme Court ruled today that the effort by several homosexual couples to legalize gay marriage was rendered moot by a 1998 amendment to the state constitution that barred such marriages.

The decision effectively terminates the move to recognize gay marriage in Hawaii, which was once regarded by gay rights activists as one of the more likely places to win legalization of homosexual unions.

That hope followed a 1993 decision from the state Supreme Court that said the state's failure to recognize gay marriages denied some citizens the rights that others have.

The ruling set off preemptive legislating around the nation. At least 30 states banned gay marriages, and Congress passed the Defense of Marriage Act, which denied federal recognition of homosexual marriage and allowed states to ignore same-sex unions licensed elsewhere.

The ruling also led Hawaii lawmakers to pass a 1994 law banning gay marriage. They later drafted a constitutional amendment that gave them the authority to pass just such a law. Last year, Hawaii voters approved the amendment 2 to 1.

* * *

December 21, 1999

VERMONT HIGH COURT BACKS RIGHTS OF SAME-SEX COUPLES

By CAREY GOLDBERG

BOSTON, Dec. 20—The Vermont Supreme Court unanimously ruled today that the state must guarantee the very same protections and benefits to gay and lesbian couples that it does to heterosexual spouses. The court left it to the Legislature to either legalize gay marriage, which no state has yet done, or adopt a domestic partnership law, which would be the most sweeping in the country.

To extend equal rights to homosexual couples "who seek nothing more, nor less, than legal protection and security for their avowed commitment to an intimate and lasting relationship is simply, when all is said and done," the ruling said, "a recognition of our common humanity."

The court found that it was unconstitutionally discriminatory in Vermont to deny marriage licenses to homosexual couples, depriving them of the myriad benefits, from inheritance rights to health insurance to tax breaks, that accrue to heterosexual married couples. It is up to the Legislature to decide whether to establish a system recognizing gay couples as do-

mestic partners, with the benefits like those of spouses, or to simply include homosexual partners in the state's marriage laws. It gave lawmakers an unspecified "reasonable period of time" to consider.

Peter Shumlin, the president pro tempore of the Vermont Senate, said today that the state's predominantly Democratic lawmakers might decide in the coming session how to respond. Mr. Shumlin said he expected it would be much easier to get votes for a domestic partnership law than one creating full-fledged gay marriages, but "both are strong possibilities," he said.

"When the court says, 'You have a class of people whose civil rights are being trampled upon,' Vermonters want to remedy that," he said.

Some state officials say they support gay marriage. But Gov. Howard Dean, a Democrat, said he thought the Legislature would pass a domestic partnership law. Same-sex marriage, he said, "makes me uncomfortable, the same as anybody else," The Associated Press reported.

William Sorrell, the Vermont attorney general, said of domestic partnership: "It would likely be a civilly sanctioned relationship that would, for all intents and purposes, have the benefits and protections a traditionally married couple would have but wouldn't be called a marital relationship. They wouldn't be called spouses, they'd be called domestic partners, and for a number of people, that makes an enormous difference."

But Beth Robinson, a lead lawyer for the plaintiffs, said that unlike marriage, domestic partnership would not entitle couples to benefits from the federal government and all private employers.

Piecemeal systems of protections and benefits for gay and lesbian couples have been enacted in recent years around the country, but advocates for gay rights said today that because the Vermont ruling would cover all possible benefits, it would put the state far ahead of all others. California and Hawaii have statewide domestic partnership systems, they said, but they pale next to what is coming in Vermont.

If Vermont chooses full-fledged gay marriage and homosexual couples begin flocking to the state to wed, their legal status in their home states would prove a very tangled issue, experts said today.

The campaign to legalize gay marriage has inspired a vigorous opposition. Since the prospect arose in a Hawaii case in 1991, nearly 30 states have passed laws against gay marriage. But gay rights advocates say it is not clear whether those laws would stand against challenges. Most likely, legal experts say, there would be state-by-state battles over recognizing same-sex marriages performed in Vermont.

Today's decision, written by Chief Justice Jeffrey L. Amestoy, exhilarated the three couples who brought the case against the state, as well as their lawyers and the many gay and civil rights groups supporting them.

"We celebrated our 27th anniversary together in October," one of the couples, Holly Puterbaugh and Lois Farnham, said in a joint statement. "We look forward to the time when we can finally make it official."

But the ruling brought expressions of dismay from religious and conservative groups and others who oppose gay marriage.

"The decision is not only troubling but it is tremendously disappointing," said Jay Sekulow, chief counsel of the American Center for Law and Justice, a national conservative group, in a statement. "While this legal decision is designed to elevate the status of same-sex couples, it really represents a slap in the face for marriage between a man and a woman."

In Vermont, Craig Bensen, an evangelical pastor and vice president of Take It to the People, a coalition that opposes gay marriage, said the group was considering a strategy like those used in Hawaii and Alaska, where opponents of gay marriage put the idea to a referendum and got enough votes to block it. The Hawaii Supreme Court dismissed as moot the gay-marriage case there on Dec. 10, because a 1998 ballot measure had authorized lawmakers to restrict the definition of marriage to man-woman unions.

"We suspect there will be momentum for a constitutional amendment to clarify the nature of marriage," Mr. Bensen said. "The difficulty is, we've got the toughest Constitution to amend in the country."

Though the ruling went against them, Mr. Bensen and those sharing his beliefs said they were happy to see the issue go to the Legislature.

Attorney General Sorrell said, "It's an important public policy question, and where important public policy should be debated and decided is in the Legislature, not the courts."

Mr. Sorrell noted that because the decision was based on the state Constitution rather than the federal one, the ruling cannot be appealed to the United States Supreme Court.

The provision of the Vermont Constitution referred to by the court was the common benefits clause, which says that the government ought to be "instituted for the common benefit, protection and security of the people, nation or community, and not for the particular emolument or advantage of any single person, family or set of persons who are a part only of that community."

Although the court's ruling focused on benefits rather than marriage itself, lawyers for the same-sex couples said today that they believed that the Legislature would ultimately choose full-fledged marriage for same-sex couples. A domestic partnership system would not go far enough to secure gay couples the exact privileges accorded heterosexual ones, like access to benefits from the federal government and private employers, they said.

"This legal status of marriage carries with it a lot of baggage," said Ms. Robinson, the lawyer for the couples. "The Legislature will come to understand that as a practical matter, you can't call it something different and have it be truly equal."

Matt Coles, director of the Lesbian and Gay Rights Project of the American Civil Liberties Union, noted that the phrase "domestic partnership" was invented only 19 years ago, when there was virtually no recognition of gay and lesbian relationships and the whole idea was so radical that when the San Francisco City Council passed a domestic partnership law, Mayor Dianne Feinstein, now a United States senator, vetoed it.

"If you think about the way law and society move," Mr. Coles said, "to go from San Francisco considering domestic partnerships too far out there in 1981, to all five justices of the Vermont Supreme Court taking equal treatment for granted in 1999—it's astonishing, it really is."

While the justices, who are appointed by the governor and can be removed by the Legislature, concurred that gay couples should be protected from discrimination, one, Denise R. Johnson, wrote that the court should order the state to let them marry. To do otherwise, she wrote, would consign them to "an uncertain fate in the political cauldron" of a moral debate in the Legislature.

The case began in 1997 when the three couples—Ms. Puterbaugh and Ms. Farnham, Stan Baker and Peter Harrigan, and Nina Beck and Stacy Jolles—filed suit after their local town clerks denied them marriage licenses. A Superior Court judge turned them down, but they appealed to the State Supreme Court, which heard their arguments last year.

The ruling, Ms. Puterbaugh told reporters today, will make this a special Christmas.

"I think there's going to be a little extra feeling of family now," she said.

* * *

February 6, 2000

A KALEIDOSCOPIC LOOK AT ATTITUDES ON GAY MARRIAGE

By CAREY GOLDBERG

MONTPELIER, Vt., Feb. 2—Imagine, nearly four hours of State House testimony late into the night and not a moment of tedium, not a single slide into the low-level murmur

Paul O. Bolsvert for The New York Times

University of Vermont supporters of freedom for gays to marry rallied on Tuesday outside the Vermont State House in Montpelier, Vt.

that means the chamber's attention has drifted, not a seat or a spot on a railing left vacant.

Such is the experience of watching the mass public hearings that the Vermont Legislature has held twice in the last two weeks on how it should respond to the State Supreme Court's ruling that gay couples must be granted the same rights and benefits as other spouses.

Much of the widespread fascination stems from the importance of the events: Vermonters take seriously the possibility that theirs will be the first state to legalize same-sex marriage. Vermont was the first state to outlaw slavery, some point out, and it could be on the verge of a similar act of moral leadership. Others warn that the state risks degenerating into the next Sodom.

But the hearings also fascinate in that, with scores of citizens testifying for two minutes each, they provide a kaleidoscopic look at current attitudes toward the country's decade-long debate over gay marriage. And those attitudes are full of parallel arguments and competing claims.

Consider the effect of a long marriage on a man's thinking:

At Tuesday night's televised hearing, one man argued that his marriage of 39 years convinced him that marriage was meant to be only between a man and a woman. "No matter how far back it goes, to the Bible, marriage has been one man, one woman. That's all. Not one man, one man, one woman, one woman."

But another man, Kenneth Wolvington, said, "Mrs. Wolvington and I have been married for 52 years" and "for the life of us, we can't imagine how gay marriage would adversely affect anyone in our family."

Or the question of Scripture:

Those who spoke against gay marriage, repeatedly cited a verse in Leviticus that calls sex between men "an abomination."

"God's words were that some sexual relations were indeed immoral," Jon Freeman said, arguing that children should be taught the difference between moral and immoral behavior. A Unitarian who spoke pointed out that the Bible cannot always be taken by its ancient word in this modern time: for example, he noted, it condoned slavery, which no one today would justify. The central tenet in the Bible, he said, is to love your neighbor as yourself—whether or not your neighbor is gay.

Weighty political questions are also at play in the debate, among them, the separation of church and state, and the issue of when a majority's opinion should be overridden in favor of a minority's rights.

A proponent of gay marriage argued that "the state is not in the business of giving people their morality," it is meant "to pass laws based on what's good for the community."

Those opposing gay marriage argued that the nation's founders established the country based on Judeo-Christian morality, and that the morality inherent in the biblical concept of marriage could not be separated from the law.

The question of majority versus minority stems in part from a poll indicating that most Vermonters disapprove of the idea of gay marriage.

Those who back gay marriage recalled past racial issues: Most Americans did not support ending the ban on interracial marriages, they said, and school integration was not supported by most Southerners, yet the courts are now deemed right in both mandates because they protected the equal rights of a minority.

"This is similar to the objections to interracial marriages a few decades ago," Molly Goldberg, a high school student, said. "Lawmakers had to move one step ahead of the people and pave the way for more tolerance."

Opponents of gay marriage countered that the question of gay marriage was so important to so many that the truly democratic method would be to put it to a popular vote in the state, through a referendum on a constitutional amendment.

"Let the people answer this issue," Anthony Kenny said.

And Robert Charlesworth argued: "The government is responsible for protecting minorities. It's not responsible for imposing minority values on the majority."

Even nature came into the argument, used by each side. An opponent of gay marriage remarked that "each fall, we see the majestic white-tailed buck chasing and mating with females, not with each other."

One backer of gay marriage countered that if procreation were the point of marriage, infertile couples would not be allowed to wed. Several lesbians testified that they had not chosen to be gay, but that they now had relationships every bit as committed as any marriage.

"What you are debating is not just policy and law," said Susan Clark, "what you are debating is my life, my partner's life."

The two sides also disagreed over the best analogies for the issue.

Some opponents said gay marriage should be compared to polygamy, or worse:

"We're not homophobes," one man said, "We'd be equally offended by attempts to legislate incest, rape or child molestation." (That remark drew the only muffled groan of the evening from the gay marriage camp.)

Backers of gay marriage drew parallels most often to the struggle for civil rights.

Ultimately, both sides argued that the future of the state, its children, and more, were at stake. One opponent of gay marriage said that "the downfall of every civilization is preceded by homosexuality." Others predicted an influx of gays into the state, which, they asserted, would damage its moral fiber.

Proponents of gay marriage called for leading the way to improve the climate for gays who now fear persecution, and for allowing Vermont's children to grow up in a state that does not discriminate.

"My hope," said Julie Wilson, who runs a high school gay-straight alliance, "is that my students, when they're old enough to be married, will be able to marry whoever they want."

* * *

March 17, 2000

VERMONT'S HOUSE BACKS WIDE RIGHTS FOR GAY COUPLES

By CAREY GOLDBERG

MONTPELIER, Vt., March 16—A bill to create "civil unions" giving gay and lesbian couples virtually all the benefits of marriage cleared its most critical legislative hurdle and gained final approval in the Vermont House of Representatives tonight, setting the stage for the state to adopt the most sweeping set of rights for same-sex couples in the country.

The pivotal 76-to-69 vote came after hours of emotional debate on topics like insurance and morality and on the heels of an equally close and hard-fought preliminary vote on Wednesday night. The bill, which gives same-sex couples spousal rights and privileges, is expected to pass more easily in the Senate next month, and Gov. Howard Dean has said he will sign it despite the deep schism the issue has created among Vermonters.

Meant to respond to a Vermont Supreme Court ruling that same-sex couples deserved all the same rights as heterosexual spouses, the bill stopped short of calling the same-sex unions marriage, and in fact, specified that marriage could only be between a man and a woman.

Though the bill, laboriously forged by the House Judiciary Committee over recent weeks, makes a distinction between same-sex unions and marriage, the benefits are virtually the same in providing state recognition for same-sex couples who cannot marry.

Couples may apply for a license from a town clerk and receive a certificate of civil union, the bill says. They then carry all the benefits and responsibilities that spouses do, and if they separate, their union must be dissolved in a family court.

For members of civil unions, the bill lists two dozen areas in which the law would consider their roles to be just like those of spouses, including child custody law, probate law, workers' compensation, family leave benefits and immunity from being compelled to testify.

Supporters of the bill said they did not expect other states to recognize the legal status of Vermont's civil unions, so it did not appear to raise any of the questions about recognition across state lines that a law allowing actual marriage would. Legal experts have also testified that the civil unions would not be portable.

"The state," the bill said, "has a strong interest in promoting stable and lasting families, including families based upon a same-sex couple."

The state may, but a great many of its citizens remain opposed to the idea of same-sex unions, and locked in hot debate with the many citizens who support it.

Complaining that it was marriage in all but name, opponents of the bill even distributed small yellow plastic ducks to lawmakers, symbols of their advertisements on radio and in newspapers arguing that if something looks, talks and swims like a duck, then it is a duck. Several ducks could be seen tonight sitting demonstratively on opponents' desks.

Backers of the bill said that though it fell short of actual marriage, it marked real progress.

"It's a big step in the right direction," said Nina Beck, a partner in one of the three same-sex couples whose suit challenging the state's refusal to let them marry led to the State Supreme Court's decision.

"It's not what we set out to do," said Ms. Beck, who stood to rock her 4-month-old son beneath the chamber's gilt-framed portrait of George Washington during the debate, "but it's many steps ahead of where we are now."

Asked if she and her partner, Stacy Jolles, would go to their town clerk to request a civil union certificate, she said, "Sign us up!"

In an interesting sidelight to the issue of same-sex marriage, the bill also provides a more limited set of benefits to blood relatives in another institution it calls reciprocal beneficiaries. Dealing mainly with medical decisions and funeral arrangements, it was meant to address situations in which, for example, widowed sisters live together and are effectively life partners, yet the state recognizes no special relationship between them.

The bill also provides for an oversight commission that would follow the results of the civil union law, "note its strengths and shortcomings," and report on them.

The campaign to legalize gay marriage has aroused controversy across the nation. California and Hawaii have statewide domestic partnership systems, but these pale in their scope next to the new Vermont law. Nearly 30 states have passed laws against gay marriage, and California voters this month approved a proposition declaring that marriage could legally exist only between a man and a woman.

In tonight's debate, Representative Frank M. Mazur of South Burlington warned that Vermont's moves toward recognizing same-sex couples left him worried about whether it might hurt the state's business climate and concerned "about whether there'll be a boycott against the state."

"Vermont is not an island," Mr. Mazur said. "We depend upon other states," and many of those states have made their views clear by passing Defense of Marriage Acts that specify that they would not recognize same-sex marriages if another state ever approved them.

A diametrically opposed argument came from Representative Marion C. Milne, a Republican, who contended that the Legislature must respect the State Supreme Court's finding that same-sex couples had been enduring unconstitutional discrimination.

"I will vote for this bill because I believe it is constitutionally mandated, but more importantly, because I believe it is the right thing to do," Ms. Milne said. She invoked the future, noting that the results of the vote would linger long after she and her fellow lawmakers were gone.

Minutes later, another representative, Nancy Sheltra, a Republican of Derby, invoked the future differently: "It's going to be very hard for me to explain to the next generation why the State Legislature decided to define marriage in a different manner and take away the moral standards we have stood for in this state," Ms. Sheltra said.

Bill Lippert, the only openly gay member of the Legislature, offered a vision of a different future: "Those of you who vote no on this bill for a variety of reasons, I'm sorry for your fear," Mr. Lippert said. "I'm sorry because we gay and lesbian couples are not a threat," as opponents will discover with time.

"I look forward to living together and to living in growing fairness in the state of Vermont," he said.

In the more immediate future, the bill now goes to the Democrat-dominated Senate, where leaders have said they believe they have the votes to get it passed. The Legislature is hoping to finish its current session by mid- or late April, and its leaders have said they wanted to respond to the Supreme Court ruling by session's end.

A lobbyist for opponents of the bill, Bill Shouldice, said tonight that he expected the bill to undergo more changes in its time in the Senate, and that, in fact, his side had been saving some of its fire until then.

There is another reason for the bill to cruise ahead in the Legislature: The same-sex issue is likely to have repercussions on this fall's elections in Vermont, and some politicians have said they would like to get it behind them well in advance.

* * *

July 2, 2000

IN VERMONT, GAY COUPLES HEAD FOR THE ALMOST-ALTAR

By CAREY GOLDBERG

SOUTH BURLINGTON, Vt., July 1—From Burlington to Brattleboro, with public hoopla or private solemnity, a scattering of gay couples across Vermont became the first in the country today to legally take on all the rights and responsibilities of marriage, in the first state to let them.

On this, the day that Vermont's new law creating marriagelike civil unions officially came into effect, most town clerks were closed for the weekend, so there could be no broad rush to the almost-altar.

But a handful of clerks opened their offices in response to requests from gay couples, very roughly estimated at perhaps two dozen, from both in and out of state, who wanted to pay their $20 fee, sign their certificates and get all-but-married the moment they could after years of unofficial union.

For Lois Farnham and Holly Puterbaugh, who have been together nearly 28 years and were plaintiffs in a 1997 suit against the state that led to the civil unions law, such a moment was once so unimaginable that they had a soloist sing "The Impossible Dream" at their church ceremony before about 200 guests today.

"Twenty-seven and a half years, that's a long engagement," Ms. Farnham said at the South Burlington municipal office, where the couple received their license and a wet-eyed hug from the city clerk, Margaret Picard. "It's nice after all this time to say Holly's my spouse."

Paul O'Boisvert for The New York Times

Margaret Picard, left, issued a civil union license yesterday to Lois Farnham, center, and Holly Puterbaugh in South Burlington, Vt.

In Brattleboro, Carolyn Conrad, 29, and Kathleen Peterson, 41, were so eager to get "C.U.-ed" that they went to the town clerk's office at midnight and filled out the paperwork. Witnessed by a cheering crowd of about 100 and a handful of protesters, they exchanged vows minutes later before a justice of the peace, making them the first in the country to be civilly united (or "civilly unionized," or "unified," or maybe "civilized"—there is still some confusion here over verbs, couples say).

As eager as the couples were to unite, others are as eager to see the outcome of all this civil joining. Opponents of civil unions predict legal tangles when out-of-staters try to get their Vermont civil unions recognized in their home state. Gay rights advocates say they are eager to show that the sky will not fall.

"Same-sex couples will be forming civil unions and the state's not going to fall apart," said Beth Robinson, a lead lawyer in the case that prompted the civil unions law. "It's just going to be better, and that's going to be the most helpful part of this dialogue. Because the longer we go with the law in effect, the more incredible the claims of our opponents will be exposed as being."

Over all, although today was mainly a day of joyful celebration for uniting couples, the broader picture in this pastoral state remains one of unusual turmoil—particularly turmoil centered on November's elections and the effect the civil unions issue will have on them.

Ever since the State Supreme Court ruled last December that denying gay couples the benefits of marriage amounted to unconstitutional discrimination, the question of gay unions has sundered the state, fanning atypical rancor. After months of difficult debate, the Legislature passed a civil unions law in April, and Gov. Howard Dean, a Democrat, promptly signed it. But the turbulence continues on several fronts.

A few town clerks have said they would resign rather than issue civil union certificates, though most appear willing to abide by the law.

"It's not that I'm not sympathetic to people and their needs, but I need to draw the line," said Gerry Longway, town clerk in Fairfield since 1980 and one of those considering resignation. "It just doesn't seem right or fair."

Opponents of the law are also suing to overturn it, claiming it should be invalidated because as it was coming up for a vote in the Legislature, several lawmakers placed small bets as to what the margin would be. Their efforts to get a judge to block the law from taking effect failed, but they say they plan to pursue their legal battle.

They are also forming a variety of small groups with names like "Who Would Have Thought" and "Standing Together and Reclaiming the State" to try to bring down lawmakers who voted for civil unions in the coming elections.

Already, some opponents have placed attack advertisements in Vermont's newspapers, including a black-bordered full-page advertisement in The Burlington Free Press on June 18 that denounced "the insufferable hubris of the narcissistic gay lobby that would place personal pleasures before public order." It argued that it is "probably no coincidence" that financial markets began to slide as the same-sex marriage debate began here in February.

Because Vermont's procedure for referendums is so cumbersome, few believe the civil unions law could be overturned that way; but if the composition of the Legislature changes, there is a chance that the new body could vote to alter the law. In that case, it would be up to the State Supreme Court to decide whether the law still complied with the court's ruling that gay couples must be given the same benefits as heterosexual couples.

Advocates of civil unions have started their own political action committee, called Vermonters for Civil Unions, and plan to continue efforts at public education about gay marriage.

Legal experts say it is not clear what will happen when out-of-staters get civilly united in Vermont and then ask their home states to recognize the Vermont union.

Couples seeking civil unions must register with a town and have their unions solemnized by a member of the clergy or justice of the peace. Partners seeking to dissolve their unions must go through the Family Court just as divorcing couples do.

Already, there are signs of a nascent gay wedding industry—nothing fancy or flashy, but little in this green state of 600,000 ever is.

A new Web site, www.gayweddingguide.com, offers everything from a fledgling gift registry for gay couples to a selection of inns, and the Web site of Vermont's gay newspaper, Out in the Mountains, offers a list of justices of the peace who are friendly to civil unions. People in the Vermont wedding industry say they expect a surge of civil unions in the coming days and weeks because of a long-pent-up demand.

Marc Awodey, a justice of the peace in Burlington, said that he was booked for one civil union on Monday and three others in July, two of them for out-of-state couples. He had heard of about 50 planned for the coming week, and about two dozen to be performed today.

Estimates of the number of unions were difficult, however: Consider the spur-of-the-moment decision by Chuck Turner and Bill Miller, lounge owners from New Orleans who have been together 29 years and had happened to be traveling in Canada in a motor home on a long vacation with their mothers.

They decided to dip down into Vermont on a quick break from their itinerary, lined up a justice of the peace, stopped at a mall for rings, and showed up, mothers in tow, in the South Burlington clerk's office this morning for their union.

"Now," Mr. Miller said, "we finally get to send wedding invitations to all those people who've been sending them to us for 30 years."

* * *

GUARDIANSHIP

August 7, 1988

GAY GROUPS ARE RALLIED TO AID 2 WOMEN'S FIGHT

BY NADINE BROZAN

Today, the eve of her 32d birthday, as Sharon Kowalski lies in a nursing home in Hibbing, Minn., demonstrators across the country will be demanding that her family let her see Karen Thompson, who says they intended to spend their lives as a couple.

The case has inspired advocates of gay rights and disability rights, and on "National Free Sharon Kowalski Day" processions and vigils will be held in 21 cities, including New York, Boston, Washington and San Francisco.

"There are other cases that pit blood relatives against loved ones," said Thomas B. Stoddard, executive director of the Lambda Legal Defense and Education Fund, which promotes the rights of homosexuals and people with AIDS. "But there is no other case that approaches this one in symbolic importance."

Couple Exchanged Rings

Ms. Thompson, a college professor, said she and Ms. Kowalski bought a house in St. Cloud, Minn., a city of 43,000 people 60 miles northwest of Minneapolis, exchanged rings and considered themselves married. On Nov. 13, 1983, a drunken driver's automobile struck one driven by Ms. Kowalski. It left her disabled. Her family prevailed on courts to keep Ms. Thompson away.

Ms. Kowalski, a high school teacher of physical education and health, has an injured brain stem. She cannot walk and only occasionally speaks a word or two, but responds to questions about her wishes by typing and gesturing.

For more than four years her parents and Ms. Thompson, now 41 years old, have fought over her diagnosis, care and rehabilitation and her right to choose visitors and her lawyer. Her father says she is not a lesbian and Ms. Thompson has interfered.

Families Not Informed

The struggle began shortly after the accident, when Ms. Thompson invited the Kowalskis to stay at the couple's home near Ms. Kowalski, in a St. Cloud hospital. Ms. Thompson said neither she nor Ms. Kowalski had told her family of the relationship.

"We were extremely closeted," Ms. Thompson said. "We never discussed being gay, never said the word out loud. I played the game that I had fallen in love with Sharon because of certain characteristics and that, had I found those characteristics in a man, I would have fallen in love with him."

But she said of that denial, "If Sharon's parents had known about us before the accident, then four years after they could not still be claiming that their daughter was not a lesbian."

Legal Documents Urged

She urges gay couples to draw up powers of attorney, wills and other protective legal documents or they have no legal right to "spousal" property or decision-making. In her case, she allowed no documentation; the house, she said, was in her name for secrecy. Ms. Thompson said she soon sensed that the Kowalskis knew of the relationship, and decided "to come out to them, in the form of a letter."

The Kowalskis, a middle-aged couple from the Iron Range of northern Minnesota, were stunned. "When they received it, they said I was sick and crazy and they never wanted to set eyes on me again," Ms. Thompson said.

Fearful that they would move their daughter to Hibbing, a five-hour drive from St. Cloud, she filed for guardianship. Mr. Kowalski counterfiled, and in April 1984 an out-of-court pact was reached. He would be guardian, but Ms. Thompson would have generous visitation rights and an equal voice in medical decisions. The pact did not last.

Physicians Back Parents

"I taught Sharon to type," said Ms. Thompson, an associate professor of physical education and recreation at St. Cloud State University. "I helped her with reading, writing, math problems, short-term memory skills, with flexibility and exercise. To listen to them, you would think we're talking about a totally helpless, incompetent patient who cannot possibly express her wishes."

Physicans testified for the Kowalskis that Ms. Thompson left Ms. Kowalski depressed. Dr. William Wilson, the family physician, wrote the court, "Visits by Karen Thompson at this time would expose Sharon Kowalski to a high risk of sexual abuse."

In July 1985 a district court in Stearns County, Minn., granted Donald Kowalski, a 57-year-old retired mining company foreman, unconditional guardianship. "Within 24 hours, Donald Kowalski said I was never to be allowed to visit Sharon again," Ms. Thompson said in an interview in Buffalo where she was addressing the National Organization for Women.

Visits Linked to Depression

Mr. Kowalski said in an interview: "Karen Thompson kicked herself out of there by being so aggressive and by driving Sharon into a deep depression. She told Sharon she was being held prisoner, that she was in a dangerous environment. If you couldn't talk and you were lying there, wouldn't that put you in a depression?"

"She never gave us any indication" of a lesbian relationship, he said, "and she would have told our other daughter of such a relationship. So who are we supposed to believe? Karen Thompson has lied about everything."

Ms. Thompson seeks support for her cause and funds for her legal costs, $120,000 so far. Last summer she was a marshal of the Gay-Lesbian Pride Parade in New York. In October she was a keynote speaker at the gay rights rally of 200,000 people in Washington.

According to Mr. Stoddard of Lambda, the case "has touched the deepest nerve in the gay community across the United States because it triggers the two deepest fears of every gay person: a fight among loved ones and denial of personal wishes."

Nan D. Hunter, a lawyer and director of the American Civil Liberties Union's Lesbian and Gay Rights Project, said: "I don't think we've had any case that is so dramatic, or in which the conflict has been so extended. But there have been many instances of tension between surviving partners of men dying of AIDS and their family members. Then the situations have run the gamut from unease and discomfort to litigation and open warfare."

Advocates of disability rights also say the case raises fundamental issues concerning a disabled person's right to a voice in his or her destiny.

"Essentially, this is a classic example of a disabled person being entirely denied the right to control her life," said Marilyn Golden, a policy analyst with the Disability Rights Education and Defense Fund.

Psychiatric Tests Scheduled

Ms. Thompson has filed numerous legal appeals from the order barring her. Now the door to a reunion has been opened slightly, depending on the findings of a competency evaluation to be done this month by a psychiatrist and a specialist in communication disorders.

If Ms. Kowalski is judged capable of deciding, her right to do so may be partly or totally restored. The tests, for which she will be taken to the Miller-Dwan Medical Center in Duluth, will make up the first comprehensive assessment of her condition in four years.

Jack Fena of Hibbing, a lawyer for Donald Kowalski and his wife, Della, tried to block court-ordered tests on the ground that it will be harmful to move Ms. Kowalski out of familiar surroundings. In his view, evaluation is unnecessary. "If you get your leg cut off, how many doctors must tell you that your leg is cut off?" he said.

Ms. Thompson says she keeps remembering that at their last meeting, Ms. Kowalski typed: "Help me Karen, get me out of here."

"I made a commitment to Sharon," she said. "Sharon may have limitations, but those only make her different than she was before, not less. I still think we could have a good life together."

*   *   *

February 8, 1989

WOMAN'S HOSPITAL VISIT MARKS GAY RIGHTS FIGHT

By NADINE BROZAN

Karen Thompson walked into Sharon Kowalski's room at the Miller-Dwan Medical Center in Duluth, Minn., last week and said quietly: "Hi, Sharon. Do you remember me?"

Ms. Thompson said the meeting, their first in three and a half years, was "an emotionally overwhelming moment." The two women had exchanged wedding bands and shared a home in St. Cloud until Ms. Kowalski was paralyzed and suffered brain injuries in an automobile accident in November 1983.

Behind the reunion was a series of bitter court battles between Ms. Thompson, a 41-year-old associate professor of physical education and recreation at Saint Cloud State University, and Ms. Kowalski's parents, Donald and Della Kowalski. The dispute was over who had the right to make decisions for the 32-year-old Ms. Kowalski, who once taught high school classes in physical education and health.

Processions and Vigils

The case became a cause celebre and an important symbol around the country for groups who advocate gay rights, rights for the disabled and women's rights. Processions and vigils were organized in 21 cities on Aug. 7 to mark "National Free Sharon Kowalski Day."

The conflict over Ms. Kowalski began soon after the accident when Ms. Thompson told the Kowalskis about the nature of her relationship with their daughter. In an out-of-court agreement, Mr. Kowalski became guardian but Ms. Thompson retained broad visiting rights. In July 1985, asserting that Ms.

Thompson was a detrimental and depressing influence, as he has throughout the case, Mr. Kowalski sought and received unconditional guardianship.

In 24 hours he had Ms. Thompson and other friends barred from any contact with Ms. Kowalski, including mail. In the ensuing years Ms. Thompson went to state and Federal courts on numerous occasions seeking revokation of Mr. Kowalski's guardianship, but losing at every level until last year.

In September, under court order, Ms. Kowalski was moved from the Leisure Hills Nursing Home in Hibbing, Minn., to the Miller-Dwan Medical Center for an evaluation of her competency by a team of physicians and mental health experts.

Day Evaluation Ordered

As a result of their report, Judge Robert T. Campbell of St. Louis County District Court ordered that a more comprehensive evaluation of Ms. Kowalski be performed for a 60-day period beginning Jan. 17 and that she undergo variety of physical, psychological and occupational therapy treatments not offered in the nursing home.

The Kowalskis had opposed this, arguing that the move would be detrimental and that there was nothing new to be learned from further testing or to be gained from augmented therapy.

Ms. Thompson's lawyer, M. Sue Wilson, said, "The initial evaluation showed that Sharon Kowalski can intereact with others, that she understands what is going on, that she can reliably express her wishes about who shall visit her and that she would very much benefit from rehabilitation that is more intensive and focused than what was going on in the nursing home."

The judge also said it was up to the hospital to decide who could visit Ms. Kowalski, to be determined according to "her reliably expressed wishes."

So, Ms. Thompson and three other friends were permitted to visit Ms. Kowalski. Ms. Thompson said she arrived Thursday and stayed all day Friday, Saturday and Sunday and was asked to participate in psychological, speech and occupational therapy sessions.

Psychologists at the hospital had prepared Ms. Kowalski for the encounter but Ms. Thompson said: "She seemed shocked at first. She immmediately got tears in her eyes and I broke down, though I had vowed to remain calm. But for the rest of the weekend, she was all smiles and laughs."

Ms. Kowalski communicated mainly through whispering, shakes of the head, a keyboard that can be programmed to say sentences and an alphabet board.

"I told her I needed to know what she thought of me before I could pursue the fight for her, and she spelled out the word, 'lover,'" Ms. Thompson said. "It was very clear and very consistent that she thinks of me as her partner and wants to come live with me."

Father Is Disbelieving

Donald Kowalski said yesterday, as he has many times before, that he refused to believe that his daughter was a lesbian. "I've never seen anything that would make me believe it, and I will not change my mind until Sharon is capable of telling me in her own words," he said in a telephone interview. "And I do not believe the reports that she was happy to see Thompson."

Mr. Kowalski said he did not agree that the move was in his daughter's best interest, explaining his views this way: "My daughter was taken from a place where she was getting good care and improving, and I went to visit her a week ago, and she was so confused by all the new people. She didn't know where she was. If her doctor had thought she needed the higher form of rehabilitation, believe me he would have said so."

Ms. Kowalski's testing and treatment at Miller-Dwan are scheduled to continue through mid-March, at which time another report will be filed with Judge Campbell and he will decide where she will go next.

Mr. Kowalski, a retired miner, said he could no longer afford to fight legal battles for jurisdiction over his daughter. "I have no lawyer and I can't afford one," he said.

* * *

April 26, 1991

2 SIDES ARE BYPASSED IN LESBIAN CASE

By NADINE BROZAN

After a five-year legal battle in Minnesota between the parents of a paralyzed, brain-damaged woman and her lesbian lover, a judge has chosen a third party to act as the disabled woman's legal guardian.

In his ruling in the case Judge Robert Campbell of the St. Louis County District Court in Duluth, Minn., likened the paralyzed woman, Sharon Kowalski, now 34 years old, to a child over whom divorcing parents do battle.

"The two wings of her family were unable to reach agreement on her care and visitation, matters which will serve her best interests," he wrote in an opinion issued Wednesday. "She must enjoy the love and comfort of both wings of her family for her complete well-being and her long-term rehabilitation."

Those goals can be accomplished, he said, only through the appointment of a "neutral third party."

Closeted before the accident, the couple became a cause celebre, the subject of parades and vigils. They came to symbolize the struggle for equal rights of homosexuals and people with disabilities.

Judge's Ruling Denounced

The woman's lover, Karen Thompson, 43, immediately denounced Judge Campbell's ruling, accusing him of appointing a guardian who was just a "stand-in" for Ms. Kowalski's parents.

And a spokesman for lesbian and gay groups called the ruling "deeply offensive" and predicted it would "resonate throughout the law."

The case began in 1983 after Ms. Kowalski, a high school gym teacher, was severely injured in a car collision with a drunken driver. Until then she and Ms. Thompson, with

whom she had exchanged wedding bands, lived in a house they had bought. Ms. Thompson said the house was in her name because of their desire for secrecy.

Shortly after Ms. Thompson told the parents about her relationship with their daughter—they have continued to deny that she is a lesbian—the Kowalskis took steps to end the relationship.

Ms. Kowalski's father, Donald Kowalski, a retired mining foreman, obtained sole guardianship in July 1985. He moved his daughter to a nursing home in Hibbing, Minn., a five-hour drive from Ms. Thompson's home in Clearwater, a village near St. Cloud in south-central Minnesota, and had her barred from visiting the younger woman.

Numerous Appeals Filed

Over the next three years Ms. Thompson filed numerous appeals in local, state and Federal courts, trying to have the guardianship revoked and contending that Ms. Kowalski was being denied accesss to therapy intended to advance her physical and mental capacity.

Last summer Mr. Kowalski resigned his guardianship, citing two heart attacks that he said had been provoked by the strain of repeated legal challenges.

And now Judge Campbell has appointed Karen Tomberlin as Ms. Kowalski's guardian. Ms. Tomberlin is a teacher and coach at Greenway High School in Coleraine, a small town in the Iron Range region of northern Minnesota near Nashwauk, where the Kowalskis live.

In his court order Judge Campbell described Ms. Tomberlin as "a close friend of Sharon and Sharon's parents" who has known Ms. Kowalski since 1973.

The judge is on vacation and is unreachable, according to members of his staff.

Ms. Kowalski's mother, Delia, reached at her home, said she had no comment.

Decison to Be Appealed

Speaking from Atlanta, where she is attending a national lesbian rights conference, Ms. Thompson, an associate professor of physical education, recreation and sports science at St. Cloud State University, said she would appeal Judge Campbell's decision.

"Karen Tomberlin is just a stand-in for the parents," Ms. Thompson said. "She took up their cause when they became too tired and sickly."

Ms. Thompson said she had briefly told Ms. Kowalski about the latest decision before leaving for Atlanta. "Sharon was clearly upset, moved and concerned," she said.

Ms. Tomberlin could not be reached for comment yesterday.

In 1988 Judge Campbell ordered that a comprehensive evaluation of Ms. Kowalski be conducted in Duluth, and she was moved there. He also ruled that Ms. Thompson be permitted to visit.

After Mr. Kowalski resigned his guardianship and the evaluation found that Ms. Kowalski was able to determine with whom she wished to live, new hearings on her guardianship were held.

'Commitment and Devotion'

In his order, Judge Campbell wrote that Ms. Thompson "has demonstrated commitment and devotion to the welfare of Sharon Kowalski." He noted that she had particpated in Ms. Kowalski's therapy and counseling and was familiar with her "medical, material and social needs."

The judge also wrote, "In the past two years, when asked where she would like to live, Sharon has consistently said, 'St. Cloud with Karen.'"

But in a section of his decision subtitled "outing," the judge said Ms. Thompson had violated Ms. Kowalski's privacy by disclosing her sexual orientation "to Sharon's parents and the world without Sharon's consent." And he cited as a consideration the fact that Ms. Thompson now has "other domestic partnerships."

She does not deny that. "I said on the stand that two and a half years after being away from Sharon, I decided to leave myself open to other relationships," Ms. Thompson said. "Sharon comes home with me all the time, and some of that time the other person is there. She really likes the person I am with, and has never asked."

Ms. Thompson added: "The system separated us for three and a half years, and we became strangers. For Sharon, I will always be what I was years ago. She can never know me as I am today, but I will love her for the rest of my life."

Thomas B. Stoddard, executive director of the Lambda Legal Defense Fund, a gay rights legal affairs group, called Judge Campbell's decision "a deep offense not only to all lesbians and gay men, but to all Americans who choose their partners and households by their own terms and not the legal rules imposed by society."

"The idea of neutrality does not apply in any other area of family law," he continued. "Sharon chose her family. But the judge doesn't agree, so he imposed his own vision on her."

* * *

December 18, 1991

DISABLED WOMAN'S CARE GIVEN TO LESBIAN PARTNER

By TAMAR LEWIN

After a seven-year legal battle that became a rallying cause for gay rights groups, a Minnesota appeals court yesterday granted guardianship of Sharon Kowalski, a 35-year-old woman left brain-damaged and quadriplegic in a 1983 car accident, to her lesbian lover.

"This seems to be the first guardianship case in the nation in which an appeals court recognized a homosexual partner's rights as tantamount to those of a spouse," said M. Sue Wilson, the lawyer for Ms. Kowalski's lover, Karen Thompson.

Ms. Thompson had fought since 1984 to be named guardian, over the objections of Donald and Della Kowalski, who said their daughter had never told them she was a lesbian and who barred Ms. Thompson from visiting their daughter's nursing home for several years after the accident.

A Cause Taken Up

Ms. Thompson's fight to be reunited with her lover became a cause celebre among groups advocating gay rights and rights for the disabled. These groups organized vigils and processions in 21 cities on Aug. 7, 1988, which was called "National Free Sharon Kowalski Day."

"This case exemplifies the difficulties lesbians and gay men have in safeguarding our relationships," said William Rubenstein, director of the American Civil Liberties Union's Lesbian and Gay Rights Project. "The remarkable thing about this case is not that Karen Thompson finally won guardianship, but that it took her seven years to do so, when guardianship rights for a heterosexual married couple would be taken for granted."

Mr. Rubenstein said the Thompson case had struck a responsive chord among homosexuals, coming just as many gay men whose partners had died of AIDS were finding that they had no legal rights to stay in their apartments, share in the estates or decide where their partners would be buried.

"This case, and AIDS, have been the defining events of the 1980's in this area," Mr. Rubenstein said. "It's underscored why we need legal protection, and created a terrific incentive to fight for these kinds of marital rights and recognition of domestic partnership."

The Minnesota Court of Appeals said the St. Louis County District Court in Duluth had abused its discretion in denying Ms. Thompson's petition to become Ms. Kowalski's caretaker and instead appointing a third party, who was a close friend of Ms. Kowalski's parents.

"Thompson's suitability for guardianship was overwhelmingly clear from the testimony of Sharon's doctors and caretakers," the appeals court said.

A Battle's History

Ms. Kowalski, a former high school gym teacher, has required around-the-clock care since the automobile accident left her nearly paralyzed, with severe short-term memory loss and impaired ability to speak.

Her father, a retired mining foreman, won sole guardianship in July 1985, moved his daughter to a nursing home in Hibbing, Minn., and barred any visits by Ms. Thompson, a 44-year-old physical education professor at St. Cloud State University.

Over the next three years, Ms. Thompson filed appeals in local, state and Federal courts, seeking to change the guardianship decision and charging that Ms. Kowalski was being denied access to the therapy she needed.

In September 1988, Judge Robert Campbell of the St. Louis County District Court ordered a comprehensive evaluation of Ms. Kowalski, and she was moved to a Duluth nursing home, where Ms. Thompson was allowed to resume visits to the woman with whom she had exchanged wedding bands.

368 THE GAY RIGHTS MOVEMENT

Last year, Mr. Kowalski resigned his guardianship, citing heart problems and weariness with the extended court proceedings. In April, Judge Campbell awarded guardianship to a third party, Karen Tomberlin, Ms. Kowalski's high school track and volleyball coach.

Judge Campbell likened Ms. Kowalski to a child over whom divorcing parents were battling and concluded that she could not express a reliable preference for guardianship. But in reversing that decision, the appeals court disagreed.

Deciding Kowalski's Choice

"All the medical testimony established that Sharon has the capacity reliably to express a preference in this case, and she has clearly chosen to return home with Thompson if possible," the court said. "This choice is further supported by the fact that Thompson and Sharon are a family of affinity, which ought to be accorded respect."

The appeals court also noted that Ms. Thompson was the only person willing or able to care for Ms. Kowalski outside an institution and that she had built a house fully accessible by wheelchair.

The court also rejected Judge Campbell's finding that Ms. Thompson had acted contrary to Ms. Kowalski's best interests by making public their lesbian relationship.

Ms. Tomberlin, reached yesterday at Greenway High School in Coleraine, Minn., said she had not seen the opinion or decided whether she would appeal.

"The worst thing about the decision is that Karen apparently wants to bring Sharon home to St. Cloud, but because of the years of hurt and pain, Sharon's parents have said they will never go see her again if she lives there," she said. "The void is too deep."

Ms. Tomberlin said she had not been able to reach the Kowalskis to discuss the opinion, and a call to their home was answered by a machine. Ms. Thompson's lawyer said yesterday that her client did plan to bring Ms. Kowalski to St. Cloud, about 60 miles northwest of Minneapolis, where they had lived together before the crash.

"This decision came out on the 12th anniversary of the commitment ceremony where they exchanged rings and promised to love each other their whole lives," said Ms. Wilson, the lawyer. "Karen and Sharon talked today about what they were going to do to celebrate. Sharon doesn't have the short-term memory to remember what happened an hour ago, but she does remember Karen and the past, and that she is a lesbian."

* * *

PART VII

HOMOPHOBIA AND INTOLERANCE

Fear and Hatred

December 17, 1963

GROWTH OF OVERT HOMOSEXUALITY IN CITY PROVOKES WIDE CONCERN

By ROBERT C. DOTY

The problem of homosexuality in New York became the focus yesterday of increased attention by the State Liquor Authority and the Police Department.

The liquor authority announced the revocation of the liquor licenses of two more homosexual haunts that had been repeatedly raided by the police. The places were the Fawn, at 795 Washington Street near Jane Street, and the Heights Supper Club at 80 Montague Street, Brooklyn.

The city's most sensitive open secret—the presence of what is probably the greatest homosexual population in the world and its increasing openness—has become the subject of growing concern of psychiatrists, religious leaders and the police.

One division of the organized crime syndicate controls bars and restaurants that cater to the homosexual trade. Commenting yesterday on the situation, Police Commissioner Michael J. Murphy said:

"Homosexuality is another one of the many problems confronting law enforcement in this city. However, the underlying factors in homosexuality are not criminal but rather medical and sociological in nature.

"The police jurisdiction in this area is limited. But when persons of this type become a source of public scandal, or violate the laws, or place themselves in a position where they become the victims of crime they do come within our jurisdiction.

"This matter is of constant concern to us in our efforts to preserve the peace and protect the rights of all the people. It has been given, and will continue to be given, special attention."

The two latest places to be put out of business by the liquor authority were described by Donald S. Hostetter, authority chairman, as "notorious congregating points for homosexuals and degenerates."

Mr. Hostetter said the Heights Supper Club had a signal-light system that "warned the boys to stop dancing with one another" when a newcomer was suspected of being a policeman.

The Fawn has a back room to which an admission was charged and where as many as 70 to 80 deviates had parties on Friday and Saturday nights. Most of the patrons were males, but on occasion police found women dancing with women.

There were 19 police visits this year resulting in summonses and complaints of a noisy jukebox, disorderly premises, insufficient lighting and dancing without a cabaret license, and an arrest for degeneracy.

Both places were so wary about nonmembers of the "fraternity" that the police used specialists known in the department as "actors" to get evidence.

Closed Since Oct. 29

The Heights Supper Club license was in the name of the 80 Montague Restaurant, Inc., with Martha Leaver listed as sole owner and president. William Leaver was listed as a director.

The club has been closed since Oct. 29 on an S.L.A. suspension order. The new penalty makes it impossible to apply for a new license for two years with no indication that it would be granted then.

Vincent Zito of 259 Bleecker Street was listed as sole owner of Belpe Restaurant, Inc., in whose name the license for the Fawn had been issued.

Homosexual bars are only a small part of the homosexual problem in New York. For more than a month, this reporter has discussed the problem with city officials, physicians, social workers and homosexuals themselves.

Sexual inverts have colonized three areas of the city. The city's homosexual community acts as a lodestar, attracting others from all over the country. More than a thousand inverts are arrested here annually for public misdeeds.

Yet the old idea, assiduously propagated by homosexuals, that homosexuality is an inborn, incurable disease, has been exploded by modern psychiatry, in the opinion of many experts. It can be both prevented and cured, these experts say.

Out of the Shadows

It is a problem that has grown in the shadows, protected by taboos on open discussion that have only recently begun to be breached.

The overt homosexual—and those who are identifiable probably represent no more than half of the total—has become such an obtrusive part of the New York scene that the phenomenon needs public discussion, in the opinion of a number of legal and medical experts.

Two conflicting viewpoints converge today to overcome the silence and promote public discussion.

The first is the organized homophile movement—a minority of militant homosexuals that is openly agitating for removal of legal, social and cultural discriminations against sexual inverts.

Fundamental to this aim is the concept that homosexuality is an incurable, congenital disorder (this is disputed by the bulk of scientific evidence) and that homosexuals should be treated by an increasingly tolerant society as just another minority.

This view is challenged by a second group, the analytical psychiatrists, who advocate an end to what it calls a head-in-sand approach to homosexuality.

They have what they consider to be overwhelming evidence that homosexuals are created—generally by ill-adjusted parents—not born.

They assert that homosexuality can be cured by sophisticated analytical and therapeutic techniques.

More significantly, the weight of the most recent findings suggests that public discussion of the nature of those parental misdeeds and attitudes that tend to foster homosexual development of children could improve family environments and reduce the incidence of sexual inversion.

Leaving the subject exclusively to barroom jesters, policemen concerned with public aspects of the problem and the homosexuals themselves can only perpetuate the mystery and misconceptions that have grown in the dark, according to expert opinion.

The statement that the city has what is probably the greatest concentration of sexual inverts anywhere in the world rests on observed and inferential evidence. There are no statistics.

No one pretends to know how many men there are in the city who seek sexual partners of their own sex. (This study has been confined to male homosexuality. Some observers believe the female deviation—lesbianism—is also on the increase here.)

Experts' Views Differ

Estimates range from an avowedly conservative 100,000 by one leading psychiatrist to a probably exaggerated 600,000 by the homosexual president of the Mattachine Society of New York, the organization dedicated to education of the general public on "the problems of the sexual deviant."

Some experts believe the numbers of homosexuals in the city are increasing rapidly. Others contend that, as public attitudes have become more tolerant, the homosexuals have tended to be more overt, less concerned with concealing their deviant conduct.

In any case, identifiable homosexuals—perhaps only half of the total—seem to throng Manhattan's Greenwich Village, the East Side from the upper 40's through the 70's and the West 70's. In a fairly restricted area around Eighth Avenue and 42d Street there congregate those who are universally regarded as the dregs of the invert world—the male prostitutes—the painted, grossly effeminate "queens" and those who prey on them.

In each of the first three areas the homosexuals have their own restaurants and bars—some operated for them under the contemptuous designation of "fag joints" by the organized crime syndicate.

They have their favored clothing suppliers who specialize in the tight slacks, short-cut coats and fastidious furnishings favored by many, but by no means all, male homosexuals.

There is a homosexual jargon, once intelligible only to the initiate, but now part of New York slang. The word "gay" has been appropriated as the adjective for homosexual.

The 'Gay' Life

"Is he gay?" a homosexual might ask another of a mutual acquaintance. They would speak of a "gay bar" or a "gay party" and probably derive secret amusement from innocent employment of the word in its original meaning by "straight"—that is, heterosexual—speakers.

The homosexual has a range of gay periodicals that is a kind of distorted mirror image of the straight publishing world.

Thus, from the Mattachine Society and other serious homophile organizations, the homosexual can get publications offering intellectual discussion of his problems.

Newsstands offer a wide range of magazines and papers designed to appeal to inverted sexual tastes. These include many of the so-called body building publications presenting, under the guise of physical culture, photos of scantily-clad, heavily-muscled men, and others peddling outright homosexual pornography in text and illustration.

In summer, the New York homosexual can find vacation spots frequented by his kind—notably parts of Fire Island, a section of the beach at Jacob Riis Park, and many others.

In fact, a New York homosexual, if he chooses an occupation in which his clique is predominant, can shape for himself a life lived almost exclusively in an inverted world from which the rough, unsympathetic edges of straight society can be almost totally excluded.

It is this phenomenon, existing only in a few big cities and pre-eminently in New York, that draws homosexuals here. They arrive to find escape from the legal and social harassment in their smaller home communities, where their deviancy can be hidden only at the price of self-denial.

Here they have to fear only the law, which punishes homosexual conduct variously as a crime or a misdemeanor.

Accordingly, it has become a prime objective of the homophile movements to obtain repeal of laws that forbid private homosexual acts between consenting adults, even though these are seldom enforced.

In this, they have the support of psychiatrists and some legal authorities. All, including the homosexuals, agree that enforcement of bans on homosexual conduct constituting a public nuisance or involving minors should be rigorously continued.

In each of the last four years, 1,000 to 1,200 men have been arrested in New York for overt homosexual activity. Most—about two thirds—were arrested under the disorderly conduct statute for soliciting male partners.

Spokesmen for the Mattachine Society complain bitterly against alleged entrapment of homosexuals by plainclothes policemen sent into homosexual haunts. The homophile groups have won some support from civil rights groups in their campaign to outlaw the uncorroborated testimony of an arresting officer as proof of cases of entrapment for soliciting.

Open to Entrapment

The tendency of homosexuals to be promiscuous and seek pick-ups—a tendency recognized even by the gay writer, Donald Webster Cory, in his book "The Homosexual in America"—makes them particularly vulnerable to police entrapment.

Any sexual contact between persons of the same sex is punishable under the sodomy statute. If the action involves any use of force or threat of force or if one of the participants is a minor, sodomy is a felony. There have been about 250 such arrests annually in recent years, with about two-thirds of them coming to indictment and trial.

In all other cases, notably acts between consenting adults, sodomy is a misdemeanor. There have been an average of 120 arrests here annually under this section, most often for acts in public.

First Deputy Police Commissioner John F. Walsh says the Police Department has limited itself to an effort to suppress solicitation in bars, public lavatories and Turkish baths and any approaches to minors by homosexuals. No attempt is made, he says, to enforce the theoretical ban on private homosexual conduct between consenting adults.

Blackmail Feared

Homosexuals and some legal authorities argue that this prohibition, even if unenforced, should be removed from the statute books. Its mere existence, they contend, offers a foundation for possible blackmail of homosexuals.

The British Government's Report of the Committee on Homosexual Practices and Prostitution—the so-called Wolfenden Report—strongly urged removal of legal penalties for private homosexual acts between consenting adults, but Parliament refused to act on the recommendation. In this country, only Illinois has acted in the sense urged by the Wolfenden Report.

There have been 40 to 70 arrests a year in New York for homosexual offenses involving minors—usually young men in their late teens rather than juveniles.

Parental concern over this aspect of the problem probably is excessive, according to most psychiatrists and public officials. In the first place, it is observed, truly psychotic inverts who prey upon pre-adolescent boys are no more common than molesters of girl juveniles.

The Borderline Cases

Secondly, prevailing psychiatric opinion is that a single homosexual encounter would be unlikely to turn a young man toward homosexuality unless a predisposition already existed in the individual.

Police Commissioner Michael J. Murphy, who said jurisdiction was limited.

There is general belief, however, that strict enforcement of the law against seduction of minors is important to protect borderline cases from adult influences that could swing them toward homosexual orientation when heterosexual adjustment was still possible.

Commissioner Walsh, officials of the State Liquor Authority and New York homosexuals agree that there is evidence that the crime syndicate had moved into the operation of bars and night-spots for homosexuals as early as 1957.

The police and the liquor authority have closed, temporarily or permanently, scores of places—more than 30 last year alone—where disorderly conduct involving homosexuals was established.

"There is no direct proof of syndicate operation, but on more than one occasion we have had the same persons employed in this type of place as manager, bartender or doorman, indicating some sort of organization," Commissioner Walsh says.

He acknowledges that this may involve some low-level police pay offs but says it is unorganized on the police side.

The Commissioner's confidential unit cracks down on such practices whenever they can be established, he says.

Two names have recurred in the behind-the-scenes operation of these places. One is an ex-convict with a long record of arrests for offenses ranging from juvenile delinquency to assault. He has long been known as an associate of a lieutenant of Vito Genovese, the reputed head of the Cosa Nostra crime syndicate.

Silent Partner

The ex-convict has owned or operated a succession of places that catered to homosexuals. His license for operation of a West Side bar was not renewed several years ago but he has appeared in the management of other homosexual haunts since then.

Syndicate interest in such operations is financial. Homosexuals are traditionally willing to spend all they have on a gay night. They will pay admission fees and outrageous prices for drinks in order to be left alone with their own kind to chatter and dance together without pretense or constraint.

Homosexuals are victimized frequently by "fag workers"—young hoodlums who specialize in leading homosexuals on and then robbing and beating them, sometimes fatally.

A homosexual who had achieved good progress toward cure under psychoanalysis recently told his analyst that at certain hours on certain evenings he could identify as homosexual approximately one man out of three along Third Avenue in the 50's and 60's. This was probably an exaggeration, but the area named unquestionably has a relatively large homosexual population.

Some homosexuals claim infallibility in identifying others of their kind "by the eyes—there's a look that lingers a fraction of a second too long."

Most normal persons believe they have a similar facility in spotting deviates. This is true only of the obviously effeminate type—the minority who either openly proclaim their orientation or who make only perfunctory efforts to disguise it.

"The homosexual community cuts entirely across society—from the Bowery bum to the corporation executive," says a spokesman for the Mattachine Society, himself an invert. He is the owner of his own trade publication business and serves the society under his own name, but was unwilling to be identified by name.

Heterosexual Masquerade

"Many homosexual men carry out a successful lifetime masquerade—with wives, children and entirely masculine appearance," he says.

In Greenwich Village, a center for the bohemians of the homosexual world, one real estate management concern estimated that about one-fourth of the 245 apartments in its 18 West Village buildings were rented to homosexuals.

In some areas of the East Side the "middle-class" homosexuals lead outward lives that are prosperous and even gay, in the original sense, built around tasteful apartments and weekend cocktail parties. The West 70's are home to a less prosperous class of homosexuals who drift through the rooming-house neighborhoods between the park and Broadway.

An all-night restaurant on Broadway in the 70's was described by officials of the Mattachine Society as "the bottom of the barrel"—the haunt of exhibitionist queens and eccentrics. A visit there disclosed that even at noon there were half a dozen obvious homosexuals killing time over coffee and jukebox music.

Impossible Dream

Many homosexuals dream of forming a permanent attachment that would give them the sense of social and emotional stability others derive from heterosexual marriage, but few achieve it.

The absence of any legal ties, plus the basic emotional instability that is inherent in many homosexuals, cause most such homosexuals partnerships to founder on the jealousies and personality clashes that a heterosexual union would survive.

Hence, most homosexuals are condemned to a life of promiscuity—the cruising of bars seeking casual partners.

It is miscalculation in this almost inevitable phase of their lives that most often brings homosexuals into conflict with the law. This peril, however, is becoming less menacing.

"From homosexual subjects treated 25 years ago we learned that finding a paramour was a difficult and dangerous undertaking," wrote Dr. Abram Kardiner, a leading authority in the field, nine years ago. "Today [1954] we learn they are plentiful, in all walks of life, with no risks involved. They are to be found in bars, restaurants, theaters, public toilets, in the factories and universities."

Found Everywhere

Inverts are to be found in every conceivable line of work from truck driving to coupon clipping. But they are most concentrated—or most noticeable—in the fields of the creative and performing arts and industries serving women's beauty and fashion needs.

Their presence in creative activity is not, as an old myth fostered by homosexuals would have it, because inverts tend to have superior intellect and talent. Most students of the subject agree that the significant factor in homosexual colonization of some of the arts is that men who would find difficulty in winning acceptance from fellow workers in more prosaic activities naturally gravitate toward solitary, introspective endeavor.

The list of homosexuals in the theater is long, distinguished and international. It is also self-perpetuating.

There is a cliquishness about gay individuals that often leads one who achieves influential position in the theater—as many of them do—to choose for employment another homosexual candidate over a straight applicant, unless the latter had an indisputable edge of talent that would bear on the artistic success of the venture.

Not Immune to Women

There is a popular belief that homosexuals are immune to sexual attraction by women. Dr. Irving Bieber, director of the most recent extensive study of homosexuality, disputes this view and cites the presence of large numbers of inverts in occupations that bring them into close personal contact with women to prove the reverse.

He asserts that homosexual men receive sexual stimulation from women. But, because their capacity for normal erotic expression has been crippled psychically, Dr. Bieber believes female attraction produces a reaction of fear and search for homosexual outlet.

The tendency of high-fashion designers to produce styles that minimize or suppress womanly curves—styles that can be worn really well only by hipless, bosomless mannequins—has often been interpreted as an expression of homosexual hostility toward women. In Dr. Bieber's opinion, it is, rather, another expression of fear.

The practice of homosexuality is regarded as sin by all three of the main branches of western religion—Roman Catholicism, Protestantism and Judaism.

Religions Condemn It

Leaders of all three reprove homosexual acts, just as they condemn illicit heterosexual conduct, but recognize that the homosexual needs both the support of the church and phsychiatric treatment to help him overcome his deviant impulses.

"The increase in homosexuality is only one aspect of the general atmosphere of moral breakdown that has been going on around us," says Monsignor Robert Gallagher of the Youth Counseling Service of the Roman Catholic Archdiocese of New York.

"I believe there are some signs of recognition of the nature of this breakdown and of reaction against it. We refuse to let homosexuals say they are irresponsible. We try to help them to exercise human responsibility and give them the encouragement that religion has to offer. Parish priests are advised under our pastoral counseling program to urge homosexuals to seek psychiatric help."

This expressed the general approach of other churchmen consulted.

Family Ties Studied

In a nine-year study— "Homosexuality—a Psychoanalytic Study of Male Homosexuals"—that won international attention last year, Dr. Bieber, associate clinical professor of Psychiatry, New York Medical College, and nine associates in the same field published evidence that the roots of homosexuality lay in disturbed early family relationships.

They studied 106 male homosexuals undergoing psychoanalysis and, for comparison, 100 heterosexual males also under treatment.

They found significant differences in the family patterns of the homosexual group as compared with the heterosexual sample.

In almost every homosexual case, they found some combination of what they termed a "close-binding, intimate" mother and/or a hostile, detached or unrespected father, or other parental aberrations.

"The father played an essential and determining role in the homosexual outcome of his son," the Bieber group reported flatly. "In the majority of instances the father was explicitly hostile . . .

"We have come to the conclusion [that] a constructive, supportive, warmly related father precludes the possibility of a homosexual son; he acts as a neutralizing, protective agent should the mother make seductive or close-binding attempts."

The group reported that 27 percent of the homosexuals under treatment by the group achieved a heterosexual orientation.

"Our findings are optimistic guideposts not only for homosexuals but for the psychoanalysts who treat them," the report concluded. "We are firmly convinced that psychoanalysts may well orient themselves to a heterosexual objective in treating homosexual patients rather than adjust even the more recalcitrant patient to a homosexual destiny."

The organized homosexuals dispute the validity of psychiatric findings on deviants. They argue that the medical students of the problem see only those homosexuals who are disturbed enough to seek treatment. Therefore, they say, findings based on that sample cannot be applied to the majority of "adjusted" homosexuals.

To this, Dr. Bieber replies that, during his wartime service, he interviewed intensively about 75 homosexuals discovered by military authorities. Among these involuntary subjects for study he found no basic differences in their psychopathology from that of the voluntary group under treatment, except that the former were more defensive and resistant to recognizing their deviancy.

Hostility a Key Factor

Dr. Bieber differs from some of his colleagues on the probable effect of a sudden—and highly unlikely—removal of all of the legal and social hostility to homosexuality.

"Public acceptance, if based on the concept of homosexuality as an illness, could be useful," he says. "If, by a magic wand, one could eliminate overnight all manifestations of hostility I think there would be a gradual, important reduction in the incidence of homosexuality."

He believes that wiping out negative attitudes would contribute to healing homosexuality rather than creating it.

But he does not approve the attempt by organized homosexuals to promote the idea that they represent just another minority, since their minority status is based on illness rather than on racial or religious factors.

He notes the contrast between this attitude and that of Alcoholics Anonymous, which is based on recognition of alcoholism as a disease and the determination to do something about it.

Dr. Charles W. Socarides, a New York analyst with wide experience in treating homosexuals is worried about the drive by homosexuals to win social acceptance for their deviancy as a kind of "normal abnormality" and over the consequences of success.

'Homosexual Is Ill'

"The homosexual is ill, and anything that tends to hide that fact reduces his chances of seeking and obtaining treatment," Dr. Socarides says. "If they were to achieve social acceptance it would increase this difficulty."

Confronting these generally accepted scientific conclusions that homosexual development can be both averted and cured is the strange, ambivalent attitude of the homosexuals toward themselves, as reported by Randolfe Wicker.

He is a young man in his middle 20's, under his real name a free-lance writer, who founded the New York League of Homosexuals, now merged with the Mattachine Society. He asked 300 homosexuals to answer two questions: "If you had a son would you want him to be homosexual?" and "If a quick, easy cure were available, would you take it?"

Eighty-three per cent indicated basic dissatisfaction with the life of a homosexual by saying they would not want a son to follow that path. Only 2 percent answered the first question affirmatively and the rest said they would leave the choice up to the hypothetical son.

But an overwhelming 97 percent told Mr. Wicker they would not change, even if change were easy. Why? The 44-year-old president of Mattachine gave his answer.

"I have been a homosexual for 30 years," he said. "I have none of the social and emotional background of the straight world—no history of normal dating. I would be lost in the world of heterosexuals."

* * *

April 24, 1987

FEAR OF AIDS STIRS NEW ATTACKS ON HOMOSEXUALS

By DIRK JOHNSON
Special to the New York Times

CHICAGO, April 22—In the Bohemian neighborhood of New Town on this city's North Side, several shops and bars that are popular among homosexuals here have recently been scrawled with obscene slurs and the imperative: "Die!"

The graffiti articulate, however crudely, what sociologists and homosexual rights advocates here view as growing intolerance in a time of widespread fear and anger over AIDS.

"Homophobia, which seemed to be falling for several years, appears to be on the rise again," said David McKirnan, a psychologist at the University of Illinois at Chicago. He recently conducted a survey of 3,500 homosexuals here that found that 20 percent of homosexual men had encountered at least one physical attack in their lifetime.

"Fear of gays among straights has always been based on the sense that they're going to do something to you," he said. "And AIDS does so in terms of a threatening disorder that satisfies all the requirements of a biblical plague."

Last month the editor of The Windy City Times, a publication serving homosexuals here, was beaten with a baseball bat by an intruder who burst into his office. The editor, Jeffrey McCourt, suffered a broken arm and severe back bruises. Nothing was stolen from the office.

Threats in Recent Months

It was the most violent of antihomosexual acts reported here in recent months. Some of the threats have been delivered by an underground group here, "The Great White Brotherhood of the Iron Fist."

That group recently ran a newspaper advertisement soliciting homosexual companionship, and then sent letters to the families and employers of those who responded. The letter warned about contracting the deadly acquired immune deficiency syndrome, and enclosed a copy of the response to the ad as proof of homosexuality.

At the University of Chicago, a campaign involving late-night telephone threats and obscene mail has been directed at dozens of students and faculty members. Hundreds of virulent leaflets have been distributed on campus. "Death to Faggots" bumper stickers have been plastered on the doors of teachers and students believed to be homosexuals, or their allies.

"We're hearing story after story of vicious harassment of gays on college campuses across the country," said Kevin Berrill, director of the antiviolence project for the National Gay and Lesbian Task Force in Washington. "We're accustomed to thinking of colleges as islands of tolerance. And in some ways, they are. For gays on campus, these are the best of times and the worst of times. There are more gay rights organizations and programs than ever. At the same time, we're seeing an unprecedented report of incidents directed against gays."

For example, Mr. Berill said, last year a Yale University student, Wayne Dick, sponsored "Bestiality Awareness Days," a mockery of the school's "Gay Awareness Week." Also last year, students at the University of Massachusetts at Amherst began a "Heterosexuals Fight Back Week."

Increasing Harassment

The experience on college campuses, Mr. Berrill said, reflects the mood in society generally. In 1986, reported incidents of harassment against homosexuals in New York increased by 83 percent, he said. Nationally, homosexual rights groups last year recorded about 5,000 incidents of assault ranging from verbal ridicule to homicide.

Some of the increase in documented cases of assault, he said, is probably the result of better reporting, although homosexuals report only a fraction of such incidents. Not all the increase in attacks can be attributed to the specter of AIDS, he said.

"As we've become more visible, we've become more vulnerable to people who hate us," he said. "What AIDS has done is simply give the bigots and bashers the justification to attack gays."

Despite the perception of increased attacks, a recent Gallup Poll found that antihomosexual sentiment had not increased perceptibly since last fall. The poll reported that about 33 percent favor and 55 percent oppose the legalization of consenting homosexual relations, virtually unchanged from last fall.

However, last year's study marked the first time that a majority of those surveyed opposed legalized homosexual acts. In 1982, about 45 percent favored legalization and 39 percent opposed it. The newest poll, a telephone survey of 1,015 adults from March 14 to March 18 had a margin of sampling error of plus or minus four percentage points.

Tension at U. of Chicago

In the wake of the harassment campaign at the University of Chicago, school officials have hired a private investigator and appointed an administrative liaison representative to work with representatives of homosexuals on campus.

"We deplore these acts of harassment," said Hanna Gray, the university president, in a statement released earlier this month."And we are doing everything possible to determine who is responsible for them."

But homosexual rights groups on campus say university officials responded slowly to the problem. They criticized the administration for allowing conservative student groups to use a table in the student center to disseminate literature on homosexuals that some consider inflammatory.

"Had any group been passing out anti-black or anti-Jewish literature, they would not be allowed to continue," said Jonathan Katz, a graduate student who is a former president of the Gay and Lesbian Alliance. "But we don't count for very much."

In part, harassment of homosexuals has attracted more attention in recent years because homosexuals are increasingly unwilling to endure the attacks silently, according to groups that advocate homosexual rights.

* * *

January 1, 1989

VIOLENT RACISM ATTRACTS NEW BREED: SKINHEADS

By WAYNE KING

There are four of them, and they dress in a manner best described as bristling: hair close-cropped, heavy boots with trousers bloused, black leather jackets and epaulets. They wear ties, and the look is neat, but a little Germanic, circa 1939. Two have earrings, but they say that is not part of the look, the skinhead look.

The four are bright, serious, anti-drug, anti-gay, anti-communist and militantly pro-American, and they are part of New York's small but apparently growing skinhead population. Denizens of the streets and clubs of the East Village, devotees of a militantly working-class music called

"Oi!," they represent a disparate, rebellious appendage of the ever-evolving youth subculture.

So far, New York's skinheads have cultivated the style of violence far more than its substance. Still, a growing list of skinhead attacks throughout the nation points up the danger in the skinheads' belief in violence as a way of life.

Skinheads have joined forces with old-line racist groups like the Ku Klux Klan and newer neo-Nazi groups in a score of states and have been charged with racist violence, including beatings, stabbings and three killings, in California, Florida and Oregon.

New York Incident

There are estimated to be several hundred skinheads in New York City—the four interviewed anonymously put the number at about 800—but the great majority are neither racist nor neo-Nazi, according to police officials, civil rights groups and skinheads themselves.

Indeed, the only reported incident of racial violence involving skinheads in New York City came last month, when four skinheads from Philadelphia and New Jersey attacked a white couple with an infant son in a PATH station in Manhattan.

Likewise, the Anti-Defamation League of B'nai B'rith says there are thousands of skinheads nationwide, but only about 2,500 actively racist skinheads, concentrated in 21 states.

But there is general agreement that the skinhead youth culture forms a fertile ground for recruiting by racist and anti-Semitic groups.

Such recruiting is being done by the Klan and neo-Nazi organizations like the California-based White Aryan Resistance, which has been organizing skinheads into racist cadres, called War Skins, on the West Coast and elsewhere.

'They're Violent'

White Aryan Resistance is led by a former Ku Klux Klan Grand Dragon, Tom Metzger, whose 20-year-old son, John, seeks to snare skinheads into the racist movement through his own organization, the Aryan Youth Movement.

"It is the one segment of the white racist movement in America that is growing," said Irwin Suall, fact-finding director of the Anti-Defamation League, the leading agency monitoring the rapid growth of racist skinhead groups across the country. "They're not only young; they're violent."

And he cautioned: "New York does not have a fence around it. There is no reason to believe New York is going to be immune to the racist variety of skinheadism."

Even avowedly nonracist skinheads in New York—some of whom are organized into groups like SHARP (Skinheads Against Racial Prejudice)—concede that the racist appeal can be effective.

'It Can Become White Pride'

"Skinheads have an intense feeling about whatever it is they believe in," said a 15-year-old Irish-American skinhead in New York who says racism is "un-American, and skinheads are pro-America."

"So someone who is not sure about his beliefs, you instill that pride in them, it's easy to convert to racism. Pride for yourself, it can become white pride."

They proclaim a belief in violence as a way of life and concede that the usually steel-toed English workboots they affect—Dr. Martens brand—represent more than a fashion statement.

"The reason Dr. Martens come into this," said a 15-year-old skinhead who disavows any racism, "is they're really comfortable boots, they're easy to work in, they have air holes, they're really bendable."

British Phenomenon

And, said his brush-cut companion, "You can kick the hell out of people."

"To say we are not violent would be a lie, O.K.," said the first youngster, who is Jewish.

The American skinhead movement grows out of a British phenomenon of the late 60's and early 70's in which white working-class London youth, angry and xenophobic, rebelled against society in general, while some blamed an influx of blacks and other minority group members for an impending bleak future.

Some began to shave their heads in defiance of "long-haired hippyism," and, for some, the movement began to take on a fascist overlay, fed eventually by blatantly racist "white power" bands like Skrewdriver and No Remorse.

The movement found its way to America, with "American skins" affecting the British workboots, cropped hair or shaved heads, braces and bloused trousers.

'Major Thing Is Anger'

Their music, a major unifying factor, ranges from a nonracist brand of Cockney rock called "Oi!" (a Cockney greeting), reflecting working-class unity and rebellion, to racist "white power" music typified by Skrewdriver, whose repertory includes such titles as "Race and Nation" and "White Power."

"Their major thing is anger," said Gary Lustgarten, a proprietor of Pyramid, an East Village cabaret at Tompkins Square that has some skinhead clientele and occasionally books bands that appeal to the "skins," as they are often called. "They feel something is owed them they never received, but they don't want to get it from their parents or from the Government. They're angry, their music reflects that."

The anger is a generalized anti-establishment emotion. But in addition to the discontent of what skinheads like to describe as "working class youth," there are some well-established conservative phobias. "We hate Jane Fonda," one young skinhead said.

War Zone and other skinhead bands also perform at CBGB, another Lower East Side club, often at Sunday matinees that attract younger "skins" in their mid-teens.

Venus, a Manhattan record store that stocks "Oi!" and other music that appeals to skinheads, carries albums by perhaps 50 skinhead-oriented bands, British and American. American groups have names like Youth Defence League, the Kicker

Boys, Bootboys and Immoral Discipline. There are song titles like "Strong Free Nation," "American Heritage," "I Hate Hippies" and "Boots and Braces, Stars and Stripes."

The militance of the music, said a skinhead, reflects a belief in "positive violence" and "the fact that we appreciate America."

* * *

July 10, 1990

HOMOPHOBIA: SCIENTISTS FIND CLUES TO ITS ROOTS

By DANIEL GOLEMAN

A rise in hostile actions against homosexuals can be traced primarily to hatred based on fear and self-righteousness rather than to the AIDS epidemic, researchers are finding. Although polls show more Americans are beginning to accept homosexual men and women and support their rights, there has been a great increase in reports of anti-gay bias since the beginning of the epidemic. But rather than creating the new hostility, researchers have found, the disease has given bigots an excuse to act out their hatred.

In studying the virulence and tenacity of anti-gay feelings, psychologists are finding clues to the deeper sources of homophobia. The new findings confirm the theory that some men use hostility and violence to homosexuals to reassure themselves about their own sexuality. But the greatest portion of anti-homosexual bias, psychologists now say, arises from a combination of fear and self-righteousness in which homosexuals are perceived as contemptible threats to the moral universe.

Such attitudes are supported, researchers say, by the fact that unlike any other minority, homosexuals still find themselves the target of institutionalized bias. They are barred from the armed services, and in many states sodomy laws make their sexual activities illegal. Until 1980, the official psychiatric diagnostic manual listed homosexuality as a mental disorder.

"It's as though our very existence is somehow a threat," said Naomi Lichtenstein, a social worker at the New York City Gay and Lesbian Anti-Violence Project who counsels victims of attacks.

One of the most troubling findings for those trying to combat anti-gay bias is data showing the hostility is far more accepted among large numbers of Americans than is bias against other groups. In surveys, about three-quarters of homosexuals say they have been harassed by people calling them names, and as many as one in four say they have been physically assaulted.

"Anti-gay violence is still acceptable because while leaders decry racial and religious bigotry, they ignore violence against gays and lesbians," said Matt Foreman, executive director of the New York City Gay and Lesbian Anti-Violence Project.

A 1988 study by the State of New York for the Governor's Task Force on Bias-Related Violence concluded that of all groups, "the most severe hostilities are directed at lesbians and gay men."

In "one of the most alarming findings" the report found that while teen-agers surveyed were reluctant to advocate open bias against racial and ethnic groups, they were emphatic about disliking homosexual men and women. They are perceived "as legitimate targets which can be openly attacked," the report said.

In a survey of 2,823 students from 8th to 12th grade, three-quarters of the boys and half the girls said it would be bad to have a homosexual neighbor. The feelings were as strong among 12-year-olds as among 17-year-olds. Many students added gratuitous vicious comments about homosexuals; that was not the case with other groups.

Scientists who study attitudes toward homosexuals say the largest group among people who are biased are those for whom homosexuals "stand as a proxy for all that is evil," said Dr. Gregory Herek, a psychologist at the University of California at Davis.

"Such people see hating gay men and lesbians as a litmus test for being a moral person," said Dr. Herek, who has done extensive research on attitudes toward homosexuals. Often they act out of adherence to religious orthodoxy in faiths that hold homosexuality to be a sin.

Dr. Herek does not see AIDS as having increased anti-gay feelings as much as offering "a convenient hook on which they can hang their pre-existing prejudices."

The affirmation of one's own values through anti-gay sentiment, his research has found, is the most common motive. For instance, in a study of attitudes toward homosexuals in 248 college students, Dr. Herek found this was the source of hostility in just over half those who held an anti-gay bias.

Bob Altemeyer, a psychologist at the University of Manitoba who has developed a scale measuring attitudes toward homosexuals, has found that those with the most intense hostility have an extreme fear that the world is an unsafe place and that society is at risk, and a self-righteousness that leads them to judge those who hold different values as morally inferior.

"They see homosexuality as a sign that society is disintegrating and as a threat to their sense of morality," said Dr. Altemeyer. "Their self-righteousness makes them feel they are acting morally when they attack homosexuals. It overcomes the normal inhibitions against aggression."

Religion Makes Change Difficult

Dr. Altemeyer tells his students that he is gay. "For most, over the course of the year it makes their attitudes toward gays more positive," he said. "But if their hostility toward gays is based on religion, their views are hardest to change."

Once a person has an anti-gay bias, it is difficult to change, Dr. Herek said, "even when reality contradicts it." Thus the stereotypes of gay men as feminine and lesbians as masculine persists in people's minds even though most gay men and lesbians do not, in fact, conform to those images.

In an article to be published later this year in "Homosexuality: Social, Psychological and Biological Issues" (Sage Publishers), Dr. Herek reviewed a case in point: the

tenacity of the belief that homosexuals should not be teachers because they might sexually molest children.

Persistence of Stereotypes

Citing studies showing that child molesters are overwhelmingly heterosexual or simply fixated on children, not homosexual, Dr. Herek notes that despite the facts, many people continue to believe that gay men are child molestors.

"Once parents perceive a threat to their children," Dr. Herek said, "their emotionality makes them prone to simplistic thinking. It is such emotionality that makes anti-gay stereotypes so hard to change."

In a classic study of stereotpying, Mark Snyder, a psychologist at the University of Minnesota, gave people a description of the life history of a woman named "Betty K." After reading the history, some were told that Betty later had a lesbian relationship and lived with her female lover. Others were told that Betty married a man.

"It made a dramatic difference in how people remembered and interpreted her life," said Dr. Snyder. While there was nothing negative in what people remembered, Dr. Snyder found that people selected facts that supported stereotypes about lesbians and ignored those that might contradict them. That normal tendency, he said, can build into a bias.

Negative Attitudes Snowball

"If your attitude is negative, it snowballs, and you only notice and remember facts that are negative, until it becomes a full-blown prejudice," said Dr. Snyder. "And you tend to assume everyone feels as you do. As you become more convinced, you are more likely to take the next step and put your beliefs into actions like outright discrimination or violence, whether it's against blacks or gays."

Defensiveness about their own sexuality is another common source of people's hostility toward homosexuals. In Dr. Herek's research, for instance, this was the second most common motive, accounting for about 40 percent of those hostile to homosexuals.

This explanation for homophobia is the oldest, dating back at least to a 1914 essay by Sandor Ferenczi, one of Freud's original followers who proposed that feelings of disgust toward gay men by heterosexual men are defensive, a reaction against their own similar attraction to other men. That view stems from Freud's theory that all people are originally bisexual in early childhood, and repress their attraction to the same sex as they grow.

"Homophobia has much to do with the stereotypic perception of gays as feminine: the more feminine a gay man appears, the more hostility he evokes in other men," said Dr. Richard Isay, a psychiatrist at Cornell Medical College and author of "Being Homosexual."

Dr. Peggy Hanley-Hackenbruck, a psychiatrist at Oregon Health Services University and president of the Association of Gay and Lesbian Psychiatrists, said, "In insecure heterosexual women, a lesbian can arouse fears of their own latent homosexual feelings, and so provoke hostility."

But Dr. Isay said, "Seeing a feminine man evokes a tremendous amount of anxiety in many men; it triggers an awareness of their own feminine qualities, such as passivity or sensitivity, which they see as being a sign of weakness. Women, of course, don't fear their femininity. That's partly why men are more homophobic than women, and why those biases are so strong in groups where men are selected for their masculine qualities, such as the army or sports."

Other psychoanalysts see the expression of anti-gay bias by men as being a way to reassure themselves that they are not homosexual.

"By hating gays, they can reassure themselves they are not gay," especially if they harbor doubts about their sexual orientation, said Dr. Jennifer Jones, a psychologist at the Sexuality Research Program at the State University of New York at Albany.

Both factors can be at play. "In gangs of teen-age boys who go out looking for gays to attack, the gay symbolizes an outsider," said Dr. Herek. "The attack solidifies the attackers' membership in their group, and affirms their shared values. But it's also crucial that it is their sexuality that defines homosexuals as outsiders. If you feel insecure about your own sexuality, as so many adolescents do, you can reassure yourself by attacking gays."

A Steady Rise in Violence

An exact accounting of such violence against gays is difficult, since many victims are reluctant to contact the police. But there were three times more attacks against gays reported to the New York Police Department Bias Crime Unit in the first half of 1990 as against the same period the year before.

In 1989 just over 7,000 incidents of violence and harassment were reported against gay men and lesbians in the United States, including 62 bias-motivated murders, according to a report released last month by the National Gay and Lesbian Task Force. The figures through the 1980's show a steady rise, peaking in 1988 and remaining at about the same level in 1989.

While most racial attacks are matters of turf in which people are attacked when they enter into another group's neighborhood, that is not so with homosexuals. Those who attack gays more often travel to a gay neighborhood to attack, Ms. Lichtenstein said. The most frequent pattern of attack, according to Ms. Lichtenstein, is against a lone man or two men walking together.

As with other bias crimes, the most frequent attackers are young men 21 or under who act in groups, according to a study of 331 incidents, to be published in an article by Kevin T. Berrill, director of the anti-violence project of the National Gay and Lesbian Task Force, in the September issue of The Journal of Interpersonal Violence.

"The attacks are intended to drive us back to the invisibility and isolation of the closet," Mr. Berrill said.

"Coming out" is one of the most powerful strategies for attacking anti-gay prejudice, Dr. Herek said. This approach is particularly effective on those whose anti-gay attitudes are based on a negative stereotype that has never been challenged by socializing with someone who is gay. Paradoxically, that approach may also lead to a rise in anti-gay incidents, gay rights leaders say.

"Although the data might suggest that intolerance is gaining ground, I believe the opposite is true," Mr. Berrill said. "In the years to come, I think that lesbian and gay people will experience both increased acceptance and increased violence."

* * *

July 9, 1993

FIGHTING HOMOSEXUALITY WITH WORDS

By WALTER GOODMAN

20/20
ABC, tonight at 10
(Channel 7 in New York)
"Janet Reno," produced by Chris Harper; "A Gospel of Hate," produced by Barbara Baylor; Victor Neufeld, executive producer; Hugh Downs and Barbara Walters, anchors.
WITH Catherine Crier and John Stossel, correspondents.

Meet the Rev. Fred Phelps, whose method of fighting homosexuality is to call one opponent "a Jezebellian, switch-hitting whore" and another "a fat, ugly sodomite" and still another, a county district attorney, "a depraved, adulterous, whorish woman." On tonight's edition of "20/20" he characterizes his approach as "moral persuasion."

Mr. Phelps operates out of a Baptist church in Topeka, Kan., with a congregation of his nine grown children and their spouses and children. They attack by fax, picket those they find objectionable (including people who have died of AIDS) and to judge by John Stossel's vivid report, make life a torment for anybody on their list.

The least you can say for Mr. Phelps is that he minces no words. "God hates fags!" he is heard yelling at the gay-rights march in Washington in April. "Fags are worthy of death!" That is also the most you can say for him. Mr. Stossel inquires into the difficulties of cracking down on behavior that many in Topeka find offensive but is probably not illegal. The efforts by the aforementioned district attorney to get at the Phelpsians via an old Kansas defamation statute do not seem promising.

The report has a happy ending of sorts. Topekans now picket the picketers, and last month they filled the town auditorium for a love-thy-neighbor day. Their language may not have quite the biblical fire of the Phelps family faxes, but they seem more in the Christian spirit.

Also on "20/20" tonight is a tepid interview with Attorney General Janet Reno, evidently intended for people who have not seen or read her many other interviews in recent weeks. The toughest question put by Catherine Crier, who does the massaging, is whether Ms. Reno is "running the show" at the Justice Department. When nothing approaching an answer is forthcoming, Ms. Crier ambles amiably on to the next question.

She gives Ms. Reno yet one more opportunity to wring her hands over the dubious decision to attack the Branch Davidians in Waco, Tex., but does not ask about more topical matters like the treatment of Sheik Omar Abdel Rahman, the Islamic cleric who may or may not be implicated in terrorist activities. Ms. Crier does inquire whether the unmarried Ms. Reno is a lesbian, noting that she was called one by a political opponent in 1988. Mr. Phelps may be comforted by her description of herself as "just an awkward old maid with a very great affection for men."

* * *

October 14, 1998

HOMOPHOBIA OFTEN FOUND IN SCHOOLS, DATA SHOW

By JAMES BROOKE

DENVER, Oct. 13—Last Saturday morning, while Matthew Shepard lay comatose from a beating, a college homecoming parade passed a few blocks from his hospital bed in Fort Collins, Colo. Propped on a fraternity float was a straw-haired scarecrow labeled in black spray paint, "I'm Gay."

Few people missed the message. Three days earlier, Mr. Shepard, a gay University of Wyoming freshman, was savagely beaten and tied to a ranch fence in such a position that a passer-by first mistook him for a scarecrow.

Today, officials at Colorado State University in Fort Collins reacted with outrage, opening an investigation and disciplinary procedures against the fraternity, Pi Kappa Alpha. The fraternity chapter immediately suspended seven members and said they had acted independently.

But in a week when candlelight vigils for Mr. Shepard were being held on campuses across the nation, the scarecrow incident highlighted how hostility toward homosexuals often flourishes in high schools and universities, gay leaders said today.

"People would like to think that what happened to Matthew was an exception to the rule, but it was an extreme version of what happens in our schools on a daily basis," said Kevin Jennings, executive director of the Gay, Lesbian and Straight Education Network, a New York group dedicated to ending anti-gay bias in the schools.

Mr. Shepard, a slightly built 21-year-old, was beaten so severely that he died on Monday. He never regained consciousness after being discovered on Oct. 7, 18 hours after he was lashed to the fence. Two men, Russell A. Henderson, 21, and Aaron J. McKinney, 22, were arraigned on first degree murder charges late Monday night. Their girlfriends, Chasity V. Pasley, 20, and Kristen L. Price, 18, have been arraigned as accessories after the fact.

In response to the killing, about 50 candlelight vigils were scheduled this week, from Texas to Vermont, from Wayne, Neb., to New York City.

Rocky Mountain Collegian

A scarecrow on a fraternity float in Fort Collins, Colo., last weekend was labeled 'I'm Gay,' mocking a gay freshman's beating in Wyoming.

At the Poudre Valley Hospital in Fort Collins where Mr. Shepard was in intensive care for five days, his parents, Dennis and Judy Shepard, received about 6,000 electronic messages of condolences. Today, when funeral arrangements were announced for Friday in Casper, Wyo., the hospital Web site received 30,000 hits an hour.

University friends in Laramie, Wyo., have set up the Matthew Shepard Memorial Fund to raise money to pressure the state Legislature to pass legislation against hate crimes.

"I see his name going down in gay history as a catalyst for renewed activism," said Matt Foreman, a former Wyomingite who directs Empire State Pride Agenda, a gay political organization in New York.

From around the nation today, gay leaders emphasized that campus homophobia was not restricted to college towns in the Rocky Mountain West.

Last year, in a survey of almost 4,000 Massachusetts high school students, 22 percent of gay respondents said they had skipped school in the past month because they felt unsafe there, and 31 percent said they had been threatened or injured at school in the past year. These percentages were about five times greater than the percentages of heterosexual respondents. The survey was conducted at 58 high schools by the Massachusetts Department of Education.

In a separate study of nearly 500 community college students in the San Francisco area, 32 percent of male respondents said they had verbally threatened homosexuals and 18 percent said they had physically threatened or assaulted them. The study was conducted this year by Karen Franklin, a forensic psychologist who is a researcher at the University of Washington.

Surveys of gay college students conducted in the late 1980's at Yale University, Oberlin College, Rutgers University and Pennsylvania State University found that 16 percent to 26 percent had been threatened with violence, and that 40 percent to 76 percent had been verbally harassed, said the

National Gay and Lesbian Task Force, a lobbying group based in Washington.

Last year, a Des Moines student group, Concerned Students, recorded hallway and classroom conversations at five high schools on 10 "homophobia recording days." They estimated that the average Des Moines high school student heard about 25 anti-gay remarks every day.

"Nine out of 10 'teaching tolerance' courses weed out gays," Mr. Foreman said. "There are a lot of people preaching anti-racism and anti-Semitism. But it is still very much O.K. to make anti-gay jokes, to express anti-gay sentiments."

A survey of the nation's 42 largest school districts found that 76 percent did not train teachers on issues facing gay students and 42 percent lacked policies to protect students from discrimination based on sexual orientation, said the Gay, Lesbian and Straight Education Network, which did the study last month.

In Fort Collins, while the hospital officials struggled with an electronic avalanche of condolences, city police detectives were investigating a different kind of E-mail.

On Monday, hours after Mr. Shepard's death, two gay organizations, the Rainbow Chorus and the Lambda Community Center, received identical messages applauding the killing of Mr. Shepard. The messages closed with the words, "I hope it happens more often."

* * *

June 13, 1999

GAYS AND MONSTERS

By JESSE GREEN

Some of Abner Louima's most vocal supporters want Justin Volpe's lawyer to apologize—but for what, exactly? Surely we don't hold him responsible for the actions of his client, the New York cop who sodomized Louima with a broomstick after a brawl. Nor do we expect him to say he is sorry for accusing Louima of lying about it: that's what lawyers do in defense of defenseless clients. No, it was Marvyn Kornberg's lurid explanation for Louima's injuries that precipitated a furor. Louima, he argued, had not been tortured in the station house, but had engaged in consensual anal intercourse earlier that night at Club Rendez-Vous: he had sex with a man. Al Sharpton called this accusation "a second rape."

The outrage over the supposed slight shows that Kornberg was onto something, though. Absurd as his defense seems, it cleverly played on the expectation that a jury of ordinary Americans would still see homosexuality as vile, and see violence as normal in a homosexual act—at least in preference to seeing sadism as normal in a heterosexual arrest. How else explain a torn rectum and bladder? If it could be suggested that Louima were gay (though he was at the club that evening indulging in archetypal straight behavior: flirting with other women while the wife stayed home), he might be deserving of the treatment he got, whoever may have done it, in love or fury.

The tactic failed, but not because it was despicable or even because it was a lie; what defeated Volpe was the testimony of other cops. Still, Kornberg's easy recourse to assumptions about the violence and depravity of gayness—accompanied by a Seinfeldian not-that-there's-anything-wrong-with-that shrug—proved that homosexuality is still America's favorite goblin. It may have shaken off the last dust of the closet, but public tolerance for it is superficial at best. More than that, the subject has become so much a part of popular discourse that it is available to anyone, however cynical or unscrupulous, to define and use as he wishes.

Kornberg isn't the worst of the opportunists. In several other recent cases, lawyers and hucksters have managed, with even less justification, to create around gayness a nimbus of culpability. "Pushed to the edge by school athletes who shoved them around and called them 'faggots,' " The National Enquirer wrote of the Columbine killers, "the two outsiders finally snapped from this final humiliation." Though the article doesn't even bother to suggest that the boys were actually homosexual, it echoes what Jerry Falwell, fresh from his important Tinky Winky crusade, had been saying on television. The headline: "Gay Secret That Made Them Kill."

What gay secret? That they weren't gay?

When I was in high school, homosexuality was utterly invisible. Just as my father had searched for the Sandy Koufaxes of this world to normalize his Jewishness, I spent hours hoping to discover that anyone, anywhere might be gay. (The sole fruit of my search: Liberace.) Homosexuality was still a slow, vaporous force, like Mann's Venetian plague, coming stealthily upon young men and leaving them literally demoralized. Being called a "fairy"—my bullies had not gone to law school—wasn't something you publicized; instead of driving me to go on a rampage, it drove me to study the oboe.

Now that gayness is public domain, the delicate fairy has largely been eclipsed by the predatory queer. This is especially evident in the story that started circulating after the murder of Matthew Shepard. Shepard, who was gay, was said to have provoked his own demise by flirting with his attackers—in effect, by threatening them. The lawyers for another murderer also blame the gay victim. After Scott Amedure revealed (during an unbroadcast episode of "The Jenny Jones Show") his romantic interest in Jonathan Schmitz, Schmitz shot him dead. It was Amedure's insult to Schmitz's heterosexuality, the lawyers argued, that caused their client to kill. Indeed, a jury recently ordered Warner Brothers, which owns the show, to pay Amedure's family $25 million for having failed to predict that murder was a reasonable response to the unbearable insult of a gay crush.

No jury would buy that argument if a straight pair were involved. A man who shot a female admirer would be called a psychopath, not the victim of a heterosexual humiliation. The TV show on which such an encounter occurred would be held harmless—and die of poor ratings. But make the crush homosexual and the valentine becomes a mode of attack, the heart becomes a shiv.

The closet was a terrible place, but at least you could decorate it according to your own taste. Now everyone feels free to hold forth (usually incorrectly) on what it really means to be gay. Alas, public falsehoods are little improvement over private truths. Liberace may not have been the best role model for what I knew in my heart as a child, but better him than the current crop of fictional gay monsters (especially the straight ones) brandishing terrible secrets, lethal crushes and outrageous phalluses. The worst Liberace ever did was make me cringe. Now, who knows? Maybe inside that suspect purse, Tinky Winky is packing heat.

Jesse Green is a regular contributor to the magazine. His memoir, "The Velveteen Father: An Unexpected Journey to Parenthood," has just been published.

* * *

HATE CRIMES

November 20, 1980

GUNMAN KILLS ONE AND WOUNDS 7 IN VILLAGE

By JOSH BARBANEL

One man was killed and seven others cut down by bullets when a man in a white Cadillac fired a into a bar frequented by homosexuals and at groups of men standing on two nearby streets in the West Village, the police said.

The wounded were taken to St. Vincent's Hospital, where a spokesman said early today that two were in surgery and one of these was not expected to live.

The dead man, who was carrying no identification, was not immediately identified. A man was arrested a few minutes after the attacks and charged with the shootings. The police recovered an Uzi submachine gun and two automatic pistols in the Cadillac, which had been stolen last Sunday.

At a news conference at 2:30 A.M. Lieut. John Yuknes, of the Sixth Precinct, said that the suspect, identified as Ronald Crumpley, 38 years old, of West 11th Street, "indicated a dislike of homosexuals."

Police sources said Mr. Crumpley made statements implicating himself in the shooting, and told them that his father was a minister. They said the suspect appeared to be intoxicated on liquor or drugs. He was charged with weapons possession and auto theft in addition to homicide.

2 Police Officers Injured

Two police officers were injured on 12th Street near the Avenue of the Americas when their car collided with another as they pursued the Cadillac, along with two other police cars and an unmarked Federal Bureau of Investigation vehicle.

The officers, identified as Louis Troche and Paul Warren of the 13th Precinct, were in satisfactory condition in Bellevue Hospital early this morning.

The police said the Federal officers were returning from another case when they heard shots fired, spotted the Cadillac and gave chase. Mr. Crumpley was found moments later, hiding under a moving van parked nearby, and was arrested.

Not Necessarily a Suspect

The police said the first shooting occurred at 10:50 P.M. in front of the Ramrod Bar at 394 West Street near 10th Street. The Cadillac pulled in front the bar and, according to the police, Mr. Crumpley sprayed machine gun bullets at men standing in front and inside.

The car then made a U-turn and Mr. Crumpley got out of his car and fired again, the police said. They said he fired more than 40 bullets in all.

Five men were wounded both inside and outside the bar, including the man who died, as other patrons ducked for cover and rushed to the back of the bar.

"I heard what I thought was firecrackers and saw a lot of people fall down," said John Gamrecki, who was one of 150 patrons in the Ramrod Bar at 394 West Street when the shots were fired.

"A rain of bullets came through the window," one witness said later. "Somebody next to me fell. I didn't stop, I just ran for it," said Terry Kline, a patron in the Ramrod. "We all ran to the back but we couldn't open the door."

"He fired at the bar indiscriminately—it didn't matter who he hit," said Police Officer Fred Elwick of the public information unit.

The suspect then drove to West 10th Street and Greenwich Street, where he fired at several other men, but none was injured. Moments later, according to the police, the same man opened fire at a group of men standing outside an all-night delicatessen at 690 Washington Street. The police said that at least 10 bullets were fired, striking three men.

The shooting victims and their conditions are: George Wentz, in extremely critical condition with wounds in the stomach, back, leg and shoulder; Tom Ross, shot in the shoulder; Rene Martucci, multiple wounds, in serious condition; John Litaker, discharged with a superficial shoulder wound; Richard Huff, arm and chest wounds, and Olaf Graveson, wounded in the right arm.

Lee Pietrangelon, manager of the Ramrod, said: "It's frightening to me. It's frightening for everyone to think that there are people sick enough to go around doing this kind of thing."

* * *

November 23, 1986

VIOLENCE AGAINST HOMOSEXUALS RISING, GROUPS SEEKING WIDER PROTECTION SAY

By WILLIAM R. GREER

Attacks on homosexuals appear to have increased sharply around the nation in the last three years as homosexuals have become more vocal in their pursuit of civil rights and more visible because of publicity surrounding the spread of AIDS.

Law-enforcement agencies do not record crimes against homosexuals as a specific category. In several cities, however, homosexuals have formed organizations to document what they say is growing violence against them, to lobby for more protection and to counsel the victims.

At a hearing last month before the House Judiciary Subcommittee on Criminal Justice, these groups presented surveys they had conducted at the local, state and national levels that seemed to document a rise in such violence and suggest some of the underlying causes.

"It seems clear from the testimony," said Julian Epstein, a spokesman for Representative John Conyers Jr., the Michigan Democrat who heads the subcommittee, "that there have been dramatic increases in violence directed against gay men and lesbians, and the violence seems to be connected with the AIDS problem and a general hostility directed against the gay and lesbian population."

New York Cases Said to Double

David M. Wertheimer, executive director of the New York City Gay and Lesbian Anti-Violence Project, formed in 1980 after a series of gang attacks on homosexuals in Manhattan's Chelsea section, testified that the project had counted 351 incidents, from homicides to verbal attacks, aimed at homosexuals in the first nine months of 1986, as against 167 incidents in that time last year.

So far this year the group has counted 17 homicides where the victim appeared to have been selected because he was a homosexual, Mr. Wertheimer said.

The homosexual rights groups say that homosexuals have always been victims of violence but that the attacks have become more brutal and more frequent and that the assailants have increasingly referred specifically to acquired immune deficiency syndrome, which cripples the body's immune system.

In the United States most AIDS victims have been male homosexuals or intravenous drug users and their sexual partners. AIDS is spread through sexual intercourse or exchanges of blood.

Taunts Accompany Attacks

In 28 percent of all New York incidents reported in 1985, Mr. Wertheimer said, assailants taunted their victims with comments about AIDS. He estimated that the percentage of such cases was roughly the same this year.

"We're in the middle of an epidemic of violence against gay men and lesbians," Mr. Wertheimer said.

A San Francisco group, Community United Against Violence, said at the hearing that through September, 150 homosexuals reported being physically assaulted by attackers who shouted insults related to homosexuality, a 23 percent increase over the 116 such assaults in the same period last year.

The surveys presented at the hearing indicate that homosexuals are more often the victims of violent crimes than the general public. Surveys in cities from Richmond to Minneapolis to Des Moines, and in states from Maine to Alaska, found that 15 to 20 percent of homosexuals interviewed said they had been beaten in incidents related to their sexual orientation

A survey of 2,074 homosexuals in eight cities by the National Gay and Lesbian Task Force found that 1 in 5 homosexual men and 1 in 10 homosexual women reported having been physically assaulted in their lifetimes because of their homosexuality.

A Matter of Perception

Some of these victims said they were perceived to be homosexuals because they were walking arm in arm with a partner or leaving a bar frequented by homosexuals, but others could not explain why they were selected. The survey also found that some heterosexuals, including a married couple walking together in Queens, had been attacked by assailants shouting epithets about homosexuality.

As Matthew Holloway, a homosexual who works for a major financial institution in San Francisco, waited for his roommate outside a supermarket last December, a teen-age man and woman began to shout at him.

"We should kill you first, because you're gonna give us AIDS," Mr. Holloway said they shouted. He said that a few minutes later, as he and his roommate drove from the parking lot, they were attacked by the couple and a dozen other young people. His roommate, David Johnson, was dragged from the car and beaten with chains and skateboards. He suffered three broken ribs, a broken jaw and bruises. Mr. Holloway fought to stay in the car and was unharmed. The attackers fled before the police arrived; no suspects were arrested.

Police Don't Separate Data

Because the police do not systematically collect statistics on crime against homosexuals specifically, as the police and the homosexual rights groups acknowledge, a rise in such violence cannot be officially documented.

Moreover, such incidents are often not reported—some surveys say 90 percent go unreported—and the way the police classify crimes that result from bias differs from the way the groups classify them.

Mr. Epstein, the aide to Representative Conyers, said that as a result of the hearing, the Congressman planned to ask the Justice Department to compile statistics on such crimes. He said Mr. Conyers would also include protection for homosexuals in the civil rights provisions of the Federal criminal code, like provisions for blacks and other minority groups.

Federal Protection Sought

Such a change would allow the Federal Bureau of Investigation, United States Attorneys and other Federal agencies to intervene in cases as investigators and prosecutors, Mr. Epstein said. "The response on the part of local law enforcement has not been adequate," he said. "Most other groups that have been particularly targeted for violence because of who they are and what they believe enjoy Federal protection. Gays and lesbians don't."

The New York City and Washington police departments have assigned special units to investigate crimes against homosexuals in the way they investigate crimes against blacks or Jews. The Boston Police Department is considering similar measures. Robert M. Morgenthau, the Manhattan District Attorney, has appointed a prosecutor and a liaison officer for homosexual groups to handle cases of violence.

Since last July, when the Bias Unit of the New York City Police Department expanded its responsibility for crimes resulting from ethnic or religious bias to include bias based on sexual orientation, it has classified only 13 cases as such, according to its commanding officer, Capt. Donald J. Bromberg.

He said some incidents reported to the homosexual rights groups would not be classified by the police as crimes resulting from bias. "Our statistics do not show any type of increase for the most part," he said. "We also are aware that there are many cases out there that aren't reported to the police."

Brooklyn Man Recalls Beating

A homosexual man said in an interview that he walked around the corner from his Brooklyn apartment at 8 A.M. one Saturday last summer and three young men grabbed him. As his assailants shoved him back and forth, punching him in the chest and midsection, he said, they shouted: "Faggot! You faggots give us AIDS."

No one came to help, recalled the man, who works in the Mayor's office and asked that his name not be used to protect his privacy. He later reported the case to the police.

Since then, he said, he has been taunted twice by other groups and once was struck by a thrown bottle.

"What I find frightening is these groups don't seem to have any fear of verbally or physically assaulting people in the middle of the day, in a shopping center, in front of businesses, with hundreds of people around," he said. "Somehow they've gotten the message that their action will be condoned or at least ignored."

Social psychologists and psychiatrists who counsel victims of violence against homosexuals say AIDS has led to an increase in such violence by providing people a justification for their existing hostility to homosexuals. News about the disease has also forced some people to confront a population that they had ignored.

Dr. Gregory M. Herek, an assistant professor of social psychology at the City University of New York Graduate Center, said, "Homophobia also occurs at the institutional level when churches, the popular media, the schools and government pretty much teach people that there is something wrong with homosexuality and in fact it is appropriate to do bad things to them." Dr. Herek is chairman-elect of the American Psychological Association's Committee on Lesbian and Gay Concerns.

Vatican Letter Angers Groups

Homosexual rights groups say a statement by the Vatican last month in a letter on homosexuality to Roman Catholic bishops, for example, as well as speeches by religious fundamentalists have led some people to rationalize aggression against homosexuals.

The Vatican letter deplored crimes against homosexuals but said that "when civil legislation is introduced to protect behavior to which no one has any conceivable right," people should not be surprised when "irrational and violent reactions increase."

Dr. Herek said the violence toward homosexuals was similar in some respects to the increase in violence against blacks in the 1960's at the peak of the civil rights movement.

But, he said, violence against homosexuals differs significantly from violence against other groups. Most attackers of homosexuals, he said, are adolescents seeking both to gain acceptance among their peers and to alleviate anxieties they may have about their own sexuality.

* * *

July 3, 1988

ARE HOMOSEXUALS FACING AN EVER MORE HOSTILE WORLD?

By JAMES KIM

A flurry of recent studies have confirmed what many gay-rights groups say they already knew: Harassment and crimes against homosexuals are increasing. Moreover, gay-rights advocates say, the incidents are becoming more violent.

They acknowledge that their conclusions are based on a surge in the number of reports, which does not necessarily mean an increase in the number of attacks. Statistics are hard to come by because the police generally do not classify assaults according to motivation. Even where they keep track of bias-related crimes, as in New York City, the circumstances of an attack are often ambiguous, and many go unreported. But recent studies by both government and advocacy groups have found hostile incidents to be rising.

The problem seems to stem from a complex mix of circumstances, including anxieties and resentment about the AIDS epidemic.

"AIDS is a convenient new excuse to attack the gay community," said David M. Wertheimer, the executive director of the New York City Gay and Lesbian Anti-Violence Project.

Several weeks ago, a man in Chicago had to be hospitalized after an assailant attacked him with a bottle, screaming epithets with references to AIDS. In New York, a man suffered nearly fatal stab wounds when a gang of 10 people at-tacked him in Central Park, taunting him with anti-gay slurs.

"The problem is emerging as one of the most serious so-cial problems of the decade," said Mr. Wertheimer. Kenneth B. Morgen, a psychologist in Baltimore who has studied the issue, said, "This is a crime that is coming out of the closet."

In a report issued last month, the National Gay and Lesbian Task Force, a Washington-based lobbying organization, said that last year it received reports of 7,008 anti-gay incidents, 42 percent more than in 1986. Verbal abuse accounted for 78 per-cent of the incidents, physical assaults for 12 percent and van-dalism for 5 percent.

Kevin T. Berrill, director of the organization's anti-violence project, notes that of the 64 local groups that provided data for the report, 23 said anti-gay attacks were more frequent last year than in 1986. Eleven said they were less frequent, and 30 said they were not sure.

A study that Mr. Morgen conducted in Baltimore found that 16 percent of homosexuals had been harassed or assault-ed at least once by someone who mentioned AIDS, and 14 percent experienced this in the last year.

The number of people who seek counseling after being harassed or assaulted is also rising. Mr. Wertheimer's group in New York served 14 percent more people last year than in 1986. A San Francisco group, Community United Against Violence, reported 11 percent more victims over the same pe-riod and said the number of attacks requiring medical atten-tion rose 22 percent.

"There is no escaping the conclusion that anti-gay vio-lence is a serious problem," Mr. Berrill said.

Recent government reports, including those issued by the New York Governor's Task Force on Bias-Related Violence and the National Institute of Justice, have reached similar conclusions.

"Although it's very, very difficult to document, we sense there's been an increase in these attacks," said Catherine M. Abate, chairwoman of the New York State Crime Victims Board and former executive deputy commissioner of the New York State Division of Human Rights.

Political Progress

At the same time, there is evidence of increased accep-tance of homosexuality. In the last decade, some states and cities have adopted anti-discrimination laws and voters have elected some openly gay candidates. President Reagan's AIDS commission has recommended Federal action to bar discrimination against those infected with the virus.

In New York City, many gay people say they have detect-ed signs of greater acceptance by heterosexuals, especially well-educated professionals. But the extent of sympathy among other groups is less clear.

For example, the Governor's task force report found, "One of the most alarming findings in the youth survey is the open-ness with which the respondents expressed their aversion and hostility toward gays and lesbians." More than 30 percent of the junior and senior high school students surveyed said they

had witnessed harassment of students and teachers thought to be homosexual.

People who have studied the problem say it is obscured in part because so many incidents go unreported. An October 1987 study commissioned by the National Institute of Justice said that homosexuals rank with Southeast Asians as the least likely to report bias crimes.

The House of Representatives has passed a bill requiring the collection of statistics by local authorities. A companion bill is awaiting action by the Senate. At least three states, Connecticut, Minnesota and Maryland, now have similar laws.

"We can do surveys until we're blue in the face," Mr. Berrill said. "What we really need is more official documentation of the problem."

* * *

November 15, 1991

AN UNLIKELY MARTYR FOCUSES GAY ANGER

By DONATELLA LORCH

Julio Rivera, his friends say, was the most improbable gay martyr—a Hispanic drug user from Queens who lived on the far fringes of gay society.

Yet the stabbing death of this 29-year-old man in July 1990 has served to rally gay people throughout New York City. And the killing's impact has been especially strong in Mr. Rivera's neighborhood of Jackson Heights, which has with little outside notice become home to the city's second-largest gay community.

Since Mr. Rivera's death in what prosecutors call a gay-bashing attack, there have been rallies, candlelight vigils, even an attempt to storm Gracie Mansion. Three new gay rights groups have been formed in Queens, and the borough had its first-ever gay rights march.

"It took Julio's death to really galvanize the gay communi-ty," said Alan Sack, 39, an interior designer who described in court last week how his friend bled to death in his arms in a Queens schoolyard. Mr. Sack was in large part responsible for initiating the movement, by reaching out to gay advocacy groups that had previously been shunned in Jackson Heights.

"Many in the gay community are appalled and terrified about coming out," he said. "Now we are all realizing there is a certain social and political consciousness to being gay."

'You Exist'

The alliance of gay people that has developed around the Rivera case has worked to focus public attention on the esca-lating violence against gay people throughout the city. And it has given a strong public voice to gay New Yorkers outside the largely white world of the city's traditional gay center, Greenwich Village.

"One thing it did was put a brown face to gayness in the city of New York," said Rafael Ruiz-Ayala of the Latino Gay Men of New York City. "There are a lot of people who think

A poster circulated in Jackson Heights, Queens, shows defendants in the fatal stabbing of Julio Rivera, who, the police say, was a victim of a gay-bashing attack.

Julio Rivera

that Latino gays are twice the scum of the city. This has created a new awareness. It acknowledges you exist."

For gay advocates, the trial of two men charged in the slaying has become the gay equivalent of the Howard Beach case, in which a black man was chased to his death by a group of whites. That case became a rallying point for many blacks in New York; gay rights groups who fought for a year to have the Rivera killing classified as a bias crime say the trial is similar watershed in the lives of the city's homosexuals.

"This is the first time there is a clear-cut example of how gay bashing works," said Ed Sederbaum, organizer of Queens Gays and Lesbians United.

Mr. Rivera, who prosecutors say was stabbed and beaten by three men looking for a gay man to attack, was one of two gay men killed in 1990 in what the police labeled bias incidents. Mr. Rivera's case is also the first such homicide to come to trial in New York State, said Matt Foreman, executive director of the New York City Gay and Lesbian Anti-Violence Project.

Reports of anti-gay violence are on the rise. Mr. Foreman said that 511 gay and lesbian bias-related crimes were reported to his group through October of this year, compared with 223 in 1989, a 129 percent increase. The count kept by the police is lower, said Inspector William Wallace, commander of the bias unit, in part because of the stigma that many attach to such crimes. He said 74 gay bias incidents were reported to the Bias Unit in 1991 through October and 96 incidents in

1990, following a 115 percent increase in such cases between 1989 and 1990. He attributed the increase to the efforts by gay rights groups to promote the reporting of bias crimes.

A Quieter World

Jackson Heights, where Mr. Rivera lived for 10 years, has had its share of such crimes, said Mr. Sack. Gay advocacy groups say the area has been home to a large number of homosexuals, including many Hispanic homosexuals, for more than 25 years. The gay community is concentrated within an eight block radius that runs from 74th Street to 77th Street and along stretches of row houses between 37th Road and 37th Avenue. The are eight gay bars in the neighborhood.

The gay people who live here say the neighborhood is a world away from Greenwich Village. Gay residents here are mostly working class and older people, many of whom live there for the lower rents and the more suburban lifestyle.

The main issue among homosexuals here has always been privacy, and few Jackson Heights residents belonged to or approved of more radical movements like Queer Nation or Act Up.

Some are reticent out of choice, some out of anxiety, gay advocates say. "It's easy to be gay in the Village," Mr. Ruiz-Ayala said, but harder in Jackson Heights, especially for Hispanic men from working class families. "For Latino gays, seeing Julio Rivera is seeing their face on paper."

Mr. Sacks agreed that Jackson Heights "is considerably more closeted."

"It is not political," he said. "We try to keep a low profile."

But there is another side as well. At the heart of the neighborhood is a cruising strip, near where Mr. Rivera was killed, that is famous among homosexuals throughout New York City. And the man who stabbed him to death—who pleaded guilty to a lesser charge in return for testimony against his two friends—said he and his friends went to the schoolyard where Mr. Rivera was killed because they knew it as a site where cruising homosexuals congregated. A jury in state Supreme Court in Queens is expected to begin deliberations on Monday on charges against the two defendants, Estat Bici, 19, and Erik Brown, 21.

Mr. Sack described his friend as a handsome and charming but deeply troubled man, a part-time bartender who supported a cocaine habit. He loved to dress well and "play macho," Mr. Sack said. Mr. Rivera had moved to Jackson Heights 10 years ago and had shared houses with a variety of lovers.

But while his life style did not fit in with the image that many gay residents of Jackson Heights seek for their community, he had a wide range of friends, Mr. Sack said. The friendships remained after his death. In the weeks after he was murdered, the neighborhood was plastered with posters asking for help to solve the crime. They are still there.

'May as Well Organize'

Mr. Rivera's death and Mr. Sack's anger have broken the neighborhood's insularity. After the killing, Mr. Sack contacted Mr. Foreman and Queer Nation and asked for help and advice. "I had only heard about Queer Nation on Oprah Winfrey and Phil Donahue," Mr. Sack said. With their help, fliers were distributed and marches organized—and gay people began to listen. On one candle-light march this August, 350 gay men and women walked to the schoolyard as store owners cheered them on.

"If you recognize you are still not safe by keeping a low profile in your neighborhood," said Mr. Sedarbaum, "you may as well organize to make your presence felt among the wider community in which you live."

Now, 19 months after Mr. Rivera was killed the momentum of the movement is being felt. Gay organizations are being joined by Hispanic men and women, who have previously been almost invisible in the movement, Mr. Ruiz-Ayala said.

Mr. Foreman is organizing sensitivity training for officers at the 115th Precinct in Jackson Heights. Joe Cooper, a member of Queer Nation, is planning to train people for a local version of his organization's "Panther Patrols," that walk the streets to deter violence. Mr. Sedarbaum and Mr. Sack have formed yet another organization in Queens called Queens Gay and Lesbians United that held its fourth meeting this week and is getting involved in community activities.

The movement has also gone beyond the issue of anti-gay violence, into broad questions of social acceptance and specific programs like a Meals-on-Wheels project for homebound AIDS patients.

"The energy couldn't be maintained if it was only about gay bashing," Mr. Sedarbaum said. "There are a number of personal and political needs fulfilled in staying together."

* * *

March 20, 1992

ANTI-GAY CRIMES ARE REPORTED ON RISE IN 5 CITIES

Special to The New York Times

WASHINGTON, March 19—Incidents of violence against homosexuals rose 31 percent last year, according to a survey made public today by a homosexual rights group. The group blamed political, religious and entertainment industry leaders for fostering a homophobic climate.

The survey of five cities by the group, the National Gay and Lesbian Task Force Policy Institute, found 1,822 reported incidents in 1991, as against 1,389 the previous year.

The incidents, compiled by victim assistance agencies in New York, San Francisco, Chicago, Boston and Minneapolis-St. Paul, included harassment, threats, physical assaults, vandalism, arson, police abuse and murder. More than three-quarters of the victims were male.

"The wide scope of anti-gay violence in 1991 should come as no surprise, given the stench of bigotry that routinely emanates from Hollywood, the halls of Congress, the pulpits of the religious right and other venues," said Kevin Berrill, director of the institute's Anti-Violence Project who wrote the report.

There are 24 million gay and lesbian Americans, Mr. Berrill said.

The report also complains of anti-gay comments by Patrick J. Buchanan, the conservative columnist who is challenging President Bush for the Republican nomination for President; Senator Bob Kerrey, the Nebraska Democrat who recently dropped out of the race for his party's nomination, and David Beckwith, Vice President Dan Quayle's press secretary.

Senator Kerrey was criticized for telling a sexual joke involving lesbians to Gov. Bill Clinton of Arkansas, who is seeking the Democratic Presidential nomination. The Nebraska Senator later apologized for his "inappropriate" remarks. The joke involved a fictitious account of another Democratic candidate approaching two lesbians in a bar.

Mr. Beckwith, referring to the public reaction to Mr. Kerrey's joke, said, "The good news is that the lesbians are upset with Kerrey. The bad news is that they'll be coming our way to support us." He also publicly apologized for his remarks.

Mr. Buchanan has been singled out for criticism on several occasions by gay and lesbian groups. In a column, he once wrote in reference to the AIDS disease: "The poor homosexuals. They have declared war on nature and now nature is exacting an awful retribution." And a 30-second Buchanan campaign commercial, showing footage from a documentary about homosexuals, attacks President Bush for approving funds for the National Endowment of the Arts, which underwrote some sexually explicit projects.

The task force report said that movies like "Silence of the Lambs" and "Basic Instinct," which opens in theaters tomorrow, defamed homosexuals.

Movie Protests

Last year, protesters in San Francisco disrupted the filming of "Basic Instinct," a movie about a detective trailing a bisexual, female murder suspect. Members of gay organizations have shown up at preview screenings to protest the movie and say they plan to distribute leaflets or perhaps give away the movie's ending when it opens in theaters.

In the five metropolitan areas surveyed, physical assaults rose 15 percent, to 775; police abuse increased 29 percent, to 146 incidents; and vandalism swelled 51 percent, to 125 incidents, according to the study. It said there were eight anti-gay murders, compared with three the year before.

Threats and harassment were the most frequently reported types of incident with 1,255 episodes reported.

The task force statistics, broken down from each metropolitan area, found: New York had 592 incidents in 1991, up 17 percent from 1990; San Francisco, 473, up 11 percent; Boston, 209, up 42 percent; Chicago, 210, up 6 percent; and Minneapolis-St. Paul, 338, up 202 percent.

The police departments in the five metropolitan areas reported 362 anti-gay crimes in 1991, a 41 percent increase over the number documented the previous year, the report says.

The institute said its figures were higher than similar figures compiled by police departments because many victims of anti-gay crimes go to victim assistance agencies rather than the police.

Police departments in Boston and New York reported a drop in such crimes last year, of 21 percent and 14 percent respectively.

* * *

March 12, 1993

RISE IN GAY BIAS CRIMES REPORTED

By RONALD SULLIVAN

An advocacy group that monitors bias attacks against homosexuals said yesterday that the number of incidents in which gay men and women were victims rose 12 percent last year, and the intensity of violence nearly doubled.

In its sixth annual report on hate crimes against gay people, the New York City Gay and Lesbian Anti-Violence Project said 662 gay men and women were victims of anti-homosexual crimes last year, compared with 592 in 1991. The increase follows a 16 percent rise from the year before, the group said.

At the same time, the group said the number of victims requiring medical attention rose about 41 percent last year, to 112 from 79.

The Police Department, which tracks attacks on homosexuals as bias crimes, said there were 86 such attacks last year, 2 fewer than it recorded in 1991.

But the advocacy group sharply disputed the police figures, arguing that many homosexual victims are reluctant to report attacks to the police because the victims consider the justice system to be unresponsive.

And the group said even its own figures, which it collects from people who volunteer information, did not accurately reflect the scope of bias incidents involving homosexuals because many victims simply did not report attacks or because such attacks were classified by the police as drug-related or domestic disputes.

The Anti-Violence Project, a nonprofit agency that has been recording incidents of bias against homosexuals and helping victims for six years, said there was a surge of violence against gay men and women during the final months of last year when efforts to introduce a gay-awareness component into the public schools curriculum and the debate over allowing homosexuals in the armed forces produced a backlash against homosexuals.

The group said that about half of the crimes in its report involved discrimination and that the rest involved various kinds of assaults.

* * *

September 12, 1993

WHAT THE NAVY TAUGHT ALLEN SCHINDLER'S MOTHER

By JESSE GREEN

Not far from the laminated portrait of Elvis, high on a shelf in her tumbledown house, sits the only photograph Dorothy Hajdys has of her father, who died in prison when she was 5: a dashing sailor with faraway eyes serving his country in World War II. The pictures of her first husband—a man named Allen Schindler who decided he was John the Baptist and, she says, nearly drowned her in the bathtub to prove it—are not on display. Water is a running theme in the family: Frank Hajdys, her second husband, was a Navy man as well; before he died in 1985 he regaled their young son, Billy, and his three stepchildren—Dorothy's two girls and one boy—with tales of his adventures aboard the battleship Arizona. The stepson, "little Allen," so called to distinguish him from his biological father, must have taken Frank Hajdys's stories to heart because in 1988, at the age of 18, he signed up and shipped out. "I thought I was the most proudest mother in the nation," Dorothy has said.

"I thought I was the most proudest mother in the nation," Dorothy was shouting into a microphone set up in front of the

Capitol last April. A sad curiosity to the general public, which might have caught her on the evening news, Dorothy Hajdys (pronounced HAY-jiss) was a hero to the hundreds of thousands of people gathered before her at the gay-rights march on Washington. Earlier in the day they had cheered her wildly, this 47-year-old grandmother with the door-hinge voice and battleship proportions, marching at the head of a contingent of veterans and clutching a photograph of her son like a shield.

"Cheering me!" she said later. "Me who didn't even know a homosexual until January!" Yet that seemed to be what the crowd was responding to—not the tragedy of her son's brutal murder but the swift education that had opened her eyes, opened her mouth and brought her here. If the Salvation Army bookkeeper from Chicago Heights, Ill., was scandalized by the Dykes on Bikes gunning their engines and the Gays in the Millinery prancing in fancy hats, she kept her disapproval to herself. Still, she seemed frozen, as if bracing for a blow; when the crowd started roaring, she just stared back, until a friend had to prompt her: "Wave, Dorothy, wave!" Which she immediately did, as if to a ship.

"I am finally going to a special place," radioman Allen Schindler wrote on the first page of a pale green notebook he bought two years after entering the Navy. The special place was the aircraft carrier Midway—"the mighty, mighty Midway," he called it—and the notebook was to be a record of his happiness on board. Evidently he expected an abiding happiness, for he numbered the bottoms of the pages from 1 to 192. But in 1991 he was transferred to the Belleau Wood, a smaller ship with a reputation for mayhem. As his progressively less legible entries attest, Allen was miserable. At Christmas Dorothy saw he had removed stitches from the logo on his cap, turning the B in Belleau into an H. What she didn't know was that the hell he was suffering was the hell of a gay man in fear for his life.

Indeed, Allen Schindler would never get past page 64 of his journal. Two months before his 23rd birthday, on Oct. 27, 1992, while on shore leave in Sasebo, Japan, he was followed into a park bathroom shortly before midnight by two drunken shipmates, one of whom, Airman Charles Vins, watched and occasionally joined in while the other, Airman Apprentice Terry Helvey, kneed Schindler in the groin, struck him in the face and then, cradling his head in the crook of his arm, punched him repeatedly while lowering him to the floor. There, Helvey began stamping on him with the heel of his foot, striking blows from head to crotch that resulted, according to the pathologist who performed the autopsy, in abrasions, contusions and lacerations of the forehead, eyes, nose, lips, chin, neck, Adam's apple, trachea, lungs, liver—which was pulped "like a smushed tomato"—and penis. The pathologist compared the damage to that of a "high-speed auto accident or a low-speed aircraft accident" and said it was the most severe trauma he'd ever witnessed—even worse than a case he'd seen of a man trampled to death by a horse.

A sailor who happened upon the scene but could only make out shadows through a window in the bathroom door described Helvey's footwork another way: "It seemed like he was dancing."

Dorothy hated to lie. She would teach her children never to lie. But with Allen Sr. unemployed because of a mysterious back problem, she needed a job to help pay the mortgage. And John's frozen pizza, a girlfriend told her, would not hire the mother of a newborn—little Allen was just 1 month old. So Dorothy lied and got the job. But it wasn't enough. Two years later, with money still short, she took on another, at Burger King. Now she could fry fries from 10 A.M. to 2:30 P.M., change uniforms and dash across town to John's, where, from 3 P.M. to 1 A.M., she tossed pepperoni onto frozen pizzas as they whizzed past relentlessly. In the little time remaining she slept, and kept dreaming this image: Allen's bottle of milk emerging frozen among the pizzas on the endless conveyor belt.

His real bottle she rarely saw; it was her aunt Marie, living in the small apartment at the back of the house, who took care of Allen. Marie helped him through Dorothy's divorce from Allen Sr.; through Dorothy's marriage to Hajdys, her Burger King boss; through Allen's disappointment that his stepfather had plenty of time and money for Billy but none for his stepson. And so it was an understandably miserable 12-year-old who, upon Marie's death, lashed out at his mother, blaming her for ruining the family. "I said, 'If you think this is so terrible, go stay with your father for a week,'" Dorothy recalls. "But Allen Sr. slammed the door in his face, saying, 'You're her problem now.' That did the trick! Allen and me weren't real, real close, but after that I was his mother and father and we never had a problem again."

When Dorothy got home from the Salvation Army at 6:30 on Oct. 27, 1992, Billy had already left for his job at the Haunted House in nearby Park Forest. "I figured I wasn't going nowhere," she remembers. "So I just put on a nightshirt and did some work for this lady at church." What happened next, as she sat on the floor cutting crosses out of plastic to make bookmarks, she would hardly be able to relate if she hadn't at once begun dictating a journal of each day's events to her daughter Kathy. "Two sailors came to my door in dress blues," the log begins that night. "They told me that my son had been assaulted by two men in a park in Sasebo, Japan, and that he was dead." Ten pages and seven months later, it ends with "Allen's stone was put in at the cemetery." In between, in homely prose, it records Dorothy's struggle to bury her son and understand why he died—a pursuit in which the Navy all but abandoned her. "Oct. 30: Heard nothing." "Nov. 1: Still heard nothing."

Waiting for answers, or even the body, she barely slept. It wasn't until the arrival, on Nov. 4, of the coffin—bearing a corpse unrecognizable except by tattoos on its pale arms—that Dorothy was finally told her son's assailants were shipmates. "But why would shipmates want to beat him so badly?" she wanted to know. "Nov. 9," the journal records, "No new information." It was left for a reporter from Pacific Stars and Stripes, an independent military newspaper, to tell her that Allen was gay, that he had met with a legal officer in hopes of getting off the Belleau Wood and that, according to a letter sent to the paper by three gay men who knew him in Japan, Allen's death was the result of violence encouraged, if not permitted, by a climate of bigotry aboard ship.

Dorothy at first denied her son was gay but soon realized that the reporter's scenario was credible, and that the Navy, in its stonewalling, was not. Previously she'd tended to be submissive in the face of mistreatment. "Oh yeah, anybody could do anything to me," she now says. It's a part of family folklore that as a child she had allowed some cousins (who, by a trick of remarriage, were also her half-brothers) to tie her to a homemade stake and set her on fire. And then there were the men in her life, who jilted her, sponged off her, told her lies to get their way. Frank Hajdys, it turned out, was not sterile from a "Navy injury," as Billy's birth proved. "And Allen Sr. wasn't all that faithful," Dorothy adds. "The night little Allen was born, he was in a tavern with a girl, and she actually came and stayed in our house!" She pauses. "But I will say she cleaned up." Allen Schindler Sr. could not be reached for comment.

But within weeks of the murder, Dorothy's reserve of humility was spent. The pronouncements of her Government and its agencies, which she had formerly either ignored or accepted, she now treated with suspicion bordering on scorn. When, in November, the accomplice, Vins, was tried without her knowledge and sentenced to what amounted to only four months in the brig, she was angry but not surprised. Nor did it surprise her to learn, in March, that a senior Navy official was leaking a story, later disproved, that her son's murder was the result of a romance with Helvey gone bad.

By then, Dorothy knew about disinformation. She had begun her own inquiry, working the phone and filling scrapbooks with relevant articles. When the first reporter had called, she was barely able to speak, but now she cultivated the press, prodding them to follow up on inconsistencies and feeding them pieces of one another's stories. "If one more reporter calls me with information before you do," she told the Navy commander in charge of the case, "you haven't even heard me scream!" It wasn't long before Dorothy began wondering who cared more about her son: the Navy, in which three generations of her family had served, or the gay community, which she had not until recently even known she was part of.

The organized gay community is no more organized—and no more a community—than any other affiliation of people who have, at best, only one thing in common. A dysfunctional family, its various representatives spend a lot of time backbiting and defending their turf. But they all recognized a useful symbol when they saw one, and immediately began squabbling for Dorothy's attention like a brood of 7-year-old boys.

Dorothy, having lost a son, responded to the attention, albeit warily. When Michael Petrelis, an organizer for the voluble gay-rights group Queer Nation, called her six weeks after the murder, she was still uncomfortable with the word homosexual. Was she aware, he asked in his New Jersey honk, that gay activists were rallying around her son's cause, hoping to make him the gay Rodney King? "He scared the living daylights out of me, with his voice and all," Dorothy recalls.

"There was no way he was getting me involved in no queer nations." But soon representatives of more polite groups began calling. The Human Rights Campaign Fund asked if it could fly her to a candlelight vigil in Washington. Not knowing it was a gay organization—or that the vigil had been organized, in part, by Petrelis—she said yes. Soon, the Campaign for Military Service, whose goal was to lift the ban on homosexuals, asked if she would sign a letter telling her story, as part of a mass-mail fund-raising effort. Yes, she said; and yes to the news conferences, the memorials, the crystal awards and sympathy plaques. After all, she brought home only $190 a week; she could never afford the kind of publicity these groups were willing to pay for. If they wanted to fly her and Kathy and Billy to some city they'd never seen, put them up in a nice hotel, pay for meals, let her say her piece, why should she refuse? It was more attention than she'd ever gotten from anyone in her life. And if they were using her only to further their aims, as some claimed, she would use them to further hers.

"I was like a refrigerator who didn't want to be moved," Dorothy recalls of her first meeting with Jim Jennings, whom press reports, to her horror, had identified as her son's one-time lover. "I hate that word lover," she says. "And I didn't want to go. Meet all these gay people? I figured they were weird, like Klinger from 'M*A*S*H,' dressing like women, with their pinkies in the air." But Jennings had invited her to a memorial service in San Diego in honor of Allen, and Dorothy decided she had to attend. "And guess what? They were nice! None of them looked like Klinger."

In the months following Allen's death, Dorothy achieved what parents of living homosexuals often fail to, even after years of effort: an acceptance of her child's sexuality. Unfortunately, she now lives with the regret that it took a brutal murder to do it. For Allen had told her, in a phone call from San Diego long before he died, that he was gay. "I thought it was just him trying to get me," she says. "He was always doing things to drive me crazy. He sent a picture of himself in a white tux with some girl from the Philippines in a white dress and told me they got married—he had me going for a long time with that, and it wasn't until later Kathy told me the girl was a guy. So I didn't believe him when he said he was gay. I thought if I just didn't take the bait, he'd give up. But right after, we went to Kings Island near Cincinnati, a really neat amusement park. We were in line to get on the roller coaster and this guy behind me said, 'Look at the faggot up there with the tattoos on his arms trying to make people think he's a macho man.' That really hurt me. And I didn't understand."

How could she understand? Allen looked nothing like Klinger: he was well built, handsome, with thick blond hair and blue eyes. He wore an earring, "but doesn't everyone?" Dorothy says. She ignored the incident, and over the next few years, if Allen mentioned men he liked, she didn't respond. But reading his journal, she knew she'd been wrong. The final entry, in purple ink, describes Allen's crush on a man he had met while on shore leave in Sasebo a few days before his

390 THE GAY RIGHTS MOVEMENT

death. Eric Underwood, who danced on Broadway in "La Cage aux Folles" and was now performing at a theme park commemorating the first Dutch settlement in Japan, was apparently everything Allen wanted. Everything except single; Underwood had a lover stateside. Still, their hours of conversation over several days left the enamored sailor feeling a bit less lonely. "I guess that means we are everywhere," he wrote, and for the last time closed his journal—which bore on its cover a heart-shaped sticker and the legend "Be Kind to Me, I Gave Blood Today."

"Terrible things went on that ship," Dorothy believes. "Gay sailors being lost at sea, which really means thrown overboard." Dorothy has constructed a version of her son's last weeks aboard the Belleau Wood from the sometimes contradictory accounts of shipmates, reporters and her new gay friends. In Dorothy's mind it is better that Helvey be assigned the likely, if unprovable, motive of gay-bashing than that he have no motive at all, as the Navy seems to hold. It is better to think that Helvey was acting out a Navy-wide hatred than to think that, in essence, he acted alone.

One of Dorothy's best new friends—and major informants—is Eric Underwood. It was Underwood, along with two other performers at the theme park, who wrote the letter to Pacific Stars and Stripes. In his five months in Japan, he had heard plenty of stories about gay sailors being punched in the face while sleeping, or doused with lighter fluid and ignited. According to him, the Belleau Wood was the worst ship of all. "So bad," he says, "that Allen, after we talked, had a hard time going back to that environment. I'd have to coax him to the door. He said that people harassed him 24 hours a day."

The Navy says Schindler never reported any harassment, but harassed or not, he was scared. "More people are finding out about me," he wrote three weeks before he died. "You never know who will want to harm me or cease my existence." Still, in the struggle between circumspection and revelation, revelation had won. He now ate with a group of gay sailors who called themselves the Fab Five. He told the chaplain he was gay and wanted a discharge. And then, apparently desperate to announce the truth, Radioman Schindler broadcast what the Navy calls "an unauthorized statement" over the Pacific Command: "I'm too cute to be straight."

Whoever else may have heard the comment on the wide ocean, Schindler's shipmates now knew, if they hadn't before, that he was gay. One month later, he had his last talk with Underwood. Now Underwood has long talks with Dorothy instead. "She's like another mom to me," he says. Certainly she brags about him like a mother, showing visitors a photo he uses for modeling auditions. "Look at him in the bathing suit," she says a bit lubriciously. "He says he would have went for Allen." With that match impossible, Dorothy has dreamed up another: in the TV movie about her life—now in development at Quest Entertainment—she hopes Underwood will play her son. "He's a knockout," she says. "Blond and blue-eyed like Allen." Or, she might have added, like Helvey.

In the beginning I wanted nothing but to go to Japan and stomp Helvey's head as he had stomped my son's, but I didn't want his mother to have to go through what I'm going through." Dorothy was speaking at the Fourth Annual Homicide Memorial, a day of sermons and singing and light politicking sponsored by the Cook County State's Attorney's office. It was a blistering day, threatening rain, but Dorothy had made the trip to Grant Park in Chicago, on the shores of Lake Michigan, because talking about her son has virtually become her profession. (Having flown only twice before Allen died, she has since racked up more than 40,000 miles.) The Salvation Army hadn't seen a full week of her since kettle-counting time at Christmas. And now that Dorothy had expanded her venues to include non-gay events, it didn't seem likely that her schedule would abate. She didn't want it to: it scared her when a week went by with no calls from the press or requests for her presence. "You need to release your anger or it can build inside you," she told the hangdog audience of survivors, who sat at picnic tables, sobbing into their soft drinks. "And if that happens, you can become something terrible. Thanks to the media, I was able to tell my anger over and over and over."

It does sometimes seem that Dorothy has only a half-dozen phrases to describe her feelings and beliefs—phrases that roll out of her in rotation, as identical as bullets, or pills. "The Pledge of Allegiance says justice for all," goes her brief for gay civil rights, "not justice for all except homosexuals." Another favorite is: "You can mess around with a lot of things, but don't mess around with my kids!" Simplistic as they are, these unscripted formulations, expounded by a woman who calls herself "the stupidest person on earth," always hit home. Certainly no one is intimidated by her vocabulary, her manner or her attire. "If she were a New York sophisticate and wore clothes by Galanos," says Thomas Stoddard of the Campaign for Military Service, "it wouldn't have the same effect."

Ellen Meyers, who arranged for Dorothy's appearance at the memorial, puts it more bluntly. "Dorothy's spectacular," she says. "I mean, her child is dead from a hate crime. And down in Springfield she's been lobbying for the state gay-and-lesbian-rights bill. Usually we have professional queers spouting statistics, but to have a mother! And a mother from a white, working-class Republican town—how could you beat that?"

It was hard to beat. Hearing her testimony—"Allen was my son but he could have been the son of any of you here"—the Judiciary Committee of the Illinois House of Representatives, wiping back tears, approved the bill for consideration on the floor, where it also passed. "It was like maybe Allen's death had finally done some good," Dorothy exulted. Two months later, however, the bill was killed by a State Senate committee.

On March 30, William Bracken, a lawyer Dorothy retained on the advice of Miriam Ben-Shalom, a lesbian veteran, filed a Federal tort claim of $8 million against the Navy for the wrongful death of Allen Schindler. Bracken likens the atmosphere aboard the Belleau Wood to "willful endangerment." The Navy, which must deny or accept the claim by Sept. 26 or risk a full-blown lawsuit, has not yet responded, though it has conducted an investigation into the "conditions and attitudes which prevailed at the time of the murder." The investigators concluded that "the ship, the command and those senior personnel responsible for the ship actively discouraged violence, threats and illegal discrimination of any type, including against homosexuals."

If the Navy nevertheless agrees to a settlement, Dorothy may find herself a rich woman. She says the TV movie, if it is made, will bring her $100,000; an agent has dangled before her the prospect of $2,000 per night on the lecture circuit. In anticipation, Kathy has urged her mother to move to a nicer house, but, planted in her armchair, glancing first at her curio cabinet crammed with dolls, then at a boomerang and a black velvet map brought back from one of Allen's adventures, Dorothy appears unable to move.

Not that she loves Chicago Heights, a woeful town of 36,000 some 30 miles from Chicago. Once, when the steel mills prospered, there was probably a good side of the tracks, but that was long ago. In any case, Dorothy lives virtually on the tracks, 50 yards from the railroad's deafening rattle. There she has tried to make a home of a grimy 100-year-old frame house that cost $10,900 in 1969 and might not fetch much more today. A rainbow banner flies from the porch; a plastic goose and a miniature windmill stand sentry in the pebbled front plot. Inside, the house hardly seems large enough for Dorothy and 18-year-old Billy to move around in, but hovel or not, it's the only house Allen knew. To leave it would erase him further. His tiny room has been preserved as it was, except for the emptying of the fish tank, the "adopting out" of the parrots and the removal of the huge cage in which Allen kept his three-foot-long monitor lizard, Junior—named, it would seem, after himself. "Allen wanted to work in a zoo, or at Sea World," Dorothy says. "When he got home from the Navy." She spends little time in his room—unnerved, perhaps, by the photographs of the Midway lovingly arranged on the sea-blue walls.

Visitors attending Terry Helvey's court-martial last May at the Naval base in Yokosuka, Japan, were directed to opposite sides of a small gallery in the courtroom, as if for a wedding. On the left sat the defendant's party: Helvey's mother, Regena, and aunt Sheryl Sarchette. On the right, the victim's: Dorothy, Kathy and, not incidentally, most of the press. Separated from onlookers by a partition, Helvey and his lawyers on one side were not quite mirrored by the prosecutor and an empty seat on the other—a seat that seemed to stand for the absent victim himself. Also absent from the ceremony were any of the many fathers, stepfathers and paternal surrogates associated with the event. Allen Schindler Sr., who according to Dorothy's sworn testimony never paid child support, took no interest in the case beyond attempting to claim half of his son's life insurance. As for Helvey, his father, a tattoo artist, had long since decamped. So had his stepfather; Regena Helvey testified at the court-martial that, among other disci-

plinary acts, he had forced Terry to eat his own excrement and amputated half of his left middle finger by slamming it in a door when the boy was 6.

Dorothy was painfully aware of the symmetries and asymmetries in the room. Her background was strikingly similar to Regena Helvey's: small towns, hard lives, bad men. Like Dorothy, Regena had scraped by with factory and fast-food jobs (in her case, at Kentucky Fried Chicken); she had left her son in the care of Aunt Sheryl. But Regena Helvey was clearly a different kind of woman from Dorothy; slim, almost sultry, refusing all interviews, she seemed to be trying to take up as little space on earth as possible, but to take it up attractively. Reporters were thrilled by the prospect of the mothers meeting, but Regena wasn't about to let that happen; during recesses, she rushed outdoors to smoke, making herself scarce before Dorothy lumbered into the hall. And Dorothy wasn't keen on meeting Regena, either. As the trial began and the defense outlined its intention to pin the blame on Helvey's terrible upbringing, Dorothy turned toward the reporters behind her and, only half whispering, said: "We had a bad life too, but my son wasn't a murderer."

Although the press was literally on Dorothy's side, it was hard not to sympathize with Regena Helvey and even to some extent with her son, who shaved neatly for each day of the trial, occasionally wore glasses and looked utterly bereft. When he rose to speak on the third day—the court permitted him to make an unsworn statement—he virtually decomposed before the jury's eyes, stuttering, crying, choking back yelps of pain, spitting out pieces of apology until, collapsing back into his seat by the window, he ducked his head under the Venetian blinds. His defense was barely more coherent: some mumbo jumbo about steroid use from a robotic psychiatrist, a photomontage of Helvey's high-school sports team, a two-hour testimonial video from his hometown. "Our little dog, who didn't like anyone, loved Terry," said a girlfriend. "Well groomed," said a minister. "Shared his pizza."

By the time the eight-officer panel began deliberations, Helvey's fate no longer seemed to be the dominant issue. Having avoided the possibility of the death penalty by pleading guilty to a lesser charge, the defense suggested a sentence of 21 years—since, at 21, this was all of life Helvey knew. But whether 21 years or 60, his life was ruined. Something else was on trial: the American family, and all in all the proceedings did not constitute much of a vindication. Marriage had brought happiness to no one; men were "lazy rats," as Dorothy put it; mothers were left to mourn and fight and pay the consequences. Regena Helvey took the stand to corroborate the defense's contention that she had been an inadequate mother—even admitting she had tried LSD while pregnant with Terry—hoping that her confession would somehow mitigate his sentence. Dorothy took the stand to describe again her son's ruined body, hoping to earn Helvey a life in prison. In the end, the court-martial was indeed a kind of marriage, for the two families would forever be locked together in regret, one mother participating in her own character assassination in order to save her son's life, the other reliving her son's murder over and over in order to save her own. And Helvey, if there was any justice, would spend a long time dreaming of the man he had danced upon.

The mothers, as it turned out, did meet. Minutes after the jury sentenced Helvey to be confined for the length of his natural life, Dorothy was led into a small room where the convict was waiting behind a table. Once inside, she began screaming. He had destroyed her life. He had destroyed her family. Her 8-year-old granddaughter could not fall asleep without clutching her picture of Uncle Allen. "I'm sorry," Helvey stammered, over and over, unable to look at her directly. It was then that his mother came into the room; Helvey motioned her away, but she stayed and put her arm around his waist—"like she really cared," says Dorothy sarcastically.

The three of them remained in the room a few more minutes, Dorothy yelling, Terry repeating his two pathetic words. Regena Helvey, perhaps aware that words are sometimes worthless, said nothing.

Dorothy sits in her chair at home, sorting through the blue nylon knapsack returned to her at the end of the trial. Inside it, her son's belongings have been stored in plastic sandwich bags, as evidence. "What kind of evidence is this?" she asks, holding up a bottle of shampoo. Also in the knapsack are keys and a checkbook, snapshots and loose change, some drawings of lizards and a pink-triangle pin with the caption "Non-Breeder." She begins to tremble. Not that Dorothy hasn't gotten what she wanted: back in Yokosuka she had been so elated that she even embraced Queer Nation's Michael Petrelis. "If there's a place in the Guinness Records for the woman kissed most by gay men, I'm it!"

She has embraced Petrelis's methods, too. She has learned the lessons of the loudmouths: without them, justice would not have been done. Having become a loudmouth herself, however, she is faced with the realization that she can never stop. She spends her days waiting for more chances to "tell her anger"—to broadcast unauthorized statements, as Allen did. The subject doesn't matter much: how the military ban helped kill her son, how gay marriages would be beneficial. What matters is that she is at war, and will be at war, one way or another, for the rest of her life. After all, Helvey's mother still has Helvey; he might even be paroled someday. Allen is now just a bag of mementos—another man gone.

Billy clomps into the house on a new pair of Rollerblades. Dorothy points her thumb at him. "The Navy called here trying to recruit him—can you believe it?" she snorts. "Weeks after Allen was killed. But no way are they going to get their hands on him."

Perhaps it was once possible to think of the Navy as a substitute father for America's lost boys, but no longer. In this regard, the Navy failed Helvey as much as Schindler. In his unsworn testimony at the court-martial, Helvey said that all he had ever wanted was a family, and that the Navy, with all its "fights, typhoons and hurricane warnings," provided it. But what kind of family, Dorothy likes to ask, would reject a lov-

ing son merely for being what he is? And that's how the Navy failed Allen Schindler. He loved the Navy, and died of unrequited love; it shipped him back, an anonymous pulp, unrecognizable even to his mother, except for the insignia tattooed on his right arm—of the U.S.S. Midway.

Jesse Green is the author of "O Beautiful," a novel.

* * *

November 21, 1993

3 MEN ARE CHARGED WITH MURDER IN NEW ORLEANS ANTI-GAY ATTACK

By The Associated Press

NEW ORLEANS, Nov. 20—Three men have been accused of beating and stabbing two men, one fatally, while shouting anti-homosexual epithets in the French Quarter.

The victim, Joe Balog, 22, of Gulfport, Miss., was chased, beaten and fatally stabbed on Nov. 11 as he and a friend returned to their car in the early morning after visiting several bars. Mr. Balog's friend, whose identity has not been made public, was seriously injured.

On Thursday, the three suspects, Grant Wayne Gunderson and Ronald D. Graves, both 24, and Mingo Graham, 23, all of the New Orleans suburb of Metairie, were charged with murder. They were jailed without bond, and no hearing date was scheduled.

Advocates for gay rights here say the attack is the latest in a series of harassing incidents and attacks on homosexuals in the French Quarter.

The Wrong Signals

"It used to be just harassment, but it's gotten worse in the last few years," said Lin-Tod Soldani, a liaison between homosexuals and the Police Department. "I think people are getting the signal from the government on down that gays are second-class citizens, and it's O.K. to treat them any way at all."

Mr. Soldani said the attackers mistakenly believed Mr. Balog and his friend were homosexuals. He estimated that more than 50 percent of the men on streets of the French Quarter late at night are homosexual.

While homosexuals believe that crimes against them are increasing, the police here say it is hard to tell because separating hate crimes from other attacks is often difficult. Also, homosexuals are sometimes reluctant to report crimes against them.

Bryan Sanchez, a 22-year-old college student, said he was kicked and taunted by a group of six well-dressed young men in the French Quarter exactly a year before the attack on Mr. Balog. Mr. Sanchez, who is homosexual, suffered a ruptured ear drum in the attack.

"After they had all hit and kicked me, they stood over me calling me names and shouting things at me," Mr. Sanchez said. "It was terrifying, and it happened for no reason other than they wanted to hurt someone who was gay."

Mr. Soldani said a hostile attitude toward homosexuals had been worsened by the reversal of a city decision to extend health insurance to the domestic partners of gay city workers.

*   *   *

August 30, 1994

WITH FOUR GAY MEN SLAIN, TEXAS REVISITS ISSUE OF HATE CRIME

By SAM HOWE VERHOVEK
Special to The New York Times

HOUSTON, Aug. 29—In Irving, near Dallas, three gay men have been brutally slain this last year in separate incidents, all involving repeated stabbings well beyond those that caused death. A suspect was taken into custody last weekend and has been charged in one killing.

In Houston, the police recently arrested four football stars from a local high school and charged them with the July murder of a gay man outside a nightclub here. The police said the teen-agers were looking for money to buy clothes and had decided that a gay man would be their easiest mark.

These slayings, along with what gay-rights leaders say are dozens of incidents in which gay men and lesbians have been robbed or assaulted in recent months, have drawn wide public attention and prompted advocates for homosexuals to renew calls for increased police protection of homosexuals and for increased penalties for crimes that arise from anti-gay bias.

The string of slayings has also revived criticism of a broad hate-crime law enacted by the Texas Legislature last year. While the law provides for increased penalties for crimes motivated by "bias or prejudice," its legal use in cases of anti-gay activity remains murky. An early version of the bill, which specifically referred to bias based on sexual orientation, was revised after several conservative legislators said they would not vote for that.

Concerns About Society

Dianne Hardy-Garcia, the executive director of the Lesbian/ Gay Rights Lobby of Texas, said in an interview today that anti-gay violence should be specified as protected in the law because, she said, many people still believed that harassment of homosexuals was acceptable.

Many cases of such harassment come at the hands of teen-age boys, like the ones now accused in the Houston murder, Ms. Hardy-Garcia said.

"They do not have this hatred inborn," she said. "They have been taught somehow that it is O.K. to target lesbians and gays for violence. Anti-gay rhetoric is so common and when you teach and preach hatred, it produces violence."

The three slain in Irving were all gay men who frequented bars in a nearby Dallas neighborhood and who were stabbed to death in a similar, grisly fashion. Still, the police in Irving said today that they were not prepared to classify the killings officially as anti-gay violence and that one man might have died in a dispute over drugs, not his sexual orientation.

Last Friday, police officers from Dallas and Irving captured 33-year-old Edwin Bernard Perkins, who was on parole from Arkansas after serving sentences for aggravated robbery, attempted murder and carrying a prohibited weapon.

The police charged Mr. Perkins with the Aug. 18 murder of Larry David Allen, a gay man who was stabbed to death with a steak knife and thrown through the plate-glass window of a motel near Texas Stadium in Irving.

Capt. Travis Hall, the head of the criminal investigations division for the Irving police, said that the police now considered Mr. Perkins a suspect in the June 22 killing of Leopoldo Quintanilla Jr. and the Jan. 25 slaying of Larry Leggett.

"The three slayings all have similarities," he said. "All the victims had homosexual life styles. All three of them were known to frequent the same clubs in the Oak Lawn area of Dallas. And the suspect is also known to frequent those areas. All had multiple stab wounds."

Killing Sparks Concern

In the Dallas area, gay-rights leaders said that while the apparent serial slayings of the gay men had attracted attention for obvious reasons, more common incidents of robberies and harassment of homosexuals were often unreported, sometimes by those affected.

The killing in Houston's Montrose neighborhood of 29-year-old Michael J. Burzinski, on July 30, generated considerable concern here about the dead man and the suspects, four teen-agers who starred last year on the football team at Aldine High School just outside the city. Two were headed for junior college on football scholarships, but now all are in custody on charges of the capital murder.

Police officers said three youths expressed remorse in their confessions, in which they described the incident as stemming from a robbery for spending money on clothes. The youths beat Mr. Burzinski, a photo processor, then kidnapped him, forcing him to withdraw $400 from a bank machine. According to police reports, two youths said the robbery turned into a killing when the one with a gun said Mr. Burzinski had to be shot because he could identify them.

Some gay-rights leaders here said they were disturbed that far more attention had been focused on how the youths' promising lives had turned to ruins than on the brutality of the crime.

"The thing that has appalled me is the absolute vacuum of moral leadership," said Hiram Butler, an art dealer in Houston. "People say: 'Oh, the poor guys that killed him, they had things going for them. They might have done something with their lives.' But no religious leader, no politician, no one with any standing in this community has stood up and said: 'This is wrong. We will not stand for this.'"

*   *   *

November 11, 1997

CLINTON BACKS EXPANDING DEFINITION OF A HATE CRIME

By JAMES BENNET

WASHINGTON, Nov. 10—Uncertain of the scope of the problem or how best to address it, President Clinton convened a White House Conference on Hate Crimes here today, saying that such acts "strike at the heart of what it means to be an American."

In an address starting the daylong conference, Mr. Clinton endorsed forthcoming legislation that would add crimes committed against people because they are gay, lesbian, female or disabled to the list of Federal hate crimes.

Federal hate crimes now include crimes committed against people because of their race, religion, color or national origin. The new legislation, sponsored by Senators Edward M. Kennedy, Democrat of Massachusetts, and Arlen Specter, Republican of Pennsylvania, would also eliminate a requirement that the crime occur while the victim is engaged in a "federally protected" activity—enrolling in school, for example.

Mr. Clinton also announced a package of modest Federal initiatives to combat hate crimes. And he took advantage of the setting—an auditorium at George Washington University crowded with civil rights advocates, educators, law enforcers and victims of hate crimes—to restate his support for Bill Lann Lee, his contested nominee for assistant attorney general for civil rights.

Mr. Clinton said that members of the Senate Judiciary Committee were blocking the nomination of Mr. Lee "because he supports his own President's position on affirmative action."

"All I ask the Senate committee to do is just to send his name out," he said. "They don't even have to make a recommendation; just let the Senate vote." On Sunday, Senator Orrin G. Hatch, the Utah Republican who is chairman of the committee, called the nomination "dead."

In 1996, there were 8,759 hate crimes reported to the Justice Department, up from 7,947 in 1995. But since jurisdictions define hate crimes differently and reporting is voluntary, White House officials cautioned that those numbers were unreliable. They said that there were no statistics to indicate whether organized hate groups, like the Ku Klux Klan, were on the rise or dissipating.

The decision to hold today's conference grew out of preparations for Mr. Clinton's yearlong initiative to improve race relations.

Mr. Clinton participated in an hourlong workshop this afternoon, listening as a California legislator, a New York educator, a Seattle student and others talked about grappling with hate crimes and discrimination. He appealed to them for advice, receiving in return mostly praise for steps he had already taken in underscoring the problem.

Arturo Venegas Jr., chief of the Sacramento Police Department, warned that there was "no magic bullet" to end hate crimes.

While several participants emphasized that schools could teach children the dangers of prejudice, Tammie Schnitzer, who as a private citizen in Billings, Mont., rallied her city against a rash of anti-Semitic crimes four years ago, said education was not sufficient.

"This problem is far deeper," Ms. Schnitzer said. "I have to teach my grandparents before I teach my kids."

Mr. Clinton announced today that all United States attorneys would "establish or expand working groups" to focus on combatting hate crimes. He said the Justice Department would assign at least 50 more Federal Bureau of Investigation agents and prosecutors to enforce the hate crimes laws. And he said the Department of Housing and Urban Development would provide for stiffer fines against people who discriminate in housing.

* * *

September 18, 1998

REPORTS OF ANTI-GAY CRIMES INCREASE BY 81 PERCENT

By MICHAEL COOPER

Reports of bias crimes against gay men and lesbians have risen 81 percent this year, the police said yesterday, even as overall crime has dropped sharply and other types of bias attacks have fallen slightly.

There have been 76 crimes reported so far this year that the police have labeled as anti-gay bias crimes, up from 42 during the same period last year, said Lieut. Stephen Biegel, a Police Department spokesman. During the same period the overall number of bias crimes has dropped 3 percent, to 368 from 381, he said.

Advocates for gay causes joined with politicians yesterday in City Hall Park to denounce the violence and call on the Police Department to do more to protect gay men and women. "The police bias unit is doing a great job after the fact, after someone has been a victim," said Christine Quinn, the executive director of the New York City Gay and Lesbian Anti-Violence Project. "What we need is a law-enforcement response that will deter this crime and send a message that there is zero tolerance for this type of hatred in New York City."

Police Commissioner Howard Safir said yesterday that he had increased the number of officers in the Sixth Precinct in Greenwich Village in late August after three murders and several anti-gay bias crimes were reported there. "We're always concerned when there's an attack that involves bias," he said. "But certainly we do not have an epidemic."

But Ms. Quinn noted that most of the new officers assigned to the Sixth Precinct were plainclothes officers who were sent there to crack down on prostitution. "Prostitution clearly is not the biggest problem facing the lesbian, gay, bisexual and transgendered community at this moment," she said, calling for more uniformed officers in the area.

And she said that many attacks had occurred elsewhere. Since September, Ms. Quinn said, her group has documented

12 more anti-gay attacks, not all of which were reported to the police, in neighborhoods around the city, from the Bronx to Rego Park, Queens. They included the slashing of a woman in Park Slope, Brooklyn, by two men yelling anti-gay epithets, and the gunpoint robbery of a man in the Bronx by three men who used an anti-gay slur.

City Comptroller Alan G. Hevesi said that too few officials had denounced anti-gay bigotry.

"As the crime rates have dropped enormously, crime rates where the victims are gay men or lesbians are going up," he said. "The reason for that is in our society. Even here in New York City, which has to be the most tolerant city in the world, there is an acceptability to expressing bigotry against gays and lesbians. And that is a terrible tragedy."

*   *   *

October 12, 1998

AFTER BEATING OF GAY MAN, TOWN LOOKS AT ITS ATTITUDES

By JAMES BROOKE

LARAMIE, Wyo., Oct. 11—As a gay college student lay hospitalized in critical condition after a severe beating here, this small city, which bills itself as "Wyoming's hometown," wrestled with its attitudes toward gay men.

On Saturday, at the University of Wyoming's annual homecoming parade, "Pistol Pete" and his uniformed brass band were overshadowed by the largest group of marchers: 450 people, many wearing yellow armbands and carrying signs in support of the student, Matthew Shepard, 21, who suffered severe head injuries in the attack last week.

"Hate Is Not a Small Town Value—No to Violence and Evil," read one sign, as watchers applauded. With passers-by spontaneously joining the protest group, two women held another sign that read, "No Hate Crimes in Wyoming."

Two candlelight vigils were held tonight at churches near the campus. At the Poudre Valley Hospital in Fort Collins, Colo., where Mr. Shepard's health continued to deteriorate, the hospital has received so many flowers that nurses have started to distribute bouquets to other patients. A vigil at the hospital on Saturday evening drew about 500 people.

"We live in the Equality State," Shannon Rexroat wrote on Friday in a special edition of The Branding Iron, the campus newspaper. Referring to Wyoming's pioneer heritage as the first state to grant women the right to vote, Ms. Rexroat, the newspaper's editor added: "That means nothing to me anymore. We live in a state where a young man was brutally beaten because he is gay."

But others recalled today another side of "Wyoming's hometown," which has a population of 27,000.

Associated Press

On Saturday, a candlelight vigil for Matthew Shepard was held at the hospital in Fort Collins, Colo., and marchers in a University of Wyoming parade in Laramie protested the beating.

On Friday, Jamie Lewis, another editor, was handing out copies of the special edition, when, "One guy just put his hands up in the air and said to me, 'faggot-lover.'"

Last week's assault bubbled out of a climate of hostility toward gay men and lesbians, leaders of the local Unitarian church said in a letter published today in the city's newspaper, The Laramie Daily Boomerang.

"This incident was atypical in its brutality, but not in its underlying motive," wrote Jeffrey A. Lockwood and Stephen M. Johnson. Gay people in Laramie, they wrote, "are frequently assaulted with derision, intolerance, insult and hostility—if not guns and ropes."

Ric Turley, who dropped out of college here after one year in the 1970's, recalled driving here to see his family for Christmas in 1993 and seeing a vandalized billboard on the main highway running north out of Colorado. Under a brace of pistols, an advertising appeal for a state history museum had been changed he said, from "Shoot a Day or Two," to "Shoot a Gay or Two."

Mr. Turley, who is gay, said he had complained to the museum. But returning a month later, he found the message had not been erased. After complaining to the museum again, he said he took a can of black spray paint and blotted out the word "gay."

"It was this kind of complacency and apathy that allowed this to happen," he said of the beating in which two local men, Russell Henderson and Aaron McKinney, have been charged. Two women, Kristen L. Price and Chastity V. Pasley, have been charged as accessories after the fact to attempted first-degree murder.

According to the local police and prosecutors, the two men lured Mr. Shepard out of a bar by saying they were gay. Then, the Laramie police say, the pair kidnapped Mr. Shepard, pistol-whipped him with a .357 Magnum, and left him tied to a ranch fence for 18 hours until a passing bicyclist spotted Mr. Shepard, who was unconscious.

Today, the Laramie police said that Mr. McKinney was arrested on Thursday at the same hospital in Fort Collins where Mr. Shepard was being treated. Mr. McKinney was being treated for a "minor" skull fracture, unrelated to the fracas with Mr. Shepard, said Ben Fritzen, a Laramie Police detective.

President Clinton has condemned the attack, saying on Saturday, "I was deeply grieved by the act of violence perpetrated against Matthew Shepard." Mr. Clinton urged Congress to pass the Federal Hate Crimes Prevention Act, saying, "There is nothing more important to the future of this country than our standing together against intolerance, prejudice and violent bigotry."

Wyoming is 1 of 10 states that does not have a hate crime law. The latest attempt died in the Legislature in Cheyenne in February. On Saturday, Gov. Jim Geringer said he was "outraged and sickened" by the attack.

In Laramie, Mr. McKinney's father, Bill, also condemned the attack. But he complained about the attention by the national media.

The national press "blew it totally out of proportion because it involved a homosexual," Mr. McKinney was quoted as saying in an article on Sunday in The Denver Post. "Had this been a heterosexual these two boys decided to take out and rob, this never would have made the national news."

Ms. Price, the girlfriend of Aaron McKinney and the mother of their 4-month-old son, Cameron, also was quoted in the article. Ms. Price told The Post that her boyfriend had said that on Tuesday night Mr. Shepard made passes at him at a local bar, the Fireside.

"He embarassed him and Russ in front of all their friends and everybody at the Fireside," said Ms. Price, who was not at her apartment here today. "Later on, Aaron did say he told him he was gay just to rob him, because he wanted to take his money for embarrassing him."

Ms. Price said that after the three men got in the pickup and drove for a mile, "Aaron told him: 'Guess what? I'm not gay—and you just got jacked.'"

Mr. Shepard grew up in Casper until his sophomore year in high school, when his father, an oil rig safety engineer, was transferred to Saudi Arabia. The young man completed high school at a boarding school in Lugano, Switzerland.

On Saturday, his parents, Dennis and Judy Shepard, released a statement thanking "the American public for their kind thoughts."

"He is a trusting person," the Shepards wrote. "He has always strongly felt that all people are the same, regardless of their sexual preference, race or religion."

*　　*　　*

October 21, 1998

KILLING SHAKES COMPLACENCY OF THE GAY RIGHTS MOVEMENT

By MICHAEL COOPER

For some of the younger marchers, the demonstration Monday night that paralyzed parts of midtown Manhattan was their first political rally. For some older protesters, though, the march—to express outrage over the killing of a gay college student in Wyoming—was a return to the angry street protests that had so often symbolized the militancy of the gay rights movement.

As the chaotic denouement of the march and the police response was debated yesterday, one thing seemed clear: the size of the loosely organized protest showed how the killing of Matthew Shepard has galvanized gay men and lesbians in New York and around the country as has no other single event in recent years.

The demonstration began at 6 P.M. as a rally in front of the Plaza on 59th Street near Central Park, then swelled to 5,000 people on Fifth Avenue, blocking traffic. Confrontations with police officers resulted in about 110 arrests.

While the size of the protest in midtown surprised even its organizers, the evocation of anger and sadness on the streets of New York was not unique. Candlelight vigils have been held across the country, from Washington to Grand Junction, Colo., Raleigh, N.C., and Lubbock, Tex. In San Francisco, the giant rainbow flag in the Castro district that symbolizes the gay rights movement was lowered to half staff. The Internet has been filled with discussion of the crime. Last night, 1,000 people attended an hourlong prayer service for Mr. Shepard at the Cathedral of St. John the Divine in Manhattan.

The cause of the passion, participants say, is a sense that even as gay people have become more accepted than ever, there are reminders of the hatred and violence of the not-so-distant past. Well before Mr. Shepard's killing, an increase in police reports of anti-gay crimes in New York City had unsettled gay people, shaking them out of complacency in the years since the height of AIDS activism.

Recent protests over issues like benefits for domestic partners and the right to march in the St. Patrick's Day Parade have lacked the drama of the guerrilla street tactics of AIDS activists. Some gay men and lesbians contend that their success in drawing attention to AIDS gave some a false feeling of acceptance, especially in the city with the largest gay population in the country.

"There was a sense, I think, in the gay community, particularly living in a certain segment of it in New York City, that we can live in a kind of bubble and feel relatively safe and feel as if we've arrived," said Tim Allis, 37, a magazine editor. "A sense that gay rights are there, that we are so much a part of the mainstream in so many ways, so visible, with so many role models on television. It's a bit of an illusion."

Thomas Ruble, 45, had been to two gay pride rallies and parades, but never to a large protest march until Monday night. "Sometimes, in our little gay lives in the middle of America, I think we have forgotten that they kill us," he said. "They hate us."

In more than 20 interviews with gay men and lesbians in the past week, many people said that the killing of Matthew Shepard had struck a strong emotional chord. Some cited his clean-cut image. Others spoke of the brutality of the crime, in which he was left, severely beaten, lashed to a fence in near-freezing temperatures to die.

Jay Blotcher, who was a spokesman for Queer Nation, a street protest group, in the early 1990's, said that in recent years, his group and other militant organizations had run out of steam and were failing to attract young members.

"We were looking to younger people to pick up the mantle and it wasn't really happening," he said. "I attributed that to that fact that a new generation came of age and said: 'I don't have to be a gay activist, I'm just a gay person. It doesn't have to be an issue.'"

"I think something like this reminds us that it still is an issue," he added. "There were lots of young people at the rally on Fifth Avenue. And there were people I know there who had hung up their activist mantles and gone into semiretirements."

In New York City, there were 82 anti-gay bias crimes reported this year through Oct. 4, compared with 46 during the same period last year, representing a 78 percent jump,

said Deputy Inspector Barbara A. Sicilia, the commander of the Bias Unit. Overall bias crimes rose by 2 percent, to 384 from 374.

Although the most incidents were reported in lower Manhattan, where they usually occur, more incidents were also reported in Queens, the Bronx and Staten Island.

In the latest attack, two men shouted anti-gay remarks at a 31-year-old man on the streets of the Dyker Heights section of Brooklyn yesterday evening, then hit him in the head with an unspecified object, the police said. The man was not seriously injured.

Carl Locke, the director of client services at the Gay and Lesbian Anti-Violence Project, a nonprofit organization that helps victims of bias crimes, said the spread of bias crimes across the city shows the extent to which gay people are becoming more visible outside their usual neighborhoods, Greenwich Village and Chelsea in Manhattan and Park Slope in Brooklyn.

"Most gay-related crimes have people come to your neighborhood and seek you out to hurt you," he said. "Now people don't have to come downtown. As we are more visible outside of Manhattan, we have also seen an increase in crimes in those neighborhoods."

While many activists believe that anti-gay crimes are on the rise across the country, statistics are difficult to come by. The National Coalition of Anti-Violence Projects, which collects data from 14 organizations across the country, reported that violent crimes against gay people rose 2 percent, to 2,445 incidents, in 1997, the last year for which statistics are available. In 1996, the report said, anti-gay crimes rose by 6 percent.

But those figures reflect incidents labeled bias crimes by local organizations, which often use different standards than the police when determining motivation.

Jack Levin, a professor of sociology and criminology at Northeastern University and an author of "Hate Crimes: The Rising Tide of Bigotry and Bloodshed" (Plenum Press, 1993), said it was not unusual for anti-gay crimes to buck the trends of other bias crimes.

"Most hate crimes respond to economic factors like the unemployment rate, but not gay-bashing," he said. "Gay-bashing has nothing to do with money, with economic survival. That's why so many perpetrators are teen-agers and come from every point among the economic continuum. It is typically done by young people, with their hormones raging, feeling confusion about sexual identity. Young guys in denial about their own homosexual feelings who see the very presence of a gay person as a threat."

Nineteen states, including New York, do not have legislation that specifically prohibits anti-gay hate crimes. In these states, someone who assaults a gay man or a lesbian can be convicted of assault, but not a bias-related assault. New York does have a law, aggravated harassment in the first degree, that outlaws harassing people because of "the race, color, religion or national origin of such person," but it makes no reference to sexual orientation.

The Democratic-controlled State Assembly has repeatedly passed bills that would outlaw anti-gay crimes, but the Republican-controlled State Senate has failed to act on them. This year, Gov. George E. Pataki, a Republican, renewed his call to pass the bill, saying that "passing the bias-crime legislation, including a provision protecting those who would be discriminated against based on sexual orientation, is very important."

Mr. Allis, the magazine editor, said that Mr. Shepard's killing put recent history into a new light.

"There was that sense of connecting the dots," he said. "Between the well-publicized murders, the less-publicized hate crimes that we hear about across the country, Trent Lott's words calling homosexuality a disease, and small acts of intolerance, there were all sorts of indications. But the murder of Matthew Shepard brought the picture into relief."

* * *

February 5, 1999

ROCKY MOUNTAIN STATES RESISTING MOVE TO BROADEN HATE-CRIME LAWS

By JAMES BROOKE

DENVER, Feb. 4—Last fall, national revulsion over the killing of Matthew Shepard, a gay college student in Wyoming, seemed strong enough to push legislatures in the Rockies to expand hate-crime laws to include sexual orientation.

But this winter lawmakers in Colorado, Idaho, Montana and Utah have defeated bills that would add sexual orientation to categories of people protected by existing hate-crime laws. In Wyoming legislators have defeated all efforts to pass that state's first hate-crime law.

In New Mexico, which has the region's lone Democratic-controlled legislature, lawmakers are expected to pass a hate-crime bill that includes sexual orientation. But Gov. Gary E. Johnson, a Republican, has vowed a veto, saying, "All crimes are hate crimes."

Kerry Lobel, executive director of the National Gay and Lesbian Task Force, a Washington group that pushes for hate-crime legislation, said: "We are incredibly disappointed. We looked to the Wyoming Legislature for leadership and legislation, not lip service."

The votes came as the Federal Bureau of Investigation on Jan. 21 released its latest tally of hate crimes. In 1997, sexual orientation was the motivation for 14 percent of reported hate crimes, or 1,102 crimes out of 8,049, the bureau said. Under the bureau's voluntary reporting system, police departments covering about 80 percent of the country's population report their hate crimes.

Forty states have some kind of hate-crime legislation, generally laws that increase fines and add jail time for crimes motivated by hatred of a specific group. Of those states, 19 have laws that specify sexual orientation as a category for protection. Ten states, largely in the South and Southwest, do not have any hate-crime legislation.

Outside the Rockies, legislatures in Hawaii, Oklahoma, and Virginia are considering hate-crime bills that include sexual orientation.

Antipathy toward hate-crime legislation seems to stem from several factors, including a belief that the laws would confer special rights on the groups named and a backlash against publicity resulting from the Shepard killing.

Sally Vaughan, a resident of Remington, Wyo., complained two weeks ago at a legislative hearing in Cheyenne about what she called "the vicious smear campaign" by the national press in its coverage of Shepard killing. Wyoming became the true victim of bias crime, Ms. Vaughan said.

Doug Thompson, who recently formed a Wyoming group called Citizens for Equal Protection, urged lawmakers in Cheyenne to protect all citizens "and not just a few groups who claim victim status."

Gov. Jim Geringer, a Republican, gave general support to a hate-crime bill but also warned legislators about yielding to "external pressure."

In the end, a hate-crime bill that six weeks ago seemed destined for passage died yesterday in the Senate Judiciary Committee.

"The part of the bill that made people the most uncomfortable was the provision for sexual orientation," State Senator John C. Schiffer, a Republican who is the committee chairman, said today, adding, "My feeling right now is that the committee is tired of discussing bias crimes."

A Democratic member of the committee, Senator Rae Lynn Job, said, "A lot of people felt that by passing this we were going to give some people more protection than others."

In Montana, a bill to add sexual orientation to an existing hate-crime bill last week died in committee. In its place, the State Senate passed a bill that would allow a judge to increase penalties for a crime motivated by hate, but it did not specify any protected groups.

"The language is over broad, vague, lacking in specific terms and will be constitutionally challenged," State Senator Steve Doherty, a Democrat, said. "It is nice-sounding fluff."

The campaign to add sexual orientation to the list of hate crimes has been hampered by the reluctance of the Shepard family to allow their son to become a martyr for a political cause.

"It's a very frightening concept as a parent that your son now becomes a martyr, a public figure for the world," Mr. Shepard's mother, Judy Shepard, told "Dateline NBC" in an interview that is to be broadcast on Friday night. "He's just our son."

In December, Mrs. Shepard and her husband, Dennis, set up the Matthew Shepard Foundation, saying in a statement, "The foundation will be dedicated to the principle of helping people move beyond tolerance to embrace and rejoice in diversity."

Last month, in Casper, Wyo., the family's hometown, Mrs. Shepard announced an International Hike Against Hate and

Violence to stretch 2,500 miles from Skagway, Alaska, to Laramie, Wyo., this summer.

In an interview for the March issue of Vanity Fair, Mrs. Shepard described Matthew as having the posture of a victim.

"He was the kind of person whom you just look at and know if you hurt him that he's going to take it, that there's nothing he can do about it, verbally or physically," she said.

* * *

April 6, 1999

GAY MURDER TRIAL ENDS WITH GUILTY PLEA

By JAMES BROOKE

LARAMIE, Wyo., April 5—In a case that has focused national attention on violence against homosexuals, a 21-year-old roofer pleaded guilty today to kidnapping and murdering a gay college student and was sentenced to serve two consecutive life sentences.

Escaping a possible death penalty, Russell A. Henderson was sentenced by District Judge Jeffrey A. Donnell for his part in the beating, robbery and murder of the student, Matthew Shepard, here six months ago. Police said Mr. Henderson and another man had pretended to be gay to lure Mr. Shepard to his death.

"You are deserving the fullest punishment this court can mete out," Judge Donnell said, accepting a plea agreement two days before opening arguments were to begin. In his only reference to Mr. Shepard's sexual orientation, the judge said the killing was "part because of his life style, part for a $20 robbery."

During an emotional hearing at the Albany County Courthouse here, Mr. Henderson turned to Judy and Dennis Shepard and apologized for murdering their 22-year-old son.

Mr. Henderson then turned on his former friend, Aaron J. McKinney, saying that Mr. McKinney was the mastermind of the Oct. 6 kidnapping of Mr. Shepard from a bar here. Lawyers observing the case speculated that prosecutors had dropped their bid for a death sentence in return for Mr. Henderson's testimony at Mr. McKinney's trial this August on the same charges. After listening impassively to this testimony, the judge turned to Mr. Henderson and said, "This court does not believe you feel any true remorse in this matter."

Conceding that he faced an "academic choice," Judge Donnell chose the harsher alternative, two life sentences to be served consecutively, rather than concurrently. In his final comments before the defendant was led away, the judge told him, "You are not a victim here, Mr. Henderson, you are a perpetrator."

Wyoming legal experts said today that there was virtually no chance that Mr. Henderson would ever be eligible for parole. His only hope of release would be a governor's pardon.

"It is my hope that Mr. Henderson will die in the Wyoming State Penitentiary," Cal Rerucha, the Albany County Attorney, said after the sentencing. "The only time

he leaves the Wyoming State Penitentiary is when they bury him."

Recently, a Wyoming coalition of clergy and a national coalition of gay groups spoke out against applying the death penalty in the Shepard case, in keeping with their opposition to capital punishment.

Compressing an enormous amount of drama into a one-hour hearing, the court proceedings included the Shepards telling Mr. Henderson of their deep pain, the defendant giving his first public account of the crime and his grandmother telling of a loving young man who grew up in a household free of hate.

Dressed in black pants, a gray shirt and a black and white paisley tie, Mr. Henderson had let his hair grow out, shunning the skinhead look he favored at the time of his arrest.

"It was 10 P.M., and me and Aaron decided to go out to a bar," Mr. Henderson testified, responding to questions by his lawyer, Wyatt Skaggs. After drinking "a few pitchers of beer" at the first bar, Mr. Henderson said, they went to the Fireside bar. There, while drinking another pitcher, he said, Mr. McKinney noticed the college student.

"Aaron had mentioned to me that he wanted to take him out and rob him," Mr. Henderson testified in a clear if subdued voice. "I disagreed with this."

He said that Mr. McKinney told him to drive the pickup truck borrowed from Mr. McKinney's father, where to drive and where to park.

"Aaron McKinney, he pulled out a gun and told Matthew Shepard to give him his wallet," continued Mr. Henderson, who said that while he drove, his friend beat Mr. Shepard. After parking in a field near a subdivision where Mr. Henderson had once lived, Mr. McKinney "pulled Matthew out of the truck and continued to hit him" with the pistol, he said.

"Aaron told me to go get a rope out of the truck," Mr. Henderson said as the Shepards stared grimly ahead. "Aaron told me to tie his hands" to a fence pole.

"Matthew looked really bad, I told him to stop," Mr. Henderson said. "Mr. McKinney hit me above the mouth. I returned to the pickup truck."

After driving away, leaving Mr. Shepard tied to a fence in temperatures that dropped below freezing, Mr. Henderson said, he and his friend got in another fight. When caught by a Laramie police officer, Mr. Henderson said, he lied about what he had been doing that evening.

Instead of calling for medical help for Mr. Shepard the next day, Mr. Henderson said, he and his girlfriend, Chasity Pasley, and Mr. McKinney's girlfriend, Kristen LeAnn Price, drove 50 miles east to a truck stop in Cheyenne with his bloody clothing "and put it in a dumpster to cover up that I was out there when Matthew was beaten."

Ms. Pasley pleaded guilty in December to being an accessory after the fact to first degree murder and faces sentencing. Ms. Price faces a trial on those charges in May.

After Mr. Henderson spoke, it was the turn of Lucy Thompson, his maternal grandmother, who has reared him since he was a baby.

"Our hearts ache for the pain and suffering that the Shepards have gone through," Mrs. Thompson said. "We have prayed for you many, many times. You have showed us such mercy."

Mrs. Thompson, who reared Russell until he dropped out of Laramie High School near the end of his senior year, described him as "a survivor" whose "mother was young and not ready to be a mother." Three months ago, at age 40, Cindy Thompson Dixon, Russell's mother, froze to death on a rural road outside of Laramie after a night of drinking.

Saying that her grandson had a "loving and kind" side, she recalled him playing on the floor with his young cousins. "Even as a teen-ager, Russell was never embarrassed to give me a hug or to kiss me on the forehead in front of his peers," she said.

Noting that the case had "developed into a hate crime," Mrs. Thompson said that she had never preached hatred in her household and that "Russell has never been a hateful individual."

Mr. Henderson's lawyer, Mr. Skaggs, denied today that Mr. Shepard had been targeted because he was gay. "This crime has never been a hate crime," he said.

In closing, Mrs. Thompson begged the judge not "to take Russell out of our lives forever." Turning to the Shepards, she said, "I want to thank all the Shepards. I love you even though I have never known you."

After his grandmother's appeal, Mr. Henderson, who had hoped to earn a slim chance of one day winning parole, addressed the dead man's family.

"Mr. and Mrs. Shepard, there is not a moment that doesn't go by that I don't see what happened that night."

"I know what I did," he continued, turning back to Judge Donnell. "I'm very sorry for what I did. I am ready to pay for what I did."

Then it was the turn of Mr. and Mrs. Shepard, who had traveled from their home in Saudi Arabia, where they had moved from Caspar, Wyo., several years ago for a job.

Mrs. Shepard recalled her son's interest in theater, politics and international cultures.

"He wasn't my son, my first born anymore," she said, recalling hugs and late-night talks. "He was my friend, my confidant, my constant reminder of how good life can be."

She said that the last time she saw him he was covered with bandages and wired with tubes in a hospital intensive care unit.

"One of his eyes was partially open," she recalled. "I could see the clear blue of his eye. But the twinkle of his life wasn't there anymore."

The stress on the Shepard family was so great, she continued, that within a month of Matthew's funeral, his paternal grandfather died.

"At times, I don't think you are worthy of addressing," Mrs. Shepard said, turning to Mr. Henderson. "We won't allow you to kill our family."

Mr. Shepard, looking drawn, said he had thrown away the remarks he had written on the plane.

"My son was born blind," he said in an impromptu speech. "Not physically blind, but blind to people's differences—short or tall, black, brown or white, religion or ethnic backgrounds. His friends included gays and so-called straights."

Summing up his remarks to Mr. Henderson, a 175-pound man who had helped to kill his 105-pound son, Matthew's father said, "It takes a brave man to tie up another man, who did not know how to clench a fist until he was 13 years old."

After the Shepards had spoken, Cal Rerucha, the Albany County Attorney, kept his remarks brief. Turning to the defendant, he said, "Mr. Henderson you have created hell on earth—for a family, for our community, for the state."

* * *

May 16, 1999

HATE CRIMES BILL DIES IN TEXAS SENATE

By The Associated Press

AUSTIN, Tex., May 15—Texas lawmakers have abandoned a hate crimes bill with specific protections for homosexuals, and critics are blaming Gov. George W. Bush for its failure, accusing the Republican Presidential prospect of showing no leadership.

The bill, named for James Byrd Jr., the black man dragged to death behind a truck in East Texas last June, would have increased the penalties for hate crimes and specifically included homosexuals as a protected class for the first time.

Asked about the bill, Governor Bush has said only, "I will look at the bill when it makes it to my desk, if it makes it to my desk."

The bill sailed through the Democratic-led House but languished for weeks in a committee of the Republican-controlled Senate. It was abandoned late on Friday. The Legislature adjourns on May 31.

A spokeswoman for Mr. Bush, Karen Hughes, said the Governor's office had tried to break the stalemate, but critics were not convinced.

Dianne Hardy-Garcia, executive director of the Lesbian and Gay Rights Lobby of Texas, attacked Mr. Bush's neutrality, saying, "His unconscionable, immoral lack of leadership on this issue is both tragic and exasperating."

* * *

June 9, 2000

ATTACKING HATE CRIMES

It has been a source of shame that year after year New York State has failed to enact a meaningful hate-crime law even as violence against gays and minority groups has become more common. More than 40 other states have approved some form of hate-crime legislation.

This week the State Senate finally approved a bill that will increase punishments for those convicted of crimes motivated by hatred. These lawmakers are sending an important message that such crimes harm entire communities as well as individual victims, and therefore deserve greater punishment. The Senate bill would increase sentences for crimes in which the victims are singled out because of their race, gender, religion, national origin, age, disability or sexual orientation.

For more than a decade the Republican Senate has blocked such legislation. Gov. George Pataki has been supportive of tougher penalties for bias-related crimes and has offered his own program in recent years. But Senate Republicans have consistently refused to include sexual orientation in any bill, even though crimes against gays are a fast-growing segment of bias crimes. This year Joseph Bruno, the Senate majority leader, perhaps sensitive to election-year pressures, allowed the governor's bill to be put to a floor vote. The bill passed by a vote of 48 to 12.

The Assembly, which has approved hate-crime legislation for the past 11 years, passed a similar bill in February. Though the two bills are different in procedure, they both significantly increase criminal penalties. There should be little difficulty in reaching a compromise for the governor to sign. It is time New York took a strong step against violence directed toward specific groups.

* * *

THE RELIGIOUS RIGHT

October 4, 1981

FLORIDA CURB ON HOMOSEXUALS SURVIVES A TEST

Special to the New York Times

TALLAHASSEE, Fla., Oct. 3—State Representative Tom Bush was not surprised that a Florida law barring state aid to any university that gives funds, meeting space or recognition to any group advocating "sexual relations between persons not married to each other" survived its first judicial test, in a state circuit court last week.

"It was a very carefully drafted and handled piece of legislation," said the 33-year-old Republican legislator from Fort Lauderdale, who sponsored the measure with State Senator Alan Trask of Winterhaven. "Contrary to what the gays might say, we are not a couple of Bible-thumping idiots who parked our brains outside of the Legislature before enacting this."

The law drafted by Representative Bush and Senator Trask, a 47-year-old Democrat who says he is a born-again Christian, was passed in May as an amendment to the state budget. It has again divided the state on the issue of civil rights for homosexuals, reminiscent of when Anita Bryant, the singer, led efforts to kill a 1977 Dade County ordinance guaranteeing homosexuals equal rights in jobs, housing and public accommodation.

The state education commissioner, Ralph Turlington, challenged the amendment in court, asserting it violated a state constitutional ban on the inclusion of substantive non-fiscal legislation in the budget. He has appealed the circuit court ruling, and the state Court of Appeals for the First District has asked the Florida Supreme Court to take the case under advisement.

No state university has had its funds cut as a result of the law, but homosexual rights groups say the amendment has had a chilling effect, and at least one group has also filed suit. In addition, there have been student protests on some campuses.

Measure Began as Separate Bill

The measure began as a separate bill that its authors acknowledge was designed to force homosexual rights groups off university campuses. The broader language involving unmarried people was added to improve the legislation's chances at surviving the inevitable court challenges, since a 100-year-old Florida law already prohibits what it defines as fornication.

The bill was dying in a Senate committee last spring when Mr. Trask, who had lost a fight to keep a homosexual rights group out of a community college in his district, found a way to circumvent the Legislature's committee system.

In a heated budget debate on the Senate floor in May, Mr. Trask brandished a brochure of alternative courses sponsored by students at Florida State University listing such offerings as "Future Sex" and "Lesbian and Gay Rap Sessions."

Condemning such activities as "antifamily," Senator Trask dared his colleagues, as television cameras rolled, to vote against the measure, which he then proposed as an amendment to the state's $9.3 billion budget.

Few senators opposed the amendment, although many later said they resented being put into a position of either voting for the measure or appearing to condone illicit sex.

Representative Bush later used the same tactic in the Florida House, saying: "If homosexuals want to be homosexuals in their own homes, fine. But I don't want my taxes spent to support them."

'Fear' a Reason for Votes

"Everybody was afraid to vote against it, particularly with the Moral Majority looking at those kinds of votes," said Ken Megill, president of the United Faculty of Florida, referring to the fundamentalist group headed by the Rev. Jerry Falwell. The faculty union called the Bush-Trask amendment an insult to academic freedom.

Gov. Bob Graham, although indicating he opposed the amendment, declined to veto the bill, saying that he would have had to kill the whole budget to do so.

After Mr. Turlington filed suit, two other Cabinet members, Secretary of State George Firestone and Gerald Lewis, state comptroller, in pretrial hearings challenged Mr. Turlington's legal right to spend taxpayer's money to sue the Legislature.

* * *

November 19, 1981

'MAJORITY' VS. GAYS

By LARRY BUSH

WASHINGTON—Even a quick look at events in Washington and around the country shows that the Christian right's attack on gay civil rights is taking on new life and intensity. The outcome is uncertain, but two things are clear: The Moral Majority will stop at nothing to make scapegoats of gay people, and the gay community is becoming more united as a result. In this climate, nothing less than extending civil rights laws to cover gays will end the political and moral outrages coming into view.

The clearest signal of the Moral Majority's intentions came Oct. 1 when it persuaded the House of Representatives to overturn a revised sex-assault bill recently passed by the District of Columbia city council that decriminalized sodomy between consenting adults in private. The measure, which had been requested by Congress and was similar to measures already in effect in at least 25 states, drew support from a coalition that included the National Conservative Political Action Committee and Washington's "Mother of the Year." There was no reason to believe that Congress would intervene to block the act during the pro forma 30-day waiting period before it became law.

The Congressional veto was prompted by the Rev. Jerry Falwell's claims that gay men and lesbians are exerting too much influence in local Washington politics. Unable to counter their political weight in a city where the Moral Majority has no strength, Mr. Falwell wanted Congress to rule that their private lives are criminal. What he asked for and got from his supporters in the House was a veto that virtually excommunicates gays from the body politic in Washington.

Nor is that the only sign of increasing hostility toward gays. Attorney General William French Smith recently took a public swipe at "so-called fundamental rights," including the "right to sexual privacy"—and now President Reagan's Justice Department will be expected to define the limits of such rights.

The White House has also confirmed that it is considering backing even more extreme legislation proposed by the Moral Majority. The "Family Protection Act" now pending in Congress would, among other things, deny all Federal funds to any person or group that even "suggests" that homosexuality is an acceptable "life style" and effectively deny matching Federal funds to any candidate for public office who supports gay civil rights.

While most Americans are unaware of this assault on civil liberties, lesbians and gay men are increasingly concerned—and are organizing. That is their only protection against the hostility gaining strength throughout the country. In January, Austin, Tex., will consider a referendum that sanctions discrimination against gays by landlords and real estate agents; gays in cities everywhere feel that the police are turning a blind eye to street assaults on people taken to be homosexuals. Those assaults now include rapes of gay men as well as lesbians who are kidnapped as they leave local bars, knife slayings on the street, and even shooting deaths of unarmed gay men by police officers in Houston and Los Angeles. Many gays believe that this violence is linked to the rise in anti-gay political rhetoric. Both the street assaults and the political attack will be at issue in New York City today and tomorrow; tonight, gay men and lesbians will gather on the first anniversary of the death of two men shot by a machine gun through a window of the West Village's Ramrod Bar. Tomorrow, the City Council is to hold hearings on a bill to forbid discrimination based on sexual orientation.

The increasing prejudice and violence is forcing gays to accept that their private lives are a political issue. They are caught in the bind noted recently by Mayor-elect Andrew Young, as he acknowledged the new political power of Atlanta's gay community: "The objective is to get rid of the intrusion of the state and society. The irony is that in order to do that you've got to make it a public issue."

Gays are also gaining political power in other cities, for example in Houston where they won a commitment from the newly elected mayor to fire the police chief, and in Wisconsin where the Assembly recently passed a bill forbidding discrimination against them. The Wisconsin measure, which is expected to be approved and made law by the state Senate early next year, is supported not only by the gay community but also by the state's religious leaders, including the Roman Catholic Archbishop of Milwaukee.

Such cooperation acknowledges that what is at stake is not only protecting gays from abuse but reafffirming that prejudice is unacceptable. The question is not whether gays are winning and Jerry Falwell is losing. But if the anti-gay campaign is rejected, the victory will be for the principle that a person's sexuality is private, and that it cannot be abused and exploited by those who would use it as a ready source for fund-raising, hate campaigns, cheap votes, and political posturing.

Larry Bush writes about national issues for The Advocate and The New York Native, both biweekly papers.

* * *

September 26, 1985

FALWELL ORDERED TO PAY THE $5,000 HE OFFERED

SACRAMENTO, Calif., Sept. 25—The Rev. Jerry Falwell was ordered by a judge Tuesday to honor a $5,000 offer to a homosexual who proved that Mr. Falwell had attacked his church.

Mr. Falwell, head of Moral Majority, had denied making an attack on the homosexual-oriented Universal Fellowship of the Metropolitan Community Church in a sermon in 1984.

He offered Jerry Sloan, a former pastor, $5,000 to produce a tape recording.

Mr. Sloan presented the tape "almost immediately," binding Mr. Falwell to "his unilateral contract," Judge Michael Ullman of Municipal Court ruled. Mr. Sloan filed suit last year to collect.

The tape was of a sermon Mr. Falwell delivered in an Old Time Gospel Hour broadcast on two Sacramento stations in March 1984. In July 1984, Mr. Falwell, on a television show, denied the attack and made the offer.

The judge said Mr. Falwell referred to the homosexual church as "brute beasts, part of a vile and satanic system." Mr. Falwell was ordered to pay court costs and the $5,000, with interest. His lawyer could not be reached.

Mr. Sloan said he and Mr. Falwell were schoolmates at Baptist Bible College in Springfield, Mo.

* * *

August 17, 1992

HOMOPHOBIC? RE-READ YOUR BIBLE

By PETER J. GOMES

CAMBRIDGE, Mass.—Opposition to gays' civil rights has become one of the most visible symbols of American civic conflict this year, and religion has become the weapon of choice. The army of the discontented, eager for clear villains and simple solutions and ready for a crusade in which political self-interest and social anxiety can be cloaked in morality, has found hatred of homosexuality to be the last respectable prejudice of the century.

Ballot initiatives in Oregon and Maine would deny homosexuals the protection of civil rights laws. The Pentagon has steadfastly refused to allow gays into the armed forces. Vice President Dan Quayle is crusading for "traditional family values." And Pat Buchanan, who is scheduled to speak at the Republican National Convention this evening, regards homosexuality as a litmus test of moral purity.

Nothing has illuminated this crusade more effectively than a work of fiction, "The Drowning of Stephan Jones," by Bette Greene. Preparing for her novel, Ms. Greene interviewed more than 400 young men incarcerated for gay-bashing, and scrutinized their case studies. In an interview published in The Boston Globe this spring, she said she found that the gay-bashers generally saw nothing wrong in what they did, and, more often than not, said their religious leaders and traditions sanctioned their behavior. One convicted teen-age gay-basher told her that the pastor of his church had said, "Homosexuals represent the devil, Satan," and that the Rev. Jerry Falwell had echoed that charge.

Christians opposed to political and social equality for homosexuals nearly always appeal to the moral injunctions of the Bible, claiming that Scripture is very clear on the matter and citing verses that support their opinion. They accuse others of perverting and distorting texts contrary to their "clear" meaning. They do not, however, necessarily see quite as clear a meaning in biblical passages on economic conduct, the burdens of wealth and the sin of greed.

Nine biblical citations are customarily invoked as relating to homosexuality. Four (Deuteronomy 23:17, I Kings 14:24, I Kings 22:46 and II Kings 23:7) simply forbid prostitution, by men and women.

Two others (Leviticus 18:19-23 and Leviticus 20:10-16) are part of what biblical scholars call the Holiness Code. The code explicitly bans homosexual acts. But it also prohibits eating raw meat, planting two different kinds of seed in the same field and wearing garments with two different kinds of yarn. Tattoos, adultery and sexual intercourse during a woman's menstrual period are similarly outlawed.

There is no mention of homosexuality in the four Gospels of the New Testament. The moral teachings of Jesus are not concerned with the subject.

Three references from St. Paul are frequently cited (Romans 1:26-2:1, I Corinthians 6:9-11 and I Timothy 1:10). But St. Paul was concerned with homosexuality only because in Greco-Roman culture it represented a secular sensuality that was contrary to his Jewish-Christian spiritual idealism. He was against lust and sensuality in anyone, including heterosexuals. To say that homosexuality is bad because homosexuals are tempted to do morally doubtful things is to say that heterosexuality is bad because heterosexuals are likewise tempted. For St. Paul, anyone who puts his or her interest ahead of God's is condemned, a verdict that falls equally upon everyone.

And lest we forget Sodom and Gomorrah, recall that the story is not about sexual perversion and homosexual practice. It is about inhospitality, according to Luke 10:10-13, and failure to care for the poor, according to Ezekiel 16:49-50: "Behold, this was the iniquity of thy sister Sodom, pride, fullness of bread, and abundance of idleness was in her and in her daughters, neither did she strengthen the hand of the poor and needy." To suggest that Sodom and Gomorrah is about homosexual sex is an analysis of about as much worth as suggesting that the story of Jonah and the whale is a treatise on fishing.

Part of the problem is a question of interpretation. Fundamentalists and literalists, the storm troopers of the religious right, are terrified that Scripture, "wrongly interpreted," may separate them from their values. That fear stems from their own recognition that their "values" are not derived from Scripture, as they publicly claim.

Indeed, it is through the lens of their own prejudices and personal values that they "read" Scripture and cloak their own views in its authority. We all interpret Scripture: Make no mistake. And no one truly is a literalist, despite the pious temptation. The questions are, By what principle of interpretation do we proceed, and by what means do we reconcile "what it meant then" to "what it means now?"

These matters are far too important to be left to scholars and seminarians alone. Our ability to judge ourselves and others rests on our ability to interpret Scripture intelligently. The right use of the Bible, an exercise as old as the church itself, means that we confront our prejudices rather than merely confirm them.

For Christians, the principle by which Scripture is read is nothing less than an appreciation of the work and will of God as revealed in that of Jesus. To recover a liberating and inclusive Christ is to be freed from the semantic bondage that makes us curators of a dead culture rather than creatures of a new creation.

Religious fundamentalism is dangerous because it cannot accept ambiguity and diversity and is therefore inherently intolerant. Such intolerance, in the name of virtue, is ruthless and uses political power to destroy what it cannot convert.

It is dangerous, especially in America, because it is anti-democratic and is suspicious of "the other," in whatever form that "other" might appear. To maintain itself, fundamentalism must always define "the other" as deviant.

But the chief reason that fundamentalism is dangerous is that, at the hands of the Rev. Pat Robertson, the Rev. Jerry Falwell and hundreds of lesser-known but equally worrisome clerics, preachers and pundits, it uses Scripture and the Christian practice to encourage ordinarily good people to act upon their fears rather than their virtues.

Fortunately, those who speak for the religious right do not speak for all American Christians, and the Bible is not theirs alone to interpret. The same Bible that the advocates of slavery used to protect their wicked self-interests is the Bible that inspired slaves to revolt and their liberators to action.

The same Bible that the predecessors of Mr. Falwell and Mr. Robertson used to keep white churches white is the source of the inspiration of the Rev. Martin Luther King Jr. and the social reformation of the 1960's.

The same Bible that anti-feminists use to keep women silent in the churches is the Bible that preaches liberation to captives and says that in Christ there is neither male nor female, slave nor free.

And the same Bible that on the basis of an archaic social code of ancient Israel and a tortured reading of Paul is used to condemn all homosexuals and homosexual behavior includes metaphors of redemption, renewal, inclusion and love—principles that invite homosexuals to accept their freedom and responsibility in Christ and demands that their fellow Christians accept them as well.

The political piety of the fundamentalist religious right must not be exercised at the expense of our precious freedoms. And in this summer of our discontent, one of the most precious freedoms for which we must all fight is freedom from this last prejudice.

Peter J. Gomes, an American Baptist minister, is professor of Christian morals at Harvard.

* * *

November 12, 1995

GAY ADVERTISING CAMPAIGN ON TV DRAWS WRATH OF CONSERVATIVES

By DAVID W. DUNLAP

If a new television campaign by Parents, Families and Friends of Lesbians and Gays had only its dramatic scenes— a teen-age girl contemplating suicide with a handgun and a young man being beaten by a gang as the attackers shout slurs—it would be controversial enough.

But because these scenes are interspersed with actual clips of the Rev. Pat Robertson and other conservatives deploring homosexuality, the campaign has drawn the wrath of Mr. Robertson's Christian Broadcasting Network, which is threatening legal action against stations that broadcast the two 30-second advertisements.

The campaign, which began on Wednesday, is intended to make the point that anti-gay rhetoric bears some relation to assaults against homosexuals and to suicides among lesbian and gay youth.

"We wanted to say, 'Wake up and join us in opposing hate speech,'" said Mitzi Henderson of Menlo Park, Calif., the president of the board of the nationwide parents' group, which is known as P-Flag.

But on the day the campaign began, the associate general counsel of the Christian Broadcasting Network, Bruce D. Hausknecht, wrote an open letter addressed to "all General Managers" in which he declared:

"The spots contain defamatory material and cast Pat Robertson and CBN in a false light by implying that Pat advocates/ promotes heinous crimes against gays or directly caused the suicide of one or more homosexual persons. This is outrageously false and severely damaging to the reputation of Dr. Robertson and this ministry."

Mr. Hausknecht warned that if the advertisements were televised, the Christian Broadcasting Network would "immediately seek judicial redress against your station," including injunctions and monetary damages.

As a result, P-Flag officials said, the campaign has been rejected by eight stations in Houston and Atlanta, and by the Cable News Network. Two stations and two cable companies in Tulsa and Washington have accepted the advertisement that shows a beating. No station or cable company has accepted the suicide scene.

At CNN, the vice president for public relations, Steve Haworth, said the advertisement had been tentatively accepted for "Larry King Live" until it was reviewed by a senior corporate lawyer, whom Mr. Haworth did not identify.

"He maintained that the message was overly ambiguous," Mr. Haworth said, "and did not meet our standards for advocacy advertising." Local cable companies were at liberty to run the advertisement, Mr. Haworth added, so CNN viewers in some cities may see it.

The executive director of P-Flag in Washington, Sandra Gillis, said the group had chosen Tulsa, Atlanta and Houston "because they're heartland America."

One advertisement intersperses scenes of a beating with grainy, televised images of Mr. Robertson and the Rev. Jerry Falwell. The evangelists' voices are also heard over the scenes of violence.

"Homosexuality is an abomination," Mr. Roberston says. "The practices of these people is appalling. . . . Many of those people involved with Adolf Hitler were Satanists; many of them were homosexuals. The two things seem to go together. . . . It is a pathology, it is a sickness."

And Mr. Falwell says, "God hates homosexuality."

Appearing at the end of the advertisement is Nancy Rodriquez of Warner Robbins, Ga., whose 27-year-old son, Paul Broussard, was beaten to death in Houston four years ago. "The F.B.I. said it was a gay bashing," she says.

Mr. Haworth, of CNN, said the problem was that the message could be interpreted either as "words drive thugs to commit hate crimes against gays" or "words create an atmosphere in which others, due to no complicity by the speakers of the words, commit crimes."

In the other advertisement, a young girl is seen rifling desperately through drawers, a wardrobe and a chest, accompanied by the words and images of Mr. Robertson, Mr. Falwell and Senator Jesse Helms, Republican of North Carolina. She finds the gun she is looking for, and as the advertisement ends, is seen holding it and weeping. An announcer says, "It is estimated that 30 percent of teen-age suicide victims are gay or lesbian."

Further complicating the P-Flag campaign, Ms. Rodriquez said on Friday that she had been dismissed from her full-time job at Mike Houston Auto Care in Warner Robbins, which she said was because of her public involvement with the campaign.

* * *

November 29, 1995

DISNEY'S HEALTH POLICY FOR GAY EMPLOYEES ANGERS RELIGIOUS RIGHT IN FLORIDA

By MIREYA NAVARRO

MIAMI, Nov. 28—Florida has become a battleground for the conservative Christian assault on the Walt Disney Company, whose recent decision to extend health benefits to the live-in partners of gay employees has fueled complaints that it can no longer be trusted to provide wholesome entertainment.

In mid-November the Florida Baptist Convention passed a resolution at its annual meeting stating that "Disney's moral leadership has been eroded." It asked its one million members to "seriously and prayerfully reconsider their continued purchase and support of Disney products," and it plans to seek adoption of a similar measure at the annual meeting of the Southern Baptist Convention in June.

Now David Caton, Florida director of the American Family Association, says he is organizing a boycott of Disney products and theme parks through radio, direct mail campaigns to Christian churches and the group's publications, which reach 35,000 members in Florida and half a million nationwide.

Mr. Caton, whose group has been a major force in efforts to repeal ordinances around the country guaranteeing civil rights to gay people, accused the company of losing its "moral compass" as it grew and allowing itself "to be a vehicle to influence American society regarding homosexuality being mainstream or normal."

The Rev. Tim Benson, pastor of the West Kendall Baptist Church here and vice president of the Florida Baptist Convention, said today: "We're disheartened. Our main impetus behind this is to encourage Disney to take a good look at who they are and what they represent to America."

Mr. Benson's group, which stopped short of calling for a formal boycott, is an association of more than 2,000 churches in Florida.

The new criticism of the internationally known bastion of family entertainment was triggered by Disney's announcement last month that it would extend health coverage to the live-in partners of gay employees, a move Mr. Benson called "just another step in the direction of making the traditional family meaningless." Disney officials say the action, which also prompted a reprobative letter to the company from several Florida state legislators, brought health benefits in line with a corporate policy against discrimination.

But critics say the action was the last straw after a series of other objectionable practices by Disney, including allowing an annual "gay day" celebration at Disney World in Orlando that draws thousands of homosexuals and using promotional tie-ins between the theme park and cruise ships that offer alcohol and gambling.

The religious conservatives also have complained of subliminal sexual messages in animated movies like "The Lion King" and found fault with books, movies and television programming produced by Disney subsidiaries like Miramax, which this year distributed the film "Priest," about a gay Roman Catholic priest.

With its scheduled acquisition of Capital Cities/ABC in January, they say, Disney would also become entangled with "N.Y.P.D. Blue," a television program that has been controversial for its sexually explicit scenes.

Although not expected to make a dent in profits, the protests are grating for a company that is identified around the world with children. Walt Disney World receives 30 million visitors a year out of the 34 million people who visit Orlando.

John Dryer, a Disney spokesman, would not address the criticism point by point but said that the company's theme parks did not discriminate against groups of people and that "we regret that people are offended by a decision to provide health care to our employees."

Mr. Dryer also said that as an entertainment company Disney produces some material for mature audiences, but that such material is not labeled or marketed with the Disney name, which continues to be used for family oriented products.

Richard Jennings, executive director of Hollywood Supports, a Los Angeles group that works with the entertainment industry on AIDS and gay-bias issues, said health benefits for domestic partners were "really a matter of equal pay for equal work" and were already offered by other entertainment giants like Universal and Paramount Pictures. But he said the protests from conservatives were expected.

"The homophobic elements of the radical right seem to be emboldened by their support in government," he said. "They're moving even harder now."

But critics say they are only reacting to Disney's deviation from its wholesome core as it grows.

Financial analysts said the boycott efforts were unlikely to have much effect, citing Disney's $12.1 billion in revenue in 1995, a figure that is expected to jump to nearly $20 billion after the acquisition of Capital Cities/ABC is completed.

"It's a waste of their time," said Harold Vogel of Cowen & Company, an investment firm in New York. "Disney has a high-quality reputation for everything they do. Consumers around the world trust them."

* * *

October 14, 1998

THE ROAD TO LARAMIE

By FRANK RICH

On the same day Americans learned last week that Matthew Shepard, a 5-foot-2, 105-pound gay college student, had been tortured, strung up like an animal and left to die on a fence outside Laramie, Wyo., the Family Research Council was co-hosting a press conference in Washington. It was the latest salvo in a six-month campaign by the religious right, with the tacit, even explicit, approval of Republican leaders, to demonize gay people for political gain in this election year.

This particular press conference was to announce a new barrage of ads—a TV follow-up to a summer print campaign—in which alleged former homosexuals who have "changed" implore others to do likewise "through the power of Jesus Christ." The commercials, gooey in style, end with a slogan: "It's not about hate . . . It's about hope."

But it's really about stirring up the fear that produces hate. If these ads were truly aimed at gay people, they wouldn't be broadcast at extravagant cost to the wide general audience reached by TV, and they wouldn't be trumpeted in Washington, insuring free national exposure, three weeks before Election Day. The ads themselves, despite the sugar-coating of "hope," ooze malice. In one of them, homosexuality is linked to drug addiction and certain death by AIDS; all of them implicitly posit that homosexuality is itself a disease in need of a cure.

Matthew Shepard has now been "cured," that's for sure. As his uncle, R. W. Eaton, told The Denver Post, the 21-year-old Matt, who aspired to a career in diplomacy and human rights, was "a small person with a big heart, mind and soul that someone tried to beat out of him." Of his nephew's shattered body Mr. Eaton said, "It's like something you might see in war." And a war it is. Go to the Family Research Council's Web site

and you will find a proud description of its readiness to "wage the war against the homosexual agenda and fight to maintain the traditional meaning of 'family.'"

The head of the Family Research Council is Gary Bauer, a G.O.P. power broker and putative Presidential candidate, who disingenuously goes on talk shows to say that his organization hates no one and deplores violence. But if you wage a well-financed media air war in which people with an innate difference in sexual orientation are ceaselessly branded as sinful and diseased and un-American seekers of "special rights," ground war will follow. It's a story as old as history. Once any group is successfully scapegoated as a subhuman threat to "normal" values by a propaganda machine, emboldened thugs take over.

Two weeks after James Byrd was savagely dragged to his death from a pickup truck in Texas in June, I wrote a column about an ugly incident outside the G.O.P. state convention in Fort Worth, where a mob threatened a group of gay Log Cabin Republicans who were protesting discriminatory treatment by their own party. The gay-bashers had been directly preceded by steady saber-rattling from Republican politicians: Senator James Inhofe of Oklahoma had likened James Hormel, a gay nominee to an ambassadorship, to David Duke; Pat Robertson had wondered on TV if God might wreak havoc on Disney World for its "Gay Days"; the Texas G.O.P. spokesman had likened Log Cabin to the Ku Klux Klan.

Just two days after this near-brush with violence in Fort Worth, Trent Lott was on TV seconding the religious right's condemnation of gay people as sinful and sick. A frightened gay Texas Republican who had been at the convention melee asked when I interviewed him then: "Do you have to have someone hurt and beat up and dragged from a truck to stop this?"

Months later not even the murder in Laramie has moved Senator Lott to apologize for his words, and still no major G.O.P. leader dares take on its "religious" wing and its crusade against people like Matthew Shepard.

In one of the new ads in that supposedly hate-free crusade, an ostensibly loving mother condemns her son for the "bad choice" of being gay. Is it that mother who speaks for American values, or is it Matthew's? "Go home, give your kids a hug," Judy Shepard said in a message read by a tearful hospital spokesman who announced her child's death early Monday morning, "and don't let a day go by without telling them you love them."

* * *

October 23, 1999

FALWELL FINDS AN ACCORD WITH GAY RIGHTS BACKER

By GUSTAV NIEBUHR

Two months ago the Rev. Jerry Falwell, well known for conservative political and theological views, took the unusual step of agreeing with the Rev. Mel White, a supporter of gay rights, to convene a meeting bringing together 200 of each man's associates.

The goal was simple: a civil exchange of views between two groups that disagree profoundly over gay rights in church and state. The two ministers also promised to avoid harsh language on the issue in the future.

The meeting is to take place today at Mr. Falwell's Thomas Road Baptist Church in Lynchburg, Va. It has generated controversy for weeks, with plans for protests by some gay rights supporters, who say nothing can be gained from meeting with Mr. Falwell, and by some gay rights opponents.

In a telephone interview, Mr. Falwell said he thought the gathering significant for its occurring at all, for the fact that conservative evangelicals who believe homosexual activity a grave sin would break bread with gay men, lesbians and their supporters.

"To my knowledge, it's never happened before," he said, adding that the occasion was so historic it would be "remembered in the same way the formation of Moral Majority is remembered." That was Mr. Falwell's political organization, founded in 1979, a high-profile effort to persuade religious conservatives to take part in politics.

In the 1980's, Mr. Falwell wrote an autobiography, using a ghost writer recommended by his publisher. The writer was Mr. White, a former seminary professor and, at the time, a married man. Six years ago Mr. White declared that he is gay and said he had come to terms with that after a long struggle.

Since then, he has met with Mr. Falwell twice, most recently in August, when he complained that language about homosexuals in fund-raising letters from Mr. Falwell's organizations was so harsh that it could provoke antigay violence. Mr. Falwell, in turn, said he had been a target of aggressive, threatening language, some of it from gay groups.

The 90-minute meeting today, to begin at 4 P.M., will be closed to the press but will be followed by a news conference. Mr. Falwell said he would affirm at the meeting that neither he nor his associates would ever change their view that the Bible makes homosexual activity wrong, or ever support legal recognition of same-sex unions.

But although he said he did not believe that language from his ministry had contributed to violence against homosexuals, he acknowledged Mr. White's criticism that the language had sometimes been strident.

"We plead guilty to that, and we will try to do better," he said, "and I will use what influence I have across the evangelical landscape" to encourage others to do likewise.

"Most Christians believe the gay life style is wrong," Mr. Falwell said. But "we've got to, in the next century, make the world believe we love the sinner more than we hate the sin."

Mr. White, ordained but not a church pastor, is chairman of Soulforce, a group devoted to nonviolent action to advance gay rights. In an interview, he said Mr. Falwell would "set the pace" today by speaking first.

"And he's going to say we're sinners," Mr. White said. "And that's what we disagree on. But what we agree on is this conversation has gotten out of hand."

Mr. White said he would respond by maintaining that his sexuality was a gift from God. And others in his group will also speak: parents and friends of homosexuals, gay men and lesbians themselves, a few of them graduates of Liberty University, where Mr. Falwell is chancellor.

"They all loved Liberty," Mr. White said, "and they're going to say, 'Jerry, you gave us a great education.'"

Both men said they hoped protests would not overshadow the meeting.

"My prayer," Mr. Falwell said, "is the good thing that's happening inside the building will not be lost outside on the sidewalks."

Paper on Antigay Violence

While the Falwell-White meeting has been in the works, another initiative, to rally religious voices against antigay violence, has been undertaken by Bishop Steven Charleston, president and dean of Episcopal Divinity School in Cambridge, Mass. On Oct. 1, Bishop Charleston wrote the Cambridge Accord, a statement to circulate among bishops of Anglican churches around the world.

The document has three points: that no gay person "should ever be deprived of liberty, personal property or civil rights because of his or her sexual orientation," that an appeal to Christian faith can never be used to justify such discrimination, or violence, and that everyone is equal in God's sight and deserves respect.

As of Wednesday, nearly 80 bishops had signed the statement, the best-known of them the retired Archbishop of Cape Town, Desmond Tutu.

The document is posted on the Web site of the divinity school, www.episdivschool.org.

PART VIII

LAW, POLITICS AND PUBLIC POLICY

LAW AND LAW ENFORCEMENT

August 16, 1960

POST OFFICE WINS IN OBSCENITY CASE

WASHINGTON, Aug. 15 (UPI)—Federal Judge George L. Hart Jr. ruled today that the Post Office might bar from the mails magazines designed primarily to appeal to male homosexuals.

He said in effect that the department might ban any material as obscene if it aroused the "prurient" interest of a single segment of society.

The Supreme Court has ruled that the effect of the material on the average person should be the yardstick for determining obscenity.

Judge Hart upheld the Post Office's ruling against the magazines "Manual," "Trim" and "The Grecian Guild Pictorial," all published by Herman L. Womack of Washington.

Defense Attorney Stanley M. Dietz said he would appeal. He said homosexuals were entitled to the rights of other citizens. If a normal male can buy magazines with photos of nude women, he asked, "Isn't a homosexual entitled to get magazines with pictures of semi-nude men if that's what interests him."

* * *

December 1, 1960

CAFE DRIVE TURNS TO HOMOSEXUALS

*Police Vow a Close Look at Cabaret Help in 'Village'
for License Violations*

By IRA HENRY FREEMAN

An intensified investigation of Greenwich Village cabarets that employ homosexuals was promised yesterday by Deputy Police Commissioner Edward J. McCabe.

In another, entirely separate, phase of the widespread investigation of the city's night clubs and cafes, the police were balked again yesterday in their efforts to interrogate Sherman Billingsley, who established the Stork Club.

Commissioner McCabe said the regulations gave the police discretionary right to deny police identity cards to ex-convicts, narcotic addicts, racket suspects and homosexuals. Since these cards are required by law of all cabaret owners and employes who come in contact with the public, denial of a card means exclusion from employment.

Careful Scrutiny Promised

Commissioner McCabe was then asked about some Village night spots that employed apparent homosexuals as entertainers and waiters. The Commissioner said these places would be investigated more closely now.

He said that in the last three months a "good number" of night-club workers previously arrested in other states for grand larceny, armed robbery, rape and narcotics and sex offenses had been discovered. They got police identity cards here, he said, by concealing their police records, but the Federal Bureau of Investigation fingerprint file in Washington turned them up.

Contrary to a report by opponents of the regulations, Commissioner McCabe said, fingerprints of cabaret workers are taken only once and are now checked against the master file in Washington.

When the Stork Club case was called before Commissioner McCabe yesterday morning, Mr. Billingsley was not present for questioning. The Commissioner demanded of Roy M. Cohn, counsel for the nightclub, why Mr. Billingsley was absent after promises on Monday to appear yesterday.

"Because the Police Department obviously regards Mr. Billingsley as a defendant," Mr. Cohn replied. "But we do not."

Stork Witness Heard

Commissioner McCabe contradicted this, saying he wanted to determine Mr. Billingsley's status in the Stork Club and, therefore, whether he should be required to carry a police identity card.

Later John J. Farrell, who said he was president of the nightclub, testified that Mr. Billingsley had no status in the Stork Club, although his name has been synonymous with it for twenty-five years.

Mr. Farrell testified that the nightclub was owned by Mr. Billingsley's wife Hazel and some other relatives. Mr. Billingsley was manager until four years ago, when he relinquished that job and his police identity card, according to Mr. Farrell.

Under questioning by Sgt. Frank Nolan, who is presenting the department's case, Mr. Farrell said Mr. Billingsley, as co-owner of Cigone, Inc., a perfume company, rented an office in the Stork Club. He "hung around" the club almost nightly, Mr. Farrell conceded, "entertaining customers for his perfume business and friends."

Watching over his wife's interest, Mr. Farrell said, Mr. Billingsley might "call my attention to a curtain that was crooked, or if the service was slow, or there was a dish on the menu he didn't like."

Commissioner McCabe gave Mr. Cohn until 10:30 A. M. today to decide whether Mr. Billingsley would testify voluntarily or be subpoenaed. Mr. Cohn said he would take court action to nullify any subpoena.

While Mr. Farrell was in the police license division at 56 Worth Street for the hearing, he was served with a subpoena to appear "forthwith" before Louis I. Kaplan, city Commissioner of Investigation, with all records. Mr. Kaplan is inquiring into charges that the police extorted bribes from nightclub entertainers.

By telephone, Mr. Cohn arranged to produce Mr. Farrell before Commissioner Kaplan next Monday.

* * *

August 30, 1964

JURIST PARLEY ASKS EASING OF PENALTIES ON SEXUAL BEHAVIOR

THE HAGUE, Aug. 29 (Reuters)—The ninth International Congress on Penal Law ended six days of sessions here today with a plea for fewer penalties on sexual behavior.

The congress, attended by more than 500 jurists from 54 countries, adopted a resolution declaring that adultry and fornication should not be considered criminal offenses.

It said homosexual behavior between consenting adults should not be prohibited by criminal law.

It said the distribution of birth control information and contraceptive devices should be regarded as an offense only if it violated laws on pornography and obscenity, or interfered with measures to protect young people.

The congress called for possibilities for obtaining legal abortions in countries that prohibit them.

It said criminal law should not prohibit artificial insemination unless performed without the consent of both the woman concerned and her husband.

Family Study Is Urged

The congress recommended the establishment of a comprehensive committee of experts to study the problem of nonsupport of families. It said this problem had assumed wide proportions as a result of greater mobility of labor.

The congress adopted an 1,800-word resolution dealing with the international effects of penal judgments.

It called for international recognition of convictions for traffic offenses. It stressed that foreign criminal proceedings should be conducted in conformity with the fundamental principles of states ruled by law, if judgments were to be recognized by other countries.

It also called for consideration of foreign convictions and penalties served abroad in the case of a new prosecution for the same offense in another state.

The congress recommended that states in which ex-convicts resided should undertake supervision of paroles and probations of foreign jurisdictions.

* * *

January 30, 1965

HEMPSTEAD PLANS PATROL TO COMBAT INFLUX OF DEVIATES

By RONALD MAIORANA
Special to The New York Times

HEMPSTEAD, L. I., Jan. 29—The Town of Hempstead will move next week to create a special force to repel what has been described as an invasion by sexual deviates and narcotics pushers.

Presiding Supervisor Palmer D. Farrington said today that "the public demands and has the right to assurance of strict surveillance of public facilities," including parks and beaches.

"We don't want to take over police duties and responsibilities," Mr. Farrington said. "But we have been invaded by queers and dope pushers who are preying on our youngsters."

Mr. Farrington said the proposed Safety Department would consist of about 70 men and cost the town $300,000 annually. Members of the force will wear blue uniforms, carry nightsticks and work on a 24-hour basis in close cooperation with the Nassau County Police Department, if the plan is approved.

Training by County

Although members of the proposed Safety Department would be trained by the Nassau County Police Department, the Acting County Police Commissioner, Francis B. Looney, said that his department had "no record of any activity by sexual deviates or narcotics pushers or addicts in Hempstead Town parks."

Mr. Farrington, who made the announcement at a news conference in his office at Town Hall, said the nucleus of the safety force had been formed in the last year on an experimental basis.

A public hearing for the adoption of a local law to establish the department will be held Tuesday at the Town Hall.

The Town of Hempstead has a population of more than 800,000 and within the borders of its 132 square miles are 1,650 miles of roadways, including the Southern State Parkway, Jones Beach 10,000 acres of waterways and a number of communities including Valley Stream, Levittown, Malverne and Garden City.

* * *

June 4, 1965

ASSEMBLY PASSES A TOTAL REVISION OF THE PENAL LAW

Homosexual Acts Remain as Crimes Under Amendment—
Adultery Issue Open

By JOHN SIBLEY

Special to The New York Times

ALBANY, June 3—The Assembly voted approval today of a complete revision of the Penal Law, which lawyers agree has become a bewildering morass since its last major overhaul in 1881.

After intricate parliamentary maneuvering, however, the Assembly left uncertain the outcome of the most controversial issues in today's debate: whether adultery and homosexuality should be treated as matters of law or of morality.

As put forward by a special commission that worked four years to redraft the law, neither adultery nor homosexual acts between consenting adults would be treated as crimes.

From both sides of the aisle today there were applause and lavish praise for the commission chairman, Republican Assemblyman Richard J. Bartlett of Glens Falls. Though there was criticism of specific provisions of the proposed new law, virtually every speaker credited the Bartlett Commission with a brilliant job of tightening and clarifying the penal law as well as bringing it into conformity with current judicial and social thinking.

Churchmen's Fears Cited

From the beginning, there was no doubt that the commission's version would be overwhelmingly approved. After its adoption, the House turned to two bills that would retain adultery and homosexuality in the criminal law.

These measures were introduced by Assemblyman Julius Volker, an Erie County Republican who is a member of the Bartlett Commission. Mr. Volker said his bills were "inspired by the entreaties of churchmen who fear we would be appearing to give passive approval to deviant sexual practices."

The Volker amendment to retain homosexual acts as crimes was passed by a vote of 115 to 16.

Then the Assembly voted, 73 to 49, in favor of the bill to retain the crime of adultery. This was a defeat, however, since a majority of the entire Assembly, 76 of the 150 members, is needed to pass a bill.

Mr. Volker was allowed to table the bill, which means he may bring it up for a vote again at any time. It is expected that when more members are present he will be able to get the 3 more votes he needs and that adultery will therefore remain a crime.

Under present law both adultery and acts of homosexuality involving consenting adults are punishable by up to one year in jail. But the penalties have rarely been imposed

The new code would take effect Sept. 1, 1967.

The main bill, as introduced by the commission, had originally passed by a vote of 113 to 17, when Mr. Volker's adultery amendment was defeated, however. Assemblyman Donald J. O'Hara, Niagara Falls Democrat, moved to reconsider the vote on the main bill.

Margin Reduced

On the second vote, the commission bill's victory margin was reduced but still substantial, 106 to 24.

Should Mr. Volker's adultery amendment ultimately prevail, and if the Senate also approves the commission bill and both amendments, Governor Rockefeller will have the choice of putting into effect a new penal law with or without the inclusion of adultery and homosexual acts as crimes.

Mr. Bartlett voted against the Volker amendments today. But during the debate, he had promised that if they succeeded, he would urge the Governor to sign them.

Mr. Bartlett explained that the commission majority felt that sexual behavior was a matter of private morality, not of law, and that it was pointless in any case to continue a law that was virtually never enforced.

Later, outside the Assembly Chamber, the commission chairman voiced disappointment that this controversy had dominated the debate.

"Whatever happens to the Volker bills," Mr. Bartlett said, "there'll be no changes in practice."

Mr. Bartlett takes more pride in some of the other substantive changes in the commission's draft, as well as the "tidying-up" achieved by editing, reclassifying and weeding out dozens of provisions of the present law that are not truly criminal in character but administrative or civil.

One of the substantive changes is the elimination of the present two degrees of murder. The concept of premeditation, the essential ingredient in first degree murder, has become fuzzy and misunderstood, even by lawyers, he said.

Under the new law, murder would be made a single crime, with intent to kill as the essential element.

The draft law also narrows the definition of kidnapping. Under the present statute, for example, a burglar may be guilty of kidnapping if he moves his victim from one room to the next. Or a father may be found guilty of kidnapping his own children from the mother who has been given legal custody.

Under the new law, kidnapping would be limited to the commonly understood situation in which the victim is held for ransom. The other acts would be made lesser offenses, titled "false imprisonment" and "custodial interference."

The commission made two changes involving burglary. It eliminated "breaking" as an element of burglary, noting that the courts have declared "every opening of an unlocked door or window to be a breaking."

Instead, the new law would make unlawful entry and intent to commit a crime as the two essential elements of burglary.

Also, the draft creates a new offense of "criminal trespass" in three degrees, all below the fourth degree of burglary. Since intent to commit a burglary is difficult to prove, defendants have frequently gone free for lack of a lesser offense on the books.

The commission's bill would make the customer of a prostitute, as well as the prostitute herself, liable to prosecution.

On the other hand, the gambling statutes are revised to exclude players from criminal liability. Only the operator or promoter would be guilty of a crime.

The proposed law makes sweeping changes in sentencing procedures. Generally, it would do away with mandatory sentences, on the theory that a judge at the time of sentencing cannot predict when a convict will be ready to return to society. Greater discretion would be given to parole boards.

About one-third of the existing penal law would be transferred to other bodies of law. For instance, the section dealing with cruelty to animals would be incorporated in the agriculture and markets law.

Other sections to be transferred deal with matters such as seizure and destruction of gambling equipment, pornographic material, dangerous weapons, licensing and civil aspects of gambling and prostitution.

Crimes are classified under logical categories rather than in alphabetical order as at present, a system under which related matters are often widely separated.

* * *

April 2, 1966

GARELIK URGES PUBLIC TO REPORT POLICE TRAPPING OF HOMOSEXUALS

By ERIC PACE

Chief Inspector Sanford D. Garelik said yesterday that he hoped the public would report cases in which policemen lure homosexuals into breaking the law and then arrest them.

Chief Garelik's appeal, made in an interview, followed similar remarks that he made Thursday night at a neighborhood meeting held under the auspices of the Judson Memorial Church, on Washington Square South.

The chief appeared there to discuss the police clean-up campaign in Greenwich Village and Times Square. Both areas are gathering points for homosexuals.

The New York Civil Liberties Union has charged that the practice of luring homosexuals into breaking the law, known as entrapment, is widespread. However, a high police officer contended yesterday that "we don't encourage people to commit a crime that they weren't going to commit."

Chief Garelik declined to appraise the extent, if any, of such actions, but said that "I'm very severe in my condemnation of entrapment."

The chief said he hoped the public would report entrapment incidents as they would crimes. A Police Department rule stipulates that "members of the force . . . shall not use practices known as 'entrapment' to obtain evidence."

The question of how policemen should treat homosexuals has become increasingly controversial during recent years as growing tolerance by the general community has made it eas-

The New York Times

Sanford D. Garelik

ier for homosexuals to assert themselves in public. The police crackdown, which is directed at illegal and disorderly behavior in general, prompted the Civil Liberties Union last month to protest that it seemed aimed at infringing on homosexuals' rights.

A spokesman for the group said yesterday that Chief Garelik's appeal "shows a certain naiveté."

"It's alarming to think that the chief inspector doesn't know that a large number of police spend their duty hours dressed in tight pants, sneakers and polo sweaters . . . to bring about solicitations," the spokesman added.

A provision of the State Penal Law makes it an offense if "any person, with intent to provoke a breach of the peace or whereby a breach of the peace may be occasioned . . . frequents or loiters about any public place soliciting men for the purpose of committing a crime against nature or other lewdness."

A spokesman for the Mattachine Society, Inc., of New York, an organization that provides legal and medical aid for homosexuals and information about them, questioned the worth of Chief Garelik's appeal.

"The last thing homosexuals are going to do is complain about something," the society spokesman said. "They'll just sit there like a possum, they're so afraid of their families' finding out or losing their jobs."

The New York society, which reports a membership of 1,000, is an offshoot of the Mattachine Society of San Francisco, which was founded 15 years ago.

In moving against homosexuals, Chief Garelik said, "We are not carrying out a vendetta against social behavior. . . . We are only enforcing the law, and until such time as the law is changed, we have to accept our responsibility."

He said that plainclothes men in general dressed to fit their surroundings and that offenses by homosexuals were of only minor concern to them.

He also asserted that the homosexual problem was a minor problem in Greenwich Village, compared with the total problem of narcotics, crowd control and other matters.

* * *

March 9, 1970

HOMOSEXUALS HOLD PROTEST IN 'VILLAGE' AFTER RAID NETS 167

About 200 radical women and men homosexuals demonstrated in Sheridan Square last night against what they termed the increasing repression of homosexuals in Greenwich Village by the police.

The protesters, members of the Gay Liberation Front and a number of women's liberation organizations, protested the arrest of 167 people in a predawn raid on a bar that the police said was frequented by homosexuals.

One of those arrested was in critical condition at St. Vincent's Hospital after he jumped from a second-story window at the Charles Street station house and was impaled on a iron spike fence below, according to the police.

The demonstrators gathered in Sheridan Square at Seventh Avenue at about 8:30 P.M. and marched to the Charles Street station house.

After a brief march there, they moved on to St. Vincent's Hospital, at Seventh Avenue and 11th Street, to conduct a "death vigil" for the injured man, identified by the police as Diego Vinales, 23 years old, of East Orange, N. J.

The Fire Department's rescue squad was forced to cut out a section of the fence, with Mr. Vinales still impaled on it, and to transport both the fence and the injured man to the hospital. There surgeons asked the firemen to don surgical gowns and assist in the surgery. Five spikes were removed from the injured man's thigh and pelvis.

By late evening the demonstrators had left the hospital and were marching through the West Village area in orderly fashion, according to the police.

The raid, at 5 A.M., took place at The Snake Pit, 213 West 10th Street, which the police said had been operating illegally after hours.

All of those arrested except Mr. Vinales were given summons for disorderly conduct and released. Mr. Vinales was booked for resisting arrest.

* * *

March 26, 1970

KOCH ACCUSES POLICE HERE OF HARASSING HOMOSEXUALS

Representative Edward I. Koch has accused Police Commissioner Howard R. Leary of permitting the Police Department to resume a policy of harassing homosexuals with illegal arrests.

Mr. Koch, a Democrat-Liberal from Manhattan, made the statement in a letter to Commissioner Leary asking him to explain the arrest of 167 men in a Greenwich Village after-hours club on March 8.

Two weeks later, according to David S. Worgan, executive assistant district attorney for Manhattan, virtually all of the charges of disorderly conduct made against the men were dismissed in court because "the police could not make a legal case."

Deputy Inspector Seymore Pine, the police official in charge of enforcing gambling, prostitution and liquor laws in lower Manhattan, said the arrests had been made to curb the after-hours club and not to harass homosexuals.

* * *

January 8, 1971

REPEAL OF LAWS ON SEX IS URGED HERE

By ELEANOR BLAU

City Investigation Commissioner Robert K. Ruskin called yesterday for the repeal of all state criminal laws regulating sexual conduct between consenting adults.

Testifying at 270 Broadway at a hearing on discrimination against homosexuals, Mr. Ruskin, who stressed that he was not speaking as a city official, said the laws do not serve "the public interest or any useful social purpose."

In fact, he said, the laws creates a climate for corruption. Mr. Ruskin reported that his department had investigated many cases in which corrupt law-enforcement officers as well as individuals posing as policemen, had used the threat of arrest and disclosure on these laws for blackmail.

The one-day hearing was conducted by two Democratic Assemblymen, Stephen J. Solarz of Brooklyn and Antonio G. Olivieri of Manhattan, in advance of a legislative proposal on the problem. They said they hoped to submit the proposal to the Legislature in a few weeks.

"Unspoken prejudices and archaic laws currently restrict the rights and lives of homosexuals in this city," they said in a statement.

These laws must be repealed, they declared, but, in addition, they said, laws must be passed to protect the rights of homosexuals.

The Assemblymen said they believed this was the first time such a hearing had been held by state legislators.

Other witnesses included City Councilmen Eldon R. Clingan and Carter Burden, who jointly introduced a bill yesterday to extend the city's Human Rights Law to ban discrimination in housing, public accommodation and employment based on sexual orientation.

Elaborating on charges he made yesterday, Mr. Burden cited cases in which he said the Columbia Broadcasting System and the International Business Machines Corporation had discriminated against homosexuals in their hiring practices.

At C.B.S., he asserted, a man was dismissed from the scheduling department when an investigation of his draft record revealed homosexual tendencies. At I.B.M., Mr. Burden said, a man was asked directly whether he had homosexual tendencies, and was told homosexuality was considered reason for dismissal.

Both corporations yesterday denied any discrimination in hiring practices.

Also addressing the hearing were members of several male and female homosexual organizations, most of whom urged the abolition of laws against sodomy and solicitation. Many reported cases of what they described as police harassment, brutality, entrapment and bribery.

* * *

March 25, 1971

U.S. CITIZENSHIP IS WON BY HOMOSEXUAL

An order to grant United States citizenship to a 24-year-old homosexual from Cuba was issued in Federal District Court here yesterday over the opposition of the Immigration and Naturalization Service.

Judge Walter R. Mansfield ruled that the applicant's private homosexual acts did not bar him from citizenship, although resident aliens have been denied citizenship because of homosexuality.

Immigration authorities said they would have to study the ruling by Judge Mansfield before deciding whether to appeal it or determining what effect it would have on their policies concerning homosexuals.

Judge Mansfield stressed in his 12-page decision that the man had never corrupted the morals of others, preyed on minors or engaged in publicly offensive acts, limiting his homosexuality to consenting adults in private.

"Without condoning the purely private conduct here involved," the judge said, "we accept the principle that the naturalization laws are concerned with public, not private, morality."

The Immigration and Naturalization Service had contended that the petitioner—Manuel Labady, a Manhattan hairdresser—failed to establish that he was "a person of good moral character" because of his homosexuality.

Under the naturalization laws, the required good moral character is specifically precluded by habitual drunkenness, adultery, perjury and crimes that result in imprisonment for 180 days or more during the five years prior to applying for citizenship.

A petition for naturalization can be denied for other reasons, but Judge Mansfield ruled that Mr. Labady met the requirements by leading "a quiet, peaceful, law-abiding life as an immigrant in the United States."

Mr. Labady had informed immigration authorities that he was a homosexual when he entered the United States legally as a permanent resident in 1960 at the age of 14.

Judge Mansfield observed that he lived with his mother, maintained gainful employment and was highly regarded by his employer and associates.

"Under all of the circumstances," the judge said, "setting aside our personal moral views, we cannot say that his conduct has violated public morality or indicated that he will be anything other than a law-abiding and useful citizen

* * *

October 2, 1971

CONNECTICUT EASES HOMOSEXUAL LAW

Special to The New York Times

HARTFORD, Oct. 1—A new Connecticut Penal Code permitting homosexual relations between consenting adults went into effect today.

The code, which was approved by the 1969 session of the General Assembly, repealed several statutes that carried penalties for lascivious carriage and fornication. Penalties for conviction under these statutes were a fine of $100, six months in jail, or both.

The new code eliminates any reference to lascivious carriage or fornication.

To celebrate the new law, homosexuals from throughout Connecticut plan a Gay Liberation Festival here this weekend.

* * *

March 26, 1977

RIGHTS, FRIGHTS AND LIMBO

No, No, Anita!

Not long ago we expressed pleasure that Miami singer Anita Bryant retained her TV job despite an anti-Anita campaign brought on by her opposition to a Dade County ordinance that prohibits discrimination against homosexuals. Now, due largely to Miss Bryant's efforts, the county has scheduled a special June election to reconsider the measure, and we hope the voters will uphold it. Some correspondents interpreted our support for Miss Bryant's right to speak as support for what she has been saying. Far from it. Miss Bryant's arguments—such as her charge that homosexuals are out to recruit converts among children—are absurd as well as benighted, and county officials are to be commended for extending the area of civil rights to an often abused group. It is good that Miss Bryant is keeping her job; it would be better if she lost her campaign.

* * *

March 27, 1977

HOMOSEXUAL LEADERS MEET AT WHITE HOUSE WITH PRESIDENTIAL AIDE TO DISCUSS DISCRIMINATION IN FEDERAL LAW

WASHINGTON, March 26 (UPI)—Leaders of the homosexual rights movement met with a Presidential aide at the White House today to lobby for an end to discrimination against homosexuals in Federal law.

"This is the first time in the history of this country that a President has seen fit to acknowledge the rights and needs of some 28 million Americans," Jean O'Leary of the National Gay Task Force said of the meetings with Margaret Costanza, Mr. Carter's assistant for public liaison.

About two dozen homosexual rights activists from all over the nation participated, asking for the right to serve in the military, for more homosexuals in the State Department, the Federal Bureau of Investigation and the Central Intelligence Agency and tax-free status for their organizations.

In a statement, the group called the White House meeting "a happy milestone on the road to full equality under law for gay women and men."

Marilyn Haft, a Costanza aide, said that she did not know President Carter's personal views on the issue, but added: "The point is they are being discriminated against; the point is not their sexual views."

Mr. Carter has expressed concern for preserving the traditional values of the American family and has urged Federal workers living out of wedlock with a member of the opposite sex to get married. The President was at Camp David, Md., when the meeting took place in the White House Roosevelt Room.

The participants expressed concern about Federal policy barring homosexuals from serving in the Armed Forces and discharging those discovered to be homosexual, including those who won Purple Hearts, with less-than-honorable status and without veterans benefits.

They also asked for changes in Federal prison regulations to allow homosexual prisoners to receive homosexual publications, to have more recreational opportunities and to be free from abuse and assault.

They asked that the President support a bill outlawing discrimination against homosexuals and demanded more Federal grants for homosexual social and research programs, expansion of Federal Communications Commission rules to require broadcast access for the homosexual community, and an end to housing discrimination and to the ban on the granting of United States citizenship to homosexual immigrants.

Miss O'Leary said the group was "highly optimistic" that the meeting would soon lead to complete fulfillment of President Carter's pledge to end all forms of Federal discrimination on the basis of sexual orientation.

*   *   *

May 10, 1977

MIAMI DEBATE OVER RIGHTS OF HOMOSEXUALS DIRECTS WIDE ATTENTION TO A NATIONAL ISSUE

By B. DRUMMOND AYRES JR.
Special to The New York Times

MIAMI, May 9—A dispute over rights for homosexuals, building locally for the last several months, is focusing attention on a national issue.

As far as the Miami area is concerned, the argument will be settled on June 7, when residents vote to repeal or uphold a county ordinance that bars discrimination against homosexuals in employment, housing and public accommodations.

But both sides in the fight have vowed to continue the struggle elsewhere in the country whatever the outcome of the Miami referendum. National committees are being organized and fund drives are under way in "gay" bars and fundamentalist churches from here to San Francisco.

The Miami dispute is not the first of its kind. At least three dozen other communities have debated the issue, with varying results. Other national committees have also existed for some time, including several that are lobbying for Federal legislation and White House support.

But no other homosexual debate has caught the national attention like the Miami dispute. No other debate has involved so many people, resulted in so much spending, stirred so many editors, made so many talk shows or generated so many bumper stickers and emblazoned T-shirts. Why?

Personalities at Issue

The answer lies primarily in personalities and the particular twist of the Miami issue. The main figure in the dispute is Anita Bryant, the Miami television singer known nationwide for her sunny purveying of Florida orange juice and her devoutly patriotic rendering of "The Battle Hymn of the Republic." A fervent Southern Baptist, the 37-year-old mother of four school-age children, heads Save Our Children Inc., the main anti-homosexual group.

"If homosexuality were the normal way, God would have made Adam and Bruce," she says. "This has become a national fight. I've spoken all around the country. We've gotten more than 20,000 letters and taken in about $40,000 from more than 40 states. It won't stop here in Florida. We're setting up to go nationally."

Save Our Children was organized a few months ago after Miami homosexuals persuaded the county commission to pass a homosexual rights ordinance. Miss Bryant's group contends that the ordinance would force schools to hire homosexual teachers and that the teachers would then proselytize and possibly molest children. It warns that similar laws are being considered in other cities around the country and on Capitol Hill.

"Those arguments are all just a lot of homophobia," counters Robert Kunst, a Miami homosexual who helped organize the Miami Victory Campaign, one of several groups trying to preserve the ordinance.

"We've heard from just as many people, taken in just as much money, been on just as many talk shows," he adds. "The truth is that Anita Bryant is the best thing that has ever happened to us. She's really stirred it good, gotten it in the national limelight once and for all with that trash about child molestation. This is a human rights fight and we're prepared to take it all over the country. She knows as well as we do that child molestation is usually heterosexual."

Right or wrong, the Save Our Children argument has proved potent. To force the commission-passed law onto the ballot for a referendum, Miss Bryant's group needed 10,000 petition signatures. It got 60,000, many by approaching parents in local churches.

In Charlotte, N.C., members of the Jesus Is Lord Club, a Bible study group, heard of the petition drive and mailed checks for $10 and $20. An Alabama woman sent $1,000.

"Support is coming in from everywhere," says Mike Thompson, a Miami advertising executive who helped organize Save Our Children. "One day I'm on the phone to Minnesota, talking to legislators there about how to defeat a gay rights bill. The next night I'm on the 'Tomorrow' show in New York. This thing is leap-frogging."

Askew Joins Fight

A few days ago, the anti-homosexual forces received an important boost from Gov. Reubin Askew of Florida, a man who shuns alcohol and tobacco and is sometimes referred to by critics and supporters alike as "Reubin the Good."

"I've never viewed the homosexual lifestyle as something that approached a constitutional right," Governor Askew said at a news conference. "So if I were in Miami. I would find no difficulty in voting to repeal the ordinance. I do not want a known homosexual teaching my child."

The pro-homosexual forces in Miami are split about how to preserve the ordinance. One group, the Coalition for Humanistic Rights of Gays, offered at one point to foot the $300,000 bill for the referendum, apparently fearing that otherwise the vote might not be called. The offer infuriated Robert Kunst and others, who split to form their own lobby, arguing that the county was responsible for referendum costs.

As matters now stand, the county will pick up the tab.

Bob Basker, the executive director of the coalition, says that the June 7 vote will be "a very strong precursor" of what may happen elsewhere in the country. He predicts that defeat would result in a national "witch hunt" against homosexuals.

To help Miami homosexuals head off defeat, a number of leading homosexual activists have visited the city, among them Leonard Matlovich, the Air Force sergeant who was discharged when he disclosed his homosexuality. Homosexuals in New York recently held a fund-raising rally at the Waldorf Astoria Hotel and are planning several other rallies.

In San Francisco, homosexuals have set up a "Miami Support Committee." The operators of several dozen "gay" bars have ordered a "gaycott" of Florida orange juice. Bumper stickers proclaim,"A day without human rights is like a day without sunshine," a twist of Miss Bryant's juice ad that says "A day without orange juice is like a day without sunshine."

Has the "gaycott" had any effect on sales of Florida juice or endangered Miss Bryant's $100,000-a-year television advertising contract with the Florida Department of Citrus?

"Sales are up," says Arthur Darling, a department spokesman. "There's no way of knowing about contracts at this point. Obviously, we'd have been better off if the whole thing had never come up. But as long as she doesn't get involved on our time or with our name, we have no right to deny her First Amendment rights to speak out."

Miss Bryant says that her bookings for entertainment not related to selling citrus are down about 70 percent. "But I have to carry on this fight," she adds.

One of her agents is Richard Shack, husband of Ruth Shack, the county commissioner who proposed the homosexual rights ordinance. He said he and Miss Bryant talk only business, not politics.

With the referendum vote a month away, most surveys give the homosexual forces a slight edge. However, a considerable number of voters remain undecided and the turnout remains an imponderable in a community made up, in good part, of conservative churchgoers and retired liberals from the Northeast.

On neither side does anyone pretend to understand a bumper sticker that reads:

"A Day Without Gays is like a Day Without Anita."

* * *

June 8, 1977

MIAMI VOTES 2 TO 1 TO REPEAL LAW BARRING BIAS AGAINST HOMOSEXUALS

By B. DRUMMOND AYRES JR.
Special to The New York Times

MIAMI, June 7—In a decision almost certain to have national impact, residents of the Miami area voted by a margin of more than 2-to-1 today to repeal a law that protects homosexuals from discrimination in employment, housing and public accommodation.

The vote, a referendum on an ordinance enacted more than four months ago by the Dade County Commission, was the first of its kind in a major United States city. It came at the end of a heated campaign that focused national attention on the long-smoldering question of what legal and social status should be given the 5 to 10 percent of the nation's population that practices homosexuality.

Both the winners and the losers in the campaign vowed to continue their struggles elsewhere in the country.

Anita Bryant, the pop singer and television personality who led the repeal forces, celebrated the victory by dancing a jig at her Miami Beach home. Later, she told newsmen that she was establishing a national committee to fight homosexuality and added:

"All America and all the world will hear what the people have said, and with God's continued help, we will prevail in our fight to repeal similar laws throughout the nation which attempt to legitimize a life style that is both perverse and dangerous."

Robert Kunst, a leading figure in the Miami homosexual community, contended that the vote was "not a disappointment."

"We started from ground zero and got around 100,000 people to support us," he said. "This is just the beginning of the fight."

With the votes of all of Miami's 446 precincts tabulated, the referendum results were 202,319 votes for repeal and 89,562 for retention of the ordinance. Slightly more than 40 percent of eligible voters went to the polls, an unusually high turnout for a referendum.

John W. Campbell, another leading member of Miami's homosexual community, also attempted to view the defeat optimistically. At a "victory dance" at the Fountainebleu Hotel on Miami Beach, as hundreds of homosexuals chanted "We Shall Overcome," he said:

"The campaign has motivated gay people politically, not merely in Florida but all across our nation and even in Europe. We're going national now. We've got more than $50,000 left over, more than any gay group has ever had before.

"For decades," he continued, "homosexuality was 'the love that dare not speak its name.' Now the whole world is talking about our cause. We are everywhere. We are not going to go away. And we are going to win. We didn't get the votes we expected. But we got one heck of a lot."

Ruth Shack, the county commissioner who originally proposed the ordinance, said the vote was "three times worse than I ever expected."

"They came out of the woodwork," she said of the law's opponents. "It was a huge step back nationally. We even lost heavily among Jewish liberals on Miami Beach. My political future? I'll be back to work again tomorrow. Life goes on."

Jean O'Leary, an executive director of the National Gay Task Force, said after the vote: "The defeat for human rights in Dade County is all the evidence anyone could need of the extent and virulence of prejudice against lesbians and gay men in our society, and of the necessity to redouble our efforts to end such prejudice and the discrimination it inspires."

Miami's homosexual community was not particularly large or vocal before homosexual rights erupted as an issue. The community, situated in the Coconut Grove section of the city, just south of the business district, became a national focal point for homosexual politics mainly through the efforts of Miss Bryant.

Miss Bryant became an outspoken opponent of homosexuality early this year after the Dade council adopted the ordinance.

A number of smaller cities around the country have adopted similar bans in recent years as homosexuals, encouraged by the civil rights progress made by blacks, have begun to press their own case for legal and social recognition. But only in Miami did the extension of rights run into implacable opposition.

Miss Bryant, a devout Baptist, formed an anti-homosexual group that she named Save Our Children. She argued that the Miami ordinance was a religious abomination and license for homosexuals to recruit and molest children. She demanded that the ordinance be rescinded and persuaded 60,000 people—six times the required number—to sign petitions that subjected it to today's countywide referendum.

Using her national reputation and church ties, she helped Save Our Children raise almost $200,000 in campaign funds. Much of the money came from beyond Florida.

"If homosexuality were the normal way," she asserted time after time, "God would have made Adam and Bruce."

Miss Bryant's campaign cost her a number of entertainment engagements. It also infuriated and mobolized homosexuals all over the country.

To work for preservation of the ordinance, Miami homosexuals formed two groups, the Coalition for Human Rights and the Victory Campaign.

The two groups disagreed a bit over strategy, but they agreed totally on the ultimate goal and on Anita Bryant. "She's the best thing that ever happened to gays," they asserted repeatedly.

In San Francisco and New York, cities with large homosexual communities, thousands of dollars were raised for the Miami struggle.

Political organizers came from several other cities to help the homosexual cause. Using a war chest of some $300,000, they devised a campaign that relied heavily on television and newspaper advertisements. Most of the ads asserted that homosexuals were not child molesters and were being subjected to bigotry and a Nazi-style witch hunt.

* * *

February 21, 1978

SECULAR BOOKINGS OFF, ANITA BRYANT SINGS AT REVIVALS

By GEORGE VECSEY
Special to The New York Times

SAN ANTONIO, Feb. 19—Anita Bryant's "victory" has been costly.

Last year she was booked for 80 secular concerts at $8,500 and up; this year she sings mainly at revivals, sharing whatever people drop in the cardboard buckets that are passed around.

"We were at the top of the list," Miss Bryant said last night. "Now we'll take what we can, and praise the Lord for changing our directions. But I'll admit, this was a struggle for me, not to get bitter." Then the red-haired singer went out to deliver her hymns and her religious witness in an athletic center, before about 3,500 people.

Although some in the audience were stimulated into spiritual frenzy by the revival, most seemed to be there to see the woman who has gone from pop performer to national symbol since she led a crusade to keep homosexuals out of public jobs in Dade County, Fla.

While the evangelist Cecil Todd exhorted the audience to put prayers back in public schools and keep homosexual teachers out of them—and suggested that the first step would be to put $10 or $100 into the container—Miss Bryant sat in the cement-block locker room that smelled of basketball players and talked about the great changes in her life in the last year.

Sang for Billy Graham

According to her husband and manager, Bob Green, she used to command about $8,500 for a one-night show, sometimes more for conventions or corporate meetings. She sang love songs, secular songs and tossed in a few of the best-known neutral gospel tunes.

The former Miss America runner-up also sang at Billy Graham rallies and other religious meetings as part of her spiritual life, but she says: "I never used to charge religious groups. It hurts me to do it now."

Last year when the Miami area was embroiled in a controversy over homosexuals in public jobs, Miss Bryant volunteered to join a fight to overturn an equal opportunity law by a referendum. She became such a lightning rod in the controversy that a panel of religion writers for Christian Century magazine picked her as the ninth most influential person and the leading woman in United States religion.

The law was overturned by a 2-to-1 margin, and Miss Bryant has been marked as an enemy by homosexuals ever since. She has been heckled frequently, has had her show disrupted several times and has been hit at least once by a thrown pie.

Orange Juice Boycott

A recent article in the Gay Community News of Boston began, "We should not rest until Anita Bryant is utterly destroyed." The writer, Donald Cameron Scot, urged homosexuals to continue boycotting Florida orange juice, whose growers pay her $100,000 a year for her endorsement and commercials.

"Nobody had ever said a bad thing about me in my life," Miss Bryant says. "It was hard to understand the viciousness. All of a sudden, nobody would touch me."

Miss Bryant says she lost every secular booking and was dropped as a commentator for the Orange Bowl television show. Her main source of income is the Florida Citrus Commission, which retained her late last year after some nervous moments.

"I understand they have lost half their income," says Mr. Todd, the evangelist, who pays her out of the money he collects from the people who attend his rallies.

"We are thinking of changing our life style," says Mr. Green, Miss Bryant's husband, referring to their 27-room home on Biscayne Bay. "We feel we could live with less. This has made us more free. But it has affected us already: We had a fellow with us 13 years as musical arranger who had to take another job."

Pickets Greet Singer

Most of Miss Bryant's appearances are like last night's, when she was the feature act for Cecil Todd's Revival Fires evangelical group, based in Joplin, Mo.

At the Blossom Athletic Center on the outskirts of town, Miss Bryant was greeted, as usual, by a circle of 50 orderly pickets singing, "Jesus Loves Me" and carrying signs that said, "Judge Not Lest Ye Be Judged," or "Straights for Gay Civil Rights."

Most of the audience seemed to be factory or farm people, dressed up for a Saturday night's entertainment. At least a quarter of them were from the large Mexican-American community here. Some waved their hands, chanted "Amen" or prayed silently with moving lips for much of the evening.

After a male gospel quintet sang and Mr. Todd preached, Miss Bryant, singing in a strong, deep and pleasant voice, delivered 11 hymns, interspersed with at least two outright plugs for Florida orange juice. Once she said: "But I know something even better than vitamin C—try Christ. He'll make the difference in your life."

Near the end, she appealed to any homosexuals in the audience, as well as "idolators, fornicators and adulterers."

"If you are willing to look at this sin, you will have God's forgiveness. You are washed. You are sanctified." Mr. Green said later that they received "at least one letter a day from people who stopped," but nobody stepped forth last night.

After Miss Bryant sang, Mr. Todd urged people to "get saved" and about 25 people came to the front. By then, wearing a fur coat, Miss Bryant was preparing for the long drive to El Paso for another performance today.

"These revivals are a whole new area for me," Miss Bryant said, "and as a performer, I do like singing for secular shows. I can't deny that. But maybe God is using me to reach all the Christians this way, and I'm not afraid of what is happening."

* * *

June 24, 1980

ADMINISTRATION OPPOSING BAN ON HOMOSEXUAL ALIENS

By ROBERT PEAR

WASHINGTON, June 23—The Carter Administration has endorsed a proposal to repeal a section of the immigration law that prohibits the entry of homosexual aliens into the United States.

In a letter sent last week to several persons interested in homosexual rights, Anne Wexler, an assistant to President Carter, said that the Administration's position was "premised upon the President's human rights policies and the nation's responsibility to be consistent with our immigration expectation of other countries."

She noted that the United States, as one of 35 countries that signed the Helsinki agreement in 1975 had promised to ease restrictions on travel as one way of promoting human rights. Some people, including Patricia M. Derian, Assistant Secretary of State for human rights, have seen the ban on homosexuals as possibly inconsistent with the commitment made at Helsinki.

Assistant Attorney General Alan A. Parker, in a separate letter to Senator Alan Cranston, Democrat of California, said that the Justice Department supported the objective of his bill to repeal statutory language requiring the Immigration and Naturalization Service to exclude suspected homosexual aliens.

The two letters constituted the first statement of the Administration's position on the issue. Justice Department lawyers concluded last December that "the I.N.S. is statutorily required to enforce the exclusion of homosexual aliens" because the ban was enacted by Congress in 1952 and upheld by the Supreme Court in 1967.

In practice, according to a spokesman for the immigration service, homosexuals have been admitted in recent months because the Public Health Service would no longer certify aliens as being victims of a mental disease or defect solely on the basis of their homosexuality. But the homosexuals were "paroled" into the country, with no decision as to whether they were legally entitled to enter.

33 Grounds for Exclusion

The Immigration and Nationality Act of 1952, also known as the McCarran-Walter Act, as amended, lists 33 grounds for automatically excluding aliens, including paupers, prostitutes and polygamists. The Select Commission on Immigration and Refugee Policy, a 16-member study group, is likely to recommend changes in this section of the law, which applies to foreigners trying to come here either as visitors or permanent residents.

A recent Library of Congress study said that the McCarran-Walter Act was passed at the height of the cold war and was "basically a restrictionist measure," designed to keep out Communists, subversives and other immigrants seen as a potential danger to the nation.

Senator Edward M. Kennedy, a member of the select commission, has called for repeal of all 33 subsections of the law listing grounds for exclusion. "Had these sections applied to American citizens, rather than to aliens, they would undoubtedly have been thrown out in court years ago," he said. They should be replaced with "reasonable and humane" provisions, he added.

A Congressional aide who characterized the exclusions as "an accumulation of prejudices" said that wholesale revision of this portion of the law would be more feasible politically than selective repeal of the ban on homosexuals.

Charles F. Brydon, co-executive director of the National Gay Task Force, which is based in New York, said that there was "a substantial gay group" among the Cuban refugees who had come to the United States in the last nine weeks.

Some, according to Verne Jervis, the immigration service spokesman, said that they had been in prison because they were homosexuals. They have been allowed to enter this country like other homosexuals, he said.

Representative Anthony C. Beilenson, Democrat of California, has introduced in the House a bill that is similar to Mr. Cranston's. No immediate action is expected on either measure, according to aides on Capitol Hill.

* * *

February 15, 1981

NO CHANGES SOUGHT ON EXCLUDING ALIENS

By ROBERT PEAR
Special to the New York Times

WASHINGTON, Feb. 14—The Select Commission on Immigration and Refugee Policy has decided not to recommend any change in the law that bars certain classes of aliens, including Communists and homosexuals, from the United States.

The 16-member commission decided, in effect, to sidestep one of the main functions it was expected to perform, apparently because the subject was too controversial. In its final report, to be issued Feb. 27, the commission urges Congress to re-examine the criteria for excluding aliens, but avoids making specific proposals on the subject.

Congress, in creating the commission three years ago, had asked for a comprehensive review of immigration law, together with "legislative recommendations to simplify and clarify" it. The commission has voted to recommend a general amnesty for illegal aliens now in the United States, a comprehensive revision of how visas are allocated and stiff penalties for employers who hire illegal aliens in the future.

At the final meeting of the commission last month, several members characterized the current list of exclusions as archaic, but said the commission would be going too far if it urged Congress to "modernize" the criteria. "The less said, the better," Senator Alan K. Simpson, Republican of Wyoming, told his colleagues on the commission.

Defining Grounds for Exclusion

Allen E. Kaye of New York, president of the Association of Immigration and Nationality Lawyers, said yesterday he was "distressed and disappointed" that the commission had not said more about the grounds for exclusion. "It seems like such a cop-out," he said.

William Fliegelman, former chief immigration judge for the Federal Government, said that commission members "failed to measure up to their responsibility" to help eliminate what he called outmoded, unworkable features of the law concerning exclusion of aliens.

The existing law explicitly forbids the issuance of visas to 33 classes of aliens, including those who are mentally retarded or insane; those afflicted with "sexual deviation" or a "dangerous contagious disease"; paupers, vagrants, polygamists and prostitutes; aliens who are "likely at any time to become public charges," and aliens who have been convicted of drug violations, even minor marijuana offenses.

One section of the law contains a 1,000-word description of the political and ideological grounds for excluding anarchists, Communists, those "affiliated with any organization that advocates the economic, international and governmental doctrines of world Communism" and those who publish or circulate materials advocating the use of force to overthrow the Federal Government.

Popular Support Cited

Despite the exclusions, the United States still takes a larger number of legal immigrants each year than any other country. Although none of the commissioners publicly defended the exclusions, several members said privately that there was popular support for many of the restrictions and that with a more conservative mood in Congress, it would be difficult to change this aspect of the law.

The influx of 125,000 Cubans last year, including at least 1,700 criminals, the demonstrations by Iranian students and growing concern about illegal aliens were all cited as reasons for what was called a "restrictionist" climate in Congress.

Commission staff members recommended major changes in the law, noting that respected scholars and artists had been denied visas because of their political views. Other aliens, according to the staff members, have been excluded because of medical conditions that pose no threat to public health and because of minor misconduct in the distant past.

"An alien convicted of stealing a loaf of bread and firewood in Italy during World War II to keep from starving and freezing is still inadmissible to the United States," said Sam Bernsen, director of legal research for the commission and former general counsel of the Immigration and Naturalization Service.

In 1979, according to the State Department, consular officers denied more than 600,000 visa applications.

'Anachronistic Remnants'

The American Association for the Advancement of Science, the American Association of University Professors and the Association of the Bar of the City of New York urged the commission to recommend repeal of the so-called ideological exclusions. "Our reputation for allowing expression free from unnecessary governmental restraint will continue to be tarnished by these anachronistic remnants of a fearful era," the bar association said.

The Attorney General may grant a waiver to a member of a proscribed political organization, but there is often a delay, and many aliens dislike the disclosure requirements concerning political beliefs.

Commission members said they feared that any recommendation to liberalize the rules against homosexual aliens would overshadow their other proposals. Representative Romano L. Mazzoli, Democrat of Kentucky, the new chairman of the House Judiciary Committee panel on immigration, said, "I can think of nothing that will more quickly blow this really quality work product out of the water and breach it forever than to get too deeply into this subject."

The section of the law barring homosexual aliens has become difficult to enforce. The Public Health Service, noting changes in the medical view of homosexuality, will no longer certify aliens as being victims of a mental disease or defect on the basis of homosexuality. The commission, created by Congress in 1978, consisted of 16 members headed by the Rev. Theodore M. Hesburgh, president of the University of Notre Dame. There were four members from the House, four from the Senate, four Cabinet officers from the Carter Administration and four members from the public at large.

* * *

February 14, 1986

IT ISN'T A 'GAY RIGHTS' BILL

By THOMAS B. STODDARD

The deep feelings across New York City and in the City Council triggered by the bill to outlaw discrimination in employment, housing and public accommodations on the basis of "sexual orientation"— incorrectly called the "gay rights bill"—are often triggered by misconceptions about its scope and nature.

One Council member, Noach Dear, rails against the bill, which is up for consideration for the 15th consecutive year, because he believes, incorrectly, that it would authorize marriage between two men or two women. It would not. Indeed, it could not, since New York State's marriage statutes lie solely within the Legislature's jurisdiction.

John Cardinal O'Connor of the Roman Catholic Archdiocese of New York and Bishop Francis J. Mugavero of the Brooklyn diocese have issued a joint statement opposing the bill, asserting that it "primarily and ultimately" seeks to achieve "the legal approval of homosexual conduct and activity." This criticism, too, misses the mark. The bill specifically states it shall not be construed to "endorse any particular behavior or way of life." Furthermore, it applies not only to homosexuals but to heterosexuals as well. "Sexual orientation" is made an improper basis for discrimination in either instance.

Some employers seem to fear the bill would impose hiring quotas on them or otherwise undermine their authority to judge employees on merit. Yet the bill explicitly upholds employers' right to enforce "bona fide job-related qualifications of employment" and bars the use of quotas.

What has gotten lost in the debate is the justification for the bill. Ask a man whom we will call John Doe. Several years ago, he worked as a clerk in a Manhattan hardware store. One evening he stopped for drinks at a bar frequented by homosexual men. On the street, one of his supervisors noticed him leaving. That week, the supervisor made several plainly bigoted remarks in his presence, at one point even stating to his face, "I don't like having faggots working for me." Shortly afterward, despite an exemplary work record, Mr. Doe was dismissed.

When Mr. Doe went to the New York City Commission on Human Rights to file a complaint, he was told he had no remedy. The law permits most private companies to fire someone on the basis of "sexual orientation" or "perceived sexual orientation," whether accurate or not. John Doe is not alone. From the middle of November 1984 through the end of October 1985, the commission received 320 complaints of discrimination on the basis of actual or perceived "sexual orientation." These complaints comprised nearly one-third of all discrimination complaints of any kind coming to the commission's attention over that period—the largest category of documented discrimination in New York City.

The Human Rights Commission's statistics are consistent with other studies of the issue. In a 1980 survey of homosexual men and lesbians living in New York City conducted by the National Gay Task Force, fully 21 percent of the respondents answered that they had encountered discrimination on the job because of their sexual orientation. In addition, 61 percent expressed the view that they would in the future face discrimination if their homosexuality were somehow disclosed.

Such discrimination is all too real. It transcends malicious jokes about "fags," "fairies" and "dykes." It causes suffering and loss. Men and women who call themselves "gay" or "lesbian" are a varied population. They are old and young, black and white, immigrant and native-born. Some are well-to-do but others have to struggle to survive. Whatever their differences, they all risk substantial loss for being who they are.

The City Council bill would help to limit the threats to their personal survival, as law has done previously for other Americans who have suffered prejudice as a class. The bill is a traditional civil rights measure, neither more nor less, and one squarely within the American conceptions of individual liberty and equality.

Thomas B. Stoddard is executive director of the Lambda Legal Defense and Education Fund, a national organization that works to protect homosexuals' rights. He is an author of the bill before the New York City Council to prohibit discrimination on the basis of sexual orientation.

* * *

June 3, 1990

AGENCY TO USE DORMANT LAW TO BAR HOMOSEXUALS FROM U.S.

By PHILIP J. HILTS
Special to The New York Times

WASHINGTON, June 2—On the eve of a major international AIDS conference in San Francisco, the Immigration and Naturalization service is preparing to invoke a little-enforced law that bars the entry of homosexuals to the United States as sexual deviants, agency officials say.

The officials said Friday that they had taken steps to enforce the law after being told that some gay groups from abroad were going to test the law by declaring themselves homosexuals when they arrived for the Sixth International Conference on AIDS in San Francisco on June 20.

Homosexual rights groups in the United States said they knew nothing of a plan to test the statute. Tom Stoddard, executive director of the Lambda Legal Defense and Education Fund, a rights organization, said the idea behind the immigration service's assertion was nonsense.

"They are living in a fantasy world," Mr. Stoddard said. He said that the law was not being enforced and that his organization did not want to challenge it because of the conservative makeup of the Supreme Court.

Action Is Called Reluctant

An immigration service spokesman, Duke Austin, said the agency was taking the action reluctantly. "We didn't want to implement the statute, but we are under a court order to do that," he said. Even though the court ruling Mr. Austin referred to came in 1983, Mr. Austin said the immigration service felt compelled to act now in the face of an open challenge.

The gay organizations were shocked and puzzled over the agency's move. They cited the Bush Administration's new policies making it easier for people infected with the AIDS virus to travel to the United States to attend international meetings.

"This is a sudden, irrational and unexpected move in another direction," Mr. Stoddard said.

Geoffrey Knox, a spokesman for the Gay Men's Health Crisis in New York City, said: "This will exacerbate rather than defuse the problems at the conference. It is unbelievable that they are going to do something like this."

The Public Health Service also seemed embarrassed by the plans. A spokesman for the agency, James Brown, said Secretary Louis W. Sullivan of the Department of Health and Human Services and Assistant Secretary James Mason "along with many others from the Public Health Service will attend this important conference and want it to be a success."

Memorandum Discloses Plans

The immigration service's plans came to light this week in a memorandum written by a Federal health offical in which he warned his superior that Public Health Service doctors would have to be involved in enforcing the law and that the agency faced potential embarrassment as a result. Before a homosexual can be barred by the immigration service, a Public Health Service doctor must certify the alien to be afflicted with a "sexual deviation, or a mental defect."

The requirement that a doctor's certification be issued before the law could be enforced was a result of a 1983 ruling by the United States Court of Appeals for the Ninth Circuit, in California. The court let stand the Federal law that had been on the books since the 1950's that barred homosexuals, but at the same time it ruled in favor of the challenge to the statute that had been brought by the Lesbian Gay Freedom Day Committee of San Francisco.

The committee had contended that a Public Health Service doctor's certificate declaring an alien a homosexual was required before the law, which bars homosexuals even for a visit, could be enforced. The appeals court agreed. In addition to California, the decision affects the states of Alaska, Arizona, Idaho, Montana, Nevada, Oregon, Washington and Hawaii.

The immigration service did not appeal the decision.

The agency contends that a doctor's certificate is not necessary to bar homosexuals' entry to this country in states outside the Ninth Circuit. But in most places the immigration service avoids enforcing the law, by not asking people if they are homosexual. When people declare themselves homosexual, an immigration service official who spoke on the condition of anonymity said, the service simply defers action on the case for the duration of the person's visit.

The law was amended in 1965 to describe people who should be barred from entry to the United States as those "with psychopathic personality, or sexual deviation, or a mental defect." The Supreme Court ruled in 1967 that homosexuals could be barred from the country as sexual deviants.

It was not immediately clear how many doctors the immigration service would need to enforce the law, but the Public Health Service said doctors would be available at any airport where they were required.

Official Cites Concern

In the memorandum by the Federal health official, dated May 22, Dr. John West, Acting Regional Health Administrator for the Health and Human Services in the Western States, said the department had been requested to make available "a P.H.S. medical officer to conduct examinations of aliens who enter the U.S. and who self-profess to be homosexuals."

He suggested in the memo that involvement by the Public Health Service could be embarrassing because the Bush Administration had been working to make the conference a success and because Public Health Service itself was involved. "I want to alert you to a potentially sensitive matter which relates to the Sixth International AIDS Conference in San Francisco and will affect public perceptions of P.H.S.," Dr. West wrote to Dr. James Allen, Director of the National AIDS Program Office. "I am bringing this to your attention given the heightened sensitivities about our agency's participation in various aspects of the conference."

He wrote in the memorandum: "In conducting these examinations, a P.H.S. medical officer would ask several questions, including, 'Are you a homosexual?' Then the medical officer would certify a form and return it to I.N.S. for whatever action I.N.S. deems is warranted."

'Inspectors Have No Choice'

Mr. Austin of the immigration agency said the issue was an old one and was not about AIDS. But he said, "If the inspectors get a guy who is coming into that conference and he wants to make an issue, make that kind of proclamation at the border, the inspectors have no choice."

If the I.N.S. bars the entry of a homosexual, the person has the right to appeal to an administrative law judge.

Mr. Brown, the Public Health Service spokesman, said, "We do not want to issue these certificates, but we were told

by the Department of Justice that the circuit court ruled that we must do it because it is the law."

This ruling by the Justice Department was made not long after the 1983 court decision requiring the doctor's certificate before a homosexual could be barred.

The Public Health Service stopped issuing certificates declaring a person a homosexual after the American Psychological Association officially stopped listing homosexuality as a mental disorder in 1979.

Gay organizations had thought they would not have to worry about homosexuals being barred from the country after the appeals court decision, which said, "Because the P.H.S. refuses to issue medical certificates on the basis of homosexuality per se, and because we today hold that the I.N.S. may not exclude homosexual aliens without such certificates, it is completely speculative that any aliens will be excluded in the future on the basis of their homosexuality per se."

* * *

June 9, 1990

A.C.L.U. AND GAY GROUPS VOW LEGAL TEST ON IMMIGRATION POLICY

By PHILIP J. HILTS
Special to The New York Times

WASHINGTON, June 8—The American Civil Liberties Union and homosexual groups said today that they would take legal action to stop Federal immigration and health officials if they try to bar self-declared homosexuals from entering the United States to attend an AIDS conference this month in San Francisco.

Gay groups said today that some people coming to the Sixth International Conference on AIDS would declare themselves in order to test a law under which homosexuals can be barred from the country. The conference begins on June 20.

The civil liberties union and the gay groups said the policy under which the Immigration and Naturalization Service and the Department of Health and Human Services planned to enforce the law was "disturbing and illegal." The groups asked the agencies to reverse the policy. If it is not reversed, they said, they will defend in court one or more of those detained by the immigration service in a test case.

The groups made their views known in a letter to Dr. Louis W. Sullivan, the Secretary of Health and Human Services. Besides the A.C.L.U., they are the Lambda Legal Defense Fund, the National Gay Rights Advocates, the National Gay and Lesbian Task Force and the Human Rights Campaign Fund.

Under Federal law, anyone with a "psychopathic personality, or a sexual deviation or a mental disorder" may be barred from entry to the United States. The Supreme Court ruled in 1967 that homosexuals can be barred as sexual deviates.

The issue does not ordinarily arise because immigration officials do not normally ask people arriving in the United States about their sexual orientation. But when confronted with a challenge to the law by people who declare themselves to be homosexual, immigration officials said their service feels obliged to take steps to determine if they should be barred from the country.

In the area covered by a 1983 appeals court ruling, which includes California, the immigration service policy is to detain professed homosexuals at the airport, ask a Public Health Service doctor to issue a certificate saying they are homosexual, and then to turn them over to a judge for a hearing on whether they should be excluded from the United States. The court ruling requires the I.N.S. to take these steps, officials say.

"We will enforce the law," said Duke Austin, a spokesman for the immigration service.

Mr. Austin said that while the immigration service would enforce its policy, the agency had made "no special plans whatsoever in regard to the AIDS conference." Recent discussion of enforcement, he said, came from the Public Health Service, the Department of Health and Human Services and gay leaders, not the I.N.S.

A few weeks ago the Public Health Service took steps to locate doctors who could issue certificates. In March, the immigration service issued a legal opinion saying that a policy first laid down in 1984 still held: In most jurisdictions, homosexuals can be barred from the country based on their self-declaration; in the area covered by the 1983 court decision, immigration officials can exclude them only after obtaining a certificate of homosexuality from a Public Health Service doctor.

Law Is Sharply Assailed

"The law on this was enacted in a time when homosexuality was regarded as an illness," said Urvashi Vaid, a spokeswoman for the National Gay and Lesbian Task Force. "We now understand that it is not a medical condition, not an illness, not a criminal condition."

Tom Stoddard, executive director of the Lambda Legal Defense and Education Fund, said the statute "leads to actual discrimination, and even more than that casts an aura of untouchablity on lesbian women and gay men in the United States as well as abroad."

Both the immigration service and the health service have said they are only reluctantly enforcing the law.

"We didn't want to implement the statute, but we are under a court order to do that," said Mr. Austin.

*   *   *

June 25, 1990

JEERS AT AIDS GATHERING DROWN OUT HEALTH CHIEF

By PHILIP J. HILTS

SAN FRANCISCO, June 24—Drowned out by a deafening roar of shouts, whistles and air horn blasts from more than 500 protestors, the Secretary of Health and Human Services, Dr. Louis W. Sullivan, stood before the closing session of the Sixth International Conference on AIDS today for 15 minutes, giving a speech that no one could hear.

The conference had drawn 11,000 people to the Moscone Convention Center over the past week for hundreds of scientific sessions that proceeded without disruption. But protesters angry at immigration prohibitions against homosexuals and at the pace of Federal spending on AIDS research had said they would keep Dr. Sullivan from speaking.

The introduction to the Health Secretary had barely gotten to the word "Sullivan" when a group from the AIDS Coalition to Unleash Power ran to the front of the hall shouting and unfurling a pink banner that read, "He talks, we die."

For more than 20 minutes, the noise was so loud that many of the 6,000 people in the audience pressed their fingers to their ears. But five minutes into the pandemonium, Dr. Sullivan went to the lectern and began what department officials later said was his speech. Those on the floor of the convention center could hear virtually none of it and were left with the impression that he was only moving his lips. Some protesters threw wads of paper at the stage, but none came close to hitting the secretary.

Words of Unity Unheard

In his prepared text, the secretary said: "We must learn to listen to each other, to learn from each other and to work together. Our frustration must never drive us to close our ears or our hearts."

The written speech ended: "The AIDS epidemic can divide us—or it can unite us. It can lure us into accusation, blame, or hostility—or it can show us our own and one another's frailty, fallibility and mortality."

Kay James, assistant secretary for public affairs at the Health Department, said the secretary showed "courage to do what he did today, refusing to be silenced just like the activists do."

Ms. James said she believed that the secretary intended to read from a letter he sent in May to the Speaker of the House, Thomas S. Foley, criticizing a proposed change to the Americans with Disabilities Act, which prohibits discrimination against the disabled, including those infected with human immunodeficiency virus that causes AIDS.

'Policy Based on Fears'

In the letter, Dr. Sullivan criticized an amendment that would explicitly eliminate all those in food-handling jobs from coverage under the act. He wrote: "Infections such as HIV are not transmitted during the preparation or serving of food or beverages. . . . Any policy based on fears and misconceptions about HIV will only complicate and confuse disease control efforts without adding any protection to the public health."

Before the meeting, 36 organizations, including AIDS advocacy groups, The American Public Health Association, and the American Psychological Association sent Dr. Sullivan a letter saying, "The United States still suffers without leadership from the White House and the Department of Health and

Human Services on those issues most directly shaping the future of people with HIV infection and AIDS."

The groups criticized United States immigration restrictions on people with the AIDS virus and asked Dr. Sullivan to support AIDS legislation pending in Congress. The administration has opposed the bills, which offer disaster relief to the cities hardest hit by the epidemic and money to pay for counseling, testing, and early treatment of those infected with the AIDS virus.

Conference organizers and AIDS advocacy groups had expressed hope that Dr. Sullivan would deal with these issues and announce new policy on them, but there was no comment on them in his printed speech.

Other speakers in the closing ceremonies of the meeting attacked two immigration policies—restrictions on free travel of homosexuals and of AIDS-infected people to the United States.

AIDS advocacy groups had expected that someone coming into the country would challenge the law by declaring himself homosexual to border officials and then fighting in court any attempt to exclude him. No one has so far made that challenge.

Outside, It's Parade as Usual

Outside the convention hall, at the annual Freedom Day Parade organized by the gay and lesbian community, the Act-Up protest group played a minor role. There was an Act-Up contingent among the marchers, but the Market Street parade belonged to the bands and dancers, the professional groups and service organizations, the transvestites and politicians who turn out every year.

Hundreds of thousands of people, homosexuals and heterosexuals alike, lined the route from the Ferry Building to City Hall, where an al fresco festival continued until dusk. The parade began, as it always does, with a pack of lesbians on motorcycles, gunning their motors and baring their breasts to the cheering crowd. Behind them, for more than two hours, came groups like the Arab Lesbian/Bisexual Women, the Companions of People Living With Aids, the Hookers From Hell, the Gay Rodeo Association, the Sons of Orpheus Drumming Troop and the Bisexual Cat Lovers Against the Bomb.

The loudest applause was reserved for the AIDS service providers: the volunteers who do laundry and run errands for the sick and the dying, the nurses and orderlies on the AIDS ward at San Francisco General Hospital, the hospice that rents a cable car each year to carry the weakest patients along the half-mile parade route.

* * *

September 15, 1991

THE SENIOR G-MAN

By DAVID M. OSHINSKY

J. EDGAR HOOVER: The Man and the Secrets
By Curt Gentry
Illustrated. 846 pp. New York: W. W. Norton. $29.95.

FROM THE SECRET FILES OF J. EDGAR HOOVER
Edited by Athan Theoharis
370 pp. Chicago: Ivan R. Dee. $24.95.

Shortly after his election victory in 1968, Richard Nixon made a most traditional move. Following the lead of every incoming President since Franklin D. Roosevelt, he ordered an adviser, John Ehrlichman, to establish immediate White House contact with the Federal Bureau of Investigation. Mr. Ehrlichman phoned J. Edgar Hoover, the bureau's legendary Director, who invited him to his office. Greeted at a fortress-like reception desk by a black "F.B.I. agent" (Hoover's personal valet), Mr. Ehrlichman was marched through the Director's many "trophy rooms" to a large paneled office. A door opened, and he entered yet another room, 12 or 13 feet square. From above came the purplish glow of an insect-repelling light, which the Director, a notorious hypochondriac, had installed, he said, to "electrocute" dangerous germs. "When he stood," Mr. Ehrlichman recalled in his memoirs, "it became obvious that he and his desk were on a dais about six inches high. . . . J. Edgar Hoover looked down on me and began to talk." As he rambled on about Congress, Communists and the Kennedys, Mr. Ehrlichman grew irritable and bored. How could anyone take this old man seriously?

A few weeks later, Hoover phoned the President. There were rumors, he said, about homosexual activity "at the highest levels of the White House staff." They came from a bureau informant, who had mentioned Ehrlichman. Of course, the F.B.I. would check out these rumors if the President so ordered. He did. The rumors proved false. But Hoover had sent his calling card. Mr. Ehrlichman would not take him lightly again.

The Director had been playing this game for years. His great advantage over others, as Curt Gentry makes clear in "J. Edgar Hoover: The Man and the Secrets," was his unlimited access to information and his genius at doling it out. When he died in 1972, the 77-year-old Hoover had been Director of the bureau for 48 years, serving eight Presidents and 18 attorneys general.

Mr. Gentry, a journalist and a co-author of "Helter Skelter," a best-selling account of the Charles Manson case, is a master of detail and description. What he lacks—in this book, at least—is a willingness to analyze his subject or the culture in which he lived. He tells us much that Hoover said and did in his long career, but he rarely goes beyond that. All judgments are left to the reader, and many questions arise. Why was Hoover so obsessed with cleansing America of radicals and subversives—loosely defined? Why did he wash his hands every few minutes and go numb whenever an insect touched his body? Is there, perhaps, a connection between questions one and two?

The list goes on. Why would a lifelong bachelor, who was never seen in the company of a woman other than his mother, spend so much energy prying into the sex lives of others? And what about his fear and loathing of minorities? During his years as Director, the handful of black agents spent their time driving his limousine, handing him towels and manning the flyswatter. An occasional Hispanic agent could be found on what was called the "taco beat" in the rural Southwest. As late as 1970, Hoover remarked: "You never have to bother about a President being shot by Puerto Ricans and Mexicans. They don't shoot very straight. But if they come at you with a knife, beware."

Oddly, given both the bulk of his book and the inroads made by other scholars in this field, Mr. Gentry spends only a few pages on Hoover's formative years. In 1987 the historian Richard Gid Powers provided a compelling portrait of the young Hoover in "Secrecy and Power." In his view, Hoover was a natural product of his environment: "Southern, white, Christian, small-town, turn-of-the-century Washington." His neighborhood was homogeneous—and closed. In "The Boss," published in 1988, John Stuart Cox and Athan Theoharis took a rather different view. Their J. Edgar Hoover was molded by a family life reminiscent of a Dickens novel. Yet they, too, portrayed him as a captive of his parochial culture—a man of narrow interests and "homely tastes." Even late in his life, when he was told in a memorandum that "Jean-Paul Sartre promised to take an active part in the French 'Who Killed Kennedy Committee,' Mr. Hoover scribbled a five-word response: 'Find out who Sartre is.'"

Now, in "From the Secret Files of J. Edgar Hoover," Mr. Theoharis has collected some previously unreleased documents that indicate the kind of information Hoover gathered about people and used against them for five decades.

Hoover's career as America's most dangerous file clerk began in 1919, when the Attorney General, A. Mitchell Palmer, appointed him chief of the Justice Department's newly organized General Intelligence Division. Palmer believed that a crackdown on Bolsheviks would be his ticket to the White House. He left the details to Hoover, a 24-year-old recent graduate of law school. Within three months, Hoover had set up an index system listing virtually every radical leader and organization in the United States. By 1921, the system contained upward of 400,000 names. Hoover led the mass roundups (the Palmer Raids) of 1919-1920 and directed the deportation of Emma Goldman, Alexander Berkman and other foreign-born revolutionaries. When a number of prominent lawyers signed a petition condemning the Justice Department's "continued violation of the Constitution," Hoover opened a file on each signer.

As the fear of radicalism ebbed in the 1920's, Hoover's future looked grim. What saved him from obscurity was the Teapot Dome scandal. Beginning in the early 1920's, it swept through the Federal bureaucracy, providing upward mobility

to those who escaped indictment and jail. The new Attorney General, Harlan Fiske Stone, was looking for someone to run the old corruption-plagued Bureau of Investigation. He chose Hoover, who seemed intelligent and scandal-free. As Mr. Gentry demonstrates, Hoover ruthlessly rebuilt the bureau. For the first time, agents were chosen on merit; many were college graduates; all attended a special training school. Before long, the bureau, its name augmented by the preface "Federal," had a crime lab, a fingerprinting system and a rigid chain of command. Hoover also created the Crime Records Division to handle public relations. Headed by Louis B. Nichols, a publicity genius, it turned the Director and his "G-men" into national heroes.

Every "public enemy" of the 1930's—from Ma Barker to John Dillinger to Pretty Boy Floyd—was tracked down by the F.B.I. All movie and radio scripts about the bureau were cleared by Lou Nichols's office. And no criticism ever went unanswered. When a national magazine had the temerity to describe the director as short, fat and effeminate, Nichols planted an article in a rival publication assuring Americans that Hoover's "compact body . . . carries no ounce of extra weight—just 170 pounds of live, virile masculinity."

Stone had warned Hoover about abuses of power. "The Bureau of Investigation is not concerned with political or other opinions of individuals," he said in a public statement. But in Hoover's view, one defended America by shielding its citizens from subversive opinions and ideas. So he went underground, increasing the bureau's surveillance activities in all sorts of new ways. The agency's most sensitive material, gathered through wiretaps, bugs and break-ins, was carefully separated from general files. This information hoard included an "Obscene File," a "Sex Deviate File" and a "confidential" file in the office of the bureau's Associate Director, Clyde Tolson, Hoover's inseparable companion. But the most explosive documents—labeled "Official and Confidential" and "Personal and Confidential"—were supervised by Helen Gandy, Hoover's administrative assistant. An official familiar with part of the "O/C" file described it as "12 drawers full of political cancer."

The disease spread rapidly. In 1936, President Roosevelt asked the F.B.I. to investigate "communist and fascist activities" in the United States. His oral authorization allowed Hoover to expand the Bureau's surveillance operation under a White House umbrella. The F.B.I. tapped the telephones and bugged the hotel rooms of diplomats, journalists, labor leaders and political activists. In the name of "national security," it harassed critics whom F.D.R. considered isolationists and spread slanderous stories about their pasts. In time the White House relied on Hoover for all sorts of things—such as finding the President's alcoholic cousin, Kermit Roosevelt, who had disappeared for several months with a mistress; or tailing the wife of Roosevelt's adviser Harry Hopkins, who was suspected of leaking political secrets to the press.

Moreover, the Bureau kept growing—from about 2,000 special agents in 1940 to more than 7,000 by 1952. As the cold war heated up, Hoover became the country's backstop against subversion. While historians would surely disagree with Mr. Gentry's bluster that "'McCarthyism' was, from start to finish, the creation of one man, F.B.I. Director J. Edgar Hoover," it is clear that information from the Bureau's secret files, fed selectively to politicians and journalists, became the lifeblood of the anti-Communist right. What is missing from Mr. Gentry's account, however, is a sense of Hoover's deep commitment. It is no doubt true that he had a stake in keeping the Communist threat alive. But he was no McCarthy. His fear of radicalism had very deep roots.

Mr. Gentry never pierces Hoover's mind. His account of Hoover's later years is fact-filled, episodic and detached. He provides many details about the F.B.I.'s treatment of Martin Luther King Jr. but barely a word about the civil rights movement or its devastating impact on Hoover's 19th-century world view. He gives an excellent description of the F.B.I.'s counterintelligence program (Cointelpro), but almost nothing about its primary targets: the Communist Party, the Black Panthers and the New Left. Indeed, the closest Mr. Gentry gets to Hoover's feelings about the tumultuous changes of the 60's is a random (but revealing) remark Hoover made after he visited the wife of Ramsey Clark, then Attorney General. She was "nothing but a hippie," Hoover sneered. "I went over there and she was barefoot! What kind of a person is that?"

By the 1970's, there was public talk of replacing Hoover, and private maneuvering as well. In the Nixon White House, a memorandum was prepared calling for his immediate removal. (The author was G. Gordon Liddy, a former F.B.I. agent best remembered at the bureau for having run a security check on his future wife.) But Nixon backed away. He did not want to offend Hoover. He was hardly alone. As Athan Theoharis notes in "From the Secret Files of J. Edgar Hoover," the Director thrived on people's uncertainty. "While Congressmen suspected that Hoover had information that could ruin their careers," he writes, "they hesitated to challenge him." The samples he offers from Hoover's surviving files range from the sensational (a wiretap conversation between Ensign John F. Kennedy during World War II and a lover, Inga Arvad, a suspected Nazi spy) to the mundane (a "strictly confidential" memo noting that Senator Claude Pepper charged a dress shirt to the account of a businessman friend).

What is most appalling about these files is the amount of malicious misinformation in them. In 1952, for example, a memo noted that Gov. Adlai Stevenson of Illinois, the Democratic Presidential nominee, was one of "the two best known homosexuals in the state." It hardly mattered to Hoover that the informant was a college basketball player under indictment for fixing a game or that his evidence was based only on rumor. What did matter was that Stevenson had spoken out against loyalty oaths, criticized Joe McCarthy, and vetoed a bill that would outlaw the Communist Party in Illinois.

The Crime Records Division of the F.B.I. leaked the homosexual charge to selected members of the press. Rumors flew wildly across the Presidential campaign. And Hoover refused to let go. Almost a decade later, when Stevenson visited

Lima, Peru, as the American Ambassador to the United Nations, the F.B.I. added this to his bulging file: "Stevenson made a point of visiting the National Museum of Archaeology, which has a collection of highly pornographic Inca statuettes. That particular collection is kept closely guarded and not available to the public."

In a bizarre way, these secret files victimized J. Edgar Hoover as well. Mr. Gentry shrewdly compares him to the "embezzling bank clerk" who could never take a vacation because he feared his crimes would be discovered while he was away. Relentlessly, he fought every hint that he retire. He instructed Helen Gandy to shred his "Personal and Confidential" file the moment he died. She did her job well. Within days of Hoover's death in 1972, she moved dozens of file drawers to his home. She claimed they contained his personal correspondence, and no one questioned her story. The Acting Director of the bureau, L. Patrick Gray 3d, assured skeptical reporters that "there are no dossiers or secret files. There are general files, and I took steps to keep their integrity." In Hoover's basement, meanwhile, the shredders worked on.

The complete story of Hoover's F.B.I. can never be told. In 1977, Bureau officials added more gaps to the paper trail by destroying the 300,000 pages in the "Sex Deviate Program." To their credit, Mr. Theoharis and Mr. Gentry in these new books have provided much material about J. Edgar Hoover and the autonomous fiefdom he ruled for almost 50 years. The Director couldn't hide it all. But his deepest secrets, one suspects, have followed him to the grave.

David M. Oshinsky is a professor of history at Rutgers University and the author of "A Conspiracy So Immense: The World of Joe McCarthy."

* * *

February 13, 1992

CITING GAY BIAS, U.S. MOVES TO DROP CASE

By The Associated Press

The Government has moved to drop charges against three men who say they were singled out by a Federal prosecutor for arrest because they are gay, court papers disclosed yesterday.

A review of the drug and tax case by the Justice Department's Public Integrity Section found that "evidence was apparently falsified," the papers said, adding that "this circumstance warrants that the pleas of guilty be vacated and that the charges against these defendants be dismissed."

The defendants—Bruce Mailman, Boris Fedushin and Carlos Insignares—asked a judge last week to force the Government to turn over results of its investigation into an assistant United States Attorney, James McGuire, and an Internal Revenue Service agent, Frank Primerana, who has resigned. Mr. McGuire was suspended in a separate matter.

Mr. Mailman's lawyer, James M. LaRossa, said in motion papers that the two "exhibited a deep-seated personal bias against gays and sought to target gays for prosecution simply because of their sexual preference."

* * *

June 21, 1992

LEGAL VICTORIES FOR GAY WORKERS

By BARBARA PRESLEY NOBLE

Gay activism has come a long way since those raucous evenings in the 1950's when a pony dancer used to jump onto the bar at a gay hangout in San Francisco and lead the crowd in choruses of "God Bless Us Nellie Queens." As the gay community prepares to celebrate its annual "pride week," which will culminate next weekend with marches in several cities, gay rights advocates say the effects of years of organizing and educating are finally being seen, nowhere more clearly than in the workplace.

Not only are gay men and lesbians variously stepping, sidling and leaping out of the closet—according to personal style and the degree of risk they perceive to themselves—many are no longer willing to tolerate the anti-gay policies and behavior endemic in some workplaces. "They are more willing to assert their rights than they ever were," said Paula L. Ettelbrick, legal director of the Lambda Legal Defense and Education Fund, a New York-based group that does test-case litigation.

Lambda just won a suit on behalf of a deputy sheriff in Florida who had been dismissed for being gay. In a Federal district court in Atlanta, a lesbian whose job offer from the Georgia Attorney General's office was withdrawn after she disclosed she had married her female partner in a religious ceremony won the right last month to challenge the agency's decision. And in Massachusetts 10 days ago, a ruling recognizing the legal standing of an unmarried heterosexual couple in benefit claims laid the groundwork for a challenge by gay groups.

Paralleling successes in litigation are incremental victories in state legislatures. The rights of gay people remain a "balkanization of protections," said Kevin M. Cathcart, Lambda's executive director. But since 1989, five states have included sexual orientation among the protected categories in their civil rights laws, bringing the total to six: Wisconsin, Vermont, New Jersey, Hawaii, Massachusetts and Connecticut, plus the District of Columbia. More than 85 cities now have ordinances forbidding job discrimination on the basis of sexual orientation.

And though the ultimate goal, a Federal anti-discrimination law, is likely to remain in its state of suspended animation at least until a more sympathetic political party moves into the White House, significantly more people are protected than they were when the first state law was passed in Wisconsin in 1982. "Besides the practical effects, there is the symbolism of the states," said William B. Rubenstein, director of the American Civil Liberties Union's National Lesbian and Gay Rights Project, which is litigating the Georgia case. "It's an implicit signal to Congress that a Federal law is more realistic."

Mr. Rubenstein attributes the acceleration of gains to the increasing focus on family issues among gay men and lesbians. "The AIDS crisis and the Sharon Kowalski case have made it clear for a lot of gay people the consequences of our relationships not being recognized by the law," Mr. Rubenstein said. "Hospitals have visitation policies for family members. A lover may not be considered a family member." After an eight-year legal battle with the family of Sharon Kowalski, a Minnesota woman who was left disabled by a car accident in 1983, her companion Karen Thompson was recently appointed Ms. Kowalski's guardian.

In the workplace, lack of recognition may not have life-or-death consequences, but it raises questions of fairness. Several groups report an explosion of calls from unmarried gay and straight employees interested in obtaining benefits for members of their households. Only a handful of companies offer benefits—a form of compensation—to nonmarried partners. "It's as if a job posting said, 'Lesbians and gay men: $30,000; heterosexuals: $40,000,'" Mr. Rubenstein said.

The demand for spousal benefits runs against a trend in business toward cutting benefits—and against the might of conventional insurance plans. But the reason for corporate resistance gives gay-rights advocates cause for hope. "For most employers, it's not that they don't want to recognize gay and lesbian rights," said Ms. Ettelbrick of Lambda. "They find the arguments compelling, but they don't want to shell out."

But many companies face polite pressure from internal gay employee groups, and from heterosexual co-workers. "I see much more consciousness among straight employees," Ms. Ettelbrick said. Companies may eventually find that the price of the lock on the closet door is far too high.

A Patchwork of Judicial Rulings

The extension of rights to gay men and lesbians is a quilt of litigation stitched together issue by issue and jurisdiction by jurisdiction. Gay rights advocates got more fabric to work with earlier this month when a Massachusetts court ruled in favor of a heterosexual woman who filed for unemployment benefits when she left her job to follow her unmarried partner of 13 years to the site of his new business.

In the case, Reep v. the Department of Employment and Training, the Massachusetts Supreme Judicial Court ruled against the state's claim that only married people were entitled to the benefits. "They said you can't use marriage as a bright-line test," said Mary L. Bonauto, a staff attorney at Gay and Lesbian Advocates and Defenders, a Boston-based group. The court provided a list of factors to consider in evaluating the significance of a relationship.

Ms. Bonauto expects the ruling to be as significant as New York's landmark Braschi case, which allowed the lover of a deceased man to take over an apartment lease. "Now we have a building block in place to show that nonmarital gay and lesbian families also merit the protection of the law," she said.

* * *

August 9, 1993

CLINTON'S GAY RIGHTS FORAY MAY MISCARRY; LANDMARK ASYLUM CASE

To the Editor:

In a landmark decision this month, an immigration judge in San Francisco granted political asylum to a Brazilian gay man. Citing numerous abuses by antigay death squad gangs, who are often joined by the police in their massacres of gays, the judge decided that homosexuality classifies as a social group, is immutable or a characteristic an asylum applicant should not be compelled to change.

Thus, the judge ruled in essence that gay men and lesbians who fear persecution in their home country should receive no more nor less protection than any other person who is persecuted as part of a social group.

One hopes the judge's decision toward gay and lesbian foreigners who fear persecution abroad will be followed by other immigration judges throughout the country. One would also hope this rare, enlightened attitude toward foreign gays and lesbians can be extended to gay and lesbian Americans fighting to lift the military ban and who, like their foreign counterparts, only ask to be treated equally.

TANIA M. ALVAREZ
San Francisco, July 29, 1993
The writer is an immigration lawyer.

* * *

December 12, 1994

GAY RIGHTS BATTLE FLARES IN FLORIDA

By MIREYA NAVARRO
Special to The New York Times

GAINESVILLE, Fla.—Nancy Clayton says she is no Archie Bunker. She says she has gay friends.

But she was among those who voted on Election Day to repeal an ordinance in Alachua County that granted gay people protection from discrimination in housing and employment. Mrs. Clayton, 34, says the law singled out homosexuals for "special" rights—rights that went beyond those afforded to her as "the mother of 2.5 kids."

"We're all different," she says. "We shouldn't make issues bigger than they should be."

Votes on gay rights laws have become increasingly common in recent years and often, as in the case of Alachua County in northern Florida, gay rights lose.

Gay rights advocates say this trend, spurred by religious conservatives, shows that people are still easily swayed by anti-gay arguments because of misconceptions and ignorance about homosexuals and the extent of the unfair treatment they receive, legally. That gap in knowledge, the advocates say, threatens the local and state laws that, along with judicial rulings, form the patchwork of legal protection for homosexuals around the country.

Phillippe Frederich for The New York Times

Florida's Alachua County has voted to repeal a law protecting homosexuals from discrimination. "There's a tremendous fear of homosexuals," said Damian Pardo, left, a Miami banker who with Fran Bohnsack heads a gay rights group in Florida. Roger Huckelberry also belongs to the group.

In Florida, the battleground over gay rights is spreading after a long lull. Not since the singer Anita Bryant undertook her successful "save our children" campaign in the 1970's to eliminate a Dade County gay rights ordinance have homosexuals seen such an organized effort to reverse their gains, gay groups say.

Now, there are efforts to put gay rights ordinances to the ballot test in two of the six other jurisdictions that have them, Tampa and West Palm Beach, while officials in a third, Hillsborough County, say they will repeal their gay rights law. There are also efforts to get a statewide vote on a measure to repeal existing local laws on gay rights and prohibit the enactment of new ones, similar to one passed in Colorado but found unconstitutional by the Colorado Supreme Court.

The fact that even Alachua County voters in a relatively liberal city like Gainesville, home of the University of Florida, strongly opposed gay rights, gay groups say, shows the need for campaigns to show why homosexuals need civil rights laws.

Already, groups in Dade and Broward Counties in South Florida plan a three-month educational campaign starting in January to show homosexuals as having many of the same cares and concerns as the people who are fighting gay rights laws in the name of family values.

"If your child were gay, would your love be less?" is a question that will be posed in advertisements on the side of 100 public buses.

"There's a tremendous fear of homosexuals," Damian Pardo, a Miami banker who heads one of the groups, said of voters. "They need to understand to make an informed choice."

So far, the gay rights ordinances enacted around the country have served mainly a symbolic purpose, according to a study by professors at the University of Florida. The study found that few claims had been filed under them, partly because many gay men and women are reluctant to reveal their sexual orientation publicly.

Alachua County officials said that during the year and a half the ordinance was in effect, no discrimination claim was filed under it, nor did any employer complain of being forced to hire a homosexual. But supporters of the laws say they serve as a deterrent to discrimination and have encouraged similar policies in the private sector. Eight states, the District of Columbia and about 130 counties and cities have gay rights laws.

In Alachua County, with a population of about 186,000, most of them Democrats, 57 percent of those who cast ballots voted to repeal the ordinance. An amendment to the county charter to prevent similar ordinances in the future passed with 60 percent of the vote.

Support for the repeal came from churches and conservative Christian groups like the American Family Association. Opponents were a loose coalition that included gay groups, business owners and some members of the clergy.

Those in favor of repealing the law contended that the law was part of a broader gay agenda. A leaflet distributed by the one group, Concerned Citizens of Alachua County, included a listing of what it asserted were examples of "major demands by homosexual activists," including publicly financed artificial insemination programs for lesbians and relaxation of laws "that protect minors from being sexually exploited."

Those opposed to repeal of the law had a range of concerns, from civil rights to the bad publicity that an image of intolerance would bring to the county. The Rev. Jesse Jackson and Coretta Scott King urged county residents to stand behind the ordinance, drawing parallels between homosexuals and blacks in their struggle for equal rights.

John Tarayos, 41, a medical student at the University of Florida, said he had received telephone calls from campaign volunteers pushing for repeal who asked: "How would you like your children to live next to a same-sex couple and see them being affectionate with each other?" He said he became enraged when he found out that his Roman Catholic Church had given out his unlisted telephone number.

After hanging up, he said, he sent a check for $75 to the opposing camp.

"I didn't perceive it as special rights but equal rights," he said. "Why go backward?"

But Steve Summerlin, an insurance business owner who was a leader in the campaign to repeal, said, "No one's sexuality should take legal precedence over my right to choose what's best for my family, business or property interest."

Still, polls show that most Americans oppose discrimination against homosexuals. But the same polls also show that most people believe gay Americans are already protected.

In fact, lawyers say, many employers and landlords legally can discriminate against homosexuals.

"There's nothing in the Constitution that prohibits restaurants from throwing out people because they are black," said William B. Rubenstein, director of the American Civil Liberties Union's Lesbian and Gay Rights Project. "That's why the Civil Rights Act of 1964 had to be passed."

Gay rights advocates assert that conservative extremists are using anti-gay initiatives as an organizing and fund-raising tool. But the initiatives have also given impetus to gay rights movements whose members are now enlisting support from local politicians, minority groups and others.

In Alachua County, the battleground is moving to the courts, where a legal team from the Lambda Legal Defense and Education Fund plans to challenge the county amendment prohibiting passage of other gay rights ordinances. It is one of several legal fights by gay groups in Florida.

"Civil rights and human rights should never be put to a popular vote," said Bryan Hushon, 23, a senior at the University of Florida, and a homosexual who said he was "embarrassed on behalf of the county" for repealing its gay rights ordinance.

"It's just not ethical," he said. "I just want what everybody else has in this county, and I don't feel I have that now."

* * *

October 31, 1998

TRIAL IS TESTING LOUISIANA'S SODOMY LAW

By RICK LYMAN

NEW ORLEANS, Oct. 28—Jim Wiltberger, an accountant and political activist, remembered what it was like to be a gay man traveling outside the French Quarter into the more conservative and unwelcoming parishes of Louisiana.

Gay men identified themselves with code words, he said. They signaled one another by twisting their pinkie rings. They had colored handkerchiefs sticking out of their pockets to advertise their sexual orientation, with different colors connoting particular proclivities.

"But then there got to be something like 54 different colors and nobody could remember what the code was and, besides, at a bar you couldn't see the color in the dark," Mr. Wiltberger said from the witness stand today in Civil District Court in New Orleans, a wobbly air-conditioner fan clanging in the background.

Even as religious conservatives and some Republican politicians have intensified their criticism of homosexuality and urged states to strengthen or more strictly enforce their anti-sodomy laws, advocates for gay and lesbian have continued a decade-old strategy of attacking the 19 remaining state anti-sodomy statutes, one state at a time. The current battle is in Louisiana.

In a case that opened on Monday and was expected to run at least a week, John D. Rawls, a gay New Orleans lawyer, is arguing that the state's antisodomy law is incompatible with the Louisiana Constitution.

The trial began with a veterinarian describing how some 460 species of mammals have been known to exhibit some form of homosexual behavior. It continued with a discussion of how "crime against nature" statutes date to 12th-century ecclesiastical laws. And it included the testimony of several homosexuals about how the law had been used to discriminate against them in Louisiana.

The Louisiana law against "unnatural carnal copulation" makes it a felony punishable by up to five years in prison and applies to both homosexual and heterosexual couples.

Mr. Rawls said he would prove that the law was invalid because it was religious in nature, that it discriminated against people whose rights were protected by the State Constitution and that there was no rational scientific basis for it.

"Of course that's what he's going to do, that's what he ought to do, that's the smart thing to do," said Charles Braud, who is defending the law for the state Attorney General's office. "But this statute has been on the books in Louisiana for 150 years and it's the Attorney General's job to defend the Constitution and the state's laws. I believe all we have to do is show that the legislators had a rational reason for enacting the law."

Mr. Braud said the state would wait until Mr. Rawls finished his arguments before deciding whether to call its witnesses, including mental health experts and the leaders of groups that believe homosexuality is a chosen life style that, with counseling, can be unchosen.

The Lambda Legal Defense and Education Fund has led some of the efforts to overturn antisodomy laws and is assisting in this case.

"Back in the early 1960's, every state in the union had some form of antisodomy statute," said Suzanne B. Goldberg, a lawyer with the organization. "Now there are 19 states that still have them, 14 that outlaw sodomy and oral sex between all couples and 5 that outlaw it only for same-sex couples."

The issue, gay activists say, is not so much the arrest of people for engaging in such sex acts but the other ways in which the laws are used to discriminate against or clamp down on homosexuals.

"Sodomy laws are used to brand gays and lesbians as criminals, and they are also used as the basis for all sorts of other discrimination," Ms. Goldberg said. "There have been instances, in Texas, Florida and Georgia, where they were used to deny jobs to gay applicants, and in North Carolina and Virginia such laws were used as a basis for denying custody in divorce cases. It's also often used as a means of keeping gays out of the political process."

Even more important, she said, was the social climate that such laws create in a community, perhaps encouraging those disposed to violence against homosexuals.

Many states repealed their anti-sodomy laws in the late 60's and early 70's. In 1986, though, the Supreme Court, in a 5-to-4 vote, ruled in a case involving a gay Georgia man arrested while engaging in oral sex in his own home that there was no privacy protection under Federal law that invalidated the Georgia statute. As a result, gay groups have moved into the state courts and legislatures in the last decade, because state constitutions sometimes guarantee more specific and widespread rights than does the Bill of Rights.

Since that Supreme Court decision, Nevada and the District of Columbia have voted to repeal their antisodomy laws, and state courts have overturned them in Kentucky, Montana and Tennessee.

But not all efforts to have the laws repealed have succeeded. In Texas, an appeals court declined to rule on the constitutionality of that state's law. In Missouri, a state court upheld the state's antisodomy law, arguing in part that Missouri had a public health interest in outlawing anal and oral sex, since such acts could spread the AIDS virus.

Gay activists say they are already looking beyond the Louisiana case, to battles in Arkansas and Maryland.

"The issue in every state is always the same, whether that state's courts are willing to tear up their state constitution or throw out their sodomy laws," Mr. Rawls said. "This is a continuing, galling insult to all lesbian, gay, bisexual and transgender persons."

* * *

November 21, 1998

2 MEN FINED $125 EACH FOR SODOMY IN PRIVATE

By The Associated Press

HOUSTON, Nov. 20—Two men caught having sex in a private home were each fined $125 today after pleading no contest in a case they said will challenge the sodomy law in Texas.

The two men, John Geddes Lawrence, 55, and Tyrone Garner, 31, said they would contest the fine, imposed by Justice of the Peace Mike Parrott, and appeal the case.

On Sept. 17, Harris County deputies walked in while the two were having consensual intercourse in Mr. Lawrence's unlocked apartment east of Houston. The deputies were investigating a complaint about an armed intruder at the apartment. The authorities say they believe that the complaint was filed by someone who was angry with the men.

The two were arrested and charged with sodomy, one of the few times the 119-year-old state law has been enforced. The law makes homosexual oral and anal sex a Class C misdemeanor, punishable by a maximum fine of $500.

Of the 19 states that have a sodomy statute barring consensual anal or oral sex, Texas is one of five that focuses on same-sex partners. The other four are Arkansas, Kansas, Missouri and Oklahoma, according to Lambda Legal Defense and Education Fund of New York.

* * *

March 23, 1999

GAY COUPLES SPLIT BY IMMIGRATION LAW; UNDER 1996 ACT, PERSONAL COMMITMENTS ARE NOT RECOGNIZED

By ANDREW JACOBS

A dozen roses in hand and butterflies in his stomach, Kent McCoy stood in the arrivals area at Kennedy International Airport last summer waiting for his companion, Samer Yahya, to return from a monthlong visit with relatives in Italy.

But as the last passengers trickled out of the customs area that August evening, Mr. McCoy's anticipation turned to panic. Three hours later, with the terminal deserted and the roses wilting, an immigration agent appeared and told Mr. McCoy that his partner of four years had been detained for carrying a flawed visa. "We've got your friend," Mr. McCoy said the officer told him. "We're sending him back."

Mr. Yahya, 29, a theater major at Trinity College in Hartford, says he did not know that his student visa had been improperly issued in the United States when it should have been issued in Rome. Still, he said he was strip-searched, dressed in a prison jumpsuit and shackled to a bench overnight at the airport. He and Mr. McCoy were not allowed to speak, and the next day, he was put on a plane to Rome. Seven months later, the two men are still separated. The American Embassy in Rome denied Mr. Yahya a new student visa, saying that although he was a legitimate student, he was likely to stay in this country illegally after finishing his studies.

Like thousands of gay Americans in relationships with foreigners, Mr. McCoy discovered that although he considered himself married, his relationship with Mr. Yahya had no legal standing and offered him no protection against deportation.

While heterosexuals in similar circumstances can marry and automatically gain residency rights for their spouses—even if the spouse entered the country illegally—gay men and women who would be willing to make a similar legal commitment to one another cannot.

And since 1996, when Congress passed a collection of new immigration laws, the few provisions that once were interpreted to allow gay partners to stay in this country have been eliminated. These laws were aimed, in general, at slowing the tide of illegal immigrants coming to this country, not in particular at this group. But gay couples have been caught up in its strict enforcement.

For example, judges, who previously had the discretion to waive a deportation on humanitarian grounds and might have allowed someone like Mr. Yahya to stay, are now obliged to deport such illegal immigrants—even when they and their partners share mortgages, businesses, homes and children.

As a result, immigration lawyers estimated, tens of thousands of relationships have been thrown into jeopardy or broken apart by the new deportation drive, which has sent nearly 290,000 immigrants back to their countries since 1997, more than double the number from the previous two years.

"It doesn't matter that we've been sharing a home and a life for years, that we're essentially married," said Mr. McCoy, 46, an architect who lives in Hartford. "We've been torn apart."

Elaine Komis, a spokeswoman for the Immigration and Naturalization Service, said there was nothing her agency could do. "We don't make the laws," she said. "Congress does. This would be a major change to the immigration preference system, one that requires an act of Congress."

But advocates of rights for gay people said a Congress that passed the 1996 Defense of Marriage Act, legislation that withholds Federal benefits from the partners of gay men and

Larry Davis for The New York Times

Bruce MacDonald has applied to Canada for immigrant status so he can bring in his Thai partner, whom the United States has refused to admit.

women, is unlikely to change immigration law to help couples like Mr. Yahya and Mr. McCoy.

Representative Bob Barr, a conservative Republican from Georgia, agreed that such legislation would stand little chance. "It never ceases to amaze me the off-the-wall things people come up with," he said. "How would immigration officials distinguish between life partners and sex partners? How would they even know who is homosexual and who isn't? There would be so much room for abuse."

Need for Luck, Guile and Law-Breaking

For many couples, staying together requires a combination of luck, guile and, sometimes, a willingness to break the law. Foreigners with special skills may qualify for work permits, but such visas are hard to get and last only six years. Some remain here on tourist visas, which allow them to come and go but are issued with the expectation that the visa holder will live in his or her home country and visit the United States occasionally. And so every few months, as a way of pretending that they do not actually live here, such people leave the country, hoping that a border agent will not turn them back on their return.

For a handful, there is asylum, but that option is available only to those who can prove that returning to their home country would expose them to some form of persecution.

There is also the "green card marriage," a fake union to someone of the opposite sex. Such an arrangement is a felony, however, with penalties of imprisonment, fines and a lifetime ban on re-entering the country.

Many who are desperate simply ignore the laws and remain here illegally when their proper documents expire.

And for many, moving to the partner's country, even if the American is willing to give up family and career, is impossible in the face of similar or even more severe immigration restrictions.

Edward Keating/The New York Times

Michel Buffet, left, and Robert Mogel have been together for nine years, but when Mr. Buffet gets his Ph.D., and is no longer a student, he faces deportation to France.

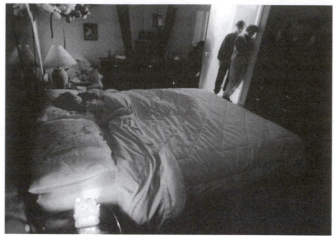

Laura Pedrick

Christiana Pacheco, right, and Alexandra Sousa have raised Ms. Pacheco's daughter, Katie, 8. Ms. Sousa has been ordered out of the country before summer.

When all else fails, there is Canada, one of 10 countries that grant immigration rights to same-sex partners. A growing number of gay Americans are moving there, though many say they do so bitterly.

Bruce MacDonald, 48, a medical social worker in Seattle, has applied to the Canadian Government for immigrant status. If granted, he will have the right to bring in his partner, a Thai national who has been repeatedly denied a visitor's visa by the United States. So far the process has taken two years and cost Mr. MacDonald $4,000 in legal fees.

"Imagine being forced by your government to leave behind family and friends because your relationship has no value," Mr. MacDonald said. "It's wrenching."

Sitting in the fluorescent glare of an Immigration Court waiting room in Newark last month, Christiana Pacheco and Alexandra Sousa anxiously held hands while a Federal immigration judge decided their future. With a ticket to Lisbon in her pocket, Ms. Sousa was prepared for the worst.

For the last eight years, the two women have shared a modest ranch house in a Philadelphia suburb, where they have been raising Katie, Ms. Pacheco's 8-year-old daughter from her former marriage.

Born in Portugal, Ms. Sousa, 29, came to the United States with her family as a teen-ager. When her parents returned home several years ago, she was already involved with Ms. Pacheco and decided to stay, even though she was not here legally. "At that point, I had a family of my own," she said.

When the new immigration laws were passed three years ago, Ms. Sousa, a software designer, decided to deal with her undocumented status. On the advice of a lawyer, she filed an asylum claim, citing anti-gay persecution at home. She now realizes it was a mistake.

'Isn't There Some State?'

During a hearing last year, Judge Nicole Y. K. Kim found no grounds for asylum and suggested the women find another way to preserve their family. According to the women and

their lawyers, the judge asked, "Isn't there some state where you two can get married?" No, there is not, and even if there were, the 1996 Federal law denies gay couples any benefits of marriage under immigration rules.

On this February morning, Judge Kim was deciding whether Ms. Sousa should be deported immediately—which would have meant being barred from re-entry for up to 10 years—or allowed to leave and preserve her right to return someday. The judge granted her 120 days to leave, the maximum, and wished her good luck.

"I feel like I'm dying," Ms. Sousa said as the couple and their lawyers left the courtroom. The most harrowing thing, she said, was having to break the news to the child she had raised since infancy. "She won't understand that I don't have the proper papers, that I have to go far away," she said.

Tom Hogan and Alex Lopez were caught trying to skirt the legal limitations of a tourist visa three weeks ago, at the American border near Montreal. Mr. Hogan, an Irish national with a 10-year tourist visa, was stopped by immigration officials as he and Mr. Lopez, his partner of two and half years, tried to drive back to their home in New Jersey.

Mr. Hogan had already come and gone a half-dozen times last year, in an attempt to show that he was not really living in the United States. The last time he had passed through immigration, however, an alert official said that he was spending too much time here and warned that it would be his final visit.

Fearing rejection that Saturday night, Mr. Hogan hoped to take advantage of lax checks at the Canadian-United States border by posing as an American, and he offered up a driver's license and credit cards to prove it. The ruse failed. During seven hours of questioning, Mr. Hogan confessed that he did actually live here with his partner. His passport was stamped with a five-year re-entry prohibition and he was immediately deported.

Speaking from Ireland the other day, Mr. Hogan said he had no idea how to rejoin Mr. Lopez. He said he was particularly worried about the health of his partner, who has AIDS.

"The worst thing," said Mr. Hogan, a nurse, "is that if he were to get sick tomorrow, I can't just get on a plane to take care of him."

Mr. Lopez, 38, a garment industry executive, said that he, too, was at a loss. "I'm a good American," he said. "I pay my taxes. Why don't I have a right to be with the person I love?"

Representative Jerrold L. Nadler, who has taken up the case, said he hoped to introduce legislation that would give same-sex partners immigration rights. But Mr. Nadler, a Democrat from New York, said he was not optimistic that such a bill would pass.

"In a Republican Congress, the chances are zero to none," he said. "Anything you do to help gay people deal with real-life problems they see as an affirmation of the gay life style."

The Lesbian and Gay Immigration Rights Task Force, which has about 7,000 members and seven branches nationwide, has started a lobbying campaign to change the law, but its leaders acknowledge that it might be years before the changes gain favor in Congress. It has been only a decade, they point out, since Congress repealed a law that barred gay men and women from entering the United States at all.

Like many foreigners desperate to stay with their partners, Rebecca, a human resources executive from Israel, said she took a secretarial job because the employer was the only one willing to sponsor her for a work visa. Rebecca, 37, who said she was afraid to give her last name, shares a house in New Brunswick, N.J., with her partner of two years, who owns a home renovation business. If she loses her job, she loses her visa. That equation, Rebecca said, encourages her employer to work her harder and longer than other employees.

"My back is really to the wall, and I'm always so nervous about losing my job," she said.

Yoshi Ito and his partner, Jay McMillan, learned how tenuous a work visa can be. To help close a budget gap, Mr. Ito's employer, a New Jersey software company, laid him off this month. Mr. Ito, 29, who had spent eight months in Japan separated from Mr. McMillan while he waited for the visa, said he would go back home in April, apply to American graduate schools and hope to return on a student visa.

'All We Want Is to Be Together'

"Everyone talks about gay marriage, but all we want is to be together," said Mr. McMillan, 40, a sales representative for a food manufacturer, who lives in Detroit. Because he could find no other employer willing to sponsor him, Mr. Ito took the job in New Jersey even though it meant driving 10 hours each way on weekends to be with Mr. McMillan.

Despite the insecurity of holding a temporary student visa, Michel Buffet, a 29-year-old French national, bought a house this month in Montclair, N.J., with his American partner, Robert Mogel, a vice president of a medical supply company. The couple, who have been together for nine years, are also planning to adopt a child.

As he comes to the end of his doctoral program in organizational psychology at Columbia University, Mr. Buffet hopes to get a work visa by persuading officials he has skills that are needed in this country—the only way he can stay here legally. "I don't think either of us will ever feel relaxed," Mr. Buffet said, "until I have that paper in my hand."

Although he has no clear strategy for bringing him back, Kent McCoy keeps Samer Yahya's voice on his answering machine's outgoing message. The two communicate several times a day by E-mail, and though Trinity College continues to hold Mr. Yahya's scholarship, Mr. McCoy says he is starting to lose hope.

At the moment, moving to Canada looks like the only viable option, but Mr. McCoy cringes at the thought of giving up his architectural practice, his friends and his home. "I'm the third generation in Hartford," he said. "I have an elderly mother to look after. My whole life is here."

He mentioned a friend who recently met a woman during a vacation in Russia. After a brief romance, they were married, and six weeks later, she was living in the United States.

"I'm not asking for special rights," he said. "All I want is to be treated like everyone else."

* * *

June 27, 1999

STONEWALL VETERANS RECALL THE OUTLAW DAYS

By DAVID KIRBY

The Stonewall Inn, where a police raid in June 1969 sparked an uprising by a handful of drag queens and rabble-rousers and ushered in the modern gay rights movement, is by far the best known hangout from the days when being gay meant being a social outlaw. But Greenwich Village had other spots, too, where gay men and lesbians sought a modicum of safety and privacy. Many of these places have perished, as have many Stonewall veterans who frequented them. But a few remain.

Walk into Fedora Restaurant on any given night, for example, and you enter another era. Faded pictures recall bygone days when gay men packed the place on West Fourth Street with laughter, song and the camaraderie that comes from being in a refuge from a hostile world. Today, fewer of the regulars from those days stop in. But there are those who still do, gentlemen of a certain age, some with ascots and walking sticks. Others pop in only occasionally, for nostalgia's sake.

"It's exactly the same," marveled Bob Kohler, 73, a longtime Villager who witnessed the Stonewall uprising and still considers himself a "radical gay activist."

Mr. Kohler said he patronized Fedora "when it was the only game in town." Now, he said during an interview at the restaurant, "I eat here on strange and special occasions." He added, "Last time, I had a friend dying of AIDS who wanted to come for one last, memorable meal."

The menu, with its chicken tetrazzini and eggs a la russe, has changed little since Fedora opened in 1952 (the prix fixe dinner, originally $1.75, is now $10.95). The owner, Fedora Dorato, a vivacious woman full of memories, played hostess for her husband, Henry, who ran the place until he died in 1997. "Every night at 8, Fedora would make her entrance and everybody would stop and applaud," Mr. Kohler recalled. "Sometimes straight people would be there, and they'd ask why. Well, in those days, most people weren't very nice to gay people. Fedora was."

Warren Allen Smith, 77, who owned a recording studio in the Village in the 60's, said he was eating at Fedora on the second night of the disturbances, when a big commotion erupted at the Stonewall, around the corner.

"I thought it was a happening," he said. "I was in my 40's, and I was a businessman and closeted. So I stayed in the park across the street watching. I didn't want to mix with those dregs causing problems."

Life for gay men and lesbians before Stonewall, even in the liberal Village, was challenging at best. It was a time psychiatrists regarded them as mentally ill and the police regularly raided their bars, which were often seedy dives.

"They were at once admirable and scary," said Martin Duberman, author of the book "Stonewall" (Dutton, 1993), which recounts the uprising and its participants. "Though they were all we had, gay bars were frightening. You never knew what might happen, especially with police raids. The cops treated customers like scum. They threw us up against walls. If you didn't have ID, you were arrested. And management never interfered."

By all accounts, fear of the police was rampant among gay people of the day. "I was more afraid of being entrapped by a plainclothes cop than being mashed by some tough from Jersey City, which is the big fear now," Mr. Duberman said. "They would choose the hunkiest young cops and dress them in the standard gay uniform of the day—chino pants, penny loafers and T-shirt—and send them out to entrap gay men. The guy would come up and say, 'Hey, what're you doing tonight?' And because they were generally gorgeous, you said: 'Nothing. What are you doing?' And then, snap! On went the handcuffs. Just like that."

"You always went out with anxiety," Mr. Duberman said. "Danger and trepidation were built into the scene."

Julius's, a bar at West 10th Street and Waverly Place that dates to the 19th century, also became popular with gay people in the 60's. Hanging on the wall is a copy of an older Walter Winchell column with the headline "Where to Go and Why," which refers to the wood-paneled watering hole as a "society bar," though it would hardly be described that way now. These days it is still a gay bar, with a crowd rang-

ing from Stonewall veterans to people who were born well after 1969.

But back then, concern about the police led to a policy forbidding patrons from turning their back to the bar, which was taken as a sign of sexual availability. In 1967, Julius's temporarily lost its liquor license after an undercover patrolman arrested, on degeneracy charges, a young man who, according to a yellowed New York Times article behind the bar, "wore tight clothes and walked with a mincing gait."

"Julius's was a place where nobody was gay until they had a couple of drinks," said Jim Fouratt, a longtime Villager who participated in the riots. He spent long liquid afternoons at the smoky old bar, which also drew gay artists and writers, like Allen Ginsberg. "Nobody called themselves gay," Mr. Fouratt said. "You were either a 'beatnik' or 'bohemian.' Those were the code words."

But Julius's patrons weren't as radical as Stonewall's, some Village veterans said. "On the second night of rioting, we walked over to Julius's and said: 'Come out! Come out!' But nobody did," Mr. Fouratt said. "They were very proper compared to Stonewall, which, incidentally, was an awful place. But for all its tackiness and tawdriness, it was a place where people who really felt bad about being gay could feel really good and free. It was a release from the outside world and all the baggage people carried around."

Joan Egan, 67, says the Village is a different place for gay people these days. "The character of the Village today is for tourists," she said. "Nobody I know goes to the Village to be gay anymore. But in the past, that's exactly why they went there."

"There were many more bars for women back then," Ms. Egan said. "Though today, fortunately, we have other places to meet." She remembered watching the Stonewall disturbances. "It was exhilarating and terrifying, and the noise was unbelievable," she said.

Bitter disputes still simmer over who was where when, and there are at least two competing groups of Stonewall veterans. But many agree that a lot of young gay people are woefully unaware of the hardships of gay life in the pre-Stonewall era, and unappreciative of their struggles.

"You feel betrayed by your own people," Mr. Kohler said. "The assimilation and the apathy in the gay community today saddens me. So many just want to party, party, party. And that, after fighting for 30 years, is very discouraging."

*   *   *

Constitutional Law

August 18, 1984

U.S. COURT UPHOLDS NAVY'S DISCHARGE OF A HOMOSEXUAL

By STUART TAYLOR JR.
Special to the New York Times

WASHINGTON, Aug. 17—Ruling that "private, consensual homosexual conduct is not constitutionally protected," a Federal appeals panel today upheld the Navy's discharge of a petty officer who acknowledged engaging in homosexual acts.

Judge Robert H. Bork wrote for the unanimous three-judge panel that while several Supreme Court decisions had recognized a vaguely defined constitutional "right of privacy," the Court "has never defined the right so broadly as to encompass homosexual conduct."

The 21-page ruling today was the broadest and most ringing repudiation a Federal appeals court had given to the view of some libertarians that laws penalizing homosexual conduct are unconstitutional.

Precedent Somewhat Unclear

While some lower Federal courts have suggested that private homosexual conduct enjoys a degree of constitutional protection, the Supreme Court in 1976 affirmed a lower court decision suggesting the contrary. Because the Supreme Court issued no opinion in that case, its importance as a precedent is somewhat unclear.

Stephen V. Bomse, a San Francisco lawyer representing the homosexual plaintiff in the case before the three-judge panel, said today that he had not seen the court's opinion or spoken with his client.

"Assuming he wants to pursue it," Mr. Bomse said, "we will pursue it," by asking the full 11-judge United States Court of Appeals for the District of Columbia to rehear the case.

Demand for Legislation Likely

Coming at a time when homosexual rights activists have gained political strength in the Democratic Party and in many communities, the ruling is likely to fuel demands for state and Federal legislation to protect homosexuals against discrimination.

The case grew out of the 1981 discharge of James L. Dronenburg, who, Judge Bork noted, had "an unblemished service record and earned many citations praising his job performance" in nine years as a Korean linguist and cryptographer with a top-security clearance.

A 27-year-old petty officer at the time of his honorable discharge, Mr. Dronenburg first denied, but later acknowledged, allegations by a 19-year-old seaman recruit that he repeatedly engaged in homosexual conduct in a Navy barracks while attending the Defense Language Institute in Monterey, Calif. William G. Cole, the Justice Department lawyer who handled the appeal, said today that he did not know whether any action had been taken against the recruit.

After his discharge, Mr. Dronenburg filed a suit charging that the Navy's policy mandating discharge of all homosexuals violated his constitutional rights to privacy and equal protection of the laws.

Judge Bork stressed that "legislation may implement morality" in sexual matters and that the courts had no business creating new constitutional rights to engage in sexual activity.

Governmental penalties against homosexual conduct could logically be struck down, he said, only if "any and all private sexual behavior" was constitutionally protected, "a conclusion we are unwilling to draw."

Judge Bork's opinion did not discuss whether private, consensual heterosexual activity would enjoy any special constitutional protection in the military or elsewhere. Many states still have laws prohibiting certain heterosexual acts.

'Moral Choices of the People'

"If the revolution in sexual mores that appellant proclaims is in fact ever to arrive," Judge Bork wrote, "we think it must arrive through the moral choices of the people and their elected representatives, not through the judicial ukase of this court."

The Federal appeals court here is widely viewed as the most powerful in the nation after the Supreme Court. Judge Bork, a leading scholar, an exponent of judicial restraint whom President Reagan appointed to the appeals court in 1982, is often mentioned as a possible Supreme Court appointee if Mr. Reagan wins a second term.

Aside from ruling that the constitutional right to privacy did not encompass homosexuality, Judge Bork said in the decision that there had been no equal protection violation because the Navy policy "is plainly a rational means of advancing a legitimate, indeed a crucial, interest common to all our armed forces."

"The effects of homosexual conduct within a naval or military unit are almost certain to be harmful to morale and discipline," Judge Bork said. He added that homosexual liaisons were sure "to call into question the even-handedness of superiors' dealings with lower ranks, to make personal dealings uncomfortable where the relationship is sexually ambiguous, to generate dislike and disapproval among many who find homosexuality morally offensive, and, it must be said, given the powers of military superiors over their inferiors, to enhance the possibility of homosexual seduction."

Opinion Is Unanimous

His opinion was joined by Judge Antonin Scalia, another Reagan appointee to the appeals court, and Federal District Judge David W. Williams of Los Angeles, sitting specially on the appeals court here.

Their decision upheld an earlier ruling by Federal District Judge Oliver Gasch rejecting Mr. Dronenburg's suit.

Judge Bork said in his opinion that while in his personal view "no court should create new constitutional rights," beyond those that were "fairly discoverable in the Constitution," he was obliged as a lower court judge to follow Supreme Court precedents since 1965 creating a new "right of privacy."

But he said these decisions, which have struck down laws limiting use and sale of contraceptives and have created a constitutional right to have an abortion, "contain little guidance for the lower courts" and establish no general principle protecting all private sexual behavior.

In the absence of such a general principle or a specific constitutional provision protecting homosexual conduct, Judge Bork said, courts should defer to the elected branches of Government.

He also said that lower courts should heed a 1976 decision in which the Supreme Court summarily affirmed a ruling by a lower court that had upheld a Virginia law making it a crime to engage in private consensual homosexual conduct.

Because of the Supreme Court's failure to explain the basis for its decision in that case, and the possibility that it involved doubts as to the plaintiffs' standing to sue, some experts contend that the Supreme Court has not resolved the issue decided the appeals court today.

* * *

September 2, 1984

COURT RULING SPURS HOMOSEXUALS' ANTIDISCRIMINATION EFFORT

Civil rights activists seeking laws to forbid discrimination against homosexuals say that a high court's upholding of the Navy's discharge of a homosexual was a setback, but one that would give them added motivation to work harder for their goals.

The enactment of antidiscrimination measures by municipalities and states flagged after the election of President Reagan in 1980 signaled a conservative groundswell, but homosexual rights activists cite a number of state and municipal victories in the past couple of years as indicating renewed strength.

A three-judge panel of the United States Court of Appeals for the District of Columbia, ruling Aug. 17, upheld the Navy's discharge of a petty officer because he had had sexual relations with another man.

"Private, consensual homosexual conduct is not constitutionally protected," Judge Robert H. Bork wrote. A change in what the judge perceived as societal condemnation of homosexuality would have to come "through the moral choices of the people and their elected representatives," he said, not through judicial command.

Laws in 56 Places

Virginia Apuzzo, executive director of the National Gay Task Force, suggested that homosexual activists were likely to take up Judge Bork's virtual invitation to increase pressure on state and local governments.

"Every time we've encountered a setback such as this," she said, "it's motivated us to work even harder." Her organization counts 56 cities, counties or states that now have laws or executive orders prohibiting at least some forms of discrimination against homosexuals.

Leaders of the rights movement count five legislative victories so far this year, on top of four last year and five in 1982.

Stressing the relative youth of the homosexual rights movement, which is widely considered to have been born in 1969, Thomas B. Stoddard, legislative director of the New York Civil Liberties Union who is co-author of a book on the civil rights of homosexuals, called the progress "nothing short of a miracle."

Mayors' Group Urges Action

An important recent success was the United States Conference of Mayors' approval of a resolution recommending that "all levels of government adopt legal protections for the rights of gay and lesbian Americans."

By passing that resolution in June, the mayors enabled homosexual organizations to "raise the issue in city after city," Miss Apuzzo of the National Gay Task Force said. "We have raised the dialogue; now we will have the local organizations bring it to the political representatives and their constituents."

Mayor Arthur J. Holland of Trenton, one of the sponsors of the measure, said: "Gays and lesbians are human beings, too. Average gays and lesbians are so inclined by their nature and just want what every other person wants."

But what success there has been in gaining such legislation is not unalloyed. Many of the laws apply only to public employment, and many lack enforcement provisions. And, more importantly, lawmakers may not have the final word.

Big Setback in California

As in the watershed 1977 referendum in Dade County, Fla., where Anita Bryant and antihomosexual organizations achieved the repeal of a rights ordinance, laws recently approved in Houston and Montgomery County, Md., face possible challenges this fall at the ballot box.

The homosexual rights movement suffered a significant loss in California in March, when Gov. George Deukmejian vetoed a statewide measure outlawing job discrimination.

"A person's sexual orientation should not be a basis for the establishment of a special protected class of individuals," Mr. Deukmejian said, "especially in the absence of a compelling showing of need."

"The proponents have been unable to provide compelling evidence that there is, in fact, widespread employment discrimination based upon sexual orientation," he concluded.

Moral Majority Opposition

Conservative Christian organizations are often a strong voice against the passage of measures that specifically mention sexual orientation or homosexuality.

"Homosexuals deserve protection under the law just like any other person," said Stephen Heuston, a legislative assistant with Moral Majority in Washington. "Homosexuality is not a special class. Homosexuality, unlike race and unlike gender, is a choice."

Similarly, opponents of the Houston measure ran a full-page advertisement in The Houston Chronicle that said: "The other guarantees in the ordinance forbid discrimination on the basis of race, color, religion, age, disability, sex and national origin. They are acts of God. Homosexuality is a conscious selection of a lifestyle that deviates from the social norm. Should such a deliberate selection be lumped together with acts of God?"

Many homosexual activists, however, with the support of many psychologists, dispute these opponents' assertion: Homosexuality is not a matter of choice, they say, but part of an individual's basic makeup that is determined at an early age.

Mondale Supports Amendment

Activists hope, Miss Apuzzo said, that work on the local level will build a "groundswell" toward getting Congress to add sexual orientation to the protected classes of race, religion and sex in the 1964 Civil Rights Act.

An attempt to so amend the act has languished since 1975 in the House of Representatives, with 79 legislators currently signed on as co-sponsors. In the Senate, a similiar version has nine co-sponsors.

"It's not how many we need, but who we need," said Vickey I. Monrean, executive director of the Gay Rights National Lobby. Backers must find a "cross section of political support" before they can hope to move the bill forward.

President Reagan, asked at a news conference June 14 if he supported the amendment, said, "Well, I just have to say that I am opposed to discrimination, period." Pressed further, the President said he wanted to "see what else they have in there."

Walter F. Mondale, his Democratic opponent, has said he supports the legislation.

Broad Measure in Wisconsin

The rights advocates' first statewide victory came in 1982, when Wisconsin approved a comprehensive law forbidding discrimination against homosexuals in employment, public accommodations, housing, education, real estate practices, credit and union practices.

Illinois and Michigan prohibit discrimination in public housing, and in California, New York, Ohio and Pennsylvania executive orders ban some forms of discrimination.

On the municipal level, some cities with working-class, conservative reputations, including Detroit and Columbus, Ohio, approved ordinances as early as 1979. In New York City, however, with probably the most homosexuals in the country, proponents of a rights ordinance have failed each year since 1975.

Elsewhere in New York, the cities of Buffalo, Rochester, Ithaca, Troy and Alfred have laws protecting the rights of homosexuals. In Connecticut, where a statewide measure has failed several times, a Hartford ordinance prohibits employ-ment discrimination against homosexuals. No municipalities in New Jersey have such ordinances, though an antidiscrimination bill is pending in the State Assembly.

* * *

July 1, 1986

HIGH COURT, 5-4, SAYS STATES HAVE THE RIGHT TO OUTLAW PRIVATE HOMOSEXUAL ACTS; DIVISION IS BITTER

By STUART TAYLOR JR.
Special to the New York Times

WASHINGTON, June 30—A bitterly divided Supreme Court ruled 5 to 4 today that the Constitution does not protect homosexual relations between consenting adults, even in the privacy of their own homes.

The Court held that a Georgia law that forbids all people to engage in oral or anal sex could be used to prosecute such conduct between homosexuals.

The majority said it would not rule on whether the Constitution protected married couples and other heterosexuals from prosecution under the same law. Associate Justice John Paul Stevens, however, said in a dissent that such laws were "concededly unconstitutional with respect to heterosexuals" under the reasoning of previous Supreme Court rulings.

Weakens Legal Position

The decision is unlikely to curb the growing visibility of homosexuality as a fact of daily life in America, but it weakens the legal arguments of homosexual activists against various forms of discrimination.

This does not necessarily mean it would allow discrimination against homosexuals in other contexts. However, both homosexual groups and their opponents agreed the ruling would slow the advancement of homosexual rights.

The announcement of the decision was unusually dramatic, with Associate Justices Byron R. White, author of the majority opinion, and Harry A. Blackmun, author of an impassioned dissent, both reading detailed passages from the bench.

Limits Effect of Past Rulings

The ruling limited past Supreme Court decisions by rejecting what Justice White called the view "that any kind of private sexual conduct between consenting adults is constitutionally insulated from state proscription."

While the Court has previously upheld a vague right of sexual privacy for heterosexuals, it has never specified, and did not say today, whether that right protects oral or anal sex between men and women.

Criminal prosecutions for private sexual conduct between consenting adults are rare in the case of homosexuals, the Court noted today, and almost unheard of in the case of heterosexuals.

The case ruled on today was a civil suit challenging the Georgia sodomy law brought by Michael Hardwick, a homo-

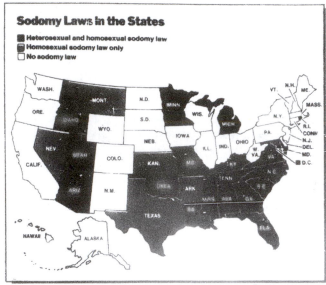

Sodomy Laws in the States

■ Heterosexual and homosexual sodomy law
■ Homosexual sodomy law only
□ No sodomy law

sexual who had been arrested in his Atlanta bedroom while having sexual relations with another man.

The law defines sodomy as "any sex act involving the sex organs of one person and the mouth or anus of another."

A police officer had gone to his home to serve a warrant because Mr. Hardwick had not paid a fine for public drunkenness. The officer was given permission by someone who answered the door to the enter the house and find Mr. Hardwick.

Was Not Prosecuted in Case

Mr. Hardwick was not prosecuted, but he challenged the law on the ground that it violated his constitutional right to privacy.

Justice White's opinion declined to extend to homosexuals a line of decisions involving heterosexuals—in particular a 1965 decision striking down a Connecticut law against contraception—in which the Court has recognized constitutional rights to sexual privacy. While the court did not specifically refer to homosexual acts between women, its reasoning would apparently apply to such acts.

Justice White stressed the "ancient roots" in English common law of statutes criminalizing homosexual relations, noting that all 50 states outlawed homosexual sodomy until 1961 and that 24 states and the District of Columbia still do.

"The Court is most vulnerable and comes nearest to illegitimacy when it deals with judge-made constitutional law having little or no cognizable roots in the language or design of the Constitution," Justice White said in explaining why it should not create a right to homosexual sodomy.

Justice Blackmun, in his dissent, said, "The right of an individual to conduct intimate relationships in the intimacy of his or her own home seems to me to be the heart of the Constitution's protection of privacy."

Justice Stevens, in a separate dissent, said the Court's rationale, like the Georgia statute and the English common law from which it was derived, "applies equally to the prohibited conduct regardless of whether the parties who engage in it are married or unmarried, or of the same or different sexes."

He said that the court's prior decisions indicated the Constitution barred governmental intrusion into private heterosexual relationships, and that the same protections should apply to homosexuals.

Severity of Punishment Cited

One member of the majority, Associate Justice Lewis F. Powell Jr., said in a separate concurrence that while states may criminalize homosexual sodomy, those who commit such acts may enjoy some protection from the Eighth Amendment's ban on "cruel and unusual punishments."

Noting that the Georgia law authorizes prison sentences of one to 20 years for a single homosexual act, he said, "In my view, a prison sentence for such conduct—certainly a sentence of long duration—would create a serious Eighth Amendment issue."

Others joining the majority opinion were Chief Justice Warren E. Burger and Associate Justices William H. Rehnquist and Sandra Day O'Connor.

Associate Justices William J. Brennan Jr., Thurgood Marshall and Stevens joined Justice Blackmun's dissent. The first two also joined Justice Stevens's dissent.

Twenty-six states have decriminalized sodomy, and five of the 24 that still make homosexual sodomy a crime have decriminalized heterosexual sodomy, at least in some contexts.

The New York Court of Appeals, in a 1980 decision apparently in conflict with today's Supreme Court decision, held the state's law barring sodomy unconstitutional. But a state official said the ruling would have no direct bearing on New York law.

"The New York State statute was struck down by our own state court of appeals, and that statute remains unconstitutional," said Timothy Gilles, a spokesman for State Attorney General Robert Abrams. Mr. Gilles said the Supreme Court had declined to rule on the New York case in 1981, letting stand the state court ruling.

New Jersey and Connecticut have decriminalized sodomy by legislation.

Noncommittal on Desirability

Justice White stressed today that the case, Bowers v. Hardwick, No. 85-140, "does not require a judgment on whether laws against sodomy between consenting adults in general, or between homosexuals in particular, are wise or desirable," or about whether states should repeal such laws.

"The issue presented is whether the Federal Constitution confers a fundamental right upon homosexuals to engage in sodomy and hence invalidates the laws of the many states that still make such conduct illegal and have done so for a very long time," he said.

Justice White said that homosexual activity was not protected by previous decisions that have interpreted the 14th Amendment right not to be deprived of "liberty" without "due process of law" as including various "fundamental rights" not specified in the Constitution. He said these rights were limited to those "deeply rooted in this nation's history or tradition" or "implicit in the concept of ordered liberty."

In light of the law's longstanding condemnation of homosexual conduct, Justice White said, it would be "at best, facetious" to suggest that homosexual conduct qualified as a "fundamental right."

Privacy Argument Rejected

Justice White also rejected the argument that homosexual conduct should be protected at least where it occurs in the privacy of the home. "Otherwise illegal conduct is not always immunized whenever it occurs in the home," he said, citing laws against possession of narcotics and stolen goods as well as "adultery, incest and other sexual crimes."

In response to arguments that the Constitution bars majorities from imposing their view of morality on minorities, he said the law "is constantly based on notions of morality, and if all laws representing essentially moral choices are to be invalidated under the Due Process Clause, the courts will be very busy indeed."

A Federal appellate court in Atlanta had held that the Georgia law "infringes upon the fundamental constitutional rights of Michael Hardwick" to have private sexual relations, indicating it was likely to strike the law down after further proceedings. The state appealed to the Supreme Court.

Justice White noted that a husband and wife who had challenged the law along with Mr. Hardwick had been held by the lower courts not to have standing to sue because they had never been arrested.

He said: "The only claim properly before the Court, therefore, is Hardwick's challenge to the Georgia statute as applied to consensual homosexual sodomy. We express no opinion on the constitutionality of the Georgia statute as applied to other acts of sodomy."

* * *

July 3, 1986

CITY'S HOMOSEXUALS PROTEST HIGH COURT SODOMY RULING

By WILLIAM G. BLAIR

The Supreme Court ruling this week that upheld sodomy laws has generated anger and demonstrations in New York City's homosexual community.

Leaders said a rally, held Tuesday night at Sheridan Square in Greenwich Village, would be followed with another there tomorrow.

A leader of the protest, Eleanor Cooper, said the rally would start at noon and probably include "a march, but just where we don't know yet."

Ms. Cooper, executive director of the Coalition for Lesbian and Gay Rights, which includes 50 homosexual and other groups, said a permit for the demonstration would be sought today from the Police Department. A department spokesman said the request would be considered when it was received.

'Not a Throwaway Minority'

Ms. Cooper said the demonstration was "intended to express our anger and to make it clear that we're not a throwaway minority of some sort."

She said that the protest was intended not only to coincide with the day the nation celebrates its independence, but also to convey the anger of homosexuals to Chief Justice Warren E. Burger and President Reagan, both of whom are to be in the city for the Liberty weekend festivities.

The decision that has infuriated homosexuals around the nation came on Monday when a bitterly divided Supreme Court upheld Georgia's sodomy law and ruled that the Constitution did not protect such conduct between consenting adults.

The executive director of the National Gay and Lesbian Task Force, Jeff Levi, said by telephone from Washington that he did not know of any nationally coordinated demonstration tomorrow. He observed, however, that spontaneous demonstrations by homosexuals occurred Tuesday in several cities around the country as soon as details of the Supreme Court's 5-to-4 ruling became widely known.

Sitdowns in the Street

One demonstration, involving nearly 1,000 people and lasting five hours, took place Tuesday night in and around Sheridan Square. The protest had a permit, and there were no arrests.

The rally featured sitdowns on Seventh Avenue at Sheridan Square and on the Avenue of the Americas at West Eighth Street. A dozen speakers addressed the crowd, and their words were frequently accompanied by such chants as "It's time for militancy" and "No more nice guys."

A flyer was distributed that promised homosexual activists would "disrupt traffic, snarl subways and show our rage" during the July 4 celebrations.

Among the speakers was the assistant director of the Lambda Legal Defense and Education Fund, Nancy Langer, who told the crowd: "We're going to stop July 4. We all know what's going to happen July 4, Warren Burger will be in town."

Another speaker was the State Commissioner of Human Rights, Douglas H. White, who is also vice chairman of a homosexual-rights task force established in 1984 by Governor Cuomo.

Mr. White described the High Court's decision as one "in keeping with Gestapo or K.G.B. tactics." He said "any person suspected of variant sexual activity would be fair game for overzealous police officers and spiteful neighbors."

He reaffirmed his support for a statewide homosexual rights bill like the one recently adopted by New York City.

New York State's law barring anal or oral sex was struck down by the State Court of Appeals, the state's highest tribunal, in 1980. New Jersey and Connecticut also have revoked sodomy laws, placing them among the 26 states that have no such laws. Twenty-four states and the District of Columbia outlaw homosexual sodomy.

* * *

July 5, 1986

HOMOSEXUALS, UPSET BY RULING, PLAN DRIVE TO ABOLISH ANTI-SODOMY LAWS

By ROBERT LINDSEY
Special to the New York Times

SAN FRANCISCO, July 4—Leaders of homosexual groups angered over a Supreme Court decision upholding the right of states to ban sodomy say they are considering economic boycotts, lawsuits, mass protests and a lobbying campaign to legalize homosexual acts between adults in the 24 states that ban sodomy.

"If we are going to be relegated to second-class citizenship, then we'll teach the nation we are equal and we can retaliate," said John Wahl, a San Francisco lawyer who is among many homosexuals here who favor an economic boycott aimed at overturning laws against sodomy.

"We're going to take whatever action is necessary, and we'll escalate that action as much as necessary until we have equal treatment in this land," he added.

Jeff Levy, executive director of the National Gay and Lesbian Task Force in Washington, said the decision Monday in which the High Court ruled that a Georgia law prohibiting anal and oral intercourse did not violate the constitutional right to privacy "had really galvanized people."

'Incredible Anger Out There'

"There is an incredible anger out there—people are really prepared to come out and fight," he said.

Mr. Levy said organizations of homosexuals, besides staging protests in several cities, including one that drew more than a thousand protesters in New York today, would soon begin lobbying to overturn anti-sodomy laws in the 24 states and the District of Columbia where they are still on the books. And he said the laws would be challenged in some places on the ground that they are barred by state constitutions.

At a meeting here Thursday, leaders of several homosexual groups said they were considering organizing a nationwide boycott of products from Georgia, including Coca-Cola, to protest the state's anti-sodomy law. The corporate headquarters of the soft drink company is in Atlanta.

"There are a lot of gay dollars out there," Terry Anderson, coordinator of the proposed boycott, said. "Most gays have relatively high incomes; there are a lot of two-income households out there. Until Coca-Cola helps us get these antiquated laws off the books, we're going to continue to boycott it."

Decision on Boycott

In an interview today, Mr. Anderson indicated some homosexual leaders were uncertain about the boycott and that a final decision would not be made until at at least Tuesday, when a strategy meeting is scheduled.

In the mid-1970's, San Francisco was one of the nation's first cities in which large numbers of homosexuals joined forces to gain political power. Later, along with New York, it became one of the first cities where physicians detected large numbers of cases of AIDS, the lethal disease that mainly affects homosexual men and drug abusers.

Leaders of homosexual groups said that recent Government efforts purportedly intended to limit the spread of AIDS, but which they see as evidence of bias toward homosexuals, combined with this week's Supreme Court decision, had enraged homosexuals. They said the actions caused more anger in their community than anything since 1979 when a San Francisco Supervisor, Dan White, was sentenced to prison for less than six years for the murder of Mayor George Moscone and Supervisor Harvey Milk. The supervisor was a homosexual.

And, saying that they would no longer accept governmental interference in their private lives, they asserted that the Supreme Court's decision was a catalyst that would galvanize them to resist such interference.

California decriminalized sexual behavior between consenting adults in 1975, so the High Court's decision on sodomy had no effect here.

A Pattern Is Seen

But spokesmen for homosexual groups attacked the ruling as part of what they contended was as a broader pattern of efforts by political conservatives and religious fundamentalists, sometimes under the guise of efforts to control AIDS, to end sexual relationships between people of the same sex and to eliminate gains homosexuals had made in the past decade or so.

Among other examples of the trend, they say, is a new Justice Department opinion declaring that employers can legally discharge workers infected with AIDS if they do so to protect other employees.

They also cited a referendum that is being placed on the November ballot in California as a result of a petition campaign by followers of the political extremist Lyndon H. LaRouche Jr. If approved by voters, it would prohibit the employment of AIDS victims and carriers in schools, restaurants and other places, and it would allow state officials to quarantine them in hospitals or sanitariums.

Such actions disregard scientists' assurances that the disease cannot be transmitted except through sexual contact or direct exchange of blood.

Besides considering a boycott of Georgia companies, members of homosexual groups here said they would expand political efforts against candidates who were insensitive to their interests, including the Rev. Pat Robertson, the television evangelist who is a possible 1988 Republican Presidential candidate.

They also said they were planning a protest rally when Associate Justice Sandra Day O'Connor of the Supreme Court makes a speaking appearance here July 17. They said they hoped to attract thousands of homosexuals to protest her vote upholding Georgia's anti-sodomy law.

"We think the right wing has inordinate influence in the present Administration," Mr. Wahl said. "The right wing is using the AIDS epidemic to oppress our people. I hate this kind of warlike talk, but you're going to have warfare if they try to intern our people."

* * *

August 12, 1986

HUNDREDS PROTEST SUPREME COURT SODOMY RULING

As members of the American Bar Association held a dinner inside, hundreds of protesters gathered last night on the plaza of Lincoln Center to protest the recent Supreme Court ruling that Constitutional guarantees to privacy do not protect homosexual sex.

The demonstration was an extension of a rally held earlier in the day in front of the New York Hilton, where Chief Justice Warren E. Burger was addressing the bar group in his last speech as the nation's Chief Justice. During the speech, about 400 demonstrators gathered outside the hotel in a protest organized by the Coalition for Gay and Lesbian Rights. Demonstrators held placards reading "Human rights begin at home," and chanted "Keep the courtroom out of the bedroom."

The civil rights lawyer Alan M. Dershowitz, who said he had walked out of the Chief Justice's speech in protest of the recent ruling, told the crowd outside the Hilton that the decision would open the way for the persecution of all people, regardless of their sexual preference.

"When it comes to the issue of legitimacy, when it comes to the issue of quarantine, we are all gay, because what happens to gays today will happen to us tomorrow," Mr. Dershowitz said.

He said that Chief Justice Burger "will be remembered in infamy for the insensitivity he has shown to all." In the recent decision, which upheld a Georgia sodomy law, the Chief Justice wrote a separate concurring opinion.

* * *

September 22, 1987

PACKWOOD, SEEING THREAT TO PRIVACY, OPPOSES BORK

By LINDA GREENHOUSE
Special to the New York Times

WASHINGTON, Sept. 21—Senator Bob Packwood, saying he believed Judge Robert H. Bork would do "everything possible" to overturn the Supreme Court's decisions on abortion and the right to privacy, today became the first Senate Republican to oppose Judge Bork's confirmation to the Supreme Court.

Mr. Packwood, a moderate from Oregon who is one of Congress's firmest supporters of abortion rights, said he would take a leading role in the fight against confirmation. He said he would aim his efforts at the 10 to 15 Republicans he estimated were open to persuasion.

Judge Bork's views on abortion law, and on privacy rights were a dominant theme of the questions put to the nominee by Judiciary Committee members last week, and that concern was evident again today as the senators began hearing other

Demonstrators at Lincoln Center last night protesting Supreme Court ruling on sodomy laws.

witnesses. Among them were black leaders like William T. Coleman Jr., the former Secretary of Transportation, who said a Justice Bork would turn back the clock on civil rights. Other witnesses, however, described the judge as a distinguished jurist who would be an ideal addition to the Court.

Opposition Not a Surprise

Because of his outspokenness on the abortion issue, Senator Packwood had been counted by both sides as leaning strongly against the Bork confirmation, so his announcement at a news conference today was not a surprise. But his stand could have considerable influence, not simply because he is opposing the nomination but because of the terms in which he framed his opposition.

Mr. Packwood said that in two meetings with Judge Bork, he had probed the nominee for assurances that the constitutional right to privacy, and the Court's abortion rulings that are based on that right, would not be in jeopardy if Judge Bork were confirmed. The Senator, a lawyer who is not a member of the Judiciary Committee, said he had also scrutinized the judge's testimony on these issues last week.

Having done that, Senator Packwood said, "I am convinced that Judge Bork feels so strongly opposed to the right of privacy that he will do everything possible to cut and trim, and eliminate if possible, the liberties that the right of privacy protects."

No Explicit Mention

In his testimony last week, as in his earlier writings, Judge Bork maintained his criticism of the Court's privacy decisions on the ground that the Constitution does not explicitly mention a right to privacy.

Pressed by several senators on whether he would go beyond academic criticism to an effort to overrule Roe v. Wade, the Court's leading abortion case, Judge Bork did not answer directly. He said he would take several factors into account, including whether the lawyers seeking to uphold the decision could find a basis for abortion rights elsewhere in the Constitution.

Judge Bork's supporters on the Judiciary Committee cited that response as evidence that the nominee would approach the question with an open mind.

Because he speaks with considerable authority on the privacy issues, Mr. Packwood's contrary conclusion makes it less likely that undecided senators can find reassurance in Judge Bork's testimony.

'Mask' Is Off Testimony

Senator Packwood's analysis "takes the mask off" Judge Bork's testimony, said Kate Michelman, director of the National Abortion Rights Action League, one of the organizations lobbying against the Bork confirmation.

"It tells other senators: 'don't be misled,' " she added. "We hope it will inform the other moderate Republicans and encourage them to stop and look at the record for themselves."

In July, speaking to the abortion-rights group, Senator Packwood said of Judge Bork: "If I conclude that there is any possibility that he will overturn Roe vs. Wade, I will not only oppose him, I will not only filibuster, but I will lead a filibuster."

Today, however, while the Senator said he would participate in a filibuster, he stopped short of saying he would lead a filibuster or conduct one singlehandedly if Democratic opponents decide against that strategy, which could allow a minority of the Senate to prevent Judge Bork's confirmation.

Senator Packwood said he had not yet talked to any other senators and could not predict the fate of the nomination. But he said that by the time the full Senate is ready to vote, there would not be more than one or two senators who are actually undecided.

* * *

December 21, 1990

GAY GROUPS TURN TO STATE COURTS TO WIN RIGHTS

By ROBB LONDON

Three times this year, state judges have struck down laws forbidding sodomy. In doing so, most recently in Texas, each judge has said such a law violates the civil rights of homosexuals under the state's constitution.

These rulings are the latest examples of a strategy that is being used with success, not just by gay-rights groups but by other interest groups. Civil rights advocates are using the strategy to win legal recognition of rights that many Federal judges—especially the Justices who make up the current conservative majority on the Supreme Court—are reluctant to find in the United States Constitution.

The interest groups are pursuing claims under state constitutions in those state courts that are now perceived to be more liberal than the Federal courts.

Reversing a Decade-Old Trend

"This clearly reverses the trend of a generation ago, when state courts were seen as conservative, and the Federal courts as the only hope for expansive rulings in civil rights cases," said A. E. Dick Howard, a professor of constitutional law at the University of Virginia.

State courts have also recently recognized other legal rights that the Supreme Court has not been willing to grant, in certain free speech cases, environmental disputes, abortion rights cases and lawsuits seeking redistribution of state funds from rich school districts to poor ones, Professor Howard said.

Several state courts, including California's, have recognized a state constitutional right to demonstrate in public places that are privately owned, like shopping malls. By contrast, the Supreme Court has held that the owners of shopping centers can eject people who try to use the premises as public forums.

Redistribution of Tax Money

The Supreme Court has also refused to find a Federal constitutional right of poor school districts to demand some of the money of wealthier districts. But courts in New Jersey,

Montana, Kentucky and Texas have now recognized a right to some redistribution of state tax money under their own constitutions.

Abortion rights advocates, too, say they are increasingly resorting to state courts, asserting that some state constitutions permit the right to abortion.

"We were forced to begin looking at our options under state law 10 years ago when the Supreme Court held that the Federal Government didn't have to provide Medicaid funds for abortion except to save a woman's life," said Eve Paul, vice president for legal affairs of the Planned Parenthood Federation of America in New York City. "So we brought challenges under state constitutions in New Jersey, California and Massachusetts and got courts there to affirm a right to state Medicaid funds in those places."

Several state courts have also discovered in their constitutions a right to a decent environment, which no Federal court has yet acknowledged, Professor Howard said.

Regulating the Environment

"An environmentalist who comes into Federal court seeking some kind of relief had better be armed with a specific Federal statute that gives him what he wants," he said. "If it can't be found there, then it's usually no dice. But many state constitutions have strong environmental entitlements."

Many state judges have long argued that lawyers have failed to take advantage of state courts and constitutions. In the 1970's, Hans Linde, a Justice of the Oregon Supreme Court, published a series of articles and lectures that caused a sensation in legal circles around the country, arguing that lawyers have a responsibility to bring cases initially in state courts and under state constitutions.

"Many state constitutions contain explicit textual guarantees of certain personal liberties that the Federal Constitution is much more vague about," Mr. Linde, who is now retired from the bench, said in an interview yesterday. "One of the reasons is that most lawyers are trained right from the beginning of law school to do their research in Federal case law, and they never learn to take state courts as seriously."

The result, Mr. Linde said, has been a Federal docket clogged with many appeals that could have been resolved at the state level. "Much of the stuff that goes to the Supreme Court would never have to go there," he added, "if lawyers abandoned this notion that the Federal courts are the big leagues and the state courts are the farm teams."

Six states still have laws on the books banning homosexual sodomy exclusively, said Paula L. Ettelbrick, legal director of the Lambda Legal Defense and Education Fund, a national gay rights group with headquarters in New York City. Sixteen states plus the District of Columbia still maintain laws banning sodomy generally, whether heterosexual or homosexual, she said.

Ms. Ettelbrick said it was extremely rare for prosecutions to be brought under these laws. But she said the laws harmed gay people simply by being on the books, stigmatizing them and hindering public acceptance of homosexuality.

3-for-3 in Rulings

Buoyed by their victory in Texas last week, gay-rights lawyers said they would offer similar challenges to sodomy laws in other states.

"We're three for three since the Supreme Court went against us in 1986, and we're going to keep going," Ms. Ettelbrick said. "Everywhere except Missouri, that is. We don't really know why, but Missouri is probably hopeless for the foreseeable future, because judges there have been particularly unsympathetic to gays and lesbians and other types of cases, like the right to adopt children."

The gay rights advocates who won the Texas case last week say they began to consider going to the state courts in 1985, after they failed in an attempt to have the Texas sodomy statute invalidated in the Federal courts. "It was just assumed that the first try should be in the Federal courts," said J. Patrick Wiseman, the lawyer for the five homosexual plaintiffs.

In fact, a Federal court in Texas did strike down the state's sodomy law. But the United States Court of Appeals for the Fifth Circuit reversed that decision, in a 9-to-7 vote in 1985, holding that the constitutional right to privacy and equal protection of the laws did not extend to homosexual sodomy.

"That definitely started us thinking about other avenues," Mr. Wiseman said. "Up to that point, I think many had a sense that the Federal courts were like the cavalry. We'd seen them ride to the rescue in the school desegregation cases of the 50's and 60's, and we figured they were our best chance."

Opponents of sodomy laws were even more disillusioned a year later, when the Supreme Court decided the case of Bowers v. Hardwick, ruling 5 to 4 that the Constitution does not protect homosexual relations between adults even in the privacy of their own homes. The case was brought by Michael Hardwick, who had been arrested in his Atlanta bedroom while engaging in sex with a man.

Prosecutors declined to charge Mr. Hardwick after his arrest, but he challenged Georgia's sodomy law anyway on the ground that it violated his Federal constitutional right to privacy.

After the Bowers decision, gay leaders decided to try state courts. Some pointed to a passage in the Bowers opinion that almost seemed to invite such challenges, or at the very least seemed to anticipate them: The decision, the Court said, did not raise any question about the right or propriety of state court decisions invalidating sodomy laws on state constitutional grounds.

In Lexington, Ky., a man who had been arrested in 1986 by an undercover vice officer challenged Kentucky's sodomy statute under the state's Constitution. The Kentucky statute was virtually identical to the Texas law.

Greater Protection in Kentucky

The man, Jeffrey Wasson, claimed the statute violated his rights to privacy, to equal protection of the laws and to be free from cruel and unusual punishment, as interpreted by Kentucky courts. In response, prosecutors, citing the Bowers case, argued that the Kentucky Constitution did not grant a greater right to privacy than the Federal Constitution did and that the Bowers decision ought to control.

In June, however, Judge Charles Tackett of Fayette County Circuit Court ruled in favor of Mr. Wasson, finding that the Commonwealth was free to grant its citizens greater protection of privacy rights than under the Federal Constitution. And he added that Kentucky's courts had consistently protected its citizens' rights when the act occurred in the privacy of the home and did not injure or affect the rights of others.

In Michigan, Judge John A. Murphy of Wayne County Circuit Court issued a similar opinion in March in a case brought by a group challenging that state's sodomy law. The Michigan Constitution granted the plaintiffs a right of privacy in their homes, he ruled, saying, "and this interest does not vary depending on the activities engaged in."

5 Challenge Texas Law

In Texas, five homosexual men and women filed a civil suit in 1989 in Travis County District Court seeking to have the state's sodomy law declared unconstitutional and barring officials from further enforcement of it on the ground that it violated Texas's constitutional guarantees of privacy, equal rights and due process.

None of the plaintiffs had ever been arrested for violating the law, but they challenged it anyway on the ground that it subjected them to stigmatization, fear and emotional stress, discrimination in the judicial system and frequent harassment by law-enforcement officials. The statute also tacitly encouraged hate crimes against homosexuals, they said, by enshrining in the law a negative view of homosexuality.

Through its Attorney General, Jim Mattox, Texas argued that its courts should follow the Federal law in this area, citing the Bowers case and the Fifth Circuit court's earlier ruling upholding the sodomy law. If the law should be changed, the state argued, it should be changed by the Legislature, not the courts.

A spokesman for the Attorney General's office said that a decision on whether to appeal the judge's ruling has not yet been made.

* * *

December 26, 1990

MILESTONE ANNIVERSARY FOR THE RIGHT TO PRIVACY

By LINDA GREENHOUSE
Special to The New York Times

WASHINGTON, Dec. 25—One hundred years ago this month, the Harvard Law Review printed an article by two Boston lawyers, Samuel D. Warren and Louis D. Brandeis, entitled "The Right to Privacy."

The article's publication was a major event in the history of American law. Its title was brilliant in its simplicity. Its argument for legal recognition of a "general right of the individual to be let alone" proved to have a generative force far beyond the context its authors had in mind.

Its echoes are heard today both in impassioned political debate and in courts all over the country, including the Supreme Court, where one of its young authors went on to a distinguished 23-year tenure as a Justice.

Yet even in a country that seems to mark the anniversary of any occurrence to which a date can be fixed, the centennial of the privacy right is passing without benefit of fireworks. It is a birthday filled with ambiguity and contradictions.

The article struck a chord nearly universal in its appeal, perhaps even more so in the modern computer state than in the genteel world of turn-of-the-century Boston that the authors inhabited. Warren and Brandeis did not invent the notion of a legally enforceable right to privacy. Their breakthrough was to wrest the concept of privacy from its traditional mooring as an aspect of the common-law right of private property, and to place it on new legal ground as an aspect of an individual's "inviolate personality."

But privacy is one thing as an abstract value, another in specific application. Privacy today is often a political and legal battleground, whether the issue is abortion, gay rights or drug testing. A list of 5-to-4 Supreme Court decisions is not the stuff of which centennials are made.

In fact, to read the article itself in light of today's concerns is a bit disconcerting. Here is no ringing defense of the individual against the state. The threat to privacy that concerned the authors came not from the Government but from gossip mongers and snooping journalists.

"The press is overstepping in every direction the obvious bounds of propriety and of decency," they said. "Gossip is no longer the resource of the idle and of the vicious, but has become a trade, which is pursued with industry as well as effrontery."

The article came in for considerable criticism at a centennial conference held this fall at the University of California at Berkeley. Floyd Abrams, a First Amendment lawyer, said Warren and Brandeis had displayed a "rather breathtaking preoccupation with trivia" and seemed to "believe that information is a kind of contagious disease from which we must protect the masses."

Once launched, it took much of the next century for that 1890 notion of privacy to evolve, in a series of Supreme Court cases, into the modern constitutional right against intrusion by the Government in the most personal aspects of an individual's life. The Court's 1973 abortion decision, Roe v. Wade, may well have been the high-water mark for the constitutional right to privacy.

Whether the Supreme Court ever formally renounces that decision, as many believe it will, it is at least safe to say that the future of the right to privacy, at the moment of its centennial, is a clouded one.

In refusing four years ago, in Bowers v. Hardwick, to find a constitutional right to homosexual privacy, the Court indicated that it would extend the right to privacy into no new territory. The Court rather pointedly rested Cruzan v. Missouri, its 1990 decision recognizing a constitutional basis for the right to refuse life-sustaining treatment, not on the right to privacy but on the 14th Amendment's explicit protection of "liberty."

And yet, for those searching for something to celebrate on this anniversary, the news is that the right to privacy still carries political and legal weight. Judge Robert H. Bork said there was no such right, and the defeat of his Supreme Court nomination three years ago indicated the dim prospects for nominees who do not offer at least the cautious endorsement Judge David H. Souter gave this year.

Three state courts in the last few months have found a right to privacy in their own state constitutions to protect homosexual conduct.

So the centennial of the right to privacy is a bittersweet birthday at best. But it should not go unmarked, for it is at least an occasion to wonder at the power of an idea that may, or may not, have run its course.

* * *

June 20, 1995

THE NEW YORK PARADE

Hibernians See Vindication In Emphasis on Free Speech

By DAVID W. DUNLAP

By upholding the exclusion of a gay, lesbian and bisexual group from the St. Patrick's Day Parade in Boston, the Supreme Court vindicated the Ancient Order of Hibernians in its long-running efforts to keep a gay contingent out of the line of march in New York City, lawyers for the Hibernians said yesterday.

For their part, gay and lesbian organizations in New York were disappointed and angered by the Supreme Court decision, but several said they took comfort that the Justices had strongly supported the right of free speech while avoiding a broad ruling on gay civil rights. One group, the Lambda Legal Defense and Education Fund, said the decision might be helpful to its challenge of the military's policy on homosexual service members.

Yesterday's decision echoes a 1993 ruling by Judge Kevin Thomas Duffy of Federal District Court in Manhattan, who said it was unconstitutional for New York City officials to require the Hibernians, a Roman Catholic fraternal order, to include the Irish Lesbian and Gay Organization in the St. Patrick's Day Parade.

"Judge Duffy's decision was only binding on the parties to that case," said Ernest L. Mathews Jr., a lawyer for the Hibernians. "The Supreme Court has now enunciated the law for the whole country."

John P. Hale, another lawyer for the Hibernians, said the Supreme Court had "vindicated the correctness" not only of Judge Duffy's ruling but also of the decision earlier this year by Judge John F. Keenan of Federal District Court in Manhattan to deny the gay group a permit to hold its own protest march.

Mr. Hale said he hoped the new decision would "end the bitter public confrontation" and "restore a measure of civic harmony now that everyone is aware what the law of this land requires."

But Paul O'Dwyer, a lawyer for the Irish gay group, said the courts had turned the parades into "private events run by small groups whose only purposes are propagating their homophobic and bigoted views."

He added, however, that the new ruling might help the effort to stage a protest next year, as the Justices acknowledged that "a march is expressive in nature and that you have a right to have that message heard by a target audience."

The legal director for the Lambda group, Beatrice Dohrn, said the decision might buttress its challenge to the Pentagon's "don't ask, don't tell" policy, which requires gay troops to keep their sexual orientation private, at the risk of discharge.

Lambda has argued that this amounts to the unconstitutional prohibition on free expression, and Ms. Dohrn said the Supreme Court seemed to recognize in the Boston case that "coming out" as a homosexual is a significant message.

The ruling is not likely to directly affect efforts by a gay and lesbian synagogue, Congregation Beth Simchat Torah, to march as a contingent in the annual Salute to Israel Parade, sponsored by the American Zionist Youth Foundation.

Prof. Arthur S. Leonard of the New York Law School, who belongs to the gay temple, said the congregation agreed that "the way to get into the parade is through lobbying and education," rather than litigation.

Professor Leonard said yesterday's opinion, by Justice David H. Souter, "should generate a collective sigh of relief among the lesbian-gay legal groups."

"We all feared that this case, in the hands of a Scalia or Thomas, could well rip a big loophole in gay rights laws all over the country," he said, referring to the conservative Justices Antonin Scalia and Clarence Thomas. "Instead, we have a carefully crafted opinion that narrowly addresses the issue of the parade, while at the same time upholding the authority of the state to ban sexual-orientation discrimination."

William A. Donohue, president of the Catholic League for Religious and Civil Rights, a lay group with an office in the headquarters of the Archdiocese of New York, said he was delighted by the Court's decision on the Boston parade.

Mr. Donohue's group recently opened a new gulf in relations between Catholic and gay groups in New York by trying to persuade city officials to move the starting point for next Sunday's gay and lesbian march so that it does not pass St. Patrick's Cathedral on Fifth Avenue in Manhattan, as it has in past years.

"The whole purpose of the march is to insult Catholics," Mr. Donohue said. Some marchers walked naked past the cathedral last year, he added, while others dressed as nuns and priests, and shouted obscenities or chants like, "Confess, confess, the Cardinal wears a dress."

Marty Algaze, an aide to Deputy Mayor Fran Reiter, said yesterday, as he did on Sunday, that the city had already approved the route and granted the parade permit to the Heritage of Pride organization and had no intention of changing it at the last moment.

But Mr. Donohue said Mayor Rudolph W. Giuliani would pay a high political price if the parade was not moved. "I'm going to make this his Crown Heights," Mr. Donohue said, referring to the racial disturbances in 1991 that damaged Mayor David N. Dinkins's political fortunes.

* * *

May 21, 1996

EXCERPTS FROM COURT'S DECISION ON COLORADO'S PROVISION FOR HOMOSEXUALS

By The New York Times

WASHINGTON, May 20—Following are excerpts from the Supreme Court's decision today in Romer v. Evans, declaring unconstitutional a Colorado state constitutional provision that nullified civil rights laws singling out homosexuals for protection. Justice Anthony M. Kennedy wrote the majority opinion, which was joined by Justices John Paul Stevens, Sandra Day O'Connor, David H. Souter, Ruth Bader Ginsburg and Stephen G. Breyer. Justice Antonin Scalia's dissenting opinion was joined by Chief Justice William H. Rehnquist and Justice Clarence Thomas.

From the Decision by Justice Kennedy

One century ago, the first Justice Harlan admonished this Court that the Constitution "neither knows nor tolerates classes among citizens." Plessy v. Ferguson (1896) (dissenting opinion). Unheeded then, those words now are understood to state a commitment to the law's neutrality where the rights of persons are at stake. The Equal Protection Clause enforces this principle and today requires us to hold invalid a provision of Colorado's Constitution.

The enactment challenged in this case is an amendment to the Constitution of the State of Colorado, adopted in a 1992 statewide referendum. The parties and the state courts refer to it as "Amendment 2," its designation when submitted to the voters. The impetus for the amendment and the contentious campaign that preceded its adoption came in large part from ordinances that had been passed in various Colorado municipalities. . . . What gave rise to the statewide controversy was the protection the ordinances afforded to persons discriminated against by reason of their sexual orientation. Amendment 2 repeals these ordinances to the extent they prohibit discrimination on the basis of "homosexual, lesbian or bisexual orientation, conduct, practices or relationships."

Yet Amendment 2, in explicit terms, does more than repeal or rescind these provisions. It prohibits all legislative, executive or judicial action at any level of state or local government designed to protect the named class. . . .

Soon after Amendment 2 was adopted, this litigation to declare its invalidity and enjoin its enforcement was commenced in the District Court for the City and County of Denver. . . .

The trial court granted a preliminary injunction to stay enforcement of Amendment 2, and an appeal was taken to the Supreme Court of Colorado. Sustaining the interim injunction and remanding the case for further proceedings, the State Supreme Court held that Amendment 2 was subject to strict scrutiny under the 14th Amendment because it infringed the fundamental right of gays and lesbians to participate in the political process. . . . On remand, the state advanced various arguments in an effort to show that Amendment 2 was narrowly tailored to serve compelling interests, but the trial court found none sufficient. It enjoined enforcement of Amendment 2, and the Supreme Court of Colorado, in a second opinion, affirmed the ruling. Evans v. Romer. We granted certiorari and now affirm the judgment, but on a rationale different from that adopted by the State Supreme Court.

The state's principal argument in defense of Amendment 2 is that it puts gays and lesbians in the same position as all other persons. So, the state says, the measure does no more than deny homosexuals special rights. This reading of the amendment's language is implausible. . . .

Sweeping and comprehensive is the change in legal status effected by this law. So much is evident from the ordinances that the Colorado Supreme Court declared would be void by operation of Amendment 2. Homosexuals, by state decree, are put in a solitary class with respect to transactions and relations in both the private and governmental spheres. The amendment withdraws from homosexuals, but no others, specific legal protection from the injuries caused by discrimination, and it forbids reinstatement of these laws and policies. . . .

We cannot accept the view that Amendment 2's prohibition on specific legal protections does no more than deprive homosexuals of special rights. To the contrary, the amendment imposes a special disability upon those persons alone. Homosexuals are forbidden the safeguards that others enjoy or may seek without constraint. . . . We find nothing special in the protections Amendment 2 withholds. These are protections taken for granted by most people either because they already have them or do not need them. . . .

The 14th Amendment's promise that no person shall be denied the equal protection of the laws must co-exist with the practical necessity that most legislation classifies for one purpose or another, with resulting disadvantage to various groups or persons. We have attempted to reconcile the principle with the reality by stating that, if a law neither burdens a fundamental right nor targets a suspect class, we will uphold the legislative classification so long as it bears a rational relation to some legitimate end.

Amendment 2 fails, indeed defies, even this conventional inquiry. First, the amendment has the peculiar property of imposing a broad and undifferentiated disability on a single named group. . . . Second, its sheer breadth is so discontinuous with the reasons offered for it that the amendment seems inexplicable by anything but animus toward the class . . .

By requiring that the classification bear a rational relationship to an independent and legitimate legislative end, we insure that classifications are not drawn for the purpose of disadvantaging the group burdened by the law.

Amendment 2 confounds this normal process of judicial review. It is at once too narrow and too broad. It identifies persons by a single trait and then denies them protection across the board. . . .

It is not within our constitutional tradition to enact laws of this sort. Central both to the idea of the rule of law and to our own Constitution's guarantee of equal protection is the principle that government and each of its parts remain open on impartial terms to all who seek its assistance. Respect for this principle explains why laws singling out a certain class of citizens for disfavored legal status or general hardships are rare. A law declaring that in general it shall be more difficult for one group of citizens than for all others to seek aid from the government is itself a denial of equal protection of the laws in the most literal sense. "The guaranty of 'equal protection of the laws is a pledge of the protection of equal laws.'" Skinner v. Oklahoma ex rel. Williamson (1942) (quoting Yick Wo v. Hopkins (1886)). . . .

Laws of the kind now before us raise the inevitable inference that the disadvantage imposed is born of animosity toward the class of persons affected. "[I]f the constitutional conception of 'equal protection of the laws' means anything, it must at the very least mean that a bare . . . desire to harm a politically unpopular group cannot constitute a legitimate governmental interest." Department of Agriculture v. Moreno (1973). Even laws enacted for broad and ambitious purposes often can be explained by reference to legitimate public policies which justify the incidental disadvantages they impose on certain persons. Amendment 2, however, in making a general announcement that gays and lesbians shall not have any particular protections from the law, inflicts on them immediate, continuing, and real injuries that outrun and belie any legitimate justifications that may be claimed for it. We conclude that, in addition to the far-reaching deficiencies of Amendment 2 that we have noted, the principles it offends, in another sense, are conventional and venerable; a law must bear a rational relationship to a legitimate governmental purpose, and Amendment 2 does not.

The primary rationale the state offers for Amendment 2 is respect for other citizens' freedom of association, and in particular the liberties of landlords or employers who have personal or religious objections to homosexuality. Colorado also cites its interest in conserving resources to fight discrimination against other groups. The breadth of the amendment is so far removed from these particular justifications that we find it impossible to credit them. . . .

We must conclude that Amendment 2 classifies homosexuals not to further a proper legislative end but to make them unequal to everyone else. This Colorado cannot do. A state cannot so deem a class of persons a stranger to its laws.

Amendment 2 violates the Equal Protection Clause, and the judgment of the Supreme Court of Colorado is affirmed.

From the Dissent By Justice Scalia

The Court has mistaken a Kulturkampf for a fit of spite. The constitutional amendment before us here is not the manifestation of a "bare . . . desire to harm" homosexuals, ante, but is rather a modest attempt by seemingly tolerant Coloradans to preserve traditional sexual mores against the efforts of a politically powerful minority to revise those mores through use of the laws. . . .

In holding that homosexuality cannot be singled out for disfavorable treatment, the Court contradicts a decision, unchallenged here, pronounced only 10 years ago, see Bowers v. Hardwick (1986), and places the prestige of this institution behind the proposition that opposition to homosexuality is as reprehensible as racial or religious bias. Whether it is or not, is precisely the cultural debate that gave rise to the Colorado constitutional amendment (and to the preferential laws against which the amendment was directed). Since the Constitution of the United States says nothing about this subject, it is left to be resolved by normal democratic means, including the democratic adoption of provisions in state constitutions. This Court has no business imposing upon all Americans the resolution favored by the elite class from which the members of this institution are selected, pronouncing that "animosity" toward homosexuality, ante, is evil. I vigorously dissent.

The central thesis of the Court's reasoning is that any group is denied equal protection when, to obtain advantage (or, presumably, to avoid disadvantage), it must have recourse to a more general and hence more difficult level of political decision-making than others. . . . [I]t seems to me most unlikely that any multi-level democracy can function under such a principle. For whenever a disadvantage is imposed, or conferral of a benefit is prohibited, at one of the higher levels of democratic decision-making (i.e., by the state legislature rather than local government, or by the people at large in the state constitution rather than the legislature), the affected group has (under this theory) been denied equal protection. . . . The Court's entire novel theory rests upon the proposition that there is something special . . . in making a disadvantaged group (or a nonpreferred group) resort to a higher decision-making level. That proposition finds no support in law or logic. . .

The case most relevant to the issue before us today is not even mentioned in the Court's opinion: In Bowers v. Hardwick we held that the Constitution does not prohibit . . . making homosexual conduct a crime. . . . If it is constitutionally permissible for a state to make homosexual conduct criminal, surely it is constitutionally permissible for a state to enact other laws merely disfavoring homosexual conduct. . . . And a fortiori it is constitutionally permissible for a state to adopt a provision not even disfavoring homosexual conduct, but merely prohibiting all levels of state government from bestowing special protections upon homosexual conduct. . . .

No principle set forth in the Constitution . . . prohibits what Colorado has done here. But the case for Colorado is much stronger than that. What it has done is not only unprohibited, but eminently reasonable. . . .

The Court's opinion contains grim, disapproving hints that Coloradans have been guilty of "animus" or "animosity" toward homosexuality. . . . Of course it is our moral heritage that one should not hate any human being or class of human beings. But I had thought that one could consider certain conduct reprehensible—murder, for example, or polygamy, or cruelty to animals—and could exhibit even "animus" toward such conduct. . . . The Colorado amendment does not, to speak entirely precisely, prohibit giving favored status to people who are homosexuals; they can be favored for many reasons—for example, because they are senior citizens or members of racial minorities. But it prohibits giving them favored status because of their homosexual conduct . . .

[T]hough Coloradans are, as I say, entitled to be hostile toward homosexual conduct, the fact is that the degree of hostility reflected by Amendment 2 is the smallest conceivable. The Court's portrayal of Coloradans as a society fallen victim to pointless, hate-filled "gay-bashing" is so false as to be comical. Colorado not only is one of the 25 states that have repealed their anti-sodomy laws, but was among the first to do so. But the society that eliminates criminal punishment for homosexual acts does not necessarily abandon the view that homosexuality is morally wrong and socially harmful. . . .

There is a problem, however, which arises when criminal sanction of homosexuality is eliminated but moral and social disapprobation of homosexuality is meant to be retained. . . . Because those who engage in homosexual conduct tend to reside in disproportionate numbers in certain communities, have high disposable income and of course care about homosexual-rights issues much more ardently than the public at large, they possess political power much greater than their numbers, both locally and statewide. Quite understandably, they devote this political power to achieving not merely a grudging social toleration, but full social acceptance, of homosexuality. . . .

I do not mean to be critical of these legislative successes; homosexuals are as entitled to use the legal system for reinforcement of their moral sentiments as are the rest of society. But they are subject to being countered by lawful, democratic countermeasures as well.

That is where Amendment 2 came in. It sought to counter both the geographic concentration and the disproportionate political power of homosexuals by (1) resolving the controversy at the statewide level, and (2) making the election a single-issue contest for both sides. It put directly, to all the citizens of the state, the question, Should homosexuality be given special protection? They answered no. The Court today asserts that this most democratic of procedures is unconstitutional. . .

Today's opinion has no foundation in American constitutional law, and barely pretends to. The people of Colorado have adopted an entirely reasonable provision which does not even disfavor homosexuals in any substantive sense, but merely denies them preferential treatment. Amendment 2 is designed to prevent piecemeal deterioration of the sexual morality favored by a majority of Coloradans, and is not only an

appropriate means to that legitimate end, but a means that Americans have employed before. Striking it down is an act not of judicial judgment, but of political will.

* * *

March 24, 1998

CALIFORNIA JUSTICES ALLOW SCOUTS TO BAR GAY AND ATHEIST MEMBERS

By TODD S. PURDUM

LOS ANGELES, March 23—The California Supreme Court ruled today that the Boy Scouts of America can exclude homosexuals, agnostics and atheists from its ranks because it is a private membership group not covered by the state's civil rights law.

In a pair of unanimous decisions, the court held that under California's 1959 civil rights law, the Scouts are not a business establishment and so are free, as is any private club, to set membership policies as they see fit.

Civil rights and gay groups expressed disappointment at the ruling, which cannot be appealed because it did not turn on any claim of Federal constitutional law. But they pointed to other pending challenges to the membership policies of the Scouts, including a ruling by a divided New Jersey appeals court earlier this month that the Scouts are a public accommodation and cannot exclude members because of sexual orientation.

"This is the end of the line for this decision, but not for this question nationally," said Jon Davidson, supervising lawyer for the Western regional office of the Lambda Legal Defense and Education Fund, a gay rights group.

Challenges to the Scouts' ban against gay participants are pending under other local anti-discrimination statutes in Chicago and the District of Columbia, and one may well wind up in the United States Supreme Court. In Chicago, for example, the city's Human Relations Commission recently ruled that the Scouts' policy against admitting gay members violated the city's anti-discrimination ordinance. There is no Federal anti-discrimination law that bars discrimination in public accommodations on the basis of sexual orientation.

While the plaintiffs in today's case sued only under the California law, the Boy Scouts had asserted claims of a constitutional right of free association, and would have been prepared to appeal to the United States Supreme Court on those grounds if they had lost, spokesmen for both sides said. In the New Jersey case, the Boy Scouts are appealing this month's loss at the appeals court to the state's Supreme Court and, if they lose there, will doubtless continue the challenge to the United States Supreme Court, which could resolve the issue nationally.

"We're very pleased, obviously," a national spokesman for the Scouts, Gregg Shields, said of the California ruling. "For 88 years, the Boy Scouts of America has brought the moral values of the Scout oath and law to American boys, helping them to achieve the objectives of scouting. Since its inception in 1910, the Boy Scouts has been a voluntary association, and those who meet the standard of membership are welcome."

In the past, the California Supreme Court has ruled that such organizations as Boys Clubs and a private country club were business establishments because their buildings and programs were open to the public. But the justices ruled today that the Scouts are a private, selective organization, whose camps, hikes, training and programs are available only to members, although the Scouts sell some goods and publications to the public.

Chief Justice Ronald George, in the court's lead opinion, said that "Scouts meet regularly in small groups (often in private homes) that are intended to foster close friendship, trust and loyalty."

Chief Justice George added, "The Boy Scouts is an expressive social organization whose primary function is the inculcation of values in its youth members."

Two other justices, Stanley Mosk and Janice Rogers Brown, said in separate opinions that they would support the court's going even further and overruling its previous decisions in the golf club and Boys Club cases by narrowing its definition of business establishments.

The pair of rulings, in separate cases that were argued together, involved two distinct issues. In one, Timothy Curran, now a documentary film maker who lives in Miami, challenged his rejection as a teen-age assistant Scoutmaster by a Contra Costa County Scout organization in 1981, after it learned that he was gay. The other case involved 9-year-old twin brothers, Michael and William Randall, now 16, who were barred by an Orange County Cub Scout den in 1990, after they refused to declare a belief in God.

"I just hoped that the Boy Scouts had the honesty and integrity that my sons have shown," said James G. Randall, their father and their lawyer, who choked back tears at a press conference here today.

Mr. Randall said he feared that the decision could have broader implications and allow "the largest youth organization in the world to discriminate based on race and sexual orientation."

In fact, the rulings held that while the provisions of the California civil rights act do not extend to the Scouts' membership policies, the organization was not "free to exclude boys from membership on the basis of race, or on other constitutionally suspect grounds, with impunity," because other laws, including Federal tax laws granting tax-exempt status, would apply.

At various times in the past, Scout groups have barred members of some races or have segregated troops, though the organization no longer does that. By contrast, the Boy Scouts contend that being gay is immoral, not in keeping with the Scout pledge to be "morally straight," and that gay men would not be good role models. They also contend that the Scout oath's pledge of "duty to God" is central to the organization's mission.

The Randall twins were dismissed for their refusal to use the word "God" in the oath, and their father said they were

agnostics, who were still working out their religious beliefs. They had been allowed to continue in the organization after lower court rulings in their favor, and recently applied to earn the rank of Eagle Scout, the organization's highest honor, but Mr. Shields, the Scouts spokesman, said that they were no longer Scouts, unless they agreed to swear the standard oath.

"It is sad to see that the Scout law that is so valued can be tarnished by a few people," said Michael Randall, who with his brother broke into tears at the press conference today. "I find it difficult to believe that in this country we still have discrimination.

"Once a Scout, always a Scout," he said. "There are no former Scouts."

* * *

October 14, 1998

JUSTICES LEAVE INTACT ANTI-GAY MEASURE

By LINDA GREENHOUSE

WASHINGTON, Oct. 13—Two years after overturning an anti-gay rights amendment to the Colorado Constitution, the Supreme Court today left intact a similar measure barring protective legislation for homosexuals in Cincinnati.

The Court refused to hear a challenge to the Cincinnati charter amendment, which the voters adopted in 1993 and which a Federal appeals court found last year to be constitutional. On the surface, the Justices' action sent a confusing signal about whether the Court still meant what it said, by a 6-to-3 majority in the Colorado case, about the Constitution not permitting homosexuals to be stripped of legal protection and made "strangers to the law."

However, although the Court's disposition of the Cincinnati case today was evidently unanimous, three Justices took the unusual step of explaining the action in a separate statement that put the case in a different and less suggestive light.

While the three—Justices John Paul Stevens, David H. Souter and Ruth Bader Ginsburg—spoke only for themselves, they offered a rare window into the Court's internal deliberations over whether to take up a new case, deliberations that usually end only with a published order of "granted" or "denied."

In this case, the three Justices said, the actual meaning of the Cincinnati amendment was sufficiently ambiguous, and sufficiently different from the Colorado amendment struck down in Romer v. Evans, as to make the case a poor vehicle for a Supreme Court decision.

The Justices noted that in upholding the measure last year, the United States Court of Appeals for the Sixth Circuit had interpreted it as barring only "special protection" for gay men and lesbians, as opposed to taking the more sweeping step of depriving gay people of the general anti-discrimination protections available to other groups.

In the Colorado case, by contrast, the Supreme Court said Colorado's Amendment 2 could fairly be read as depriving gay men and lesbians "even of the protection of general laws," amounting to "a denial of equal protection of the laws in the most literal sense."

While the gay-rights groups challenging the Cincinnati amendment insisted that it was essentially identical to the Colorado provision, the Sixth Circuit found otherwise. In its 1997 decision, the appeals court, which sits in Cincinnati, said there was a "stark contrast" between the two provisions, with the Colorado provision having excluded gay people "from the protection of every Colorado state law" while Cincinnati's charter amendment "merely prevented homosexuals, as homosexuals, from obtaining special privileges and preferences," like affirmative action.

In their statement today, Justices Stevens, Souter and Ginsburg said the dispute over what the Cincinnati amendment actually meant "counsels against granting the petition." They said, "This Court does not normally make an independent examination of state law questions that have been resolved by a court of appeals," adding that the denial of review should not be taken as an indication of the Court's views on the underlying issues. The case was Equality Foundation of Greater Cincinnati v. City of Cincinnati, No. 97-1795.

Suzanne B. Goldberg, a lawyer with the Lambda Legal Defense and Education Fund, a gay-rights group that challenged both the Colorado and Cincinnati amendments, said today that the Supreme Court's action cast no doubt on the nondiscrimination principle the Court adopted in the Colorado decision of two years ago. However, she said in an interview, her group would monitor the situation in Cincinnati to make sure that the amendment, known locally as Issue 3, was indeed as "meaningless" as the Sixth Circuit opinion found it to be. "This is not the end of the battle over Issue 3," she said.

While the litigation that led to today's case challenged the amendment on its face, rather than in any particular application, specific cases could come up next, she said. One Cincinnati ordinance, enacted before the voters adopted Issue 3, prohibits discrimination in city employment on the basis of race, sex, religion, disability, national origin and sexual orientation. If a gay city employee challenges an adverse employment action as discriminatory, the Ohio state courts will have to decide whether Issue 3 is as narrowly drawn as the Sixth Circuit found it to be.

If the Sixth Circuit was right, Issue 3 would be irrelevant to the operation of a general anti-discrimination law, which would continue to protect gay people on the same basis as other protected groups. But if Issue 3, properly interpreted, does carve gay people out from such generally worded protection, then a new case would move back up through the courts with the amendment in a different light.

Neither the Court's action today nor the Cincinnati dispute bears on the further, and distinct, question of whether sexual orientation should be included as a protected category in hate-crimes legislation. Such laws are newly in the spotlight following the recent murder of a gay college student in Wyoming. While 40 states have some form of hate crimes legislation, only 21 include crimes based on sexual orientation.

Cincinnati voters adopted Issue 3 by a margin of 62 percent to 38 percent. It is titled: "No special class status may be granted based upon sexual orientation, conduct or relationships." It is the only such provision on the books anywhere in the country, said Ms. Goldberg, co-author of a newly published book on the Colorado case called "Strangers to the Law" (University of Michigan Press, 1998).

Issue 3 provides that the city, including various boards and commissions, "may not enact, adopt, enforce, or administer any ordinance, regulation, rule or policy which provides that homosexual, lesbian or bisexual orientation, status, conduct, or relationship constitutes, entitles, or otherwise provides a person with the basis to have any claim of minority or protected status, quota preference or other preferential treatment."

The charter amendment was adopted after a campaign by a Cincinnati group called Equal Rights, Not Special Rights. That group's lawyer, Michael Carvin, said in an interview today that he interpreted the Court as sending a signal that while under the rule of the Colorado case, states could not bar gay-rights legislation at the state level, localities could do so. "Local citizen initiatives can overturn gay-rights laws even if states cannot," he said, adding that the action today demonstrated that "the Court will not extend Romer v. Evans to the facts of this case."

This was the second time Cincinnati's Issue 3 was before the Supreme Court. The Sixth Circuit had initially upheld the amendment in 1995, a year before the Supreme Court's ruling in the Colorado case. After overturning Colorado's Amendment 2 in Romer v. Evans, the Justices vacated the Cincinnati decision and told the Sixth Circuit to reconsider the case in light of the Colorado ruling.

Justice Antonin Scalia, Chief Justice William H. Rehnquist and Justice Clarence Thomas dissented from that action, saying that the Sixth Circuit decision should either be left intact or taken up for full review. In an opinion by Justice Scalia, the three Justices said that citizens at the local level should be free to decide "in democratic fashion, not to accord special protection to homosexuals" and that the Romer decision had not addressed that issue. The Sixth Circuit proceeded to uphold Issue 3 a second time, in the ruling that the Court let stand today.

* * *

November 24, 1998

GEORGIA'S HIGH COURT VOIDS SODOMY LAW

By KEVIN SACK

ATLANTA, Nov. 23—Twelve years after the United States Supreme Court upheld Georgia's anti-sodomy statute in a landmark decision, Georgia's own Supreme Court invalidated the law today by ruling that private consensual sodomy between adults is protected under privacy rights guaranteed by the State Constitution.

Although top courts in other states have struck down similar laws, the ruling today held special symbolic meaning for gay rights advocates because it was Georgia's anti-sodomy law that had prompted the United States Supreme Court to declare that "the Constitution does not confer a fundamental right upon homosexuals to engage in sodomy."

"This is especially sweet," said Stephen R. Scarborough, a lawyer with the Lambda Legal Defense and Education Fund, a gay rights organization that filed a friend-of-the-court brief challenging Georgia's law. "I think that it really sends the signal to other states who may be considering similar challenges that we are in a day and age where the government simply does not belong in bedrooms."

Georgia's became the fifth top state court to reject anti-sodomy laws since the United States Supreme Court, on a vote of 5 to 4, upheld the Georgia law in its 1986 decision, Bowers v. Hardwick, Lambda officials said. In each case, state courts ruled that their state constitutions afforded more extensive privacy rights than those guaranteed by the United States Constitution.

Georgia's Chief Justice, Robert Benham, noted in the decision today that "it is a well-recognized principle that while provisions of a state constitution may not be judicially construed as affording less protection to that state's citizens than a parallel provision in the Federal Constitution may provide, the state constitution may provide more protection than the U.S. Constitution."

The 6-to-1 ruling leaves 18 states with anti-sodomy laws of some kind. Thirteen prohibit both homosexual and heterosexual sodomy, while five ban only same-sex sodomy. Georgia's law, which dated from 1833, defined sodomy as "any sexual act involving the sex organs of one person and the mouth or anus of another."

Anti-sodomy statutes existed in every state as recently as the early 1960's. Twenty-five states, including New Jersey and Connecticut, have repealed their anti-sodomy laws, while top courts have struck down the laws in seven states, New York among them. Legal challenges are winding through the courts in several other states, including Texas, Arkansas and Louisiana.

Paradoxically, the successful challenge to Georgia's law came in a case involving heterosexual activity. In 1996, Anthony San Juan Powell was convicted of sodomizing his 17-year-old niece after both testified that he had had sexual intercourse with her and performed oral sex on her.

Mr. Powell was originally indicted on charges of rape and aggravated sodomy because his niece maintained that the sex had not been consensual, an accusation he denied. The jury acquitted him of those charges but convicted him of sodomy after the trial judge had made that option available. He was sentenced to five years in prison and served 14 months before being released on bond pending the outcome of his appeal, said his lawyer, Steven H. Sadow.

The United States Supreme Court's decision in 1986 focused on homosexual sodomy, with Warren E. Burger, who was then Chief Justice, writing that protecting homosexual sodomy as a fundamental right would "cast aside millennia of moral teaching." But the Georgia decision made clear that any sexual activity that is consensual, adult and private would be protected under privacy rights that, though not made explicit by the State Constitution, have been recognized by Georgia courts since 1905.

That recognition, Justice Benham wrote, does not mean that the court condones homosexuality. But he added, "While many believe that acts of sodomy, even those involving consenting adults, are morally reprehensible, this repugnance alone does not create a compelling justification for state regulation of the activity."

The lone dissenter, Justice George H. Carley, accused his colleagues of "acting as social engineers rather than as jurists." He said the decision would call into question any criminal statute proscribing a consensual act that does not harm anyone but the participants, including laws against consensual incest and drug use.

Lou Sheldon, the chairman of the conservative Traditional Values Coalition, echoed that concern.

"It seems that the Georgia Supreme Court is willing to allow incestual relationships and moral indecency to occur all in the name of 'privacy,' " he said in a statement. "Apparently laws can be discarded if they are broken privately."

Although prosecutions under Georgia's sodomy statute have been rare, gay rights advocates said the statute had been used to stigmatize homosexuals and to deny them jobs and child custody and visitation rights. Indeed, in 1991, Michael J. Bowers, then the Georgia Attorney General, rescinded a job offer to a lawyer, Robin J. Shahar, after learning that she is a lesbian. Among other reasons given for his decision, Mr. Bowers said his office's ability to enforce state laws would be compromised by hiring someone who, he assumed, was breaking the sodomy statute.

Today Ms. Shahar, a senior assistant city attorney in Atlanta, said she was thrilled by the ruling.

"Sodomy has really been used as a tool by people who want to discriminate against us, even when the statute doesn't apply," she said. "And the courts have been letting them get away with it."

* * *

August 5, 1999

NEW JERSEY COURT OVERTURNS OUSTER OF GAY BOY SCOUT

By ROBERT HANLEY

TRENTON, Aug. 4—Equating the Boy Scouts with such public accommodations as restaurants, libraries, schools and theaters, the New Jersey Supreme Court ruled today that the organization's expulsion of a gay Eagle Scout in 1990 violated the state's antidiscrimination law.

In a unanimous 7-to-0 decision, the court first rejected the Boy Scouts' arguments that it is a private organization and that its decision to remove the scout, James Dale, was pro-

The New York Times

James Dale, center, who was expelled from the Boy Scouts in 1990, leaves a news conference after the New Jersey Supreme Court struck down the Scouts' ban on gay members. At right is his lawyer, Evan Wolfson.

tected by the First Amendment. The court also dismissed the Scouts' contention that homosexuality is immoral, comparing that view to discrimination against women and blacks.

After saying Mr. Dale's dismissal was "based on little more than prejudice," the Chief Justice, Deborah T. Poritz, wrote: "The sad truth is that excluded groups and individuals have been prevented from full participation in the social, economic and political life of our country. The human price of this bigotry has been enormous. At a most fundamental level, adherence to the principle of equality demands that our legal system protect the victim of invidious discrimination."

The case of Mr. Dale, who is now 29, is the second one to have reached the highest court in a state. But the result is just the opposite of the earlier case. In March 1998, the California Supreme Court ruled that the Scouts could expel homosexuals, agnostics and atheists. That court held that the Boy Scouts were a private organization not covered by California's civil rights law and that the organization had constitutional rights of freedom of association and freedom of expression to expel homosexuals.

In a concurring opinion in the New Jersey decision today, Justice Alan B. Handler, widely considered the court's staunchest liberal, said he agreed with much of his colleagues' legal reasoning. Then Justice Handler, who is retiring after this term, concluded his 44-page opinion with something of a sociological and philosophical lecture. "One particular stereotype that we renounce today is that homosexuals are inherently immoral," Justice Handler wrote. "That myth is repudiated by decades of social science data that convincingly establish that being homosexual does not, in itself, derogate from one's ability to participate in and contribute responsibly and positively to society.

"In short, a lesbian and gay person, merely because he or she is a homosexual, is no more or less likely to be moral than a person who is heterosexual."

Paul Stevenson, a public-affairs spokesman for the Boy Scouts of America at their national headquarters in Dallas, expressed disappointment with the New Jersey ruling and said

the group planned to appeal it to the United States Supreme Court.

The California ruling was not appealed because it did not turn on any claim of Federal constitutional law.

"The Boy Scouts of America is a private organization with the right to set our membership and leadership standards," Mr. Stevenson said. He contended that New Jersey's anti-discrimination law did not supersede the organization's First Amendment rights of association. Consequently, he reasoned, New Jersey's high court had used the state's anti-discrimination law to discriminate against the Boy Scouts.

Mr. Dale, who was an assistant scoutmaster at Troop 73 in Matawan, N.J., when he was expelled, said he was elated with the ruling.

"The Supreme Court of New Jersey is wonderful," he said as he appeared with his lawyer at the headquarters of the Lambda Legal Defense and Education Fund in Manhattan. "This is what Scouting taught me: Goodness will prevail."

The lawyer, Evan Wolfson, called the ruling "a strong, clear powerful decision by one of the nation's most respected state supreme courts."

"The decision we got today is a win-win decision," Mr. Wolfson said. "It's a victory for Jim Dale and it's a victory for other gay men like him."

Gov. Christine Todd Whitman applauded the ruling during a public appearance in Bergen County. She said she did not believe in discrimination "in any form" and said a person's sexual orientation was a private matter. "If the troop leader is a good leader, there's no reason to worry" about his sexual orientation, Governor Whitman said.

Mr. Dale, who lives in Manhattan and helps arrange health fairs for people with AIDS, said he wanted to return to Scouting. The ruling ordered his reinstatement and instructed a lower New Jersey court to take up his request for compensatory and punitive damages against the Boy Scouts.

Mr. Dale joined Scouting in 1978 at age 8, obtained more than 25 merit badges and Scouting's highest rank—Eagle Scout—and eventually became assistant scoutmaster. The Boy Scouts considered him an exemplary member, the ruling said.

But in July 1990, his photograph appeared in a local newspaper identifying him as co-president of the Lesbian/Gay Alliance at Rutgers University. Soon afterward, the Scouts sent him a letter informing him of the expulsion and saying that the Scouts' standards for leadership forbade membership to homosexuals.

Today's decision said Mr. Dale asked various Scout executives for a copy of the standards of leadership but was never given one. In late 1990, the organization's lawyers told him that the Boy Scouts "does not admit avowed homosexuals to membership." He began his legal fight soon afterward.

During court arguments over nine years, the Scouts argued that the organization believed homosexuality was immoral and that belief was both explicit and implicit in the Scout Oath that a scout is "morally straight" and in the Scout Law that a scout is "clean."

The court disagreed with that argument in its 89-page ruling.

In finding that the Scouts were a "public accommodation" as defined by the state's antidiscrimination law and not a "selective" private organization, Chief Justice Poritz wrote that Congress had chartered the organization, that 87 million boys and men had joined Scouting since its inception in 1910, and that churches and police and fire departments routinely sponsor local troops.

"Most important," she wrote, "it is clear that Boy Scouts does not limit its membership to individuals who belong to a particular religion or subscribe to a specific set of moral beliefs."

She said the Boy Scouts teach tolerance and the understanding of differences in others and that the group's charter and bylaws do not permit exclusion of any boy.

"Boy Scouts is not 'distinctly private' because it is not selective in its membership," the Chief Justice wrote. Largely because of its broad membership and large size, she dismissed the Boy Scouts' arguments that First Amendment freedom of "intimate association"—usually reserved for family relationships and small groups whose members share common thoughts and beliefs—shielded the organization from the antidiscrimination law.

In dismissing the argument that the First Amendment right of "expressive association" allowed the dismissal of Mr. Dale, the Chief Justice said the organization's ability to disseminate its message would not be impaired if he was a member.

"Boy Scout members do not associate for the purpose of disseminating the belief that homosexuality is immoral," she wrote. "Boy Scouts discourages its leaders from disseminating any views on sexual issues; and Boy Scouts includes sponsors and members who subscribe to different views in respect of homosexuality."

The Chief Justice said the court agreed with the Scouts' espousal of moral values. But she said it disagreed with the contention that the Scout Oath's principle of "morally straight" and its admonition that a scout be "clean" meant that homosexuality is immoral.

"The words 'morally straight' and 'clean' do not, on their face, express anything about sexuality," she wrote. Thus, she said, Mr. Dale's membership does not violate the Scouts' right of expressive association.

That, she concluded, "suggests that Dale's expulsion constituted discrimination based solely on his status as an openly gay man."

Expelling him was not justified by the need to preserve the organization's expressive rights, she said. And she held that expulsion solely on the ground of sexual orientation was "inconsistent with the Boy Scouts' commitment to diverse and representative membership."

Justice Handler, in his concurring opinion, said the Boy Scouts' legal contention in the Dale case that homosexuality is immoral is out of touch with current law, public policy and social mores.

"Boy Scouts' adherence to 'traditional moral values,' its 'belief in moral values,'" Justice Handler said, "remain undisturbed and undeterred by Dale's open avowal of his homosexuality."

* * *

April 16, 2000

BATTLE LOOMS WHEN SUPREME COURT HEARS PLEA OF BOY SCOUTS TO BAR GAYS

By LINDA GREENHOUSE

WASHINGTON, April 15—For anyone wanting a front-row seat at the next battle in the culture wars, the place to be is the Supreme Court later this month when the justices hear the case of Boy Scouts of America v. James Dale.

Neither the Boy Scouts nor Mr. Dale, an Eagle scout and former assistant scoutmaster whom the Scouts expelled after learning from a newspaper article that he was gay, come into court alone.

The case has galvanized the religious right, on the Boy Scouts' side, and organizations like the American Bar Association and the National Association for the Advancement of Colored People on Mr. Dale's. Religions have been split by the case: Orthodox Jewish groups for the Scouts, Reform Judaism for Mr. Dale; the United Methodist Church for Mr. Dale, a dissident group of Methodists for the Boy Scouts.

Dozens of organizations, including medical and education professionals, bar groups and state and local officials, have filed briefs. The dispute—for the weight of its competing arguments, the doctrinal challenge it presents for the court and its overall cultural resonance—is plausibly the most compelling case on a docket already weighty with potential landmark rulings.

The Boy Scouts are appealing a decision last August by the New Jersey Supreme Court that Mr. Dale's expulsion from the troop he had served with distinction for half his life violated New Jersey's anti-discrimination law. The five-million-member organization argues that what is at stake is the freedom of a private, voluntary organization to "create and interpret its own moral code"—in this instance, by excluding avowed homosexuals—and that without such freedom, "American society would be fundamentally transformed."

"A society in which each and every organization must be equally diverse is a society which has destroyed diversity," the Boy Scouts assert in their brief, warning that the logical result of the New Jersey court's ruling would be for a Croatian cultural society to have to admit Serbs or for a gay rights group to be unable to exclude a biblical fundamentalist. The argument is based on the First Amendment right to freedom of association and its corollary, the freedom to not associate.

The Supreme Court has agreed with the kind of arguments the Boy Scouts are making—sometimes.

Mr. Dale and his lawyers at the Lambda Legal Defense and Education Fund are arguing that freedom of association has never been regarded as an absolute free-floating right, but

454 THE GAY RIGHTS MOVEMENT

rather as a right to associate for a purpose, to advance a cause or belief. Even assuming that people have a right to come together for the purpose of opposing homosexuality, his brief says, that is not a description of the Boy Scouts.

The common interests that bring its millions of members together "are not about homosexuality or sexual orientation," Mr. Dale says. Consequently, he argues, New Jersey's "vital government interests" in prohibiting discrimination outweigh any incidental burden on the expressive interests of a major civic organization that is chartered by Congress and stitched tightly to government at all levels.

The Supreme Court has agreed with the kind of argument Mr. Dale is making—sometimes.

"There is an undeniable, inevitable tension between the right of a private group to define who it wants as members, and the right of the state to prevent invidious discrimination," David D. Cole, a professor at Georgetown University Law Center, who filed a brief on Mr. Dale's behalf, said in an interview the other day. "There is no easy answer."

With no clear way to resolve the tension, Professor Cole said, the Supreme Court has dealt with it by establishing two categories of cases: On the one hand, the court has rejected efforts by government to limit what a private group can say, or to force a private group to yield control over its message. This category was exemplified by a 1995 decision holding that the organizers of the Boston St. Patrick's Day parade, the South Boston Allied War Veterans Council, could not be required, despite a state anti-discrimination law, to accept the participation of a group whose members wanted to march under a banner of gay pride.

On the other hand, Professor Cole said, the court has held that exclusion from an organization based simply on someone's group status or identity, is not constitutionally protected. In a trilogy of cases in the mid-1980's, the court rejected claims by all-male organizations, including the Jaycees and the Rotary Club, to a First Amendment right to continue excluding women.

In all these cases, the St. Patrick's Day parade case as well as the all-male club trilogy, the justices were unanimous, in outcome although not necessarily in their reasoning. Unanimity on such touchy issues is "remarkable," Professor Cole said, reflecting the court's success in placing the cases in one analytical box or the other and thereby avoiding the struggle of reconciling the tensions inherent in each case.

Basically, the court found that the clubs existed for a commercial purpose and that the exclusion of women was not part of their self-described mission.

Not surprisingly, each side in the current case, Boy Scouts v. Dale, No. 99-699, to be argued on April 26, invokes the precedent that supports its desired outcome. The Boy Scouts assert that the case is controlled by the St. Patrick's Day parade case, Hurley v. Gay, Lesbian & Bisexual Group of Boston (G.L.I.B.). "By donning the uniform of an adult leader in scouting," the Boy Scouts' brief says, Mr. Dale would "celebrate his identity as an openly gay scout leader in precisely the same way that the G.L.I.B. marchers wished to conscript the

parade to celebrate their identity" and to claim social acceptance within the Irish community.

Mr. Dale asserts that the trio of all-male club cases, beginning with Roberts v. United States Jaycees in 1984, governs his case; just as the clubs could not keep out women simply for being female, without regard to any views they might hold on the clubs' mission, they cannot exclude him simply upon learning his identity as a gay man. The New Jersey Supreme Court found that under the state's Law Against Discrimination the Boy Scouts were a "public accommodation" to which the law could properly be applied.

The disclosure of Mr. Dale's sexuality was not connected to his Boy Scout activities, but rather came in a newspaper article about a gay students' group in which he was active at Rutgers University, where he was an undergraduate. Within days after the article, with his picture, appeared in The Newark Star-Ledger, the Monmouth Council of the Boy Scouts revoked his membership in Troop 73, telling him that it was Boy Scout policy to "specifically forbid membership to homosexuals."

Given the dueling precedents, the fate of the case may well turn on whether the court sees a statement of gay identity as an inherently expressive act, one that conveys a message beyond a simple self-description. The Boy Scouts, looking to place Mr. Dale in the position of the would-be St. Patrick's Day parade's marchers, assert that being openly gay conveys not only an identity but a built-in message of disaffection with the "scouting values" that a troop leader is supposed to transmit.

Mr. Dale, on the other hand, asserts that "learning that someone is gay tells you nothing about his or her political party, religious beliefs, lifestyle, or moral code" and that consequently his exclusion amounted to the same discrimination based on status that the court rejected in the all-male club cases. If reinstated, his brief says, "Dale is prepared to be bound by the same directives and limitations placed on all scoutmasters."

Underneath the legal arguments is the fact that the case concerns not just any mass-membership organization, not a businessmen's dinner club, but the Boy Scouts—described by Lord Robert Baden-Powell, who founded the organization in England in 1907, as a "character-factory." What impact will that fact have on the justices?

Both sides strive for the high ground. "In an age when we laugh and mock what we used to honor and venerate," the Family Research Council, a conservative Christian organization, says in its brief, "the Boy Scouts of America stands against a cultural tide" and should not be "sacrificed on the altar of a civil right that belies its name."

On the other hand, the American Public Health Association tells the court that Boy Scouts' "central role in so many communities" makes it all the more important to make sure the organization does not rely on "discredited myths and stereotypes to justify excluding gay scouts simply because of their status."

Correction: An article last Sunday about a Supreme Court case over the Boy Scouts' right to expel a gay scout leader referred incorrectly to the United Methodist Church. As a denomination, the church took no position. Two Methodist organizations did file briefs, on opposing sides—the United Methodist Board of Church and Society opposing the Scouts' policy and the General Commission on United Methodist Men favoring it.

The article also referred incorrectly to the commission. It is an official church group, not a dissident group.

* * *

April 27, 2000

JUSTICES EXPLORE SCOUTS' EXCLUSION OF GAY MEMBERS

By LINDA GREENHOUSE

WASHINGTON, April 26—The question before the Supreme Court today was whether the Boy Scouts have a constitutional right to exclude gay members, but the justices did not seem particularly interested in either Boy Scout policy or the future of gay rights.

Rather, what clearly concerned the court were the implications of ruling for one side or the other. If the Boy Scouts cannot exclude gays, can they still exclude girls, the justices wanted to know. Would a Jewish social group be forced to accept non-Jewish members, or a gay organization to include heterosexuals?

More generally, the justices asked, if an organization deems a particular kind of exclusivity to be central to its identity, must courts take that assertion at face value? If not, by what standard are they to judge it? If so, might that not be the equivalent of giving a free pass from the anti-discrimination commands of civil rights law?

The questions came thick and fast for the lawyers representing the Boy Scouts of America and James Dale, who was an Eagle Scout assistant scoutmaster when his troop in Monmouth County, N.J., expelled him 10 years ago, after learning from a newspaper article that he is gay.

The Boy Scouts "specifically forbid membership to homosexuals," he was told. Mr. Dale, who as the article reported was co-president of a student gay rights organization at Rutgers University, sued under New Jersey's anti-discrimination law, which includes protection for sexual orientation. Last year the New Jersey Supreme Court ruled that the Boy Scouts are a "public accommodation," to which the state law applies, and rejected the argument that the First Amendment guarantee of freedom of association shielded the Scouts' policy.

The justices' questions today reflected their effort to decide where to slot this case into an array of First Amendment precedents that offer ammunition to both sides. For example, several justices asked in different ways whether Mr. Dale's termination reflected the simple fact of his sexual orientation, as opposed to scouting officials' conclusions that he was engaged in "public advocacy," as Justice Anthony M. Kennedy put it.

"It's about the message that would go to youth in the program," replied George A. Davidson, the Boy Scouts' lawyer.

"Being openly homosexual communicates the concept that this is O.K.," he said, adding that "coming out" as a gay person, "in the culture in which these statements are made, is a statement fraught with moral meaning."

The issue of whether being gay inherently conveys a message is important, given one of the court's precedents, a 1995 decision that the organizers of Boston's St. Patrick's Day parade had a First Amendment right to exclude gay marchers. The court ruled in that case, which the Boy Scouts have cited prominently, that the organizers did not have to turn their parade over to an unwanted message, in that instance to an expression of gay pride.

But Mr. Dale's lawyer, Evan Wolfson of the Lambda Legal Defense and Education Fund, maintained that what was at issue in Mr. Dale's case was "identity-based discrimination, the equation of a human being with an assumed message," without reference to anything Mr. Dale had said or done.

"A human being is not speech, other than 'I am who I am,'" Mr. Wolfson said.

His assertion that there is no message inherent in Mr. Dale's sexual orientation was an effort to invoke, rather than the case of the St. Patrick's Day parade, a trio of sex discrimination cases from the 1980's. In those cases, the court rejected claims that all-male organizations, including the Jaycees and the Rotary Club, had a constitutional right to exclude women, with the court noting that the women simply sought to join and were not trying to change the essential nature of groups organized around business networking.

The lesson from those cases, Mr. Wolfson said, is that scouting must show that its own "expressive purposes in bringing its members together are significantly burdened" by a requirement to admit gays. The Scouts have failed to meet that test, he said, because the Boy Scouts are not organized around a principle of opposition to gay rights.

"Who," Justice Kennedy said to Mr. Wolfson, "is better qualified to determine the expressive purpose of the Boy Scouts: the Boy Scouts or the New Jersey courts?"

Mr. Davidson, representing the Scouts, conceded that excluding gays did not appear in the organization's official manuals. But that makes no difference, he said, noting that "the Boy Scouts are so closely identified with traditional moral values that the phrase 'He's a real Boy Scout' has entered the language."

Mr. Davidson said the policy was based on the Scouts' "moral code," as expressed in the phrase "morally straight" in the Scout Oath and the word "clean" in the Scout Law.

Justice John Paul Stevens asked whether the Boy Scouts took the position that a person who engages in homosexual activity "cannot fit that definition."

"That's correct," Mr. Davidson replied.

The lawyer said the Scouts were in an even stronger position than the organizers of the St. Patrick's Day parade, who won their case even though, he said, there was "no readily apparent message in the parade."

"Here we have a moral code," Mr. Davidson said.

But Justice David H. Souter, who wrote the court's unanimous opinion in that 1995 case, Hurley v. Irish American Gay Group of Boston, disputed Mr. Davidson's analysis.

"The problem in simply drawing a parallel to Hurley," Justice Souter said, "is that we're not at the point where anyone is proposing to use the Boy Scouts" for expressing his own message. Mr. Dale wanted to rejoin scouting and was "not proposing to carry a banner," the justice said.

Mr. Davidson replied: "He put a banner around his neck when he appeared in the newspaper."

Mr. Wolfson, arguing for Mr. Dale, said the Boy Scouts, "one of the least private public accommodations in the country," had not justified an exclusion from a "neutral civil rights law of general applicability."

Some justices suggested that perhaps none of the court's precedents was really a good fit for this case.

Justice Sandra Day O'Connor told Mr. Wolfson that "I can well understand" why public accommodations law should apply to organizations that have a commercial purpose, like the Jaycees or the Rotary Club in the earlier cases. "But should the weight we give it in the context of a First Amendment claim be the same for private organizations?"

Chief Justice William H. Rehnquist asked whether members of a Roman Catholic organization could limit the group to Catholics on the basis that "we just feel much more comfortable with Catholics, and we do Catholic work." He asked Mr. Wolfson whether, in light of the Constitution's protection for freedom of association, "they need a more expressive message than that."

Mr. Wolfson replied that freedom of association was not "free floating" but rather was entitled to recognition only to the extent that it served the ability of an organization's members to express their message. As simply a free-floating right, he said, it could be invoked "as a defense against civil rights laws that would swallow civil rights laws."

While most members of the court appeared uncertain how to decide this case, Boy Scouts v. Dale, No. 99-669, Justice Antonin Scalia left little doubt of his view.

"To require the Boy Scouts to have as a scoutmaster someone who embodies a contradiction of their message—how can that be?" Justice Scalia asked Mr. Wolfson.

He said the Constitution "prevents a state from diluting or imperiling the message an organization wants to convey, whether by speech or by dropping a bomb."

A decision is expected by early summer.

* * *

April 27, 2000

GOOD CAUSES MAKE BAD LAW

By CHARLES FRIED

The Supreme Court heard two cases this term that seem to take the measure of our society—one, for the way we treat homosexuals and the other for the way we protect women from barbarity.

In Boy Scouts of America v. Dale, argued yesterday, the court will decide whether the scouts can ban gay troop leaders. In United States v. Morrison, the government and the NOW Legal Defense and Education Fund have asked the court to uphold the constitutionality of the Violence Against Women Act, which allows victims to file federal lawsuits against those who treat them violently.

Advocates say these cases involve vital protections of the rights of women and homosexuals. But also at stake are important legal principles, and these principles should preclude the court from ruling for gays in the Boy Scouts or for the constitutionality of the Violence Against Women Act.

The national government has only those powers that the Constitution assigns to it. For instance, the federal government can "tax and spend for the general welfare," regulate interstate commerce and enforce constitutional amendments, but it has no power to regulate just because something seems to need regulating. That is the job of the states.

The Violence Against Women Act, then, is plainly unconstitutional. The act's proponents, however, as their main argument, resort to a familiar sophistry to argue that the law is a regulation of interstate commerce: They claim that violence against women lowers their earning power, discourages them from traveling between states and subtracts them from the national labor force. (Full disclosure: I was of counsel to the other side of the case.)

If that argument were accepted, then almost any activity would also be susceptible to federal regulation. A street-corner mugging, for instance, could become grounds for a federal lawsuit.

The Boy Scouts case is also about the basic structure of our government. In that case, the New Jersey Supreme Court ruled last year that the state law forbidding discrimination against homosexuals prevents the Boy Scouts from denying a leadership position to an openly gay man. The scouts argue that the state and federal governments cannot coerce their choice of leaders.

This contest is not about states' sovereignty, as the lawsuit over the Violence Against Woman Act is, but about the sovereignty of the individual. This sovereignty is enshrined in the First Amendment's freedoms of speech, thought and association, and the Supreme Court has acknowledged it in decisions protecting the right of individuals to use contraceptives and the right of women to choose abortion. And it is the very principle gay rights advocates must invoke to overturn cruel laws criminalizing consensual adult homosexual relations.

But the Boy Scouts case pushes an argument that undercuts that fundamental principle of individual liberty. The right to join with others in associations, expressing personal values, is as much a part of individual liberty as the right to abortion. It cannot be up to the government, at any level, to decide which values individuals may choose to join together to express. Just as the Nazis were rightly allowed to march in Skokie, Ill., and just as the organizers of the St. Patrick's Day parade in Boston were allowed to exclude marchers carrying gay-pride banners, so the scouts should be allowed to inculcate their values, however much we may disapprove.

There are two arguments being used against the Boy Scouts, which are being pressed with the sophistry that is now a hallmark of the teaching in most law schools. First, the Boy Scouts are being compared to a Junior Chamber of Commerce, which the Supreme Court has said is a commercial association and therefore forbidden from excluding women. Second, the scouts are said not to be really a private group, but, because of their numbers, a state actor and susceptible to regulation as such.

Both arguments are unacceptable. By this logic, any large organization could be characterized as commercial and as involved with government in some way or another. Indeed these same claims could easily be made on behalf of gay or women candidates for the priesthood. Or for that matter, for male leaders in the National Organization for Women.

Our legal principles might lead us to outcomes that we don't always desire. But we must trust that our society is robust enough that we need not sacrifice our constitutional principles, which keep us free and diverse, for the sake of gratifying pronouncements that may come back to haunt us.

Charles Fried, a law professor at Harvard, is a former Solicitor General.

* * *

June 29, 2000

EXCERPTS FROM THE SUPREME COURT'S RULING ON GAYS AND THE BOY SCOUTS

By The New York Times

WASHINGTON, June 28—Following are excerpts from the Supreme Court's ruling today that the Boy Scouts of America can exclude gay members. The vote in the case, Boy Scouts of America v. Dale, was 5 to 4. Chief Justice William H. Rehnquist wrote the decision; Justice John Paul Stevens wrote the dissent.

From the Decision by Chief Justice Rehnquist

The forced inclusion of an unwanted person in a group infringes the group's freedom of expressive association if the presence of that person affects in a significant way the group's ability to advocate public or private viewpoints. But the freedom of expressive association, like many freedoms, is not absolute. We have held that the freedom could be overridden "by regulations adopted to serve compelling state interests, unrelated to the suppression of ideas, that cannot be achieved through means significantly less restrictive of associational freedoms."

To determine whether a group is protected by the First Amendment's expressive associational right, we must determine whether the group engages in "expressive association." The First Amendment's protection of expressive association is not reserved for advocacy groups. But to come within its

ambit, a group must engage in some form of expression, whether it be public or private. . . .

The general mission of the Boy Scouts is clear: "To instill values in young people." The Boy Scouts seeks to instill these values by having its adult leaders spend time with the youth members, instructing and engaging them in activities like camping, archery, and fishing. During the time spent with the youth members, the scoutmasters and assistant scoutmasters inculcate them with the Boy Scouts' values both expressly and by example. It seems indisputable that an association that seeks to transmit such a system of values engages in expressive activity. . . .

The values the Boy Scouts seeks to instill are "based on" those listed in the scout oath and law. The Boy Scouts explains that the scout oath and law provide "a positive moral code for living; they are a list of 'dos' rather than 'don'ts.'" The Boy Scouts asserts that homosexual conduct is inconsistent with the values embodied in the scout oath and law, particularly with the values represented by the terms "morally straight" and "clean."

Obviously, the scout oath and law do not expressly mention sexuality or sexual orientation. And the terms "morally straight" and "clean" are by no means self-defining. Different people would attribute to those terms very different meanings. For example, some people may believe that engaging in homosexual conduct is not at odds with being "morally straight" and "clean." And others may believe that engaging in homosexual conduct is contrary to being "morally straight" and "clean." The Boy Scouts says it falls within the latter category.

The New Jersey Supreme Court analyzed the Boy Scouts' beliefs and found that the "exclusion of members solely on the basis of their sexual orientation is inconsistent with Boy Scouts' commitment to a diverse and 'representative' membership [and] contradicts Boy Scouts' overarching objective to reach 'all eligible youth.'" The court concluded that the exclusion of members like Dale "appears antithetical to the organization's goals and philosophy." But our cases reject this sort of inquiry; it is not the role of the courts to reject a group's expressed values because they disagree with those values or find them internally inconsistent.

The Boy Scouts asserts that it "teaches that homosexual conduct is not morally straight," and that it does "not want to promote homosexual conduct as a legitimate form of behavior." We accept the Boy Scouts' assertion. We need not inquire further to determine the nature of the Boy Scouts' expression with respect to homosexuality. But because the record before us contains written evidence of the Boy Scouts' viewpoint, we look to it as instructive, if only on the question of the sincerity of the professed beliefs. . . .

At least as of 1978, the year James Dale entered scouting, the official position of the Boy Scouts was that avowed homosexuals were not to be scoutleaders.

A position statement promulgated by the Boy Scouts in 1991 (after Dale's membership was revoked but before this litigation was filed) also supports its current view:

"We believe that homosexual conduct is inconsistent with the requirement in the scout oath that a scout be morally straight and in the scout law that a scout be clean in word and deed, and that homosexuals do not provide a desirable role model for Scouts." . . .

As we give deference to an association's assertions regarding the nature of its expression, we must also give deference to an association's view of what would impair its expression. That is not to say that an expressive association can erect a shield against antidiscrimination laws simply by asserting that mere acceptance of a member from a particular group would impair its message. But here Dale, by his own admission, is one of a group of gay scouts who have "become leaders in their community and are open and honest about their sexual orientation." Dale was the copresident of a gay and lesbian organization at college and remains a gay rights activist. Dale's presence in the Boy Scouts would, at the very least, force the organization to send a message, both to the youth members and the world, that the Boy Scouts accepts homosexual conduct as a legitimate form of behavior.

"Hurley" is illustrative on this point. There we considered whether the application of Massachusetts's public accommodations law to require the organizers of a private St. Patrick's Day parade to include among the marchers an Irish American gay, lesbian and bisexual group, GLIB, violated the parade organizers' First Amendment rights. We noted that the parade organizers did not wish to exclude the GLIB members because of their sexual orientations, but because they wanted to march behind a GLIB banner. We observed:

"A contingent marching behind the organization's banner would at least bear witness to the fact that some Irish are gay, lesbian, or bisexual, and the presence of the organized marchers would suggest their view that people of their sexual orientations have as much claim to unqualified social acceptance as heterosexuals. The parade's organizers may not believe these facts about Irish sexuality to be so, or they may object to unqualified social acceptance of gays and lesbians or have some other reason for wishing to keep GLIB's message out of the parade. But whatever the reason, it boils down to the choice of a speaker not to propound a particular point of view, and that choice is presumed to lie beyond the government's power to control."

Here, we have found that the Boy Scouts believes that homosexual conduct is inconsistent with the values it seeks to instill in its youth members; it will not "promote homosexual conduct as a legitimate form of behavior." As the presence of GLIB in Boston's St. Patrick's Day parade would have interfered with the parade organizers' choice not to propound a particular point of view, the presence of Dale as an assistant scoutmaster would just as surely interfere with the Boy Scouts' choice not to propound a point of view contrary to its beliefs.

The New Jersey Supreme Court determined that the Boy Scouts' ability to disseminate its message was not significantly affected by the forced inclusion of Dale as an assistant scoutmaster because of the following findings:

"Boy Scout members do not associate for the purpose of disseminating the belief that homosexuality is immoral; Boy Scouts discourages its leaders from disseminating any views on sexual issues; and Boy Scouts includes sponsors and members who subscribe to different views in respect of homosexuality."

We disagree with the New Jersey Supreme Court's conclusion drawn from these findings.

First, associations do not have to associate for the "purpose" of disseminating a certain message in order to be entitled to the protections of the First Amendment. An association must merely engage in expressive activity that could be impaired in order to be entitled to protection.

Second, even if the Boy Scouts discourages scoutleaders from disseminating views on sexual issues, a fact that the Boy Scouts disputes with contrary evidence, the First Amendment protects the Boy Scouts' method of expression. If the Boy Scouts wishes scout leaders to avoid questions of sexuality and teach only by example, this fact does not negate the sincerity of its belief discussed above.

Third, the First Amendment simply does not require that every member of a group agree on every issue in order for the group's policy to be "expressive association." The Boy Scouts takes an official position with respect to homosexual conduct, and that is sufficient for First Amendment purposes. In this same vein, Dale makes much of the claim that the Boy Scouts does not revoke the membership of heterosexual scoutleaders that openly disagree with the Boy Scouts' policy on sexual orientation. But if this is true, it is irrelevant. The presence of an avowed homosexual and gay rights activist in an assistant scoutmaster's uniform sends a distinctly different message from the presence of a heterosexual assistant scoutmaster who is on record as disagreeing with Boy Scouts policy. The Boy Scouts has a First Amendment right to choose to send one message but not the other. The fact that the organization does not trumpet its views from the housetops, or that it tolerates dissent within its ranks, does not mean that its views receive no First Amendment protection. . . .

We have already concluded that a state requirement that the Boy Scouts retain Dale as an assistant scoutmaster would significantly burden the organization's right to oppose or disfavor homosexual conduct. The state interests embodied in New Jersey's public accommodations law do not justify such a severe intrusion on the Boy Scouts' rights to freedom of expressive association.

From the Dissent by Justice Stevens

New Jersey "prides itself on judging each individual by his or her merits" and on being "in the vanguard in the fight to eradicate the cancer of unlawful discrimination of all types from our society." Since 1945, it has had a law against discrimination. The law broadly protects the opportunity of all persons to obtain the advantages and privileges "of any place of public accommodation." . . .

The majority holds that New Jersey's law violates B.S.A.'s [Boy Scouts of America's] right to associate and its right to free speech. But that law does not "impose any serious burdens" on B.S.A.'s "collective effort on behalf of its shared goals," nor does it force B.S.A. to communicate any message that it does not wish to endorse. New Jersey's law, therefore, abridges no constitutional right of the Boy Scouts. . . .

It is plain as the light of day that neither one of these principles, "morally straight" and "clean," says the slightest thing about homosexuality. Indeed, neither term in the Boy Scouts' law and oath expresses any position whatsoever on sexual matters.

B.S.A.'s published guidance on that topic underscores this point. Scouts, for example, are directed to receive their sex education at home or in school, but not from the organization. . . .

B.S.A. never took any clear and unequivocal position on homosexuality. Though the 1991 and 1992 policies state one interpretation of "morally straight" and "clean," the group's published definitions appearing in the Boy Scout and scoutmaster handbooks take quite another view. And B.S.A.'s broad religious tolerance combined with its declaration that sexual matters are not its "proper area" render its views on the issue equivocal at best and incoherent at worst. . . .

B.S.A. has, at most, simply adopted an exclusionary membership policy and has no shared goal of disapproving of homosexuality. B.S.A.'s mission statement and federal charter say nothing on the matter; its official membership policy is silent; its scout oath and law and accompanying definitions are devoid of any view on the topic; its guidance for scouts and scoutmasters on sexuality declare that such matters are "not construed to be scouting's proper area," but are the province of a scout's parents and pastor; and B.S.A.'s posture respecting religion tolerates a wide variety of views on the issue of homosexuality. . . .

The only apparent explanation for the majority's holding, then, is that homosexuals are simply so different from the rest of society that their presence alone unlike any other individual's should be singled out for special First Amendment treatment.

That such prejudices are still prevalent and that they have caused serious and tangible harm to countless members of the class New Jersey seeks to protect are established matters of fact that neither the Boy Scouts nor the court disputes. That harm can only be aggravated by the creation of a constitutional shield for a policy that is itself the product of a habitual way of thinking about strangers. As Justice Brandeis so wisely advised, "we must be ever on our guard, lest we erect our prejudices into legal principles."

If we would guide by the light of reason, we must let our minds be bold. I respectfully dissent.

* * *

June 29, 2000

VICTORY HAS CONSEQUENCES OF ITS OWN

By ANDREW JACOBS

In convincing the Supreme Court that it should have the right to bar gays from its ranks, the Boy Scouts of America has definitively established itself as an organization that considers homosexuality a detriment to the well-being of its young members.

But as the public becomes more tolerant of lesbians and gay men—and less accepting of discrimination against them—some civil rights advocates said yesterday that the Boy Scouts' victory could ultimately harm the group.

Though the organization's membership has grown to nearly 5 million, from 4.3 million in 1997, its aggressive legal campaign to exclude gay leaders has provoked disenchantment from religious groups, school boards and parent volunteers around the country.

A dozen municipal governments, including Washington, Chicago and San Francisco, have severed relationships with the scouts or are considering measures to keep the group from using public buildings. In Connecticut last month, authorities removed the group from its list of charities eligible for state payroll deductions. And after learning of the decision yesterday, the United Methodist Church, which sponsors 15 percent of Boy Scout troops, said it would encourage local congregations to sever ties.

"The Boy Scouts have a hollow, Pyrrhic victory," said Ruth Harlow, deputy legal director for Lambda Legal Defense and Education Fund, which argued the case of James Dale, an Eagle Scout assistant scoutmaster whose troop expelled him after learning he was gay.

"Their leaders and lawyers have convinced five members of the Supreme Court of their narrow, discriminatory vision," Ms. Harlow said. "Now they have to live with that vision."

Boy Scout officials dismissed the notion that the decision would spark a backlash against the group. "We feel that American families never left the values that the Boy Scouts never left," said Gregg Shields, a spokesman for the group. Membership grew, Mr. Shields noted, even as the scouts waged a 10-year legal battle to retain the ban. Even if donors or sponsors pulled out, he said, the scouts would find other support. "We'll be just fine," he said.

But David A. Rice, vice president of Scouting for All, a group that opposes the scouts' policy, said the ruling would force corporate sponsors and cities with antidiscrimination laws to review their relationships with the group.

"This narrows the organization and pushes it more firmly into the hands of religious conservatives and the right wing," Mr. Rice said. "Many public-spirited companies will find they can no longer be involved with the scouts."

So far, defections have been minimal. Fewer than a dozen United Way chapters have withdrawn financing, among them the United Way of Somerset County, N.J., which last month pulled its annual $30,600 gift after the local scout council refused to sign its nondiscrimination policy.

New York City officials said they would try to stop the scouts from using school buildings or receiving support from any publicly financed agency. Christine Quinn, a member of the City Council, said that by accommodating scout meetings, the city was violating its human rights law.

In Monmouth County, N.J., where Mr. Dale served until his ouster in 1990, reaction was mixed. Some, like Dolores Dalzell, 62, a former den mother, expressed relief. "I don't think it's proper," she said about gay scout leaders. "I wouldn't want my children exposed to them."

Others said they were disturbed that the Boy Scouts could now legally discriminate. Lynda Montague, 28, a secretary from Sayreville, said the ruling persuaded her to prevent her 8-year-old son from joining the scouts when he gets older. "I don't want him to belong to a group that promotes bigotry," she said.

* * *

June 29, 2000

EXCERPTS FROM THE PRESIDENT'S NEWS CONFERENCE AT THE WHITE HOUSE

Following are excerpts from President Clinton's news conference yesterday at the White House, as recorded by The New York Times:

Q. Mr. President, what do you think of the justices' ruling this morning that allows the Boy Scouts to bar gays as leaders? And if you disagree with it, can you justify your role as honorary president of the Boy Scouts, which discriminates against gays and atheists?

A. Well, first of all, the court's ruling, I noticed it with interest. I haven't read it yet, but I did get a pretty good report on it. I noted with interest that they seemed to go out of their way to draw the ruling quite narrowly and to limit it strictly to the question of whether the Boy Scouts could pick the people who were going to be scout leaders.

I generally, I have to tell you, you know, I'm generally against discrimination against gays. I think it's—and I think that the country has moved a long way and I'm proud of things that we've been able to do and I'm disappointed we haven't been able to do more in some areas. But I think we're moving in the right direction. And I think that's all I should say. I mean, the Boy Scouts still are a—they're a great group, they do a lot of good. And I would hope that, you know, this is just one step along the way of a movement toward greater inclusion for our society, because I think that's the direction we ought to be going in. . . .

* * *

THE POLITICAL ARENA

October 27, 1970

3 CANDIDATES SUPPORT RIGHTS OF HOMOSEXUALS

Three of the major statewide candidates have issued statements in support of the Gay Activists Alliance platform on homosexual civil rights.

Arthur J. Goldberg, the Democratic-Liberal candidate for Governor, Senator Charles E. Goodell, the Republican-Liberal incumbent for the United States Senate, and his Democratic opponent, Representative Richard L. Ottinger, have issued similar statements calling for an end to discriminatory laws and practices against homosexuals.

According to Mark Rubin, a spokesman for the alliance, this is the first time that any political candidate has taken an official position on homosexual rights.

* * *

July 13, 1972

MCGOVERN FORCES SHAPE PLANKS TO SUIT CANDIDATE

By JOHN HERBERS
Special to The New York Times

MIAMI BEACH, July 12—In an 11-hour session that ended at sunrise today, the Democratic National Convention rejected strong efforts to write into the party platform a series of New Left stands on such issues as abortion, homosexual rights, tax reform and guaranteed income. The forces of Senator George McGovern were firmly in control.

The convention, operating at full strength despite the hour, turned back by a wide margin an appeal by Gov. George C. Wallace of Alabama for planks against busing and Government spending and for a stronger military, a citizen's right to bear arms and prayer in public schools.

In the end, Senator McGovern got almost exactly the kind of platform he wanted to run on against President Nixon in November—a 24,000-word document with a liberal, Populist tone and direction, but one so worded that he could shape his own stand on the major issues of the day.

The McGovern forces did not so much fear tying the Senator's hands with a New Left platform drawn for his constituency in the primaries as they did providing targets for the

Republicans to use against him in their appeal to the center of the electorate.

Only two of 20 minority reports to the document drafted by the Platform Committee in Washington last month were approved by the convention—one to extend more land rights to Indians and one to offer stronger military support for Israel.

The McGovern leaders in effect gave way on these two relatively mild planks in return for delegate unity on ones that they felt could cost the South Dakotan large numbers of votes in the election, the chief of which was abortion.

The platform calls for "immediate and complete withdrawal of all U.S. forces in Indochina"; amnesty for Vietnam draft evaders "when the fighting has ceased and our troops and prisoners of war have returned"; abolition of the present welfare system and enactment of a guaranteed income of about $3,900 for a family of four; full employment with the Government as employer of last resort; tax reform on a gradual basis, and enactment of a number of new social programs, from day care to massive aid to the cities. It also calls for a reduction in military spending.

The platform debate opened at 10 P.M. yesterday. An hour later, Governor Wallace, in a wheelchair, made his appearance and gave a nine-minute address, which received a polite but restrained reception. Then, after two hours of speeches for and against his proposals, the convention voted down all eight of the Wallace planks with a thundering chorus of noes. No effort was made to obtain a roll-call vote on them.

Then came a tax reform proposal that had the McGovern forces worried. Supported from the rostrum by Senator Fred R. Harris, the self-styled Populist from Oklahoma it would have endorsed a specific plan for a more sharply graduated income tax and removal of many exemptions and loopholes.

From the press gallery and elsewhere in the hall, the yeas sounded as loud as the noes. But Yvonne Braithwaite Burke, a forceful black woman who is vice chairman of the Democratic National Committee, ruled that the noes had won. There were no objections until after she had moved to the next item of business, at which time she ruled that it was too late to take another vote.

The first roll-call came on the National Welfare Rights Organization's plan for a $6,500 minimum income for a family of four. It was defeated, 1,852.86 to 999.75. By voice vote the convention rejected a proposal to freeze rents at their level on Aug. 14, 1971.

Then came the seemingly mild report sponsored by the Women's Caucus: "In matters relating to human reproduction, each person's right to privacy, freedom of choice and individual conscience should be fully respected, consistent with relevant Supreme Court decisions."

The convention came to life. The McGovern forces had carefully gauged the situation and released as many of their delegates as possible to vote their conscience while holding enough to win. Shirley MacLaine, the actress, endorsed the meaning of the report but asked delegates to vote against it to save the McGovern candidacy.

The vote was 1,569.80 to 1,103.37 against the proposal. Another motion to adjourn was shouted down and the Gay Liberation report, calling for repeal of all laws regarding sexual acts between consenting adults, was put before the convention.

The plank was defeated by voice vote.

A plank saying "we support allocation of Federal surplus lands to American Indians on a first-priority basis" carried by an overwhelming margin.

The delegates were trying to keep alert. Still, they shouted down attempts to adjourn. In rapid order, they rejected plans to oppose busing to inferior schools or when it involved long distances, leaving the platform with a pro-busing position, and link withdrawal from Vietnam to a release of American prisoners.

They overwhelmingly approved maintenance of a military force in Europe and the Mediterranean "ample to deter the Soviet Union from putting unbearable pressure on Israel," a proposal offered by supporters of Senator Henry M. Jackson of Washington.

The platform was adopted at 6:15 A.M. At 6:21 A.M. it was all over, and the delegates struggled out into the dawn.

* * *

November 14, 1974

SEXUALITY ISSUE PUT TO REST, ELAINE NOBLE IS READY FOR OFFICE

By JOHN KIFNER
Special to The New York Times

BOSTON, Nov. 13—She grew up poor in a Pennsylvania mining town, escaping on a scholarship that, along with cocktail waitressing, took her through Boston University. Now 30 years old, she has two master's degrees, college teaching jobs behind her, a record of community activity including a post on the Governor's Commission on the Status of Women, and a reputation for being outgoing, tough, able and articulate.

So maybe it was not altogether surprising that in last week's election she won a seat in the State Legislature.

Except that Elaine Noble is a lesbian—believed to be the first avowed homosexual elected to a state office.

"There was a lot of pressure from some of my supporters in the community not to mention it," Miss Noble recalled. "But I thought it was necessary to state that politically. I mean, we're not purple, right?"

Produced Program

So, along with her recently acquired master's degree in education from Harvard and her membership in the Women's Political Caucus, Miss Noble's campaign literature also listed among her qualifications her work in producing a radio program called "Gay Way," on a local FM station.

But, more prominently, the literature talked about "neighborhood security" in the frequently fearful and victimized area, the need for comprehensive health care and decent housing and "the uneven level of city services, like transportation and trash pickup."

"When I decided to run, it was because I'm the most qualified for this job," she was saying over a beer at Steve McGrail's bar, a neighborhood place with shamrocks on the menu. And I figured the worst thing that can happen is that I lose."

The Sixth Suffolk—Boston's Fenway/Back Bay—is a new district, carved out of the tail ends of two adjoining districts. It covers sprawling Boston University and a pack of hospitals, medical schools and colleges.

Its people are the elderly, many of them women scraping out the ends of their lives alone, the transient community of students, gay people, clusterings of some 24 nationalities,

What enabled Miss Noble to win the district was a campaign that stressed her community work and the fact that she had met so many of the voters face to face. It started, however, as an amateur undertaking.

Opponent a Bar Owner

Her campaign in both the Democratic primary and the election was made up of old friends and community activists, gay and straight, so inexperienced, she recalled, that the first thing they did was get every book they could from the library on how to run a campaign.

Her opponent in the general election was Joseph P. Cimino, part-owner of Daisy Buchanan's, one of a chain of singles bars. Miss Noble has been active with residents trying to restrict the number of bars opening in the area.

The community work, the basis for her campaign, included, among other things, helping the elderly and the blind, particularly in housing, organizing pressure for rent control, lobbying, fighting the use of a school playground as a parking lot for Red Sox baseball games and organizing a garbage cleanup coupled with a threat to dump the refuse at City Hall unless service was improved. Boston's crisis over court-ordered school busing for integration was at full peak during the campaign, and, typically, Miss Noble spent much of her time working to ease tensions rather than politiking.

"Even in a crowd where there were hecklers, there were always two or three people that I've helped," she said.

Miss Noble won by 1,730 to 1,201.

The seat in the legislature is a long way from Natrona, Pa., where there was a salt mine at the end of Miss Noble's street. After working in a factory for a year after high school, she won a partial scholarship to Boston University.

After graduation, there was a job at a two-year women's school where Miss Noble came to terms with her lesbianism.

"It was a totally female environment. God, it was great, a fantastic experience," she recalled.

Returning to Boston, she taught in the speech department at Emerson College. And, more important, she took up again the community work she had begun as an undergraduate working in a South End settlement house.

The New York Times/Arthur Grace

Elaine Noble last week won a seat in the Massachusetts State Legislature.

'Breaking Stereotypes'

"She's going to walk around this place breaking stereotypes just by her own style and intelligence. To meet her face-to-face dispels stereotypes," said State Representative Barney Frank, a friend who represents the neighboring Beacon Hill-Back Bay District. "It sounds condescending and I don't mean it to be, but you could not have a better individual to be the first openly gay person in office."

There is still pain from the rebuffs she feels lesbians have gotten from the women's movement, but now her office walls are lined with congratulatory telegrams, including one from the city police superintendent.

Street Reaction

People stop to shake her hand on the street and she hugs them and the old men come out of their small shops to congratulate her. Louis, the barber, says, "If you do good, we'll move you on up."

Years ago, when she was leaving the neighborhood, a group of retired veterans she had helped had Louis give her a haircut as a present because her long hair blew in her eyes on her motor scooter.

She cried then, she remembered, "because I was paranoid, really afraid of looking like a lesbian."

"We're proud of you, honey," an elderly dry-cleaning-man was saying. "Now you'll have a good career. Just don't let anybody bother you."

On the corner, there were two old women. One, who used to shout "Sodom! Gomorrah!" at her turned and walked away. But the other stayed to chat a minute. Then, as she picked up her brightly-colored shopping bag, she remarked to Miss Noble: "It's so heavy. I have such a heavy thing to carry."

"So do I, lady," Miss Noble said under her breath.

*   *   *

January 12, 1978

SAN FRANCISCO LEGISLATORS MEET IN DIVERSITY

By LES LEDBETTER
Special to The New York Times

SAN FRANCISCO, Jan. 11—The San Francisco Board of Supervisors that met Monday for the first time is the most diverse and unpredictable governing body that anyone here can recall seeing or hearing about anywhere in the country.

A switch from at-large to district elections last year brought five new members to the 11-person local legislature and retained six independent incumbents.

"You're going to see a lot of 6 to 5 votes and a lot of strange alliances," said Quentin Kopp, a re-elected incumbent.

One of the new members is Harvey Milk, an avowed homosexual who walked to City Hall with hundreds of supporters and told the city establishment, "I want to introduce my lover," after other supervisors had introduced wives, husbands and blood relatives.

The election of Mr. Milk, a former New Yorker and a former Navy officer, is perceived to be a clear indication of growing political strength of the homosexual community here. His first legislative act was to introduce a bill that would bar discrimination against homosexuals.

A Machine of Minorities

And the new supervisors also include the first black woman elected to that post, Ella Hill Hutch; the first Chinese-American, Gordon Lau; the first unwed mother and feminist, Carol Ruth Silver; and the first former fireman, Dan White, who was also a local policeman.

San Franciscans have always boasted of the diverse cultures nourishing here, from the well-known groups such as Chinese and Italians to Samoans and Basques.

But these boasts have been tempered in recent years as minority groups, liberal activists and homosexuals formed what their opponents call a machine, to challenge the established power centers of business and finance and upper-middle-class families. This coalition is credited with electing the current administration and winning passage of the district elections.

Establishment leaders warn, as they have for several years, that the social demands of this new coalition are chasing industries and middle-class taxpayers out of the city.

The re-elected supervisors include two-potential challengers to Mayor George Moscone and several establishment-oriented lawmakers who are struggling to come to grips with the new political realities emerging in this city.

"I think it will be a very independent board, one that cannot be defined until eight or nine months have passed," said Diane Feinstein, a re-elected incumbent who was elected president of the Board Monday and who is a potential candidate for the post of Mayor in 1979. Mr. Kopp is another potential challenger.

Diversity Shows in Speeches

"I think it will be a better, more responsive board that I can work with," said the Mayor, smiling. The new arrange-

The 11-member San Francisco Board of Supervisors is a diverse and unpredictable group. At left, Harvey Milk takes oath of office from Judge Ollie Marie-Victoire. An announced homosexual, he tried to introduce his lover in ceremony at City Hall. At center, Carol Ruth Silver, the board's first unwed mother, speaks to her feminist supporters. At right, Gordon Lau, the first Chinese-American elected to the board, holds his daughter, Diane, at the installation ceremonies.

ment is expected to increase Mr. Moscone's power because he can deal with individual board members while the previous board, elected by citywide voting, had a sense of unity.

The Mayor, who often fought the previous supervisors and used his veto 18 times in the past two years, is the only man who can put projects in the city budget. The supervisors can only delete.

"I think this board will, the new members especially, be cooperative," said the Mayor in an interview. "They want results, they need results, that's why they ran."

The diversity of the supervisors and the schisms that separate groups in this city were perhaps nowhere better demonstrated Monday than in the introductory speeches by the new supervisors.

Supervisor White, 31, spoke of his pride "as an American" and of his achievements, while his grandmother, who immigrated from Ireland, watched with other relatives.

Supervisor Milk criticized a state law banning homosexual marriages and tried to introduce as his lover a young man who had left the overflowing chambers just before Mr. Milk spoke.

Supervisor Silver introduced her housemate, a male, to her colleagues, and then she introduced her children. Her way of living might once have been strange even in this cosmopolitan city, but her reputation as a tough advocate and Mr. Milk's more flamboyant style eclipsed even the mildest murmurs.

Supervisor Hutch is a long-time staff worker for the International Longshoremen's and Warehousemen's Union and may have a deciding vote on many issues that pit liberals against conservatives or downtown business against poor neighborhoods.

On Monday, she teamed up with a conservative who successfully sought a board president independent of the Mayor and his allies. This was considered surprising, since she was supported by Congressmen John and Philip Burton, Democratic allies of the Mayor.

The Mayor's new ability to court individual supervisors is double-edged, since he could garner enemies by opposing their pet projects.

Additional powers in the city should also accrue to the Chief Operating Administrative Officer, former supervisor Roger Boas.

Old Forces Dominate

But if the district elections produced a new political force on the Board of Supervisors—one more closely allied to the Mayor and the coalition of labor, minorities and liberals that have demonstrated increasing political muscle in the last 25 years—that new force still has not established its dominance.

The election of Supervisor Feinstein as board president over Supervisor Lau by a vote of 6 to 5 clearly indicated this.

Supervisor Kopp had been board president since 1976 and used that post to challenge the mayor on many occasions. When he saw his own re-election was improbable, he helped Mrs. Feinstein in opposition to Mr. Lau, who was supported by the Mayor, Supervisors Milk and Silver and incumbent Supervisors Robert Gonzales and John Molinari.

Board President Feinstein yesterday named Supervisor Kopp chairman of the finance committee, the key committee of the board. Also appointed to the finance committee were two Feinstein supporters, Lee Dolson, a conservative college professor with experience representing the white establishment here, and Supervisor Hutch.

* * *

November 28, 1978

SAN FRANCISCO MAYOR IS SLAIN; CITY SUPERVISOR ALSO KILLED; EX-OFFICIAL GIVES UP TO POLICE

SUSPECT SOUGHT JOB
Moscone Had Been Asked to Reappoint Him as a Board Member

By WALLACE TURNER
Special to The New York Times

SAN FRANCISCO, Nov. 27—Mayor George Moscone was shot to death in his office at City Hall this morning, and a few minutes later Supervisor Harvey Milk, the city's first acknowledged homosexual official, was shot and killed in an office on the other side of City Hall.

About an hour after the killings, Dan White, who stepped aside Nov. 10 as a Supervisor but sought to withdraw his resignation and remain in office, surrendered to the police. He was booked on two counts of murder.

Dianne Feinstein, President of the Board of Supervisors, was sworn in as Mayor and will serve until the board selects a replacement for Mr. Moscone.

Replacement Chosen

Initial reports turned up no one who saw either shooting, but Mr. White, a 32-year-old former fireman, was seen at 10:15 A.M., in Room 200, the reception area of the Mayor's office.

Mr. Moscone had scheduled a news conference for 11:30 A.M., when he was to announce the selection of Don Horanzy, a real estate broker, bank analyst and former Federal employe, to replace Mr. White as Supervisor.

When Mr. White came into the reception room of the Mayor's suite this morning and asked to see Mr. Moscone, the Mayor came out personally to greet him and said that of course he would see him, witnesses recalled.

Change in Procedure

Mayor Moscone had made it a practice to have someone present during interviews, usually Mel Wax, his press secretary. But today, when Cyr Copertini, the Mayor's secretary, asked Mr. Moscone if someone should be in the meeting with Mr. White, the Mayor said no.

Mr. Moscone escorted Mr. White down the long corridor past the offices of the staff and into the public office, a large room about 30 feet square where mayors usually met reporters and visitors. Then, witnesses said, the two men went into a smaller, private meeting room accessible only through the public office.

The secretary heard noises shortly afterward and nervously went to a window, she said, expecting to see a truck that had backfired. She and others in City Hall were nervous because of the possibility of assassination connected with the People's Temple, which had had a controversial history in this city. It was a possibility that the police discounted.

At 11 A.M., Deputy Mayor Rudy Nothenberg went to the Mayor's private office and found Mr. Moscone dead, shot three times in the head and arm.

The Mayor's suite faces onto Polk Street, with windows opening to views of Civic Center Plaza, but because space is cramped, the supervisors' offices are removed from the Mayor's office, and no one could be found immediately who had witnessed Mr. White's exit.

Mr. White was next seen some distance away, at Room 250. To get there would have required passing through the public office and out one of three doors along that corridor into the main corridor. A walk of 50 feet or so would have led to a turn in the corridor to the left for 35 feet, down seven marble steps, across 70 feet of marble tile past the carved marble railings that overlook the City Hall Rotunda, up seven steps, across 35 feet, a right turn, and 105 feet to Room 250.

The sign on the door says "Administrative Assistants to Members of the Board of Supervisors." A second sign, in smaller gold lettering, says "For entry, see Room 235," but City Hall reporters say the door is never locked.

Recognized the Voice

Stan Yee was working in Room 250 which is the work area for the supervisors' staffs. He had his back to the door, he said, and, "I heard Dan White come in here screaming for a key to the supervisors' offices."

That is Room 237. Mr. Yee said he was at a typewriter and did not turn around to see the man, but recognized his voice. He said Denise Acaer, an aide to Mr. White, gave the man a key and that he "ran back into the hall and down the corridor."

Mr. Yee said the next thing he knew, sheriff's deputies with rifles were running up the stairs.

Peter Nardoza, an aide to Supervisor Feinstein, said she had told him earlier today that she wanted to see Mr. White. Mr. Nardoza contacted Mr. White's staff, which still worked despite his resignation in the hope he would be reappointed.

"His staff said he was in transit but would come to see her," Mr. Nardoza said. Later Mr. White called, he recounted, and said he was en route to the Mayor's office.

"I happened to meet him in the hallway outside the Mayor's office," Mr. Nardoza said. "I asked him if he were ready to see and talk with Supervisor Feinstein, and he said, 'In a couple of minutes. I have something to do right now.' "

Went Into His Office

Mr. Nardoza said Mr. White went into the office that he had used as a supervisor and had continued to use as he tried to get reinstated.

"Later I saw Dan run out and run back down the hall to his aides' offices," Mr. Nardoza said. "And then I learned that White came into the area where the supervisors' offices are and asked Harvey Milk to come into White's old office for a couple of minutes. After a while I looked into that room, and I could see Harvey Milk face down on the floor."

Mr. Milk was elected at the same time as Mr. White. The slain Supervisor was a declared homosexual who walked in parades with his male lover and even sought to introduce him to the audience on the day the new board was sworn in. The lover has since committed suicide.

Mrs. Feinstein's office is a few feet away from the offices of Mr. Milk and Mr. White. She was in her office when Mr. Milk was shot, and it was she, with tears in her eyes, who first told reporters from the City Hall press room a few doors down the corridor about it. She has withheld any description of what she saw.

Two armed guards were on duty in the reception area of the Mayor's office at the time of the shootings because security had been reinforced in the light of the People's Temple deaths. Mr. Moscone was politically close to the Rev. Jim Jones, founder of the temple, and once appointed him chairman of the San Francisco Housing Authority, a minor job.

Police Chief Charles Gains said, however, that he knew of no connection between the People's Temple and the City Hall shootings.

Even before City Hall security was increased, for months in fact, visitors had been required to pass through a metal detector, but Supervisors were exempt, and an officer said Mr. White, as a recent Supervisor, would not have been searched.

It was on Nov. 14, only four days after he resigned, that Mr. White decided he wanted to reconsider and withdraw his resignation, but the City Attorney's opinion was that it could not be withdrawn but that the Mayor could, if he wished, reappoint Mr. White.

Mr. White then began to campaign for reappointment, but Mayor Moscone was noncommittal.

He told Mr. White, who had been elected with strong backing from the firemen's and policemen's unions, to get a showing of support from his supervisoral district, a largely white, middle-class section that is hostile to the growing homosexual community of San Francisco. But Mr. White had alienated his constituency in a year in office.

Whether Mr. White knew that he would not be reappointed was unclear.

Mr. Wax, the Mayor's press secretary, said: "It is not known if Mayor Moscone broke the news to him." However, three persons who had been interviewed by the Mayor's staff for the appointment received telegrams this morning. "I hope you will give the new supervisor your full support," the Mayor wired to them.

When Mr. White took office last January, he said it was "the realization of my grandmother's dream." She was an Irish immigrant who worked as a servant in the homes of rich San Franciscans.

As Supervisor, Mr. White made it clear that he saw himself as the board's defender of the home, the family and religious life against homosexuals, pot smokers and cynics.

When Mr. White announced his resignation he said he could not support his wife and himself on the $9,600 salary for the part-time supervisor's job. Also, he has been criticized for his role in efforts to develop a tourist center on an old pier at Fishermen's Wharf.

Warren Simmons, an entrepreneur, was successful in getting his plans for the development through the Port Commission, which controls the docks, and through various city offices. Many of those who helped Mr. Simmons, allegedly including Mr. White, had leases to operate shops in the development. Mr. White had a place called The Hot Potato, which was closed today. It was one of the places he was sought before he surrendered.

Mr. White's Fire Department colleagues, who served with him from Jan. 21, 1974, until his resignation on Dec. 9, 1977, to take his supervisorial duties, were stunned at his arrest.

Assistant Chief John Scherrate, who knew Mr. White from the time he was in the firemen's academy as a recruit, following the steps of his father and stepfather, said, "Dan was a very intense person. Everything he did, he did with zeal."

Michael Mulesky, 27, worked with Mr. White at Engine Co. 43 for 18 months. "I liked him, and enjoyed working with him," Mr. Mulesky said. "He was really sharp and took the job seriously. Everything he did, he did full out."

Was to Receive Award

He said Mr. White was to receive the Class C Meritorious Service award at a ceremony next Thursday. The award was for helping another fireman rescue a woman and child from the 17th floor of a burning apartment house on Aug., 4, 1977, when he was running for Supervisor but still working his fireman's shift.

Mr. Mulesky said, "He never really got excited or nervous. He really had his act together."

In July 1977, Mr. White and his wife moved into a modest home at 150 Shawnee Street in the Mission. It is a stucco-fronted row house much like others in the working-class neighborhood. They paid $70,000 for it.

Neighbors said they did not know Mr. White very well, although they saw him jogging most mornings and found him friendly enough. He had them in for the christening of his first-born son four months ago.

But in the gay bars of Polk and Castro streets, Mr. White was remembered unkindly as the sole supervisor to vote against an ordinance forbidding discrimination on the grounds of sexual orientation. He also voted against closing Polk and Castro streets to traffic for the gaudy homosexual Holloween party that has become a tradition in San Francisco.

Mrs. Feinstein presided at a heavily guarded 2 P.M. meeting at which the Supervisors paid tribute to the two dead officials, then adjourned.

"I think we all share the sense of outrage and shame and sorrow and anger," Mrs. Feinstein said. She said San Francisco should go into a "state of very deep and meaningful mourning, express its sorrow with dignity and inner examination. I would call on the people of San Francisco to carry out this course of action."

She asked the board members to stand and pray silently for the wife and family of the late Mayor and for the friends and colleagues of Mr. Milk. "We need to be together and bring out what is good in each of our hearts," she said.

* * *

November 28, 1978

HARVEY MILK, LED COAST HOMOSEXUAL-RIGHTS FIGHT

By JOHN M. CREWDSON
Special to The New York Times

SAN FRANCISCO, Nov. 27—Harvey Milk, the 48-year-old San Francisco Supervisor who was shot and killed today, was this city's first acknowledged homosexual official. He had been instrumental earlier this year in the passage of a homosexual rights ordinance that is considered the most stringent in the nation.

Dan White, the former Supervisor who has been taken into custody in connection with the shooting deaths of Mr. Milk and Mayor George Moscone, was the only one of the city's 11 supervisors to vote against the ordinance.

Mr. Milk and Mr. White were elected to the board in November 1977. Mr. Milk's district, the fifth, encompasses most of the Haight-Ashbury and Upper Market Street areas, where much of this city's homosexual population is concentrated.

Mr. Milk first campaigned for Supervisor in 1973, a decision he attributed to anger generated by the televised Senate Watergate hearings. He made his homosexuality known from the start, and received only a token number of votes.

He Defeated 16 Others

He campaigned unsuccessfully again in 1975, then won last year over 16 other candidates with 30 percent of the vote.

The son of Russian-Jewish immigrants, Mr. Milk was born in New York City and received his bachelor's degree in 1951 from the Albany State College for Teachers. He had worked as a financial analyst on Wall Street and moved here in 1969 to take a similar position in this city's financial district.

Mr. Milk, who called himself a liberal Democrat and often referred to City Hall as "Silly Hall," campaigned on a broad platform that embraced expanded child-care facilities, free municipal transportation, low-rent housing and a civilian police-review board, rather than primarily the issue of homosexual rights.

Like Mayor Moscone and a number of other prominent California politicians, Mr. Milk had, until the time of the murders and suicides in Guyana last weekend, publicly endorsed the People's Temple and its founder, the Rev. Jim Jones.

In an interview a few days before his death, Mr. Milk said that he had spoken at the Temple once or twice, principally because early on it had supported the homosexual rights movement. He said he had been invited to visit Jonestown, the cult's settlement in Guyana, by Mr. Jones, but had declined.

"Some day this will make a great opera and I'd sure like the rights to it," he said. "Guyana was a great experiment that didn't work. I don't know, maybe it did."

* * *

May 22, 1979

EX-OFFICIAL GUILTY OF MANSLAUGHTER IN SLAYINGS ON COAST; 3,000 PROTEST

By WALLACE TURNER
Special to The New York Times

SAN FRANCISCO, May 21—Dan White, a former San Francisco Supervisor, was found guilty of voluntary manslaughter today in the shooting deaths of Mayor George Moscone and Supervisor Harvey Milk, and the verdict touched off a confrontation between the police and demonstrators at City Hall.

Mr. White, 32 years old, had been charged with first-degree murder in the Nov. 27 slayings, and the prosecutor had asked for the death penalty. Instead, Mr. White faces a minimum sentence of five years in prison and a maximum sentence of seven years, eight months.

Within an hour after the verdict was announced, an angry crowd of about 3,000 demonstrators marched to City Hall, where they surged against the front doors, breaking panes of glass. Many of the demonstrators were homosexuals, as was Mr. Milk.

Protesters Beat on Doors

The demonstrators at City Hall, chanting "Remember Harvey" and "Dump Dianne," a reference to Mayor Dianne Feinstein. The protesters beat against the ornate glass and wrought iron doors with their fists. Police officers burst through two glass panels adjacent to the doors in an effort to aid two colleagues.

About two hours after the demonstration began, dozens of police officers swept into the crowd, pushing the protesters away from the building as a cloud of tear gas hung over the scene. Two policemen were injured, and a San Francisco Supervisor, Carol Ruth Silver, was struck by a flying object as she stood nearby. The extent of her injuries was not immediately known.

Retreating demonstrators burned eight automobiles, according to witnesses. There were no immediate reports of arrests.

Earlier, the District Attorney, Joseph Freitas Jr., said of the verdict, "I'm very, very disappointed." The jury of seven women and five men had deliberated for 36 hours over six days. "It was a wrong decision. The jury was over-whelmed by emotions and did not sufficiently analyze the evidence that this was deliberate, calculated murder," Mr. Freitas said.

Douglas Schmidt, Mr. White's attorney, said, "It's the verdict that was supported by the evidence. It was voluntary manslaughter. It was an awful thing, and I don't want to make light of it." He said Mr. White "is filled with remorse and I think he's in very bad condition." Mr. White was crying when they parted, Mr. Schmidt said.

The issue for the jury was never whether Mr. White killed Mr. Moscone and Mr. Milk. The prosecution played for the jury a tape recording in which the former Supervisor admitted that he had shot the two men in their offices on opposite sides of City Hall, and the defense did not contest the validity of the confession.

The issue for the jury became whether Mr. White was in control of his actions, or whether he was so distraught that he was not responsible.

Mr. Freitas's statement expressing disappointment was echoed by Supervisor Silver, who said she was "stunned, shocked" and "very, very sad" at the verdict. Mayor Dianne Feinstein said she received word of the verdict "with disbelief."

Earlier, Harry Britt, a homosexual appointed by Mayor Feinstein to succeed Mr. Milk, said, "This insane jury has legitimatized the immorality of this killer. Every gay will know that this man's act represented intense homophobia."

The 25-minute-long tape recording played for the jury was made within two hours of the time around 11 A.M. Nov. 27 when the two men were shot to death. Mr. White told two homicide inspectors that he had hoped to be reappointed to a Board of Supervisors seat from which he had resigned, and lost control of himself when be learned that Mayor Moscone had decided to name someone else.

The two men were alone in the Mayor's private office. Mr. White shot Mr. Moscone three times in the body, and then fired two shots into his head as he lay on the floor.

Then Mr. White hurried across City Hall to the area where the Supervisors have small offices. He asked Mr. Milk into the office Mr. White had used before be resigned, began to talk to him, and shot him because "Harvey smirked."

Members of the jury declined to be interviewed as they left the Hall of Justice. They received their instructions last Wednesday after hearing 22 defense and 26 prosecution witnesses in 10 days of testimony.

Superior Court Judge Walter Calcagno set June 19 for a presentence report by the probation department.

The killings of Mayor Moscone and Supervisor Milk occurred as San Franciscans were attempting to comprehend the mass deaths, just nine days before, of more than 900 members of the People's Temple at Jonestown, Guyana. Most members of the religious group were from the San Francisco area.

The emotional shock of the Moscone and Milk killings was compounded by its coming so soon after those tragedies, as well as by the unusual positions that the Mayor and the Supervisor had held in public affairs here.

Lifelong San Franciscan

Mr. Moscone, 50, was a lifelong resident of the city and had served as a Supervisor and State Senator before his election as Mayor in 1975. He had announced plans to run for re-election this year.

He was survived by a wife and four children. A benefit fund approaching $500,000 has been raised to provide an annuity for the family.

Mr. Milk, 48, was a symbol to thousands of homosexuals here because he openly lived a homosexual life. The night after the killings, thousands of homosexuals and others paraded through the Civic Center Plaza in front of City Hall, carrying lighted candles, to commemorate Mr. Milk's place in their lives.

Mr. White also was admired by a large segment of the city. The son of a city fireman, he served in Vietnam, worked as a San Francisco policeman and resigned a job with the fire department to serve on the Board of Supervisors.

When he resigned Nov. 10, he explained that he could no longer afford the part-time job and its $9,600-a-year salary because it took all his time.

But then he decided he wanted to stay on the board, and asked the Mayor to reappoint him. Supervisor Milk was one of those who opposed his reappointment.

The prosecutor asked for a finding that the killings constituted first-degree murder with "special circumstances," which would permit the death penalty under terms of a capital punishment law adopted in a statewide referendum last November.

The "special circumstances" cited were that Mayor Moscone had been killed to block an official action—naming another person to the seat Mr. White had resigned but wanted back—and that more than one person had been killed.

* * *

November 1, 1980

IF WE GAY MEN AND LESBIANS' STAND UP

By ANDREW HUMM and BETTY SANTORO

The way politicians seize upon the issues affecting lesbians and gay men at election time, it's difficult to believe that ours was once the love that dared not speak its name.

Some attack lesbian and gay voters; others avoid rabid statements but oppose gay rights; and a new group responds to us as a constituency and seeks to win our votes.

The first group, spiritual descendants of Senator Joseph R. McCarthy, assumes that no one has ever met a gay person and that we can be conveniently linked with any exisiting evil—inflation, crime, declining Scholastic Aptitude Test scores, the loss of the Panama Canal. Devotees of this gay-equals-decadence approach try to tar their political opponents with a link to homosexuality, and assume that the electorate will share their horror.

Gay-baiters have tried to pin a homosexual tag on candidates from James Buchanan in 1856 to Edward I. Koch in 1978—two cases where it didn't stick—but a lot of political ruins and suicides were provoked in between.

The Republican candidate for the Senate, Alfonse D'Amato, has said that his Democratic opponent Elizabeth

Holtzman and some of his journalist critics at The Village Voice are "part of the meandering conspiracy of gay liberation/ultra-left organizations out to destroy the middle class." Mr. D'Amato, a suburban town supervisor who didn't have a stand on the subject of lesbian and gay rights before his statewide race, is now making every effort to put lesbian and gay voters on the other side as he carves out a constituency for himself.

The second group has been to the big city and has usually met a few gay people who don't have horns. Still, they're unwilling to sanction the rights of gay people for fear of being seen as approving a variant life style. Thus, Ronald Reagan says that his campaign guidebook, the Bible, is against homosexuality, so he guesses he's against it, too. George Bush, a heartbeat to his left, says he doesn't believe in codifying our rights, "but I don't think those people should be harassed." Thanks, George.

The emergence of more out-of-the-closet lesbians and gay men in the 1970's has brought a more reasoned response from the third group of politicians. They see us not as a threat to the middle class but as a part of it, as well as of the rich and the poor; not as political embarrassments but as partners in the political process.

Jimmy Carter approved the appointment of Virginia Apuzzo, a lesbian community activist, to his party's platform committee. For the first time in American history, a major national party, the Democrats, adopted a plank calling for an end to discrimination on the basis of sexual orientation. The party's Gay Vote '80 project has registered thousands of lesbians and gay men in key districts. Our neighborhoods are being targeted by many candidates from both parties for special appeals. John B. Anderson even went so far as to sign on as a co-sponsor of the House gay-rights bill in the midst of his campaign for the Republican Presidential nomination.

Despite this progress, the Moral Majority draws more negative attention to the fight for lesbian and gay rights than the positive attention that we in the movement are able to draw. Two prominent conservatives in the House—Robert E. Bauman of Maryland and Jon Hinson of Mississippi—recently have been in the news in connection with homosexually related incidents, but now decry their homosexual inclinations as evil. They are campaigning to keep their jobs by denying that they are part of the group whose rights they have worked against. Sadder yet, their anti-gay constitutents apparently so enjoy this spectacle of repentance that they may just return them to Congress to continue the fight against lesbian and gay rights. If we gay men and lesbians will stand up for ourselves in contrast to these men, there may be some surprises on election day.

Andrew Humm and Betty Santoro are representatives of the Coalition for Lesbian and Gay Rights, which consists of 47 groups.

* * *

November 8, 1983

THROUGHOUT THE COUNTRY, HOMOSEXUALS INCREASINGLY FLEX POLITICAL MUSCLE

By DUDLEY CLENDINEN

DES MOINES, Nov. 1—Here on the rolling farmland of the Midwest, where Grant Wood painted "American Gothic" and other commentaries on plain values and the upright life, the streets of San Francisco and Greenwich Village seem far away.

In his law office downtown, Stephen W. Roberts, a former Republican state chairman, thought about it and said he only knew of one friend in his whole acquaintance who was "openly gay."

"Being gay, at least in Iowa at this point, is not totally acceptable," he explained.

Ready or not, Des Moines, like a number of other cities and towns coast to coast, is beginning to feel the effects of a rapidly maturing effort by homosexuals to use the political system to create space and respect for themselves in American society.

From its first few big-city successes five years ago, this effort has now spread into political activity at city, county, state and national levels. The results have been mixed; sexual intolerance, as leaders of the homosexual rights movement admit, remains strong in most of the nation.

A Methodist and Executive

Here in Des Moines, the friend Mr. Roberts spoke of, Rich Eychaner, 34 years old, is making plans to seek the Republican nomination for Congress from the Fourth District, which includes Des Moines. He is the owner of the largest moving van company in the state, an officer of the Iowa Cubs baseball team, a Methodist Sunday school teacher and a television talk show host.

"I'm not running as a gay person for Congress," he said. "I'm running for Congress as a qualified person who happens to be gay."

Realistically, no one in politics here except Mr. Eychaner seems to think he has a chance to beat the incumbent, Neal Smith, a Democrat, in next year's general election.

"He's doing all the right things," said Rolf V. Craft, the state Republican chairman. "He's committed. He has a poll. He's going to all the county meetings. He's been very active in the community. In all ways but one, I guess you'd call him a traditional Republican candidate."

Political Money and Armies

That Mr. Eychaner's proposed candidacy is being treated with such respect is indicative of the evolving efforts by openly homosexual citizens, individually and in groups, to flex their political muscle.

"To me, it's been evident for quite a while that what politicians are looking for from you are two things: money and armies," said James M. Foster, a homosexual activist and polit-

The New York Times/Ira Wyman and Ken Love

Rich Eychaner, right, is seeking the Republican nomination for Congress from Des Moines. David Scondras, left, is a candidate for the Boston City Council.

ical strategist who was Senator Edward M. Kennedy's northern California campaign manager in 1980.

"In the late 1960's and early 1970's we began the process of putting together the army," he said. "In the late 1970's we began the process of putting together the money."

Marion S. Barry Jr., running as an underdog for Mayor of Washington in 1978, was an early beneficiary of the effort, said Sybil Hammond, deputy director of the city's Office of Community Services and Mr. Barry's "liaison to the gay community."

"In his first race, he was expected to finish third out of three," she said, "and with his coalition of women and gays, he won." Mayor Barry's experience as a black, Miss Hammond said, made him empathetic to the discrimination homosexuals encounter.

The Barry administration tried to draw homosexuals into the structure of the city by reminding readers of newspapers aimed at homosexuals that the city has an open-hiring policy and by inviting them to apply for city jobs.

"We have two openly gay policemen and two firemen," Miss Hammond said. "There have been probably up to 60 appointments to various boards and commissions in the city."

Effective political support has brought homosexuals greater access to the system in other cities. "They work very hard," says William Oiler, legislative coordinator for Ernest N. Dutch Morial, the Mayor of New Orleans. "They will send letters to all the people on their mailing list. They will make phone calls. They will try to get out their vote."

"So they get board appointments," said Mr. Oiler. "They get departmental appointments. They get access. And that breeds more influence."

Candidates Woo Support

In Houston, 1981 is the election year that political observers point to as the turning point for homosexual influence. Frank Mann, a City Councilman who had sneered at homosexuals, was defeated. Kathy Whitmire, who courted the vote of Houston's large homosexual community, won the mayoralty by a wide margin.

Clintine Cashion, the Mayor's campaign manager, said that in the current election campaign, "We saw all the mayoral candidates seeking that endorsement."

In Sacramento, Calif., in 1982, Sheriff Duane Lowe lost his office by 993 votes out of a total 320,000 cast, a defeat for which the county's homosexual community is widely credited. "Duane Lowe said he would not hire any gays as deputy sheriffs," says James K. Graham, editor of The Sacramento Star, a newspaper that aims at homosexuals.

His opponent, Robbie Waters, said he would treat homosexuals equally in law enforcement and hiring policies. An organization called "Gay Vote 82" registered 1,000 new voters and campaigned for Mr. Waters.

"I certainly feel they were a factor in my election," Sheriff Waters said. "I did extremely well in those precincts with a large gay population."

That same year a national political action committee dedicated to furthering homosexual civil rights began making substantial cash contributions in Congressional races around the nation. Drawing from mailing lists and from local committees set up around the country, the Human Rights Campaign Fund raised $609,000, said its executive director, Vic Basile. For the elections next year, it will try to raise $1 million.

"Politicians are getting much less shy about dealing with us in an up-front way," Mr. Basile said. "Candidates not only want our money, they want to be on the dais. They want to be seen." Former Vice President Walter F. Mondale spoke at its first dinner at the Waldorf Astoria, and the Rev. Jesse Jackson was the keynote speaker this year.

In 1982, the fund made contributions to 119 different Congressional candidates, Mr. Basile said, and 80 percent of them won. Representative Thomas M. Foglietta, Democrat of Philadelphia, courted the homosexual vote and received $6,000 from the fund. He then became one of the 73 co-sponsors of the Gay and Lesbian Civil Rights Act in the House.

In campaigning for Governor last year, Mario Cuomo pledged to sign an executive order banning discrimination against homosexuals in state government. In the general election, Mr. Cuomo defeated Republican Lewis E. Lehrman by the rather narrow margin of 51 to 47 percent.

The extent of a homosexual turnout at the polls is almost impossible to quantify, admitted Peter Vogel, co-chairman of the National Association of Gay and Lesbian Democrats. But "in terms of the precincts where we know there are high concentrations of lesbians and gay men," Mr. Vogel said, the vote was "overwhelming for Cuomo."

In Philadelphia, W. Wilson Goode, who is favored to be elected Mayor on Nov. 8, has held two or three events in private homes and bars to raise money from homosexuals, according to Bill Epstein, his campaign manager.

The effort by homosexuals to assert their political influence has proceeded in fits and starts. Even in San Francisco, Mayor Dianne Feinstein vetoed an ordinance that would have extended insurance and other benefits to live-in lovers of city employees.

A student on the University of Oklahoma campus in Norman was beaten after posting "Gay Awareness Week" signs. When news of the beating was published, he was dismissed from his job. The City Council then considered an antidiscrimination ordinance, but it was defeated 7 to 2 last week.

Despite the high concentration of homosexuals in Greenwich Village, opposition from representatives of the outer boroughs on New York's City Council has consistently led to the defeat of a proposed ordinance to bar discrimination against homosexuals in jobs and housing.

Some black politicians are beginning to embrace the movement for homosexuals' civil rights, but the National Gay Task Force found itself at arm's length just before the 20th anniversary in August of the civil rights march on Washington.

Virginia Apuzzo, executive director of the National Gay Task Force, said a few black rights leaders balked at supporting homosexual rights until considerable pressure was brought.

'Rainbow Coalition' Cited

Nevertheless, some black politicians are striving to include homosexuals as part of a "rainbow coalition." The groups in the coalition also include women as well as Hispanic, elderly, poor and handicapped voters, and Mr. Jackson stressed it in his announcement for the Democratic Presidential nomination.

Such a coalition is a functional alliance in places like Boston, where it is the basis of strength for Melvin H. King, the first black to enter a runoff for Mayor.

Mr. King's opponent, Raymond Flynn, a City Councilman from South Boston of Irish descent and populist views, is trying hard to attract the homosexual vote, too.

And David Scondras, a college instructor and neighborhood activist, is the first openly homosexual man to run for city office there. He has been endorsed in his bid for the City Council by Mr. King, the Black Political Task Force, the city's two elected black officials, the teachers' union and several women prominent in politics.

Hope and Caution

"There's an acknowledgment, an understanding among blacks and women, that an openly gay person has a whole history of experience in what it's like to be left out, to feel hostility, to be devalued because you're different," Mr. Scondras said.

Like Mr. Eychaner in Iowa, he is optimistic. "The age of bigotry is eclipsing, and the age of coalition-building is beginning," Mr. Scondras said.

Miss Apuzzo's concern is that the alliance hold together out of mutual understanding, not just a passing sense of political expediency.

"The veracity of the rainbow coalition for us is the consistency with which lavender is a part of it," she said. "We are no longer the stepchild of the movement that shapes and inspires our own."

* * *

September 15, 1989

BARNEY FRANK'S PUBLIC AND PRIVATE LIVES: LONELY STRUGGLE FOR COEXISTENCE

By MICHAEL ORESKES
Special to The New York Times

WASHINGTON, Sept. 14—When he was first elected to the State Legislature from the Back Bay of Boston in 1973, Barney Frank's friends told him that if he was going to be a politician he would have to spruce up. His hair was a mess, his shoes were unpolished, and, to be blunt, he was fat.

Barney Frank, aggressive to the point of irritating, brilliant to the point of arrogant, responded in a classically Barney Frank manner. Instead of losing weight, cutting his hair or polishing his shoes, he produced a campaign poster. Above a huge picture of a bloated Barney, his black hair tousled (but his shoes at least unseen), was the headline "Neatness isn't everything. Re-elect Barney."

Today that poster has the most prominent spot on the wall in the Washington office of Representative Barney Frank, Democrat of Massachusetts.

Mr. Frank points up at the poster as he explains what was wrong with his life back then—how he tried to divide his public from his private life, how he could not handle the strain of this and, finally, how he made a personal blunder that threatens now to wreck a political career more successful than he ever imagined possible as a boy growing up in Bayonne, N.J.

Mr. Frank is a homosexual. In 1987, he became the first member of Congress to voluntarily acknowledge this, answering honestly a question that he had instructed a reporter to ask him. That moment, he said, was the end of a long struggle for him to stop "conceding on the private side and having people judge me wholly on the public side."

Looking Back Over a Lifetime

In a political time when things that were once nobody's business have now become everybody's business, the exploration of the Massachusetts Democrat's private life, now under way on the front pages of newspapers and in the House ethics committee because of his relationship with a male prostitute, is singular, forcing not just the public but Barney Frank himself to delve back over his life. "I'd always been interested in public policy," he said in his office this week, "I had not thought growing up that I was likely to be an elected official. I was Jewish and gay and I knew that."

He pumped gas at his father's truck stop in Jersey City. He went to Harvard. He took every politics course there was. He tried to write a doctoral thesis, but did not have the pa-

tience. He went to work in Kevin White's victorious mayoral campaign and then went with him as executive assistant to Boston's City Hall. With the encouragement of friends, he won a seat in the Legislature.

Through these years, and on to Congress in 1980, Mr. Frank did not so much conceal his private life as abandon even trying to have one, he said. Mr. Frank, who is approaching 50, says he thinks younger gay men understand better how to make a life than he did. "In my case it was compounded by the fact that I was overweight," he said. "My sense of personal self-esteem was pretty low. My estimate of my social skills was pretty low."

Publicly, success followed success. In 1979, the Rev. Robert F. Drinan was told by the Pope to leave Congress. Mr. Frank ran for the seat and won. "I was enjoying my public life a lot," Mr. Frank recalls, but felt "a sense of desperation at the state of my personal life."

Facing a Long-Delayed Issue

So in 1983, after winning election to a second term in the House, he said, "I began to think about how I would deal with the personal side and tried various combinations and permutations." But he had waited so long to seek a private life, that when he finally tried, he said, he did not really know how.

"It wasn't just being gay," he said. "It was having this sense of being awkward, of being an outsider, of being a minority in so many ways."

So, he said, his efforts were tentative and, in one case, disastrous—his involvement with Stephen L. Gobie, a male prostitute who then conducted his business from Mr. Frank's Capitol Hill apartment. Many supporters of Mr. Frank are trying to understand why, as one of them put it, a man as smart as Barney is did something so dumb.

"It is generally not understood that gay people often have a prolonged social adolescence," said Mr. Frank's friend and supporter, Thomas Stoddard, executive director of the Lambda Legal Defense and Education Fund, the oldest national gay rights group in the country. "They have to deal with questions of dating and sexual adolescence at a later stage. This was part of Barney discovering who he was. Most people understand when it happens to an 18-year-old heterosexual male. It's the same phenomenon."

Barney Frank has outgrown the man of the campaign poster. As part of his effort to put his personal life together he has slimmed down, is neater. His suits are better. His hair, now graying, is somewhat neater, although his shoes could still use some polish. He lives in a stable relationship with another man.

Haunting Experience

But the personal struggles of the old Barney Frank have come back to haunt him, particularly the day in 1985 when he answered an ad in a gay newspaper. At the other end of the telephone was one Stephen L. Gobie, young, strapping, smooth-talking. Mr. Frank, by his own account, paid him $80 for sex, and then befriended him, hoping he could turn Mr. Gobie away from drugs and prostitution. He wrote letters on behalf of Mr. Gobie to his probation officer. Mr. Gobie called Mr. Frank "sweet and low"—sweet guy, low on cash.

Two years after the two men parted company, Mr. Gobie has decided to tell his tale, mostly in a series of interviews with The Washington Times. Each time the story begins to lag, he adds new details. Not only did he use Mr. Frank's Capitol Hill apartment for prostitution, which Mr. Frank says he did not know, but Mr. Gobie also serviced Congressional wives, he says. He said he used Mr. Frank's car for trysts and that Mr. Frank quashed the parking tickets by sending them to the House clerk; Mr. Frank says he is gathering up all his canceled checks to the District of Columbia parking bureau to disprove this. It is ironic that Mr. Frank's sexual orientation—or at least the public acknowldgment of it—would have kept him from office in earlier days, because as a politician he is something of a throwback. He can walk out on the floor of the House and debate ideas, live and in person, with wit and intelligence. He does not read speeches.

"He is about the quickest mind I've ever met," said Representative Charles E. Schumer, Democrat of Brooklyn.

His ability to synthesis situations or ideas made him a prominent spokesman for the liberal wing of his party. In a debate over abortion, he accused the anti-abortion forces of believing that life begins at conception, and ends at birth.

Fond Memories of Childhood

He draws his oratorical inspiration not from Clay or Webster but from Shemp Howard, who was one of the Three Stooges and the husband of his father's cousin. Some of his fondest memories of childhood, he said, were when his mother took him to the comedy movies in Newark where they would laugh together at Laurel and Hardy, Abbott and Costello and Moe, Larry and Curly.

"It's precisely because things that we talk about are so deadly serious that humor is essential," Mr. Frank said.

Once, he asked Mr. Stoddard if he would like to come as his date to a White House dinner, where perhaps Senator Bob Dole and his wife, Elizabeth, one of Washington's most prominent couples, would also be attending. "We'll be the gay Doles," Mr. Frank said. Mr. Frank can be a little too sharp-edged, however. "I am impatient," he said. "The impatience has come across as arrogance." Even Mr. Frank's explanation has that edge as he says he sometimes feels that in Washington "there are hundreds of people and part of what they get paid for is to waste my time."

Arrogance, even a streak of hubris, is what some of his colleagues perceive when Mr. Frank does things like filing an ethics complaint against Representative Gus Savage, Democrat of Illinois, asking that the committee investigate charges that Mr. Savage accosted a woman in the back seat of a Government car while he was on an offical visit to Africa just a few weeks before Mr. Frank's own troubles started.

Mr. Frank draws a strict distinction between public and private activity, maintaining none of his problems ever affected his work. "People are capable of having messed up careers and wonderfully successful private lives and vice versa," he

said. "It may be that you would have bad judgment that would negatively affect both. But my answer would be that during the period I was feeling weakest about my private life, people were saying nice things about my public life."

Friends See Improvements

Actually, friends say, they have noticed improvements since he came to Congress. At first, they recall, he bounced from issue to issue. Now he focuses more, in the last few years, helping to usher through the 1987 housing act and playing an important role in the debate on last year's immigration law.

Mr. Frank's usual buoyancy was missing as he sat in his office the other day trying to talk. He rubbed his hands together and often held them over his mouth as he spoke, like an insecure boy. The intercom buzzed. "Take a message and hold the calls," he says, "unless it's Herb or Ann."

Ann is his sister, Ann Lewis, the Democratic consultant. Herb is Herb Moses, his companion, who is an economist. Things would be much worse without him, Mr. Frank said.

"One of the things that happens when you are public and you are dealing with it is you can get to meet people," Mr. Frank said. "I met somebody who is a throughly thoughtful and sensible guy. He's younger than I am, but he's more mature. He's been a wholly positve influence. I thought I'd managed by '87 to put some of that personal craziness behind me. I guess I didn't fully do that."

* * *

August 20, 1992

THE GAY VOTE; GAY RIGHTS AND AIDS EMERGING AS DIVISIVE ISSUES IN CAMPAIGN

By JEFFREY SCHMALZ
Special to The New York Times

HOUSTON, Aug. 19—Homosexual issues, which for months were derided with winks and nods by Republicans as they talked of family values, have flared into the open at the party's national convention here and on the streets outside the Astrodome.

Beginning with a speech by Patrick J. Buchanan on Monday night and continuing with remarks by other Republicans over the last two days, the party made it clear that it would make its opposition to homosexual rights a major issue in the campaign, portraying Bill Clinton and the Democrats as wanting to give preferential treatment to gay men and lesbians.

The Republican comments—coming after a strong endorsement of gay rights by Mr. Clinton during the primary season and by Democrats at their convention last month—means that for the first time, the Presidential candidates are engaging in open debate over sharply different views on gay rights and AIDS.

"It could be the wedge issue of this campaign, the Willie Horton issue," said William Schneider, a political analyst with the American Enterprise Institute. "It's risky for the

Les Romero/The New York Times

Justin Wood of Fort Worth, Tex., demonstrating with Act Up protesters as the Rev. Jerry Falwell spoke to delegates at a hotel in Houston.

Republicans. They can't appear repressive. But polls show people are uncomfortable with it. They don't approve of it. The Democrats can't be perceived as promoting it. It's not clear how it's going to play out, because we've never had it in a Presidential race like this before."

This year, unlike four years ago, representatives of homosexual-rights groups were not permitted to speak before the Republican platform committee. And unlike four years ago, the 1992 platform includes a passage referring to homosexuals: "We oppose efforts by the Democratic Party to include sexual preference as a protected minority receiving preferential status under civil rights statutes at the Federal, state and local level."

In some ways, there are parallels between the convention's handling of the gay-rights and abortion questions. In both cases, conservatives prevailed in disputes over uncompromising platform planks. Aides to Gov. William F. Weld of Massachusetts said he had wanted to include a discussion of gay rights in his address to the convention on Tuesday night but had been asked by party officials not to.

Gays in 'God's Country'

Mr. Buchanan, in his speech on Monday night, pointed out that Gov. Robert P. Casey of Pennsylvania, who opposes abortion rights, had not been allowed to speak at the Democratic National Convention in New York last month. Then he added: "Yet a militant leader of the homosexual rights movement could rise at that convention and exult: 'Bill Clinton and Al Gore represent the most pro-lesbian and pro-gay ticket in history.' And so they do."

Mr. Buchanan went on to include homosexual rights in a list of negatives that he said Mr. Clinton would impose on the nation, along with abortion on demand and women in combat. "It's not the kind of change we can tolerate," he said, "in a nation that we still call God's country."

Homosexual-rights groups, most of which have endorsed Mr. Clinton, responded today with outrage, saying they had expected to be attacked, but not so blatantly or ferociously.

"This is the most explicitly anti-gay campaign we've ever seen," said Urvashi Vaid, the executive director of the National Gay and Lesbian Task Force and a Clinton supporter. "It's hateful. The party is saying, 'We don't want you.' We're the only ones left to attack. Communism is gone. There's too much support for women's issues. The Los Angeles riots make it impossible to attack blacks, and the party is wooing them anyway. That leaves us as the ones to beat on to divert attention from the economy and other failings."

In their public comments today, Republican officials were cautious in their remarks on gay issues. At the party's official morning briefing on the day's family-values convention theme, they avoided questions about gay men and lesbians.

But privately top Bush campaign officials said they would hit the issue hard in the campaign, portraying Mr. Clinton as a promoter of homosexuals. Campaign aides said radio ads were being considered that would run only in the South and would portray a Clinton victory as sure to lead to more gay teachers in the schools.

The campaign officials argued, however, that Mr. Bush was not antihomosexual and that he merely opposed giving gay men and lesbians special treatment. They pointed out that he had signed legislation ordering a Federal study of hate crimes, including attacks on homosexuals, the first time a Federal law had extended civil rights on the basis of sexual orientation.

'A Willie Horton Issue'

Representative Newt Gingrich of Georgia, the second-ranking Republican in the House, said: "You can look at the issue three ways—tolerance, repression and promotion. Repression and promotion are equal extremes. Every American should be protected from violence. But no American deserves to have special privilege."

George Stephanopoulos, Mr. Clinton's communications director, said the Democrats did not support quotas. Referring to Mr. Gingrich's comments, he said it was not clear what Republicans meant by "promotion."

Governor Clinton, interviewed tonight on NBC News, said he did not advocate giving recognition to homosexual marriages, as some Republicans have maintained. "What I have advocated is the absence of discrimination in employment," he said. "And the fact that status alone should not be enough to kick someone out of the military who has otherwise served well. They ought to argue those issues, not these bogus issues that they keep bringing up."

Mr. Clinton, who turned 46 years old today, has been more outspoken on gay issues than previous Democratic Presidential candidates, in part because he grew up at a time when homosexuals were growing more open about their sexual orientation.

Before Mr. Clinton, the party had never pressed the matter at the Presidential level. Four years ago, Michael S. Dukakis seemed uncomfortable with gay issues, even though the party's official position was to support gay rights. There was little difference between Mr. Dukakis's stand on AIDS, for example, and Mr. Bush's position.

This time, the two candidates are at odds over such issues as whether to allow openly gay members of the military, which Mr. Clinton supports and Mr. Bush opposes.

Tonight, the Rev. Pat Robertson picked up on that issue, telling the convention that Mr. Clinton "would destroy the traditional family" and citing as evidence that the Democratic candidate would "repeal the ban on homosexual's in the military and appoint homosexuals to his cabinet."

Both inside and outside the Astrodome, the difference in tone between the Republican and Democratic conventions is striking. There are no openly gay delegates here, only two alternates. Gay Republicans said they had trouble finding gay people to run on slates for Mr. Bush or Mr. Buchanan. At the Democratic convention, there were 110 openly gay delegates. In New York, signs throughout the convention hall proclaimed lesbian and gay rights. Here there are signs like "Family Rights Forever/Gay Rights Never."

Perhaps the only kind word at the convention about homosexuals came tonight when Mary Fisher addressed the gathering about her infection with the virus that causes AIDS. "I am one," she said, "with the lonely gay man sheltering a flickering candle from the cold wind of his family's rejection."

Protests and Demonstrations

Throughout this week, Act Up, the AIDS advocacy group, has made its presence felt strongly. Some 2,000 people marched on the convention hall Monday night, burning Mr. Bush in effigy before being dispersed by mounted police in a confrontation in which a half dozen demonstrators were clubbed as they chanted: "We're here! We're queer! We're not gonna go!" Mr. Bush was disrupted twice today by Act Up hecklers while speaking at a Republican National Committee event, and the Rev. Jerry Falwell was disrupted while speaking at another event.

But for no other gay group here has the Republican stand on homosexual issues been more painful than for gay Republicans. At a meeting over the weekend, representatives of the Log Cabin Federation, which represents 6,000 gay Republicans throughout the country, voted not to endorse Mr. Bush. Many expressed support for Mr. Clinton, but the group's by-laws prohibit endorsing a Democrat.

Group members couldn't help smiling as they cited what they called the hypocrisy of the party leaders. "There are plenty of gay people working for George Bush and around him," said Tony Zampella of San Diego. "We know it. He knows it. Who's kidding who?"

* * *

FAMILY VALUES

By WILLIAM SAFIRE

Integrity, Courage, strength"—those were the family values as defined by Barbara Bush at the Republican convention in Houston. She added "sharing, love of God and pride in being an American." Not much controversy in that definition.

But on "family values night," as Marilyn Quayle described the session dominated by Republican women, the values took on an accusatory edge: after recalling that many in the baby boom had not "joined the counterculture" or "dodged the draft," the Vice President's wife made clear to cheering conservatives what she felt was at the center of family values: "Commitment, marriage and fidelity are not just arbitrary arrangements."

Pat Robertson, the religious broadcaster who sought the Presidential nomination four years ago, eschewed such innuendo and slammed home the political point: "When Bill and Hillary Clinton talk about family values, they are not talking about either families or values. They are talking about a radical plan to destroy the traditional family."

We have here the G.O.P.'s political attack phrase of the 1992 campaign. When Mario Cuomo stressed the words family and values in his speech to the 1984 Democratic convention, he used them in a warmly positive sense. But this year, packaged in a single phrase, the terms are an assertion of moral traditionalism that carries an implicit charge: the other side seeks to undermine the institution of the family by taking a permissive line on (a) abortion rights, (b) homosexual rights and (c) the "character issue," code words for marital infidelity.

Sometimes pot smoking is included, but sex is most often the common denominator, and the pointing finger includes women who do not center their lives inside the home: the defeated candidate Pat Buchanan includes "radical feminist" in his angry denunciation of those who lack what he considers to be family values.

The use of family as an attributive noun in its modern sense can be traced back to the 18th century, as in Samuel Johnson's 1781 sales pitch for his dictionary: "This Lexicon . . . might become a concomitant to the Family Bible." In that decade, family man was coined, followed a generation later by family circle. The word family is based on the Latin famulus, "servant"; in 1400, a man's servants included his wife, children and domestic help. "His family," goes a report of a 1621 Star Chamber case, "were himself and his wife and daughters, two mayds, and a man." You do not have to be a radical feminist to know that this sense has been lost. The poet John Milton first used family in the sense of "parents and children" in "Paradise Lost" in 1667, with Jesus as the head of the family of Man: "As Father of his Familie he clad/ Thir nakedness."

The family being used as the attributive, or modifying, noun today is the traditional family, by which is usually meant a father and mother (of opposite sexes), legally married, with children under 18 living at home. According to the Census Bureau, 26 percent of American households now meet these criteria.

This group is also known as the nuclear family, a coinage of the anthropologist George P. Murdock in 1949—"a married man and woman with their offspring"—perhaps taken from the 1913 "nucleus-complex" discussed by the psychoanalyst Carl Jung, combining the lust of sons for mothers and lust of daughters for fathers. (How did we get here? Back to politics.) In 1966, Daniel T. Jenkins wrote of "the extended, as distinct from the nuclear, family," and Barbara Bush in 1992 used that term to expand her meaning of family: "When we speak of families, we include extended families. We mean the neighbors, even the community itself."

The earlier term for something similar to family values was social issue, a 1970 coinage by Richard M. Scammon and Ben J. Wattenberg in their seminal work, "The Real Majority." The authors argued that rather than being primarily concerned with the old bread-and-butter issue of economics, the voters were turning their attention to the drug culture, angry dissenters and changing moral standards. Like the social issue, the term family values calls attention to a cultural rather than an economic interest, as Republicans are especially eager to do this year; the difference is that the use of family values focuses more sharply on abortion, gay rights and the pre- and extramarital activities that go under the name of playing around or hanky-panky. (Another sexual issue, harassment, is not included in most definitions of family values, presumably because it usually takes place at the office and not within plain sight of the family; besides, opposition to sexual harassment is a cause more associated with feminists and libertarians than with traditionalists.) And now, for etymologists at least, to the jackpot question: Who is the coiner of family values in its current sense? The earliest use of the phrase I can find is in "The Education of Catholic Americans," a 1966 book by the Rev. Andrew M. Greeley and Peter H. Rossi: "Marriage and family values do show some relationship with Catholic education; however, the relationship is in most instances not a strong one." (Greeley, now also a well-known novelist, has just published "Wages of Sin," its title taken from a grammatically disagreeable line in the Book of Romans: "For the wages of sin is death.") The first official political use of family values was in the 1976 Republican Party platform: "Divorce rates, threatened neighborhoods and schools and public scandal all create a hostile atmosphere that erodes family structures and family values."

Lexicographic Irregulars are invited to submit earlier citations; more to the point, however, is the search for the modern political operative who first sent his principal a memo about how the public can be distracted from slow economic growth by a concentration on family values. Even the most confidential White House interoffice memorandums will be accepted in this purely lexicographic quest.

The campaign theme is powerful, but it can backfire. At the Houston convention, as a score of the members of the Bush family gathered around the President and Barbara Bush to display family values in all their solidarity, the background music inexplicably chosen for this moving moment in the Astrodome was "The Best of Times" from "La Cage aux Folles," a Broadway musical that broke new ground in the straights' acceptance of homosexuality.

* * *

October 29, 1993

AMERICA WITHOUT CLOSETS

By TORIE OSBORN

WASHINGTON—To outward appearances, the gay and lesbian rights movement is in trouble.

We suffered a bitter defeat in the White House and on Capitol Hill over the military ban on homosexuals; just this week, in a painful and ironic twist, the Administration asked the Supreme Court to block a lower-court order lifting the ban. The far right continues to step up local attacks: three cities face anti-gay ballot measures next week and as many as 10 states are gearing up for Colorado-style referendums next year to ban local gay rights laws.

Any internal organizational ferment, including my own decision to step down next week as head of the National Gay and Lesbian Task Force, has been taken as a sign that the movement is in disarray.

But these widely publicized storm clouds conceal a much brighter outlook. Lesbian and gay Americans have never had a better chance to become a mainstream political movement—if we can come up with the right strategy.

The stage has been set by precisely those events that have led people to conclude that we're in trouble. For this once hidden minority, widespread visibility is the absolute condition for all progress. And with every front-page event—the battle over the military ban, the huge march on Washington last April—the denial blanketing the very existence of gay men and lesbians is being thrown off forever.

Poll after poll shows that Americans' tolerance on these issues correlates with personally knowing someone who is gay. And every day, more and more people do. A vast new migration into the mainstream is taking place, from out of the closets of regular middle- and working-class lesbian and gay Americans.

How is the gay rights movement to take advantage of this growing visibility? For 20 years, the movement has been almost entirely reactive, careering from event to event—a court victory here, an electoral loss there. Now we need to unify as never before, working across organizational lines and consolidating resources to develop a national plan of action—that gay agenda we've been accused of promoting. That's why I am leaving the day-to-day management of the task force: to work with others to develop a broad political vision for the movement.

We need state-of-the-art market research to design winning messages. We need think tanks and national media strategies to counter the disinformation efforts of the right, now sugar-coating its hate agenda with mainstream language like the battle cry "no special rights." Never has it been more apparent that gay and lesbian people lack the most basic civil rights than in the case of Sharon Bottoms of Virginia, who lost custody of her child solely on the basis of her sexual orientation.

A powerful grass-roots political structure must be built to support local and national efforts, using voter-identification techniques borrowed from electoral campaigns and high-tech communications tactics to organize, educate and mobilize the huge numbers of newly "out" gay men and lesbians, as well as the thousands of local organizations flourishing across the country.

Gay men and lesbians must also take the time to work on overcoming our own activist culture's aversion to power, success and leadership. This fear, born of being marginalized and ostracized, diminishes our potential by promoting narrow, purist thinking as well as destructive attacks on leaders and organizations. The politics of protest must become the politics of taking power, or we will be outsiders forever.

Our journey through the agony of AIDS, and through the self-loathing of the closet and out the door, has forged a new and potent force—based on a belief in the courage of community, a rage at systemic injustice and a new spirit of hopefulness. When it is fully articulated, it can be a gift to mainstream America as well as ourselves. It can help reinvigorate this country and its vision of a truly pluralist democracy.

Torie Osborn is a columnist for The Advocate, the national gay news magazine, and author of the forthcoming "Coming Home to America."

* * *

November 12, 1995

GAY POLITICIANS AND ISSUES WIN MAJOR VICTORIES

By DAVID W. DUNLAP

Except for the biggest prize of all, the San Francisco mayoralty, lesbian and gay politicians were able to claim victory last week in most races they had entered, as well as in a key referendum on civil rights.

A ballot initiative in Maine that would have denied civil rights protections to homosexuals was rejected, 53 to 47 percent. It was the first time that a statewide gay rights referendum had been considered in the East. Similar measures were rejected last year in Oregon and Idaho, by narrower margins.

At the same time, however, voters in Northampton, Mass., which has a large and influential lesbian and gay population, overturned an ordinance to grant limited recognition to domestic partners, homosexual and heterosexual. The margin was 87 votes out of 9,453.

While Roberta Achtenberg placed third in the mayoral race in San Francisco (population 723,959), Bill Crews was re-elected mayor of Melbourne, Iowa (population 669). He attracted national attention when he disclosed his homosexuality in the 1993 gay rights march in Washington, and this was his first race since then.

"I think it's important that after coming out, I was re-elected," Mr. Crews said. "And it feels greater." He received 167 of the 289 votes cast.

Buffalo elected its first openly lesbian official, as Barbra Kavanaugh, a 40-year-old lawyer, won a seat on the City Council. She has represented poor clients in housing cases and said that housing and education would be her chief concerns. She and her companion, Lynn Edelman, have two young boys in public school.

LAW, POLITICS AND PUBLIC POLICY 477

Openly homosexual candidates won at least 10 other races around the nation, including the mayoralty of Carrboro, N.C., and lost three others, according to the Gay and Lesbian Victory Fund, a political action committee based in Washington.

"When a person discloses their sexual orientation, it enhances their standing in the eyes of the public," said David Clarenbach, executive director of the Victory Fund, "not because they're gay or lesbian but because they're being honest."

The most closely watched contests were in Maine and San Francisco.

The Maine initiative, Question 1, would have nullified and prohibited local laws protecting homosexuals from discrimination. It asked whether civil rights safeguards should be conferred solely on the basis of 11 characteristics like race, sex, religion and age. Sexual orientation was excluded from that list.

With 99 percent of the ballots tallied by the end of the week, the vote was running 219,090 against Question 1, 192,397 in favor. The measure failed in 11 of Maine's 16 counties.

The opposition was led by Maine Won't Discriminate, a coalition of political, business, religious and community groups. "We have a political framework now that didn't exist before," said the chairwoman, Patricia A. Peard. "These are all people who care about justice issues, from Kittery to Presque Isle. We held back the radical right and built something inside Maine."

The leading advocate of Question 1, Carolyn H. T. Cosby, chairwoman of Concerned Maine Families, also saw a "substantial mandate to go forward," since opponents had outspent supporters by about 10 to 1 and still wound up in a close race.

* * *

VATICAN DENOUNCES GAY-MARRIAGE IDEA

By The Associated Press

VATICAN CITY, March 28—The Vatican has appealed to voters not to support politicians who endorse same-sex marriages.

The Rev. Gino Concetti, a moral theologian, wrote in the Vatican's official newspaper on Wednesday that homosexual marriages would "undermine the foundation of the family model upon which human civilization was built."

Father Concetti recalled that in 1994 Pope John Paul II denounced a European Parliament resolution that said homosexual couples should be allowed to marry and adopt children. The Pope said at the time that such a development would legitimize "moral disorder."

"If unions of homosexuals are a moral disorder," Father Concetti wrote in L'Osservatore Romano, "neither can they ever be legitimate on the legal or civil level."

Also open for "moral censure," he wrote is "the action of that citizen, who, with his choice, favors the election of the candidate who has formally promised to translate into law the homosexual demand."

* * *

CLINTON IS GREETED WARMLY AS HE SPEAKS TO GAY GROUP

By JAMES BENNET

WASHINGTON, Nov. 8—It is rare that a politician can draw an ovation with such a stock line as "I'm delighted to be here."

But, in becoming the first President to address a gay and lesbian organization with a speech here tonight, Bill Clinton was rewarded with thunderous applause for that simple statement.

And as he deftly turned aside occasional hecklers with enthusiastic assists from the crowd of 1,500, Mr. Clinton was also thunderously applauded upon restating his support for a law to protect homosexuals from discrimination in the workplace, and upon issuing a peppery defense of Bill Lann Lee, his contested nominee to be Assistant Attorney General for Civil Rights.

Speaking at a sold-out dinner held by the Human Rights Campaign, Mr. Clinton said that Mr. Lee "is being discriminated against," not because of his qualifications but "because some members of the Senate disagree with his views on affirmative action."

"Now," Mr. Clinton continued, "if I have to appoint a head of the office of civil rights who is against affirmative action, it's going to be vacant a long time."

The White House had played down Mr. Clinton's speech in advance, comparing his appearance at this dinner to his routine stops on the rubber-chicken interest-group circuit. But Mr. Clinton did not make a routine speech tonight, instead calling for a redefinition "of the immutable ideals that have guided us from the beginning" to include acceptance of gays and lesbians.

Mr. Clinton has had deep differences with gays and lesbians, disappointing many at the beginning of his first term by backing down in efforts to fully integrate homosexuals into the military, and disappointing them again at the end of that term by signing legislation intended to prevent single-sex marriage.

But gays and lesbians overwhelmingly supported Mr. Clinton for re-election last year, and audience members tonight repeatedly called out "We love you, Bill."

Elizabeth Birch, the executive director of the Human Rights Campaign, said in introducing the President tonight: "Because our needs were almost as great as our expectations, it was inevitable that we—you and this community—would experience both shared disappointment and some disagreement. But Mr. President, you have played a brave and powerful and indispensable role in the march toward justice for us."

She called Mr. Clinton "the first President in history to stand up for our civil rights."

Other speakers hailed Mr. Clinton's presence here as a milestone in acceptance of gays and lesbians. "Tonight, because of the President's address, we will be visible across America," declared Bob Baublitz, one of the organizers of the dinner.

But, in his speech, the President was cautious.

Marty Katz for The New York Times

President Clinton was greeted last night by Elizabeth Birch, the executive director of Human Rights Campaign, a gay and lesbian group.

Mr. Clinton did not express an opinion about the fact that the television comedy series "Ellen" recently portrayed its lead character as coming out the closet, even though Ellen DeGeneres, the actress who portrays Ellen, was in the audience to receive an award tonight.

Vice President Al Gore recently came under fire from conservatives for praising "Ellen" in a Hollywood speech.

Mr. Clinton did not appear publicly at the dinner with Ms. DeGeneres, who, like her character, has come out of the closet. The President left before Ms. DeGeneres accepted her award. He did pose backstage for a photograph with her and her girlfriend, Anne Heche, but White House officials were quick to point out that the photograph also included numerous officials from the Human Rights Campaign. The photograph will not be released publicly, the White House said.

In his speech, Mr. Clinton did not address the group's continuing complaints that gays are harassed in the military, or its objection to the legislation opposing gay marriage. Instead, he focused on his support for the Employment Non-Discrimination Act, which is the top legislative goal of the Human Rights Campaign. Polling has shown broad support for the notion of equal protection for homosexuals under the law.

Mr. Clinton said that "Being gay, the last time I had thought about it, seemed to have nothing to do with" the ability to "fix a broken bone or change a spark plug." The crowd gave him a standing ovation for that line, as well as for his subsequent statement that discrimination in the workplace "is wrong, and it should be illegal."

Mr. Clinton faced at least three hecklers. The first, a man, cried out "People with AIDS are dying!" The crowd shushed

him, but Mr. Clinton chuckled. "I'd have been disappointed if you hadn't been here tonight," he said.

He added, "People with AIDS are dying, but since I became President we're spending ten times as much" combating the disease. Mr. Clinton's words were drowned by applause that quickly turned into yet another standing ovation.

* * *

August 2, 1998

CHASING THE POLLS ON GAY RIGHTS

By RICHARD L. BERKE

WASHINGTON—Senator Trent Lott, the Republican leader, sounded harsh when he likened homosexuality to kleptomania and alcoholism. But through a prism of pragmatic politics, his comments seemed to make sense: The latest Gallup Poll shows that 59 percent of Americans say that homosexual behavior is morally wrong. In his own party, Mr. Lott played to a particularly receptive audience because Republicans are far less accepting of homosexuality than Democrats.

Given the pounding President Clinton took in 1993 when he tried to overturn the ban on homosexuals in the military, he, too, seemed to be asking for trouble recently when he issued an executive order barring Federal agencies from discriminating against homosexuals. But Mr. Clinton's move may have been shrewd as well: The most pronounced shift in attitudes toward homosexuals in recent years has been a steady increase in support for equal rights in employment, housing and job protections. A survey by the President's pollsters, released last week by the Human Rights Campaign, a gay group, showed that 70 percent of Americans support Mr. Clinton's order.

Public opinion about homosexuals is so fluid, and often so seemingly contradictory, that it can be treacherous for any politician to take a stand on anything related to homosexuality. For years Democrats and Republicans have been skittish about the issue, and not only because many people are uncomfortable about delving into private lives. Attitudes toward homosexuality are so complex that they cannot easily be transformed into yes or no party platforms.

The subject has been so verboten that it was considered a triumph for homosexual organizations when, early in Mr. Clinton's first term, the White House released a photograph of the President meeting with leaders of the groups.

Ads About 'Reforming'

But now, homosexuality has sprung to the lead of political dialogue on more fronts than ever. Last week, the House approved a measure that would deny Federal housing money to San Francisco because of its support of homosexual partners; a measure, also passed, would take $21 million from housing programs for people with AIDS and give it to veterans. The House will also consider a measure that would deny Federal money to carry out Mr. Clinton's order regarding gay Federal employees. And Republicans have succeeded in blocking his nomination of a wealthy gay contributor, James C. Hormel,

More Tolerant, But Still Disapproving

Americans are more tolerant toward homosexuals than they were 25 years ago, but overall do not approve of homosexuality.

A growing number of Americans believe that nature is more important than nurture in determining homosexuality ...

*In your view, is homosexuality something a person is born with or is homosexuality due to other factors such as upbringing or environment?**

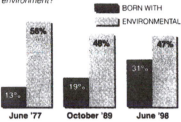

■ BORN WITH
▨ ENVIRONMENTAL

June '77 — 13% / 56%
October '89 — 19% / 48%
June '98 — 31% / 47%

... and also believe homosexuals should have equal job opportunities.

*In general, do you think homosexuals should or should not have equal rights in terms of job opportunities?**

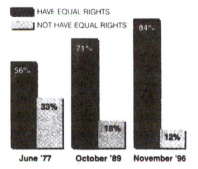

■ HAVE EQUAL RIGHTS
▨ NOT HAVE EQUAL RIGHTS

June '77 — 56% / 33%
October '89 — 71% / 18%
November '96 — 84% / 12%

But a poll conducted in June found most Americans believe homosexuality is morally wrong ...

Do you personally believe homosexual behavior is morally wrong or is not morally wrong?

DON'T KNOW/ NO ANSWER 6%
WRONG 59%
NOT WRONG 35%

... and a June 1997 poll found most Americans do not believe homosexual couples should raise children.

Is it generally a good thing for our society or a bad thing for our society or doesn't it make much difference that more gay and lesbian couples are raising children?

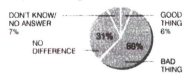

DON'T KNOW/ NO ANSWER 7%
GOOD THING 6%
NO DIFFERENCE 31%
BAD THING 56%

*Figures do not include replies indicating both causes, no cause or no opinion.

*Sources: Gallup Organization (first three questions)
Princeton Survey Research Associates for the Pew
Research Center March 1997 (fourth question)*

The New York Times

Associated Press

Boston's 28th annual Gay Pride Parade, with 60 floats, was held on July 11.

as ambassador to Luxembourg. The debate intensified when conservative groups began running full-page newspaper advertisements featuring "reformed" homosexuals.

Homosexual groups responded with their own advertisements, including one that featured smiling Republican parents and their lesbian daughter.

Democrats, too, are becoming more visible on gay issues. Mr. Clinton was the guest of honor at a fund-raising event Saturday in East Hampton sponsored by gay Democrats. Vice President Al Gore and Representative Richard Gephardt, the Democratic leader, are increasingly willing to back gay issues. Mr. Gore will be the featured speaker in September at the annual dinner of the Human Rights Campaign. And five openly gay Democrats are running for Congress this year, a record number.

For both parties, the debate is intended to bring out voters on the fringes next November. Surveys show that the most conservative Republicans are particularly uncomfortable with homosexuality, just as the most liberal Democrats are most likely to embrace gay rights. But a deeper explanation is that with the increasing aggressiveness of the gay political movement and the greater visibility of gays in pop culture, there is an assumption that tolerance is on the rise.

"We are talking about these issues as Americans as we never have before," said Richard Socarides, a senior White House adviser who is the principal liaison on gay issues. "I'm sure that the changes in public opinion are quite frightening to conservatives—but they're irreversible."

Wishful Thinking

That may be wishful thinking. While attitudes seem, slowly, to be drifting toward acceptance, the conundrum is that most people still do not approve of homosexuality.

"The contradiction is that Americans are strongly in favor of equal opportunities—even for a situation they don't necessarily approve of," said Frank Newport, the editor of the Gallup Poll.

As an example, the proportion of Americans who think homosexuals should be hired as elementary school teachers has steadily increased, to 55 percent in 1996 from 27 percent in 1977, according to the Gallup Poll. But there is still a sizable proportion who do not want homosexuals teaching elementary students. And in the view of many Americans, homosexual behavior is now more acceptable than adultery. But people still lump the two in the same category.

Survey after survey shows a generational divide. Seven out of 10 people who are 65 and older say homosexual behavior is wrong, according to the Gallup Poll; only five out of 10 who are between 18 and 29 have that view. While a recent Gallup Poll found that more people think homosexuality is a product of environment and upbringing rather than a biological trait, more and more Americans think homosexuality is not a choice.

Because attitudes toward homosexuals are evolving, politicians can draw the wrong conclusions from poll findings that seem to back their views. The proliferation of AIDS made the public less sympathetic toward homosexuals in the 1980's, but by the time of Mr. Clinton's election in 1992, tolerance had increased immensely. But Mr. Clinton may have mistakenly concluded that an increase in support for gay rights meant that people would support homosexuals in the military. They did not.

Mr. Clinton was more mindful of the polls in his re-election campaign, when he signed a bill that opposed gay marriages. The move enraged homosexual organizations but was intended to help him rebuild good will with conservative Democrats. Politically, it was a no-lose position because even most Democrats who believe homosexual behavior is morally acceptable do not believe that homosexuals should be allowed to marry.

Republicans are now finding that despite public discomfort with homosexuality, sharp oratory may not be welcome either. Some are now distancing themselves from Mr. Lott's comments, fearing they could make the party appear intolerant and carry a political toll in November.

"I don't think it helps to have public leaders engaged in that kind of dialogue," Speaker Newt Gingrich said. Gary Bauer, a prominent conservative who heads the Family Research Council said he wished the debate would focus on policy matters like gay adoptions (which polls show most Americans do not favor)—not on whether homosexuality is a sin. But he also said, "On the sin issue, I don't want to undercut Trent in any way." Ed Goeas, a Republican pollster, said he did not share the view of some Republicans that criticism of homosexuals by people like Mr. Bauer made his party appear insensitive. He said he worried more about Senator Alfonse M. D'Amato of New York, who as part of his aggressive courtship of gay voters has condemned many of his fellow Republicans.

"Someone like D'Amato saying we're intolerant hurts us far more than anything Gary Bauer says," Mr. Goeas said, "because it plays into the label of intolerance."

That Republicans are even debating how not to appear intolerant is perhaps the best evidence of how the perception of public attitudes toward homosexuals has evolved.

* * *

October 20, 1998

GAY PHILANTHROPIST'S NOMINATION TO BECOME AMBASSADOR TO LUXEMBOURG DIES IN THE SENATE

By PHILIP SHENON

WASHINGTON, Oct. 19—The Senate has effectively killed the nomination of James C. Hormel to be Ambassador to Luxembourg, an appointment that would have made him the first openly gay American ambassador, Congressional officials said today.

The officials said the Senate's Republican leadership had decided not to act on the nomination of Mr. Hormel, 65, a San Francisco philanthropist, before adjourning for the year.

They said his nomination would be allowed to die in the Senate along with those of Kent M. Wiedemann to be Ambassador to Cambodia and Diane E. Watson as Ambassador to the Federated States of Micronesia.

Twenty-seven of President Clinton's other nominees for ambassadorships or for the Federal bench are expected to be approved by the Senate before lawmakers leave Washington for the year.

Mr. Hormel, an heir to the Hormel meat-packing fortune and a former dean at the University of Chicago Law School, had received broad bipartisan support in the Senate, and Congressional officials agreed that he might well have been confirmed for the Ambassador's post in Luxembourg had there been a Senate vote.

But Senator Trent Lott of Louisiana, the Senate majority leader, refused to allow a vote by the full Senate. Earlier this year, Mr. Lott captured headlines when in an interview he described homosexuals as sinners who, like alcoholics and kleptomaniacs, could overcome their afflictions.

"This shows that anti-gay bias continues in the United States Senate," said Winnie Stachelberg, a lobbyist for the Human Rights Campaign, the nation's largest gay-rights group. "A small minority of Senators have taken away the opportunity for an up-or-down vote on Jim Hormel, which is all that people were asking for." Barry Toiv, a White House spokesman, said that it was "extraordinary that the Republican leadership refuses to move a nomination that a strong majority of Senators support just because the nominee is gay."

He said the President "will consider all of his options," including possibly renominating Mr. Hormel next year.

Mr. Hormel's nomination was aggressively opposed by a conservative organization, the Traditional Values Coalition, that provided Senators with copies of sexually explicit material available in a special gay-research center named for Mr. Hormel at the San Francisco Public Library. Mr. Hormel has long provided financial support to gay-rights causes.

Congressional officials said they did not know exactly why the Senate Republican leadership had decided not to act on the nominations of Mr. Wiedemann as Ambassador to Cambodia and Ms. Watson as Ambassador to the Federated States of Micronesia, a group of tiny Pacific islands.

One Senate aide speculated that Mr. Wiedemann's nomination had been sacrificed as a protest to the Government of Prime Minister Hun Sen of Cambodia, who seized full control in a violent coup last year. "Since we don't have a legal government, why should we honor Hun Sen with an ambassador," the aide said.

Mr. Wiedemann, a career diplomat who speaks four languages, had served most recently as the senior diplomat in the American Embassy in Myanmar, formerly known as Burma.

Ms. Watson, a veteran Democratic state legislator in California and the first African-American woman elected to the state senate, was one of the state's most vociferously liberal lawmakers, and Congressional aides said she may have simply proved too liberal to be acceptable to the Senate's Republican leaders.

Correction: An article yesterday about the nomination of James C. Hormel to be Ambassador to Luxembourg, an appointment that would have made him the first openly gay American ambassador, misidentified the home state of Trent Lott, the majority leader, who refused to allow a vote by the full Senate. Mr. Lott is from Mississippi, not Louisiana.

* * *

January 13, 1999

CLINTON RENAMES GAY PHILANTHROPIST AS ENVOY

By PHILIP SHENON

WASHINGTON, Jan. 12—President Clinton has defied senior Republican lawmakers by renominating a prominent San Francisco philanthropist as Ambassador to Luxembourg, a post in which he would be the first openly gay American envoy, White House and Congressional officials said today.

They said the nomination of the businessman, James C. Hormel, 66, was quietly resubmitted last week to the Senate, where it died last year because the majority leader, Trent Lott, refused to put it before the full Senate for a vote.

"Mr. Hormel is eminently qualified and he had solid bipartisan support in the last Congress," said a White House spokesman, Barry Toiv. "We were confident then and we are confident now that if the nomination were brought to the floor of the Senate and there were a fair up-or-down vote, he would be confirmed. We hope that is what will happen this year, and soon."

The nomination of Mr. Hormel, heir to the Hormel family meat-processing fortune and a former dean at the University of Chicago Law School, had received broad bipartisan support in the Senate. Congressional officials agreed that he probably would have been confirmed in a full Senate vote.

The nomination was approved by the Senate Foreign Relations Committee, which is led by Senator Jesse A. Helms, a North Carolina Republican who is generally considered no friend to the gay rights movement.

A spokesman for Mr. Lott, Republican of Mississippi, had no immediate comment on the renomination.

Mr. Lott decided to refuse to allow a vote on the nomination last year after an interview in which he described homosexuals as sinners who like alcoholics and kleptomaniacs could overcome their affliction.

Mr. Hormel's nomination was aggressively opposed by a conservative religious organization, the Traditional Values Coalition, which provided senators with copies of sexually explicit material from a special gay-research center named for Mr. Hormel at the San Francisco Public Library.

Mr. Hormel, who has said he had nothing to do with the selection of books and magazine for the library, has long provided financial support to gay-rights causes. He has also given large donations to causes like breast-cancer treatment and the San Francisco Symphony.

The Government of Luxembourg, where discrimination on the basis of sexual orientation is outlawed, has said it would welcome Mr. Hormel's confirmation.

Although he has refused to give interviews about the nomination, Mr. Hormel answered some Republican critics last year in a letter to the Senate in which he said, "I will not use, nor do I think it appropriate to use, the office of the ambassador to advocate any personal views that I may hold on any issue."

San Franciscans who know Mr. Hormel have been indignant over his treatment by the Senate. George P. Shultz, who returned to San Francisco after having been Secretary of State in the Reagan Administration, has said Mr. Hormel would be a "wonderful representative of our country."

* * *

June 5, 1999

CLINTON APPOINTS GAY MAN AS AMBASSADOR AS CONGRESS IS AWAY

By KATHARINE Q. SEELYE

WASHINGTON, June 4—Over Republican objections, President Clinton today appointed James Hormel as Ambassador to Luxembourg, employing a rarely used executive privilege to make him the nation's first openly gay envoy.

Mr. Hormel, a San Francisco philanthropist and heir to a meat-packing fortune, was first nominated to the post by Mr. Clinton in October 1997. The Senate Foreign Relations Committee approved the nomination, but Senate conservatives, led by the majority leader, Trent Lott of Mississippi, blocked it from a vote on the Senate floor.

Mr. Clinton, who pledged months ago to gay advocacy groups that he was determined to make the appointment, did so today through a constitutional device available to the White House when Congress is in recess. Congress returns from its 10-day Memorial Day vacation on Monday.

Under the provisions of a so-called recess appointment, Mr. Hormel, 65, could remain in the job until the end of the next session of Congress, probably in October of next year, effectively installing him through the duration of the Clinton Administration.

White House officials said Mr. Clinton had decided to use the recess appointment when it was clear that all public and private strategies for a vote had failed.

Mr. Lott, who has said homosexuals are sinners, like alcoholics or kleptomaniacs, said through a spokesman today that he opposed the appointment.

"Senator Lott opposes the nomination of someone who has supported an extremist, anti-Catholic group to represent the United States," said the spokesman, John S. Czwartacki. "Mr. Hormel's refusal to condemn this brand of religious intolerance makes his appointment by the Clinton-Gore Administration a slap in the face to Catholics everywhere."

He was referring to Mr. Hormel's refusal to condemn the activities of the Sisters of Perpetual Indulgence, a San Francisco acting troupe featuring men who wear nuns' habits. Luxembourg is 99 percent Catholic.

Marc Thiessen, a spokesman for Senator Jesse Helms, the North Carolina Republican who is chairman of the Foreign Relations Committee, said Mr. Clinton's move was intended for political gain.

"It shows the President's contempt for the constitutional process, No. 1," Mr. Thiessen said. "This is an effort to get political gain out of certain Presidential constituencies."

Conservative and religious groups also expressed outrage.

"Clinton does unpopular things in sneaky ways," said Robert Knight, a spokesman for the Family Research Council. "This appointment was not going to fly, so he imposed it on the country. And it means that he's using this nation to make the case to the world for sodomy and adultery."

David M. Smith, a strategist for the Human Rights Campaign, a gay advocacy group, rejected the suggestion that Mr. Clinton had acted purely for political gain or to benefit his political heirs, Vice President Gore, who is running for President, and Hillary Rodham Clinton, who is likely to run for the Senate from New York. "He wanted to make a very strong statement that this type of discrimination was not going to be tolerated," Mr. Smith said.

Richard Socarides, who oversees gay and lesbian issues for the White House, said Mr. Gore and Mrs. Clinton would probably do well with gay and lesbian voters anyway. Mrs.

Clinton is participating in a private fund-raising dinner on Wednesday night in New York for gay men and lesbians sponsored by the Democratic National Committee.

* * *

August 11, 1999

GAY VOTERS FINDING G.O.P. NEWLY RECEPTIVE TO SUPPORT

By KATHARINE Q. SEELYE

WASHINGTON, Aug. 10—Prominent Republican candidates for President are creating an atmosphere that is subtly but fundamentally more inviting to gay and lesbian voters than party leaders have been in recent memory.

Gov. George W. Bush of Texas, Senator John McCain of Arizona and Elizabeth Dole, former president of the American Red Cross—who combined have the lion's share of support among Republicans in early polls—have all signaled an openness to gay supporters, including a willingness to appoint them to positions like ambassadorships in their Administrations.

The new receptivity toward gay voters follows a similar nonantagonist approach by leading Republicans on abortion. While they still oppose abortion and are by no means converts on other gay rights issues like same-sex marriage, the most prominent candidates are offering a lower-key, more inclusive approach designed to appeal beyond the conservative base of the party to independent and Democratic voters. It also reflects the continued growing political influence of gay donors and gay voters across party lines.

The new message on gay supporters is a far cry from 1996, when Bob Dole, the Republican nominee, returned a $1,000 donation from the Log Cabin Republicans, a group of gay party members, and from 1992, when the dominant voice on the issue from Republicans was that of Patrick J. Buchanan, whose declaration of a "culture war" was aimed squarely at homosexuals.

Many of the more conservative candidates have not changed their views, and even Mr. Bush, Senator McCain and Mrs. Dole have not embraced a broader agenda that includes adoptions by gay people and a less punitive approach toward homosexuals in the military. But gay political leaders say the difference in attitude is striking nonetheless.

"The tone has totally changed," said Rich Tafel, executive director of the Log Cabin Republicans. "What I hear is gay Republicans enthusiastic about the tone being set by the leading candidates. It looks like Republicans for the first time are saying, 'This is a community I'm not going to alienate and maybe I want to reach out to it.' That's kind of a shocking revelation."

Democrats, of course, have courted gay voters for years, and this year both Vice President Al Gore and former Senator Bill Bradley, the two rivals for the Democratic nomination, are competing for their support. Both campaigns have fund-raisers working expressly with gay donors, who tend to be generous financially and active politically.

On the Republican side, though, this rapprochement is new. Mr. Bush, so far the run-away favorite in the Republican field, has said he would have no qualms about hiring homosexuals. "If someone can do a job, and a job that he's qualified for, that person ought to be allowed to do his job," he said earlier this year.

Senator McCain, who has appointed Representative Jim Kolbe of Arizona, the only openly gay Republican in the House, to his national steering committee, has similarly said he would hire on merit alone. He has supported anti-hate-crimes legislation that would protect victims of crime not only because of their race but their "sexual orientation." He has said that someday he could envision a gay President.

Mrs. Dole has said she would appoint to her Administration anyone who was qualified, emphasizing in an NBC interview last month that "all people are welcome" and adding: "I'm inclusive." Of the contribution her husband spurned in 1996, Mrs. Dole said that if she received a check from the same group, "I would not turn it away."

William Kristol, who was chief of staff to Vice President Dan Quayle and now is editor of the conservative Weekly Standard, said that the mainstream Republican candidates this year were unhappy under the banner of strident, anti-gay language.

"The Republican establishment does not want to fight the conservative culture war," Mr. Kristol said, "partly because they think it's a losing fight but more importantly, they don't believe in it."

Outside the party establishment, some conservatives remain adamantly opposed to gay rights. Gary Bauer and Alan Keyes make their rejection of homosexuality a major plank of their platforms. Mr. Bauer said recently that when he heard Senator McCain say the party should be "a big tent that admits everybody," the phrase sounded to him "like fingernails on a chalkboard."

Steve Forbes, the wealthy publisher and candidate, flatly opposes any concessions to gay voters. He frequently says he wants "equal rights for all, special rights for none." Asked if Mr. Forbes would appoint an openly gay person to his Administration, his campaign manager, Bill Dal Col, said: "If the person is qualified for the job, that's fine as long as it is not a statement on a life style or promoting a life style." As for gay adoptions, Mr. Dal Col said: "There are plenty of heterosexual couples out there," and existing laws against hate crimes are enough.

The Rev. Louis P. Sheldon, a staunch conservative who heads a national group called the Traditional Values Coalition and who has denounced homosexuals often in his career, denied that there was an effort among Republicans to reach out to gay voters.

Noting that the Republican Presidential candidates oppose homosexuals in the military and same-sex marriages, Mr. Sheldon said that "there aren't that many Log Cabin voters out there." He added: "There is nothing immutable about sexual behavior—it is chosen."

Still, anti-gay sentiment is less strident this year. Many Republicans avoid the matter. Brian Kennedy, the national political director for former Gov. Lamar Alexander of Tennessee, said: "He neither brings up those issues in his stump speech nor do we ever recall him being asked about it. It doesn't seem to be on the radar screen for the '99 cycle."

Bob Adams, spokesman for Mr. Buchanan, said that although the candidate "has certainly not abandoned the culture war," the anti-gay sentiment of past campaigns had changed. "It hasn't come up, and we haven't been making it an issue," he said.

Even Mr. Quayle, a social conservative who has aggressively promoted "family values," has shown moderation toward homosexuals. Asked on a radio program last month what he would do if one of his children were homosexual, he said he would support them "whatever they are."

While he avoided answering specific questions about homosexuals in the military and gay adoptions, Mr. Quayle also said: "Life-style orientation really makes no difference to me at all. Believe me, I don't inquire what one's sexual preference may or may not be." He repeated his view that homosexuality is a choice but did not say, as he did in 1992, that it was "a wrong choice."

Mr. Kristol said most Republicans were still being careful in their statements because they did not want to alienate the grass-roots conservatives who believe homosexuality is a sin. But the candidates' tempered tone, he said, poses a dilemma for conservative voters. "The question is, Do conservatives want to win so badly that they will accept this kind of establishment leadership?" he asked. "Or have they, too, given up on the culture war? Do they want a political champion for their views?"

Since gay voters emerged several years ago as a significant voting bloc, Republicans ceded them to the Democrats. About 5 percent of voters in 1996 identified themselves in polls of people leaving voting booths as homosexual—"about the same percentage as Hispanics and larger than the Jewish vote," said Elizabeth Birch, executive director of the Human Rights Campaign, the nation's largest gay and lesbian lobbying group.

Mr. Tafel, who is organizing gay Republican voters to participate in the Iowa straw poll on Saturday and is seeking a slot for an openly gay speaker at the Republican national convention next year, said that the party was finally recognizing the influence of the gay electorate. "It's the first time we haven't been taken for granted" as likely Democrats, he said. His group has yet to make an endorsement or give any money to any candidate, but it plans to do so closer to next year's convention.

Also making the gay vote more available to Republicans this year is the fact that liberal Democrats have not been entirely happy with the Clinton Administration's record on gay issues. They have complained about the level of financing for the treatment of AIDS, the opposition to gay marriage and the murky "don't ask, don't tell" policy that has allowed a record number of discharges of homosexuals from the military. Such discharges increased 86 percent over the last five years.

Alert to the potential appeal of Republicans who refrain from broad cultural attacks, Democrats are warning that the Republicans are not as tolerant as they may appear. Pat Ewing, a senior adviser at the Democratic National Committee, said of Mr. Bush: "He is purposefully vague, not moderate. Bush denied Texans protection from hate crimes and let it be known that he opposed any provision to protect gays and lesbians from these crimes. His platitudes are meant to obscure."

Karen Hughes, a spokeswoman for Mr. Bush, said he objected to the hate-crimes legislation because "all violent crime is motivated by hate" and Texas already has a law that covers such crimes. But, she said, he also did not believe that sexual orientation should be singled out for special rights. "He doesn't believe in granting legal rights based on sexual orientation," she said.

Mr. Gore has made an extra effort to appeal to homosexuals. In one of his rare departures from Clinton orthodoxy, he has called for a more "compassionate"—though unspecific—approach to homosexuals in the military.

In California, which is likely to have a ballot initiative next year to outlaw same-sex marriage, Mr. Gore said he favored legal protections for same-sex partners, like health benefits and hospital visitation rights, but he opposed "a change in the institution of marriage as we now know it between men and women."

The Vice President would leave gay adoptions up to adoption professionals on an individual basis, his spokesman, Chris Lahane, said.

Democrats acknowledge that Mr. Gore and Mr. Bradley have virtually identical records on gay issues. Eric Hauser, a spokesman for Mr. Bradley, said he supported a review of the "don't ask, don't tell" policy on gays in the military. He also supports gay adoptions and extending legal rights, including health benefits and hospital visitation, to same-sex partners as "common sense" measures.

When Mr. Bradley was in the Senate, he voted for the so-called defense of marriage act, which said no state had to recognize the same-sex laws of another state. Likewise, President Clinton signed the bill into law, and Mr. Gore "stood beside him" in supporting it, Ms. Birch said.

Although Mr. Gore has been outspoken in favor of gay issues, he has also been subjected to gay demonstrators. AIDS activists have turned up, noisily, at several campaign events, accusing him of siding with drug companies and trying to block South Africa's access to cheaper generic drugs to fight H.I.V. His staff says this is an international patent issue and he is trying to work it out.

* * *

October 4, 1999

GAY AND LESBIAN GROUP OFFERS THANKS TO CLINTON

By JOHN M. BRODER

LOS ANGELES, Oct. 3—Eight years ago this week, Bill Clinton, then Governor of Arkansas, sat down with a small group of gay and lesbian advocates in Hollywood and made modern political history by becoming the first major-party Presidential candidate to court gay support openly.

Seven months later, as the presumptive Democratic nominee, he left many of his gay supporters in tears at the Palace Theater in Los Angeles when he fervently declared to a large crowd, "I have a vision of America, and you are part of it."

Never before had gay and lesbian political power and personal identity been acknowledged so strikingly, and Mr. Clinton was handsomely rewarded. Gay men and lesbians raised nearly $4 million for the Clinton-Gore campaign in 1992, and the Democratic ticket received more than 80 percent of their votes.

Despite rocky moments in the relationship—particularly Mr. Clinton's inability to make good on his promise to end the prohibition on gay people serving in the military—gay voters have remained deeply loyal to the President.

On Saturday night in Los Angeles, Mr. Clinton repaid their faith with an appearance at a black-tie fund-raising dinner sponsored by the largest gay political group in California.

The President received a two-minute standing ovation when he rose to speak at the dinner, sponsored by Access Now for Gay and Lesbian Equality, or Angle. His half-hour speech was frequently interrupted by applause.

Mr. Clinton gave a version of his standard stump speech but concluded with a meditation on the persistence of fear and violence based on race, ethnicity or sexual orientation. He cited the recent deaths of Matthew Shepard, a 21-year-old gay college student killed in Wyoming, and James Byrd, a black man dragged to his death in Texas, as evidence that America still had a lot to learn about tolerance.

"The biggest problem we've got is the primitive, age-old fear and hatred and dehumanization of the other—people who aren't like us," Mr. Clinton said.

"People are still scared of people who aren't like them," he added. "And other people are scared of themselves, and they're afraid they won't count unless they've got somebody to look down on. And if you have to find somebody to look down on, it must be somebody that is different from you."

Mr. Clinton was warmly received even though he had angered many gay men and lesbians with his acceptance of the "don't ask, don't tell" compromise on homosexuals in the military and with his signing, in 1996, of the Republican-sponsored Defense of Marriage Act, which denied Federal recognition of same-sex marriages.

David Mixner, Los Angeles's premier gay political impresario, organized Saturday's event as a sort of homecoming party for the President, an expression of gratitude for his efforts to move homosexuals into the social and political mainstream of America. Dozens of openly gay officials serve in the Clinton Administration, and Mr. Clinton has moved to end antigay employment discrimination in the Government's civilian agencies, including the Federal Bureau of Investigation and the Central Intelligence Agency.

"We have had an extraordinary journey the last two decades," Mr. Mixner said in his emotional remarks introducing the President. "It has been a trail of tears. We have buried our dead and manned the barricades of liberty."

In a tribute to Mr. Clinton, a friend of his for 30 years, Mr. Mixner said: "Ever since 'The Canterbury Tales'—strange crew that was—people have been judged by their traveling companions. And we picked a good one in 1992."

Mr. Mixner said 286 of his friends had died of AIDS, and he spoke of the "rocky journey" gay people have had with the sympathetic but politically flexible President. Nonetheless, he said to the President, "It is time for us to say thank you tonight."

Nearly 1,000 people attended the dinner, held in the flower-bedecked ballroom of the Beverly Hilton Hotel. The event raised about $850,000 for the Democratic Congressional Campaign Committee.

Mr. Mixner said in an interview that he and other gay leaders had decided to devote their energies and money to electing a Democratic House of Representatives. He said he had been appalled by the way House Republicans treated the President during impeachment proceedings and sickened by senior House Republicans' overt and subtle gay-bashing.

Mr. Mixner was jailed for his role in a 1993 protest in Washington over Mr. Clinton's position on the issue of gay people in the military. But he said the President had redeemed himself with gay voters over the course of his Presidency.

"I would be a fool indeed, one, not to speak up when I disagree, and two, not to acknowledge and celebrate the victories we have made and to offer thanks," Mr. Mixner said. "I am not a fool on either account."

Many of the leading Presidential candidates have recognized the power and wealth of gay voters and are explicitly seeking their support. Vice President Al Gore and former Senator Bill Bradley are courting votes and contributions. On the Republican side, Gov. George W. Bush of Texas, Senator John McCain of Arizona and Elizabeth Dole have all signaled an openness to gay supporters—a major change from 1996, when Bob Dole, the Republican nominee, returned a $1,000 donation from the Log Cabin Republicans, a gay group.

Mr. Mixner said in the interview that he supported Mr. Gore because of the Administration's record on gay issues, but that Mr. Bradley had made inroads with a declaration last month in support of the expansion of gay rights, including the right to serve openly in the military. Mr. Bradley repeated that declaration in a speech in Michigan on Saturday.

But Saturday night's dinner here was chiefly devoted to an expression of gratitude to Mr. Clinton as his tenure in office ticks down. The President acknowledged that he had been stymied in his efforts to broaden acceptance of gay men and lesbians by the opposition of Republicans in Congress, senior

Associated Press

David Mixner introduced President Clinton on Saturday at the Access Now for Gay and Lesbian Equality fund-raising dinner in Los Angeles.

officers in the military and even some conservative Democrats, like former Senator Sam Nunn of Georgia.

"I wish I could have done better," Mr. Clinton said wistfully. "But we've done pretty well. And we're a long way from where we were."

* * *

April 17, 2000

BUSH MISCALCULATES ON GAY REPUBLICANS

By JONATHAN RAUCH

WASHINGTON—So, George W. Bush finally held a meeting with a dozen openly gay Republicans. Afterward, he announced that while his mind had not been changed on the issues, he was a "better person" for listening.

Glad to hear it. But the more interesting question is: Did the meeting make him a better candidate? A better potential president?

Yes, a little. Meeting with gays is certainly better than not meeting with them. And it is better if the Republican Party treats homosexuals as respectable citizens instead of pariahs.

But the meeting was also part of a larger pattern that Governor Bush set early on during the primaries, a pattern that is less heartening. His every move seems based on political calculation rather than personal belief.

From the very beginning, his often maladroit maneuvering on gay issues has looked more like triangulation than principle. Before the early primaries he forswore meeting with a gay Republican group; then, just before California, he said he would reconsider.

He had first said a year ago that he would be willing to appoint openly gay officials, then seemed to backtrack in a talk with conservatives. Last week, he said that sexual orientation "is not a factor" in naming someone to a job. He opposes adoption rights, anti-discrimination protections and hate-crimes laws for homosexuals, while also trying to sound less harsh than his similarly positioned competitors to the right.

In short, he has chosen his path with a mincing delicacy that suggests fear of being wrongfooted politically. "Gotta play this right," he seems to be saying. The carefully choreographed meeting with homosexuals seemed just another move in the game.

True, politicians are usually political; it's their job. But not always. In 1978, Ronald Reagan, the former California governor and Republican presidential front-runner, met quietly with a gay delegation. The group wanted him to come out against the so-called Briggs Initiative, which would have barred homosexuals from teaching in public schools.

Mr. Reagan listened, and what he did after the meeting was not so quiet. He issued a robust statement. The initiative, he said, had "the potential of infringing on basic rights of privacy and perhaps even constitutional rights." Mr. Reagan single-handedly turned the tide against the measure.

It was precisely Mr. Reagan's backbone that gave him broad national appeal. He seemed capable of deciding what he thought was right and then doing it, never mind the politics or the conventional wisdom.

The Republicans need some of that spine on gay issues. The party's right is still wedded to a hopelessly outdated strategy: marginalizing gays or dealing with them only at arm's length and with rubber gloves.

But, in 2000, that is not a strategy at all; it is just denial. Today it seems silly to anathematize gays. Television shows are full of openly gay characters. Companies, many localities and some states grant partner benefits.

The pity is that Republicans today are in a good position to seize the new center that is emerging on homosexuality. The new gay agenda stresses commitment over frolic and responsibility over liberation. Republicans could claim this middle ground by welcoming gay people who want to live stable, responsible lives.

Yes, Mr. Bush probably couldn't bring the Republican Party to a detente with homosexuality in 2000, but he could move the party to the center, folding homosexuals into his vision of "compassionate conservatism."

But there, precisely, is the problem. Mr. Bush's slogan has no real vision behind it; none, at least, that the candidate seems prepared to articulate, or to advance against his party's entrenched interests. So, in the end, his meeting with gay Republicans was about positioning. Too bad. The meeting could have been about so much more. Perhaps the candidate still could be.

Jonathan Rauch, a contributing writer of the Independent Gay Forum, is the author of "Government's End: Why Washington Stopped Working."

* * *

PUBLIC EMPLOYMENT

April 19, 1950

PERVERTS CALLED GOVERNMENT PERIL

Gabrielson, G.O.P. Chief, Says They Are as Dangerous as Reds— Truman's Trip Hit

Special to The New York Times

WASHINGTON, April 18—Guy George Gabrielson, Republican National Chairman, asserted today that "sexual perverts who have infiltrated our Government in recent years" were "perhaps as dangerous as the actual Communists."

He elevated what he called the "homosexual angle" to the national political level in his first news letter of 1950, addressed to about 7,000 party workers, under the heading: "This Is the News from Washington."

Giving National Committee support to the campaign of Senator Joseph R. McCarthy, Republican of Wisconsin, against the State Department, but without mentioning him by name, Mr. Gabrielson said:

"As Americans, it is difficult for us to believe that a National Administration would go to such length to cover up and protect subversives, traitors, working against their country in high Governmental places. But it is happening. If there is but one more (Alger) Hiss or (Judith) Coplon still in a key spot, he should be ferreted out. It's no red herring.

"Perhaps as dangerous as the actual communists are the sexual perverts who have infiltrated our Government in recent years. The State Department has confessed that it has had to fire ninety-one of these. It is the talk of Washington and of the Washington correspondents corps.

"The country would be more aroused over this tragic angle of the situation if it were not for the difficulties of the newspapers and radio commentators in adequately presenting the facts, while respecting the decency of their American audiences."

Mr. Gabrielson's letter, appearing over his signature and made available to reporters, did not expand on his assertion that "sexual perverts" were "perhaps" as dangerous as Communists in Government. He was out of the city today and could not be reached for elaboration.

The chairman's letter also attacked President Truman for labelling his trip to the West Coast next month as "nonpolitical," saying that this was "simply a device to carry on politics at the expense of the taxpayers" and "is 'Pendergastism' at its worst."

"We must insure in every way at our command that the people understand the nature of this trip; that the President, in these critical times, spent one month in Florida preparing for another junket away from his White House duties while Congress wallows leaderless," he asserted.

* * *

May 20, 1950

INQUIRY BY SENATE ON PERVERTS ASKED

Hill and Wherry Study Hears There Are 3,500 Deviates in Government Agencies

By WILLIAM S. WHITE
Special to The New York Times

WASHINGTON, May 19—A Senate investigation of alleged homosexuals in the Executive Branch of the Government was recommended unanimously today by a Senate Appropriation subcommite of ten members.

Perverts are described by intelligence officers as poor security risks because of their vulnerability to blackmail.

The inquiry was proposed on the basis of a private, preliminary study made by Senators Lister Hill, Democrat of Alabama, and Kenneth S. Wherry of Nebraska, the Republican floor leader, during which a Washington police vice officer said it was his "own judgment" that 3,500 perverts were employed in Government agencies.

The officer, Lieut. Roy E. Blick, testified, it was disclosed this afternoon in the publication of a partial transcript of his evidence, that he thought 300 to 400 of these persons were in the State Department.

"A Quick Guess," He Says

This, he said at one point, was a "quick guess," in the sense that it was based upon his experience that arrested persons not connected with the State Department sometimes would say:

"Why don't you go get so-and-so and so-and-so? They all belong to the same clique."

"By doing that," Lieutenant Blick added "their names were put on the list and they were catalogued as such, as a suspect of being such."

Mr. Wherry had wanted the resolution for a formal Senate investigation, which would be made by any "appropriate" body of the Senate, to specify that "the Department of State and other departments and agencies" were to be the fields of the inquiry.

The Democratic members of the Appropriations Subcommittee balked, however, at singling out the State Department and the language ultimately adopted was simply "the departments and agencies of the Government."

12 "Whereases" Struck Out

Struck out also were twelve "whereas" paragraphs, in one of which Senator Wherry had recalled that the State Department itself had disclosed last Feb. 18 that in the past ninety-one persons had been asked to resign because of perversion or suspected perversion.

After this disclosure, which came prior to the opening of the current Senate investigation of Senator Joseph R. McCarthy's charges of Communist infiltration of the State Department, Senators Hill and Wherry called many witnesses in closed hearings.

While Messrs. Hill and Wherry agreed on the necessity for an investigation, they differed sharply on the implications of some of the information they had received in their own preliminary study.

Accordingly, they filed separate reports to their Appropriations subcommittee colleagues. Both quoted a letter from Dr. R. H. Felix, Director of the National Institute of Mental Health, stating that the available data indicated that perhaps 4 percent of the white male population of the country were "confirmed homosexuals."

Finds Deviates Everywhere

"While corresponding data for females are lacking," Dr. Felix added, "the prevalence is probably about the same." The letter continued:

"All available evidence indicates that homosexuality can be found in all parts of the country, both urban and rural, and in all walks of life. I have been unable to find any evidence whatsoever which indicates that homosexuality is more prevalent in the District of Columbia than in other sections of the country."

Senator Hill's report stressed Dr. Felix's statement that homosexuality was no more prevalent in Government than elsewhere, and he proposed that one of the subjects of the investigation be that of medical treatment and rehabilitation.

Senator Wherry, for his part, asserted that by Dr. Felix's "reasoning one could argue, but not very intelligently, that because there are an estimated 55,000 Communists in the United States the Federal Government should have a pro rata share, and that because there are a million criminals in the country none should complain if the Government has its share."

* * *

December 16, 1950

FEDERAL VIGILANCE ON PERVERTS ASKED

Senate Group Says They Must Be Kept Out of Government Because of Security Risk

WASHINGTON, Dec. 15 (AP)—A Senate investigating group labeled sexual perverts today as dangerous security risks and demanded strict and careful screening to keep them off the Government payroll. It said that many Federal agencies had not taken "adequate steps to get these people out of Government."

Filing a report to the Senate after a six-month investigation by an Expenditures subcommittee, the chairman, Senator Clyde R. Hoey, Democrat of North Carolina, declared:

"If Government agencies will investigate properly each complaint of sex perversion and thereafter follow the present adequate Civil Service rules, these perverts can be put out of Government and kept out."

Many perverts have been ousted, Mr. Hoey said, and he pledged that his subcommittee would keep a close check on the situation.

Stressing the risk that the Government takes in employing a sex deviate or keeping one on the payroll, the subcommittee said:

"The lack of emotional stability which is found in most sex perverts, and the weakness of their moral fiber, makes them susceptible to the blandishments of foreign espionage agents."

Called 'Prey to Blackmailers'

The report also noted that perverts were "easy prey to the blackmailer." It said that Communist and Nazi agents had sought to get secret Government data from Federal employes "by threatening to expose their abnormal sex activities."

The subcommittee criticized the State Department particularly for "mishandling" ninety-one cases of homosexualism among its employes. It said that many of the employes were allowed to resign "for personal reasons," and that no steps were taken to bar them from other Government jobs.

The Senate authorized the investigation last June after an Appropriations subcommittee had estimated there were about 3,750 homosexuals on the Federal payroll in Washington alone. In addition, Senator Joseph H. McCarthy, Republican of Wisconsin, had charged that sexual perverts were employed in the State Department, where they were especially dangerous security risks.

The full-scale investigation was assigned to an Expenditures subcommittee including Senators Hoey, Herbert R. O'Conor of Maryland, James O. Eastland of Mississippi, John L. McClellan of Arkansas, Democrats, and Karl E. Mundt of South Dakota, Margaret Chase Smith of Maine and Andrew Schoeppel of Kansas, Republicans. All of them signed today's report.

Tightening Laws Urged

The committee said that it was unable to determine accurately how many perverts now held Federal jobs. It added, however, that since Jan. 1, 1947, a total of 4,954 cases had been processed, including 4,380 in the military services and 574 on Federal civilian payrolls.

Between April 1 and Nov. 1 this year, the committee reported, the most cases of perversion turned up in any one agency was ninety-seven in the Veterans' Administration. The Commerce Department had forty-nine in the same period and the State Department thirty-seven. Four cases were found among Congressional employes, and fifteen at the Library of Congress.

In addition to strict enforcement of Civil Service rules about firing perverts, the subcommittee recommended tightening of the District of Columbia laws on sexual perversion, closer liaison between the Federal agencies and the police and a thorough inquiry by all divisions of the Government into all reasonable complaints of perverted sexual activity.

*   *   *

April 28, 1951

F.B.I. CHECKS 3,225,000 FOR U.S. JOBS; 299 OUSTED

By The United Press

WASHINGTON, April 27—The Federal Bureau of Investigation has checked on 3,225,000 present or prospective Government employes and turned up 14,484 instances of "derogatory information," according to J. Edgar Hoover.

A House Appropriations subcommittee today made public testimony by the head of the F. B. I. in which Mr. Hoover said that of the 14,484 cases in which the F. B. I. had initiated an investigation, the Federal Loyalty Board removed or denied employment to 299 individuals.

He said 2,941 resigned while their cases were under scrutiny. The Loyalty Board retained 8,060 after their cases had been investigated by the F. B. I.

Relative to what he described as "sex diviates in government service," Mr. Hoover said that since April 1, 1950, his agency had identified 406 in this category.

*   *   *

April 13, 1953

U. S. OUSTED 425 ON MORALS

WASHINGTON, April 12 (AP)—"Homosexual proclivities" have led to the dismissal of 425 State Department employes since 1947. The figures were given recently to the House Appropriations Committee, which made them public today, by John William Ford, director of the department's Office of Security. Mr. Ford also said that last October about twenty-six persons were released following an investigation of the Voice of America offices in New York.

* * *

April 28, 1953

NEW SECURITY PLAN ISSUED; THOUSANDS FACE RE-INQUIRY

Eisenhower Program Discards Truman Idea of Loyalty Distinction—Review Boards Dropped—McCarthy Is Enthusiastic

By ANTHONY LEVIERO
Special to The New York Times

WASHINGTON, April 27—The Eisenhower Administration today announced a new, stricter security program for Federal employes, discarding the dual Truman system that had made a distinction between loyalty and security.

The new program will go into effect May 27 with the aim of assuring that all employes of the Executive Branch of the Government are "reliable, trustworthy, of good conduct and character, and of complete and unswerving loyalty to the United States."

President Eisenhower stated this aim in the preamble of a five-page Executive Order that will subject all present and future employes to a character scrutiny based on seven specified standards of conduct.

The outright traitor and a tipsy Federal employe, talking about his work in a bar, alike are subject to dismissal under the new program. The tipsy employe might receive a chance in another, less sensitive Federal job. Essentially, the Truman system did the same thing, but the traitor would be branded disloyal and the loose-talking drinker would be labeled a security risk.

Under the new system no provision is made for a distinction between disloyalty and borderline or misconduct cases, unless department heads, who will have the final adjudication authority, indicate it.

The new program will require a new investigation of many thousands of employes previously investigated, as well as many more thousands who have had no security check. The Truman system had started as a loyalty program, requiring a finding of disloyalty as a cause for dismissal.

Then came the case of William W. Remington, former Commerce Department economist, in which the Loyalty Review Board on Feb. 10, 1949, decided that a finding of disloyalty against him would be "a travesty of American justice." Subsequently, Remington was convicted in Federal court for perjury in lying about his Communist associations.

That case caused a sharp change in the loyalty program. It was modified to add the "security" aspect, to permit the dismissal of any person about whom there was reasonable doubt of loyalty or who had been indiscreet in his associations or conduct.

Under the first or loyalty phase, only persons in "sensitive" jobs were investigated. That left many thousands of uninvestigated persons in Federal employ and some of these were able to transfer to sensitive agencies such as the State and Defense Departments without being investigated.

The new system requires an investigation of any employe not previously investigated and of all new applicants for positions. Usually the investigation for nonsensitive jobs involves a name check in Federal personnel files and, if this turns up derogatory information, the case is referred to the Federal Bureau of Investigation for what is called a full-field investigation, which may take three to nine months.

Under the old system there were 18,901 cases that had gone through the full-field inquiry as a result of adverse data, and the President's order today specified that these cases should be "re-adjudicated." In addition, there are 1,831 full-field investigations now in process that developed out of adverse data.

It should be stressed that many Federal employes were required to submit automatically to full-field investigation because they held highly important positions involving national security, and not because of derogatory information. The order did not call for a reinvestigation of these persons.

Discarded with the old system are the Loyalty Review Board of the Civil Service Commission and the regional boards consisting of leading citizens unconnected with the Federal service. Replacing this "court of appeals" outside the Federal service will be "hearing boards" consisting of three Federal officials who are not employes in the same department as an accused person.

Held 'More Workable'

These comparative features of the new and old systems were brought out in an hour-long press conference held by Herbert Brownell Jr., the Attorney General, in the office of James C. Hagerty, White House press secretary. With Mr. Brownell were the Deputy Attorney General, William P. Rogers, Bernard M. Shanly, acting special counsel of the President, and Philip Young, chairman of the Civil Service Commission.

"We believe this machinery is much more workable and therefore an employe's case can't be dragged along for several years," Mr. Brownell said.

Asked why he thought so, Mr. Brownell replied: "Because the standards and rules are much more explicit."

In opening the news conference, Mr. Brownell reminded the press of President Eisenhower's views in his Message on the State of the Union. The President had said he desired a security program that would make certain that the nation's security was "not jeopardized by false servants," that would clear the air of unreasoned suspicion, rumor and gossip, and to make it unnecessary for "another branch of the Government" to police the Executive Branch.

The reference to "policing" by another branch was understood to mean that the President desired to reduce to a minimum the investigations of Federal loyalty by Congress and the resultant quarrels.

The new security program won approving comments from the three leading investigators in Congress—Senator Joseph R. McCarthy, Republican of Wisconsin, chairman of the Senate Government Operations Committee and long the chief investigator of loyalty in the State Department; Senator William E. Jenner, Republican of Indiana, chairman of the Senate Internal Security subcommittee, and Representative Harold H. Velde, Republican of Illinois, chairman of the Un-American Activities Committee of the House of Representatives.

Recognizing their interest in the loyalty and anti-Communist field; President Eisenhower invited the three investigators to the White House this morning to take part in his usual Monday morning conference with Congressional leaders.

McCarthy Approves

General Eisenhower reviewed the new program for the committee chairmen and afterward Senator McCarthy said:

"I think it is a tremendous improvement over the old method. Altogether it represents a pretty darn good program. I like it. It shows that the new Administration was sincere in the campaign promises to clean house."

When Senator Robert A. Taft, Senate Majority Leader, and Speaker Joseph W. Martin Jr., were asked what they thought of it, Speaker Martin replied, "We didn't have any vote but I heard no criticism."

A prime source of dispute has been Congressional efforts to get carte blanche to examine loyalty files, and Presidents since Washington have resisted that.

There was nothing explicit in the President's order denying access to the records to persons outside the Executive Branch. Asked about this, Mr. Brownell said the privacy of the files had been preserved by a provision of the Executive Order that stated that they shall be "maintained in confidence."

This provision requires that loyalty information shall belong to the investigating agency that developed it but, "subject to considerations of national security," may be retained by the department concerned. It may be passed on to other executive departments or agencies if the investigating agency, normally the Federal Bureau of Investigation, is willing.

Criteria of Security

Seven numbered criteria for security were established by the President, but actually the total was twelve, because the first point had five subdivisions. All five subdivisions of Point No. 1 dealt with problems of behavior involving trustworthiness, misrepresentations, criminal and immoral acts, including drug addiction and sexual perversion, insanity or neurological disorder, and susceptibility to coercion.

The other six points dealt directly with loyalty, including acts of sabotage, espionage and treason; association with saboteurs, spies, traitors, seditionists, anarchists or revolutionists; advocacy of force to overthrow the Government; membership in any organization that was totalitarian, Fascist, Communist or subversive; intentional, unauthorized disclosure of information relating to national security; performing one's work in a manner that would serve the interests of another Government in preference to United States interests.

The new system stresses the authority of department heads. When derogatory information is turned up against an employe, his chief may decide the case is insubstantial and put him back to work; or, if adverse with ameliorating circumstances, transfer him to a nonsensitive job, pending final adjudication; or suspend him.

A suspect who is suspended or placed temporarily in a nonsensitive job then receives a hearing before a three-man board chosen by his chief from a roster of Federal officials maintained for the purpose by the Attorney General. After a hearing, this board makes recommendations and the case goes back to the department chief, who may accept or reject the recommendations.

No Judicial Review

Under the old system, the department head made the final decision, too, but he could be influenced by two boards. First, a suspect received a hearing before a board drawn from his own department.

The case was then reviewed by a panel drawn from the lists of lawyers, educators and other selected citizens of the Loyalty Review Board. The recommendations of the Loyalty Review Board were not binding but were usually accepted. The board will complete the cases it now has in process.

Neither the old system nor the new provides any form of judicial review. Any employe who felt he was dismissed unfairly would have no recourse beyond his department head unless he could find a basis for litigation. The President's order made clear, however, that working for the Government was a privilege and not a right.

It appeared from a reading of the order and of the twelve pages of a sample of security regulations sent to all departments and agencies by the Justice Department that an accused person under the new system—as under the old—might be dismissed on the basis of a case initiated after accusations from anonymous accusers.

The sample regulations state that rules of evidence are not binding on the hearing boards, but that they should take into consideration the situation when the accused "is handicapped by the nondisclosure to him of confidential information or by lack of opportunity to cross-examine confidential informants."

When Mr. Brownell was asked if it was not correct that a person could be dismissed without ever knowing his accusers, he replied:

"Only if you assume bad faith on the part of everybody involved."

In his order the President specified that the Civil Service Commission and the National Security Council should keep the new system under review in order to eliminate deficiencies that appear, as well as any tendency "to deny to individual employes fair, impartial and equitable treatment at the hands of the Government, or rights under the Constitution and laws of the United States or this order."

Bingham Approves

Hiram Bingham, former Republican Senator from Connecticut and chairman of the Loyalty Review Board, declared of the new system:

"It puts into effect some of the things I tried to get President Truman to put into effect. I asked the former President several times to go beyond the field of loyalty and allow us to get rid of people we thought were undesirable and unsuitable but not disloyal. He never would allow us to do that. So far as it extends the dismissal authority it is excellent.

"I am sorry that there is no appeal allowed from the decisions of the heads of sixty departments. I have been in the program for two and a half years and have found that people who make decisions in departments on firing do not always do so justly. We have reversed a good many cases where the lower boards have found people to be ineligible.

"I think it is a mistake to extend the character of 'sensitive' to such agencies as the Department of Agriculture, the Post Office Department, the Interior Department, etc. There are hundreds of thousands of jobs in such agencies which are not sensitive and where employes should be allowed to appeal.

"Because of this extension people can be put out because somebody doesn't like them. There are 1,500,000 people who are in agencies which are not sensitive and their rights of appeal have been taken away.

"I think there should be appeals allowed to nongovernmental bodies like the Loyalty Review Board, not composed of Government employes."

* * *

October 15, 1964

PRESIDENT'S AIDE QUITS ON REPORT OF MORALS CASE

*Jenkins Was Arrested Last Week in Capital Y.M.C.A.—
Is Sent to Hospital*

By MAX FRANKEL
Special to The New York Times

WASHINGTON, Oct. 14—Walter W. Jenkins resigned tonight as a special assistant to President Johnson after it became known that he had been arrested here last week on a charge of disorderly conduct involving "indecent gestures."

The White House press secretary, George E. Reedy, announced the resignation in New York, where President Johnson was spending the night.

The arrest of Mr. Jenkins, as well as a record of his arrest in January, 1959, under similar circumstances, is in the records of the Morals Division of the Washington Metropolitan Police Department.

The charge against him in the 1959 arrest read "disorderly conduct (pervert)."

Associated Press

QUITS POST: Walter W. Jenkins, White House aide, resigned after his arrest was made known yesterday.

Free Access to Data

Mr. Jenkins, who has served Mr. Johnson for 25 years, has been a confidant and close associate of the President in the White House. He is thought to have had free access to much if not most of the information available at the White House but it could not be determined this evening what degree of clearance he held for the handling of materials affecting the national security.

Mr. Jenkins' arrest last Wednesday became known here this evening in a manner that is not entirely clear. Local reporters were somehow advised of the police record after Dean Burch, chairman of the Republican National Committee, had called attention to "a report sweeping Washington that the White House is desperately trying to suppress a major news story affecting the national security."

Within an hour, the White House staff in New York disclosed that Mr. Jenkins had been hospitalized here to be treated for "extreme fatigue."

Led to Questioning

The Republican party's statement was distributed here at about 6 P.M. and led to questioning all major Government departments, including the White House staff in New York. Mr. Jenkins' hospitalization was disclosed at about 7 P.M.

By 8:30, reporters here had examined the record of arrests for last week and addressed new questions to the White House. Mr. Reedy announced the resignation at 10:30 P.M. at a hurriedly called news conference in the Waldorf-Astoria Hotel.

A White House source said President Johnson had known nothing about Mr. Jenkins' hospitalization or arrest until his staff received questions from newsmen.

Mr. Jenkins, 46 years old, has been a personal aide to Mr. Johnson since 1939. In recent years, the relationship between the two men appears to have involved close professional, political, business and personal associations. One of Mr. Jenkins' six children is named Lyndon.

A man of compact build, a slightly florid face, with heavy, graying hair, Mr. Jenkins has been described as a "nervous type." But he was also known for extremely hard work on behalf of the President.

As a special assistant at the White House, he performed many administrative and political services, advising on speeches, expediting material for the President's interest, taking notes for him at meetings of the National Security Council and sitting in on Cabinet meetings.

Mr. Jenkins was reported by the George Washington University Hospital to be suffering from "hypertension and nervous exhaustion." He was not available for comment.

Officials at the Republican National Committee refused, after their first cryptic comment, to make any statement. Presumably, their statement was a reference to the Jenkins case and it was intended to imply that a person in his condition in such high office might compromise the national security.

It could not be determined this evening whether Mr. Jenkins had been given a security clearance by the Federal Bureau of Investigation or whether such a clearance is customary for close associates of a President drawn into service on his personal staff.

A White House source said he assumed there was a security clearance but did not say how high a classification it carried. The source said he did not wish to rely on memory and therefore could not say whether Mr. Jenkins had participated in meetings of the National Security Council.

The F.B.I. refused to comment when asked whether Mr. Jenkins' arrest in 1959 had been noted during security investigations.

The first White House statement in New York said that Mr. Jenkins had been hospitalized. It said he had been "suffering from extreme fatigue for some time" and had been sent to George Washington University Hospital by his physician, Dr. Charles Thompson.

At 8:25 P.M., United Press International carried the story of Mr. Jenkins's arrest last Wednesday. It did not disclose how it had come to examine the police arrest record for that date, saying only that "rumors swept Washington political circles" and that "an unidentified tipster" had told unnamed reporters where they could find further information.

Account Is Checked

Other reporters were then able to corroborate the account by checking the arrest records of the Morals Division in Room 5058 of the Municipal Building here.

Under the date of Oct. 7, they found an entry, listed as Case 2208, recording the arrest at 8:35 P.M. of Walter Wilson Jenkins, of 3407 Huntington Street, Northwest.

His birthplace was listed as Jolly, Texas. His occupation, clerk.

The place of arrest was given as the Young Men's Christian Association—which is two blocks from the White House. The charge was recorded as "disorderly (indecent gestures)."

The collateral posted was said to have been $50 and a rubber stamp entry, "elects to forfeit," indicated that Mr. Jenkins chose to forfeit the $50 instead of appearing in court to fight the case. Such a choice is not an admission of guilt and does not amount to a conviction.

The complainant in the arrest was listed as R. L. Graham and the arresting officer as L. P. Drouillard. Both are members of the Washington police force.

Another entry in the same book showed that Andy Choka, a 60-year-old member and resident of the Soldiers' Home for Disabled Veterans, was arrested at the same time in the same place on the same charge. He, too, was said to have forfeited $50 of collateral.

The same two officers were listed on the entry, except that Mr. Graham was listed as the arresting officer and Mr. Drouillard as the complainant.

Government records list the Walter W. Jenkins who has worked for the President as residing at the same address as that of the police record. Biographical records show the President's aide to have been born in Jolly, Tex., on March 23, 1918.

Rules of House Cited

A telephone operator at the soliders' home said Mr. Choka was one of about 2,000 residents. But rules of the home prevented any call or visitors to his quarters this evening.

As this information became known, word spread of a previous arrest of Mr. Jenkins and this, too, was found in the police records.

An entry under the date of Jan. 15, 1959, showed that at 10:20 P.M., a Walter Wilson Jenkins of 3704 Huntington Street, Northwest, was arrested on a charge given as "disorderly conduct (pervert)."

His birthdate was recorded as 3/23/1918, his birthplace as Jolly, Tex., his race as white, and his occupation as clerk.

The place of arrest was the Y.M.C.A—there is only one in Washington.

A rubber stamp entry showed that he had elected to forfeit a required collateral of $25. The complainant was listed as C. J. Morda, the arresting officer as C. E. Rinaldi.

There was no indication in the 1959 record that any other person had been arrested at the same time and place by the same officers.

The police said the morals division arrest records were open for public inspection, but they refused to answer other questions or help newsmen to locate policemen or detectives who might have a recollection of either incident.

The records did not show whether the arrests were made inside or outside the Y.M.C.A. building or any other surrounding circumstances.

In New York Mr. Reedy appeared before reporters at about 10:15 P.M. and read the following statement:

"As I told some of you earlier today, Walter Jenkins, who has been suffering from fatigue, went into the hospital this afternoon at the orders of his doctor.

"Walter Jenkins submitted his resignation this evening as special assistant. The resignation was accepted and the President has appointed Bill D. Moyers to succeed him."

Mr. Moyers, also a Texan and associate of the President, has been a special assistant at the White House.

The press secretary said the resignation had been submitted "just shortly before" his announcement.

Other questions were answered by a man who would allow himself to be identified only as a White House source.

He said that President Johnson had not spoken with Mr. Jenkins today and that he first learned about the situation shortly before he went to see Mrs. John F. Kennedy, between 6:30 and 7 P.M.

The source said that the President had inquiries made about Mr. Jenkins' condition when he returned from the visit with Mrs. Kennedy. After that, the source added, Mr. Jenkins submitted a written resignation.

Effective Immediately

The resignation was described as being effective immediately. The actual document of resignation was said not yet to have reached the Presidential party in New York.

When asked about the reported arrest on Oct. 7, the White House source said that "the first we knew of any of these matters was when the newspaper queries came this evening."

The White House source was questioned closely about security clearances for Mr. Jenkins, but he said he did not know anything about them. He also said that he did not wish to rely on his memory about Mr. Jenkins's relationship to the National Security Council and other sensitive Government assignments.

The Presidential party's check on Mr. Jenkins's condition, the source said, led to word that he had suffered a breakdown resulting from complete fatigue.

Mr. Jenkins' physician, Dr. Thompson, could not be reached for direct comment. He was, however, quoted during the evening by The Associated Press as saying that Mr. Jenkins was suffering from "insomnia, tensions and agitation" and that he was "just worn out."

The physician was said to have left orders that only Mr. Jenkins' wife was to be permitted to see him. She is the former Marjorie Whitehill, whom Mr. Jenkins married in 1945. They have two daughters and four sons.

Mr. Jenkins attended Wichita Falls High School and a junior college in the same city. Later he attended but did not complete courses at the University of Texas in Austin.

One biographical account said that his association with Mr. Johnson began in 1939, when the 18-year-old Walter Jenkins went to the LBJ Ranch near Austin with a friend who was seeking a job. Instead, the job went to the young Jenkins. He was first a Capitol policeman here and shortly thereafter in the office of Mr. Johnson, then a member of the House of Representatives.

Served in Africa

Mr. Jenkins has been with Mr. Johnson since, except in World War II, when he served with the Army in Africa, Corsica and Italy, rising to the rank of major. He also took a brief leave in 1951 to seek a House seat in the 13th Congressional District in Texas, but failed and returned to Washington as Mr. Johnson's principal aide.

He served Mr. Johnson through his years in the Senate, was his principal assistant in the office of the Vice President from 1961 until 1963 and moved to the White House with Mr. Johnson after President Kennedy's assassination last Nov. 22.

Mr. Jenkins's name came up several times during the recent investigation by the Senate Rules Committee of the business affairs of Robert G. Baker, the former secretary to the Senate Democratic majority. Republicans on the committee wanted Mr. Jenkins to testify before them about allegations that it was at his suggestion that Don B. Reynolds, a Washington insurance salesman, purchased advertising time on the Johnson family's television station in Austin after selling a life insurance policy to Mr. Johnson in 1957.

Mr. Jenkins denied in a sworn affidavit to the committee that he knew anything about the arrangements leading to Mr. Reynolds's purchase of advertising time. The Senate committee, controlled by Democrats, never called Mr. Jenkins to testify.

* * *

November 21, 1964

FEDERAL JOB CORPS TO EXCLUDE YOUTHS HAVING POLICE RECORDS

An official of the Office of Economic Opportunity said here yesterday that boys with police records or homosexual tendencies would not be accepted for youth camps planned in the Federal antipoverty campaign.

The restriction was not written into the law establishing the agency, said the official, Dr. Lewis D. Eiger, director of the agency's Office of Program Development and Analysis of the Job Corps, but was made a regulation.

Dr. Eiger's announcement, made before a group of social workers and officials, brought criticism from some members of the audience. They thought the agency would be losing a good chance for rehabilitation by excluding "kids who have records."

"I know youngsters now who have benefited from such a residential training program even though they had a record," said one woman, who identified herself only as being with the New York City Youth Board.

Dr. Eiger said the ban included boys convicted of assault, of a sex crime, of narcotics addiction or of homosexual activity.

Dr. S. Michael Miller, professor of sociology and a senior research associate of the Youth Development Center at Syracuse University, said the regulation was acceptable for a limited time "if it is a tentative measure to get public support," but he thought it should not be permanent.

There has been opposition to the establishment of Job Corps centers in some areas because of expressed fears that they would be filled with juvenile delinquents. A campaign led by The Richmond (Va.) News-Leader was waged against a proposed camp in York County, Va., on those grounds.

There were about 125 persons from the East, Midwest and South, but mostly from New York State, at yesterday's meeting, of the National Committee on Employment of Youth, a private organization. It was held in the Brotherhood Building, 40th Street and Seventh Avenue.

Dr. Eiger said that when the program was in full swing next July there would be about 126 centers housing about 33,000 young men and women in cities and rural areas. They will be taught trades, given remedial reading lessons and medical and dental care where it is needed.

* * *

June 4, 1965

QUERIES ABOUT SEX LIFE DROPPED FOR U.S. JOBS

WASHINGTON, June 3 (UPI)—Questions about sex attitudes, religion and family life have been eliminated from examinations for persons seeking a Government job, it was announced today.

John W. Macy, chairman of the Civil Service Commission, said most job applicants would no longer be required to take personality tests or be asked questions about their private affairs.

He made the disclosure in testimony before a House Government Operations subcommittee investigating official and unofficial investigating.

Mr. Macy said the tests had failed to determine how well a person applying for a job could perform the work. Results were undependable, could be "grossly misinterpreted" and "seriously jeopardize" a person's right to privacy, he said.

Civil Service offices were instructed last week to drop the tests.

* * *

May 9, 1969

CITY LIFTS JOB CURB FOR HOMOSEXUALS

The city's Civil Service Commission has agreed that homosexuality is no longer a barrier for all jobs under its jurisdiction.

The policy declaration was made by the commission and approved Monday by Federal Judge William B. Herlands. It came as a result of an action brought by two men who had passed Civil Service examinations for case workers in the Department of Welfare (now the Department of Social Services) but were turned down for the jobs.

The case originated in 1967 after Ronald B. Brass of 105 East 10th Street and Frederick Teper of 645 Ocean Avenue, Brooklyn, passed the caseworker examinations.

One of the men received a letter from the commission saying: "It is our policy to disqualify homosexuals for employment as caseworkers, hospital care investigators and children's counselors." The second man was also denied a position on the grounds of homosexuality.

Accusations Denied

Both men denied they were homosexuals and asked for a hearing or appeal on their disqualification. Their request was denied by the commission.

According to court papers the commission determined that one of the men was a homosexual on the basis of an Army deferment issued to him on the ground of "homosexual tendencies." This reportedly was based on a psychiatric interview in which the man described dreams.

The second man was said to belong to a club of homosexuals and this information became known to the commission.

After the men's request for a hearing was turned down, the New York Civil Liberties Union brought suit to force the commission to give them jobs.

The order settling the case specifically states: "The City Civil Service Commission has re-evaluated the qualifications of the named plaintiffs, and finds them qualified for the position of caseworker in the Department of Social Services."

In the document spelling out its policy, the commission said:

"The City of New York does not have a policy of absolute disqualification for homosexuality. The only exclusion it utilizes are those provisions which authorize disqualification for either mental or physical disability or for guilt of a crime or infamous or notoriously disgraceful conduct. Each case of homosexuality is carefully examined to determine whether or not it falls into any of these categories.

"Policy dictates that with reference to a homosexual applicant, the commission would be required to determine the personal qualities reasonably considered indispensable to the duties of the position, and then to reasonably determine whether the applicant's condition is inconsistent with the possession of these qualities to the extent of rendering him unfit to assume the duties of the position."

Stand Explained

In an amplification of this, the commission explained in the statement of policy that "an admitted homosexual, when the acts are frequent and recent, would probably not be qualified for the position of Correction Officer, whose duty it would be to guard prisoners in one of the city penitentiaries."

"Nor would such a person be probably qualified as a children's counselor or playground attendant," it added.

Aryeh Neier, the director of the New York Civil Liberties Union, said he knew of no other similar written policy by a state concerning jobs and homosexuals.

Mr. Neier said it was the experience of the Civil Liberties Union that prior to the order a known homosexual could not obtain a Civil Service job after passing a written test.

Federal officials here said they knew of no Federal law barring employment on the ground that the applicant is a homosexual. But the Federal Civil Service Commission has a regulation that bars employment for Federal jobs for immoral conduct; homosexuality is regarded in this category by the Federal commission.

The case involving the applicants for the welfare jobs was brought to Federal Court because it concerned the abridgement of due process, making it a question of Constitutional law.

* * *

January 7, 1971

SCHOOLS ACCUSED OF HOMOSEXUAL BIAS

A City Councilman accused the Board of Education and two major corporations yesterday of discriminating against homosexuals in their hiring practices.

The charges were made by Carter Burden, Democratic-Liberal of Manhattan, at a City Hall news conference following the introduction of legislation to extend the protection of the city's human-rights law to ban discrimination in housing, public accommodation and employment "based on the sexual orientation of an individual."

In addition to the Board of Education, Mr. Burden accused the International Business Machines Corporation and the Columbia Broadcasting System.

The bill was introduced in the Council by Mr. Burden and the minority leader, Councilman At Large, Eldon R. Clingan, a Manhattan Liberal. Mr. Burden said he would offer proof of his charges today at a hearing on discrimination in housing and employment conducted by Assemblyman Stephen J. Solarz of Brooklyn.

At the Columbia Broadcasting System, a representative denied any discrimination in hiring practices. He said applicants were judged "on the basis of qualification for a job, not on any specific standard of behavior."

A spokesman for the International Business Machines Corporation said: "We know of no evidence to support this charge. Our policy is to hire the best-qualified applicants."

Efforts to reach the Board of Education for comment were unavailing.

* * *

October 19, 1971

CITY AIDE BACKS HOMOSEXUAL BILL

Measure Would Bar Bias in Housing and Jobs

By ALFONSO A. NARVAEZ

Eleanor Holmes Norton, chairman of the City Commission on Human Rights, said yesterday that the Lindsay administration supported passage of a bill prohibiting discrimination against homosexuals in housing and employment and that she expected Police and Fire Department officials to support the job aspect of the measure.

During testimony at a hearing conducted by the City Council's Committee on General Welfare at City Hall, Mrs. Norton said that the bill was "a logical extension of the existing code," which bars discrimination because of race, creed, national origin, sex, age and physical handicaps.

Officials Unavailable

"It is time we recognize the fact that there is yet another group in our society which suffers analogous prejudice and which faces unconstitutional deprivation of jobs, housing and other rights due any citizen of this country," Mrs. Norton said.

Police and Fire Department officials were unavailable for comment yesterday on the proposed measure.

When asked by Councilman Michael DeMarco, Democrat of the Bronx, if she spoke for the Lindsay administration and for the Police and Fire Departments Mrs. Norton replied that she spoke "only for the Mayor and myself," but added, "I have no reason to believe that any member of the Mayor's Cabinet has a different policy than the administration."

Councilman DeMarco asked the committee's chairman, Councilman Saul S. Sharisson, to request that Fire Commissioner Robert O. Lowery and Police Commissioner Patrick V. Murphy testify to give their views on the subject.

Mr. DeMarco questioned the propriety of allowing homosexual males into the Fire Department where they would be living in close proximity with other men in firehouses. Mr. DeMarco said later that he was opposed to the bill.

Mrs. Norton urged the committee to pass the bill without delay. "To hesitate," she said, "is to encourage the continuance of present unacceptable and unconstitutional forms of harassment and discrimination against citizens of our city who deserve the same protection we regularly afford to others."

Although most of those who testified favored the bill, strong opposition was voiced by the commander of the Queens County Catholic War Veterans.

"This bill, as I understand it, proposes to legislate immorality," Robert D. Goff said. "I believe these people are sick and should be treated as such."

Mr. Goff charged that the bill was being steamrollered through the Council and that the public was unaware of the consequences of the bill.

"This bill has been in committee for nine months," replied Councilman Carter Burden, one of the measure's sponsors.

* * *

December 21, 1971

A.C.L.U. SUIT FIGHTS FEDERAL DISMISSALS FOR HOMOSEXUALITY

Special to The New York Times

WASHINGTON, Dec. 20—The American Civil Liberties Union filed suit in the United States District Court here today to stop the Federal Government from dismissing employes solely because they are homosexuals.

The class action suit asks for a permanent injunction against the Civil Service Commission and the Government that would stop all investigations of the sexual activities of Federal employes or of those applying to work for the Government.

In addition, the suit requests the court to rule that the practice of using homosexuality as the sole basis for disqualifying an individual from Federal employment is unlawful.

Florence Isbell, executive director of the A.C.L.U. here, said that the suit was the first class action brought on behalf of former Government employes who had been dismissed for being homosexuals. She noted that two cases recently brought by the organization had resulted in decisions limiting the Government's power to dismiss individuals because they were homosexuals. But she said that those decisions had not been accepted as policy by the Government.

Plaintiffs in the suit are Charles W. Baker and Donald P. Rah Jr., formerly clerk-typists in the National Bureau of Standards; David F. Carpenter, formerly a substitute mail handler at the United States Post Office in San Francisco, and Max W. Loop, formerly a clerk-carrier at the Post Office in Nashville, Ind.

All four, the suit alleges, were dismissed from their Government positions because detailed investigations had determined that they were either homosexuals, reputed to be homosexuals or had associated publicly with persons known to be homosexuals.

The suit contends that all four had received satisfactory ratings for the Government work and were properly carrying out their jobs when dismissed. Saying that there is "no compelling governmental interest" in the sexual practices of Federal employes, the suit asks the court to order the reinstatement of the plaintiffs and to expunge any references to their sexual activities from their personnel records.

Named as defendants in the suit are Robert Hampton, Jayne Spain and L. J. Andolsek, who are, respectively, chairman, vice-chairman and commissioner of the Civil Service

Commission; Maurice Stans, Secretary of Commerce; Lewis Barnscomb, director of the National Bureau of Standards, and E. T. Klassen, Postmaster General.

* * *

July 4, 1975

HOMOSEXUAL HIRING IS REVISED BY U.S.

WASHINGTON, July 3 (UPI)—The United States Civil Service Commission is taking a new approach on the suitability of homosexual applicants for government employment.

The commission issued new guidelines today to be distributed to government department heads, to determine which applicants are "suitable" for Federal service.

"A significant change from past policy—resulting from court decisions and injunctions—provides for applying the same standard in evaluating sexual conduct, whether heterosexual or homosexual," the commission said.

The guidelines say that court decisions require that persons cannot be disqualified from Federal employment "solely on the basis of homosexual conduct."

The commission concluded: "While a person may not be found unsuitable based on unsubstantiated conclusions concerning possible embarrassment for the Federal service, a person may be dismissed or found unsuitable where the evidence exists that sexual conduct affects job fitness."

* * *

July 16, 1975

SHEDDING BLINDERS

The United States Civil Service Commission has struck an important blow against the glacier of bias that imprisons the vast majority of homosexuals in America. It issued new guidelines—affecting the great bulk of Federal civilian employes—which forbid employment discrimination "solely on the basis of homosexual conduct," and require that there be no differentiation in treatment between homosexuals and heterosexuals.

The new guidelines still carry a bit of the baggage of old taboos by exempting the Central Intelligence Agency and the Federal Bureau of Investigation. Homosexuals are alleged to have both a lesser capacity to withstand stress and a greater vulnerability to blackmail and are thus deemed unsuited for sensitive positions or work in sensitive agencies. The American Psychiatric Association demolished the stress theory in a resolution passed in 1973 which reads in part: "Homosexuality per se implies no impairment of judgment, stability, reliability or general social or vocational capabilities. . . ." The blackmail theory does not withstand scrutiny. Blackmail of homosexuals has been a possibility only because of formal or informal employment practices discriminating against them but, even so, most successful blackmail attempts have involved heterosexual activity.

Whatever its shortcomings, the Civil Service Commission ruling is an enormously constructive step. Its greatest impact is apt to be the influence it has on other public and private employers across the nation.

The New York City Council could profit from the Federal example when the bill banning discrimination against homosexuals in employment, housing and public accommodations comes before it later this year. This legislation, which fell victim last year to zealous opposition, has now attracted broad public and religious support. Perhaps the Federal leadership will help the City Council understand that it is the whole community that gains when irrational and unfair strictures are removed from any segment of the population.

* * *

October 4, 1977

TEACHERS IN WEST AND NEW JERSEY LOSE DISPUTES OVER HOMOSEXUALITY

By GRACE LICHTENSTEIN

The United States Supreme Court yesterday let stand a Washington State court ruling that teachers can be dismissed for being homosexuals.

The Court declined to review the case of James Gaylord, a Tacoma high school social studies teacher who was dismissed on grounds of "immorality" when school officials learned of his homosexuality in 1972. He had been teaching for nearly 13 years and was not accused of engaging in improper conduct.

The decision set no precedents, according to supporters of organizations for the rights of homosexuals, but it outraged those groups and civil liberties groups. It was praised by Anita Bryant, the singer and orange juice promoter who led the successful campaign against homosexual rights in Florida last June.

The Court also declined to review a case involving a homosexual teacher in New Jersey, John Gish, who was shifted from his teaching duties. After he became president of the New Jersey Gay Activist Alliance in 1972, the Paramus Board of Education ordered him to undergo a psychiatric examination. Mr. Gish contended that that violated his rights to privacy, liberty, freedom of expression and equal protection under the law.

Yesterday's ruling spotlights a highly emotional issue that involves parents, unions, politicians, courts, school boards and homosexual students, as well as thousands of homosexual teachers.

Homosexual Rights Upheld

The rights of homosexual teachers have been upheld in recent state court decisions in California, Maryland, Oregon and Delaware, according to the National Gay Task Force, a New York-based umbrella group.

Moreover, several cities including New York have active professional organizations of homosexual teachers, which have the support of the two major teachers unions.

In New York, the Gay Teachers Association consists of about 250 active members who serve in public, elementary, junior and high schools. The Board of Education's executive director of personnel, Frank C. Arricale 2d, told the group in a letter in 1975:

"You can be assured that homosexuality is not a bar to entrance into teaching in New York City nor to the continuation of teaching. Frankly, we are not particularly interested in whether or not teachers are homosexual or not."

Last week, in response to a question, a board spokesman reiterated that support. "Simply the fact of his sexual orientation is not enough to bar a teacher," the spokesman said.

Similarly, the United Federation of Teachers; its parent union, the American Federation of Teachers; the National Education Association and the New York State United Teachers have all expressed support for homosexuals within their ranks.

"We don't believe teachers' lives out of the classroom should be a cause for dismissal," a U.F.T. spokesman said yesterday.

Yet homosexual teachers were the focus of Miss Bryant's crusade against the Dade County (Miami) antidiscrimination ordinance. Upon hearing about the high court decision yesterday she said:

"Now I have greater hope that God has given America a space to repent and that this will slow down the forces that are attempting to destroy the foundations of this country—the family unit."

In the summer, a Gallup poll showed that while a majority of people approved of equal job rights for homosexuals in general, 65 percent of those polled believed that homosexuals should not be allowed to teach.

The Tacoma case is Gaylord v. Tacoma School District, No. 77-01. The New Jersey case is Gish v. Board of Education, No. 77-3.

Sexual Role Minimized

Homosexual teachers contend that their sexual preference has nothing to do with their competence. But they acknowledge that there are biases against them they must strive to overcome.

"There's a discernible fear among parents of the myth of child molesting," said Marc Rubin, a leader of the Gay Teachers Association in New York. "They push the same connotive button when they call it proselytizing or 'harm to the family.' There are plenty of heterosexual school teachers who lead polygamous lives or are not married but that's not considered a danger."

Meryl Friedman, another New York leader, voiced concern yesterday that the Supreme Court's decision not to rule on homosexual teacher questions "is going to open doors" for school board dismissals of teachers in other locations.

"We've got to educate them to the fact that there have been gay teachers from time immemorial; Socrates, for instance," she said.

In Tacoma, Mr. Gaylord, the 39-year-old teacher involved in the case, took the Court action philosophically. "Needless to say, I'm disappointed," he said. "For me it is the end of the road. I'm not terribly happy about losing, but someone else will win, believe me."

Mr. Gaylord was dismissed after school officials, prompted by a former student, confronted him about his suspected sexual orientation. He did not deny it. The officials said this preference would impair the school's learning atmosphere. A Phi Beta Kappa graduate of the University of Washington, Mr. Gaylord now works for the American Federation of Teachers.

* * *

March 11, 1992

JUDGE AFFIRMS SUIT BY LESBIAN OVER WITHDRAWAL OF JOB OFFER

By TAMAR LEWIN

A Federal district judge in Atlanta yesterday let stand a lawsuit brought against the Georgia Attorney General by a lesbian lawyer whose job offer was rescinded after she disclosed that she was planning to marry another woman.

In her lawsuit the lawyer, Robin Joy Shahar, is seeking monetary damages and a reinstatement of the job offer.

Ms. Shahar, a 1991 graduate of Emory University Law School, had worked for the Georgia Department of Law the summer before her graduation and was offered a permanent job in the department after her graduation. She accepted the job and was told to report for work last Sept. 23.

But after telling the Deputy Attorney General that she planned to marry another woman and to take the last name of her partner, Ms. Shahar received a letter withdrawing the offer because of the "purported marriage between you and another woman."

Georgia is one of 24 states that outlaw sodomy.

'Public Perception' Cited

Ms. Shahar and her partner participated in a Jewish wedding ceremony on July 28, a few weeks after the letter was delivered. She then filed suit against the State Attorney General, Michael J. Bowers, in October, asserting that he had violated her constitutional right to freedom of association, equal protection, due process and freedom of religion.

Responding to Ms. Shahar's lawsuit, Mr. Bowers asserted that regardless of whether she had actually committed sodomy, the fact of her participation in a wedding ceremony to another woman gave him ground to withdraw the offer of employment "to insure public perception" that his department was enforcing the state's laws.

Mr. Bowers successfully defended Georgia's anti-sodomy law in a 1986 Supreme Court challenge, Bowers v. Hardwick.

Mr. Bowers also sought to have her claims of religious freedom dismissed on the ground that the ceremony is not fundamental to her faith.

The judge, Richard C. Freeman, rejected those arguments. Judge Freeman, who was named to the Federal bench by President Richard M. Nixon in 1971, ruled that Ms. Shahar could go ahead with her lawsuit. She is now working in a law firm in Atlanta.

William B. Rubenstein, director of the American Civil Liberties Union's lesbian and gay rights project, who is among those representing Ms. Shahar, said: "What this means is that lesbians and gay men who are open about their sexuality do not lose their constitutional rights, or their right to public employment. It's a major victory for lesbians and gay men, and it's part of a recent trend toward respecting our rights."

Mr. Rubenstein said that in a similar case last month in San Francisco, a Federal judge refused to dismiss the lawsuit of Frank Buttino, a special agent with the Federal Bureau of Investigation who said his constitutional rights had been violated when he lost his job after the bureau learned of his homosexuality. He had worked for the F.B.I. for 20 years.

"Since there is so little law establishing gay men and lesbians' rights, and almost half the states still have anti-sodomy laws, these are very important decisions," Mr. Rubenstein said.

* * *

October 20, 1995

CLINTON BACKS BILL TO PROTECT HOMOSEXUALS FROM JOB BIAS

By STEVEN A. HOLMES

WASHINGTON, Oct. 19—Two years after being politically wounded by the issue of homosexuals in the military, President Clinton has decided to back a bill outlawing job discrimination against homosexuals, White House officials said today.

In a letter sent today to Senator Edward M. Kennedy, Democrat of Massachusetts and a chief sponsor of the anti-discrimination legislation in the Senate, Mr. Clinton noted that in 41 states it is legal for a person to be dismissed from a job because of sexual orientation.

Those who face this kind of job discrimination have no legal recourse, in either state or Federal courts," Mr. Clinton wrote. "This is wrong."

Gay rights leaders who have been lobbying the White House for Mr. Clinton's endorsement of the bill conceded that his backing would have little immediate practical effect because the Republican Congress was dead set against the measure, which would apply to public and private employment.

"We won't even get hearings on it," said Representative Barney Frank, Democrat of Massachusetts, one of three openly gay members of Congress.

Still, Mr. Clinton's endorsement is the first by a sitting President involving a major piece of legislation to secure equal rights for homosexuals. And it is likely to guarantee that gay rights will become an issue in next year's Presidential campaign.

"I'm sure Pat Robertson and Pat Buchanan will try to make hay of this," said George Stephanopoulos, a senior adviser to Mr. Clinton. "But the President believes it's the right thing to do, and I believe that most Americans agree that discrimination is wrong for whatever reason."

The bill, the Employment Non-Discrimination Act, would extend to sexual orientation the same Federal protection against bias in hiring, promotions or dismissals that currently exists on the basis of race, sex, religion, color or national origin. But to try to gather more support and trump critics' argument that they are seeking "special rights" for homosexuals, the drafters of the bill carved out several exemptions.

The measure would not cover the armed forces, businesses with fewer than 15 employees and religious institutions, including sectarian schools. The measure would not require businesses to provide health or other benefits to domestic partners of employees, and it would prohibit employers from giving anyone preference in hiring or promotion because of sexual orientation.

If enacted, the measure would cover Congress. It would cover heterosexuals as well because it would prohibit discrimination as a result of sexual orientation.

Even with the exemptions, social conservatives have condemned the bill, and they criticized Mr. Clinton today for his endorsement.

"I'm not surprised," said Robert H. Knight, director of cultural studies at the Family Research Council, a conservative advocacy group. "He's tried to give them everything they've wanted. This seems to be the one issue area where the Clinton Administration doesn't flip-flop. They have been relentlessly pursuing the homosexual agenda within the Federal Government and the military. And this would extend it to the private sector with grave consequences."

Gay rights leaders were thrilled with Mr. Clinton's endorsement despite the dim prospects for the bill in Congress.

"I feel that it's an excellent move, and it's in keeping with his broader message of healing the country," said Elizabeth Birch, executive director of the Human Rights Campaign, the country's largest gay rights organization. "While others continue to be engaged in the politics of division, I feel that he's staking out some moral high ground."

Though Mr. Stephanopoulos concedes that the bill will have rough sledding in Congress, he said he believed that the Administration would attract more support for the goal of ending discrimination against homosexuals in the workplace than it did in trying to lift the ban in the military.

"Part of the power of the argument that the military had was that the military is different," he said. "It has special problems of morale and discipline that require different standards. We didn't agree with the argument, but we understood it, and the President had to act in a way that was consistent with maintaining morale and discipline. But this bill is about the simple bedrock judgment that you shouldn't discriminate against people because of who they are, and we think the public will support that."

Backers of the measure say public opinion polls consistently show that a large majority of Americans do not favor discrimination against homosexuals. The advocates say the polls also indicate that most Americans do not know that in most states, homosexuals have no protections against being dismissed.

"The right wing says what these people want is special rights," Mr. Frank said. "And people are prepared to believe that we are asking for special rights because they assume we already have the protections we are asking for, and so we must be asking for something more."

* * *

September 6, 1996

ANTI-DISCRIMINATION PROPOSAL DELAYS SENATE VOTE ON BILL OPPOSING SAME-SEX MARRIAGE

By ERIC SCHMITT

WASHINGTON, Sept. 5—The Senate today postponed a vote on a bill to bar Federal recognition of same-sex marriages after Republicans and Democrats failed to agree on which amendments could be offered to the bill.

The main sticking point is an amendment that would prohibit discrimination against homosexuals in the workplace. The measure, offered by Senator Edward M. Kennedy, Democrat of Massachusetts, and Senator James M. Jeffords, Republican of Vermont, would bar an employer from using sexual orientation as a basis for hiring, firing, promoting or demoting an employee.

This week Senator Trent Lott of Mississippi, the majority leader, called the amendment a "distraction" and said he would use a procedural maneuver to prevent Democrats from offering the amendment to the marriage bill.

But Senator Kennedy threatened to attach the measure to any one of a number of appropriations bills that Senator Lott wants to approve if Republicans block his amendment to the marriage bill.

"Bigotry in any form in the workplace is unconscionable and unacceptable," Mr. Kennedy said today. "If Republicans practice the inclusion they preached in San Diego, the Employment Non-Discrimination Act will pass."

A vote on the overall marriage bill was put off until next week. Gay rights groups and their Senate backers said 32 senators had promised to support the anti-discrimination amendment, and they were within reach of the votes needed to approve the amendment. Besides Mr. Jeffords, at least two other Republican Senators support it: John H. Chafee of Rhode Island and Alfonse M. D'Amato of New York.

"My position is clear: People should be judged on the basis on their ability," Senator D'Amato said in a telephone interview. He predicted that despite the leadership's opposition, the Senate would ultimately approve the amendment.

The underlying bill, called the Defense of Marriage Act, would allow each state to ignore same-sex marriages in any other states. These marriages are not legal in any state now. But if Hawaii, where the law is being challenged, or any other state permits them, other states would be obliged under the Constitution to recognize them as well.

Whenever the bill comes to a vote in the Senate, even its opponents concede that it will pass. The House approved the bill by a vote of 342 to 67 on July 12. President Clinton has angered gay groups by promising to sign the bill, but this has denied Bob Dole and other Republican candidates a campaign issue.

Passage of the gay rights amendment in the waning days of a Republican-controlled Congress would be a stunning victory for homosexuals and would culminate an effort that started in 1975, when Bella S. Abzug, then a Representative from Manhattan, introduced the first Federal anti-gay job discrimination bill.

Job discrimination against homosexuals is already barred in nine states: California, Connecticut, Hawaii, Massachusetts, Minnesota, New Jersey, Vermont, Wisconsin and Rhode Island

In an effort to defuse opposition, Mr. Kennedy's amendment specifically prohibits preferential treatment or quotas for homosexuals in the workplace, and exempts the armed forces, religious organizations and employers with fewer than 15 workers. The measure would take effect 60 days after enactment.

But many conservative Republicans oppose the amendment, which would face a strong challenge in the House even if it wins Senate approval. One leading critic, Don Nickles of Oklahoma, the second-ranking Republican in the Senate, says the amendment would permit openly gay men and lesbians to be Boy Scout and Girl Scout leaders.

Mr. Nickles has offered three amendments to the marriage bill that Democrats strongly oppose. One would require labor unions to obtain written consent of employees before their union dues could be used for political purposes. Another would reimburse the legal expenses of the White House travel office employees who were dismissed in May 1993. The third amendment would cancel the District of Columbia's exemption from certain welfare rules.

The other Democratic amendments would make hate crimes against homosexuals a Federal crime, and would make it illegal for anyone convicted of domestic violence to own or buy a handgun.

A third Democratic proposal, requiring insurers to allow mothers to stay in the hospital for up to 48 hours after childbirth (96 hours after Caesarean delivery), was adopted today by the Senate in a voice vote as an amendment to a fiscal 1997 appropriations bill for veterans, housing and other programs.

* * *

August 6, 1998

HOUSE SUPPORTS BAN ON BIAS AGAINST GAY FEDERAL EMPLOYEES

By LIZETTE ALVAREZ

WASHINGTON, Aug. 5—The House today soundly rejected a measure that would have blocked President Clinton's directive banning job discrimination against Federal workers who are gay.

In an emotional, heartfelt debate that prompted some conservatives to side with liberals, the House, by a vote of 252 to 176, rejected arguments that Mr. Clinton's directive would lead to affirmative action for homosexuals and defeated the opposing measure, which was attached as an amendment to a spending bill.

The vote also revealed a degree of discomfort among some Republicans toward the party's recent salvos against homosexuality.

"If a person does an honest day's work for an honest day's pay, that's all I can ask," said Representative Thomas J. Bliley Jr., a Virginia Republican, who added that he "unequivocally opposes" discrimination.

The amendment, sponsored by Representative Joel Hefley, Republican of Colorado, would have undone Mr. Clinton's May 28 executive order adding homosexuals to groups that may not be discriminated against in Federal employment. The executive order sought to make uniform a Federal employment policy that is already in effect at many agencies.

Mr. Hefley said he sought to rein in Mr. Clinton. He said he believed that the President had abused his power in issuing a blizzard of executive orders during his two terms.

"This amendment is not about homosexuality, and it's not about discrimination," Mr. Hefley said. "It's about the misuse of the executive order process. The process is not designed to circumvent the Congress."

Mr. Hefley also said that this particular executive order banning discrimination would lead to affirmative action, quotas and special privileges for homosexuals, a contention that a number of conservative Republicans rejected.

Only a handful of Republicans tonight chose to speak out in support of the amendment. Instead, several Republicans took the floor to criticize the measure, including those who object to homosexuality on moral and religious grounds.

"Homosexuals are taxpayers, too, and deserve an equal break in terms of fairness in employment," said Representative Dana Rohrabacher, a conservative California Republican, amused that he stood in the unfamiliar company of Democrats. "There is no reason for the Federal Government to discriminate for or against an individual."

Representative Christopher Shays, Republican of Connecticut, said he was "outraged" that Republican leaders "sought to make this a political issue."

Gay rights advocates viewed Mr. Hefley's amendment as an election-year ploy to appease social conservatives who have accused Republican leaders of neglecting causes like abortion, homosexuality and affirmative action.

"They are throwing political bones to the extreme right wing of the party in advance of the '98 elections," said David M. Smith, a spokesman for the Human Rights Campaign, the nation's largest gay and lesbian political organization. "They perceive it to be good politics in a low-turnout election. And they need to energize their base."

This is the second time in as many weeks that the House has grappled with issues relating to homosexuality. Last week, the House passed a measure that would prevent San Francisco from using Federal housing money to implement the city's policies supporting live-in homosexual partners. The amendment passed by two votes.

The two proposals are part of a larger effort on the part of some Republicans to take a more vocal stance against homosexuality. Senator Trent Lott of Mississippi, the majority leader, recently compared homosexuality to kleptomania. House Republicans also joined the fray, quoting Scripture to make their point.

Republicans have also succeeded in blocking the nomination of the wealthy Democratic contributor James C. Hormel, who is gay, as ambassador to Luxembourg.

Conservatives intensified the debate when they began running full-page newspaper advertisements featuring "reformed" homosexuals.

Mr. Hefley's amendment was attached to the spending bill earmarking $34 billion for the Departments of State, Commerce and Justice.

* * *

The Military

August 31, 1952

NAVY OUSTS SEX OFFENDER

Accused Officer Resigns—
24 Sailors Also Being Dismissed

BOSTON, Aug. 30 (AP)—A Navy spokesman said today an officer allegedly involved in homosexuality had been relieved of his ship command and had submitted his resignation from the service.

Lieut. Comdr. Bernard S. Solomon, First Naval District Public Information Officer, said that twenty-four enlisted men at the Newport, R. I., Naval Base also involved in the case were being discharged by administrative decree under conditions "other than honorable."

He did not identify the ship nor the names of the individuals concerned. Fleet units as well as shore installations are said to be involved in the reported incidents. A Navy spokesman said the alleged offenses occurred in the last few weeks, but gave no details. Newport is the home base of the Atlantic destroyer fleet.

* * *

April 17, 1966

WAR ROLE SOUGHT FOR HOMOSEXUALS

Groups to Aid Deviates Ask End to Pentagon Ban

By PETER BART
Special to The New York Times

LOS ANGELES, April 16—A national campaign to end the exclusion of homosexuals from the armed forces was set in motion here this week.

The campaign will culminate in a series of parades and demonstrations in major cities on Armed Forces Day, May 21.

The organization staging the campaign contends there are 17 million homosexuals in the nation, most of whom would be eager to fight for their country. The organization, called the Committee to Fight Exclusion of Homosexuals From the Armed Forces, argues that an end to the ban would ease the shortage of manpower available for service in Vietnam.

Donald Slater, a spokesman for the committee, which is based here, said the drive represented the first manifestation of a new militancy in "the homosexual movement." The campaign, he said, grew out of a convention of homosexual organizations held Feb. 19-20 in Kansas City.

The convention, which was formally called the National Planning Conference of Homosexual Organizations, is said to have represented the first major effort of homosexual groups throughout the nation to organize a unified self-improvement program.

About 40 homosexuals representing 15 groups attended the two-day meeting, among them members of the Council on Religion and the Homosexual of San Francisco; the Janus Society of America, Philadelphia; the Mattachine Society of New York, and One, Inc., of Kansas City.

The homosexuals also agreed to set up a national legal fund to defend homosexuals who are in legal difficulties and to fight against "restrictive" sexual laws.

Mr. Slater discussed the aims of his organization in the small, sparsely furnished offices of Tangents magazine, a homosexual literary periodical of which he is the editor. Tangents, an outgrowth of a defunct publication called One, has a circulation of 5,000, according to its editor, a small, slender man with graying hair. The walls of the office are lined with books dealing with homosexuality. A seminude male adorns a calendar on the wall.

Mr. Slater said he was encouraged to find an increased willingness of homosexuals across the nation to discuss their situation publicly.

He said he did not believe that the homosexual population was increasing relative to the total population but conceded that "it may seem that way because of the trend toward more open discussion."

The campaign on military policy, Mr. Slater said, will focus on distributing leaflets to the public and encouraging people to write to the President. To attract public attention, homosexual groups around the country will seek to go on radio and TV programs and to engage in public debates.

* * *

February 11, 1988

HOMOSEXUAL BAN IN ARMY REJECTED BY APPEALS COURT

By TAMAR LEWIN

A Federal appeals court in San Francisco struck down the Army's ban on homosexuals yesterday, ruling that homosexuals are entitled to as much protection against discrimination as members of racial minority groups.

The United States Court of Appeals for the Ninth Circuit ruled 2 to 1 that the discrimination that homosexuals face "is plainly no less pernicious or intense than the discrimination faced by other groups."

The ruling was the first by a Federal appeals court prohibiting a branch of the armed services from excluding people on the basis of sexual orientation. The Army had argued that homosexuals would impede recruitment and create problems of morale and discipline.

Legal Experts See an Appeal

The Defense Department had no immediate comment on the ruling. The decision was hailed by a representative of the gay rights movement, who said it could have implications far beyond the military if it is upheld.

Richard K. Willard, head of the Justice Department's civil division, said he could not say whether there would be an appeal until he saw the decision.

Legal experts said an appeal was almost certain.

Whether the ruling would stand on appeal is unclear, however. In recent years, the United States Supreme Court has not been receptive to homosexual rights cases. In 1986, in Bower vs. Hardwick, the Court upheld a Georgia anti-sodomy law allowing criminal prosecution for private homosexual acts.

Judge Kennedy Could Be Key

And Anthony M. Kennedy, who is to join the Supreme Court next week, upheld the Navy's right to exclude people for homosexual conduct in a case he decided in 1980 when he was a judge on the the same court that issued yesterday's decision.

However, several legal experts said Judge Kennedy's reasoning in that case was so nuanced that it was impossible to be sure how he would rule in the current case. This case is different from the earlier one in that it does not involve charges of specific sexual conduct but a solider's statement that he is homosexual.

Judge William A. Norris, in the 60-page decision, which was joined by Judge William Canby, drew a distinction between the Georgia sodomy case and the military ban on homosexuality, holding that the High Court's 1986 ruling did not necessarily apply to the case at hand, since the sodomy laws were based on actual conduct, while the military ban was based simply on "sexual orientation."

Judge Norris said the Army ban would apply even to those who desired homosexual contact but committed no sexual act, while heterosexuals who engaged in homosexual acts while intoxicated might not come under the ban.

"If a straight soldier and a gay soldier of the same sex engage in homosexual acts because they are drunk, immature or curious, the straight soldier may remain in the Army while the gay soldier is automatically terminated," the decision said. "In short, the regulations do not penalize soldiers for engaging in homosexual acts; they penalize soldiers who have engaged in homosexual acts only when the Army decides that those soldiers are actually gay."

The majority said the military rules therefore violate the Fifth Amendment, which bars discrimination by the Government without compelling justification.

Judge Norris wrote that the ban on homosexuals in the military was just as offensive, legally, as the old laws against miscegenation.

"Laws that limit the acceptable focus of one's sexual desires to members of the opposite sex, like laws that limit one's choice of spouse (or sexual partner) to members of the same race, cannot withstand constitutional scrutiny absent a compelling governmental justification," he said.

'Most Important Opinion'

Thomas Stoddard, executive director of the Lambda Legal Defense and Education Fund, said: "This is the most important judicial opinion issued in the history of the gay rights movement. I'm sure that it will be appealed to the Supreme Court, but if it stands, it will have an impact far beyond the military. The court's broad endorsement of gay people's constitutional rights would affect custody and immigration cases involving homosexuals, and make it easier for gay people to work in the F.B.I or the C.I.A."

In a dissenting opinion, Judge Stephen Reinhardt said that while he felt the military ban was unconstitutional, the High Court's decision in the sodomy case left him no choice but to uphold the ban.

Dissent Cites High Court

"Like the majority, I believe that homosexuals have been unfairly treated both historically and in the United States today," he said in his opinion. "Were I free to apply my own view of the meaning of the Constitution and in that light to pass upon the validity of the Army's regulations, I too would conclude that the Army may not refuse to enlist homosexuals."

Judge Reinhardt said that although he was certain that Bowers v. Hardwick "will be overruled by a wiser and more enlightened Court," the decision as it stands appeared to him to uphold the legality of the military ban.

"Homosexuals are defined by their conduct—or, at the least, by their desire to engage in certain conduct," Judge Reinhardt said. "With other groups, such as blacks or women, there is no connection between particular conduct and the definition of the group. When conduct that plays a central role in defining a group may be prohibited by the state, it cannot be asserted with any legitimacy that the group is specially protected by the Constitution."

Judge Reinhardt said that because of the Bower v. Hardwick decision, he could not agree with the majority opinion that homosexuals must be treated as a class entitled to special protection under the Constitution.

Case Sent Back to Trial Court

Exactly how widely yesterday's ruling will apply was unclear. In its ruling, the appeals court sent the case back to the trial court, with instructions to declare the Army regulations constitutionally void. Technically, the ruling applies only to the states in the Ninth Judicial Circuit: California, Oregon, Washington, Idaho, Arizona, Nevada, Montana, Alaska and Hawaii.

But lawyers specializing in constitutional litigation said that as a practical matter, the Army would probably stop enforcing the regulations nationwide, as would other branches of the military, which apply the same policies on homosexuality.

In Bowers v. Hardwick, the High Court ruled 5 to 4 that neither the 14th Amendment guarantee of liberty, nor the constitutional right to privacy created a right to engage in homosexual sodomy.

The fifth vote for the majority came from Lewis F. Powell Jr., the Justice whose place Judge Kennedy will take.

Yesterday's ruling came in the case of Perry Watkins, a career soldier who repeatedly acknowledged his homosexuality, starting with a statement on a preinduction medical form he filled out when enlisting in 1967.

At the time, the Army's policy was to discharge soldiers for sodomy, but not simply for being homosexuals.

Sergeant Watkins was not found to have committed any specific sexual acts and the Army never contended that his job performance was impaired, but the Army regulations were changed in 1981 to require that all homosexual be discharged. Sergeant Watkins was discharged in 1984, four years short of the 20 years required for a pension.

The decision ordered the Army to reconsider Mr. Watkins's application for re-enlistment.

1,400 Homosexuals Discharged

About 1,400 men and women a year are discharged from the military on the grounds of homosexuality.

The Watkins case, brought by the American Civil Liberties Union of Seattle, has been in the courts for several years. In fact, the same appeals court that issued yesterday's opinion upheld the military's right to discharge homosexuals in a 1983 ruling in Mr. Watkins's case. That decision was not based on the constitutional arguments, but was limited to arguments that the Army was barred from discharging him on the grounds of homosexuality since he had disclosed his homosexuality at the time he joined the military.

Judge Norris dissented in the court's 1983 decision.

In the decision yesterday, Judge Norris said that the Army's argument that homosexuals in the military would hurt morale and discipline was no more acceptable legally than the similar concerns military officials used to offer to justify racial segregation in the ranks.

Mr. Stoddard of Lambda Legal Defense Fund said the military adopted an explicit policy against homosexuals in the late 1940's.

"It was very closely tied to the McCarthy business and the fear of communism, the notion that homosexuals are unstable and dangerous because of their terrible secret," he said. "I say that with irony."

* * *

September 9, 1988

WHAT THE NAVY'S ANTI-GAY PREJUDICE COSTS

To the Editor:

"A Bad Deal for a Good Soldier" by Robert A. Bernstein (Op-Ed, Aug. 8) was a fitting appraisal of the wastefulness of discharging military personnel based solely on their sexual orientation. In a military as technologically advanced as ours, the cost of training is extremely high. It is not unusual for training costs for an individual to run into the hundreds of thousands of dollars. With the Navy alone discharging more than 2,500 people a year for homosexuality, and the other services just slightly fewer, the cost of discharging gays from the military runs into hundreds of millions every year. Waste of this magnitude makes petty the fuss over $250 ashtrays and $700 hammers.

I have had the misfortune of experiencing this waste firsthand. In July 1983, I was inducted into the class of 1987 at the United States Naval Academy. After four years of intensive military training and work toward my undergraduate degree, I was questioned about allegations concerning my homosexual orientation and did not deny them.

I was then one of the 10 highest-ranking midshipmen at the Academy, and had excellent performance and conduct records. I was immediately forced to resign, weeks before graduation, and was denied the opportunity to complete my degree and serve in the capacity for which I had been trained at a cost of over $110,000. As in Perry Watkins's case with the Army, no consideration was paid to the character of my service.

Although the military says homosexuality is "contrary to good order," it is obvious to me that the real problem is not homosexuality, but rather, the military's open and officially supported prejudice against homosexuals who have the desire and capability to serve their country.

This sanctioned prejudice is unconscionable. I intend to take whatever steps are necessary to regain my degree and the career I spent four years training for.

JOSEPH STEFFAN
Fargo, N.D., Aug. 23, 1988

* * *

April 8, 1990

GAY SOLDIERS: THEY WATCHED THEIR STEP

By DORIS KERNS GOODWIN

COMING OUT UNDER FIRE: The History of Gay Men and Women in World War Two
By Allan Berube
Illustrated. 377 pp. New York: The Free Press. $22.95.

In recent weeks, the Supreme Court refused to consider two constitutional challenges to the military's policy of barring homosexuals from service. The first case involved a male Navy officer, the second a female Army sergeant, both of whom were discharged for displaying "a propensity to engage in homosexual conduct." In neither case did the military present evidence of such conduct; the "propensity" alone was considered sufficient grounds for discharge. In the wake of the passions generated by this controversial issue, Allan Berube's historical account of gay soldiers in World War II, "Coming Out Under Fire," provides a timely and valuable perspective.

In theory, during the war, homosexuals were supposed to be screened out at induction centers on the grounds that they would make poor combat soldiers and that their presence would threaten discipline and morale. (The same rationale was applied at the outset against blacks as well.) The screening devices typically used with male inductees included observation of female bodily characteristics and mannerisms, answers to questions regarding occupational choice (men who checked off interior decorator or dancer were immediately suspect) and responses to the question: How do you like girls?

But in practice, Mr. Berube argues, since the pressure to meet unfilled quotas was so great, the examinations were often perfunctory. As a result, hundreds of thousands of homosexuals, perhaps a million or more, made their way into the armed forces, serving in all branches of the military—as tank drivers and clerks, riflemen and bombardiers, messmen and gunnery officers.

"Coming Out Under Fire," the product of more than 10 years of research, of digging into archives and interviewing scores of veterans, is the story of how—out of necessity—the military coped with this large influx of homosexuals, and how gay men and women coped with the military. It is the conten-

tion of Mr. Berube, a historian of homosexuals in the United States, that the majority of gay male soldiers experienced an unexpected, if somewhat uneasy, acceptance by fellow soldiers so long as they refrained from aggressively pursuing uninterested men. Inspired by the necessity of living together in close quarters, heterosexuals developed "their own pragmatic ethic of tolerance: 'I won't bother you if you don't bother me.'" To be sure, some gay soldiers were harassed and abused by straight soldiers, but if a homosexual performed a useful function in his unit, that generally took precedence over the suspicion or even the knowledge that he was gay.

Necessity also played a role in relaxing the policy of discharging homosexual soldiers if they were caught having sex. Whereas in World War I, solely on the discovery of a love letter written by another soldier, a young Navy man was convicted of sodomy and sentenced to 15 years in prison, the more common practice in World War II was to send offenders to sick bay, where psychiatrists and other doctors attempted to distinguish "experimenters" from "confirmed perverts." Since the long public trials of the type conducted during World War I were considered too costly in time and energy, a simpler procedure was adopted: the "experimenters" were generally returned to duty, while the "perverts" were subjected to administrative discharge. "There was a war on," said Ted Allenby, a gay Marine who fought at Iwo Jima. "Who in the hell is going to worry about this . . .?"

The book is at its best in describing the experience of gay soldiers who had never admitted, perhaps even to themselves, that they were gay. Thrown together with their buddies in secluded places, with the constraints of small-town mores and family life left behind, many homosexual soldiers came to terms for the first time in their lives with their sexual inclinations. (Interestingly, the recruits who had acknowledged they were gay before entering the service were often the most reluctant to have sex; their fear of exposure was more finely tuned.) Although Mr. Berube's main focus is on gay men, he also deals provocatively with the experience of homosexuals in the Women's Army Corps. He makes the assertion that "butch" women—identified by mannish builds, close-cropped hair and the absence of makeup—occupied a more respected status within the armed forces than did effeminate men, since aggressive, masculine traits more comfortably fit the stereotype of the good soldier. Indeed, he says, such women were more likely to assume responsibility and become the leaders of their units.

Mr. Berube vividly portrays the painful choices many veterans had to confront, once the war was over, in deciding whether to commit themselves to heterosexual marriage and children or to follow a homosexual life. A great many veterans who had formed their first gay relationships during the war chose marriage and raised families. Others, believing their identity as homosexuals to be integral to their lives, continued their gay existence and settled in the cities. A handful began to speak out. Organizations formed. The early sounds of opposition to discrimination and persecution against homosexuals began to be heard not long after the war was over.

Mr. Berube tells his story with a clear and remarkably even-handed voice. At times the absence of modern social science techniques left this reader wishing for more conclusive evidence, and at times I wished the author had opted to look in depth at the life stories of five or six veterans instead of painting a broad canvas. Nevertheless, particularly in the context of today's debate over who has the right to fight and die for his or her country, "Coming Out Under Fire" is well worth reading.

Doris Kearns Goodwin, the author of "The Fitzgeralds and the Kennedys," is working on a book about Franklin and Eleanor Roosevelt and the American home front during World War II.

*   *   *

May 18, 1990

MILITARY MAKES PREJUDICE A POLICY ON GAYS

To the Editor:

It is no wonder the Department of Defense refuses to defend its bar on gays in the military and Reserve Officers Training Corps (news article, May 6). The bar is morally indefensible. The department's policy reads:

"The presence of [homosexual] members adversely affects the ability of the armed forces to maintain discipline, good order and morale, to foster mutual trust and confidence among service members, to insure the integrity of the system of rank and command, to facilitate assignment and world-wide deployment of service members, who frequently must live and work under close conditions affording minimal privacy, to recruit and retain members of the armed forces and to maintain the public acceptability of military service and to prevent breaches of security."

None of these rationales are based on the ability of gay soldiers to fulfill the duties of their stations. Indeed none of them are based on gays doing anything at all. Their force relies exclusively on current widespread bigoted attitudes toward gays. They appeal to the bigotry and consequent disruptiveness of nongay soldiers who are made uptight by the mere presence of gay soldiers and officers.

The country, indeed the military, has rejected such illegitimate bootstrapping of prejudice into policy in the case of blacks. Moral consistency requires that it should now be rejected in the case of gays.

The claim of gay security breaches is a red herring. The courts have noted that there is simply "no evidence" of gay-caused breaches of security (688 F. Supp. 1361, 1375), yet the armed forces have not barred heterosexuals from military employment despite the documented record of the heterosexually enhanced selling of the country down the river by the Walker family spy ring and by heterosexual marines showing their Communist paramours around the parts of our Moscow embassy they were supposed to be securing from spies. In any case, the fine young men whom the military is now tossing out of the R.O.T.C. are openly gay and so are incapable of being blackmailed for being gay.

The nominal function of the armed forces is to defend what the country is, but as the sad racial and gender histories of the armed forces have shown, the actual function of the armed forces is to define what the country is. It is because of the role gays have been assigned in the way the country defines itself to itself, rather than because of any legitimate policy or strategic concerns, that gays are unjustly denied the right to defend their country.

RICHARD D. MOHR
Urbana, Ill., May 7, 1990
The writer, professor of philosophy at the University of Illinois, is the author of "Gays/Justice—A Study of Ethics, Society and Law" (1988).

*   *   *

September 2, 1990

ADMIRAL PRAISES LESBIANS BUT URGES THEIR DISMISSAL

By JANE GROSS

The commander of the Navy's surface Atlantic fleet has characterized lesbian sailors as "among the command's top performers" but told his officers that homosexual women must be vigorously rooted out of the service.

The instructions, in a message from Vice Adm. Joseph S. Donnell to the officers in charge of nearly 200 ships and 40 shore installations in the Eastern half of the nation, offer a rare look at the reasoning behind the Pentagon policy that bars gay men and women from the armed forces.

The message says rooting out female homosexuals is particularly difficult because lesbians are "more aggressive than their male counterparts" and thus "intimidating" to those who might turn them in. In addition, the message says, investigations may be "pursued halfheartedly" by officers because lesbian sailors are generally "hard-working, career-oriented, willing to put in long hours on the job and among the command's top performers."

Critics Seize on Message

Opponents of the Pentagon ban on homosexuals said the message pointed up hypocrisy of the policy. "With a document like this, the Navy almost caricatures itself," said Representative Gerry E. Studds, a Massachusetts Democrat and a homosexual, who made the message available. "Dear God, if it is the Navy's policy to root out top performers, what is going on here? When any remotely fair-minded person thinks about this for two minutes, it collapses under its own weight. This is a telling example, and in and of itself a repudiation, of a bankrupt policy."

The message was sent to Mr. Studds and to several feminist organizations and gay rights advocacy groups, by lesbian sailors on the East Coast who are alarmed by what seemed a newly aggressive posture.

The spokesman for the admiral, Lieut. Comdr. Ryland Dodge, said the message was not meant as a signal that women would be targets of special enforcement. "I don't read it that way," he said. "But I can see how someone might."

The message ends with instructions to officers: "Demonstrate equality in the treatment of male and female homosexuals. The problem won't just go away, so we must deal with it sensibly, and fairly, with due regard for the privacy interests of all."

Sent Out in July

While the message was dated July 24, before the Iraqi invasion of Kuwait, many critics of the Pentagon policy said it was ironic that the Navy was investing time and energy in getting rid of talented, experienced sailors at a time of military buildup in the Persian Gulf.

"This says that the policy is more important than the mission, and that is heresy," said James W. Woodward, a former Navy officer who challenged his discharge for homosexuality all the way to the Supreme Court, which refused to hear the case last winter.

The Department of Defense policy, which has been upheld by the courts, states that "homosexuality is incompatible with military service," and that "separation is mandatory" if a member of the Armed Forces is found to be gay. According to Pentagon data, about 1,400 gay men and women are forcibly discharged each year, with lesbians let go at three times the rate of gay men.

The Pentagon directive says: "The presence of such members adversely affects the ability of the armed forces to maintain discipline, good order and morale; to foster mutual trust and confidence among service members; to insure the system of rank and command; to facilitate assignment and worldwide deployment of service members who frequently must live and work under close conditions affording minimum privacy; to recruit and retain members of the armed forces; to maintain the public acceptablity of military service; and to prevent breaches of security."

'Predator' Image Disputed

Pentagon spokesmen routinely decline to elaborate on the policy, and Lieut. Greg Smith, a Navy spokesman in Washington, said Friday that the directive spoke for itself. But Admiral Donnell, in his message, went beyond the directive, saying lesbians had an "adverse impact" on those "who must live and work in close proximity" to them. Specifically, the admiral warned of a "predator-type environment," in which "more senior and aggressive female sailors" exert "subtle coercion" or "outright sexual advances" on their "young, often vulnerable" female colleagues.

Gay rights advocates were angered at the description of lesbians as predators. "I liken that to the myth that male homosexuals are child molesters," said Sandra Lowe, a staff lawyer for the Lambda Legal Defense and Education Fund in New York.

Ms. Lowe said the admiral's characterization of lesbians as "aggressive" and "intimidating" was a subtle attack on all women in non-traditional jobs, homosexual or heterosexual. "There is a gender component to this," Ms. Lowe said. "Women are always suspect who are competent. They don't want any of us, and here is one group they can get rid of."

The admiral's message said, "There is a perception by many that female homosexuality is somewhat tolerated while male homosexuality is dealt with swiftly and sternly." But he cited Navy statistics, from 1985 to 1989, that he said showed lesbians were discharged at twice the rate of gay men.

Changing Times at Sea

Commander Dodge was asked why, given that rate of discharges, it was necessary to urge more scrupulous enforcement of the rules against lesbians. He said the reason was the increasing number of women in the Navy—about 6,000 of a total force of 600,000—and the fact that officers "maybe don't have as much experience with that side of the story."

* * *

September 1, 1991

GAY SOLDIERS, GOOD SOLDIERS

Do homosexual personnel, male and female, threaten the effectiveness of the armed forces? Or is it shortsighted prejudice for the military services to ban homosexuals and to discharge those discovered in its ranks?

That long-festering issue has emerged with new force in recent weeks, requiring Defense Secretary Cheney to explain anew to Congress and the public just why homosexuals are deemed "incompatible with military service."

Mr. Cheney showed little appetite for the task, with good reason. The ban deprives the armed forces of talent and the discharges damage thousands of careers and lives. All for a policy with not a shred of hard evidence to support it.

Much of the opposition to homosexuals reflects a deep-seated fear that gay personnel would make sexual advances on their heterosexual comrades, provoking fights or starting affairs that would destroy discipline. But that wrongly brands all homosexuals as sexual aggressors. The same specter of unrestrained sexuality was raised when women were first admitted to military service. Yet women have been successfully accommodated, and they performed valiantly in the Persian Gulf war.

The Defense Department is actually two-faced on the subject of homosexuality. Homosexuals are allowed to serve in civilian jobs, even at the highest and most sensitive levels, under civil service rules that outlaw sexual orientation as a criterion for employment. That is why Secretary Cheney has no trouble retaining a trusted aide who was identified as homosexual by a gay magazine.

But the department bans homosexuals from military service and has discharged more than 13,000 people as homosexuals since 1982. Many, sad to say, have been outstanding. Some have won bronze or silver stars. One was a naval cadet near the top of his class at Annapolis. Underscoring the absurdity of the

Public Approval Of Homosexuals In the Military

Percentage of Americans who believe that homosexuals should be allowed in the armed forces.

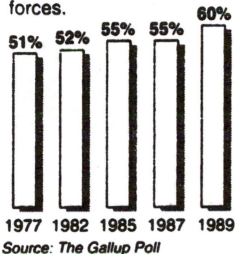

1977	1982	1985	1987	1989
51%	52%	55%	55%	60%

Source: The Gallup Poll

policy, the commander of the surface fleet in the Atlantic last year urged, in a message to his subordinates, that investigations of lesbians not be "pursued halfheartedly" just because lesbians are generally "hard-working, career-oriented, willing to put in long hours on the job and among the command's top performers."

The official justification for the ban is a single sweeping paragraph in the Defense Department's administrative discharge directive. It asserts, with dubious accuracy, that the presence of homosexuals "seriously impairs the accomplishment of the military mission" in seven areas, including morale and recruitment.

The Pentagon may be retreating from one claim—that homosexuals are a security risk, peculiarly subject to blackmail. Unpublished studies for the military in 1957 and 1988 concluded that homosexuals were a negligible security risk, and Secretary Cheney dismissed the allegation as "a bit of an old chestnut."

Other assertions that the presence of homosexuals makes it difficult to maintain morale and insure the integrity of the command system sound like worst-case projections based on outdated stereotypes. Polls show that most Americans think homosexuals should be allowed in the military.

The most emotional reason for excluding homosexuals is that service members, in contrast to civilians in the Defense Department, "frequently must live and work under close conditions affording minimal privacy." Perhaps some heterosexual servicemen fear they would be propositioned in the showers. But that possibility could be managed with regulations proscribing sexual harassment. And what consenting adults do on their own time is their business, not the military's.

The military and its civilian overseers need to reexamine the case; there's no evident justification for discrimination on the basis of sexual orientation.

* * *

October 3, 1991

SUNY'S GAY RIGHTS DILEMMA

The military's policy of barring gays and lesbians from active service puts college administrators in a tough spot. If they permit military recruiters on campus, as most do, they appear to encourage discrimination that has no evident benefit for national security. But if they bar military recruiters, they risk violating state and Federal laws. They could also lose scholarships and research funds if the Pentagon chose to sever ties.

The issue was raised sharply when New York State's Division of Human Rights ruled, in a case filed by a lesbian law student, that the State University's Buffalo campus must refrain from providing space or other help to military recruiters. Aiding the recruiters, the division said, violates Gov. Mario Cuomo's executive order that bars state agencies from discriminating against homosexuals in hiring or use of state resources.

The university will appeal. Its officials say they have no legal authority to ban recruiters and that a university should not bar a group simply because it finds its policies odious.

Governor Cuomo also challenges the ruling, saying his anti-discrimination order is superseded by a state law that requires state schools to provide access to military recruiters "on the same basis" as private employers. Yet that wording simply requires equal treatment of all employers.

Mr. Cuomo is on firmer legal ground in noting that recent decisions by the state's highest court, the Court of Appeals, raise serious doubts about his authority to impose the state's internal anti-discrimination rules on parties outside government.

Those people rightly troubled by discriminatory recruitment on campus would have a better chance to make their argument in a court case if the New York State Legislature would enact a law banning discrimination against homosexuals. But the Legislature continues to balk.

Some gay rights activists are outraged at Mr. Cuomo for serving up his negative legal analysis only hours after the ruling was issued, in an apparent rush for political damage control. But the real villains are the State Legislature and a military that refuses to shed its unjust and shortsighted opposition to homosexuals.

* * *

November 19, 1992

R.O.T.C. USES OATH ON HOMOSEXUALITY

By ERIC SCHMITT
Special to The New York Times

WASHINGTON, Nov. 18—The Naval Reserve Officers Training Corps is requiring all R.O.T.C. midshipmen to sign a new affidavit saying they can be discharged and forced to pay back their scholarship if they are found to be homosexual.

The military services and service academies have for years required their members to say whether they are homosexual and whether they had ever engaged in homosexual activity. But the new Navy policy seems to reinforce the policy and make it clear that it means to recoup education and training costs if an officer is discharged for homosexuality.

The timing of the new policy has prompted gay and lesbian advocates to accuse the Navy of a vindictive campaign against gay men and lesbians in the military in the waning days of the Bush Administration. Bill Clinton has promised to lift the 48-year-old ban on homosexuals in the military after he becomes President on Jan. 20.

"I consider this inquisitorial affidavit a totally unwarranted intrusion in the private lives of American citizens," Patricia Schroeder, Democrat of Colorado and a senior member of the House Armed Services Committee, said in a statement.

Ms. Schroeder sent a letter to Defense Secretary Dick Cheney on Tuesday protesting the affidavits and asked that the Pentagon suspend the requirements that R.O.T.C. students at colleges and universities sign the document. There are 7,109 midshipmen in training programs, according to the Navy. They are commissioned as active-duty and reserve officers.

Army and Air Force Policies

Other gay advocates said the policy represented an increase in efforts to enforce the recoupment policy. It costs an average of $52,967 to train a R.O.T.C. midshipman, the Navy said.

"I've never seen them be so specific about recoupment in terms of discharges for homosexuality," the director of the American Civil Liberties Union's National Lesbian and Gay Rights Project, William Rubenstein, said. "It's ironic they're seeking money from people who are willing to serve in the military."

A spokeswoman for the Navy, Lieut. Cate Mueller, said the affidavit was developed "as an effort to establish a method similar to ones already in use by the Army and the Air Force and to insure that R.O.T.C. students understand Department of Defense policy regarding homosexuality."

An Army and Air Force form has for many years required R.O.T.C. students to answer questions about homosexuality. The service academies use the same form.

Question No. 61 on the form, between queries about exposure to tuberculosis and venereal disease, reads, "Have you ever had or do you now have homosexual activity?"

Retreat by the Army

The services have threatened to force students discharged over homosexuality to pay back their scholarships. But legal experts said they believed that none of the services had recouped money.

One Army R.O.T.C. cadet at Washington University in St. Louis, James M. Holobaugh, was discharged in 1990, when the Army learned that he was homosexual. Shortly after the discharge the Army sent him a bill for his $25,000 scholarship. Mr. Holobaugh enlisted the help of the A.C.L.U., which told the Army that he would serve his military obligation or the Army would forfeit the money. After about six months the Army backed down.

Navy planners proposed the language for the affidavit in February, and the Chief of Naval Operations, Adm. Frank B. Kelso 2d, approved it in June. R.O.T.C. units began requiring all midshipmen to sign it when they returned for the fall semester this year.

The affidavits drew attention after The Cornell Daily Sun, the Cornell University student newspaper, published an article on Nov. 13 about student protests over the affidavit. A lawyer contacted the A.C.L.U. about the affidavit, and an R.O.T.C. midshipman at Cornell contacted Ms. Schroeder's office here.

'More of a Change in Style'

The commander of the Navy R.O.T.C. at Cornell, Capt. Gerald Corcoran, said the affidavit represented "more of a change in style than in substance" from what students had been required to sign before.

"The timing of all this, admittedly, is absolutely horrible," Captain Corcoran said in a telephone interview. "But we're not out to change people's attitudes or opinions on this."

Captain Corcoran said a few of the 104 midshipmen at Cornell had objected to the affidavit and had been allowed to insert the phrase, "according to the Department of Defense's policy," in describing how homosexuality is incompatible with military service.

"It's a travesty," Joseph L. Barrios, the representative of lesbian, gay and bisexual interests representative to the Cornell Student Assembly, told The Daily Sun. "The affidavits reflect a lot of ignorance on the part of the Navy. They are insensitive, ignorant and unaware of the harm in expelling qualified people on the basis of their sexual orientation."

* * *

December 1, 1992

MILITARY'S GAY SUBCULTURE: OFF LIMITS BUT FLOURISHING

By ERIC SCHMITT
Special to The New York Times

JACKSONVILLE, N.C.—Every Friday and Saturday night, scores of off-duty marines flock to a small bar here to shoot a game of pool, cure a bout of loneliness or dance until the wee hours.

Randy Davey for The New York Times

An off-duty marine playing pool at Friends Lounge, a gay bar that Camp Lejeune, the largest Marine Corps base on the East Coast, has declared off limits to the installation's 43,000 marines and sailors.

By the book, they are risking stiff fines or even jail time, since Camp Lejeune, the largest Marine Corps base on the East Coast, has declared the bar, Friends Lounge, off limits to the installation's 43,000 marines and sailors. It is a gay bar and conflicts with the military's ban on homosexual behavior.

But for many of the gay marines here who keep their sexual orientation secret, Friends Lounge is one of the few public places in this conservative military town where homosexuals—once they are safely past the locked front door and inside—can temporarily set aside their fears of being discovered and drummed out of the Marine Corps they proudly serve.

Adapting to the Forbidden

"Straight people know this as a place that's off limits, but for gays it's a safe haven," said Alan D., a 23-year-old lance corporal who, like all the homosexuals on active duty interviewed for this article, spoke only on the condition that his full name not be published.

The bar at Camp Lejeune, and the many others like it, demonstrate that there is a flourishing gay subculture in the military, despite the official ban on homosexuals in uniform. It underscores the way the military has already adapted to something its leaders say is impossible even to contemplate.

Senior military leaders, arguing that it would lead to severe morale problems and weaken combat effectiveness, loudly protested when President-elect Bill Clinton said he would lift the ban on homosexuals. They said heterosexual soldiers, sailors and marines cannot coexist with gay ones.

But at Camp Lejeune and many other military bases, they already coexist. Individual base commanders vary widely in how strictly they enforce the ban on the thousands of gay men and lesbians in the services, particularly when it involves gay bars and organizations that are situated off base.

The commanders of Camp Lejeune are clearly aware of the bar's existence but have not done anything to shut it down or round up its patrons for years. "We don't sit and stake out these places and harass people," said Maj. Jay Farrar, a camp spokesman.

This does not mean that being a gay marine at Camp Lejeune is entirely without risk. Gay marines here must still keep their sexual orientation officially secret, since if they are exposed, they face discharge under the Marine Corps rules.

Because the rules against homosexuals are still in force, gay service members say they are forced to live a stealthy life style. And in an effort to help them deal with the hostility they face, an underground network of gay military groups, as well as a string of bars and clubs, has sprung up to lend support and provide contacts to homosexuals at bases around the country.

The network has evolved in a variety of ways, from exchanging telephone numbers on computer bulletin boards to working together at AIDS-prevention clinics. A few years ago, 20 junior Navy officers formed the San Diego Gay Naval Officers Association, an informal social club. A West Point graduate in Falls Church, Va., Michael W. Gary, recently started an association of gay alumni from the service academy.

Big-City Advantages

In large metropolitan areas, like Washington or Atlanta, gay soldiers say it is easier to blend in and tap gay civilian advocacy and support groups. The majority of the 125 members of American Legion Post 448 in San Francisco, for example, are homosexual and helped support Petty Officer Keith Meinhold of the Navy when he declared his homosexuality on national television earlier this year.

But many installations, particularly Army bases, are in small, rural towns hours from a big city. In these cases, gay soldiers say that dinner parties at friends' houses become the center of their social lives, with occasional trips out of town to clubs where they will not be recognized.

Even in larger cities, gay soldiers must be extremely discreet. "When I was at Fort Bliss in El Paso, I drove six hours to a gay bar in Tucson because I was so paranoid of being seen in town," said Mr. Gary, 29, who served five years in the Army.

Loneliness can be a constant companion for young service members struggling to come to terms with their sexual identity. Tim Rump, a 26-year-old former Air Force radio-intercept analyst, was stationed at Wheeler Air Force Base in Hawaii for three years. Mr. Rump said that when he joined the service he was not sure if he was gay and felt isolated.

"While I associated with people in the office, I was very secretive about what was going on in my own life and didn't make that many close friends," said Mr. Rump, who was discharged from the Air Force when an acquaintance turned him in.

Other gay soldiers and sailors say that tight-knit circles of friends reach out when a member transfers to a new base.

"When I went to San Diego from Norfolk, my friends here called their friends there, and I had a ready-made network when I arrived," said a 34-year-old Navy lieutenant commander who is now in the Washington area.

Aid From National Groups

In addition, an array of large national organizations, from the American Civil Liberties Union to the Lambda Legal Defense and Education Fund, offer advice and legal counseling to gay members of the military who are threatened with being discharged for homosexuality.

"Don't tattle," advises one pamphlet distributed by the Gay and Lesbian Military Freedom Project, an umbrella group of gay rights organizations. "Giving names may actually make things worse for you. Investigators may try to bluff you into thinking that giving names will help you, when in truth, they may have nothing against you unless you give names."

Other groups, like the Gay/Lesbian/Bisexual Veterans of America, which has 30 chapters around the country, lobby to change national and state laws to gain more rights for homosexuals.

Here in Jacksonville, gay men and lesbians say there are several small groups of gay enlisted personnel and officers. Military regulations prohibit fraternization between enlisted personnel and officers, whether they are homosexual or heterosexual.

'We're All a Family'

One social group of about 30 gay marines and civilians, called Oasis, serves as a social anchor and a fund-raising organization for some of the area's gay men. New members are closely screened to prevent military investigators posing as gay service members from infiltrating the group. "There's a camaraderie here," said one 30-year-old sergeant who belongs to Oasis. "It's like we're all a family, and we can understand what each other is going through."

Three miles from Camp Lejeune's main gate, Friends Lounge is another social hub for many gay marines. A single-story, white cinder block building emblazoned with a pink triangle and Lambda symbol, both signs of gay pride, the bar is set back from the main road, just behind a service station.

Patrons are checked before a locked door is opened. Inside, Friends Lounge looks like your average bar: two pool tables, a long wooden bar and bar stools, several tables and a dance floor. By 1:30 A.M., the music is rocking, and male and female couples are dancing, embracing or sharing a drink at the bar.

"People come here to meet the crowd," said Gary Hendricks, 25, a homosexual who left the Marine Corps in August 1991 after six years. "if it weren't for this bar, it'd be hard for other gays to know who the community is."

Unofficial Toleration

In the mid-1980's, military investigators and the sheriff would park across from the bar and pull people over when they left, said Danny Leonard, 47, the bar's owner for 10 years.

But he said that since then, as long as Friends Lounge kept a low profile, the Marine Corps has unofficially tolerated its existence and not prosecuted the bar's military clientele.

Mr. Leonard, who does a female impersonator act on Friday nights, said that for the last four years neither the police nor the Marine authorities had bothered him or his patrons. "They can be themselves here and then go back to the base

and do their jobs," said Mr. Leonard, who added that 70 percent of his 200 patrons on weekends are in the military.

Still, many homosexuals said that frequenting gay bars was too risky. Tanya Domi, a former Army captain who is a lesbian, said: "Enlisted personnel may go to bars, but it's really dangerous for officers. What if a subordinate sees you there?"

Bar Visit Brings Allegations

A 29-year-old staff sergeant at Fort Meade, Md., recalled being summoned by Army criminal investigators after he visited a bar in Texas that was popular with homosexuals as well as heterosexuals. The investigators had apparently jotted down his license plate while cruising the club's parking lot.

"They dumped it on me that I was a homosexual, they had witnesses, and that I should sign a paper saying so," said the sergeant. "I was so scared, I was almost sick. They treated me like I was a criminal, but presented no evidence. It was guilt by association."

The sergeant said he refused to sign the document, and the investigators dropped the allegations.

At the Oar House, a gay bar two miles from the Norfolk Navy base in Virginia, the bar's president, Frank Belcher, said surprise visits by the Naval Investigative Service ended seven years ago.

"Usually we had a call from the base telling us they were coming," said Mr. Belcher. "Homosexuals are everywhere in the military."

* * *

December 8, 1992

SUPREME COURT ROUNDUP

Homosexuals in the Military

By LINDA GREENHOUSE
Special to The New York Times

In another action today, the Court refused to hear a Bush Administration appeal from a lower court ruling that rejected the military's rationale for its exclusion of homosexuals.

As a result, the military will now have to choose a new defense to a lawsuit brought by a woman who was denied a promotion to major and then dismissed from the Army Reserve after the Army learned that she is a lesbian. The woman, Carolyn D. Pruitt, had revealed her homosexuality in a newspaper interview.

Ms. Pruitt's constitutional challenge to the military's policy was dismissed by a Federal District Judge in California, but was reinstated last year by the United States Court of Appeals for the Ninth Circuit, in San Francisco.

The appeals court said Ms. Pruitt was entitled to go forward with her contention that the policy violated the constitutional guarantee of equal protection of the laws. In sending the case back to the District Court for further hearings, the appeals court said the Defense Department would not be permitted to defend the policy on the ground the presence of homosexuals in the military would create tension and hostility. The "prejudice of others against homosexuals" was not a valid justification for the military's policy, the appeals court said.

In its Supreme Court appeal, Cheney v. Pruitt, No. 92-389, the Administration said the appeals court should have deferred to the military rather than "second-guess the judgment of military officials as to what categories of persons should be barred from military service in order to promote an effective and disciplined fighting force."

* * *

January 31, 1993

HOMOSEXUALS WAKE TO SEE A REFERENDUM: IT'S ON THEM

By JEFFREY SCHMALZ

So jubilant were gay and lesbian Americans on election night that many actually danced in the streets, celebrating the victory of Bill Clinton and the beginning of a new era that would, at last, accept them as part of the nation's family.

Last week, not even three months after that euphoric night and just days after gay celebrations at the Clinton inaugural, reality hit home. President Clinton's plan to end the ban on homosexuals in the military ran into a firestorm of protest from the military, from Democrats and Republicans alike in Congress and, most important, from the American people. Mr. Clinton was forced to retreat, putting off for at least six months an executive order to lift the ban.

Almost lost in the nitty-gritty of the battle over the military was the larger issue: The gay struggle for individual rights is running head-on into America's deep ambivalence about homosexuality.

The dispute over gay men and lesbians in the military reflects a kind of continuing national referendum on homosexual rights, revealing just how tenuous support can be despite big political and social advances and polls showing that a majority of Americans oppose job discrimination against homosexuals. It is being played out over and over: In Colorado, in efforts to overturn a statewide referendum barring local gay-rights measures. In New York, in a battle over the "rainbow curriculum," which encourages tolerance toward homosexuals.

"I thought all along that the Willie Horton issue of the campaign would be gays and Clinton's support of gay rights," said William Schneider, a political analyst with the American Enterprise Institute. "Well, instead of happening in the campaign, it has come true now."

The outcry over the President's military proposal stunned gay-rights leaders, who had expected opposition but nothing like this. After being blinded by their vision of Mr. Clinton as the white knight, they realized that having the President on their side was not enough.

Without question, the religious right, still stinging from the defeat of George Bush and its losses on abortion, fueled

Mustered Out	
People removed from active duty in fiscal year 1992 because they were gay.	
Per 10,000 troops	
Total armed forces	3.9
Navy	7.4
Marines	3.1
Air Force	2.4
Army	2.3
All women	8.1
All men	3.4
Enlisted people	4.6
Officers	0.3
Source: Defense Department	

The New York Times / Agence France Presse

Senators Sam Nunn, right, and George J. Mitchell, the majority leader, discussing President Clinton's decision on homosexuals in the military.

the furor, flooding call-in shows and Congressional phone lines with vehement opposition to the Clinton plan.

'A Groundswell of Feelings'

But members of Congress said they were hearing from average citizens, too. The office of Senator John Glenn, Democrat of Ohio, said calls early in the week were running 10 to 1 against lifting the ban. By Friday, after gay groups began to muster their phone banks, the ratio had dropped, but it was still 4 to 1.

Representative Jim Leach, an Iowa Republican, said: "The majority of the Christian right may have a particular perspective, but the debate appears to have tapped a groundswell of feelings in Americans of all walks of life."

As is often the case with gay rights, it became clear that even middle-of-the-road Americans who said they opposed discrimination were still uncomfortable with homosexuality. "I'm sorry," a caller said apologetically last week to a Detroit radio station. "I don't think I'm a bigot. We shouldn't deny them their rights. But I think gay people want society to say they're normal and it just isn't so."

Gay and lesbian Americans reacted with anger, hurt and even fear. Many questioned Mr. Clinton's allowing the issue to become a confrontation so quickly. But in random conversations with almost two dozen homosexuals, all were in favor of pressing the fight. And though a bit rattled, all took some pride in the events of the last week: Their issues, all but unmentionable not so long ago, were on the national stage, and championed by the President himself.

'My People' on Page One

"I fault Clinton's timing, but I feel close to him," said Bill Goldstein, a 32-year-old editor at a Manhattan publishing house. "When I read the newspaper in the morning, I can't believe that my people are on the front page. I can't help thinking, 'Damn it, we're not going to let them stop thinking about us.'"

But there was also hurt and rage, emotions expressed by David Goodhand, 29-year-old computer software designer in Seattle. "Now every gay man, every gay woman in America knows where we stand. They hate us," he said. "It's like being a black and hearing the Government debate pro-slavery."

Lynn Greer, 35, a property manager in Columbus, Ohio, put it this way: "I'm a little sad. We've gone from euphoria and feeling like part of the process to finding we're not at the table. Now we have to start again with our neighbors, one by one."

Gay groups were ecstatic with the 1992 campaign, in part because Republicans backed off the gay-bashing comments prominent at the party's Houston convention in August. But as a result, gay issues never got an airing in the campaign.

Political strategists say President Bush had to back off because mainstream Americans perceived the religious right as running away with the party. Gay rights, like abortion and single parents, became a topic to be avoided. And with the issue not engaged, Mr. Clinton seemed to get a false sense of confidence.

"Americans don't want to glorify minorities, but they don't want to persecute them, either," said Mr. Schneider. "The Republicans, at the convention, crossed into persecuting gays. Now, people seem to feel Clinton has crossed into glorifying them."

What made matters worse, analysts agree, was that the American armed forces were involved. The dispute had the effect of pitting the gay agenda of social change against favorable feelings about the military, perceived by many Americans as one part of the Government that works. Pentagon officials said the presence of open homosexuality would undermine cohesion in the ranks.

"I think the election created a false security," said Representative Barney Frank, a Massachusetts Democrat and one of two openly gay members of Congress. "Sometimes winning can be bad for you."

National gay-rights groups in Washington, already stretched thin by the fight on AIDS, seem overwhelmed and confused. Preoccupied with preventing passage of an anti-gay measure last year in Oregon, they didn't concentrate enough effort in Colorado, and the measure there passed.

It is because of the groundwork done by the national organizations that the issue of homosexuals in the military advanced at all. Now, however, the groups are being criticized for not lobbying quickly and thoroughly enough: They let the Pentagon run away with the issue as a military one. They failed to drive home the message that it was a civil-rights fight. And they failed to muster strong support from natural allies, like those in the pro-choice movement.

"We have lost much of our experience and leadership through AIDS and movement burnout," said Thomas B. Stoddard, a gay-rights lawyer. "There's no reservoir of experienced leadership. All of our national organizations are weak and bereft of people with substantial experience."

Meanwhile, one of the biggest fights ever is looming.

"There's no going back," said David B. Mixner, a gay corporate consultant in Los Angeles who advises the White House on gay issues. "This isn't about just the military. This is about homophobia in America. It's the beginning of a two-year, a three-year fight in 11 states or more and in school-board rooms around the country."

The Rev. Lou Sheldon, national chairman of the Traditional Values Coalition, representing 25,000 churches, agreed. "Lifting of the ban is just the tip of the iceberg of the homosexual agenda. We are in the research stage on how to proceed, to find what people are thinking, to find out what will fly."

* * *

February 1, 1993

TRUMAN'S LEGACY TO CLINTON

By LUCIAN K. TRUSCOTT IV

LOS ANGELES—Isn't it paradoxical that on the day President Clinton and Vice President Al Gore attended the funeral service for Thurgood Marshall, Mr. Clinton found himself in the situation Harry S. Truman occupied in 1948 in the months leading up to his executive order integrating the military?

I grew up in the integrated Army. One day, schools, housing—the Army itself—were segregated; the next day they weren't. Six years would pass before Thurgood Marshall successfully argued Brown v. Board of Education before the Supreme Court. Ten more years would be wasted before Congress found the courage to pass the Civil Rights Act of 1964.

But in July 1948, the courage of one man, Truman, ended the decades of dishonor represented by a segregated military in a democratic society. That February, he announced that he had ordered the Secretary of Defense to eliminate discrimination in the armed forces as soon as possible. A storm of protest, especially from Southern Congressmen, ensued: There would be a potential for violence. Whites didn't want to live in the same barracks with blacks.

The day after Truman issued his order, Gen. Omar N. Bradley, the Army Chief of Staff, reportedly said: "The Army is not out to make any social reform. The Army will not put men of different races in the same companies. It will change that policy when the nation as a whole changes it." That rebellion went nowhere.

Others raised questions: Would a white take orders from a black sergeant or lieutenant? What about bathroom facilities? Would—gasp!—whites and blacks share toilets, showers and sinks? What about the feelings of white families who might not want their boys living with blacks? Wouldn't this hurt the retention of soldiers and damage recruitment?

Oh, it was admitted that black units had served with distinction in World War II and before. So long as the black units remained separate but equal, things would be fine, it was said. It was the mixing that would damage the Army: blacks serving side by side with whites would be detrimental to good order and discipline, and destructive of morale.

Substitute "gays" for "blacks," and you've pretty much got the situation facing President Clinton. The same chorus of protest, resistance to change, fear of the unknown.

The idea of segregating gay soldiers in barracks and combat, now under study in the Pentagon, is as anathema as segregating black soldiers. Whether in the military or in schools, separate but equal is inherently unequal.

Reading the reactions of senior military officials, especially that of Gen. Colin L. Powell, Chairman of the Joint Chiefs of Staff, you would think time had stopped, that Truman's courageous stand never happened.

Opponents of gays in the military say smugly that these two things are not analogous, because integration of the military dealt with skin color, and allowing gays in deals with a "life-style choice." Specious hogwash! Discrimination and segregation based on sexual preference are as unacceptable and plain stupid as the treatment of blacks before Truman.

It may take Congress, the national headquarters of risk aversion, years to pass the gay rights equivalent of the Civil Rights Act of 1964. But the principle is the very one Truman faced, and Bill Clinton knows this.

"The issue is whether men and women who can and have served with real distinction should be excluded from military service solely on the basis of their status, and I believe they should not," Mr. Clinton said Friday when he announced the July 15 deadline to draft an order allowing gays to serve in the military.

He will face stiff Capitol Hill opposition. Congressmen who make antebellum noises about this issue should be ashamed, and Mr. Clinton should tell them so. But integration will happen, perhaps beginning in July. Straight soldiers will learn to serve next to, catnap with, sleep near and use the same restrooms as gay soldiers. Officers who resist carrying out the order should be fired.

The equality Truman ordered was inevitable; so is the equality Bill Clinton wants for gay soldiers, sailors, airmen and women.

As my father told me, it doesn't matter what color they are, what sex they are or what their sexual preference is. The only thing that counts is whether or not they can soldier.

Lucian K. Truscott IV, a West Point graduate, is author of "Dress Gray." His two grandfathers (a four-star general and a colonel) and father (a colonel) were career soldiers.

* * *

April 11, 1993

PUBLIC STAGES; MEN IN UNIFORM

By FRANK RICH

There is no solid proof for the transvestism charges leveled against J. Edgar Hoover in Anthony Summers's best seller, "Official and Confidential." But we can dream, can't we?

For connoisseurs of hypocrisy, it is hard to beat the spectacle of our No. 1 G-man—the puritanical, blackmailing spy on the sex lives of Martin Luther King and the Kennedys, the malicious persecutor of "sex deviates" and any other nonconformists he deemed subversive—getting all dolled up in outfits reminiscent of Marie Dressler in "Dinner at Eight."

But if Hoover the cross-dresser is just too deliciously ironic to be true, Hoover the presumed homosexual is not. If anything, Summers would have written a far more shocking book had he endeavored to prove that his subject was a flaming heterosexual. Even in Hoover's lifetime there were few Americans, or worldly ones anyway, who failed to recognize the F.B.I. Director's 42-year-long constant companionship with Clyde Tolson for what it was, even without knowledge of the racy photographs that Summers says someone says he once saw.

Whatever sexual activities did or did not accompany Hoover and Tolson's relationship, the sad part was not their intimate bond, which seems their one source of joy, but the ferocity with which the F.B.I. Director punished those who might whisper about it. Like his friend and red-baiting acolyte, Roy Cohn, who was still camouflaging his widely known homosexuality when he died of AIDS, Hoover overcompensated for his secret by hounding any prominent liberal homosexuals in sight. Both men, such terrifying icons in life, stand revealed in death as cliched examples of how homophobia can start the moment men frightened of their own sexuality refuse to face themselves in the mirror.

The denial of homosexuality is malignant whether it festers in individuals, especially those with Cohn or Hoover's power to punish others, or in the country as a whole. Such denial is at the heart of the firestorm that ambushes President Clinton's halting efforts to lift the ban on homosexuals in the military: there is still a deeply ingrained American inclination to will homosexuality out of sight and mind. ("We don't ask any questions, and you don't give any answers" is the policy Senator Sam Nunn proposed as he held hearings on the issue.) No one even argues anymore that the ban has kept, or will ever keep, homosexuals out of the service. The ban fans are reduced to arguing instead that gay soldiers must keep lying about who they are—at least until they reach the gay bar just beyond the base's gates—lest an open admission of their sexuality prompts them to pounce willy-nilly and, lesbians excepted, to dress up in one of the cunning little cocktail ensembles supposedly favored by J. Edgar.

Besides denying gay service men and women their dignity and civil rights and encouraging hate crimes, this ban that is not really a ban asks us to fund a farcical fantasyland where gay soldiers must pretend to be straight and straight soldiers must pretend to be idiots, blind to eternal human differences. Should the President's instantly punctured trial balloon of a sexually segregated armed forces somehow be realized, the farce would continue in the "heterosexual" barracks. Who in America believes that any workplace is exclusively heterosexual? Only those who believe that Hoover really did carry a torch for Ginger Rogers's mother.

Anyone looking for some welcome comic relief during the bitter gays-in-the-military debate can find it on television newscasts. Every mention of the controversy requires a ritualistic airing of the same two pieces of stock footage. First there is the tape of transvestites bumping and grinding in a gay rights parade in San Francisco. This tape, we're told, is being soberly examined by grown men in the Pentagon as evidence of the nightmare in store for an out-of-the-closet military. Should this ludicrous specimen of military intelligence typify that which the Pentagon is receiving about genuine menaces like Iraq, our security is in greater jeopardy than we thought.

Then there is that ubiquitous, grainy film of naked soldiers filing into a shower to show just how vulnerable American heterosexual boys are to homosexual attack. Exactly what is this "Privates on Parade" about? It has no informational value whatsoever—we do know what showers and male backsides look like—but it could pass for soft-core gay porn. Am I imagining that the local anchor is smirking salaciously when he introduces this footage? And if so, who is getting the last laugh: homophobes who think the film is about the sanctity of heterosexuality or gay men who think the film smuggles gay eroticism into the straight American bloodstream?

Either way, this march of buttocks is the silliest example yet of how disingenuousness can become a cultural art form in a society in which otherwise rational adults insist on denying the sexual facts of life. It's the New Camp—a witless degeneration of the old—and even PBS is subscribing to it. When "Frontline" aired a sober documentary using Summers's findings, it lavished homophobic attention on the "special shade of pink" applied to the roses on the wallpaper in Hoover's home, but then illustrated spoken testimony about Hoover and Cohn's supposed orgies in the Plaza Hotel with a homoerotically titillating visual tour of an empty hotel room, complete with Champagne bucket and frilly double bed, all bathed in pink light.

Aside from taking a tour of what a New Yorker cartoonist recently relabeled the "Jaye Edgar Hoover Building," my only brush with the F.B.I. occurred when, as a novice journalist just out of college, I had published a magazine profile of Daniel Ellsberg, of the Pentagon Papers case. Tracked down in London, I soon found myself in a back room in the American Embassy, where I refused on legal grounds to answer some innocuous questions from a pair of agents in crew cuts and white wash-and-wear short-sleeve shirts.

What I remember most about this brief encounter is the office's alien decor—no pink wallpaper but many glowering portraits of the Director's bulldog face and an arsenal of mounted guns. At the time, this shrine to F.B.I. machismo was intimidating, as was intended, but in retrospect it seems a crude parody of heterosexual posturing. The American denial of homosexuality not only oppresses homosexuals, after all, but heterosexuals, who are presented with unattainable straight role models whose inflated bluster may be less an expression of masculinity than a repression of sexual ambivalence.

Is it too much to hope that the military will rethink its obsolete code before some general is found trying to squeeze into a size 14 at Saks?

* * *

April 18, 1993

THE ODD PLACE OF HOMOSEXUALITY IN THE MILITARY

By CATHERINE S. MANEGOLD

Until 1942, no specific proviso barred homosexuals from serving in the military. That year, military psychiatrists, new to the ranks, warned of the "psychopathic personality disorders" that would make homosexuals unfit to fight. Then they devised supposedly foolproof guides to ferret them out: an effeminate flip of hand or a certain nervousness when standing naked before an officer.

It never really worked. Homosexuals served throughout World War II and after. In the repressive atmosphere of the 1950's, discharges for homosexuality soared; at the height of the Vietnam War, when recruitment drives were at their peak, enforcement was lax.

That military tradition of keeping out homosexuals could end on July 15, when President Clinton has said he will lift the ban. Pentagon officials, who had been notably recalcitrant in cooperating with the plan, said last week that they are rushing through several studies to address key matters like housing.

As things have stood, homosexuals could serve so long as they could hide. In the 1940's, if something untoward occurred, it was ascribed to "emergency" or "deprivation" homosexuality, according to John Costello in "Virtue Under Fire," a 1985 study of changing sexual mores brought about by World War II. Homosexual interludes were discounted as sparked by frustration. The armed forces thus maintained the facade of sexual purity (read: heterosexuality).

With President Clinton's announcement in January that the ban on homosexuals in the military would be lifted, a military tradition became harder to keep. Gay advocacy groups like the Campaign for Military Service saw the issue rapidly expand into a national debate on the worthiness of homosexuals. They have spent millions of dollars on a neatly packaged, well-advertised battle, underscored by a march on Washington next Sunday, to win inclusion in the ranks as blacks and women did before them.

Polls show that the nation remains divided, working its way through a subject as fiery as abortion yet imbued with more primal fears and deep social and religious constraints. The result has often been the rhetorical equivalent to the fog of battle, a fog in which women have been peculiarly absent, the ghosts of the debate.

Sex and Puritanical Roots

The argument has many voices. Some say it's a question of civil rights. Others say combat effectiveness. Or fear. Or homophobia and a surge in gay bashing that would devastate unit cohesiveness. Perhaps it is really about control and what would happen to one of the last bastions of American traditionalism if its defining social order were tampered with.

The argument is also, inevitably, about sex. That may be why keeping the subject hidden has always had a certain intrinsic appeal in a country with puritanical roots.

Military leaders who reject the civil rights analogy say the controversy is not about sex or even equal rights, but the agenda of a special interest group. They fear that complying with President Clinton's orders would set a precedent, inviting demands for inclusion by everyone from the mentally handicapped to other sexual minorities like transsexuals. They also argue that it is a privilege to serve in the fighting forces, not a right. "It's a nightmare as far as the military is concerned," said Bernard E. Trainor, a retired Marine lieutenant general. "It threatens the strong, conservative, moralistic tradition of the troops."

Not everyone in the military agrees. Adm. William J. Crowe Jr., a former Chairman of the Joint Chiefs of Staff, told The Washington Post recently that the argument was fueled "more by emotion than by reason." He said that the armed forces' culture of strict discipline is, in fact, uniquely suited to control the behavior of both homosexuals and the heterosexuals who might bash them—more so than civilian society.

Randy Shilts, the author of "Conduct Unbecoming," a new history of homosexuality in the military, points to the armed forces' policies on AIDS to illustrate how well the four services can cope with thorny problems when they must. "The armed forces has some of the most enlightened policies on H.I.V. in the country," he said. Discounting fears that wounded AIDS-infected soldiers might bleed on their buddies, he cited as an example the fact that regulations already prevent those soldiers from going into combat.

But even if the military can manage the transition, that does not necessarily mean the controversy will fade. There is a deeper source of discontent: "They want us to move faster than the country," said a former general who did not wish to be identified. Sodomy laws based on religious proscriptions against sex for sex's sake are still on the books in 24 states. The District of Columbia recently moved to drop its sodomy law, but Congress, which has final say, blocked a similar attempt in 1981.

The Supreme Court, too, was disinclined to undo a taboo that it says dates to biblical times. In its 1986 decision Bowers v. Hardwick, the Court upheld Georgia's sodomy law.

So for months now, Americans have been watching ominous shower shots on the nightly news and wrestling with their fears. Women soldiers have voiced support for the policy change and do not express the fear of being attacked by same-sex predators that preoccupies some men. Many of their male comrades, some of whom still believe that women are ancillary to the fighting troops, have made macho threats about just what they would do if they found a gay man in their midst.

Another widespread objection is that it would feminize a male club. Enduring images of homosexual men depict them as effeminate, therefore weak, therefore a drain upon a mighty fighting force. Yet that ignores the role of a dominant participant in homosexual sex, a partner who takes the aggressive "male" role. The argument also raises the question whether anything could have feminized the force more than women. And women are already there.

Yet some soldiers are so perturbed by the prospect of including gay men in the ranks that they are willing to break the rules by assaulting fellow soldiers. Their explanation is that they fear attack or unwanted sexual advances—sexual harassment—as if they really don't believe that no means no. It is likely, too, that some fear their own reactions and the prospect that they might respond sexually. "Hatred of gay men," Ken Corbett, a psychologist, wrote in an Op-Ed article for The New York Times in February, "is based on fear of the self, not of an alien other." For decades, psychologists have said that at the core of homophobia is repressed fear and latent homosexuality.

Psychologists point to a rich history of songs, drag shows and jokes in the military that serve to neutralize powerful feelings. As early as 1941, the psychiatrist William Menninger described the typical soldier's wartime relationship as one of "disguised and sublimated homosexuality," a theme given voice in the popular war song, "My Buddy": "I miss your voice and the touch of your hand, my buddy."

That intense companionships were both so common and so acceptable in pop culture must have alleviated some soldiers' fears about unexpected longings. With those fears neutralized and the relationships the cause of celebration, the military became a safe place for the emotional intimacy so compelling to men and women facing the chaos and terror of war.

Seen from a distance, the logic of the military's denial of homosexuality in the ranks was simple: as long as no homosexuals were enlisted, soldiers could play at being lovers (and even consummate the roles) without ever having to acknowledge those feelings. Whatever happened, happened. There was a war on.

The implied double standard was made official in 1982. The Department of Defense regulations adopted that year allow a heterosexual to have homosexual sex and to be exonerated—so long as he or she states that the incident was a lapse. Gay and lesbian soldiers, by contrast, are discharged just for identifying themselves as such.

Women More Vulnerable

Col. Margarethe Cammermeyer, a much-decorated nurse in the Army National Guard who was discharged last May for her sexual orientation, says the ban has left women particularly vulnerable. "There is a tremendous amount of lesbian-baiting in the service," she said. "Any straight man who propositions a woman and she's not interested, well, it can't be because he's not attractive. So it must be because she's a lesbian. It's used as a threat all the time."

Because homosexuals now have to hide, anyone in the armed forces, she says, can sabotage the career of another by making allegations about their sexuality. If homosexuals were allowed to be open, that disruption would disappear. Though men are equally susceptible to such accusations, they are less likely than women to be dismissed because of their orientation. Lesbians are discharged at a rate from two to six times higher than gay men, depending on the branch of the service.

Several books, but most notably Allan Berube's "Coming Out Under Fire," trace the start of a gay rights movement in America to the military itself. They argue that the relative openness of gay and lesbian relationships in the military in World War II eventually led to those veterans settling in port cities like San Francisco and New York where, for the first time, they established identifiable subcultures.

Depending on its own convenience, the military operated with a double standard: while there were purges and discharges during that war, scores of written accounts show an easy acceptance among the Allied forces (German S.S. officers, in contrast, faced death by firing squad). Women in particular were likely to escape punishment. The Women's Army Corps actually dealt with lesbianism as a normal part of life. "A lecture to WAC officer candidates on homosexuality, prepared by the Surgeon General's Office and revised by WAC officials," wrote Mr. Berube, included the observation that "every person is born with a bisexual nature." In that corps, discharge was used only as a last resort in cases that disrupted a unit.

Men, too, often seemed to accept their gay comrades. Ben Small, a gay Army Air Corpsman stationed near New Guinea, once wrote away for a pile of dresses for a drag show. When the dresses arrived, he recounted in Mr. Berube's study, "Well, here's everybody in the office from the lieutenant on down trying on dresses! Everybody suddenly becomes a drag queen!"

Such tolerance would not last through the cold war. By the 1950's, Senator Joseph McCarthy was well into a civilian witch hunt that would quickly bleach the military's ranks as well. At the time, Senator McCarthy's right-hand man, Roy Cohn, and J. Edgar Hoover of the Federal Bureau of Investigation, both closeted themselves, presented the argument that homosexuals were the agents of communism. "One homosexual can pollute a Government office," concluded a report authorized by the Senate in 1950. Military discharges based on sexual orientation doubled in the 1950's and then increased by half again in the 1960's.

When recruitment demands were high during the Vietnam War, the situation loosened. Cal Anderson, an Army court reporter who would later join the Washington State Assembly, recalled in "My Country, My Right to Serve," that he was once caught in the act. The commander's reprimand was short and mild: "Now, I don't care what people do in their own time," he told the terrified young soldier. "But the Army doesn't feel that way, so in the future, be more discreet."

Klinger in Drag

By 1972, the popular television show "M*A*S*H" featured a soldier who almost always appeared in drag: Corporal Klinger, played by Jamie Farr. Though the show stopped short of explicitly dealing with his sexuality—always leaving open the question that he was merely trying to get a discharge—the character became one of the most beloved in the series.

Today, many senior officers see the issue in a long historical perspective. Steeped in military lore that traces homo-

sexuality to pre-Christian history, they point to tales of homosexuality on the front lines from the Sacred Band of Thebes in 338 B.C. (where each soldier was said to be a lover of another) to such military giants as Alexander the Great, Richard the Lion-Hearted and T. E. Lawrence (popularly known as Lawrence of Arabia). Seen in that context, said a retired general, the issue becomes more a matter of management than revolution.

In an open letter to his soldiers printed in the Marine magazine "Leatherneck" last month, Gen. Carl E. Mundy Jr., the Marine Corps Commandant, advised: "We are made up not of individuals who seek self-identity, but of selfless men and women who place country and corps ahead of self . . . whatever their privately held preferences or belief may be." He urged tolerance: "We treat all marines with firmness, fairness and dignity."

Those comments were supportive, but typically oblique. General Trainor, who now directs the national security program at Harvard's Kennedy School of Government, may have encapsulated the military's gut reaction best. Given half a choice, he said, the military would have looked long and hard at the matter and then decided: "Listen, I'd rather not deal with it."

* * *

May 12, 1993

COMPROMISE ON MILITARY GAY BAN GAINING SUPPORT AMONG SENATORS

By ERIC SCHMITT
Special to The New York Times

WASHINGTON, May 11—Senior Senate Democrats and Republicans are beginning to coalesce around a proposal that would end the military's efforts at unmasking homosexuals but would continue to bar gay men and women from serving if they are open about their sexuality.

Senator Sam Nunn, the Georgia Democrat who heads the Armed Services Committee, summarizes the policy as, "Don't ask, don't tell." It would mean that the military would not ask new recruits about their sexual orientation or conduct investigations meant to ferret out homosexuals.

But it would also impose a strict code of conduct that would address such questions as harassment, holding hands on base and same-sex dancing.

Opposed by Clinton

The Clinton Administration and gay-rights groups oppose the plan, which would essentially make permanent an interim Defense Department policy worked out by President Clinton and Senator Nunn in January. The temporary plan stopped the practice of asking recruits their sexual orientation, but it still allows the armed services to place declared homosexuals in a special-reserve status until Mr. Clinton issues a new policy.

The proposal, which still lacks specific details, today received the endorsement of the commander of American forces in the Persian Gulf war, Gen. H. Norman Schwarzkopf. "Open homosexuality is the problem," the retired general told a hearing of the Armed Services Committee.

General Schwarzkopf told senators that allowing declared gay men and lesbians to serve in the armed forces would result in disheartened troops. Testifying in his familiar booming voice, General Schwarzkopf likened such demoralized soldiers to the Iraqis "who sat in the deserts of Kuwait" when allied forces rolled through.

Supported by Sailors

The compromise, enthusiastically received by scores of Navy sailors whom senators interviewed at the Norfolk Navy Base on Monday, has suddenly gained momentum. Senators John W. Warner, Republican of Virginia, and Jim Exon, Democrat of Nebraska, today lent their support to the proposal.

"What this says is that people can't identify themselves as being gay and stay in the military," said one Pentagon official. "It contradicts the President's commitment and his order to the military to draft a policy that lifts the ban."

Defense Secretary Les Aspin must present a draft executive order to Mr. Clinton by July 15. The Pentagon has two groups—about 50 military officers and the Rand Corporation—studying how to carry out the directive. Senior aides to Mr. Aspin say they will begin consulting with advocacy groups, military leaders and lawmakers in early June.

Gen. Colin L. Powell, Chairman of the Joint Chiefs of Staff, and the other military service chiefs would almost certainly support the compromise since it would codify the interim policy they have already approved.

Thomas B. Stoddard, coordinator of the Campaign for Military Service, a gay-rights group, said Senator Nunn's proposal would not end discrimination against gay service members.

'A Lawyer's Tinkering'?

"'Don't ask, don't tell' is a lawyer's tinkering with a policy that must be rooted out in its entirely if equal protection of the law means anything," said Mr. Stoddard.

It is unclear how deep support for the compromise runs in the Senate Armed Services Committee, which has been holding hearings on whether homosexuals should be allowed to join the military since late March. Senator Nunn and the panel's ranking Republican, Strom Thurmond of South Carolina, both favor the plan.

A spokesman for Senator Dan Coats, one of the ban's strongest proponents, said the Indiana Republican has sensed a shift toward the compromise but is waiting to hear more testimony.

Senator Edward M. Kennedy, Democrat of Massachusetts, and Senator Carl Levin, Democrat of Michigan, strongly oppose the compromise. "Members of the armed forces, like any other Americans, should be judged by their ability, not by the prejudice of others," said Mr. Kennedy's spokeswoman, Pamela Hughes.

Senate Backing Predicted

One senior Senate aide said, "We haven't done any kind of a head count, but my feeling is that the compromise would get a heck of lot more votes than Clinton's position."

Supporters of the compromise acknowledged that defining homosexual behavior posed a brier patch of hypothetical situations to untangle. A spirited exchange between General Schwarzkopf and Senator Levin illustrated the point.

Seated alongside two Marine Corps officers and a senior Navy enlisted officer at the witness table, General Schwarzkopf summarized: "Don't ask the question, but don't tolerate any homosexual activity or behavior in the organization."

When Senator Levin asked if reading a magazine that catered to homosexuals constituted homosexual activity, General Schwarzkopf said, "No."

A Barracks Scenario

But then General Schwarzkopf added that if a soldier was reading the magazine "in the barracks on a continuous basis to the point where it caused all those around you to be concerned about your sexual orientation and it started to cause polarization within your outfit," the offending service member should be removed.

Several gay people, some on active duty and others who have left the service, testified at the Senate hearing and took issue with General Schwarzkopf and Senator Nunn's compromise.

"As long as there's a regulation out there, someone will have the power to use that threat against me," said Margarethe Cammermeyer, a former colonel and chief nurse in the Washington State National Guard. She was discharged last year for acknowledging that she is a lesbian.

A Father's Discovery

The hearing's most emotional moment was provided by a Marine colonel, Fred Peck, who became familiar to Americans as the military spokesman for the multinational operation in Somalia.

Colonel Peck, who returned last week from five months in Somalia, told senators that if the military ends its ban on openly gay members he would tell his sons to stay out—especially the one who is homosexual. Colonel Peck said he would fear for the life of his 24-year-old son, Scott, an aspiring journalist at the University of Maryland.

"I love him as much as I do any of my sons," said Colonel Peck, who later told reporters he learned of his son's sexual orientation just five days ago.

* * *

July 20, 1993

'DON'T ASK, DON'T TELL.' DON'T BELIEVE IT.

By WILLIAM B. RUBENSTEIN

The "don't ask, don't tell" policy that President Clinton seems to have endorsed yesterday is a failed attempt to lift the ban on gays in the military. With the issue now shifting back to the courts, the political branches should be aware that the constitutional defense of any policy short of full equality will also fail.

The constitutionality of the ban has been litigated for more than 25 years. While it has survived, interim decisions, including a case now on appeal to the Court of Appeals for the Ninth Circuit, have declared it unconstitutional. Courts have shown increasing willingness to take seriously the constitutional claims of lesbians and gay men. Just yesterday, the Colorado Supreme Court struck down a measure enacted by the voters in November barring gay rights protections.

"Don't ask, don't tell" would violate the First Amendment and the Equal Protection Clause of the Fifth Amendment. While First Amendment challenges were unsuccessful in the past, the political debate that has just taken place will bolster them. Previously the courts rejected the argument that "coming out" was protected speech, ruling that gay service members were not discharged for their speech but because their speech revealed information rendering them unfit for service.

The politicians are no longer arguing that homosexuality renders one unfit to serve, and everyone acknowledges there are lesbians and gay men in the military. The political debate has clarified that homosexuality is not incompatible with service; what is incompatible, in the new view, is talking about one's homosexuality.

The policy violates the First Amendment in that it permits speech about sexual orientation that reveals a heterosexual orientation but not a homosexual orientation. This is content-based censorship, like permitting Christian soldiers to identify their religion publicly but not permitting Jewish soldiers to do so.

The Government's central defense will be that the courts have a longstanding policy of deferring to the military on personnel questions, that speech rights of those in the service are limited and that the disruption that openly gay people would supposedly cause is satisfactory justification for the restrictions. These are difficult hurdles, but they are surmountable.

In the Supreme Court decision striking down the hate speech ordinance in St. Paul, Minn., Justice Antonin Scalia wrote for the Court that content-based censoring distinctions, even regarding what has been traditionally considered unprotected speech, trigger the closest judicial scrutiny. Thus, while soldiers' speech rights may be limited, the military is not entitled to censor expressions of sexual orientation on the basis of viewpoint.

A policy that does not grant equality to gay service members also violates the Equal Protection Clause, which here requires that individuals be judged according to their abilities and not the group to which they belong. Courts put government to the test of justifying group-based distinctions and would require the Administration to demonstrate that its discrimination against gays is rationally related to a legitimate Government interest. The Supreme Court has emphasized that catering to the prejudices of others is not such a legitimate interest.

Applying this reasoning, one appellate court last year reinstated an equal protection challenge to the discharge of a lesbian under the old military policy, holding that the Government must show that its policy is not based on prejudice. A Federal district court has also struck down the old regulations on this theory, in a case now before the Ninth Circuit.

Several other appellate courts have rejected equal protection challenges to the old military regulations, ruling that the military's litany of "discipline, good order and morale" was a legitimate basis for banning gays. Those courts did not truly focus on how the "good order" argument is linked to prejudice: "Good order" will be upset by gay soldiers because of others' prejudices. The "don't ask, don't tell" solution also concedes that gay people are not disruptive unless others know we are among them.

Ultimately, this question will go before the Supreme Court. In the meantime, politicians should know of the danger ahead if the ban is not lifted. If courts do their jobs correctly, they will overrule prejudicial public policies and guarantee full equality to lesbians and gays.

William B. Rubenstein is director of the American Civil Liberties Union's Lesbian and Gay Rights Project.

* * *

July 8, 1994

GAY IN WORLD WAR II: ABUSE BY THE MILITARY

By STEPHEN HOLDEN

COMING OUT UNDER FIRE
Directed and produced by Arthur Dong; written by Allan Berube and Mr. Dong; director of photography, Stephen Lighthill; edited by Veronica Selver; music by Mark Adler; released by Zeitgeist Films. At Quad Cinema, 34 West 13th Street, Greenwich Village. Running time: 71 minutes. This film is not rated.

At the core of "Coming Out Under Fire," Arthur Dong's quietly devastating documentary film about homosexuality in the military during World War II, are interviews with 10 gay men and women who served in the armed forces.

Some, like Phillis Abry, a radio technician in the Women's Army Corps, were able to carry on homosexual relationships without being detected and received honorable discharges. Others, like Marvin Liebman, who was in the special services of the United States Army Air Corps, were identified as gay, having "psychopathic" personalities, and were discharged as undesirable.

In the witch-hunt atmosphere that pervaded the military toward the end of the war, people suspected of being gay were relentlessly interrogated and manipulated into identifying other homosexuals. Many were sent to psychiatric hospitals or imprisoned for months in "queer stockades." Discharged as undesirable, they often found themselves pariahs, unwelcome in their hometowns and unable to find work.

Mr. Liebman was interrogated when military censors read a letter he had written to a friend whom he addressed as "darling" in the campy language of Dorothy Parker. Another veteran, identified as Clark, was an Army clerk and typist who helped create a mimeographed newsletter, The Myrtle Beach Bitch. The campy publication, which was circulated privately among gay servicemen, eventually got him into trouble. He was court-martialed and served nine months in prison. He has spent years challenging his undesirable discharge status.

These and many other personal testimonies are skillfully woven into an absorbing portrait of 1940's military life that brings in Army training films, newsreels and period documents.

"Coming Out Under Fire," which opens today at the Quad Cinema, traces the hardening of the military's anti-homosexual attitudes as the war progressed. At the start of the war, the military hoped to exclude homosexuals from service simply by asking new recruits about their sexual orientation and excluding those who said they "liked" members of their own sex. As it became clear that thousands of gay men and lesbians had chosen to serve, a climate of relative tolerance abruptly gave way to an atmosphere of paranoia and denunciation that increased even after the war ended. The witch-hunting reached its peak in the early 50's in the McCarthy era when the State Department dismissed hundreds of gay and lesbian employees as alleged security risks.

The film, which is based on Allan Berube's history of gay men and women in World War II, also has scenes suggesting that despite the official condemnation of homosexuality, gay and straight servicemen and women could co-exist harmoniously. The armed services liberated lesbians from the traditional attitudes and trappings of femininity.

Servicemen staged drag entertainments for one another in which many of the performers were gay. As Tom Reddy, who served in the Marines, recalls: "I went in at 17 and came out at 21, and I knew I was a man. It took nerve to put on a dress and run out there in front of 500 or 1,000 of your peers that were all pretending to be so macho."

For all the feelings of pride and self-esteem that are expressed in the stories, "Coming Out Under Fire" has a bitter undertone. Even those who went undetected and received honorable discharges recall that when the witch hunts began they had to modify their behavior and start looking over their shoulders.

The film sets these events against a backdrop of the Congressional hearings last year on homosexuals in the military. As these scenes make abundantly clear, the Pentagon's view of homosexuality as incompatible with military service remains implacable.

* * *

March 20, 1996

MILITARY RECRUITING BAN ON A CAMPUS IS UPHELD

By GEORGE JUDSON

STAMFORD, Conn., March 19—Connecticut's highest court upheld a permanent ban on military recruiters at the University of Connecticut School of Law today, ruling that the Pentagon's policy on homosexuals violates the state's Gay Rights Law barring discrimination on the basis of sexual orientation.

The 3-2 decision by the Connecticut Supreme Court cannot be appealed, because it is based on a state law. The university, which is based in Storrs, had no comment on whether it might extend the ban beyond the law school or seek a change in the law. The law school has its own campus in Hartford.

In New York, military recruiters have been barred from campuses of the State University of New York since 1994, when SUNY decided not to appeal a similar ruling by a lower state court that recruitment on campus violated an executive order barring discrimination at state institutions.

While some private universities have long banned military recruiters, often in decisions dating from the Vietnam War era, and several law schools have barred them on the basis that they discriminate against homosexuals, Connecticut is one of only nine states that have laws prohibiting such discrimination by all employers.

A key to the decision handed down today, said civil rights lawyers who represented gay and lesbian students at the law school, was that the Pentagon was considered to be an employer like any other, and the Connecticut law requires any employer that discriminates to be barred from campus.

"As we continue to get rid of the ban on homosexuals altogether, this means that at least some courts will apply their existing nondiscrimination laws to the military like they do everyone else," Marc Elitov, staff counsel for the American Civil Liberties Union, said.

The University of Connecticut case began in 1992, when the law school's Gay and Lesbian Students Association, under Connecticut's 1991 Gay Rights Law, sought to bar military recruiters who were about to visit the campus. A Superior Court judge granted a temporary injunction that was later made permanent, and the university's trustees appealed.

While the trustees argued that the students' complaint was with the military, for not hiring homosexuals, rather than with the university, the decision today, by Justice Joette Katz, agreed with the lower court that the law school violated state law by accommodating a discriminatory employer.

The homosexual students, Justice Katz wrote, "had been denied equal placement opportunities because the career services office had allocated resources to the military, which would not, regardless of their abilities and talents, hire them."

"The defendants," she wrote, "sanctioned impermissible discrimination that caused the plaintiffs' members to have feelings of shock, anger, humiliation, frustration and helplessness."

The Attorney General's office, representing the trustees, had argued that a state law requiring the university to provide access to military recruiters should take precedence over the Gay Rights Law.

But the Supreme Court majority again agreed with the lower court—and the plaintiffs—that that law in fact required the university to bar military recruiters. The law, enacted in 1984 after the Board of Trustees had itself banned military recruiters, was intended only to ensure it the same access as other employers, not to give it special privileges, Justice Katz wrote.

"Because the law school may not permit civilian employers to recruit on campus if they discriminate," Justice Katz wrote, "it may not permit the military, which does so discriminate, to recruit on campus."

In the decision, the majority cited a similar 1994 decision by New York's high court, the Court of Appeals, that allowed local school districts to bar military recruiters because of discrimination, as long as they barred all employers that discriminate.

Philip D. Tegeler, a lawyer with the Connecticut Civil Liberties Union who represented the students, said the decision today applies only to the law school campus. "We hope," he said, "that the Attorney General will make the appropriate review of practices on other campuses."

The Attorney General, Richard Blumenthal, issued a brief statement. "We respect the court's decision and opinion in this case, although our position was to the contrary," he said. "We will discuss with the university its future course of action consistent with the reasoning and outcome of this case."

One of the witnesses for the plaintiffs was a University of Connecticut law professor, John Brittain, who is an expert in school desegregation cases.

Since even the Clinton Administration's "don't ask, don't tell" policy regarding homosexuals effectively bars them from being hired, he said, "the military's presence had a detrimental psychological impact on the gay students, leaving them with a feeling of exclusion, a feeling of 'do not apply here,' similar to the feelings that blacks had during the era of Jim Crow segregation.

"The decision vindicates the feelings among the gay law students," he said. "Ironically, their equal rights have been vindicated now by the exclusion of the military."

* * *

April 6, 1996

COURT UPHOLDS CLINTON POLICY ON GAY TROOPS

By NEIL A. LEWIS

WASHINGTON, April 5—A Federal appeals court in Richmond today upheld the Clinton Administration's "don't ask, don't tell" policy for homosexuals in the military, saying it was inappropriate for the Federal courts to tell Congress and the President how to deal with such an issue.

In a 9-to-4 decision, the full United States Court of Appeals for the Fourth Circuit became the highest court yet to rule on the issue of how homosexuals may be treated by the military. The majority opinion emphasized that the policy as set by the White House was based on a law enacted by Congress and that courts were traditionally obligated to defer to the other branches of Government, particularly when the matter involved military policy.

The ruling continues the march to the Supreme Court by gay members of the military and former service members who have brought a fusillade of lawsuits in courts across the nation challenging the regulations that embody the policy.

The two other cases furthest along are in the Second Circuit, in New York, and the Ninth Circuit, in San Francisco, both considered far more liberal than the Fourth Circuit and therefore more likely to reject the policy.

A ruling by either of those other courts against the "don't ask, don't tell" policy is likely to insure Supreme Court consideration to settle the disagreement.

The court in Richmond ruled in the case of a former Navy lieutenant, Paul Thomasson, who was dismissed from the service last June after giving a letter to his commanding admiral in 1994 stating, "I am gay."

Mr. Thomasson said in an interview today that he found the new policy unbearably hypocritical, especially because at the time he was working in the Office of Naval Personnel, which was charged with carrying it out.

"I could not abide the hypocrisy of my Government saying it was O.K. for me to go into harm's way," Mr. Thomasson said, "but I could not try to overcome the prejudice or ignorance people have involving my homosexuality."

Mr. Thomasson, who lives in the Washington area and works as a temporary employee for a military-related company, said his commanding officer, Adm. Albert Konetzni, and other admirals for whom he had worked were supportive of his Navy career even after the disclosure of his homosexuality.

The current policy was the product of heated debates within the Clinton Administration and in Congress. On taking office in 1993, Mr. Clinton tried to impose a blanket moratorium on discrimination against homosexuals in the military, but he was forced to back down in the face of heated opposition from the military and some members of Congress.

Under a compromise put into effect in 1994, homosexuals are permitted to serve as long as they keep their homosexuality a secret, and commanders are barred from asking service members questions about their sexual orientation. The military retained its longstanding prohibition of homosexual acts, and commanders are still allowed to open investigations of military personnel if there is evidence, including statements they might make, that they are homosexual.

The military has always argued that the presence of homosexuals could harm a unit's cohesion.

Mr. Thomasson's lawyer, Allan B. Moore, said he and his client were still deciding whether to seek review from the Supreme Court.

Judge J. Harvie Wilkinson 3d, who wrote for the majority, said he could not agree with Mr. Thomasson's argument that the policy was unconstitutional.

"To do so would not only overturn the efforts of the elected branches of Government to resolve a significant question of national military policy, it would also violate much plain and settled Supreme Court precedent," Judge Wilkinson wrote.

He said the record showed that the policy had been fully debated by the House and Senate.

"What Thomasson challenges, therefore, is a statute that embodies the exhaustive efforts of the democratically accountable branches of American Government and an enactment that reflects months upon months of political negotiation," Judge Wilkinson wrote, adding, "The courts were not created to award by judicial decree what was not achievable by political consensus."

Judge Kenneth K. Hall wrote in a dissent that Mr. Thomasson was being punished for "nothing more than an expression of his state of mind."

"The expression was not illegal," Judge Hall wrote, "and the fact admitted is not a ground for discharge."

The Administration has resolutely defended the policy, both in court and in public statements. "We believe that the current policy is working well," Kenneth Bacon, the Defense Department's chief spokesman, said in a recent interview. Mr. Bacon said the policy was one that balanced an individual's right to privacy with the military's need to maintain unit cohesion and readiness.

Underlying the debate is just what the Administration policy intends to prohibit. Many of the gay members of the service who have brought suit, including Mr. Thomasson, have argued that the policy does not punish homosexuality, but speech.

In the New York case, Judge Eugene H. Nickerson of Federal District Court in Brooklyn ruled last year that the policy violated a service member's First Amendment right to free speech and Fifth Amendment right to equal treatment under the law.

"The policy is not only inherently deceptive," Judge Nickerson wrote, "it also offers powerful inducements to homosexuals to lie."

The case was appealed by the Administration and argued in January before a three-judge appeals panel.

Under the current policy, if an investigation reveals that a service member has displayed a propensity for homosexual behavior through, for example, statements, the individual is summoned before a military hearing board and is presumed to be in violation of the military's code prohibiting homosexual acts.

Today's majority opinion by Judge Wilkinson said that by using speech as an indicator of a propensity to commit a homosexual act, a person was not being penalized for speech. Moreover, he wrote, members of the military have long been held to have reduced First Amendment rights.

Joining Judge Wilkinson in the majority were Donald S. Russell, H. Emory Widener Jr., Francis D. Murnaghan Jr., William W. Wilkins Jr., Paul V. Niemeyer, Clyde H. Hamilton, J. Michael Luttig and Karen J. Williams. Of them, Judges Wilkinson and Wilkins were appointed by President Ronald Reagan, Judges Russell and Widener by President Richard M. Nixon, Judge Murnaghan by President Jimmy Carter and Judges Niemeyer, Hamilton, Luttig and Williams by President George Bush.

In dissent, in addition to Judge Hall, were Chief Judge Sam J. Ervin 3d, and Judges M. Blane Michael and Diana G. Motz. Of them, Judge Hall was appointed by President Gerald Ford; Judge Ervin by President Carter and Judges Michael and Motz by President Clinton.

* * *

December 9, 1999

KILLER'S TRIAL SHOWS GAY SOLDIER'S ANGUISH

By FRANCIS X. CLINES

FORT CAMPBELL, Ky., Dec. 8—The graphic story of the harassment and bludgeon slaying of an Army private who feared expulsion from the service for being homosexual emerged here today at a court-martial that gay rights proponents say lays bare the grave flaws in the military's "don't ask, don't tell, don't pursue" policy.

The 21-year-old victim, Pfc. Barry Winchell of Kansas City, Mo., was beaten to death with a baseball bat as he slept in his barracks bed early last July 5 after what fellow soldiers testified was months of vile name calling, rumor mongering and an inquiry into his private life that was supposed to be forbidden under military policy.

The court heard one of the accused, Pvt. Calvin Glover, 18, of Sulphur, Okla., enter a plea of guilty to a lesser charge of unpremeditated murder. But his trial went forward on the separate charge of premeditated murder with details unfolding on the final months of Private Winchell's life as a soldier subjected to derision.

The court of five officers and enlisted men tonight pronounced him guilty of premeditated murder, solely measuring how calculating Private Glover had been in the assault. He will be sentenced on Thursday and could face life in prison.

Witnesses testified that the victim, fearful that protesting the harassment to superiors meant risking expulsion from the service as a homosexual, had been taunted by Private Glover into a fist fight. Private Winchell won the fight handily at the end of a night of barracks drinking. But the humiliated loser, Private Glover, retaliated with a baseball bat two days later as Private Winchell slept.

In pleading guilty to the lesser charge and hoping for leniency, Private Glover accused a second defendant, Specialist Justin Fisher, 25, of Lincoln, Neb., of supplying the baseball bat and goading him into the assault.

"I was just so drunk," Private Glover tearfully told the court on Monday. "I had no intent for him to die."

The court-martial, replete with testimony about widespread drunkenness and barracks harassment and routine denunciations of Private Winchell by fellow soldiers as "a faggot," "a queer," and "a homo," was treated by the prosecution as purely a murder trial.

The Army has made no comment on the case's possible implications for its controversial policy toward gays.

But gay rights organizations contend that the slaying is a classic example of a hate crime rooted in homophobia, and that the Clinton administration's "don't ask" policy, far from making life easier for gays and lesbians in the armed services, has left many to suffer in silence or leave the service.

Since its inception, the policy has seen a doubling of discharges of gay service members, to 312 last year, and a comparable increase in complaints of homosexual harassment, gay rights organizations say.

"This murder has shut down any illusions soldiers had," said Michelle M. Benecke, co-executive director of the Servicemembers Legal Defense Network, a gay rights organization that monitors military justice.

"Every day, service members in every service must endure anti-gay epithets and threats," Ms. Benecke said in underscoring the Pentagon's failure to circulate guidelines on its gay policy until after the slaying of Private Winchell.

In testimony at the trial and in a preliminary inquiry here last summer, witnesses said that Private Glover, after being struck in the face and thrown to the ground in his challenge to Private Winchell, seethed with embarrassment, shouted homophobic curses and threatened a killing, declaring, "It ain't over."

Witnesses said that Private Winchell, a machine gunner in the 101st Airborne Division, had been initially labeled a homosexual by his roommate, Specialist Fisher, who is facing a separate court-martial on Monday on charges that he was an accomplice in the slaying and had lied to investigators.

Private Glover's defense team sought to bring out from witnesses that Specialist Fisher was a dominant, manipulative individual while the accused private was subservient and a braggart.

The presiding judge, Col. Gary Holland, told the court that the critical question was whether Private Glover, amid a long weekend of barracks drinking, partying and bickering, had opportunity to "cool off" from a point of initial rage and premeditate the assault.

Of Specialist Fisher, the judge stressed it had been stipulated as fact that "he's the one who handed the accused the bat" and "told him to go out and mess up" Private Winchell.

On the morning of the slaying, a military policeman testified, Specialist Fisher, his clothes covered in blood, stood by the ambulance shouting, "Let him die! Let him die!" as Private Winchell was taken to the hospital. In the earlier hearing, Specialist Fisher swore that Private Glover spewed homophobic epithets before the assault and confessed to the slaying as he hurriedly washed blood from the bat. When the two checked on the stricken Private Winchell, Specialist Fisher said, Private Glover lifted his bloodied head and said, "Yes, he is dead."

Witnesses testified that the assault was so severe that Private Winchell's face was unrecognizable, with his eyes swollen shut and his head cracked open. Private Glover fled the scene, according to testimony, and threw bloody evidence in a trash bin. He was later arrested in his room by investigators, who said they had found blood stains on the door and on his clothing.

Last March, Specialist Fisher accompanied Private Winchell to the Connection in Nashville, a nightclub favored by gays, witnesses said, and gossip soon went around the post that the Private Winchell was homosexual. Testimony established that Private Winchell had dated a female impersonator at the club, Cal Addams, a former Navy medic known as Calpernia, who eulogized Private Winchell last July as "a kind, calm gentleman."

"Pretty much everybody in the company called him derogatory names," Private Winchell's platoon sergeant, Michael Kleifgen, testified at the pretrial hearing. "They called him a 'faggot' and stuff like that, I would say on a daily basis. A lot of times, he was walking around down in the dumps."

Despite the military's "don't ask" stricture, Sergeant Kleifgen testified last summer that he decided to informally investigate after Specialist Fisher described the nightclub visit without identifying Private Winchell. The sergeant said he suspected that Private Winchell was gay but Private Winchell denied this. The sergeant dropped the matter, he testified, finally acknowledging to the amazement of some in his audience, that "the military has a policy of 'don't ask, don't tell.'"

At the same time, the sergeant said he did nothing to enforce Army regulations against the sort of harassment that Private Winchell was suffering. "Everybody was having fun," the sergeant said in explaining his reasoning.

In the welter of harassment and epithets, several witnesses testified, a few soldiers complained of homophobic denunciations of Private Winchell by ranking superiors. But nothing came of their complaints that Army policy had been violated, the witnesses said. "We did a formal I.G. complaint and nothing was done, sir," Sergeant Kleifgen testified today, referring to the inspector general's office here. The Fort Campbell public affairs office said it would inquire into the reported complaint to see what might have happened.

Under the policy introduced by the Clinton administration, the military cannot inquire into a soldier's sex life unless there is clear evidence of homosexual conduct. But gays who volunteer this information can be discharged for being homosexual. After the Winchell slaying and reports of white supremacists in the Army, President Clinton signed an executive order in October that amends the court-martial manual to allow judges to weigh hate-crime factors in meting out sentences.

Correction: Articles yesterday about the conviction of an Army private, Calvin Glover, in the murder of Pfc. Barry Winchell and about Hillary Rodham Clinton's criticism of the "don't ask, don't tell" policy of the military misstated the number of gay service members discharged last year because of the policy. The number was 1,149; discharges from the Army account for 312.

* * *

December 19, 1999

CLOSE QUARTERS:
HOW IS THIS STRATEGY WORKING?
DON'T ASK.

By ERIC SCHMITT

WASHINGTON—The string of denunciations of the military's "don't ask, don't tell" policy, triggered by Hillary Rodham Clinton and quickly followed by President Clinton and Vice President Al Gore, don't tell Americans that the policy will be tough to change and don't ask why it hasn't worked.

The policy is law, and not just a mere regulation to wipe away with a new president's signature on an executive order. And there are no signs that Congress, even if Democrats regain control of one or both chambers in next year's election, will change the compromise lawmakers hammered out with President Clinton in 1993.

Underlying the debate is a more fundamental question: Why hasn't the "don't ask, don't tell" policy worked? The military has been far more effective in integrating blacks and women into the armed forces than it has with gays. The recent court-martial of an Army private convicted of brutally murdering a gay soldier has also turned up the political heat on the policy.

Pentagon officials insist that the policy is fine, but that its enforcement needs improvement. "What we haven't done is adequately police the harassment," said one senior military official who follows the policy closely.

Last week Defense Secretary William S. Cohen ordered the Pentagon's inspector general to investigate major military bases to determine whether gay members are harassed. Each of the armed services is also preparing new training programs to educate troops on the five-year-old policy.

The military's experience with integrating blacks and women offers some lessons in effective approaches for changing a culture that strives for an esprit de corps. The two examples, however imperfect, show how the military had to overcome deep prejudices largely for practical reasons. Blacks were needed to fill the ranks during the Korean War. Women were needed for the new all-volunteer force in the early 1970's after the Vietnam war. Senior commanders publicly supported both changes.

These changes took years to carry out, and there have been plenty of bumps along the way. President Harry Truman's 1948 executive order speeded desegregation of the ranks, but it wasn't until the 1960's that the number of black sergeants and officers grew significantly. There are still relatively few black generals and admirals.

A quarter century after large numbers of women were brought into the military, sexual harassment persists, and women are still restricted from several combat positions. The Navy continues to bar women from nuclear-powered submarines on the grounds that putting men and women side by side in such tight confines would wreak havoc with the crew's war-fighting ability.

The military draws a sharp distinction between racial and sexual intolerance: race carries no behavioral implications; sex does. That is why the military can condemn racial bigotry and sexual harassment but separate men and women in living quarters: sex between service members could seriously disrupt morale.

Military officials argue that most Americans—and, therefore, most soldiers—don't actually approve of or tolerate homosexuality. And while gay service members make up only a tiny fraction of the 1.4 million-member military (compared with 20 percent blacks and 14 percent women), commanders fear that forcing heterosexual members to live, or fight, side by side with homosexuals—and possibly be exposed to gay sex—would be disruptive, and undermine the military's mission to fight and win the nation's wars.

"Open homosexuals would paralyze a unit, and degrade unit cohesion and erode combat readiness," Gen. Merrill McPeak, the Air Force chief of staff, told a Senate hearing in 1993, summing up a sentiment prevalent among top uniformed officers today.

Gay rights advocates say the same argument was used to exclude blacks and women. More than 60 percent of Americans opposed racial integration when President Truman issued his executive order. The prejudices were overcome not with sensitivity training but with the enforcement of strict codes of conduct.

But when President Clinton tried to lift the ban on gay service members in 1993, he faced a near-rebellion from the Joint Chiefs of Staff and resounding defeat in a Congress controlled by Democrats.

"Don't ask, don't tell" was the weak compromise that was designed to permit gay men and lesbians to serve without fear of harassment or expulsion as long as they kept their orientation to themselves. The policy has been carried out unevenly and has, arguably, caused more harm than good. Gay rights groups say it has encouraged harassment in some units.

The number of service members discharged for homosexuality soared to 1,145 in the 1998 fiscal year, which is nearly double the number in 1993, when the policy was hotly debated. The Pentagon says most of those discharges involve young soldiers who volunteered information as a way to get out of the military. But gay rights advocates say gays are seeking escape from harassment or improper investigations.

Most military officials insist that, in general, "don't ask, don't tell" is working. But critics, including those who disagree on whether to allow gays to serve openly, say the policy has failed.

"'Don't ask, don't tell' was a compromise that never could have worked without sustained leadership at the highest levels," said Representative Martin T. Meehan, a Massachusetts Democrat on the House Armed Services Committee who has long supported allowing gays to serve openly.

Representative Stephen E. Buyer, an Indiana Republican on the same committee and a lieutenant colonel in the Army reserve, said the military should ask recruits about their orientation. "With 'don't ask, don't tell,' we're living in a gray area," he said.

The Pentagon, however, is sticking to its guns. "I do not expect the policy to be changed—certainly not during this administration," Secretary Cohen said last week.

But with public opinion polls showing Americans more accepting of gays in the workplace, the American military may be one of the last major battlegrounds of gay intolerance left in society. Just last week, Britain became the latest NATO ally to end its ban on gays in the military, acting under pressure from the European Court of Human Rights. Under its new policy, which American gay rights groups advocate, sexual behavior involving on-duty personnel will be a punishable offense but a member's sexual orientation will not.

There are signs that hostility in the military toward gays may be easing. Gay rights groups say there are fewer mass investigations and criminal prosecutions.

An anecdotal survey of troops in Bosnia last year conducted by the sociologists Charles Moskos of Northwestern University and Laura L. Miller of the University of California at Los Angeles found that 26 percent of the servicemen said gay men and lesbians should be allowed to serve openly, compared with 15 percent in 1993, when the policy was under debate. Women seem more accepting, with 52 percent saying gay men and lesbians should be allowed to serve, compared with 33 percent in 1993.

Still, any policy shift seems a long way off. "Public attitudes and military attitude change slowly on these issues," said Edwin Dorn, a former top Pentagon personnel official. "Whether we like it or not, the political reality is there are a lot of folks who believe that homosexuality is wrong."

* * *

February 2, 2000

PENTAGON ORDERS TRAINING TO PREVENT HARASSMENT OF GAYS

By ELIZABETH BECKER

WASHINGTON, Feb. 1—Every member of the armed forces, from four-star generals to privates, will undergo training by the end of the year to prevent anti-gay harassment, the Pentagon announced today in a sweeping admission that its "don't ask, don't tell, don't harass" policy is poorly understood in the ranks.

In the wake of the murder of a gay private in Kentucky last July, Secretary of Defense William S. Cohen ordered each of the armed services to prepare training programs and asked the senior civilian and military leaders of the Army, Navy, Air Force and Marines to send letters to their commanders this month emphasizing that anti-gay threats and harassment will not be tolerated.

"What this does is try to make the training more regular and to emphasize, from the top down, that this is a priority of all the services and to make this emphasis stronger and clearer than it was before," said Kenneth H. Bacon, a Pentagon spokesman.

While the policy is five years old, the armed forces have never made it a subject for universal training of its members. Nor has the Pentagon sent out messages to the field specifically ordering full compliance.

Although the policy appears straightforward—that gay men and lesbians may serve in the military so long as they keep their sexual orientation to themselves and do not engage in homosexual acts—the military has been plagued with instances of gays being harassed until they admitted their sexual orientation, ending their military careers.

Gay and lesbian activists applauded the new program.

"This is a victory to finally have this training and to have this message sent out to the field but it's a shame it took the murder of a private at Fort Campbell to get them to do this," said Michelle Benecke, co-director of the Servicemembers Legal Defense Network, which has lobbied for the changes.

It also took the intervention of presidential politics. President Clinton said in a radio interview in December that the military's policy was "out of whack" following the conviction of an Army private in the murder of Pfc. Barry Winchell in their barracks at Fort Campbell, Ky.

Within days, Vice President Al Gore called for the outright elimination of the policy, which was already the position of former Senator Bill Bradley, his rival for the Democratic nomination.

The Pentagon also announced today that the number of service members discharged because they were homosexuals dropped in the fiscal year that ended on Sept. 30—to 1,034 from 1,145 the year before.

The core of the new training sessions, which run about an hour, will be a slide presentation detailing what the policy does and does not allow. The services also plan to use video presentations, role playing exercises and pamphlets to hammer home that slurs and innuendos are forbidden.

"We're going to ensure everyone in every command has this training," said Cmdr. Greg Smith, a Navy spokesman. "This hasn't quite risen to the level of annual sexual harassment training, but it's clearly important."

The Army said it hoped to give the courses to all of its members within 90 days. "Every four-star general on down," said Edwin Viega, an Army spokesman.

The Air Force plans to complete its training within six months, a spokesman said, and the Navy will be done in one year.

The Pentagon said it had no immediate estimate of the cost of the additional training. P. J. Crowley, a Defense Department spokesman, said the expense would be measured in hours rather than dollars.

"It will cost more in effort than in money," Mr. Crowley said. "How long it takes to get to the entire force will be a function of time and opportunity."

Only the Army has begun training. Its presentation knocks down the widely held assumption that a service member can be investigated as gay if he or she goes to a gay bar, reads gay magazines or has gay friends.

One of the 14 slides shown in the training reads: "zero tolerance for harassment." In bold letters on another slide, the Army tells its members that "derogatory, persistent, threatening or annoying behavior" is unacceptable in any form, on or off duty, from anonymous threats to graffiti in latrines.

According to a draft of the Navy's presentation, instructors will be asked to use a standard exercise in sensitivity training that develops trust and respect for all sailors in the service. Then the instruction will show slides defining anti-gay harassment and reminding sailors that their commanding officers are under orders to "take immediate steps to protect the safety of the victim, stop the threatening behavior, and hold those responsible for the harassment accountable."

In the fuller Army presentation, soldiers are told that they should not fear coming under investigation themselves if they report anti-gay harassment. That protection was missing at Fort Campbell when Private Winchell was beaten to death with a baseball bat after months of harassment by his comrades, who openly reviled him with the full knowledge of his superiors.

Today's announcements are meant to ensure that the military's basic policy is carried out. "What adds teeth is the message sent out from the leaders that we will tolerate no harassment," said Lt. Col. Russ Oakes, an Army spokesman.

To measure ill will against gays in the military, Mr. Cohen commissioned the inspector general of the Defense Department to visit 38 military bases in this country and overseas and do extensive interviews on the subject. The report is due in March.

PART IX

THE INTERNATIONAL SCENE

EUROPE

December 3, 1937

12 CZECH NAZIS ON TRIAL

Members of Youth Organization Face Homosexual Charges

Wireless to The New York Times

PRAGUE, Czechoslovakia, Dec. 2—Twelve members of Konrad Henlein's Sudeten German party's youth organization appeared in court today to answer charges of homosexuality which were chiefly directed against the absent thirteenth codefendant—the "Foreign Minister" of the Sudeten German party, Heinz Rutha, who killed himself soon after his arrest early in November.

The only politically prominent man answering charges today was Walther Rohn, editor of the party's monthly organ.

Counsel for five of the accused requested a hearing in camera.

The prosecutor objected on the grounds that the Henlein press is attempting to prove the motives of the accusation are political. After consideration the court decided on an in camera hearing except for the reading of the indictment, judgment and sentence. The indictment says that although Rutha maintained his innocence the confessions of several others of the accused implicated him.

* * *

March 25, 1954

MORALS CASE JAILS PEER

Montague Sentenced to Year, 2 Others Get 18 Months Each

WINCHESTER, England, March 24 (AP)—Lord Montagu of Beaulieu, 27-year-old bachelor, was sentenced today to a year's imprisonment on three charges involving homosexuality.

Montagu's 37-year-old farmer cousin, Michael Pitt-Rivers, and Peter Wildeblood, 30, a London newspaperman, were sentenced to eighteen months. The cases of all three involved two Royal Air Force men.

It was the first time a peer of the realm had been found guilty in a criminal court since the abolition some years ago of the right of peers to be tried in the House of Lords. Justice Benjamin Ormerod passed sentence.

* * *

April 29, 1954

BRITISH SEX STUDY DUE

Special Group Will Be Named to Review Present Laws

Special to The New York Times

LONDON, April 28—A Government appointed committee will examine laws relating to homosexuality and prostitution, Sir Hugh Lucas-Tooth told the House of Commons today.

The Parliamentary Secretary for the Home Office said the membership of the committee and its terms of reference would be announced in "some little time." He said these were "difficult and controversial problems" and added:

"I think there will be general agreement that the criminal law in this respect ought to provide for the protection of the young and the preservation of the public order and decency.

"The question is: should the law confine itself to securing these two objectives or be amended so as to permit unnatural relations between consulting adults in private? Such activities are no crime in many countries in the world."

* * *

December 17, 1955

BRITISH PANEL FINDS WIDE SEX DEVIATION

LONDON, Dec. 16 (AP)—A team of experts on medicine and crime said today sex deviation was so widespread in Britain there were "practicing homosexuals" in Parliament.

Reporting on an investigation made for the British Medical Association, the experts said the number of male perverts in the United Kingdom might exceed half a million, perhaps 2 to 3 percent of all British males.

The investigation was made by a panel of twelve doctors, psychiatrists and criminologists. Dr. Ronald Gibson, a medical officer at Winchester Prison, headed the group. It was set up to give the Government the medical association's views on possible legislation to curb homosexuality and prostitution.

The report said known homosexuals were active "in church, Parliament, civil service, armed forces, press, radio, stage and other institutions." It said there was a danger that homosexuals in positions of authority might give preferential treatment to others of their kind and might fall prey to blackmailers.

"The real safeguard against homosexual activity," the panel said, "is public opinion. Measures to promote a healthy attitude toward sex should be promoted by all possible means."

*   *   *

November 7, 1958

BRITISH CENSOR LIFTS HOMOSEXUALITY BAN

Special to The New York Times

LONDON, Nov. 6—Britain's stage censor has lifted the ban on homosexuality as a subject for public dramatic presentations.

Plays touching on the subject, such as Arthur Miller's "A View From the Bridge" or Tennessee Williams' "Cat on a Hot Tin Roof," have been produced in London but only at private theatre clubs. They have been barred from public theatres by the Lord Chamberlain, whose office exercises official censorship.

The Earl of Scarborough, who is Lord Chamberlain, informed Charles Killick, chairman of the Theatres National Committee, that the ban was lifted in a letter than said in part:

"This subject is now so widely debated, written about and talked of that its complete exclusion from the stage can no longer be regarded as justifiable. In future, therefore, plays on this subject which are sincere and serious will be admitted, as will references to the subject which are necessary to the plot and dialogue and which are not salacious or offensive."

*   *   *

May 25, 1965

LORDS VOTE TO EASE HOMOSEXUALITY BAN

By ANTHONY LEWIS
Special to The New York Times

LONDON, May 24—The House of Lords approved in principle tonight a bill to remove from criminal law all penalties for homosexual conduct by consenting adults in private.

The vote was 94 to 49. The result was a considerable surprise and could lead to early passage of a reform that has been debated for years.

The House of Commons is scheduled to debate the homosexual law reform on Wednesday. The vote in the Lords was arranged first as a test of sentiment on an issue that politicians have treated gingerly.

The general expectation has been that the House of Lords would be more resistant to change in this area than the Commons. This was because of its public reputation as maintainer of the conservative traditions of a stiff-lipped old Britain.

The debate in the Lords did not turn out that way at all. There were some ringing calls for old-fashioned morality, notably one from Viscount Montgomery of Alamein, but most speeches went the other way.

There was special drama when the 35-year-old Marquess of Queensberry rose for his maiden speech in the House.

It was his great-grandfather, the ninth Marquess, who denounced Oscar Wilde as a homosexual in 1895. Wilde went to prison in the most notorious case ever brought under the laws that the present bill would repeal.

"I do not believe that our laws on this subject are a solution," the young Marquess said. "They have, if anything, helped to produce a nasty, furtive underworld which is bad for society and bad for the homosexual.

"The best possible solution is that he should be allowed to lead a quiet, ordered life, finding, if he must, sexual satisfaction with another adult man.

"I shall support the bill wholeheartedly."

The legislation would carry out a recommendation made in 1957 by a committee under Sir John Wolfenden. No government since then has been willing to endorse the proposal as its own, but the present Labor regime has indicated that it will allow time for consideration of a private bill.

The vote was on second reading, which approves a bill in principle and sends it on for committee scrutiny. If the House of Commons acts affirmatively on Wednesday, its draft rather than the Lords' bill may become the final legislation.

The Earl of Arran, who writes a newspaper column, among other activities, was the author of the Lords bill. He opened the debate by appealing to "this House to show itself the place I believe it to be—a place of progress and compassion."

Earl Attlee, the former Labor Prime Minister, also urged approval, saying the measure would end confusion between sin and crime.

"It is false to imagine that doing away with this as a criminal offense will in any way extend the evil," he said.

Viscount Montgomery, the field marshal of World War II, was the main opposition speaker. "One might just as well condone the devil and all his works," he said.

Two former Conservative Lord Chancellors, the Earl of Kilmuir and Viscount Dilhorne, opposed the bill. The former said it would encourage homosexuals to proselytize others in "sodomite societies and buggery clubs that everyone knows exist."

*   *   *

December 12, 1966

COMMONS ENDORSES A MEASURE TO REFORM HOMOSEXUALITY LAW

By ANTHONY LEWIS
Special to The New York Times

LONDON, Feb. 11—The long-debated bill to reform Britain's law on homosexual conduct won a dramatic victory today in the House of Commons.

By a vote of 164 to 107, members gave the bill its second reading. Twice before in recent years similar measures had been defeated in the Commons.

The legislation would repeal all criminal penalties against homosexual acts committed in private by consenting adults. This was the proposal made in 1957 by a committee under Sir John Wolfenden, in a report bearing his name.

Second reading constitutes approval in principle. There must still be committee decision, but today's margin should assure passage through the Commons eventually unless opponents manage a parliamentary maneuver.

The House of Lords approved an identical bill last year, so final approval of the Wolfenden recommendation is now in sight.

The vote indicated the sharp change in public and political opinion over the last few years. In 1960 the Commons defeated a similar measure, 213 to 99. Last year the Commons turned back another, 178 to 159.

Churches have been in the forefront of the demand for reform. The Church of England and Roman Catholic and Methodist groups have all called for adoption of the Wolfenden recommendation.

Approval by the House of Lords, formerly considered a center of opposition to social reforms, gave the campaign for change a big push. And recent public-opinion polls have shown nearly a two-thirds majority for this legislation.

The Labor Government took no official position on the bill, which is of a kind usually left to nonparty votes. It was introduced by Humphry Berkeley, a Conservative.

But an important speech for the legislation was delivered by the Home Secretary, Roy Jenkins. He emphasized that he was speaking as an individual, not for the Government, but his views carry weight in the House.

Mr. Jenkins estimated that somewhere between one male in 20 and one in 40 is "in some sense an active homosexual." That would make the total number in Britain about 500,000 to 1,000,000.

"The spread in the community is much more even than is sometimes imagined," Mr. Jenkins said, "and is not concentrated in any particular social class or occupational group." He added:

"The great majority of homosexuals are not exhibitionist freaks but ordinary citizens. Homosexuality is not a disease but is more in the nature of a grave disability for the individual, leading to a great deal of loneliness, unhappiness, guilt and shame."

A main argument of proponents was that present law condemns men for a condition that is not a matter of their choice, and for impulses that are almost impossible to control.

Depending on the nature of the act, the maximum sentence can be as severe as a life term. In recent years the penalty usually has been between one and a half and three years.

For offenses against minors, the bill prescribes a maximum sentence of three to five years.

Mr. Berkeley, who noted that he was a Roman Catholic, said that among the strong supporters of reform were "those who have voluntarily undertaken to lead lives of chastity, such as ordained priests and monks."

"They know from their own experience as men of God," he said, "that prayer, meditation, access to the strong sacraments and strong determination are required to lead a life of absolute chastity from the start of adult life to the grave."

The present law is, in any event, unenforceable except in a selective, arbitrary way, Mr. Berkeley said. He said that of the probable millions of homosexual acts between consenting adults in private, only about 100 led to criminal prosecutions each year. The opportunities for blackmail are severe, he argued.

A principal opponent, Sir Cyril Osborne, said that if the bill passed, "the tendency will be for the number of homosexuals to increase."

"I am rather tired of democracy being made safe for the pimps, the prostitutes, the spivs and the pansies, and now the queers," he said.

* * *

December 20, 1966

COMMONS APPROVES BILL ON HOMOSEXUALS

By W. GRANGER BLAIR
Special to The New York Times

LONDON, Dec. 19—The long-debated bill to reform and liberalize Britain's law on homosexual conduct was accepted by the House of Commons tonight without a dissenting vote.

The House approved without a vote the second reading of the measure, virtually assuring the bill's eventual passage in the remaining legislative stages.

The bill, based on a report published in 1957 by a committee under Sir John Wolfenden, has been twice debated and defeated since that time.

The present measure would repeal virtually all criminal penalties against homosexual acts if committed in private by consenting adults. However, it also provides for the penalty of life imprisonment for homosexual offenses against a boy under the age of 16.

An act of gross indecency against a youth between the ages of 16 and 21 could bring five years' imprisonment and a public act of indecency could be punished by two years in prison.

The measure had been approved by the House of Lords and had passed its second reading in the Commons last February when Parliament was dissolved for the March general elections.

All bills in the legislative hopper at the time died automatically. The homosexuality bill was reintroduced when the new Parliament convened after the elections. Today's debate produced virtually no new arguments for or against the measure.

*   *   *

May 10, 1969

BUNDESTAG VOTES PENAL REFORM; ENDS MOST SEX-CRIME PENALTIES

By RALPH BLUMENTHAL
Special to The New York Times

BONN, May 9—A far-reaching penal reform that eliminates the penalties for homosexuality between consenting adults for sodomy and for adultery was approved without serious opposition today in West Germany's Bundestag, the lower house of parliament.

The Bonn republic's first major revision of criminal statutes dating from 1871 also eliminates almost all jail sentences of less than six months replacing them with a system of fines based on ability to pay as well as the gravity of the violation.

The measure also does away with the distinction between jails, which now usually house minor offenders, and penitentiaries, now for those convicted of more serious offenses.

If, as expected, the Bundesrat, or upper house, adds its approval, the sex-law reforms will go into effect Sept. 1, the elimination of the penitentiary designation and of sentences of less than six months on April 1, 1970, and the remaining provisions in October, 1973.

The reform has been called "the work of a century." The old Prussian laws have been modified over the years, but it was only in 1953 that a parliamentary committee began to review the outdated statutes comprehensively. The first draft of the reforms was prepared in 1962.

The emphasis throughout is on punishment directed toward rehabilitation instead of reprisal. A Justice Ministry pamphlet explaining the bill leads with a quotation from Seneca: "Only this proves wisdom—to punish not because a crime occurred yesterday but rather that it will not occur tomorrow."

Reform of the laws on sex offenses, a key part of the bill, starts with this assumption by the Justice Ministry: "Not everything that is distasteful by religious, ethical or moral standards can be punishable."

Thus sodomy and homosexuality between consulting adults will no longer be punishable by jail terms. The penalty of up to six months jail for adultery will also be dropped, as will all present penalties against adults who knowingly permit their children to engage in extramarital sexual relations.

"Adultery," notes the commentary on the bill, "is not the cause of a marriage splitup, but more the effect. Neither punishment nor state authority has ever cemented a marriage."

Some Penalties Retained

However, the penalties for sexual relations with a minor or forced relations with an adult remain strict, in some cases 10 years imprisonment or more. Under the new plan, chronic sexual offenders can, with their agreement, be sterilized.

The measure eliminates almost all prison sentences of less than six months—some now are as short as a day. The new system of fines that allows violators to remain on their jobs and with their families, reformers feel, will hasten rehabilitation.

The fines are scaled to the seriousness of the offense and the resources of the violator. For example, a theft for which a poor man might be fined $100 might cost a millionaire $90,000.

A fine may also replace some sentences of longer than six months.

The distinction between jails and penitentiaries will be eliminated because the variety of crimes and criminals has already clouded the difference. Furthermore, the reformers say, the stigma of having been in a penitentiary tends to embitter inmates and hamper their reintegration into society.

The Bonn Republic has never had the death penalty.

Liberalization in Britain

Special to The New York Times

LONDON, May 9—In the last few years Britain has legalized abortion and homosexuality between consenting adults and a bill is now before Parliament to broaden the grounds for divorce.

A 1967 act provided for suspension of sentences of less than two years and widened the parole system.

Depending on the offense, a 10-year sentence may be served in a high-security prison or in an "open" prison, with the facilities for rehabilitation.

In Britain, adultery is not a criminal offense, but sodomy is, as are sexual relations with a minor, under 15, even with the consent of the minor.

A State Matter in U. S.

In the United States, such legislation is a state matter. Homosexual acts, even when conducted in private between consenting adults, are forbidden except in Illinois, which revised its criminal code recently to exempt consenting adults.

In New York State homosexual acts or sodomy between consenting adults are misdemeanors with penalties of up to three months in jail. Such an act with anyone under 17 years of age is a felony and can bring up to four years in jail.

Adultery also is a misdemeanor with penalties of up to three months in jail.

*   *   *

July 16, 1986

A MISREAD TREATISE ON HOMOSEXUALITY

To the Editor:

It is supremely ironic that Chief Justice Burger should cite "Homosexuality in the Western Christian Tradition," by

Derrick Sherwin Bailey, in his concurrence with the Supreme Court's decision that the Constitution does not protect homosexual relations between consenting adults (news story June 30).

Mr. Bailey's book of 1955 is generally acknowledged to have been a motivating force in the decriminalization of homosexualacts in Great Britain.

His detailed historical analysis of the relevant material from the biblical and Western legal tradition left the reader to conclude that such precedents as the story of Sodom (Genesis 19) and the Levitical proscriptions (18:22 and 20:13) as well as the very laws Chief Justice Burger cites from the Justinian and Theodosian codes cannot be used as prooftexts for criminal legislation in the last quarter of the 20th century.

To reject these precedents is not, as Chief Justice Burger says, "to cast aside millennia of moral teaching" but simply to acknowledge the historicity and conditionedness of human existence. To do otherwise is tantamount to accepting the penalty of stoning for the crime of adultery.

FRANK OVEIS
Bronx, July 2, 1986

* * *

October 2, 1989

RIGHTS FOR GAY COUPLES IN DENMARK

By SHEILA RULE
Special to The New York Times

COPENHAGEN, Oct. 1—In what gay rights advocates hailed as the first unions of their kind in the world, six homosexual couples were legally joined today in "registered partnerships" that gave them most rights of married heterosexuals, but not the right to adopt or obtain joint custody of a child.

Associated Press

One of six homosexual couples who were united yesterday under a new Danish law. Eigil, left, and Axel Axgil, who have lived together since 1950, celebrated after the ceremony in Copenhagen.

Each of the couples entered a small room in the ornate City Hall, and in civil rites that differed from those of heterosexuals only in the description of the union were asked by Mayor Tom Ahlberg if they wanted to be "in partnership" with each other. After saying "I do," the couples, all of them male, were given certificates of their partnership.

The ceremonies, followed by the traditional throwing of rice and confetti, were held on the day a new national law went into effect making Denmark the first country to legalize homosexual unions.

Members of Parliament passed the measure in May by a vote of 71 to 47, after a 40-year campaign by gay rights advocates. In this country where Government has traditionally been sympathetic toward minorities, opposition has come mainly from the small Christian People's Party, which called the legislation unnatural, unethical and dramatically at odds with the laws of other countries.

Unions Not Called Marriages

Although the law stops short of calling the unions marriages, it gives homosexual couples most of the advantages and disadvantages of marriage. Partners—at least one must be a resident Danish citizen—are liable for each other's maintenance. They also have the automatic right to inherit the other's property, and must undertake legal divorce proceedings to dissolve the partnership. They can also be forced to pay alimony, and in some circumstances, a partner can be held responsible for the other's tax liabilities.

But the couples cannot be married in the state Danish People's Church, which is Evangelical Lutheran and to which more than 90 percent of the population of 5 million belong. The church does not recognize such unions.

Lesbians in particular object to the law's failure to grant the right to adopt or obtain joint custody of a child. Some gay-rights advocates saw this as the main reason that no women took part in today's ceremonies.

Advocates said that Sweden last year became the first country to provide some minimum rights to homosexual couples, including rights involving inheritance, but that the Swedish law equates homosexual couples with unmarried heterosexual couples.

In the United States, San Francisco will have a measure on the November ballot that would give legal recognition to the "domestic partnership." The measure would allow couples in nontraditional relationships to register their partnerships with the city, in much the same way that couples apply for marriage licenses.

New York's highest court expanded the legal definition of a family in July, ruling that a gay couple who had lived together for a decade could be considered a family under New York City rent-control regulations.

At the ceremony here today, Eigil and Axel Axgil, who have lived together since 1950 and taken syllables from their first names to form a common surname, were among those legally united. Axel Axgil founded the first national association for homosexuals in 1948, after which he was dismissed from his job and became the target of other discrimination.

"The only way to be able to move anything is to be open about it," said Eigil Axgil, 67 years old. "You have to say that this is the way I am so society can be open to you. If everyone follows this lead in Denmark, if everyone goes out and says this is the way they are and go out of the closet, this event will also happen in the rest of the world."

The Christian People's Party, which has four of the 179 seats in Parliament, unsuccessfully tried to force a referendum on the issue but hopes to make the law an issue in the next election, which must be held by 1992.

Flemming Kofod-Svendsen, the party's chairman, said in an interview that his party opposed the law for several reasons, including its impracticality. The law is not recognized in any other country, he said.

Also, Mr. Kofod-Svendsen said, the Bible makes it clear that marriage can only be between man and woman.

"We also oppose the law for family reasons," the legislator said. "The foundation for family life and society is marriage which, it is my understanding, is between a man and a woman."

Members of the Rev. Ivan Larsen's 11,000-member Evangelical-Lutheran parish in Copenhagen apparently disagree. The cleric said that when he told parishioners he would be joining in a homosexual partnership today with Ove Carlsen, a school psychologist, they wished the couple "good luck."

Bishops in the state church are apparently at odds over the law. Local newspapers reported that some favored being able to bless homosexual couples united in partnership. But other bishops were quoted as saying that because the law stated that homosexual couples were entering into a partnership and not a marriage, the debate was irrelevant because the church could bless only marriages.

But Else Slange, chairman of the Danish National Organization for Gays and Lesbians, said the fact that Denmark became the first country to adopt such a law had "something to do with our religious traditions."

"I think the Lutheran Church has more and more opened itself up to different kinds of things," she said. "I think that does something to the community, that thoughts get more free."

* * *

January 6, 1991

AS IRELAND BATTLES AIDS, THE CHURCH IS CALLED A ROADBLOCK

By SHEILA RULE
Special to The New York Times

DUBLIN—This nation is playing out the tragic drama of AIDS, and tradition, Roman Catholic orthodoxy and ignorance are among the grim protagonists, advocates in the fight against the disease say.

Ireland does not appear to have as serious a problem as many other countries; it has proportionally far fewer cases than the United States and even fewer than other European countries, official statistics indicate. But advocates say the situation is troubling because conservative attitudes arising from Roman Catholicism both predispose this country to the spread of AIDS and hamper its prevention.

Catholicism dominates Irish society, with 90 to 95 percent of the population of 3.5 million people professing affiliation with the church. Efforts to promote the use of condoms have been opposed because they clash with the church's teachings. The distribution of clean needles to drug addicts has run into similar church-led opposition on the ground that it promotes drug abuse.

'Attitudes Have to Change'

In line with church teachings, abortion is illegal here, making it more likely that mothers with AIDS will pass on the disease to babies. Homosexuality is outlawed as well, leading some campaigners against AIDS to conclude that many gay men are disguising their sexual orientation by marrying and having children, and perhaps further helping the disease's spread.

Some political observers say that the election in December of Mary Robinson, a political outsider, as the first woman to be Ireland's President may signal a liberalizing of attitudes, although the presidency is a largely ceremonial post. A member of the small, leftist Labor Party, Mrs. Robinson campaigned hard for the liberalization of laws on divorce, contraception and homosexuality.

"Attitudes have to change in Ireland," said Brian Murray, chairman of a voluntary organization, Cairde, that helps AIDS victims. "Otherwise, there will not be tolerance of the use of condoms or clean needles. Attitudes arising from Catholicism have produced a very conservative moral ethos that decries the use of condoms in any context. Governments try to fall in behind public opinion and public opinion is led by the church on these issues."

The Government says it is working hard to stem the disease's spread and points to its compulsory AIDS education program in secondary schools and its financing of a drug-treatment center in Dublin that offers condoms, clean needles and counseling.

The church, too, offers materials to help teachers educate students about the dangers of AIDS. It emphasizes monogamy and abstinence.

Church and Morality

"The Catholic Church, as is widely known, promotes the view that sexual morality, if observed, would prove to be a great antidote to the spread of AIDS," said Des Cryan, a spokesman in the Catholic Press and Information Office. "And the general attitude in Ireland, not just among Catholics, but the general attitude is that they basically oppose free, clean-needle schemes because they think it would contribute to drug abuse."

Government statistics put the number of people here diagnosed as having AIDS at 172 as of October. Nearly 1,000 more were said to be infected with the HIV virus, which causes the disease, but doctors and advocates say that there could actually be three times as many cases.

World Health Organization figures show that for 1989 there were 1.3 diagnosed cases of AIDS reported here for every 100,000 people while the United States had 13.3 per 100,000.

Here, about 60 percent of people with the virus and nearly half of those with AIDS are intravenous drug users, representing the sad legacy of cheap heroin dumped into the poor housing projects of Dublin and other European cities in the early 1980's.

The spread of the disease among homosexual men is viewed by officials as a lesser problem and statistics show only 135 infected with the virus.

Those active in fighting AIDS say the country's conservative, church-influenced attitudes have led to the failure both by church and Government to develop practical and comprehensive programs against the disease.

The state-financed program for drug users, which includes outreach workers, is faulted for its location in a fashionable section of Dublin, which critics say leaves it inaccessible to people in deprived areas where drug abuse flourishes.

Sexual Orientation Disguised

The Government has not directed an AIDS education campaign at homosexual men. James Walsh, the state AIDS coordinator, said the rate of homosexual infection slowed in Ireland as it did in other countries after gays started employing safer sexual practices in the mid-1980's.

But some advocates say the actual number of cases of AIDS infection among gay men is not 135 but closer to 2,000. Because homosexuality is illegal, they say, many homosexuals disguise their sexual orientation, marry and have children.

Official statistics are also viewed as misleading in another way. Anti-AIDS campaigners say that because of large-scale emigration, especially among people between the ages of 18 and 35, many Irish citizens infected with the virus could be in other countries.

The Irish characterize their country as a large village of sorts—family-oriented, relatively slow to change but edging toward greater secularism.

Many young people who ignore the church's moral arguments against risky sexual and drug activities still share traditional values like the importance of having a family.

At St. James's Hospital, which treats most of Dublin's AIDS cases, the state's only AIDS consultant said that half of the 120 women there infected with the virus wanted to get pregnant, despite counseling about the disease. The consultant, Dr. Fiona Mulcahy, said the other half insisted that they did not want to get pregnant, but less than a third used contraception.

Amniocentesis Unlikely

Scientists think that about 40 percent of babies of infected mothers will themselves be born with the AIDS virus and die, and that the rest will lose their mothers. Official statistics show that Ireland has 69 babies infected with the AIDS virus.

Family planning experts say it is still nearly impossible to obtain amniocentesis—the medical procedure that can trace fetal abnormalities—because detection of defects could lead to a woman seeking an abortion.

Similarly, until 1979 it was illegal to provide contraceptive services and information; condoms can now be legally sold only at pharmacies, doctors' offices, clinics that treat sexually transmitted diseases, state health boards and family planning centers.

The Roman Catholic Church offers what it calls a "resource pack" as a guide to help teachers discuss AIDS with secondary school students.

The material says that condoms, if used correctly, reduce the risk of infection but provide nothing like complete protection. It says that "sexual intercourse expresses the total, unconditional self-giving of husband and wife, with openness to the procreation of new life," and that the "use of contraceptives contradicts this truth and is, therefore, morally wrong."

The Government began its AIDS education program this school year over the objection of Catholic bishops who viewed it as morally aimless. Mr. Walsh said that the program seeks to promote mutual fidelity in sexual relationships. Students are advised that if they do take risks, condoms provide highly effective prevention.

A Challenge to the People

Mr. Walsh says that some people have criticized this approach from the opposite extreme of the bishops, as slanted too heavily toward trying to instill sexual morality.

Campaigners against AIDS say that to prevent the disease from taking a grim toll, the Irish must challenge the church and other symbols of authority.

David Esson, who runs a self-help group for AIDS victims called Irish Frontliners, said, "Irish people are conditioned in such a way that no matter how big the biggest wrong, they do not speak out against authority, be it the church, a Government minister, a policeman or a teacher."

"They accept what is happening," he said. "This means that we have lost quite a lot of people so far to AIDS and we are going to lose quite a lot more."

* * *

November 7, 1993

THE HIGH PRIEST OF APOSTASY

By ISABELLE DE COURTIVRON

GENET: A Biography
By Edmund White
With a chronology by Albert Dichy
Illustrated. 728 pp. New York: Alfred A. Knopf. $35.

When I studied Proust, Gide, Genet, Cocteau, Rimbaud, Verlaine in graduate school, homosexuality was treated as an anecdote. I was aware that Proust's Albertine was really Albert, I knew about Verlaine's shooting of Rimbaud in

Brussels, I took notes on Gide's fascination with young Arab boys; but having dutifully mentioned these facts in their lectures, our professors quickly switched back to their habitual literary analysis as if sexual preference, and homosexual desire and sensibility, had not made much of an impact on these authors' visions or on their style. And yet this was during the heady days of the early 1970's when sexual liberation seemed to dominate not only our consciousness of the world but also our reading of texts.

Of course, even in the early 70's no professor could treat the works of Jean Genet without touching on the subject of homosexuality; Genet, one of France's most original and forceful novelists and playwrights, had made it the center of his autobiographical fiction. Moreover, we had read Kate Millett's "Sexual Politics," in which she argued that "femininity" was constructed independently of biological attributes and was systematically considered of lesser value, a thesis that she illustrated by way of Genet's gay pairings. Still, in the classroom we did not discuss the world of pederasty, sadomasochism, transvestism, gay prostitution and drag queens. When we went on to study the extraordinary theater of Jean Genet, we reverted to discussions about race and class relations, about roles and functions; the world of homosexuality was once more relegated to the literary closet.

Edmund White's "Genet," a monumental biography that places Genet's personal and literary vision squarely in his exclusively homosexual experience, helps us measure how far criticism (and social consciousness) has come in the past 20 years. At times Mr. White comes perilously close to reducing his subject's complex works to an overinterpretation in light of this particular reading; but his biography is so meticulously researched and detailed, his understanding and illumination of the works is so rich, that the book ultimately succeeds in resisting the nagging temptation of reductionism.

Mr. White, an American novelist who lives in Paris, poses the principal challenge: "The chronicler of Genet's life must grab at any explanation of how someone who left school at the age of 12 became a master of the French language." Indeed, this is one of the great enigmas of French literature, one that Genet himself helped to cultivate as he constructed his own legend through exaggeration, obfuscation, self-transformation and mythification. The real story, however, even when re-established accurately, remains unparalleled; and although the explanation sought by Mr. White is never satisfactorily reached, the process of this extraordinary transformation is what makes his biography so fascinating.

Genet was a child of public welfare and remained a ward of the state until he was 21. Born in 1910 to a 22-year-old unwed mother, he was abandoned by her when he was 30 weeks old and placed with foster parents who lived in a small village in the Morvan, a poor and backward region in east-central France. According to Mr. White's sources, he was doted on by this family, especially its women. But in order to establish his credentials as an outcast and as the apostle of the wretched, he later turned his foster parents into monsters and described his status in the village as that of a despised orphan.

Genet, who was a voracious reader, was sent at the age of 13 directly from school to an educational center run by the public welfare system outside of Paris to study typography. He ran away almost immediately, and after a series of such escapes, of failures in placement in homes and institutions, of arrests for theft and of pseudoscientific attempts to "diagnose" his criminal behavior, he was finally consigned, at the age of 15, to the penal institution of Mettray.

His experience of Mettray and of the barbaric conditions of incarceration were to be fictionalized in "Miracle of the Rose." However, contrary to the strategy he adopted when he demonized his ostensibly felicitous childhood, Genet idealized his incarceration at Mettray, which became the first model of his feudal penchant for small all-male societies organized around strict hierarchies (this penchant and his admiration for all-male societies structured along Nietzschean lines, Mr. White rightly suggests, predisposed him toward fascism; but he was consistently attracted by men of the left who steered him in the opposite direction).

It was at Mettray that he began to realize his destiny as a writer, that he forged his conception of homosexuality as a violent role-playing sexual world and that he conceptualized the themes of honor and treason, of domination and submission, of authenticity and illusion that were to inform all of his writings.

Genet enlisted in the army in 1929 and was sent to Beirut and Damascus. This was his first experience of French colonialism, and what he witnessed in the Middle East immediately resonated with the oppression he associated with the Morvan and with Mettray. It was also the only time in his life he acted as a representative of the French society he so despised. For this reason, he would later minimize the amount of time he spent in the army, the most conventional moment in his life. He re-enlisted several times and finally deserted in 1936.

Back in France, he continued to steal (handkerchiefs or books—as Mr. White states, "he was a highly literary thug") and was arrested numerous times. However, the years 1940-47 saw the writing of his most powerful fiction; two of those novels were written while he was behind bars ("Our Lady of the Flowers" and "Miracle of the Rose"). Mr. White's comparisons of Genet with Proust (one of the most important influences on Genet) and with Gide in terms of class and sexuality are compelling. He shows how Genet's vagabond peregrinations were a search for survival—unlike the great tradition of the middle class, which sought exotic escape from inner conflicts (a la Gide). He also emphasizes the degree to which Genet differed from these two major authors in the full (if painful) acceptance of his sexuality and of its antisocial implications. Genet rejected the traditional pleas for understanding, or the rational assignment of blame, in favor of presenting homosexuality as entirely evil, and as an element in the trio of virtues he was to establish with theft and treachery. Evil became his own code word for an outsider's morality. One longs for a much-overdue biography of Gide that would be informed by such trenchant analysis.

Jean Cocteau, in the early 40's, was to inaugurate Genet's public career just as, a few years later, Sartre would consecrate it. After a number of stays in France's most notorious prisons for repeated thefts, Genet had become a strange hybrid: half criminal and half literary celebrity. Though his name was on everyone's lips in Paris, his books were published clandestinely. He eventually moved from Cocteau's fashionable Right Bank circles to Sartre's Left Bank existentialist family. Because he continued to be threatened with imprisonment, in July 1948 Sartre and Cocteau joined forces to ask for a presidential pardon for the writer, which was granted in 1949. "This letter," the author writes, "quickly became one of the cornerstones of the public and permanent Genet legend" (the "noble outlaw"). By 1952 Sartre had written his book "Saint Genet: Actor and Martyr" and in doing so had canonized Genet.

Genet had completed five novels, all the poetry he would write and several plays. His works were published under the prestigious Gallimard imprint. He had been pardoned by the president of France. In 1949, nearing 40, he sank into a deep depression: "Canonized, pardoned, consecrated, assimilated, Genet was no longer society's scourge. He had become its pet."

Only in the mid-50's did Genet, who was capable of great regeneration, begin transforming himself from a novelist to a playwright; he changed his image from a dandy to a thug, ceased being a Cocteau fan and became an admirer of the ascetic Giacometti and turned from preoccupations with the self in his writing to obsession with the dispossessed of the world. This phase saw the birth of his plays "The Balcony," "The Blacks," "The Screens," in which he explored identity and difference, illusion and authenticity, reciprocity and imitation, in order to reveal the mechanisms of power and the social dynamics of a system he reviled. This productive period also coincided with his love for a young circus acrobat, Abdallah Bentaga. Silence set in again in 1964, at the time of Abdallah's suicide. In 1967 Genet himself attempted suicide.

Genet's third transformation came in 1968, under the guise of political activism. From that time on, he refused to speak of his writing and threw himself into political causes like those of the Black Panthers and the Palestinians. Mr. White judiciously interprets the reasons why someone as fiercely anarchistic as Genet would have been attracted to strictly organized political groups. He explains that Genet's belief in the hollowness of experience and the interchangeability of human beings, as well as his monastic insistence on ridding himself of all material possessions, led him to political causes that themselves were constructed around something that was missing, to virile all-male groups that had no land and no country. Genet, however, always thought that once revolutions were accomplished, the new victors imitated their predecessors, and he often stated that if the Palestinians gained a homeland he would no longer be on their side. During those years he wrote mostly political essays, traveled to the Middle East (where he stayed in Palestinian camps) and to North Africa and supported German terrorist groups. At the same time, in his private life he continued to be attracted to young (usually heterosexual) men, creating "families" with these men, their mothers, their wives and children, all of whom he continued to support at great expense. Throat cancer having been diagnosed in 1979, Genet, the cultured outcast, the erudite thief, the unassimilable poet, died in 1986, a few months after his play "The Balcony" had been staged (one might say enshrined) at the Comedie Francaise.

Edmund White's research is impressive and abundant and constitutes a treasure for scholars. For less specialized readers, however, this abundance sometimes gets in the way of the narration. It is as if the biographer had been reluctant to exclude any small bit of information gathered through great effort over the past six years. Some parts of the book, especially those that deal with later years when so many more witnesses are alive to be interviewed (and when the activities of the main subject are more diffuse and less interesting), are cluttered by anecdotes strung together for no apparent reason and by many minor characters who appear and disappear without purpose except to show whom Genet knew, liked, worked or slept with (and, inevitably, betrayed). Some cutting would have been in order here to make the biography less cumbersome.

There are also many original contributions: Genet's extraordinary sensibility to art, particularly to Rembrandt and Giacometti, about whom he wrote eloquent essays; his hilarious adventures with Allen Ginsberg, William Burroughs and Terry Southern at the 1968 Democratic National Convention in Chicago, where Genet supported the hippies but was attracted to the cops; the favorable reception of his works in England and in the United States (where, although his plays were critical successes, he could not obtain a visa, according to Mr. White, because of his association with the Communist Party, his criminal record and his homosexuality).

The French are a people historically torn between passionate individualism and collective adherence to strictly codified traditions, and they have always made room for those two characteristics in their literary pantheon: on one hand the venerable Academie Francaise, on the other the poetes maudits who, in challenging the French bourgeoisie with their insults, their penchant for drugs and alcohol, their sexual provocations and, most important, their incandescent writings, have become its darlings. Edmund White's biography reminds us that Jean Genet was a spectacular poete maudit.

Isabelle de Courtivron, chairwoman of the department of European and comparative literatures at the Massachusetts Institute of Technology, is the co-editor, with Whitney Chadwick, of "Significant Others: Creativity and Intimate Partnership."

Correction: A biographical note on page 1 of The Times Book Review today with a review of "Genet: A Biography" misstates the reviewer's title. She is head of the department of foreign languages and literatures at the Massachusetts Institute of Technology.

* * *

February 23, 1994

POPE DEPLORES GAY MARRIAGE

By ALAN COWELL
Special to The New York Times

ROME, Feb. 22—Fueling a debate in the United States and Europe over homosexual matrimony, Pope John Paul II chastised such unions today as "a serious threat to the future of the family and society" and said they could not be "recognized and ratified as a marriage in society."

The Pope's comments were made in a 100-page letter on family values that not only restated the Vatican's familiar views on contraception, divorce and abortion but also sent a message to Catholics to refrain from supporting the notion of gay or lesbian marriage.

The document was issued two weeks after the European Parliament in Strasbourg offered support for the idea of homosexuals' marrying and adopting children.

Several cities in Italy permit local officials to perform public marriages uniting gay and lesbian couples. Some legislators have proposed a national law legalizing such weddings, even though opinion surveys show most Italians oppose the idea.

Gay Adoptions Opposed

The question of adoption of children by homosexuals is even more contentious in Italy, according to surveys showing few Italians favor the idea.

The Pope's letter, addressed to Catholics rather than to clergymen, was drafted long before the European Parliament vote and was timed to coincide with the United Nations Year of the Family. However, since the vote on Feb. 8, the Pope has taken issue strongly with the nonbinding resolution, telling worshipers here on Sunday that the assembly was wrong in "inappropriately conferring an institutional value on deviant behavior."

In his letter, the Pope said, "Marriage, which undergirds the institution of the family, is constituted by the covenant whereby a man and a woman establish between themselves a partnership for their whole life."

"Only such a union can be recognized and ratified as a marriage in society. Other interpersonal unions which do not fulfill the above conditions cannot be recognized, despite certain growing trends which represent a serious threat to the future of the family and society itself."

*　*　*

June 26, 1995

PERSONALIZING NAZIS' HOMOSEXUAL VICTIMS

By DAVID W. DUNLAP

WASHINGTON—Transformed by homosexuals from a mark of Nazi persecution into an emblem of gay liberation, the pink triangle gained great currency but lost its link to personal experience.

Today, after a half century, the symbol can be associated once again with one man's name, with his voice, with his story.

Josef Kohout is the name; prisoner No. 1896, Block 6, at the Flossenburg concentration camp in Bavaria, near the Czech border. At the age of 24, he was arrested in Vienna as a homosexual outlaw after the Gestapo obtained a photograph he had inscribed to another young man pledging "eternal love." Liberated six years later by American troops, Mr. Kohout returned to Vienna, where he died in 1994.

Among his personal effects was a fragile strip of cloth, two inches long and less than an inch wide, with the numbers 1896 on the right and a pink triangle on the left. It is the only one known to have been worn by a prisoner who can be identified, said Dr. Klaus Muller of the United States Holocaust Memorial Museum here.

Together with Mr. Kohout's journal and the letters his parents wrote to the camp commander in a fruitless effort to visit him, the badge has been given to the museum by Mr. Kohout's companion.

"I find it very important that the pink triangle is connected with the people who were forced to wear it," said Dr. Muller, the museum's project director for Western Europe.

In its mission, the museum embraces not only the Jewish victims of the Holocaust, but other groups who were persecuted, like the Gypsies, the disabled, Jehovah's Witnesses and Russian prisoners of war.

It has begun a $1.5 million campaign to locate homosexual survivors and document their experiences, following a suggestion from David B. Mixner, a corporate consultant in Los Angeles who is active in gay causes. The campaign coordinator, Debra S. Eliason, said $350,000 has been pledged so far.

Patrons of the museum are given identification cards of victims to personalize the otherwise vast historical narrative, and of the victims identified in the cards, a handful were homosexuals. On his first visit, Representative Gerry E. Studds of Massachusetts, one of three openly gay members of Congress, coincidentally received the card of Willem Arondeus, a homosexual Dutch resistance fighter who was killed in 1943. "For me to get that card was just stunning," Mr. Studds said.

"Of the many places we never existed, certainly the Holocaust was one, in most people's minds," Mr. Studds said. "The supreme triumph in the last generation, in terms of the struggle of gay and lesbian people, is recognition of the simple fact that we exist."

The donation of Mr. Kohout's mementoes to the museum will contribute to that recognition, but he is not the only homosexual victim of Nazism whose presence is being felt. Gradually, at the twilight of their lives, a handful of survivors are stepping forward to press gingerly their own claims for recognition, having all but given up hope for restitution.

"The world we hoped for did not transpire," said a declaration signed earlier this year by eight survivors, now living in Germany, France, Poland and the Netherlands. They called for the memorializing and documenting of Nazi atrocities against homosexuals and others.

They pleaded for "the moral support of the public."

The signers included Kurt von Ruffin, now 93, a popular actor and opera singer in Berlin during the 1930's who was sent to the Lichtenburg camp in Prettin, and Friedrich-Paul von Groszheim, 89, who was arrested, released, rearrested, tortured, castrated, released, rearrested and imprisoned in the Neuengamme camp at Lubeck.

Between 10,000 and 15,000 homosexuals may have been incarcerated in the camps, Dr. Muller said, out of approximately 100,000 men who were arrested under Paragraph 175 of the German criminal code, which called for the imprisonment of any "male who commits lewd and lascivious acts with another male." (The law was silent on lesbianism, although individual instances of persecutions of lesbians have been recorded.)

Perhaps 60 percent of those in the camps died, Dr. Muller said, meaning that even in 1945, there may have been only 4,000 survivors. Today, Dr. Muller knows of fewer than 15.

Their travails did not end at liberation. They were still officially regarded as criminals, rather than as political prisoners, since Paragraph 175 remained in force in West Germany until 1969. They were denied reparations and the years they spent in the camps were deducted from their pensions. Some survivors were even jailed again.

Old enough to be grandfathers and great-grandfathers, the survivors scarcely courted attention as homosexuals, having learned all too well the perils of notoriety. "It is not easy to tell a story you were forced to hide for 50 years," Dr. Muller said.

In their collective declaration this year, the survivors acknowledged as much. "Today," they wrote, "we are too old and tired to struggle for the recognition of the Nazi injustice we suffered. Many of us never dared to testify. Many gay men and lesbian women died alone with their haunting memories."

One of the first men to break his silence was the anonymous "Prisoner X. Y.," who furnished a vividly detailed account of life as a homosexual inmate in the 1972 book, "The Men With the Pink Triangle," by Heinz Heger, which was reissued last year by Alyson Publications.

By a coincidence that still astonishes him, Dr. Muller said, Prisoner X. Y.—"the best documented homosexual inmate of a camp"—turned out to be Mr. Kohout.

After his arrest in 1939, Mr. Kohout was taken to the Sachsenhausen camp and served at the Klinker brickworks, which he called "the 'Auschwitz' for homosexuals." Prisoners who were not beaten to death could easily be killed by heavy carts barreling down the steep incline of the clay pits.

In 1940, he was transferred to Flossenburg. On Christmas Eve 1941 inmates were made to sing carols in front of a 30-foot-high Christmas tree on the parade ground. Flanking it were gallows from which eight Russian prisoners had been hanging since morning. "Whenever I hear a carol sung—no matter how beautifully—I remember the Christmas tree at Flossenburg with its grisly 'decorations,' " he wrote.

Mr. Kohout died in March 1994, at the age of 79. A month later, in an apartment in Vienna, his surviving companion submitted to an interview by Dr. Muller, who had tracked him down through a gay group in Austria and pressed him for more and more information.

As Dr. Muller recalled it, the companion finally said: "If you're so interested in all these details, I have some material in two boxes and, honestly, I didn't have the strength to go through it because I'm still struggling with his death. But if you want to, we could look at these."

The first thing the companion unpacked was Mr. Kohout's pink triangle badge. The first thing Dr. Muller thought was, "This is impossible."

"We had searched for a pink triangle for years," he said, "one that would not only document the Nazi marking system but also could be reconstructed as a part of one individual story."

Included in the donation from Mr. Kohout's companion were letters written by Amalia and Josef Kohout, the prisoner's parents. On Dec. 28, 1943, they asked the commander at Flossenburg for permission to visit their son, whom they had not seen in four and a half years.

Two months later, having heard nothing, they wrote again. This time, they despaired because their son had failed to notify them that he had received a package of bread and marmalade they had sent. Dr. Muller said the Kohouts were brave not to have signed these letters with the customary "Heil Hitler."

The letters and the triangle itself are still in storage, but part of Mr. Kohout's journal is now on display at the museum. It is the page on which he wrote simply of his liberators' arrival on April 24, 1945: "Amerikaner gekommen."

* * *

March 26, 1998

THE IDEAL MARTYR: OSCAR WILDE HAS THE LAST LAUGH

By MATT WOLF

LONDON, March 25—Nearly 100 years after his death and vilification, Oscar Wilde is suddenly and somewhat surprisingly back in everyone's good graces here, and the object of apparently endless fascination.

Why such regard from the country that famously reviled the Irishman during his life as a bon vivant, poet, playwright and esthete?

The establishment, it seems, embraced Wilde's plays only insofar as it could tolerate his life, and once that life became bound up with tales of male prostitutes and charges of perversion, even the most elegantly spun epigram could not forestall his premature and despairing end.

As Wilde says in Moises Kaufman's "Gross Indecency: The Three Trials of Oscar Wilde," the piece of theatrical reportage that has become an Off Broadway hit, "One day you'll be ashamed of your treatment of me."

Shame may play its part in the current explosion in Britain of interest in Wilde that includes two new plays and a film about him as well as various television shows, stage revivals and film adaptations of his plays, and what promises to be the fullest museum exhibition of his manuscripts. Currently in

London, one can see Tom Stoppard's "Invention of Love" at the Royal National Theater, in which Wilde makes an 11th-hour appearance (played by Michael Fitzgerald), and the new film biography "Wilde." Liam Neeson opened last week to mixed reviews in a West End run of "The Judas Kiss," the David Hare play about Wilde, that is to travel on to Broadway.

But a collective feeling of guilt by itself cannot explain an intensity of focus surpassing even the recent and similar immersions in Virginia Woolf and the rest of the Bloomsbury group. It's as if Wilde's 46 years had become a sort of Rorschach test, a uniquely English crucible, fusing issues of cultural, national, and sexual identity, from which artists and commentators can extract what they like.

"We do pour into Oscar Wilde a lot of things we want him to have and want him to be," said Stephen Fry, the 40-year-old actor who has the title role in "Wilde," an English film from the director-producer team of "Tom and Viv" that is scheduled to open in the United States on May 1. (The British premiere was on Oct. 16, Wilde's birthday.) "To some, he's a gay martyr. To others, his Irishness is central. There are those who see him as an icon of artistic independence."

Indeed, there are as many Wildes as there are people writing about him. One play, "The Secret Fall of Constance Wilde" by Thomas Kilroy, which had its premiere last fall at the Abbey Theater in Dublin, centers on Wilde's widow, Constance. In "The Invention of Love," Mr. Stoppard contrasts the flamboyant Wilde with the terminally repressed A. E. Housman, the English poet and classicist who is the true subject of the play. Wilde is there as a figure of antithesis, Mr. Stoppard, said, "someone who crashed in flames at a very young age," while the beloved Housman lived to be 77.

By Mr. Hare's own reckoning, "The Judas Kiss," too, is an act of imaginative empathy, not a chronicle of events in the manner of "Gross Indecency."

"I'm effectively saying, 'This is poetry,'"Mr. Hare said. "The play's purpose in existing is not really to tell us about Oscar." He said his play bore no relation to his screenplay about Wilde, "Feasting With Panthers," which was never filmed. "Thirty-five million dollars was an awful lot to spend on a tragic gay subject," Mr. Hare said, "what's worse, a 19th-century tragic gay subject."

This time, he said, he was drawn to Wilde's life as a way of completing an ad hoc dramatic trilogy that includes "Skylight" and his ongoing West End hit "Amy's View": three plays, he said, "about love and sacrificial love."

Richard Eyre, the former artistic director of the National, is the director of both the Stoppard and Hare plays, and he said he had been surprised to find himself working within the space of six months on two plays involving the same literary figure. "Both Tom and David are heterosexual writers drawn towards a man sort of crucified for his sexuality," he said. "You do feel that, given Wilde's own time, somebody conspicuously not heterosexual is a liberating way of writing

about the phenomenon of romantic love, of loving someone hopelessly. Wilde was famously a victim of romantic love."

Indeed, the Wilde allure may simply lie in the appeal to any artist of a life story that involves scandal, doomed romance, a rebel and a fatal flaw: his pursuit of a lawsuit against his lover's fiercely unrepentant father, the Marquess of Queensberry.

"His was the ur-scandal, the prototypic scandal," Mr. Fry said. "Now we're realizing that if his art was serious, maybe his life was, too."

Wilde will also live on in other ways. Three separate film adaptations are planned of his 1895 play "An Ideal Husband," which has had renewed prominence since Peter Hall's acclaimed 1992 revival. The play has been on and off the West End, including a visit to Broadway, for more than 1,500 performances.

Oliver Parker, who directed the 1995 film of "Othello," with Laurence Fishburne and Kenneth Branagh, said he wanted a June start for his own $11 million adaptation of "The Ideal Husband." A rival $3.5 million version is set to begin filming on May 11, with the co-producer, Zygi Kamasa, touting James Wilby, Peter Ustinov and Amanda Donohoe or Jennifer Ehle as possible cast members; the first-time filmmaker Bill Cartlidge will write and direct.

Not to be outdone, the English clothing designer John Pearse said he had written a contemporary screenplay, set in the United States, of Wilde's "Picture of Dorian Gray," adapted in the very free style of the new film version of "Great Expectations." Mr. Pearse said the $20 million venture was "bubbling along," with Mike Figgis ("Leaving Las Vegas") planning to direct, perhaps as early as the fall. Those who prefer to read Wilde can head in 2000 to the British Library, which is preparing the most complete display yet of his manuscripts and letters.

Amid what one can only call Wilde mania, can there be too much of a good thing? "It's a bit late in the day," said Alan Bennett, the playwright, who considered a biographical screenplay on Wilde but decided against it. "The battle, as it were, is won. I think I find all this just slightly self-righteous."

Merlin Holland, Wilde's grandson and himself a writer and journalist, said he was "frightened about overexposure, that people will get Oscar sickness and feel there's been a surfeit of him."

But Mr. Holland, 52, whose book, "The Wilde Album," is to be published in the United States by Henry Holt on April 7, said he was pleased "that England was finally coming round to the conclusion, and not before time, that the man was an artist as well as a homosexual."

Mr. Fry said: "The story of Wilde will always move people of each generation in the same way as the story of Christ or Socrates. He will retain that position as one of the great men of the century."

* * *

February 18, 1999

U.S. WRITER ON GAY TOPICS IS BADLY BEATEN IN AN IRISH CITY

By JAMES F. CLARITY

DUBLIN, Feb. 17—A prominent American writer on gay themes who was beaten on Jan. 31 was in critical but stable condition here tonight, hospital officials said.

The writer, Robert Drake, 36, of Philadelphia, received "severe head injuries" in Sligo, the police said. No one has been arrested.

On Feb. 3, two men in their early 20's, accompanied by a lawyer, made a statement in the case to the police in Sligo. They have not been charged.

Friends of Mr. Drake's in the United States say the two young men had told the police that they beat him senseless in his apartment, where he was working on a book, after he had made sexual overtures to them.

The police did not confirm that today. The national headquarters said the case had been referred to the Director of Public Prosecutions in Dublin.

Mr. Drake won a Lambda award last year for an anthology in 1997, for which he was a co-editor, "His 2: Brilliant New Fiction by Gay Writers." His most recent book is "The Gay Canon: Great Books Every Gay Man Should Read." In the mid-90's, he wrote a novel about a gay man who is murdered because of his sexual orientation.

Mr. Drake's former partner, Dr. E. Scott Pretorius, a radiologist at the Hospital of the University of Pennsylvania, has written to friends of Mr. Drake, asking them to help provide $10,000 to fly him back to the United States. Dr. Pretorius wrote that when he visited Mr. Drake at William Beaumont Hospital here, Mr. Drake was barely conscious most of the time.

Dr. Pretorius also wrote to friends and officials of gay organizations: "Robert's family, friends and I are outraged by this unimaginable act of violence against this gentle and kind individual. It is my hope that the parties responsible will be zealously prosecuted to the furthest extent of Irish law. Crimes such as these are the natural byproduct of a culture which continues to relegate gay men and lesbians to second-class citizenship. We are seen as less than human by the terrorists who commit crimes such as these."

The police here do not keep statistics on crimes specifically against homosexuals. A spokesman said such crimes were rare in Ireland.

Homosexuals march without controversy in St. Patrick's Day parades in Dublin, Cork and other large cities. Parliament has several openly gay members, some of whom have been Cabinet ministers. Gay bars and nightclubs operate openly here. And the plays of one of Ireland's most famous gay men, Oscar Wilde, are frequently performed.

"It would be an isolated crime," the police spokesman added.

* * *

April 15, 1999

THREE GAY GUYS ON BRITISH TV: WHAT'S THE FUSS?

By SARAH LYALL

LONDON, April 14—It burst onto British television in February, an explosion of graphic language, male nudity and explicit sex guaranteed to offend as many people as it enthralled. It was called "Queer as Folk," and it set out to venture where British television had not gone before, chronicling the lives and loves of a trio of gay men from Manchester who were not role models, victims or martyrs.

If that was not radical enough, the series seemed determined to shock. Its first episode, which daringly included a 15-year-old boy having sex with a 29-year-old man, generated outrage from all sides, not least from gay-rights groups who said it played to antigay stereotypes. Meanwhile conservatives said they were horrified, both by the act and by the audacity of depicting it on television.

But as "Queer as Folk" continued its eight-week run, a strange thing happened. It began to mellow into a compelling drama that many viewers began to find as absorbing as any late-night soap opera. Never mind the homosexuality: after a few weeks, it seemed, the three million or so people who tuned in each week—more than half of them women—were drawn simply by the story.

"Quite apart from anything else, the pace of the script is so fast, funny and brave," wrote Barbara Ellen in The Observer of London. And writing in The Independent, Allison Pearson called the series "smart, funny, beautifully acted and squelchingly explicit."

But the discussion did not go away. And this week, as "Queer as Folk" finishes its first run with the promise of a second season, most likely next year, viewers, critics and programmers are still debating what if anything the series says about the state of homosexuality and the state of television in Britain.

The series' co-creator and writer, Russell T. Davies, said he knew he was making history of sorts when Channel Four hired him to write a series about gay men whose sexuality was accepted as a matter of course rather than as a novelty or an anomaly. The title derives from an old Yorkshire saying, "There's nowt so queer as folk," meaning there's nothing so odd as people.

Channel Four, a commercial competitor of the BBC whose mandate in part is to appeal to nonmainstream constituencies, had been looking for a way to make a series in which "heterosexuals barely get a look-in," as Gub Neal, the station's head of drama, put it.

It's not that homosexuals haven't appeared on British television. But to the extent that gay characters have been featured in popular shows like the soap opera "Brookside," they have usually been AIDS sufferers, victims of social and employment discrimination or vehicles onto which others can project their fears and prejudices. And other shows, like Armistead Maupin's "Tales of the City," have tended to focus on the political aspects of being homosexual.

"Most of the gay drama we've had on British television has dealt with big statements: victimization, the political agenda, AIDS," Mr. Neal said. "But this group of characters doesn't think they're victims at all. They're not even aware that they're a minority. They simply exist and say, 'Hey, we don't have to make any apologies, and we're not going away.' The series has given us a chance to simply reveal gay life, to some extent, in its ordinariness."

But how ordinary are the characters in "Queer as Folk"? The setting is a small but thriving urban gay community in Britain's heartland, and the plot concerns a group of night-club-loving young men who are affluent, unattached and generally revel in their promiscuity. Among other things, the series shows them bare-chested and dancing, kissing and having sex with strangers and making bawdy jokes about their sexuality and romantic conquests.

It was this kind of behavior that upset many critics, even those who said they supported homosexual rights. "No one in 'Queer as Folk' is remotely admirable," wrote John Macleod in The Herald of Glasgow, listing all the things he found distasteful about the series: "promiscuity, age-exploitation, unlawful drug use, deception, filthy language, drunkenness, infidelity, betrayal and callousness."

And that summarized the left's initial objection to the series. While conservative-minded people said it was terrible to air graphic depictions of gay sex—some scenes were "little short of pornographic," wrote Tim Lusher in the right-leaning Daily Mail—advocates of gay rights worried that "Queer as Folk" could only endanger their cause.

"It didn't challenge any stereotypes," said Angela Mason, director of Stonewall, a gay-rights lobbying group. "It was ridiculous. I thought the explicit sex scenes with a youthful 15-year-old did smack of sensationalism."

Many of the criticisms focused on the behavior of Stuart, one of the main characters, a charming, good-looking Lothario with a ravenous sexual appetite and a studied indifference to the feelings of others. He doesn't care that Nathan, the drop-dead handsome 15-year-old he sleeps with in the first episode, wants a real relationship. Nor does Stuart care that Vince, his best friend, has been in love with him for years. All Stuart wants, he says, is to have a good time with as many men as he can.

"Every libel hurled at the gay community over the years," Mr. Macleod wrote, "seems vindicated by 'Queer as Folk.'"

But in Mr. Davies's view, the characters should not have to be representative or admirable. "What straight drama sets out by saying, 'We must depict the whole of straight life'?" he asked. "This is a very, very narrow slice of gay life. To criticize it for not depicting everyone is like watching a current-affairs documentary and saying, 'Why isn't there more cookery?'"

Mr. Davies, who is homosexual, said he found it liberating to write about characters who live hedonistically at times without excuse and without apology. Nathan is "out, and he's proud, and he's happy," Mr. Davies said. "That seems to be what some people found so shocking. I think they would have

been happier if I'd done a story about a 15-year-old who is gay and who goes out and hangs himself."

To be sure, Mr. Neal said, Mr. Davies's characters are much more interesting to watch than, say, a monogamous middle-aged gay couple would be. "It wouldn't have been that exciting to show them doing things like cooking for each other and going out for Sunday lunch," Mr. Neal said. "The series doesn't have to make big comments about life. It does what British drama has done for years, to say that we can follow the small details of people's lives and find that very interesting."

By the end of the series this week (in the final episode, on Tuesday, Stuart discovers rejection for the first time), many of the original critics had begun to accept, and even embrace, "Queer as Folk."

"I think it's been good that we've had it because it's pushed back a lot of boundaries and opened up a lot of issues," said Mark Watson, a spokesman for Stonewall. "And it's genuinely good for the gay community in that it doesn't have us all agonizing over our sexuality or dying of AIDS. I hope it will make producers think they can get away with making more dramas about lesbians and gay people and can develop them more freely."

Mr. Neal, too, said he hoped "Queer as Folk" would prove a turning point. "There's never been anything that was this explicit or graphic or sustained in its depiction of gay characters," Mr. Neal said. "We've come a long way when every gay character on television doesn't have to be a positive stereotype."

* * *

October 14, 1999

FRANCE GIVES LEGAL STATUS TO UNMARRIED COUPLES

By SUZANNE DALEY

PARIS, Oct. 13—The French Parliament passed a new law today giving legal status to unmarried couples, including homosexual unions.

The Socialist Government proposed the law nearly two years ago, touching off protests by conservatives and the Catholic Church.

The law allows couples, of the same sex or not, to enter into a union and be entitled to the same rights as married couples in such areas as income tax, inheritance, housing and social welfare.

Legalization of the unions, or "civil solidarity pacts," known here by the acronym PACS, stems from a promise that Prime Minister Lionel Jospin made to recognize gay relationships.

But during the idea's gestation, it grew to include virtually any two people sharing a home, be it brother and sister or even a priest and his housekeeper.

Indeed, the Government has gone out of its way to say that PACS are not marriages but a new form of legal coupling that recognizes the needs of people today.

Defending the new statute, the Justice Minister, Elizabeth Guigou said it would force "the retreat of homophobia" and offer "a solution to the five million couples who live together without being married."

The law passed in the National Assembly by a vote of 315-249. But conservative lawmakers, who delayed passage several times, immediately said they would ask the Constitutional Council to decide whether it is unconstitutional, in which case it would become void.

The new law makes France the first traditionally Catholic nation to recognize homosexual unions. But even as the law proceeded through its last debate, protesters staged a noisy demonstration outside the National Assembly.

Conservatives and the Catholic Church have denounced the legislation as an assault on the family, an unraveling of the moral fabric of society and a license for debauchery. Debates over the bill were among the stormiest the country has seen as impassioned legislators railed at each other.

Earlier this year, more than 200,000 people marched through Paris to protest the law. One group, the Future of Culture, bombarded Mr. Jospin with 60,000 postcards, saying the plan would "destroy the remains of civilization still separating us from barbarism." About half the country's 36,000 mayors said at the outset that they would have nothing to do with officiating at gay unions.

Yet surveys showed that nearly half of the French people supported PACS for homosexuals and even more wanted them for other relationships. Supporters of the law argued that it was a long overdue acknowledgment of modern relationships in a country where an estimated two million heterosexual people live together outside of marriage and 40 percent of the children are born to unwed parents.

Supporters say the bill will help not only gay couples, but also young heterosexual couples, and older people and relatives who want to live together and pool their resources. "Voulez-vous PACS-er avec moi?" became a hot joke here for a while.

Among the provisions in the law, employers will have to take couples' joint vacation plans into account. Partners will be able to help foreign partners enter the country and each partner will become liable for the other's debts.

Couples who want to enter into PACS will sign up before a court clerk. The contract can be revoked by either party with a simple declaration, made in writing, which gives the partner three months' notice. It does not extend any rights to homosexuals wanting to adopt children or expand any parental rights.

In the end, however, the new law has not entirely satisfied gay organizations, who are unhappy that the PACS consign homosexual unions to a lower status than marriage and make no mention of adoption.

Many people expressed disappointment that the law requires that they register their union and live together for three years before they can get the benefits of filing a joint tax return.

* * *

January 13, 2000

BRITISH, UNDER EUROPEAN RULING, END BAN ON OPENLY GAY SOLDIERS

By SARAH LYALL

LONDON, Jan. 12—The government announced a code of conduct for the military today that ends its ban on openly gay men and women serving in the armed forces.

The action follows a European court ruling last fall that Britain could no longer keep the exclusion. It ends a decades-old practice of subjecting gays in the military to intrusive investigations and dishonorable discharges.

The change brings Britain into line with almost all other NATO nations, including France, Canada and Germany, which allow openly gay men and lesbians to serve in their armed forces.

The United States, with its "don't ask, don't tell" policy, is at variance with that trend. The policy, adopted by the Clinton administration, allows gays to serve provided they do not disclose or discuss their sexuality. President Clinton himself has objected to the results of the policy.

In the American presidential campaign, both contenders for the Democratic nomination have said they would work to change the policy so that gays could serve openly, while leading Republicans stand by the policy. The topic has become more charged since the killing of a gay soldier at a Kentucky base last summer.

The new British policy sets out a code of conduct for all manner of social and sexual relations, whether heterosexual or homosexual.

Under the guidelines, "unacceptable social conduct" that might result in disciplinary action includes sexual harassment; overt displays of affection that might offend others; and taking sexual advantage of subordinates.

The code determines that commanders have the right to be aware of and to intervene in the personal lives of their subordinates. "In the area of personal relationships," it says, there is an "overriding operational imperative to sustain team cohesion and to maintain trust and loyalty between commanders and those they command."

That "imposes a need for standards of social behavior which are more demanding than those required by society at large," the statement says.

The about-face in British policy became inevitable on Sept. 27 when the European Court of Human Rights in Strasbourg, France, unanimously ruled in favor of four former servicemen and -women who were discharged in the mid-1990's because of their homosexuality. In ruling against the British government, the court found that its ban violated the fundamental human right to privacy, as set out in the European Convention on Human Rights.

In cases where Britons argue that their rights have been violated, Strasbourg serves as a court of last resort, much the way the Supreme Court functions in the United States.

Britain signed the European convention, with 40 other countries, and thus obliged itself to abide by the court's rul-

Defense Secretary Geoffrey Hoon announcing in the House of Commons that Britain is dropping its ban on the openly gay serving in the military. The change brings Britain in line with almost all other NATO countries.

ings, even to the extent of changing its laws if necessary. Previous cases have forced Britain to end corporal punishment in schools and to give greater rights to prisoners and to suspected terrorists.

Today's announcement follows a decision on Tuesday by the European Union's highest legal body, the Court of Justice in Luxembourg, which ruled in favor of a woman who argued that Germany's constitutional ban against women bearing arms amounted to unlawful sex discrimination.

In the House of Commons this afternoon, Geoffrey Hoon, the defense secretary, acknowledged that the human rights court's ruling had left the government with no choice but to end the ban. "The European Court of Human Rights ruling makes very clear that the existing policy in relation to homosexuality must change," he said.

"As all personal behavior will be regulated by the code of conduct," he said, "there is no longer a reason to deny homosexuals the opportunity of a career in the armed forces."

The British Defense Department has long argued that the presence of gays in the military would depress morale among the 210,000 uniformed personnel and disrupt the services' effectiveness as fighting forces. In defending its ban, it has also pointed to surveys that it says show that members of the armed services are reluctant to serve with gay men and lesbians.

Responding to today's announcement, Iain Duncan Smith, the Conservative Party's defense spokesman, said that there was no reason to believe that people in the armed services would be more willing to accept gays than they had in the past.

"I believe and have always believed," Mr. Duncan Smith said, "that we should follow the advice of the armed forces, which had always been that lifting the ban would adversely affect operational effectiveness."

But supporters of gay rights and civil liberties applauded the change, saying that it was overdue.

Angela Mason, the executive director of the gay-rights group Stonewall, said: "When I first came to Stonewall seven years ago, I was shocked that lesbians and gay men in the

armed forces were treated so brutally. I am very proud that as from today they will be able to serve their country with dignity and respect."

And Roger Garford, a member of Rank Outsiders, a support group for gay men and lesbians who are serving or have served in the military, said he welcomed the news that no one in the armed forces could now be forced to go through what he did in the early 1980's, when rumors that he had had a homosexual relationship with a civilian reached his commanding officer. A chief technician in the Royal Air Force, Mr. Garford had then served for about 20 years.

The Special Branch was called to investigate, he said, and interrogated him for nine hours. After he broke down and admitted he had had an affair with a man, Mr. Garford, who was married at the time, was released by the officers. But they then embarked on a long investigation of his friends and colleagues in an effort to amass further evidence that he was gay.

Finally, Mr. Garford said, they gave him a dishonorable discharge, four months before he was to become eligible for a pension. He soon divorced, and is currently waiting, along with some 60 others who were dismissed by the military because of their homosexuality, to see whether he is entitled to compensation.

* * *

March 23, 2000

GERMANY: MAKING AMENDS TO GAYS

By TERENCE NEILAN

Lawmakers proposed making amends to a long-neglected group of Nazi victims: thousands of men sent to concentration camps for being gay. The governing Social Democratic and Green parties introduced a bill to acknowledge Nazi persecution of gays and ask the government to review whether to annul convictions under a Nazi-era anti-gay law that remained on the books until 1969.

* * *

June 3, 2000

DUELING FESTIVALS: GAY PRIDE AND VATICAN COLLIDE

By ALESSANDRA STANLEY

ROME, June 2—World Pride Roma, a global gay pride festival, is expected to draw gays from all over the world to Rome on July 1 for a week's worth of conferences, fashion shows, a gay pride parade, and a concert featuring Gloria Gaynor and The Village People.

The Vatican, which is host to Holy Year events for religious pilgrims at the same time, is not amused.

But when the Roman Catholic Church sought this week to block the World Pride event, it inadvertently turned it into one of the most politically charged—and closely watched—events on Rome's Jubilee calendar. The clash between the

Vatican and World Pride organizers has noisily spilled over into national—and even international—politics and has filled newspaper front pages, talk shows and parliamentary debate.

Italy's center-right opposition, gearing up for elections next year, has molded the timing of the gay event into a political bludgeon, deepening divisions within the already frayed center-left government.

Prime Minister Giuliano Amato, breaking with his predecessor, Massimo d'Alema, and some of his own cabinet members, chimed in last week, saying the scheduling of a gay event during a Jubilee was "inopportune."

The furor drove one cabinet official to come out of the closet. Alfonso Pecoraro Scanio, Italy's minister of agricultural policy, said in the current issue of the weekly magazine Panorama that he is bisexual, a rare breach of privacy that he said was inspired by what he considered the unjust attacks on gay pride events.

But the politician who has drawn the most fire is Rome's liberal mayor, Francesco Rutelli, who first welcomed the World Pride event, then this week withdrew the city's support, alienating many within his own center-left constituency while failing to appease the church.

By stepping forward, then back, Mr. Rutelli helped make the World Pride event into an international cause celebre.

"They advertised it far better than we ever could," Leigh Christopher, an organizer from San Francisco, said at the World Pride offices in the Mario Miele Center, an Italian gay rights association. Organizers say they are expecting as many as 300,000 to attend.

The decision to hold the World Pride festival in Rome was made in 1997, although some in the organization argued that the event should be held in a city better known for gay rights, like Amsterdam or New York. But the lure of Rome during a Jubilee of the Roman Catholic Church, which condemns homosexual acts as sinful, won out. "There was a compelling argument for the opportunity provided by a Jubilee year to open discussion on religion and homophobia," said Deborah Oakley-Melvin, a former president of the San Francisco Gay Pride association who is helping organize the Rome event. The response was worse, and therefore better, than she had expected.

With ill-masked delight, Ms. Oakley-Melvin said, "this is turning into another Stonewall," a reference to the 1969 uprising of gays against a police raid on the Stonewall Inn in Greenwich Village. That event was considered the beginning of the modern gay-rights movement in the United States.

But in Italy, a country that never had anti-homosexual legislation, even under Mussolini, gay rights has not had the political or social resonance found in the United States or Germany. It never experienced a Stonewall riot.

"Italy is a classic example of a Catholic country—everyone does everything, but the important thing is not to say it," said Massimo Consoli, a historian of gay rights.

"Italian homosexuals never had to fight the kind of government repression found in other countries, so there has never been a strong gay movement here—until now." He added,

"The Vatican is giving us a visibility that nobody has accorded us in centuries."

The church was first to express dismay over the propriety of holding a gay pride festival during a Holy Year. Cardinal Camillo Ruini, president of the Italian Conference of Bishops, complained publicly in January. He was soon followed by Cardinal Angelo Sodano, the Vatican secretary of state. "The authorities know that Rome is a Holy City," Cardinal Sodano said.

Vatican officials and some political leaders worried that, among other things, the gay festival would attract drag pontiffs to the streets of Rome. But the Amato government's desire to curb the gay event has incurred the wrath of many groups, including Italian Jews. "We Jews are really sorry about this debate against homosexuals," Amos Luzzatto, president of the Union of Italian Jewish Communities, told the Roman newspaper Il Messaggero. He said he wanted to express solidarity with homosexuals sent by the Nazis to death camps alongside Jews.

Few politicians, right or left, have expressed outright homophobia, insisting that the timing of the gay pride event is the problem. But conservative politicians who fiercely oppose the city's being host to a gay festival during the Jubilee have not warmed to Prime Minister Amato's efforts to distance himself from the event.

"He cannot wash his hands of it," Silvano Moffa, president of the province of Rome, and a member of the right-wing party, National Alliance, said of Mr. Amato. "In this Jubilee, Amato is turning into the Pontius Pilate of the year 2000."

Thursday night, representatives of the Christian Democratic Center, a small center-right opposition party, held a protest rally against the World Pride festival, showing cautionary video clips of a recent San Francisco gay pride event that featured men dressed as nuns, "The Sisters of Perpetual Indulgence." Only a few dozen people showed up.

After the Vatican made its feelings known, Mayor Rutelli asked organizers in February to postpone their festival for a week, arguing that the parade, fashion show, and other outdoor events could conflict with religious Jubilee events. "There was no pressure from the church," Mr. Rutelli explained in an interview. "There was opposition from the church."

Ms. Oakley-Melvin said the organizers refused to change their schedule, having already unilaterally decided not to begin the festival the last week in June, which is the anniversary of the Stonewall riots, but which also coincides with the June 29 feast day of SS. Peter and Paul, a Roman holiday. They also canceled a planned drag queen contest to spare Roman sensibilities.

"Its just a provocation," she said. "They didn't think we would respond in any other way than 'yes.'"

Mr. Rutelli said he was outraged by what he described as an uncooperative attitude by the event's organizers. "I didn't tell them not to do it, I just asked them to postpone it by just one week," the mayor said. He said that the $150,000 the city pledged to help pay for cultural events within the festival would instead go to cover municipal expenses, such as police protection and trash removal. And the organizers would no longer be allowed to display the city logo. "The event will take place," he added, "but without city sponsorship."

Mr. Rutelli, who publicly urged the organizers to spare the feelings of "an aging pope," said he had sought a postponement because the week of July 1 includes several important Jubilee events, including a Polish pilgrimage.

"The World Pride rally is complicated and delicate because there is going to be a Jubilee with 200,000 Polish pilgrims," he said. "Rome is a free and open city, but there is also a question of public order."

The Rev. Stanislaw Heymo, a Dominican priest who organizes all Polish pilgrimages, said that in fact, fewer than 50,000 Poles would come to Rome on July 6 and 7, and would hold an evening prayer meeting at the Colosseum on July 7, the same evening as the festival's "Leather World Pride Party." He was not pleased by the coincidence.

"This is a very bad thing," he complained. "It would be better to spend money on the poor and immigrants, because homosexuals are rich, from rich families. They do nothing other than travel throughout the world, flaunting their sickness."

* * *

July 4, 2000

FRENCH BISHOP, DISCIPLINED OVER 'GAY PRIDE' ISSUE, STILL SPEAKS OUT IN ROME

By ALESSANDRA STANLEY

ROME, July 3—Skirting a Vatican order to withdraw from a gay pride seminar on religion and homosexuality, Bishop Jacques Gaillot sat on a couch outside the hotel conference room today and explained where he thinks the Roman Catholic Church has erred.

"The church should not have second-class citizens," said Bishop Gaillot, who is from France. "Homosexuals have the same right to tolerance and dignity as any other group." He said he was called on Sunday by his French superiors and told that the pope had asked that he not take part in the seminar, just one event in the seven-day gay pride festival called World Pride Roma 2000.

"I am being loyal and obedient to the pope," said Bishop Gaillot, who skipped the seminar but instead discussed the order with the news media. "But the pope has done me a great service in creating an event out of me." The bishop, who was removed from his diocese in Evreux in 1995 for his leftist views, added with a twinkle, "Nobody would be asking me for interviews had it not been for the pope's intervention."

World Pride Roma 2000, which opened on Saturday, was timed to coincide with a Holy Year of the Roman Catholic Church. Vatican opposition elevated the gay event into a tense political battleground, pitting church leaders and many right-wing groups against organizers and defenders of gay rights.

The Vatican's efforts to postpone the festival, and most recently, its effort to silence a bishop whose views do not reflect its own, have focused attention less on gay pride than on the state of tolerance inside the Holy See.

"There is a big difference in how the Vatican and American church leaders approach homosexuality," said Francis De Bernardo, a member of New Ways ministry, a religious association for gay Catholics. "U.S. bishops want outreach."

He said he was not surprised by Rome's cold shoulder, citing the Vatican's efforts to silence Jeannine Gramick and Robert Nugent, a nun and priest who were ordered to end their ministry to gay men and lesbians in 1999. "But this thing with Bishop Gaillot is disturbing. It shows there is not going to be even the hint of a conversation between the church and the gays gathering here."

So far, there has mainly been conflict between the two sides.

On Saturday, as the Italian movie star Maria Grazia Cucinotta cut a rainbow-colored ribbon, alongside Vladimir Luxuria, Italy's best known drag queen, at the opening ceremony in the garden of the Philharmonic Academy in Rome, about 700 demonstrators marched trough central Rome with the neo-Fascist group Forza Nuova. As the riot police looked on, the group paraded noisily, with Fascist salutes and and banners that read, "no gay pride."

A Catholic association, Centro Culturale Lepando, and a right-wing party, National Alliance, organized a torchlight seven-mile walk by 1,000 people to offer "penance" for the gay pride event.

At the Church of Saint Teresa of Avila in Rome, a small group of believers organized by the Committee for a Christian Rome recited a rosary to atone for the city's decision to allow the gay pride event.

Today, riot policemen and bomb squads lined the entrance of the Hotel Cicerone, near the Vatican, where gay pride meetings were being held.

The event, which organizers expect to draw more than 200,000 gay men and women to Rome, was planned three years ago and initially won the support of the city. But after the Vatican protested earlier this year, Mayor Francesco Rutelli tried to persuade World Pride organizers to postpone the event for a week. He contended that its schedule—which includes conferences, drag fashion shows and a parade through Rome this Saturday—could disturb the church's events for this Jubilee year.

When the organizers refused, Mr. Rutelli said the events would go on as planned, but he withdrew the city's endorsement and its logo from the banners. Prime Minister Giuliano Amato broke with many leaders of his center-left coalition by saying the timing of the gay pride festival during a Holy Year was "inopportune."

The Catholic Church does not teach that homosexuality is a sin, but that homosexual acts are sinful, just as adultery is. And the Vatican views the timing of the gay pride event as an offense to the church and to family values—as well as a political cudgel.

Agence France-Presse

The scene on Sunday at an information stand at World Pride Roma 2000. The gay event began on Saturday.

"It pains me to see that young people are being told that the church is their enemy," said Cardinal Ersilio Tonini, an emeritus archbishop who was one of the few church officials to address the issue on television over the weekend. "For us, they are always our brothers and sons. But shouting about pride in this public event is not right. The church has to tell the truth, even if that truth is not fashionable."

The event expected to draw the most protest is the gay pride parade on Saturday, and the Colosseum has become the focus for the controversy.

Organizers say they will march to the Colosseum and form a ring around it in defiance of the city, which refused to approve the streets around it as part of the parade route.

Right-wing groups have said they will block marchers from surrounding the structure, which they view as a shrine to Christian martyrs. The Colosseum has also been adopted this year by human rights groups and the Catholic Church as a symbol in their fight against the death penalty.

Historians say that no early Christians were actually fed to the lions in the Colosseum, but church lore and Hollywood movies have kept the legend alive. At the neo-Fascist counterdemonstration on Saturday, protesters held banners reading, "Gays at the Colosseum? Only with Lions!"

* * *

July 9, 2000

GAY PARADE, OPPOSED BY VATICAN, PASSES PEACEFULLY IN ROME

By ALESSANDRA STANLEY

ROME, July 8—Defying the Vatican and right-wing political groups, tens of thousands of demonstrators marched peacefully in a gay pride parade through central Rome today.

The parade was one of the last and most contested events of the weeklong World Pride Roma 2000, an international gay festival that was timed to coincide with a Holy Year of the Roman Catholic Church and that the Vatican fiercely opposed. As it turned out, however, the parade was calm, peaceful and, according to some participants, a little duller than recent gay pride parades in New York, Paris and London.

Police officers had braced themselves for possible violence after Forza Nuova, a neo-Fascist group, vowed to stage a counterdemonstration and to prevent gay marchers from approaching the Colosseum. But Forza Nuova canceled its plans this week, citing the death of the 13-year-old daughter of a leader of the group. Many center-left politicians marched in the parade, and so did a few center-right politicians.

The city of Rome, which had approved the parade three years ago, withdrew its support after the Vatican made its opposition known. City officials had said marchers would not be given permission to march around the Colosseum. But late in the week, Rome officials and parade organizers reached a compromise on the parade route, agreeing that the marchers would file past the Colosseum but not circle it entirely.

"I was expecting more disturbances—this is much calmer than gay pride parades in New York," Michael Lavelle, 48, a telecommunications manager from New York City, said as he marched back to Circus Maximus, Rome's oldest sports arena, which has been the headquarters of the World Pride event. Mr. Lavelle, who was in a group of 150 New Yorkers, said he and others had decided to come to Rome "once we heard there was a problem with the church."

Parts of today's parade, which included many of the sights and sounds that the Vatican dreaded—drag queens, scantily clad male gladiators, topless women and outrageous floats—were broadcast live by Italian television, along with panels of commentators fiercely arguing the church's position and that of gay rights advocates.

But some marchers said the Rome parade was bland compared with other gay pride events. "Paris was a lot more fun—there was more music, more dancing," said a Belgian who would give his name only as Patrick and who said he had taken part in gay pride parades in France, the Netherlands and Germany this year. "I am a little disappointed. I guess that is because this is Rome and the pope has a lot of power."

The gay rights movement in Italy—a country that never had anti-homosexual legislation, even under Mussolini--has never been as powerful as it was in the United States or Britain and Germany, and the World Pride festival and the controversy around it brought new attention to gay rights issues in Italy.

By the standards of Italian society, which tends to be permissive as long as people keep their activities private, the sight of so many gay marchers was startling.

"I don't think the Vatican should have tried to prevent this," said Marina Fidanza, 65, a grandmother who watched from a park above the Colosseum. "I am a Catholic, but how can you stop it. This is Rome after all." She was watching, as she put it, to "get a sense of what all this fuss is about."

She added, "But this whole showing off of sexual orientation seems a bit much to me."

*   *   *

AFRICA

November 18, 1997

IN A NEW SOUTH AFRICA, OLD ANTI-GAY BIAS PERSISTS

By DONALD G. MCNEIL JR.

JOHANNESBURG, Nov. 17—Busi Kheswa, chairwoman of a black lesbian organization in Soweto, was dancing with her girlfriend at a downtown nightclub recently when a stranger started shouting at them.

"He said my parents hadn't performed the proper rituals when I was born, and that's why I was abnormal," she said.

Zanele Mphika, a policewoman, was walking with her girlfriend in a black township when a thug drew a gun on them. "He told me he knew who I was, and he was going to rape my girlfriend in front of me to teach us what happens to people like us," she said. Caught without her own weapon, she fought him off barehanded.

Meanwhile, Hugh McLean, chief fund-raiser for the Coalition for Gay and Lesbian Equality, says that in the 25 years or so that he has been openly gay, he has "never met open hostility from any quarter."

And Police Sgt. Dennis Adriao, who came out of the closet to found a gay police organization in 1994, shortly after he was named the force's Officer of the Year, said he has won support from the chief of the force, which once spied on and dismissed anyone thought to be gay.

South Africa, which kept morality so buckled down under the former Calvinist Afrikaner Government that everything from gambling to kissing someone of another race was illegal, has seen a tidal wave of change in the last decade. Now, that wave is breaking against scattered boulders of resistance on one of the last issues: gay rights.

The country's new, post-apartheid Constitution, ratified last December, bans discrimination on the basis of sexual orientation. But achieving full legal protection for homosexuals is proving a slow process, and even when laws change, anti-gay attitudes persist.

The old laws must still be challenged in each of the nine provinces, before judges who are not, on average, as liberal as the nation's Constitutional Court. And in the political arena, a backlash is growing, particularly among Christian and Muslim conservatives and traditional black Africans.

In October, for example, Parliament approved a policy change for the armed forces, barring discrimination against homosexuals. The army officer who drafted it, Col. Jan Kotze, expressed pride that South Africa's policy is so much clearer than the American compromise of "don't ask, don't tell." But he said some commanders resent it and, since the anti-sodomy laws are still on the books, gay soldiers may be at risk of criminal charges even though military policy presumably accepts gay sex within the same limits it accepts heterosexual sex.

Sodomy, in fact, remains a Schedule 1 crime, meaning that a private citizen can arrest someone he suspects of it and even use deadly violence to do so. Last June, in a case concerning consensual sex between two prisoners, a Cape Town judge ruled the law unconstitutional. But his decision does not apply to the other eight provinces, and dozens of prisoners are still charged each year.

Another law, the Sexual Offenses Act, prohibits any act between men "at a party" that leads to sexual gratification—in-

Graham Williams for The New York Times

Some gay police officers within South Africa's national force report no bias. An officer, center, joined a recent gay pride march in Johannesburg.

cluding kissing or touching. The law was passed in the 1960's after a vice raid on a men's party at a home in Johannesburg.

Legal discrimination survives in other areas. A doctor may not artificially inseminate an unmarried woman, so lesbians who want to bear children must find other means. Gay couples are not permitted to adopt children. Gay relationships are generally not recognized for pension or medical benefits. Some judges have denied divorced lesbians custody of their children and even visits when their female partner is present.

Meanwhile, in the social arena, bigotry persists. Some gay whites are "out," but many remain in the closet, fearing they would be subtly shunned in a society where demeaning jokes are still common. Blacks, and especially African lesbians like Ms. Kheswa and Ms. Mphika, face far worse—open hostility and threats.

The gay rights movement here is new and strives not to offend. There have been gay pride marches for eight years, but they attract fewer than 4,000 marchers; New York City, by contrast, has held them for 27 years with as many as 200,000 participants. South Africa's first walk-in legal-advice center for homosexuals opened only in September.

The governing African National Congress is a strong advocate of human rights, so the Constitution's equality clause "was handed to us on a platter," said Jonathan Berger, the legal center's coordinator. But in practice, he added, "we're light-years behind the States. Quite prominent people in the A.N.C. have made homophobic remarks."

The coalition and the Human Rights Commission recently sued to overturn the sodomy law. To their surprise, Justice

Minister Dullah Omar opposed them on a technicality. Mr. Omar is an A.N.C. appointee, but his power base is among Muslims in Cape Town, where fundamentalist imams hold sway.

Changing public attitudes may prove harder than changing laws. The gay coalition's budget is now financed entirely with donations from Norwegian and Dutch organizations. Mr. McLean said South African corporations politely but inevitably refuse his requests to help gay causes. A few wealthy individuals helped some years back, he said, but he could not release their names.

"You're talking about gay men who are making it in business," he said. "They don't want to be up front."

There are gay bars in Johannesburg and Cape Town, which the police do not raid, even though sex takes place in dark corners.

"We get some celebrities," said a bartender at one of them, Gotham City. "But they're not out."

Perhaps the best example of how attitudes are changing is in the South African Police.

In 1985, Capt. Corrie van Niekerk was a constable, working with two other lesbians at the front desk of a police station. She said the commander tried to flirt with them and then, rebuffed, heard that they were homosexuals, who at that time were barred from the force.

"He had my phone bugged," she said. "He sent police social workers to stake out my house. When I switched off the lights at night, they knocked on my door to see who was with me."

Producing evidence that they were lesbians, he ordered all three to resign quietly or face dishonorable discharges. They quit, she said, and one then committed suicide.

Ms. van Niekerk joined a small force in the black township Soweto that was open to whites and did not ask about her sexuality. When it was reabsorbed into the national force, she rose to captain.

Her younger male colleague Sergeant Adriao said he came out after his 1993 award allowed him to study police work in Europe. "The commanding general had just boasted that there were no queers on the force," he said. "Then three months later, he was shaking my hand. But he didn't know."

When he returned the next year, a new Government was in place. Sergeant Adriao came out, first to a gay magazine, then on national television. His colleagues, he said, "have been fine about it." He has gay-pride parade posters in his office and led the police contingent in the Johannesburg parade last month. One Johannesburg commander briefly tried to insist that they not march in uniform. But, citing a directive issued in 1994 by the national commander saying that the force would tolerate no anti-gay discrimination, they had him overruled.

Black society has deep homophobic streaks, based less on religion than on the overwhelming emphasis on having children to continue the family line. Ignorance in rural culture also plays a role. Sexuality is rarely discussed at home or school, so myths abound.

"If you tell people you are gay, the first question is, 'How do you have sex?' They think you have a penis and a vagina," Ms. Kheswa said. "At high school, if the boys suspect another boy, they will pull off his clothes to see what's happening with him."

* * *

October 10, 1998

SOUTH AFRICA STRIKES DOWN LAWS ON GAY SEX

By DONALD G. MCNEIL JR.

JOHANNESBURG, Oct. 9—Citing a provision in the new Constitution, South Africa's highest court struck down the country's sodomy laws today.

In theory, gay rights have been protected here since the country passed its provisional constitution in 1994. But many of the Calvinist-era laws remained on the books. The suit decided by the Constitutional Court today was brought by the National Coalition for Gay and Lesbian Equality and was not opposed by the African National Congress Government.

"Obviously, we're happy," said Mazibuko Jara, the coalition's national manager. "We welcome the decision as confirming the values and principals of our constitution."

South Africa's constitution—the world's most liberal—bans "unfair" discrimination on the basis of race, gender, sex, pregnancy, marital status, ethnic origin, color, age, disability, religion, conscience, belief, culture, language and birth, as well as sexual orientation.

The harsh laws that the court overturned classified sodomy as a Schedule 1 offense, like murder or rape, punishable by life imprisonment.

A more esoteric law also struck down today, Section 20A of the Sexual Offenses Act, which was written after a vice raid on a gay men's party in the 1960's, outlawed any behavior "at a party"—defined as a gathering of more than two men—that led to sexual gratification. Under that law, gay activists said, a man could be jailed for giving another man a come-hither glance, if seen by a third man, who could be the arresting officer.

Such laws were seldom enforced in recent years, and there have been Gay Pride marches for a decade now. But two Cape Town prisoners who engaged in consensual sex were charged with sodomy last year, and the threat of such prosecutions still existed, particularly in prisons and the army under conservative commanders, activists said.

South Africa has become increasingly liberal since the days when army officers tried to change homosexuals by giving gay recruits electric shocks while showing them pictures of naked men. Military and police codes of conduct now ban anti-gay discrimination, and a few government-owned corporations like the national electric company recognize same-sex marriages.

But most corporations and government departments do not, and other laws prevent, for example, adoption by gay couples. A spokesman for the gay rights coalition said today's broad ruling might be used to challenge those laws and policies.

The ruling was written by Judge Lori Ackerman with a concurring ruling by Judge Albie Sachs, who wrote that it should be seen as "part of a growing acceptance of difference in an increasingly open and pluralistic South Africa."

* * *

August 23, 1999

A CULTURE OF RIGHTS

By ANTHONY LEWIS

JOHANNESBURG—One of the most remarkable institutions in post-apartheid South Africa is the Constitutional Court, created to enforce the rules of the new democracy. In its courtroom the other day there was an argument that threw dramatic light on the way this country, and the world, has changed.

The case was this. South African immigration law provides that a foreign "spouse" of someone here may be admitted as an immigrant. Gay and lesbian individuals and organizations challenged the law's constitutionality, arguing that it discriminated against same-sex couples who were committed partners but could not legally marry.

The new South African Constitution includes a sweeping Bill of Rights. It forbids discrimination on grounds, among others, of race, gender, religion, "marital status" or "sexual orientation."

Arguing for the Government, Essop Patel urged the court to uphold the immigration law despite those constitutional guarantees. He said the concept of sovereignty gave Parliament plenary power over immigration.

"Can the immigration law be inconsistent with the Constitution?" the court's president, Arthur Chaskalson, asked. Mr. Patel struggled to escape that and similar questions but finally answered, "No."

If there was discrimination, Mr. Patel said, it was allowable as a way for the state to protect the institution of the family. "Aren't you protecting stereotypes," Justice Laurie Ackermann asked, of what sexual relations and family should be?

"What is really needed in this country," Mr. Patel said, "is a law recognizing domestic partnerships." He asked the court to give Parliament time to act. The judges asked how much time. He could not say.

Counsel for those challenging the law, Wim Trengove, was asked by the judges what they should do if they agreed with him that the law was unconstitutionally discriminatory. Should they strike down the benefit for alien spouses? Or read into the statute a like advantage for same-sex partners? What about unmarried heterosexual couples?

Mr. Trengove said the court should confine itself to this complaint and read into the law a benefit for homosexual life partners. Members of the court expressed concern that that might put them in too legislative a role.

One notable aspect of the argument was the understanding, respectful view that everyone took of homosexuality. South African society, black and white, was in the past deeply homophobic. But even the Government's lawyer spoke critically of "homophobia." And an editorial about the case in a conservative newspaper, The Citizen, mocked objections to same-sex relationships and even marriages.

Even more striking—profoundly so—was the commitment of the judges and lawyers to the very process of constitutional law. For not long ago the idea that a South African government would submit itself to the decisions of a court on issues of civil rights and liberties was unimaginable.

Until 1994 South Africa had no written constitution. Judges were bound to enforce whatever Parliament enacted.

And the apartheid Government turned law into a mechanism of oppression.

So the scene in that courtroom was a world turned upside-down. Everyone accepted the principle of judicial review. Everyone was comfortable with the idea that judges should have the last word on what the Government can and cannot do.

From an authoritarian country, South Africa has become one concerned with individual rights. Someone near the top of the Government said to me, "After what we suffered, we want a culture of rights."

In looking to a Bill of Rights and judges to enforce it, South Africa is part of an international trend. In this argument, the lawyers and judges discussed cases in Canada, Europe and Australia.

There is some talk here of combining the Constitutional Court with the longstanding appeals court for non-constitutional issues. Perhaps someday there should be a single court of last resort. But for now only the Constitutional Court has the legitimacy to build the legal foundation of the new South Africa.

All segments of society seem to have confidence in the Constitutional Court. Its membership is diverse. Five of 11 judges are black, 6 white. Two are women. One is blind. They include professors and practitioners. Together, they are trying to do in a few years what American judges have done over 200: bring a constitution to life.

* * *

September 30, 1999

UGANDA: HOMOSEXUALS FACE ARREST

President Yoweri Museveni has ordered the arrest of homosexuals in Uganda, saying United Nations human rights conventions do not necessarily apply to Africa, the Government-owned New Vision newspaper quoted him as saying. Homosexual acts are illegal in Uganda and carry a maximum punishment of life imprisonment. (AP)

* * *

RUSSIA

January 5, 1992

OUTING PETER ILYICH

By PAUL GRIFFITHS

TCHAIKOVSKY: The Quest for the Inner Man
By Alexander Poznansky
Illustrated. 679 pp. New York: Schirmer Books.

All biographers, whether or not they are in quest of inner men or inner women, have to voyage from the terra firma of

chronicled fact onto the seas of supposition. Tchaikovsky's case is unusual only in that we know that parts of the factual coastline, including no doubt some interesting departure ports, are hidden from view, for reasons that are all too banal. So far every edition of his letters and diaries has been bowdlerized, and even scholars of unimpeachable seriousness have been denied access to the original documents, evidently because those who were responsible in Russia have not wanted the details of the composer's homosexual life to enter the public domain.

Thus history, in a gesture of sad irony, has perpetuated the distinction between private and public existence that caused

Peter Ilyich Tchaikovsky such self-doubt, bitterness and pain, even if at the same time it encouraged the introspection without which his music might not have been possible. What we see in the published letters is what he allowed the world to see: the working musician, the devoted elder brother and uncle, the international traveler, the passionate friend. What we cannot yet know is what he himself kept concealed, and disclosed only to his diary or to his brothers, especially to Modest, who was a second self: also homosexual and also an artist, being a minor playwright, a librettist for his brother and an early biographer, well placed in so many respects to provide the composer with a tidy image.

In "Tchaikovsky," Alexander Poznansky leaves his readers in no doubt that the inner man he seeks is precisely the one who has been censored out of sight. That, of course, produces a difficulty. Since the evidence is not available, conclusions about Tchaikovsky's secret life have to be largely a matter of guesswork. Mr. Poznansky, however, is quite some guesser, and brazen enough even to leave it quite apparent how his guesses are guided by three fixed ideas—ideas whose motivations and relative priorities in his mind one would have to guess at oneself (the task can be left to those who go in quest of the inner Poznansky).

First there is an animus against anything coming out of the Soviet Union, especially emigres who left later than himself (he came to the United States in 1977, and works as a librarian at Yale University). Then there is the conviction that Tchaikovsky did not commit suicide, which dismisses the story brought to the West by the Russian musicologist Alexandra Orlova in 1979 and subsequently supported by independent sources. Finally there is the certainty that Tchaikovsky was not, as has long been supposed, a tortured if perhaps also rather ready victim of guilt and despair, but that on the contrary he enjoyed an active sex life with a variety of fellow musicians, male prostitutes, bathhouse attendants, domestic servants, coachmen and family members.

There is, of course, no documentary support for any of this; the censors would certainly have slipped up if there were to be, and Mr. Poznansky's tottering castle of unwarranted, indelicate extrapolations must count as the best argument yet that the longstanding embargo on the Tchaikovsky archive should be lifted. Given the present mood in Russia, that seems more than likely to happen anyway. Meanwhile, fortunately, this book is not going to mislead anybody, since its tactics are so blatant.

Most open of all are the simple disingenuous avowals that the truth is something other than what every shred of evidence suggests it is. Mr. Poznansky quotes extensively, for instance, from a well-known letter in which Tchaikovsky appears to be blaming his homosexuality for his feelings of estrangement from society; but the author then blithely affirms that there are "many other letters and writings in which he took his sexual tastes as quite natural for his individual constitution and as a source of enjoyment." Needless to say, nothing is cited in support of this attractive piece of wishful thinking; as before, if such citation had been possible to lo-

cate, it would have been made impossible by the censors. And Mr. Poznansky is well aware of that, not hiding the fact that he takes any show of a cut in the documents as evidence of a deleted homosexual reference.

But he has other ways of hearing something in the sources' silences. There are long passages, for example, where we leave Tchaikovsky for a moment in order to survey what Mr. Poznansky is fond of calling "the homosexual milieu," before jumping back to argue from the general to the specific. The bathhouse story is a case in point. After a long paragraph from the confessions of a servant lad, suggesting that St. Petersburg in the 1870's had something in common with San Francisco a century later, terse comments from Tchaikovsky's published diary can have only one meaning: "With Timosha. Somehow wasn't any fun. It's not the same anymore." But Mr. Poznansky offers no evidence that this Timosha was a bathhouse attendant, and even if he was, imagine how the same diary entry would read after a page on swimming instruction or the bracing delights of coal tar soap.

Sometimes one can watch Mr. Poznansky maneuvering from supposition into fact in the very tenses of his prose. He wants some reason for Tchaikovsky's prostration in the wake of his brief and ill-advised marriage to a woman he barely knew, and for his later loathing of her. "It would seem likely," we are told, that all this was due to some change in the wife's behavior. But the change on display is in the writing. By the next sentence, "she had, no doubt, decided that the probation period had lasted long enough and that it was now time to demand fulfillment of her conjugal rights." Now it is just a short step into the unconditional past: "Here, of course, lay her fateful blunder. . . .Tchaikovsky's masculine pride was severely wounded."

It certainly makes a compelling scene. After 10 weeks of marriage, most of that time spent alone while Tchaikovsky was visiting his sister in order to get over the shock of the ceremony, the not so newly wed and frustrated Mrs. Tchaikovsky dares to make her claim. It would seem likely that she loosens her corset. No doubt she smiles. And the composer rushes headlong and horrified from the room. . . . But no. We need no cheap drama to understand why Tchaikovsky, having precipitated himself into marriage at the age of 37, should almost immediately have recoiled, nor why he should have developed an extreme distaste for a woman who kept pestering him with financial claims.

This whole episode in Mr. Poznansky's book may suggest a peculiarly Russian view of the iconic power of words, the power to make things true retrospectively. Certainly when it comes to reading Tchaikovsky's writings (as opposed to reading the gaps in Tchaikovsky's writings), Mr. Poznansky seems easily convinced that what is written must have been so, with no allowance necessary for literary habits and conceits. When the composer, as he often does, expresses the wish in a letter to smother someone with kisses, this is taken as a declaration of erotic passion. Nor does Mr. Poznansky take due note of how the Tchaikovsky stories that have come down to us are a part of Russian literature of the period: there is an awful lot here about people spending long bored summer weeks at their dachas, and about young men killing themselves. More could be said of the semblances, in Tchaikovsky's biography as in his music, with the work of Pushkin, Turgenev, Tolstoy and Chekhov (the last of them nearly, as Mr. Poznansky fails to point out, the author of a Tchaikovsky libretto).

But what is most lacking here is any sense that Tchaikovsky spent a great deal of his life composing music. Not so surprisingly, he too wrote about the existence within himself of an "inner" being, notably in a long letter (of which Mr. Poznansky makes nothing) to his distant patroness Nadezhda von Meck. For him, though, the inner man was the one responsible for the symphonies, concertos, ballets, operas, quartets, songs and so much that Mr. Poznansky skims in quest of something else.

Paul Griffiths, the music critic of The Times of London, is the author of "The Jewel Box," a libretto for music by Mozart, and a novel, "The Lay of Sir Tristram."

* * *

February 10, 1993

RUSSIA'S GAY MEN STEP OUT OF SOVIET-ERA SHADOWS

By JILL J. BARSHAY
Special to The New York Times

MOSCOW, Feb. 9—After decades of enduring persecution and intimidation in the old Soviet Union, homosexuals in Russia are emerging into the open for the first time, even though they say they continue to feel mistreated and threatened by hostile public attitudes and by old laws that remain on the books.

Today, gay groups are officially registered and gay newspapers are published under municipal government laws. In addition, a handful of homosexuals organized a demonstration in front of the United States Embassy at the time of President Clinton's inauguration last month.

The few homosexual activists are largely ignored by the mainstream, however, and gay newspapers are only circulated privately.

There is also no organized movement among homosexuals or their supporters to demand that laws banning homosexuality be repealed, but a few officials say there is a chance that the laws can be quietly eliminated.

While hoping and in some cases pressing for legal changes, homosexual groups say that their problem is less with the law than with social attitudes and ignorance.

'Russian Walls Are Thin'

"I'm more afraid that my friends and family will find out than the law," said a successful businessman who is 28 years old. "Your socio-economic stature can protect you from the authorities. It is unfair, but true, that most of the gays in prison are from the lower classes."

Gleb Kosorukov for The New York Times

Homosexuals in Russia are still dealing with longtime laws banning homosexuality and are mistreated by social attitudes and ignorance. Gay couples danced at a closed party last month at a club in Moscow. Such gatherings are held sporadically and are unpublicized.

He lives alone in a comfortable, one-bedroom apartment. But even at home, he keeps up his guard, asking to speak quietly during an interview.

"Russian walls are very thin," he said. "If my neighbors knew I was gay, they would look at me differently and use it against me."

Under Article 121 of the criminal code, a holdover from the Soviet era, "sexual relations between men are punishable by prison terms of up to five years." Lesbian sexual relations are not mentioned and thus legal. The Government sentenced 10 people to prison for homosexual relations in the first half of 1992.

Quiet Pressure for Change

Among those seeking to change the law are a few people in the Government, although they apparently have taken no overt action on the matter.

"Homosexuals are in a quasi-legal situation," said Sergei B. Romazin, head of judicial reform at the Justice Ministry. "My personal opinion is that we need to change this situation immediately. Article 121 should be repealed, except when rape is involved."

In the fall, a proposed new criminal code omitted the language on the "crime of homosexuality," but it is considered possible that it could be reinstated.

Ukraine Law Repealed

The Ministry of Justice could not provide reliable statistics on the present number of prisoners convicted for homosexuality, but Mr. Romazin said he would "release those in prison immediately as soon as the law is changed."

There is some precedent for removing the legal ban on homosexuality. The Parliament in Ukraine, the most populous state outside Russia in the Soviet Union, decriminalized homosexuality last year.

However, in order to get the old law off the books, a new law was enacted that requires compulsory testing for exposure to the AIDS virus for prostitutes, drug addicts, foreigners, and other "high-risk" groups. Because homosexuals could be included, many say this new law allows some of the old sanctions to remain in effect.

Endemic Homophobia

Homophobia is strong throughout Russia, especially in the provinces. A 31-year-old journalist at an independent newspaper in Kazan, Tatarstan, said that in his home province "very few people know I'm gay."

"Tatars are not Americans," he added. "They wouldn't understand.

Russian society has a long history of official discrimination. A 1964 Soviet sex manual instructs, for example: "With all the tricks at their disposal, homosexuals seek out and win the confidence of youngsters. Then they proceed to act. Do not under any circumstances allow them to touch you. Such people should be immediately reported to the administrative organs so that they can be removed from society."

During the Soviet period, the threat of Article 121 was employed by the K.G.B. to end careers, destroy reputations, or blackmail artists and writers into staying within the bounds of the party line.

Sergei Paradzhanov, one of the Soviet Union's greatest directors and a homosexual, was arrested under Article 121 in 1974 and sentenced to five years in a labor camp. Colleagues believed that he was really paying the price for his controversial films.

Inflexible Attitudes

Attitudes have not changed much since. In a 1991 public opinion poll conducted in Chelyabinsk, an industrial city in the Urals, 30 percent of the respondents aged 16 to 30 years old felt that homosexuals should be "isolated from society," 5 percent felt they should be "liquidated," 60 percent had a "negative" attitude toward gay people and 5 percent labeled their sexual orientation "unfortunate."

One of the many abuses of the old regime was the "gay list." The police used to conduct "raids in places where gays met to do document checks," said Pavel Masalsky, a former prisoner convicted for homosexuality and no other crime.

From these checks, the Ministry of Internal Affairs compiled lists of suspected homosexuals. At trial, a name on this list was sufficient proof of guilt. Even today proof of actual sexual relations is not required.

Mr. Masalsky, 29, an electrical technician, was a victim of the "gay list" as well as what he said was the medical profession's ignorance. He was sentenced in 1984 to three years—an average term—after a friend betrayed him to the authorities.

'A Nightmare to Remember'

After the arrest, he said, "I was first subjected to a physical during which the doctor concluded I was gay. The main evidence against me at the trial was the Ministry of Internal Affairs' 'gay list.' It's a nightmare to remember it all."

In the army, which until recently was obligatory for all young men, gay troops face consequences ranging from physical harassment by fellow recruits to court martial.

Public tolerance and visibility are improving, however, slowly undercutting the stigma of homosexuality. In the past, homosexuals were forced to hide out in underground clubs and public bath houses. The more adventurous would stroll about the well-known fountain in front of the Bolshoi Theater. Now there are more respectable places for gay men, particularly in Moscow and St. Petersburg.

A Moveable Disco

An openly gay discotheque, financed by American gay businessmen, floats around Moscow every weekend. Sometimes it is moved across town at the last minute to avoid harassment from anti-gay thugs, known as "repairmen" in Russian slang.

Kevin Gardner, an American who is head of the Moscow chapter of the United States-based International Gay and Lesbian Human Rights Commission, said that there are hundreds of gay organizations throughout Russia.

In Moscow, there are a half dozen officially registered gay publications such as Impulse and Risk, which cover topics from homosexual life abroad to AIDS issues. In St. Petersburg, the gay organizations Krylia (wings) and the Tchaikovsky Foundation (Tchaikovsky was homosexual) are registered with the city government. Even in Russia's industrial heartland in the Ural Mountains, an organization called Rights of Sexual Minorities has existed for years.

"These groups don't have an organized political agenda," said Mr. Gardner. "A few activists have made appeals to repeal Article 121, but many are afraid to come out politically until Article 121 is repealed." Many gay organizations, trying to circumvent the legal prohibition, publicly emphasize AIDS awareness over gay rights as a more acceptable agenda.

Homosexuals say they fear that attitudes in Russia are so deeply ingrained that they will probably never enjoy the freedoms found in the United States. One of the Russian businessmen interviewed, for example, dreams of creating a male family with an adopted child but acknowledges that it could probably never happen.

"The law would forbid the adoption and society is not ready to accept a permanent gay relationship," he said. "There is no gay district in Moscow where gays can openly live like Castro Street in San Francisco. Even if the law were repealed, my life wouldn't really change for the better."

*   *   *

May 29, 1993

RUSSIA ENDS GAY BAN

Special to The New York Times

MOSCOW, May 28—Russia has repealed its Soviet-era law banning homosexuality, according to a long list of changes to the Criminal Code that was published on Thursday by Parliament's newspaper, Rossiskaya Gazeta.

Homosexuality had been a crime punishable with up to five years in prison since 1960, when the code was enacted, and the law has been enforced as recently as last year.

* * *

November 20, 1993

RUSSIA STILL IMPRISONS MEN FOR HOMOSEXUALITY

To the Editor:

If more attention had been paid to the translation of Arkady Bronnikov's "Body Language" (Op-Ed, Nov. 6), about tattoos in Russian prisons, it might have been more enlightening on the subjects of Russian prisons and Russian homophobia.

In Russian, the word "pederast" is often used as a synonym for homosexual. This is the usage of Mr. Bronnikov, when he states that "the pederast is a complete outcast." Not only is this deeply offensive to gay people, but in addition it distorts Mr. Bronnikov's description of prison conditions.

The status of the prison outcast—the one who sleeps next to the latrine, does all the dirty work, eats separately and is raped, tormented and forcibly tattooed—is the fate that is reserved for everyone who is perceived to be homosexual.

Last summer's International Gay and Lesbian Human Rights Commission's fact-finding mission to Russia, for which I was project coordinator, found that more than 1,000 men are suffering the fate of the outcast in Russia's 744 prison facilities.

Though the country's sodomy law was repealed last May, they may include men who were imprisoned simply because they are gay.

When the law was repealed, 73 men were serving time for consensual gay sex and 192 more were in prison under the sodomy law in combination with another charge (which was often trumped up), according to Ministry of Internal Affairs statistics. No mechanism for reviewing their cases was put in place, and many of these men continue to be incarcerated.

These are the prisoners that Mr. Bronnikov means when he writes of "pederasts."

MASHA GESSEN
San Francisco, Nov. 10, 1993

* * *

July 8, 1995

GAY RUSSIANS ARE 'FREE' NOW BUT STILL STAY IN FEARFUL CLOSET

By MICHAEL SPECTER

ST. PETERSBURG, Russia—At first glance Aleksandr Korotkov seems like the happiest man in Russia. Packed tightly into a black leather jumpsuit and dancing as if a disco beat had taken hold of his soul, once a week he becomes an openly gay man in a society that has never had much use for openness or for homosexuality.

Mr. Korotkov, who is 27, earns enough as a graphics designer to live here in a comfortable apartment. He owns a car, and every Saturday he spends $30 for the privilege of entering Mayak, this city's most fashionable gay nightclub.

But that is pretty much where the good times end. When dawn breaks and it is time to leave, he runs right to his car and jumps into jeans and a sweatshirt. He never parks far from the entrance, where five armed guards insure the tranquillity of the clientele, and he varies his routes home because he does not want anyone knowing where he has been.

"I know we are supposed to be free now," he said glumly, listening in the ornate former czarist ballroom to the quickening pulse of a new version of the James Brown classic "It's a Man's World."

"I mean we are free now," he said, speaking in English. "At least it seemed that way for a while. They can't lock us up anymore. But that's about it. We are still considered scum here. I think we always will be."

As much as is possible for one man, Mr. Korotkov's outlook and his way of life typify the contradictory world of gay life in Russia today.

He enjoys liberties that until recently could not even have been imagined. But he is fairly sure that if his boss knew he was gay, he would be dismissed on the spot. He can meet gay friends at clubs, at gay film festivals and through political organizations. But he says he is considering marrying and having children because the strain of this kind of life is often too much to bear.

In a way that is eerily reflective of the rest of Russian society today, gay activists are confused, finding it hard to figure out what they want from their new world and increasingly afraid that their brief burst of freedoms is starting to end.

Like reformers in other fields, they have become bitter about the American models they once eagerly embraced. Today, most want nothing to do with the West. They find the idea of coming out of the closet—crucial to the gay movement in the United States—naïve.

And while homosexuals here have become knowledgeable about AIDS, the disease has never had the politicizing effect that it has had in America. There it drove angry advocates into the streets by the thousands. Here, homosexuals often see the disease as another way to identify them with something they wish to hide.

Despite the problems, it would be impossible for any homosexual to make light of the progress that came with the fall of the Communist state in 1991. Sodomy is no longer against the law, a law that was used from the time of Stalin until 1993 to intimidate people and send them to the camps. Personal ads from advertising sections labeled "Man to Man" are as frank and easy to find as they are in New York.

But unofficial discrimination and fear are still rampant. Even today, and even for many homosexuals themselves, the idea of an open gay identity for Russians is ludicrous.

Otto Pohl for The New York Times

Homosexuals in Russia enjoy liberties that until recently could not even have been imagined, but fear and secretiveness are also common. Russians relaxed at Pyramida, one of Moscow's largest gay clubs.

"It would be foolish to interpret some new freedoms as tolerance," said Igor Kon, a sociologist who is Russia's best-known expert on sexual practices and whose book, "The Sexual Revolution in Russia," has just been published in the United States.

"To understand what is going on with gay life here, you have to understand what is going on with the rest of life here," he said.

For many years Soviet society portrayed itself, though fooling no one, as sexless. In the 1920's huge debates took place in Moscow over the concepts of free love, fidelity and sexual morality. By the time Stalin took control, however, Freud was banned, sex surveys were suppressed and sexual freedoms ended for half a century. It can surprise nobody that a sexual revolution is under way in Russia today, and that it is moving very fast.

But not always for homosexuals. Despite changes in the laws, old attitudes toward sexuality, minorities—and anything that combines the two—die very hard.

In 1989, 31 percent of the Russian population said in polls that homosexuals ought to be executed, and 32 percent said they should be isolated. Only 12 percent said they ought to be left alone. While the figures are shifting, they still have along way to go: in 1994, 23 percent in a poll said homosexuals should be killed, 24 percent said they should be isolated, and 29 percent said they ought to be left alone.

"We got all excited, and then we woke up and realized we are a deeply hated minority," said Yuri Yureyev, president of the St. Petersburg Tchaikovsky Fund, named after the composer, who was gay.

"Of course there is a lot of anger and disappointment," Mr. Yureyev said. "Maybe like every other group in this country we expected too much from the West and too much from ourselves. We had no models of how to be a community. Nobody knew how to do it. So we put on leather and opened bars like they have in San Francisco and in New York. It was foolish. It will take decades before we can be that open. Maybe it will never even happen here."

Many of the bars and clubs are shuttered now. Others, almost always owned by people who are not gay, charge far more for tickets than normal nightclubs. In some parts of town—here and in Moscow, the only other city with an obvious gay subculture—private clubs are like American speak-easies of the Prohibition era. You need a password to get in. To get out without being beaten by thugs, many patrons stay all night.

Tension has not always brought homosexuals together. Unwilling to be public, unsure of how to stay private, gay groups now fight bitterly among themselves, so much so that in Kiev, Ukraine, in May, representatives of most major gay organizations from former Soviet republics voted at the end of a conference to agree that the conference never took place. It was the only motion on which they could agree.

"An incredible amount has changed for the better," said Yelena Zabadikena, a lesbian who works at Center for Gender Issues here. "But it takes a long time to create a cohesive movement."

"In some ways it has been easier for lesbians and other ways harder," she said. "The penalties and discrimination have never been quite as harsh as for men. But we have not received the same attention in the media, and in Russia women always have fewer funds and less capacity to organize."

Long waits for housing and strict rules about who can live where make the idea of a gay enclaves, like those in Greenwich Village or the Castro, highly unlikely. And if problems are large for advocates and the rich, they are mammoth for the many gay people who live in the provinces and cannot even dream of life in the fast lane.

"I work in a factory, and I live with my mother," said a short, balding young man who agreed to be identified only by his nickname, Misha. "There is no space, no money, no choice."

Sitting in his kitchen in an ugly Soviet-era high-rise 10 minutes from the center of St. Petersburg, he served tea and described a gay life that is far more common than ones that feature discos and bars. A gay rights advocate called him and asked if he would agree to speak with a reporter. He said yes only because he felt certain that nobody he knows will ever see his comments.

"At work, trashing gays is a favorite pastime," he said. "Nobody knows what I am. I think they would kill me if they did. I don't mind them that much. I just mind feeling like I can never be free. The only place for me to go is the cruising area of the city. But it's dangerous there."

Like most people in Russia today, gay or not, Misha has little interest in politics. He laughed at the suggestion that if all homosexuals just announced who, and what, they were the need for secrecy would diminish.

"I make enough to live," he said. "Not much more. I know about how in America they all admit they are gay and tell on others. You people have different standards. Privacy is important here."

Although Westerners often point out that the Russian language has no word for privacy, it can in fact be one of the world's most secretive cultures. Homosexuals have long known how to live secretly. Until recently a gay man or a lesbian would never even mention the fact to the closest of friends.

"What everyone here knows—gay or straight—is how to have a private life that is different from their public life," said David Tuller, an American journalist who is writing a book about gay life here.

"In the West we would call that living a lie," he said. "Here they don't think that way. This is not a talk-show culture. Nobody is ever going to appear on television to talk about wanting to sleep with short men or tall women. They just want to be able to have their lives and not be bothered. For people here that would be a big step."

* * *

March 25, 2000

STATE TV TIES A PUTIN RIVAL TO JEWS, GAYS AND FOREIGNERS

By MICHAEL R. GORDON

MOSCOW, March 24—Russia's state-owned television has broadcast reports that the nation's leading liberal challenger to Vladimir V. Putin is supported by Jews, homosexuals and foreigners.

The three prime-time reports by the ORT television network were clearly intended to exploit the anti-Semitism, homophobia and suspicion of foreigners that still pervade Russian society, as well as its enthusiasm for conspiracy theories.

The reports, broadcast Thursday night, indicated that the forces behind Mr. Putin were trying to make sure that he would win more than 50 percent of the votes cast Sunday. He needs that many to avoid a runoff, which would be held April 16.

The candidate against whom the broadcasts were aimed, Grigori A. Yavlinsky, the leader of the liberal Yabloko faction, is generally held to have no chance in the election. But though Mr. Yavlinsky, who is part Jewish, is running a distant third out of 11 candidates, he stands to siphon the most votes from Mr. Putin. He therefore poses the greatest danger to the acting president's chances of winning a mandate on the first round. Hoping to score a decisive victory, Mr. Putin implored Russians today to go to the polls and pick a leader who could restore the country's prestige and command its nuclear arsenal. The Russian Orthodox patriarch Aleksy II also urged a high turnout.

But the televised reports had a different tone. Kseniya Ponomaryova, deputy head of Mr. Putin's election headquarters, said she saw nothing wrong with the reports, which she said the campaign had not orchestrated.

"ORT has shown that gays support Yavlinsky, and that there are grounds to consider that his campaign is financed by persons who do not have Russian citizenship," she said. "What can I say about it?"

But others said the reports made a mockery of the Kremlin's pledge to take the high road.

"Putin promised no dirty tricks during the presidential campaign," said Georgi A. Arbatov, a longtime specialist on Russia's relationship with the West. "But now they are turning all the propaganda against Yavlinsky during the last days of the campaign. Putin's whole style reminds me of a policeman in the provinces."

The Russian government owns 51 percent of ORT, whose reports are seen throughout Russia. Boris A. Berezovsky, the tycoon, master political intriguer, Putin supporter and Yavlinsky foe, is also a major owner and has an played an influential behind-the-scenes role at the network.

Certainly, ORT has not hesitated in the past to join the political fray. Before parliamentary elections in December, Sergei Dorenko, the host of one of the network's most watched news affairs shows, conducted attacks against Yevgeny M. Primakov, the former prime minister, and Yuri M. Luzhkov, the Moscow mayor, both Putin rivals.

The relentless criticism was one reason Mr. Primakov and Mr. Luzhkov fell way behind Mr. Putin in the opinion polls and decided not to take part in the presidential campaign. But the broadcast Thursday night was exceptional even by ORT standards.

One of its reports charged that the candidate was bankrolled by powerful Jewish businessmen, specifically Vladimir V. Gusinsky, the head of the NTV, Russia's only independent television network. He is one of Russia's most prominent Jewish citizens.

Mr. Gusinsky has dual Russian and Israeli citizenship. ORT's report, however, emphasized his Jewish background. It showed Mr. Gusinsky at a banquet with Hasidic leaders, who were wearing black fedoras and skullcaps.

Mr. Gusinsky has made it no secret that he thinks Mr. Yavlinsky is the best candidate for Russia. But ORT suggested darkly that Mr. Yavlinsky was secretly being financed by "Israeli citizens." It was a striking attack in light of Mr. Putin's vows to battle anti-Semitism.

The network also charged, without producing any evidence, that Mr. Yavlinsky's campaign was receiving financial support from two German research organizations. But its most eye-catching report was about gay Russians who ostensibly are backing Mr. Yavlinsky.

There is little tolerance in Russia for homosexuals, who have not been a visible or important factor in the nation's political life. So the report that a gay group had organized a press conference in the "Blue Heart Club" created a stir. "Blue" is Russian slang for "gay."

The ORT report cautioned that the press conference might be part of a disinformation campaign, but not until it had first broadcast the effusive declarations of support for Mr. Yavlinsky.

Along with ORT, Russia's other state-owned television network, RTR, attended the event. NTV said that it had not been invited and that the entire episode appeared to have been staged.

That was hardly the only mud that has been slung at Mr. Yavlinsky. ORT has also charged that he secretly underwent plastic surgery.

Tonight, ORT's coverage of him was more restrained. It continued to criticize him, but also mentioned a letter he had written denying that his campaign had received foreign funds.

In addition, the two German research groups featured in the ORT report told the Russian press they were not underwriting Mr. Yavlinsky's presidential bid.

For all its unsavoryness, the logic of ORT's attacks on Mr. Yavlinsky is clear. Mr. Yavlinsky is only expected to receive 5 percent to 10 percent of the vote. But Mr. Putin could use those voters, many of them from Russia's emerging middle class, to achieve the majority he is seeking in the first round.

Igor Malashenko, a senior executive at Mr. Berezovsky's media conglomerate, said there were several explanations for ORT's broadcast. Mr. Berezovsky, he said, might be going out of his way to demonstrate his loyalty to Mr. Putin. And Mr. Putin's campaign team, he said, is anxious to avoid a runoff.

"People are not terribly excited by the election," Mr. Malashenko said. "So they want to demonstrate that there is some sinister conspiracy against Putin—basically, a Jewish conspiracy."

Otto Latsis, a political analyst at the daily Izvestia, said he doubted that Mr. Putin has personally authorized the broadcasts and described them as despicable and foolish.

"Whoever made the decision was trying too hard," he said.

Correction: Because of an editing error, a front-page article on Saturday about reports by the state-owned ORT television network that a candidate in the Russian presidential election was supported by Jews, homosexuals and foreigners misstated the affiliation of Igor Malashenko, a media executive who commented. He works for Vladimir V. Gusinsky, who is chairman of Media Most, the conglomerate that includes the independent NTV network. He does not work for Boris A. Berezovsky, a major partner in the state-owned channel.

* * *

THE MIDDLE EAST

January 23, 1984

IN JORDAN, CONGRATULATIONS ARE IN ORDER

By JUDITH MILLER

AMMAN, Jordan, Jan. 17—This capital has been filled of late with the sounds of "a thousand congratulations."

Ever since King Hussein shuffled his Cabinet last week, prominent Jordanians have traveled across town, in some cases across the kingdom, to say, as Bedouin tradition dictates, "A thousand congratulations" to the new ministers and palace advisers.

The visit lasts 5 to 10 minutes. The well-wisher extends "a thousand congratulations" in Arabic to the official. Kisses on both cheeks are exchanged. The visitor is seated and offered a miniature cup of Arabic coffee, a bitter ceremonial brew. He sips it while offering praise for the official's talents, best wishes for his success and a request for his assistance should the need or an appropriate occasion arise.

After the cup is empty, the visitor shakes his wrist back and forth, the traditional sign that he has had enough coffee, and returns the cup to the coffee server. A few more pleasantries are exchanged, along with a few more kisses, and the visit is over.

A cardinal rule of these encounters is that no actual business is to be conducted. Reporters who tried to ask ministers a few substantive questions were gently but firmly informed that the session was over.

After office hours, visits continued at officials' homes, often late into the night.

"I'm exhausted," said Adnan Abu-Odeh, the already-influential Information Minister, who was promoted to one of the two most powerful advisory posts in the palace.

The most popular radio show in Amman is "Direct Line," a call-in program broadcast at 9 o'clock every morning.

Last week, many listeners were stunned to hear the voice of a surprise participant—King Hussein. He called in from his hospital bed to say that he was feeling much better and would soon be going home to the palace.

He spoke for only a minute or two. But it was enough to reassure an obviously jittery public that he was alive, if not yet well.

Doctors said this week that the King was not, as originally announced, suffering from a bleeding peptic ulcer but from a minor and common undisclosed problem that had been worsened by too little rest.

Every night at 7:30, Jordanians can watch the news in Hebrew. The broadcast does not come from Israel but from Jordan TV, widely regarded as the highest quality television in the Arab world. Mohammed Kamal, the founder and director general of Jordan TV, said he decided to broadcast news in Hebrew, in addition to Arabic, French and English, because so many Israelis were viewers.

"We try to be objective and very balanced," Mr. Kamal said. "The main problem is finding newscasters who speak Hebrew well enough."

Jordan TV has five broadcasters who speak the language, and he said he hoped to hire Palestinians from the West Bank.

"Their Hebrew after all these years of occupation is quite good," Mr. Kamal said.

Israelis say the Hebrew on Jordan TV is sometimes a tad archaic. In a recent broadcast, Iraqis were reported in Hebrew to be "smiting their Iranian enemies," for example.

A survey last February in Israel by the Hebrew University's Institute of Communication concluded that Israelis watched

Jordanian news more out of curiosity than a desire to be informed.

But the survey, a copy of which was provided by Jordan TV, also found that Jordanian television was, on balance, far more popular than its Israeli competition.

Mr. Kamal asserted that the wide variety and quality of programming offered on Jordan's two color stations—its Arabic and foreign programs—accounted for its appeal.

'Dallas' Is Broadcast

Jordan TV was first in the Arab world to broadcast the celebrated American series "Dallas." But Jordan decided not to broadcast "Dynasty," another American series similar to Dallas. Mr. Kamal said many people here felt the program promoted homosexuality because several of its episodes focused on a homosexual member of the clan.

Mr. Kamal said Jordan TV was the only Arab station to broadcast live the speech delivered in the Israeli Parliament in 1977 by President Anwar el-Sadat of Egypt. "It was news and we showed it, despite criticism," Mr. Kamal said.

Among the most vocal critics was Syria, which routinely jams Jordan's news broadcasts—in Arabic, not in Hebrew.

Mr. Kamal asserted that programing was objective. But he said the Government committee that screens programs decided last February against broadcasting "The Winds of War," a multipart series based on the novel by Herman Wouk.

"The book has a Jewish author," Mr. Kamal said, adding that it was felt that the series promoted sympathy for Israelis.

He said that, in view of Israel's invasion of Lebanon and its settlement activities in the West Bank, it was felt that the timing was wrong.

* * *

June 5, 1989

AYATOLLAH RUHOLLAH KHOMEINI, 89, RELENTLESS FOUNDER OF IRAN'S ISLAMIC REPUBLIC

By RAYMOND H. ANDERSON

The life of Ayatollah Ruhollah Khomeini was so shadowy, with such an overlay of myth and rumor, that there was lingering disagreement or uncertainty about his ancestry, his true name and his date of birth.

But when he returned in triumph to Teheran on Feb. 1, 1979, after almost 15 years in exile, the imposing man in a black robe with a white beard and intense dark eyes left little doubt about who he was, or what he wanted for his ancient land.

Ayatollah Khomeini felt a holy mission to rid Iran of what he saw as Western corruption and degeneracy and to return the country, under an Islamic theocracy, to religious purity.

The Islamic Shiite leader's fervor helped drive Shah Mohammed Riza Pahlevi from the Peacock Throne on Jan. 15, 1979, and into foreign exile. The Shah's eventual arrival

in the United States for cancer treatment was the spark that set off the American hostage crisis of 1979-81.

Hostility for the West

Under the Ayatollah, Iran was wrenched backward from widespread economic development and social change and onto a path that was broadly hostile to the Western world.

The Ayatollah's path also led to eight years of grisly, costly, inconclusive war between Iran and its Arab neighbor, Iraq. He demanded that his country fight unrelentingly after Iraq invaded Iran in September 1980, but he eventually accepted a truce in 1988.

Many longtime Iranian opponents of the Shah hoped that the Ayatollah would turn over power and allow a democratic society to emerge. But he held to his dream of an Islamic republic and retained his Islamic fervor—scuttling a tentative economic and political opening to the West in February 1989 with his call for the killing of a British author, Salman Rushdie, whose novel "The Satanic Verses" was deemed to have blasphemed the faith.

A month later, he dismissed Ayatollah Hussein Ali Montazeri, a relative moderate who had been designated as his political heir.

A Leader Beyond Challenge

There was no one in Iran with sufficient authority to challenge the Ayatollah successfully. In the aftermath of the revolution, he moved relentlessly toward his theocratic goal, consolidating power and silencing the opposition.

In a frenzy of political retribution and Islamic purification, thousands of people were executed in public, including torturers, criminals, homosexuals, prostitutes and the Shah's officials.

A 1987 report of the United Nations Commission on Human Rights estimated that as many as 7,000 people were shot, hanged, stoned or burned to death after the 1979 revolution.

Amid Iranian demands that the Shah be returned to Iran to stand trial for abuse of power, President Carter intervened to allow the Shah to enter the United States for cancer treatment. In a fury, Iranians clambered over the walls of the American Embassy in Teheran on Nov. 4, 1979, seizing diplomats, staff members and military personnel as hostages to trade in exchange for the Shah.

The hostage crisis caused agony, fear and humiliation in the United States. There was well-founded dread that the captors, mostly student militants, might start shooting hostages to dramatize their demand for the Shah.

Under growing pressure, President Carter endorsed a desperate military rescue mission in April. The mission was abandoned at a desert site southeast of Teheran after three of eight helicopters had problems, leaving too few for a safe operation. As the rescuers rushed to get away before dawn, a helicopter crashed into a C-130 transport and exploded. Eight men died in the fire.

For the Ayatollah and most Iranians, the collapse of the rescue mission was cause for jubilation. Crowds celebrated in the streets. But for Mr. Carter, as he conceded later, it was the ignominious beginning of the end for his Presidency.

It was not until Jan. 20, 1981, Inauguration Day for Ronald Reagan, that the hostages were released, after 444 days. They flew out of Iran's airspace at almost the very moment that Mr. Reagan was taking the oath of office.

The seizure of the hostages was an assertion of defiance that had rallied Iranians behind the Ayatollah and helped insure approval of his new Constitution establishing Iran as an Islamic republic.

Lifelong supreme authority was vested in the Ayatollah, with the title Velayat Faghi, or Religious Leader.

Wide Dissent in the Land

Despite approval of the Islamic republic by an overwhelming majority, there was opposition to the Ayatollah among liberals, rival religious leaders and many of Iran's ethnic minorities.

Ayatollah Khomeini repeatedly used hatred of the United States—he called it "the Great Satan"—to bolster support for his revolution, amid signs of increasing internal disagreement over the continuing holding of the American Embassy hostages.

Another motive for the Ayatollah's anti-Americanism was his vision of spreading his fundamentalist revolution throughout the Islamic world.

"This is not a struggle between the United States and Iran," he declared. "This is a struggle between Islam and blasphemy."

The Iranian regime's hatred for the United States played itself out many times in the Ayatollah's years. On July 31, 1987, thousands of chanting Iranian pilgrims in the holy city of Mecca, in Saudi Arabia, rampaged and fought with the Saudi riot police. Many were killed and wounded. "Death to America! Death to France! Death to Israel!" they shouted.

The Ayatollah's regime accused the United States of having plotted the violence.

Deep Divisions Over the U.S.

But there were occasional reports of differences in Iran on the issue of relations with the United States, and these hints of emerging "moderation" in Iran led to the greatest foreign- policy debacle of the Reagan years: the Iran-contra afffair.

Some Americans in the Reagan White House spoke of "moderates" in Teheran who looked to a time when the Ayatollah would pass from the scene. It was to such "moderates" that the White House turned in 1985, seeking influence to win the release of Americans being held in Lebanon by Shiite fundamentalist groups loyal to the Ayatollah.

Complex deals of arms for hostages were played out, with disastrous results for the United States. The Reagan Administration was deeply embarrassed in 1986 when it became public that it had been trading arms for hostages in direct violation of its own anti-terrorism policy.

In a troubling twist that was ultimately deemed illegal, the profits from the sales of American arms to Iran—mostly missiles that Iran used to good effect in its long and fierce war with Iraq—went to support the Nicaraguan rebels.

Iran had tweaked the "Great Satan" once again. But in the fall of 1986, Ayatollah Khomeini criticized Iranians who had taken part in the dealings with Washington, calling them "Satan-oriented."

"I never expected such things from such people," he said.

Conflicting Birthdates

The man who became the Islamic ruler of Iran and a force in much of the world was born, by varying accounts, in 1900, 1901 or 1902. Iranian accounts put his age at 86, but May 27, 1900, has become the most accepted date for the Ayatollah's birth, making him 89 at the time of his death.

His birthplace was the town of Khomein, about 180 miles south of Teheran. His father was a mullah, or religious leader.

Little is known of the Ayatollah's childhood except for one event that possibly influenced his character. When he was an infant, his father was murdered, apparently in a dispute with a landowner over irrigation rights.

The Ayatollah's supporters have asserted that his father was killed on orders of Riza Khan, the officer who seized power in 1921, assumed the throne as Riza Shah in 1925, took the dynastic name Pahlevi and changed the name of Persia to Iran, for its prehistoric Aryan roots.

Studies Theology And Takes a Bride

Raised by his strong-willed mother and an aunt, Ruhollah Khomeini began religious studies in Khomein. According to various accounts, he continued his studies at the Marvi Theological School in Teheran, in the Shiite shrine city of Najaf in Iraq and in Isfahan and Arak.

In the 1920's, he followed his tutor to Qum, where he completed his studies, worked as a teacher and became interested in Islamic mysticism and Plato's "Republic," which may have helped shape his vision of an Islamic state led by a philosopher-king.

It was during these years that he married, reportedly a woman from Qum. They had a daughter who died in infancy and a son, Mustafa, whose death in the 1970's provoked speculation that he had been killed by the Shah's secret police.

According to some accounts, Ruhollah Khomeini's first wife died and he then married the daughter of a wealthy landowner. They had, it was said, three daughters and a son, Ahmad, who went on to serve as his father's chief aide.

Dissent Stirred in 1941

Ruhollah Khomeini apparently concentrated on theology through most of Riza Shah's reign, for there are no accounts of opposition activity until 1941, the year that the old Shah, pro-German and anti-British, was deposed by British forces in favor of his son, Mohammed Riza. The cleric was unequivocal when he did speak out, in a book called, "Unveiling the Mysteries."

"The orders of the dictatorial state of Riza Shah," he declared, "are valueless, and all laws approved by the Parliament must be burned."

The book, foreshadowing the Ayatollah's later campaign, accused Riza Shah of persecuting the clergy, destroying Islamic culture and submitting to foreign domination. It also had the first known outline of the Khomeini conception of the Islamic state, which he came to regard with increasing fervor as the only legitimate form of government.

"God," he wrote, "has formed the Islamic Republic. Obey God and his Prophet and those among you who have authority. It is the only government accepted by God on Resurrection Day. We don't say that the Government must be composed of the clergy but that the Government must be directed and organized according to the divine law, and this is only possible with the supervision of the clergy."

Polemics Attracted the Young

The book created an uproar. Students applauded it, but the older, more conservative mullahs were uneasy.

Although he continued to speak out and was gaining a zealous following, the Khomeini campaign was overshadowed in 1951 when the National Front Government of Mohammed Mossadegh came to power and when, in 1953, the Shah was briefly driven into exile. The Khomeini faction sympathized with the opposition to the Shah, but regarded the Mossadegh Government as too secular and yearned for an Islamic state.

It was in the years after the Shah was restored to the throne by the C.I.A. that Ruhollah Khomeini acquired the honorific Ayatollah, or Reflection of Allah, a title that is bestowed by acclamation of a mullah's followers. It is held by more than a thousand mullahs in the Shiite world.

By the time he took the lead in the opposition to the Shah, he had received the title of Grand Ayatollah, held by only six other mullahs in Iran at the time. That was 1962, when the Ayatollah led a general strike against a ruling that witnesses in court no longer had to swear by the Koran.

Opposed Shah's Goal of a Modern Society

In 1963, the Shah announced his White Revolution to modernize Iran swiftly and from top to bottom, a program that included emancipation of women and seizure of the vast lands controlled by the clergy. The Ayatollah spoke out forcefully against it.

He won support from the students at Teheran University, who distributed as many as 200,000 copies of his statements, marking the first link between the religious leader and young intellectuals opposed to the Shah.

In June, when the Ayatollah, preaching to 100,000 at a Qum mosque, demanded that the army depose the Shah, he was arrested. Riots followed.

Released from jail, he was kept under house arrest for almost a year and then detained again in November 1964 when he vehemently protested an agreement exempting American servicemen in Iran from the jurisdiction of the country's courts.

When he was brought before Prime Minister Hassan Ali Mansour and refused a last-minute appeal to drop his opposition to the Government, the Prime Minister reportedly slapped him and ordered him into exile.

Weeks later, Prime Minister Mansour was assassinated by a young gunman carrying the Ayatollah's picture.

A Relentless Campaign

The Ayatollah went first to Turkey but then moved his base to Iraq, settling in Najaf and continuing his relentless campaign against the Shah.

Because of the Shah's control of Iranian politics and such institutions as the press, it was to the mullahs, with their traditional role as champions of the downtrodden, that the discontented turned for leadership.

As an exile in neighboring Iraq with more freedom to speak out than people at home, Ayatollah Khomeini provided the polemics and inspiration.

The Shah, backed by the army and the country's oil wealth, ignored the constant denunciations, but as the Ayatollah's influence grew—fed by growing disenchantment with corruption, repression and the cultural upheavals of modernization—the Government grew ever more concerned.

In January 1978, an article mildly critical of the Ayatollah was planted in a Teheran newspaper and proved an immediate and costly mistake.

In response, demonstrators carrying pictures of the Ayatollah poured into the streets of virtually every city and town in the country. The yearlong battle for Iran was on. By September the revolt had spread to the oilfields, where workers began a crippling strike, leading the Shah to declare martial law.

For the Shah, It Was Too Late

The next month, Iraq, reportedly acting at the request of Iran, stationed policemen around Ayatollah Khomeini's house, provoking more demonstrations. The Shah, finally recognizing the Ayatollah's influence, switched tactics and proclaimed an amnesty that would have let him and thousands of other exiles to return home. It was too late. The Ayatollah refused, saying he would not return until the Shah was gone.

When the Ayatollah was expelled from Iraq, he moved to France and set up headquarters in the Paris suburb of Neauphle-le-Chateau. There, he and his aides coordinated the activities of hundreds of mullahs in Iran by telephone.

In the frantic days of December 1978, the Ayatollah refused offers of compromise, insisting on the Shah's ouster.

When the Shah left Iran on Jan. 16, the Ayatollah denounced the new Government that the Shah had appointed.

Attempts to Thwart Return

Caught between the Ayatollah's intransigence and a powerful army still loyal to the Shah, Prime Minister Shahpur Bakhtiar first closed Teheran airport to thwart the Ayatollah's return, then relented.

Finally, on Feb. 1, Ayatollah Khomeini flew home, reclining on a carpet on the floor of an Air France plane.

Within days, the Bakhtiar Government had faded away and the Ayatollah was in full control.

He told the Iranians, "The remaining one or two years of my life I will devote to you to keep this movement alive."

Insisting at first that he would defer to the provisional secular Government he established, the Ayatollah went to Qum but was soon undercutting his own ministers at virtually every turn, ridiculing the Prime Minister, Mehdi Bazargan, as weak and ruling increasingly through a secret, mullah-dominated Islamic Revolutionary Council and similar bodies.

To the dismay of the National Front and other secular groups that had helped lead the struggle against the Shah and hoped to establish a modern democracy, the Ayatollah moved to impose Islamic rule.

Orders Women To Wear Veils

He ordered women to wear veils and chadors, the full-length gowns. He allowed no criticism of his rule, and when his Oil Minister resisted demands for a purge of non-Islamic workers among the industry's 40,000 employees, he dismissed him as a traitor.

Asked by the Italian journalist Oriana Fallaci in 1979 about reports of executions of homosexuals, prostitutes and adulterers, the Ayatollah said: "If our finger suffers from gangrene, what do you do? Do you let the whole hand, and then the body, become filled with gangrene, or do you cut the finger off?"

The Ayatollah described music as "no different from opium" and banned it from television and radio. Music, he said, "stupefies persons listening to it and makes their brain inactive and frivolous."

Because of Iran's increasing isolation in the Khomeini era, it was often difficult to assess the precise role of the Ayatollah in ruling the country. But his influence as interpreter of the divine will and symbol of the Islamic Republic was strong and durable. In the years after his rise to power, his Government endured an ineffective Western arms embargo, rebellion by Kurdish and Baluchi minorities and a wave of assassinations in 1981 when the People's Mujahedeen, a Marxist group, moved against him.

Backing to Terrorists

After 1980, the Government began financing and supporting local rebel groups in Persian Gulf countries, including Kuwait, Bahrain and Saudi Arabia, and according to the United States, it gave backing to terrorist bombings and hostage taking.

The Ayatollah's hopes that his revolution would spread were not fulfilled. But as the Baghdad-born University of London scholar Elie Kedourie wrote in May 1989 in the Times Literary Supplement, a British weekly, an abiding goal of the Iranian Islamic Republic is "to liberate the disinherited masses of the Muslim world, whether these live in independent states like Egypt or Saudia Arabia or Morocco or the Emirates of the Gulf, or whether they are under non-Muslim rule, as in the Soviet Union or Israel."

Not a few Western analysts of the Middle East came to believe that the Ayatollah's Iran was inflexibly bent on expanding its brand of revolutionary fundamentalism across the Arab world—and were then surprised at how easily Iran adjusted to the truce in the Gulf war in 1988.

A War Without Victory or Defeat

That the Ayatollah's regime managed to survive that grueling conflict was a striking success of sorts. After the initial Iraqi invasion, the Iranian Army, with the help of Revolutionary Guards, threw itself into the defense of the country. Volunteer suicide squads and masses of young conscripts retook land with human wave attacks, and then lost it again, and the Ayatollah's Government used the nationalist fervor to consolidate its rule. The war was fought to a stalemate.

Casualties on both sides were immense and the financial cost enormous. The war threatened a new international oil crisis as attacks increased on tankers in the gulf. In July 1987, the United States put naval forces in the gulf to escort Kuwaiti tankers.

Despite the suffering and cost, Ayatollah Khomeini urged his people to fight on until victory over Iraq. Speaking in February 1987, he called the war a "divine cause."

"Almost every day, Iran is hit, and many children, youngsters, old men and ordinary people see their homes fall in on them," he said. "But as soon as they clamber from the rubble, they speak of the need for us to make war until victory."

But in the months that followed, it became more and more evident that Iran's larger army would not bring it victory over Iraq, which remained largely on the defensive but controlled the air with its warplanes and sometimes made telling use of missiles and even poison gas.

Peace a 'Deadly Poison'

It was on a note of Islamic fatalism that the Ayatollah finally, in July 1988, announced his acceptance of the truce. "I had promised to fight to the last drop of my blood and to my last breath," he noted in a statement reported by the Teheran radio.

"Taking this decision was more deadly than taking poison," he went on, "I submitted myself to God's will and drank this drink for his satisfaction."

With the hostilities ended, there followed a surge in political crosscurrents and bickering in Iran. Ayatollah Khomeini's ouster of Ayatollah Montazeri as his successor-designate in March 1989 came after that cleric suggested that the Iranian revolution was off course: in radio and television messages he had criticized aspects of the regime, including its view that those who did not unquestioningly support it were foes of Islam.

In the months that followed, Ayatollah Khomeini's son Ahmad came to be seen, amid a welter of rivalries, as a chief candidate to assume his father's leadership role. No new heir was appointed until the day after his death, when the Iranian President, Hojatolislam Ali Khamenei, was named supreme leader.

* * *

November 22, 1992

GAY SOLDIERS CUT THE MUSTARD ABROAD

While military leaders resist President-elect Clinton's pledge to include homosexuals in the armed services, many foreign forces have successfully incorporated gay personnel. The experience abroad suggests that gay soldiers can indeed function effectively in military units that are enlightened enough to accept their service.

The lamentable current American policy bans homosexuals, both male and female, from military service and requires discharging those discovered while serving. The rationale is that the presence of known homosexuals would undermine morale and discipline and would unfairly invade the privacy of heterosexuals who do not want to share close quarters with individuals of the same sex who might find them sexually attractive.

Those fears appear grotesquely exaggerated when measured against the more rational policies in many other nations.

A report by the General Accounting Office issued in June found that Austria, Denmark, Italy, Japan, Luxembourg, the Netherlands, Norway, Spain and Sweden all allow homosexuals to serve in the armed forces without restriction.

True, some of these nations discharge homosexuals if they engage in sexual harassment or if their sexual orientation interferes with their duties. But that puts the emphasis where it belongs, on behavior rather than sexual orientation.

Critics minimize these examples because not one of the nations involved is a military power. Still, all military forces, no matter how small, face the same privacy issues. And it is harder to dismiss two larger examples, France and Israel.

France, a nuclear power, tolerates homosexuals in its armed forces, albeit grudgingly. Homosexuality there is deemed a medical problem, and doctors must judge whether a homosexual is fit for military service. If the doctors O.K. the individual, French commanders routinely advise even the fit to resign; but they cannot force homosexuals to leave the service.

The Israeli Army, among the most effective fighting forces in the world, requires military service of all able-bodied citizens, including homosexuals. Israeli spokesmen say there is no discrimination against gay soldiers. Homosexuals are not denied promotion because of their sexual orientation; they are allowed to become career soldiers; they serve in even the most elite fighting units, on critical frontiers.

Some homophobic Israeli commanders are thought to harass homosexuals or deny them promotions. Many gay Israeli soldiers, in turn, seek transfers to bases where they can work during the day and sleep at home. But some commanders so value their gay soldiers that they try to block such transfers.

Each nation must judge how best to reconcile its own cultural attitudes with fairness to homosexual citizens. The lesson from abroad is that, with good will and effort, America can do it too.

* * *

February 21, 1993

HOMOSEXUALS IN ISRAELI ARMY: NO OFFICIAL DISCRIMINATION, BUT KEEP IT SECRET

By CLYDE HABERMAN
Special to The New York Times

JERUSALEM, Feb. 20—For 15 years, Prof. Uzi Even had done top-secret research for the military. In the 1967 and 1973 wars he was assigned as an intelligence officer with combat units in Sinai and on the Golan Heights.

Then, after a security check 10 years ago turned up that he was living with another man, he decided he would no longer hide his homosexuality.

"It was as though an iron curtain came down between me and my colleagues," said Professor Even, chairman of the chemistry department at Tel Aviv University. "They were ordered not to speak to me."

In short order, his security clearance was canceled, he was stripped of his rank, which even now he does not reveal for security reasons, and he was given office chores on reserve duty.

No Official Discrimination

Officially, there is no discrimination against homosexuals in the Israeli armed forces. Virtually all Israeli men and women, except for Arabs and ardently Orthodox Jews, enter the service at the age of 18, and homosexuals are no exception. Conscripts are not asked about sexual orientation, and people who are openly gay are not drummed out of the service because of it.

But as Professor Even's experience suggests, the Israeli Army may be something less than the model of tolerance and openness supposed by some who cite Israel's example in advocating an end to the ban on homosexuals in the military in the United States.

By coincidence, at the same time that the United States has been enmeshed in the issue, Israel has recently been engaging in a rare and occasionally intense public debate on attitudes toward homosexuality in its army.

Pressure to Hide Homosexuality

Although homosexuals serve with everyone else in the military in Israel, many Israeli homosexuals say that in reality they feel pressures to hide their orientation, both in active service and the reserve duty that most men perform for a month or two each year until the age of 51.

"Israeli society is a macho society, and the army is a mirror of that," said Rafi Niv, who writes on homosexual issues for a local newspaper in Haifa. "Most gay soldiers I know are in the closet."

Generally speaking, homosexuality is not considered acceptable in a country where the family is central and where strict religious values shape public policy on personal behavior, from cradle to tomb. There is an incipient gay rights movement, but it is not large and the issue itself is far from dominant for most Israelis.

Despite the fact that gay Israelis are conscripted, for example, those soldiers who are found to be homosexuals, or who declare that fact openly, are required to undergo psychological testing and security checks, an indication that the Army still regards them with distrust and concern that their orientation might reflect emotional disorders.

The requirement of security checks appears also to reflect concern about blackmail for those who have kept their homosexuality to themselves.

Risks in Psychological Testing

While nothing negative necessarily results from the psychological testing, homosexuals say they find the process intrusive and threatening. Indeed, there are real risks: Some Army professionals acknowledge that those men's chances of being assigned to highly classified work or to certain combat units are highly reduced.

"Maybe we are more afraid than we really have to be," said a 34-year-old insurance-company supervisor in Haifa who insisted on not being identified. "But I don't serve with the same people each time I do reserve duty. When I'm stuck for 30 days with people and I don't know how they will react, it is better that I don't come out."

Professor Even argues that his experience bears out these concerns.

"I was openly gay," he said in a interview. "Nobody could say that I was subject to blackmail because by that point there was nothing to blackmail me with."

The fact that homosexuals are accepted in the Israeli armed forces may have something to do with the role played by the army in Israeli society. Because of universal conscription, banning homosexuals would be seen as a discriminatory act against one group.

Common Rite of Passage

Even in an age when it is not the revered institution it once was, the military remains the one common denominator in a fractious country. Service is generally regarded as a critical rite of passage. Important relationships are forged in the Army, and the type of unit one serves in often can determine success later in life.

"Saying you can't serve because you're a homosexual is saying you can't be a part of society, period," said Lieut. Col. Moshe Fogel of the army.

The Israeli Defense Forces, as the army is officially called, have been accepting homosexuals with no questions asked at least since the 1970's. They were years ahead of Parliament, which eliminated sodomy as a crime only in 1988, and banned job discrimination on the basis of sexual orientation in late 1991.

There is no military code specifically governing homosexual conduct. Regulations prohibit sexual activity in general on military bases, although the rules are often ignored at least between men and women.

The code also forbids officers—usually men—from coercing subordinates—usually women—into sexual rela-

Rina Castelnuovo for The New York Times

After a security check by the Israeli military 10 years ago revealed that he was living with another man, Prof. Uzi Even, right, shown at home with his companion, Amit, decided he would no longer hide his homosexuality. As a result, his security clearance was cancelled, and he was stripped of his rank.

tions, a rule that many Israeli women complain is also routinely violated. Presumably, these codes would apply as well to homosexual activity. But the day-to-day reality, Colonel Fogel says, is that gay soldiers keep their orientation to themselves, and so the issue does not arise.

Army Issues Statement

After Professor Even's testimony, the army issued a formal statement rejecting charges of bias and saying that homosexuals are not prohibited, as a group, from sensitive assignments.

Officers who argue that the army is tolerant of homosexuals cite the case of Col. Doron Meisel, who held senior positions in the medical corps under three chiefs of staff, all of whom knew he was gay.

Colonel Meisel's death from cancer two years ago, at the age of 46, left open, however, the question of whether his homosexuality would have stood in the way of future promotion.

Another gay reservist, a professor at Hebrew University in Jerusalem, does his annual duty in an intelligence unit, and often has access to top-secret material. He says that several other people in his unit are also gay, and their homosexuality is known to everyone with whom they work.

"It's not an issue," he said. But then after a pause he added, "in my unit."

"If the security people knew about it then it could become an issue," he acknowledged.

Evaluation Mandatory

Psychological evaluation of known homosexuals has been mandatory since 1983, and few would say that it works to their advantage. Army officials said they had no explanation why the evaluations were instituted at that time.

"Soldiers declared or found to be homosexuals will be restricted from serving in highly sensitive units like intelligence," Reuven Gal, a former Army chief psychologist, said in an interview last week with Israel Radio. "Or they might be excluded from some combat units that are highly condensed or under high stress or may serve for long periods of time in seclusion."

Much seems to depend on the attitude of the soldier's commanding officer toward homosexuality, and the arbitrariness is one reason that several gay groups are campaigning to scrap the 1983 regulations.

"If being gay is disqualifying for sensitive positions, it's wrong to keep gays in the service," said Liora Moriel, head of one such group. "But if it's not a disqualifying factor, these rules should be taken off the books."

But it may take more than rule-book changes to purge anti-gay attitudes from the military, given the degree to which it reflects the larger society.

The impact of this matter was made clear by a recent parliamentary hearing that Professor Even addressed: While it was under way, lawmakers from Orthodox Jewish parties refused even to enter the Parliament building.

Prime Minister Yitzhak Rabin, a former Army chief of staff, says he sees no reason for anti-gay discrimination, and he promises an inquiry to see if Professor Even should be returned to his former position.

Thus far, the professor has not heard back. But he says the public's verdict is in and, judging from the press reaction and from phone calls, it is sympathetic. "I was expecting some crank calls," he said. "But I got only one."

*   *   *

August 30, 1993

FUNDAMENTALIST CRITIC ARRESTED IN TEHERAN

Special to The New York Times

TEHERAN, Iran, Aug. 29—Prosecutors of the Islamic Revolutionary court have arrested Abbas Abdi, editor of Salam, a newspaper that promotes Islamic fundamentalism.

Salam reported today that Mr. Abdi was taken into custody Thursday during an outing with his family. His whereabouts remain unknown.

Islamic Revolutionary courts handle espionage or "anti-revolutionary" cases. In the early years of the revolution, they arrested and executed virtually all opponents to the Government.

Salam has been critical of centralized decision-making and has urged a multiparty system. The hard-line fundamentalists, who lost their majority in Parliamentary elections last year, claim to support cultural and political openness.

Editorials have opposed physical punishment in schools, promoted freedom of the press and encouraged a discussion on homosexuality in Iran.

But Mr. Abdi's most prominent distinction, thought to be a safeguard regardless of Salam's negative reporting, was his contribution to the Iranian revolution: as an engineering student, Mr. Abdi led the takeover of the United States Embassy in Teheran, holding more than 50 Americans hostage for 444 days.

In another attack on Salam, the publisher, Hojatolislam Mohamad Mussavi Khoeini, was summoned today to appear before the Special Clerical Court, where he reportedly faces charges of slander.

*   *   *

July 23, 1996

IN EGYPT, ON-SCREEN SEX RECEIVES MIXED REVIEWS

By NEIL MACFARQUHAR

CAIRO, July 22—In this summer's hit movie here, three working women from a poor Cairo neighborhood fret about their meager choice of marriageable louts.

Aside from routine problems like bagging a longtime fiancé seemingly allergic to commitment or warding off the boss's gropings, much of the plot of the movie, "Oh Life, You Are My Love," revolves around a shop clerk insisting that any man she marries must love her despite her lost virginity. When suitor after suitor flees, her friends convince her that some restorative surgery will fool all future mates.

The days are over when a girl's honor was like a matchstick, it could only burn once," one of the women says in the movie, mocking a famous adage. "Now it's like a lighter, you click it on and it burns, you click it again and it burns."

These are days of ferment in the Egyptian arts, with Government censors allowing a more forthright examination of social problems and habits in movies, in plays and on television. The Government eased its restrictions as part of the showdown with religious militants seeking to establish strict Islamic rule, and also to combat public grumbling that senior officials live completely removed from common problems.

Parallel with more relaxed Government rules, however, there has been an outbreak of freelance attempts to ban works deemed morally suspect. And while things like kissing may now be common on television and in the movies, writers and directors still haggle with censors, and religious institutions and the police are allowed to vet many materials.

"If one person from the police wakes up in the morning and decides he doesn't like something, he can try to get it banned," said Marlyn Tadros, deputy director of the Legal Research and Resource Center for Human Rights, a private, nonprofit group. "It is scary, because you don't know what is coming."

Egyptian intellectuals accuse the Government of working both sides of the fence. They say President Hosni Mubarak has stressed that his Government is not in the business of banning artistic works, yet it does not rein in Government institutions that target specific works.

"On the one hand the Islamic Research Institute is a Government authority, but on the other hand the Government is giving some freedom in these artistic areas," said Rawia Abdel Azim, the director of Sinai House, a publisher whose works have been denounced by religious officials. "They are doing that to absorb the anger on the streets, not for the sake of real liberalization."

Newspapers remain stringently controlled. Journalists largely avoid writing anything about the military, national security, religion or the character of the President out of fear they will be taken to court and face recently inflated fines. Like the newspaper law, the censorship law bans works that damage the public interest or religion, using vague terms that can be interpreted widely.

"There are certain scenes that do not go along easily with the principles of a religious society, things that cannot be seen as intellectual creativity," said Abdel Qader Al-Nashar, the legal consultant to the Minister of Culture, whose ministry reviews every movie, television program, play or song distributed in Egypt. "We cannot condone vice or delinquency or homosexuality and then show that to the society."

Sheik Youssef Al-Badry, a Muslim cleric famous for confronting actors and writers, said he had yet to see "Oh Life, You Are My Love" but frowned on the idea of a woman deceiving her husband.

"It shows people how to get rid of their mistakes, but not through repentance and returning to Allah," he said. "This movie publicizes and legitimizes what has previously been done in secret."

Both this movie and the newly released "Asphalt Demons," which tells the story of three minibus drivers who spend their off hours engaged in adultery with various neighbors and relatives, are considered marked departures because they talk about the ambitions, thoughts and problems of ordinary people.

"One of the censors actually told us that there are more beautiful people around, people from better classes, why didn't we talk about them," said Mohammed Hilmi Hillel, the scriptwriter of "Oh Life, You Are My Love," noting he had to make 44 dialogue cuts to get the script approved.

"Oh Life, You Are My Love" includes one of the most daring Egyptian sex scenes ever, featuring a newly married couple. Tame by Western standards, the bedroom shots of backs and intertwined hands shocked the audience during one recent screening, with one woman yelling, "Shame!"

The movie includes one misguided figure in the form of an Islamic militant, something of a stock character these days. His conversion took place some time after he stole the shop clerk's virtue, an act he now calls sin and he demands that she take the veil. Such figures are always dupes.

"Egyptians are all profoundly religious and even with the terrorism this country has experienced they could not accept a sheik as a villain," said Rafric Sabran, a scriptwriter and prominent critic.

That attitude induces considerable self-censorship, as does the fact that producers depend on rich Persian Gulf backers for financing. Most financiers arrive with a long list of prohibitions necessary to make any work palatable back home. They range from not having an unmarried man and woman alone in a room together (a proverb states that the third person always present is the devil) to not using common expressions like 'By God.'

Those who test the limits do so not only with their choice of subject matter, but with plots that avoid the usual sugar-coated endings. Each woman in "Oh Life, You Are My Love" makes a troubling sacrifice to get what she wants.

"It is the first time you have three women as central characters, heroes really, in a film and it is the first time we talk frankly about their problems on the screen," said Attiat El-Abnoudi, an Egyptian documentary maker. "One of them is deceiving the man she wants to marry. In the old times a girl with a problem like that would have ended the movie in a Cairo cabaret working as a prostitute."

* * *

June 4, 2000

MATAN HAS TWO MOMMIES, AND ISRAEL IS TALKING

By DEBORAH SONTAG

JERUSALEM, June 3—Four-year-old Matan Berner-Kadish, the center of a swirling debate about alternative families, is not at all conflicted about his identity. He knows he is a Power Ranger, fiercer than any Ninja warrior by far.

Towheaded with floppy bangs, Matan was completely nonplused by the photographs of his parents on the front page of Israeli newspapers earlier this week. "Mommy," he said, pointing to Nicole Berner-Kadish, "and Eema," he added, using the Hebrew word for mommy and pointing to Ruti Berner-Kadish.

For Matan, there has never been any question. He has always had two mothers, or, to be precise, one mom who is American-born and speaks to him in English and one eema who is Israeli-born and speaks to him in Hebrew.

But it was not until Monday that the state of Israel accepted that basic fact of his existence, with a watershed court ruling that drew howls of outrage—but not much more—from the religious right.

The Israeli High Court ordered the government to register Nicole Berner-Kadish, an American-Israeli who adopted Matan in California, as his second mother and to list him on her national identity card. Matan—whose name means "gift"—was conceived and planned as both women's child. But after Ruti Berner-Kadish, who was artificially inseminated, gave birth to him, Israel, unlike California, refused to recognize Nicole's parental rights.

A classic Israeli idiom, which means to proclaim that there's no one like mom, says, "There is only one mother." And the government felt that the catch phrase should be taken literally: it was biologically impossible, the government insisted, for anyone to have more than one.

The two women, who hold dual nationality, expected this. But as children of the 1960's who both spent their formative years in California, and many of them in Berkeley, they were raised to do battle for their rights and everybody else's.

Nicole, 35, a lawyer, and Ruti, 36, an academic, say they felt well positioned to charge ahead on an issue that makes many Israelis squeamish. Fresh-faced, well-scrubbed professionals, they put people at ease because they themselves are at ease, even in religious, conservative Jerusalem.

"We're what's known as white-picket-fence lesbians, or whatever the Israeli equivalent would be," Nicole Berner-Kadish said. "We're like perfect poster children for alternative families."

Represented by the Association for Civil Rights in Israel, they petitioned the High Court two years ago. While their case was pending, Nicole Berner-Kadish was artificially inseminated and gave birth in Israel to the couple's second son, Naveh. He is the next legal battle.

In a society that spent many decades trying to forge a collective identity, individual variants were long considered obstacles on the path to nation-building. Israel promoted conformity as a Zionist ideal.

Until 1988, the state outlawed homosexual acts in its criminal code, and gay life was extremely closeted. Even the gay and lesbian advocacy group had a euphemistic name: the Association for Personal Rights. Gay and lesbian bars moved furtively from one location to another.

In the 1990's, gays and lesbians began to assert themselves and nurture a visible culture. It is now sufficiently developed for Tel Aviv to have issued a map of the city's gay meeting places last week.

At the same time, the gay and lesbian communities also made significant civil rights' advances. Discrimination on the basis of sexual orientation was outlawed and a couple of major court cases—against El Al, the state airline, and the army—set the precedent for benefits to be awarded to gay spouses and widows.

In the lesbian community, the 90's ushered in a baby boom, and every issue of a lesbian newsletter includes several "Mazel Tovs" to new mothers.

Since it involves hospitals, schools and other public institutions, motherhood kind of forced the community out into the open, although the Berner-Kadishes say that many of their friends still speak indirectly about "our situation."

"There's still a tremendous amount of fear about being found out," Ruti said. "Here I am, totally out, and sometimes I hear a remark and. . ." Nicole interrupted, "You come home and burst into tears." "Sometimes, I compare it to being Jewish in America," Ruti said. "I think people are really polite to my face and inside, on some level, they think I have horns."

Last spring, when Matan was 3, he and a playmate were strapped into their child seats, riding in the back of the couple's car. Matan's friend suddenly said, "Where's Matan's daddy?" And, while Ruti held her breath, Matan answered, "I don't have a daddy. I have an eema and a mommy. You're the one who has a daddy."

A few days later, provoked by the question, Matan asked his mother why he did not, after all, have a father. Then he asked why he did not have a sister, and why he did not have a pet. Having long anticipated the moment, his mothers launched into an speech about how there are all different kinds of families, and not long into their explanation, Matan nodded his head and asked for a fruit smoothie.

In pursuing their case, the women had the powerful documentary support of a California adoption certificate. That allowed the case to be argued on technical issues, separating legal definitions from biological ones.

Israeli case law says that the Interior Ministry has to register citizens as they define themselves if they can show an official document supporting what they claim—a marriage certificate from Cyprus, for instance, to prove they are married.

A three-judge panel rejected the government's argument. But the decision was a narrow one, addressing the registration alone and not the principle.

Still, the dissenting judge—the only man on the panel—and almost everyone else saw it to have broader social implications. Judge Abd al-Rahman Zouabi said that registering Nicole Berner-Kadish as Matan's second mother would create an "abnormal family unit."

The Berner-Kadishes had fought successfully to keep their case from being secret; the state not only listed Nicole as Jane Doe but sought to bar media coverage. And when they won on Monday, on the sixth anniversary of their unofficial wedding ceremony, they were jubilant.

Gay groups called it a momentous day, but religious groups were outraged.

Avraham Ravitz, a strictly Orthodox legislator, said the High Court was turning Israel into a "Sodom and Gomorrah, in which every possible perversion is sanctioned by law."

But Emuna Elon, who is a religious, right-wing pundit, tried to calm the debate in an op-ed piece. "This precedent-setting ruling does not turn 'Eema and Mommy' into a married couple," she wrote. "But it does grant security and satisfaction to two good and loving women who have decided to be life partners and to raise children, and there isn't anything wrong with that according to Jewish law, either."

With the speed of the Israeli news cycle, Matan became part of popular culture in a day. This happened even at a time when Israel was still reeling from the quick withdrawal from Lebanon, which had been fought for by a grassroots group called the Four Mothers Movement, started by soldiers' mothers.

A cartoon showed a little boy telling an Israeli soldier, "I have two mothers!" And the soldier said, "I've got four!"

Matan did not have a clue that he was caricatured in the newspaper. Sitting on a couch with a plastic sword in his lap, he watched "Bambi." Occasionally, he and a friend jousted.

"Pow," Matan said, thrusting his fists through the air. "Pow, pow."

* * *

ASIA

April 5, 1991

JAPAN DENIES IT HAS AN AIDS PROBLEM

To the Editor:

The Japanese Ministry of Health's decision to continue banning birth control pills (news article, March 19), arguing that they may discourage condom use and lead to an increase in AIDS, is another example of the Japanese Government's oblique and unresponsive approach to AIDS.

My colleagues and I, on a recent trip to Japan to speak about human immunodeficiency virus education and prevention, were worried by the lack of Government and corporate support for public information programs and testing. Local health and gay activists told us of futile attempts to help those with AIDS because hospitals segregate the patients and do not allow volunteer visitors or, in some cases, AIDS patients are not told of the diagnosis.

Newspapers are reluctant to report on the subject, and though AIDS in Asia has been mostly transmitted heterosexually, only the Japanese gay press has actively publicized the disease. AIDS is still considered a foreigners' disease, and efforts to exclude them from bathhouses and brothels are only false assurances of escaping infection.

Seven million Japanese traveled abroad last year, of whom 750,000, mostly men, went to Thailand, a country with about 400,000 infected cases, mostly among prostitutes. Almost half of these male travelers to Thailand, when polled, said that they had engaged the services of a prostitute. An increasingly large number of imported prostitutes in Japan have tested H.I.V. positive. Japan had 405 reported AIDS cases as of last Aug. 31, a small number compared with the West and Africa, but the largest number in the Asian-Pacific region outside Thailand and Australia.

The Japanese gay organization Occur has filed suit against the Tokyo Metropolitan Government for denying it use of a public facility for youth counseling and AIDS programs. My organization has recently begun to offer services to H.I.V.- infected Japanese nationals who have nowhere else to go.

JOHN L. SILVA
Exec. Director, Gay Asian Pacific
Alliance Community H.I.V. Project
San Francisco, March 23, 1992

* * *

November 18, 1992

ASIAN AIDS CASES SOON TO PASS AFRICA'S

To the Editor:

Your Nov. 8 special report on AIDS in Asia predicts that reported cases in Asia will multiply in the millions, and the reputation of AIDS as a gay disease will be forgotten. There is, unfortunately, a growing trend to scapegoat gay people as the principal carriers of this disease.

Recently, China attributed a jump in AIDS cases to drug addiction, prostitution and homosexuality. A recent gay Asian regional conference held in the Philippines had its conference site changed when the hotel owners realized AIDS was a principal topic. In Japan, where AIDS cases through homosexual transmission is almost double that of heterosexual transmission, new Government pamphlets on human immunodeficiency virus awareness do not directly address the gay population. There is a prevailing notion that AIDS is a result of the gay liberation movement, and any educational materials directed to gays may only increase the AIDS caseload.

The World Health Organization's AIDS surveillance report notes homosexual and bisexual AIDS cases represent 50 percent to 75 percent of the cases in Australia, New Zealand, Singapore, Hong Kong, Malaysia, French Polynesia, New Caledonia and the Philippines.

You speculate that Asian governments have not responded to the AIDS crisis because of fears of offending local standards, of driving away international investors, local denial or plain ignorance of the problem's seriousness. These reasons let many countries off the hook much too easily. Their ruling parties and elites know full well what AIDS is, and their health ministers have attended many world AIDS conferences.

For the less developed and poorer Asian countries, AIDS is inextricably linked to poverty, and if these governments, many of them corrupt, have not addressed basic health issues of their poor before AIDS, there is little reason they will address this disease now. Thailand is the sole exception with its Government backing a successful H.I.V. education program. With more than 35 countries in the region and 25 of these countries reporting H.I.V. and AIDS cases, W.H.O. predicts cumulative AIDS cases in the region will exceed Africa's by the year 2000.

You end by citing how the lingering denial of AIDS in Asian countries will have catastrophic effects on their economies when significant numbers of the work force succumb to the disease. In this global economy, the United States, Japan and Western European nations have significant investments, manufacturing plants and factories in Asia. California alone has a $40 billion yearly trade with Asia.

The economic health and well-being of Asia has profound effects on the Western nations and Japan, and our own denial is exemplified by an absence of sharing resources and experiences in combatting AIDS.

For the second year in a row, the San Francisco AIDS surveillance unit has recorded a decline in the number of reported Asian Pacific Islander AIDS cases, reflecting the same decline as that of the white gay male population. Culturally sensitive and gay-positive educational materials, early intervention and testing and sexual behavior changes have been responsible for this decline. Replicating and sharing these programs in Asia will be one invaluable step in helping to stem an AIDS epidemic there.

JOHN L. SILVA
Exec. Dir., Community HIV Project
Gay Asian Pacific Alliance
San Francisco, Nov. 12, 1992

* * *

July 18, 1996

PREVENTING AIDS IS STILL THE BEST INVESTMENT

To the Editor:

Gabriel Rotello, in "The Risk in a 'Cure' for AIDS" (Op-Ed, July 14), misses the point when he writes that prevention efforts have "faltered." There is powerful evidence, much of it reported at the international AIDS conference in Vancouver, of the effectiveness of prevention strategies developed in the past decade.

In Thailand, aggressive condom promotion and enforcement of condom use in brothels have led to a significant decrease in H.I.V. transmission in men. In sub-Saharan Africa, condom sales rose from fewer than one million annually in 1988 to more than 167 million in 1995.

In Uganda, education campaigns have helped reduce the level of H.I.V. infection rates among the 15- to 19-year-old age group. In Australia and New Zealand, prevention programs created by partnerships between gay organizations and government have helped lower H.I.V. prevalence within the gay population.

Prevention remains underfinanced, and support from international donors is also dwindling. Yet it's the best investment governments can make to slow the spread of AIDS.

PETER LAMPTEY, M.D.
Arlington, Va.
July 15, 1996
The writer is director of the AIDS Control and
Prevention Project.

* * *

AUSTRALIA

November 4, 1973

AUSTRALIA ISSUE: HOMOSEXUALITY

Stigma Lessens, but Debate About Status Goes On

Special to The New York Times

SYDNEY, Australia, Nov. 3—A few days ago a cabinet minister declared in the Australian Parliament that beating up homosexuals was "virtually a recognized civilian team sport" here.

Dr. Moss H. Cass, the Minister for Environment and Conservation in the present Labor Government, was supporting a motion by a former Liberal Prime Minister, John G. Gorton, to remove the stigma of criminality from homosexual acts by consenting adults in private.

The motion was adopted by 64 votes to 40. Legislation to change the present harsh statutes on homosexuality is expected to follow.

However, a subsequent development has raised the question of whether Australia is ready to have homosexuality presented to the young as an acceptable alternative way of life.

Number of Lectures Given

The question came up when newspapers disclosed this week that "gay liberation" activists had been giving lectures on homosexuality in a number of Sydney and Melbourne high schools.

Spokesman for the homosexual organizations stated that the lectures had been given at the request of teachers, with the approval of the school authorities. State education officials said that this was the first they had heard of the lectures, and ordered an investigation.

The reaction among teachers, students, parents and others has been varied. A homosexual candidate in the New South Wales state elections this month, running on a "gay liberation" platform, has adopted the question as a campaign issue.

Persons convicted of homosexual acts can still be jailed for 14 years in New South Wales, and up to 21 years in Victoria, a more conservative state.

Attitudes toward homosexuals in this country, which has long regarded itself as a bastion of rugged masculinity, have changed drastically since the time when a person could be sentenced to life imprisonment for what old legal terminology defined as "the abominable crime" of sodomy.

Homosexual Marriages Noted

A synod of the Anglican Church in Sydney urged last month a review of harsh laws affecting homosexuals.

The Congregational Church, in its annual assembly here, also supported a more tolerant attitude toward homosexuals.

A Congregation minister in Perth, the Rev. Mario Shoenmaker, has performed marriage ceremonies for male and female homosexual couples this year.

A Roman Catholic weekly in Sydney, while describing homosexuality as "a psychological aberration," recently published a two-page academic article on the subject "to stimulate discussion."

Martin Smith, a 41-year-old independent candidate running in the new South Wales election on a "gay liberation" platform, told reporters that a team of 15 homosexual lectures had spoken on the subject at 30 state and private schools in Sydney "without opposition."

'No Moral Judgments'

"We are not trying to tell the children that homosexuals are any better or worse than heterosexuals," said Mr. Smith. "We make no moral judgments—we leave that up to the children."

G. L. Cramer, chairman of an organization private school heads in Victoria State, declared that it was "a grave mistake" to expose "impressionable adolescents" to the views of homosexuals.

But a spokesman for the Victoria State Department of Education said that the lectures in the Melbourne schools had been part of "an over-all social awareness program."

"As far as I know, there has been only one complaint from parents," he added.

* * *

November 24, 1992

AUSTRALIA ENDS A PROHIBITION ON HOMOSEXUALS IN MILITARY

By The Associated Press

CANBERRA, Australia, Nov. 23—The Cabinet has ended its ban on homosexuals in the military, a spokeswoman for Prime Minister Paul Keating said today.

The ban was supported by the officers of the Australian Defense Force and by the Armed Forces Federation, which represents the rank and file.

Military officials had persuaded Defense Minister Robert Ray in June to continue the ban, citing what they called the potential threat to morale. But in September, a special Labor Party committee recommended that the prohibition be ended.

Attorney General Michael Duffy's desire to overturn the ban was bolstered by the commitment of President-elect Bill Clinton to allow homosexuals to serve, and by a similar decision earlier this year by Canada.

* * *

CANADA

May 16, 1969

BROAD CRIMINAL-CODE CHANGES VOTED BY CANADIAN COMMONS

By JAY WALZ
Special to The New York Times

OTTAWA, May 15—Prime Minister Pierre Elliott Trudeau won House of Commons approval last night for sweeping changes in Canada's criminal code.

The bill embodying the changes legalizes abortions and some homosexual acts. It also covers a wide range of criminal law.

A motorist must soon subject himself to a breath test if a policeman suspects him of driving while under the influence of liquor. If the breath analysis shows a level of alcohol in the blood of more than 0.08 percent, the driver faces, on first offense, penalties up to three months in jail and a $500 fine.

The new law restricts the use of firearms, making it an offense to use them "in any way dangerous to the safety of any person."

While the provision is general, it is aimed particularly at hunters who range the Canadian wilds in large numbers. A hunter who shoots at sounds or unfamiliar sights has until now been charged only with criminal negligence.

There are also provisions designed to keep weapons out of the hands of the mentally ill, and sections establishing categories of prohibited and restricted weapons.

Present probation laws will be liberalized. Other provisions revise the outdated penal system, outlaw harassing telephone calls and make it an offense to be cruel to animals.

Another amendment provides stiffer penalties for obtaining Canadian passports fraudulently, as James Earl Ray, convicted of the assassination of the Rev. Dr. Martin Luther King Jr., did in Toronto a year ago.

Lotteries and games of chance will be legal if they are conducted by federal or provincial governments, or by organizations licensed by a government.

The bill must be acted on by the Senate, where it will be debated in the next few days, but approval there is taken for granted. It must also have the assent of the Governor General of Canada, but the Commons vote was the last major hurdle.

Mr. Trudeau made the criminal code amendments with their politically controversial abortion and homosexual clauses the first real test of strength in the Commons since the election 10 and a half months ago. The vote of 149 to 55 crossed party lines.

Robert L. Stanfield, leader of the Conservative Opposition, who had sought to have the omnibus measure broken apart to let Tories support the Government on "noncontroversial" sections, finally voted with Mr. Trudeau. So did 11 other Conservatives.

But 34 of Mr. Trudeau's Liberals absented themselves to avoid going on record against the Government or for the legalization of abortion and homosexuality.

Trudeau Explained Purpose

Defending the removal of some homosexual practices from the list of criminal offenses, the Prime Minster once said the purpose was "to take the government out of the bedrooms of the nation."

Many doctors and sociologists, however, do not consider the new provisions as radical as they sound. At present, an abortion is an offense unless a doctor, supported by a consulting physician, determines that a woman's life is at stake.

The new law will permit abortions where the woman's health is endangered but requires the decision on the operation to be made by a three-member hospital panel.

On homosexuality, the new law declares that it shall no longer be a criminal offense for consenting adults to commit homosexual acts in private. On other sexual offenses, present law is changed to keep anyone from being placed in preventive detection simply because he might commit a further sexual offense even though the offense causes no harm to anyone else.

* * *

October 11, 1991

CANADA ENDING ANTI-GAY ARMY RULES

By CLYDE H. FARNSWORTH
Special to The New York Times

TORONTO, Oct. 10—Responding to the pressure of court cases, the Government is about to end a policy of barring homosexuals from joining the armed forces, senior military officials say.

The officials, who include the Defense Minister, Marcel Masse, the Chief of the Defense Staff, Gen. John de Chastelain, and the Associate Defense Minister, Mary Collins, informed members of Parliament of the impending change in recent days, parliamentary officials said.

But the Ministry of Defense has yet to issue a formal announcement. "All of the matters haven't been finalized," Associate Defense Minister Collins told reporters today.

Parliamentary officials said the announcement had been held up by objections from some Conservative members. One Tory backbencher from the Toronto area, Don Blenkarn, said that rules had to be introduced to make sure of "decent" behavior on ships or in military barracks.

Nicholas Swales, a member of the staff of the House of Commons Standing Committee on National Defense, called the policy change "inevitable."

"Following a decision to admit women to all branches of the armed forces, except submarines, and into combat roles, it was only a matter of time before they came round to this sort of conclusion," he said.

The move was hailed as long overdue by gay advocates and human rights supporters. "It's a simple employment-equity issue," said Christine Donald, spokeswoman for the Coalition for Lesbian and Gay Rights in Ontario. "This has been a case of systemic barriers against disadvantaged groups."

Philip MacAdam, an Ottawa lawyer and former director of the Association of Lesbians and Gays of Ottawa, said the Government should now pay compensation to "possibly hundreds" of lesbians and gays discriminated against by the military.

Under existing Canadian military rules, homosexuals are not "knowingly" enrolled as serving members of the armed forces. In those cases where after joining the armed services people have been identified or have identified themselves as homosexuals, they cannot under these rules be forced out, though in practice they are made pariahs by being declared ineligible for training courses, promotion or re-enlistment.

The policy has been subjected to court challenges as a violation of the 1982 Charter of Rights and Freedoms, a document equivalent to the United States Bill of Rights that is part of the Canadian Constitution and that guarantees equal benefit and equal protection under the law.

The impending decision on the military sets Canada apart from the United States and several other leading nations.

According to a Pentagon policy statement, "homosexuality is incompatible with military service." Defense Secretary Dick Cheney reaffirmed the policy after the Supreme Court in February left standing an appeals court ruling upholding the prohibition on the ground that rights of free speech and equal protection under the law were not violated.

Britain also excludes homosexuals from its armed forces, although a parliamentary committee last spring said the policy should change because the services had lost "some men and women of undoubted competence and good character."

The Soviet Union's criminal code, which applies to members of the military as well as civilians, provides that sexual relations of a man with another man "shall be punished by deprivation of freedom for a term not exceeding five years."

Yet several other countries have already moved in the direction of Canada. France has no law barring homosexuals from military service. Homosexuality is not a reason for exclusion in Japan, although it may be used as grounds for discharge or other punishment if a soldier is impaired or fails to "maintain the military's dignity."

* * *

January 31, 1993

THE GAY TROOP ISSUE

Little Trouble in Canada When Its Gay Ban Ended

Special to The New York Times

TORONTO, Jan. 29—In Canada it has been almost a nonevent. The decision three months ago to end all barriers to the enlistment and promotion of homosexuals in Canada's armed forces has barely caused a stir.

Although a definitive assessment has yet to be made, Capt. Brett Boudreau, a Defense Department spokesman, said, "Important indicators lead us to believe the policy is accepted." He added: "There are no known reports of incidents involving physical abuse, harassment or gay bashing. There have been no resignations as a result of the change in policy and no open declarations of sexual preference by any of our members."

Canada's decision last Oct. 27 was taken after a Federal court declared that the armed forces' policies against homosexuals violated Canada's 1982 Charter of Rights and freedom, a document equivalent to the American Bill of Rights.

Pressure to Resign

Under earlier policies, homosexuals were pressured to resign. Those who refused were ostracized, receiving no promotions, no education to further a military career and no security clearances. Many chose to leave, but some sued the military.

A decision in one such case precipitated the October ruling. It involved the resignation, under protest, of an acknowledged lesbian officer, Michelle Douglas, at the Canadian Forces Base in Toronto.

Justice Andrew MacKay of Federal Court ruled in her favor. Within minutes of his decision, the Government reached a settlement with the former officer, agreeing not only to end the anti-homosexual policy, but to pay her $100,000 and her legal costs.

"For us now," Captain Boudreau said, "it just doesn't seem to be a problem. The Federal court said the old policy was against the Charter of Rights and Freedoms and that's all there is to it."

* * *

February 26, 1993

GAY COUPLE IN CANADA LOSE A BATTLE FOR FAMILY BENEFITS

By Reuters

OTTAWA, Feb. 25—Canada's Supreme Court rejected family benefits for a gay couple today, declining to recognize homosexual couples as legally married.

The court ruled 4 to 3 that gay couples do not constitute families under the country's Human Rights Act. The ruling ended a seven-year legal battle by Brian Mossop, a translator in Toronto, to claim a day of paid leave to attend his lover's father's funeral.

Federal employees are entitled to take a off to attend funerals of members of their immediate families, including fathers-in-law of married heterosexuals.

* * *

May 10, 1996

LEGISLATURE ACTS TO WIDEN GAY RIGHTS IN CANADA

By CLYDE H. FARNSWORTH

TORONTO, May 9—Fulfilling promises by governments over the past decade, the House of Commons today overwhelmingly passed landmark legislation banning discrimination against homosexuals.

An amendment to the Human Rights Act of 19 years ago would add the words "sexual orientation" to the list of characteristics that may not be used to discriminate in hiring or promoting the one million people employed by the federal civil service, or those working in regulated businesses like banks, railways, airlines, telecommunications and broadcasting. Together, these groups account for about 10 percent of the Canadian work force.

Discrimination is currently forbidden on the grounds of age, sex, race, religion or disability.

But depending on court interpretations, today's measure could affect areas beyond employment, including housing, some legal experts said.

The legislation now goes to the Senate, which has already supported a similar measure. To become law, the amendment also needs the formality of a royal assent.

The Government stressed the limited nature of the change, and said explicitly that it was not intended to give legal status to same-sex marriages. But opponents said it would eventually force businesses to extend employment benefits to same-sex partners, lead to recognition of same-sex marriages and encourage what some called a dissolute and unhealthy style of living.

Seven provinces have already prohibited discrimination on the basis of sexual orientation, but passage of a national law would carry far greater significance.

Prime Minister Jean Chretien allowed members to vote freely on the issue rather than follow a party directive; the vote was 153-76.

Gay rights activists welcomed the progress of the bill, while conservative groups voiced anger.

"We're very pleased the federal Government has affirmed the rights of lesbians and gays to be treated equally," said John Fisher, executive director of Equality for Gays and Lesbians Everywhere, in Ottawa.

But Diane Watts, spokeswoman for a conservative group known as REAL Women, said the Government had caved into special interests. "It will alter Canadian society fundamentally," she said.

The debate was so contentious that it led to disciplinary action against some Members of Parliament. Two members of the Reform Party, which tends to take a conservative line on social and economic issues, were disciplined for suggesting that it is acceptable for employers to discriminate against gays. A third was disciplined for criticizing the way Preston Manning, leader of the party, handled the issue.

Mr. Manning said he feared the bill was the first step toward a requirement for spouses' benefits for homosexuals or official sanction of same-sex marriages. "We and I believe the vast majority of Canadians do not want to start down that slippery slope," he said.

But Justice Minister Allan Rock insisted the bill conveys no special rights. The Supreme Court has ruled that extension of benefits to same-sex partners does not automatically follow the banning of discrimination.

"This bill is about equal rights," said Mr. Rock. "It's not about special rights."

Canada would join Norway, Sweden, the Netherlands, Slovenia, Israel and South Africa among the countries that have national bans on discrimination against homosexuals. But only South Africa has the protection enshrined in its Constitution, said Rachel Rosenbloom, an associate at the International Gay and Lesbian Human Rights Commission in San Francisco.

There is no such federal legislation in the United States, where the issue has been equally divisive and contentious, but anti-discrimination provisions have been adopted in nine states: California, Connecticut, Hawaii, Massachusetts, Minnesota, New Jersey, Rhode Island, Vermont and Wisconsin.

In the United States the issue has probably stirred most controversy in Colorado, which four years ago shattered its image of tolerance with an amendment to the state constitution specifically forbidding state and local governments from adopting measures to protect homosexuals.

* * *

May 21, 1999

CANADA RULES 'SPOUSE' INCLUDES HOMOSEXUALS

By Reuters

OTTAWA, May 20—The Supreme Court of Canada, in one of the most far-reaching homosexual-rights rulings anywhere, today struck down a heterosexual definition of the word "spouse."

In an 8-to-1 decision, the court ruled that Ontario's Family Law Act was unconstitutional in denying homosexuals the right to apply for alimony from each other.

"The Supreme Court has overturned centuries of social tradition," said Darrel Reid, president of Focus on the Family Canada, which intervened in the case to argue against expanding gay rights.

The case involved two lesbians, identified only as M and H. Denied spousal support after separating from her partner,

M asked the courts to strike down the provision in Ontario's spousal law that limited the right to claim alimony to married or common-law heterosexual couples.

Supreme Court Justice Peter Cory, writing for the majority, said, "The exclusion of same-sex partners from the benefits of" the act "promotes the view that M, and individuals in same-sex relationships generally, are less worthy of recognition and protection."

The court, stressing that it was not changing "traditional conceptions of marriage," noted that the Ontario law had already expanded the definition of spousal support in allowing it to apply to heterosexuals in common-law relationships. But it said its decision "may well affect many other statutes that rely on a similar definition of the word 'spouse.'"

Federal and provincial laws, including those governing adoption, marriage and taxes, contain hundreds of references to spouses.

In January, one gay-rights lobbying group began a challenge to 58 federal laws, and the federal Government has been quietly trying to introduce changes that would eliminate legal differences between homosexuals and heterosexuals.

Martha McCarthy, M's lawyer, praised Canada's 1982 Charter of Rights and Freedoms, on which the high court's decision was based, and said the ruling was "the first time that gays and lesbians can say that the charter's promise of equality for them and for their relationships has been fulfilled."

Ms. McCarthy's client had already settled out of court with H, but Ontario had continued the case.

Another intervener in the case, the Evangelical Fellowship of Canada, said that if "spouse" is to cover all domestic partnerships, it becomes useless in addressing "the unique needs of marriage and heterosexual spousal relationships."

The Supreme Court gave Ontario, Canada's most populous province, six months to change its law. But Canada's provinces and the federal Government are permitted under the Charter of Rights to invoke a clause to ignore the decision.

Ontario's Premier, Mike Harris, indicated he would not fight the ruling. "My sense is that I think across the country governments will comply," he said on a radio show.

* * *

LATIN AMERICA

April 16, 1965

CUBAN GOVERNMENT IS ALARMED BY INCREASE IN HOMOSEXUALITY

By PAUL HOFMANN
Special to The New York Times

HAVANA, April 15—Homosexuality has become "an alarming political and social matter" in Cuba, a leading

newspaper of Premier Fidel Castro's Government warned today.

In an article titled "Revolution and Vices," El Mundo of Havana said that sexual deviates were blatant in Cuban cities and had infiltrated intellectual and art life.

The article singled out the ballet and suggested it was better to disband some dance troupes than to tolerate them as known centers of immorality.

Homosexuals are conspicuous in some neighborhoods of Havana, particularly the part of 23d Street known as La Rampa (the ramp), leading from the waterfront to the Havana Libre Hotel, formerly the Havana Hiltion. They also congregate in some numbers in parts of Santiago de Cuba.

On La Rampa effeminate young men parade in the afternoon and evening hours. Sexual perverts are also said to gather in some of the many night clubs that the Government's tourist department keeps going. The regime is reviewing what remains of Havana's once notoriously uninhibited night life, and reportedly is considering closing some night spots.

Art Academy Scandal

A homosexual scandal in the Havana Art Academy earlier this year led to a faculty reshuffle. A foreign leftist writer who visited Cuba some time ago was expelled on charges of homosexuality.

At an international theatrical congress in Havana last year a participant from Britain caused an uproar when he unsuccessfully proposed a motion to condemn "persecution" of homosexuals.

El Mundo described homosexuality as a legacy of capitalism. The newspaper quoted Premier Castro as having said that "the countryside does not produce homosexuals" and that sexual deviation was a big-city phenomenon.

The article commented: "The virility of our peasantry does not permit that abominable vice. But in some of our cities it is rampant. There, homosexuals unite and form a clan."

The newspaper stressed that the Castro revolution would fight vice until it was banished from "our virile country, which is locked in a fight for life or death with Yankee imperialism."

The article declared that "no homosexual represents the revolution, which is a movement of he-men."

El Mundo said that the revolution would not persecute homosexuals but would break their "positions, procedures and influence" by applying "revolutionary social hygiene." This was understood as a warning that homosexuals would be rounded up and sent to labor camps.

* * *

August 12, 1993

IN LIVE-AND-LET-LIVE LAND, GAY PEOPLE ARE SLAIN

By JAMES BROOKE
Special to The New York Times

RIO DE JANEIRO, Aug. 11—A Brazilian paradox—tolerance of homosexuality and violence against homosexuals—has been highlighted by the granting of political asylum in the United States to a Brazilian homosexual on the ground that he would be persecuted if returned home.

The ruling late last month by a San Francisco immigration judge, Philip Leadbetter, represented the first time that a homosexual had won asylum in the United States on the ground that homosexuals were a persecuted social group in the country of origin, said Julie Dorf, executive director of the International Gay and Lesbian Human Rights Commission, a private group in San Francisco.

Marcelo Tenorio, a 30-year-old house painter, told the judge that he had left Brazil after he had been stabbed and badly beaten outside a gay bar on a Rio beachfront in 1989. A Brazilian gay rights campaigner who testified in favor of Mr. Tenorio's request said 1,200 homosexuals had been slain in Brazil since 1980.

But Brazil is also renowned for its tolerance of gay life.

Transvestite shows, where many of the performers are gay, are considered family entertainment, and transvestites play an integral part of Rio's Carnival. Caetano Veloso and Gilberto Gil, two of Brazil's most famous singers, openly flaunt their bisexuality and wear dresses in public.

Rio's gay bars and gay Carnival balls have long attracted tourists from Europe, the United States and Brazil's more conservative South American neighbors.

'A Very Ambiguous Opinion'

"Brazil displays a very ambiguous opinion about homosexuality," said Luiz Mott, president of the Gay Group of Bahia, Brazil's oldest and most prominent gay rights group. "On one hand it is a nation with a very exuberant gay culture, exporting transvestites to Italy and France, attracting tourists for Carnival. On the other hand, one homosexual is murdered in Brazil every five days."

Relying on newspaper reports, Mr. Mott's group tabulated 1,200 killings of homosexuals since 1980, and Mr. Mott believes the real number is twice as high. Of the recorded killings, only 10 percent led to arrests, he said.

David I. Harrad, a spokesman for the Dignity Group, a gay rights group in Curitiba, in southern Brazil, said: "In Curitiba, we have had 20 murders of homosexuals over the last 10 years, and only one was solved. The one that was solved was only cleared up because the family paid the police to keep on the case."

"More people practice homosexuality in Brazil than in most countries, but very few people reveal their condition," said Mr. Harrad, a Briton. "People have a great fear of revealing their homosexuality for fear of machismo."

In Rio, 38 killings of homosexuals were recorded in the first half of this year, according to the Atoba Group, a gay rights group here. Most of the suspected killers are male prostitutes. In a recurring scenario, a young street hustler goes home with an older man, has sex, kills the man while he is sleeping, then loots his apartment.

'Extermination Groups'

Mr. Mott's group has also identified 12 "extermination groups," including a Sao Paulo skinhead group with T-shirts reading "Death to Homosexuals."

But the Government and some mainstream newspapers say homosexuals are not victims of organized attacks here.

"Judge Tricked: Gay Wins Asylum in U.S.A. With Lie About Brazil," was the headline on an article this week in Veja, the nation's largest-selling newsweekly.

"There is no conspiracy or evidence that could indicate an organized practice," Veja wrote of the killing of homosexuals here. "In the hands of the noisy American pink lobby, Tenorio's cause became a festival of demagoguery—and of Brazil-bashing."

Since there are no separate statistics on the killing of homosexuals, whether they are disproportionately victims cannot be proved. But the sometimes sordid circumstances of the deaths attract a lot of attention.

In one of this year's most shocking killings, Renildo Jose dos Santos, a town councilman in Alagoas State, was kidnapped, tortured and decapitated in early March.

Six weeks earlier, Mr. Santos had revealed his bisexuality in a radio interview in his town, Coqueiro Seco. The council immediately voted to bar him from office. When the councilman started to receive death threats, the Gay Group of Bahia tried to win political asylum for him in Canada. Before a response came, Mr. Santos was kidnapped and killed. After his severed head was discovered in an adjoining state, five men, including the town's Mayor, were arrested.

March Draws Only 100

Gay campaigners say they hope that the United States asylum case will stir Brazilian public opinion to call for an end to impunity in gay killings. Next month representatives of 38 gay groups are to meet in Sao Paulo to devise a strategy to lobby Brazil's Congress. In October, Congress will start to revise the Constitution, and the lobbyists hope to win approval of an amendment explicitly banning discrimination on sexual grounds.

Brazil's gay rights movement suffers from a lack of foot soldiers. A gay pride march on a Rio beach in June drew only 100 people.

"Brazil's gay movement is relatively weak and disorganized, in part because there are no laws prohibiting homosexuality to organize around," said Richard Parker, an American anthropologist who works with AIDS prevention groups here. Brazil decriminalized most homosexual acts in 1823.

In a recent DataFolha poll, 44 percent of respondents nationwide said they "totally agreed" that "homosexuals should be accepted like anyone else."

"In the United States, friendship networks of gay men are largely gay men," continued Mr. Parker, who has written two books on Brazilian sexuality. "Here in Brazil, their lives are much more integrated with their families; their friendships tend to be much more mixed."

But the impunity enjoyed by those who kill homosexuals appears to stem from the closeted nature of gay activity here.

"In many cases, the families don't want to expose themselves to ridicule," he said of killings of gay men that go unsolved.

* * *

January 4, 1997

GAY RIGHTS, PREJUDICE AND POLITICS IN MEXICO

By SAM DILLON

GUADALAJARA, Mexico—Since Pedro Preciado came out as a homosexual 18 years ago, he says, the police here have arrested him a dozen times, often punching and kicking him before hauling him off to jail and imposing a fine for violating "public morals and good customs."

So when it comes to harassment, Mr. Preciado, a co-founder of Guadalajara's first gay rights organization, knows what he is talking about. And he was not terribly concerned when the municipal government here in Mexico's third largest city passed an ordinance early in December outlawing "abnormal sexual behavior." He considers the new ordinance an improvement over the one it replaced.

Not everyone agrees. Passages regulating sexuality in the Guadalajara law, which prohibits everything from painting graffiti on public walls to allowing pets to soil the street, have set off a new debate about discrimination against homosexuals in Mexico.

Some academics and journalists have portrayed the measure darkly as the first move in a new campaign of anti-gay repression, but Mr. Preciado sees the opposite trend.

"Slowly but steadily, respect for homosexual rights is building across Mexico," he said.

The ordinance has come under special scrutiny because Guadalajara, whose metropolitan area includes more than three million residents, is governed by the National Action Party, or PAN. A right-of-center opposition party, the PAN already controls a third of Mexico's cities and towns and, according to opinion polls, could extend its influence in nationwide elections in 1997. Some critics argue that the PAN's vision of Mexico's future is based on a past in which homosexuals were repressed.

"The PAN leaders think they're going to win new power and so, pushed by the Catholic Church, they think now is the time to moralize the society," said Carlos Monsivais, an essayist who has criticized what he calls the Roman Catholic Church's repressive cultural hegemony in Mexico.

Mr. Monsivais recalled that at the turn of the century, 41 prominent Mexican intellectuals were detained, accused of being homosexual and sent to a forced labor camp in Yucatan State. As recently as the 1950's, he said, people accused of homosexual activity were sometimes consigned to a prison colony on the Marias Islands in the Pacific Ocean.

In recent decades, most official brutality has disappeared, he said, although vestiges of the country's past bias have continued in cities like Guadalajara in the form of ordinances outlawing "moral failures," or other vaguely described crimes. The laws have permitted the police to arrest homosexuals, or, more frequently, to extort money from them.

It was after the police repeatedly arrested him and other homosexuals for holding hands in public or for similar "infractions" that Mr. Preciado helped found Guadalajara's Gay

Pride Liberation Group in 1981, he said. Lesbians started a parallel organization, and, by the end of the 1980's, the twin organizations had scores of members, he said.

The most serious confrontation with bias in Guadalajara came in 1991, when an attempt to hold an international congress of gay men and lesbians aroused angry condemnations from political, religious and business leaders. The Mayor even threatened to revoke the operating license of any hotel offering lodging to gay visitors. In the face of that and other threats, the congress was rescheduled for Acapulco, Mr. Preciado said.

During that confrontation, Guadalajara was controlled by the Institutional Revolutionary Party, or PRI, the governing party in Mexico for nearly seven decades.

In February 1995, Cesar Coll Carabias, a businessman from the PAN, won election as Mayor of Guadalajara and his party also won a majority on the City Council. Because of the ties of the party to the Catholic Church and its conservative reputation, its rise in Guadalajara alarmed many homosexuals, Mr. Preciado said.

In nearly two years in office, Mr. Coll has several times given critics an opportunity to portray him as an intolerant moralist. He has, for example, urged secretaries in municipal offices not to wear miniskirts and pressed the Playtex company to remove billboards showing a woman in an alluring brassiere.

So on Dec. 5, when Guadalajara's PAN-dominated City Council approved language in its new Police and Good Government Ordinance prohibiting "public practices that imply the development of an abnormal sexual life," a chorus of broadcasters, newspaper columnists and academics condemned the statute.

"This is a repressive ordinance aimed at satisfying a hard-core clerical clique within the PAN," said Javier Hurtado, a political science professor at the University of Guadalajara.

But according to Jorge Zepeda Patterson, the editor of the Guadalajara newspaper Siglo 21, some facts have been obscured in the debate, especially the origin of the new ordinance; it is a revised version of a series of municipal statutes that have been on Guadalajara's books for several decades. And virtually all the offensive passages in the new law were already included in the old, he said.

In an interview at his City Hall office, Mr. Coll said the ordinance had been systematically distorted by PRI officials, "whose strategy it is to discredit all of our initiatives."

The city's intention was to modernize statutes that had long given police legal cover to extort and abuse not only homosexuals but also prostitutes, he said. He insisted that the words "abnormal sexual life," which were also included in Guadalajara's previous law, were not meant to describe homosexuality.

"We've found there are people who make love with animals in parks, and we have to be able to detain them," Mr. Coll said.

Mr. Preciado said that whatever the city's intentions with the phrase, biased police officers or judges could easily interpret it to harass homosexuals.

But Mr. Coll's administration has demonstrated more tolerance toward homosexuals than PRI governments, Mr. Preciado said. In 1995, for example, Mr. Coll met with Mr. Preciado in his office, and "he treated me very cordially," Mr. Preciado said. Furthermore, the city's dozen gay bars and discos have been allowed to operate without harassment or extortion, he said.

Mr. Preciado said critics had failed to notice that the new ordinance has eliminated several previous Guadalajara statutes used against homosexuals; one that was stricken prohibited "any act that violates public morals or good customs." Furthermore, several new civil rights guarantees were added in the new ordinance, including one obligating the police to allow detained persons to get in touch with a lawyer, he said.

"The new ordinance," he said, "is not worse than the old one."

* * *

October 16, 1999

AT 41, A FATHER FIGURE TO CHILE'S GAY RIGHTS CAUSE

By CLIFFORD KRAUSS

SANTIAGO, Chile, Oct. 11—As a rebel student leader opposing the Pinochet dictatorship 20 years ago, Carlos Sanchez Soto lived a double life fraught with danger.

He used to duck the police in the middle of the night to paint the walls of Santiago with revolutionary graffiti. He was briefly jailed. And he was expelled from his university in 1981 after joining other dissidents in a daring hunger strike in the Metropolitan Cathedral.

But those were relatively breezy days, Mr. Sanchez says, compared with what he faces now as the most visible homosexual civil rights leader in Chile.

"During the dictatorship I knew who the enemy was," Mr. Sanchez said. "Now the opposition we face is much broader, more subtle and harder to identify."

Nine years after Gen. Augusto Pinochet stepped down as President, political protests are tolerated, but Chile remains Latin America's most culturally conservative society. Divorce is still prohibited, and abortion is illegal even in cases involving rape or the survival of the mother. Movies and videos are censored.

And as far as homosexuality goes, it is rarely talked about. Gay activists estimate that only about 1 percent of the homosexual population is openly gay—less than anywhere else in the region.

Mr. Sanchez says no company will hire him to ply his trade as a computer technician now that his picture has appeared in the newspapers as a gay activist. He lost most of his old friends when he came out of the closet six years ago. His relationship with his only daughter also changed and remains somewhat strained.

When he calls news conferences, usually only the alternative press shows up. When he goes to Congress to lobby, conservative legislators refuse to see him. And then there is the tiny gay movement itself, which activists describe as a pit of jealousy and intrigue, rife with arguments over tactics and financing.

Now 41, his wispy Trotsky-style beard graying, Mr. Sanchez is a father figure in a movement that is young and politically inexperienced. He gives advice to young gay Chileans about their love lives and how to deal with their parents.

But more than anything else, he balances between those in the movement who want to shock with their militancy and those who want to fit into society as comfortably as possible by shunning demonstrations and isolating those on the fringes, like gay prostitutes and transvestites.

"The dictatorship period was my political school," he said. "I learned how to organize, how to negotiate and when to break off a negotiation."

At a recent planning session at the headquarters of the Unified Movement of Sexual Minorities, of which he is one of eight directors, a more radical leader spoke in favor of the Communist Party presidential candidate and suggested that the group invite all of the candidates competing in the December election to present their views.

Mr. Sanchez shot down the idea, explaining later that he knew that the main presidential contenders would decline, leaving only fringe candidates to make their case. "I don't want us to be marginalized," he said, adding that sexual orientation and civil rights crossed ideological lines.

Mr. Sanchez's pragmatism has enabled him to work with the Health Ministry, which gives the Unified Movement of Sexual Minorities small grants to produce videos for AIDS prevention. His quiet but persistent lobbying in Congress helped lead to the recent repeal of a 19th-century law that made gay sex illegal as sodomy.

But Mr. Sanchez can be very direct when necessary. Working closely with Silvia Parada, 30, a transvestite leader, his latest focus has been on guaranteeing humane treatment and health care for homosexuals in prison and protesting police brutality against transvestites and gay prostitutes.

On a recent Monday afternoon, Mr. Sanchez put on a staid double-breasted gray suit jacket and rode the subway with Silvia Parada to San Miguel prison to visit German (Mariana) Rodriguez, a transvestite prisoner who has AIDS. When they visited the dim visiting pen in the prison's Tower 1, the section of the jail where 60 gay prisoners are segregated, they were told that he had been taken to the prison clinic sick and in great pain.

Mr. Sanchez huddled with a group of prisoners, first inquiring about Mr. Rodriguez's symptoms and about the care he was receiving and then about how the prisoners were being treated by guards. The prisoners described a wide assortment of harassment.

"They treat us like dogs, not like we're human beings," said a 20-year-old transvestite named Manuel. Mr. Sanchez, his face tightening into an angry grimace, shot back, "Don't ever forget you are a human being."

Helen Hughes for The New York Times

Carlos Sánchez Soto was a rebel student during the Pinochet dictatorship. Now he is the most visible homosexual civil rights leader in Chile.

"This is what we need to do: make an accusation and make it publicly, so various reporters will start asking questions," Mr. Sanchez said.

From the prison, Mr. Sanchez and Silvia Parada hailed a taxi to take them to the Supreme Court building, where a demonstration they had organized was starting.

With police officers laughing behind them, seven transvestites stood at the top of the stone entrance steps and spoke out against what they described as systematic police brutality. One had fresh bruises across his arms and chest, and stitches above one swollen eye and below his nose.

"We're not a plague!" Michel Clemente, 30, pleaded to more than 50 people who gathered to listen, many with faces of amused astonishment. "We're part of this society whether you like it or not!"

Mr. Sanchez looked on with a broad smile. "This is perfect," he said. "The 'girls' will be safe from the beatings for 10 or 15 days at least. It's another small step."

* * *

June 10, 2000

BRAZIL GRANTS SOME LEGAL RECOGNITION TO SAME-SEX COUPLES

By LARRY ROHTER

RIO DE JANEIRO, June 9—In an action that gay groups describe as the first of its sort in Latin America, the Brazilian government has extended de facto legal recognition to same-sex relationships by granting such couples the right to inherit each other's pension and social security benefits.

"This decision is historic and unprecedented, not just for Brazil but for all of Latin America," said Toni Reis, director of Dignidade, a gay rights group based in the southern city of

Curitiba. "It creates a model and a reference point for other gay movements in Latin America to begin pressuring their governments for recognition of their civil rights."

As the result of new regulations announced on Thursday, applicants who can prove that theirs is a "stable union" will be treated by the National Social Security Institute no differently than a married couple in cases of retirement or death. The policy also allows people in same-sex relationships to declare their partners as dependents on income tax returns.

The government decree, which resulted from a recent court decision, comes while a much broader measure, first introduced in 1995, remains stalled in the Brazilian Congress.

That legislation would formally create "civil partnerships" for homosexual couples who wished to have their relationships recognized by law. But with an election less than four months away, lawmakers aligned with conservative Protestant and Roman Catholic groups are lobbying against it.

"We're cowards when it comes time to decide," said Roberto Jefferson, a congressman who is one of the sponsors of the bill. "Because of a half-dozen religious radicals, the proposal doesn't get voted on."

Catholic Church authorities had no comment today on the decree. But in the past, the National Conference of Brazilian Bishops has condemned the proposed law as "hostile to the Brazilian family," saying that "it is no different from abortion, which though legal in some coutries continues to be immoral."

The legislative impasse illustrates "the state of contradiction in which Brazil lives" in regard to homosexuality, said Claudio Nascimento, secretary general of the Brazilian Association of Gays, Lesbians and Transvestites. "We have an image of being a liberal country, the country of Carnival and tolerance, but at the same time that we see advances in some areas, there are also attitudes against homosexuality that are deeply ingrained."

Gay rights groups here point, for instance, to the high level of violence against homosexuals and what they say is the impunity enjoyed by those who engage in it. By their calculations, 1,831 homosexuals have been killed in Brazil because of their sexual orientation in the last 10 years, with only 8 percent of the cases having gone to court.

At the same time, Mr. Nascimento said, 77 municipalities have enacted laws prohibiting various forms of discrimination against gay men and lesbians. The conservative city of Juiz de Fora, for instance, recently decriminalized public displays of affection between same-sex couples, with its mayor, Tarcisio Delgado, declaring that his community wanted to be seen as socially "advanced and in solidarity with minorities."

In addition, the state of Rio de Janeiro last month approved a law imposing fines as high as $5,500 against individuals or institutions found to discriminate against homosexuals. The law also permits the authorities to close hotels, restaurants and nightclubs that repeatedly deny their services to gays.

Marta Suplicy, the country's leading sexologist and the member of Congress who was the main sponsor of the original domestic partnership legislation, said the new regulations "increase the chances that my bill can be approved after the elections."

A recent poll indicates that 54 percent of Brazilians approve of some form of legal status for homosexual couples, compared with just 7 percent in 1994.

"This isn't Sweden or Holland, where the rights of homosexuals are totally recognized," said Mr. Reis, the director of Dignidade. "But we are making progress."

Brazil is a socially conservative country: women here did not obtain the right to vote until the 1930's, and divorce was prohibited until the 1970's. But Ms. Suplicy said it would be simplistic to attribute such delays solely to a heritage of machismo and Roman Catholicism.

"Those are the same everywhere," she said today. "It is harder to effect this sort of change in Latin America mainly because the notion of civil rights is not as strongly developed as in Europe or the United States."

SUBJECT INDEX

BYLINE INDEX